WORDSWORTH LITERARY LIVES

General Editor: Keith Carabine

THE LIFE OF TOLSTOY

The Life of
TOLSTOY

A BIOGRAPHY BY
AYLMER MAUDE

Introduction by
HENRY CLARIDGE

A man so various that he seemed to be
Not one, but all mankind's epitome.

DRYDEN

WORDSWORTH EDITIONS

In loving memory of
MICHAEL TRAYLER
the founder of Wordsworth Editions

I

Readers who are interested in other titles from
Wordsworth Editions are invited to visit our website at
www.wordsworth-editions.com

For our latest list and a full mail-order service, contact
Bibliophile Books, 5 Datapoint, South Crescent, London E16 4TL
TEL: +44 (0)20 7474 2474 FAX: +44 (0)20 7474 8589
ORDERS: orders@bibliophilebooks.com
WEBSITE: www.bibliophilebooks.com

First published in 2008 by Wordsworth Editions Limited
8B East Street, Ware, Hertfordshire SG12 9HJ

ISBN   978 1 84022 561 7

Typeset in Great Britain by Antony Gray
Printed and bound by Clays Ltd, St Ives plc

Contents

THE LIFE OF TOLSTOY

Part One – The First Fifty Years

1 *Ancestry and Parentage*

Ancestors. Count Peter. Paternal grandparents. Maternal grandparents. Púshkin. Tolstoy's father. His mother. First recollections. Auntie Tatiána. Antecedents.

2 *Childhood and Early Manhood*

Yásnaya Polyána. Auntie Tatiána. K. I. Mauer, tutor. The brothers: Nikoláy, Sergéy and Dmítri – and sister Márya. Dúnechka. The Ant-Brothers and the Green Stick. The house-serfs. Beethoven's Sonata Pathétique. Pilgrims and saints. Death of father and grandmother. Flying. Personal appearance. Corporal punishment. Originality. Riding lessons. Countess Osten-Saken. Aunt P. I. Yúshkov. Books. Abstract speculations. Kazán University. Diary. Dmítri. Rousseau and Dickens. Yásnaya again. The serfs. Petersburg. Rudolph the musician. Women. Gambling. Money difficulties. Moscow. The freedom of Russian nobles.

3   *The Caucasus*

4   *The Crimean War*

5   *Petersburg. The Country. A Love Affair*

6   *Travels Abroad*

7   *At Yásnaya again. Turgénev. Arbiter. Magazine*

Nations. My doubts about Non-Resistance laid before Tolstoy. Gladstone. Tolstoy's relation to political reformers. Prince D. N. Shakhovskóy. *The Empty Drum*. 'Tell him Count Tolstoy called.' Henry George. Semënov on the change in Tolstoy. 'Zaccheising'. A. P. Ivánov, his copyist. Police supervision. *Non-Acting*. Zola and Dumas. *Art and not-Art*. Armenian students and the Social Democrats. Amiel. Guy de Maupassant. Drózhzhin's refusal of military service. The clash between Christianity and Patriotism.

14   *The Doukhobórs*

Congress of Naturalists. Bicycling. Death of Gay. Mary. Semënov buys some land. Henry George. A masquerade. The mingling of grave and gay. The Tolstoyans' treatment of the Countess. *Preface to Guy de Maupassant's stories*. *Christianity and Patriotism*. Articles on religion. Three groups of religions. Nicholas II. 'Insensate fancies'. Death of Iván. 'A man and wife are not separate beings.' *Master and Man*. Semënov on life at Yásnaya Polyána. *Shame! A Persecution of Christians in Russia*. Tolstoy's opinion of the Doukhobórs. Peter Verígin in exile. 'The seed sown by Christ'. Refusals of military service. Chertkóv. Tolstoy's letters to Verígin. Verígin's letters. Tolstoyan exiles. Tolstoy's gratitude to Chertkóv. *Help!* J. C. Kenworthy. 'An inexhaustible purse'. Anton Chékhov. 'Shakespeare did write plays better than you!' 'Two kinds of people'. Tolstoy's charm, his way with children. *The Archive*. To serve a local Government is wrong. Jane Addams – visit to Yásnaya Polyána. Letters to Khilkóv. Jane Addams's letter. 'What class is your excellency pleased to travel?' 'A quiet room to work in'. 'Money I have earned.' Lawn tennis. Chess. The Holy Synod's booklet and Pears' Soap. *The Demands of Love. A Letter to E. H. Crosby. How to Read the Gospels. What is Art?* Submitting Tolstoy's teaching to the test he put to Churches and Governments.

15   *Excommunication*

What is Art? Correspondence with Tolstoy. The main theme of the book. Bernard Shaw. A. B. Walkley's comments. Why the Tolstoy movement disintegrated. The Purleigh Colony. The *odium theologicum*. The Doukhobór migration. Prince D. A. Khilkóv. 7,636 Doukhobórs go to Canada. Verígin's letters sent to the Canadian Doukhobórs. Nudity parades. Chertkóv. *A Handbook*. Chertkóv's disapproval of my book. L. Sulerzhítski. *An Open Letter* from the Sons of Freedom. Gandhi. Non-Resistance. Lack of definiteness.

Introduction

Aylmer Maude's *The Life of Tolstoy* is one of the outstanding examples of a biography whose subject was both alive and knew the biographer at the time of its first publication, and whose contribution to the subsequent biographies (particularly those in English) of a writer regarded by many as the greatest of all novelists is inestimable. *The Life of Tolstoy: First Fifty Years* was published in 1908 by Constable in London; *The Life of Tolstoy: Later Years* followed in 1910. A revised edition of the two volumes was published by Oxford University Press (the text used here) in 1930; Maude thus published a biography of Tolstoy whilst he was still alive and a revised biography some twenty years after his death. As he notes in his Author's Preface to the edition of 1930: 'Much has been published about him since he died and additional matter is incorporated in these volumes'; thus the revised edition is a more authoritative and comprehensive account of Tolstoy's life and works than its predecessor. By 1930 Maude and his wife, Louise, were considerably advanced with their project of translating Tolstoy's complete works into English, and translations of the two great novels *Anna Karénina* and *War and Peace* had appeared, respectively, in 1918 and 1922; and the revised biography naturally, therefore, benefits from the augmentation and deepening of knowledge about Tolstoy's art and his philosophy of life that these two translations would have provided. For the revision Maude also had the co-operation of Tolstoy's eldest daughter, Tatiána Sukhotín-Tolstoy. In his Introduction to *The Final Struggle: Being Countess Tolstoy's Diary for 1910* (the year of her husband's death), Maude wrote that his 'own acquaintance lasted from 1888 till his death in 1910'. Maude met Tolstoy in Moscow through the offices of his brother-in-law, Dr P. S. Alexéev (1849–1913), who was married to his wife's sister, Lucy, and in his 'Recollections of Tolstoy' in the *Slavonic Review* (1929) he recalled that during the winters of 1895–6 and 1896–7 he visited the novelist almost every week. (Maude's account of his first meeting with Tolstoy can be found in Chapter 9 of Part Two of the biography.) Maude and his wife returned to England in 1897 but he made further visits to Russia to see Tolstoy, staying with him at his estate at Yásnaya Polyána (literally 'Clear Glade'), in Túla, some hundred and forty miles south of Moscow. It was on his visit in 1902 that Maude was 'authorised' by Tolstoy to write his biography and in his Author's Preface he notes that 'Tolstoy contributed a good deal of matter'. Maude also knew Pavel Ivanovich Birukóv [Paul Birukoff] (1860–1931), whose four-volume *The Life of Tolstoy* (1906–23) was the first comprehensive biography, and Maude, like the French novelist Romain Rolland who also wrote a biography of Tolstoy (*Vie de Tolstoy*, 1911), drew on Birukóv's researches. Tolstoy's correspondence with Maude, it might be noted, is the most extensive he conducted with any Englishman.

AYLMER MAUDE

Aylmer Maude was born in Ipswich on 28 March 1858. His father, Francis Henry Maude, was the vicar of Holy Trinity Church in Ipswich; his mother, Lucy, was from a Quaker family. Maude was a boarder at Christ's Hospital in Horsham, Surrey, from 1868 to 1874. Leaving Christ's Hospital at the age of sixteen he went to the Lyceum in Moscow which he attended between 1874 and 1876. He remained in Moscow after finishing his studies, first of all finding work as a private tutor and then joining the carpet department at the Scottish-owned Muir and Mirrielees department store in Moscow (the store is now the Tsum building on Petrovka Street). He left Muir and Mirrielees to join the Anglo-Russian Carpet Company, for which he acted as business manager and, latterly, director. It was while he was with the Anglo-Russian Carpet Company that he met and married Louise Shanks. Louise, though English, was Moscow-born, her father, James Stewart Shanks, being a partner in a British-owned jewellery business with offices in Moscow. Her Russian was utterly fluent, and, one assumes, entirely idiomatic, and her role in the translation of Tolstoy's works (of which we have more to say below) has, arguably, been considerably underestimated. Maude met Tolstoy when the novelist had, to all intents and purposes, abandoned the writing of novels, though not of fiction, and when his reputation as a teacher and moral philosopher was beginning to penetrate not only Russian intellectual circles (particularly after the assassination of Alexander II in 1881) but also those in Western Europe and North America. Maude was some thirty years Tolstoy's junior, and, given his partly Quaker background, it was not surprising that he was drawn both to Tolstoy's formidable intelligence and to his pacifism. Though the Countess Sófya Andréevna Tolstoy (Tolstoy's wife) found Maude 'a ponderous and dull man', he maintained regular contact with Tolstoy whilst pursuing his business interests, but in 1897, having spent thirty-six years in Moscow, Aylmer and Louise retired to England intending to live on investment income, residing first at the Brotherhood Church in Croydon, a Tolstoyan community founded by J. C. Kenworthy, and then at Wickham's Farm in Danbury, near Purleigh, Essex, close to a branch of the Brotherhood Church, founded in 1896, to which the Maudes gave financial support. The Maudes moved to Great Baddow, near Chelmsford, in 1902, shortly after the dissolution of the Purleigh commune, and it was here that *The Life of Tolstoy* was substantially written. Once established at Great Baddow, Maude and his wife now devoted themselves to the translation of Tolstoy's works and the promulgation of his ideas. Maude returned to Russia on several occasions to interview Tolstoy, but he also served in the British Expeditionary Force to North Russia in 1918–19 (sent after the Russian Revolution to prevent Allied war materials, stock-piled in Archangel, from falling into German or Bolshevik hands and, also, more broadly, to thwart the spread of Bolshevism), where, given his fluent Russian, he was employed as a liaison officer. He was closely associated with the Fabian Society (for which he wrote a pamphlet on 'Municipal Trading' published by the society in 1908) and the Co-Operative Movement (Louise Maude was president of the Chelmsford Cooperative Women's Guild), and his devotion to progressive causes informs his interest in the work of Dr Marie Stopes (1880–1958), the campaigner for women's rights and a pioneer of family planning. Maude wrote two books about her, *The Authorised Life of Marie C. Stopes* (1924) and *Marie Stopes: Her Work and Play* (1933). In 1932 Maude was granted a Civil List Pension in recognition of his services to literature and also to alleviate the increasingly penurious circumstances in which he and his wife found themselves. The Maudes lived to see the twenty-one volumes of the Tolstoy Centenary Edition published in their life-times: Aylmer died aged eighty on 25 August 1938; his wife, Louise, survived him by barely a year, dying in 1939.

It was during Aylmer's Maude's residence at Wickham's Farm that he undertook his most substantial personal and political contribution to the dissemination of Tolstoy's ideas. The Doukhobórs (or 'Dukhobórs'; the word means 'spirit-wrestlers') were an eccentric, dissenting religious sect towards whom Tolstoy found himself increasingly sympathetic (particularly for their pacifism, vegetarianism and their renunciation of property). Worshipping God in the spirit they rejected the Russian Orthodox Church, and believing in the gospel of love they repudiated violence and held all people equal as brethren. They refused to serve the state and thus refused military service. Tsar Alexander I had exiled the Doukhobórs to the Caucasus in the 1830s but under the increasingly stern regime of Tsar Nicholas II they were punished for their pacifism by Cossack infantrymen. By early 1898 their situation was so dire that Tolstoy addressed a long letter to foreign newspapers describing their sufferings and soliciting aid for their emigration. He counted their members at some twelve thousand and made preliminary calculations as to the costs their emigration would entail. (His close friend Vladimir Grigoryevich Chertkóv [1854–1936], with whom Maude would later disagree over matters of biography and translation, had himself been sent into administrative exile for supporting the Doukhobórs, during which time he had lived with his wife and child at the Brotherhood Church under Kenworthy in Croydon.) Tolstoy's vigorous advocacy of their cause persuaded the Russian government to approve their emigration and, with Maude's help at the British end, some six thousand Doukhobórs left for Canada in 1899, their numbers augmented by later migrations. Maude's account of them and his involvement in their re-settlement was published as *A Peculiar People: The Doukhobórs* in New York in 1904.

The 'Maude Translations'

Because Tolstoy eschewed copyright he could raise no objections to the translations of his work. In 1883, so his son Sergéy tells us, he gave full power of attorney to his wife, Sófya Andréevna, to manage his affairs and estate, and in 1891 he relinquished copyright on anything published after 1881. He invited his publishers outside Russia to take advantage of the absence of copyright arrangements between Russia and other nations to publish his works in whatever translations they could effect without any reference to his intellectual, moral or legal rights. The consequences of this (as Maude recalled in Appendix 2, 'English Translations of Tolstoy', of *The Life of Tolstoy: First Fifty Years*, Constable, 1908) were, in literary terms, disastrous. For the English-reading market, the edition of *War and Peace* that appeared in the Everyman series was a translation by Edward Vizetelly of a French translation of Tolstoy's great novel. Vizetelly's translations of Emile Zola's novels were known to be particularly unreliable and his *War and Peace* was, at best, a paraphrase. An American translation by Nathan Haskell Dole was guilty of many grammatical and linguistic errors, but was, above all, marred by its egregious attempt to 'Americanise' Tolstoy. Constance Garnett's translations, however, were praised by Joseph Conrad and D. H. Lawrence. Her translation of *Anna Karénina* (1917) appeared a year before Maude's and in his first edition of *The Life of Tolstoy* Maude wrote positively of her work, remarking in the Appendix that 'it belongs to a different and much superior category', but he changed his mind in the light of more careful research and concluded that 'she falls short of doing Tolstoy full justice'. Later commentators, comparing her renditions of Dostoévski, Tolstoy and Turgénev, have remarked on their similarity, Mrs Garnett's making these three novelists sound the same despite the considerable differences between them in technique and narrative style. It was in an attempt to rectify what had clearly become an undesirable situation with respect to the understanding and appreciation of one of the greatest authors of the modern era that George Bernard Shaw early in 1922 wrote a letter to the English press seeking to secure a complete edition of Tolstoy's works. Signatories to the letter (which was appended to the revised edition of Maude's *The Life of Tolstoy*) included Arnold Bennett, Edward Carpenter, Jerome K. Jerome, Somerset Maugham, Sir Bernard Pares (the great English historian of imperial Russia), Arthur Rackham, H. G. Wells and Rebecca West. Shaw's letter advertised the claims that Maude had already made on the translation of Tolstoy, though he pointed out that Maude's edition was projected for the centenary of Tolstoy's birth in 1928 (under the auspices of Oxford University Press). This letter did much to promote the authority of Maude's work and to encourage his and his wife's labours. But it is better to quote Tolstoy's own judgements: in February 1901 (by which time *What is Art?* and *Resurrection*, very largely translated by Louise Maude, had appeared), he wrote of 'your and your wife's splendid translations . . .' and ten years later he added: 'the edition of your translations of my writings can only give me pleasure, because your translations are very good and I do not desire better ones . . .'

THE LIFE OF TOLSTOY

Maude's biography is not, strictly speaking, the life of a writer. Though Tolstoy's reputation as the greatest of novelists is virtually unchallenged, it rests on relatively few novels. His contemporary Fyodor Dostoévski (1821–81), for example, wrote twelve novels, and a range of novellas and short stories, whereas Tolstoy wrote only three novels (though they are works of some magnitude), if one excludes his early unfinished work, *The Cossacks*, which is closer to a novella than a novel: they are *War and Peace*, *Anna Karénina* and *Resurrection*. There are, of course, many short stories, some of them amongst the finest ever written, and works of autobiography such as *Childhood*, *Boyhood* and *Youth* that are characteristically Tolstoyan in both their intelligence and their effortless narrative pace. The publication of *Anna Karénina* in 1877 effectively marks the first stage of a major turning point in Tolstoy's personal life, and the comparative fictional 'silence' of his later years is explained by the increasing intensity of his preoccupations with religious belief and, above all, with the teachings of Christ (and, indeed, with the refutation of what he called the 'false understanding' of Christ's ministry). Accompanying this was a sense of the uselessness of art when construed entirely by way of aesthetic criteria and a growing conviction that the function of art was essentially religious. This simple fact as to how much of Tolstoy's life was *not* taken up with the writing of fiction needs restating if only to emphasise that much of what occupies Maude is not the quotidian world of a writer who goes about the business of arranging experience, real and imagined, into narrative art. Tolstoy was a public figure much as were Rudyard Kipling and George Bernard Shaw (of whose works he had a low opinion; he considered Shaw 'clever-foolish'); but whilst they enjoyed fame in the English-speaking world, Tolstoy's fame was international. Maude's account of Tolstoy's engagement with the great moral, spiritual and political challenges facing both nineteenth-century Russian society and the wider world is particularly impressive, and more than compensates for his relative lack of interest in psychological analysis and explanation and his silence about the sources of Tolstoy's creativity. This can be demonstrated by looking at Maude's account of Tolstoy's military service in the Crimea (first published in 1908 and subsequently revised for the 1930 edition) and comparing it to the treatment given to the same in Birukóv's biography of 1911, also titled *The Life of Tolstoy*. The latter's account is perfunctory and insubstantial: Biryukov wants to get Tolstoy out of the army as quickly as he can before he moves on to the more important matters of Tolstoy's writings and his educational and social activities. Maude, by contrast, despite his growing intellectual and moral attachment to Tolstoy's Christian pacifism, understands how important Tolstoy's military service was to his later life and career. Thus in his chapter on the Crimean War in Part One he writes: 'At twenty-five years of age it fell to Tolstoy's lot to take part in a great European war and extend the range of his experience in a way that considerably affected his subsequent life and writings.' Few things provide the novelist with more material than the experience of war and physical combat, and in an aristocratic society such as that of Russia in the nineteenth-century no institution other than the army would have presented Tolstoy with the variety and intensity of life he encountered first in the Caucasus, where he was initially posted, and then at Sevastopol during the famous siege of 1854. It was out of these experiences that the early writings (notably *The Sevastopol Sketches*) grew and it was, of course, the palpable contact with the futility of war that shaped his pacifism. Maude devotes nearly eighty pages to Tolstoy's army years, much of it constructed out of the extensive correspondence with his brother Sergéy and his Aunt Tatiána (their correspondence written in French); the latter had been a considerable influence on Tolstoy's life after the death of both his parents whilst he was still a child. Even though Maude is seduced by the *post hoc, ergo propter hoc* temptations of the biographer in this chapter ('if I may anticipate and speak of conclusions not definitely expressed by him till much later . . . '), he powerfully evokes both the horrors of battle and the pleasures and distractions of military life.

Maude's method is to let Tolstoy speak very much for himself, as is evidenced by the chapter on Tolstoy in the Crimea. Given the prodigious amount of autobiographical writing that Tolstoy essayed (the letters, diaries, the early sketches and *Childhood* [1852], for example), there is much from which Maude can, uncritically, quote. (The Maudes, in fact, began the task of translating Tolstoy's diaries, and a diary of the years between 1853 and 1857 was published in 1927, but the project as a whole was left incomplete at their deaths.) Maude drew extensively on Birukóv's 1906 biography (though in the appendices Maude noted the superiority of the Russian original over the English translation) and on the work of Nikolai Nikolaévich Gúsev, whom Chertkóv had recommended as Tolstoy's secretary in his declining years and who resided on the estate at Yásnaya Polyána. Gúsev's *Lev Nikolaévich Tolstoi, 1828-1862* was published in Moscow in 1927; Maude, of course consulted the work in the Russian. But for a good deal of our time in reading *The Life of Tolstoy* we hear the words of its protagonist. This trust in the authenticity and sincerity of the written (and in some cases spoken) words of his subject might seem naïve, for modern biography is eager to challenge our assumption that there is an easy correspondence between what one says about oneself and what one did, and what is true. Tolstoy himself recognised this. Writing in 1902 to P. (Pavel) I. Birukóv, who had broached the matter of his writing a life of Tolstoy, he spoke of the Charybdis of self-praise and the Scylla of cynical frankness that discolour autobiographical reminiscence. Tolstoy, was painfully aware of the ways in which the lives of great men might frequently disappoint us when we learn of the shabbiness (often sexual) that accompanies greatness. 'People will say,' he wrote to Birukóv, 'there's a man whom many people rate highly, and look at what a scoundrel he was!' Unsurprisingly, the novelist in Tolstoy is acutely aware of the lack of correspondence between the self we present to society and the inner self uniquely revealed in fiction. The sentiment, however, can be rephrased by way of Dr Johnson's observation that it comforts us to learn that the eminent experience many of the same difficulties and discomforts in life that we do. Tolstoy was convinced of 'the insincerity which is characteristic of every biography', but he conceived of biography in nineteenth-century terms, as something hagiographical rather than biographical: the lives of great men put on a pedestal for others to emulate, biography, in other words, as *exempla*. Maude follows the Victorian convention of 'Life and Letters' but despite the absence of anything that could be construed as 'Freudian' or psychoanalytic, any appeal to the unconscious in other words, in his account of Tolstoy Maude anticipates in several ways the practices of the modern biographer.

Despite his immense admiration for Tolstoy and his relentless dedication to the promotion of his works, Maude retained a disinterested and impartial view both of his life and his work, and his imaginative writings. Maude's experience of the experiments in communal living with the Brotherhood Church communities in Croydon and Purleigh taught him to be sceptical of the practical applicability of many of Tolstoy's social and economic teachings, and of his involvement with the Doukhobórs he remarks that he found the 'Tolstoyans' the least administratively efficient of all the groups with which he dealt (his account can also be found in Part Two of the biography). To those who say of Tolstoy's fiction (particularly of *Anna Karénina* and *War and Peace*), 'All human life is there', Maude had a cogent response. Himself a man of a mercantile background, he notes:

> What Tolstoy does not show us is what he did not know – the middle-class world: the world of merchants, manufacturers, engineers, and men of business. Of course these in Russia a hundred years ago played a comparatively small part; there was practically no political activity such as that of our County Councils, Borough Councils and Parliament. But that all this was absent from Tolstoy's mind, and that his outlook on life was confined to the aristocracy which consumed and the peasantry which produced will . . . help us to understand the social teaching to which he ultimately came.

(Anton Chékhov, who greatly admired Tolstoy, criticised his prejudiced portrayal of doctors, something which he attributed to Tolstoy's ignorance of the medical profession.) Maude was a 'Westerner', whereas Tolstoy's criticism of Western values (dramatised particularly well, as E. B. Greenwood has demonstrated, in the short story 'Lucerne', first published in 1857) increasingly took on a Slavophil character, with its emphasis on the superiority of the mystical over the rational, the superiority of peasant intelligence to that of the educated, the rejection of individualism and the rejection of industrialisation. As he remarks in Part One in his discussion of Tolstoy's educational work, 'That he had been somewhat influenced by the Slavophils is indicated by his readiness to assume that Russia may advance along a line of her own entirely different from the one Western nations have travelled.' Tolstoy's adoption of peasant dress in his later years (Ilya Répin's famous full-length painting of 1901, 'A Portrait of Tolstoy', brilliantly evokes this; one of his more intimate portraits of Tolstoy is to be found on the cover of this edition) is among the more obvious outward signs of his anti-Western thinking. Maude was critical of Tolstoy's wholesale rejection of politics and attempts at social and economic reform. He recognised that modern society was becoming increasingly technical and managerial, and that the growth of an administrative class (a civil service) was a necessary condition of the governance of complex societies. Tolstoy dismissed this outright as can be memorably evidenced in Part 7 of *Anna Karénina* when Kitty thinks of how her husband, Levin (the closest Tolstoy comes in his fiction to an autobiographical portrait), seems restless and on his guard in the town, whereas on his estate, among his family and the peasants, his life is harmonious and ennobling. The town, of course, embodies government bureaucracy (the *Dúma*, which, in the nineteenth-century, were the elected municipal parliaments) and the trappings of high society. In Part Two of the biography Maude recalls some impassioned correspondence with Tolstoy in which he argued the virtues of incremental constitutional change and his conviction that Western liberal democracies had done much to foster 'a juster and kindlier society . . .'

*   *   *

It would be churlish to criticise Maude for the errors and *lacunae* in *The Life of Tolstoy*. Whilst biography, like most of the arts, can't be said to *progress* it is unavoidable for the work of one biographer not to build on the achievements of another, even if the 'building' is a matter of correction and emendation. The biographer is, moreover, no matter how hard he or she tries to evade it, just another first-person. Maude was a member of the Fabian Society, one of the pre-eminent intellectual movements in the United Kingdom advocating the transition to a form of full socialism by gradualist, as opposed to revolutionary, means. He was particularly active for the Fabians during the years 1907 to 1912 when he was a member of the society's executive, the very years during which the first edition of his *Life* appeared, and some of this attachment to rational and scientific reform of society and its institutions, as I have shown, colours his account of Tolstoy's anti-political, anti-economic thinking. This can't be faulted as such, but the modern reader might find it intrusive and in-appropriately evaluative. He reads the fiction, above all, for what it contributes to our understanding of Tolstoy's ideas and what it con-tributes to biographical knowledge; his approach to it, by and large, is descriptive. He is not a particularly good literary critic but, it might be argued, it is unfair to expect him to be, and he maintains a judicious, 'Johnsonian' distance between the biographical enterprise, which has its own intrinsic interests, and the critical one. More importantly, how-ever, Maude is somewhat weak as an intellectual historian, though here he is in the company of many of his Tolstoyan contemporaries. It was

Sir Isaiah Berlin who pointed out that many of Tolstoy's commentators, among them Birukóv, Stefan Zweig, Derrick Leon and, of
course, Maude himself, were strangely silent about the theory of history
articulated in *War and Peace* (notably in the First and Second Epilogue,
but also dramatised in the novel itself) and of the degree to which
his thinking about human nature and society was influenced by the
writings of Joseph de Maistre (1753–1821), the Savoyard lawyer noted
for his reactionary Catholicism, his counter-revolutionary arguments,
and his defence of the *status quo* during the years of the Bourbon
Restoration. More recent biographies, for example those of Troyat and
Wilson, attach greater importance to Tolstoy's reading of de Maistre.
There is, finally, an over-arching aspect of *The Life of Tolstoy* that needs
to be briefly addressed, one that both explains its strengths and its
weaknesses. Maude knew Tolstoy. As I have remarked, he was thirty
years Tolstoy's junior: when they met in 1888 Maude was thirty and
Tolstoy was sixty. The great fictional achievements of *War and Peace*
(1865–9) and *Anna Karénina* (1877) were already past and Tolstoy was
at the height of his international fame as a writer (Tolstoy belongs to a
very élite company, that of the artist whose works are known to his
contemporaries to be destined for greatness and permanence, something not known, for example, to Shakespeare, but known to Mozart).
The situation is akin to that of James Boswell when he met Samuel
Johnson and the temptation to feel flattered by the indulgence of those
who are already eminent can often colour the biographical record. The
biographer's interest in his subject naturally arises from the position of
importance that his subject has arrived at and the life is, as it were, read
backwards for genetic explanations of present conditions and circumstances. Maude is theoretically unexercised about the advantages
and disadvantages of knowing his subject, and the necessarily selective
nature of his subject's recollections. Broadly speaking he seems to
concur with Johnson's remark to Boswell that no one can write the
life of a man 'but those who have eat and drunk and lived in social
intercourse with him'. This proximity leads Maude to speak, somewhat
unreflectively, in his Author's Preface of his being 'qualified' to write
Tolstoy's life, as if not knowing him were, somehow, a *dis*qualification,
and to advert to his impartiality.

It is, as we have seen, a certain kind of 'Western' scepticism about
Tolstoy's ideas that keeps *The Life of Tolstoy* insulated from the provoc-
ations towards hagiography. In his Author's Preface, Maude writes 'of

certain things that Tolstoy overlooked which seem to knock big holes in some of his cherished "principles" '. This scepticism gathers particularly for Maude around Tolstoy's conviction as to the immorality of government and most forms of political organisation, and the futility of attempts at constitutional change. 'To most of us in the Western world,' Maude asserts, 'such a thesis appears quite unreasonable.' Even Maude's agreement with Tolstoy about the immorality of war – 'I regard it as on a par with slavery, duelling, and cannibalism . . . ' – did not persuade him that Tolstoy's advocacy of the non-payment of taxes and refusal of military service were commendable or desirable actions, for this 'has the grave disadvantage that if successful it would disintegrate the state, and if attempted by all humane people, would throw the control of affairs into the hands of those who were not humane'. Maude understands that it is the essential intractability of nineteenth-century Russian society, its resistance to most forms of ameliorative constitutional and social reform, that informs Tolstoy's views of political and socio-economic change, but he intelligently points to the intellectual weakness of this stance in his chapter on the Doukhobórs in Part Two, contrasting Tolstoy's 'impulsive, strenuous nature and his tendency to theorise . . . ' with Jane Addams' 'practical American character . . . ' and her successes in improving the condition of the poor in the Chicago of the 1890s and early 1900s (Addams was a social reformer; she visited Tolstoy at Yásnaya Polyána in 1896). Maude's critique of the impracticability of many of Tolstoy's ideas (it comes across, particularly, in his accounts of the emigration of the Doukhobórs and of the collapse of the communitarian experiment at Purleigh) may seem devastating to many readers but it is made quite independently of the moral and spiritual intelligence that went into the articulation of the ideas themselves.

A striking feature of the revised biography of 1930 is the degree to which the revision had been shaped by the monumental events of October 1917. The details of the revision cannot be explored at any length here but one example of Maude's attitude to the Russian Revolution can be found in his 'Editor's Note' to the translation of *The Kingdom of God and Peace Essays* (1935) in the Tolstoy Centenary Edition. Here he reminds us that these works are banned both in Stalin's Soviet Union and Hitler's Germany, and that Tolstoy's protests 'against the suppression of personal freedom and of liberty of the press and of speech . . . ' are now more urgent than when they were written. At the time of writing the first edition (1908–1910), Maude had only the most indistinct adumbration of the way in which Russian society would change. However, he was acutely aware of the impact the defeat of Russia in the war with Japan in 1904–05 would have on popular political sentiment and attitudes to Tsar Nicholas II.

*　　*　　*

Despite our now knowing so much more about Tolstoy, both his works and his world, and the exponential growth of our knowledge of Russian society through the period of the late nineteenth-century and the Russian Revolution that has resulted from the access to archival resources in Moscow and St Petersburg following the collapse of Soviet communism, Maude's biography remains a work of prodigious and compelling scholarship. It is a work of immense detail, the accuracy of which has been subsequently attended by little in the way of correction or emendation. There have, of course, been interpretive differences with Maude's account and, as we have seen, some enlargement of both the social and the intellectual historical contexts of Tolstoy's life and work. But in most substantive respects Maude's biography remains unchallenged. It impresses, most notably, for its communication of a moral intelligence that in many ways seems coextensive with that of its subject. This is felt most forcefully at the end of the concluding chapter, where, having reported on the details of Tolstoy's death, Maude writes: 'The love and gratitude that followed him were abundantly earned, for if he was dogmatic – and the letter killeth – he was inspired, and the spirit giveth life.' The French critic Sainte-Beuve said of the writings of François-René de Chateaubriand, one of the central figures of French Romanticism, that he could enjoy the work, but 'found it hard to judge in isolation from the man who wrote it'. For the modern reader *The Life of Tolstoy* bridges the gap between the great Russian novelist and the life he led, and movingly evokes a man whom his biographer found of a 'heroic, inflexible, and profoundly religious nature'.

Further Reading

John Bayley, *Tolstoy and the Novel*, Chatto & Windus, London, 1966

Isaiah Berlin, *Russian Thinkers*, The Hogarth Press, London, 1978

Paul Birukoff, *The Life of Tolstoy*, Cassell, London, 1911

R. F. Christian, *Tolstoy: A Critical Introduction*, Cambridge University Press, Cambridge, 1969

R. F. Christian (ed.), *Tolstoy's Diaries*, 2 vols, Charles Scribner's Sons, New York, 1985

R. F. Christian (ed.), *Tolstoy's Letters*, 2 vols, Athlone Press, London, 1978

Henry Gifford, *Tolstoy*, Oxford University Press ('Past Masters' Series), Oxford, 1982

E. B. Greenwood, *Tolstoy: The Comprehensive Vision*, J. M. Dent, London, 1975

Michael J. Holman, 'Half a Life's Work: Aylmer Maude brings Tolstoy to Britain', *Scottish Slavonic Review*, 4 (Spring, 1988), pp. 39–53

Malcolm Jones (ed.), *New Essays on Tolstoy*, Cambridge University Press, New York, 1978

Derrick Leon, *Tolstoy : His Life and Work*, Routledge, London, 1944

Hugh McLean (ed.), *In the Shade of the Giant: Essays on Tolstoy*, University of California Press, Berkeley, 1989

Aylmer Maude, *Tolstoy and His Problems*, G. Richards, London, 1901

Ernest J. Simmons, *Leo Tolstoy*, Little Brown, Boston, 1946

Ernest J. Simmons, *Introduction to Tolstoy's Writings*, University of Chicago Press, Chicago, 1968

George Steiner, *Tolstoy or Dostoevsky*, Faber & Faber, London, 1960

Leo Tolstoy, *Anna Karenina* (translated by Louise and Aylmer Maude), Wordsworth Classics, Ware, Hertfordshire, 1995

Leo Tolstoy, *War and Peace* (translated by Louise and Aylmer Maude), Wordsworth Classics, Ware, Hertfordshire, 2004

Nikolai Tolstoy, *The Tolstoys: Twenty-Four Generations of Russian History, 1353–1983*, Hamish Hamilton, London, 1983

Henri Troyat, *Tolstoy* (translated by Nancy Amphoux), Doubleday & Company, New York, 1967

Edward Wasiolek, *Tolstoy's Major Fiction*, University of Chicago Press, Chicago, 1978

A. N. Wilson, *Tolstoy*, Hamish Hamilton, London, 1988

THE LIFE OF TOLSTOY

Author's Preface to the Revised Edition

I wrote this book because so many people are interested in Tolstoy and so few seem to understand him. An English *Life* of him seems therefore to be needed, and having lived in Russia for twenty-three years, known Tolstoy well for several years, visited him often in Moscow and stayed with him repeatedly at Yásnaya Polyána, I am perhaps qualified to write it, especially as I have made a long and careful study of his views. My wife and I have translated most of his works, have known people closely connected with him, and have taken part in an unsuccessful 'Tolstoy' Colony; I also went to Canada at his wish to arrange the Doukhobór migration of which I subsequently wrote the history.

Moreover I am impartial. That is to say, I have taken pains to understand Tolstoy's views and to recognise the good in them, but being a Westerner, I am also aware of certain things Tolstoy overlooked which seem to knock big holes in some of his cherished 'principles'.

To my first *Life of Tolstoy*, which appeared in 1908 and 1910, Tolstoy himself contributed a good deal of matter, and it had the advantage of being carefully revised by his wife, Countess S. A. Tolstoy, who rendered me assistance both verbally and in writing: I have now cordially to thank his eldest daughter, Countess Tatiána Tolstoy (Madame Sukhotín), for very kindly reading and correcting the present amended work.

I owe thanks also to my friend P. I. Birukóv, Tolstoy's Russian biographer, and to N. N. Gúsev, of whose very reliable and careful works, *Tolstoy in Youth* and *Tolstoy in the Flower of his Artistic Genius*, I have made free use. Tolstoy has been fortunate in both his Russian biographers, who have dealt with the facts of his life clearly and conscientiously. If they and I do not see eye to eye on some of his later opinions, the difference probably arises chiefly from the fact that I am English while they are Russian.

There is a matter of typography which needs some explanation. I have sought to tell as much of the story as possible in Tolstoy's own words, and have had occasion to quote other writers. At times the Russian text quoted contains allusions or expressions which might perplex an English reader unless a word or two of explanation were added. To introduce paragraphs of explanation would interrupt the narrative, besides lengthening the book. To have recourse to frequent footnotes, in cases where two or three words of explanation are all that is required, is unsightly and unsatisfactory; so I have adopted the plan of using square brackets [ ] to enclose such explanations or where, for clearness' sake, words are added that are not contained in the original. The ordinary round parentheses ( ) I have kept for their common use.

In its first form this book was published while Tolstoy was still alive. Some brief account of his home-leaving and death was introduced in subsequent editions, but they were not dealt with in due proportion to the rest of the narrative, or in a way to show the tragic influence his 'principles' had on the final event.

Much has been published about him since he died and additional matter is incorporated in these volumes; but I have not found many errors to correct. The difficulty of making room for the new matter and for a fuller account of his last days within the existing limits, has chiefly been met by omitting passages quoted from translations now available, to which I have referred the reader where necessary.

The years that have passed since the work first appeared have confirmed my belief in the importance of understanding Tolstoy's outlook on religion, social problems, art, and life generally. He was not always right, but he was always thoughtful, and stated important matters plainly and impressively. No writer of comparable power has handled so wide a range of great questions so profoundly, sincerely, and persuasively. To follow his thought, broadens and deepens our comprehension of life, and if at times we are forced to join issue with him and to find reasons for this disagreement, the effort is valuable and invigorating.

To be able to say this much of one who stands in the forefront of the world's novelists, dramatists and short-story writers, is to claim for him an amazing range both as artist and as thinker, but the claim is fully justified.

While still a young officer fighting in Sevastopol, he was keenly conscious of man's need of guidance in life and of the impossibility of any one man supplying all that is needed.

A conversation about Divinity and Faith [he wrote in his Diary] has suggested to me a great, a stupendous idea, to the realisation of which I feel myself capable of devoting my life. This idea is the founding of a new religion corresponding to the present state of mankind . . . a practical religion . . . giving bliss on earth. I understand that to accomplish this the conscious labour of generations will be needed. One generation will bequeath the idea to the next, and someday fanaticism or reason will accomplish it. Deliberately to promote the union of mankind by religion – that is the basic thought which, I hope, will dominate me.

Those words were written before he was twenty-seven. His subsequently expressed outlook on life and indictment of war were in keeping with that early aspiration, and did more than was done by any other man of his time to prepare men's minds for the League of Nations and such proposals as Mr Kellogg put forward to cause wars to cease.

Tolstoy's ardour and truthfulness were such that his life and works continually acted and reacted on one another. We cannot fully appreciate or understand his works without knowing his life, and the story of his life must be told with constant reference to his books.

His desire was that truth should prevail over error, and the ultimate achievement of that aim depends on the number and quality of those who with like sincerity and independence of mind co-operate in the pursuit of that purpose, neither credulously accepting nor lightly rejecting the guidance he offered, but thinking with their own heads and accepting or rejecting as their reason demands.

AYLMER MAUDE
Great Baddow,
Chelmsford
12th July 1930

Author's Note to the Revised Edition

Much fresh information about Tolstoy has appeared since the issue of the first edition of my *Life of Tolstoy* just before Tolstoy's death, and Countess S. A. Tolstoy's *Later Diary* in particular has caused me to add much fresh matter.

Her *Diary*, though valuable as a corrective of some misapprehensions, is so biassed that it has occasioned much misconception. An illustration of this has quite recently presented itself, and may be cited, not as a specially glaring example but as a characteristic instance of the way in which many English writers are inclined to treat Tolstoy, as an artistic genius but a poor thinker – a man of such inferior intellectual calibre that they can only treat him *de haut en bas*. Several journalists have adopted that attitude, and shown as much ignorance of the subject and as lively an imagination as the writer of the article here referred to. The following letter explains itself.

To the Editor of the *Daily Express*

SIR – That legends should grow up around great men is perhaps natural, but it is a curious experience to see them grow before our eyes.

As I was just completing my *Life of Tolstoy*, I noted some statements in Mr St John Ervine's article on Tolstoy in your paper which conflict with the information at my disposal. He says: 'Her [the Countess's] house was continually occupied by the "dark ones", a motley gang who fed Tolstoy's vanity and devoured his substance.' The house belonged to the Countess, who refused to admit Tolstoy's chief friend and was quite capable of not admitting anyone she disliked. There never was any 'motley gang' at Yásnaya Polyána to 'devour his substance', and the 'hordes of hungry disciples to be fed and housed' are an invention. 'He pretended to live like a peasant' is untrue. Tolstoy never lived or pretended to live like a peasant.

The statement that Tolstoy 'actually made a spade to dig up a cornfield because a plough was much too sophisticated an implement to use' cannot be substantiated. It is apparently based on a mistranslation in the recently published book *The Countess Tolstoy's Later*

Diary, where her remark: 'He has got a spade ready and wants to dig the ground' has been mistranslated into, 'He has now manufactured a spade and wants to dig up a cornfield.' This is an excellent example of the evolution of legend by a series of errors no one of which aimed at mendacity.

Yours truly,

AYLMER MAUDE

No fact relating to Tolstoy is more firmly established than that he was very fond of ploughing and regarded it as an excellent exercise and occupation. From *Anna Karenina* to *Essays and Letters* we have abundant evidence of this, apart from the incidents and conversations recorded in the present volume. The critic, however, alleges that Tolstoy considered the plough 'too sophisticated an implement to use'. An irritable entry in the wife's *Diary*, when in her eyes anything Tolstoy did was wrong, exaggerated by a mistranslation such as easily occurs in a book of the kind, is seized on by a critic who embroiders it and from his inner consciousness supplies a curious explanation of a non-existent fact.

To me who try to enable the English-reading public to see Tolstoy as he was, every fresh legend about him circulated in a widely distributed newspaper is regrettable. Tolstoy's work will certainly endure after much of the rubbish now piled up to obscure it from our view has been forgotten; but fantastic legends, such as this of Tolstoy as a metalworker who 'actually made a spade', or as a man 'who pretended to live like a peasant', are apt to endure. They have a strong appeal to the credulous and infantile elements in human nature, and belong to the domain of the father of lies.

Mr St John Ervine has himself very kindly written an introduction for one of the volumes of the Tolstoy Centenary Edition, and I hope I have made it plain that even in the article above referred to he has done no worse than many other critics, for Countess Tolstoy's *Diary* furnished a series of traps into which it must have been hard for any reviewer not well acquainted with Tolstoy and his work to avoid falling.

I owe cordial thanks to Tolstoy's eldest daughter, Madame Tatiana Sukhotín-Tolstoy, for help she has rendered me in the preparation of this book, and to Miss Helen Jessiman, whose assistance I have found very useful. I am also grateful to Mr A. C. Fifield for expert proofreading as well as for useful comments and to Miss L. E. Elliott, Secretary of the Tolstoy Society, for many excellent suggestions.

AYLMER MAUDE
Great Baddow,
Chelmsford
12th July 1930

Note on the Pronunciation of Russian Names

The spelling of Russian names in Latin letters in a work of this kind presents difficulties.

On the one hand a man has a right to decide how he will have his name spelt, but on the other hand the employment of different systems of transliteration in one book tends to confusion.

I have, in general, followed the transliteration scheme of the British Academy. In pronouncing the names the reader should note the following:

1   Stress the syllable marked with an accent.

2   Vowel sounds are broad and open:
    a as in f*a*ther.
    e as *a* in f*a*te, but *e* initial and unaccented is pronounced *ye*.
    ë as *yo* in *yo*lk.
    i as *ee* in m*ee*t.
    o as in l*o*ch.
    u as *oo* in b*oo*t.
    In diphthongs the broad sounds are retained:
    ya as *in ya*rd,
    ye as in *ye*s.
    yo as in *yo*re.
    yu as *u* in *u*sury.
    ay as *eye*.
    ey as in th*ey*
    oy as in b*oy*.

3   *y* with a vowel forms a diphthong. It also stands for the difficult Russian letter Ы which sounds something like *we* thickly pronounced.

4   Consonants:
    g is hard, as in *g*o.
    zh is like *z* in a*z*ure.
    r is sounded strongly, as in *r*ough, ba*rr*en.
    s is sharp, as in *s*eat, pa*ss*.

PART ONE

THE FIRST FIFTY YEARS

I

Ancestry and Parentage

Count Leo Tolstoy was born on 28th August (old style)* 1828, on the estate of Yásnaya Polyána (Clear Glade) in the province of Túla, about a hundred and thirty miles south of Moscow.

In the annals of the Russian nobility it is recorded that a man named Indris came from 'the lands of Caesar', that is to say, from the Holy Roman Empire, in the year 1353 with two sons and three thousand followers, and settling at Chernígov in the Ukraine was received with favour by the reigning Grand Duke, who granted him much land. A great-grandson of his, Andrew by name, migrated to Moscow, where he was well received by the reigning Grand Duke Vasíli (1435–62), who conferred upon him the surname of Tolstoy.

As, however, the annals of the Russian nobility were to a large extent concocted about the time of Peter the Great, it is doubtful whether this story is true. Be that as it may, it is certain that Peter Tolstoy, born in 1645, distinguished himself in the service of the State. During the struggles which preceded the acquisition of power by Peter the Great he made the mistake of allying himself with that autocrat's ambitious half-sister, Sophia. The defeat of her Guards, the Streltsí, caused him quickly to transfer his allegiance to Peter, whose favour he eventually managed to secure. When drinking with his chosen companions in later days, the Tsar would often pat Tolstoy's head, saying, 'Head, head, it would have been time for you to come off your shoulders long ago, had you not been so clever.'

---

* Till the Revolution, Russia retained the old-style calendar, abandoned in England since 1752. There was, therefore, a twelve days' difference during the nineteenth century, and the Russian 1st January was our 13th January. In the twentieth century the difference increased to thirteen days. In this book the dates are given old style, except in the chapter telling of his travels in western Europe, where (as there mentioned) the new style is adopted.

This Peter Tolstoy held a commission in the Guards and fought in the Azov campaign of 1696, but later on was sent abroad by Peter to study shipbuilding. In 1701 he was sent as Ambassador to the Sublime Porte, and when war broke out between Turkey and Russia in 1710, he twice suffered imprisonment, for nearly two years in all, in the Seven Towers – the stronghold wherein the Sultan occasionally confined the ambassadors of States with whose conduct he felt dissatisfied. Returning to Russia in 1714, Tolstoy obtained the favour of Prince Ménshikov and became a Minister of State. He accompanied Peter the Great to Holland and France, and did him an important though discreditable service. Peter the Great's son, the refractory Aléxis, who disliked his father's reforms, had escaped from Russia and was living with his mistress Euphrosyne at St Elmo, near Naples. By threats and promises, and by the aid of this woman, Tolstoy induced the unfortunate Tsarévich to return to Russia, and when he had got him there took a leading part in his trial and secret execution.

For this service Tolstoy received large estates and was promoted to the headship of the Secret Chancellery.

On the day of the coronation of Peter's second wife, Catherine [August 30th 1725], Tolstoy became a Count. His coat of arms shows seven towers, in memory of his imprisonment by the Sultan, and is appropriately supported by two wolfhounds rampant, looking outwards.

On the death of Peter the Great, Tolstoy actively supported Ménshikov in securing the throne for Catherine I, and was one of the seven members of the Upper Secret Council which practically ruled Russia. On the question of choosing a successor to Catherine he ventured, however, to oppose Ménshikov. The latter was too powerful for him, and, forfeiting his title of Count and deprived of all offices, rewards and estates, Tolstoy, at the age of eighty-two, was banished to the Solovéts Monastery on an island in the White Sea [May 6th 1727]. Here, two years later, he died. Ménshikov himself, one may remark in passing, finished his life that same year in Siberia, having been banished by an order signed by the boy he had placed on the throne. To be a Russian Minister of State in those days was almost as dangerous as it would be today, in Russia, to oppose the Dictatorship of the Proletariate.

The title of Count was revived in the family in 1760 for the benefit of Peter Tolstoy's grandson, Andrew, who while still a youth married a Princess, Shchetínin, who bore him twenty-three children. One of these was Count Ilyá Tolstoy who figures in *War and Peace* as the elder Count

Rostóv. He married a Princess Gorchakóv and was Leo Tolstoy's grandfather.

There is one matter it may be as well to explain at the outset, as English readers are often puzzled by it: I refer to Russian titles of nobility, which have been abolished since the Revolution, but often occur in this book and in Tolstoy's works. The only really Russian title is that of *Knyaz*, commonly translated 'Prince'. It was borne by descendants of Rúrik, by descendants of the Lithuanian Prince Ghedimín, and by descendants of various Tartar Khans whose dominions Russia annexed. It was also conferred by Imperial Decree on a dozen or more other Russian families. Though *Knyaz* is translated 'Prince', *Velíki Knyaz*, curiously enough, is not translated 'Great Prince', but 'Grand Duke', and this indicates how difficult it is to find suitable equivalents for these titles. Not till the time of Peter the Great were the German titles, Count (*Graf*) and Baron, introduced into Russia. Both of these became common among the Russo-German landlords of the Baltic Provinces, but less so among real Russians.

It must be borne in mind that there was no law of primogeniture in Russia. Each son and daughter inherited the family title, so that there were usually several, and sometimes many, people with equal rights to the same title. Though springing from one stock they might be but distantly connected. There were, for instance, other Counts Tolstoy, contemporaries of Leo Tolstoy and distant cousins of his. One of these, his third cousin the poet Count Aléxis Tolstoy, was a well-known author and dramatist. Many other members of the family were also writers or artists.

Tolstoy's grandfather already mentioned, Count Ilyá Tolstoy, was an easy-going, generous, trustful, and extravagant man, who married a wealthy Princess Gorchakóv, but ran through her money and his own, and at last, to secure a means of livelihood, procured the post of Governor of Kazán. This he was able to do thanks to his family influence. It is recorded to his credit that, contrary to the general custom of the time, he accepted no bribes (except from the Government contractor, who was considered the natural financial prop of a Provincial Governor), though his wife accepted presents without his knowledge. His son, Count Nicholas Tolstoy, was Leo Tolstoy's father. Ilyá Tolstoy's career as Governor came to an unhappy conclusion. The representatives of the nobility of the province were hostile to him and denounced him to Alexander I's all-powerful Minister Arakhchéev. A committee of investigation was appointed which was controlled by personal enemies of his, and as a result of their report, on 5th February 1820, an Imperial decree was issued dismissing Count Ilyá Tolstoy from his post. He was so distressed by this that he fell ill and died within a month. No serious misconduct was in fact proved against him, beyond the fact that he had borrowed 5,000 rubles of Treasury money, which it was illegal to do. There were probably few provincial Governors of the time against whom more serious offences could not have been proved.

The Tolstoys were a prolific family. Klyuchévski, the historian, told Tolstoy's wife that of all the families ennobled under Peter the Great and Catherine the Great they were the only family that had survived.

Count Ilyá Tolstoy's eldest daughter married a Count Osten-Saken. She became guardian to Leo Tolstoy and his brothers and sister after the loss of their parents. Another daughter married V. I. Yúshkov, and Leo Tolstoy was under her charge when he lived in Kazán and studied at that University.

The first fact known to us about Leo Tolstoy's father is characteristic of the manners of his class and day. When he was only sixteen his parents arranged a *liaison* between him and a peasant girl, such connections being considered necessary for the health of young men. A son was born, and Tolstoy records his 'strange feeling of consternation when (in after years) this brother of mine, fallen into destitution and bearing a greater resemblance to my father than any of us, used to beg help of us and was thankful for the ten or fifteen rubles we used to give him'.

Nicholas Tolstoy was not yet eighteen when Napoleon invaded Russia; but despite his parents' efforts to dissuade him, he insisted on entering the army. He went through the campaigns of 1813 in Germany, and on his way to rejoin the army after being sent with dispatches to his mother's cousin, Prince Gorchakóv, Minister of War, in Petersburg, he and his orderly were captured by the French. The orderly managed to hide his master's gold coins in his boots, and for months never risked taking them off, though his feet grew sore and he suffered extreme discomfort. Thanks to this devotion, Nicholas Tolstoy, after reaching Paris, was able to live in comfort.

After the war was over Nicholas was appointed Adjutant to Prince Andrew Gorchakóv, a General in command, and a brother of the Minister of War. The family connection with the Gorchakóvs was, later on, of use to Leo Tolstoy at the time of the Crimean War.

Nicholas retired in 1819 with the rank of Lieutenant-Colonel, and entered the Civil Service, in which he served till January 1824.

Count Ilyá, on his death in 1820, left his estate so encumbered that his son declined to accept the inheritance. The young man had to face the task of providing for his old mother who was accustomed to great luxury, as well as for a sister and a distant cousin, Tatiána Alexándrovna Érgolski, who had been adopted into the family; and so his relations arranged a marriage for him with the wealthy but plain Princess Márya Volkónski.

His father's life, Tolstoy tells us, was then

passed in attending to the estate, a business in which he was not very expert but in which he exercised a virtue great for those days: he avoided cruelty, and even perhaps lacked firmness. During his lifetime I never heard of corporal punishment. If it ever was administered to the serfs the cases were so rare and my father took so little part in them that we children never heard them mentioned. It was after his death that I learnt for the first time that such punishment ever took place at home.

Like most men who served in the army in the early years of Alexander's reign, he [Count Nicholas Tolstoy] was not what is now called a Liberal, but out of self-respect he considered it impossible to serve during the latter [reactionary] part of Alexander's reign, or under Nicholas I. During all my childhood and youth our family had no intimate relations with any Government official. I of course understood nothing about this in childhood, but I understood that my father never humbled himself before anyone, nor altered his brisk, merry, and often chaffing tone. This feeling of self-respect which I witnessed in him increased my love and admiration for him.

Leo Tolstoy's mother's family, the Volkónskis, were descendants from Rúrik (the first ruler mentioned in Russian history) as well as from St Michael the martyr, Prince of Chernígov; and through them, even more than on his father's side, Tolstoy was connected with many of the leading families of the Russian aristocracy. Prince Nicholas Volkónski, his mother's father, came into conflict with the most powerful of the favourites of Catherine the Great. Tolstoy tells us that 'having attained the high position of *Général en Chef*, he lost it suddenly by refusing to marry Potëmkin's niece and mistress, Varvára Engelhardt. To

Potëmkin's suggestion that he should do so, he replied: "What makes him think I will marry his strumpet?" '

There is, however, some mistake here, for Volkónski did not attain the rank of *Général en Chef* under Catherine the Great, but later under Paul, when Potëmkin was no longer in power. He served as an officer in the Turkish campaign of 1780, and as Ambassador-Extraordinary at Berlin in 1793, and he was actually dismissed from the army in 1797 by Paul for failing to attend a review. He was readmitted eighteen months later and appointed Military Governor of Archangel. There he served for less than a year, and, after reaching the rank of *Général en Chef* in June 1799, retired into private life in November and settled on his estate of Yásnaya Polyána, where he died in 1821.

He had married a Princess Catherine Trubetskóy. She died in 1799, leaving her husband an only daughter nine years of age, who was Tolstoy's mother. This Princess Trubetskóy, who was Tolstoy's grandmother, was also the great-granddaughter of a certain Márya Glébova, the poet Púshkin's great-great-grandmother, so that Tolstoy was Púshkin's third cousin once removed.

Tolstoy writes of his grandfather, Prince N. Volkónski:

He was regarded as a very exacting master, but I never heard any instance of his being cruel or inflicting the severe punishments usual in those days. I believe such things did happen on his estate, but the enthusiastic respect for his importance and cleverness was so great among the servants and peasants whom I have often questioned about him, that though I have heard my father condemned, I have heard only praise of my grandfather's intelligence, business capacity, and interest in the welfare both of the peasants and of his enormous household.

Later, a strange chance brought Prince Volkónski again into touch with Varvára Engelhardt whom he had refused to marry. She married a Prince Sergéy Golítsin, who consequently received promotions and decorations and rewards; and Tolstoy tells us: 'With this Sergéy Golítsin and his family my grandfather formed so close a friendship that my mother from her childhood was betrothed to one of his ten sons . . . This alliance, however, was not destined to be consummated, for the young man died prematurely of fever.'

In a portrait of Prince N. Volkónski, which has been preserved, there is much that corresponds to Leo Tolstoy's own appearance. 'Both,' as his brother-in-law remarks, 'have high, open foreheads and large organs of the creative faculty, and in both the organs of musical talent are exceedingly prominent and are covered by thick overhanging eyebrows, from beneath which small, deep-set grey eyes pierce the soul of the man on whom they are turned.'

It was after his death that his daughter Márya married Count Nicholas Tolstoy, who was then twenty-eight, she being thirty-two [1822]. Her dowry included 800 serfs, as well as the estate of Yásnaya Polyána. In *War and Peace* Tolstoy has described her – as he pictured her to himself from what he heard from relations and servants and could learn from her letters and diary – as Princess Márya. He tells us in his *Reminiscences*:

> I do not remember my mother. I was a year and a half old when she died. [He was actually nearly two.] By some strange chance no portrait of her has been preserved, so that as a real physical being I cannot picture her to myself. I am in a way glad of this for in my conception of her there is only her spiritual figure and all that I know about her is beautiful. I think this has come about not merely because all who spoke to me of my mother tried to say only what was good, but because there actually was much good in her.

She was well educated, spoke five languages, played the piano well, and had a wonderful gift for improvising tales in the most delightful manner. It is said that at balls her young lady friends would leave the dance and gather in a dark room to hear her tell a story, which shyness induced her to do where she could not be seen. Tolstoy remarks that 'her most valuable quality was that they hot-tempered she was yet self-restrained. "She would get quite red in the face and even cry," her maid told me, "but would never say a rude word." ' She had in particular one quality Tolstoy valued very highly – that of never condemning anyone. It was a characteristic shared by her eldest son, Nicholas; and Leo Tolstoy says: 'In the *Lives of the Saints* by D. Rostóvski, there is a short story which has always touched me exceedingly, of a certain monk who to the knowledge of all his brethren had many faults, but whom an old monk, in a dream, saw occupying a place of honour among the saints. The old man asked in astonishment, "How could this monk, so unrestrained in many ways, deserve so great a reward?" The answer was: "He never condemned anyone." '

Tolstoy adds: 'If such rewards did exist, I think my brother and my mother would have received them.'

Another feature Tolstoy records of his mother is 'her truthfulness and the simple tone of her correspondence'. He tells us that in his imagination his mother 'appeared to me a creature so elevated, pure, and spiritual, that often in the middle period of my life, during my struggles with overwhelming temptations, I prayed to her soul, begging her to aid me; and such prayer always helped me much'.

Yet another quality Tolstoy says showed itself in his mother's letters and was inherited by his eldest brother. This was 'indifference to other people's opinions of them and a modesty which even caused them to try to conceal their mental, educational, and moral superiority. It was as though they were ashamed of those advantages.'

Five children were born to Nicholas and Márya Tolstoy. First four sons, of whom Leo was the youngest. His name in Russian is Lyóv Nikoláevich (Leo, son-of-Nicholas) Tolstoy. Leo Tolstoy is the way he signed himself when using the Latin alphabet; and when pronouncing his name it should be remembered that the accent falls on the second syllable, and that it rhymes with 'boy'. The fancy spellings Tolstoi and Tolstoï are due to the fact that the early translators relied on French versions, and did not know how Tolstoy spelt or pronounced his name. He was born on 28th August 1828 (o.s.) at Yásnaya Polyána, with a caul – which in Russia, as in England, is considered a sign of good fortune.

A year and a half later a daughter, Márya, was born on 7th March 1830, and five months later the mother died.

Pilgrims, monks, nuns, and various half-crazy devotees were frequent visitors at the house, and even took up their abode there. One of these was a nun, Márya Gerásimovna, who in her youth had made pilgrimage to various holy places dressed as a man. After the birth of four boys Tolstoy's mother longed for a daughter, and promised that if one were granted her, she would take as the baby's godmother the first pilgrim who should be met by her messenger on the neighbouring high road. The next child really was a daughter, and the first pilgrim met was Márya Gerásimovna who was travelling dressed as a boy. Thereafter Márya Gerásimovna, though she lived partly in the Túla convent, was free of the Tolstoy's house and spent much of her time there.

Tolstoy gives us his earliest reminiscences in an autobiographical fragment published in 1878.

These are my first recollections. I cannot arrange them in order for I do not know which come first or last. Of some of them I do not even know whether they happened in a dream or when I was awake. I lie bound* and wish to stretch out my arms, but cannot. I scream and cry, and my screams are disagreeable to myself but I cannot stop. Someone – I do not remember who – bends over me. This all happens in semi-darkness. I only know there were two people there. My cries affect them: they are agitated by my screams but do not untie me as I want them to, and I scream still louder. To them it seems necessary that I should be bound, but I know it is unnecessary and I wish to prove this to them and again burst into cries which are unpleasant to myself but are yet unrestrainable. I feel the injustice and cruelty – not of people, for they pity me, but – of fate, and I pity myself. I do not know and shall never know what it was all about: whether I was swaddled while still a baby at the breast and struggled to free my hands; whether they swaddled me when I was more than a year old to prevent my scratching some sore, or whether I have gathered into this one recollection (as one does in a dream) many different impressions. The one sure thing is, that this was the first and strongest impression of my life. And what remains on my memory is not my cries nor my suffering, but the complexity and contradictoriness of the impressions. I desire freedom, it would harm no one, but I who need strength am weak, while they are strong.

The next impression is a pleasant one. I am sitting in a tub and am surrounded by a new and not unpleasant smell of something with which they are rubbing my tiny body. Probably it was bran put into the water of my bath; the novelty of the sensation caused by the bran aroused me, and for the first time I became aware of, and liked, my own little body with the visible ribs on my breast, and the smooth dark wooden tub, the bared arms of my nurse, the warm steaming swirling water, the noise it made, and especially the smooth feel of the wet rim of the tub as I passed my hands along it.

My next recollections belong to the time when I was five or six, and there are very few of them, and not one that relates to life outside the walls of the house. Nature, up to the age of five, did not exist for me. All that I remember happened in bed or in our rooms. Neither grass,

* Russian babies are usually swaddled tightly with bands, making them look like fresh mummies.

nor leaves, nor sky, nor sun, existed for me. It cannot be that no one ever gave me flowers and leaves to play with, that I never saw any grass, that they never shaded me from the sun, but up to the time when I was five or six years old I have no recollection of what we call Nature. Probably, to see it one has to be separate from it, and I was Nature.

The recollection that comes next after the tub is that of Ereméevna. 'Ereméevna' was the name with which they used to frighten us children. Probably they had long frightened us with it, but my recollection of it is this: I am in bed and feel well and happy as usual, and I should not remember it but that suddenly the nurse, or some one of those who made up my life, says something in a voice new to me, and then goes away; and in addition to being happy I am also frightened. And besides me there is someone else like me. (Probably my sister Márya, whose crib stood in the same room.) And I now remember a curtain near my bed; and both my sister and I are happy and frightened at the strange thing happening to us, and I hide in my pillow: hide, and glance at the door from behind which I expect something new and merry. We laugh, and hide, and wait. And then someone appears in a dress and cap quite unknown to me, but I recognise that it is the same person who is always with us (whether my nurse or aunt I do not remember), and this someone says something about bad children and about Ereméevna in a gruff voice which I recognise. And I squeal with fear and pleasure and really am frightened, and yet am glad to be frightened and do not want her who is frightening me to know that I have recognised her. We become quiet, but presently begin whispering to one another again on purpose that Ereméevna may come back.

I have another recollection similar to this of Ereméevna (but as it is clearer it probably belongs to a later date) which has always remained inexplicable to me. In this recollection the chief part is played by our German tutor, Theodore Ivánich, but I am sure I was not yet in his charge, so the event must have taken place before I was five. It is my first recollection of Theodore Ivánich, and it took place at so early an age that I can remember no one else: neither my brothers nor my father nor anyone. If I have some notion of some one individual person, it is only of my sister, and this only because she, like me, was afraid of Ereméevna. With this recollection is joined my first conception of the fact that our house had an upper story. How I climbed there – whether I went by myself or whether someone carried me – I have quite forgotten, but I remember that many of us are there and we all form a circle holding each other's hands; among us are some women I did not know (for some reason I remember that they were washerwomen), and we all begin to go round and to jump; and Theodore Ivánich jumps, lifting his legs too high and too loudly and noisily, and I at one and the same instant feel that this is wrong and depraved and notice him and (I believe) begin to cry – and all is over.

That is all I remember up to the age of five. I remember neither my nurses, aunts, brothers, sister, nor my father, nor the rooms, nor my toys. My more distinct recollections begin from the time I was moved downstairs to Theodore Ivánich and the elder boys.

When I was moved downstairs to Theodore Ivánich and the boys I experienced for the first time, and therefore more strongly than ever since, the feeling which is called the sense of duty, the consciousness of the cross every man is called upon to bear. It was hard to leave what I was accustomed to from the beginning of things, and I was sad, poetically sad, not so much at parting from people: sister, nurse, and aunt, as at parting with my crib, the curtain, and the pillow; and I feared the new life into which I was entering. I tried to see the jolly side of this new life awaiting me; I tried to believe the caressing words with which Theodore Ivánich lured me to him. I tried not to see the contempt with which the boys received me – the youngest boy. I tried to think it was a shame for a big boy to live with girls, and that there was nothing good in the life upstairs with nurse; but my heart was terribly sad, I knew I was irreparably losing my innocence and happiness, and only a feeling of personal dignity and the consciousness of doing my duty upheld me. (Often in afterlife I have experienced similar moments at the parting of crossroads, when entering on a fresh course.) I experienced quiet grief at the irreparability of my loss; I was unable to believe that it would really happen, though I had been told that I should be moved to the boys' rooms. I remember that the dressing-gown with a cord sewn to its back, which they put on me, seemed to cut me off for ever from upstairs, and I then for the first time observed – not all those with whom I had lived upstairs, but – the chief person with whom I lived and whom I did not remember before. This was my Auntie Tatiána Alexándrovna Érgolski. I remember her short, stout, black-haired, kindly, tender, and compassionate. It was she who put the dressing-gown on me and, embracing me and kissing me, tied it round my waist; and I saw that she felt as I did, that it was sad, terribly sad, but had to be; and for the first time I felt that life is not a game but a serious matter.

'Auntie' Tatiána Alexándrovna Érgolski, mentioned in the above reminiscences, was a very distant relative, who being left an orphan, had been brought up by Tolstoy's paternal grandparents. She was very attractive and affectionate. She loved Count Nicholas, Leo's father, but stood aside that he might marry the rich Princess Márya Volkónski and repair the family fortunes. Six years after his wife's death Count Nicholas asked Tatiána to marry him and be a mother to his children. Not wishing (Tolstoy tells us) to spoil her pure, poetic relations with the family, she refused the first but fulfilled the second of these requests.

The joyousness of Tolstoy's boyhood was largely due to the care and affection of this excellent woman, and in the most firmly rooted of his principles – such as his detestation of corporal punishment and his approval of complete chastity – it is easy to trace her unconscious influence.

Here, for instance, is one episode:

We children were returning home from a walk with our tutor, when near the barn we met the fat steward, Andrew, followed by the coachman's assistant, 'Squinting Kuzmá' as he was called, whose face was sad. He was a married man and no longer young. One of us asked Andrew where he was going, and he quietly replied that he was going to the barn where Kuzmá had to be punished. I cannot describe the dreadful feeling these words and the sight of the good-natured crestfallen Kuzmá produced on me. In the evening I told this to my Auntie Tatiána, who hated corporal punishment and wherever she had influence never allowed it for us any more than for the serfs. She was greatly revolted at what I told her, and rebuking me said, 'Why did you not stop him?' Her words grieved me still more . . . I never thought that we could interfere in such things and yet it appeared that we could. But it was too late and the dreadful deed had been done.

To sum up what we know of Tolstoy's antecedents: on both sides he came of people who had little sympathy either with the reactionary autocratic rule that succeeded the liberal tendencies of the early years of Alexander I, or with the harsh treatment to which the serfs were sometimes exposed. A cousin of Tolstoy's mother was one of the Decembrist conspirators, and on the accession of Nicholas I in 1825 took part in their abortive attempt to overthrow the autocracy. He was exiled to Siberia for thirty years, doing hard labour in irons part of the time. His wife (another Princess Márya Volkónski) voluntarily accompanied him, as Nekrásov has told in a well-known Russian poem. Towards the end of their lives several members of the family retired into convents or monasteries.

We find strong family love pervading the households of Tolstoy's parents and grandparents, and even after their death Tolstoy's nature ripened in a congenial atmosphere of family affection, and many of his most pronounced sympathies and antipathies were not peculiar to himself but were shared by other members of the family.

2

Childhood and Early Manhood

As already mentioned, Yásnaya Polyána (Clear Glade), where Tolstoy was born, had been an ancestral estate of the Volkónskis and belonged to his mother, Princess Márya. It is situated ten miles south of Túla, in a pleasantly undulating country. The estate is well wooded and has many avenues of lime trees, a river, and four ponds. In Tolstoy's grandfather's time, sentinels kept guard at the small, round, brick towers which now stand neglected at the entrance of the main birch avenue leading to the house. Something of the great confidence in himself and readiness to despise others, which despite all his efforts to be humble characterised Tolstoy, may have been due to the fact that he was born and grew up on an estate where for generations his ancestors had been the only people of importance.

'Auntie' Tatiána Alexándrovna Érgolski had been brought up by Tolstoy's paternal grandmother in an equality with her own children. She (Tatiána) was resolute, self-sacrificing, and, says Tolstoy,

> must have been very attractive with her enormous plait of crisp, black, curly hair, her jet-black eyes, and vivacious, energetic expression. When I remember her she was more than forty and I never thought about her as pretty or not pretty. I simply loved her eyes, her smile, and her dusky broad little hand with its energetic cross vein.
>
> We had two aunts and a grandmother; they all had more right to us than Tatiána Alexándrovna, whom we called Aunt only by habit (for our kinship was so distant that I could never remember what it was), but she took the first place in our upbringing by right of love to us (like Buddha in the story of the wounded swan), and we felt her right.
>
> I had fits of passionately tender love for her.
>
> I remember once, when I was about five, how I squeezed in behind her on the sofa in the drawing-room and she caressingly touched me with her hand. I caught it and began to kiss it and to cry with tender love of her . . .
>
> Auntie Tatiána had the greatest influence on my life. From early

childhood she taught me the spiritual delight of love. She taught me this joy not by words, but by her whole being she filled me with love. I saw, I felt, how she enjoyed loving, and I understood the joy of love. This was the first thing.

Secondly, she taught me the delights of an unhurried, quiet, life.

Another though much less important influence was that of the tutor, Theodore Rössel (who figures as Karl Iványch Mauer in Tolstoy's early story, *Childhood*). Tolstoy owed his excellent knowledge of German and French to the fact that his father, following a custom common among well-to-do Russians, engaged foreign teachers and let his children learn languages not so much from books as by conversation while they were still quite young. Rössel's 'honest, straightforward, and loving nature' helped to develop the boy's good qualities.

Tolstoy got on well too with his three brothers, who were five, two and a half, and one year and four months, older than himself, as well as with his little sister Márya, his junior by a year and a half.

He not only loved, but deeply respected, his eldest brother Nicholas (pet name, Nikólenka), whose influence lasted until, and even after, his death in 1860. Of him Tolstoy says:

He was a wonderful boy, and later a wonderful man. Turgénev used to say of him, very truly, that he only lacked certain faults to be a great writer. He lacked the chief fault needed for authorship – vanity, and was not at all interested in what people thought of him. The qualities of a writer that he possessed were, first of all a fine artistic sense, an extremely developed sense of proportion, a good-natured, gay, sense of humour, an extraordinary inexhaustible imagination, and a truthful and highly moral view of life; and all this without the slightest conceit. His imagination was such that for hours together he could tell fairy-tales or ghost stories or amusing tales in the style of Mrs Radcliffe, without a pause and with such vivid realisation of what he was narrating that one forgot it was all invention . . . When he was not narrating or reading (he read a great deal) he used to draw. He almost invariably drew devils with horns and twisted moustaches, intertwined in the most varied attitudes and engaged in the most diverse occupations. These drawings were also full of imagination.

It was he who, when I was five and my brothers Dmítri six and Sergéy seven, announced to us that he possessed a secret by means of which, when disclosed, all men would become happy: there would be no more disease, no trouble, no one would be angry with anybody, all would love one another, and all would become 'Ant-Brothers' . . . We even organised a game of Ant-Brothers, which consisted in sitting under chairs, sheltering ourselves with boxes, screening ourselves with shawls, and cuddling against one another while thus crouching in the dark . . . The Ant-Brotherhood was revealed to us but not the chief secret – the way for all men to cease suffering any misfortune, to leave off quarrelling and being angry, and become continuously happy – this secret he said he had written on a green stick buried by the road at the edge of a certain ravine, at which spot (since my body must be buried somewhere) I have asked to be buried in memory of Nikólenka. Besides this little stick there was also a certain Fanfarónov Hill, up which he said he could lead us if only we would fulfil all the appointed conditions. These were: first, to stand in a corner and not think of a white bear. I remember how I used to get into a corner and try (but could not possibly manage) not to think of a white bear. The second condition was to walk without wavering along a crack between the boards of the floor; and the third was, for a whole year not to see a hare, alive or dead or cooked; and it was necessary to swear not to reveal these secrets to anyone. He who fulfilled these and other more difficult conditions which Nikólenka would communicate later, would have one wish, whatever it might be, fulfilled.

Nikólenka, as I now conjecture, had probably read or heard of the Freemasons – of their aspirations towards the happiness of mankind, and of the mysterious rites of initiation to their order; he had probably also heard about the Moravian Brothers [in Russian *ant* is *muravéy*].

Writing when he was over seventy, Tolstoy added:

The ideal of ant-brothers lovingly clinging to one another, though not under two armchairs curtained by shawls but of all mankind under the wide dome of heaven, has remained unaltered in me. As I then believed that there existed a little green stick whereon was written the message which would destroy all evil in men and give them universal welfare, so I now believe that such truth exists and will be revealed to men and will give them all it promises.

When he died, Tolstoy was actually buried on the spot endeared to him by the imaginary green stick and by the longing for human brotherhood aroused by his eldest brother's story.

It was, however, Tolstoy's second brother, Sergéy (pet name, Serëzha), whom Tolstoy in his young days most enthusiastically admired and wished to imitate. Sergéy was handsome, proud, straightforward, and singularly sincere. Of him Leo Tolstoy says:

I loved and wished to be like him. I admired his handsome appearance, his singing (he was always singing), his drawing, his gaiety, and especially (strange as it may seem to say so) the spontaneity of his egotism. I myself was always aware of myself and self-conscious; I always guessed, rightly or wrongly, what other people thought or felt about me, and this spoilt my joy in life. This probably is why in others I specially liked the opposite feature – spontaneity of egotism. And for this I specially loved Serëzha. The word *loved* is not correct. I loved Nikólenka; but for Serëzha I was filled with admiration as for something quite apart from and incomprehensible to me.

Of the third brother, Dmítri (pet name, Mítenka), only a year older than himself, Tolstoy tells us:

I hardly remember him as a boy. I only know by hearsay that as a child he was very capricious. He was nearest to me in age and I played with him oftenest, but did not love him as much as I loved Serëzha, nor as I loved and respected Nikólenka. He and I lived together amicably. I do not recollect that we quarrelled. Probably we did, and we may even have fought . . . As a child I remember nothing special about Mítenka except his childish merriment.

A girl, Dúnechka Temeshóv, was adopted as a member of the family. She was the natural daughter of a wealthy bachelor friend of Tolstoy's father.

I remember how when I had already learnt French I was made to teach her that alphabet. At first it went all right (we were both about five years old), but later she probably grew tired and ceased to name correctly the letters I pointed out. I insisted. She began to cry. I did the same, and when our elders came we could say nothing owing to our helpless tears.

In his later recollections of her he says:

She was not clever, but was a good, simple girl; and, above all, so pure that we boys never had any but brotherly relations with her.

The relations between the family and its servants, who were serfs and of whom there were about thirty, were, as in many a Russian family, often really affectionate. One instance of a serf's devotion has already been quoted, and such cases were not rare. In *Childhood*, under the name of Natálya Sávishna, mention is made of the old housekeeper, Praskóvya Isáevna, who was completely devoted to the welfare of the family, and Tolstoy says: 'All that I there wrote about her was actual truth.'

Here is another example illustrating both kindly toleration of minor offences committed by a serf, and the family affection which sweetened life:

My pleasantest recollections of my father are of his sitting with grandmother on the sofa helping her to play patience. My father was polite and tender with everyone, but to my grandmother he was always particularly tender and submissive. They used to sit – Grandma playing patience and from time to time taking pinches from a gold snuff-box. My aunts sit in armchairs, and one of them reads aloud. We children come in to say good-night, and sometimes sit there. We always take leave of Grandma and our aunts by kissing their hands. I remember once, in the middle of a game of patience and of the reading, my father interrupts my aunt, points to a looking-glass and whispers something. We all look in the same direction. It was the footman Tíkhon, who (knowing that my father was in the drawing-room) was going into the study to take some tobacco from a big leather folding tobacco-pouch. My father sees him in the looking-glass and notices his figure stepping carefully on tiptoe. My aunts laugh. Grandmama for a long time does not understand, but when she does she too smiles cheerfully. I am enchanted by my father's kindness, and on taking leave of him kiss his white muscular hand with special tenderness.

In *Childhood* the following passage occurs, which certainly expresses his own feeling:

Happy, happy, irrevocable days of childhood! How can one fail to love and cherish their memory? Those memories refresh and elevate my soul and are the source of my greatest delight . . . What time can be better than that in which the two finest virtues – innocent joy and an unbounded need to love – are the only motives in one's life?

And in his *Recollections* Tolstoy tells us that:

All who surrounded me in childhood, from my father to the coach-man, seem to me to have been exceptionally good people. Probably my pure, loving feeling, like a bright beam, revealed to me the best qualities in people (such qualities always exist); but to regard them as exceptionally good was much nearer the truth than it would have been to see only their faults . . .

Tolstoy's sister, Márya, tells us that his enjoyment of life was remark-able; he was like a ray of light. He would run into the room with a happy smile as if he had made a discovery about which he wished to tell everyone. He was fond of jests: was always tender, kindly, yielding, and never rude. If he were petted, tears would come into his eyes; if his brothers offended him he would go away and cry. If someone asked him: 'What is it, Lëvochka? What is the matter?' he would reply: 'They offend me,' and would go on crying.

He always cried very easily, and was nicknamed *Lëva-Rëva*, 'Leo Cry-baby'.

In his *Recollections* he tells us how, when he was about eight years old, his father once made him read Púshkin's poems *To the Sea* and *Napoleon*, of which he, Leo, was fond and which he had learnt by heart. He says:

He was evidently struck by the feeling with which I recited the verses, and exchanged significant glances with Yazykov [Leo's godfather] who was there. I understood that he saw something good in my reading, and this made me very happy.

From childhood to the end of his life Tolstoy was quite exceptionally susceptible to music. In one version of *Childhood* he describes how in the evening 'Mama' played Field and Beethoven, and the feelings of little Nikólenka as he listened to her performance, sitting with his feet up on an easy-chair in the drawing-room.

Mama finished Field's Concerto, rose from the round stool, took another book of music, opened it on the music-stand, drew the candles nearer, and after adjusting her dress again sat down to the piano. By the care with which she did all this and the thoughtfully severe expression of her face it seemed that she was preparing for something very serious. 'Something is going to happen,' thought I, and again closed my eyes, pressing my head into the corner of the armchair. The smell of the dust I disturbed in turning round tickled my nostrils, and the familiar sounds of the piece Mama was playing produced in me a sweet impression and at the same time disturbed me. She was playing Beethoven's Sonata Pathétique. Though I knew the whole Sonata so well that there was nothing new to me in it, it disturbed me so that I could not fall asleep. What if it suddenly went not as I had expected? The restrained, majestic, but agitated, *motif* of the Introduction, which seems to fear to express itself, made me hold my breath. The more beautiful and more complex the musical phrase the stronger became the feeling of fear lest anything should disturb this beauty, and the stronger the feeling of delight when the phrase was harmoniously resolved.

I only became tranquil when the *motif* of the Introduction has said everything and resolved itself loudly and harmoniously into the Allegro. The commencement of the Allegro is too usual, and therefore I was not fond of it. Listening to it, one rested from the strong sensations of the opening pages. But what could be better than the place where the questions and answers begin? At first the conversation is quiet and tender: but suddenly, in the bass, someone utters two stern phrases full of passion, to which it seems as if there could be no reply . . . But no! There is a reply, and the reply becomes better and better and yet stronger, until at last everything mingles into a kind of obscure, disquieting murmur. That part always surprised me; and the feeling of surprise was as strong as though I were hearing it for the first time. Afterwards, amid the noise of the Allegro, an echo of the Introduction is suddenly heard. Then the conversation is again repeated, again comes the echo, and suddenly, at the moment when one's soul is so agitated by these constant alarms that it begs for rest, it all finishes, and finishes so unexpectedly and beautifully . . .

During the Andante I drowsed; one's soul was tranquil, joyful, one was ready to smile, and one had a dream of something light, white, and transparent. But the Rondo in C minor aroused me. 'What is he speaking about? Where is he asking to go? What does he want?' And one wishes it all to finish quicker, quicker, quicker; but when he had ceased to weep and to entreat I wanted still to hear the passionate expression of his sufferings.

Childhood is a story and not an autobiographical work, and Tolstoy's mother died long before he could appreciate the Sonata Pathétique, but we can hardly be wrong in assuming that this description, written when Tolstoy was twenty-three, describes his own sensations as a child, and probably the lady who really performed the piece was Tolstoy's sister's governess, who in later years taught her to play this Sonata herself.

An important feature of the life in which Tolstoy grew up was furnished by the half-crazy saints who swarmed in Russia in those days. Readers of *Childhood* will remember Grísha, an admirable specimen of that class, about whom Tolstoy makes the following characteristic note in his memoirs:

> Grísha is an invented character. We had many of these half-crazy saints at our house, and I was taught to regard them with profound respect, for which I am deeply grateful to those who brought me up. If there were some among them who were insincere, or who experienced periods of weakness and insincerity, yet the aim of their life, though practically absurd, was so lofty that I am glad I learned in childhood unconsciously to understand the height of their achievement. They accomplished what Marcus Aurelius speaks of when he says: 'There is nothing higher than to endure contempt for one's good life.' So harmful and so unavoidable is the desire for human glory which always contaminates good deeds, that one cannot but sympathise with the effort not merely to avoid praise but even to evoke contempt. Such a character was Márya Gerásimovna, my sister's godmother, and the semi-idiot Evdokímushka, and some others in our house.

How deeply these early impressions were engraved on Tolstoy's mind is obvious from his earliest as well as his latest writings. Take for instance the lines from *Childhood* referring to Grísha's prayer overheard by the children.

> Much water has flowed since then, many memories of the past have lost their meaning for me and become dim recollections, even the pilgrim Grísha has long since completed his last pilgrimage; but the impression he made on me and the feeling he evoked, will never die in my memory.

In Tolstoy's later life we shall again and again find this medieval note recurring (with whatever of truth or falsity it contains), and the assertion that it is not the usefulness or uselessness of a man's life that matters so much as his self-abnegation and the humility of his soul.

To complete the picture of Tolstoy's early boyhood at Yásnaya Polyána, we must think of him as interested in his father's dogs and horses and hunting (in *Childhood* he tells the true story of how he hunted his first hare), and also in the games and masquerades with which the family and visitors, as well as the servants, amused themselves, especially at New Year.

Despite his sensitive introspective nature, Tolstoy's childhood was a happy one, and to it he always looked back with pleasure. He speaks of 'that splendid, innocent, joyful, poetic period of childhood, up to fourteen', and tells us that the impressions of early childhood, preserved in one's memory, grow in some unfathomable depth of the soul like seeds thrown on good ground, till after many years they thrust their bright, green shoots into God's world.

When Tolstoy was eight years old the family moved to Moscow for his elder brothers' education. The following summer they lost their father, who, having gone to Túla on business, fell down in the street on his way to visit his friend Temeshóv, and died of apoplexy. What money he had with him was stolen, but some unnegotiable bonds were brought back to the Tolstoys in Moscow by an unknown beggar. The funeral took place at Yásnaya Polyána; and Leo, who did not attend it, long fancied that his father was not really dead. Looking at the faces of strangers in the streets of Moscow, he felt almost certain he might at any moment again meet him alive.

This event brought the problems of life and death vividly to the boy's mind, and nine months later the impression was intensified by the death of his grandmother, who never recovered from the shock of her son's death. Hers was the first death Tolstoy witnessed, and he never forgot the horror he felt when, as she lay dying of dropsy, he was admitted to kiss her swollen white hand and saw her, dressed in white, lying motionless on a high white bed. But he says:

> I remember that new jackets of black material braided with white were made for all of us. It was dreadful to see the undertaker's men hanging about near the house and then bringing in the coffin with its lid covered with glazed brocade, and my grandmother's stern face with its Roman nose, and her white cap and the white kerchief on her neck, lying high in the coffin on the table; and it was sad to see the tears of our aunts and of Páshenka; but yet the new braided jackets and the soothing attitude adopted towards us by those around gratified us . . . I remember how pleasant it was to me to overhear during the funeral the conversation of some gossiping female guests, who said, 'Complete

orphans; their father only lately dead and now the grandmother gone too.'

Some time after this, an event occurred that is recorded on the first page of Tolstoy's *Confession*:

I remember how, when I was about eleven, a boy Vladímir Milútin, a Grammar School pupil, visited us one Sunday and announced as the latest novelty a discovery made at his School. The discovery was that there is no God and all that we are taught about Him is a mere invention. I remember how interested my elder brothers were in this news. They called me to their council and we all, I remember, became animated, and accepted the news as something very interesting and fully possible.

Various stories have been preserved relating to Tolstoy's boyhood and some of them are sufficiently characteristic to be worth repeating.

One incident which made a strong impression on the lad, keenly sensitive as he always was to any shade of injustice, was the following:

Soon after the death of their father and grandmother, the orphan Tolstoys, then living in rather straitened circumstances owing to their property being left in trust, were invited to a Christmas Tree at the house of an acquaintance, and the young Princes Gorchakóv, nephews of the then Minister of War, were also among the guests. All the children received presents; but whereas the Gorchakóvs had expensive ones, the Tolstoys, to their annoyance, received cheap common ones.

Other stories, told by Tolstoy himself or by the family, illustrate his impulsive, imaginative, strenuous, and rather erratic nature at this period.

When he was about seven or eight years old he had an ardent desire to fly, and persuaded himself that it was possible to do so. It was only necessary to sit down on your heels clasping your arms firmly round your knees, and the tighter you held them the higher you would fly. As Tolstoy was always ardent to put his beliefs into practice it is not very surprising that one day, soon after the family had moved to Moscow, he stayed behind in the class-room when he should have come down to dinner, and climbing out on to the window-sill, some six yards from the ground, threw himself out. He was picked up unconscious. The ill results of his fall were fortunately confined to a slight concussion of the brain, and after sleeping for eighteen hours on end he woke up again quite well.

As already mentioned it would be a mistake to take his story, *Childhood*, as autobiographical; but it contains many passages one knows from other sources to be true of his own life, and one such is that in which (speaking in the character of Nikólenka) he says:

I knew very well that I was not good-looking . . . so that every reference to my appearance offended me painfully . . . There were moments when I was overcome by despair: I imagined that there could be no happiness on earth for one with such a broad nose, such thick lips, and such small, grey eyes as mine; and I asked God to perform a miracle, and make me handsome, and all I then had and everything I might have in future I would have given for a handsome face.

In fact his personal appearance caused the sensitive lad much concern, but his efforts to improve it were unsuccessful. On one occasion he clipped his eyebrows, and the unsatisfactory results occasioned him great grief.

He records in his *Reminiscences* the following incident which certainly intensified his lifelong antipathy to corporal punishment:

I do not remember for what, but for something quite undeserving of punishment, St Thomas (the resident French tutor who succeeded Rössel) first locked me in a room and then threatened to flog me. I thereupon experienced a dreadful feeling of anger, resentment, and disgust, not only towards St Thomas himself but towards the violence with which I was threatened.

When quite a small boy he conceived an attachment for the nine-year-old daughter of his father's friend, Islénev, and being jealous of her for daring to talk to others, he angrily pushed her off a balcony, with the result that she limped for a long time afterwards. A quarter of a century later, when he married this lady's daughter, his mother-in-law used laughingly to remind him of the incident and say, 'Evidently you pushed me off the balcony in my childhood that you might marry my daughter afterwards!'

His sister relates that once when they were driving in a troika (i. e. with three horses abreast) to Yásnaya, Leo got down during a break in the journey and went forward on foot. When the carriage started again and began to overtake him he took to running, and when the horses went faster he also increased his speed, racing as hard as he could. He was not overtaken till he had gone about two miles and was completely tired out. He was lifted back into the carriage gasping for breath, perspiring, and quite exhausted. Those not endowed with the remarkable physical vigour that, in spite of frequent attacks of ill-health, characterised Tolstoy through life, would probably have done themselves serious injury had they taxed their vital resources as recklessly as he often did.

All accounts agree in representing him as an original and odd little fellow, unwilling to do things like other people. He would for instance enter a drawing-room and, carefully placing his feet together and bending his head, make his bow backwards, saluting each of the company in turn.

Two incidents are recorded relating to the love of riding which remained a characteristic of his through life.

When his brothers were sent to a riding-school, Leo (in spite of his father's assurances and those of the riding-master that he was too small to begin and would tumble off) also obtained permission to learn to ride. At his first lesson he duly tumbled off, but begged to be replaced in the saddle and did not fall off again, but quickly became an expert rider. In one of the short stories he wrote many years later for the use of schoolchildren, he tells how he once wished to ride the old horse Raven after his brothers had each had a turn on it, and how Raven being too tired to move from the stables, he beat it till he broke his switch on its sides. He then demanded a stouter switch from the serf in charge, but the man replied:

'Ah, master, you have no pity! Why do you beat him? He is twenty years old and is tired out; he can hardly breathe. Why, for a horse, he is as old as Timoféich [a very old peasant living at the place]. You might as well get on Timoféich's back and drive him beyond his strength like that with a switch. Would you feel no pity for him?'

I thought of Timoféich and listened to the man. I got off the horse's back; and when I noticed how its steaming sides were working and how heavily it breathed through its nostrils, swishing its thin tail, I understood how hard it was for it. Till then I had thought that it was as happy as I was myself. And I felt so sorry for Raven that I began to kiss his sweaty neck and to beg his pardon for having beaten him.

Since then I have grown up, but I always have pity on horses and always remember Raven and Timoféich when I see horses ill-treated.

He does not appear to have been very good at his lessons, and some-where mentions the dictum of a student who used to coach his brothers and himself, and said of their aptitude for learning:

Nicholas wishes and can, Sergéy can but won't, Dmítri wishes but can't (this was not true), and Leo neither wishes nor can. (That, I think, was perfectly true.)

On the other hand, St Thomas, the French tutor already referred to (he figures in *Childhood* as St Jérôme), must have noticed the lad's capacity, for he used to say, 'Ce petit a une tête: c'est un petit Molière' [This little one has a head: he is a little Molière].

After the father's death the family property passed under the control of the Court of Wards, and expenses had to be cut down [1838]. It was therefore decided that though the two elder brothers must remain in Moscow for the sake of their education, the three younger children should return to Yásnaya Polyána, where living was cheaper, in the charge of their much-loved Auntie Tatiána. Their legal guardian, the Countess Alexándra ('Aline') Ilynishna Osten-Saken, remained in Moscow with the elder boys.

This lady had made what seemed a brilliant marriage with the wealthy Count Osten-Saken, whose family was among the first in the Baltic Provinces, but her married life was a terrible one. Her husband went out of his mind and tried to kill her. While he was confined in an asylum the Countess gave birth to a stillborn child. To save her from this fresh shock, a girl born of a servant was substituted for the stillborn baby. This girl, Páshenka, lived with the Tolstoy family and was already grown up when Tolstoy was quite a child. Subsequently the Countess Alexándra lived first with her parents and then with her brother, Tolstoy's father. She was a devotee of the Orthodox Russo-Greek Church of which Tolstoy eventually became so fierce an opponent, but much in her character and conduct accords with the precepts laid down in his later writings, and it is evident that certain aspects of his understanding of the Christian character which strike most Englishmen as peculiar, far from being invented by him, are derived from a deeply-rooted Russian and family tradition. He tells us:

My aunt was a truly religious woman. Her favourite occupation was reading the Lives of the Saints, conversing with pilgrims, half-crazy devotees, monks and nuns, of whom some always lived in our house while others only visited my aunt . . . She was not merely outwardly religious, keeping the fasts, praying much, and associating with people of saintly life, but she herself lived a truly Christian life, trying not only to avoid all luxury and acceptance of service, but herself serving others as much as possible. She never had any money for she gave away all she had to those who asked. A servant related to me how, during their life in Moscow, my aunt used carefully on tiptoe to pass her sleeping maid when going to Matins, and used herself to perform all the duties which in those days it was customary for a maid to perform. In food and dress she was as simple and unexacting as can possibly be imagined. Unpleasant as it is to me to mention it, I remember from childhood a specific acid smell connected with my aunt, probably due to negligence in her toilet: and this was the graceful poetic Aline with beautiful eyes, who used to love reading and copying French verses, who played on the harp, and always had great success at the grandest balls! I remember how affectionate and kind she always was, and this equally to the most important men and women and to the nuns and pilgrims.

Tolstoy goes on to tell how pleasantly she bore the jests and the teasing that her devotion to the priests brought upon her.

I remember her dear good-natured laugh and her face shining with pleasure. The religious feeling which filled her soul was evidently so important to her, so much higher than anything else, that she could not be angry or annoyed at anything, and could not attribute to worldly matters the importance others attach to them.

In the summer of 1839 the whole family assembled at Yásnaya Polyána, but they had returned to Moscow by September when the Emperor Nicholas I visited Moscow to lay the foundation-stone of the Cathedral of Our Saviour (built to commemorate the liberation of Russia from Napoleon in 1812). Tolstoy witnessed the ceremony from the window of a neighbouring house, and judging by an apparently autobiographical passage in one of the drafts of *Childhood* he was also in a crowd which cheered the Emperor as he drove from the Krémlin palace. No doubt the scene in *War and Peace* where Pétya Rostóv sees Alexander I pass in the Krémlin was based on that experience.

The next year, 1840, was a famine year. The crops were so poor that corn had to be bought to feed the serfs, and to raise funds for this purpose one of the Tolstoys' estates had to be sold. The supply of oats for the horses was stopped, and Tolstoy remembers how he and his brothers, pitying their ponies, secretly gathered oats for them in the peasants' fields, quite unconscious of the crime they were committing.

In the winter of that year the whole family moved to Moscow, returning to Yásnaya for the following summer. The next autumn their guardian, the kind good Countess Alexándra Osten-Saken, died in the Convent, or 'Hermitage', founded by Óptin (a robber chief of the fourteenth century) in the Government of Kalúga, to which she had retired.

After her death her sister, Pelagéya Ilyníshna Yúshkov, became their guardian. She was the wife of a Kazán landowner. Auntie Tatiána and she were not on friendly terms; there was no open quarrel between them, but V. I. Yúshkov (Pelagéya's husband) had been a suitor for Tatiána's hand in his youth and had been rejected. Pelagéya could not forgive her husband's old love for Tatiána.

The change of guardianship led to the removal of the family to Kazán in the autumn of 1841, when Leo Tolstoy was thirteen, and the children were separated from Auntie Tatiána, much to her grief, but returned to Yásnaya Polyána every summer.

The books which up to the age of fourteen most influenced Tolstoy were, he tells us, the Story of Joseph from the Bible, the *Forty Thieves* and *Prince Camaralzaman* from the *Arabian Nights*, various Russian folk-legends, Púshkin's *Tales* and his poem *Napoleon*, as well as *The Black Hen* (a fairy tale) by Pogorélski. The influence the story of Joseph had on him, he says, was 'immense', and in later life he instanced it as an example of the 'brevity, simplicity, and sincerity' characteristic of that supreme art which has the widest appeal.

In his aptitude for abstract speculation, as in other respects, the boy was truly father to the man, and in a passage, certainly autobiographical, in *Boyhood*, he says:

> It will hardly be believed what were my favourite and most constant subjects of reflection during boyhood, so incompatible were they with my age and position. But in my opinion the incompatibility of a man's position with his moral activity is the surest indication of his searching for truth . . .
>
> At one time the idea occurred to me that happiness does not depend on external causes, but on our relation to those causes, and that a man

accustomed to endure sufferings cannot be unhappy – and to inure myself to hardship, regardless of the severe pain I felt, I used to hold Tatíschev's dictionaries out at arm's length for five minutes at a time, or went into the box-room and lashed my bare back with a rope so painfully that tears involuntarily appeared in my eyes.

At another time, remembering that death awaited me any hour and any minute, I understood, wondering why people had not understood it before, that one can only be happy by enjoying the present and not thinking of the future, and, for three days, under the influence of this idea, I neglected to learn my lessons and did nothing but lie on my bed, enjoying myself by reading a novel, and eating gingerbread made with honey, on which I spent my last coins . . . But by none of my philosophical tendencies was I so carried away as by scepticism, which at one time led me to the verge of insanity. I imagined that besides myself nobody and nothing existed in the universe, that objects were not objects at all, but images which appeared only when I paid attention to them, and as soon as I left off thinking of them, these images immediately disappeared. In a word, I coincided with Schelling in the conviction that not objects exist, but my relation to them. There were moments when, under the influence of this *idée fixe*, I reached such a state of insanity that I sometimes looked rapidly round to one side, hoping to catch nothingness (*néant*) unawares where I was not . . .

The philosophical discoveries I made flattered my vanity extremely: I often imagined myself a great man, discovering new truths for the benefit of mankind and, with a proud consciousness of my own worth, regarded the rest of humanity: but strangely enough when I encountered those other mortals, I felt shy of each of them, and the higher I set myself in my own estimation, the less was I capable not only of exhibiting the consciousness of my own dignity, but even of accustoming myself to avoid being ashamed of my simplest words and movements.

At the time of the move to Kazán a serf-lad of about his own age was presented to each of the young Tolstoys to attend on him. One of these, Vanúsha, later on accompanied Tolstoy to the Caucasus, and was still living in Túla, at a good old age, when last I heard of him.

For five and a half years, from the autumn of 1841 to the spring of 1847, the brothers lived at Kazán, returning each summer to Yásnaya for the vacations. They all entered Kazán University. The aunt who was their guardian and with whom they lived the greater part of the time, was a kind but not particularly clever woman. Her husband was wealthy and the house was the centre of much hospitality and gaiety.

Leo Tolstoy, with the idea of becoming a diplomat, prepared to enter the faculty of Oriental Languages, in which a knowledge of Arabic and Turco-Tartar was required. He worked hard, and matriculated in May 1844, before he was sixteen, passing excellently in French (for which he received the mark 5 +; 5 being in an ordinary way the highest mark, and the + indicating exceptional distinction); German, Arabic, and Turco-Tartar very well; and in English, Logic, Mathematics, and Russian Literature, well; but he did indifferently in Latin, and failed completely in History and Geography, getting the lowest mark, a 1, for each of these. Of History he says, 'I knew nothing,' and of Geography 'still less'; adding, 'I was asked to name the French seaports, but could not name a single one'. At the end of the summer vacation he was admitted for re-examination in the subjects in which he had failed, and then passed successfully.

We may assume that a passage such as the following from *Boyhood* records his own dreams at this age.

> I was then nearly sixteen. Tutors still visited me and I was reluctantly and grudgingly preparing for the University . . .
> At that period, which I regard as the end of boyhood and beginning of youth, my dreams were based on four feelings: love *of her*, the imaginary woman of whom I always dreamt in one and the same way and whom I expected at any moment to meet somewhere . . . The second feeling was the love of being loved. I wanted everybody to know me and love me, I wanted to tell my name . . . and for everybody to be struck by this information, to surround me and thank me for something. The third feeling was hope of some unusual, vainglorious good-fortune, and was so strong and firm that it verged on insanity. The fourth and chief feeling was self-disgust and repentance, but repentance so mingled with hope of happiness that it had nothing sad about it . . . I even revelled in my repulsion for the past and tried to see it blacker than it really was. The blacker the circle of my recollections of the past, the clearer and brighter stood out the clear, bright point of the present, and the fairer streamed the rainbow colours of the future. That voice of repentance and passionate desire for perfection was the main new sensation of my soul at this period of

my development, and it was this that laid a new foundation for my views of myself, of mankind, and of God's universe.

Oh, beneficent and comforting voice that hast so often since then – in sad times when my soul has silently submitted to the powers of worldly deceit and debauch – suddenly and boldly risen up against all falsehood, virulently denounced the past, showing me, and making me love, the bright point of the present, and promising welfare and happiness in the future – beneficent, comforting voice! – can it be that you will ever cease to make yourself heard?

The winter season when Tolstoy, as a student at the University and a young man of good position, entered Kazán society was a particularly gay one [1844–5]. He attended many balls, given by the Governor of the Province, by the *Maréchal de la Noblesse*, and by private people, as well as many masquerades, concerts, tableaux-vivants, and private theatricals. He was long remembered by old inhabitants as having been 'present at all the balls, soirées, and aristocratic parties, a welcome guest everywhere, and always dancing; but far from being a ladies' man he was distinguished by a strange awkwardness and shyness'. At Carnival time in 1845 he and his brother Sergéy took parts in two plays which were given very successfully for some charitable object.

As to the nature of Kazán society and of his surroundings there, accounts are contradictory. On the one hand, we have his own state-ment that (imitating his brother Sergéy in this as in other matters) he became 'depraved', and Zagóskin, a fellow-student of Tolstoy's at the University, says that the surroundings in which the latter moved were demoralising and must have been repellent to him. On the other hand, on seeing Zagóskin's remarks, Tolstoy (in whom there was often observable a strong spirit of contradiction) replied:

I did not feel any repulsion but was very glad to enjoy myself in Kazán society which was then very good. I am on the contrary thank-ful to fate that I passed my first youth in an environment where a young man could be young without touching problems beyond his grasp, and that I lived a life which, though idle and luxurious, was yet not evil.

The explanation of these contradictions, no doubt, is that the family circle in which Tolstoy lived was an affectionate one, and he himself not only enjoyed his life but formed friendships and made efforts to which in later years he looked back with satisfaction. Yet there was assuredly much in his life and in the life around him which (except when others were severe on it) he recalled with grave disapproval, a disapproval plainly expressed in his *Confession*.

To come as near as we may to the truth we must allow for the personal element which in Tolstoy's case was violent and fluctuating.

With constant amusements going on around him it is not surprising that at the end of his first University year he failed in his examinations. The failure does not however appear to have been entirely his fault, for he tells us:

> Ivanóv, Professor of Russian History, prevented me from passing to the second course (though I had not missed a single lecture and knew Russian History quite well) because he had quarrelled with my family. The same Professor also gave me the lowest mark – a 'one' – for German, though I knew the language incomparably better than any student in our division.

Instead of remaining for a second year in the first course of Oriental Languages, Tolstoy preferred to leave that faculty, and in August 1845 he entered the faculty of Law. During the first months of this new course he hardly studied at all, throwing himself more than ever into the gay life of Kazán society. Before midwinter however he began, for the first time as he tells us, 'to study seriously, and I even found a certain pleasure in so doing'. Comparative Jurisprudence and Criminal Law interested him, and his attention was especially arrested by a discussion on Capital Punishment. Meyer, Professor of Civil Law, set him a task which quite absorbed him; it was the comparison of Montesquieu's *Esprit des Lois* with Catherine II's *Great Nakáz*. The conclusion to which he came was that in Catherine's *Nakáz* Montesquieu's Liberal ideas are found mixed with an expression of Catherine's own despotism and vanity, and that the *Nakáz* brought more fame to Catherine than good to Russia.

Of this study Tolstoy remarked to his German biographer that it was perhaps the chief cause of his leaving the University prematurely. He felt little interest in the subjects the Professors lectured on. It was his way to devote himself ardently to whatever he took up, and he read innumerable books, but always at any one time in one and the same direction. When a subject interested him he turned neither to the right nor to the left but tried to acquaint himself with all that could throw light on it. So it was at Kazán, and he found the University curriculum an obstacle to mastering the matters that occupied his mind.

He passed his examinations successfully in May 1846, and was duly admitted to the second year's course of Jurisprudence. Some time previously he and another student had disputed which of them had the better memory, and to test this each of them learnt by heart the reply to one examination question in History. Tolstoy's task was to learn the life of Mazéppa, and as luck would have it that was the very question he happened to draw at his examination, so that he naturally obtained a 5, the highest mark.

From the autumn of 1846 the brothers ceased to live at their aunt's and settled in a flat of their own, consisting of five rooms.

A fellow-student, Nazárev, has given us his impression of Tolstoy as a student. He says:

> I kept clear of the Count, who from our first meeting repelled me by his assumption of coldness, his bristly hair, and the piercing expression of his half-closed eyes. I had never met a young man with such a strange, and to me incomprehensible, air of importance and self-satisfaction . . .
>
> At first I seldom met the Count, who in spite of his awkwardness and bashfulness had joined the small group of so-called 'aristocrats'. He hardly replied to my greetings, as if wishing to intimate that even here we were far from being equals, since he drove up with a fast trotter and I came on foot . . .

One gathers that Tolstoy was in those days particularly careful of his personal appearance, his clothes indicating his aristocratic pretensions. But though externally the Tolstoy of 1846 differed greatly from the Tolstoy of forty years later, his conversation ran on much the same lines as in later life, and was uttered with the intensity of conviction and the flashes of dry humour which later on made even the most didactic of his writings so readable.

It so happened that Nazárev and Tolstoy were both late for a lecture on History one day, and were incarcerated together by order of the Inspector, that being a usual punishment for such unpunctuality. Their conversation in their place of confinement having led to some mention of Lérmontov's poem, *The Demon*, Tolstoy took occasion to speak ironically of verse generally, and then, noticing a volume his companion had of Karamzín's *History of Russia*, he attacked History as the dullest and almost the most useless of subjects. A collection of fables and useless details, sprinkled with a mass of unnecessary figures and proper names . . . Who wants to know that the second marriage of John the Terrible, with Temrúk's daughter, took place on 21st August 1562; and his fourth marriage, with Anna Alexéevna Koltórskaya, in 1572? Yet they expect me to grind all this, and if I don't, the examiner gives me a 'one'.

Later on, says Nazárev,

the, to me, irresistible force of Tolstoy's doubts fell upon the University and on University teaching in general. The phrase 'The Temple of Science' was constantly on his lips. Remaining perfectly serious himself, he portrayed our professors in such a comical light that in spite of all my efforts to appear indifferent I laughed like one possessed . . . 'Yet,' said Tolstoy, 'we both had a right to expect that we should leave this temple useful men, equipped with knowledge. But what shall we really carry away from the University? . . . What shall we be good for, and to whom shall we be necessary?'

Nazárev says that in spite of the feeling, half of dislike, half of perplexity, that Tolstoy evoked in him, he well remembers that he was dimly conscious of something remarkable, exceptional, and at the same time inexplicable, about him.

From the educational articles Tolstoy wrote sixteen years later we know that he disapproved of examinations, of the restricted groove of studies marked out for the students in each faculty, and of the system which made it necessary for the professors to deliver original lectures of their own and obliged the students to listen to those lectures and study them however incompetent the professors might be.

During his second year in the Faculty of Law Tolstoy attended lectures very irregularly and received bad marks for 'diligence' from the professors generally at the half-yearly examination.

The fact that his brother Sergéy had finished his studies and was leaving, strengthened Tolstoy's dissatisfaction with the University. It also happened just at this time that the division of the family estates between the brothers and their sister was settled, and Leo inherited Yásnaya Polyána with four other estates, about 5,400 acres of land and 330 male peasants besides their womenfolk. A sense of responsibility for their welfare attracted him to Yásnaya Polyána, and finally, without waiting for the May examinations, we find him, soon after Easter 1847, applying to have his name removed from the University roll 'on account of ill health and family affairs'. He really had been in hospital in March, but the plea of ill health was a mere excuse.

His failure to take a degree was a source of great annoyance and disappointment to him, and it must not be supposed that he left Kazán with any idea of taking life easily or neglecting further study.

Tolstoy kept a private Diary during the greater part of his life, and the first volume that has been preserved begins on 17th March 1847, when he was in hospital at Kazán. On its first page he notes that he is entirely alone, and adds:

The chief advantage is that I have come to see clearly that the irregular life which the majority of fashionable people suppose to be an outcome of youth is really an outcome of early spiritual depravity. A man living in society finds solitude as beneficial as one not living in society finds social intercourse . . . It is easier to write ten volumes of philosophy than to put a single precept into practice.

A month later he notes:

Of late I have failed to conduct myself as I should wish; of which the cause has been, first, my removal from hospital, and secondly, the company in which I am beginning increasingly to move . . .

I find myself confronted by the question: 'What is the aim of man's life?' and . . . I invariably arrive at the conclusion that the purpose of our human existence is to afford a maximum of help towards the completest development of everything that exists.

Here he had propounded a question that always seemed to him supremely important, but to which he found quite a different answer in later years. On the same day he writes:

I should be the unhappiest of men if I could not find a purpose for my life – a purpose both general and useful . . . So now my whole life will be an active and constant striving towards that single aim.

Here are some rules he set himself at that time:

1 To fulfil what I set myself, despite all obstacles.
2 To fulfil well what I undertake.
3 Never to refer to a book for what I have forgotten, but always to try to recall it to mind myself.

4 Always to make my mind work with its utmost power.
5 Always to read and think aloud.
6 Not to be ashamed of telling people who interrupt me that they are hindering me: letting them first feel it, but (if they do not understand) telling them, with an apology.

Deciding to settle at Yásnaya for two years, he drew up a list of studies he intended to pursue for his own mental development and to qualify for a University degree; and this list was, as the reader will see, appalling in its scope.

1 To study the whole course of law necessary to get my degree.
2 To study practical medicine, and to some extent its theory also.
3 To study: French, Russian, German, English, Italian, and Latin.
4 To study agriculture, theoretically and practically,
5 To study History, Geography, and Statistics.
6 To study Mathematics (the High School course).
7 To write my [University] thesis.
8 To reach the highest perfection I can in music and painting.
9 To write down rules (for my conduct).
10 To acquire some knowledge of the natural sciences, and
11 To write essays on all the subjects I study.

Such rules and resolutions abound in Tolstoy's Diary. After failing to act up to them, he again and again gathers his energies and maps out for himself plans of life and courses of study sufficient to tax the energies of an intellectual giant.

During the last year of his life at Kazán he made close friends with a student named Dyákov (the Dmítri of *Boyhood*), and under his influence had developed

an ecstatic worship of the ideal of virtue, and the conviction that it is man's destiny continually to perfect himself. To put all mankind right and to destroy all human vices and misfortunes appeared a matter that could well be accomplished. It seemed quite easy and simple to put oneself right, to acquire all the virtues, and to be happy.

As to his religious opinions at this time, he tells us that having believed in the doctrines of his Church as a boy and confessed and taken Communion devoutly, by the time he was fourteen:

I began to reflect on life in general and came up against religion which did not coincide with my theories, and of course I considered it a good thing to get rid of it.

[Letter to his Aunt, Alexándra Tolstoy, in 1859]

I was baptised and brought up in the Orthodox Christian faith. I was taught it in childhood and all through my boyhood and youth. But when I left the University in my second year, at the age of eighteen, I no longer believed anything I had been taught.   [*Confession*]

His Diary nevertheless shows that he prayed frequently and earnestly; the fact no doubt being, that though intellectually he discarded the Orthodox Russo-Greek Church, in times of trouble or distress he instinctively appealed to God for help. His opinions were wavering and immature, as he himself tells us in another passage:

The religious beliefs taught me in childhood disappeared . . . and as from the age of fifteen I began to read philosophical works, my rejection of those beliefs became a conscious one at a very early age. From the time I was sixteen I ceased to go to Church or to fast of my own volition. I did not believe what had been taught me in childhood, but I believed in something. What it was I believed in I could not at all have said. I believed in a God, or rather I did not deny God; but I could not have said what sort of God. Neither did I deny Christ and his teaching, but what his teaching consisted in I again could not have said.

   Looking back on that time I now see clearly that my faith – my only real faith, that which apart from my animal instincts gave impulse to my life – was a belief in perfecting myself. But in what this perfecting consisted and what its object was, I could not have said. I tried to perfect myself mentally – I studied everything I could, anything life threw in my way; I tried to perfect my will, I drew up rules which I tried to follow; I perfected myself physically, cultivating my strength and agility by all sorts of exercises and accustoming myself to endurance and patience by all kinds of privations. And all this I considered to be the pursuit of perfection. The beginning of it all was of course moral perfection; but that was soon replaced by perfection in general: by the desire to be better not in my own eyes or those of God, but in the eyes of other people. And very soon this effort again changed into a desire to be stronger than others: to be more famous, more important and richer than others.   [*Confession*]

At one time his special desire was to become the strongest man in the world, and he devoted himself ardently to gymnastics for a number of years. His muscular strength and dexterity remained remarkable till he was well advanced in years, and visitors at Yásnaya Polyána long after his marriage were often amazed at his agility.

In an early draft of his *Confession* the following passage occurs:

> I remember that on the day of my first examination at the University, walking near the Black Lake I prayed God to enable me to pass the examination, and while learning the words of the Catechism I saw clearly that the whole Catechism was false.

That relates to 29th May 1844.

When speaking of Tolstoy's relations with women, it should be borne in mind that incontinence for young men was considered so natural that few in his position would have felt any serious qualms of conscience about such visits to houses of ill-fame as he lets us know that he began to pay at this time. His brother Dmítri, however, led a chaste life, and alternating with gross lapses of conduct we find Leo noting down for his own guidance such resolutions as the following:

> To regard the society of women as an inevitable evil of social life and to avoid it as much as possible. From whom indeed do we learn sensuality, effeminacy, frivolity in everything, and many other vices, if not from women? Whose fault is it, if not women's, that we lose our innate qualities of boldness, resolution, reasonableness, justice, etc.? Women are more receptive than men, therefore in virtuous ages women were better than we; but in the present depraved and vicious age they are worse than we are.

During his years at the University, Tolstoy saw much of his brother Dmítri, of whom he says:

> I remember also that when my elder brother Dmítri, who was then at the University, suddenly in the passionate way natural to him devoted himself to religion and began to attend all the Church services, to fast, and to lead a pure and moral life, we all – even our elders – unceasingly held him up to ridicule and called him, for some unknown reason, 'Noah'. I remember that Músin-Púshkin, the then Curator of Kazán University, when inviting us to a dance at his house ironically persuaded my brother (who had declined the invitation)

by using the argument that even David danced before the Ark. I sympathised with these jokes made by my elders, and drew from them the conclusion that though it is necessary to learn the catechism and go to church one must not take such things too seriously.

[*Confession*]

Again we read of this brother:

His peculiarities became manifest and are impressed on my mind from the time of our life at Kazán. Formerly in Moscow I remember that he did not fall in love, as Serëzha and I did, and was not fond of dancing or of military pageants, but studied well and strenuously . . . At Kazán I, who had always imitated Serëzha, began to grow depraved . . . Not only at Kazán but even earlier I used to take pains about my appearance. I tried to be elegant and *comme il faut*. There was no trace of anything of that kind in Mítenka. I think he never suffered from the usual vices of youth; he was always serious, thoughtful, pure, and resolute, though hot-tempered, and whatever he did he did to the best of his ability . . . He wrote verse with great facility. I remember how admirably he translated Schiller's *Der Jüngling am Bache*, but he did not devote himself to this occupation . . . He grew up associating little with others, always except in moments of anger, quiet and serious. He was tall, rather thin, and not very strong, with long, large hands and round shoulders. I do not know how or by what he was attracted at so early an age towards a religious life, but it began in the very first year of his University career. His religious aspirations naturally directed him to Church life, and he devoted himself to this with his usual thoroughness.

In Mítenka there must have existed that valuable characteristic which I believe my mother to have had and which I knew in Nikólenka, but of which I was altogether devoid – complete indifference to other people's opinion about oneself. Until quite lately (in old age) I have never been able to divest myself of concern about people's opinion, but Mítenka was quite free from this. I never remembered on his face that restrained smile which involuntarily appears when one is being praised. I always remember his serious, quiet, sad, sometimes severe, almond-shaped hazel eyes. Only in our Kazán days did we begin to pay particular attention to him, and then merely because while Serëzha and I attached great importance to what was *comme il faut* – to externalities – he was careless and untidy and we condemned him for this.

We others, especially Serëzha, kept up acquaintance with our aristocratic comrades and other young men. Mítenka on the contrary selected out of all the students a piteous-looking, poor, shabbily dressed youth, Poluboyárinov [which may be translated half-noble] – whom a humorous fellow-student of ours called Polubezobédov [half-dinnerless] – and consorted only with him, and with him prepared for the examinations . . . We brothers, and even our aunt, looked down on Mítenka with a certain contempt for his low tastes and associates; and the same attitude was adopted by our frivolous comrades.

After their University days were over Tolstoy saw little of his brother Dmítri; so it will be convenient here to sacrifice chronological sequence and relate what more there is to tell of the latter's life and death. The material is again supplied by Tolstoy's *Reminiscences*.

When we divided up the family property, Yásnaya Polyána, the estate where we lived, was, according to custom, given to me (the youngest). Serëzha, as a lover of horses and according to his wish, received Pirogóvo, where there was a stud. To Mítenka and Nikólenka were given the two other estates: to Nikólenka, Nikólskoe, to Mítenka, the Kursk estate, Sherbachóvka. I have kept a note of Mítenka's showing how he regarded the possession of serfs. The idea that it is wrong, and that serfs ought to be liberated, was quite unknown in our circle in the 1840s. The hereditary possession of serfs seemed a necessary condition of life, and all that could be done to prevent its being an evil was to attend not only to their material but also to their moral welfare. In this sense Mítenka wrote very seriously, naïvely, and sincerely. Thinking he could not do otherwise, he, a lad of twenty, when he left the University took it upon himself to direct the morality of hundreds of peasant families, and to do this (as Gógol recommended in his *Letters to a Landowner*) by threats of punishments and by punishments . . . But besides this duty to his serfs there was another duty which at that time it seemed impossible not to fulfil: namely, Military or Civil service. And Mítenka decided to enter the Civil Service.

Tolstoy proceeds to tell how his brother, desiring to be useful to his country, chose legislation as his speciality, and going to Petersburg astonished the Head of the Department as well as certain aristocratic acquaintances by asking where he could find a place in which he could be *useful*. The friend to whom he went for advice regarded the service of the State merely as a means of satisfying ambition, and 'such a question had probably never occurred to him before'. Eventually we find Dmítri returning home discouraged, and taking up some local work. All this to some extent helps us to understand Leo Tolstoy's sceptical attitude towards the institution of Government, and his strong belief that men in Government service are solely actuated by selfish motives.

Tolstoy continues:

After we had both left the University I lost sight of him. I know he lived the same severe, abstemious life, knowing neither wine, tobacco, nor above all women, till he was twenty-six, which was very rare in those days. I know also that he associated with monks and pilgrims . . . I think I was already in the Caucasus when an extraordinary change took place. He suddenly took to drinking, smoking, wasting money, and going with women. How it happened I do not know; I did not see him at the time. I only know that his seducer was a thoroughly immoral man of very attractive appearance, the youngest son of Islénev [an uncle of the lady Leo Tolstoy subsequently married].

In this life Mítenka remained the same serious religious man he was in everything. He ransomed from the brothel a prostitute named Másha, who was the first woman he knew, and took her into his house. But this life did not last long. I believe it was less the vicious and unhealthy life he led for some months in Moscow than his mental struggle and his qualms of conscience that suddenly destroyed his powerful organism. He became consumptive, went to the country, was doctored in the provincial town, and took to his bed in Orël, where I saw him for the last time just after the Crimean war. He was in a dreadful state of emaciation: one could even see how his enormous hand joined on to the two bones of his lower arm; his face was all eyes, and they were still the same beautiful serious eyes with a penetrating expression of enquiry in them. He was constantly coughing and spitting, but was loth to die and reluctant to believe he was dying. Poor pockmarked Másha, whom he had rescued, was with him and nursed him. In my presence, at his own wish, a wonder-working icon was brought. I remember the expression of his face when he prayed to it . . . He died a few days later.

Readers of the didactic works of Tolstoy's later years will notice how closely his injunctions to a man to keep to the first woman, whoever she may be, with whom he has had intimate relations, correspond with the course actually followed by his brother Dmítri.

When Tolstoy left the University, however, these things were still unthought of. Let us, before returning to the events of his own life at that time, notice some books which he read between the ages of fourteen and twenty-one. They included:

The Sermon on the Mount from St Matthew's Gospel.

Rousseau's *Confessions* and *Émile*,

Dickens's *David Copperfield*,

Gógol's *Vii*, which all had an 'immense' influence on him.

In another category came works which he says had 'very great' influence. These were:

Rousseau's *Nouvelle Héloïse*.

Sterne's *Sentimental Journey*.

Púshkin's *Eugéni Onégin*.

Schiller's *The Robbers*.

Gógol's *Dead Souls*.

Turgénev's *A Sportsman's Notebook*.

Druzhínin's *Pólenka Sax*.

Grigoróvich's *Antón Gormeyka*, and the chapter *Tamán* from Lérmontov's *A Hero of Our Times*.

In a third category he mentions some of Gógol's Shorter Stories and Prescott's *Conquest of Mexico*, as having had 'great' influence.

In these works one finds many ideas which have been congenial to Tolstoy throughout his life and his adhesion to which only became firmer with age. In illustration of this, take a couple of passages from Dickens which many readers may have passed without much attention, but which to Tolstoy represented the absolute truth of the matters they touch on. David Copperfield says of Parliament:

> I considered myself reasonably entitled to escape from the dreary debates. One joyful night, therefore, I noted down the music of the parliamentary bagpipes for the last time, and I have never heard it since; though I still recognise the old drone in the newspapers without any substantial variation (except, perhaps, that there is more of it) all the livelong session.

To most Englishmen with memories of Pym and Hampden, or

personal knowledge of the lives of men who have devoted themselves disinterestedly to public affairs, parliamentary or local, Dickens's sneers at Parliament as 'the national dust-yard', and his account of the Eatanswill election in *The Pickwick Papers*, seem merely humorous; but to Tolstoy, with his inherited dislike of government, this testimony from a great English writer who had served as a parliamentary reporter, seemed irrefutable evidence of the futility of parliaments. This, I think, was of importance later on, when Tolstoy's outlook on life led him to condemn governments in general, for it predisposed him to extend that condemnation to parliamentary as well as to autocratic government and to refuse any support to the Cadet Party which tried in the Dúma to introduce responsible parliamentary government; an attempt which, had it succeeded, might have averted the Bolshévik revolution – which both by its methods and its results would have horrified Tolstoy.

Take, again, a passage in which Dickens hits a nail adroitly on the head:

Mr Micawber had a relish in this formal piling up of words, which, however ludicrously displayed in his case, was, I must say, not at all peculiar to him. I have observed it, in the course of my life, in numbers of men. It seems to me to be a general rule. In the taking of legal oaths, for instance, deponents seem to enjoy themselves mightily when they come to several grand words in succession, for the expression of one idea – as, that they utterly detest, abominate, and abjure, and so forth – and the old anathemas were made relishing on the same principle. We talk about the tyranny of words, but we like to tyrannise over them too. We are fond of having a large superfluous establishment of words to wait upon us on great occasions; we think it looks important, and sounds well. As we are not particular about the meaning of our liveries on State occasions, if they be but fine and numerous enough, so the meaning or necessity of our words is a secondary consideration, if there be but a great parade of them.

No modern writer has ever more carefully eschewed the practice Dickens here attacks than Tolstoy did throughout his career. Indeed, he is far stricter than Dickens himself in this respect.

But much more important than the influence of Dickens was that of Rousseau, of whom Tolstoy once remarked:

I have read the whole of Rousseau – all his twenty volumes, including his *Dictionary of Music*. I was more than enthusiastic about him, I worshipped him. At the age of fifteen I wore a medallion portrait of him next my body instead of the Orthodox cross. Many of his pages are so akin to me that it seems to me that I must have written them myself.

Another writer who influenced Tolstoy, though to a much smaller extent, was Voltaire, of whom he says:

I also remember that I read Voltaire when I was very young, and his ridicule [of religion] not only did not shock me, but amused me very much.

Everything Tolstoy did in his life he did with intensity; and that this applies to the way in which he read books in his youth, is shown by the fact that we find him in *What is Art?* written when he was seventy, according the highest praise to books he had read before he was twenty-one, or even before he was fourteen.

It was in the spring of 1847 that Tolstoy, who was not yet nineteen, returned to his estate of Yásnaya Polyána, to live with his dear 'Auntie' Tatiána; to 'perfect' himself, to study, to manage his estate, and to improve the condition of his serfs. The last part of this programme at any rate, was not at that time destined to have much success. Though one must never treat Tolstoy's fiction as strictly autobiographical, yet *A Landlord's Morning* gives a very fair idea of his own efforts to improve the lot of his serfs and of the difficulties and failures he encountered in the course of that attempt. In that story Prince Nekhlyúdov decides to leave the University and settle in the country, and writes to his aunt:

As I already wrote you I found affairs in indescribable disorder. Wishing to put them right I discovered that the chief evil is the truly pitiable, wretched condition of the serfs, and this is an evil that can only be remedied by work and patience. If you could but see two of my serfs, David and Iván, and the life they and their families lead, I am sure the sight of these two poor wretches would convince you more than all I can say in explanation of my intention.

Is it not my plain and sacred duty to care for the welfare of these seven hundred souls for whom I must account to God? Will it not be a sin if following plans of pleasure or ambition, I abandon them to the caprice of coarse Elders and stewards? And why should I seek in any other sphere opportunities of being useful and doing good, when I have before me such a noble, brilliant, and intimate duty?

Not only is this letter just such as Tolstoy himself may have written, but the difficulties Nekhlyúdov encounters when he tries to move his peasants from the ruts to which generations of serfdom had accustomed them are just those Tolstoy himself met with: the suspicion shown by the serfs towards any fresh interference on the part of the master, and the fact that ways to which a community have grown accustomed are not easily changed by the sudden effort of a well-intentioned but inexperienced proprietor. Serfdom was so unsatisfactory a condition, the physical, mental, and moral needs of the serfs were so urgent, Tolstoy's efforts to improve their condition produced such poor results, and the serfs were so intractable, that far from his exertions yielding him moral satisfaction, they only produced 'a mixed feeling of weariness, shame, impotence, and regret', as readers of *A Landlord's Morning* may well understand.

After spending two summers at Yásnaya, Tolstoy went to Moscow in October 1848 and passed that winter idly amusing himself in Moscow society, to which he had ready access. Early in 1849 he went to Petersburg where he entered for examination at the University of that city.

On 13th February he wrote to his brother Sergéy:

I write you this letter from Petersburg, where I intend to remain *for ever* . . . I have decided to stay here for my examinations and then to enter the service . . .

In brief, I must say that Petersburg life has a great and good influence on me: it accustoms me to activity and supplies the place of a fixed table of occupations. Somehow one cannot be idle; everyone is occupied and active; one cannot find a man with whom one could lead an aimless life and one can't do it alone . . .

I know you will not believe that I have changed, but will say, 'It's already the twentieth time and nothing comes of you – the emptiest of fellows.' No, I have now altered in quite a new way. I used to say to myself: 'Now I will change,' but at last I see that I have changed, and I say, 'I have changed.'

Above all, I am now quite convinced that one cannot live by theorising and philosophising, but must live positively, i.e. must be a practical man. That is a great step in advance and a great change; it never happened to me before. If one is young and wishes to live, there is no place in Russia but Petersburg for it . . .

On 1st May he wrote again to his brother, in a very different strain:

Serëzha! I think you already say I am 'the emptiest of fellows', and it is true. God knows what I have done! I came to Petersburg without any reason and have done nothing useful here, but have spent heaps of money and got into debt. Stupid! Insufferably stupid! You can't believe how it torments me. Above all, the *debts*, which I *must* pay *as soon as possible*, because if I don't pay them soon, besides losing the money I shall lose my reputation . . . I know you will cry out; but what's to be done? One commits such folly once in a lifetime. I have had to pay for my freedom (there was no one to thrash me, that was my chief misfortune) and for philosophising, and now I have paid for it. Be so kind as to arrange to get me out of this false and horrid position – penniless and in debt all round.

He goes on to mention that he had passed two examinations at the University, but that he had altered his mind, and now instead of completing his examinations wanted to 'enter the Horse Guards as a Cadet'. (A Cadet was a young man who volunteered for the army. Before receiving a commission a Cadet lived with the officers, while preparing to become one of them.)

God willing, I will amend and become a steady man at last. I hope much from my service as a Cadet, which will train me to practical life, and *nolens-volens* I shall have to earn the rank of officer. With luck, i.e. if the Guards go into action, I may get a commission even before the usual two years are up. The Guards start for the front at the end of May. At present I can do nothing: first, because I have no money (of which I shall not need much, I fancy), and secondly, because my two birth-certificates are at Yásnaya. Have them sent on as soon as possible.

Before long, Tolstoy was again writing to his brother:

In my last letter I wrote much nonsense, of which the chief item was that I intended to enter the Horse Guards; I shall act on that plan only in case I fail in my examinations and if the war is a serious one.

The war in question was Russia's share in quelling the Hungarian rebellion. Not a thought of the justice of the cause seems at that time to have crossed the mind of the man who in later life became so powerful an indicter of war.

This is Tolstoy's own summary, written many years later, of the period we are now dealing with:

It was very pleasant living in the country with Auntie Tatiána, but an indefinite thirst for knowledge drew me away to a distance. This was in 1848, and I was still uncertain what to undertake. In Petersburg two roads were open to me. I could either enter the army, to take part in the Hungarian campaign, or I could complete my studies at the University to enter the Civil Service. My thirst for knowledge conquered my ambition, and I again began to study. I even passed two examinations in Law, but then all my good resolutions broke down. Spring came, and the charm of country life again drew me back to my estate

Of the two examinations he passed that April he says:

In 1848 I went to pass the examinations for my degree at Petersburg University, knowing literally nothing, and reading up only for a week or two. I worked day and night; and passed with Honours in Civil and Criminal Law after giving only one week to each subject.

But in spite of this success he did not take the remaining examinations, and returned to Yásnaya without having obtained a degree – finally abandoning the attempt to do so.

In later times when Tolstoy's reputation was worldwide, critics often amused themselves by detecting inconsistencies in his conduct and questioning his sincerity. But the proof of his sincerity is writ large in the story of his life. Time after time, from the earliest pages of his Diary, we find him vehemently resolving never more to do certain things but always to do other things, and again and again confessing in the greatest distress that he had failed to carry out his intentions; yet in spite of everything he returns, and again returns, to his earliest ideals, and gradually shaping his life into accord with them, eventually forms habits which when he first extolled them appeared utterly beyond his reach. Not insincerity, but impetuosity retrieved by extraordinary tenacity of purpose, characterised him. It was the same with his thirst for knowledge as with his yet deeper thirst after righteousness. Often as he was swayed by the lures of life, each of those two great desires found its satisfaction at last.

The letters quoted above show some consciousness of the fact that there is a practical side to life not to be mastered by theorising; but the duty of learning by experience as well as by ratiocination is one Tolstoy seldom dwelt on, and never, I think, realised at all fully.

Another characteristic matter alluded to in these letters is the difficulty he found himself in for lack of his birth-certificates and other papers. Russia had long suffered from a superabundance of red tape which contrasted strongly with the slipshod habits of its people and promoted the hatred of officialism which is still so general there. The fact that Tolstoy was on several occasions put to great inconvenience for lack of certificates which it was not in his nature methodically to keep in readiness, seems a small matter, but it probably had its share in increasing his dislike of governments.

From Petersburg he brought back with him to Yásnaya a gifted but drunken German musician named Rudolph, with whom he chanced to make acquaintance and whose talent he discerned. For some time Tolstoy devoted himself passionately to music, acquiring sufficient skill to become an excellent and sympathetic accompanist on the piano, and at one time he even apparently thought of becoming a professional musician. He was always most susceptible to the influence of music, and in music as in literature had strong sympathies and antipathies. Rudolph supplies the principal figure in his story *Albert*, written some years later.

Aunt Tatiána, who had played the piano excellently in youth but had quite given it up for nearly thirty years, and who was now fifty-three years of age, resumed its practice and, Tolstoy tells us, played duets with him and often surprised him by the accuracy and beauty of her execution.

Tolstoy's life is full of events in which he played a public part, and these necessarily so overshadow his private recreations, that there will be but scant opportunity to dwell on the influence music had on him from his youth to his old age. Suffice it to say that besides Weber (especially his Sonata in A flat major), Mozart, Haydn, Schubert, Schumann, Bach, Chopin, Beethoven's earlier works, and Wieniawski, Tolstoy was particularly partial to Russian folk songs, such as *Down along our Mother Vólga*, to Cossack and soldier songs, and to those that used to be sung by the Gypsy choirs. He maintained that Gypsy singing was sincere and infected the hearers, so that it was true art, even though it might be art of an inferior order.

Readers who want to know more about Tolstoy's likes and dislikes in music are referred to the very thorough treatment of it by his eldest son, Count Sergéy Tolstoy, in his article on 'Music in Tolstoy's Life'.*

For the next three years Tolstoy lived partly at Yásnaya and partly in Túla and in Moscow, and led a life alternating between the asceticism of his brother Dmítri and the self-indulgence of his brother Sergéy, giving way to dissipation, hunting, Gypsy-girl singers, and, he tells us, 'above all to cards: I lost heavily and deranged my affairs' – which, indeed, became seriously involved. But even here we find him, in the summer of 1850, resuming his Diary with penitence and self-reproach and drawing up a timetable of how his days are in future to be spent: estate-management, bathing, diary-writing, music, dinner, rest, reading, bathing, and again estate-business to close the day. This curriculum was, however, neglected. Gusts of passion often swept away his good resolutions.

At this time [1849] he made his first attempt to start a school for the peasant children of Yásnaya, but it was closed again two years later when he was in pecuniary difficulties; and it was not till 1862 that he discovered that he had infringed the law by opening it without official permission.

In relation to women Tolstoy's ideal was a regular and affectionate family life. Women were for him divided into two groups: those sacred ones who could be looked on as possible wives or sisters, and those who could be paid for and possessed for short periods. His animal passions were very strong, and late in life he told me that neither drinking, cards, smoking, nor any other bad habit, had been nearly so hard for him to overcome as his desire for women. But he never doubted that that desire was a bad one. To judge him fairly it must be remembered how loose was the general tone of the society in which he lived, and that the advice given him at this critical time of his life by those who were his natural guides was not that he should live a chaste life, but that he should attach himself to a woman of good social position. In his *Confession* he tells us:

> The kind aunt with whom I lived, herself the purest of beings, always told me that there was nothing she so desired for me as that I should have relations with a married woman: *Rien ne forme un jeune homme, comme une liaison avec une femme comme il faut* [Nothing so forms a young man as an intimacy with a woman of good breeding]. Another

* See *Family Views of Tolstoy*, Allen and Unwin, 1926.

happiness she desired for me was that I should become an aide-de-camp, and if possible aide-de-camp to the Emperor. But the greatest happiness of all would be that I should marry a very rich girl and become possessed of as many serfs as possible.

We never find Tolstoy involved in any family scandal or called on to fight a duel about women; but his Diary at this period contains many traces of his struggles and his falls, as when, calling in his pride as an aid to his conscience, he writes:

Men whom I consider morally lower than myself do evil better than I . . . I live an animal life, though not quite debauched. My occupations are almost abandoned and I am greatly depressed in spirit.

His pecuniary affairs having become disordered owing to his gambling habits, towards the end of 1850 he thought of trying to earn money by taking a contract to run the post-station at Túla, which before railways were built was an undertaking of some importance. Varied, however, as Tolstoy's abilities unquestionably were, Nature never intended him for a man of business, and this plan fortunately came to nothing.

The winter of 1850–51 he passed for the most part in Moscow, and as a foretaste of the simplification of life which was to be such a prominent feature of his later years, we find him writing to his aunt at Yásnaya: *Je dîne à la maison avec des stchi et kasha dont je me contente parfaitement* [I dine at home on cabbage soup and buckwheat porridge, with which I am quite contented]; and he goes on to say that he only awaits the preserves and home-made liqueurs [which she no doubt sent him] to have everything as he was accustomed to have it in the country.

We find Auntie Tatiána warning him against card-playing. Tolstoy replies in French:

All that you say about the perversity of play is very true, and I often think about it, and that is why I believe that I shall gamble no more . . . 'I believe,' but I hope soon to tell you for certain.

In March 1851 he returned to Moscow after visiting Yásnaya, and he notes in his Diary that he went there with the treble aim of playing cards, getting married, and entering the Civil Service. Not one of these three objects was attained. He took an aversion to cards. For marriage he considered a conjunction of love, reason, and fate, to be necessary, and none of these was present. As to entering the service, it was again the fact that he had not brought the necessary documents with him that barred the way.

In March he writes to Auntie Tatiána, and says he believes it to be true that spring brings a moral renovation. It always does him good, and he is able to maintain his good intentions for some months. Winter is the season that causes him to go wrong. Happening to read a Life of Benjamin Franklin, and borrowing an idea from him, Tolstoy, besides his Diary, started a 'Franklin Journal', in which was a tabulated list of the virtues and qualities he aimed at acquiring with ruled spaces for each day of the week, in which spaces he marked with a cross day by day those against which he had transgressed.

Next came a period of religious humility: he fasted diligently and composed a sermon, which of course was never preached. He also tried unsuccessfully to write a Gypsy story and an imitation of Sterne's *Sentimental Journey*. He even at this time began the early drafts of what eventually, after several revisions, became his first published work, *Childhood*; and the astonishing thing is that, as a recently published fragment entitled *The Story of Yesterday* shows, from the very first he showed himself master of a new style of fiction destined to play a great role in subsequent literature, and to which reference must be made in a later chapter.

This period of his life was brought to a close by the return from the Caucasus, on leave of absence, of his eldest brother Nicholas, who was by this time an artillery officer.

Anxious to economise and pay off debts contracted at cards, especially one of 4,000 rubles to Ogaróv, a gendarme officer who owned a small estate near Yásnaya, Leo resolved to accompany his brother on the latter's return to the Caucasus, and this he did at the end of April 1851. He entrusted his estate to the care of his brother-in-law (Márya's husband), who was to pay his debts and allow him only 500 rubles (then equal to about £80) a year to live on, and he gave his word not to play cards any more.

Tolstoy had another reason, to which allusion has already been made, for wishing to escape from his accustomed surroundings. His brother Sergéy was very fond of the Gypsy choirs, famous in Russia for their musical talent. These choirs used to visit Yásnaya, and Leo Tolstoy, who shared his brother's susceptibility to the fascinations of the Gypsy girls, saw a means of safety in flight to the Caucasus.

Before closing this chapter let us note the extraordinary freedom enjoyed by young men of Tolstoy's class in those days of serfdom. Economically, serfdom supplied them with means, at the expense of a class deprived of almost all rights and absolutely dependent on their owners. Even if a member of the aristocracy ruined himself, family interest or a prudent marriage often retrieved the position for him. Religious restraint counted for little, for side by side with superstition, scepticism was common among the educated. The standard of morals expected of a young man was elastic and ill-defined. No irksome sense of public duty pressed on his attention. Politics, in our sense of the word, were forbidden; and though he had to enter the State service (civil or military), this was regarded either as a way of making a career for himself or as a mere formality.

The detachment from the real business of life in which young Russians grew up and the comparative isolation in which they lived on their country estates, explain the extremely radical conclusions often arrived at by those of them who wished to make the world better. Chain a man to the heavily laden car of social progress and he can only advance very slowly, though any advance he does accomplish represents much effort and is of practical importance. Detach him from that car and he may easily and pleasantly fly away on the wings of speculation to the uttermost realms of the highest heaven without its producing any perceptible result on the lives of his fellow men. I mean, that the less a man is involved in practical work the easier and pleasanter it is for him to take up extreme positions; I do not mean to deny that activity in the realm of thought and feeling exerts an unseen yet potent influence on other minds, and ultimately on practical affairs.

A knowledge of the social surroundings in which Tolstoy developed makes it easier to understand the doctrines he subsequently taught. It was partly because he grew up in a detached and irresponsible position that the state of his own mind and soul were to him so much more important than the immediate effect of his conduct on others, and the same cause led him to remain in ignorance of lessons every intelligent man of business among us learns of necessity.

His independent position made easier the formation of that state of mind, free from intellectual prejudice, which enabled him later on to examine the claims of the Church, of the Bible, of the economists, of governments, and of the most firmly established manners and customs of society, untrammelled by fear of shocking or hurting other people, though all the time his feelings were so sensitive that it was never possible for him to doubt or question the goodness of lines of conduct he had admired and approved when in childhood he saw them practised by people near and dear to him.

Contrasting his moral attitude with that of a young Englishman anxious to do right in our day, I should say that Tolstoy had no adequate sense of being a responsible member of a complex community with the opinions and wishes of which it is necessary to reckon. On the contrary, his tendency was to recognise with extraordinary vividness a personal duty revealed by the working of his own conscience and intellect, apart from any systematic study of the social state of which he was a member.

He thus came to see things in a way we do not see them, while he remained blind to some things with which we are quite familiar. That is one reason why he is so extraordinarily interesting: he puts things in a way no Englishman would ever dream of putting them, and yet we feel how near akin we of the Western twentieth-century world are to this nineteenth-century Russian nobleman, who has so much in common with the medieval saint and the Oriental fatalist; and this helps us to realise that all nations and classes of men are indeed of one blood.

Later on, when we have to deal with Tolstoy's peaceful anarchism and his conviction that no external regulation of society is necessary, but that all men would naturally do right were they not hampered by man-made laws, it will be useful to bear in mind that his own strength grew through having to steer unaided through the stormy seas of passion, and from finding his own way to a haven the lights of which had first shone on him in childhood. Like the rest of mankind, he judged others by himself.

3

The Caucasus

The brothers Nicholas and Leo left Yásnaya Polyána on 20th April 1851, and spent a couple of weeks in Moscow. The frankness of Leo's intercourse with his Aunt Tatiána is illustrated by the following letter which he wrote telling her of a visit he paid to Sokólniki, a pleasant outskirt of Moscow on the borders of a pine forest, where a fête is held on May Day.

He wrote in French, for Tatiána, like many Russian ladies educated early in the nineteenth century, knew French better than she did Russian, but this is its translation.

I went to the fête at Sokólniki in detestable weather, which was why I did not meet any of the society ladies I wished to see. As you say I am a man who tests himself I went among the plebs in the Gypsy tents. You can easily imagine the inward struggle I there experienced, for and against. However, I came out victorious: that is to say, I gave nothing but my blessing to the gay descendants of the illustrious Pharaohs. Nicholas considers me a very agreeable travelling companion, except for my cleanliness. He is cross because, he says, I change my linen twelve times a day. I also find him a very agreeable companion, except for his dirtiness. I do not know which of us is right.

On leaving Moscow, instead of travelling to the Caucasus by the usual route via Vorónesh, Nicholas Tolstoy, who liked to do things his own way, decided that they would drive first to Kazán. Here they stayed a week visiting their acquaintances, and that was long enough for Leo to fall in love with a young lady to whom his shyness prevented his expressing his sentiments. He left for the Caucasus bearing the secret with him, and it was not long before she married someone else.

From Kazán they drove to Sarátov where they hired a boat large enough to take their travelling carriage on board, and with a crew of three men they made their way down the Vólga to Astrakhán, sometimes rowing, sometimes sailing, and sometimes drifting with the stream.

The scorn of luxury and social distinctions so prominent in Tolstoy's later philosophy was at this time more to the taste of his brother Nicholas. A gentleman drove past them in Kazán leaning on his walking-stick with ungloved hands, and that was sufficient to cause Leo to refer to him contemptuously, whereupon Nicholas, in his usual tone of good-natured irony, wanted to know why a man should be despised for not wearing gloves.

From Astrakhán they had still to drive some two hundred and seventy miles by post-chaise, but reached Starogládov, where Nicholas Tolstoy's battery was stationed, by the end of May. The whole journey from Moscow, including the stay in Kazán, had taken them nearly a month.

It will be convenient here to explain why the Russians were then fighting in the Caucasus.

After the conquest of the Tartar Khanates of Kazán and Astrakhán by Russia in the sixteenth century, the Tartar tribes were gradually pushed back to the south, until the Russians came in contact with the wild hill-tribes inhabiting the northern slopes of the Caucasian mountains. As an outpost against these tribes by the commencement of the nineteenth century a line of Cossack stations had been formed along the northern banks of the rivers Térek, flowing into the Caspian Sea, and of the Kubán, flowing into the Black Sea. Meanwhile Georgia, situated to the south of the Caucasian Mountains, had been voluntarily annexed to Russia in 1799, to escape Persian oppression; and it therefore became politically desirable for Russia to subdue the tribes that separated her from her newly acquired dependency. During the first half of the nineteenth century this task proceeded very slowly, but at the time we are dealing with, Prince Baryátinski, in command of the Russian forces stationed on the northern bank of the Térek, was undertaking a series of expeditions against the native tribes. Till then the Russians had held hardly anything south of the Térek and north of the Causasian Mountains, except their own forts and encampments, and their greatest difficulty was in dealing with the warlike Chéchen tribe which occupied the wooded ravines on the south side of the Térek and the mountainous defiles of Ichkériya. Here Tolstoy was engaged during his army service in the Caucasus. What this warfare was like we learn from his stories *The Raid, The Cossacks, The Wood-Felling,* and *Meeting an Acquaintance in the Detachment.** In less than another decade Baryátinski had captured

* All these stories are included in *The Cossacks and other Tales of the Caucasus.*

Shámyl (the famous leader who so long defied Russia) and subdued the whole country.

Soon after the brothers Tolstoy arrived at Starogládov, Nicholas was ordered to Stáry-Yurt, the fortified camp at Goryachevódsk ('Hot Springs'), an advanced post recently established to protect invalids who availed themselves of those mineral waters.

Here Leo Tolstoy first saw, and was deeply impressed by, the beauty of the magnificent mountain range he so well describes in *The Cossacks*. In July 1851 he wrote to his Aunt Tatiána:

> Nicholas left within a week of his arrival and I have followed him, so that we have now been almost three weeks here, lodging in a tent. But as the weather is fine and I am getting accustomed to this kind of life, I feel very well. There are magnificent views here, beginning where the springs are situated. It is an enormous mountain of rocks one upon another, some of which are detached and form, as it were, grottoes; others remain suspended at a great height. They are all intersected by torrents of hot water which fall noisily in certain parts, and especially in the morning cover the whole upper part of the mountains with a white vapour which this boiling water continually gives off. The water is so hot that one can boil eggs hard in three minutes. In the middle of this ravine, by the chief torrent, stand three mills one above the other built in a quite peculiar and very picturesque manner. All day long, above and below these mills, Tartar women come unceasingly to wash clothes. I should mention that they wash with their feet. It is like an ant-hill, always in motion. The women for the most part are beautiful and well formed. In spite of their poverty the costumes of Oriental women are graceful. The picturesque groups formed by the women, added to the savage beauty of the place, furnish a really admirable *coup d'œil*. I very often remain for hours admiring the view. Then again, in quite a different way, the view from the top of the mountain is even more beautiful. But I fear to weary you with my descriptions.
>
> I am very glad to be at the springs, for I benefit by them. I take ferruginous baths and no longer have pain in my feet.

As showing how hot these springs were, it may be mentioned that a dog belonging to Nicholas fell into the water and was scalded to death.

The officers Tolstoy met he found to be men without education, and he wrote:

At first many things in this society shocked me, but I have accustomed myself to them without, however, attaching myself to these gentlemen. I have found a happy mean in which there is neither pride nor familiarity.

He was helped by the fact that Nicholas was popular with everyone; and by adopting the plan of having vodka, wine, and something to eat, always ready for those who dropped in to see him, he succeeded in keeping on good terms with these men though he did not care to know them intimately.

The following extract from his Diary* preserves the record of rapidly changing moods he experienced in those days. Soon after reaching the Caucasus he noted:

Stáry-Yurt. 11th June, 1851

Yesterday I hardly slept all night. Having posted up my Diary, I prayed to God. It is impossible to convey the sweetness of the feeling I experienced during my prayer. I said the prayers I usually repeat by heart: 'Our Father', 'To the Virgin', &c., and still remained in prayer. If one defines prayer as a petition or as thanksgiving, then I did not pray. I desired something supreme and good; but what, I cannot express, though I was clearly conscious of what I wanted. I wished to merge into the Universal Being. I asked Him to pardon my crimes; yet no, I did not ask that, for I felt that if He had given me this blissful moment He had pardoned me. I asked and at the same time felt that I had nothing to ask, and that I cannot and do not know how to ask; I thanked Him, but not with words or thoughts. I combined in one feeling both petition and gratitude. Fear quite vanished. I could not have separated any one emotion – faith, hope, or love – from the general feeling. No, this was what I experienced yesterday: it was love of God, lofty love, uniting in itself all that is good, excluding all that is evil. How dreadful it was to me to see the trivial and vicious side of life! I could not understand its having any attraction for me. How I asked God with a pure heart to accept me into His bosom! I did not feel the flesh . . . But no, the carnal, trivial side again asserted itself, and before an hour had passed I almost consciously heard the voice of

---

* An English edition of *The Diaries of Leo Tolstoy*, *1847–52*, has been published (1917) by Dent & Sons, but the translations here given are from the original.

vice, vanity, and the empty side of life; I knew whence that voice came, knew it had ruined my bliss! I struggled against it and yet yielded to it. I fell asleep thinking of fame and of women, but it was not my fault, I could not help it.

Two days later he writes:

I am still indolent, yet am satisfied with myself except in regard to sensuality. Several times when the officers have been talking of cards I have wished to show them that I too can play; but I have always refrained. Even if they ask me to play, I hope I shall decline.

The next entry is on 3rd July:

I wrote the above on 13th June, and have quite wasted my time since, for that very day I was so carried away that I lost at cards 200 rubles of my own, 150 of Nikólenka's, and 500 on credit – a total of 850 rubles. However I am keeping myself in hand and living prudently, except that I have ridden over to Chervlënaya and got drunk there . . . This is bad and troubles me greatly. Indeed I have never spent more than two months well or so that I could feel satisfied with myself . . .

Another day after writing down reflections on suffering and death, he concludes:

How strong I seem to myself to be against all that can happen; how firm in the conviction that one must expect nothing here but death; yet a moment later I am thinking with pleasure of a saddle I have ordered, on which I shall ride dressed in a Cossack cloak, and of how I shall carry on with the Cossack girls; and I fall into despair because my left moustache is higher than my right, and for two hours I straighten it out before the looking-glass.

On 8th July he remarks that if love be what he has read and heard said of it, it is a thing he has never experienced. And he goes on to say:

There was a time when I used to see a girl-student named Zinaída [Molostvóva] whom I liked; but I got to know her only a little. I stayed a week in Kazán, and if you asked me why I did so or what I there found so agreeable, or why I was so happy there, I should say that it was not because I was in love – for I do not know love. Yet such ignorance is, I fancy, the chief feature and the whole charm of love. How morally light-hearted I was during that time! None of the burden of mean passions which now spoils all the pleasure of life for me did I then feel. I did not utter a word of love, yet felt assured that she knew my feelings and that if she liked me it was due to the fact that she understood me . . . My relations with Zinaída have remained at the stage of a pure yearning of two souls for one another . . . Shall I never see her again? . . . Not yet abandoned are my schemes for journeying to marry her, and though I am not sure that she would constitute for me happiness, I am in love . . . Do you remember the Archbishop's garden, Zinaída – the side path? It was on the tip of my tongue to make a declaration, as it was on yours; it was for me to take the initiative, but do you know, why I said nothing? It was because I was so happy that I had nothing to wish for and feared to spoil not my, but our, felicity . . . To the end that gracious period will remain the best of my life's recollections.

On 10th August he accuses himself of a pernicious tendency to discursiveness, and goes on to say of an author whom he admired sufficiently to translate part of the *Sentimental Journey* into Russian:

Even my favourite author, Sterne, for all his immense talent in narration and clever prattle, is tediously discursive.

After this he goes off at a tangent to say:

No one who has had much to do with the Gypsies will have failed to form the habit of singing Gypsy songs, and whether he sings them well or ill he will find that so doing gives him pleasure and recalls vivid memories . . .

   I was singing such a Gypsy song at my window, *Tell me Why?* a song which, though not one of my favourites, Kátya sang to me one evening when, seated on my knee, she declared that I was the only man she loved, and that the reason she showed favour to others was because her comrades [the others in the choir she belonged to] required it of her, but that she allowed to no one but me liberties that required concealment behind the curtain of modesty. With all my soul I believed her artful Gypsy prattle, and I was in a good frame of mind, as I had not been vexed by the arrival of any *visitor*. That is why I love the song and the evening.

He goes on to explain how upset he was when someone listening under his window mistook what he was singing for a Calmuck song.

By August he was back again at Starogládov and, full of energy, risked his life as a volunteer in expeditions against the Chéchens. Meeting Ilyá Tolstoy, an officer and a relation, he was introduced by him to the Commander-in-Chief, General Baryátinski. The latter had noticed Leo Tolstoy during one of the expeditions, and on making his acquaintance complimented him on his bravery and advised him to enter the army. Ilyá Tolstoy urged the same advice, Leo accepted it, and towards the end of October made a tiresome but beautiful seven days' journey to Tiflis with a view to passing examinations enabling him to enter the service as a Cadet. From there he wrote to his Aunt Tatiána a letter containing the first intimation of the vocation that was ultimately to make him far more famous than Baryátinski himself:

> Do you remember, dear Aunt, the advice you once gave me – to write novels? Well, I am following your advice, and the occupation I mentioned to you consists in producing literature. I do not know if what I am writing will ever be published, but it is work that amuses me and in which I have persevered too long to abandon it.

The work he was engaged on was *Childhood*, which he seems to have begun while still in Moscow.

An entry in March 1852 in the Diary – which he had neglected for seven months – tells us:

> I spent September at Starogládov, journeying to Grózny and Stáry-Yurt, hunting, running after Cossack women, or drinking, writing a little, and translating. In October my brother and I went to Tiflis for me to enter the Service; and there I spent a month in doubt what to do and with vain and foolish plans in my head. Beginning in November I underwent a treatment and spent two months, till the New Year, indoors. But the time, though tedious, passed quietly and usefully, for during it I wrote the whole of Part I [of *Childhood*].

At Tiflis he lived in the 'German' suburb, paying 5 rubles a month for a two-roomed lodging. The main obstacle to his entering the army was that he had neglected to bring with him to the Caucasus a copy of his birth-certificate and other documents. While at Tiflis he played billiards assiduously at a public table. He says:

> I played for points with a marker and lost about a thousand to him – indeed, I might have lost my all.

When making this entry, in March 1852, he was able to say that he had then not played cards for six months, and apparently the 'points' for which he played billiards were nominal ones.

On 23 December 1851, having passed an examination to qualify as a Cadet, he wrote to his brother Sergéy announcing that in a few days he expected to receive an appointment to the 4th Battery of Artillery, and that on the day he received it he would set out for Starogládov and from there go on campaign, and to the best of his ability 'assist with the aid of a cannon in destroying the predatory and turbulent Asiatics'. He goes on to tell of hunting. He had been out nine times, and had killed two foxes and about sixty grey hares. He had also hunted wild boar and deer, but had not killed any.

In the same letter Tolstoy mentions Hadji Murád, the hero of a tale he wrote more than fifty years later and left for posthumous publication. He says:

If you wish to show off with news from the Caucasus, you may recount that a certain Hadji Murád (the second man in importance to Shámyl himself) surrendered a few days ago to the Russian Government. He was the leading daredevil and 'brave' in all Circassia, but was led to commit a mean action.

A little later, on 6th January 1852, we find him still in Tiflis, writing in French to Aunt Tatiána.

I have just received your letter of 24th November, and reply at once (as I have formed the habit of doing). I wrote to you lately that your letter made me cry, and I blamed my illness for that weakness. I was wrong. For some time past all your letters have had the same effect on me. I always was 'Leo Cry-baby'. Formerly I was ashamed of this weakness, but the tears shed when thinking of you and of your love for us are so sweet that I let them flow without any false shame. Your letter is too full of sadness not to produce the same effect on me. It is you who have always given me counsel and, though unfortunately I have not always followed it, I should wish all my life to act only in accord with your advice. For the moment permit me to tell you the effect your letter has had on me and the thoughts that have come to me while reading it. If I speak too freely I know you will forgive it on account of the love I have for you. By saying that it is your turn to leave us to rejoin those who are no more and whom you have loved so much, by saying that, you ask God to set a limit to your life, which seems to you so insupportable and isolated – pardon me, dear Aunt, but it seems to me that in so saying you offend God and me and all of us who love you so much. You ask God for death, that is to say, for the greatest misfortune that could happen to me. (This is not a phrase, for God is my witness that the two greatest misfortunes that could come to me would be your death and that of Nicholas – the two persons whom I love more than myself.) What would be left me if God granted your prayer? To please whom should I then wish to become better, to have good qualities, and a good reputation in the world? When I make plans of happiness for myself, the idea that you will share and enjoy my happiness is always present. When I do anything good, I am satisfied with myself because I know you will be satisfied with me. When I act badly, what I most fear is to cause you grief. Your love is everything to me, and you ask God to separate us! I cannot tell you what I feel for you, words do not suffice to express it. I fear lest you should think I exaggerate, and yet I shed burning tears while writing to you.

In the same letter he tells of one of those remarkable 'answers to prayer', instances of thought-transference, or (if the reader pleases) simple coincidences, which have played so great a part in the history of all religious bodies.

Today one of those things happened to me which would have made me believe in God if I had not for some time past firmly believed in Him.

In summer at Stáry-Yurt all the officers who were there did nothing but play, and play rather high. As living in camp we have to meet frequently, I was very often present at play, but in spite of persuasions kept steady for a month; but one fine day, for fun, I put down a small stake. I lost, staked again, and lost again. I was in bad luck; the passion for play reawoke in me and in two days I had lost all the money I had, and what Nicholas gave me (about 250 rubles), and another 500 rubles besides, for which I gave a note-of-hand payable in January 1852.

I should tell you that near the camp there is an Aoul [native village] inhabited by Chéchens. A young fellow (a Chéchen) named Sádo used to come to the camp and play; but as he could neither reckon nor write, there were scamps who cheated him. For that reason I never wished to play against Sádo and I even told him that he ought not to play, because he was being cheated; and I offered to play for him. He was very grateful to me for this and presented me with a purse; and as it is the native custom to exchange presents, I gave him a wretched gun I had bought for 8 rubles. I should tell you that to become a *kunák*, that is to say, a *friend*, it is customary to exchange presents and afterwards to eat in the house of one's *kunák*. After that, according to the ancient custom of these peoples (which hardly exists now except as a tradition) you become friends for life and death: that is to say, if I asked of him all his money, or his wife, or his weapons, or all the most precious things he has, he must give them to me, and I also must not refuse him anything. Sádo made me promise to come to his house and become his *kunák*. I went. After having regaled me in their fashion, he asked me to choose anything in his house that I liked: his weapons, his horse – anything. I wished to choose what was of least value and took a horse's bridle with silver mountings, but he said I was offending him, and obliged me to take a sword worth at least 100 rubles.

His father is a rather rich man, but keeps his money buried and does not give his son a cent. The son, to have money, goes and steals horses and cows from the enemy. Sometimes he risks his life twenty times to steal something not worth 10 rubles, but he does it not from greed but because it is 'the thing'. The greatest robber is most esteemed, and is called *Dzhigít*, 'a Brave'. Sometimes Sádo has 1,000 rubles, sometimes not a cent. After one visit to him I gave him Nicholas's silver watch and we became the greatest friends in the world. He had proved his devotion several times by exposing himself to danger for my sake; but that is nothing to him – it has become a habit and a pleasure.

When I left Stáry-Yurt and Nicholas remained there, Sádo used to go to him every day, saying that he did not know how to get on without me and that he felt terribly dull. I wrote to Nicholas saying that as my horse was ill I begged him to find me one at Stáry-Yurt. Sádo having learnt this, must needs come to me and give me his horse in spite of all I could do to refuse it.

After the folly I committed in playing at Stáry-Yurt, I did not touch a card again and I was always lecturing Sádo, who is devoted to gambling and though he does not know how to play always has astonishing luck. Yesterday evening I was engaged in considering my money matters and my debts and thinking how I was to pay them.

Having long thought of these things, I saw that if I do not spend too much, all my debts will not embarrass me but can be paid off little by little in two or three years; but the 500 rubles that I had to pay this month threw me into despair. It was impossible for me to pay it, and at the moment it embarrassed me much more than did previously the 4,000 to Ogaróv. After having contracted those debts in Russia, the stupidity of coming here and adding fresh ones made me despair. In the evening while saying my prayers I asked God – and very fervently – to help me out of this disagreeable scrape. 'But how can I get out of this scrape?' thought I as I lay down. 'Nothing can happen that will make it possible for me to meet that debt.' I already pictured all the unpleasantnesses I should have to go through because of it: how when he presents the note for collection, the authorities will demand an explanation as to why I did not pay, &c. 'Lord, help me!' said I, and fell asleep.

Next day I received a letter from Nicholas enclosing yours and several others. He wrote me: 'The other day Sádo came to see me. He has won your notes-of-hand from Knorring and has brought them to me. He was so pleased to have won them, and asked me so often, "What do you think? Will your brother be glad that I have done this?" that I have grown very fond of him. That man is really attached to you.'

Is it not astonishing to see one's petitions granted like this the very next day? That is to say, there is nothing so wonderful as the divine goodness to one who merits it so little as I do. And is not the trait of Sádo's devotion admirable? He knows I have a brother Sergéy who loves horses and, as I have promised to take him to Russia when I go, he tells me that, if it costs him his life 100 times over, he will steal the best horse to be found in the mountains and will take it to him.

Please have a 6-barrelled pistol bought in Túla and sent to me, and also a musical-box if that does not cost too much. These are things which will give him much pleasure.

In explanation of this letter one has to mention that Sádo was a 'peaceful' Chéchen, that is, one friendly to Russia, though his tribe in general were hostile.

A few days later we find Tolstoy on his way back to Starogládov, and while stopping at the post-station of Mozdók, again writing to his aunt a long letter in which he says:

Religion and the experience I have of life (however small it may be) have taught me that life is a trial. In my case it is more than a trial, it is also an expiation of my faults.

It seems to me that the frivolous idea I had of journeying to the Caucasus was an idea with which I was inspired from above. It is the hand of God that has guided me – I do not cease to thank Him for it. I feel that I have become better here (and that is not saying much for I was very bad) and I am firmly persuaded that all that can happen to me here can only be for my good since it is God himself who has so willed it. Perhaps it is a very audacious notion, nevertheless it is my conviction. That is why I bear the fatigues and physical privations I have mentioned (they are not physical privations – there are none for a fellow of 23 who is in good health) without resenting them, and even with a kind of pleasure in thinking of the happiness that awaits me.

This is how I picture it: After an indefinite number of years, neither young nor old, I am at Yásnaya; my affairs are in order, I have no anxieties or worries. You also live at Yásnaya. You have aged a little, but you are still fresh and in good health. We lead the life we used to lead. I work in the morning but we see one another almost all day. We have dinner. In the evening I read aloud something which does not weary you, and then we talk. I tell you of my life in the Caucasus, you tell me your recollections of my father and my mother; and you tell me the 'terrible tales' we used to listen to with frightened eyes and open mouths. We remind each other of those who were dear to us and are now no more; you will weep, I shall do the same, but those tears will be sweet; we shall talk about my brothers, who will come to see us from time to time; of dear Márya, who with all her children will also spend some months of the year at Yásnaya which she loves so much. We shall have no acquaintances – no one will come to weary us and tell tales. It is a beautiful dream, but it is not all that I let myself dream – I am married. My wife is a gentle creature, kind and affectionate; she has the same love for you that I have. We have children who call you Grandmamma; you live upstairs in the big house, in what used to be Grandmamma's room. The whole house is as it was in Papa's time, and we recommence the same life, only changing our rôles. You take the rôle of Grandmamma, but you are still better; I take Papa's place, though I despair of ever deserving it; my wife, that of Mamma; the children take ours; Márya, that of the two aunts (except their misfortunes) . . . but someone will be lacking to take the part you played in our family – never will anyone be found with a soul so beautiful, so loving, as yours. You have no successor! There will be three new characters who will appear from time to time on the scene – the brothers, especially the one who will often be with us, Nicholas: an old bachelor, bald, retired from service, as good and noble as ever.

I imagine how he will, as of old, tell the children fairy tales of his own invention, and how they will kiss his greasy hands (but which are worthy of it), how he will play with them, how my wife will bustle about to get him his favourite dishes, how he and I will recall our common memories of days long past, how you will sit in your accustomed place and listen to us with pleasure; how as of yore you will call us, old men, 'Lëvochka' and 'Nikólenka', and will scold me for eating with my fingers and him for not having clean hands.

If they made me Emperor of Russia or gave me Peru: in a word, if a fairy came with her wand asking me what I wish for – my hand on my conscience, I should reply that I only wish that this dream may become a reality.

He returned to Starogládov, and at the end of January 1852, and during nearly all February, was engaged on an expedition as a Cadet in the artillery. On 17th and 18th February he took part in fierce fighting and in the capture of a village, an event which he described much later, in Chapters XVI and XVII of *Hadji Murád*.

The kind of warfare he was engaged on is also well described in *The Raid* and *The Wood-Felling*. A detachment would set out to seize a Tartar village, make a clearing in a forest, or capture cattle. It would exchange cannon-shot with Tartar skirmishers and would lose perhaps half a dozen men killed or wounded before accomplishing its object; but the more serious part came when the expedition retired to its fortified camp. As soon as the retreat commenced, Tartar sharpshooters would swarm out trying to cut off stragglers and inflicting as much damage as possible. Even after the Russians were beyond musket-range a chance cannon-ball from the Tartars might reach them within sight of their own quarters.

To see a single man one knows struck down by a deadly bullet may impress an observer as vividly as the myriad corpses of a great battle-field, and in Tolstoy's earliest war-sketches one feels the horror of war just as strongly as when, later on, he describes the far bloodier struggle at Sevastopol.

Having left home with no idea of entering the army he had not brought with him a certificate of discharge from the Civil Service, which he now needed, and for lack of which he missed receiving a St George's Cross awarded to him for bravery.

Writing to his Aunt Tatiána he says:

During this expedition, I twice had the chance of being presented to receive a St George's Cross, but was prevented from receiving it by that confounded paper being a few days late. I was nominated to receive it on 18th February (my name-day), but it had to be refused me for lack of that paper. The list of nominations was sent off on the 19th, the paper came on the 20th. I frankly confess that of all military honours, that little cross is the only one I have the vanity to desire.

On that 18th February his life had been in imminent danger, for an enemy shell struck the carriage of a gun he was training, smashed it, and exploded at his feet. Strangely enough Tolstoy was not wounded.

Subsequently two more crosses were sent to his battery, and one of them was at his disposal; but at a hint from Alexéev, the kindly Colonel, instead of keeping it for himself Tolstoy let it go to an old and deserving private, to whom it meant a life-pension.

He had a third chance of obtaining the cross during the winter campaign of 1852–3, but this time, having played chess till late at night he omitted to go on duty next morning and the commander of the division, noticing his absence, placed him under arrest and cancelled the award which had been already drawn up in his favour.

While under arrest he heard the band playing and the drums beating while the awards were being distributed and, as he told his wife years later, 'I yielded to utter despair.' In his Diary he noted: 'That I have not got the cross grieves me much. Am even sorry I did not decline to apply for a commission.'

Hope again revived and was again disappointed, for just before leaving the Caucasus (on 20th January 1854) he notes in his Diary: 'The news that I am not to be awarded a cross hurt me very much, but strange to say an hour later I had recovered my spirits.'

Chess, I may here mention, was always a favourite game of Tolstoy's and is frequently mentioned in his Diaries. He never studied the game from books, but he played much and with ingenuity and skill.

On 29 March 1852 he notes:

The pettiness of my life worries me. True I feel this because I am myself petty, but I have the capacity in me to despise myself and my life. There is something in me that forces me to believe that I was not born to be what other men are. What does this come from? From lack of concord and absence of harmony among my faculties, or from the fact that I really do stand on a higher level than ordinary men? I have reached maturity, the season of development is passing or has passed, and I am tortured with a hunger – not for fame – but to acquire great influence for the furthering of the happiness and benefit of mankind.

There is repeated mention in the Diary of the fact that his brother Nicholas, for whom in all other respects Leo had the highest esteem, drank too much. On 31st March 1852, an entry runs:

Got to Alexéev's [the commander of his regiment] when everyone else had sat down to table, and my brother was in a pitiable condition. So painful was it to see him that I left as soon as the meal was over and settled down to my writing. I finished one chapter. Nikólenka arrived, still in the same condition. I went out shooting and learnt later from Bálta that he [Nicholas] had run amok on the parade ground. It is a pity that he does not know how grieved I am to see him drunk. I feel sure that, since drunkenness gives him little pleasure, he would then refrain.

When not on campaign Tolstoy was generally stationed at the Cossack village of Starogládov, where he lived more or less the life vividly described in *The Cossacks*. The Grebénsk Cossacks located there were descended from Russian Dissenters (Old-Believers) who had fled from the persecution of former Tsars and settled among the Mohammedan Chéchens near the river Térek. They retained the purity of their Russian speech and remained nominally Christian, but had intermarried with the natives and adopted many of their manners and customs. Love of freedom, idleness, robbery, hunting, and war, were their most prominent characteristics. They considered them-selves altogether superior to the semi-savage Mohammedan natives and to the tame, disciplined, Russians. Drunkenness was not so much a weakness of these men as 'a tribal rite, to abandon which would have been considered an act of apostasy'. The work was done by the women, or by hired Nogái-Tartar labourers. The women were physically better developed than the men and were celebrated for their beauty, combining the purest type of Circassian features with the powerful build of Northern women. In their relations with men, especially before marriage, they enjoyed absolute freedom.

There was much that attracted Tolstoy in the simple life of these people: their frankness, their skill in hunting, their contempt for everything artificial or weak, and their freedom from such moral struggles as tormented him. By one beautiful girl, Solomónida (the Mariána of *The Cossacks*) he was greatly attracted, but she remained indifferent to the attentions of Russian cadets and officers who were inferior in the arts of war and hunting to the young men of her own tribe. His courtship failed (as Tolstoy says of his hero in *The Cossacks*) because he could not, like a dashing young Cossack, 'steal herds, get drunk on Tchikir wine, troll songs, kill people, and when tipsy climb in at her window at night without thinking who he was or why he existed'.

One must always be on one's guard against taking Tolstoy's stories as autobiography, but there are passages in *The Cossacks* which certainly apply to himself and give a vivid idea of his moods at this time as well as of his way of life while living as a cadet at Starogládov.

On one occasion Olénin (the hero of the story) is out hunting in the woods and asks himself:

'How must I live so as to be happy, and why was I formerly not happy?' And he remembered his previous life, and felt disgusted with himself . . . And suddenly a new light seemed revealed to him. 'Happiness,' said he to himself, 'consists in living for others. That is clear. The demand for happiness is innate in man and therefore it is legitimate. If we seek to satisfy it selfishly, by seeking wealth, fame, comforts, or love, circumstances may render the satisfaction of these desires impossible. It follows that they are illegitimate, but not that the demand for happiness itself is illegitimate. But what desire is there that can always be satisfied despite external conditions? What desire? Love, self-sacrifice!' He was so glad and excited at discovering this, as it seemed to him, new truth, that he jumped up and began impatiently seeking for someone for whom he might quickly sacrifice himself, to whom he might do good, and whom he could love. 'Yes; I need nothing for myself!' he kept mentally repeating: 'Then why not live for others?'

In the same story Tolstoy tells us that his hero lived monotonously and regularly.

He had little to do with his commander or fellow-officers. In the Caucasus the position of a cadet with means of his own was in this respect peculiarly favourable. He was not sent to drill nor kept at work. As a reward for going on an expedition he was recommended for a commission, and meanwhile he was left alone. The officers considered him an aristocrat, and therefore in their intercourse with him bore themselves with dignity. Card-playing and the officers' carousals with singers, of which he had had experience when on service with the detachment, seemed to him unattractive and he avoided the officers' society.

Again he tells us that his hero

often thought seriously of abandoning all else, enrolling himself as a Cossack, buying a cottage and marrying a Cossack girl . . . and living with Uncle Eróshka, going with him to hunt and fish and with the Cossacks on expeditions. 'Why don't I do this? What am I waiting for?' he asked himself . . . But a voice told him to wait and not decide. He was restrained by a dim consciousness that he could not fully live the life of Eróshka and Lukáshka because he had another happiness – he was restrained by the thought that happiness lies in self-sacrifice . . . He continually sought an opportunity to sacrifice himself for others, but it did not present itself.

In the same story the Cossack Lukáshka kills a Tartar 'brave' at night and rises greatly in popular esteem and in his own; and the hero thinks to himself:

'What nonsense and confusion! A man kills another and is as happy and satisfied as though he had done an excellent deed. Does nothing tell him there is here no great cause for rejoicing? That happiness consists not in killing others but in sacrificing oneself?'

We have a yet safer record of Tolstoy's feelings in his Diary, in which about this time he noted down reflections to the following effect concerning the three chief faults he was conscious of in himself: 'The passion of gaming is a covetous passion, gradually developing into a craving for strong excitement. Against this passion one can struggle. Sensuality is a physical need, a demand of the body excited by imagination. It increases with abstinence and therefore the struggle against it is very difficult. The best way is by work and occupation.

Vanity is the passion least harmful to others and most harmful to oneself.' In another place, indicating quite a different phase of consciousness, he writes:

> For some time past repentance for the loss of the best years of life has begun to torment me, and this since I commenced to feel that I could do something good . . . There is something in me which compels me to believe that I was not born to be like everybody else.

In May we find him going on furlough to Pyatigórsk to drink the mineral water and to be treated for rheumatism. This is his description of Pyatigórsk, written nearly twenty years later in his *Reading Book for Children:*

> Pyatigórsk (Five Hills) is so called because it stands on Mount Besh-tau. *Besh* means in Tartar 'five', *tau* means 'hill'. From this mountain flows a hot sulphur stream. The water is boiling and over the places where it springs from the mountain there is always steam as from a samovar.
>
> The whole place where the town stands is very gay. From the mountain flow hot springs, and at the foot of the mountain flows the river Podkúmok. The mountain slopes are wooded, all around are fields, and afar off one sees the great Caucasian mountains. On these the snow never melts, and they are always as white as sugar. When the weather is clear, wherever one goes one sees the great mountain Elbrus, like a sugar-cone. People come to the hot springs for their health, and over the springs arbours and awnings have been erected, and gardens and paths have been laid out all around. In the morning a band plays and people drink the waters, or bathe, or stroll about.

Here he found his sister Márya and her husband. She, too, had come to Pyatigórsk to be cured of rheumatism. She tells how her brother was at this time attracted by Spiritualism, and would sometimes even borrow a table from a café and have a *séance* on the boulevard. He remained in Pyatigórsk till 5th August and then returned to Starogládov.

He mentions that for some time past he had acquired a taste for reading history, and says that he perseveres in his literary occupations. He had already three times rewritten a work he had in hand (*Childhood*), and intended to rewrite it again. He felt much more content with himself at this period and adds:

There was a time when I was vain of my intelligence, of my position in the world, and of my name; but now I know and feel that if there is anything good in me, and if I have anything to thank Providence for, it is for a good heart, sensitive and capable of love, which it has been pleased to give me and to preserve in me.

On 19th June 1852 from Pyatigórsk he writes:

I have till now committed no follies in this place. It will be the first town from which I shall carry away with me no repentance; so I will not blame myself for petty weaknesses or indiscretions.

Later that month he writes:

I have never lived more blamelessly or felt myself morally more satisfied than during the last months, since I was at Tiflis.

He was rereading Rousseau who had greatly influenced him in his student days, and he notes:

Began to read the *Confessions*, which, unfortunately, I cannot help criticising.

Later he writes:

Read Rousseau and feel how far higher he stands in culture and in talent than I, though lower in self-respect, firmness, and judgement.

At the end of June owing to his financial difficulties he notes:

I may lose Yásnaya, which, despite all philosophy, would be a terrible blow to me.

In August he instructs his brother Sergéy to sell the large wooden house in which they had been born, as he needed the money to pay his debts. The house was a well-built, three-storey one containing forty-two rooms, and was sold for 5,000 assignation rubles (about £230), to be pulled down. It was re-erected by the purchaser about twelve miles away. The following literary notes made at different times are worth recording:

8th October 1852: I must for ever abandon the idea of writing without correction: three or four times over is still not enough.

And the corrections must first of all consist of abbreviation, the excision of all that is unnecessary, superfluous, and weak.

On a later occasion:

No talented addition can improve a work as much as it can be improved by deletions.

1st December 1853: Literary success satisfying oneself is only obtained by working at every aspect of a subject. But the subject must be a lofty one for the labour always to be pleasant.

On 2nd July 1852 he completed *Childhood*, and a few days later dispatched the manuscript, signed only with the initials L. N., to the best Petersburg monthly, *The Contemporary*. On 28th August he received a reply from the editor, the poet Nekrásov, saying he would publish the story and thought its author had talent. Another letter, dated 5th September, followed, in which Nekrásov said that having reread the story in proof he found it 'much better than I had realised at first. I can say definitely that its author has talent'. He added that it would appear in the next number of his magazine.

Tolstoy notes in his Diary: 'Received letter from Nekrásov; praise, but no money.'

Nekrásov's next letter was dated 30th October and explains that it is not customary to pay authors for their first work, but that he hopes Tolstoy will send him more stories, and that in future he will pay him as much as to the very best-known writers, namely, 50 rubles (about £7 at that time) per sheet of sixteen pages. He mentioned also that *Childhood* had been very well received by the public.

When Tolstoy received the *Contemporary* containing his story he was, however, much annoyed to find that its title had been altered to *The History of My Childhood*. On 27th November he wrote to Nekrásov:

Without mentioning small changes I will note two which struck me most disagreeably . . . The title *Childhood* and my *few words of preface*, *explained the idea of the work*; but the title *The History of My Childhood* contradicts it. Who wants to be bothered with a history of *my* childhood! The alteration is especially disagreeable because, as I wrote to you in my first letter, I wished *Childhood* to form the first part of a novel.

Much injustice has been done to Tolstoy by faulty editions of his works, and unfortunately the 'Everyman' series still supplies its readers with a version which begins with *The History of My Childhood* and contains a preface which represents the work as being autobiographical, despite Tolstoy's emphatic repudiation of that suggestion.

From the first he had adopted a style which suited him – the psychological novel, the chief interest of which lies not in the events that occur but in the feelings which prompt the actions of the characters.

On the nature of Tolstoy's early works I cannot do better than summarise what was said by Prince D. S. Mirsky in a lecture he gave to the Tolstoy Society.

He remarked that it is impossible to write a history of the novel without giving Tolstoy his place in it, for his place is one of the most central. He may be said to stand at the crucial point where the modern novel begins. Everything before Tolstoy belongs to a prehistoric stage of the novel – and much that comes after him. If there is a dividing line between the old and the modern novel, Tolstoy marks it. His immediate predecessors in the development of the modern novel were the great French analytical novelists – Rousseau and Stendhal. Tolstoy always mentions these two when speaking of those who influenced him. He himself heralds a change in the texture of the narrative from the old dramatic method (which is still the method of Dostoévski) to a new method, 'the point of view method'. The dramatic method consists of giving the actions and words of the characters without an explanation. Tolstoy, in his earlier period, never gives the actions or words of his characters without an explanation. With him the psychological explanation is the important thing. What is important is not what his people do, it is why they do it that matters . . . But this applies only to the early Tolstoy.

In the first period Tolstoy was preparing himself for his great works, he was forming a certain technique of analysis by which he could lay his finger on the mechanism of the internal preparation of human action. He was gradually perfecting an instrument of analysis which allowed him to go far deeper than anyone before him into the deeper layers of the consciousness. He goes to the original fact, and by a new combination of these divided particles of reality creates a new concrete reality. This preparatory period is, on the whole, free from all consideration of construction. When Tolstoy does turn to construction he gives his stories a moralistic construction, as for example in *The Two Hussars*.

Tolstoy kept his authorship a secret, revealing it to no one except Nicholas and Aunt Tatiána. His sister Márya was by this time back at her husband's estate, situated near Turgénev's village of Spásski. There

Turgénev came one day to visit her, bringing with him the last number of the *Contemporary*. Full of praise of a new story by an unknown author he began reading it aloud, and to her great astonishment Márya recognised several incidents from her own childhood. Her first guess was that Nicholas must have written it.

Among writers who at once acclaimed Tolstoy's genius was Panáev, co-editor of the *Contemporary*. He, Turgénev pretended, had to be carefully shunned by his friends on the Névski (the chief street in Petersburg) lest he should insist on reading them extracts from the new story. Before long the work reached Dostoévski in Siberia, and he was so struck by it that he wrote to a friend asking him to find out who the talented L. N. was.

Meanwhile, Tolstoy continued his military career in the Caucasus. On his return to Starogládov in August 1852 he had noted in his Diary: 'Simplicity – that is the quality which above all others I desire to attain.'

He had to pass an unpleasant month in consequence of the autumn manoeuvres, about which he wrote: 'It was not very pleasant to have to march about and fire off cannons, especially as it disturbed the regularity of my life'; and he rejoiced when it was over and he was again able to devote himself to 'hunting, writing, reading, and conversation with Nicholas'. He had become fond of shooting game, at which – as at all physical exercises – he was expert; and he spent two or three hours a day at it. He writes to his Aunt Tatiána:

> At 100 paces from my lodging I find wild fowl, and in half an hour I kill 2, 3, or 4. Besides the pleasure, the exercise is excellent for my health, which in spite of the waters is not very good. I am not ill, but I often catch cold and suffer from sore throat, or from toothache, or from rheumatism, so that I have to keep to my room at least two days in the week.

One of the forms of sport he enjoyed during his stay in the Caucasus was shooting steppe grouse. Before they migrate in mid-August these birds assemble in enormous flocks and are extremely wild and difficult of approach. It is hardly possible to get within two hundred, or two hundred and fifty, yards of such a flock. Tolstoy had a horse that was specially trained for this particular sport. On it he used to ride at a foot-pace two or three times round a flock, carefully narrowing the circle till he got as near as possible without alarming the birds. Then he would dash forward at full gallop with his gun ready. The moment the birds rose he dropped his reins on the horse's neck and the well-trained animal would instantly stop, allowing its master to take aim.

On his birthday, 28th August 1852, he notes:

> Am now 24, yet have accomplished nothing. I feel that not in vain have I for eight years struggled with doubt and with my passions. For what am I destined? The future will reveal it.

On 19 October 1852 he notes:

> Simplicity is the first condition of moral beauty. For readers to sympathise with a hero they must recognise in him their weaknesses as well as their virtues: virtues that are possible, weaknesses that are inevitable.

One knows that in his own works Tolstoy did not hesitate to display his weaknesses as well as his good qualities.

While away from home on a hunting expedition with some officer acquaintances, Tolstoy came upon the last number of the monthly *Fatherland Notes*, containing a highly appreciative notice of *Childhood*. Years later he told his wife:

> I lay on a bunk in a hut, with my brother and another officer there, and I read it, feasting with delight on its praise; and thought to myself: 'Nobody knows, not even those fellows there, that it is I who am being so praised.'

His military career was not giving him satisfaction. He had been in the Caucasus nine months before entering the army, and having left home without any definite plans he had, as already mentioned, neglected to bring his birth-certificate and other necessary papers. The result of this was that instead of becoming an officer within eighteen months as he expected to do when he entered the army, he now, after serving for ten months, received notice that he would have to continue another three years before he could have a commission.

In this difficulty he applied to his aunt P. I. Yúshkova, who by application to an influential friend eventually succeeded in somewhat hastening his promotion. Meanwhile however, Tolstoy – who had made up his mind to retire from the army as soon as he got his commission – almost lost patience.

On 29th October he wrote a letter to Auntie Tatiána in which, after describing his infatuation with hunting, he mentions the unsatisfactory state of his health, and adds:

Do not imagine that I am concealing anything from you. I have a strong frame but have always had weak health.

During the year 1852 he had generally kept himself well in hand, had not played cards at all, had been industrious, and, as is shown by his Diary, had thought much and deeply on religion and the duty of man, and his opinions fluctuated, as they did during the next thirty years. Here are some notes from his Diary during 1852.

20th March: Not less than before do I believe and doubt . . . I confess that one of the chief aspirations of my life has been to attain a firm and unalterable belief in something.

29th June: Read *Profession de Foi du Vicaire Savoyard* [from Rousseau's *Emile*]. It is full of contradictions, of obscure abstract passages, and of exceptional beauty. The main point I have got from it is conviction of the non-immortality of the soul. If for the idea of immortality the idea of recollection of a former existence is required, then we are not immortal. And my mind refuses to comprehend endlessness at one end. Someone has said that the sign of truth is clarity. One may dispute this, yet clarity remains the best token, and by it one must always verify one's opinions. *Conscience* is our best and most reliable guide. But where are the signs that distinguish it as a voice from other voices? For pride speaks with equal force, as for instance when an injury calls for revenge.

He whose aim is his own happiness, is bad; he whose aim is the good opinion of others is weak; he whose aim is the happiness of others, is virtuous; he whose aim is God, is great . . . *That is bad for me which is bad for others; that is good for me which is good for others*. So conscience always speaks . . . *The aim of life is goodness*. It is a sentiment inherent in our souls. *The way to good living is by knowledge of good and evil . . . We are good only when our whole strength is constantly directed to that aim* . . . Is, then, every diversion, every pleasure which brings no advantage to others, an evil? I do not find my conscience reproach me for such things, but on the contrary it commends me for them. Hence that voice is not the voice of conscience. Early or late, conscience reproaches me for every moment not utilised to advantage, even if no harm be done.

13th July: *The desire of the body is for personal good. The desire of the soul is for the good of others*. One cannot decline to admit the immortality of the soul, but one can decline to admit the soul's annihilation. *If the body separated from the soul perishes, yet where is the evidence that the soul perishes? Suicide is the most striking expression and evidence of the soul, and its existence is an evidence of its immortality. I have seen that a body dies; so I assume that mine will do so; but nothing proves to me that the soul dies, and so I say that, according to my understanding, it is immortal.*

18th July: I pray like this: O God, deliver me from evil, i.e. from the temptation to do evil, and dower me with good, i.e. with capacity to do good. Will good or evil befall me? Thy will be done.

Can it be that I shall never reach a conception of God as clear as the conception of goodness? That is now my strongest desire.

17th August: Nothing has so convinced me of the existence of God and of our relation towards Him, as the thought that the capacities of all animals are given them in accord with the needs which they have to satisfy. Not more, and not less. For what has the capacity to conceive of cause, eternity, infinity, and omnipotence, been given to man? The assumption of the existence of God is an hypothesis supported by indications. And faith, in accordance with man's development, complements the correctness of that hypothesis.

14th November: Have drawn up a short formula of my creed, as follows: 'I believe in the one, good, and incomprehensible God, in the immortality of the soul, and in eternal recompense for our deeds. What though I do not understand the mysteries of the Trinity and of the birth of the Son of God? I honour, and do not reject, the faith of my fathers.'

On 24th December 1852, he completed the sketch entitled *The Raid: A Volunteer's Story*, and two days later posted it to the *Contemporary*, in which magazine it appeared in March 1853. The following passage occurs in this his first story of war, and foreshadows the attitude he ultimately made his own. He is describing a march through Caucasian scenery to a night attack on a Tartar *Aoul*, and he says:

Nature, beautiful and strong, breathed conciliation.

Can it be that people have not room to live in this beautiful world, under this measureless starry heaven? Can feelings of enmity, vengeance, or lust to destroy one's fellow beings, retain their hold on man's soul amid this enchanting Nature? All that is evil in man's heart should, one would think, vanish in contact with Nature – this immediate expression of beauty and goodness.

From the very start we find Tolstoy hampered in his work by that incubus of all Russian writers, the Censor. In a letter to his brother Sergéy in May he writes: '*Childhood* was spoilt and *The Raid* simply ruined by the Censor. All that was good in it has been struck out or mutilated.' In comparing Tolstoy's literary achievement with that of Western writers one should make a large allowance for the continual annoyance, delay, mutilation, and suppression, inflicted on him by that satellite of despotism.

At the New Year [1853] the battery in which Leo Tolstoy served went once more on active service against Shámyl. The expedition assembled at Fort Grózny, where scenes of debauchery occurred.

That campaign in general had a demoralising effect on Tolstoy, and on 20th January 1853 he notes:

My life is extremely disorderly, so that I do not recognise myself and am ashamed to live like this. Have played cards, lost 40 rubles, and shall play again.

And next day:

What of the much-extolled good the Caucasus was to do me, when I am leading such a life as this?

On 16th February at night and on the 17th, on the eve of his name-day, curiously enough almost exactly a year after the day on which his life had been in great danger, he was again engaged in a sharp fight in which Shámyl was heavily defeated.

The conditions of life referred to continued for several months, and on 25th June 1853 he notes:

I have latterly begun to turn attention on myself and have become intolerably repulsive to myself . . . This damned army detachment has completely jolted me out of the path of goodness on which I had entered so well and which I wish to resume at any cost because it is the best path. Lord, teach and direct me

Not till towards the end of the year did he again settle down to a life of regular industry and self-control.

In May we find him writing to his brother Sergéy that he had applied for his discharge and hoped in six weeks' time to return home a free man. Difficult as his admission to the army had been, he found however that to retire was a yet harder matter, destined to take not weeks but years.

On 25th June his life was again in danger, owing to an adventure which supplied him with the subject-matter he utilised later on in *A Prisoner in the Caucasus*.*

It being dangerous to travel between the Russian forts without an escort, non-combatants as well as stores and baggage were periodically convoyed from one post to another. On these expeditions it was forbidden to detach oneself from the main body; but the intolerable slowness of the infantry march on a hot day frequently tempted those who were mounted to ride on, even at the risk of being attacked by the Tartars. On one such occasion five horsemen, including Tolstoy and his friend Sádo, disobeyed the regulations and rode ahead. The two friends ascended a hillside to see whether any foes were visible, while their three companions proceeded along the valley below. Hardly had they reached the crest of the ridge than they saw thirty mounted Tartars galloping towards them. As there was not time to rejoin their companions in the valley, Tolstoy shouted them a warning and raced off along the ridge towards Fort Grózny which was their destination. The three did not at first take his warning seriously, but wasting some precious moments before turning to rejoin the column were overtaken by the Tartars, and two of them were very severely wounded before a rescue party from the convoy put the enemy to flight. Meanwhile Tolstoy and Sádo, pursued by seven horsemen along the hill-ridge, had to ride nearly three miles to reach the fort. It happened that Tolstoy was trying a young horse of Sádo's, while Sádo was riding Tolstoy's ambler which could not gallop. Though Tolstoy could easily have escaped on Sádo's fiery horse, he would not desert his comrade. Sádo had a gun, unluckily not loaded, and so he could only make pretence of aiming at his pursuers. It seemed almost certain that both fugitives would be killed; but apparently the Tartars decided to capture them alive – wishing perhaps to revenge themselves on Sádo for being a pro-Russian – and therefore did not shoot them down. At last a sentinel at Grózny espied their plight, gave the alarm, and some Cossacks from the garrison galloped to their rescue. At sight of these the Tartars made off, and the fugitives escaped uninjured.

It may here be mentioned that one of the impressions Tolstoy left on those who knew him in the Caucasus was that of his fine horsemanship and boldness as a rider.

* in *Twenty-Three Tales*

From the middle of July to October, Tolstoy again stayed at Pyati-górsk, and then returned to Starogládov, and during the last months of his sojourn in the Caucasus he seems again to have settled down to a life of industry and self-restraint.

A companion he had brought with him to the Caucasus was his black bulldog Búlka. He intended to leave it at home, but after he had started the dog broke a pane of glass and escaped from the room in which it was confined, and when Tolstoy after stopping at the first post-station was just resuming his journey, he saw something black racing along the road after him. It was Búlka, who rushed to his master, licked his hand, and lay down panting in the shade of a cart. The dog had galloped nearly fourteen miles in the heat of the day and was rewarded by being taken to the Caucasus, where it was destined to meet with many adventures.

On one occasion it boldly attacked a wild boar and had its stomach ripped open by the latter's tusk. While its wound was being sewn up the dog licked its master's hand.

On another occasion when Tolstoy was sitting at night with a friend in the village street, intending to start for Pyatigórsk at daybreak, they suddenly heard a sucking-pig squeal and guessed that a wolf was killing it. Tolstoy ran into the house, seized a loaded gun, and returned in time to see the wolf running straight towards him from the other side of a wattle-fence. The wolf jumped on to the top of the fence and descended close to Tolstoy who, almost touching it with the muzzle of his gun, pressed the trigger. The gun missed fire, and the wolf raced off chased by Búlka and by Tolstoy's setter, Milton. The wolf escaped, but not till it had snapped at Búlka and inflicted a slight wound on his head. Strange to say, the wolf ventured to return a little later into the middle of the street and again escaped unhurt.

Not long after, in Pyatigórsk shortly before Tolstoy left the Cau-casus, while drinking coffee in the garden of his lodging, he heard a tremendous noise of men and dogs, and on enquiry learnt that convicts had been let out of gaol to kill the dogs of whom there were too many in the town, but that orders had been given to spare dogs wearing collars. As ill luck would have it Tolstoy had removed Búlka's collar; and Búlka, apparently recognising the convicts as his natural enemies, rushed out into the street and flew at one of them. A man had just freed the long hook he carried from the corpse of a dog he had caught and held down while his companions beat it to death with bludgeons. He now adroitly hooked Búlka and drew the unfortunate dog towards him calling to his mate to kill it, which the latter prepared to do. Búlka however bounded aside with such force that the skin of his thigh burst where the hook held it, and with tail between his legs and a red wound in his thigh he flew back into the house and hid under Tolstoy's bed. His escape was not of much use. The wolf that had snapped at him six weeks before must have been mad, for Búlka after showing premonitory symptoms of rabies, disappeared and was never heard of more.

Tolstoy's state of mind during the latter part of this year is indicated by his letters. To his brother Sergéy he wrote on 20th July 1853:

I think I already wrote you that I have sent in my resignation. God knows however, on account of the war with Turkey, whether it will be accepted, or when. This disturbs me very much, for I have grown so accustomed to happy thoughts of soon settling down in the country, that to return to Starogládov and again wait unendingly – as I have to wait for everything connected with my service – will be very unpleasant.

In December 1853 he writes from Starogládov:

Please write about my papers quickly. This is necessary. *'When shall I come home?'* God only knows. For nearly a year I have been thinking only of how to sheathe my sword, but still cannot manage it. And as I must fight somewhere, I think it will be pleasanter to do so in Turkey than here, and I have therefore applied to Prince Serge Dmítrievich [Gorchakóv] about it, and he writes me that he has written to his brother, but what the result will be I do not know.

It will be remembered that Tolstoy's paternal grandmother was a Gorchakóv. Through her he was nearly related to Prince S. D. Gorchakóv and to his brother, Prince Michael Dmítrievich Gorchakóv, who had been a friend of his father's in the war of 1812 and was now in command of the Russian army on the Danube.

The letter continues:

At any rate by New Year I expect to change my way of life, which I confess wearies me intolerably. Stupid officers, stupid conversations, and nothing else. If there were but a single man to whom one could open one's soul. Turgénev is right: 'What irony there is in solitude' –

one becomes palpably stupid oneself. Although Nikolenka has gone off with the dogs – Heaven knows why (Epíshka* and I often call him 'a pig' for so doing) – I go out hunting alone for whole days at a time from morning to evening, with a setter. That is my only pleasure – and not a pleasure but a narcotic. One tires oneself out, gets famished, sleeps like the dead, and a day has passed. When you have an opportunity, or are yourself in Moscow, buy me Dickens's *David Copperfield* in English, and send me Sadler's *English Dictionary* which is among my books.

Tolstoy spent more than two and a half years in the Caucasus, and during the last year wrote *Boyhood*, and *Reminiscences of a Billiard-Marker*, besides continuing *The Cossacks*, and beginning *A Landlord's Morning* and *The Wood-Felling*. His dissatisfaction with himself is strongly reflected in *Reminiscences of a Billiard-Marker*.

On 13th September 1853, he notes:

Felt terribly dull this morning. After dinner walked . . . Then had an idea: *The Reminiscences of a Billiard-Marker* – wonderfully good. Wrote, went to look at the Assembly, and again wrote *Reminiscences of a Billiard-Marker*. It seems to me that I am only now beginning to write with ardour.

14th September: Finished a rough draft and in the evening made a fair copy of a sheet. I write with such enthusiasm that it is even distressing. My heart fails and I tremble on taking up the notebook.

15th September: Wrote in the morning and went without dinner. Went for a walk . . . Wrote from 8 to 11. It went well, but the style is too irregular. I have written more than half of it.

16th September: Am a brick, and work excellently. Have finished!

On the 17th he sent it to Nekrásov saying that he valued it more than *Childhood* or *The Raid*, and that it must be published exactly in its present form. The occurrences in the story are for the most part fiction, but the feelings of repentance, self-dissatisfaction, and almost of despair which it expresses were certainly such as Tolstoy had at that time been experiencing.

The whole story therefore, based on his own experiences at Tiflis, took only four days, but though he had worked at it with such

---

* The Cossack hunter Epíshka, the original of Eróshka, who figures prominently in *The Cossacks*. Nicholas Tolstoy had lodged with him.

enthusiasm he was not quite satisfied with it when it was finished, for he sent a letter with it to Nekrásov expressing dissatisfaction with its hasty workmanship. It did not appear till more than a year later.

In the Diary he generally uses several names for each of his stories before deciding on the one under which it was published. To avoid confusion, when mentioning them I keep in each case to the title finally adopted.

Not till January 1854 did the long-expected order arrive, allowing him to pass the examination (a pure formality) entitling him to become an Ensign. On the 19th he left for home, and travelling with post-horses, reached Yásnaya on 2nd February, where he enjoyed a three weeks' stay with his Aunt Tatiána, his three brothers, and a friend. On this journey, when some sixty miles north of Novocherkássk, he encountered a severe storm, to which we owe *The Snow Storm*, published a couple of years later, and also much of the storm described in *Master and Man*, some forty years later.

The Russo-Turkish war had now begun in earnest, and as a result of his own application, he received orders to join the army of the Danube.

Apart from his letters, the main source of information concerning this period of his life is his private Diary in which he hastily and briefly jotted down a day-by-day record of his actions, as well as comments on people and events, scraps of information, rules of conduct, bitter self-reproaches for failure to observe them, and general reflections, some of which contrast, while others coincide, with the opinions he expressed in later life. His Diary was intended for himself alone and did not aim at any literary quality. In his last years he expressed the opinion that only certain passages in it were worth publishing, but his literary executors have, not unnaturally, given it to the world, and from it we gather the following information.

His impressions of army life were unpleasant. On 6th January 1853 he had noted:

> Stupid people. All – especially my brother – drink, and it is very unpleasant for me. War is such an unjust and evil thing that those who wage it try to stifle their consciences. Am I doing right? Oh God, teach me and forgive me if I am doing wrong.

Writing solely for himself and with the object of restraining himself and amending his ways, he jots down with perfect frankness the records of his gambling, his drunkenness – which was rare – and his dissolute conduct. The notes of this latter have for the most part been suppressed in the published Diary.

13th–16th January 1853: My throat has been aching, but on the 14th I got drunk with Arinévski . . . Played today for trifling amounts, but the bump of play is developing. This is a stupid life.

18th–20th January: My life is extremely disorderly so that I do not recognise myself and I am ashamed to live like this.

24th January–10th February: I have debts. I have lost more than I have in hand. Have lost my gun to Bálta. My brother is drinking, which distresses me. I will stop playing after tomorrow, and when the campaigning is over will finish with the service.

16th April: God help me! I am now experiencing for the first time an exceedingly sad and depressing feeling – regret at having wasted my youth without pleasure or advantage; and I feel that it has passed. It is time to bid it farewell.

He was then not yet twenty-five.

4th–7th May . . . I must have a woman. Desire does not give me a moment's peace.

8th–15th May: Have done nothing these seven days. I was at Birdie's and drank, though several times I wished to stop.

15th–22nd May: I had a Cossack girl twice. It is bad! Have let myself deteriorate greatly. Have abandoned the story, and am writing *Boyhood* with the same eagerness with which I wrote *Childhood*. I hope it will be equally good. My debts are now all paid. A brilliant literary career is open to me. I ought to get a commission. I am young and clever. What more, one would think, should I wish for? I must work and exercise self-restraint and may yet be happy.

25th June . . . Played cards and lost Sultan [a horse]. I was almost taken prisoner, but on this occasion behaved well though I was too effusive. [This is the only mention in the Diary of the incident recounted a few pages back.] On getting back I decided to remain here a month to finish *Childhood*, but I have conducted myself all the week in such a disorderly fashion that I have become very sad and depressed as always happens when one is dissatisfied with oneself . . . It suddenly became incomprehensible to me how I could have behaved so badly all this time. If I wait for circumstances in which I can easily be virtuous and happy I shall never attain them. I am convinced of this. Girls have led me astray. As far as I can I will try to be useful and industrious and will certainly not act frivolously or do evil. I thank God for this disposition, and I pray: 'Creator, support me.' I have done much evil latterly . . . I have spent money on trifles, and wasted time which I might have used to advantage. I have boasted, disputed, and been angry.

The aim of my life is clear: it is goodness, the duty I owe to my serfs and fellow-countrymen. I owe a duty to the first of these because I own them, and to the second because I possess mind and talent. The latter duty I can fulfil now, but to accomplish the first I must use all available means.

My first thought (long ago) was to draw up for myself rules of life, and now I must return to that . . . From this evening, in whatever circumstances I may be, I pledge myself to do this every evening. False shame has often hindered me in it. I undertake as far as possible to overcome that. *Be straightforward, even if rude; be frank with everybody, not childishly, unnecessarily frank. Restrain thyself from wine and women.* The pleasure is so brief, so cloudy, and the remorse so great. *Give thyself completely to whatever affair thou undertakest. On receiving a strong impression restrain thyself from action; but having considered it, even though mistakenly, act resolutely.*

Today I did not finish my prayers, being shy of Alexéev. I wrote little and without reflection. Ate too much, and fell asleep from laziness. Stopped writing on account of Arslan Khan's arrival. I boasted of my connection with Gorchakóv. Insulted Yanushkévich without apparent reason. Wanted to have women. Boasted a good deal to Gróman, to whom I read the story of Karl Iványch.

On 26th June he notes:

After dinner I went to the Ukrainians, but did not find an opportunity to do a good deed. I disobeyed my conscience . . . This compulsory continence, it seems to me, gives me no rest and hinders my work, and the sin is slight, since the unnatural position in which fate has placed me excuses it . . . After dinner I was idle. Might at least have thought things out, if not written. The wenches hinder me.

Previously, in May 1852, he had written:

Have I talent in comparison with the newer Russian writers? Assuredly not.

But on 12th October, as a contrast to his frequent notes of self-condemnation and self-depreciation we come upon the following recognition of his own latent powers:

Read a work on the literary characterisation of genius today and this awoke in me a conviction that I am a remarkable man both as regards capacity and eagerness to work. From today I will take to it. In the morning write *Boyhood*, and after dinner and in the evening *The Fugitive*.

On 4th–6th October he notes:

Saw Valerián and Másha off yesterday and spent the night with a girl. Am terribly depressed. Tomorrow will try to get rid of this depression by activity.

A remark he notes down on 24th October 1853 is this:

When reading a work, especially one that is purely literary, one is chiefly interested by the character of the author which shows itself in it; but there are works in which the author affects a point of view, or changes it several times. The pleasantest books are those in which the author seems, as it were, to try to hide his opinion yet remains true to it wherever it is shown. The most insipid books are those in which the author's point of view changes so often that it is quite lost.

On 26th October he makes an observation which helps to explain why, knowing the Russian peasants as well as he did, and occasionally – as subsequently in *The Power of Darkness* – depicting all the horrors of which they were capable, he yet often presents them as superior to other sections of the community. He says:

The common people are so far above us by the work they accomplish and by the privations in their lives, that it seems wrong for one of us to write anything bad about them. Evil there is in them, but it is better to say of them, as of the dead, only what is good. Therein lies Turgénev's merit and the deficiency of Grigoróvich in his *Fishers*. Who can be interested in the faults of this miserable but worthy class? There is more of good than of evil in them, and it is also more natural and more generous to seek the causes of the former than of the latter.

This indicates that in this case he swerved from his general rule of looking at things and stating them precisely as they really are, and deliberately allowed sympathy and pity for the peasants to bias his judgement – thus ultimately laying himself open to the reproach of appearing to misunderstand them.

On 31st October 1853 he enters some notable observations:

Read *The Captain's Daughter* and must, alas, admit that Púshkin's prose works are already old-fashioned, not in language but in the way the story is told . . . The new tendency is for interest in feelings to predominate over interest in the events themselves. Púshkin's stories seem rather bare.

It is strange that we all conceal the fact that one of the main springs of our life is money. As if that were shameful! Take novels, biographies, or stories – they all try to avoid questions of money, whereas in it lies the chief interest of life (or if not the chief, the most continual) and by it a man's character is best shown.

Other comments made the same day are the following:

Self-confidence and aplomb depend not on the brilliance of one's position, but on success in the path one has chosen however insignificant it may be.

I am frequently held up when writing by routine expressions which are not quite correct, true, or poetic, but the fact that one meets them so frequently makes me often write them. These unconsidered, customary expressions, of the insufficiency of which one is aware but which one tolerates because they are so customary, will be to posterity a proof of bad taste. To tolerate such expression means to go with one's age, to correct them means to go in advance of it.

This remark contains the key to the failure of most translators to express Tolstoy's thoughts adequately. He aimed at a direct simplicity of statement such as many writers carefully avoid.

Alternating strangely with his emphatic self-condemnation and punctilious record of failings great and small, we at times come on similarly strenuous disapproval of other people, as well as on recognition of his own intellectual and moral superiority to them. Thus the next entry, a couple of days later, is this:

Almost every time I meet a new man I experience a painful feeling of disappointment. I imagine him to be like myself, and study him applying that standard. Once for all I must become accustomed to the thought that I am an exception and ahead of my age, or that I am one of those incompatible, unadaptable natures that never are satisfied. I must adopt a different standard (lower than my own) and measure people by it. I shall less often be mistaken. I long deceived myself by imagining I had friends who understood me. Nonsense! I have not yet met a single man who was morally as good as I, or who believed that I do not remember an instance in my life when I was not attracted by what is good and was not ready to sacrifice everything for it.

And the next day he writes:

Am perfectly convinced that I ought to acquire fame, this even causes me to take so little pains: I am convinced that all I need is to wish to work up the material I feel within me.

In November he writes:

There are thoughts the application of which is endlessly varied. Therefore the more general the expression of such thoughts the more food they afford for the mind and heart, and the more profoundly can they be felt.

I am replacing all the prayers I have composed by the Lord's Prayer alone. Any petition I can make to God is expressed more loftily, and in a way more worthy of Him, by the words, 'Thy will be done on earth as in Heaven.'

Another remark the same day is:

I have never made a declaration of love, but recollecting the terrible nonsense which, with a smile of subtle meaning, I talked to people who attracted me, I blush at the very remembrance. The conversations one reads in our fashionable novels *pour tout de bon* [in real earnest] are as like as two peas to what I said. I must realise that idleness and a disorderly life (that is, a life that lacks order) is not merely harmful in practical affairs but may cause most terrible vices and actions on my part, as I have experienced today. I am so weak. I must fear idleness and lack of order as I do cards.

About the same time he notes:

I have often been amazed to note how people find inner satisfaction in their own phrases devoid of thought – just in the mere words – as at a higher stage they find satisfaction in thoughts.

Rules he lays down for himself later that month are:

Every time you feel annoyance and anger, avoid all intercourse with people, especially with those dependant on you. Avoid the company of people who are fond of drunkenness, and drink neither wine nor vodka.

Avoid the society of women whom you can easily have, and try to exhaust yourself by physical labour when you feel strong desire. I must note down every day the number of times these rules have been infringed.

An indication of his sharp observation of himself is given by another remark the same day:

The tone of a man I am talking with always reacts deplorably on me. If he speaks pompously, so do I; if he mumbles, so do I; if he is stupid, so am I; if he speaks French badly, so do I.

On 1st December he makes a matter-of-fact note on soldiering, which served him later in life as an item in his denunciation of militarism and the army system generally:

Discipline is essential for the existence of a military class, and to create discipline drill is essential. Drill is a way of bringing men to a state of mechanical obedience by means of petty threats, so that the cruellest punishments do not produce such obedience as is obtained by the drill habit.

Detached reflections and observations are jotted down from time to time which indicate the activity of his mind apart from any particular moral or other tendency. For instance, on 16th December one finds him making this remark:

With the shape of a hand – especially a beautiful one – the idea of power is somehow associated. Sometimes when looking at a beautiful hand one thinks: 'What if I were dependent on that man?'

And farther on, that same day:

As I was being shaved today I vividly imagined how a mortal wound inflicted on one already wounded would instantly change his state of mind – from one of despair to resignation.

On a previous occasion he had noted:

Every work to be good must, as Gógol expressed it in his *Farewell Tale*, be sung from its composer's soul.

The greater part of the Diary however is a brief and hasty record of events. Notes of expenditure, losses at cards, the amount of work he had done that day, and brief notes on incidents, expressions, or encounters he wished to remember, fill most of its pages.*

Of the two and a half years he spent in the Caucasus, as of his University days, Tolstoy has at different times expressed himself differently. To Birukóv, in 1905, he spoke of it as one of the best times of his life notwithstanding all deflections from his dimly recognised ideals. He added that the latter part of his military career and especially the period of his subsequent literary activity in Petersburg, was a time of gradual moral deterioration, and that not till he returned to Yásnaya Polyána and devoted himself to the peasant children did he again recover and his spirit reassert itself.

In 1903, writing of the four periods of his life, he had spoken of 'the terrible twenty years of coarse dissipation, the service of ambition, vanity, and above all, of lust', which followed after the age of fourteen.

As Tolstoy in his later years judged himself by a very high standard and always expressed himself forcibly, his words give an impression of his conduct that is probably worse than the facts of the case justify.

When he left the Caucasus, he had served for nearly two years as a Cadet, and it was only then that he obtained his commission as an Ensign. On reaching home he noted in his Diary:

Reached Yásnaya Polyána on 2nd February tired and ill. Found affairs in good order, and myself out-of-date, reformed, and aged ... On the 6th [February 1854] I was *in* Túla ... and heard of my promotion.

While visiting his sister he made a will, and was only able to stay a couple of weeks, before he had to set off to join the Russian army in Turkey.

---

* The above quotations are from *The Private Diary of Leo Tolstoy*, 1853–57, William Heinemann & Co.

4

The Crimean War

At twenty-five years of age it fell to Tolstoy's lot to take part in a great European war and extend the range of his experience in a way that considerably affected his subsequent life and writings.

He tells us that his first understanding of war came from Stendhal. To Paul Boyer, Tolstoy once spoke of Stendhal's novels as inimitable works of art, adding, 'I am greatly indebted to him. He taught me to understand war. Reread the description of the battle of Waterloo in *La Chartreuse de Parme*. Whoever before so described war? Described it, that is, as it is in reality? Do you remember Fabrice riding over the field of battle and understanding "nothing"?'

Tolstoy's brother Nicholas, though fond of war, also disbelieved in the popular romantic view of it and used to say: 'All *that* is embellishment, and in real war there is no embellishment.' 'A little later, in the Crimea,' added Tolstoy in his talk with Boyer, 'I had a grand chance to see with my own eyes that this is so.'

Of the causes that led to the war it need only be said that the rule of the Turks over Christian populations had long kept a dangerous sore open in Europe, and the consequent diplomatic difficulties were complicated by the indefiniteness of two lines in the Treaty of Kainardji which Catherine the Great imposed upon Turkey in 1774. There was also friction between the Eastern and Western Churches with reference to the custody of the Places in Palestine rendered holy by their traditional connection with the Prince of Peace. Nicholas I, who had well-nigh drilled all intelligence out of those near him in his Government and his army, was unaccustomed to being thwarted. Dimly conscious of the first faint symptoms of that growth of Liberalism which a few years later, in the early 1860s, led to sweeping reforms in Russia, he felt inclined to demonstrate the beneficence of his rule not by allowing changes at home but by inflicting reforms on Turkey. Failing to get his way by diplomatic pressure, he rashly proceeded to occupy the Danubian Principalities as a 'material guarantee' of Turkey's compliance with his demands.

He was opposed by Austria and Prussia as strongly as by England and France, and the pressure exerted by the four Powers sufficed to compel him to withdraw his army from Turkish soil. Thereupon the war, which had as yet been waged only between Russia and Turkey, might well have ended, had not England and France undertaken a quite needless invasion of the Crimea: an enterprise in which Austria and Prussia refused to join. The end did not justify the proceedings, for in spite of success in this war, Napoleon III's dynasty crumbled to dust within twenty years, while within a like period after Palmerston's death Lord Salisbury frankly admitted that we had 'put our money on the wrong horse'. As to Nicholas I, his pride was bitterly mortified by the results of an enterprise which failed of its immediate object and by that very failure hastened the coming of those reforms in Russia against which he had set his face. Even Turkey did not really benefit by being allowed to oppress her subject-races for a couple of generations longer.

It was the influence of Napoleon III, as Kinglake has pointed out, that led England to take part in the war. Having by treachery and murder made himself Emperor of the French, that monarch found himself for a time dangerously isolated from people of good repute. In consultation with Palmerston he decided to subordinate the traditional Eastern policy of his country to that of England if thereby he might succeed in being publicly paraded as the friend and ally of Queen Victoria. As soon as he had secured an alliance with England, by Palmerston's aid and helped by the extraordinary war fever which seized the English nation, he quickly forced the peacefully disposed Lord Aberdeen down an inclined plane which ultimately landed both nations in a war for which no sufficient motive, justification, or excuse, existed.

Hostilities between Russia and Turkey had begun in October 1853, but France and England did not break off negotiations with Russia till the end of March 1854, the very month in which Tolstoy reached Bucharest on his way to join the army of the Danube.

From there, on 13th March, he wrote to his aunt telling of his journey. The roads after he had passed Khersón, and especially after he had crossed the frontier, were abominable. His journey lasted nine days, and as he wrote to his aunt, he 'arrived almost ill with fatigue'. In his Diary next day he notes: 'Reached Bucharest two days ago . . . for a week past I have been ominously ill.'

On 17th March he mentions his first interview with Gorchakóv:

Prince Gorchakóv was not here. He arrived yesterday, and I have just come from his lodgings. He received me better than I expected – quite as a relation. He embraced me and made me promise to dine at his house every day, and he wants to keep me near him, but this is not yet decided.

Forgive me, dear Aunt, for writing but little to you – I have not yet collected my wits; this large and fine town, all these presentations, the Italian opera, the French theatre, the two young Gorchakóvs who are very fine lads . . . so that I have not spent two hours at home and have not thought of my duties.

On 22nd March he adds: 'I learnt yesterday that I am not to remain with the Prince but am to go to Oltenitza to join my battery.' He stayed with the battery however only for a couple of weeks, and the next mention of the matter in his Diary reads: 'My transfer to the Staff came just when I had quarrelled with the Battery Commander, and it flattered my vanity.'

In May he wrote:

While you are fancying me exposed to all the dangers of war, I have not yet smelt Turkish powder but am very quietly at Bucharest, strolling about, playing music, and eating ices. In fact all this time, except for two weeks I spent at Oltenitza where I was attached to a battery, and one week passed in journeys in Moldavia, Wallachia and Bessarabia by order of General Serzhputóvski on whose Staff I now am by special appointment, I have been at Bucharest; and to speak frankly, the rather dissipated, quite idle, and very expensive kind of life that I lead here displeases me very much. Formerly it was the service that kept me here, but now for three weeks I have been kept here by a fever contracted during my journey, but from which, thank God, I have for the present recovered sufficiently to be able in two or three days' time to rejoin my General who is in camp near Silistria. Apropos of my General, he appears to be a very fine fellow, and though we know one another very slightly, seems well disposed toward me. What is also agreeable is that his Staff consists for the most part of gentlemen.

We shall find Tolstoy modifying this opinion a little later; but we may note that at this time he was glad to be on the Staff and much preferred to associate with *gens comme il faut*.

By June 1854 the military and political situation was as follows. The Russians had advanced through Moldavia and Wallachia to the Danube, had crossed that river, and were besieging Silistria. Austria, supporting the other great powers, had massed a powerful army on the Turkish frontier, and a glance at the map will show that the Russian army, far removed from its base, was in imminent danger of being cut off by the Austrians, who peremptorily summoned Russia to evacuate the Principalities, and on 14th June concluded a formal alliance with the Porte. These circumstances explain the sudden abandonment of the siege of Silistria mentioned in the following letter, which Tolstoy addressed to his Aunt Tatiána and his brother Nicholas conjointly; though when he wrote it the causes which produced that result were a mystery to him.

I am going to tell you of my recollections of Silistria. I there saw so much that was interesting, poetic, and touching, that the time I passed there will never be effaced from my memory. Our camp was on the farther side of the Danube, i.e. on the right bank, on very high ground amid splendid gardens belonging to Mustafa Pasha, the Governor of Silistria. The view from there was not only magnificent but of the greatest interest to us all. Not to speak of the Danube, its islets and its banks, some occupied by us, others by the Turks, one could see the town, the fortress, and the little forts of Silistria, as on the palm of one's hand. One heard the booming of cannon and musket-shots unceasingly day and night, and with a spyglass could distinguish the Turkish soldiers. It is true it is a queer sort of pleasure to see people killing one another, yet every evening and every morning I got on to my cart and remained for hours at a time watching, nor was I the only one who did so. The sight was really fine, especially at night. At night my soldiers usually undertake trench-work, and the Turks fling themselves upon them to hinder them; then you ought to see and hear the fusillade! The first night I passed in camp this dreadful noise awoke and frightened me: I thought an assault had begun. I very soon had my horse saddled; but those who had been already some time in camp told me that I had only to keep quiet: that this cannonade and fusillade was an ordinary affair and they jestingly called it 'Allah'. Then I lay down again; but not being able to sleep I amused myself, watch in hand, counting the cannon-shots, and counted 110 reports in a minute. And yet at close quarters all this did not look as terrible as might be supposed. At night when nothing was visible it was a case of who could burn most powder, and with all these thousands of cannon-shots at most some thirty men were killed on each side . . .

This then was an ordinary performance we had every day, and one in which I took part when sent to the trenches with orders; but we also had extraordinary performances such as the one on the eve of the attack, when a mine of 240 puds [8,600 lb.] of gunpowder was exploded under one of the enemy's bastions. On the morning of that day the Prince had been to the trenches with all his Staff (and as the General to whom I was attached belongs to it, I was there too) to make final arrangements for next day's assault. The plan – too long for me to explain here – was so well arranged, all was so well foreseen, that no one doubted its success. Apropos of this I must tell you further that I am beginning to feel admiration for the Prince [Gorchakóv] (for that matter you should hear how the officers and soldiers speak of him: not only have I never heard him spoken ill of, but he is generally adored).

That morning I saw him under fire for the first time. You should see his tall rather absurd figure, his hands behind his back, his cap on the back of his head, his spectacles, and his way of speaking like a turkey-cock. One could see that he was so preoccupied with the general trend of affairs that the balls and bullets did not exist for him. He exposes himself to danger so simply that one would say he was unconscious of it, and involuntarily one feels more alarmed for him than for oneself, and he gives his orders with such clearness and precision and is at the same time always so affable with everybody. He is a great man, i.e. a capable and honest man, as I understand the word: one who has dedicated his whole life to the service of his country, and not from ambition but for the sake of duty. I will give you a trait of his character connected with the story I had begun to tell you of the assault. After dinner that same day, the mine was sprung, and nearly 600 guns opened fire on the fort we wished to take, and this continued the whole night. It was such a sight and such an emotion as one never forgets. That evening the Prince, amid all the commotion, went to sleep in the trenches that he might personally direct the assault, which was to begin at 3 o'clock the same night.

We were all there, and as usual on the eve of a battle we all pretended not to think of the morrow more than of any other day, and we all, I am sure, at bottom felt our hearts contract a little (and not a little but a great deal) at the thought of the assault. As you know, the time before a fight is the most disagreeable: it is only then that one has time to be afraid, and fear is a most disagreeable feeling. Towards morning, the nearer the moment came the more the feeling diminished, and towards 3 o'clock when we were all expecting to see a shower of rockets let off which was the signal for the attack, I was so well inclined for it that I should have been much disappointed if anyone had come to tell me that the attack was not to take place. And there! Just an hour before the time for the attack, an aide-de-camp comes from the Field-Marshal [Paskévich, who for a time took over the supreme command of the army of the Danube] with orders to raise the siege of Silistria! I can say without fear of making a mistake, that this news was received by all, soldiers, officers, and generals, as a real misfortune; the more so as we knew from the spies – who very often came to us from Silistria and with whom I very often had occasion to speak – that once we had taken this fort (about which none of us felt any doubt) Silistria could not have held out for more than two or three days. Is it not true that if this news was calculated to pain anyone it must have been the Prince, who having all through this campaign arranged everything for the best yet saw, in the very middle of the action, the Field-Marshal override him and spoil the business? Having this one chance to repair our reverses by this assault, he received counter-orders from the Field-Marshal at the moment of commencing! Well, the Prince was not put out of temper for a moment. He, who is so impressionable, was on the contrary pleased to be able to avoid that butchery, the responsibility for which he would have had to bear; and during the whole time of the retreat – which he directed personally, not wishing to cross (the Danube) before the last of the soldiers – which took place with remarkable order and exactitude, he was gayer than he has ever been . . .

Yes, dear Aunt, I should much like your prophecy to come true. What I desire most is to be aide-de-camp to such a man as he, whom I love and esteem from the bottom of my heart. Adieu, dear and kind Aunt. I kiss your hands.

The retreat from Silistria began at the end of June, and the army retired to Bucharest. Here, at an officers' ball, Tolstoy, as he told me himself, seized an opportunity to beg Gorchakóv to have him transferred to where service would be most active.

He had been in bad health all this time, and while in Bucharest had to submit to an operation under chloroform, and to undergo treatment for six weeks. On leaving there the army retired to Russia, but delayed by his illness, it was September before Tolstoy left Turkey and reached Kishinëv.

His Diary, besides a bare and irregular chronicle of events, shows how his feelings and conduct fluctuated. On 15th June, summarising his conduct for the previous three months, he says:

> I have several times had women, have lied, boasted, and what is most horrible of all, did not behave under fire as I expected of myself.

And on 23rd June:

> During the march from Silistria to Moi I rode to Bucharest, gambled, and was obliged to borrow money – a humiliating position for anyone and particularly for me . . . I still do not know what to set to work at, and therefore am doing nothing. I fancy that best of all would be to work at *A Landlord's Morning* . . .
>
> 3rd July: . . . As soon as I am alone and criticise myself I involuntarily return to my former idea – that of perfecting myself; but the chief mistake, the reason I have been unable to go quietly along that road, was that I confused perfecting oneself with perfection . . .
>
> One must take oneself as one is and try to correct the corrigible faults. A nature naturally good will lead me to what is good without a notebook, which has all along been my nightmare. Mine is a character which desiring, seeking, and ready for all that is excellent, is for that very reason incapable of being consistently good.

On 7th July he writes in his Diary:

> I lack modesty. That is my great defect. What am I? One of four sons of a retired lieutenant-colonel, left orphan at seven years of age in the care of women and strangers, having neither a social nor a learned education, and becoming my own master at seventeen years of age; without any large fortune, without any social position, and chiefly without principles: a man who has mismanaged his affairs to the last degree, has spent the best years of his life aimlessly and without pleasure, and who finally banished himself to the Caucasus to escape

from his debts and above all from his habits, and from there, by availing himself of connections that had existed between his father and the Commander of the army, was transferred to the army of the Danube; a twenty-six-year-old ensign almost without means except his pay (for what means he has he must use to pay his remaining debts), without influential friends, without capacity to live in Society, without knowledge of the service, without practical abilities, but with enormous ambition. Yes, that it my social position. Let us see what I myself am like.

I am ugly, awkward, untidy, and socially uneducated. I am irritable, tiresome to others, not modest, intolerant, and shamefaced as a boy. I am almost an ignoramus. What I know I have somehow learnt by myself, in snatches, disconnectedly, unsystematically, and it amounts to very little. I am incontinent, irresolute, inconstant, and stupidly vain and passionate like all characterless people. I am not brave, I am not methodical in life, and am so lazy that idleness has become an almost unconquerable habit of mine.

I am intelligent, but my intelligence has as yet never been thoroughly tested on anything. I have neither practical, social, nor business, ability.

I am honest – that is, I love goodness and have formed a habit of loving it and when I swerve from it I am dissatisfied with myself and return to it with pleasure; but there is something I love more than goodness – fame. I am so ambitious, and so little has that feeling been gratified, that between fame and virtue I am afraid I often might choose the former if the choice presented itself.

Yes – I am not modest, and therefore am proud at heart but shame-faced and shy in society.

That is a grossly unfair estimate of himself, but shows just the sort of eager injustice to anyone who fails to reach the high standard he set up, that always characterised him. The account is inaccurate in details. For instance, he was not seven, but nearly nine, when his father died. He had not wrecked his affairs to the extent he suggests. Though his studies had been desultory he had read widely, with a quick under-standing and retentive memory. He was master of the Russian, French, and German languages, besides having some knowledge of English, Latin, Arabic, and Turco-Tartar. (Later in life he added a knowledge of Italian, Greek and Hebrew.) As for not yet having tested his cleverness

– he had published stories for which the editor of the best Russian magazine paid him the rate given only to the foremost writers; while his awkwardness in society did not depend on ignorance: on the contrary, he had grown up among people who paid much attention to manners, and he was himself gifted with social tact which became evident as soon as he attained self-confidence. Any defect in his manners must have been merely a result of that nervous shyness natural to highly-strung sensitive natures conscious of powers that society scantily recognises. Yet when all is said his description gets home: over-emphatic and unfair, like much of his other writing, it still leaves you in no doubt as to what he meant and hits the real weaknesses of the victim he is attacking.

On 15th August he notes:

I repeat what I had written before: I have three chief defects: (1) lack of character, (2) irritability, and (3) laziness, of which I must cure myself. Will watch these three faults with all possible attention and note them down.

And on 22nd–23rd August the entry runs:

Two marches from Berlad to Aslui. Two days of terrible toothache and complete idleness. Reproaches for these two days (besides inactivity which I might have mastered) consist of irritability [with fellow-officers and his serf Alëshka].

From 9th to 12th September he read *Uncle Tom's Cabin* every day in spite of toothache that was troubling him severely. Read at a moment when the question of the abolition of serfdom was presenting itself seriously to Russian landowners, the book interested him greatly and he sympathised with the feelings it expressed. Other authors read during his service in Turkey and the Crimea were: Goethe, Alphonse Karr, Lérmontov, Púshkin, Dickens (*Bleak House*), Schiller (*Die Rauber* and other plays, as well as some poems), Ostróvski, George Sand, Heine, Thackeray (*Henry Esmond*, *Vanity Fair*, *Pendennis*), and 'a stupid novel' by Balzac.

On 17th September he notes: 'Have behaved badly. Did nothing in the evening, ran after girls – going out contrary to my intention.'

Early in October he notes: 'Little by little I am becoming steadier,' but on 21st of that month the entry is: 'Have lost all my money at cards.'

Tolstoy, who had been promoted to a sub-lieutenancy in September,

in Kishinëv, on 1st November renewed his application for an appointment in the Crimea, and was ordered to Sevastopol, which he reached
on the 7th of that month.

The situation there at this time [1854] was as follows. The Allies had
landed in the Crimea to the north of Sevastopol on 14th September
n.s. and had defeated the Russian army under Ménshikov on the 20th at
Alma. Instead of marching straight into the town, which was almost
undefended, they had then gone round and encamped on the south
side, where they remained inactive till 17th October, by which time
Totleben, an engineer of rare genius, had thrown up earthworks and
mounted guns (many of them taken from the Russian ships that were
sunk at the entrance to the roadstead). Ménshikov had practically
abandoned the town, withdrawing the bulk of his army northward; but
the situation was saved by the patriotism of just that section of the
Russian forces which had been least exposed to the deadening influence
of Nicholas I's militarism – namely, by the officers and men of the fleet.
Inspired by the example of the heroic Admiral Kornílov (who lost
his life during the siege) they rallied to the defence with remarkable
devotion. Their example awoke enthusiasm throughout Russia and
compelled Ménshikov to supply reinforcements which enabled the
town to hold out for eleven months, despite the great superiority of the
Allies in rifles, artillery, and other modern equipments of war.

Tolstoy reached Sevastopol when the defence was already fully
organised and when (in spite of the repulse experienced at Inkerman)
the garrison had gained confidence in their powers of resistance and
had settled down to a dogged defence.

Of the hospitals, in which the wounded saw the limbs of others
amputated while waiting their own turn; of the Staff-officers, who
managed to amuse themselves pretty well during the siege; of the
commissariat-officers flourishing amid the general havoc; as well as of
the line officers and the non-commissioned officers and privates upon
whom the greatest hardships fell, Tolstoy gives vivid glimpses in the
Sketches he wrote during the siege.

A fortnight after his arrival he writes from outside the town to his
brother Sergéy, apologising for not having sent him a letter sooner, and
adds:

So much have I learnt, experienced, and felt, this year that I positively
do not know what to begin to describe, nor how to describe it as I

wish to . . . Silistria is now ancient history and we have Sevastopol, of which I suppose you all read with beating hearts, and where I was four days ago. Well, how can I tell you all I saw there, and where I went, and what I did, and what the prisoners and wounded French and English say; and *whether it hurts them and hurts very much*,* and what heroes our enemies are, especially the English? I will tell all that later at Yásnaya or at Pirogóvo; and you will learn much of it from me through the press. How this will happen I will explain later; but now let me give you an idea of the position of affairs in Sevastopol. The town is besieged from one side, the south, where we had no fortifications when the enemy approached it. Now we have on that side more than 500 heavy guns and several lines of earthworks, positively impregnable. I spent a week in the fortress and to the last day used to lose my way among that labyrinth of batteries as in a wood. More than three weeks ago the enemy advanced his trenches at one place to within 200 yards, but gets no farther. When he makes the smallest advance he is overwhelmed with a hailstorm of shot and shell.

The spirit of the army is beyond all description. In the times of ancient Greece there was not such heroism. Kornílov making the round of the troops, instead of greeting them with 'Good health to you, lads!' says: 'If you have to die, lads, will you die?' and the troops shout, 'We'll die, Your Excellency! Hurrah!' and they do not say it for effect. On every face one saw that it was not jest but earnest, and 22,000 men have already fulfilled that promise.

A wounded soldier, almost dying, told me how they captured the 24th French Battery but were not reinforced; and he wept aloud. A company of Marines nearly mutinied because they were to be withdrawn from batteries in which they had been exposed to shellfire for thirty days. The soldiers extract the fuses from the shells that fall. Women carry water to the bastions for the soldiers. Many are killed and wounded. The priests with their crosses go to the bastions and read prayers under fire. In one brigade, the 24th, more than 160 wounded men would not leave the front. It is a wonderful time! Now however, after the 24th [24th October, o.s. = 5th November, n.s. – the Battle of Inkerman] we have quieted down; it has become splendid

---

* This refers to a family joke, and occurs in other letters home apropos of people who were killed or wounded.

in Sevastopol. The enemy hardly fires and all are convinced that he will not take the town; and it is really impossible . . . I have not yet succeeded in being in action even once, but thank God that I have seen these people live in this glorious time. The bombardment of the 5th [17th October, n.s., when the first attack on Sevastopol, a very fierce one, took place] remains the most brilliant and glorious feat not only in the history of Russia, but in the history of the world. More than 1,500 cannon were in action for two days against the town and not only did not cause it to capitulate, but did not silence one two-hundredth part of our batteries. Though I suppose this campaign is unfavourably regarded in Russia, our descendants will place it above all others; do not forget that we, with equal or even inferior forces and armed only with bayonets and with the worst troops in the Russian army (such as the 6th corps) are fighting a more numerous enemy aided by a fleet, armed with 3,000 cannon, excellently supplied with rifles, and with their best troops. I do not even speak of the superiority of their Generals.

Only our army could hold its ground and conquer (we shall yet conquer, of that I am convinced) under such circumstances. You should see the French and English prisoners (especially the latter): they are each one better than the other – morally and physically fine fellows. The Cossacks say it is even a pity to cut them down; and alongside of them you should see some Chasseurs or others of ours: small, lousy, and shrivelled up.

Now I will tell you how you will get printed news from me of the deeds of these lousy and shrivelled heroes. In our artillery Staff, which is composed, as I think I wrote you, of very decent and nice fellows, the idea has arisen of publishing a war periodical [a weekly paper], the aim of which would be to maintain a good spirit in the army. It would be a cheap paper (three rubles a year) and a popular one, that the soldiers may read it. We drew up a plan of the paper and submitted it to the Prince. He was very pleased with the idea and submitted the project and a sample number, which we also drew up, for the Emperor's approval. The money for its publication will be advanced by myself and by Stolypin.* I am chosen editor together with a certain Konstantínov who . . . has had experience in such matters.

---

* Father of P. A. Stolypin, who became Premier of Russia in 1906.

In the paper, we should publish descriptions of battles – not such dull ones and not such inaccurate ones as are given in other papers – courageous deeds, biographies, and obituary notices of worthy, and especially of unknown men; military stories, soldiers' songs, and popular articles on engineering and artillery, &c. This plan pleases me very much: in the first place I like the work; and secondly, I hope the paper will be useful and not too bad. It is as yet merely a project until we know the Emperor's reply, about which I confess I have my fears. In the specimen number sent to Petersburg we rashly inserted two articles, one by me and one by Rostóvtsev, not quite orthodox. For this business I want 1,500 rubles, which I have asked Valerián to send me.

I, thank God, am well, and live happily and pleasantly since I returned from Turkey. In general my army service divides up into two periods: beyond the frontier – horrid: I was ill, poor, and lonely. This side of the frontier – I am well and have good friends, though I am still poor: money simply runs away.

As to writing, I do not write; but, as Auntie teases me by saying, I 'test myself'. One thing disquiets me: it is that for four years now I have lived without female society; and I may become quite coarse and unsuited for family life which I so enjoy.

During the year then closing he worked at *Youth* and *The Wood-Felling: A Cadet's Story*, but his army service and the frequent moves from place to place hindered his writing, and neither of these stories was completed in 1854.

On 6th January he wrote to his Aunt:

There is no more fighting in the open country because of the winter which is extraordinarily rigorous particularly just now; but the siege still goes on . . . I think I have mentioned an occupation I had in view which promised very well – as I may say now that it is settled. I had the idea of starting a military newspaper. This project, at which I worked with the cooperation of many very distinguished men, was approved by the Prince and submitted to His Majesty for his consent, but he has refused.

This disappointment has, I confess, distressed me greatly and has much altered my plans. If God wills that the Crimean campaign should end well, and if I do not receive an appointment that satisfies me, and if there is no war in Russia, I shall leave the army and go to the Military Academy in Petersburg. I have formed this plan, (1) because I do not want to abandon literature, at which it is impossible to work amid this camp life; (2) because it seems to me that I am becoming ambitious, but I want to do some good; and to do it one must be something more than a Sub-Lieutenant, and (3) because I shall see you all, and all my friends.

On 23rd January 1855 he notes in his Diary:

I have been to Sevastopol, received money, talked with Totleben, visited the Fourth Bastion, and played cards. Am greatly disgusted with myself.

The next entry, on 28th January, is:

Have played *stoss* for two days and two nights. The result is evident – the loss of the house at Yásnaya Polyána. It seems useless to write: am so disgusted with myself that I should like to forget my own existence.

While he was in the Caucasus he had written to his brother to sell the big house at Yásnaya Polyána, and it is not clear whether the sale was then effected or not, and whether Tolstoy here merely means that he had lost as much as the house had fetched.

On 12th February in a mood of depression, he writes:

Time, the time of youth, visions, thoughts, is all being lost, leaving no trace. I do not live, but waste my years. My losses compel me to bethink myself a little.

On 11th March he noted in his Diary:

Gorchakóv has arrived with the whole Staff; I have been to see him and was well received, but of a transfer to the Staff, which I have long desired, there is no news. I will not ask for it, but will wait for him to do it of his own accord or for my aunt to write a letter.

On 11th April the entry is:

Fourth Bastion.* Have written very, very little of *Youth* or *Sevastopol*

---

* The Fourth Bastion to which Tolstoy was sent was the most southern and the most dangerous of the defences of Sevastopol. English writers call it the Flagstaff Bastion.

during these days. My cold and feverish condition were the cause of this. Besides that, I am vexed (especially now when I am ill) that it does not occur to anybody that I am good for anything except *chair à canon* [cannon-fodder], and of the most useless kind. Feel inclined to fall in love with a nurse I saw at the Ambulance.

In May he wrote again to his brother, recapitulating what had happened during the previous six months:

From Kishinëv on 1st November I petitioned to be sent to the Crimea, partly in order to see this war and partly to break away from Serzhputóvski's Staff which I did not like, but most of all from patriotism, of which at that time, I confess, I had a bad attack. I did not ask for any special appointment, but left it to those in authority to dispose of my fate. In the Crimea I was appointed to a battery in Sevastopol itself, where I passed a month very pleasantly amid simple, good companions, who are specially good in time of real war and danger. In December our battery was removed to Simferópol and there I spent six weeks in a squire's comfortable house, riding into Simferópol to dance and play the piano with young ladies, and in hunting wild goats on the Chatyrdág [the highest point of the chain of mountains running across the southern part of the Crimea] in company with officials. In January there was a fresh shuffling of officers and I was removed to a battery encamped on the banks of the Belbék, seven miles from Sevastopol. There I got into hot water: the nastiest set of officers in the battery; a commander who, though good-hearted, was violent and coarse; no comforts, and it was cold in the earth huts. Not a single book, nor a single man with whom one could talk; and there I received the 1,500 rubles for the newspaper, sanction for which had already been refused; and there I lost 2,500 rubles, and thereby proved to all the world that I am still an empty fellow; and though the previous circumstances may be taken into account in mitigation, the case is still a very, very bad one. In March it became warmer, and a good fellow, an excellent man, Bronévski, joined the battery. I began to recover myself; and on 1st April, at the very time of the bombardment, the battery was moved to Sevastopol and I quite recovered myself. There, till 15th May, I was in serious danger, i. e. for four days at a time, at intervals of eight days, I was in charge of a battery in the Fourth Bastion; but it was spring and the weather was excellent, there was abundance of impressions and of people, all the comforts of life, and we formed a capital circle of decent fellows; so that those six weeks will remain among my pleasantest recollections. On 15th May Gorchakóv, or the Commander of the Artillery, took it into his head to entrust me with the formation and command of a mountain platoon at Belbék, 14 miles from Sevastopol, with which arrangement I am up to now extremely well satisfied in many respects.

Apparently it *had* occurred to someone that Tolstoy might be used better than as food for cannon. It has been said – I myself formerly accepted and repeated the statement – that this transfer to Belbék was the result of an order given by Alexander II (Nicholas I died on 2nd March, n.s.) after reading *Sevastopol in December* to 'take care of the life of that young man'. It is true that Alexander was impressed by that sketch, for he gave instructions to have it translated into French; but as the transfer to Belbék was made on 15th May and the sketch only appeared in the June number of the *Contemporary* it is doubtful whether the transfer was made at the Emperor's instigation.

A vivid description of what going to the Fourth Bastion and living in it was like is given in *Sevastopol in December 1854*, and men who were in the trenches in Flanders during the Great War sixty years later tell me that Tolstoy's description very closely resembles their own experiences, both of the kind of warfare and of the feelings of those who fought.

On 12th April, during his sojourn in the Fourth Bastion, Tolstoy writes in his Diary:

The same Fourth Bastion, which I am beginning to like very much. Am writing a good deal. Today have finished *Sevastopol in December* and written a little of *Youth*. The constant charm of danger, observing the soldiers with whom I am living, the sailors, and the methods of war, is so pleasant that I do not want to leave here, especially as I should like to be present at the assault, if there is to be one.

Two days later he writes:

O Lord, I thank Thee for Thy continual protection. How surely Thou leadest me to what is good, and how insignificant a creature should I be if Thou shouldst abandon me! Leave me not, O Lord, help me, not for the satisfaction of my insignificant aims but for the eternal, great, and unknown aim of existence of which I am conscious.

Tolstoy had by now reached the conclusion that the influence exercised by the Staff on the conduct of a war is usually pernicious. It is a view merely indicated in his subsequent novels, but which fitted into a general view of life he ultimately arrived at and that must be dealt with later. For the moment let it suffice to mention that whereas he shows a keen appreciation of Admiral Kornílov's achievement in rousing the spirit of the garrison, he nowhere praises Totleben's achievement in organising the defence of the town and improvising that 'labyrinth of batteries' in which Tolstoy used constantly to lose his way. He says, for instance:

> Now you have seen the defenders of Sevastopol . . . The principal joyous thought you have brought away is a conviction of the strength of the Russian people; and this conviction you gained, not by looking at all these traverses, breastworks, cunningly interlaced trenches, mines, and cannon, one on top of another, of which you could make nothing; but from the eyes, words and actions – in short, from seeing what is called the 'spirit' of the defenders of Sevastopol.

To everything a man can do off his own bat and by his own effort Tolstoy was keenly alive and sympathetic; but when it comes to a complex co-ordinated plan, involving the subordination of many parts of one whole, he was suspicious and even hostile. Had he remained a subordinate officer, or even a novelist, it would not have been necessary to note this peculiarity; but that we may understand his later teachings it is important to see all the roots of feeling from which they grew, and this one among the rest.

To get on however with our tale. One evening while Tolstoy was sitting with the adjutants of Count Osten-Sáken, commander of the garrison, Prince S. S. Urúsov, a brave officer and the best Russian chess-player of his day, who was a friend of Tolstoy entered the room and wished to speak to the General. An adjutant took him to Osten-Sáken's room, and ten minutes later Urúsov passed out again, looking very glum. After he had gone, the adjutant explained that Urúsov had come to suggest that a challenge should be sent to the English to play a game of chess for the foremost trench in front of the Fifth Bastion: a trench that had changed hands several times and had already cost some hundreds of lives. Osten-Sáken had naturally refused to issue the challenge.

Tolstoy suffered a good deal off and on from ill health. For instance he notes, in 1855, in his Diary:

30th July: Rode on horseback; dined at Stolypin's, did absolutely nothing. My health is bad. Fever and headaches. Prepared for departure. Idleness.

31st July. Health seems bad, feverishness and terrible weakness. Because of this I have done nothing.

On 16th August, n.s., Tolstoy took part in the battle of the Chérnaya (Black River) in which the Sardinian contingent, which had arrived in May to reinforce the Allies, highly distinguished itself. This last attempt to relieve Sevastopol failed as its forerunners had done. Three days later Tolstoy wrote to his brother saying that he had not been hurt, and that 'I did nothing, as my mountain artillery was not called on to fire'.

After this battle the officers of the battery were sitting round a camp-fire. One of them suggested that they should compose a song, as had previously been done by some Staff officers apropos of the battle of Alma. Each in turn was to make up a verse. But the attempt was unsuccessful and the verses they composed were worthless. Next day Tolstoy read them some he had composed, and these were received with delight by his fellow-officers who began singing them, and before long they were to be heard throughout the army and copies of them found their way all over Russia.

There has been some confusion about these verses, written by Tolstoy, and others previously written about the battle of Alma – in the composition of which he had little or no part for he only reached Sevastopol after that battle had been fought. In the account given in the first edition of this book I was led astray by following what seemed to be an authoritative account of the matter given in the *Rússkaya Stariná*, and I quoted the Alma verses instead of the following, which are those that refer to the fight Tolstoy took part in at the river Chérnaya. The translation is my wife's.

> 'Twas in August, on the Fourth
> That the devil sent us forth
> That there hill to take.
>
> General Baron Vrévski, he,
> Gorchakóv would not let be,
> Being rather screwed.

'Prince, if you don't take that hill,
'Twixt us two 'twill make ill-will;
I'll denounce you soon.'

So they all in Council met,
Each big-wig and epaulet,
E'en Bekók of the police,

Police-Master of the place,
Could not think in this here case
What he'd better say.

So they pondered, racked their brains,
Drew up plans with care and pains
On a large white sheet.

All so smooth without a blot –
But some ravines they clean forgot
Which we had to cross!

Princes, Counts, and big-wigs start –
The topographers take part –
'Gainst this great redoubt.

Says the Prince: 'You go, Liprandé!'
But Liprandé: 'Wait, *attendez*;'
Muttering, 'Think I'd go?

'Any fool will do; you had
Better send out there Reyád,
And let me look on.'

Reyád, not troubling of his pate,
To the bridge then led us straight:
'Now then, shout "Hurrah!" '

'Wait,' then Martinau did pray,
'Till r'inforcements come our way.'
– 'No, we'd better go!'

So 'Hurrah' we all did shout –
I don't know how't came about –
No supports were sent!

Bélovtsev – our General – took
And a banner fiercely shook –
Tho' it didn't suit his face;

In full Regiments started we,
But in all some Comp'nies three
Reached Fedúkin's heights.

Of the French there were a lot –
Three times more than we had got,
And r'inforcements – heaps!

We a column to our aid
Did expect, and signals made
To the garrison.

But while General – you know who –
With long prayers made great ado
We had to retreat . . .

That same week he notes in his Diary:

Went to Bakhchisaráy, bought a horse, fornicated, and generally
behaved badly, not to mention my laziness which I have still not
mastered. My health is not good . . .

The end of the siege was now approaching, and on 27th August,
o.s. [8th September, n.s.] Tolstoy, having volunteered for service in
Sevastopol, reached the Star Fort on the north side of the roadstead
just in time to witness the capture of the Malákhov by the French, as he
has described in *Sevastopol in August*.

On the north side of the roadstead at the Star Fort, near noon, two
sailors stood on the 'telegraph' mound; one of them, an officer, was
looking at Sevastopol through the fixed telescope. Another officer
accompanied by a Cossack, had just ridden up to join him at the big
Signal-post . . . Along the whole line of fortifications but especially on
the high ground on the left side, appeared, several at a time, with
lightnings that at times flashed bright even in the noonday sun, puffs
of thick, dense, white smoke, that grew, taking various shapes and
appearing darker against the sky. These clouds, showing now here
now there, appeared on the hills, on the enemy's batteries, in the

town, and high up in the sky. The reports of explosions never ceased, but rolled together and rent the air.

Towards noon the puffs appeared more and more rarely and the air vibrated less with the booming.

'I say, the Second Bastion does not reply at all now!' said the officer on horseback; 'it is quite knocked to pieces. Terrible!'

'Yes, and the Malákhov, too, sends hardly one shot to three of theirs,' said he who was looking through the telescope. 'Their silence provokes me! They are shooting straight into the Kornílov Battery and it does not reply.'

'But look there! I told you that they always cease the bombardment about noon. It's the same today. Come, let's go to lunch; they'll be waiting for us already. What's the good of looking?'

'Wait a bit!' answered the one who had possession of the telescope, looking very eagerly towards Sevastopol.

'What is it? What?'

'A movement in the entrenchments, thick columns advancing.'

'Yes! They can be seen even without a glass, marching in columns. The alarm must be given,' said the seaman.

'Look! Look! They've left the trenches!'

And, really, with the naked eye one could see what looked like dark spots moving down the hill from the French batteries across the valley to the bastions. In front of these spots dark stripes were already visibly approaching our line. On the bastions white cloudlets burst in succession as if chasing one another. The wind brought a sound of rapid small-arm firing, like the beating of rain against a window. The dark stripes were moving in the midst of the smoke and came nearer and nearer. The sounds of firing, growing stronger and stronger, mingled in a prolonged, rumbling peal. Puffs of smoke rose more and more often, spread rapidly along the line, and at last formed one lilac cloud (dotted here and there with little faint lights and black spots) which kept curling and uncurling; and all the sounds blent into one tremendous clatter.

'An assault!' said the naval officer, turning pale and letting the seaman look through the telescope.

Cossacks galloped along the road, some officers rode by, the Commander-in-Chief passed in a carriage with his suite. Every face showed painful excitement and expectation.

'It's impossible they can have taken it,' said the mounted officer.

'By God, a standard! . . . Look! look!' said the other, panting, and he walked away from the telescope: 'A French standard on the Malákhov!'

The loss of the Malákhov rendered the further defence of the town impossible, and the following night the Russians set fire to it and blew up and destroyed such munitions of war as they could not remove from the bastions. Tolstoy was deputed to clear the Fifth and Sixth Bastions before they were abandoned to the Allies. When telling me of this he added: 'The non-commissioned officers could have done the work just as well without me.' While the destruction was proceeding the Russian forces crossed the roadstead by a pontoon bridge which had been constructed during the siege. The town south of the roadstead was abandoned and the defenders established themselves on the north side, where they remained till peace was concluded in February 1856.

To his Auntie Tatiána Tolstoy wrote on 4th September:

On the 27th a great and famous action occurred in Sevastopol. I had the fortune and misfortune to arrive at the town just on the day of the attack, so that I was present and even took some part in the action as a volunteer. Do not be alarmed: I was hardly in any danger. The 28th, my birthday, was for the second time in my life a memorable and mournful day: the first time, fourteen years ago, it was the death of Aunt Alexándra Ilínishna; now it is the fall of Sevastopol. I wept when I saw the town wrapped in flames and French standards on our Bastions; and in general in many respects it was a very sorrowful day.

The last entry in his Diary before leaving the Crimea was on 27th October:

Yesterday lost 500 rubles . . . Terrible idleness. It is essential for me to get out of this rut of military life which harms me.

Some notes made in September by an artillery Colonel, P. N. Glébov, who was attached to Headquarters, gives us an idea of how Tolstoy was there regarded.

Count Tolstoy, a Sub-Lieutenant of artillery, is in command of two mountain batteries, but he himself roams anywhere he pleases. On 4th August [i.e. at the battle of the Chérnaya] he attached himself to me, but I could not make use of his pistolets [an ironical reference to his small mountain guns] in the affair, as I was holding the position with the battery guns; on 27th August [i.e. the day the Malákhov was captured by the French] he again applied to me, but this time without his guns, so owing to the shortage of officers I was able to entrust him with the command of five battery guns. This at any rate shows that Tolstoy is eager to smell powder, but only fitfully, as an irregular, avoiding the difficulties and hardships incidental to war. He travels about to different places like a tourist, but as soon as he hears firing, he at once appears on the field of battle. When it is over, he is off again at his own discretion wherever fancy takes him. Not everyone is able to make war in so agreeable a manner. It is also said of him that for lack of something to do he makes songlets, and that the song about the 4th August is his composition.

After the retreat, Tolstoy was given the task of collating the twenty or more reports of the action from the Artillery Commanders. This experience of how war is recorded helped to produce in him the supreme contempt for detailed military histories which he often expressed in later years. He says:

> I regret that I did not keep a copy of those reports. They were an excellent example of that naïve, unavoidable kind of military false-hood, out of which descriptions are compiled. I think many of those comrades of mine who drew up those reports will laugh on reading these lines, remembering how, by order of their Commander, they wrote what they could not know.

Carrying the report he had himself prepared, Tolstoy was sent as courier to Petersburg at the end of October, and this terminated his personal experience of war. He had added a year and a half of service in Turkey and the Crimea to his two years' service in the Caucasus, but his hopes of advancement in the army had come to nothing, partly in consequence of the satirical soldiers' song already referred to.

Another matter which did him no good in the eyes of his superiors was his refusal to fall in with a reprehensible practice which by long usage had become as well established as, for instance, among ourselves, was the purchase of peerages by contributions to Party funds.

Those in command of batteries used to pay for various things, such as shoes for the horses, medicine, office expenses, and certain extras for the soldiers for which no official allowance was made, and money for this was obtained by retaining, and not accounting for, surpluses which arose from the fact that the allowance issued for the purchase of stores and fodder was in excess of what was required for the purpose. The difference between the actual and estimated cost supplied a revenue different commanders used in different ways. Some spent it all for the good of the service though in a manner not shown in the accounts; others made private profit of it. Tolstoy, during his command of a battery, refused to keep any balance of cash and insisted on showing it in the accounts. He hereby evoked the displeasure of less scrupulous commanders and called down upon himself a rebuke from General Kryzhanóvksi, who did not consider that it lay with a sub-lieutenant in temporary command to upset so well-established a custom.

The following entries in his Diary show that Tolstoy did not reach his decision to forgo this source of revenue without a struggle. On 19th May he notes:

> On the 15th I was appointed commander of a mountain battery and came into camp at Belbék, 20 versts from Sevastopol. There is a lot to do. I wish to attend to the provisioning myself, and I see how easy it is to steal – so easy that it is impossible not to steal. I have many plans about this stealing, but what the result will be I do not know.
>
> 2nd June: It is abominable that I am undecided about the provisioning.
>
> 28th June: Try each month to set 200 rubles aside, partly from the provision and forage money and partly from the money for my writings, and write to the village [Yásnaya] that they should pay my debts to Z, to D, to C, and so on, and in any case I must myself collect 1,500 rubles by the New Year.
>
> 8th July: As to the surplus remaining from my command of the battery, I will certainly take it and not speak of it to anyone. If I am asked I will say that I took it, as I know it to be honest.
>
> 12th July: Have . . . been solely occupied with the new chests and have realised that there will be no Treasury money left over. Am even surprised that the thought should have occurred to me of taking any, even though it was a quite unneeded surplus. Am very glad I have devised these chests, which will cost over 100 rubles.

From his letters and memoirs we get clear indications of Tolstoy's feelings towards his brother officers; his distaste for the common run of them, and his liking for those of a better sort. Here and there in memoirs and magazine articles by other people, one finds records of the impression he in turn produced on his companions. One of them relates:

> How Tolstoy woke us all up in those hard times of war, with his stories and his hastily composed couplets! He was really the soul of our battery. When he was with us we did not notice how time flew, and there was no end to the general gaiety . . . When the Count was away, when he trotted off to Simferópol, we all hung our heads. He would vanish for one, two, or three, days . . . At last he would return – the very picture of a prodigal son! Sombre, worn out, and dissatisfied with himself . . . Then he would take me aside, quite apart, and would begin his confessions. He would tell me all: how he had caroused, gambled, and where he had spent his days and nights; and all the time, if you will believe me, he would condemn himself and suffer as though he were a real criminal. He was so distressed that it was pitiful to see him. That's the sort of man he was. In a word, a queer fellow, and to tell the truth one I could not quite understand. He was however a rare comrade, a most honourable fellow, and a man one can never forget!

On 5th March 1855 (old style) when he was just recovering from that fit of depression at Belbék which, as already mentioned, drove him to gamble, he writes in his Diary:

> A conversation about Divinity and Faith has suggested to me a great, a stupendous idea, to the realisation of which I feel capable of devoting my life. That idea is the founding of a new religion corresponding to the present state of mankind: the religion of Christ but purged of dogmas and mysticism – a practical religion, not promising future bliss but giving bliss on earth. I understand that to accomplish this the conscious labour of generations will be needed. One generation will bequeath the idea to the next, and someday fanaticism or reason will accomplish it. *Deliberately* to promote the union of mankind by religion is the basic thought which I hope will dominate me.

In that passage we have, quite clearly stated before he was twenty-seven, the main idea which actuated Tolstoy from the age of fifty onwards. Already by the literary work he accomplished amid the bustle and excitement of the siege he was half-consciously moving in the direction that attracted him.

The entries in his Diary plainly show the vacillations that went on in his mind from day to day and from month to month. On 22nd June, when he had had encouraging news of the success of his first Sevastopol sketch, the entry runs: 'Just fancy! I have nothing to reproach myself with for the whole day!' And two days later: 'Worked all day and cannot reproach myself with anything. Hurrah!'

On 25th July the entry is:

Do not know by what train of thoughts, or simply in consequence of what memories, while talking to Khonzíni today I returned to my former view of life, the aim of which is welfare, and the ideal – virtue. This return was exceedingly pleasant to me and I was horrified at how remote I have been from that view, and how material and bad my recent thoughts and rules have been . . . Yes, military society has cast its shadow on me and stained me.

But on 28th September he writes:

I positively could not write two sheets, but might have written a little, and I was not continent; that however deliberately, and I do actually feel better.

The alleged purposes of the Crimean War were lost sight of before it ended, and the conditions of the Treaty of Peace which forbade Russia to fortify Sevastopol and limited her Black Sea navy, were repudiated by her in 1871 when France and Prussia were fighting one another, and it was not worth England's while to object. But a valuable and permanent result of the war remains in the *Sevastopol* sketches, part of which Tolstoy had written while serving in the dangerous Fourth Bastion.

The war had hindered his literary activity, and not till he was stationed at Belbék, in June 1855, did he finish the third revision of *The Wood-Felling*, which had been begun before he left the Caucasus in 1853. This he dedicated to Turgénev whose style had influenced him when writing it. It appeared in the August number of the *Contemporary*, 1855. *Youth*, on which he had worked at the same time, was not completed till later. He was also at this time forming plans for *A Landlord's Morning* which were only very partially carried out, but which indicate his attitude towards the emancipation of the serfs.

On 1st August he notes:

The plan occurred to me yet more clearly than before of making four periods of *A Landlord's Morning*, and I will myself be that hero in Khabárovka. The chief idea of the story must be the impossibility in our times of a decent life for an educated landowner with slavery. All its wretchedness should be shown and the means of correcting it indicated.

Sevastopol in December 1854 and *Sevastopol in May 1855* were written during the siege, and *Sevastopol in August 1855* was begun immediately after the town had fallen, but while the war still continued. These sketches mark a phase of his career, and are highly characteristic in the change from the patriotism of the first article to the condemnation of war in the second, where it is depicted in its naked ugliness and stripped of romanticism as no writer, not even Stendhal, had done before. These sketches were precursors of the revolt against the hypnotic fascination of war which had been habitually presented as a grand, heroic, beautiful, and ennobling pursuit. From the time of the *Sevastopol* sketches the other side of the picture has more and more frequently been shown, and men's minds have been changed to such a degree that a League of Nations has become possible and finds support, which definitely aims at the abolition of war, that previously was regarded as one of the chief aims of man's existence.

The facts are remarkable. Tolstoy had volunteered for service in Sevastopol under the influence of an 'attack of patriotism', and an entry in his Diary on 6th July 1854 indicates his ambition:

> However often I tell myself that I am not ambitious, and try as I will to be sincere about it, *le bout de l'oreille se montre malgré moi* [a proverb which may perhaps be translated: The cloven hoof shows up in spite of me]. It was unpleasant to me to learn today that Ósip Serzh-putóvski . . . has been mentioned to the Emperor . . .

He chafed against the slowness of his advancement in the service and at its not occurring to anyone that he was 'good for anything except *chair à canon* of the most useless kind'. He wrote *Sevastopol in December 1854* in a genuinely patriotic mood and it was received by the public with enthusiasm, and read with approval by the Emperor who had just succeeded to the throne, and who had it translated into French. Turgénev wrote to Panáev:

> Tolstoy's article about Sevastopol is wonderful! Tears came into my eyes as I read it, and I shouted, Hurrah! I am greatly flattered by his wish to dedicate his new tale to me . . . Here his article has produced a general furore.

Tolstoy, meanwhile, had written *Sevastopol in May*, which besides showing the meaner aspects of war frankly expresses moral condemnation of it. The following sequence of dates deserves attention. On 15th June he notes: 'Received a letter and my article from Panáev. Am flattered that it has been read by the Emperor,' but four days later he begins his second sketch and, conscious that it might get him into trouble, notes, on 23rd June, that he had revised the whole 'from the point of view of the Censor'.

On 28th of that month he writes:

It seems that I am really beginning to acquire a reputation in Petersburg. The Emperor has ordered *Sevastopol in December* to be translated into French.

Yet on 4th July he writes to Panáev (co-editor of the *Contemporary*) saying:

I am sending you the Sevastopol article [*Sevastopol in May*]. Though I am convinced that it is incomparably better than the first one, I am sure it will not please. I am even afraid it will not be allowed at all.

Next day he notes: 'I have only now reached the period of real temptation by vanity. I could gain much in life if I were willing to work without conviction,' and six days later (on 11th July) he notes: 'Have only today sent off *Sevastopol in May*' – that is to say, that, after holding it back for a week, he sent off an article he knew would go right against the grain with the public, with the publishers' interests, with the Emperor, and with the whole stream of patriotic sentiment the war had aroused. Nekrásov on receiving it, writing to Turgénev says: 'Tolstoy has sent a *Sevastopol* article, but it is so full of sober and deep truth that it is useless to think of publishing it.' And his co-editor, Panáev, wrote to Tolstoy:

It is all excellent, all is sketched in masterfully, but . . . at the present time, when the scene of its action is almost sacred ground especially to those who are far away from it – the story may even produce a very unpleasant impression.

The attempt to publish it was made, however, and with a few alterations the Censor passed it, and it was already in print in the August number of the *Contemporary*, ready for publication, when it was recalled for submission to the President of the Censor's Committee, who expressed astonishment that the editor had ever ventured to submit it and that the Censor should have passed it. His decision was that 'the article is forbidden on account of its ridicule of our brave officers – the brave defenders of Sevastopol'. Eventually he changed his mind and, after himself making considerable alterations in the article, allowed its publication. His alterations were so serious that Panáev did not wish to publish the article at all, but was told that he must. 'There was no help for it,' he writes to Tolstoy, 'and your mutilated article will appear in the September number, but without the initials L. N. T., which I could not bear to see attached to it after that . . .'

Nebrásov wrote to him in September saying:

The revolting mutilation of your article quite upset me. Even now I cannot think of it without regret and rage. Your work will, of course, not be lost . . . it will always remain as proof of a strength able to utter such profound and sober truth under circumstances amid which few men would have retained it. It is just what Russian society now needs: the truth – the truth, of which since Gógol's death so little has remained in Russian literature. You are right to value that side of your gifts most of all. Truth – in such form as you have introduced it into our literature – is something completely new among us. I do not know another writer of today who so compels the reader to love him and sympathise heartily with him, as he to whom I now write; and I only fear lest time, the nastiness of life, and the deafness and dumbness that surround us, should do to you what it has done to most of us, and kill the energy without which there can be no writer – none at least such as Russia needs . . .

On the 17th of that month Tolstoy notes in his Diary:

Yesterday I received news that *Sevastopol in May* has been distorted and printed. It seems that I am under the strict observation of the Blues [the gendarmes] on account of my articles. I wish however that Russia always had such moral writers; but I never can be a sugary one, nor can I ever write 'from the empty into the void' [a familiar Russian saying] without ideas, and above all without aim. Despite a first moment of anger in which I promised myself never again to take pen in hand, my chief and sole activity, dominating all other tendencies and occupations, must be literature. My goal is literary fame and the good I can accomplish by my writings. Tomorrow I am going to Koroléz and will tender my resignation.

It is worth while to note the very different conclusions at which Kinglake the historian of this war, and Tolstoy its novelist, arrived. Kinglake holds the war to have been unnecessary, and attributes it chiefly to the unscrupulous ambition of Napoleon III; yet he blames the Peace Party very severely for protesting against it, for had they not done so, he thinks, Nicholas would not have dared to act aggressively. Kinglake feels that negotiations between rulers and diplomatists are important and that anything that prevents a Government from speaking with authority makes for confusion and disaster.

Tolstoy, on the other hand (if I may anticipate and speak of conclusions not definitely expressed by him till much later), regards all war and preparation for war as immoral, and wishes this conviction to become so strong and so general as to render it impossible for any future Napoleon to plunge five nations into war to gratify his own ambition.

Kinglake understands things as they are and knows how easy it is to do harm with good intentions, but is somewhat blind to the trend of human progress and as to what the aim before us should be. Tolstoy, on the contrary, is chiefly concerned about the ultimate aim and about the state of mind of the individual. The actual working of our political system and international relations are things he ignores. The English writer sees clearly what is, and cares little about what should be; the Russian writer cares immensely about what should be, and rather forgets that it can only be approached by slow and difficult steps to take which sure-footedly needs an appreciation of things as they are.

Neither of them manages to say the word which would synthesise their divergent views: namely, that no self-respecting people should support or tolerate as rulers men who seek to gain national advantages by means not strictly fair, honest, and even generous. That is the key to the world's peace. Kinglake's appeal to us not to hamper the government that represents us, and Tolstoy's appeal to us not to spend our energies in preparing to slay our fellow men, can both be met in that way, and perhaps only in that way.

For an ambitious young officer actually engaged in a war even partially to express disapproval of war was difficult; and forty-seven years later when speaking of it to me Tolstoy said that, contending with his desire to tell the truth about things as he saw it, he was at the same time aware of another feeling prompting him to say what was expected of him.

He, however, like the child in Andersen's story who sees that the king has nothing on when everyone else is in ecstasies over the magnificence of the monarch's robes, had the gift of seeing things with his own eyes, as well as a great gift of truthfulness. These were the qualities which ultimately made him the greatest literary power of his century; and in spite of his own hesitation and the Censor's mutilations, we may still read the description he then wrote of the way in which the French and Russian soldiers hobnobbed together in friendship during a truce to allow the dead to be buried, a description closing with these words:

> White flags are on the bastions and parallels; the flowery valley is covered with corpses; the beautiful sun is sinking towards the blue sea; and the undulating blue sea glitters in the golden rays of the sun. Thousands of people crowd together, look at, speak to, and smile at one another. And these people – Christians confessing the one great law of love and self-sacrifice – seeing what they have done – do not at once fall repentant on their knees before Him who has given them life and laid in the soul of each a fear of death and a love of goodness and of beauty, and do not embrace like brothers with tears of joy and happiness.
>
> The white flags are lowered, again the engines of death and suffering are sounding, again innocent blood flows, and the air is filled with moans and curses.

The concluding paragraphs of the sketch are:

> There, I have said what I wished to say this time. But a painful hesitation seizes me. Perhaps I ought to have left it unsaid. Perhaps what I have said belongs to that class of evil truths which, unconsciously hidden within the soul of each one, should not be uttered for fear of becoming injurious, as the dregs in a bottle must not be shaken for fear of spoiling the wine.
>
> Where in this tale is the evil shown that should be avoided? Where is the good that should be imitated? Who is the villain, who the hero of the story? All are good, and all are bad . . .
>
> The hero of my tale, whom I love with all the power of my soul, whom I have tried to portray in all his beauty, who has been, is, and will be, beautiful – is Truth.

In *Sevastopol*, and in Tennyson's *Charge of the Light Brigade* (with its rhymes about 'hundred' and 'thundered', and its panegyric of those who knew it was not their business to think, and at whom 'all the world wondered'), we have two typical expressions of conflicting views on war: the view of a man who knew it from the classics and was Poet Laureate, and the view of a man who was in the thick of it and whose eyes were connected with his brain.

Thirty-four years later Tolstoy wrote a Preface to a fellow-officer's *Recollections of Sevastopol*, and I cannot conclude this chapter better than by quoting a few sentences from it.

Speaking of the position of a young officer engaged in the Crimean war, he says:

To the first question that suggests itself to everyone, Why did he do it? Why did he not cease, and go away? – the author does not reply. He does not say, as men said in olden times when they hated their enemies as the Jews hated the Philistines, that he hated the Allies; on the contrary he here and there shows his sympathy for them as for brother men.

Nor does he speak of any passionate desire that the keys of the Church at Jerusalem should be in our hands, or even that our fleet should, or should not, exist. You feel as you read, that for him the life and death of men are not commensurable with questions of politics. And the reader feels that to the question: Why did the author act as he did? – there is only one answer. It was because I enlisted while still young, or before the war began, or because owing to inexperience I chanced to slip into a position from which I could not extricate myself without great effort. I was entrapped into that position, and when they obliged me to do the most unnatural actions in the world, to kill my brother men who had done me no harm, I preferred to do this rather than suffer punishment and disgrace . . . One feels that the author knows there is a law of God: love thy neighbour and therefore do not kill him – a law which cannot be repealed by any human artifice.

The merit of the book consists in that. It is a pity it is only felt and not plainly and clearly expressed. Sufferings and deaths are described; but we are not told what caused them. Thirty-five years ago even that was well, but now something more is needed. We should be told what it is that causes soldiers to suffer and to die – that we may know, and understand, and destroy these causes.

'War! How terrible,' people say, 'is war, with its wounds, blood-shed, and deaths! We must organise a Red Cross Society to alleviate the wounds, sufferings, and pains of death.' But, truly, what is dreadful in war is not the wounds, sufferings, and deaths. The human race that has always suffered and died, should by this time be accustomed to suffering and death and should not be aghast at them. Without war people die by famine, by inundations, and by epidemics. It is not suffering and death that are terrible, but that which allows people to inflict suffering and death . . .

It is not the suffering and mutilation and death of man's body that most needs to be diminished – but the mutilation and death of his soul. Not the *Red* Cross is needed, but the simple cross of Christ to destroy falsehood and deception . . .

I was finishing this Preface when a cadet from the Military College came to see me. He told me that he was troubled by religious doubts . . . He had read nothing of mine. I spoke cautiously to him of how to read the Gospels so as to find in them the answers to life's problems. He listened and agreed. Towards the end of our conversation I mentioned wine, and advised him not to drink. He replied: 'but in military service it is sometimes necessary.' I thought he meant necessary for health and strength and I intended triumphantly to overthrow him by proofs from experience and science, but he continued: 'Why, at Geok-Tepe, for instance, when Skóbelov had to massacre the inhabitants, the soldiers did not wish to do it, but he had drink served out and then . . . !' Here are all the horrors of war – they are in this lad with his fresh young face, his little shoulder-straps (under which the ends of his hood are so neatly tucked), his well-cleaned boots, his naïve eyes, and with so perverted a conception of life.

This is the real horror of war!

What millions of Red Cross workers could heal the wounds that swarm in that remark – the result of a whole system of education!

5

Petersburg. The Country. A Love Affair

A number of distinguished writers have recorded their opinions of the talented young officer who appeared in Petersburg before the war was quite over and immediately entered the circle then supporting the *Contemporary*. From their memoirs one sees what Tolstoy was like at this, the stormiest and least satisfactory period of his life.

The *Contemporary* was a monthly review founded by Púshkin and Pletnév in 1836. It passed in 1847 to Panáev and the poet Nekrásov, and when Tolstoy began to write was recognised as the leading and most progressive Russian literary periodical. Its chief contributors formed a group united by close personal acquaintance, by sympathy with the Emancipation movement then making itself felt, and by a common agreement (not very strictly or permanently observed) to write exclusively for the *Contemporary*. The point to be noticed is that the circle Tolstoy entered consisted of a friendly, sociable group of people who considered themselves ardent reformers; and that though his talent and his wish to have his works published threw him and them together, he never appears to have had the least inclination to co-operate on the footing of mutual toleration which is so essential in public life. Certainly he never became friendly with the more advanced men, such as Chernyshévski, and the ultra-democratic Dobrolyúbov, who were intent on spreading democratic and socialistic ideas.

It has been suggested that this was due to the fact that Tolstoy was an aristocrat and they were democrats, but one has to go deeper than that for the explanation, which lies to a considerable extent in the fact that the advanced Russian Radicals desired the carrying out of reforms by the exercise of Governmental authority, whereas Tolstoy from the very start tended to be a No-Government man, an anarchist, and objected to linking himself up with any group, since any such alliance implies some amount of compromise and some subordination of one's own opinion.

With the first aim of the progressive movement, the emancipation of the serfs, he sympathised warmly, but with the prevailing trend of the denunciatory literature of that day he was not in sympathy. In a letter of 2nd July 1856 to Nekrásov, he says:

> Among us, not in criticism only but in literature generally and even in society, the opinion is accepted that to feel indignant, splenetic, and angry, is very good . . . But I hold that it is nasty; for a splenetic, angry man is not in a normal condition. A loving man on the contrary is so, and only in a normal condition can one do good and see things clearly.

Entries in his Diary indicate his discord with his surroundings, and also his consciousness of faults on his own side. For instance:

> 5th May 1856: Dinner to Turgénev at which (foolishly offended by a verse of Nekrásov's) I said unpleasant things to everybody. Turgénev left. I am sad, especially as I am writing nothing.

On 13 November:

> To Druzhínin's after three. Goncharóv, Ánnenkov – all disgust me, especially Druzhínin, and they disgust me because I want affection and friendship – of which they are incapable.

The poet Fet, who was himself a young officer, made Tolstoy's acquaintance at this time. A couple of years later he purchased an estate at no great distance from Yásnaya Polyána and became a friend of Tolstoy – one in fact of the few people not of his own family with whom, after reaching maturity, Tolstoy formed a close personal friendship.

Fet's first acquaintance with him was however hardly auspicious. Calling on Turgénev in Petersburg at ten o'clock one morning, he saw an officer's sword hanging in the hall and asked the manservant whose it was. 'It's Count Tolstoy's sword,' replied the man. 'He is sleeping in the drawing-room. Iván Sergéevich [Turgénev] is having breakfast in the study.' During Fet's visit of an hour's duration he and his host had to converse in low tones for fear of waking Tolstoy. 'He is like this all the time,' said Turgénev. 'He came back from his Sevastopol battery, put up here, and is going the pace. Sprees, Gypsy-girls, and cards all night long – and then he sleeps like a corpse till two in the afternoon. At first I tried to put the brake on, but now I've given it up and let him do as he likes.'

Fet tells us that as soon as he met Tolstoy [1855] he noticed his instinctive defiance of all accepted opinions, and at Nekrásov's the first time he saw Tolstoy and Turgénev together he witnessed the exasperation to which Tolstoy reduced Turgénev by his biting retorts.

'I can't admit,' said Tolstoy, 'that what you say expresses your conviction. If I stand at the door with a dagger or a sword and say, "While I am alive no one shall enter here," that shows conviction. But here you all try to conceal the true inwardness of your thoughts from one another, and call *that* conviction!'

'Why do you come here?' squeaked Turgénev panting, his voice rising to a falsetto (as always happened when he was disputing). 'Your banner is not here! Go! Go to the salon of Princess Belévski-Belózereva!'

'Why should I ask you where I am to go? Besides, empty talk won't become conviction merely because I am, or am not, here,' replied Tolstoy.

Fet's stay in Petersburg at this time was a short one and he therefore saw little of Tolstoy. D. V. Grigoróvich, the novelist, however, reported to him another scene, which also occurred at Nekrásov's lodging.

You can't imagine what it was like! Great Heavens! [said Grigoróvich]. Turgénev squeaked and squeaked, holding his hand to his throat, and with the eyes of a dying gazelle whispered: 'I can stand no more! I have bronchitis!' and began walking to and fro through the three rooms. 'Bronchitis is an imaginary illness,' growls Tolstoy after him: 'Bronchitis is a metal!'

Of course Nekrásov's heart sank: he feared to lose either of these valuable contributors to the *Contemporary*. We were all agitated, and at our wits' end to know what to say. Tolstoy, in the middle room, lay sulking on the morocco sofa; while Turgénev, spreading the tails of his short coat and with his hands in his pockets, strode to and fro through the three rooms. To avert a catastrophe I went to the sofa and said, 'Tolstoy, old chap, don't get excited! You don't know how he esteems and loves you!'

'I won't allow him to do anything to spite me!' exclaimed Tolstoy with dilated nostrils. 'There! Now he keeps marching past me on purpose, wagging his democratic haunches!'

The rest of the evidence is of much the same nature. Of desire to agree there was hardly a trace in Tolstoy, who never doubted sincerity in himself but seldom credited others with it.

Grigoróvich, in his *Literary Memoirs*, tells us that knowing how out of sympathy Tolstoy was with Petersburg and how evident it was that everything there irritated him, he was surprised to find that he took permanent lodgings. Grigoróvich, himself a Contemporarian, had met Tolstoy in Moscow and coming across him again in Petersburg and hearing that he was invited to dine with the staff of the *Contemporary* but did not yet know any of them intimately, agreed to accompany him.

On the way I warned him to be on his guard about certain matters, and especially to avoid attacking George Sand, whom he much disliked but who was devoutly worshipped by many of the group. The dinner passed off all right, Tolstoy being rather quiet at first, but at last he broke out. Someone praised George Sand's new novel and he abruptly declared his hatred of her, adding that the heroines of the novels she was then writing, if they really existed, ought to be tied to the hangman's cart and driven through the streets of Petersburg.

In spite of the curious convolutions of Tolstoy's character there was a remarkable tenacity of conviction running through his whole life, and a remark in *Resurrection*, written nearly half a century later, throws a flood of light on his detestation of George Sand's emancipated heroines while himself living a loose life. In that book the hero has been attracted as well as repelled, first by Mariette, the General's wife, and then by a handsome demi-mondaine he passes in the street, and this is his reflection:

The animalism of man's brute nature is disgusting, thought he; but so long as it remains in its naked form we observe it from the height of our spiritual life and despise it; and, whether one has fallen or resisted, one remains what one was before. But when that same animalism hides under a cloak of poetry and aesthetic feeling and demands our worship – then we are swallowed up by it completely and worship animalism, no longer distinguishing good from evil. Then it is awful!

Grigoróvich in another place speaks of Tolstoy's 'readiness to contradict'. It did not matter what opinion was being expressed, and the more authoritative the speaker appeared to be the more eager was Tolstoy to oppose him and begin a verbal duel. 'Watching how he listened to the speaker and pierced him with his eyes, and noticing how ironically he pressed his lips together, one conjectured that he was preparing not a direct reply but such an expression of opinion as would perplex his opponent by its unexpectedness.'

Danílevski, the novelist, confirms this impression of Tolstoy's eagerness to oppose. They met at the house of a well-known sculptor. Tolstoy entered the drawing-room while a new work of Herzen's was being read aloud and quietly took up a position behind the reader's chair. When the reading was over he began, at first gently and with restraint, then hotly and boldly, to attack Herzen and the enthusiasm then current for his revolutionary and emancipatory works; and he spoke so convincingly and with such sincerity that Danílevski says he never afterwards saw one of Herzen's publications in that house.

Turgénev once said: 'In Tolstoy the character which afterwards lay at the base of his whole outlook on life early made itself manifest. He never believed in people's sincerity. Every spiritual movement seemed to him false, and with his extraordinarily penetrating eyes he used to pierce those on whom his suspicion fell'; and Turgénev went on to say that personally he had never encountered anything more disconcerting than that inquisitorial look which accompanied by two or three biting words was enough to goad to fury any man who lacked strong self-control.

The different sides of people's characters do not always expand simultaneously or harmoniously, and it frequently happens that men awakening to a sense of public duty remain self-indulgent in regard to wine or women, and that others become abstainers or respectable husbands while still oblivious of the political duties they owe to the community. Among the reform group there was a good deal of gluttony, drinking, gambling, and loose living, and Tolstoy – though he was often remorseful and repentant about his own excesses with wine, women, and cards – having an innate propensity to demand *all or nothing*, bitterly resented this inconsistency in others. He would no doubt have considered it hypocritical had he himself come forward as a reformer before obtaining mastery over his own appetites, and he judged others by the same strict standard.

The ill-success of the Crimean war had dealt a blow to the prestige of the autocracy and a series of wide-reaching reforms was at this time being prepared – including the reform of civil and criminal law, the introduction of trial by jury and oral proceedings in the law courts, the establishment of the Zémstvos (a system of Local Government somewhat resembling our County Councils) and some relaxation of the insensate severity of the press censorship. But though Tolstoy reached Petersburg at a moment when Russia was entering on this hopeful and fruitful period of internal reform, his published writings, apart from the implicit condemnation of serfdom in *A Landlord's Morning* and in *Polikúshka*, do not express much sympathy with the progressive movement, or show much perception of the advantage that accrues to nations whose inhabitants interest themselves in public affairs. He never realised that even if people make bad laws for themselves, the very fact of being invited to think on large practical matters and being allowed to test their conclusions in practice, fosters freedom of the intelligence and encourages action in accord with thought; and that this habit of applying the mind to the guidance of practical affairs, overflows into a nation's commerce, industry, and agriculture, ultimately causing the difference that exists between the comparative material security of our Western world and the chronic fear of famine that oppresses many Eastern lands.

But complex problems of public policy – which are always difficult and call for patience, tolerant co-operation, and a willingness to accept half-loaves when whole ones are unobtainable – never were to Tolstoy's taste. He hankered after simple, clear-cut solutions, such as are attainable only subjectively, in the mind.

A few years later he commenced a novel, *The Decembrists*, which begins with a description of these reform years. It shows how scornfully he regarded the movement for the liberation of the people and the democratisation of their institutions. These are his words:

This happened not long ago, in the reign of Alexander II, in our times of civilisation, progress, *problems*, rebirth of Russia, &c., &c.; the time when the victorious Russian army returned from Sevastopol which it had surrendered to the enemy; when all Russia was celebrating the destruction of the Black Sea fleet, and white-walled Moscow greeted, and congratulated on that auspicious event, the remainder of the crews of that fleet, offering them a good old Russian goblet of vodka and in the good old Russian way bringing them bread and salt* and bowing at their feet. This was the time when Russia, in the person of her far-sighted virginal politicians, wept over the destruction of her dream of a Te Deum in the Cathedral of St Sophia and the deep-felt

---

* Offering 'bread and salt' is a traditional Russian sign of welcome and hospitality.

loss to the fatherland of two great men who had perished during the war (one who, carried away by impatience to hear the Te Deum referred to above, had fallen on the fields of Wallachia – not without leaving there two squadrons of Hussars; and the other an invaluable man who distributed tea, other people's money, and sheets, to the wounded without stealing anything); at that time when from all sides, in all departments of human activity in Russia, great men sprang up like mushrooms: commanders, administrators, economists, writers, orators, and simply great men without any special calling or aim; at that time when at the jubilee of a Moscow actor public opinion, fortified by a toast, appeared and began to punish all, wrongdoers; when stern commissioners galloped from Petersburg to the South and captured, exposed, and punished commissariat rascals; when in all the towns dinners with toasts were given to the heroes of Sevastopol, and to those of them whose arms and legs had been torn off, coppers were given by those who met them on the bridges or highways; at that time when oratorical talents were so rapidly developed among the people that one purveyor of liquor everywhere and on all occasions wrote, printed, and repeated by heart at dinners, such powerful speeches that the guardians of order were obliged to undertake repressive measures to subdue his eloquence; when even in the English Club in Moscow a special room was set apart for the consideration of public affairs; when periodicals appeared under the most varied banners: journals developing European principles on a European basis but with a Russian world-conception, and journals on an exclusively Russian basis developing Russian principles but with a European world-conception; when suddenly so many journals appeared that it seemed as if all possible titles had been used up: *The Messenger*, *The World*, *The Discourse*, *The Eagle*, and many others; when nevertheless fresh titles presented themselves continually; at that time when pleiades of new author-philosophers appeared proving that Science is national, and is not national, and is international, and so on: and pleiades of writer-artists who described woods, and sunrises, and thunders, and the love of a Russian maiden, and the idleness of one official, and the misconduct of many officials; at that time when from all sides appeared 'problems' (as in the year 1856 every concourse of circumstances was called of which nobody could make head or tail): the problem of the Cadet Schools, the Universities, the Censor, oral tribunals, finance, the banks, the police, the Emancipation, and many others; everybody still tried to discover new questions and everybody tried to solve them; they wrote, and read, and talked, and drew up projects, and all wished to amend, destroy, and alter, and all Russians as one man were in an indescribable state of enthusiasm. That was a condition which has occurred twice in Russia in the nineteenth century: the first time was in the year '12 when we thrashed Napoleon I, and the second time was in '56 when Napoleon III thrashed us. Great, unforgettable epoch of the rebirth of the Russian people! Like the Frenchman who said that he had not lived at all who had not lived during the Great French Revolution, so I make bold to say that he who did not live in Russia in '56, does not know what life is. The writer of these lines not merely lived at that time but was one of the workers of that period. Not merely did he personally sit for some weeks in one of the casemates of Sevastopol, but he wrote a work about the Crimean War which brought him great fame and in which he clearly and minutely described how the soldiers in the bastion fired off their muskets, how in the hospitals people were bound up with bandages, and how in the cemetery they were buried in the earth.

Having performed these exploits the writer of these lines arrived at the heart of the Empire at a rocket establishment, where he reaped his laurels. He witnessed the enthusiasm of both capitals and of the whole people, and experienced in his own person how Russia can reward real service. The great ones of the earth sought his acquaintance, pressed his hands, offered him dinners, persistently invited him to come and see them, and in order to hear from him particulars about the war narrated to him their own sensations. Therefore the writer of these lines knows how to appreciate that great and memorable time. But that is not what I want to tell about.

The very day he reached Petersburg from Sevastopol, in November 1855, Tolstoy had called on Turgénev, who begged him to stay with him and introduced him to all that was most interesting in Petersburg literary and artistic circles, watching over his interests 'like an old nurse', as Turgénev himself once expressed it. He greatly appreciated Tolstoy's artistic genius, but was strangely blind to the specially Tolstoyan side of his guest's complex nature. As we have already seen, friction soon arose between the two, and though they again and again made friends, their friendship was always unstable.

Early in 1856 Tolstoy's third brother, Dmítri, died at Orël. His story has been told in Chapter 2. Tolstoy says: 'I was particularly horrid at that time. I went to Orël from Petersburg, where I frequented society and was filled with conceit. I felt sorry for Mítenka but not very sorry. I paid him a hurried visit, but did not stay at Orël, and my brother died a few days after I left. I really believe that what hurt me most was that it prevented my taking part in some private theatricals then being got up at Court, to which I had been invited.'

An entry in his Diary on 10 January runs:

I am in Orël. My brother Dmítri is dying. How the bad thoughts I used to have about him crumble to dust. Másha [the woman Dmítri had taken from a brothel] and Tatiána Alexándrovna [Tolstoy's Auntie] are nursing him.

2nd February: Am in Petersburg. Brother Dmítri is dead. I heard of it today. From tomorrow I want to spend my days so that it should be pleasant to remember them . . . My chief shortcomings are idle habits, lack of order, sensuality, and a passion for gambling. Will struggle against them.

A fortnight later comes an entry:

Dined with Turgénev. We have made it up. In the evening a demi-monde gathering at Gordéev's. My girl, Peiker, is extremely talented, but though she laughs well it seems insincere . . . Tomorrow I will work six hours and promise myself not to go to bed till I have done it.

A month later Tolstoy, for the first time, challenged a man to a duel. The entry in his Diary, on 21st March, runs:

The day before yesterday I accidentally read a letter of Longínov's and have sent him a challenge. God knows what will come of it but I shall be firm and resolute. I am making up my mind to go into the country, marry as soon as possible, and not write any more under my own name. Above all always and with everybody be reticent and careful in what I say!

This is what had happened: at a card party one evening at Nekrásov's a letter arrived from M. N. Longínov, who was a contributor to the *Contemporary*. Nekrásov, engaged at cards, handed the letter to Tolstoy and asked him to read it out. As ill luck would have it the letter con-tained an indictment of Tolstoy for lack of free-thought. Tolstoy read the letter and said nothing, but leaving the house at once sent Longínov an abrupt challenge.

Next day, instead of Longínov's seconds, Nekrásov arrived much distressed, and said: 'If you do not withdraw your challenge to Longínov you will have to exchange shots with me. I am at fault for this whole muddle and must bear the responsibility for it.' Tolstoy did not withdraw his challenge, but Longínov did not reply to it, and the affair came to nothing.

Three months later Tolstoy wrote to Nekrásov from Yásnaya Polyána: 'Can you imagine that only now, in the country, remembering the affair with Longínov, I have realised how stupidly I behaved in the whole matter. I now heartily ask your pardon and will do the same to Longínov as soon as I see him.'

On 24th May he notes in his Diary:

Someone wished to go to the Hermitage [then a famous Moscow restaurant]. I was weak enough to agree. Met Longínov there and was foolish enough to go past him purposely looking at him. Altogether, after half an hour, I carried away from there a feeling of intolerable depression.

Till 18th May – that is for half a year – Tolstoy had lived in Petersburg amid such surroundings. His best acquaintance there was with his 'Aunt', Countess Alexándra Tolstoy, with whom he maintained very cordial relations for many years.

While still in Petersburg he was concerned with plans for the liberation of his serfs; of whom he then had 309 males besides womenfolk.

In March 1856 Alexander II, in a speech to an assembly of the Moscow nobility, had remarked that the emancipation of the serfs must come about someday, and that it would 'therefore be much better for it to come from above than from below'. In the Ministry of the Interior plans for the gradual liberation of the serfs of individual proprietors were being prepared and sanctioned. Tolstoy was one of the first to set himself to find a way to accomplish this, but the case was complicated by the fact that his estate was mortgaged to a State banking institution for 20,000 rubles.

The ruble, be it noted in passing, before the Crimean war was worth about 38*d*. redeemable in silver. When that war broke out it fell, was no longer exchangeable for silver, and never afterwards recovered its former value, but fluctuated (usually between 24 and 32 pence) during the rest of Tolstoy's life, falling as low as 18 pence as a result of the Turkish war of 1878 and being fixed at about 25 pence in gold towards the end of the nineteenth century.

On 22nd April 1856 Tolstoy notes in his Diary: 'My relation to my serfs is beginning to trouble me much. I feel the need of learning, learning, and learning.'

Next evening he went to see K. D. Kavélin, who wrote for the *Contemporary* and was an advocate of emancipation. Of him Tolstoy notes:

A delightful mind and nature. The serf-question is becoming clearer. I returned from him bright, hopeful, and happy. Shall go back to the country with a ready-written project.

Next day he drafts a project for the emancipation of his serfs and listens to 'Kavélin's charming proposals'. On the 25th he visits N. A. Milútin, a prominent advocate of emancipation who, he says, 'explained much to me and showed me a project which I read while having dinner'. And on returning home Tolstoy wrote out, for submission to the Minister of the Interior, a plan for the liberation of his own serfs at Yásnaya.

Milútin took him to see Lëvshin, Assistant Minister of the Interior, who received him 'drily' and evidently did not give him much encouragement, for Tolstoy notes: 'Whatever one undertakes to do in Russia today, everything is rearranged and the rearranging is done by men who are old and therefore unsuitable.'

Next day he visits his 'Aunts' Alexándra and her sister, who were Maids of Honour at the Palace, and reads to them and their visitors his new story *Two Hussars*. He notes in his Diary that day:

Yes, the means to gain true happiness in life is, without any laws, to throw out from oneself in all directions like a spider an adhesive web of love, and catch in it all that comes: an old woman, a child, a girl, or a policeman.

The word here translated 'laws' might be rendered as 'rules', but following so closely on his rebuff at the Ministry of the Interior, it probably means that happiness is to be found in personal affection and not by legal enactments.

Next day he notes: 'Lëvshin said he had reported to the Minister, but all the same his reply was evasive. I shall write my project nevertheless.'

On 16th May he received furlough and next day went to Moscow.

On the 27th he started to drive from there to Yásnaya Polyána, which he reached next day.

> 28th May: . . . At Yásnaya it is sad, pleasant, but somehow not in harmony with my feelings. However, comparing myself with old Yásnaya memories, I felt how much I had changed in a liberal direction . . . Today I am calling a meeting, and will say what God grants . . . Have been to the meeting. Things are going well. The peasants understand gladly, consider me a speculator, and therefore believe in me.

In that meeting he read to the peasants the proposal he had written in Petersburg, and offered them their freedom.

The plan was that the land they were cultivating should be transferred from Tolstoy to the village Commune. Each household would receive 12 acres (4½ desyatíns), of which half a desyatín would be given free, and for the rest they were to pay 5 rubles a year per desyatín for about thirty years. Of this amount one ruble would go to pay off the mortgage on the land, and the other four would complete the purchase. On signing the agreement the serfs would be free from all other obligations to the proprietor. The village Commune would collect the amounts, and if there were arrears the proprietor might resume occupation of sufficient land to cover the deficit or might exact from the peasants an equivalent in work.

The serfs hesitated and took time to consider. Rumours were rife among them that at the approaching coronation the Tsar would grant them freedom and transfer the land to them without cost. To Tolstoy's surprise they therefore declined his proposals. Both in *A Landlord's Morning* and in *Resurrection* he has described just such scenes.

On 3rd June he notes:

> . . . There was no meeting in the evening, but I hear from Vasíli that the peasants suspect a fraud, and think that freedom will be given to everybody at the coronation and that I want to bind them by contract. That it is a 'sell' as he expressed it.
>
> 4th June: . . . Went to the peasants. They don't want their freedom.
>
> 7th June: In the evening talked with some of the peasants and their obstinacy drove me to anger, which I repressed with difficulty.

In a letter he drafted (but did not send) to Count Blúdov, President of the Department of Laws, Tolstoy urged the need of a prompt decree of emancipation for the serfs, even in the first instance without land, as to arrange for its transfer would take too long. He added:

A way out must be found. If within six months the serfs are not freed there will be a conflagration. Everything is ready for it; treasonable hands are not lacking to light the fire of tumult and then the fire will spread everywhere . . .

This prediction was not verified for another sixty years. What happened at the time was that the serfs were emancipated in 1861 and the succeeding years with a modest allotment of land for the loss of which the proprietors received compensation in Government bonds – the value of which the State was to recover from the taxation of the peasants over a long period of years. This was accomplished at the time without any such serious disturbances as Tolstoy anticipated.

He goes on to note the absurdity of the relations that then existed between the serfs and their proprietors and says:

It's as if two strong men were bound together by a sharp chain, it is painful to them both and when one of them moves he involuntarily cuts the other, and neither is free to work.

10th June: . . . There was a meeting in the evening. They definitely refused to sign. The quit-tax will be discussed in autumn, and I shall be in the country.

Lest a mistake made by me in the first short biography of Tolstoy I wrote, which has been cited by other writers, should continue to cause misapprehension, let me here quote from a letter Tolstoy wrote me at that time, in which he said:

I have received your book and read it with pleasure. The short biography is excellent, except the place where you, quoting the words of Sophia Andréevna [his wife] say that 'he liberated his peasants before the Emancipation'. That is wrong: I placed them on *obrók* [subject to fixed yearly payment] instead of keeping them on *bárchina* [subject to labour dues]. It was not possible to emancipate them . . .

Reverting from these matters we must now go back three months, and note that in March the war had ended. On 25th March Tolstoy wrote to his brother Sergéy:

I want to go abroad for eight months, and if they give me leave I shall do so. I wrote to Nikólenka about it and asked him to come too. If we could all three arrange to go together it would be first-rate. If each of us took 1,000 rubles we could do the trip capitally.

Please write and tell me how you like *The Snow Storm*. I am dissatisfied with it – seriously. But I now want to write many things, only I positively have no time in this damned Petersburg. Anyway whether they let me go abroad or not I intend to take furlough in April and come to the country.

On 14th May, he notes:

Found X and Y at Donan's halfway through their dinner. We went to Pavlóvsk. Disgusting! Girls, silly music, girls, an artificial nightingale, girls, heat, cigarette-smoke, girls, vodka, cheese, wild shrieks, girls, girls, girls!

Everybody trying to pretend they were jolly and that the girls pleased them, but unsuccessfully.

And the next day:

Never miss opportunities of enjoying yourself, and never seek them. I promise myself for ever – never to enter a cabaret or a b . . . Spent a pleasant evening at my Aunts' and then called in at Dusseau's and found myself at supper with S. and others and a girl. My foot shall never, never, step inside a public place except a concert or a theatre.

Among his literary acquaintances at this time one for whom (despite a remark previously quoted) Tolstoy seems generally to have felt much respect, was Druzhínin, a critic, writer of stories, and translator of Shakespeare. Druzhínin led a revolt against the *Contemporary* and attracted some of the contributors to the *Reading Library*, a rival magazine, to which in December 1856 Tolstoy contributed his story, *Meeting a Moscow Acquaintance in the Detachment, from Prince Nekhlúdov's Caucasian Memoirs*.* This long title resulted from the intervention of the Censor, who would not allow it to be called *Razhálovanny* [*The Man Reduced to the Ranks*] as Tolstoy intended.

It was not till the middle of May that he left Petersburg, and on his road home he stopped in Moscow and visited the family of Dr Behrs, a Russian of German origin who had married Miss Islávin, a friend of

* Included with *The Cossacks*

Tolstoy's childhood. The first mention one gets of his future wife is a note in the Diary relating to this visit to Dr Behrs's country house near Moscow. 'The children waited on us. What dear, merry, little girls!' Little more than six years later the second of these 'merry little girls' became Countess Tolstoy!

Three days later he writes to his brother Sergéy:

I spent ten days in Moscow . . . very pleasantly, without champagne or gypsies, but a little in love – I will tell you later on with whom.

The object of his affection at that time was not Dr Behrs's twelve-year-old daughter, but the Princess A. Obolénski, the sister of his old college friend Dyákov. An entry in the Diary on 22nd May says:

Dined at Dyákov's. Did not recognise A. Obolénski she has so changed. I did not expect to meet her and so the feeling she aroused in me was terribly acute. From there went to Aksákov's and heard the Fourth Part read. It is good, but the old man got overpraised. Returned to Dyákov's, danced a little, and left there with Alexander Sukhotín, passionately in love. Yes, it hurts me even now to think of the happiness that might have been mine and which has fallen to the share of that excellent fellow A. Obolénski.

24th May: Heard that the Obolénskis would be at the Sukhotíns'. Went there. S. was strumming Chopin and A. [Mme Obolénski] as usual came and went, and we did not talk much. Once or twice while I spoke she was all attention. No, I am not being carried away when I say that she is the sweetest woman I know. The most refined, artistic, and at the same time moral, nature.

And on 25th May:

I was late for dinner at the Dyákovs'. A.'s daughter is ill. She told Sergéy Sukotín in my presence that when she was betrothed there were no lovers. Her husband was not present. Can she have meant to tell me that she was not in love with him? Afterwards when saying goodbye she *suddenly* gave me her hand and there were tears in her eyes because she had been crying about her daughter's illness, but I felt awfully happy. After that she unexpectedly saw me to the door. Certainly since Sónechka's days [Sónya Kalóshina, a friend of his early years, described in *Youth* as Sónichka Valákhina] I have not experienced such a pure, strong, and good, feeling.

I say 'good' because though it is hopeless it gives me joy to arouse it. I want terribly to work at *Youth*; I think because in it that feeling is relived.

26th May: I went and talked with A. for three hours, sometimes tête-à-tête and sometimes with her husband. I am convinced that she knows my feelings and that she is pleased. I was awfully happy . . .

And when leaving, next day, for Yásnaya Polyána, he notes:

Obolénski came, and I might have spent another evening with A. Who knows whether it would not have been for the worse?

From Yásnaya he made a round of visits to see his married sister and other neighbours, among them Turgánev at whose house a gathering of the Tolstoys took place. Special honour was paid to Leo, who comically posed as the hero of a Triumph. He was being crowned and almost covered with flowers, leaves, grass, and anything that came handy, when the approach of an unwelcome guest – a lady neighbour of Turgénev's – was announced. Thereupon the host seized his head in despair; the triumpher, with a howl, began to turn rapid catherine-wheel somersaults through the rooms; and his brother-in-law was quickly bandaged up as an invalid, to serve as an excuse and protection from the unwelcome intruder.

The letter to Sergéy, already referred to, contains an allusion to Tolstoy's first serious matrimonial project, which is recounted here.

At one time – probably after his return from the Crimea and certainly before his marriage – Tolstoy had an affair with a peasant-woman which resulted in the birth of an illegitimate son. In later years this son, Timothy, served as coachman to one of Tolstoy's younger sons. The mother, Aksénya, figures in Tolstoy's posthumous novel *The Devil* as Stepanída. V. I. Alexéev (who lived in Tolstoy's family as a tutor and became his friend) in his reminiscences, which may be published some-day, mentions that *The Devil* was suggested by an incident in 1880 with a cook named Dómna. That, no doubt, is correct, but Dómna was only a passing incident; Tolstoy never yielded to her and it is plain that his recollection of Aksénya counted for most in the story.

This affair probably immediately preceded his nearly becoming engaged to a young lady whose guardian he was and who lived on an estate not very far from Yásnaya. It was at one time even reported among friends and relations that Tolstoy was engaged to her.

Side lights are shed on the affair by his stories *Family Happiness** and *The Devil*.

Tolstoy, as we have seen, had long looked forward to getting married, and found bachelorhood hard to endure, being much dissatisfied with his own conduct in sex matters. In Chapter V of *The Devil* he says of his hero:

> It is impossible to explain why Eugene chose Liza Ánnenskaya, as it is never possible to explain why a man chooses this, and not that, woman. There were many reasons – positive and negative. One was that she was not a very rich heiress, . . . another that she was naïve and to be pitied in her relations with her mother; then there was the fact that she was not a beauty who attracted general attention to herself, but yet was not bad looking. The chief reason was that his acquaintance with her began at a time when Eugene was ripe for marriage. He fell in love because he knew that he would marry.

An English edition of Tolstoy's letters to Valérya was published a few years ago under the title of *Tolstoi's Love Letters*. Fate seems to decree that books relating to Tolstoy which misspell his name always contain other more serious blunders, and in this case we were given 'Tolstoy's Letters to his Fiancée', though the letters themselves and the Diary both clearly show that there was, in fact, no engagement.

On 15th June 1856 he notes in his Diary:

> Gadded about with Dyákov. He gave me much practical advice . . . and above all advised me to marry Valérya. After listening to him it seems to me, too, the best thing I can do. Can it be that money restrains me? No, it's chance. Then he gave me a lift to the turning towards Sudakóvo [Valérya's home]. Valérya put on a stern appearance probably because of my letter. I was in a good mood and calmed them. Poor thing! Her aunt seems horrid. Of course the best person she knows is Vergani [a French lady-companion], but how bad that is! It is a pity she has no backbone or fire – like vermicelli.

> 18th June: Dyákov came and I persuaded him to go to the Arsénevs' with me. Valérya chattered about clothes and the coronation. She is rather frivolous. It seems to be not a passing but an enduring passion. My arrival with Dyákov was awkward, seeming to promise something.

* *Family Happiness* is in the volume entitled *The Kreutzer Sonata and Other Stories*.

26th June: . . . Drove to the Arsénevs' . . . Valérya was in a white dress. Very charming. Spent one of the pleasantest days of my life. Do I love her seriously? And can she love for long? These are two questions I should like to solve, but cannot.

28th June: Toothache worse. After dinner went to the Arsenevs'. Valérya is extremely badly educated, and ignorant if not stupid. The word *prostituer* which she uttered, Heaven knows why, grieved me greatly and, added to my toothache, disillusioned me.

30th June: . . . The Arsénevs arrived. Valérya is a splendid girl but she certainly does not please me. However if we meet so often I may suddenly marry her. That would not be a misfortune, but it is unnecessary and I do not desire it.

1st July: . . . Spent the whole day with Valérya. She had a white dress on and bare arms, and hers are not shapely. This upset me.

5th July: Woke early, bathed. A girl came there, but I was in a good frame of mind and sent her away. Played with the children, dined, had music. Turgénev arrived. He is decidedly an inconsistent, cold, and difficult person, and I pity him. I shall never get on with him. Walked about in a vague state of sensual desire till two o'clock.

12th July: Got up late with a sore throat. Did nothing. The family from Sudakóvo [the Arsénevs' estate] arrived. Valérya was nicer than ever, but her frivolity and absence of care for anything serious is terrifying. Am afraid hers is a nature that cannot even love a child. However I spent the day very pleasantly.

13th July: . . . They teased Valérya to tears about the coronation. She was not at all to blame, but I felt uncomfortable and won't go there again for a long time. Or perhaps it was that she showed me too much friendship. I am afraid of marriage as well as of baseness, i.e. of amusing myself with her. But to marry, much would have to be changed and I have still much work to do on myself. Returned late.

'Much would have to be changed' suggests a passage in Chapter VI of *The Devil* where Mary Pávlovna (the hero's mother, who is to him what Auntie Tatiána was to Tolstoy) says:

'I wanted to tell you, Jénya – of course I do not know, but in general I wanted to suggest to you that before your wedding it is absolutely necessary to have finished with all your bachelor affairs, so that nothing may disturb either you or your wife. God forbid that it should. You understand me? . . . '

'Mamma,' said Eugene suddenly, 'I know why you are saying this. You have no need to be disturbed. My future family-life is so sacred to me that I should not infringe it in any case. And as to what occurred in my bachelor days, that is quite ended. I never formed any union, and no one has any claims on me.'

28th July: . . . Went to the Arsénevs who had invited me. It is strange that I am beginning to like Valérya as a woman, when it was just as a woman that formerly she was distasteful to me. But this not always, only when I attune myself to it. Yesterday for the first time I looked at her arms, which used to disgust me.

In *The Devil* Tolstoy pictures what might have happened had he married Valérya and then again fallen under Aksénya's spell; and his acute observation of physical characteristics and retentive memory are evident. For instance, before the hero in the story married we are told that his intended was 'tall, slender, and long. Everything about her was long; her face, and her nose – not prominently but downwards – and her fingers, and her feet.' After their marriage, when he again noticed Stepanída's strong and active body, legs, arms, and shoulders, Liza, his wife, 'met him with shining face. But today somehow she seemed particularly pale, yellow, long, and weak', and later on when Stepanída – 'broad, energetic, ruddy, and merry' – was dancing with other peasant women, Liza accompanied the old ladies up to the ring, 'in a light blue dress, with light ribbons on her head, and with wide sleeves under which her long white arms and angular elbows were visible'.

12th August: Went to the Arsénevs' at ten to take leave. She was unusually simple and nice. I should like to know, am I in love or not? . . .

He had gone to 'take leave' as the Arsénevs were going to Moscow for Alexander II's coronation.

On 23rd August, having read a letter Valérya wrote to his Auntie Tatiána which disgusted him, he wrote to the 'Young Ladies of Suda-kóvo', at Moscow, as follows:

Is it possible that a current-pattern dress *de toute beauté, haute volée* and Court aides-de-camp will always be for you the height of all happiness? Really this is cruel! Why did you write it? You knew how it would rub me the wrong way . . . You must have been horrid in the currants *de toute beauté* and are certainly a million times better in travelling dress.

To love high society rather than a man is dishonourable and also dangerous, for in that sort of society more rubbish is met with than in any other, and you even place yourself at a disadvantage, for you yourself are not high society, and so your relations with it, based on a pretty little face and a currant-pattern dress, cannot be very pleasant or dignified – *dignes*. As for the Court aides-de-camp – there are in all some forty of them and I know positively that there are only two who are not scamps and fools, so there is no pleasure to be got there either. How glad I am that your currant-pattern dress was crushed at the parade, and how stupid it was of that unknown baron to save you. In his place I would gladly have been transformed into the crowd and crushed your currants on the white dress. I say this because you were certainly not in any serious danger. It was only Pickwick (whose story you have not read) who nearly perished at a parade; but that a young lady who goes to a coronation to study music should perish from such an innocent and pleasant amusement as a parade, is a thing I never heard of in my life and so it cannot have happened. Here in the country the weather is wonderful, and today I went hunting from six in the morning to eight at night and enjoyed myself as no *Ober-fourrier de la chambre* [a Court official] or young lady in any sort of damask dress could succeed in doing. So though I should much like to come to Moscow to vex myself looking at you, I will not come, but wishing you all possible showy pleasures with their usual bitter endings, I remain your most humble and most unpleasant servant

COUNT L. TOLSTOY

Avec des sentiments distingués – excuse my having forgotten to employ that charming expression, which has so much sense.

No, joking apart, if you forgive me for this letter you are a kind creature. Please, Mlle Vergani, plead my cause.

After the Arsénevs returned to the country Tolstoy notes in his Diary on 25th September:

Went to see the Arsénevs. Valérya is sweet but, alas, simply stupid – that's where the shoe pinches.

29th September: . . . They led the conversation up to Mortier [a music master in Moscow] and it turns out that she is in love with him.

Strange, it offended me. I felt ashamed for myself and for her, but for the first time experienced something like feeling for her.

1st October: What if I have not yet known love, then, judging by this small beginning which I feel now, I shall experience it with terrible force, and God forbid that it should be for Valérya. She is terribly shallow, without principle, and cold as ice, so is always being carried away . . .

An entry in his Diary on 13th October: 'Am quite at ease about K.' is perhaps an indication that he had completely broken off with Aksénya.

24th October: . . . Went to a ball. Valérya was charming. I am almost in love with her.

28th October: In the morning wrote letters to D. Ars, and went to Valérya's. She had had her hair done up in a terrible fashion and wore a purple mantle *for me*. I felt pained and ashamed and spent a sad day. Conversation did not go. Yet quite involuntarily I was in the position of a sort of *fiancé*. That irritated me.

In his letters to Valérya Tolstoy describes himself as being made up of a 'silly man' who is in love with her and wishes to marry her, and a 'wise man' who knows that they do not yet understand one another and that no good can come of an impulsive engagement.

Writing from Moscow on 2nd November he says:

. . . In you I already love your beauty but I am only beginning to love what is eternal in you and always precious – your heart, your soul. Beauty can be recognised and loved in an hour and unloved again just as quickly, but one has to learn to know the soul. Believe me nothing on earth comes without labour, not even love – the most beautiful and natural of feelings. Forgive a stupid comparison, to love as the silly man does is like playing a sonata without keeping time, without accents, with the pedal constantly down, but with feeling – not giving pleasure either to oneself or to others. But in order to yield oneself to the feeling of music one must first control oneself, labour, work – and believe me there is no pleasure in life to be had casually. Everything is obtained by work and hardship. But the severer the work and hardship the higher the reward. And we have before us an enormous work – to understand one another and maintain our love and respect for one another. Do you really think that if we yielded to the silly man's feeling we should now understand one another? It would seem to us that we did, but afterwards we should perceive a great chasm, and having spent our feeling on silly love-making we should have nothing with which to fill that gulf.

Further he writes:

Please, *walk* every day, whatever the weather may be. That is excellent, as every doctor will tell you. Also wear your stays, and put on your stockings yourself, and generally make improvements of that kind in yourself. Do not despair of becoming perfect. But these are all trifles. The chief thing is – live so that when you go to bed you can say to yourself: today (1) I did good to someone, (2) I myself began to live a little better. Try *please*, *please*, to plan the day's occupations in advance and check them off in the evening, and you will see what a tranquil and great pleasure it is to say each day to oneself: today I have been better than yesterday. Today [in music practice] I managed to do my threes against fours very smoothly, or I understood and appreciated a good work of poetry or of art, or, best of all, I did good to someone and made him love and thank God for me . . .

A turning point in his relations with her is indicated in the Diary on 4th November:

Kóstinka made me feel depressed about Valérya. I think less about her, but feel an inexpressible dejection wherever I am.

On 8th November from Petersburg he wrote her:

DEAR VALÉRYA VLADÍMIROVNA – 'What has been will come not again', says Púshkin. Believe me, nothing is forgotten, or passes away, or recurs. Never again shall I experience that quiet feeling of attachment to you, of respect and of trust, which I felt before you went to the coronation. Then I gladly yielded to my feeling but now I fear it. Just now I wrote you a long letter which I decided not to send but will show you some later day. It was written under the influence of hatred of you. In Moscow a gentleman, who does not know you, told me that you were in love with Mortier, that you went to see him every day and that you correspond with him . . .

I feel sad, dull, and depressed; everything is a failure, everything is unpleasant, but I will not on any account see you till I feel that the silly man's feeling has quite passed and that I fully believe in you, as I used to.

Next day, in a very different mood, he wrote expressing regret at having sent such a letter, and says:

How are you? Do you work? For Heaven's sake write to me. Do not laugh at the word 'work'. To *work* wisely, usefully, in order to do good, is excellent, but even to work at trifles, to shave a stick, to do anything, is the first condition of a natural, good life and therefore of happiness. For instance, I *worked* today, my conscience is at rest, I feel a small but proud self-satisfaction and so feel that I am good. Today I should on no account have written you such an angry letter as I did yesterday. Today I have a kindly feeling towards the whole world, and have for you the feeling I should like always to have. Ah, if you could feel – could reach by suffering as I have done – the conviction that the only possible, the only true, eternal, and highest happiness is obtained by three things: work, self-abnegation, and love. I know this, I carry the conviction in my soul, but I live in accord with it only some two hours in the year; but you with your honest nature would yield yourself up to that conviction as you give yourself up to people, to Mlle Vergani and others. But for two people to be united in that conviction would be the highest bliss . . .

You see, I so wish to love you that I teach you how to make me do so. And really the chief feeling I have for you is not love, but a passionate desire to love you with all my strength . . .

Tolstoy had invented a story in which he called himself Khrapovítski and Valérya, Dembítskaya, and on 12th November, still from Petersburg, he writes to her:

. . . I will write you about the Khrapovítskis' future way of life – should they be destined ever to live on earth.

The way men and women live depends on (1) their inclination, and (2) their means. Consider the one and the other. Khrapovítski is morally an old man, who in youth committed many follies for which he paid by the loss of the happiness of the best years of his life, and he has now found his path and vocation in literature. In his soul he despises *Society*, adores a quiet family moral life, and dreads nothing on earth so much as distracting society life, in which all good honourable and pure thoughts and feelings are lost and one becomes the slave of social conventions and of one's creditors.

He has already paid for such errors with the best years of his life, so that in him this conviction is not a matter of words but a conviction ingrained by suffering. Dear Mlle Dembítskaya has not as yet experienced anything of this; for her, happiness consists in balls, bare shoulders, a carriage, diamonds, acquaintance with chamberlains, adjutants-general, etc. But it so happened that Kh. and Demb. seem to be in love with one another. (Perhaps I am deceiving myself, but at this moment I love you terribly.) So these people with contradictory inclinations seem to be in love with one another. How can they arrange so as to be able to live together? First, they must make concessions to one another. Secondly, the one whose inclinations are less moral must make most concessions. I should be willing to spend my whole life in the country. I should have three occupations: love of D. and care for her happiness, literature, and estate-management as I understand it – that is, fulfilling my duty to the people entrusted to me. One thing is bad about this. I should involuntarily lag behind the times and that is wrong. D. dreams of living in Petersburg, going to thirty balls during the winter, entertaining fine friends and driving on the Névski in her own carriage. The mean between these two demands is to live five months in Petersburg without balls, without a carriage, without wonderful toilettes with *guipure* and *point d'Alençon* lace, and quite without 'society', and to live for seven months in the country. Khrapovítski has an income of 2,000 rubles from his estate (that is, if he does not as everybody does squeeze the last farthing from his unfortunate serfs); he has also about 1,000 rubles a year from his writings (but this not certainly; he may grow stupid or be unhappy, and not write anything). D. has a disputed promissory note for 20,000 rubles, from which, if it is met, she will get about 800 rubles interest: altogether they have at best, 3,800 rubles. Do you know what 3,800 rubles means in Petersburg? To live on that sum for five months in Petersburg one must put up with four rooms on the fifth floor and have not a *chef* but a woman-cook, not dare to think of having a carriage, or a poplin dress with *point d'Alençon* lace, or a light-blue bonnet – for such a bonnet *jurera* [will jar] with the rest of one's get-up. With that income one could live in Túla or Moscow and even now and then show off before the Lazarévichs – but many thanks for that! One might also live in Petersburg on a third floor, have a carriage and *point d'Alençon* lace, and hide from one's creditors and dressmakers and shopkeepers and write to the village to say that all I had arranged about lightening the peasants' burdens was nonsense, and that the utmost is to be squeezed out of them, and then return to the country and sit there in shame for years, angry with one another – but again many thanks for that! I have experienced it. There is another way of living on the fifth floor (poorly but honourably) spending what one can on domestic comfort, on the decoration of the little flat on the fifth floor, on a man-cook and the kitchen, and on wine, so that one's friends may enjoy coming to that fifth floor – and on books, music, pictures, concerts, and quartets at home, but not on any external luxury to astonish Lazarévichs, serfs, and blockheads . . .

On 17th November, still from Petersburg, he writes:

You know my habit of doubting everything, which arises not from my character but from a certain mental development. Be sure that nothing is got for nothing. If I understand more than Gimbút [a neighbour in the country] does, I no longer possess his freshness of feeling. I involuntarily see *pros* and *cons* in everything. I doubt everything in the world, except that goodness is good, and by that alone I can be led as on a string . . . Moral goodness, that is, love of one's fellow man, poetry, beauty – which are all the same – is the one thing I never doubt and always worship, though I scarcely ever practise it. And I may be attracted by you because it seems to me that you are *good*, as I understand the word. But to you this philosophy seems dull . . .

Note in passing that in this letter Tolstoy accepts 'moral goodness, that is, love of one's fellow man, poetry, and beauty' as being identical – a view he rejected later.

The letter goes on:

You make passing mention of having read something with pleasure. What was it you read with pleasure? And what did you make of it? This interests me extremely. It would not be bad for you to go to the . . . ball. It should be of interest to put yourself to the test. Do this . . . and write me your impressions sincerely. I have hardly tested myself at all, that is, I have met no women and have been nowhere, and *la main sur la conscience* I can say that these three weeks no woman has attracted my attention at all. But with your chief rival – literature – I have been much and pleasantly occupied all this time. I have written a short story for the *Library Magazine* and am preparing another for the *Fatherland Notes* . . . I have a nice quiet flat with a piano, and my N. N. pens scrape from morning to night.

On 22nd November he notes:

Got up at eleven. Wished to write but couldn't. Gymnastics. Dined at the Panáevs'. Then stayed at Kraévski's till evening. The literary atmosphere disgusts me as nothing else ever did. Wrote to Valérya. Thought much about her. Perhaps because I have not met any woman all this time.

23rd November: . . . Had a nice letter from Valérya. Answered her: thought about Anna Nikoláevna and at the same time very very much about Valérya . . .

In this letter he said:

In your excellent supplement to the Khrapovítski's plan of life it is not good that you wish to live in the country and to go to Túla. God forbid! . . . The Khrapovítskis will either see nobody or the best society in all Russia, that is, best not in the sense of the Tsar's favour or of wealth, but of intellect and culture. Their rooms will be on the fourth floor, but the most remarkable people in Russia will come there. God forbid that they should on that account be rude to Túla acquaintances and relations, but they should be avoided – they are not wanted, and, as I have said, intercourse with people who are not wanted is always harmful. Alas! you are mistaken in supposing that you have taste; or perhaps you have, but not tact. For instance, a certain style of dress, such as a light-blue bonnet with white flowers is excellent, but it suits a young lady who drives with fast trotters in English harness and ascends a staircase with mirrors and camellias, but with the modest surroundings of the fourth floor flat and a hackney cab, and so forth, such a bonnet is ridiculous – and still more so in the country and with a country conveyance . . .

There is another kind of *élégance*, modest, afraid of anything extra-ordinary or glaring, but very particular about details, such as shoes, collars, gloves, cleanliness of nails, neatness of the hair, &c., about which I stand firm as a rock – so long as it does not take too much attention from serious matters – and which no one who cares for refinement can help liking. A taste for glaring colours is excusable though ridiculous in a plain girl, but for you with your pretty face it is unpardonable to make such a mistake. In your place I should take simplicity as the rule for my toilette, but with strictest refinement in all its details.

27th November: Had a stupid letter from Valérya. She humbugs herself and I see through it and that is trying. If people could but know one another so as not to accept the other's thought direct, but to see how it acts on the other . . .

On 28th November he wrote her:

Yesterday I was at Olga Turgénev's and heard Beethoven's trio there, which is still in my ears. It is enchanting! . . . Since I left you nothing has occurred that I could not tell you of, and I do tell and shall tell everything that can interest you. That is just what I most love in my relations with you – that they help me on the path towards all that is good. What you ask me about priests reminds me of something I have long wished to say to you. Whatever our future relations may be, *let us never talk about religion and all that concerns it.* You know that I am a believer, but very likely my faith differs from yours, and this question should never be touched, especially between those who wish to love one another . . . Religion is a great thing, especially for a woman, and you have it. Keep it, never talk about it, and without exaggerating fulfil its precepts. Occupy yourself more and more, accustom yourself to work. That is the first condition of happiness in life.

This remark about not discussing religious matters is quite unlike Tolstoy's later attitude, but we find a key to it in an entry in his Diary on the preceding 14th August. 'Had a discussion with Auntie about religion. Useless. Must remember this with my future wife.'

On 6th December he wrote to his Auntie Tatiána:

Moscow. December 6th, 1856

. . . Just when I went away and for a week after that, it seemed to me that I was in love, as it is called, but for a man of my imagination that was not difficult. But now, and since then, especially since I set to work industriously, I should like, and should much like, to be able to say that I am in love, or simply love her, but it is not so. The one feeling I have for her is gratitude for her love and also the thought that of all the girls I have known or now know she would have made the best wife for me as I think of family life.

On 12th December he notes: 'Had a pained letter from Valérya and to my shame am glad of it.' The next two days he notes that 'I feel very sad', and, 'Wrote a last letter to Valérya'. It was however not the last, for on 1st January he notes: 'Wrote a short and stiff letter to Valérya.' This was, in fact, a friendly but not loving letter, written from Petersburg. In it he says:

> How can I tell you how I spent the time of my silence? Wearily and for the most part sadly – I don't myself know why. Loneliness I find hard to bear, but contact with people is impossible. I am myself bad, yet am accustomed to be exacting. Besides that I have done nothing all the time and this depresses me. I have heard a great deal of music, and yesterday I even saw the New Year in while listening to Beethoven's trio, the most delightful in the world, and I thought of you and the effect it would have had on you. I will send you the music of it – very good music – as soon as the shop opens tomorrow.

In reply she wrote forbidding him to write to her again; but he wrote again nevertheless, saying that he felt he had been to blame, but had been perfectly sincere with her and would never cease to love her as he did, that is, in friendship; that he was going to Paris and if she would write him a few lines there he would be calm and happy.

On 3rd January, following this break in his relations with Valérya, comes an entry:

> Dined at Bótkin's . . . towards midnight to the masquerade. At first it was dull, then at supper with Stolypin and Stakhóvich a 'sweet mouth' approached me. I solicited it for a long time, it came with me, and at home was very reluctant to unmask. As like A. D. as two peas but older and coarser featured . . .

In Paris on 19th February he notes: 'Received a letter from Valérya' and next day he wrote her a letter saying:

> Your letter, which I received today, dear Valérya Vladímirovna, made me very glad. It showed me that you do not regard me as some kind of villain or monster, but simply as a man with whom you nearly came into more intimate relations, and for whom you still feel friendship and respect . . . I always told you that I did not know what my feeling for you was and that it always seemed to me that something was wrong. At one time, before I left the country, my loneliness, frequent

meetings with you, and above all your lovely appearance and especially your character, made me almost ready to believe that I was in love with you; but something always told me that it was *not the thing*, as I did not conceal from you, and I even went to Petersburg on that account. There I led a solitary life but for all that, the mere fact of not seeing you showed me that I never was or should be in love with you. And to make a mistake in that matter would have been a misfortune both for me and for you. That is the whole story. It is true that such frankness was misplaced. I might have experimented on myself without attracting you; but in this matter I paid the price of inexperience, I repent of it, ask your forgiveness for it, and it torments me, but I cannot be reproached with dishonourable conduct or even with secretiveness.

. . . The French, to my great astonishment, play Beethoven divinely, and you can imagine how I enjoy myself listening to this *musique d'ensemble*, performed by the best artists in the world . . .

Family Happiness, published in 1859, is largely based on Tolstoy's relations with Valérya, he even introduces the device he had practised in his explanations with her, making the hero speak of a man A. and 'a woman we may call B.', and attributing to them the thoughts and feelings of the two who discuss them. But in the story the hero and heroine marry and suffer from their differing outlooks on life – though eventually they settle down to a life of calm content, emancipated from the passionate love they had felt.

To conclude the story of his relations with Valérya, I will here anticipate by quoting a letter he wrote later, on 17th April 1857, from Paris to his Aunt Tatiána:

I never loved her with real love, but was carried away by the reprehensible pleasure of inspiring love in her, which gave me a delight I had never before experienced. But the time spent away from her proved to me that I did not feel any wish to see her, still less to marry her. The very thought of the obligations I should have to perform towards her without loving her terrified me; so I decided to come away sooner than I had intended. I have behaved badly. I have asked God to forgive me, and I ask the same of all whom I have grieved, but to mend the matter is impossible, and nothing in the world can renew it now.

Tolstoy was ill at Yásnaya, and early in September wrote to his brother Sergéy:

> Only now, at nine o'clock on Monday evening, can I give you a satisfactory reply, for till now things went worse and worse. Two doctors were called in and administered another forty leeches, but only now have I had a good sleep and on waking feel considerably better. All the same there can be no question of my leaving the house for five or six days yet. So *au revoir*; please let me know when you go shooting, and whether it is true that your farming has been seriously neglected; and do not kill all the game without me. I will send the dogs, perhaps, tomorrow.

In Petersburg Tolstoy had other difficulties, and on 10th November writes to his brother Sergéy:

> Forgive me, dear friend Serëzha, for only writing two words – I have no time for more. I have been most unlucky since I left home; there is no one here I like. It seems that I have been abused in the *Fatherland Notes* for my war stories – I have not yet read the attack – but the worst is that Konstantínov [the General who commanded the battery to which Tolstoy had been attached] informed me as soon as I got here that the Grand Duke Michael, having learnt that I am supposed to have composed the Soldiers' Song, is displeased, particularly at my having (as rumour says) taught it to the soldiers. This is abominable. I have had an explanation with the Head of the Staff. The only satisfactory thing is that my health is good, and [Dr] Schipulínski says my lungs are thoroughly sound.

On 20th November 1856 he left the army. He had become Sub-Lieutenant after the Danube campaign and Lieutenant after the battle of Chérnaya, but despite the fact that he had private influence enough to enable him, about this time, to save from trial by court-martial the commander of the battery in which he had served, he had himself made very slow progress throughout his military service.

We have two letters of this period from Turgénev. The first is dated Paris, 16th November 1856, and is as follows:

> DEAREST TOLSTOY – Your letter of 15th October took a whole month crawling to me – I received it only yesterday. I have thought carefully about what you write me – and I think you are wrong. It is

true I cannot be quite sincere because I can't be quite frank with you. I think we got to know each other awkwardly and at a bad time, and when we meet again it will be much easier and smoother. I feel that I love you as a man (as an author it needs no saying); but much in you is trying to me and I ultimately found it better to keep at a distance. When we meet we will again try to go hand in hand – perhaps we shall succeed better; for strange as it may sound, my heart turns to you when at a distance as to a brother, I even feel tenderly towards you. In a word, I love you – that is certain; perchance from that in time all good will follow. I heard of your illness and grieved, but now I beg of you drive the thought of it out of your head. For you, too, have your fancies and are perhaps thinking of consumption – but, God knows, you have nothing of the sort . . .

You have finished the first part of *Youth* – that is capital. How sorry I am to be unable to hear it read! If you do not go astray (which I think there is no reason to anticipate) you will go very far. I wish you good health, activity – and freedom, spiritual freedom.

As to my *Faust*, I do not think it will please you very much. My things could please you and perhaps have some influence on you, only until you became independent. Now you have no need to study me; you see only the difference of our manners, the mistakes and the omissions; what you have to do is to study man, your own heart, and the really great writers. I am a writer of a transition period – and am of use only to men in a transition state. So farewell, and be well. Write to me.

On 8th December 1856 he writes again:

DEAR TOLSTOY – Yesterday my good genius led me past the post-office, and it occurred to me to ask if there were any letters for me at the *poste-restante* (though I think my friends ought all long ago to have learnt my Paris address) and I found your letter in which you speak of my *Faust*. You can well imagine how glad I was to read it. Your sympathy gladdened me truly and deeply. Yes, and from the whole letter there breathes a mild, clear, and friendly peacefulness. It remains for me to hold out my hand across the 'ravine', which has long since become a hardly perceptible crack of which we will speak no more – it is not worth it.

I fear to speak of one thing you mention: it is a delicate matter – words may blight such things before they are ripe, but when they are ripe a hammer will not break them. God grant that all may turn out favourably and well. It may bring you the spiritual repose you lacked when I knew you.

You have, I see, now become very intimate with Druzhínin – and are under his influence. That is right, only take care not to swallow too much of him. When I was your age only men of enthusiastic natures influenced me; but you are built differently and perhaps also the times are changed . . . Let me know in which numbers of the *Contemporary* your *Youth* will appear, and by the way, let me know the final impression made on you by *Lear*, which probably you have read if only for Druzhínin's sake.

About the same time Turgénev wrote to Druzhínin:

I hear that you have become very intimate with Tolstoy – and he has become very pleasant and serene. I am very glad. When that new wine has finished fermenting it will yield a drink fit for the Gods. What about his *Youth*, which was sent for your verdict?

Before quoting Druzhínin's criticism of *Youth*, it will be in place to mention the other works of Tolstoy which appeared at this period. *Reminiscences of a Billiard Marker*, giving a glimpse of temptations Tolstoy to some extent had himself experienced, was published in January 1855, while he was in Sevastopol. In January 1866 came *Sevastopol in August*. In March 1856 *The Snow Storm*. In May 1856 a rollicking tale with flashes of humour resembling Charles Lever's, entitled *Two Hussars*. It is the only story Tolstoy wrote in that particular vein, and we have in it a glimpse of such Gypsy singers as he repeatedly mentioned in his correspondence and in his books. In November he notes in his Diary:

How I long to have done with magazines, in order to write in the way I am now beginning to think about – terribly high and pure.

In December before he went abroad, two more tales were published: *Meeting a Moscow Acquaintance in the Detachment*, which has already been mentioned, and *A Landlord's Morning*, drawn from his experience when trying to better his serfs' condition. Their stolidity, their distrust, and the immense difficulty of introducing the changes he desired, are all brought out.

In a letter to Druzhínin, Turgénev wrote:

I have read his *Landlord's Morning*, which pleased me exceedingly by its sincerity and almost complete freedom of outlook. I say 'almost' because in the way he has set himself the task there still is hidden (without his perhaps being aware of it) a certain amount of prejudice. The chief moral impression produced by the story (leaving the artistic impression aside) is that so long as serfdom exists there is no possibility of the two sides drawing together despite the most disinterested and honourable desire to do so; and this impression is good and true. But beside it, like a horse cantering beside a trotter, there is another: namely, that in general to try to enlighten or improve the condition of the peasants leads to nothing, and this impression is unpleasant. But the mastery of language, the way it is told, and his character-drawing, are grand.

In January 1857 the first part of *Youth* appeared – a continuation of *Childhood* and *Boyhood*.

Druzhínin's influence with Tolstoy at this time may be judged by the tone of the letter in which he gave him his opinion on *Youth*. He writes:

About *Youth* one ought to write twenty pages. I read it with anger, with yells, and with oaths – not on account of its literary quality but because of the quality of the notebooks in which it is written, and the handwritings. The mixing of two hands, a known and an unknown, diverted my attention and hindered an intelligent perusal. It was as though two voices shouted in my ear and purposely distracted my attention, and I know this has prevented my receiving an adequate impression. All the same I will say what I can. Your task was a terrible one, and you have executed it very well. No other writer of our day could have so seized and sketched the agitated and turbulent period of youth. To those who are developed, your *Youth* will furnish an immense pleasure, and if anyone tells you it is inferior to *Childhood* and *Boyhood* you may spit in his face. There is a world of poetry in it – all the first chapters are admirable, only the introduction is dry till one reaches the description of spring . . . In many chapters one scents the poetic charm of old Moscow which no one has yet reproduced properly. Some chapters are dry and long: for instance all the stipulations with Dmítri Nekhlúdov . . . The conscription of Seménov will not pass the Censor.

Do not fear your reflections, they are all clever and original. But you have an inclination to super-refinement of analysis which may become a great defect. You are sometimes on the point of saying that so-and-so's thigh indicated that he wished to travel in India. You must restrain this tendency, but do not extinguish it on any account. All your work on your analyses should be of the same kind. Each of your defects has its share of strength and beauty, and almost every one of your qualities bears with it the seed of a defect.

Your style quite accords with that conclusion: you are most ungrammatical, sometimes with the lack of grammar of a reformer and powerful poet reshaping a language his own way and for ever, but sometimes with the lack of grammar of an officer sitting in a casemate and writing to his chum. One can say with assurance that all the pages you have written with love are admirable – but as soon as you grow cold your words get entangled and diabolical forms of speech appear. Therefore the parts written coldly should be revised and corrected. I tried to straighten out some bits but gave it up; it is work which only you can and must do. Above all avoid long sentences. Cut them up into two or three; do not be sparing of full-stops . . . Do not stand on ceremony with the particles, and strike out by dozens the words: *which*, *who*, and *that*. When in difficulties, take a sentence and imagine that you want to say it to someone in a most conversational way.

As a translator I can testify that Tolstoy never fully learned the lesson Druzhínin here set him. To the very last he occasionally intermingled passages of extraordinary simplicity and force, with sentences that defy analysis and abound in redundances.

Nearly fifty years later Tolstoy himself criticised the subject-matter of *Childhood*, *Boyhood* and *Youth* as follows:

I have reread them and regret that I wrote them, so ill, artificially, and insincerely, are they penned. It could not be otherwise: first, because what I aimed at was not to write my own history but that of the friends of my youth, and this produced an awkward mixture of the facts of their and my own childhood; and secondly, because at the time I wrote it I was far from being independent in my way of expressing myself, being strongly influenced by two writers: Sterne (his *Sentimental Journey*) and Töpffer (his *Bibliothèque de Mon Oncle*).

I am now specially dissatisfied with the two last parts, *Boyhood* and *Youth*, in which besides an awkward mixture of truth and invention, there is also insincerity: a desire to put forward as good and important what I did not then consider good and important, namely, my democratic tendency.

Before concluding this chapter it will be in place to give a list of works Tolstoy mentions as having influenced him after he left the University and before his marriage. They were: Goethe's *Hermann und Dorothea*; Hugo's *Notre-Dame de Paris*; Plato's *Phaedo* and the *Symposium* (in Cousin's French translation); and the *Iliad* and *Odyssey* in Russian versions. All these, he says, had a 'very great' influence on him, while the poems of his compatriots, Tyúchev, Kóltsov, and his friend Fet had 'great' influence.

As previously mentioned even in early childhood he had appreciated some of Púshkin's poems and learned them by heart and recited them with feeling; but, curiously enough, it was the perusal of Mérimée's French prose translation of Púshkin's *Gypsies* that, after he was grown up, aroused Tolstoy's keen admiration of Púshkin's mastery of clear, simple, direct language. Later in life Tolstoy used to say that Púshkin's prose stories, such as *The Captain's Daughter*, are his best works, but he never lost his appreciation of Púshkin's poetic gift.

On 3rd June 1856 he notes in his Diary:

Read Púshkin's *Don Juan*. Enchanting. Truth and power I never expected.

4th June: Got up at five, went for a walk with, I confess, very erotic feelings. Read Púshkin's first poems . . .

7th June: Read the second and third parts of Púshkin. *The Gypsies* are as delightful as when I first read them, and the rest of the poems, except Onégin, are dreadful rubbish.

4th January 1857: Got up after one. The article [by Belínski] on Púshkin is wonderful. Only now have I understood Púshkin. I am decidedly happy all these days. I am intoxicated by the rapidity of the moral movement – forward and forward.

The 'moral movement' referred to is evidently not his own personal progress, for in the preceding entry he had recorded his conduct, of which he certainly did not approve, at a masquerade. He is speaking of the emancipation movement and other reforms then in progress.

Of non-Russian writers, he mentions Dickens with special approval. He read *Little Dorrit* and *Pickwick*. 'Finished reading *The Pickwick Papers*. Very good!' In his notebook he wrote:

1   The first condition of an author's popularity, the prime means to make people like him, is the love with which he treats his characters. That is why Dickens's characters are the friends of all mankind: they are a bond of union between man in America and man in Peterṣburg.
2   It is well when an author stands only just outside his subject, so that one continueally doubts whether the treatment is subjective or objective.

He also read Molière, whom he esteemed very highly, and says: 'Heard the splendid comedy *Les Femmes Savantes* read.'

Of Thackeray at this time he read *The Newcomes*, but does not comment either on it or on him.

Of Prosper Mérimée he says: 'Finished reading *Carmen*. Weak, French!' Of Auerbach, whom he was to meet later in Germany, he says: 'From two to eight in the morning read Auerbach's delightful *Befehle.*'

A literary event of this year was the appearance of Druzhínin's translation of *King Lear*. Tolstoy thought the translation good, but disliked the play and Shakespeare generally. He notes: 'Read *Henry IV*, and was furious with the *Contemporary*' (which had no doubt praised it). 'Read *Lear*; it moved me but little.' And a week later: 'Dined at Bótkin's . . . Then to Ólga Turgénev. "*Lear* is delightful!" No, with Ólga I am always uncomfortable!' His reasons for dissenting from the general appraisement of Shakespeare were explained much later in his essay on *Shakespeare and the Drama* (included in *Tolstoy on Art*). He did not shrink from stating this opinion to his literary associates, and by so doing gave an early indication of a trait characteristic of him to the end of his life, namely, his distrust of prevalent opinions and readiness to defy authority and rely on his own judgement, which is alluded to in Nekrásov's mention of Tolstoy as 'a strong and truthful personality with no secretiveness or timidity'.

Of Goethe Tolstoy notes: 'Read *Werther*. Enchanting.' But in general he did not much care for Goethe.

Among Russian writers he read were Goncharóv and Ostróvski, Russia's most popular dramatist, of whom Tolstoy many years later said to Gúsev:

Ostróvski pleased me by his simple, Russian, way of life, his seriousness, and his great talent. He was an original, self-reliant man who, even in literary circles, curried favour with no one.

With the Slavophil group of writers Tolstoy felt no great sympathy. On 5th May he notes:

> Spent the evening at Obolénski's with Aksákov, Kiréevski, and other Slavophils. It is evident that they are looking for an enemy who does not exist. Their outlook is too narrow and too far from reaching the quick to meet any resistance. There is no need of it.
>
> 21st May: Dined at Aksákov's. Made Komyakóv's acquaintance. An acute man. Disputed with Constantine Aksákov about village readings, which he considers impossible. In the evening at the Gorchakóvs disputed with Sergéy Dmítrievich [Gorchakóv] about exactly the opposite: Sergéy Dmítrievich was sure that the peasantry are the most depraved class. Of course, from a Western I became a hard-crusted Slavophil.

Tolstoy tells us that artistic talent in literature influenced him more than any political or social tendency, and this was in accord both with his highly artistic nature and his general apathy towards public affairs. There was a Slavophil theory (built to justify things as they were) which proclaimed it natural for a Slav people to leave the task of governing to its rulers, while retaining its intellectual freedom to disapprove of what was done amiss; and though Tolstoy never joined the Slavophils, this was very much his own attitude on the matter, and was clearly expressed twenty years later in *Anna Karénina*.*

Dostoévski was at this time still in exile in Siberia, and so Tolstoy did not meet him.

With Chernyshévski his relations were not cordial, and *The Kreutzer Sonata*, written much later, is in fact a counterblast to Chernyshévski's novel *What to Do?*

On 31st May 1856, while visiting his sister at her estate, a day's drive from Yásnaya Polyána, he notes:

> At five in the morning rode to Turgénev's. Arrived at seven. He was not at home. His house showed me the roots from which he comes, and this explained much to me and reconciled me to him. He returned. I lunched, walked, had a very pleasant talk with him, and went to sleep . . . Should like to write the story of a horse.

This was no doubt the occasion on which while walking with

* *Anna Karénina*, Vol. II, pp. 423–30

Turgénev they saw an old horse grazing in a meadow. Tolstoy began describing what the horse's feelings must be, and did it so convincingly that Turgénev remarked: 'I am sure, Lëo Nikoláevich, that you must have once been a horse yourself.'

On 12th March, after less than four months' acquaintance, Tolstoy noted in his Diary: 'I think I have parted with Turgénev for good,' but on 10th May he writes to his Auntie Tatiána: 'Turgénev has left, whom I now feel that I have grown very fond of, though we were always quarrelling.'

His conflicts with a number of the leading writers did not prevent his taking active interest in a 'Literary Fund' Druzhínin was founding to render assistance to necessitous authors and scientists. Tolstoy drafted a constitution for the Society, and helped it otherwise.

We find him eagerly skating, riding, dancing, playing chess, and especially ardent at gymnastic classes. There had been a time when it was his ambition to become the strongest man in the world, and his strength and skill at all kinds of physical exercises was remarkable, and remained so to old age.

A pleasure and occupation of which he makes frequent mention was music, and he devoted much time to the piano. Here are a few notes on the subject from his Diary:

21st December: Got up at half-past seven, busy with proof corrections and music till two.

23rd December: Went to Kovalévski at the University. A wonderful symphony of Haydn's.

24th December: . . . Was going to Zhemchúznikov's, but Stolypin invited me to some music, and Bótkin and I enjoyed ourselves.

In January 1857 he met Kiesewetter, a talented violinist and a composer, who had taken to drink. Tolstoy took him to Yásnaya Polyána, and later on studied music ardently with him and tried to set him on his feet, but Kiesewetter, who could not endure a regular life, disappeared from Yásnaya and perished.

The incident inspired the story *Albert*, which was published in August 1858.

Despite his headstrong outbursts and many vacillations Tolstoy seems to have been a welcome guest in almost any society he cared to frequent, and none of his critics has spoken as harshly of him as he speaks of himself when describing these years in the *Recollections* he wrote when he was an old man, and referred to his

> terrible twenty years of coarse dissipation, the service of ambition, vanity, and above all of lust . . . It is true that not all my life was so terribly bad as this twenty-year period from fourteen to thirty-four; and it is true that even that period of my life was not the continuous evil that during a recent illness it appeared to me to be. Even during those years strivings towards goodness awoke in me though they did not last long and were soon choked by passions nothing could restrain.

In his *Confession*, written about 1880, when speaking of his religious beliefs, Tolstoy tells us:

> With all my soul I wished to be good, but I was young, passionate, and alone, completely alone when I sought goodness. Every time I tried to express my most sincere desire, namely, to be morally good, I met with contempt and ridicule; but as soon as I yielded to nasty passions I was praised and encouraged.
>
> Ambition, love of power, covetousness, lasciviousness, pride, anger and revenge – were all respected . . . I cannot think of those years without horror, loathing and heartache. I killed men in war, and challenged men to duels in order to kill them; I lost at cards, consumed the labour of the peasants, sentenced them to punishments, lived loosely, and deceived people. Lying, robbery, adultery of all kinds, drunkenness, violence, murder – there was no crime I did not commit, and people approved of my conduct and my contemporaries considered and consider me to be a comparatively moral man.
>
> So I lived for ten years.
>
> During that time I began to write from vanity, covetousness, and pride. In my writings I did the same as in my life. To get fame and money, for the sake of which I wrote, it was necessary to hide the good and show the evil. And I did so. How often in my writings did I contrive to hide under the guise of indifference or even of banter those strivings of mine towards goodness which gave meaning to my life. And I succeeded in this and was praised.
>
> At twenty-six years of age [Tolstoy makes a slip here: he was over twenty-seven] I returned to Petersburg after the war, and met the writers. They received me as one of themselves and flattered me. And

before I had time to look round I had adopted the class views on life of the authors I had come among, and these views completely obliterated all my former strivings to improve. Those views furnished a theory which justified the dissoluteness of my life. The view of life of these people, my comrades in authorship, consisted in this: that life in general goes on developing and in this development we – men of thought – have the chief part; and among men of thought it is we – artists and poets – who have the chief influence. Our vocation is to teach mankind. And lest the simple question should suggest itself: What do I know and what can I teach? it is explained in this theory that this need not be known and that the artist and poet teach unconsciously. I was considered an admirable artist and poet, and therefore it was very natural for me to adopt this theory. I, artist and poet, wrote and taught without myself knowing what. For this I was paid money; I had excellent food, lodging, women, and society; and I had fame, which showed that what I taught was very good.

6

Travels Abroad

After the Danube campaign of 1854 Tolstoy only left 1857 Russia twice. The first time was on 10th February 1857 (new style) when he left Moscow by post-chaise for Warsaw (from whence a railway already ran), and reached Paris on 21st February. There he met Turgénev and Nekrásov, with the former of whom he was still unable to get on smoothly. Turgénev wrote: 'With Tolstoy I still cannot become quite intimate; we see things too differently.' Tolstoy in a moment of anger even challenged his fellow-writer to a duel, but Nekrásov succeeded in patching the matter up. For the first five weeks in Paris Tolstoy enjoyed himself greatly, was very active, and led a social life. He attended lectures by Laboulaye and other celebrities, visited Fontainebleau and various places of interest, made acquaintance with some leading singers and actresses, took lessons in English and Italian, and played chess at a café. He was much attracted by a Princess Trubetskóy and still more so by a Princess Lvóv, but any thoughts of marriage he may have had did not prevent his going to cafés chantants, to the Bal de l' Opéra, to 'would-be-gay suppers', and otherwise misbehaving himself.

In March he accompanied Turgénev to Dijon and spent a few days there. During this trip Tolstoy began his story *Albert*, founded on his acquaintance with the violinist Kiesewetter, who was mentioned in the last chapter.

On 5th April he wrote to his friend V. P. Bótkin:

I have now been living in Paris nearly two months and do not foresee the time when the town will have ceased to interest me or this way of life will have lost its charm. I am crassly ignorant, nowhere have I felt so aware of it as here. If only for that reason there is every cause for me to rejoice at being here, the more so since in this town I also feel that my ignorance is not irremediable. Moreover the fine arts give me such delight: the Louvre, Versailles, the Conservatoire, the concerts, the theatres, the lectures at the Collége de France and at the Sorbonne, above all this social liberty of which we have no idea in Russia – and the result of all this is that I shall hardly leave Paris, or the suburban village I expect to move to shortly, for another two months.

The very next day he saw a man guillotined and made the following entry in his Diary:

I got up at seven o'clock and went to see an execution. A stout, robust, white neck and breast: He kissed the Gospels and then – death. How senseless! I am not a man of politics. Morals and art I know, love, and can deal with . . . The guillotine long prevented my sleeping and obliged me to reflect.

Tolstoy had always a gift of stating essential truths in few words, and never did he sum himself up better than in the sentences, 'I am not a man of politics. Morals and art I know, love, and can deal with.' There is not much room for doubt about the second sentence, and certainly none about the first, as his whole life shows.

Many years later he wrote of this event in his *Confession*:

When I saw the head part from the body and how they thumped separately into the box, I understood, not with my mind but with my whole being, that no theory of the reasonableness of our present progress could justify this deed, and that though everybody from the creation of the world, on whatever theory, had held it to be necessary, I knew it to be unnecessary and bad; and therefore the arbiter of what is good and evil is not what people say and do, nor is it progress, but is my heart and I.

The occurrence disgusted Tolstoy with Paris. The following day he notes:

Got up late and unwell. Read, and suddenly a simple and sensible idea occurred to me – to leave Paris.

That same day he wrote to Bótkin telling him of the execution and adding:

A lot of arrests were made here the other day, a conspiracy has been discovered, they wanted to kill Napoleon at the theatre; more people will be killed in a few days' time, but certainly from today I will not merely never go to see it done, but I will never anywhere serve any government.

By the 9th of April he was in Geneva and hastened to call on his 'Aunts' Lisa and Alexándra Tolstoy, of whom mention has already been made. Their grandfather had twenty-three children by one wife. His eldest son was Count Ilyá Tolstoy, Tolstoy's paternal grandfather, and his youngest son, Andrey, was the father of Lisa and Alexándra. Tolstoy was therefore actually their first cousin once removed. In Russian they would be called his 'aunts'. He however called each of them 'Grandma', saying they were too young to be his aunts – a *paradoxe à la L. Tolstoy*, as Alexándra remarked. She was eleven years his senior, and a very close friendship – an *amitié amoureuse* in his own phrase – united them for many years. It was the best, purest, closest, and most charming friendship he had with anyone outside his own immediate family circle.

She and her elder sister, Lisa, were Maids of Honour to the Grand Duchess Marie of Lichtenberg, daughter of Nicholas I. Countess Lisa Tolstoy was in charge of the education of the Grand Duchess's daughter, who eventually became Princess of Oldenburg. Subsequently, from 1866 onward, Alexándra had charge of the education of the Grand Duchess Marie Alexándrovna, the only daughter of Alexándra II. In 1876 her pupil married Alfred, Duke of Edinburgh, who afterwards became Duke of Saxe-Coburg.

In the Introduction to her published correspondence with Tolstoy, Alexándra says:

I see him quite clearly at the time of his return from Sevastopol in 1855 as a young artillery officer, and remember what a pleasant impression he made on us all . . . He was himself simple, extremely modest, and so playful that his presence enlivened us all. He very seldom spoke of himself, but observed each new acquaintance intently and with concentration, and afterwards told us his impressions, which were nearly always rather extreme. The nickname 'thin skin', bestowed on him later by his wife, exactly suited him, so strongly, favourably or unfavourably, did the slightest shade he observed act upon him. He guessed people's nature by artistic instinct and his impression often proved amazingly correct. He was not good-looking, but the appearance of his clever, kindly, and expressive eyes made up for what he lacked in elegance and, one may say, was better than beauty . . .

She mentions Tolstoy's sudden arrival in Geneva, where she and her sister were in attendance on the Grand Duchess, and says:

Not being in correspondence with him at that time, we had no idea where he was and supposed him to be in Russia.

'I have come to you straight from Paris,' he announced. 'I became so disgusted with Paris that I almost went off my head. What have I not seen there . . . First at the *maison garnie* where I stayed, there were thirty-six *ménages*, nineteen of which were irregular. That revolted me terribly. Then I wanted to test myself and went to see a criminal guillotined, after which I could not sleep and did not know what to do with myself. Fortunately I happened to hear that you were at Geneva, and have rushed headlong to you, feeling sure that you would save me.'

In fact after telling everything he soon calmed down, and we got on excellently, met every day, climbed the mountains, and enjoyed life thoroughly. The weather was wonderful, not to speak of the scenery. We delighted in it with the enthusiasm of dwellers on a plain, though Leo tried to moderate our ardour by assuring us that it was rubbish compared with the Caucasus.

Despite the difference in our upbringing and position we had one characteristic in common. We were both terrible enthusiasts and analysers, who loved goodness, but did not know how to follow it properly.

They had a number of charming Russian acquaintances in the vicinity, and her story proceeds:

One morning a group of us set out on foot for Glion, well known as the highest point above Vevey. Our path was strewn with flowers literally and figuratively. The splendour of spring lay before our eyes and intoxicated us. As I remember we were all, regardless of age, like schoolchildren out on a spree . . . Having climbed the mountain in the sweat of our brows, we found the public room in the only hotel there crowded with Englishmen, Americans, and all sorts of people.

After tea, disregarding the numerous public, Leo unceremoniously sat down to the piano and called on us to sing.

I may say without false modesty that I then had an excellent voice and devoted much time to music, and as it happened Mme Púshina also sang. She chimed in to my songs with her pure voice, and the two Michaels supplied the bass, while Leo assumed the rôle of conductor.

I do not know in how far our improvised concert was satisfactory from a strictly musical sense, but with the open windows and the wide view, all went off well and even poetically.

We sang *God save the Tsar*, Russian and Gypsy songs, in short whatever suggested itself to Leo . . . We had a brilliant success. The foreigners overflowed with compliments and thanks – each in his own language, and implored us to continue. We evidently had met a felt want: first, as wandering musicians demanding no payment, and next perhaps by dispersing their customary spleen.

The following day the same thing happened at our *pension* [she was then staying with Tolstoy at Vevey]. *Orphée attendrissant les bêtes*. The stern Englishwomen there were so softened that they did not know how to express their friendliness – handing us chairs, treating us to sweets, and so on . . .

When my leave of absence expired and I returned to Geneva . . . Leo remained at Vevey and reproached me with being unable to tear myself away from the Chimney (as he denominated the Court).

Tolstoy's substitution of the word *trubá* (chimney) for the similar-sounding word *dvorá* (Court) was, be it mentioned in passing, suggested by the fact that the most aristocratic girls' school in Petersburg was kept by a Mlle Terouba, so that the pupils of Terouba filled the Court.

After recounting various escapades he and his friends were up to, she continues:

In July we undertook a journey to Oberland with the Grand Duchess's children. We stopped for the first night in Vevey at Monet's hotel.

Hardly had we sat down to table before a waiter came to inform me in a mysterious voice that someone wanted me downstairs . . . Guessing what was up, I quickly descended to the large downstairs room, where I found them once again – wrapped in long cloaks, with feathers in their fantastic hats. Music was spread on the floor as is done by strolling players, and instruments were replaced by sticks. On my appearance an indescribable cacophony commenced, a real *tapage infernal* or cats' concert. Voices and sticks rivalled one another. I nearly died with laughing, and the Grand Duchess's children were inconsolable at having missed the performance.

Tolstoy soon settled at Clarens at the eastern end of the Lake of Geneva, and from there, on 18th May, he wrote to his Auntie Tatiána:

I have just received your letter, dear Aunt, which found me, as you

must know from my last letter, at Clarens in the neighbourhood of
Geneva, in the village where Rousseau's Julie lived . . . I will not try to
describe the beauty of this country, especially at present when all is in
leaf and flower; I will only say that it is literally impossible to detach
oneself from this lake and from these banks, and that I spend most
of my time gazing and admiring while I walk, or simply sit at the
window of my room.

I do not cease congratulating myself on the thought which made
me leave Paris and come to pass the spring here, though I have
thereby deserved your reproach for inconstancy. Truly I am happy,
and begin to feel the advantage of having been born with a caul.

There is some charming Russian society here, the Púshkins, the
Karamzíns and the Meschérskis; and they have all, Heaven knows
why, taken to liking me; I feel it, and the month I have spent here I
have been so nice and good and cosy that I am sad at the thought of
leaving.

Among the excursions he undertook was a week's tour by way of
Montreux, Les Avants, the Col de Jaman, Interlaken, Grindelwald, and
Thun, with Sásha, the son of a Russian lady he knew.

Again and again in his Diary and letters Tolstoy's vivid delight in
Nature shows itself in descriptions of the scenery:

It is wonderful, but I was at Clarens for two months, and every time –
when in the morning and especially after dinner towards evening – I
opened the shutters on which the shadows were already falling and
glanced at the lake and the distant blue of the mountains reflected in
it, the beauty blinded me and acted on me with the force of a surprise.

But together with this keen appreciation, a sort of protest comes now
and then that this grandiose Swiss mountain scenery is after all not the
Nature that most appeals to him – a yearning for the vast steppes and
forests of Russia. After ascending the Pass of Jaman and describing the
magnificent scenery and the pleasure of the climb, he adds:

It was something beautiful, even unusually beautiful, but I do not love
what are called magnificent and remarkable views: they are, as it
were, cold . . . I love Nature when though it surrounds me on all sides
and extends unendingly, I am part of it. I love it when on all sides I
am surrounded by hot air and that same air rolls away to unending
distance and those same sappy leaves of grass which I crush as I sit on

them form the green of the boundless meadows; when those same leaves, which fluttering in the wind run their shadows across my face, form also the dark blue of the distant forests, while the same air one breathes makes the deep, light blue of the immeasurable sky; when you do not exult and rejoice alone in Nature but around you myriads of insects buzz and whirl, and beetles clinging together creep about, and all around you birds overflow with song.

But this is a bare, cold, desolate, grey plateau, and somewhere afar there is something beautiful veiled in mist. But that something is so distant that I do not feel the chief delight of Nature – do not feel myself part of that endless and beautiful distance, it is foreign to me.

In June he went to Turin to join Druzhínin and Bótkin, returning partly on foot by way of St Bernard.

On 1st July he started for Berne, on his way to Lucerne, which he reached on 6th July, and there the incident occurred that is recounted in his story *Lucerne*.

Countess Alexándra Tolstoy tells us that when she reached that town a few days after Tolstoy, she found him terribly excited and flaming with indignation.

This is what he told us had happened the previous evening. An itinerant musician had played for a long time beneath the balcony of the Schweizerhof Hotel, where a considerable company of people were sitting. Everyone enjoyed the performance, but when he raised his cap for a reward, no one threw him a single sou – an unpleasant fact, certainly, but one to which Tolstoy attributed almost criminal dimensions.

To retaliate on the smart public there assembled, he took the musician by the arm and, seating him at his own table, ordered supper and champagne for him. I hardly think the guests, or even the poor musician himself, quite appreciated the irony of this action. It characterised both the writer and the man. The impression the incident made on Tolstoy was so strong that it involuntarily communicated itself to others. Even the children were keenly interested in the adventure, and having grown fond of Tolstoy implored us to invite him to join our steamer and continue his journey with us, which was satisfactorily arranged. To this day they remember how he amused them, and what an incredible quantity of cherries he consumed.

In Tolstoy's Diary we find these entries:

15th July: Called at the Schweizerhof – the whole 'chimney'. The children are sweet and make up to one. To my shame, the smell of the 'chimney' pleases me.

18th July: I scarcely managed to finish *Lucerne* by writing from seven till half-past ten. Ran to them. Drove with them. Pleasant. An unpleasant moment when I did not know whether I might dine with them or not . . . Fine illumination and music on the lake in the evening. Read *Lucerne* to them. Vavá asked me to feed him. The children are sweet.

19th July: Got up at 10.30. Bathed, ran to the Tolstoy's. Found them just going away. Without reflection I prepared to go myself. Went by boat to Küssnacht, read Brontë.

He next proceeded to Zurich and Baden-Baden. On the way there, on 23rd July, he notes:

Most important, the idea occurred to me clearly and strongly of starting a school in my own village for the whole district, and of general activity of that kind.

This intention he carried out a little later, but on reaching Baden-Baden, famous for its gambling establishments, the temptation was too strong for him and he lost all the money he had with him and even more. The comments in his Diary from the day he arrived are:

24th July: I was constantly running to the roulette. Lost a little.

25th July: Roulette from morning till night. Lost, but won at night.

26th July: Ill since morning. Roulette till six. Lost everything. Dined at home. Quite ill. In the evening looked on at all this depraved confusion pretty calmly, but am ill and weak.

27th July: Borrowed 200 rubles from the Frenchman, and lost. Wrote letters. Shall not play any more. Am calmer . . . Polónski has no money. Awkward situation.

28th July: Woke up fresh. K. brought me some money. Went to the baths and then played and lost. Pig! I gadded about stricken and ashamed. Went to a doctor. Decided to take a week's cure, but it seems useless.

29th July: Got up late . . . Did not play as I had no money. Bad, horrid! And this kind of life has gone on for a week.

31st July: Turgénev has arrived.

1st August: Borrowed money from Turgénev and lost it. It is long since anything tormented me so.

In his distress he again found comfort in the friendship of Alexándra Tolstoy, who, with the Grand Duchess, was travelling in the same direction as himself. He notes in his Diary:

3rd August: Reached Frankfurt. The Court. Demanded a lodging in the Darmstadt palace. Priceless Sásha [Alexándra Tolstoy]. A wonder! A delight! I never knew a better woman.

By 5th August he had reached Dresden, where he visited the picture gallery and noted in his Diary: 'The Madonna at once moved me deeply.' Through Berlin and by boat from Stettin to Petersburg, he reached Russia on 31st July (Russian style).

In his Diary he notes:

This is how on my journey I planned my future occupations: first literary work; next family duties; then estate management. But the estate I must leave as far as possible to the steward, softening him and making improvements, and spending only 2,000 rubles a year and using the rest for the serfs. Above all, my stumbling-block is Liberal vanity. To live for oneself and do a good deed a day is sufficient.

Farther on he says: 'Self-sacrifice does not lie in saying "Take what you like from me", but in labouring and thinking, and contriving how to give oneself.'

He read in translation the *Iliad* and the Gospels at this time, both of which impressed him greatly. 'I have finished reading the indescribably beautiful end of the *Iliad*,' he notes, and he expresses regret that there is no connection between those two wonderful works.

During his stay in western Europe he had been reading de Tocqueville and the political writings of Émile de Girardin, also *La Cousine Bette* by Balzac, of whose preface to the *Comédie Humaine* he remarks, 'shallow and self-satisfied'. After seeing the actress Ristori in Paris he comments:

A single poetic movement compensates for the falsity of five acts. Racine's drama and the like are Europe's poetic wound. Thank God we [Russians] have not got it and shall not have it.

But of Molière he says: '*Précieuses ridicules* and *L'Avare* – excellent.' Other authors he read were Las Casas (his *Mémorial de Ste-Hélène* probably) and 'a silly novel by About'; also the Swedish novelist, Fredrika Bremer ('a very bright, attractive talent though, as usual with women, too sugary'), Freytag's *Soll und Haben* ('poor'); a good deal of Charlotte Brontë; Hans Andersen, of whom he was very fond, and Goethe's *Wilhelm Meister*. He did not generally care for Goethe, but here remarks 'read enchanting Goethe', without mentioning any particular work.

He was not writing much himself, but worked from time to time at *Youth* and at *Albert* (which later he rewrote several times) and under stress of feeling he produced *Lucerne* in a few days.

By the end of July he was in Petersburg, and a week later started for Yásnaya Polyána. On 8th August, starting from Moscow at 5 a.m. and changing horses halfway, he reached home by 11 p.m. The entry in his Diary begins with four words of Púshkin:

> 'I greet thee my . . . ' delightful Yásnaya! Pleasant and sad, but Russia disgusts me and I feel how this coarse, lying life begins to encircle me on every side. At the station Zórin was being beaten and I wanted to intercede for him, but Vasíli explained to me that one must first bribe the doctor. He told me many things of that kind; they beat and flog.

One gets glimpses of his occupations at Yásnaya from entries in the Diary:

> The piano takes time . . . Began letting the domestic serfs buy their freedom . . . Few of the serfs wish to be released on quit-rent . . . Increased the Elder's wages. Sensuality again torments me. Laziness, boredom, and sadness. Everything seems useless. The ideal is un-attainable; I have already ruined myself. Work, a small reputation, money. What for? Means of enjoyment – again what for? Soon an eternal night. It always seems to me that I shall soon die . . .
>
> It is only now that I have understood that it is not the life around one that must be arranged symmetrically as one wants it, but that one must break oneself up, make oneself pliable, so as to adapt oneself to any life . . .
>
> From morning planted trees all day.

In October he accompanied his brother Nicholas and his sister Márya to Moscow, and then spent a few days in Petersburg, where he found that he had been forgotten by a world absorbed in the public reforms then impending:

> Petersburg at first mortified me, but afterwards quite restored me. My reputation has fallen, or hardly squeaks, and I felt much grieved, but now I am tranquil. I know that I have something to say and the strength to utter it strongly, and the public may then say what it will. But I must work conscientiously, applying all my strength; then . . . 'Let them spit upon the altar.' [A quotation from Púshkin.]

He returned to Moscow and settled in furnished apartments with his sister and Nicholas. Fet was also there and in his *Recollections* makes frequent mention of the Tolstoys. He tells us that the Countess Márya (an accomplished pianist) used to come to his house for music in the evenings, sometimes accompanied by both her brothers and sometimes by Nicholas alone, who would say:

> 'Lëvochka [Leo] has again donned his evening clothes and white necktie and gone to a ball.'

Tolstoy's elegance in dress was very noticeable at this time. We read of the grey beaver collar of his overcoat, of a fashionable cane he carried, and of the glossy hat he wore set on one side, as well as of his curly, dark-brown hair.

Gymnastics were fashionable in Moscow, and anyone wishing to find Tolstoy between one and two in the afternoon could do so at the Gymnasium in the Great Dmítrovka Street, where dressed in gymnastic attire he might be seen intent on springing over the vaulting-horse without upsetting a cone placed on its back. Though muscularly very strong and active his health was often unsatisfactory and in particular he suffered frequently and severely from toothache.

Among the visitors Fet met at Tolstoy's house we find the name of Saltykóv who, under the pseudonym of Schedrín, is known as one of Russia's keenest satirists. Another guest was B. N. Chichérin, philosopher and jurist, and author of works on *Science and Religion*, *Property and the State*, and other subjects Tolstoy dealt with three or four decades later. Katkóv, editor of the *Moscow Védomosti* and the monthly *Russian Messenger*, was another acquaintance. Some of Tolstoy's chief works subsequently appeared in his magazine.

In January 1858 Countess Alexándra Tolstoy visited Moscow. References to her occur frequently in his Diary. He says of her: 'In the

evening to the Tolstoys. Alexandrine is delightful! A joy and a consolation. I have never met any woman who reached to her knees.'

Writing to her on 1st May 1858 he says:

At this very moment two nightingales are singing under my
window. I am experimenting with them and, can you believe it, have
succeeded in calling them under my window by sestolets on the
piano. I discovered it by chance. The other day, as I often do, I was
strumming a sonata of Haydn's in which sestolets occur. Suddenly
in the garden and in Auntie's room (she has a canary) there was a
whistling, piping, and trilling, in answer to my sestolets. I stopped
and they stopped. I recommenced and so did they – two nightingales
and a canary. I spent about three hours at this occupation. The
balcony was open, the night was warm, the frogs took their part and
the watchman's rattle its part. It was excellent. Forgive me if this
letter is rather wild. I confess I have gone a little off my head with the
Spring and the solitude. I wish you the same with my whole heart.
There are moments of happiness stronger, but none fuller and more
harmonious than these.

When she returned to Petersburg Tolstoy accompanied her as far as
the town of Klin, and took the opportunity to visit Princess Volkónski
(a cousin of his mother) who had a small estate in those parts. He
remained some weeks with this affectionate old lady, who was able to
tell him much about his mother and her family. He greatly enjoyed his
quiet stay with her, and at her house he wrote *Three Deaths*, which
appeared the following January. It is an admirably written study of the
deaths of a rich lady, a poor post-horse driver, and a tree.

On 26th January, in Moscow, he went to a *bal masqué* and notes:
'Two masks. One of them a Samára girl. I took her, and it was horrid.'

In February he was back at Yásnaya Polyána, then he again visited
Moscow, and in March spent a fortnight in Petersburg. His love of
music was much in evidence at this period, and in conjunction with V.
P. Bótkin, Perfílief, Mortier (his late rival) and others, he founded the
Moscow Musical Society which ultimately resulted in the formation
of the Moscow Conservatoire of which Nicholas Rubinstein became
Director.

An intimate acquaintance of Tolstoy's at this time was S. T. Aksákov,
already referred to, the author of a book translated into English as *A
Russian Gentleman*, and other works.

The invigorating influence of spring shows itself in a letter Tolstoy wrote about this time to his aunt, Countess A. A. Tolstoy:

GRANDMA! – Spring!

For good people it is excellent to live in the world; and even for men such as me, it is sometimes good. In Nature, in the air, in everything, is hope, future – an attractive future . . . Sometimes one deceives oneself and thinks that happiness and a future await not only Nature but oneself also, and then one feels happy. I am now in such a state and with characteristic egotism hasten to write to you of things that are of interest only to me. When I review things sanely I know very well that I am an old, frozen, little potato, and one already boiled with sauce; but spring so acts on me that I sometimes catch myself in the full blaze of imagining myself a plant which with others has only now blossomed, and which will peacefully, simply, and joyfully, grow in God's world. The result is that at this time of year such an internal clearing-up goes on in me, such a cleansing and ordering, as only those who have experienced this feeling can imagine. All the old – away! All worldly conventions, all idleness, all egotism, all vice, all confused indefinite attachments, all regrets, even repentances – away with you all! . . . Make room for the wonderful little flowers whose buds are swelling and growing in the spring! . . .

After much more he concludes:

Farewell, dear Grandma, do not be angry with me for this nonsense, but answer with a word of wisdom imbued with kindness, Christian kindness! I have long wished to say that for you it is pleasanter to write French, and I understand feminine thoughts better in French.

In April he was again at Yásnaya, where despite repeated visits to Moscow he spent most of the summer. There was as yet no railway from Moscow southward to Túla, and the serfs' belief concerning the new telegraph posts which stood by the side of the high road was that when the wire had been completed, 'Freedom' would be sent by it from Petersburg. Even Tatiána Alexándrovna Érgolski did not understand these newfangled things, and when driving along the road one day asked Tolstoy to explain how letters were written by telegraph. He told her as simply as he could how it was done, and received the reply: '*Oui, oui, je comprends, mon cher!*' How much she had really understood was shown however half an hour later when, after keeping her eye on the wire all the time, she enquired: 'But how is it, *mon cher Léon*, that during a whole half-hour I have not seen a single letter go along the telegraph?'

Fet and his wife used to stay a day or two at Yásnaya when journeying to and from Moscow, and Fet's account of Aunt Tatiána accords with Tolstoy's own affectionate recollections of that lady. Fet says that he and his wife 'made the acquaintance of Tolstoy's charming old aunt, Tatiána Alexándrovna Érgolski, who received us with that old-world affability which puts a man at once at his ease on entering a new house. She did not devote herself to memories of times long past but lived fully in the present.

'Speaking of them all by their pet names, she mentioned that Serëz-henka Tolstoy had gone to his home at Pirogóvo, but Nikólenka would probably stay a bit longer in Moscow with Máshenka, but Lëvochká's friend Dyákov had recently visited them,' and so on.

Many years later Tolstoy jotted down his memories of the long autumn and winter evenings spent with Auntie Tatiána, to which he says he owed his best thoughts and impulses. He would sit in his armchair reading, thinking, and occasionally listening to her kindly and gentle conversation with two of the servants: Natálya Petróvna (an old woman who lived there not because she was of much use but because she had nowhere else to go) and a maid Dúnechka.

The chief charm of that life lay in the absence of any material care, in good relations with those nearest – relations no one could spoil – and in the leisureliness and the unconsciousness of flying time . . .

When after living badly at a neighbour's in Túla with cards, Gypsy girls, hunting, and stupid vanity, I used to return home and come to her, we would by old habit kiss each other's hand, I her dear energetic hand and she my dirty vicious hand, and also by old habit we greeted one another in French, and I would joke with Natálya Petróvna and would sit down in the comfortable armchair. She well knew all I had been doing and regretted it, but never reproached me, retaining always the same gentleness and love . . . I was once telling her how someone's wife had gone off with another man, and I said the husband ought to be glad to get rid of her. And suddenly my aunt lifted her eyebrows and said, as of a thing long decided in her mind, that that would be wrong of the husband because it would completely ruin the wife. After that she told me of a drama that had occurred among the serfs. Then she reread a letter from my sister Máshenka, whom she loved if not more at least as much as she loved me, and spoke of Másha's husband (her own nephew) not to condemn him but with grief at the sorrow he inflicted on Máshenka . . . The chief characteristic of her life, which involuntarily infected me, was her wonderful, general kindliness to everyone without exception. I try to recall a single instance of her being angry, or speaking a sharp word, or condemning anyone, and I cannot recall one such instance in thirty years. She spoke well of our real aunt who had bitterly hurt her by taking us away from her . . . As to her kindly treatment of the servants – that goes without saying. She had grown up in the idea that there are masters and servants, but she utilised her authority only to serve them . . . She never blamed me directly for my evil life though she suffered on my account. My brother Sergéy, too, whom she also loved warmly, she did not reproach even when he took a Gypsy girl to live with him. The only shade of disquietude she showed on our account was that when he was very late in returning home, she would say, 'What has become of our Sergéus?' Only *Sergéus* instead of *Serëzha* . . . She never told us in words how to live, never preached to us. All her moral work was done internally; externally one only saw her deeds – and not even deeds: there were no deeds; but all her life, peaceful, sweet, submissive, and loving, not troubled or self-satisfied, but a life of quiet unobtrusive love . . . Her affectionateness and tranquillity made her society noticeably attractive and gave a special charm to intimacy with her. I know of no case where she offended anyone, and of no one who did not love her. She never spoke of herself, never of religion or of what we ought to believe, or of how she believed or prayed. She believed everything, except that she rejected one dogma – that of eternal torment. '*Dieu, qui est la bonté même, ne peut pas vouloir nos souffrances . . .*' [God, who is goodness itself, cannot desire our pains . . .] She often called me by my father's name (Nicholas) and this pleased me very much because it showed that her conceptions of me and of my father mingled in her love of us both.

It was not her love of me alone that was joyous. What was joyous was the atmosphere of love of all who were present or absent, alive or dead, and even of animals . . .

After telling of her goodness and affection Tolstoy says in his Memoirs that, though he appreciated his happiness with her, he did not at the time nearly realise its full value, and he adds:

> She was fond of keeping sweets: figs, gingerbreads, and dates, in various jars in her room. I cannot forget, nor remember without a cruel pang of remorse, that I repeatedly refused her money she wanted for such things, and how she, sighing sadly, remained silent. It is true I was in need of money, but I cannot now remember without horror that I refused her.

Again, in another place after mentioning her self-devotion, he says:

> And it was to her, to her, that I refused the small pleasure of having figs and chocolate (not so much for herself as to treat me) and being able to give a trifle to those who begged of her . . . Dear, dear, Auntie, forgive me! *Si jeunesse savait, si vieillesse pouvait* [if youth but knew, if age but could], I do not mean in the sense of the good lost for oneself in youth, but in the sense of the good not given and the evil done to those who are no more.

Of Leo's life at Yásnaya at this time his brother Nicholas gave Fet the following humorous account:

> Lëvochka is zealously trying to become acquainted with peasant life and with farming, of both of which, like the rest of us, he has till now had but a superficial knowledge. But I am not sure what sort of acquaintance will result from his efforts: Lëvochka wants to get hold of everything at once without omitting anything – even his gymnastics. So he has rigged up a bar under his study window. And of course, apart from prejudice with which he wages such fierce war, he is right: gymnastics do not interfere with farming; but the steward sees things differently and says, 'One comes to the master for orders, and he hangs head downward in a red jacket holding on by one knee to a perch and swings himself. His hair hangs down and blows about, the blood comes to his face, and one does not know whether to listen to his orders or to be astonished at him!'
>
> Lëvochka is delighted with the way the serf Ufán sticks out his arms when ploughing, and so Ufán has become for him an emblem of village strength, like the legendary Mikúla, and he himself, sticking his elbows out wide, takes to the plough and 'úfanises'.

At this period, preceding the Emancipation, relations between the owners and the serfs did not go very smoothly, of which we have indications in the Diary:

19th June 1858. I do not write, or read, or think, I am engrossed in farming. The struggle is at its hottest. The peasants try it on and are obstinate. Those at Grumont are sullen, but say nothing. I am afraid of myself. A vengeful feeling I never had before makes itself felt in me – to revenge myself on the Commune. I am afraid of being unjust.

27th November, 1858. No, I have deteriorated to an impossible extent. Farming is a coarse occupation. Today Razún lied, and I was furious and, following the wretched custom, said, 'have him flogged'. I waited for him to come. I sent to have him brought back, but they did not overtake him [before he was brought to the police to be flogged]. I shall ask his pardon. Never again will I sentence anyone before two hours have elapsed . . . I have asked pardon and given him three rubles, but it has tortured me.

9th October 1859. I have twice hit a man this summer . . .

The recollection of having hit men and had them flogged tormented Tolstoy in his old age, though he had done such things very exceptionally, and in days when it was regarded as a necessary procedure.

In May 1858 he wrote to Fet:

Dearest little Uncle [or as we might say, Dear old Boy] – I write two words just to say that I embrace you with all my might, have received your letter, kiss the hand of Márya Petróvna [Fet's wife] and make obeisance to you all. Auntie thanks you very much for your message and greets you, so also does my sister. What a wonderful spring it has been and is! I in solitude have tasted it admirably. Brother Nicholas must be at Nikólskoe. Catch him, and do not let him go. I want to come to see you this month. Turgénev has gone to Winzig till August to cure his bladder.

Devil take him. I am tired of loving him. He deserts us and won't cure his bladder.

Now goodbye, dear friend. If you have no poem ready for me by the time I come I shall proceed to squeeze one out of you. – Your

Count L. Tolstoy

Another letter to Fet runs:

Ay, old fellow, ahoy! First you give no sign, though it is spring and you know we are all thinking of you, and that I, like Prometheus, am bound to a rock yet thirst for sight or sound of you. You should either come, or at least send us a proper invitation. Secondly, you have retained my brother, and a very good brother, surnamed 'Firdusi' [an allusion to Nicholas's Oriental wisdom]. The chief culprit in this matter, I suspect, is Márya Petróvna, to whom I humbly bow, requesting her to return us our own brother. Jesting apart, he [Nicholas] bids me let you know that he must be here next week. Druzhínin will also come, so mind you come too, old fellow.

On 24th October 1858 he writes to Fet:

To write stories is stupid and shameful. To write verses – well, write them; but to love a good man is very pleasant. Yet perhaps, against my will and intention, not I but an unripe story inside me compels me to love you. It sometimes seems like that. Do what one will amid the manure and the mange one somehow begins to compose. Thank heaven I have not yet allowed myself to write and will not do so . . . Thank you exceedingly for your trouble about a veterinary. I have found one in Túla and have begun the cure, but I do not know what will come of it. – And may the devil take them all – Druzhínin is appealing to me as a matter of friendship to write a story. I really want to. I will spin such a yarn that there will be no head or tail to it . . . But joking apart, how is your Hafiz getting on? [Fet was translating some poems of Hafiz.] Turn it which way you will, the height of wisdom and fortitude for me is to enjoy the poetry of others and not to let my own loose among men in ugly garb but to consume it myself with my daily bread. But at times one suddenly wishes to be a great man and it is so annoying that this has not yet come about! One even hurries to get up quicker, or to finish dinner, in order to begin . . . Send me a poem, the healthiest of those you have translated from Hafiz, *pour me faire venir l'eau à la bouche* [to make my mouth water], and I will send you a sample of wheat. Hunting has bored me to death. The weather is excellent, but I do not hunt alone.

In company Tolstoy was however a keen sportsman, and in December 1858 he nearly lost his life while out bear-shooting. He has told the story, with some embellishments, in one of the tales for children in the volume *Twenty-Three Tales*.

The facts were these: Tolstoy and his brother Nicholas had made the acquaintance of a Mr Grómeka, who shared their fondness for hunting – a sport very different in Russia from what it is in England, as readers of Tolstoy's descriptions are aware.

Grómeka having heard that a she-bear with two young had her lair in the forest near the railway at Volochók, halfway between Petersburg and Moscow, arranged with the peasants of that locality and invited the Tolstoys and others to a hunt. The invitation was accepted, and on 21st December Leo Tolstoy shot a bear. On the 22nd the members of the party, each armed with two guns, were placed at the ends of cuttings running through the forest in which the big she-bear had been surrounded. These paths or cuttings divided the wood like the lines of a chessboard. Peasants employed as beaters were stationed to prevent the animal escaping except by approaching one or other of the sportsmen. Ostáshkov, a famous professional huntsman, supervised the proceedings. The guests were advised to stamp down the snow around them to give themselves room to move freely; but Tolstoy (with his usual objection to routine methods) argued that, as they were out to shoot the bear and not to box with her, it was useless to tread down the snow. He therefore stood with his double-barrel gun in his hand surrounded by snow almost up to his waist.

The bear, roused by Ostáshkov's shouts, rushed down a cutting directly towards one of the other sportsmen, but perceiving him, suddenly swerved from her course and took a path which brought her out on to the cutting leading straight to Tolstoy. He, not expecting her visit, did not fire till the beast was within six yards, and his first shot missed. The bear was but two yards from him when his second shot hit her in the mouth. It failed to stop her rush and she knocked him over on his back in the snow. Carried past by her own impetus at first, the bear soon returned, and the next thing Tolstoy knew was that he was being weighed down by something heavy and warm, and felt his face drawn into the beast's mouth. He could only offer a passive resistance by drawing his head as much as possible between his shoulders and trying to present his cap instead of his face to the bear's teeth. This state of things lasted only a few seconds, yet long enough for the bear, after one or two misses, to get her teeth into the flesh above and below his left eye. At that moment Ostáshkov armed with a small switch came running up, shouting: 'Where are you getting to? Where are you getting to?' at which the beast promptly took fright and rushed off. Next day she was followed up and killed. Owing to the amount of blood lost and flesh torn, Tolstoy's wound at first appeared serious, but when it had been washed with snow and he had been taken to the nearest town and had had it sewn up, it proved to be superficial. He always retained a scar however as a memento of the encounter, and the bear's skin may still be seen at Yásnaya.

Family Happiness, referred to in the preceding chapter, was partly written in 1858 and was published early in 1859.

Tolstoy spent the first months of 1859 in Moscow, and on the occasion of joining the Moscow Society of Lovers of Russian Literature, on 4th February, he for the first time made a speech in public, a task for which he once told me that he had no aptitude at all and which he much disliked. He wrote it out and it was to have appeared in the *Proceedings* of the Society, but did not get printed during his lifetime. Its subject was 'The Supremacy of the Artistic Element in Literature', and in it he maintained a position quite different from that he advocated forty years later in *What is Art?*

He was answered by the Slavophil A. S. Homyakóv, who presided at the meeting and in the course of his reply said:

Allow me to remark that the justice of the opinion you have so skilfully stated is far from destroying the legitimacy of the present temporary and exceptional side of literature. That which is always right, that which is always beautiful, that which is as unalterable as the most fundamental laws of the soul, undoubtedly holds and should hold the first place in the thoughts, the impulses, and therefore in the speech, of man. It and it alone will be handed on by generation to generation and by nation to nation as a precious inheritance. But on the other hand, in the nature of man and of society there is continual need of self-indictment. There are moments, moments important in history, when such self-indictment acquires a special and indefeasible right, and manifests itself in literature very definitely and keenly . . .

Of course Art is perfectly free, it finds its justification and aim in itself. But the freedom of Art in the abstract has nothing to do with the inner life of the artist. An artist is not a theory – a sphere of thought and mental activity, but a man and always a man of his own times, often its best representative, completely imbued with its spirit and its defined or nascent aspirations. By the very impressionability of his nature without which he could not be an artist, he even more than others receives all the painful as well as joyous sensations of the society to which he is born . . .

So the writer, the servant of pure art, sometimes even unconsciously and despite of his own will, becomes an accuser. I will let myself cite you, Count, as an example. You consciously follow a definite road faithfully and undeviatingly, but are you really quite alien to the literature of indictment? If only in the picture of a consumptive post-boy dying on a stove amid comrades apparently indifferent to his sufferings [*Three Deaths*], have you not indicated some social disease, some evil? When describing that death, is it possible that you did not suffer from the callous indifference of good but unawakened human souls? Yes, you too have been, and will be, an involuntary accuser!

This question of the true position of literary art and its relation to the rest of life was one which occupied Tolstoy for many years and on which before the century closed he expressed himself in a work which all who would deal with the subject must reckon with.

In April he went to Petersburg and spent ten days very pleasantly with Countess A. A. Tolstoy. By the end of the month he was back at Yásnaya. In July, Turgénev, from France, wrote Fet a long letter in blank verse, a few lines of which indicate the relation between Tolstoy and himself at this time:

> Kiss Nicholas Tolstoy on my behalf
> And to his brother Leo make my bow,
> As to his sister also.
> In his postscriptum rightly he asserts:
> 'There is no cause' for me to write to him,
> Indeed I know he bears me little love
> And I love him as little. Too differently
> Are mixed those elements of which we're formed.

During this winter [1859–60] Tolstoy devoted much time to an attempt to organise schools on and near his estate. The education of the peasant children was one of the things Russia most needed and most neglected. Tolstoy recognised this and set himself strenuously to show how the need could be met. The work he now did was however only preliminary to that he undertook after his second visit to Western Europe. He was himself far from being at peace mentally, and at the commencement of the New Year noted in his Diary:

The burden of the estate, the burden of bachelor life, and all sorts of doubts and pessimistic feelings agitate my mind.

Writing to Fet on 23rd February 1860, he says:

I have read Turgénev's *On the Eve*. This is my opinion: to write novels is undesirable, especially for people who are depressed and do not well know what they want from life. *On the Eve* however is much better than *A Nest of Gentlefolk*, and there are in it excellent negative characters: the artist and the father. The rest are not types; even their conception, their position, is not typical, or they are quite insignificant. That however is always Turgénev's mistake. The girl is hopelessly bad: 'Ah, how I love thee . . . her eyelashes were long.' In general it always surprises me that Turgénev with his mental powers and poetic sensibility should even in his methods not be able to refrain from banality. This banality shows itself most of all in his negative methods, which recall Gógol. There is no humanity or sympathy for the characters, but the author exhibits monsters whom he scolds and does not pity. This jars painfully with the tone and intention of Liberalism in everything else. It was all very well in the days of Tsar Gorókh [a character in a fairy story] or of Gógol (though if one does not pity even the most insignificant of one's characters one should scold them so that the heavens grow hot, or laugh at them so that one's sides split, and not as our splenetic and dyspeptic Turgénev does). On the whole however there is now no one else who could write such a novel, though it will not meet with success.

Ostróvski's *The Storm* is, in my opinion, a wretched work, but will be successful. Not Ostróvski and Turgénev are to blame, but the times . . . Something else is now needed: not that we should learn and criticise, but that we should teach Jack and Jill at least a little of what we know.

This letter to Fet, who was in Moscow, ends with requests to procure some books, including a veterinary handbook, a veterinary instrument, and a lancet for use on human beings, to see about procuring six ploughs of a special make, and to ascertain the price of clover and timothy-grass, of which Tolstoy had some to sell.

At this time he was working on *The Cossacks*, the plan of which he had sketched out in 1852, but of which he did not complete the published portion till 1862.

One comes in his Diary across notes which indicate his state of mind at this time about religion. After reading a book on Materialism he notes:

I instinctively thought of prayer. To whom? What is God, imagined so clearly that one can petition Him, communicate with Him? If I even imagine Him to myself as such, He loses for me all grandeur. A God who can be petitioned and who can be served, is an expression of mental weakness. He is God just because His whole nature is such as I cannot imagine to myself. Yes, He is not a Being, but a Law and a Force.

He was a great puzzle to his friends and acquaintances – always ready to take his own line strenuously yet sometimes far from sure what that line was. Turgénev wrote to Fet:

Leo Tolstoy continues his eccentricities. Evidently it was so decreed at his birth. When will he turn his last somersault and stand on his feet?

The fact that Tolstoy, like his friend Fet, was neglecting literature, did not fail to call forth many remonstrances: one of the most urgent of these came from Druzhínin, who wrote:

Every writer has his moments of doubt and self-dissatisfaction and however strong and legitimate this feeling may be, no one on that account has yet ceased his connection with literature; everyone goes on writing to the end. But all tendencies good or bad cling to you with peculiar obstinacy; so that you more than others need to think of this and to consider the whole matter amicably . . .

On all of us lies a responsibility rooted in the immense importance of literature to Russian society. An Englishman or an American may laugh at the fact that in Russia not merely men of thirty, but grey-haired proprietors of 2,000 serfs, sweat over stories of a hundred pages which appear in the magazines, are devoured by everybody, and arouse discussions in society for a whole day. However much artistic quality may have to do with this result, you cannot explain it merely by Art. What in other lands is a matter of idle talk and careless dilettantism with us is quite another affair. Among us things have taken such shape that a story – the most frivolous and insignificant form of literature – becomes one of two things, either it is rubbish, or else it is the voice of a leader sounding throughout the Empire. By some strange instinct the Russian public has chosen from among the crowd of writers four or five bellmen whom it values as leaders, refusing to listen to any qualifications or deductions. You – partly by talent, partly by the practical qualities of your soul, and partly owing simply to a concurrence of fortunate circumstances – have stepped into this favourable relation with the public. On that account you must not go away and hide, but must work even to the exhaustion of your strength and powers. If you tear yourself off from the circle of writers and become inactive you will be dull and will deprive yourself of an important rôle in society . . .

At this time the state of health of his brother Nicholas – who (like Dmítri) had consumptive tendencies – began to disturb Leo Tolstoy. It was arranged that Nicholas should go to Germany for a cure. The following letter written by Tolstoy to Fet after Nicholas had started, refers to this and other matters:

I am greatly at sixes and sevens with myself. Farming, on the scale on which it is carried out on my estate, crushes me. To 'úfanise' [work like a peasant; the origin of this word has already been explained] is a thing I only see afar off. Family affairs, Nicholas's illness (of which we have as yet no news from abroad) and my sister's departure (she leaves me in three days' time) also occupy and crush me. Bachelor life, i.e. not having a wife, and the thought that it is getting too late, torments me from a third side. In general everything is now out of tune with me. On account of my sister's helplessness and my wish to see Nicholas, I shall at any rate procure a foreign passport tomorrow, and perhaps I shall accompany my sister abroad, especially if we do not receive news, or receive bad news, from Nicholas.

On 26th May 1860 he notes in his Diary:

Got up at five, directed the work myself, all went well and I am cheerful . . . Towards evening I was becoming angry at the manuring. I got down and started working till I was in a heavy sweat, and everything seemed good and I felt fond of everybody. It would be strange if this adoration of mine for work went for nothing.

Things were not going well with Nicholas, who wrote from Soden in Hesse-Nassau:

In Soden we joined Turgénev who is alive and well – so well that he himself confesses that he is 'quite' well. He has found some German girl and goes into ecstasies about her. We (this relates to our dearest Turgénev) play chess together, but somehow it does not go as it should: he is thinking of his German girl and I of my cure . . . I shall probably stay in Soden for at least six weeks. I do not describe my journey because I was ill all the time.

Eventually Leo Tolstoy made up his mind to accompany his sister and her children abroad, and on 3rd July 1860 (old style) they took steamer from Petersburg for Stettin *en route* for Berlin. Besides anxiety on his brother's account Tolstoy had another reason for going abroad: he wished to study the European systems of education in order to see what had been accomplished in the line to which he now intended to devote himself.

On reaching Berlin he suffered from toothache for four days and decided to remain there while his sister proceeded to join Nicholas at Soden. He consulted a doctor, as he was suffering also from headache and haemorrhoidal attacks, and he was ordered to undergo a cure at Kissingen.

He stayed only a few days in Berlin after getting rid of his toothache, and left on 14th July (old style) having found time to attend some lectures, and having visited some evening classes for artisans at the *Handwerkersverein* where he was much interested in the system of 'question-boxes'. This method of arousing the interest of audiences by allowing them to put questions to the lecturer was new to him, and he was struck by the life it brought into the classes, and the freedom of mental contact between scholars and teacher. He noticed the same thing when in London a few months later, for he told me that nothing he saw there interested him more than a lecture he attended in South Kensington, at which questions were put by working men and answered by a speaker who was master of his subject and knew how to popularise it.

In Berlin he visited the Moabit Prison in which solitary confinement was practised, and he strongly disapproved of this mechanical attempt to secure moral reform. From Berlin he went to Leipzig and spent a day inspecting schools; but he derived little satisfaction from them, as is indicated by a remark in his Diary, 'Have been in school – terrible. Prayers for the King, blows, everything by rote, frightened, paralysed children . . .' He then proceeded to Dresden, where he called on the novelist Auerbach, whose story, *Ein Neues Leben*, had greatly influenced him. The chief character in that story is a Count Fulkenberg, who after being an officer in the army gets into trouble, escapes from prison, buys the passport of a schoolmaster, Eugene Baumann, and under that name devotes himself to the task of educating peasant children. When Auerbach entered the room where Tolstoy was waiting, the latter introduced himself with the words: 'I am Eugene Baumann,' in such solemn tones and with so morose an appearance that Auerbach was taken aback, and feared that he was about to be threatened with an action for libel. Tolstoy however hastened to add: ' – not in name, but in character – ' and went on to explain how good an effect Auerbach's *Schwarzwälder Dorfgeschichten* had had on him.

After three days in Dresden he went on to Kissingen, which in those times was about five hours' journey from Soden, where Nicholas was staying. Still intent on his educational enquiries, Tolstoy *en route* read a history of pedagogics.

From Kissingen he wrote to his Aunt Tatiána that he thought the cure was doing him good, and added:

> Tell the steward to write me most minutely about the farming, the harvest, the horses, and their illness. Tell the schoolmaster to write about the school: how many pupils come and whether they learn well. I shall certainly return in autumn and intend to occupy myself more than ever with the school, so I do not wish its reputation to be lost while I am away, and I want as many pupils as possible from different parts.

While in Kissingen he read Bacon and Luther, and made the acquaintance of Julius Froebel, author of *The System of Social Politics* and nephew of the founder of the Kindergarten system. Julius Froebel was himself interested in educational matters and was a most suitable person to explain his uncle's ideas.

Tolstoy astonished his new acquaintance, with whom he used to go for walks, by the uncompromising rigidity of his views, which contrary to his attitude when in contact with the Slavophils showed a considerable tinge of Slavophilism. Progress in Russia, declared Tolstoy, must be based on popular education, which would give better results in Russia than in Germany because the Russian people were still unperverted, whereas the Germans were like children who had for years been subjected to a bad education. Popular education should not be compulsory. If it is a blessing the demand for it should come naturally, as the demand for food comes from hunger.

Tolstoy visited the country round Kissingen, and travelling northward through a part of Germany rich in scenery and in historic interest, reached Eisenach and visited the Wartburg where Luther was confined after the Diet of Worms. The personality of the great Protestant reformer interested him much, and after seeing the room in which Luther commenced his translation of the Bible, he noted in his Diary: 'Luther was great!' Twenty years later Tolstoy himself when trying to free men's minds from the yoke of an established Church, shaped his chief weapon against the Church by translating not, it is true, like Luther, the whole Bible, but the Gospels.

Meanwhile, Nicholas Tolstoy's health had grown worse rather than better. Sergéy having been unlucky at roulette decided to return to Russia, and visiting Leo at Kissingen *en route*, told him of his fears for Nicholas. Leo then spent a fortnight in the Harz Mountains, enjoying nature and reading a great deal. On 26th August he joined Nicholas and his sister and her children at Soden. The doctors had decided that Nicholas must winter in a warmer climate, and the place selected was Hyères near Toulon, on the shores of the Mediterranean.

The first stage of the journey undertaken by the family party was to Frankfort-on-Main, where Countess A. A. Tolstoy was staying. She tells the following story of Leo's visit to her on this occasion:

One day Prince Alexander of Hesse and his wife were calling on me, when suddenly the door of the drawing-room opened and Leo appeared in the strangest garb, suggestive of a picture of a Spanish bandit. I gasped with astonishment. Leo apparently was not pleased with my visitors and soon took his departure.

'Who is that singular person?' enquired my visitors in astonishment.

'Why, it is Leo Tolstoy!'

'Ah, good heavens! Why did you not tell us who it was? After reading his admirable writings we were dying to see him.'

And reproaches were showered upon me, intermingled with ecstatic praise of his talent.

Next time I saw him I told him all the flattering things that had been said about him, but his whole concern was directed to the fact that I had probably felt ashamed about him on that occasion.

'Perhaps it was so,' I unhesitatingly admitted. 'Your savage costume and grim appearance might have amazed anyone.'

'The Chimney, it is all the Chimney!' growled he in a slightly offended tone.

So his freak resulted in my getting it from both sides.

From Frankfort the party proceeded to Hyères, where Nicholas, growing rapidly worse and worse, died on 20th September 1860.

Few men have been so admired and loved as he was by all who knew him. The only thing recorded against him is that when serving in the Caucasus he, like many of his fellow-officers, was intemperate, but after returning home he recovered his self-control. I have already told of his influence on Leo in the early days of the Ant-Brotherhood, and of the green stick buried where Tolstoy's own body was eventually to lie. Such influence Nicholas retained through life, and men and women of most different temperaments make enthusiastic mention of his charm and goodness. That Leo's judgement of life remained strongly influenced by his love for and memory of Nicholas is plain to all who read his works attentively.

Turgénev once said:

The humility Leo Tolstoy developed theoretically, his brother actually practised in life. He always lived in the most impossible lodgings, almost hovels, somewhere in the out-of-the-way quarters of Moscow, and shared all he had with the poorest outcast. He was a delightful companion and narrator, but writing was to him almost a physical impossibility, the actual process of writing being as difficult for him as for a labourer whose stiff hands will not hold a pen.

Nicholas did however, as a matter of fact, contribute some very well composed *Memoirs of a Sportsman* to the *Contemporary*.

Never was anyone's death more sincerely regretted. This is the letter Leo wrote to Aunt Tatiána the night of the event:

CHÈRE TANTE – The black seal will have told you all. What for two weeks I have been expecting from hour to hour occurred at nine o'clock this evening. Only since yesterday did he let me help him undress, and today for the first time he definitely took to his bed and asked for a nurse. He was conscious all the time and a quarter-of-an-hour before he died he drank some milk and told me he was comfortable. Even today he still joked and showed interest in my educational projects. Only a few minutes before he died he whispered several times: 'My God, my God!' It seems to me that he felt his position, but deceived himself and us. Máshenka only today, some four hours before, had gone three miles out of Hyères to where she is living. She did not at all expect it to come so soon. I have just closed his eyes. I shall now soon be back with you and tell you all personally. I do not intend to transport the body. The funeral will be arranged by the Princess Golítsin, who has taken it all on herself.

Farewell, chère tante. I cannot console you. It is God's will – that is all. I am not writing to Serëzha now. He is probably away hunting, you know where. So let him know or send him this letter.

On the day after the funeral he wrote to Sergéy:

I think you have had news of the death of Nicholas. I am sorry for you that you were not here. Hard as it is, I am glad it all took place in my presence and that it acted on me in the right way – not like Mítenka's [his third brother, Dmítri] death of which I heard when I was not thinking at all about him. This however is quite different. With Mítenka only memories of childhood and family feeling were bound up, but this was a real man both to you and to me, whom we loved and *respected* positively more than anyone else on earth. You know the selfish feeling which came latterly, that the sooner it was over the better; it is dreadful now to write it and to remember that one thought it. Till the last day, with his extraordinary strength of character and power of concentration, he did everything to avoid becoming a burden to me. On the day of his death he dressed and washed himself, and in the morning I found him dressed on his bed. Only about nine hours before he died did he give way to his illness and ask to be undressed. It first happened in the closet. I went downstairs and heard his door open. I returned and did not find him. At first I feared to go to him – he used not to like it, but this time he himself said, 'Help me!'

And he submitted and became different that day, mild and gentle. He did not groan, did not blame anyone, praised everybody, and said to me: 'Thank you, *my friend*.' You understand what that meant between us. I told him I had heard how he coughed in the morning, but had not come to him from *fausse honte* [false shame]. 'Needlessly,' said he – 'it would have consoled me.' Suffering? He suffered, but it was not until a couple of days before his death that he once said:

'How terrible these nights without sleep are! Towards morning the cough chokes one unendingly! And it hurts – God knows how! A couple more such nights – it's terrible!' Not once did he say plainly that he felt the approach of death. But he only did not *say* it. On the day of his death he ordered a dressing-gown and yet when I remarked that if he did not get better Máshenka and I would not go to Switzerland, he replied: 'Do you really think I shall be better?' in such a tone that it was evident what he felt but for my sake did not say, and what I for his sake did not show; all the same I knew from the morning what was coming, and was with him all the time. He died quite without suffering – externally at all events. He breathed more and more slowly – and it was all over. The next day I went to him and feared to uncover his face. I thought it would show yet more suffering and be more terrible than during his illness, but you cannot imagine what a beautiful face it was, with his best, merry, calm expression.

Yesterday he was buried here. At one time I thought of transporting him and of telegraphing for you; but I reconsidered it. It is no use chafing the wound. I am sorry for you that the news will have reached you when out hunting, amid distractions, and will not grip you as it does us. It is good for one. I now feel what I have often been told, that when one loses someone who was what he was to us, it becomes much easier to think of one's own death.

On 13th October 1860 he notes in his Diary:

It is nearly a month since Nicholas died. That event has torn me terribly from life. Again the question: Why? Already the departure draws near. Whither? Nowhere! I try to write, I force myself but do not get on because I cannot attach enough importance to the work to supply the necessary strength and patience. At the very time of the funeral the thought occurred to me of writing a materialist Gospel, a Life of Christ as a materialist.

One sees how one after another the seeds of the work Tolstoy was to do in later years planted themselves in his mind. In early childhood came the enthusiasm for the Ant-Brotherhood, and the influence of his brother, of Aunt Tatiána, and of the pilgrims; then an acquaintance with the writings of Voltaire and other sceptics, undermining belief in the miraculous; then, at Sevastopol, the idea of 'founding a new religion:

Christianity purged of dogmas and mysticism'; then a study of Luther's Reformation, and now the idea of a rationalist life of Christ.

On 17th October he writes to Fet:

I think you already know what has happened. On 20th September he died, literally in my arms. Nothing in my life has so impressed me. It is true, as he said, that nothing is worse than death. And when one reflects well that *that* is the end of all, then there is nothing worse than life. Why strive or try, since of what was Nicholas Tolstoy nothing remains his? He did not say that he felt the approach of death, but I know he watched each step of its approach and knew with certainty how much remained. Some moments before his death he drowsed off, but awoke suddenly and whispered with horror: 'What is that?' That was when he saw it – the absorption of himself into Nothingness. And if he found nothing to cling to, what can I find? Still less! And assuredly neither I nor anyone will fight it to the last moment as he did. Two days before, I said to him: 'We ought to put a commode in your room.'

'No,' said he, 'I am weak, but not yet as weak as that; I will struggle on yet awhile.'

To the last he did not yield but did everything for himself, and always tried to be occupied. He wrote, questioned me about my writings, and advised me. But it seemed to me that he did all this not from any inner impulse but on principle. One thing – his love of Nature – remained to the last. The day before, he went into his bedroom and from weakness fell on his bed by the open window. I came to him, and he said with tears in his eyes, 'How I have enjoyed this whole hour.'

From earth we come and to earth we go. One thing is left – a dim hope that there, in Nature, of which we become part in the earth, something will remain and will be found.

All who knew and saw his last moments say: 'How wonderfully calmly, peacefully, he died'; but I know with what terrible pain, for not one feeling of his escaped me.

A thousand times I say to myself: 'Let the dead bury their dead.' One must make some use of the strength which remains to one, but one cannot persuade a stone to fall upwards instead of downwards whither it is drawn. One cannot laugh at a joke one is weary of. One cannot eat when one does not want to. And what is life all for, when tomorrow the torments of death will begin, with all the abomination of falsehood and self-deception, and will end in annihilation for one-self?. An amusing thing! Be useful, be beneficent, be happy while life lasts – say people to one another; but you, and happiness, and virtue, and utility, consist of truth. And the truth I have learned in thirty-two years is that the position in which we are placed is terrible. 'Take life as it is; you have put yourself in that position.' How? I take life as it is. As soon as man reaches the highest degree of development, he sees clearly that it is all nonsense and deception, and that the truth – which he still loves better than all else – is terrible. That when you look at it well and clearly you wake with a start and say with terror, as my brother did: 'What is that?'

Of course so long as the desire to know and speak the truth lasts, one tries to know and speak. That alone remains to me of the moral world; higher than that I cannot place myself. That alone I will do, but not in the form of your art. Art is a lie and I can no longer love a beautiful lie.

I shall remain here for the winter because I am here and it is all the same where one lives. Please write to me. I love you as my brother loved you, and he remembered you to his last moment.

A month later we find him writing in a different state of mind:

A boy of thirteen has died in torment from consumption. What for? The only explanation is given by faith in the compensation of a future life. If that does not exist there is no justice, and justice is vain and the demand for justice – a superstition.

The next day he writes:

Justice forms the most essential demand of man from man. And man looks for the same in his relation to the universe. Without a future life it is lacking. Adaptability to its purpose is the sole, the unalterable, law of Nature say the naturalists. But in the best manifestations of man's soul: love and poetry – it is absent. This has all existed and has died, often without expressing itself. Nature far o'erstepped her aim when she gave man a need of poetry and love, if adaptability to purpose be her sole law.

Nearly twenty years later, in his *Confession*, Tolstoy referred to his brother's death in the words:

Another event which showed me that the superstitious belief in pro-gress is insufficient as a guide to life, was my brother's death. Wise, good, serious, he fell ill while still a young man, suffered for more than a year, and died painfully, not understanding why he had lived and still less why he had to die. No theories could give me, or him, any reply to these questions during his slow and painful dying.

Anyone who has read the works Tolstoy wrote during the quarter of a century that succeeded his brother's death knows how long he remained in doubt on this question of a future life, and how he expressed now one and now another view.

At Hyères he continued to study the problems of education, and for that purpose made many visits to Marseilles. He also wrote; continuing *The Cossacks* and beginning an article on Popular Education. We get a glimpse of him at this period from his sister, who tells us that they had been invited to an At Home at Prince Dundukóv-Korsákov's, but Tolstoy, who was to have been the lion of the occasion, failed to put in an appearance. The company, which included all the 'best' people, were getting dull despite the hostess's efforts for their amusement, when at last, very late, Count Tolstoy was announced. The hostess and her guests immediately brightened up, but what was their astonishment to see him appear in tourist garb and wearing wooden *sabots*! He had been for a long walk, and returning late had come to the party without going to his lodgings; and no sooner was he in the room than he began assuring everybody that wooden *sabots* were the very best and most comfortable of foot-gear, and advising everyone to adopt them. Even in those days he was a man to whom all things were permitted, and the evening instead of being spoilt became all the gayer from his eccentricity. There was a great deal of singing, and it fell to his lot to play the accompaniments.

At Hyères after his brother's death Tolstoy lived with his sister and her three children in a *pension* where the only other lodgers were a Madame Pláksin and her delicate nine-year-old son Sergéy, whose lungs were thought to be affected but who lived to become a poet and to publish his recollections of Tolstoy. Pláksin describes him as having been at that time a strongly-built, broad-shouldered man, with a good-natured smile on his face which was fringed by a thick, dark-brown beard. Under a large forehead still bearing a deep scar from the wound inflicted by the bear two years before, wise, kind eyes shone out of very deep sockets. 'Tolstoy,' says Pláksin, 'was the soul of our little society and I never saw him dull; on the contrary he liked to amuse us with his stories, which were sometimes extremely fantastic.' Tolstoy rose early, and while he was at work the children were not allowed to disturb him beyond running in for a moment to say 'good-morning'. Being himself an indefatigable walker he used to plan out excursions for the company, constantly discovering new places to visit: the salterns on the peninsula of Porquerolle, the holy hill where the chapel with the wonder-working image of the Madonna stands, or the ruins of the castle called *Trou des Fées*. On these excursions they used to have with them a small ass carrying provisions, fruit, and wine.

> Tolstoy used to tell us various tales on the way. I remember one about a golden horse and a giant tree from the top of which all seas and all towns were visible. Knowing that my lungs were delicate, he often took me on his shoulder and continued his tale as he walked along. Need I say that we would have laid down our lives for him?

At dinner-time Tolstoy used to tell the French proprietors of the *pension* the strangest stories about Russia, which they never knew whether or not to believe till the Countess, or Madame Pláksina, came to their rescue by separating the truth from the fiction.

After dinner, either on the terrace or indoors, a performance commenced, opera or ballet, to the sound of the piano: the children 'mercilessly tormenting the ears of the audience' (which consisted of the two ladies, Tolstoy, and the Pláksins' nurse). Next came gymnastic exercises in which Tolstoy acted as professor. 'He would lie at full length on the floor making us do the same, and we had then to get up without using our hands.' He also contrived an apparatus out of rope, which he fixed up in the doorway; and on this he performed somersaults to the great delight of his juvenile audience.

When the latter became too turbulent and the ladies begged Tolstoy to subdue the noise, he would set the children round the table and tell them to bring pens and ink.

The following is an example of the sort of occupation he provided.

> 'Listen,' said he one day; 'I am going to give you a lesson.'
>   'What on?' demanded bright-eyed Lisa.
>   Disregarding his niece's question, he continued: 'Write . . .'
>   'But what are we to write, uncle?' persisted Lisa.

'Listen; I will give you a theme . . . !'

'What will you give us?'

'A theme!' firmly replied Tolstoy. 'In what respect does Russia differ from other countries? Write it here in my presence and don't copy from one another! Do you hear?' added he impressively.

In half an hour the 'compositions' were ready. Pláksin had to read his own as his lines were so irregular that no one else could decipher them. In his opinion Russia differed from other countries in that, at carnival time, Russians eat pancakes and slide down ice-hills and at Easter they colour eggs.

'Bravo!' said Tolstoy, and proceeded to make out Kólya's manuscript, in which Russia was distinguished by its snow, and Lisa's, in which 'troikas' (three-horse conveyances) played the chief part.

In reward for these evening exercises Tolstoy brought water-colour paints from Marseilles and taught the children drawing.

He often spent nearly the whole day with the children, teaching them, taking part in their games, and intervening in their disputes, which he analysed, proving to them who was in the right and who in the wrong.

There was at this time some mutual attraction between him and a young Russian lady, Miss Yákovleva, who was staying at Hyères, but like many other similar affairs it came to nothing.

On leaving Hyères, Tolstoy, his sister, and her children went to Geneva, and from thence he proceeded alone to Nice, Leghorn, Florence, Rome, and Naples. In Italy he says he experienced his first lively impression of antiquity, but little record remains of this journey and it is nowhere reflected in his writings.

He returned to Paris *via* Marseilles, the schools and other institutions of which he closely observed, trying to discover how man's intelligence is really best developed.

He was very unfavourably impressed by the popular schools there. The studies, he says, consisted in learning by heart the Catechism, sacred and general History, the four rules of Arithmetic, French spelling and Bookkeeping – the latter without sufficient comprehension of the use of arithmetic to enable the children to deal sensibly with the simplest practical problems requiring addition and subtraction, though they could do long multiplication sums quickly and well when only abstract figures were given. Similarly they answered questions in French

History well by rote, but when questions were asked out of their regular order they would give such answers as that Henry IV was killed by Julius Caesar.

He observed the instruction given by the Churches, and visited the adult schools of the town as well as its *Salles d'Asile*, in which, he says:

I saw four-year-old children perform, like soldiers, revolutions round benches to orders given by whistle, and raise and cross their arms to the word of command and sing hymns of praise to God and their benefactors with strange trembling voices, and I became convinced that the educational establishments of Marseilles were extremely bad.

Anyone seeing them would naturally conclude that the French people must be ignorant, coarse, hypocritical, full of superstition, and almost savage.

Yet one need only come in contact with, and chat with, any of the common people to convince oneself that on the contrary the French people are almost what they consider themselves to be: intelligent, clever, sociable, freethinking, and really civilised. Take a workman of say thirty years of age: he will write a letter without mistakes such as he made at school, sometimes even quite correctly; he has some idea of politics and therefore of recent history and geography; he knows some history from novels, knows something of natural history, and he very often draws and is able to apply mathematical formulae to his trade. Where did he get all this?

In Marseilles I recently discovered the answer by wandering about the streets, drink-shops, *cafés chantants*, museums, workshops, wharves, and bookstalls. The very boy who told me that Henry IV was killed by Julius Caesar, knew the history of *The Three Musketeers* and of *Monte Cristo* very well.

In Marseilles Tolstoy found that everybody had read Dumas's works, of which there were twenty-eight cheap editions. He estimates that every week in the *cafés chantants* at least one-fifth of the population received oral education as the Greeks and Romans used to do. Comedies and sketches were performed, verses declaimed, and for good or evil the influence of this unconscious education far outweighed that of the compulsory education given in the schools.

In January [1861] he reached Paris, where he spent a large part of his time in omnibuses, amusing himself by observing the people. He declares he never met a passenger who was not represented in one or other of Paul de Kock's stories. Of that writer, as of Dumas *père*, he thought highly. 'Don't talk nonsense to me,' he once said, 'about Paul de Kock's immorality. He is according to English ideas somewhat improper. He is more or less what the French call *leste* and *gaulois*, but never immoral. In everything he says, and despite his rather free jests, his tendency is quite moral. He is a French Dickens . . . As to Dumas, every novelist should know him by heart. His plots are admirable not to mention the workmanship. I can read and reread him, though he aims chiefly at plots and intrigue.'

In Paris he again met Turgénev, and from France he went on to London, where he remained six weeks, not enjoying his visit much as he suffered severely from toothache nearly all the time. It is characteristic of Tolstoy that, though he was often a victim to toothache and was also much tried by bad digestion, he very seldom appears to have had his teeth attended to by a dentist. A dentist's establishment seemed to him so unnatural and artificial that it must be wrong. Moreover, dentists do not always do their work well, and toothache – if one endures it long enough – cures itself, and in the past the majority of mankind has got along without dentists. So he was inclined to put up with toothache as one of the ills it is best to bear patiently.

During his stay he and Turgénev, who had also come to London, saw a great deal of Alexander Herzen, who was then editing *Kólokol* (*The Bell*) – the most influential paper ever published by a Russian exile.

One of Herzen's closest friends and co-workers during his long exile from Russia, was the poet N. P. Ogarëv, who had been his fellow-student at the Moscow University. Ogarëv, besides being a man of ability possessed an amiable character that much endeared him to his friends; but in an essay entitled *The First Step* written in 1892, we get a glimpse of what alienated Tolstoy's sympathy from the progressive movement these men represented. He there says:

I have just been reading the letters of one of our highly educated and advanced men of the 1840s, the exile Ogarëv, to another yet more highly educated and gifted man, Herzen. In these letters Ogarëv gives expression to his sincere thoughts and highest aspirations and one cannot fail to see that – as was natural in a young man – he rather shows off before his friend. He talks of self-perfecting, of sacred friendship, love, the service of science, of humanity, and the like. And at the same time he calmly writes that he often irritates the companion of his life by, as he expresses it, 'returning home in an unsober state, or disappearing for many hours with a fallen but dear creature' . . .

Thus it was half a century ago. I was contemporary with such men. I knew Ogarëv and Herzen themselves and others of that stamp, and men educated in the same traditions. There was a remarkable absence of consistency in the lives of all these men. Together with a sincere and ardent desire for good, there was an utter looseness of personal desire, which they thought could not hinder the living of a good life nor the performance of good and even great deeds. They put unkneaded loaves into a cold oven and believed that bread would be baked. And then when with advancing years they began to remark that the bread did not bake – i.e. that no good came of their lives – they saw in this something peculiarly tragic.

Of Herzen as a writer Tolstoy ultimately formed a high opinion and admitted that he exerted a very considerable influence on the mind of educated Russians.

In England, as elsewhere, Tolstoy saw what he could of the educational methods in vogue. He also visited the House of Commons and heard Palmerston speak for three hours; but he told me he could form no opinion of the oration, for 'at that time I knew English with my eyes but not with my ears'.

While in London he received news that he had been nominated Arbiter of the Peace for his own district, near Túla. The duties of the office were to settle disputes between the serfs and their former proprietors. Except for a short period of service on the Zémstvo in 1874, this was the only official position Tolstoy ever held after leaving the army.

On 3rd March 1861 (new style), the day of Alexander II's famous Manifesto emancipating the serfs, Tolstoy left London for Russia *via* Brussels. In that city he made the acquaintance of Proudhon (the author of *What is Property?*), to whom Herzen had given him a letter of introduction. Proudhon impressed Tolstoy as a strong man who had the courage of his opinions, and though Proudhon's theories had no immediate effect on Tolstoy's life, the social, political, and economic views Tolstoy expounded a quarter of a century later were deeply dyed with Proudhonism. Another writer whose acquaintance he made in Brussels was the Polish patriot Lelewel, who had taken part in the rebellion of 1830 and was at this time a decrepit old man living in great poverty. While in Brussels Tolstoy was writing *Polikúshka* which, like *A Landlord's Morning*, implies disapproval of serfdom.

Passing through Germany he stopped at Weimar, and visited the Grand Duke Carl Alexander. Tolstoy had been reading Goethe's *Reineke Fuchs* not long before, and now visited the house in which Goethe had lived, but was more interested in a Kindergarten conducted by Minna Schelholm, who had been trained by Froebel.

At Jena he became acquainted with a young mathematician named Keller, whom he engaged to accompany him to Yásnaya to help him in his educational activities. He also stopped at Dresden, where he again visited Auerbach, concerning whom he jots down in his Diary:

21st April, Dresden: Auerbach is a most charming man. Has given me a light . . . He spoke of Christianity as the spirit of humanity than which there is nothing higher. He reads verse enchantingly. Of Music as *Pflichtloser Genuss* (dutyless pleasure) . . . He is 49 years old. Straightforward, youthful, believing, not troubled by negation.

From Dresden he wrote to his Aunt Tatiána that he intended to return to Yásnaya *via* St Petersburg as he wanted to obtain permission to publish an educational magazine he was projecting.

On 22nd April 1861 he was already in Berlin, where he made the acquaintance of the head of the Teachers' Seminary, the son of the celebrated pedagogue Diesterweg, whom, to his disappointment, he found to be 'a cold, soulless pedant who thinks he can develop and guide souls of children by rules and regulations'.

On 23rd April (old style) he re-entered Russia after spending nearly ten months abroad.

He brought with him complete editions of the works of several of the greatest European writers. They were kept at the Custom House to be submitted to the Censor, and, as Tolstoy plaintively remarked nearly half a century later, 'he is still reading them'!

Among books and authors, from the time of his first to his second return from Western Europe, he read Charlotte Brontë, Homer, whom he admired more and more, the Gospels, Shakespeare: *Antony and Cleopatra* and *Midsummer Night's Dream*, Sainte-Beuve, Montluc's *Commentaires* ('a gallant Gascon'), Macaulay (whose *History* was 'too cold for me'), Montégut, Emerson, Octave Feuillet ('an immense talent'), Rabelais, Auerbach, Bacon, Richl's *Kulturgeschichte*, which he did not like, *Adam Bede* ('very tragic, though not true and full of a single idea. That is not so with me'), Michelet's *l'Oiseau* and *l'Insecte* ('mawkish and false'), *Don Quixote*, Wiseman on Popes Leo VII and Pius VIII, and an essay of Mérimée on English art. He 'tried to read Hackländer, horrid, *mal fait* and talentless'. He notes, 'Montaigne was the first clearly to express the idea of freedom in education. Again in education equality and freedom is the chief thing.' He also read *The Athenaeum* and the *Revue des Deux Mondes*.

Of Russian writers one finds him reading Turgénev ('Ásya is rubbish'), Saltikóv ('a robust talent'), and the poets Koslóv ('a delightful and immense power'), Fet, and Tyúchev. Of Katkóv, a famous publicist and editor, Tolstoy notes: 'Katkóv's limitations are such that he just suits the public,' a remark applicable not to Katkóv alone among editors.

His Diary of this period consists largely of disjointed jotting of matters he wished to recollect, but among them one comes on interesting reflections, comments, or records, such as these:

Mme Kiréeva [afterwards Olga Novikóv] is an extraordinary and peculiar fool, which results from her having been considered clever as long as she was pretty. There is a whole set of such women.

On 1st January 1859 he notes: 'I must get married this year, or never.'
He much admired a young Princess Lvóv, and after a trip to Moscow where he abandoned as puerile a project that had attracted him, he notes:

9th October 1859: Visited the Lvóvs. The recollection of that visit makes me howl. I decided that it should be the last attempt I would make to get married, but that too is a puerility.

After a discussion with Chichérin he notes:

Christ did not impose, but revealed, the moral law which for ever remains the standard of good and evil.

7

At Yásnaya again. Turgénev. Arbiter. Magazine

After the winter's snow has so far thawed that sleighing is
impracticable, there comes a time when there is still too much snow
and the roads are too soft to allow of travelling on wheels, and transit is
practically impossible, Tolstoy reached Moscow at this period of the
year, but had not to wait long before the roads dried sufficiently to
become passable. He made the journey southward to Túla in company
with Mme Fet, wife of his friend the poet. She was travelling in her own
carriage, accompanied by her maid, to the estate Fet had purchased at
some distance from Yásnaya. Tolstoy had his own conveyance, but for
company's sake changed places with the maid and travelled with Mme
Fet. In the cool of the evening he borrowed, and wrapped himself in, a
cloak of Fet's, declaring that this would certainly result in his producing
a lyric poem.

· After reaching Yásnaya he wrote, in the third week of May 1861, to
congratulate Fet on having become a landed proprietor:

How long it is since we met, and how much has happened to both of
us meanwhile! I do not know how to rejoice sufficiently when I hear
or think of your activity as a farmer, and I am rather proud to have
had at least some hand in the matter . . . It is good to have a friend,
but he may die or go away or one may not be able to keep pace with
him, but Nature to which one is wedded by a Notarial Deed or to
which one has been born by inheritance, is still better. It is one's own
bit of Nature. She is cold, obdurate, disdainful and exacting, but then
she is a friend one does not lose till death, and even then one will be
absorbed into her. I am however at present less devoted to this friend,
I have other affairs that attract me, yet but for the consciousness that
she is there and that if I stumble she is at hand to hold on to – life
would be but a sad business.

A few days later having received an invitation from Turgénev, Tolstoy
paid him a visit, the first hours of which passed off to their mutual

satisfaction. Turgénev had just finished his favourite novel, *Fathers and Sons*, and after dinner Tolstoy was to read it and give his opinion upon it. To do this more comfortably Tolstoy, left alone in the drawing-room, lay down on a large sofa. He began to read, but the story seemed to him so artificially constructed and so unimportant in its subject-matter, that he fell fast asleep.

'I awoke,' he narrates, 'with a strange sensation, and when I opened my eyes I saw Turgénev's back just disappearing.'

In spite of this occurrence and the unpleasant feeling it produced, the two novelists set out next morning to visit Fet, who was not expecting them that day.

While the visitors rested for a couple of hours recovering from the fatigue of their journey, Mme Fet saw to it that the dinner assumed 'a more substantial and inviting appearance'. During the meal the whole party began an animated conversation and Turgénev, always fond of good eating, fully appreciated the efforts Fet's excellent male-cook had made. Champagne flowed as was usual at such reunions. After dinner the three friends strolled to a wood a couple of hundred yards from the house, and lying down in the high grass at its outskirts continued their talk with yet more freedom and animation.

Next morning at the usual breakfast time, about eight o'clock, the visitors entered the room where Mme Fet presided at the samovar. Fet sat at the opposite end of the table, Turgénev at the hostess's right hand, and Tolstoy at her left. Knowing the importance Turgénev attached to the education of his natural daughter, who was being brought up in France, Mme Fet enquired whether he was satisfied with her English governess. Turgénev praised the latter highly and mentioned that, with English exactitude, she had requested him to fix the sum his daughter might give in charity. 'And now,' added Turgénev, 'she requires my daughter to take in hand and mend the tattered clothes of the poor.'

To Tolstoy the foreign education Turgénev was giving his daughter, who was quite forgetting her own language, was very distasteful, and this feeling no doubt showed itself in his question: 'And you consider that good?'

'Certainly: it places the doer of charity in touch with everyday needs.'

'And I consider that a well-dressed girl with dirty ill-smelling rags on her lap is acting an insincere, theatrical farce.'

'I beg you not to say that!' exclaimed Turgénev, with dilated nostrils.

'Why should I not say what I am convinced is true?' replied Tolstoy.

'Then you consider that I educate my daughter badly?'

Tolstoy replied that his thought corresponded to his speech.

Before Fet could interpose, Turgénev, white with rage, exclaimed: 'If you speak in that way I will punch your head!' and, jumping up from the table and seizing his head in his hands, rushed into the next room. A second later he returned and, addressing Mme Fet, said: 'For heaven's sake excuse my improper conduct which I deeply regret!' and again left the room.

Fet, realising the impossibility of keeping his visitors together after what had happened, was perplexed what to do, for they had both arrived in Turgénev's vehicle and Fet, newly established in the country, though he had horses, had none broken in to drive in the only conveyance he possessed. To get Turgénev off was easy, but it was not without some difficulty and even danger from the restive horses, that Tolstoy was conveyed to the nearest post-station where a hired conveyance was procurable.

From Novosëlki, the first country house Tolstoy reached, he wrote Turgénev a letter demanding an apology, and asked for an answer to be sent to the next post-house at Bogusl[á]v. Turgénev, not noticing this request, sent his reply to Fet's house, so that it was several hours late in reaching Tolstoy – who was so enraged by this (as it seemed to him) fresh act of discourtesy, that from Bogusl[á]v he sent a messenger to procure pistols, and wrote a second letter challenging Turgénev and stating that he did not wish to fight in a merely formal manner, like literary men who finish up with champagne, but was in earnest, and hoped Turgénev would meet him with pistols at the outskirt of the Boguslév woods.

That night was a sleepless one for Tolstoy. The morning brought Turgénev's reply to his first letter; it commenced in the formal manner of polite communications:

Gracious sir, Leo Nikoláevich – In reply to your letter I can only repeat, what I myself considered it my duty to announce to you at Fet's, namely, that carried away by a feeling of involuntary enmity the causes of which need not here be considered, I insulted you without any definite provocation and I asked your pardon. What happened this morning proved clearly that attempts at intimacy between such opposite natures as yours and mine can lead to no good results; and I the more readily fulfil my duty to you because the present letter probably terminates our relations with one another. I heartily hope it may satisfy you, and I consent in advance to your making what use you please of it.

With perfect respect, I have the honour to remain, Gracious Sir, your most humble servant.

Iv. Turgénev
Spásski, 27th May 1861

P.S. 10.30 p.m.
Iván Petróvich has just brought back my letter, which my servant stupidly sent to Novosëlki instead of to Boguslav. I humbly beg you to excuse this accidental and regrettable mistake and I hope my messenger will still find you at Boguslav.

Tolstoy thereupon wrote to Fet:

I could not resist opening another letter from Mr Turgénev in reply to mine. I wish you well of your relations with that man, but I despise him. I have written to him, and therewith have terminated all relations, except that I hold myself ready to give him any satisfaction he may desire. Notwithstanding all my apparent tranquillity I was disturbed in spirit and felt I must demand a more explicit apology from Mr Turgénev; I did this in my letter from Novosëlki. Here is his answer, which I accept as satisfactory, merely informing him that my reason for excusing him is not the opposition of our natures but one he may himself surmise.

In consequence of the delay that occurred, besides this I sent another letter, harsh enough and containing a challenge, to which I have not received any reply, but should I receive one I shall return it unopened. So there is an end of this sad story, which if it goes beyond your house should do so with this addendum.

Turgénev's reply to the challenge came to hand later and ran as follows:

Your servant says you desire a reply to your letter, but I do not see what I can add to what I have already written, unless it be that I admit your right to demand satisfaction weapons in hand. You have preferred to accept my spoken and repeated apology. That was as you pleased. I will say without phrases that I would willingly stand your fire in order to efface my truly insane words. That I should have uttered them is so unlike the habits of my whole life that I can only attribute my action to irritability evoked by the extreme and constant antagonism of our views. This is not an apology – I mean to say, not a justification – but an explanation. And therefore at parting from you for ever – for such occurrences are indelible and irrevocable – I consider it my duty to repeat once again that in this affair you were in the right and I in the wrong. I add that what is here in question is not the courage I wish or do not wish to show, but an acknowledgement of your right to call me out to fight, in the accepted manner of course (with seconds), as well as your right to pardon me. You have chosen as you pleased, and I have only to submit to your decision. I renew my assurance of my entire respect,

Iv. Turgénev

The quarrel was not however destined to die out so quickly. Even good-natured Fet got into trouble by trying to reconcile the irascible novelists. Here is one of the notes he received from Tolstoy:

I request you not to write to me again, as I shall return your letters, as well as Turgénev's, unopened.

Fet remarks: 'So all my attempts to put the matter right ended in a formal rupture of my relations with Tolstoy, and now I cannot even remember how friendly intercourse between us was renewed.'

Before four months had passed, Tolstoy repented of his quarrel. Like Prince Nekhlúdov in *Resurrection*, he used from time to time to repent of all his sins and quarrels, and undertook a sort of spring – or autumn-cleaning of his soul. It was at such a moment that, on 25th September, he wrote to Turgénev expressing regret that their relations to one another were hostile, and he added: 'If I have insulted you, forgive me; I find it unendurably hard to think I have an enemy.' Not knowing Turgénev's address in France, he sent this letter to a bookseller in Petersburg (with whom he knew Turgénev corresponded) to be forwarded. The letter took more than three months to reach its destination, nor was this the only thing that went wrong, as is shown by the following portion of a letter, dated 8th November, from Turgénev to Fet:

Apropos, 'one more last remark' about the unfortunate affair with Tolstoy. Passing through Petersburg I learned from certain 'reliable people' (Oh, those reliable people!) that copies of Tolstoy's last letter to me (the letter in which he 'despises' me) are circulating in Moscow and are said to have been distributed by Tolstoy himself. That enraged me, and I sent him a challenge to fight when I returned to Russia. Tolstoy has answered that the circulation of the copies is pure invention, and he encloses another letter in which, recapitulating that, and how, I insulted him, he asks my forgiveness and declines my challenge. Of course the matter must end there, and I will only ask you to tell him (for he writes that he will consider any fresh communication from me to him an insult) that I myself repudiate any duel, &c., and hope the whole matter is buried for ever. His letter (apologising) I have destroyed. Another letter which he says he sent me through the bookseller Davídov I never received: And now as to the whole matter – *de profundis*.

Tolstoy had noted in his Diary one day in October:

Yesterday I received a letter from Turgénev in which he accuses me of saying he is a coward and of circulating copies of my letter. I have written him that it is nonsense, and I have also sent him a letter: 'You call my action dishonourable and you formerly wished to punch my head; but I consider myself guilty, ask pardon, and refuse the challenge.'

Even then the matter was not at an end, for on 7th January [new style?] [1862] Turgénev writes to Fet:

And now a plain question: Have you seen Tolstoy? I have only today received the letter he sent me in September through Davídov's bookshop (how accurate are our Russian merchants!). In this letter he speaks of his intention to insult me, and apologises, &c. And almost at that very time, in consequence of some gossip about which I think I wrote you, I sent him a challenge. From all this one must conclude that our constellations move through space in definitely hostile conjunction and that therefore we had better, as he himself says, avoid meeting. But you may write or tell him (if you see him) that I (without phrase or joke) *from afar* love him very much, respect him, and watch his fate with sympathetic interest, but that in proximity all takes a different turn. What's to be done? We must live as though we inhabited different planets or different centuries.

Tolstoy evidently took umbrage at Turgénev's message, and visited his wrath on Fet's innocent head. To be profoundly humble and forgiving at his own command was always, it seems, easier for Tolstoy than to allow his opponent to have an opinion of his own. Tolstoy liked things to be quite clear-cut and definite and it complicates matters to have to reckon with someone else's views. At any rate Turgénev writes:

> *Paris. 14th January* [o.s.?] *1862*
>
> DEAREST AFANÁSY AFANÁSYEVICH [Fet's Christian name and patronymic] – First of all I must ask your pardon for the quite unexpected tile (*tuile*, as the French say) that tumbled on your head as a result of my letter. The one thing which somewhat consoles me is that I could not possibly have expected such a freak on Tolstoy's part, and thought I was arranging all for the best. It seems it is a wound of a kind better not touched at all.

To judge the relations between these two great writers fairly, one must remember that Turgénev was ten years the elder and until *War and Peace* appeared ranked higher in popular esteem; yet Tolstoy showed him no deference, but on the contrary often attacked him and his views with mordant irony. Turgénev was neither ill-natured nor quarrelsome. If Tolstoy had treated him with consideration, or had been willing to let him alone, there would have been no question either of insult or of challenge. But the younger man sought the elder's company and then made himself disagreeable; and this not of malice prepense but because it was his nature to demand perfection from great men and vehemently to attack those who failed to reach the high standard he set up. This was no doubt all the more trying to Turgénev because Tolstoy neither co-operated warmly with the Liberal movement then current, nor was himself much more abstemious with regard to food, wine, women, or cards, than others of the set whom he scolded; or if he were, was so intermittently and with such serious lapses as to be little entitled to condemn others with the fervour he often displayed. On the occasion of the great quarrel Turgénev was certainly the aggressor, and his prompt apology was not addressed to Tolstoy whom he had chiefly offended but to Mme Fet. It is however plain that he acted, as he said, on an irritable and momentary impulse. Tolstoy aggravated matters by sending a challenge before receiving a reply to his first letter, and also by suggesting that he despised Turgénev and pardoned him for reasons 'he may himself surmise'. Again, in relation to Fet, who merely wished to pour oil on the troubled waters, Tolstoy showed a strange irritability. No one however can read the *Recollections*

Fet wrote thirty years later without seeing that he – who not only witnessed this affair, but had been the confidant of both writers for years – respected Tolstoy far more than he respected Turgénev.

In this whole story one may detect traces of the qualities which made Tolstoy so interesting and so perplexing a personality. He cared intensely about everything with which he was occupied. Turgénev and Turgénev's opinions and conduct were of tremendous importance to him. So were his own views of how young ladies should be brought up. So was the question whether he ought to challenge his enemy; and later on the question whether he ought to forgive him, and whether Fet should be allowed to act as mediator. It is this fact – that he cared about things a hundred times more than other people care about them – that made Tolstoy a genius and a great writer. What was admirable in his conduct was not that he acted well (he often acted very badly) but that he ardently *wished* to act well.

The same spirit that made him so intolerant with Turgénev – his strong feeling that To whom much is given, of him much shall be required' – had something to do later in life with his fierce attacks on Governments, on Shakespeare, on Wagner, and on other great institutions and men. At the same time the incident throws light on that side of Tolstoy's character which brought it about that, despite the very real charm he possessed and the fact that many men and women Were immensely attracted by his writings, he had few intimate friends and was constantly misunderstood.

V. P. Bótkin, who was in touch both with Tolstoy and Turgénev, wrote to Fet after hearing of the quarrel:

The scene between him [Turgénev] and Tolstoy at your house produced on me a sad impression. But do you know I believe that in reality Tolstoy has a passionately loving soul; only he wants to love Turgénev ardently, and unfortunately his impulsive feeling encounters merely mild, good-natured indifference. That is what he cannot reconcile himself to. And then (again unfortunately) his mind is in a chaos; by which I mean that it has hot yet reached any definite outlook on life and the world's affairs. That is why his conviction changes so often and why he is so apt to run to extremes. His soul burns with unquenchable thirst; I say 'unquenchable' because what satisfied it yesterday is today disintegrated by his analysis. But that analysis has no durable and firm reagents and consequently its results evaporate *ins blaue hinein*. Without some firm ground under one's feet it is impossible to write. And that is why at present he *cannot* write, and this will continue to be the case until his soul finds something on which it can rest.

To anyone acquainted with the history of Russia at that period but not acquainted with Tolstoy's idiosyncrasies it must indeed seem strange that the story of his life can be told with so little reference to the Reform movement of the years 1860–4. Two passages written by him to Birukóv in 1904, at the time of the Revolutionary agitation during the war with Japan, state his relation to such movements with characteristic sincerity.

As to my attitude at that time [the 1860s] to the excited condition of our whole society, I must say (and this is a good and bad trait characteristic of me) that I always involuntarily opposed any external, epidemic pressure, and that if I was excited and happy at that time it proceeded from my own personal, inner motives: those which drew me to my school work and into touch with the peasants.

I now recognise in myself the same feeling of resistance to the excitement at present prevailing, which resembles what in more timid form was then current.

Tolstoy's tendency to underrate the influence of the Liberal reformers of the 1860s may be illustrated by an incident that occurred at a dinner in Túla [1861]. The local elections had taken place, and a public banquet was given in honour of those Arbiters of the Peace who were visiting the town. Tolstoy was at this dinner, and when the toast to the health of Alexander II, the 'Tsar-Liberator', was proposed, remarked to his neighbour: 'I drink this toast with particular pleasure. No others are needed, for in reality we owe the Emancipation to the Emperor alone.'

A yet more curious instance of the same tendency occurs in an article on *Progress and the Definition of Education*, which he published a year later, and in which, arguing that printing has been of little use to the people, he says that:

Even taking as an example the abolition of serfdom, I do not see that printing helped the solution of the problem in a progressive sense. Had the Government not uttered its decisive word in that affair, the press would beyond doubt have explained matters in quite a different way to what it did. We saw that most of the periodicals would have demanded the emancipation of the peasants without any land, and would have produced arguments apparently just as reasonable, witty, and sarcastic [as were produced in favour of the more Liberal solution actually adopted] . . .

If however Tolstoy did not stand in the ranks of the Reformers he was much less partisan to his own class than many of his fellow-nobles desired; and we find the Marshal of the Nobility of Túla writing to Valúev, Minister of Home Affairs, complaining of Tolstoy's appointment as Arbiter of the Peace on the ground that he was disliked by the neighbouring landowners. In consequence of this complaint Valúev made enquiries, and received a 'confidential' reply from the Governor of the Province which said:

> Knowing Count Tolstoy personally as an educated man warmly sympathising with the matter in hand, and in view of a wish expressed to me by some of the proprietors of the district that he should be appointed Arbiter, I cannot replace him by someone I do not know.

Tolstoy tried his best to act fairly between peasants and landowners, but his unsuitability for duties involving methodical care was obvious from the start.

The very first 'charter' regulating relations between a landlord and his newly liberated peasants that he sent up to the Government Board for Peasant Affairs was signed as follows: 'At the request of such-and-such peasants, because of their illiteracy, the house-serf so-and-so has signed this charter for them.' Not a single name did the charter contain! As Tolstoy had dictated the words so his servant had written them down, and the charter had been sealed and sent off without being read over.

He could at times be wonderfully patient in dealing with the peasants though they were exasperatingly pertinacious in demanding more than it was possible to grant. An eyewitness tells how Tolstoy visited a neighbouring estate on which differences had arisen as to the land to be allotted to the peasants. He received a deputation consisting of three of the leading peasants of the village, and asked them: 'Well, lads, what do you want?'

They explained what land they wished to have, and Tolstoy replied, 'I am very sorry I can't do what you want. Were I to do so I should cause your landlord a great loss'; and he proceeded to explain to them how the matter stood.

'But you'll manage it for us somehow, *bátushka*' [literally 'little father'], said the peasants.

'No, I can't do anything of the kind,' repeated Tolstoy.

The peasants glanced at one another, scratched their heads, and reiterated their 'But somehow, *bátushka*!' and one of them added, 'If only you want to, *bátushka*, you'll know how to find a way to do it!' at which the other peasants nodded their heads approvingly.

Tolstoy crossed himself, as orthodox Russians are wont to do, and said: 'As God is holy, I swear that I can be of no use at all to you.' But still the peasants repeated: 'You'll take pity on us and do it somehow, *bátushka*!'

Tolstoy at last turned vehemently to the steward who was present, and said: 'One can sooner, like Amphion, move the hills and woods than convince peasants of anything!'

The whole conversation, says the steward, lasted more than an hour, and up to the last minute the Count retained his patient and friendly manner towards the peasants. Their obstinacy did not provoke him to utter a single harsh word.

With the landowners Tolstoy had even more trouble than with the peasants. He received many threatening letters, plans were formed to have him beaten, he was to have been challenged to a duel, and denunciations of him were sent to the authorities.

After some three months of the work, in July 1861, he jotted down in his Diary: 'Arbitration has given me but little material [for literary work], has brought me into conflict with all the landed proprietors and upset my health.'

Here is a sample of the cases he had to deal with. A Mme Artukóv complained that a certain Mark Grigóryev (who had been a house-serf and was therefore not entitled to land) had left her, considering himself to be 'perfectly free'.

Tolstoy, in his reply to the lady, said:

Mark, by my order, is at liberty to go immediately, with his wife, where he likes; and I beg you to compensate him (1) for the three and a half months he has been illegally kept at work by you since the Decree was published, and (2) for the blows still more illegally inflicted on his wife. If my decision displease you, you have a right of appeal to the Magistrates' Sessions and to the Government Sessions. I shall not enter into further explanations on this subject.

With entire respect I have the honour to remain, your humble servant,

                                                    CT. L. TOLSTOY

The lady appealed to the Magistrates' Sessions and Tolstoy's decision was cancelled, but on the case being carried to the Government Sessions his view prevailed.

Before he had been a year in office we find him writing to the Government of the Túla Board of Peasant Affairs as follows:

As the complaints [here follows a list of several cases] lodged against my decisions have no legal justification, yet in these and many other cases my decisions have been and are being repealed, so that almost every decision I give is subsequently reversed, and as under such conditions, destructive both of the peasants' and the landowners' confidence in the Arbiter, the latter's activity becomes not merely useless but impossible, I humbly request the Government Board to authorise one of its members to hasten the examination of the above-mentioned appeals, and I have to inform the Government Board that until such investigations are completed I do not consider it proper that I should exercise the duties of my office, which I have therefore handed over to the senior Candidate.

The following month he resumed official work, but six weeks later, on 30th April 1862, on the ground of ill-health handed the duties over to a substitute, and on 26th May – about a year after accepting office – the Senate informed the Governor of Túla that it 'had decided to discharge the Lieutenant of Artillery, Count Leo Tolstoy, on the grounds of ill-health' from the post of Arbiter of the Peace.

His unsatisfactory experience of administrative work perhaps increased the anti-Governmental bias shown in his later works. He certainly shared Rousseau's dislike of civil and criminal law when he wrote in his *Confession*:

The justice and the inutility of my appeals left in my mind a germ of indignation against our stupid civil institutions in which the true welfare of the public and veritable justice are always sacrificed to I know not what apparent order, really destructive of all order, and which merely adds the sanction of public authority to the oppression of the weak and the iniquity of the strong.

We may at any rate be sure that tiresome, petty, administrative work, never quite satisfactory, and at best consisting of compromises and decisions based on necessity rather than on such principles of abstract justice as were dear to Tolstoy's soul, could never be a satisfactory occupation for him. He had not the plodding patience and studious moderation such work demands, nor could his impulsive genius find scope in it. It was never easy for him to submit to the direction of others or to have to reckon with their opinions and wishes. Like Rousseau, it suited him better to reform the world on paper, or even to alter his own habits of life, than to concern himself with the slow social progress, the bit-by-bit amelioration, which alone is possible to those harnessed to the car that bears a whole society of men.

Tolstoy used at this time to find recreation in hunting, and often went for days together with his friend Prince D. D. Obolénski, who describes him as a bold and active hunter, leaping all sorts of obstacles, and a wonderful man to talk to.

Concurrently with his duties as Arbiter, Tolstoy carried on an enterprise in which he had to deal with people younger and more easy to mould than the peasants and proprietors whose quarrels he found it so hard to adjust, and from the autumn of 1859 to that of 1862 he devoted himself whole-heartedly to the task of educating the peasant children of Yásnaya and the surrounding district.

As we have already seen, a chief aim of his travels abroad was to study the theory and practice of education, and he set to work on the school at Yásnaya most enthusiastically. The monthly magazine, *Yásnaya Polyána* (now a bibliographical rarity) which he produced and edited during 1862, expressed his theories of education and made known the results attained in his school. Articles published in it (and republished in his collected writings) give a vivid description of the work carried on in November and December 1861. In one edition after another of Tolstoy's writings, this article is called 'Yásno-Polyána School in Nov. and Dec. 1862', though it appeared in the first number of *Yásnaya Polyána* in February of that year. In small matters of detail of this kind Tolstoy was always careless. Like many Russian magazines. *Yásnaya Polyána* usually appeared late, and to began with the January number was several weeks behind time. It had a very limited circulation and he lost 3,000 rubles on the twelve numbers that were issued.

In his educational work Tolstoy showed the qualities and limitations that marked his activities generally. There was the same characteristic selection of a task of great importance, the same readiness to sweep aside and condemn nearly all that humanity till then had accomplished, the same conviction that he could untie the Gordian knot, and the same power of devoted genius enabling him actually to achieve much more than seemed possible, though not a tithe of what he set out to do.

His educational articles are so original and contain so much sound sense that, extreme as some of his propositions may be, they deserve careful consideration. He defines Education as: *a human activity, having for its basis a desire for equality and a constant tendency to advance in knowledge.* This he illustrates by saying that the aim of a teacher of arithmetic should be to enable his pupil to grasp all the laws of mathematical reasoning he is himself master of; the aim of a teacher of French, or chemistry, or philosophy, should be similar. As soon as that aim is attained the activity will naturally cease. Everywhere and always, teaching that makes the pupil the master's equal has been considered good. The more nearly and rapidly this is accomplished the better; the less nearly and the more slowly it is accomplished the worse. Similarly in literature (an indirect method of teaching) those books are written best in which the author succeeds in transmitting his whole message most easily to the reader.

By 'a constant tendency to advance in knowledge' Tolstoy meant that the equality aimed at in education can only be obtained on the higher and not on the lower level: that is to say, not by the teacher forgetting what he knows, but by the pupil acquiring the teacher's knowledge. Much tuition however is based not on the desire to equalise knowledge but on quite false foundations.

These are: (1) First and commonest, the child learns in order not to be punished, (2) the child learns to earn a reward, (3) the child learns in order to be better than others, (4) the child or young man learns in order to obtain an advantageous position in the world.

Referring to the practice of sending boys to school not for their natural development but that they may be moulded into a set form, Tolstoy declared that 'Education as a deliberate moulding of people into certain forms is *sterile, illegitimate, and impossible.*'

He strongly disapproved of examinations, as tending to arbitrariness on the part of the examiners and deception on the part of the pupils.

Under what circumstances, he asks, can a pupil acquire knowledge most rapidly? 'A child or man is receptive only when he is aroused, and therefore to regard a merry spirit in school as an enemy or a hindrance is the crudest of blunders.'

The pupil's state of mind is the most important condition of successful education and to secure good results freedom is indispensable. No child should be forced to learn what it does not want to or when it does not wish to.

One need only glance at one and the same child at home or in the street, and at school. Here you see a vivacious inquisitive being with a smile in his eye and on his mouth, seeking information everywhere as a pleasure and clearly and often forcibly expressing his thoughts in his own way; while there you see a weary, shrinking, creature repeating merely with his lips someone else's thoughts in someone else's words with an air of fatigue, fear, and listlessness – a creature whose soul has retreated like a snail into its shell. One need but glance at these two conditions to see which of them is the more conducive to the child's development. That strange physiological condition which I call the 'School state of mind' and which unfortunately we all know so well, consists in the higher capacities: imagination, creative power, and reflection, yielding place to a semi-animal capacity to pronounce words without imagination or reflection.

When the pupils have been reduced to this 'School state of mind' we encounter those 'not accidental but often-repeated cases' of the stupidest boy being at the top of the class and the cleverest boy at the bottom.

In short, a child's mental capacities are really active only when that child is free, and the teacher's chief task lies 'in studying the free child' and discovering how to supply him with knowledge. Therefore 'the only method of education is experiment, and its only criterion is *freedom*.'

Attempts to enforce obedience and quietness in schoolrooms convert schools into places of torture, which have a stupefying effect well called by the Germans *Verdummen*.

Schools are not arranged to make it convenient for children to learn, but to make it convenient for teachers to teach. The voices, movements, and mirth of the children, which form a necessary condition of their studying successfully, incommode the teachers, and therefore in the prison-like schools of today, questions, conversation, and movement, are forbidden.

Schools based on compulsion supply, 'not a shepherd for the flock but a flock for the shepherd'.

To deal successfully with any object it is necessary to study it, and in education the object is a free child; yet the pedagogues wish to teach in their own way – the way that seems good in their own eyes, and when this does not act they want to alter not their way of teaching, but the nature of the child . . . Not till experiment becomes the basis of the School, and every school is, so to say, a pedagogic laboratory, will schools cease to lag behind the general level of the world's progress.

For boarding-schools Tolstoy had scant respect:

At home the comforts of life – water, fires, good food, a well-cooked dinner, the cleanliness and comfort of the rooms – all depended on the work and care of the mother and of the whole family. The more work and care the greater the comfort, the less work and care the less the comfort. A simple matter this no doubt, but more educational, I think, than the French language or information about Alexander the Great. In a boarding-school this constant, vital, reward of labour is so put out of sight that not only is the dinner no better or worse, the napkins no cleaner or dirtier, and the floors no brighter or duller, because of the girl's exertion or non-exertion, but she has not even a cell or corner of her own to keep straight or leave untidy at her pleasure, and she has no chance of making a costume for herself out of scraps and ribbons.

His general charge against day-schools, boarding-schools, and universities alike is that:

At the base of them all lies one and the same principle: the right of one man, or of a small group of men, to shape other people as they please.

He adds that:

It is not enough for School to tear children away from real life for six hours a day during the best years of their life, it wishes to tear three-year-old children from their mother's influence. Institutions have been contrived (*Kleinkinder-bewahranstalten*, infant schools, *salles d'asile*) about which we shall have to speak more in detail later on. It only remains to invent a steam-engine which will replace the nursing mother! All agree that schools are imperfect; I, personally, am convinced that they are noxious.

He argues that no man or set of men has any right to force any particular kind of education on anyone else. The teacher has no right to do more than offer such knowledge as he possesses, and should respect the child's right to reject it as indigestible, or badly served up:

On what grounds does the School of today teach this and not that, and in this and not that way?

Where in our day can we get such faith in the indubitability of our knowledge as would give us a right to educate people compulsorily? Take any medieval school before or after Luther, take the whole scholastic literature of the Middle Ages, what a strength of belief and what a firm indubitable knowledge of what was true and what was false we see in them! It was easy for them to know that a knowledge of Greek was the one essential condition of education, for Aristotle's works were in Greek and no one doubted the truth of his propositions till centuries later. How could the monks help demanding the study of the Holy Scriptures, which stood on an immutable foundation? It was well for Luther to demand the compulsory study of Hebrew, being sure, as he was, that in that language God himself had revealed truth to man. Evidently as long as man's critical sense was not aroused the school had to be dogmatic, and it was natural for pupils to learn by heart the truths revealed by God, as well as Aristotle's science, and the poetic beauties of Virgil and Cicero. For centuries after, no one could imagine any truer truth or more beautiful beauty. But what is the position of the schools of our time which retain these same dogmatic principles while, in the room next to the class where the immortality of the soul is taught, it is suggested to the pupils that the nerves common to man and to the frog are what used to be called 'the soul'; and where after hearing the story of Joshua the son of Nun read to him without explanations, the pupil learns that the sun never did go round the earth; and when after the beauties of Virgil have been explained to him, he finds the beauties of Alexandre Dumas (whose novels he can buy for sixpence) much greater; when the only belief held by the teacher is that nothing is true, but that whatever exists is reasonable, and that progress is good and backwardness bad though nobody knows in what this progress, so generally believed in, consists?

In another article he says:

Luther insists on teaching the Holy Scriptures from the originals and not from the commentaries of the Fathers of the Church. Bacon enjoins the study of Nature from Nature and not from the books of Aristotle. Rousseau wants to teach life from life itself as he understands it and not from previous experiments. Each step forward in the philosophy of pedagogics merely consists in freeing the schools from the idea of teaching the younger generations what the elder generations believed to be science, and in substituting studies that accord with the needs of the younger generations.

Again he says:

It is very usual to read and hear it said that home conditions, the coarseness of parents, field labour, village games, and so forth, are the chief hindrances to school-work. Possibly they really do interfere with the kind of school-work aimed at by the pedagogues, but it is time we understood that these conditions are the chief bases of all education, and far from being inimical to, or hindrances of, the School, are its first and chief motive power . . . The wish to know anything whatever, and the very questions to which it is the School's business to reply, arise entirely from those home conditions. All instruction should be simply a reply to questions put by life. But School far from evoking questions, fails even to answer those which life suggests . . . To such questions the child receives no reply, more especially as the police regulations of the School do not allow him to open his mouth even when he wants to be let out for a minute, but oblige him to make signs, so as not to break the silence or disturb the teacher.

The great questions, Tolstoy says, are: (1) What must I teach? and (2) How must I teach it? He remarks that a couple of centuries ago neither in Russia nor in Western Europe could these questions have arisen. Education was then bound up with religion, and to become a scholar meant to learn the Scriptures. In Mohammedan countries this union of religion with education still exists in full force. To learn, means to learn the Koran and therefore to learn Arabic. But as soon as the criterion of what to learn ceased to be religion, and the School became independent of the Church, the question of what to teach was bound to arise. That it did not arise suddenly was due to the fact that the emancipation of

School from Church took place gradually. But the day has at last come when the question must be faced; and no clear guidance is given us either by philosophy or by any definite consensus of opinion among those concerned with education. In the higher schools some advocate a classical, others a scientific education, while in the primary schools, if the education is controlled by the priests it is carried on in one way, and if it is controlled by the anti-clericals in another. Under these circumstances the only possible criterion must be the wish of the pupils, or of their parents. Tolstoy goes on to maintain that the demand of the mass of the Russian people was for tuition in the Russian and Church-Slavonic languages, and in mathematics.

As to *how* to teach, he contends that this resolves itself into the problem, How to establish the best possible relations between those who want to learn and those who want to teach, and he says:

> Probably no one will deny that the best relation between a teacher and his pupil is a natural one, and that the opposite to a natural one is a compulsory one. If that be so, then the measure of all scholastic methods consists in the greater or lesser naturalness, and consequently in the more or less compulsion that is employed. The less the children are compelled the better is the method, the more they are compelled the worse is the method. I am glad it is not necessary for me to prove this obvious truth. All are agreed that it cannot be good for health to employ foods, medicines, or exercises, which create disgust or pain, and so also in learning, there can be no need to compel children to grind at anything dull or repugnant to them, and if it seems necessary to use compulsion, that fact merely proves the imperfection of the methods employed. All who have taught children have probably noticed that the worse the teacher knows the subject he is dealing with and the less he likes it the more stern he has to be and the more compulsion he has to use, while on the contrary, the better the teacher knows and loves his subject the more free and natural will be his tuition.
>
> If history be closely examined it will be found that every advance in pedagogics has consisted merely in a diminution of compulsion, a facilitation of study, and a greater and greater approximation to natural relations between teacher and pupil.
>
> People have asked, How can we find the degree of freedom to be allowed in school? To which I reply that the limit of that freedom is

naturally defined by the teacher, by his knowledge, and by his capacity to manage the school. Such freedom cannot be dictated; its measure is merely the result of the greater or lesser knowledge and talent possessed by the master. Freedom is not a rule, but serves as a gauge when comparing one school with another or when judging new methods. The school in which there is less compulsion is better than the one in which there is more. That method is good which when introduced into a school does not necessitate any increase of discipline, while that which necessitates greater severity is certainly bad.

From his main subject of Education Tolstoy digresses into a discussion of other problems, in a way which reminds one of the remarkable essays he began to pour forth a quarter of a century later.

That he had been somewhat influenced by the Slavophils is indicated by his readiness to assume that Russia may advance along a line of her own entirely different from the one Western nations have travelled. 'Progress', in which like almost all his contemporaries he had believed, he now questions, and he indulges in a sharp attack on Macaulay for the third chapter of his *History*, which he says contains no proof that any real progress has been achieved. Buckle also is roughly handled for the assumption of progress that underlies his *History of Civilisation*, but most scathing of all is his onslaught on Hegel who till Darwin appeared was the rock on which the intellectual Liberals took their stand.

Interesting, stimulating, and suggestive as Tolstoy's articles were, and valuable as was the experience gained in his school, he met with very little encouragement in educational circles.

In an article written thirteen years later, he says of his attempts in 1859–62:

At that time I met with no sympathy in the educational journals nor even with any contradiction, but only with the completest indifference to the question I was raising. There were, it is true, some attacks on a few insignificant details, but the question itself evidently interested no one. I was young at that time and this indifference galled me. I did not understand that I with my question: How do you know what and how to teach? was like a man who in an assembly of Turkish Pashas discussing the collection of taxes from the people, should say to them: Gentlemen, before discussing how much to take from each man we must first consider what right we have to collect taxes at all? Obviously the Pashas would continue to discuss the methods of collecting and would ignore the irrelevant question.

Before proceeding to tell of the actual working of the Yásnaya Polyána school there is one matter to be noted, small indeed in itself but characteristic, and helpful for an understanding of Tolstoy's later development.

His personal honour has never been questioned, and the reader will remember that at Sevastopol he had refused to take money which according to the long-standing regimental custom was at his disposal. Well, in his magazine he printed a story written by one of the schoolboys, and appraised it with enthusiasm. The father of a family, who had been wretchedly poor, returns from the army with money to spare and explains the matter to his wife by saying: 'I was paymaster and paid the soldiers. Some money used to remain over and so I put it by.'

Commenting on this, Tolstoy says:

It is revealed that the soldier has become rich and has done so in the simplest and most natural manner, just as almost everybody does who becomes rich – that is, by other people's, the Crown's or somebody's, money remaining in his hands owing to a fortunate accident. Some readers have remarked that this incident is immoral, and that the people's conception of the Crown as a milch cow should be eradicated and not confirmed. But not to speak of its artistic truth, I particularly value that trait in the story. Does not the Crown money always stop somewhere? And why should it not once in a way stop with a homeless soldier like Gordéy? . . .

The mention of the Crown money, which at first seems immoral, in our opinion has a most sweet and touching character. How often a writer of our circle, when wishing to show his hero as an ideal of honesty, naïvely displays to us the dirty and depraved nature of his own imagination! Here on the contrary the author has to make his hero happy. His return to his family would suffice for that, but it was also necessary to remove the poverty which for so many years had weighed on the family. Where was he to take money from? From the impersonal Crown! If the author is to give him wealth it has to be taken from someone, and it could not have been found in a more legitimate or reasonable way.

Tolstoy's attitude is remarkable. He always had a keen sense of personal morality, but when public morality was in question his decisions sometimes seem faulty.

Passing from the moral to the economic aspect of the matter, it sounds strange to Western ears to hear the medieval or Oriental conception so boldly announced that property 'has to be taken from some one' before it can be obtained. In our world wealth has during the last few generations been increased enormously by inventions, organisation, division of labour, and skilful utilisation of the forces of Nature, as well as by co-operation and the bringing together into one place of mutually helpful industries and individuals, and it has become impossible for us to believe that the *only* way to obtain wealth is by depriving others of what they already possess.

8

The School

After leaving the University Tolstoy had, at the end of the 1840s, started a school for the children of his serfs, in which he himself taught, but his chief educational activity was during the years 1860, '61, and '62. The results he attained were very remarkable.

The activity of which an account is here given began in the autumn of 1859, some nine or ten months before his second journey abroad, during which visit he both studied educational methods and wrote on education. It is true that his main preoccupation with the school occurred after he returned home the second time, but the school is here dealt with in a separate chapter as a matter of convenience and despite the fact that chronologically what is here narrated overlaps with events mentioned in the two previous chapters. In December 1860, when he was in the south of France after his brother's death, he wrote to Countess A. A. Tolstoy:

> What can I say about myself? You know, I am sure, about my occupation with a school since last year. I can quite sincerely say that it is now the one interest that attaches me to life. Unfortunately this winter I cannot occupy myself with it actively and on the spot, but can only prepare for the future.

As already mentioned, his magazine, besides its theoretical articles, contained others describing the work done at his school, and from these we learn in his own words how Tolstoy and his pupils, with three masters (including the young German, Keller, whom he had brought with him from abroad), were occupied in November and December 1861. The following passages are part of his description:

> No one brings anything with him, neither books nor copybooks. No homework is set them. Not only do they carry nothing in their hands, they have nothing to carry even in their heads. They are not obliged to remember any lesson, nor any of yesterday's work. They are not

tormented by thought of the impending lesson. They bring only themselves, their receptive nature, and an assurance that it will be as jolly in school today as it was yesterday. They do not think of their classes till they have begun. No one is ever scolded for being late and they never are late, except perhaps some of the older boys whose fathers occasionally keep them at home to do some work. In such cases the boy comes to school running fast and panting. Until the teacher arrives some gather at the porch pushing one another off the steps or sliding on the ice-covered path, and some go into the rooms. When it is cold, while waiting for the master they read, write, or play about. The girls do not mix with the boys. When the boys take any notice of the girls they never address any one of them in particular, but always speak to them collectively: 'Hey, girls, why don't you come and slide?' or, 'Look how frozen the girls are', or, 'Now girls, all of you against me!'

Suppose by the timetable the lesson for the youngest class is elementary reading, for the second advanced reading, and for the third mathematics. The teacher enters the room on the floor of which the boys are lying in a heap, shouting, 'The heap's too small!' or, 'Boys, you're choking me!' or, 'Don't pull my hair!' &c.

'Peter Miháylich!' cries a voice from the bottom of the heap to the teacher as he enters: 'Tell them to stop!' – 'Good-morning, Peter Miháylich!' cry others, continuing their scrimmage. The teacher takes the books and hands them to those who have followed him to the cupboard, while from the heap of boys on the floor those on top, still sprawling, demand books. The heap gradually diminishes. As soon as most of the boys have taken books, the rest run to the cupboard crying, 'Me too! Me too!' – 'Give me yesterday's book!' – 'Give me Kóltsov!' and so forth. If a couple of boys excited by their struggle still remain on the floor, those who have taken books and settled down shout at them, 'What are you up to? We can't hear anything! Stop it!' The excited ones submit and, panting, take to their books, and only just at first swing their legs with unspent excitement as they sit reading. The spirit of war flies away and the spirit of reading reigns in the room. With the same ardour with which he pulled Mítka's hair he now reads Kóltsov's works, with almost clenched teeth, with sparkling eyes, and oblivious of all around him but his book. To tear him from his reading would now need as much effort as formerly to tear him from his wrestling.

They sit where they like: on the benches, tables, window-sills, floor, or in the armchair. The girls always sit together. Friends from the same village, especially the little ones (among whom there is most comradeship), always sit together As soon as one of them decides that he will sit in a certain corner, all his chums, pushing and diving under the forms, get there too, and sit together looking about them with faces that express as much happiness and satisfaction as though, having settled in that place, they would certainly be happy for the rest of their lives. A large armchair (which has somehow found its way into the room) is an object coveted by the more independent personalities . . . As soon as one of them decides to sit in it another discerns his intention from his looks and they collide and squeeze in. One dislodges the other and, curling up, sprawls with his head far below the back, but reads, like the rest, quite absorbed in his work. During lessons I have never seen them whispering, pinching, giggling, laughing behind their hands, or complaining of one another to the teacher.

The two lower classes sort themselves in one room, the upper class in another. The teacher appears, and in the first class all surround him at the blackboard, or lie on the forms or sit on the table near him or near one of the boys who reads. If it is a writing lesson they place themselves in a more orderly way but keep getting up to look at one another's exercise books and to show their own to the teacher. By the timetable there should be four lessons before dinner, but sometimes in practice these become three or two and may be on quite other subjects. The teacher may begin with arithmetic and pass on to geo- metry, or may begin with Sacred History and end up with grammar. Sometimes teacher and pupils are so carried away that a lesson lasts three hours instead of one. Sometimes the pupils themselves cry: 'Go on, go on!' and shout contemptuously to any who are tired: 'If you're tired go to the little ones!'

In my opinion this external disorder is useful and necessary, how- ever strange and inconvenient it may seem to the teacher. Of its advantages I shall have frequent occasion to speak but of its apparent disadvantages I will say:

First, this disorder, or free order, only frightens us because we were ourselves educated in and are accustomed to something quite different. Secondly, in this as in many similar cases, coercion is used only from hastiness or lack of respect for human nature. We think the disorder is growing greater and greater and has no limit. We think there is no way of stopping it except by force; but one need only wait a little and the disorder (or animation) calms down of itself and calms down into a far better and more durable order than any we could devise.

In another place he says:

Our school evolved freely from the principles brought into it by the teachers and pupils. In spite of the predominant influence of the teacher the pupil always had the right not to go to school, and even when in school not to listen to the teacher. The teacher had the right not to admit a pupil . . .

Submitting naturally only to laws derived from their own nature, children revolt and rebel when subjected to your premature inter- ference. They do not believe in the validity of your bells, and time- tables, and rules. How often have I seen children fighting. The teacher rushes to separate them, and the separated enemies look at one another askance and even in the stern teacher's presence cannot refrain from giving one another a parting blow yet more painful than its predecessors. How often, any day, do I see some Kirúshka, clenching his teeth, fly at Taráska, seize his hair and throw him to the ground, apparently – though it costs him his life – determined to maim his foe; yet not a minute passes before Taráska is already laughing under Kirúshka. One and then the other moderates his blows, and before five minutes have passed they have made it up and off they go to sit together.

The other day, between lessons, two boys were struggling in a corner. The one, a remarkable mathematician about ten years old, is in the second class; the other, a close-cropped lad, the son of a servant, is a clever but vindictive, tiny, black-eyed lad nicknamed Pussy. Pussy seized the mathematician's long hair and jammed his head against the wall, the mathematician vainly clutched at Pussy's close-cropped bristles. Pussy's black eyes gleamed triumphantly. The mathematician, hardly refraining from tears, kept saying: 'Well, well, what of it?' But though he tried to keep up appearances it was plain he was faring badly. This went on for some time and I was in doubt what to do. 'A fight, a fight!' shouted the boys and crowded towards the corner. The little ones laughed, but the bigger ones, though they did not interfere, exchanged serious glances and their silence and these glances did not escape Pussy's observation. He understood that he was doing something wrong, and began to smile shamefacedly, and by degrees let go of the mathematician's hair. The mathematician shook himself free and, giving Pussy a push that banged the back of the latter's head against the wall, went off satisfied. Pussy began to cry and rushed after his enemy, hitting him as hard as he could on his sheepskin coat, but without hurting him. The mathematician wished to pay him back, but at that moment several disapproving voices were raised. 'There now; he's fighting a little fellow!' cried the onlookers, 'get away, Pussy!' – and therewith the affair ended as though it had never occurred, except, I think, that both combatants retained a dim consciousness that fighting is unpleasant because both get hurt.

In this case I seemed to detect a feeling of fairness influencing the crowd, but how often such affairs are settled so that one does not know what law has decided them and yet both sides are satisfied! How arbitrary and unjust by comparison are all School methods of dealing with such cases. 'You are both to blame: kneel down!' says the teacher; and the teacher is wrong, because one boy is to blame and that one triumphs while on his knees and chews the cud of his unexpended anger, while the innocent one is doubly punished . . .

I am convinced that School should not interfere with that part of education which belongs to the family. The School should not, and has no right to, reward or punish; and the best police and administration of a School consists in giving full freedom to the pupils to learn and get on among themselves as they like. I am convinced of this, and yet the customary School habits are still so strong in us that in the Yásno-Polyána school we frequently break this rule . . .

Though subsequently in his *Confession* Tolstoy referred scornfully to his educational writings, the actual working of his school was remarkably successful and the ideas expressed in his educational articles – which fill a whole volume – are highly interesting. Education has since made much progress in the direction he indicated, but his theories and practice were far more radical than any school system now existing, or likely to exist unless and until teachers are obtainable as able and as devoted to the task as he was himself.

N. V. Uspénski, the writer, narrates that he visited Yásnaya Polyána in 1862, and Tolstoy having to leave him alone for a while asked him to glance at some of the compositions the boys had written in school. Taking up one of these, Uspénski read:

One day Lëv Nikoláevich [Tolstoy] called Savóskin up to the blackboard and told him to solve a problem in arithmetic. 'If I give you five rolls and you eat one of them, how many rolls will you have left?' . . . Savóskin could nohow solve this problem, and the Count pulled his hair for it . . .

When Tolstoy returned Uspénski pointed out to him this essay, and Tolstoy, sighing heavily, crossed his hands before him and merely said: 'Life in this world is a hard task.'

Uspénski considered that he had unearthed an extraordinary contradiction between theory and practice, but no one realising the difficulty and novelty of Tolstoy's attempt and how far he was from claiming perfection for himself or his achievements, should agree with Uspénski. On the contrary, the essay proves a freedom of relation between teacher and pupil which could not have existed had the hair-pulling been other than impulsive and exceptional.

The school was closed, or nearly so, during the summer, as most of the pupils then helped their parents with field work, obtaining, Tolstoy considered, more mental development that way than they could have done in any school. To make up for this the hours of study in winter were long.

The classes generally finish about eight or nine o'clock (unless carpentering keeps the elder boys somewhat later), and the whole band run shouting into the yard and there, calling to one another, begin to separate, making for different parts of the village. Occasionally they arrange to coast downhill to the village in a large sledge that stands outside the gate. They tie up the shafts, throw themselves into it, and, squealing, disappear from sight in a cloud of snow, leaving here and there on their path black patches of children who have tumbled out. In the open air out of school (for all its freedom) new relations are formed between pupil and teacher, freer, simpler and more trustful – those very relations which seem to us to be the ideal which School should aim at.

In the volume of this edition containing *What is Art?* the reader will find a charming account of a walk Tolstoy had with the little peasant boys, Fédka, Sëmka, and Prónka, and of a discussion on the problems of art which started him on a line of reflection that, forty years later, caused him to write *What is Art?*, readers of which should bear in mind that when he declares that children, peasants, and savages, if they are capable of sharing another's feelings can be touched by art that is clear, brief, and sincere enough, he is not uttering a paradox, still less is he making a peasant's taste the criterion of art, but he is speaking of what he knew and testifying to what he had seen. It is, he says, as easy for such a man to recognise a work of art that appeals to him, 'as for an animal of unspoilt scent to follow the trace he needs . . . The animal unerringly finds *what he needs*. So also the man, if only his natural qualities have not been perverted, will without fail select from among thousands of others the real work of art *he requires* – that infects *him* with the feeling experienced by the artist.' This is not to say that the peasant child, or savage, can appreciate each and every work of art, but that a supreme artist, great enough to be quite clear and sincere, can reach all who retain 'that simple feeling familiar to the plainest man and even to a child, that sense of infection with another's feelings – compelling us to rejoice in another's gladness, to sorrow at another's grief, and to mingle souls with another – which is the very essence of art'.

One phase of Tolstoy's experience continually throws light on another, so that an acquaintance with his life helps us to see the simple sanity of opinions that might perplex readers who regarded them as abstract propositions not rooted in experience.

The peasants at first were afraid of a school run in such an unusual manner, but before long they gained confidence and the report became current among them that: 'At Yásno-Polyána school they learnt everything, including all the sciences, and there are such clever masters that it is dreadful; it is said that they even imitate thunder and lightning. Anyway the lads understand well and have begun to read and write.' Another very general opinion was that: 'They teach the boys everything (like gentlemen's sons); much of it is no use, but still, as they quickly learn to read, it is worth sending the children there.'

Naturally Tolstoy, himself in those days an ardent gymnast, had parallel and horizontal bars put up and gave the children physical training. To the effects of this on the stomach the village mothers did not fail to attribute any digestive troubles that befell their children from time to time, especially when the long Lenten fast was succeeded by a return to more appetising food, or when, after such luxuries had long been lacking, fresh vegetables came into use in summer.

In his account of the Yásno-Polyána school Tolstoy tells us there were about forty pupils enrolled, but more than thirty were rarely present at a time; among them were four or five girls, and sometimes three or four male adults who came either for a month or for a whole winter. Later on the number of pupils rose to seventy. Most of the boys were from seven to ten years old. Tolstoy found that children learn to read most rapidly, easily, and well, between the ages of six and eight.

Before the Emancipation education for serfs was rare, rudimentary, and of very poor quality, except in quite exceptional cases. In 1860 however Tolstoy aimed at the organisation of a 'Society for the Education of the People' throughout the country; but the Government would not allow it and, as he wrote to a correspondent, he alone continued to form 'a secret Society for the Education of the People'.

After the Emancipation in 1861, however, the Government began to prompt the peasants to open schools for themselves, and those in Tolstoy's neighbourhood applied to him, as Arbiter of the Peace, to find them teachers. Tolstoy procured some students who in consequence of an agitation that had then occurred had been dismissed from the University, and in 1862 there were thirteen schools in the surrounding villages with teachers recommended by him, and run on lines similar to those followed in his own school. His relations with these teachers were excellent. Speaking of them to P. I. Birukóv in 1908, he remarked: 'What fellows they were! Pure, self-sacrificing – no idea of dissatisfaction and no hesitation about living at Babúrino [a poor little village near Yásnaya] . . . How different from the young folk of today!'

They submitted to Tolstoy's influence instinctively, and were inspired by the enthusiasm with which he devoted his whole time and strength to the children. Like him they were occupied with their pupils from about 8 a.m. till late at night, and like him devoted their whole souls to the work. 'This intense daily activity absorbs me so that I have no wish to abandon it,' wrote one of them. 'I could spend the long winter evenings with the pupils, listening to their prayers and their thoughts. My life had mingled with theirs. I felt happy when they were merry,' wrote another.

The children came to love their schools. It was an example of the influence Tolstoy exercised when enthusiastic about any undertaking. It was certainly his energy and devotion that inspired these teachers to live in such poor and unaccustomed surroundings, in rough peasant huts, devoting themselves from morning to night to teaching peasant lads – for when Tolstoy ceased to devote himself to the task, these teachers all soon abandoned the work.

In the third year of the existence of the school the distrust the peasants had felt had been so completely overcome that some well-to-do peasants even brought their boys distances of twenty and thirty miles to Yásnaya Polyána. Tolstoy insisted that the success of the schools and the very rapid progress made by the pupils resulted not from any particular 'method', but from the free and natural relations that existed between teachers and pupils, and from the readiness of the teachers constantly to experiment and adapt their teaching to the changing requirements of the scholars.

There were generally from five to seven lessons a day. The teachers kept diaries of their work, and discussed matters together on Sundays, when they drew up plans for the coming week. These plans were however not strictly adhered to, but were constantly modified to meet the pupils' desires.

Tolstoy's sister told me of another Sunday occupation at Yásnaya Polyána in those days. Tolstoy used to invite the boys from all the neighbouring schools and play games with them; the favourite game being *Barres*, which I assume to be a form of 'Storm the Castle', or possibly 'Prisoners' Base'.

He came to the conclusion that teachers involuntarily endeavour to find a method of teaching convenient for themselves, but that the more convenient a method is for the teacher the less convenient it usually is for the pupil; and only *that* method is good which satisfies the pupils.

He always avoided questioning a boy separately on a lesson. When the master had finished speaking, or when something had been read, the whole class might repeat what they had understood, and only if the clamour was too great would the master ask some, or most, or all but one, of them to be quiet, that the repetition might be heard.

His theory of freedom as the basis of success in instruction was put to a rude test by the fact that his pupils, at first, made little or no headway in learning to read. In one of his articles he says:

> The simple thought that the time had not yet come for good reading and that there was at present no need of it, but that the pupils would themselves find the best method when the need arose, only recently entered my head.

After telling how the boys at first found it difficult to master the mechanical process of reading, Tolstoy goes on to tell how progress was suddenly made in the class owing to what seemed an accident.

> In the class of advanced reading some one book is used each boy reading in turn, and then all recounting its contents together. They had been joined that autumn by an extremely talented lad, T., who had studied for two years with a sacristan and was therefore ahead of them all in reading. He reads as we do, and the pupils only understand anything of the advanced reading (and then not very much of it) when he reads, and yet each of them wishes to read. But as soon as a bad reader begins the others express dissatisfaction, especially when the story is interesting. They laugh and get cross, and the bad reader feels ashamed and endless disputes arise. Last month one of the boys announced that he would, at any cost, manage within a week to read as well as T.; others made the same announcement, and suddenly mechanical reading became their favourite occupation. For an hour or an hour and a half at a time they would sit without tearing themselves away from the books, which they did not understand; and they began taking books home with them, and really within three weeks they made such progress as one could not have expected.
>
> In their case the reverse had happened of what usually occurs with those who learn the rudiments. Generally a man learns to read, and finds nothing he cares to read or understand. In this case the pupils were convinced that there *is* something worth reading and understanding, but felt that they lacked the capacity, and so they set to work to become proficient readers.

A difficulty of enormous importance was the absence of books really suitable for simple folk to read.

> The insoluble problem was that for the education of the people an ability and a desire to read good books is essential. Good books are however written in a literary language the people don't understand. To learn to understand it one would have to read a great deal, and people won't read willingly unless they understand what they read.

Connected with this difficulty of finding books suited for peasants and peasant children, was the parallel difficulty of finding literary subjects that interested them. This was best met by reading the Old Testament stories:

A knowledge of Sacred History was demanded both by the pupils themselves and by their parents. Of all the oral subjects I tried during three years, nothing so suited the understanding and mental condition of the boys as the Old Testament. The same was the case in all the schools that came under my observation. I tried the New Testament, I tried Russian History and Geography, I tried explanations of natural phenomena (so much advocated today), but it was all listened to unwillingly and quickly forgotten. But the Old Testament was remembered and eagerly narrated both in class and at home, and it was so well remembered that after two months the children wrote Scripture tales from memory with very slight omissions.

It seems to me that the book of the childhood of the race will always be the best book for the childhood of each man. It seems impossible to replace that book. To alter or abbreviate the Bible as is done in Sonntag's and other school primers, appears to me bad. All, every word in it, is right both as revelation and as art. Read about the creation of the world in the Bible and then read it in an abbreviated Sacred History, and the alteration of the Bible into the Sacred History will appear to you quite unintelligible. The latter can only be learnt by heart while the Bible presents the child with a vivid and majestic picture he will never forget. The omissions made in the Sacred History are quite unintelligible, and only impair the character and beauty of the Scriptures. Why for instance is the statement omitted in all the Sacred Histories, that when there was nothing, the Spirit of God moved upon the face of the waters, and that after having created, God looked at His creation and saw that it was good, and that then it was the morning and evening of such and such a day? Why do they omit that God breathed into Adam's nostrils the breath of life, and that having taken one of his ribs He with the flesh closed up the place thereof, and so forth? One must read the Bible to unperverted children to understand how necessary and true it all is. Perhaps one ought not to give the Bible to perverted young ladies, but when reading it to peasant children I did not alter or omit a single word. None of them giggled behind another's back but all listened eagerly and with natural reverence. The story of Lot and his daughters, and the story of Judah's son, evoked horror but not laughter . . .

How intelligible and clear it all is especially to a child, and yet how stern and serious! I cannot imagine what instruction would be possible without that book. Yet when one has learnt these stories only in childhood and has afterwards partly forgotten them, one thinks: What good do they do us? Would it not be all the same if one did not know them at all? So it seems till on beginning to teach you test on other children the elements that helped to develop you. It seems as if one could teach children to write and read and calculate, and could give them an idea of history, geography, and natural phenomena, without the Bible and before the Bible; yet nowhere is this done: everywhere the child first of all gets to know the Bible, its stories, or extracts from it. The first relations of the learner to the teacher are founded on that book. Such a general fact is not an accident. My very free relations with my pupils at the commencement of the Yásno-Polyána school helped me to find the explanation of this phenomenon.

A child or a man on entering school (I make no distinction between a ten-, thirty-, or seventy-year-old man) brings with him the special view of things he has deduced from life and to which he is attached. That a man of any age should begin to learn, it is necessary that he should love learning. That he should love learning he must recognise the falseness and insufficiency of his own view of things and must scent from afar that new view of life which learning is to reveal to him. No man or boy would have the strength to learn, if the result of learning presented itself to him merely as a capacity to write, to read, and to reckon. No master could teach if he did not command an outlook on life higher than that of his pupils. That a pupil may surrender himself whole-heartedly to his teacher a corner must be lifted of the veil which hides from him the delight of the world of thought, knowledge, and poetry, to which learning will admit him. Only by being constantly under the spell of that bright light shining ahead of him, will the pupil be able to use his powers in the way we require of him.

What means have we of lifting this corner of the veil? . . . As I have said, I thought as many think, that being myself in the world to which I had to introduce my pupils, it would be easy for me to do this; and I taught the rudiments, explained natural phenomena, and told them as the primers do that the fruits of learning are sweet, but the scholars did not believe me and kept aloof. Then I tried reading the Bible to them and quite took possession of them. A corner of the veil was lifted, and they yielded themselves to me completely. They fell in love with the book, and with learning, and with me. It only remained for me to guide them on . . .

To reveal to the pupil a new world and to make him without possessing knowledge love knowledge, there is no book but the Bible. I speak even for those who do not regard the Bible as a revelation. There are no other works – at least I know of none – which in so compressed and poetic a form contain all those sides of human thought which the Bible unites in itself. All the questions raised by natural phenomena are there dealt with. Of all the primitive relations of men with one another: the family, the State, and religion, we first become conscious through that book. The generalisations of thought and wisdom, with the charm given by their childlike simplicity of form, seize the pupil's mind for the first time. Not only does the lyricism of David's psalms act on the minds of the elder pupils, but more than that, from this book everyone becomes conscious for the first time of the beauty of an epic story in its incomparable simplicity and strength. Who has not wept over the story of Joseph and his meeting with his brethren? Who has not with bated breath told the story of the bound and shorn Samson revenging himself on his enemies and perishing under the ruins of the palace he destroys, or received a hundred other impressions on which we were reared as on our mothers' milk?

Let those who deny the educative value of the Bible and say it is out of date, invent a book and stories explaining the phenomena of Nature, either from general history or from the imagination, which will be accepted as the Bible stories are and then we will admit that the Bible is obsolete . . .

Drawn though it may be from a one-sided experience I repeat my conviction. The development of a child or a man in our society without the Bible is as inconceivable as that of an ancient Greek would have been without Homer. The Bible is the only book to begin with for a child's reading. Both in its form and in its contents the Bible should serve as a model for all children's primers and all reading books. A translation of the Bible into the language of the common folk would be the best book for the people.

When pupils came from other schools where they had to learn Scripture by heart or had been inoculated with the abbreviated school-primer versions, Tolstoy found that the Bible had nothing like as strong an effect on them as it had on boys who came fresh to it.

> Such pupils do not experience what is felt by fresh pupils, who listen to the Bible with beating heart, seizing every word, thinking that now, now at last, all the wisdom of the world is about to be revealed to them.

In reading the above passage it should be remembered that in Russian usage 'The Bible' means the Old Testament only.

Besides the Old Testament the only books the people understand and like, says Tolstoy, are those written not for the people but by the people; such as folk-tales and collections of songs, legends, proverbs, verses, and riddles. There was much in his experience which matches that of Cecil Sharp in his revival of English Folk Songs and Dances: namely, that there is an excellent literature and art which children and common folk appreciate and assimilate as eagerly and as well as anyone, and which it is the height of folly to despise. His perception of the gap separating the art and literature accessible to the people from artificial art that is beyond their reach, led him subsequently to undertake, first a series of school primers, and then the retelling of a number of folk-tales and legends (in *Twenty-Three Tales*) which have reached more readers, and perhaps benefited the world more, than anything else he wrote.

With penmanship it happened at Yásno-Polyána school, as with reading:

> The pupils wrote very badly and a new master introduced writing from copies (another exercise very sedate and easy for the master). The pupils became dull and we were obliged to abandon calligraphy, and did not know how to devise any way of improving their handwriting. The eldest class discovered a way for itself. Having finished writing the Bible stories the elder pupils began to ask for their exercise-books to take home [probably to read to their parents]. These were dirty, crumpled, and badly written. The precise mathematician P. asked for some paper and set to work to rewrite his stories. This idea pleased the others. 'Give me, too, some paper!' – 'Give me an exercise-book!' and a fashion for calligraphy set in which still prevails in the upper class. They took an exercise-book, put before them a written alphabet-copy from which they imitated each letter, boasting to one another of their performance, and in two weeks' time they had made great progress.

Grammar proved to be an unsatisfactory subject and to have hardly any connection with correct writing or speaking.

In our youngest – the third – class they write what they like. Besides that, the youngest write out in the evening, one at a time, sentences they have all composed together. One writes, and the others whisper among themselves noting his mistakes and only waiting till he has finished to denounce his misplaced *e* or his wrongly detached prefix, or sometimes to perpetrate a blunder of their own. To write correctly and correct mistakes made by others, gives them great pleasure. The elder boys seize every letter they can get hold of, exercising themselves in the correction of mistakes and trying with all their might to write correctly, but they cannot bear grammar or the analysis of sentences and, in spite of a bias we had for analysis, they only tolerate it to a very limited extent, falling asleep or evading the classes.

History on the whole went badly, except such bits of Russian history as, when told poetically, aroused patriotic feelings. On one memorable occasion the whole class went wild with excitement and eager interest. That was when Tolstoy, exercising a poet's licence, told the story of the defeat of Napoleon's invasion of Russia in 1812.

Except in this legendary manner the teaching of history to children is, in Tolstoy's opinion, useless. The historic sense develops later than the artistic sense:

In my experience and practice the first germ of interest in history arises out of contemporary events, sometimes as a result of participation in them, through political interest, political opinions, debates, and the reading of newspapers. Consequently the idea of beginning to teach history from present times should suggest itself to every intelligent master.

Of geography as a subject for the education of children Tolstoy had an even lower opinion:

In Von Vizin's comedy *The Minor*, when Mitrofánushka was being persuaded to learn geography, his mother said: 'Why teach him all the countries? The coachman will drive him where he may have to go to.' Nothing more to the point has ever been said against geography, and all the learned men in the world put together cannot rebut such an irrefragable argument. I am speaking quite seriously. What need was there for me to know where the river and town of Barcelona are situated, when for thirty-three years I have not once had occasion to use that knowledge? Not even the most picturesque description of Barcelona and its inhabitants could, I imagine, conduce to the development of my mental faculties.

In fact the sweeping conclusion at which Tolstoy arrives is that:

I not only see no use but I see great harm in teaching history or geography before the University is reached.

And he leaves it an open question whether even the University should concern itself with such subjects.

Drawing was a favourite lesson with the boys, but I must confine myself to a single extract on that subject:

We drew figures from the blackboard in the following way: I first drew a horizontal or a vertical line, dividing it into parts by dots, and the pupils copied this line. Then I drew another, or several, perpendicular or sloping lines standing in a certain relation to the first, and similarly divided up. Then we joined the dots of these different lines by others (straight or curved), and formed some symmetrical figure which as it was gradually evolved was copied by the boys. It seemed to me that this was a good plan: first, because the boy clearly saw the whole process of the formation of the figure, and secondly, because his perception of the co-relation of lines was developed by this drawing from the board much better than by copying drawings or designs . . .

It is nearly always useless to hang up a large complete picture or figure, because a beginner is quite at a loss before it, as he would be before an object from nature. But the growth of the figure before his eyes has an important meaning. In this case the pupil sees the backbone and skeleton of the drawing on which the body is subsequently found. The pupils were always called on to criticise the lines and their relation as I drew them. I often purposely drew them wrong to find out in how far their judgement of the co-relation and incorrectness of the lines had been developed. Then again when I was drawing my figure I asked the boys where they thought the next line should be added, and I even made one or other of them invent the shape of the figure himself.

In this way I not only aroused a more lively interest, but got the boys to participate freely in the formation and development of the figures, and this prevented the question, Why? which boys so naturally put when they are set to draw from copies.

The ease or difficulty with which it was understood and the more or less interest evoked, chiefly influenced the choice of the method of instruction; and I often quite abandoned what I had prepared for the lesson, merely because it was dull or seemed alien to the boys.

In the singing class, Tolstoy very soon found that notes written on the staff were not easily grasped by the pupils, and after using the staff for some ten lessons he once showed the boys the use of numbers instead, and from that day forward they always asked him to use numbers, and they themselves always used numbers in writing music. This method is much more convenient, Tolstoy considers, for explaining both the intervals and the changes of key. The pupils who were not musical soon dropped out of the class, and the lessons with those who were, sometimes went on for three or four hours at a stretch. He tried to teach them musical time in the usual manner, but succeeded so badly that he had to take that and melody separately. First he took the sounds without reference to time, and then beat the time without considering the sounds, and finally joined the two processes together. After several lessons he found that the method he had drifted into combined the chief features (though not some of the minor peculiarities) of Chevet's method, which he had seen in successful operation, among classes of workmen, in Paris. After a very few lessons two of the boys used to write down the melodies of the songs they knew and were almost able to read music at sight.

From the limited experience he had in teaching music, Tolstoy – to quote his own words almost textually – became convinced that: (1) to write sounds by means of numerals is the most profitable method; (2) to teach rhythm separately from pitch is the most profitable method; (3) in order that instruction in music may be willingly and fruitfully received, one must from the start teach the *art*, and not aim merely at dexterity in singing or playing. Spoilt young ladies may be taught to play Burgmüller's exercises, but it is better not to teach the children of the people at all than to teach them mechanically; (4) nothing so harms musical instruction as what looks like a knowledge of music: namely, the performances of choirs, and performances at examinations, speech-days, or in church; and (5) in teaching music to the people the thing to be aimed at is to impart our knowledge of the general laws of music, but not the false taste that has been developed among us.

In one of the most remarkable of his articles Tolstoy tells how he discovered that Fédka and Sëmka possessed literary ability of a high order. Composition lessons had not gone well, until one day Tolstoy proposed that the children should write a story of peasant life to illustrate a popular proverb. Most of the boys felt this to be beyond their powers and went on with their other occupations. One of them however bade Tolstoy write it himself in competition with them, and he set to work to do so till Fédka, climbing on the back of his chair interrupted him by reading over his shoulder. Tolstoy then began reading out what he had composed, and explained how he thought of continuing the story. Several of the boys became interested, not approving of Tolstoy's work but criticising and amending it, offering suggestions and supplying details. Sëmka and Fédka particularly distinguished themselves, and showed extraordinary imagination and such judgement, sense of proportion, restraint, and power of clothing their thoughts in words, that Tolstoy was carried away by the interest of the work and wrote as hard as he could to their dictation, having constantly to ask them to wait and not forget the details they had suggested. Fédka (of whom Tolstoy says that, 'The chief quality in every art, the sense of proportion, was extraordinarily developed in him: he writhed at every superfluous detail suggested by any of the other boys') gradually took control of the work, and ruled so despotically, and with such evident right, that the others dropped off and went home, except Sëmka, who continued to co-operate along his own more matter-of-fact line.

> We worked from seven in the evening till eleven. They felt neither hunger nor weariness, and were even angry with me when I stopped writing; and they set to work to do it themselves turn and turn about, but did not get on well and soon gave it up . . .
>
> I left the lesson because I was too excited.
>
> 'What is the matter with you? Why are you so pale: are you ill?' asked my colleague. Indeed only two or three times in my life have I experienced such strong emotion as that evening . . .

Next day Tolstoy could hardly believe the experience of the night before. It seemed incredible that a peasant boy hardly able to read, should suddenly display such marvellous command of artistic, creative power.

It seemed to me strange and offensive that I, the author of *Childhood*, who had achieved a certain success and was recognised by the educated Russian public as possessing artistic talent, should in artistic matters not merely be unable to instruct or help eleven-year-old Sëmka and Fédka, but should hardly be able except at a happy moment of excitement to keep up with them and understand them.

Next day we set to work to continue the story. When I asked Fédka if he had thought of a continuation, he only waved his hand and remarked: 'I know, I know! . . . Who will do the writing?' . . . We resumed the work and again the boys showed the same enthusiasm and the same sense of artistic truth and proportion.

Halfway through the lesson I had to leave them. They wrote two pages without me, as correct in feeling and as true to life as the preceding ones. These two pages were rather poorer in detail, some of the details were not quite happily placed, and there were also a couple of repetitions. All this had evidently occurred because the actual writing was a difficulty to them. On the third day we had similar success . . . There could no longer be any doubt or thought of its being a mere accident. We had obviously succeeded in finding a more natural and inspiring method than any we had previously tried.

This unfinished story was accidentally destroyed. Tolstoy was greatly annoyed, and Fédka and Sëmka, though they did not understand his vexation, offered to stay the night at his house and reproduce it. After eight o'clock, when school was over, they came and (to Tolstoy's great pleasure) locked themselves into his study, where at first they were heard laughing but then became very quiet. On listening at the door Tolstoy heard their subdued voices discussing the story and heard also the scratching of a pen. At midnight he knocked and was admitted. Sëmka was standing at the large table writing busily, his lines running crookedly across the paper and his pen constantly seeking the inkstand. Fédka told Tolstoy to 'wait a bit', and insisted on Sëmka's adding something more at his dictation. At last Tolstoy took the exercise-book, and the lads, after enjoying a merry supper of potatoes and *kvás*, divested themselves of their sheepskin coats and lay down to sleep under the writing table; their 'charming, healthy, childish, peasant laughter' still ringing through the room.

The story just mentioned, and others written by the children, were published in the magazine; and Tolstoy declares them to be, in their way, equal to anything in Russian literature. One of these written in school by Fédka and entitled *A Soldier's Wife*, can be read in *Russian Tales* (Collins's 'King's Way' series), as also another story, *Just for a Word*, written by him in later life. Readers can therefore judge of their literary quality for themselves. It was largely on the model of these peasant children's stories that, years later, Tolstoy wrote his own famous *Twenty-Three Tales*.

The rules for encouraging composition that he deduced from his experience are these:

1   To offer as large and varied a choice of themes as possible; not inventing them specially for children, but offering such as most interest the teacher and seem to him most important.

2   To give children stories written by children to read, and to offer only children's compositions as models, because these are juster, finer, and more moral, than those written by adults.

3   (Specially important.) Never when looking through the compositions make any remarks to the children about the neatness of the exercise-books, the handwriting, the spelling, or, above all, about the construction of the sentences or about logic.

4   Since the difficulty of composition lies not in size, nor in subject, nor in correctness of language, but in the mechanism of the work which consists: (*a*) in choosing one out of the great number of thoughts and images that offer themselves; (*b*) in choosing words in which to clothe it; (*c*) in remembering it and finding a fitting place for it; (*d*) in remembering what has already been written, so as not to repeat anything or omit anything, and in finding a way of joining up what has preceded to what succeeds; (*e*) and finally in so managing that while thinking and writing at one and the same time, the one operation shall not hamper the other – I, having these things in view, proceeded as follows.

At first I took upon myself some of these sides of the work, transferring them gradually to the pupils. At first out of the thoughts and images suggested I chose for them those which seemed to me best, and kept these in mind and indicated suitable places to insert them, and looked over what had been written to avoid repetitions, and I did the writing myself, letting them merely clothe the thoughts and images in words. Afterwards I let them select, and then let them revise what had been written, and finally they took on themselves the actual writing . . .

One of the profoundest convictions Tolstoy drew from his educational experiments was that the peasants and their children have much artistic capacity, and another was the immense importance of art, shown by its humanising effect upon them. Most of the works: literary, poetic, dramatic, pictorial, and plastic, now produced, are specially produced for people possessed of leisure, wealth, and an artificial training, and are therefore useless to the people. This deflection of art from the service of the millions to the delectation of the thousands, seemed to him a great evil.

He says with reference to two realms of art, music, and poetry, which he had loved passionately and with which he was very familiar, that he noticed that the demands of the masses were more legitimate than those of the classes.

Terrible to say, I came to the conviction that all that we have done in those two departments has been done along a false and exceptional path which lacks importance, has no future, and is insignificant in comparison with the demands upon and even with the samples of those same arts which we find put forward by the people. I became convinced that such lyrical compositions as, for example, Púshkin's 'I Remember the Marvellous Moment', and such musical productions as Beethoven's Last Symphony, are not so absolutely and universally good as the song 'Willy the Steward' or the melody of 'Floating down the river, Mother Vólga'; and that Púshkin and Beethoven please us, not because they are absolutely beautiful but because we are as spoiled as they, and because they flatter our abnormal irritability and weakness. How common it is to hear the empty and stale paradox that to understand the beautiful preparation is necessary! Who said so? Why? What proves it? It is only a shift, a loophole to escape from the hopeless position to which the false direction of our art, produced for one class alone, had led us. Why are the beauty of the sun and of the human face, and the beauty of the sounds of a folk-song, and of deeds of love and self-sacrifice, accessible to everyone, and why do *they* demand no preparation?

For years I vainly strove to make my pupils feel the poetic beauties of Púshkin and of our whole literature, and a similar attempt is being made by innumerable teachers not in Russia alone, and if they will observe the results of their efforts and be frank about the matter, they will admit that the chief result of this attempt to develop poetic feeling is to kill it, and that it is just those pupils whose natures are most poetic, who show most aversion to such commentaries . . .

I will try to sum up all that I have said above. In reply to the question: Do people need the *beaux arts*? pedagogues usually grow timid and confused (only Plato decided the matter boldly in the negative). They say: 'Art is needed, but with certain limitations, and to make it possible for all to become artists would be bad for the social structure. Certain arts and certain degrees of art can only exist in a certain class of society. The arts must have their special servants entirely devoted to them.' They say: 'It should be possible for the greatly gifted to escape from among the people and devote themselves entirely to the service of art.' That is the greatest concession pedagogy makes to the right of every individual to become what he wants to be.

But I consider this to be all wrong. I think the need to enjoy art and serve art is inherent in every human being to whatever race or class he belongs, and that this need has its right and should be satisfied. Taking that position as an axiom, I say that if the enjoyment and production of art by everyone presents inconveniences and inconsistencies, the reason lies in the character and direction art has taken: about which we must be on our guard lest we foist anything false on the rising generation and lest we prevent it from producing something new both in form and in matter.

Tolstoy goes so far as to doubt whether so long as no suitable literature is produced for the people, it is even worth their while to learn to read.

Looking closer at the results of the rudiments in the form in which they are supplied to the masses, I think most people will decide that the rudiments do more harm than good, taking into account the prolonged compulsion, the disproportionate development of memory, the false conception of the completeness of science, the aversion to further education, the false vanity, and the habit of senseless reading, acquired in these schools . . .

'Let us print good books for the people!' . . . How simple and easy that seems – like all great thoughts! There is only one obstacle, namely that there exist no good books for the people either here or in Europe. To print such books they must first be produced, and none of our philanthropists think of undertaking *that* work!

Before closing this rapid summary of Tolstoy's educational writings let me quote a few more sentences which sum up his essential position:

In my articles on Education I have given the oretic reasons for considering that only the freedom of the pupils to choose what they will learn and how they will learn it can furnish a sound basis for any instruction. In practice I constantly applied those rules in the schools under my guidance . . . and the results were always very good both for the teachers and the pupils, as well as for the evolution of new methods; and this I assert boldly, for hundreds of visitors came to the Yásno Polyána school and know how it worked.

For the masters the result of such relations with the pupils was that they did not consider any methods they happened to know to be the best, but tried to discover new methods and made acquaintance with other teachers whose ways they could learn. They tested fresh methods and above all were themselves always learning. In cases of failure a master never allowed himself to think it was the pupils' fault – their laziness, naughtiness, stupidity, deafness, or stuttering, but was convinced that the fault was his own, and for every defect in the pupil or pupils he tried to discover a remedy.

For the pupils the results were that they learnt eagerly, always begged to have additional lessons on winter evenings, and were quite free in class – which in my conviction and experience is the chief condition of successful teaching. Between the teachers and the pupils friendly and natural relations always arose, without which it is not possible for a teacher to know his pupils fully . . .

With reference to the methods of instruction, the results were that no method was adopted or rejected because it pleased or did not please the teacher, but only because the pupil without compulsion accepted, or did not accept it. But besides the good results that un-failingly followed the adoption of my method, both by myself and by all – more than twenty – other teachers (I say 'unfailingly' because we never had a single pupil who did not master the rudiments) – besides these results, the adoption of the principles mentioned produced this effect, that during fifteen years all the different modifications to which my method has been subjected have not only not removed it from the demands of the people but have brought it closer and closer to them . . . In my school . . . every teacher while bringing his pupils forward, himself feels the need of learning, and this was constantly the case with all the teachers I had.

Moreover the very methods of instruction themselves – since they are not fixed once for all, but aim at finding the easiest and simplest paths – change and improve in accord with what the teacher learns from the pupils' attitude towards his teaching.

The children had nothing to pay for attending the school at Yásnaya Polyána, and the relations between them and Tolstoy are illustrated by the account a visitor has given of seeing Tolstoy rush through a gate followed by a crowd of merry youngsters snowballing him. Tolstoy was intent on making his escape, but on seeing the visitor he changed his mind, acknowledged his defeat, and surrendered to his triumphant pursuers.

Long after leaving school Fédka wrote his recollections of it. He says:

One day, soon after the school was started, Leo Nikoláevich said to us: 'Do not call me "Your Excellence". My name is Leo Nikoláevich – call me so.' Before three months had passed learning was all the rage with us. In three months we were already able to read easily . . .

The flaming eagerness shown by Leo Nikoláevich heartened us and our spirits rose day by day. In the school interval we were given tea and some lunch. Then there were games and amusements.

'You want to have something to eat and to go out a little?' asked he. 'So do I. Well, which of us will get out quickest?'

With shouts and squeals we rushed down the stairs after him. He sprang three or four steps at a time, escaping from us. We followed in a bunch.

He describes how Tolstoy soon returned after lunch and would join in the snowballing and let them try to upset him. He says:

We would surround Leo Nikoláevich, catch hold of him before and behind, try to trip him up, snowball him, and rush in and climb on his back, eager to overthrow him. But he was even more determined than we, and like a strong ox would carry us on his back. After a while from weariness, or more often for fun, he would fall into the snow. Then our ecstasy was indescribable! We at once began to cover him with snow and threw ourselves on him in a heap, crying: 'The heap's too small! The heap's too small!'

So the hours passed like minutes. If one lived in such merriment one would not notice the passing of an age.

We enjoyed school and worked eagerly. But Leo Nikoláevich worked yet more eagerly than we. He worked with us so eagerly that he often missed his lunch. In school his appearance was serious. He demanded of us cleanliness, care with the school things, and truthfulness . . .

He never punished anyone for pranks, disobedience, or idleness; and if we became too noisy he only said: 'Quieter, please!'

We kept exemplary order all three years.

. . . In such pleasures and merriment, and with rapid progress in learning, we grew as close to Leo Nikoláevich as a cobbler's thread is to wax. We were sad without him and he without us. We were inseparable from him and only the night-time divided us. We spent the day in school and passed the evening at games, sitting on his balcony till late at night. He would tell us tales about the war, or of how a man-cook cut his aunt's throat in Moscow, and how he went hunting and a bear bit him, and he showed us the scar near his eye. There was no end to our talking. We told him terrible things – about wizards, and wood-demons . . . He told us tales, terrible or funny, sang songs, suiting the words to us . . . He was in general a great jester and never missed a chance to have a laugh . . .

Fifty years have passed since then. I am already an old man. But my recollections of Leo Nikoláevich's school and of himself are still clear. They always cheer me, especially when I am in trouble . . . The love of Leo Nikoláevich then kindled burns brightly in my soul and lights my whole life; and the recollection of those bright and happy days I have never lost, and never shall lose.

Teachers from his own and the neighbouring schools, as well as other pupils of Yásnaya school, fully confirm Fédka's remarks, and Tolstoy himself, both at that time and long afterwards, gave a like impression.

Writing to the Countess A. A. Tolstoy, in July 1861, he said:

It is impossible to describe what children they are – one must see them. Among those of our own sweet class I have never met anything like them. Just think, that during two years, and with a complete absence of discipline, not a single boy or girl has been punished, and there is never any idleness, rudeness, any silly tricks or improper words.

And in 1903 he wrote to Birukóv:

I owe the brightest time in my life not to the love of woman but to love of people, to the love of children. That was a wonderful time, especially after the gloom that had preceded it.

Apart from articles on education Tolstoy wrote little during the three years from the autumn of 1859, when he began his school work, to September 1862, when he married.

He does not stand before the world today primarily as a school-master, and even if I were competent to deal with the subject it would exceed the limits of this biography to attempt a criticism of his precepts and practice, but he certainly possessed, as he claims in one of his articles, 'a certain pedagogic tact', and is right in his belief that rigid discipline in schools, lack of freedom and initiative, continual demand for silence and obedience, and refusal to allow pupils to criticise the lessons they receive, have a stupefying effect.

All that he allowed at Yásnaya Polyána was denied to us when I was at Christ's Hospital in 1868–74; and I look back on those six years of mental stultification as the most wretched of my life. At the preparatory school in Hertford, so stupefied were the little boys by terror and discipline that when the headmaster (traditionally an incarnation of all the virtues) became grossly harsh and unfair, they could not see what was happening until his insanity was so pronounced that the doctors had to take him in hand, an event that occurred soon after I left for the upper school in London.

There one of the masters (who evidently did not believe that 'history is experience teaching by example') in intervals between whacking the boys on their backs or hands with a long cane, used, I remember, emphatically to announce that 'dates and names are the most important parts of history'. A Latin master, a barrister, who was usually busy at some law work when he should have been teaching us, used to set us to learn by rote rules and illustrations which we did not in the least understand. On one occasion the example given in the grammar was:

Opes irritamenta malorum effodiuntur.
Riches the incentives of crime are dug out of the earth.

The top boy had learnt the rule and illustration by heart (which I never could do); but departing from his usual routine the master unexpectedly asked which Latin word corresponded to which English. Each of the first twenty-four boys in the class in turn got caned and sent to the bottom, so that by the time I, who had been last, had come to the top and it was my turn to reply, only one possible combination remained untried and I was able to announce that *effodiuntur* meant 'are dug out of the earth'. Unluckily there was another rule that day, and over this I, in turn, came to grief and was caned and sent to the bottom.

In the drawing class I remember doing the outline of a cube to the master's satisfaction and being promoted to the shading class. I had no idea how to shade and the attempt I made was no doubt a very bad one, but instead of receiving advice or assistance my ears were boxed so violently that I should be inclined to attribute to that assault the slight deafness from which I have since suffered, were it not that such treatment was so common at Christ's Hospital that none of the victims whose hearing was impaired could be sure to which of the masters they owed that part of their preparation for the battle of life.

I feel sure the stultifying effects of such cruel and senseless treatment would have been even more serious had not the school authorities, by some strange oversight, allowed *one* really readable and interesting periodical to find a place among the Sunday magazines and other sterilised literature obtainable in the School Library. This one publication, which I read ardently during my school years, was *Chambers's Journal*. It contained novels by James Payn, and other matter suited to my powers of mental digestion. From smuggled copies of Captain Marryat's novels I also got a good deal of culture, far more I am sure than from any of the lessons we endured.

9

Marriage

To one who admires Tolstoy's educational work it is disconcerting to see how slightingly he spoke of it sixteen years later in his *Confession*. But that was always his way: the old is useless and worthless and bad; only the new, the unachieved, the fresh ideal, is admirable. For it he decries all that the past has produced – including himself and his former work. He makes his points keenly and powerfully, but to understand him we must discriminate and allow for an artistic temperament tempting him to exaggeration. Let him however speak for himself, that the reader may judge:

> On returning from abroad I settled in the country and chanced to occupy myself with peasant schools. This work was particularly to my taste, because in it I had not to face the falsity which had become obvious to me and stared me in the face when I tried to teach people by literary means. Here also I acted in the name of Progress, but I already regarded Progress itself critically. I said to myself: 'In some of its developments Progress has proceeded wrongly; and with primitive peasant children one must deal in a spirit of perfect freedom, letting them choose what path of progress they please.' In reality I was ever revolving round one and the same insoluble problem, which was: How to teach without knowing what to teach? In the higher spheres of literary activity I had realised that one could not teach without knowing what; for I saw that people all taught differently, and by quarrelling among themselves succeeded only in hiding their ignorance from one another. But here, with peasant children, I thought to evade this difficulty by letting them learn what they liked. It amuses me now when I remember how I shuffled, trying to satisfy my desire to teach while in the depth of my soul I knew very well that I could not teach anything needful for I did not know what was needful.
>
> After spending a year at school work I went abroad a second time to discover how to teach others while myself knowing nothing.

And it seemed to me that I had learnt this abroad, and in the year of the peasants' Emancipation I returned to Russia armed with all this wisdom; and having become an Arbiter, I began to teach both the uneducated peasants in schools and the educated classes through a magazine I published. Things appeared to be going well, but I felt I was not quite sound mentally and that matters could not long continue in that way. And I should perhaps then have come to the state of despair at which I arrived fifteen years later had there not been one side of life still unexplored by me and promising me happiness: that was marriage.

For a year I busied myself with arbitration work, the schools, and the magazine; and I became so worn-out – as a result especially of my mental confusion – and so hard was my struggle as Arbiter, so obscure the results of my activity in the schools, so repulsive my shuffling in the magazine (which always amounted to one and the same thing: a desire to teach everybody and to hide the fact that I did not know what to teach), that I fell ill, mentally rather than physically, threw up everything, and went away to the Bashkírs in the steppes, to breathe fresh air, drink *kumys*, and live an animal life.

Tired of and dissatisfied with his work, and thinking he detected in himself signs of consumption, which had carried off two of his brothers, he set off in May 1862 (accompanied by his servant Alexéy and two of his pupils) to undergo a *kumys* (soured and fermented mares' milk) cure in the Samára steppes east of the Vólga. He went first to Moscow, and his friend Raévski has told how Tolstoy came up to him in the Club there and mentioned with great indignation and vexation that his brother was playing cards and had lost 1,000 rubles in a few hours. 'How can men do such things?' said Tolstoy. Half an hour later Raévski saw Leo Tolstoy himself playing Chinese billiards (a game something like bagatelle, played on a board with wire impediments) and learnt that he had lost 7,000 rubles to the stranger with whom he was playing! This was, I believe, the last occasion on which Tolstoy played any game for stakes he found it difficult to pay. The episode led to the premature publication of his novel, *The Cossacks*, which had been in hand for several years but to which he still intended to add a second part. Not having 1,000 rubles available, he let Katkóv, the well-known publicist and editor of the *Moscow Védomosti* and of the monthly *Russian Messenger*, have the story for that sum paid in advance. The novel is based on

Tolstoy's Caucasian experiences. The circumstances which led to its publication made it repugnant to him, and he never completed it.

He mentioned the occurrence at the Behrs, and the young ladies of that family were already so interested in him that they wept at the news. At their home he was always a welcome and intimate guest.

From Moscow he proceeded to Tver by rail, and thence by steamer down the Vólga to Samára. From Samára he wrote to Aunt Tatiána:

27th May 1862

Today I shall start to drive ninety miles from Samára to Karalyk . . .

I have had a beautiful journey; the country pleases me very much; my health is better, i.e. I cough less. Alexéy and the boys are alive and well, as you may tell their relations. Please write to me about Sergéy, or let him do so. Greet all my dear comrades [the masters of the schools] for me, and ask them to write to me of what goes on and of how they are getting on . . .

In another letter, of 28th June 1862, he wrote:

It is now a month since I had any news of you or from home; please write to me about everybody: first, our family; secondly, the students [who acted as masters in the schools], etc. Alexéy and I have grown fatter, he especially, but we still cough a little, and again he especially. We are living in a Tartar tent; the weather is beautiful. I have found my friend Stolypin – now Atamán in Urálsk – and have driven over to see him; and have brought back from there a secretary; but I dictate and write little. Idleness overcomes one when drinking *kumys*. In two weeks' time I intend to leave here, and I expect to be home by St Elijah's day [20th July, o.s.]. I am tormented in this out-of-the-way place by not knowing what is going on, and also by the thought that I am horribly behind-hand with publication of the magazine. I kiss your hand . . .

Just when Tolstoy was leaving Karalyk an unexpected thing happened at Yásnaya, where his sister Márya was staying with Aunt Tatiána. Owing to the denunciation of a police spy who, among other lies, pretended to have discovered a secret door in Tolstoy's house, the police authorities decided to search his estate; and one morning – to the immense astonishment of the neighbouring peasants – police, watchmen, officials, and gendarmes under the command of a colonel, appeared upon the scene. In the schoolhouse a photographic apparatus was found: a thing sufficiently rare in a Russian village in those days to evoke the suspicious enquiries of the gendarme officer, to whom one of the student-teachers chaffingly volunteered the information that it was kept to photograph Herzen (the political exile, then living in London); but nowhere were any secret doors found.

The floors of the stables were broken up with crowbars to see if anything were hidden there. The pond was dragged, but nothing more incriminating than crayfish and carp was found. All the cupboards, drawers, boxes, and desks in the house were opened and searched, and the ladies were frightened almost to death. A police-officer would not allow Tolstoy's sister to leave the library till he had finished reading aloud in her presence and in that of two gendarmes, Tolstoy's Diary and letters, which contained the most intimate secrets of his life and which he had kept private since he was sixteen years old.

Finding nothing incriminating at Yásnaya, the representatives of law and order betook themselves to the other schools working in conjunction with Tolstoy, and there turned tables and cupboards upside down, seized exercise-books and primers, arrested the teachers, and spread the wildest suspicions abroad among the peasants, to whom school education was still a novelty held somewhat in suspicion.

On receiving news of this event Tolstoy at once wrote to his aunt, the Countess A. A. Tolstoy, asking her to speak to those who knew him well and had influence, and on whose aid he could rely. Said he:

I cannot and will not let this affair pass. All the activity in which I found solace and happiness has been spoilt. Auntie is so ill from fright that she will probably not recover. The peasants no longer regard me as an honest man – an opinion I had earned in the course of years – but as a criminal, an incendiary, or a coiner, whose cunning alone has enabled him to escape punishment.

'Eh, man, you've been found out! Don't talk to us about honesty and justice any more – you've hardly escaped handcuffs yourself!'

From the landed proprietors I need not say what a cry of rapture has gone up. Please write to me as soon as possible, after consulting Peróvsky [Count V. A. P.] and Alexéy Tolstoy [Count A. T., the dramatist and poet] and anyone else you like, as to how I should write to the Emperor and how best to present my letter. It is too late to prevent the injury the thing has done or to extricate myself, and there is no way out except by receiving satisfaction as public as the insult has been; and this I have firmly resolved on. I shall not join Herzen; he has his way I have mine. Neither will I hide . . . But I will loudly announce that I am selling my estate and mean to leave Russia, where one cannot know from moment to moment what awaits one . . .

At the end of an eight-page letter he mentions that the colonel of gendarmes, on leaving, threatened to renew his search till he discovered 'if anything is hidden'; and Tolstoy adds, 'I have loaded pistols in my room and am waiting to see how this matter will end.'

He also remarks:

I often say to myself, How exceedingly fortunate it was that I was not at home at the time! Had I been there, I should certainly now be awaiting my trial for murder!

Soon after this Alexander II spent some time in and near Moscow. There Tolstoy presented a letter claiming reparation, which an aide-de-camp undertook to give to the Emperor; and some weeks later the Governor of Túla transmitted to Tolstoy the Emperor's expression of regret for what had occurred.

It is easy to imagine the effect such an outrage as this police-search had on a man of Tolstoy's acute self-esteem, and how it intensified his hatred of Government.

After his return from Samára he saw more of the Behrs than ever. Fet, whom he introduced to them, thus records his impressions of the family:

I found the doctor an amiable old gentleman of polite manners, and his wife a handsome, stately brunette who evidently ruled the house. I refrain from describing the three young ladies, of whom the youngest had an admirable contralto voice. They all, notwithstanding the watchful supervision of their mother and their irreproachable modesty, possessed that attractive quality which the French designate by the words *du chien* [lively, full of go]. The service and the dinner were admirable.

Madame Behrs was on very friendly terms with Tolstoy's sister, the Countess Márya, and before he went abroad Tolstoy had frequently at the house of the latter played with the children of both families. In 1862 he constantly visited the Behrs at Pokróvksi, where they lived in a *dácha* (country house) which they occupied every summer. He nearly always walked the eight miles from Moscow, and often took long rambles with the family besides. The girls had been educated at home, but Sónya and her eldest sister, Lisa, had passed a university examination entitling them to diplomas as qualified private teachers.

The third daughter, Tánya, was a lively, attractive girl of sixteen, with a beautiful and well-trained voice.

At the beginning of August 1862, Mme Behrs and her daughters paid a two weeks' visit to her father's estate of Ívitsa, some thirty miles from Yásnaya, and *en route* spent a couple of days at Yásnaya to visit the Countess Márya. The day after their arrival a picnic party was arranged with some neighbours. It was haymaking time, and there was much haystack climbing by the picnickers. The general impression was that Tolstoy was in love with Lisa, the eldest Miss Behrs – this opinion being fostered by the idea, then common in Russia, that an elder daughter should be disposed of before a younger was courted.

A few days later Tolstoy followed the Behrs to Ívitsa, and here the scene occurred which he has utilised in *Anna Karénina* when describing Lévin's proposal to Kitty – a scene in which something approaching thought-reading takes place.

Sitting at a card-table with Miss Sónya Behrs, Tolstoy wrote the initial letters of the sentence: 'In your family a false opinion exists about me and your sister Lisa; you and Tánichka should destroy it.'

Sónya looked at the letters and gave the words they stood for.

Tánya, who had hidden in the card-room to avoid being asked to sing, was an involuntary witness of this scene, and from her we learn that Tolstoy helped Sónya with a few of the words, but even so the test was a severe one.

Tolstoy then wrote the initial letters of another sentence: 'Your youth and need of happiness today remind me too strongly of my age and the impossibility of happiness,' and again she guessed right. The two understood one another, and their fate was then wellnigh sealed, though not finally decided for some weeks.

The Behrs returned to Pokróvski in September. Tolstoy accompanied them on the carriage-journey to Moscow and visited them every day, bringing music for the young ladies, playing the piano for them, accompanying Tánya's singing, and nicknaming her 'Madame Viardot' after the famous singer.

We may judge of his state of mind at this time by an entry in his Diary, dated 23rd August: 'I am afraid of myself. What if this be only a *desire* for love and not real love? I try to notice only her weak points, but yet I love.'

On 26th August Sónya gave him a story to read, written by herself. The entry in his Diary runs:

> Went on foot to the Behrs; it is peacefully comfortable there – the girls' laughter. Sónya was vulgar and not good, but fills my mind. She gave me her story to read. What energy of truth and simplicity! The indefiniteness torments her. I read it all without heart-sinking, jealousy, or envy; but 'unusually unattractive appearance' and 'instability of conviction' hit me hard. I have calmed down. All this [love, marriage, family life, &c.] is not my affair . . . Work, and just the satisfaction of one's needs.

It may be mentioned that in his youth Tolstoy's appearance had always troubled him.

> He was convinced that he was repulsively ugly [Tánya writes in her memoirs]. I have repeatedly heard him say so. He of course did not know that what was attractive in his appearance was the spiritual strength shown by his profound look. He could not see and observe in himself the expression of his eyes and that was what gave charm to his face.

Of the novel Sónya had written, Tánya tells us that it described the state of her soul, tormented by Tolstoy's indefinite relations towards her sister Lisa and herself. In the story Tolstoy appeared under the name of Dublítski. Tánya adds:

> It is a pity my sister burnt her novel, for in it in embryo appeared the Rostóv family [subsequently depicted in *War and Peace*]: the mother, Véra and Natásha.

So that the future Countess Tolstoy had some share in suggesting her husband's great novel.

On his thirty-fourth birthday, 28th August 1862 (old style), he jotted down in his Diary the words: 'Ugly mug! Do not think of marriage; your calling is of another kind, and for that much has been given you.'

On 3rd September:

> Never has my future life with a wife presented itself to me so clearly,

joyfully, and calmly . . . Above all it seems so simple and timely, with no passions, fear, or a single moment of regret.

His Diary shows however the state of agitation and vacillation he was in. On 7th September he notes:

Today I am at home alone and reflect at leisure on my own position. Dublítski, don't intrude where youth, poetry, beauty and love are! . . . For that, young men are in place.

The next day he exhorts himself:

Nonsense. A monastery of labour, that is your job, from the height of which you may calmly and gladly watch the love and happiness of others. I have dwelt in that monastery and will return to it. Yes.

The Diary is insincere. *Arrière-pensée*. That she is with me and will sit beside me and read . . . and this is for her.

12th September:

I am in love as I did not believe it possible to love. I am a madman and shall shoot myself if it goes on like this. I spent the evening at their house. She was charming in every way. But I am the repulsive Dublítski. I should have been on guard sooner. But now I cannot stop. Granted that I am a Dublítski, I am made beautiful by love. Yes, tomorrow I will go to them in the morning. There were some moments, but I did not avail myself of them. I was afraid, but I should have spoken simply. I should like to go back and speak out before them all. Lord, help me!

13th September:

Every day I think that it is impossible to suffer more and be happy at the same time, and every day I become more insane. Again I left with depression, repentance, and happiness, in my soul. Tomorrow I will go as soon as I am up and say everything, or will shoot myself.

It was however not till the 16th that he handed her a letter containing a proposal of marriage. Tánya in her memoirs tells the story as follows:

Leo Tolstoy came to us on the 16th after dinner. I noticed that he was not his usual self. Something agitated him, now he sat down at the piano but got up again without finishing what he had begun to play, now walked about the room, going to Sónya and asking her to play a duet, and when she sat down to the piano saying: 'Better let us just sit here.'

So they sat at the piano and Sónya gently played over the valse *Il Baccio*, learning to play it as accompaniment to the song.

I saw and felt that something important had to happen that day, but I was not sure whether it would finish with his departure or a proposal.

I was going past the room, when Sónya called to me: 'Tánya, try to sing the valse. I think I have learnt the accompaniment.'

It seemed to me that Tolstoy's restlessness had conveyed itself to Sónya and oppressed her.

I agreed to sing the valse and took my place as usual in the middle of the room.

Sónya played the accompaniment with an unsteady hand. Tolstoy was sitting beside her. It seemed to me that he was discontented at her having got me to sing. I noticed this by the unpleasant expression on his face.

I was in good voice and, paying no attention to his mood, continued to sing, carried away by the graceful air of the valse.

Sónya blundered. Tolstoy slipped quietly into her seat and continuing the accompaniment at once gave life to my voice and to the words of the valse.

I no longer noticed anything, either the expression of his face or my sister's confusion. I yielded completely to the charm of those sounds and reaching the finale, where appeal and forgiveness are so passionately expressed, I resolutely took the high note with which the valse ends.

'How you sing today!' Tolstoy said in an agitated voice.

I was pleased by his praise. I had dispelled his dissatisfaction, though I had not tried to do so.

A musical mood does not come to order, but especially in singing comes when you give a fragment of your soul.

Later on I learnt that while accompanying me that evening Tolstoy was trying his fate: 'If she takes the final high note well, I must deliver the letter today (he had more than once brought with him a letter addressed to my sister). If she takes it badly I must not deliver it.'

In general Tolstoy had a habit of questioning fate by a game of 'Patience', or by various trifles: 'Shall I do so?' or, 'Will that happen?'

I went away to make tea.

A little later I saw Sónya go quickly downstairs to our room with a letter in her hand.

Tolstoy's proposal was readily accepted; but her father, displeased that the second daughter should be preferred to the eldest, at first refused his assent, though eventually he yielded to Sónya's insistence.

The bridegroom's sense of honour led him to hand his future wife the Diary in which, mingled with hopes, prayers, self-castigations, and self-denunciations, the sins and excesses of his bachelorhood were recorded. To the girl who had looked upon him as a personification of the virtues, this revelation came as a great shock; but after a sleepless night passed in weeping bitterly over it, she returned the Diary and forgave the past.

To get married it was necessary first to confess and receive the eucharist. Tolstoy's own experiences in this matter are narrated in Chapter I of Part V of *Anna Karénina*, where they are attributed to Lévin.

The marriage took place within a week of the proposal, namely on the 23rd September 1862, in the Court church of the Krémlin, the bridegroom being thirty-four and the bride eighteen years of age. When the ceremony was over the couple left Moscow in a *dormeuse* (sleeping carriage), and drove to Yásnaya Polyána, where Tolstoy's brother Sergéy and Aunt Tatiána were awaiting them.

Fet records the letter in which Tolstoy informed him of his marriage:

FÉTOUSHKA [an endearing diminutive of Fet] Uncle, or simply Dear Friend Afanási Afanásevich – I have been married two weeks and am happy, and am a new, quite a new man. I want to visit you, but cannot manage it. When shall I see you? Having come to myself I feel that I value you very, very much. We have so many unforgettable things in common: Nikólenka, and much besides. Do drive over and make my acquaintance. I kiss Márya Petróvna's hand. Farewell, dear friend. I embrace you with all my heart.

In another letter belonging to the same period he writes:

I am writing from the country and while I write, from upstairs where she is talking to my brother, I hear the voice of my wife whom I love more than all the world. I have lived to the age of thirty-four without knowing that it was possible to love and to be so happy. When I am more tranquil I will write you a long letter. I should not say 'more tranquil' for I am now more tranquil and clear than I have ever been, but I should say, 'when I am accustomed to it'. At present I have a constant feeling of having stolen an undeserved, illicit happiness not intended for me. There . . . she is coming! I hear her, and it is so good! . . . And why do such good people as you and, most wonderful of all, such a being as my wife, love me?

It did not much disturb his happiness when, before they had been married a fortnight, something happened that might easily have led to very disagreeable consequences. On 3rd October the Minister of the Interior called the attention of the Minister of Education to the harmful nature of the *Yásnaya Polyána* magazine. This is what he wrote:

A careful perusal of the educational magazine, *Yásnaya Polyána*, edited by Count Tolstoy, leads to the conviction that that magazine . . . frequently propagates ideas which apart from their incorrectness are by their very tendency harmful . . . I consider it necessary to direct your Excellency's attention to the general tendency and spirit of that magazine, which often infringes the fundamental rules of religion and morality . . . I have the honour to inform you, Sir, of this, in the expectation that you may be inclined to consider it desirable to direct the special attention of the Censor to this publication.

Fortunately the decision did not lie with the Minister of the Interior but with the Minister of Education, who on receiving this communication had the magazine carefully examined and, on 24th October, replied that he found nothing harmful or contrary to religion in its tendency. It contained extreme opinions on educational matters no doubt, but these, he said, should be criticised in educational periodicals rather than prohibited by the Censor. 'In general,' added the Minister,

I must say that Count Tolstoy's educational activity deserves full respect, and the Ministry of Education is bound to assist and co-operate with him, though it cannot share all his views, some of which after full consideration he will himself probably reject.

Other things besides the suspicion in which he was held by the Minister of the Interior tended to discourage Tolstoy. His magazine had few subscribers and attracted little attention. The year's issue was causing him a loss of about 3,000 rubles – a larger sum than he could well afford to throw away. So he decided to discontinue it after the twelfth number. The month after his marriage he also ceased to devote attention to the school, which was too great a tax on his time and energies.

It has often been said that the obstacles placed in his way by the Government turned him aside from educational work, but in speaking to me of it Tolstoy remarked that the main factor really was his marriage and preoccupation with family life.

Both he and his wife were absorbed by their personal happiness, though from time to time small quarrels and misunderstandings arose between them. So impulsive and strenuous a nature as Tolstoy's was sure to have its fluctuations of feeling, but on the whole the ties binding the couple together remained strong and close while the months passed into years.

The Countess's parents used to say: 'We could not have wished for greater happiness for our daughter.' The Countess not only loved Tolstoy dearly as a husband but had the deepest admiration for him as a writer. He on his side often said that he found in family life the completest happiness, and in Sófya Andréevna not only a loving wife and an excellent mother for his children, but an admirable assistant in his literary work, in which, owing to his careless and unmethodical habits, an intelligent and devoted amanuensis was invaluable. The Countess acquired remarkable skill in deciphering his often extremely illegible handwriting, and was sometimes able to guess in a quite extraordinary way the meaning of his hasty jottings and incomplete sentences.

One drawback to their almost complete happiness lay in the fact that, though active and possessed of great physical strength, Tolstoy seldom enjoyed any long periods of uninterrupted good health. In his correspondence we find frequent references to indisposition. In early manhood, he seems to have distended his stomach and, especially after the hardships endured during the war of 1854-5, he was subject to indigestion for the rest of his days.

Another cause of occasional distress was the strong tendency to jealousy that husband and wife both suffered from. How Tolstoy himself could behave he has described for us in chapters XI to XV of Part VI of *Anna Karénina* (though the treatment of Vásenka Veslóvsky there recounted was actually applied to an undesirable admirer of Tánya's). On her side the Countess has told how she disguised herself and went out expecting her husband to mistake her for a peasant woman and accost her. Beyond her knowledge of what had occurred before marriage she never had any real ground for suspecting his fidelity.

Town life did not attract him; still, towards the close of the year of his marriage, he and the Countess spent some weeks in Moscow.

They were however soon back at Yásnaya. In February Fet visited them there, and found them overflowing with life and happiness.

On 15th May, after they had by some chance just missed meeting Fet at the house of a neighbouring proprietor, Tolstoy wrote to his friend:

> We just missed seeing you and how sorry I am that we did! How much I want to talk over with you. Not a day passes without our mentioning you several times. My wife is not at all 'playing with dolls'. Don't insult her. She is my serious helpmate, though now bearing a burden from which she hopes to be free early in July. What won't she do afterwards? We are *ufanising** little by little. I have made an important discovery which I hasten to impart to you. Clerks and overseers are only a hindrance in the management of an estate. Try the experiment of dismissing them all; then sleep ten hours a day, and be assured that everything will get along *not worse*. I have made the experiment and am quite satisfied with its success.
>
> How, oh how, are we to see one another? If you go to Moscow with Márya Petróvna and do not visit me, it will be dreadfully offensive. (My wife, who was reading this letter, prompted that sentence.) I wanted to write much, but time lacks. I embrace you with all my heart, my wife bows profoundly to you, and I to your wife.
>
> *Business*: When you are in Orél, buy me 20 puds [720 lb.] of various kinds of twine, reins, and shaft-traces, if they cost less than 2.30 rubles per pud including carriage, and send them me by a carter. The money shall be paid at once.

Fet soon availed himself of the invitation, and after driving past the low towers that mark the entrance to the birch alley leading to the house, he came upon Tolstoy eagerly directing the dragging of a lake and taking all possible care that the carp should not escape. The Countess, in a white dress, came running down the alley with a huge bundle of barn-door keys hanging at her waist. After cordially greeting the visitor she, notwithstanding her 'exceedingly interesting condition', leapt over the low railing between the alley and the pond. It will however be better to quote Fet's own account of his visit:

---

* This word when first invented by Nicholas Tolstoy meant to work like a peasant, but it had by now come to mean farming in general.

'Sónya, tell Nestérka to fetch a sack from the barn and let us go back to the house,' said Tolstoy – who had already greeted me warmly without losing sight of the carp-capturing operations the while.

The Countess immediately detached a huge key from her belt and gave it to a boy, who started at a run to fulfil the order.

'There,' remarked the Count, 'you have an example of our method. We keep the keys ourselves, and all the estate business is carried on by boys.'

At the animated dinner table the carp we had seen captured made their appearance. We all seemed equally at ease and happy . . .

That evening was one truly 'filled with hope'. It was a sight to see with what pride and bright hope Tatiána Alexándrovna, the kindest of aunts, regarded the young people she so loved, and how turning to me said frankly, 'You see, with *mon cher Léon* of course things could not be otherwise.'

As to the Countess, life to one who in her condition leapt over fences could not but be lit up with the brightest of hopes. The Count himself, who had passed his whole life in an ardent search for novelties, evidently at this period entered a world till then unknown, in the mighty future of which he believed with all the enthusiasm of a young artist. I myself during that evening was carried away by the general tone of careless happiness and did not feel the stone of Sisyphus oppressing me.

On 28th June 1863 a son, Sergéy, was born. During the first eleven years of marriage, the Countess bore her husband eight children, and another five during the next fifteen years: making in all, thirteen in twenty-six years.

But we must turn back a few months to mention the works by Tolstoy which appeared during this year.

In the January number of the *Russian Messenger* Katkóv had published *The Cossacks*, which Tolstoy had held back to revise and had only delivered in December.

In the February number of the same magazine appeared *Polikúshka*, the story of a serf who, having lost some money belonging to his mistress, hangs himself.

These stories are referred to in the following letter from Tolstoy to Fet, undated, but written in 1863:

Both your letters were equally important, significant, and agreeable to me, dear Afanásy Afanásevich. I am living in a world so remote from literature and its critics that on receiving such a letter as yours my first feeling is one of astonishment. Whoever was it wrote *The Cossacks* and *Polikúshka*? And what's the use of talking about them? Paper endures anything and editors pay for and print anything. But that is merely a first impression; afterwards one enters into the meaning of what you say, rummages in one's head, and finds in some corner of it, among old, forgotten rubbish, something indefinite, labelled *Art*; and pondering on what you say agrees that you are right, and even finds it pleasant to rummage about in that old rubbish amid the smell one once loved. One even feels a desire to write. Of course, you are right. But then there are few readers of your sort.

Polikúshka is the chatter of a man who 'wields a pen' on the first theme that comes to hand; but *The Cossacks* has some matter in it, though poor. I am now writing the story of a pied gelding, which I expect to print in the autumn. [It did not appear till 1888.] But how can one write now? Invisible efforts – and even visible ones – are now going on; and moreover I am again up to my ears in farming. So is Sónya. We have no steward; we have assistants for fieldwork and building, but she, single-handed, attends to the office and the cash. I have the bees, the sheep, a new orchard, and the distillery. It all progresses little by little, though of course badly compared with our ideal.

What do you think of the Polish business [the insurrection of 1863 then breaking out]? It looks bad! Shall we – you, I, and Borísov – not have to take our swords down from their rusty nails? . . .

The bees, which Tolstoy here places first among his outdoor duties, occupied much of his time, and he often spent hours studying their habits.

Turgénev, writing to Fet, commented on *The Cossacks* as follows:

I read *The Cossacks* and went into ecstasies over it, so did Bótkin. Only the personality of Olénin spoils the generally splendid impression. To contrast civilisation with fresh, primeval Nature there was no need again to produce that dull, unhealthy fellow always preoccupied with himself. Why does Tolstoy not get rid of that nightmare?

Several months later he wrote:

After you left, I read Tolstoy's *Polikúshka* and marvelled at the strength of his huge talent. But he has used up too much material, and it is a pity he drowned the son. It makes it too terrible. But there are pages that are truly wonderful! It made a cold shudder run down even my back, though you know my back has grown thick and coarse. He is a master, a master!

Tolstoy was now fairly started on the life he was destined to lead for sixteen years: a quiet country life, occupied with family joys and cares. These years followed one another with so little change that the story of a decade and a half can almost be compressed into a sentence. Children came in quick succession, two great novels and an *ABC Book* were produced, a large orchard was planted with apple trees, the Yásnaya Polyána property was improved and new estates were purchased east of the Vólga.

During 1863 he wrote two plays which he did not publish. One, a farcical comedy called *The Nihilist*, was privately performed at home with success. The second, also a comedy, written on a topic of the day, was called *The Infected Family*. Hoping to have it staged, Tolstoy took it to Moscow early in 1864; but the theatrical season was then already too far advanced, and he never subsequently cared to have it either published or acted.

The Countess Tolstoy's brother, S. A. Behrs (who from 1866, when he was a boy of eleven, till 1878, spent every summer with the Tolstoys), in his *Recollections of Count Tolstoy* gives a very interesting account of the life at Yásnaya. He mentions that a proverb about the hard fate of penniless noblemen prompted Tolstoy to take all possible care to provide for his children's future; and apart from his literary work, the passage in the letter quoted above about his bees, sheep, new orchard, and distillery, shows how this care was applied.

In his *Confession*, Tolstoy says of the years now under review:

Returning from abroad I married. The new conditions of happy family life completely diverted me from all search for the general meaning of life. My whole existence was centred at that time in my family, wife, and children, and in care to increase our means of livelihood. My striving after self-perfection and progress was now again replaced by the effort simply to secure the best possible conditions for myself and my family.

Again, writing in 1903 of this middle period of his life, Tolstoy says:

Then came a third, an eighteen-year period which may be the least interesting of all (from my marriage to my spiritual rebirth) and which from a worldly point of view may be called moral: that is to say, during those eighteen years I lived a correct, honest, family life, not indulging myself in any vices condemned by public opinion, but with interests wholly limited to selfish cares for my family, for the increase of our property, the acquisition of literary success, and all kinds of pleasure.

After the Emancipation the landlords in many parts of Russia had more or less serious friction with the peasants, among whom stories were rife to the effect that the Tsar intended to give them all the land but had been deceived by the officials into only giving part; and for a time riots were not infrequent. There was no serious trouble of this sort on Tolstoy's estate, but his sister (whom I met at Yásnaya in 1902 long after her husband's death, when she, a nun, had leave from her Convent to visit her brother after he had been seriously ill) told me that on one occasion the peasants refused to make the hay, and to save it from being lost, Tolstoy, his wife, the members of the family, and the masters from eleven neighbouring schools, set to work with a will and by strenuous exertion saved the crop before the weather changed.

On settling down to married life Tolstoy planned a great novel. The epoch he at first intended to deal with was that of the Constitutionist conspiracy which came to a head on the accession of Nicholas I to the throne in December 1825. That very premature military plot was quickly snuffed out. So little were things ripe for it that many of the soldiers who shouted for a 'Constitution' (*Konstitútsia*) thought they were demanding allegiance to Nicholas's elder brother 'Constantine, who having married a Polish lady of the Roman Catholic faith had renounced his right to the throne. While planning the work, Tolstoy found himself carried back to the scenes amid which his characters had grown up – the time of the Napoleonic wars and the invasion of Russia by the French in 1812. Here was a splendid background for a novel, and laying *The Decembrists* aside he commenced *War and Peace*, a work conceived on a gigantic scale and which achieved a splendid success.

His attention, as we have already seen, was however not wholly absorbed by literature, but divided between that and the management of his property. During his stay among the Kirghíz in the Province of Samára he had noticed how extremely cheap and how fertile was the land in those parts. He therefore wished to purchase an estate there, and in the autumn of 1864 visited the district with that end in view. In October he returned to Yásnaya. In November he wrote to Fet, mentioning his laborious preparations for *War and Peace*:

I am in the dumps and am writing nothing, but work painfully. You cannot imagine how hard I find the preliminary labour of ploughing deep the field in which I must sow. To consider and reconsider all that may happen to all the future characters in the very large work I am preparing, and to weigh millions of possible combinations to select from among them a millionth part, is terribly difficult. And that is what I am doing . . .

Late in that month he again wrote:

This autumn I have written a good deal of my novel. *Ars longa vita brevis* comes to my mind every day. If one could but make time to accomplish a hundredth part of what one understands – but only a thousandth part gets done! Nevertheless the consciousness that *I can* is what brings happiness to men of our sort. You know that feeling, and I experience it with particular force this year.

The year 1864 saw the publication of the first collected edition of Tolstoy's works. The list at the end of this volume shows the twenty 'trials of the pen' which preceded *War and Peace*, and had already placed Tolstoy in the front rank of Russian writers. They filled four very substantial volumes.

One day in October Tolstoy went out for a ride on his favourite horse, an English thoroughbred named Máshka, which had long been standing. His two borzoi dogs accompanied him. After he had ridden some way, a hare started up and the dogs rushed after it. Tolstoy had not come out with the idea of hunting, but on seeing the dogs chasing the hare could not restrain himself and galloped after them, uttering the hunting cry, 'Atoú!' The weather was bad, the ground slippery, and the horse stumbled at a narrow ravine and fell, dislocating and breaking its rider's arm. The horse ran away and Tolstoy, who was quite alone and several miles from home, fainted. When he came to he managed to drag himself more than half a mile to the highroad, where he lay in great pain. Some peasant carts passed by, but at first he could not attract anyone's attention. When at last he was noticed, in order not to alarm his wife, he asked to be taken to the hut of an old wife, Akulína, famed as a bone-setter. In spite of all she and her son Iván could do – soaping, pulling, twisting, and bandaging the arm – they could not set it, and Tolstoy continued to endure great pain.

The Countess, who had meanwhile heard of the accident, reached the hut late at night. She at once arranged to have her husband taken home, and sent to Túla for a doctor, who arrived about 3 a.m. and after administering chloroform succeeded, with the aid of two labourers who were called in to assist, in setting the arm. On coming to, Tolstoy's disbelief in the efficiency of doctors prompted him to send for another surgeon. After a consultation the two physicians decided that everything had been done properly and that Tolstoy must lie up for six weeks to allow the arm to recover. When that time was past, Tolstoy asked for his gun and fired it off to test his arm. No sooner had he done so than he again felt great pain. He thereupon wrote to his father-in-law, Dr Behrs, and on his advice went to Moscow to consult specialists. These differed in opinion, but after a week's hesitation a fresh operation was decided upon, and was carried out by two competent surgeons. It was quite successful and in due course the patient completely recovered the use of his arm.

Meanwhile the Countess (now nursing her second child, a daughter named Tatiána, born on 4th October 1864) remained at Yásnaya, where her eldest child, Sergéy, was taken dangerously ill with smallpox and diarrhoea.

While in Moscow Tolstoy concluded an arrangement with Katkóv for the publication of *War and Peace* in the *Russian Messenger*.

On 23rd January 1865, when he had got over his accident, he wrote Fet another of those light-hearted letters which sometimes contain more truth than will bear saying seriously:

Shall I tell you something surprising about myself? When the horse threw me and broke my arm and when I came to after fainting, I said to myself: 'I am an author.' And I am an author, but a solitary, on-the-quiet, kind of author . . . In a few days the first part of 'The Year 1805' [so the first part of *War and Peace* was originally called] will appear. Please write me your opinion of it in detail. I value your opinion and that of a man whom I dislike the more, the more I grow up – Turgénev. He will understand. All I have printed hitherto I consider but a trial of my pen; what I am now printing, though it pleases me better than my former work, still seems weak – as an Introduction must be. But what follows will be – tremendous!!! . . . Write what is said about it in the different places you know, and especially how it goes with the general public. No doubt it will pass unnoticed. I expect and wish it to do so, if only they don't abuse me, for abuse upsets one . . .

I am glad you like my wife, though I love her less than my novel still you know she is my wife. Be sure you come to visit us; for if you and Márya Petróvna do not stay here on your return from Moscow it will really, without a joke, be too stupid!

In May 1865 one sees by a letter of Tolstoy's to Fet that one of the children had been ill and he himself had been in bed for three days and barely escaped a fever. His wife's younger sister, Tánya, she of the contralto voice, who (with some admixture of his wife) served Tolstoy as model for Natásha in *War and Peace*, was spending the summer at Yásnaya as she did every year. The Countess Márya and her children were also there. The children, he says, were well and out all day in the open air. He adds:

I continue to write little by little, and am content with my work. The woodcock still attract me, and every evening I shoot *at them*, that is generally past them. My farming goes on well, that is to say, it does not disturb me much – which is all I demand of it . . .

In reply to a suggestion from Fet he goes on to say that he will not write more about the Yásno-Polyána school, but hopes someday to express the conclusions to which his three years' ardent passion for that work had brought him. Then follows a reference to the state of agricultural affairs after the Emancipation and an allusion to the question of famine – a subject destined to make great demands on Tolstoy's attention in later years:

Our affairs as agriculturists are now like those of a shareholder whose shares have lost value and are unsaleable on 'Change. The case is a bad one. Personally I only ask that it should not demand of me so much attention and participation as to deprive me of tranquillity. Latterly I have been satisfied with my private affairs, but the general trend – with the impending misery of famine-torments me more and more every day. It is so strange, and even good and terrible. We have rosy radishes on our table, and yellow butter, and well-baked, soft bread on a clean tablecloth; the garden is green and our young ladies in muslin dresses are glad it is hot and shady; while *there* that evil hunger-devil is already at work covering the fields with goose-weed, chafing the hard heels of the peasants and their wives, and cracking the hoofs of the cattle. Our weather, the corn, and the meadows, are really terrible. How are they with you?

The letter closes with advice to Fet to transfer his chief attention from the land to literature, and a statement that Tolstoy himself has done so and is finding life less difficult.

When Tolstoy went out hunting hares and foxes with borzoi dogs, Miss Tatiána Behrs (the Tánya alluded to above) used often to accompany him.

Between this lady and Count Sergéy Tolstoy (Leo's elder brother) an attachment grew up, during the first two years after Tolstoy's marriage which caused great distress to them both, for besides being twenty-two years older than the lady, Sergéy had lived for fifteen years with, and had a family by, a fine woman who was a Gypsy. Despite his real affection for his children and their mother, he proposed to Tánya, and she hardly realising the position accepted him. It was however arranged that the marriage should be postponed, and that the couple were not to see one another for some time. When they did meet again, almost on the eve of marriage, Tánya noticed the distress Sergéy was suffering, but did not understand that it arose from the difficulty of abandoning a woman who was devoted to him. Leo Tolstoy, aware of her perplexity, explained the situation to her, and she immediately broke off the engagement, and held to her decision though it almost broke her heart to do so. Eventually she recovered from the disappointment, and in 1867 married Mr A. M. Kuzmínski with whom she had been in love when she was fourteen. At the same time Sergéy legitimised his children by marrying their mother.

A vivid account of this whole affair, and of the tact, insight, patience, and affection Leo Tolstoy showed in dealing with it is given in *Family Views of Tolstoy* (Allen & Unwin) where also its reflection in *War and Peace* is shown, and how closely Natásha Rostóva was copied from life.

In this affair again one gets a glimpse of the experience which led Tolstoy, contrary to the opinion common among the Russian 'intelligentsia', to advocate faithfulness at all costs to a woman with whom one has once united.

Towards the end of May he visited the estate of Nikólskoe (which had become his after the death of his brother Nicholas), and he had the house there repaired. In June the whole family moved to Nikólskoe, where they lived very quietly, Tolstoy continuing to write his great novel. The Countess, besides having suggested some of the characters and repeatedly copied out the work, exerted an influence on it by persuading Tolstoy to modify and curtail his references to the dissolute conduct of Hélène. His friend D. A. Dyákov's estate was only ten miles away and Tolstoy saw much of him. Dyákov was his chief adviser in agricultural matters and in his efforts to improve the stock of his cattle, pigs, and poultry. Almost the only other visitors at Nikólskoe were the Fets; and the poet records meeting there the Countess's 'charming sister' Tánya, and experiencing violent antipathy for the sour *kumys* about which Tolstoy was enthusiastic and a large tub of which stood near the front door.

While living at Nikólskoe Tolstoy was invited for a fortnight by a neighbouring landlord, Kiréevski, to a grand hunt, in which the huntsmen wore special costumes, and luxurious dinners were served in the woods. What interested Tolstoy most in all this was not the hunt, but the opportunity it afforded him of studying types of the old and new aristocracy.

At this period one hears of his playing the guitar and singing passionate love-songs.

During the autumn of 1865, accompanied by his eleven-year-old brother-in-law, he visited the battlefield of Borodinó. They left Moscow in Dr Behrs's carriage, with post-horses. When the time came for them to have something to eat, they found that the lunch-basket had been left behind, and they had only a small basket of grapes. Thereupon Tolstoy remarked, 'I am sorry, not that we have left the basket of food behind, but that your father will be upset and will be angry with his man.' The journey took only one day, and they stayed at the monastery erected in memory of those who fell in the great fight. For two days Tolstoy investigated the scene of the conflict he was about to describe, and he then drew the plan of the fight that appears in *War and Peace*. Even in 1865 there were but few survivors of the campaign of 1812 to be found in the neighbourhood.

Tolstoy used at this time to spend whole days in the Rumyántsev Museum in Moscow, studying books and manuscripts relating to the times of Alexander I, and especially to the reforming and Masonic movements which then sprang up in Russia but were subsequently suppressed on political grounds.

S. A. Behrs tells us that Tolstoy

was always fond of children and liked to have them about him. He easily won their confidence and seemed to have the key to their hearts. He appeared to have no difficulty in suiting himself to a strange child, and with a single question set it completely at ease, so that it began at once to chat away with perfect freedom. Independently of this he could divine a child's thought with the skill of a trained educationist. I remember his children sometimes running up to him and telling him they had a great secret; and when they persisted in refusing to divulge it he would quietly whisper in their ears what it was. 'Ah, what a papa ours is! How did he find it out?' they would cry in astonishment.

He also says:

Gifted by nature with rare tact and delicacy he is extremely gentle in his bearing and conduct to others. I never heard him scold a servant. Yet they all had the greatest respect for him, were fond of him, and seemed even to fear him. Nor with all his zeal for sport have I ever seen him whip a dog or beat his horse.

A servant who lived with him more than twenty years has said: 'Living in the Count's house from my childhood, I loved Leo Nikolá-evich as though he were my father'; and in another place he remarks:

The Count had a stern appearance, but treated the servants excellently and made things easy for all strangers he met. He had a very good heart, and when he was cross with me for anything I, knowing his character, used at once to leave the room, and when next he called me it was as though nothing unpleasant had happened.

Speaking of Tolstoy's later years the same servant says:

Leo Nikoláevich has now become quite a different man. From 1865 to 1870 he was active in managing the estate, took interest in the cows, bred sheep, looked after the property, and in a word attended to every-thing. At that time he was hot-tempered and impulsive. He would order the trap to be brought when he wanted to go hunting. His man, Alexéy, would bring him his hunting-boots and the Count would shout at him, 'Why have you not dried them? You are not worth your salt!' Alexéy, knowing the Count's character, would take the boots away and bring them back almost directly. 'There! now they're all right,' the Count would say, and would brighten up instantly.

His love of the country and dislike of towns sprang partly from his keen appreciation of the charm and loveliness of Nature. He saw fresh beauty every day, and often exclaimed: 'What wealth God has! He gives each day something to distinguish it from all the rest.'

Sportsman and agriculturist himself, he maintained that sportsmen and agriculturists alone know Nature. To quote Behrs again:

No bad weather was allowed to interfere with his daily walk. He could put up with loss of appetite from which he occasionally suffered, but he could never go a day without a sharp walk in the open air. In general he was fond of active movement, riding, gymnastics, but particularly walking. If his literary work chanced to go badly, or if he wished to throw off the effects of any unpleasantness, a long walk was his sovereign remedy. He could walk a whole day without fatigue, and we have frequently ridden together for ten or twelve hours. In his study he kept a pair of dumb-bells, and sometimes had gymnastic apparatus set up there.

All luxury was distasteful to him, and much that ordinary people regard as common comforts seemed to him harmful indulgence, bad for the souls and bodies of men. Nothing could well be simpler than the arrangement of his house at Yásnaya, substantial and solidly built as it was with its double windows and the Dutch stoves so necessary to warm a Russian house. Most of the rooms had plain uncarpeted board floors. Only the rooms in an annexe built when the family increased had parquet floors.

He was not at all particular about what he ate, but objected to a soft bed or spring mattress and at one time used to sleep on a leather-covered sofa. He dressed very simply, and when at home never wore starched shirts or tailor-made clothes, but adapted to his own require-ments the ordinary Russian blouse, having it made of woollen stuff for winter and of linen for summer. His outdoor winter dress was also an adaptation of the sheepskin *shúba* and peasants' *caftán* made of the plainest material; and these afforded such good protection from the weather that they were often borrowed by members of the household as well as by visitors. The great simplicity of attire which he adopted on principle in later years involved therefore no great change in the country dress he had worn by preference long before.

During the writing of *War and Peace* Tolstoy generally enjoyed good spirits, and on days when his work had gone well he would gleefully announce that he had left 'a bit of my flesh in the inkstand'. One of his chief recreations was to go out hare-hunting with borzoi dogs, and this he often did in company with a neighbouring landed proprietor, Bíbikov.

After his marriage Tolstoy only made entries in his Diary intermittently, and from October 1865 onwards ceased for many years to keep it at all. We have few records of what he read at this period, but he mentions a novel by Druzhínin, a play by Ostróvski, Marmont's *Mémoires* (useful to him for *War and Peace*), Victor Hugo – '*Les Misérables* – strong' – Guizot, Joseph de Maistre, and Prosper Merimée's *Chronique de Charles IX*. Of Merimée he notes: 'He is clever and sensitive, but not talented.'

He did not in general care much for Goethe, but when reading *Faust* notes: 'Poetry of intellect and poetry having for its object what can be expressed by no other art.' He has a number of references to Trollope:

> Good, if it were not for diffuseness . . . Read Trollope – good. There is a novelists' poetry: (1) in the interest of the arrangement of occurrences – Braddon, my (future) Cossacks [the continuation he intended to write]; (2) in the presentation of manners on an historic background – *The Odyssey*, *Iliad*, and *The Year 1805* [under which name the first part of *War and Peace* appeared]; (3) in the beauty and gaiety of a situation – *Pickwick*, *The Outlying Field* [a story he was writing, but afterwards abandoned]; (4) in people's characters – *Hamlet*, and my future work . . .
>
>   Read *The Bertrams* – famous –

and a day later:

> Trollope kills me by his mastery. I console myself that he has his and I have mine. To know one's own – or rather to know what is *not mine*, that is the chief art. I must work like a pianist.

Later he writes: 'Have finished Trollope. Too much conventional. Read stupid Julia Kavanagh.'

On Twelfth Night [1866] a grand masquerade was held at Yásnaya; the festivities were kept up till past two in the morning and were followed by a troika drive next day.

That same January the family moved to Moscow, where they hired a six-roomed apartment for 155 rubles a month, and there they remained for six weeks while the second part of *War and Peace* was being printed.

Among the friends Tolstoy saw most of at this time were I. S. Aksákov and Prince D. Obolénski. He also attended the Moscow drawing school and tried his hand at sculpture – modelling a bust of his wife. It does not appear that he continued this occupation long.

In May 1866 a second son, Ilyá, was born and an English nurse was introduced into the family.

During this summer an infantry regiment was stationed near Yásnaya, in which a young Sub-Lieutenant named Kolokoltsóv was serving whom Countess Tolstoy had known in Moscow. He visited the Tolstoys, and introduced to them his Colonel, Únosha, and his fellow-officer Ensign Stasulévich, who had been degraded to the ranks because while he was on prison-duty a prisoner had escaped. Ensign Stasulévich was middle-aged but he had only recently regained his rank as officer.

One day Stasulévich and Kolokoltsóv called on Tolstoy and told him that a soldier serving as secretary in one of the companies of the regiment had struck his Company Commander and was to be tried by court-martial. They asked Tolstoy to undertake the man's defence, which he, who always regarded capital punishment with abhorrence, readily agreed to do.

The circumstances of the case were these. The soldier, Shibúnin, was a man of very limited intelligence whose chief occupation was writing out reports. When he had any money he spent it on solitary drinking. The Captain in command of his company, a Pole, who apparently disliked him, frequently found fault with his reports and made him rewrite them. This treatment Shibúnin bitterly resented, and one day when he had been drinking, on being told to rewrite a document, he insulted and struck the Captain. By law the penalty for a private who strikes his officer was death. Tolstoy nevertheless hoped to save the man's life, and obtained permission to plead on his behalf. The trial took place on 6th June, the members of the court-martial being Colonel Únosha, Stasulévich, and Kolokoltsóv; the latter being merely a light-headed youngster.

Tolstoy, when recounting the incident to me, remarked that of the four occasions on which he had spoken in public, this was the time that he did so with most assurance and satisfaction to himself. He had written out his speech, the main point of which was that Shibúnin was not responsible for his actions, being abnormal and having, from the combined effect of intemperance and the monotony of his occupation, become idiotic and obsessed by an idea that his Company Commander did not understand report-writing and unfairly rejected work faultlessly done. The law decreed a mitigation of sentence for crimes committed by those who are not in full possession of their senses and, since this contradicted the paragraph allotting death as the sole punishment for a soldier who strikes his officer, Tolstoy argued that mercy should be extended to the prisoner.

Shibúnin was however sentenced to death. Tolstoy wished to appeal (through his aunt, the Countess A. A. Tolstoy) to Alexander II for a pardon, but with characteristic disregard of details, omitted to mention the name of the regiment in which the affair had occurred, and this enabled the Minister of War to delay the presentation of the petition until the soldier had been shot, which occurred on 9th August.

In contrast with the action of the Colonel and the Minister was that of the peasants of the district who flocked in crowds to see the prisoner, bringing him milk, eggs, home-made linen, and anything their poverty could afford. When the day of execution arrived, Shibúnin went quite impassively to his death, to all appearance incapable of understanding what was happening. The people thronged around the post to which he was to be tied – the women weeping and some of them fainting. They fetched a priest to say Mass at his grave, and paid for the service to be repeated all day. At night contributions of copper money, linen, and candles such as are burnt in Russian churches, were laid upon his grave. Next day the Masses were recommenced and continued until the police forbade any more religious services and levelled the grave that the people might not continue to visit it.

The knowledge of such a difference between the spirit of the governors and the governed, helps us once again to understand Tolstoy's ultimate conviction that Government and the administration of law are essentially evil. In later life he would certainly not have been content to base his plea for mercy on merely legal grounds.

From time to time he continued to be troubled by ill health. In July 1866, for instance, he writes that he is confined to the house with pains in the stomach which make it impossible for him to turn quickly.

In November he expresses a sense of the importance of authorship. Fet, criticising something in *War and Peace*, had quoted the words, *irritabilis poetarum gens*, but Tolstoy, replying, 'Not I,' welcomes the criticism, begs for more, and goes on to say:

What have you been doing? Not on the Zémstvo [County Council] or in farming (all *that* is compulsory activity such as we do instinctively and with as little will of our own as the ants who make an ant-hill, in that sphere there is nothing good or bad), but what are you doing in thought, with the mainspring of your being, which alone has been, and is, and will endure in the world? Is that spring still alive? Does it wish to manifest itself? How does it express its wish? Or has it forgotten how to express itself? That is the chief thing.

By the autumn of this year the railway from Moscow to Kursk had been constructed as far as Túla, making it easier to get from Yásnaya to Moscow. Yet Tolstoy comparatively seldom felt tempted to leave his much-loved, tranquil, busy, country life, in which alone he found himself able to work with a maximum of efficiency.

About this time he planted a birch wood, which has since grown up and become valuable.

During the summer of 1867, despite the dislike and distrust of doctors which he shared with Rousseau, and which he has again and again expressed in his works, he was induced by the state of his health and his wife's persuasion to consult the most famous Moscow doctor of the time, Professor Zahárin, on whose advice he drank mineral water for several weeks.

Writing to Fet he says:

If I wrote to you, dear friend, every time I think of you, you would receive two letters a day from me. But one cannot get everything said, and sometimes one is lazy and sometimes too busy, as is the case at present. I have recently returned from Moscow and have begun a strict cure under the direction of Zahárin and, most important of all, I am printing my novel at Ris's, and have to prepare and send off manuscripts and proofs every day under threat of a fine and of delayed publication. That is both pleasant and also hard, as you know.

In November 1867 we find the whole family again established for a while in a lodging in Moscow, where they seem to have remained a large part of the winter.

Here Fet visited Tolstoy and announced to him that he had decided to arrange a Literary Evening for the benefit of the famine-stricken peasants of Mtsensk, the district in which Fet's estate lay. Tolstoy met the suggestion with irony, maintaining that Fet had invented the famine, and in reply to a request that he would ensure the success of the evening by reading something, flatly refused to do so, declaring that he never had and never could do such a thing as read in public. Still, he lent Fet the chapter of *War and Peace* containing the wonderful description of the retreat of the Russian army from Smolénsk in fearful drought. This not having been published as yet, existed only in proof. (It forms Chapter V of Book X of Volume II of that work.) Read by Prince Kugúshev, the poet and dramatist, it evoked thunders of applause.

On 12th April 1868 Turgénev, writing to Fet, said:

I have just finished the fourth volume of *War and Peace*. There are things in it that are unbearable, and things that are wonderful; and the wonderful things (they predominate) are so magnificently good that we have never had anything better written by anybody, and it is doubtful whether anything as good has been written.

About the same time V. P. Bótkin wrote from Petersburg: 'Tolstoy's novel is having a really remarkable success, everyone here is reading it, and they not merely read it but become enthusiastic about it.'

The Epilogue was not completed till late in 1869. On 30th August Tolstoy writes to Fet:

Do you know what this summer has been for me? An unceasing ecstasy over Schopenhauer, and a series of mental enjoyments such as I never experienced before. I have bought all his works, and have read and am reading them (as well as Kant's). And assuredly no student in his course has learnt so much and discovered so much as I have during this summer. I do not know whether I shall ever change my opinion, but at present I am confident that Schopenhauer is the greatest genius among men. You said he had written something or other on philosophic subjects. What do you mean by 'something or other'? It is the whole world in an extraordinarily vivid and beautiful reflection. I have begun translating him. Won't you take up that work? We would publish it together. After reading him I cannot conceive how his name can remain unknown. The only explanation is the one he so often repeats, that except idiots there is scarcely anyone else in the world . . .

Tolstoy goes on to say that he was starting next day for the Government of Pénza to look at an estate he meant to buy 'in those out-of-the-way parts'. The servant who accompanied him has told how they travelled third class from Moscow to Nízhni, and how Tolstoy chatted with his fellow-travellers so that many of them took him 'for a common man'. The idea of buying the estate in Pénza was ultimately abandoned.

He had by then finished the last part of *War and Peace*, which was to appear complete in book form in November. Two volumes had been published in 1866, three more in 1868, and the sixth was not ready till 1869. (In subsequent editions the book was rearranged in fewer volumes.)

Though he had so completely conquered the laziness of which in early manhood he had accused himself as to have become a regular, indefatigable, and extremely hard worker, yet after the completion of so gigantic a task he felt the need of recuperation, and in summer wrote to Fet: 'It is now my deadest time: I neither write nor think, but feel happily stupid,' and he adds that he goes woodcock shooting and has killed eight at an outing.

That at this time he already felt a good deal of the repugnance he so strenuously expressed in later years for luxury and profuse expenditure, is indicated by his comment on the death of his acquaintance, the author V. P. Bótkin, which took place in 1869. Bótkin, a member of a wealthy family of tea-merchants, having lived with economy till he knew his death was approaching, then hired a splendid lodging in Petersburg, fitted it up with all possible comfort and luxury, engaged a chef from the Tsarévich's kitchen, paid daily attention to the dinner menu, and engaged famous musicians to perform quartets at his house. To the magnificent feasts he gave every day (at which, owing to the state of his health, he himself participated chiefly as a spectator) he gathered a select circle of friends whose conversation interested him. He told his brother that these arrangements for the close of his life gave him the keenest pleasure, and that 'birds of Paradise are singing in my soul'. On 4th October a quartet and banquet had been arranged as usual, and many guests were expected – but V. P. Bótkin lay dead in his bed.

Tolstoy, hearing of this, wrote to Fet:

I was terribly shocked by the manner of V. P. Bótkin's death. If what is told of it is true, it is terrible. How is it that among his friends not one was found to give to that supreme moment of life the character suitable to it?

Before *War and Peace* was finished the Countess had borne four children – the fourth being a boy, born on 20th May 1869, and christened Leo – nursing them all herself, as she did her subsequent children, with three exceptions mentioned later on. Her willingness to do this was exceptional among women of her class, for the employment of wet-nurses was common in Russia.

Up to the age of ten the children were taught Russian and music by the Countess, and she even found time to make their clothes herself till they reached that age. Besides managing the household, her brother tells us that during the composition of *War and Peace* she found time to copy it out no less than seven times, a statement which cannot be taken literally: for greatly as Tolstoy believed in the proverb that 'Gold is got by sifting', and indefatigably as he revised his work, not all the chapters of *War and Peace* were altered that number of times. With Tolstoy the children learnt arithmetic; and they learnt to read French out of illustrated volumes of Jules Verne.

In all that concerned the education of the children his wife at this time willingly constituted herself the executant of her husband's decisions, which were based largely on Rousseau's *Émile*, and were relaxed only in so far as the Countess was unable to carry them out and Tolstoy found himself too much occupied with other affairs to do so. Later on there was less accord between the parents.

With the first child they tried to dispense with a nurse, but the attempt was unsuccessful, and subsequently Russian nurses and foreign *bonnes* were employed.

Toys were not allowed in the nursery but much liberty was allowed the children. No violent or severe punishments were inflicted, and none but their parents might punish them. They aimed at gaining their children's confidence by timely petting and kindly treatment.

If one of the children told a falsehood, this was treated as a serious matter and the punishment usually consisted in the parents treating the child coldly. As soon however as it showed that it was really sorry, the punishment ceased; but a child was never persuaded to say it was sorry or to promise not to repeat its fault.

All the grown-up people in the house were expected to remember that children are apt to copy and imitate what they see and hear, and the children were not kept away from the adults except at lesson time. Consequently when eight o'clock came and the children went to bed, Tolstoy would often remark: 'Now we are freer!'

Partly that they might learn English, partly because Tolstoy believed education to be freer in England than elsewhere, young English gover-nesses were engaged to have charge of his children from the age of three to nine. He was extremely fortunate in his first choice, for the young lady remained with the family for six years and after her marriage continued in most friendly relations with them all.

He aimed at acquainting the children with Nature and developing their love of it, of animals, and of insects. He liked to let them realise their impotence and complete dependence on their elders, but always did this with kindly consideration.

The children were not allowed to order the servants about but had to *ask* them for anything they wanted; and that a good example might be set, everyone in the house was expected to do the same. This was the more important because the peasant servants in Russia, even after the Emancipation, were scarcely regarded as the same kind of beings as their masters, and a famous Russian author could say without any exaggeration: 'The balcony was rotten. Only servants went there; the family did not go there.' But to avoid giving a wrong impression I must here make a reservation. Though there was no idea of the two classes overlapping, and so wide a gap existed between them that they dressed quite differently (the peasants having their own costume and style of garments), very cordial and sincere good feeling often grew up between master and man or between proprietress and servant, and real human interest such as is shown in Tolstoy's descriptions of the servants in *Childhood* and in other stories. It was not at all unusual for Russian servants to join in the conversation of the family or visitors, and the whole relation between employers and employed was quite different to what it is in England, where on Sundays the maid may be mistaken for her mistress, except that she often looks more attractive.

The plan adopted in the Yásno-Polyána school, where no child was obliged to learn anything it did not care to learn, had to be abandoned in the family; but some scope was allowed to the children for rejecting what they had no capacity for, and they were never punished for neglecting to prepare lessons, though rewarded when they learnt well.

To illustrate Tolstoy's way of developing the minds of those about him, Behrs tells of his own case when as a youth he stayed at Yásnaya:

Regardless of my youth at the time, I remember that Tolstoy discussed quite seriously with me all the scientific and philosophic questions it came into my head to put to him. He always answered simply and clearly and never hesitated to admit the fact if he did not understand this or that matter. Often my talk with him took the form of a dispute, on which I embarked despite my consciousness of his immense superiority.

The children were always eager to go for walks with their father, to answer his call to practise Swedish gymnastics, and to be on his side in any game he taught them. In winter they skated a good deal; but clearing the snow off the pond under his leadership was an even greater pleasure than the skating itself.

Before breakfast he would go for a walk with his brother-in-law, or they would ride down to bathe in the river that flows on one side of the estate. At morning coffee the whole family assembled and it was generally a very merry meal, Tolstoy being up to all sorts of jokes till he rose with the words, 'One must get to work,' and went off to his study, taking with him a tumbler full of tea. While at work in his room not even his wife was allowed to disturb him, though at one time his eldest daughter, Tatiána, while still a little girl, was privileged to break this rule. The rare days (generally in summer) when he relaxed, were very welcome to the children, for their father's presence always brought life and animation with it. Generally after dinner, before resuming work, he would read a book not directly connected with the task he had in hand. It was often an English novel; and besides those writers already mentioned Mrs Henry Wood made a great impression on him. Molière's plays always appealed to him strongly. In the evening he was fond of playing duets with his sister. He used to find it hard to keep up with her in playing long pieces with which he was not quite familiar, and when in difficulties would say something to make her laugh and cause her to play slower. If he did not succeed by means of this ruse, he would sometimes stop and solemnly take off one of his boots as though that must infallibly help him out of the difficulty, and would then recommence, with the remark, 'Now, it will go all right!'

During the early years of his married life few visitors came to Yásnaya, except the numerous members of the Tolstoy-Behrs families, who stayed there chiefly in summer. The poet A. A. Fet, D. A. Dyákov, whom he had known from boyhood and had to some extent described, under the name of Nekhlyúdov, in *Youth*, N. N. Stráhov, the philosopher and critic, whose judgement he much respected and whom he frequently consulted throughout his literary career, and Prince S. S. Urúsov whom he had known during the siege of Sevastopol, seem to have been almost the only friends who visited him in the years immediately after his marriage. This suited Tolstoy very well, for to entertain many visitors would have seriously interrupted the absorbing work in which he was engaged.

Fet has been mentioned so often in this volume that a few lines must be devoted to describing a man who came in for much abuse on account of the anti-Emancipationist sympathies expressed in some of his writings. Like Tolstoy, he had grown up with no idea that it is incumbent on men of education and capacity to organise the society of which they are members, or remedy by political action such abuses as inevitably arise among human beings who do not keep the task of systematic social organisation constantly in view. Of the impression Fet's political opinions made on the Liberals one may judge by a remark Turgénev addressed to him in a letter written in 1874: 'Twenty years ago, at the height of Nicholas I's régime, you dumbfounded me by announcing your opinion that the mind of man could devise nothing superior to the position of the Russian aristocracy of that day, nor anything nobler or more admirable.' The Liberals saw in Fet a political reactionary – which he was; but anyone who reads his *Recollections* may also see how much personal worth may be combined with political indifferentism – a quality many Russians of his generation were brought up to regard as a virtue. In private life he was a really worthy man, and Tolstoy once very truly remarked to him:

> There are some people whose talk is far above their actual morality, but there are also some whose talk is below that level. You are one who is so afraid of his sermon being above his practice that you intentionally talk far below your actual practice.

While still a young cavalry officer Fet began to write poetry, for which he had real talent, and after leaving the army he continued his literary career as an Art-for-Art's-sake man, producing verse translations of the Latin poets, besides original works of his own in prose and verse, and (after Tolstoy's suggestion, already recorded) translations from the German of Schopenhauer's *The World as Will and Idea*, and of Goethe's *Faust*.

In his dislike, or perhaps one should say ignorance, of politics, commerce, and the industrial revolution of the Western World (which was its most conspicuous achievement during the last one hundred and fifty years) as well as in his love of pure art, chiefly literary, he had much in common with Tolstoy. They could talk with profound sympathy of all that related to art, and were alike in their love of country life and in their relation to agriculture, as well as in the fact that the great problems of life centred for them round their own personality rather than around the community to which they belonged. Patriotic by instinct, it was no part of their conscious philosophy to be so, at least they never dreamed of that newer patriotism which seeks to arrange the production and distribution of the national wealth so that every member of the community may have an opportunity to live in decent conditions. They had therefore much in common, and one sees by Tolstoy's letters how greatly they enjoyed each other's society, though a time was coming when their friendship would wane.

Tolstoy had a strong dislike of leaving home even for a few days. When it was absolutely necessary to go to Moscow he would grumble at his hard fate, and Behrs, when he accompanied him, noticed how town life depressed Tolstoy, making him fidgety and irritable. When returning from a journey or a hunting expedition, he would express his anxiety by exclaiming, 'If only all's well at home!' After he had been away from Yásnaya, Tolstoy never failed to give the home party full and amusing accounts of what he had seen and heard.

A distinguishing feature of Tolstoy, already remarked on, but so strongly marked that it can hardly be insisted on too much, was the ardent and whole-hearted way he threw himself into whatever occupation he took up. On this point Prince D. D. Obolénski says:

I have seen Count L. N. Tolstoy in all phases of his creative activity . . . Whatever his occupation he did it with conviction, firmly believing in the value of what he was doing, and always fully absorbed by it. I remember him as a man of the world and have met him at balls, and I remember a remark he once made, 'See what poetry there is in women's ball-dresses, what elegance, how much thought, how much charm even in the flowers pinned to the dresses!' I remember him as an ardent sportsman, as a beekeeper, as a gardener; I remember his enthusiasm for farming, for tree-planting, fruit-culture, horse-breeding, and much else.

A housekeeper who was with him for nine years said of him:

The Count himself looked after everything, and demanded extreme cleanliness in the cowhouse and in the pig-styes and in the sheep-cot. In particular he delighted in his pigs, of which he had as many as 300 paired off in separate styes . . . There the Count would not allow the least dirt. Every day I and my assistants had to wash them all and wipe the floor and walls of the styes; then the Count on passing through the piggery of a morning would be very pleased, and would remark aloud: 'What management! . . . What good management!' But God have mercy on us if he noticed the least dirt! That at once made him shout out angrily . . . The Count was very hasty and a doctor who used to come to Yásnaya said to him more than once in my presence: 'You must not get so angry, Count, it is very bad for your health.' . . . 'I can't help it,' he would reply. 'I want to restrain myself but can't do it. That, it seems, is the way I am made!' . . . His farming gave the Count a good revenue in those days. Besides the pigs and their litters he had 80 cows, 500 good sheep, and very many fowls. We used to make excellent butter, which we sold in Moscow at 60 kopeks a pound.

His management of property was characteristically personal. He never took shares in any joint-stock company, but he bought land, bred cattle and horses of good quality, planted a large apple-orchard as well as a quantity of other trees, and in general acquired property he could manage himself, or (for he entrusted his Samára estates to stewards) over which he had full control. He was always more alive to the dangers and evils of commercial companies and large engineering and industrial undertakings, than to the good they have achieved by irrigating arid lands, uniting distant realms, and lightening man's toil by making iron bear some of his burdens for him.

Tolstoy, at this period of his life, furnishes an example of the fact that men of artistic temperament are apt to be untidy. Though he acknowledged the advantages of neatness in general he often remarked that it is a quality most frequently found in shallow natures. He himself simply could not, and therefore did not try to, keep his things in order. When he undressed he let his clothes or boots drop where he stood, and if he happened to be moving about his garments remained strewn around the room, and sometimes on the floor. Behrs remarks:

I noticed that to pack his things for a journey cost him great effort and when I accompanied him I used willingly to do it for him and thereby pleased him very much. I remember that once, for some reason, I did not at all wish to pack for him. He noticed this and with characteristic delicacy did not ask me to but put his things into his portmanteau himself, and I can assert positively that no one else, were they to try, could have got them into such fearful disorder as they were in, in that portmanteau.

When kindly reading through the manuscript of this work, Tolstoy's daughter, Countess Tatiána Tolstoy (Madame Sukhotín) wrote to me: 'I may say that in my recollection my father was very accurate, tidy, and clean. It is possible that he acquired these qualities as he grew older.'

It was a peculiarity of Tolstoy that he not only liked to have his sleep out without being disturbed, but never could or would wake anyone from sleep, and in cases of absolute necessity would ask someone else to relieve him of that disagreeable task.

Behrs recounts that when they sat up late the manservant sometimes fell asleep in his chair and omitted to serve up the cold supper. Tolstoy would never allow him to be disturbed on these occasions, but would himself go to the pantry to fetch the supper and would do this stealthily and with the greatest caution, so that it became a kind of amusing game. He would get quite cross with Behrs if the latter accidentally let the plates clatter or made any other noise.

Many years later, alluding in my presence to this peculiarity of his, Tolstoy remarked, 'While a man is asleep he is at any rate not sinning.'

On 4th February 1870 Tolstoy wrote to Fet:

I received your letter, dear Afanásí Afanásevich, on 1st February, but even had I received it sooner I could not have come. You write, 'I am *alone, alone!*' And when I read it I thought, What a lucky fellow – *alone!* I have a wife, three children, and a fourth at the breast, two old aunts, a nurse, and two housemaids. And they are all ill together: fever, high temperature, weakness, headaches, and coughs. In that state your letter found me. They are now beginning to get better, but out of ten people I and my old aunt alone turn up at the dinner table. And since yesterday I myself am ill with my chest and side. There is much, very much, I want to tell you about. I have been reading a lot of Shakespeare, Goethe, Púshkin, Gógol, and Molière, and about all of them there is much I want to say to you. I do not take in a single magazine or newspaper this year and consider it very useful not to.

S. A. Behrs tells us that Tolstoy 'never read newspapers, and considered them useless, and when they contain false news even harmful. In his humorous way he would sometimes parody a newspaper style when speaking of domestic affairs.' His attitude towards journalists and critics (except his friend Stráhov) was rather scornful, and he was indignant when anyone classed them even with third-rate authors. He considered that it is a misuse of the printing press to publish so much that is unnecessary, uninteresting, and worst of all inartistic. He seldom read criticisms of his own work. 'His feeling towards periodicals in general had its source in his intense dislike of the exploitation of works of art. He would smile contemptuously at hearing it suggested that a real artist produces his works for the sake of money.'

Having said this much about his characteristics and peculiarities, let us note the extent to which his life and mode of thought at this time approximated to his later teaching. His humane relations towards the peasants, his condemnation of many of the manifestations of modern civilisation, his simplicity in household matters and dress, his exemplary family life, humane educational ideals, deep love of sincerity and of industry (including physical labour), his ardent search for truth and self-improvement, his gradually increasing accessibility to and regard for others, his undoubted love of family and hatred of violence – indicate that the ideals of his later life were not far from him even before the conversion told of in his *Confession*.

On 17th February Tolstoy writes to Fet:

I hoped to visit you the night of the 14th but could not do so. As I wrote you, we were all ill – I last. I went out yesterday for the first time. What stopped me was pain in the eyes which is increased by wind and sleeplessness. I now, to my great regret, have to postpone my visit to you till Lent. I must go to Moscow to take my aunt to my sister's and to see an oculist about my eyes.

It is a pity that one can only get to your place after passing a sleepless, cigarette-smoky, stuffy, railway-carriage conversational night. You want to read me a story of cavalry life . . . And I don't want to read you anything because I am not writing anything; but I very much want to talk about Shakespeare and Goethe and the drama in general. This whole winter I am occupied only with the drama; and it happens to me, as usually happens to people who till they are forty have not thought of a certain subject or formed any conception of it and then suddenly with forty-year-old clearness turn their attention to this new untasted subject – it seems to them that they discern in it much that is new. All winter I have enjoyed myself, lying down, drowsing, playing bézique, going on snow-shoes, skating, and most of all lying in bed (ill) while characters from a drama or comedy have performed for me. And they perform very well. It is about that I want to talk to you. In that, as in everything, you are a classic and understand the essence of the matter very deeply. I should like also to read Sophocles and Euripides.

There we see Tolstoy, as always, ardently devoting his attention to some great subject – which happens this time to be dramatic art. How real a grip he obtained of the subject with little theatre-going was shown seventeen years later, when he wrote one of the most powerful dramas ever produced and followed it up by a capital comedy; both plays so good that they became stock pieces all over Russia and achieved success in many other countries.

At the point we have reached there was no break in the manner of Tolstoy's life. He continued to live quietly as Yásnaya and to concern himself chiefly with literature and with the management of his estates and the welfare of his family. Children continued to be born in rapid succession, and with the increasing family his means increased. But we have reached the middle of that tranquil period of sixteen years which succeeded his marriage, and here, while – as one would say of another man – he was indefatigably studying the drama; or while, as one is inclined to say of him, he was resting and recuperating before under-taking his next great work, it is convenient to close this chapter.

10

Nearing the Crisis

As he grew older Tolstoy's love of outdoor exercise tended towards activity serving a productive purpose, and one finds a hint of this in the following letter to Fet, dated 11th May 1870:

> I received your letter, dear friend, when returning perspiring home from work with axe and spade, and when therefore I was a thousand miles from things artistic in general and from our business in particular. On opening the letter I first read the poem and felt a tickling in my nose. On coming home to my wife I tried to read it to her, but could not do so for tears of emotion. The poem is one of those rare ones in which not a word could be added, or subtracted, or altered: it is a live thing, and admirable . . .
>
> I have just served for a week as juryman, and found it very interesting and instructive.

The next letter refers to the fact that Tolstoy did his best literary work in winter, when he often spent almost the whole day and sometimes part of the night at it. It was the time when his 'sap flowed':

> *2nd October 1870*
>
> It is long since we met, and in my winter condition, which I am now entering, I am specially glad to see you. I have been shooting; but the sap is beginning to flow and I am collecting it as it drips. Whether it be good or bad sap it is pleasant to let it flow in these long, wonderful, autumn evenings . . . A misfortune has befallen me; the mare is ill. The veterinary says her wind has been broken, but I cannot have broken it.

The Franco-Prussian war occurred at this time and interested Tolstoy keenly. He had been in contact with the French in the Crimea, before the Napoleonic autocracy had long held sway, and he had visited France in 1857 and 1860, before the putrescent effect of the Empire had become fully apparent. Neither the idea of German national unity, nor Bismarck's and Moltke's ideal of efficient organisation and discipline, were things that much appealed to Tolstoy. So it happened that all his sympathies were on the side of the French and he felt assured of their triumph. His friend Prince S. S. Urúsov wrote letters to Katkóv's *Moscow Védomosti* demonstrating by analogies with games of chess, that the French were continually drawing the German armies into more and more desperate positions in which they must soon be destroyed. When, on the contrary, the French were utterly defeated, it came as a complete surprise; which illustrates the fact that men of great intellectual power, living isolated on their country estates, may at times go very considerably wrong in their estimate of the forces influencing the world.

On 12th February 1871 a daughter was born, who was christened Márya. In later life she, of all his children, was the most deeply influenced by her father's teaching. The Countess, who, as already mentioned, made a point of nursing her own children, owing to the neglect of an attendant became unable to do so in this instance before the child was many weeks old, and a wet-nurse was engaged; but as soon as the mother saw her child at a stranger's breast she burst into a flood of jealous tears, dismissed the nurse on the spot, and ordered the child to be fed by hand. Tolstoy when he heard what had happened declared that his wife had only the jealous affection natural to a true mother.

During that winter [1871–2] Tolstoy devoted himself strenuously to the study of Greek. On hearing this, Fet felt so sure Tolstoy would not succeed, that he announced his readiness to devote his own skin for parchment for Tolstoy's diploma of proficiency should the latter qualify himself to receive it. Accordingly, in December, Tolstoy wrote him as follows:

I received your letter a week ago, but have not answered because from morning to night I am learning Greek. I am writing nothing, only learning; and to judge by information reaching me through Borísov, your skin (to be used as parchment for my diploma in Greek) is in some danger. Improbable and astounding as it may seem, I have read Xenophon, and can now read him at sight. For Homer, a dictionary and some effort are still necessary. I eagerly await a chance of showing this new trick to someone. But how glad I am that God sent this folly upon me! In the first place I enjoy it, and secondly, I have become convinced that of all that human language has produced truly beautiful and simply beautiful, I knew nothing (like all the others, who know but do not understand); and thirdly, because I have ceased to write, and never more will write, wordy rubbish. I am guilty of having done so; but by God I won't do it any more! Explain to me, for Heaven's sake, why no one knows Aesop's fables, or even delightful Xenophon, not to mention Plato and Homer whom I still have before me? In so far as I can as yet judge, our translations, made on German models, only spoil Homer. To use a banal but involuntary comparison, they are like boiled and distilled water, while he is like water fresh from the spring, striking the teeth with its sunlit sparkle, even its specks only making it the clearer and fresher . . . You may triumph: without a knowledge of Greek there is no education. But what kind of knowledge? How is it to be got? What is the use of it? To this I have replies clear as daylight.

S. A. Behrs tells us, 'I know for a fact that he learnt the language and read Herodotus in three months.' While in Moscow that winter he visited Leóntev, then (and when I studied there three years later) Professor of Greek at the Katkóv Lyceum, to talk about Greek literature. Leóntev was not prepared to believe in the possibility of his having learnt Greek so rapidly, and proposed that they should read something at sight. It happened that they differed as to the meaning of three passages; but after a little discussion the Professor admitted that the Count's interpretations were right.

Tolstoy felt the charm of the literary art of the ancient world, and so keenly did he enter into the minds of those of whom he read, and so different to his own was the Greek outlook upon life, that the contradiction produced in him a feeling of melancholy and apathy profound enough to affect his health.

What clash of ideals produced this result we may guess when we consider how from his earliest years he had been attracted by the Christian ideal of meekness, humility, and self-sacrifice, and how little this accords with the outlook on life of the ancient Greeks. In *What is Art?* written nearly forty years later, Tolstoy tells us that 'If, as among the Greeks, religion places the meaning of life in earthly happiness, in beauty and in strength, then art successfully transmitting the joy and energy of life would be considered good art [good in regard to the feeling conveyed] but art transmitting the opposite feelings would be bad.'. Again in the same work he says that the aesthetic theory he is combating seeks to make it appear 'that the very best that can be done by the art of nations after 1,900 years of Christian teaching is to choose as the ideal of life the ideal held by a small, semi-savage, slave-holding people, who lived 2,00 years ago, imitated the nude human body extremely well, and erected buildings pleasant to look at.'

To wean him from his absorption in Greek literature, his wife at first urged him to take up some fresh literary work; and finally, becoming seriously alarmed for his health, induced him to go eastward for a *kumys* cure. He wrote to Fet at this time:

10th June 1871

DEAR FRIEND – I have not written to you for a long time, nor been to see you, because I was, and still am, ill. I don't myself know what is the matter with me, but it seems like something bad or good, according to the name we give to our exit. Loss of strength, and a feeling that one needs nothing and wants nothing but quiet which one has not got. My wife is sending me to Samára or Sarátov for two months for a *kumys* cure. I leave for Moscow today, and shall there learn where I am to go to.

In Moscow it was decided that he should go to the part of Samára he had visited before.

Railways were always an affliction to Tolstoy. Civilisation had forced them on him without his wish and, as he argued in his educational articles, to the detriment of the peasant population. Personally he complained of disagreeable sensations he experienced when travelling by rail, and compared these discomforts with the pleasure of riding on horseback. He objected both to the officious politeness of the conductors and to the way the passengers suspiciously shun one another. (This latter complaint is not one a Westerner would bring against Russians, for they seem to us the most sociable of fellow-travellers.) He used to insist on his wife always travelling first class. He himself went either first or third, but seldom second. To travel third was a more serious matter in Russia than in England, and he used purposely to choose a car in which there were peasants, and talked to all whom he met.

On this outward journey he went third class by rail to Nízhni Nóvgorod, and by steamer down the Vólga to the town of Samára. On the boat he took the opportunity to study the manners and customs of his fellow-passengers, natives of the Vólga district, and displayed his gift for making friends with people of all kinds. Before he had been two days on the boat he was on the friendliest terms with everybody, including the sailors, among whom he slept each night in the fore part of the vessel. Even when he met reserved or surly characters it was not long before he drew them out of their shells and set them chatting at their ease. One secret of this success was the unaffected interest he took in learning about other people's lives and affairs.

From Samára he went east for eighty miles on horseback, following the banks of the river Karalyk till he reached the village of that name. He had lived there in 1862 and was welcomed as an old acquaintance and friend by the Bashkírs, who always spoke of him as 'The Count'. The reader will remember that at the University Tolstoy had studied oriental languages. His knowledge of Tartar no doubt increased his popularity with the Bashkírs. He had with him a manservant and his brother-in-law, Stepán Andréevich Behrs, then a lad of about sixteen, who subsequently in his *Recollections* gave an account of this outing. They lived, not in the 'winter village' of Karalyk, but about one and a half miles away, in a *kochévka* on the open steppe. A *kochévka* is a dome-shaped semicircular tent, made of a collapsible wooden trellis-work frame covered with large sheets of felt. It has a small painted door, and is usually carpeted with soft feather grass.

On first arriving at Karalyk, Tolstoy for some days felt depressed and unwell. He complained that he lacked capacity to feel either mental or physical pleasure, and looked at everything 'as though he were a corpse' – a characteristic usually most foreign to him and which in other people always evoked his dislike. It was however not long before he recovered his spirits and energy.

There were other visitors at Karalyk who had also come for a *kumys* cure. They neither associated with the Bashkír nomads nor adopted their customs; but Tolstoy was extremely fond of the Bashkírs, associated much with them, and followed their diet strictly, avoiding all vegetable foods and restricting himself to meat and animal products. Dinner every day consisted chiefly of mutton, eaten with the fingers out of wooden bowls.

Tolstoy soon made friends with everybody, Bashkírs and Russian visitors alike, and thanks to his genial influence the whole place grew gay and lively. A professor of Greek from a Seminary for the education of priests might be seen trying a skipping-rope match with him; a procurator's assistant discussed legal and other questions, and there was a young Samára farmer who became his devoted follower.

Accompanied by Behrs and two of their new acquaintances, and taking a supply of guns and presents, Tolstoy went for a four days' drive through the neighbouring villages. The party had splendid duck-shooting by the lakes they passed, and were entertained and treated to *kumys* by the Bashkírs at the *kochévkas* in which they rested. As opportunity presented itself they made suitable acknowledgements for their entertainment by giving presents to their hosts. One serious drawback to the hospitality was the fact that their hosts insisted on feeding them with mutton and fat with their own hands without the intermediacy of fork or spoon, and it was out of the question to insult them by refusing such well-meant, though undesirable, attentions.

On one occasion Tolstoy happened to admire a horse that had separated from its herd, and remarked to Behrs, 'See what a beautiful milking mare that is.' An hour later, when they were taking leave, their host tied the animal to their conveyance, thus presenting it to his visitor. Of course on the return journey Tolstoy had to make an equivalent present in return.

Another incident of this stay in Samára was a visit to the Petróvski Fair, which was held once a year at Buzulúk, a small town some fifty miles from Karalyk. Here Russians, Bashkírs, Oural Cossacks, and Kirghíz mingled with one another, and Tolstoy was soon on a friendly footing with them all. He would chat and laugh with them even when they were drunk; but when one in that condition took it into his head to embrace the Count, Tolstoy's look was so stern and impressive that the fellow drew back his hands and let them fall, saying, 'No, never mind, it's all right!'

The following letter of 18th July 1871, to Fet, relates to Tolstoy's experience of the nomadic Bashkírs:

Thank you for your letter, dear friend! It seems that my wife gave a false alarm when she packed me off for a *kumys* cure and persuaded me that I was ill. At any rate now, after four weeks, I seem to have quite recovered. And as is proper when one is taking a *kumys* cure, I am drunk and sweat from morn to night, and find pleasure in it. It is very good here, and were it not for homesickness, I should be quite happy. Were I to begin describing, I should fill a hundred pages with this country and my own occupations. I am reading Herodotus, who describes in detail and with great accuracy these same galactophagous [milk-eating] Scythians among whom I am living.

I began this letter yesterday and wrote that I was well. Today my side aches again. I do not myself know in how far I am ill, but it is bad that I am obliged to think – and cannot help thinking – about my side and my chest. This is the third day that the heat has been terrible. In the *kibítka* it is as hot as on the shelf of a Russian bath, but I like it. The country here is beautiful, in its age – just emerging from virginity – in its richness, its health, and especially in its simplicity, and its unperverted population. Here as everywhere I look around for an estate to buy. This affords me an occupation and is the best excuse for getting to know the real condition of the district.

After a six weeks' stay Tolstoy returned to Yásnaya.

His search for an estate had been successful, and after persuading his wife that the investment was a sound one, he purchased two thousand acres.

During his wanderings on the steppe Tolstoy met many Molokáns, members of a Bible-Christian peasant sect. They based their faith on the Bible, rejecting the Greek Church with its traditions, priesthood, dogmas, ritual, sacraments, and icons. They were distinguished by an honesty and industry unusual among their Orthodox neighbours, and they abstained from all intoxicants.

It interested Tolstoy to mix with them, and he liked to discuss their beliefs, especially with a venerable leader named Aggéy. It so happened that in the neighbouring village of Pátrovka there was a very worthy young Russian priest, who was eager to convert the Molokáns and occasionally arranged debates with them on religious subjects. Tolstoy sometimes attended these debates: his object being not so much to convert the Molokáns as to understand the points on which they differed from the Russo-Greek Church. He also took an interest in the Mohammedan faith of his Bashkír friends, and on his return to Yásnaya read through a French translation of the Koran.

A few years later he associated much with the representatives of various sects and faiths, being then deeply interested in their beliefs; but at this time his interest in such matters was only beginning.

A letter of Turgénev's, written at this period, indicates how little he allowed his quarrel with Tolstoy the man to warp his appreciation of

Tolstoy the artist. Writing to Fet on 2nd July 1871 he says:

> Your letter again grieves me – I refer to what you write about L. Tolstoy. I have great fears on his account, for two of his brothers died of consumption, and I am very glad he is taking a *kumys* cure, in the reality and efficacy of which I have faith. L. Tolstoy is the only hope of our orphaned literature; he cannot and must not vanish from the face of the earth as prematurely as his predecessors: Púshkin, Lérmontov, and Gógol.

Again in November, writing from Paris, he says:

> I am very glad that Tolstoy's health is now satisfactory and that he is at work. Whatever he does will be good if only he does not himself mutilate his own handiwork. Philosophy, which he hates, has revenged herself on him in a strange way: she has infected him, and the enemy of rationalising has plunged head over ears into rationalisation! But perhaps all *that* has fallen away from him by now and left only the pure and powerful artist.

On returning home from Samára improved in health, Tolstoy turned his thoughts once more to matters educational, especially to the crying need of good primers for those learning to read. We have seen how strongly, in 1862, he had felt the lack of well-written books simple enough for beginners and peasant readers, and how he resented the monopolisation of knowledge by the cultured classes entrenched behind barriers of pedantry. We have seen, too, how under the influence of Homer he swore he would no more write 'wordy rubbish', and the time had now come for this feeling to bear fruit. The task to which he devoted his powers at their zenith was the production of an *ABC Book* for beginners, as simple, clear, and perfect in form and subject-matter as possible.

By September he was hard at work, the Countess, as usual, acting as his amanuensis.

In an impulsive, kind-hearted way she often rendered assistance to the poor, not merely among the Yásnaya Polyána peasants, but to others from a distance also, and the neighbouring peasants thought well of her.

The increase in the Tolstoy family was met this year by a considerable enlargement of their house. By way of a house-warming to celebrate the completion of the building, a masquerade was arranged at Christmas, at which Tolstoy evoked great enthusiasm by appearing as a goat.

About this time Behrs and a school friend of his became sorely troubled about the state of their souls, and thought of entering a monastery. This is what he tells us of Tolstoy's relation to the matter:

> His attitude towards my inclination was a most cautious one. I often went to him with my doubts and questions, but he always managed to avoid expressing his opinion, knowing how very great an influence it would have with me. He left it to me to work out my own convictions. Once however he spoke out with sufficient plainness. We were riding past the village church where his parents lie buried. Two horses were grazing in the churchyard. We had been talking over the only subject that then interested me.
>
> 'How can a man live at peace,' I asked, 'so long as he has not solved the question of a future life?'
>
> 'You see those two horses grazing there,' he answered; 'are they not laying up for a future life?'
>
> 'But I am speaking of our spiritual, not our earthly, life.'
>
> 'Indeed? Well, about that I neither know nor can know anything.'

Immediately after New Year [1872] he restarted his school, but the children (who often numbered thirty to thirty-five) met, not as formerly in another building, but in the hall, and other rooms, of the Tolstoys' enlarged house. In the mornings the Countess taught her own children, and in the afternoon she, her husband, and even seven-year-old Tánya and eight-year-old Sergéy, he peasant children, who came only at that time but yet made satisfactory progress, stimulated by the interest the Tolstoys took in them, by the pedagogic genius of the Count, and by a perception that education was a rare and valuable luxury which seldom came within the reach of Russian peasants.

In the *ABC Book* Tolstoy gives several stories of how he had learned to ride and of his dogs Milton and Búlka. Easy as these stories are, they are admirably written, and combine brevity, simplicity, and sincerity; though their sincerity lies not in telling the facts just as they occurred, but in the truth of the feeling conveyed to the reader. Besides these and other stories, popular historical sketches, a number of translations and adaptations from *Aesop's Fables*, and from Indian, Hebrew, and Arabic sources, the work contains popular legends or folk-stories in verse. To make these as perfect as possible, he studied and collated all the versions of them he could collect.

The section on Arithmetic gave him an immense amount of work, for he would not content himself with the usual explanations of the various operations but devised explanations of his own.

The book contains some elementary natural science, and for the preparation of this Tolstoy, besides examining all sorts of textbooks, consulted specialists on the various subjects and himself carefully performed most of the experiments he described.

To select readings in Church-Slavonic, he perused the monkish chronicles and Lives of the Saints.

Intending to include some readings on astronomy, he took up that study himself and became so interested in it that he sometimes sat up all night examining the stars.

When the news spread that Tolstoy was writing stories for his *ABC Book*, magazine editors besieged him with demands, and the first bits of the book to see the light were *A Prisoner in the Caucasus*, which appeared in one of the monthlies in February, and *God Sees the Truth*, which appeared in another in March.

Owing to some mismanagement, Tolstoy received nothing for the periodical rights of either of these stories, which in *What is Art?* he names as the best of all his works. They (as well as *The Bear Hunt*, also from the *ABC Book*) are now included in the *Twenty-Three Tales*.

With what pleasure Tolstoy looked back to this part of his life's work was indicated by a remark he made to me in 1902. Speaking of the popularity of *A Prisoner in the Caucasus* for public readings to the peasants, he added with evident satisfaction that when *A Prisoner in the Caucasus* is now mentioned it is always taken for granted that it is his story, and not Púshkin's famous poem of the same name, that is referred to.

In the following letter to Fet we get a glimpse of those thoughts on life's deepest problems which were a few years later to fill Tolstoy's mind completely.

30th January 1872

It is some days since I received your kind but sad letter, and not till today do I settle down to answer it.

It is a sad letter, for you write that Tyúchev is dying and that there is a rumour that Turgénev is dead, and about yourself you say the machine is wearing out and you want quietly to think of Nirvana. Please let me know quickly whether this is a false alarm. I hope it is, and that, in the absence of Márya Petróvna, you have taken slight symptoms for a return of your terrible illness.

In Nirvana there is nothing to laugh at, still less is there cause for anger. We all (I at least) feel that it is much more interesting than life; but I agree that however much I may think about it, I can think of nothing else than that Nirvana is nothingness. I only stand up for one thing: religious reverence – awe of that Nirvana.

There is, at any rate, nothing more important than it.

What do I mean by religious reverence? I mean this: I lately went to see my brother, and a child of his had died and was being buried. The priests were there, and a small pink coffin, and everything as it should be. My brother and I involuntarily confessed to one another that we felt something like repulsion towards ceremonial rites. But afterwards I thought, 'Well, but what should my brother do to remove the putrefying body of the child from the house? How is one to finish the matter decently?' There is no better way (at least, I could devise none) than to do it with a requiem and incense. How is it to be when we grow weak and die? Is nature to take her course, are we to . . . and nothing else? That would not be well. One wishes fully to express the gravity and importance, the solemnity and religious awe of that occurrence, the most important in each man's life. And I also can devise nothing more seemly for people of all ages and all degrees of development, than a religious observance. For me at least those Slavonic words evoke quite the same metaphysical ecstasy as one experiences when one thinks of Nirvana. Religion is wonderful in that she has for so many ages rendered to so many millions of people these same services – the greatest anything human can render in this matter. With such a task how can she be logical? Yes – there is something in her. Only to you do I allow myself to write such letters, but I wished to write, and I feel sad, especially after your letter.

Please write soon about your health.

Your

LEO TOLSTOY

I am terribly dispirited. The work I have begun is fearfully hard, there is no end to the preparatory study necessary. The plan of the work is ever increasing, and my strength, I feel, grows less and less. One day I am well, and three days I am ill.

The work here referred to as 'fearfully hard' was preparation for a novel, which however he never wrote.

On 20th February he again wrote to Fet:

... Being in Moscow, I wished to call on the Bótkins to hear about you, but I fell ill, took to my bed, and it was all I could do to get home. Now I am better. At home all is well; but you will not recognise our house: we have been using the new extension all winter. Another novelty is that I have again started a school. My wife, and children, and I, all teach and are all contented. I have finished my *ABC Book* and am printing it ...

The next letter shows that his hope that he had finished the *ABC Book* was premature:

16th March 1872

How I wish to see you; but I cannot come, I am still ill ... My *ABC Book* gives me no peace for any other occupation. The printing advances on the feet of a tortoise and the deuce knows when it will be finished, and I am still adding and omitting and altering. What will come of it I do not know; but I have put my whole soul into it.

In May 1872 the Countess gave birth to another boy, who was christened Peter.

The Moscow firm who were printing the book were not able to give Tolstoy satisfaction. Not only was the printing a matter of difficulty owing to the variety of types required for a schoolbook of the kind, but Tolstoy, as usual, revised the work time after time while it was going through the press. At last, in May, he wrote to his trusty friend and admirer, N. Stráhov, saying that after four months' labour the printing was 'not only not finished, but had not even begun', and begging Stráhov to have the book printed in Petersburg and to take on himself for ample payment the whole task of revising the proofs. After some correspondence matters were arranged, though Stráhov declined to accept payment for the help he rendered.

Tolstoy explained to his friend that he wanted to make a profit on the book if possible. As a rule all Tolstoy's later teaching seems to grow out of his experience of life; but it would be hard for anyone to work more conscientiously and well than Tolstoy laboured over this book, and yet in later life he speaks as though any admixture of mercenary motives is fatal to good literary work. We here seem, therefore, to come upon an exception to that rule.

Stráhov's assistance enabled Tolstoy (though he continued to give most careful instructions with regard to the treatment of the various sections of the book) to get a much needed change; and after having as usual worked during the winter and spring up to the very limit of his strength, he went for a short visit to his Samára estate, where he arranged about building and about ploughing up the virgin soil. A peasant from Yásnaya village was appointed steward of the new estate, and was instructed to see to the building of the house there. Being far away from home Tolstoy was anxious about his *ABC Book*; so he cut short his stay and returned to Yásnaya before the end of July. There he learned that a fine young bull of his had gored its keeper to death. The unpleasantness of such an occurrence and of the legal investigation consequent on the man's death was greatly increased by the fact that the investigating magistrate, an incompetent and arrogant young official, wrongly held Tolstoy responsible for 'careless holding of cattle', and besides commencing criminal proceedings against him, obliged him to give a written undertaking not to leave Yásnaya. Prince D. D. Obolénski tells how Tolstoy arrived one day at a meet at the Prince's estate of Schahovskóy (some thirty miles from Yásnaya) late and much upset, and told of an examination he had that morning undergone at the hands of the investigating magistrate, whose duties included those of coroner. 'Being an excitable man,' says Obolénski, 'Tolstoy was extremely indignant at the magistrate's conduct, and told how the latter had kept one of the Yásno-Polyána peasants in prison for a year and a half on suspicion of having stolen a cow, which then turned out to have been stolen by someone else. "He will confine me for a year," added Tolstoy. "It is absurd, and shows how utterly arbitrary these gentlemen are. I shall sell all I have in Russia and go to England, where every man's person is respected. Here every police-officer, if one does not grovel at his feet, can play one the dirtiest tricks!" '

P. F. Samárin, who had also come to the hunt, opposed Tolstoy with animation, arguing that the death, or even the mutilation, of a man was so serious a matter that it could not be left without judicial investigation. After long argument Samárin more or less convinced Tolstoy, and the latter before retiring to rest remarked to Obolénski, 'What a wonderful power of calming people Samárin has!'

The judicial proceedings dragged on for more than a month, and it was not till late in September that Tolstoy was again free to take a journey to Moscow. The proceedings, first against him and then against his steward, were abandoned, but not before the newspapers had taken the matter up and made a fuss about it.

At last, in November, the *ABC Book* was published. It sold slowly, and was attacked by some of the papers. Tolstoy however was not discouraged, but held to his belief that (as he expressed it to Stráhov) he had 'erected a monument' – a conviction amply justified by the ultimate success of the work. He had indeed produced a reading-book far superior to anything that had ever existed in Russia, and probably unmatched in any language. With certain modifications, to be mentioned later on, it has continued to circulate throughout Russia ever since.

In connection with his other efforts to popularise his system of instruction, Tolstoy, in October 1872, invited a dozen teachers from neighbouring schools to visit him for a week at Yásnaya. They were accommodated in his second house (called, as is customary in Russian when speaking of a subsidiary residence, 'the wing'); and a number of illiterate boys were collected from villages within reach, to be taught on Tolstoy's lines. He also formed a project of establishing a 'University in bark shoes' [country peasants wear bark shoes] or, in other words, a training college in which peasants could become teachers without ceasing to be peasants. This plan occupied his attention off and on for some years, but, owing to causes related later, never came to fruition.

About this time Fet sent Tolstoy a letter in rhyme, to which the latter replied as follows:

12th November 1872

> The causeless shame felt by the onion
>   Before the sweetly-scented rose,
> My dearest Fet, I should be feeling,
>   Were I to answer you in prose.
>
> And yet in maiden verse replying,
>   By sad misgivings I'm beset:
> The when and where, yourself please settle –
>   But come and visit us, dear Fet.
>
> Tho' drought may parch the rye and barley,
>   Yet still I shall not feel upset
> If I but spend a day enjoying
>   Your conversation, dearest Fet!
>
> Too apt we often are to worry;
>   O'er future ills let us not fret:

> Sufficient for the day, its evil –
> It's best to think so, dearest Fet!

Joking apart, write quickly and let me know when to send horses to the station to meet you. I want terribly to see you.

Having at last got his *ABC Book* off his hands, Tolstoy resumed his preliminary labours for a large novel, which was to deal with the period of Peter the Great. On 19th November 1872 the Countess wrote to her brother:

> Our life just now is very, very strenuous. All day we are occupied. Leo sits surrounded by a pile of portraits, pictures and books, engrossed in reading, marking passages and taking notes. In the evening, when the children have gone to bed, he tells me his plans and what he means to write. At times he is quite discouraged, falls into despair, and thinks nothing will ever come of it. At other times he is on the point of setting ardently to work, but as yet I cannot say he has actually written anything, he is still preparing.

A month later she wrote:

> As usual we are all of us very busy. The winter is the working time for us proprietors, just as much as summer is for the peasants. Leo is still reading historical books of the time of Peter the Great and is much interested in them. He notes down the characters of various people, their traits, as well as the way of life of the boyars and the peasants, and Peter's activity. He does not yet know what will come of it all, but it seems to me we shall have another prose poem like *War and Peace* – but of the time of Peter the Great.

A few months later [in 1873] he definitely abandoned the project. His opinion of Peter the Great ran directly counter to the popular one, and he felt out of sympathy with the whole epoch. He declared there was nothing great about the personality or activity of Peter, whose qualities were all bad. His so-called reforms, far from aiming at the welfare of the people aimed simply at his own personal advantage. He founded Petersburg because the boyars, who were influential and consequently dangerous to him, disapproved of the changes he made, and because he wished to be free to follow his immoral way of life. The changes and reforms he introduced were borrowed from Saxony, where the laws were most cruel and the morals most dissolute – all of which particularly pleased him. This, Tolstoy holds, explains Peter's friendship with the Elector of Saxony, who was among the most immoral of rulers. He also considers that Peter's intimacy with the pieman Ménshikov and with the Swiss deserter Lefort, is explained by the contempt in which Peter was held by all the boyars, among whom he could not find men willing to share his dissolute life. Most of all Tolstoy was revolted by the murder of Peter's son Aléxis, in which affair Tolstoy's own ancestor had played a very prominent part.

Almost simultaneously with the abandonment of the project to which he had devoted so much time and attention, without any special preparation he began to write his second great novel, *Anna Karénina*.

The year before, a lady named Anna who lived with Bíbikov, a neighbouring squire mentioned on a previous page, had committed suicide by throwing herself under a train out of jealousy of Bíbikov's attentions to their governess. Tolstoy knew all the details of the affair and had been present at the post-mortem. This supplied him with a theme; but it was not till March 1873, and then as it were by accident, that he actually began to write the book. One day a volume of Púshkin happened to be lying open at the commencement of *A Fragment*, which begins with the words, 'The guests had arrived at the country house.' Tolstoy, noticing this, remarked to those present that these words, plunging at once into the midst of things, are a model of how a story should begin. Someone laughingly suggested that he should begin a novel in that way; and Tolstoy at once started on *Anna Karénina*, the second sentence, and first narrative sentence, of which is, 'Everything was upset in the Oblónskys' house.'

In May, Tolstoy and his whole family went for a three months' visit to Samára, where he had recently purchased some more land.

This summer he hired a Bashkír named Mouhamed Shah, who owned and brought with him a herd of milking mares. This Mouhamed Shah was polite, punctual, and dignified. He had a workman to drive the herd, and a wife (who retired behind a curtain in his *kochévka* when visitors came to see him) to wait upon him. In subsequent years this worthy man repeatedly resumed his engagement with the Tolstoys.

This was the first year the whole estate had been ploughed up and sown. It was fortunate for the district that someone who had the ear of the public happened to be there, for the crops in the whole neighbourhood failed utterly, and a famine ensued. So out-of-the-world were the people and so cut off from civilisation, that they might have suffered and died without the rest of Russia hearing anything about it, had not Tolstoy been at hand to make their plight known in good time by an appeal for help, which the Countess prompted him to draw up and which appeared on 17th August, in the *Moscow Védomosti*.

In this article on the Samára Famine, Tolstoy describes how the complete failure of the harvest, following as it did on two previous poor harvests, had brought nearly nine-tenths of the population to destitution and hunger.

To ascertain the real state of things Tolstoy took an inventory at every tenth house in the village of Gavrílovka – the one nearest his estate; and of the twenty-three families so examined, all but one were found to be in debt, and none of them knew how they were to get through the winter. Most of the men had left home to seek for work, but the harvest being bad everywhere and so many being in search of work, the price of labour had fallen to one-eighth of its usual amount.

Tolstoy visited several villages and found a similar state of things everywhere. Together with his article he sent 100 rubles as a first subscription to a Famine Fund. This was only a small part of what he spent in relief of the impoverished peasants, for when Prugávin (well known for his valuable descriptions of Russian sects) visited the district in 1881, many of the inhabitants told him of Tolstoy's personal kindness to the afflicted, and of his gifts of corn and money during the famine.

The subscription proved a success. Tolstoy's aunt, Countess A. A. Tolstáya, mentioned the matter to the Empress, who was one of the first to contribute. Her example was largely followed, and altogether in money and in kind something like 2,000,000 rubles was contributed during 1873–4. Within a year or two, good harvests again completely changed the whole appearance of the district.

This was the first, but neither the last nor the worst, of the famines in which Tolstoy rendered help.

Before the end of August 1873 he was back at Yásnaya.

A month later he wrote to Fet, referring to Kramskóy's portrait of himself, in the blouse which even in those days he wore when at home instead of a tailor-made coat:

25th September 1873

I am beginning to write ... The children are learning; my wife is busy and teaches. Every day for a week Kramskóy has been painting my portrait for Tretyakóv's Gallery, and I sit and chat with him and try to convert him from the Petersburg faith to the faith of the baptised. I agreed to this because Kramskóy came personally and offered to paint a second portrait for us very cheaply, and because my wife persuaded me.

Up to that time Tolstoy, sensitive as to his personal appearance, and instinctively disliking any personal advertisement, had always objected to having his portrait painted, and if he ever allowed himself to be photographed, had been careful to have the negative destroyed that copies might not be multiplied. This prejudice he abandoned in later life; and after Kramskóy had broken the ice, portraits and photographs of Tolstoy became more and more common.

Kramskóy's acquaintance with him came about in this way. He was commissioned to paint a portrait of the great novelist for the collection of famous Russians in Tretyakóv's picture gallery in Moscow, but sought in vain in that town for his photograph and was too modest to ask Tolstoy (who, he knew, was living a secluded life at Yásnaya) to give him sittings. He therefore hired a country house some three miles from Yásnaya, with the intention of painting Tolstoy who often rode past there on horseback. His intention however became known, and the Tolstoys at once sent him a friendly invitation to visit them. Of the two very similar portraits which Kramskóy painted, one remained at Yásnaya.

Before Tolstoy's next letter to Fet, the angel of death had crossed the threshold of his house for the first time in his married life. On 11th November he wrote:

We are in trouble: Peter, our youngest, fell ill with croup and died in two days. It is the first death in our family in eleven years, and my wife feels it very deeply. One may console oneself by saying that if one had to choose one of our eight, this loss is lighter than any other would have been; but the heart, especially the mother's heart – that wonderful and highest manifestation of Divinity on earth – does not reason, and my wife grieves.

During the whole of 1874 Tolstoy made strenuous efforts to get his system of education generally adopted. On 15th January, overcoming his dislike of speaking in public, he addressed the Moscow Society of Literacy on the best way to teach children to read. The details of his argument need not detain us, as it will fall to the lot of few readers of this book to teach Russian children to read Russian; but briefly, the German *Lautier-methode* had been adopted by Russian pedagogues in a way Tolstoy considered arbitrary and pedantic, and his appeal was against that method.

The large hall in which the meeting took place was crowded. The President of the Society, Mr Shatílov, invited Tolstoy to open the debate, but Tolstoy preferred to reply to questions and remarks other speakers might put. In the course of the animated proceedings, in which several men prominent in the Russian educational world took part, the discussion widened out till it covered the question of the whole direction of elementary education; and Tolstoy, from the standpoint of his belief that it is harmful to force upon the people a culture they do not desire and are not prepared for – and much of which, though considered by us to be science, may yet turn out to be no better than the alchemy and astrology of the Middle Ages – denounced the education forced on the children in elementary schools, and declared that it should in the first place be confined to teaching the Russian language and arithmetic, leaving natural science and history alone. To prove the advantage of his way of teaching reading, Tolstoy offered to give a practical demonstration in one of the schools attached to the Moscow factories. This was done, with the result that the Society of Literacy decided to start two temporary schools for the express purpose of testing the rival methods during a period of seven weeks. The one school was taught by an expert in the *Lautiermethode*, while in the other school Tolstoy's method was taught by a teacher from one of the schools near Yásnaya. After seven weeks the children were examined by a committee, but the members of the committee disagreed and handed in contradictory reports. At the meeting of the Society there was again a great divergence of opinion, and Tolstoy, who considered that the test had not been made under proper conditions (most of the pupils being too young, and the constant presence of visitors having prevented the teacher from holding the children's attention), but that his method had nevertheless shown its superiority, decided to appeal to a wider public and did so by publishing a letter addressed to Shatílov.

An account of what happened from the time the dispute passed into the press has been given by the popular critic and essayist, N. K. Mihaylóvski, a colleague of Nekrásov who was at that time editing the *Fatherland Journal*. Tolstoy, who had long dropped out of touch with

Nekrásov, now asked him to let the *Fatherland Journal* take a hand in his fight with the pedagogic specialists, and to interest a wider public in his educational reforms. As an inducement he held out a prospect (never fulfilled) that he would contribute some works of fiction to their magazine. The outcome of his correspondence was that a long article by Tolstoy (his letter to Shatílov) appeared in the September number, under the title of *On the Education of the People*.

Tolstoy's educational articles in 1862, when he had issued them in his own magazine, had fallen flat and attracted no attention, but this article, by the author of *War and Peace* in a leading Petersburg magazine, though expressing similar views, received much attention and was criticised, favourably or adversely, in many other publications. Though his views were only adopted to a small extent, the shock he administered to the professional pedagogues who looked on schoolchildren as 'a flock existing for the sake of its shepherds', had a most healthy influence, and its immediate effect was indicated by the rejection from the Moscow Teachers' Seminary of one of the textbooks Tolstoy most fiercely attacked.

Following on the storm raised by this article, Mihaylóvski, in the *Fatherland Journal* for January 1875, published a long article entitled *An Outsider's Notes*, in which he took Tolstoy's part against the pedagogues, and said: 'Though I am one of the profane in philosophy and pedagogics, and am writing simply a *feuilleton*, yet I advise my readers to peruse this *feuilleton* with great attention, not for my sake but for Tolstoy's, and for the sake of those fine shades of thought on which I merely comment.'

Before this, however, Tolstoy had made another attempt to improve the state of elementary education, by promoting the establishment of that 'University in bark shoes' already alluded to.

He had found some of the boys in the Yásno-Polyána school anxious to continue their studies after finishing the school course, and an experiment in teaching them algebra had been very successful.

In his last article on Education he had pointed out that a great obstacle to the spread of efficient elementary instruction lay in the fact that the peasants could not afford the salaries (modest as these were) demanded by Russian teachers who were not peasants. It was therefore natural that he should devise a scheme for preparing teachers from among the peasants themselves; and he drew up a project for a training college to be established at Yásnaya under his own direction and control.

In the summer of this year he paid a brief visit to his Samára estate to look after its management, and took his son Sergéy with him.

On 20th November 1874 the Countess wrote to her brother:

Our usual serious winter work is now in full swing. Leo is quite taken up with popular education, schools, and colleges for teachers, where teachers for the peasants' schools are to be trained. All this keeps him busy from morning to night. I have my doubts about all this. I am sorry his strength should be spent on these things instead of on writing a novel; and I don't know in how far it will be of use, since all this activity will extend only to one small corner of Russia.

P. F. Samárin, the Marshal of the nobility of Túla Government, backed Tolstoy cordially and pointed out that the Zémstvo (County Council) had a sum of 30,000 rubles available for educational purposes, and that this might be devoted to starting a teacher's Training College. To attain this end Tolstoy, who heretofore had always refused to stand for election, consented to enter the Zémstvo, and after being returned to that body, was unanimously chosen to serve on its Education Committee.

He presented a report in the sense indicated above, which was at first favourably discussed; but one of the elder members rose, and alluding to the fact that a collection was being made all over Russia for a monument to Catherine the Great, and that it was the centenary year of the decree by which she had created the Government of Túla, proposed that the money should be devoted to a monument of their benefactress. This loyal sentiment met with approval, and though Tolstoy did not at once abandon his plan, the means to carry it out were not forthcoming and we do not hear much more of it.

If one did not know how stupidly reactionary the governing classes of Russia were at this period, it would seem extraordinary that the central and the local authorities alike should have so constantly balked and hindered Tolstoy's disinterested projects: forbidding the publication of his newspaper for soldiers, mutilating his stories, sending gendarmes to search his schools, looking askance at his school magazine, and defeating his project for a Training College. Can it be wondered at that he came more and more to identify Government with all that is most opposed to enlightenment? We know that similar causes were at that very time driving men and women of a younger generation to undertake dangerous propaganda among factory workmen and country peasants, in more or less definite opposition to the existing order of society.

His devotion to educational matters did not entirely supersede, though no doubt it delayed, his activity as a novelist. In the spring of 1874 he had taken the commencement of *Anna Karénina* to Moscow, but for some reason none of it appeared that year.

Turgénev, in collaboration with Madame Viardot, was at this time translating some of Tolstoy's stories into French. Writing to Fet in March 1874 he says:

> The season is now almost over, but all the same I will try to place his [Tolstoy's] *Three Deaths* in the *Revue des Deux Mondes* or in the *Temps*, and in the autumn I will without fail get out *The Cossacks*. The more often I read that story the more convinced I am that it is the *chef d'oeuvre* of Tolstoy and of all Russian narrative literature.

Meanwhile life and death pursued their course. In April a son was born and christened Nicholas; and soon death, having a few months previously taken the youngest, returned to claim the oldest members of the household. The first of them to go was his dearly loved Auntie Tatiána Alexándrovna, to whose good influence throughout life he owed so much. She died on 20th June, and next year his other aunt followed her.

Tolstoy never refers to his Aunt Tatiána without letting us see how he cherishes her memory. Here, for instance, are one or two of his notes relating to her:

> When already beginning to grow feeble, having waited her opportunity, one day when I was in her room she said to us turning away (I saw that she was ready to cry), 'Look here, *mes chers amis*, my room is a good one and you will want it. If I die in it,' and her voice trembled, 'the recollection will be unpleasant to you; so move me somewhere else, that I may not die here.' Such she always was from my earliest childhood, before I was able to understand her goodness.

Again referring to her death, and to the love for his father which had played so large a part in her life, he adds:

> She died peacefully, gradually falling asleep; and died as she desired, not in the room that had been hers, lest it should be spoilt for us.
>
> She died recognising hardly anyone. But me she always recognised,

smiling and lighting up as an electric lamp does when one touches the switch, and sometimes she moved her lips trying to pronounce the name Nicholas: thus in death completely and inseparably uniting me with him she had loved all her life.

When her coffin was carried through the village, there was not one hut out of the sixty in Yásnaya Polyána from which the people did not come out asking to have the procession stopped and a requiem sung for her soul. 'She was a kind lady and did nobody any harm,' said they. Tolstoy adds:

On that account they loved her, and loved her very much. Lao-Tsze says things are valuable for what is not in them. So it is with a life. It is most valuable if there is nothing bad in it, and in the life of Tatiána Alexándrovna there was nothing bad.

Except in the case of his brother Nicholas, Tolstoy was usually not greatly upset even by the deaths of those near and dear to him. The following letter to Fet shows how he took Tatiána's death:

24th June 1874

Two days ago we buried Tatiána Alexándrovna. She died slowly and gradually, and I had grown accustomed to the process; yet her death was, as the death of a near and dear one always is, a quite new, isolated, and unexpectedly stirring event. The others are well, and our house is full. The delightful heat, the bathing and the fruit have brought me to the state of mental laziness I love, with only enough mental life remaining to enable me to remember my friends and think of them.

The next letter, dated 22nd October, tells its own tale:

DEAR AFANÁSY AFANASYEVICH – I have planned to buy, and must buy, some land at Nikólskoe, and for that purpose must borrow 10,000 rubles for one year on mortgage. It may be that you have money you want to place. If so, write to Iván Ivánovich Orlóv, Nikól-skoe village, and he will arrange the affair with you independently of our relations to one another . . . How gladly would I come to see you, were I not so overwhelmed with the school, family, and estate business, that I have not even time to go out shooting . . . I hope to be free when winter comes.

A small second edition of Tolstoy's *ABC Book*, in twelve paper-bound parts, was printed this year [1875]; but he did not yet feel quite satisfied with that work and towards the close of the year revised it, abbreviating, omitting the arithmetic, and introducing graduated reading exercises. A *New ABC Book*, apart from the more advanced *Readers*, and consisting of ninety-two pages of elementary matter, was issued in 1875, at a very low price. Between one and two million copies of it have since been sold. The reading matter from his first *ABC Book* was subsequently graded into four cheap *Readers* costing 3*d.* to 4*d.* each, and though they were not recognised by the Ministry of Education, they have from that time to this circulated in large quantities, being printed of late years in edition after edition of 50,000 at a time.

The Countess in general enjoyed good health and bore the cares of her large family lightly; but during the winter of 1874–5 her condition caused her husband much concern. In January he was able to write to Fet, 'I have ceased to fear for my wife's health'; but in fact for some time longer she continued to ail.

The commencement of *Anna Karénina* appeared in the first four monthly numbers of the *Russian Messenger* for 1875.

In February the baby, Nicholas, died of inflammation of the brain, and on 4th March 1875* Tolstoy wrote to Fet:

> We have one grief after another; you and Márya Petróvna will certainly be sorry for us, especially for Sónya. Our youngest son, ten months old, fell ill three weeks ago with the dreadful illness called 'water on the brain', and after three weeks' terrible torture died three days ago, and we buried him today. I feel it hard through my wife, but for her, who was nursing him herself, it is very hard.

In the same letter he mentions *Anna Karénina*, and immediately afterwards makes allusion to the first idea of his *Confession*, which was not actually written till 1879:

> It pleases me very much that you praise Karénina and I hear that she gets praised, but assuredly never was writer so indifferent to his success as I am!
>
> On the one hand I am preoccupied with the school affairs, and on the other, strange to say, with the subject of a new work which took

* This letter evidently relates to the year 1875, though in Fet's *Recollections* it is given as belonging to 1874.

possession of me just at the worst time of the boy's illness, and with that illness itself and death ...

This summer the whole Tolstoy family went to the Samára estates, which had already been considerably increased by the last purchase and ultimately exceeded 16,000 acres. Mouhamed Shah with his herd of mares and his *kochévka* – which Tolstoy called 'our saloon' – again appeared on the scene. A second *kochévka* was set up for the use of the Tolstoys themselves, and was so much in favour that all the members of the family were eager to occupy it.

The novelty and the peculiarities of steppe farming interested Tolstoy, and he as well as other members of his household took an active part in harvesting and winnowing. How primitive were the Samára methods of agriculture may be shown by mentioning their manner of threshing. A ring of horses was formed tied head to tail. In the centre of the ring stood a driver with a long lash, and the horses were set trotting round a corresponding circle of sheaves, out of which they trod the grain.

The virgin soil was ploughed up by five or even six pair of oxen, wearing round their necks deep-toned bells, sounding in a minor key. These things, together with the pipes of the boys who watched the herds, the sultry days, and the marvellously clear moonlit nights, had a wonderful charm for the whole party, which was increased by Tolstoy's capacity to notice and direct attention to whatever was interesting or beautiful.

The whole family became interested, Behrs tells us, in their new farming, and some of them went with Tolstoy as far afield as Orenbourg to purchase cattle and horses.

He bought about a hundred Bashkír mares and crossed them with an English trotter and with horses of other breeds, hoping to obtain a good new type.

One evening his whole herd and Mouhamed Shah's as well, were very nearly stolen by some Kirghiz nomads. The invaders were, however, pursued and driven off by two mounted Bashkír labourers.

Tolstoy declared farming in Samára to be a game of chance. It cost nearly three times as much to plough up the land, sow it, and gather in a harvest, as it did to purchase the freehold of the estate; and if during May and June there was not at least one good fall of rain, everything perished; whereas if it rained several times the harvest yielded thirty- to forty-fold.

One day, at harvest time, a poor wandering Tartar, drawing two little children in a tiny cart, came up to the balcony on which the Tolstoys were sitting, and begged to be hired as a labourer. He was allowed to set up his wigwam in a field close by, and the Tolstoy children used to go there every day to feed the little Tartars.

In the neighbouring village several well-to-do Russian peasants lived, with whom Tolstoy was on very good terms. Either because they were economically independent and lived in a province where serfdom had not prevailed, or as a result of Tolstoy's tact and ability to set people at their ease, these peasants always behaved with dignity and self-respect. They shook hands when they said 'How do you do?' and seemed quite at home with the Count.

He used to notice with pleasure the good relations and complete religious toleration that existed in those parts between the Orthodox peasants and their Mohammedan neighbours; and he was also delighted that the priest at Pátrovka was on friendly terms with the Molokáns he was trying to convert.

One rainy night, after staying late at this priest's house, Tolstoy and his brother-in-law completely lost their way. It was so dark that they could not see their horses' heads. Behrs was riding an old working horse which kept pulling to the left. Tolstoy, on hearing this, told him to let the horse follow its bent. Behrs therefore tied his reins so that they hung loose, and wrapping himself from the drenching rain in his cloak, allowed the horse to go where it liked. Carefully avoiding the ploughed land, it soon brought them out on to the road and, curiously enough, to just the part of it which was distinguishable from the extraordinary sameness of the rest, so that the riders knew where they were.

The most striking event of this year's stay in Samára was a horse race arranged by Tolstoy. Mouhamed Shah was authorised to announce to the peasants and neighbours that races would be held on the Count's estate, and invitations were sent to all likely to take part. Bashkírs and Kirghíz assembled, bringing with them tents, portable copper boilers, plenty of *kumys*, and even sheep. Ural Cossacks and Russian peasants also came from the whole surrounding neighbourhood. In preparation for the race, says Behrs:

We ourselves chose a level place, measured out a huge circle three miles in circumference, marked it by running a plough round, and set up posts. Sheep, and even a horse, were prepared with which to regale the visitors. By the appointed day some thousands of people had collected. On the wild steppe covered with feather grass a row of tents appeared, and soon a motley crowd enlivened it. On the conical hillocks (locally called 'cones') felt and other carpets were spread on which the Bashkírs sat in circles, their legs tucked under them. In the centre of the circle a young Bashkír poured *kumys* out of a large *tursuk* [a leather bottle made of an animal's leg], handing the cup to each of the company in turn. Their songs and the tunes played on their pipes and reeds sounded somewhat dreary to a European ear. Wrestling, at which the Bashkírs are particularly skilful, could be seen here and there. Thirty trained horses were entered for the chief race. The riders were boys of about ten years, who rode without saddles.

This race was for thirty-three miles, and it took exactly an hour and forty minutes; consequently it was run at the rate of three minutes a mile. Of the thirty horses, ten ran the whole distance, the others giving up. The principal prizes were a horse, an ox, a gun, a gold watch, and several many-coloured silk gowns, such as the Tartars wear. The festival lasted two days, and passed off in perfect order and very gaily. To Tolstoy's delight no police were present. The guests all politely thanked their host and departed highly satisfied. 'Even in the crowd,' says Behrs, 'it seemed to me that Leo Nikoláevich knew how to evoke *entrain* combined with respect for good order.'

Readers of Tolstoy's short stories will be aware of the use to which he subsequently put his knowledge of the Bashkírs and of a hermit he met in those parts.

On 26th August, after reaching Yásnaya, he wrote to Fet:

Two days ago we arrived home safely . . .

We have had an average harvest, but the price of labour has been enormous, so that finally ends only just meet. For two months I have not soiled my hands with ink nor my heart with thoughts. Now I am settling down again to dull, commonplace *Anna Karénina*, with the sole desire to clear a space quickly and obtain leisure for other occupations – only not for the educational work I love but wish to abandon. It takes too much time.

His Samára experiences confirmed in him the feeling that not the civilisation and progress and political struggles of the Western World and of the small Westernised section of Russians were really important, but the great primitive struggle of plain people to obtain a subsistence in healthy natural conditions, and he adds in the same letter:

> Why fate took me there [to Samára] I do not know; but I know that I have listened to speeches in the English Parliament, which is considered very important, and it seemed to me dull and insignificant; but there are flies, dirt, and Bashkír peasants, and I, watching them with intense respect and anxiety, became absorbed in listening to them and watching them and felt it all to be very important.
>
> One must live as we lived, in a healthy out-of-the-way part of Samára, and see the struggle going on before one's eyes of the nomadic life (of millions of people on an immense territory) with the primitive agricultural life, to realise all the importance of that struggle.

After their return from the Government of Samára all the children had whooping-cough. The Countess caught it from them and, being in the sixth month of pregnancy, was very ill. This resulted in the premature birth of a girl, who lived less than two hours.

Tolstoy's eldest son, Sergéy, had now reached the age of twelve. Besides their English governess and a Swiss lady, the children had at different times a Swiss, a Frenchman, and a German, as tutors for modern languages. Tutors and students who acted as tutors also lodged at Yásnaya and taught other subjects. A music master came over from Túla. The eldest boy had considerable musical talent and the family as a whole were musical. As soon as they had mastered their finger exercises the Count insisted on their at once being allowed to learn serious pieces.

Every effort was made to awaken and foster the talent for drawing and painting which some of the children, and especially the eldest daughter, Tatiána, possessed, but lessons in these subjects were given only to those who showed real capacity for them.

Much as Tolstoy disliked the curriculum of the Grammar Schools ('Gymnasiums' as they were called in Russia), he did not wish to make it impossible for his sons to enter the University and they followed the usual classical course. Sergéy passed his examinations each year in Túla Gymnasium, being carefully coached at home.

In his *Recollections* Behrs tells us of Tolstoy's enlivening influence in the family:

I cannot sufficiently describe the joyous and happy frame of mind that usually reigned at Yásnaya Polyána. Its source was always Leo Nikoláevich. In conversation about abstract questions, about the education of children, about outside matters – his opinion was always most interesting. When playing croquet, or during our walks, he enlivened us all by his humour and his participation, taking a real part in the game or the walk.

With me, he liked to mow or to rake, to do gymnastics, to race, and occasionally to play leap-frog or *gorodkí* [a game in which a stick is thrown at some shorter sticks placed in a pattern], &c. Though far inferior to him in strength, for he could lift 180 lb. with one hand, I could easily match him in a race, but seldom passed him for I was always laughing. That mood accompanied all our exercises. Whenever we happened to pass where mowers were at work, he would go up to them and borrow a scythe from the one who seemed most tired. I of course followed his example. He would then ask me: Why we, with well-developed muscles, cannot mow six days on end, though a peasant does it on rye-bread and sleeping on damp earth? 'You just try to do it under such conditions,' he would add in conclusion. When leaving the meadow, he would take a handful of hay from the haycock and sniff it, keenly enjoying its smell.

Children and grown-ups alike played croquet at Yásnaya. The game generally began after dinner in the evening and only finished by candle-light. Behrs says that, having played it with Tolstoy, he considers croquet to be a game of chance. Tolstoy's commendation of a good shot always pleased the player and aroused the emulation of his opponents. The kindly irony of his comments on a miss also acted as a spur. A simple word from him, uttered just at the right moment and in the right tone, produced that *entrain* which makes any occupation interesting and infects all who come under its influence.

The sincerity of Tolstoy's nature showed itself in the frank expression of his passing mood. If, when driving to the station he saw that they had missed the train, he would exclaim, 'Ach! we've missed it!' with such intensity that everyone within earshot would first feel as though a calamity had occurred, and would then join in the hearty laughter which his own vehemence evoked in Tolstoy. It was the same when he made a bad miss at croquet, and also if, when sitting at home, he suddenly remembered some engagement he had forgotten. If, as sometimes happened, his exclamation alarmed his wife, he would half-jokingly add, like a scolded child, 'I'll never do it again!'

His laughter, which began on a high note, had something wonderfully infectious about it. His head would hang over on one side and his whole body would shake.

His good-natured irony constantly acted as a stimulant to those about him. If for instance someone was in the dumps about the weather, Tolstoy would say: 'Is your weather behaving badly?'

When he felt it wise to reject an extra cigar, or a second helping of some favourite dish, he would remark to those present: 'Wait till I am grown up, then I will have two helpings,' or 'two cigars', as the case might be.

'If,' says Behrs, 'he noticed any of the children making a wry or affected face, he generally called out, "Now then, no grimacing, you'll only spoil your phiz." '

Behrs also tells us that:

> What he called 'the Numidian cavalry' evoked our noisiest applause. He would unexpectedly spring up from his place and, raising one arm in the air with its hand hanging quite loose from the wrist, he would run lightly through the rooms. All the children and sometimes the grown-ups also would follow his example with the same suddenness.

Tolstoy read aloud very well, and would often read to the family or to visitors.

His contempt for doctors and medicine is plainly indicated both in *War and Peace* and *Anna Karénina*. Like Rousseau he considered that the practice of medicine should be general and not confined to one profession, and this opinion inclined him to approve of the folk-remedies used by the peasants. But he did not go the length of refusing to call in a doctor when one of the family was seriously ill.

Before the year closed, his aunt, Pelagéya Ilynishna Yúshkov, with whom he had lived in his young days in Kazán, also passed away. She had been separated from her husband before his death in 1869 and for a long time had not even seen him, though they remained quite friendly towards one another. She was very religious in an Orthodox Church way, and after her husband's death retired to the Óptina nunnery. Subsequently she moved to the Túla nunnery, but arranged to spend much of her time at Yásnaya, where in her eightieth year she fell ill and died. She was in general a good-tempered though not a clever woman, and all her life long strictly observed the ceremonies of the Church and thought that she firmly believed its teaching about redemption and resurrection, yet she was so afraid of death that on her deathbed she was reluctant to receive the eucharist because it brought home to her the fact that she was dying; and her suffering at the fear of death caused her to become irritable with all about her.

A servant, Sergéy Arbúzov, who lived in the house at the time, tells us that while at Yásnaya, Pelagéya used on the first of each month to send for a priest. As soon as he arrived and began the usual ceremony of blessing with holy water, Tolstoy would escape and hide himself. Not till the gardener, Semën – whom he used to send into the conservatory to reconnoitre – brought word that the priest had gone, would Tolstoy reappear.

About that time, however, his attitude towards Church ceremonies altered. His servant (who saw only the external signs of the complex inner struggle that went on in Tolstoy) tells us:

Suddenly a wonderful change came over him, of which I was a witness. In 1875 a priest, Vasíly Ivánovich, from the Túla Seminary, used to come to teach theology to Tolstoy's children. At first, Leo Nikoláevich hardly ever talked to him, but once a snowstorm obliged Vasíly Ivánovich to stop the night at our house. The Count began a conversation with him and they did not go to bed till daylight. They talked the whole night.

From that day Leo Nikoláevich became very thoughtful and always talked with Vasíly Ivánovich. When Lent came round, the Count got up one morning and said, 'I am going to do my devotions and prepare to receive communion. You can go back to bed, but first tell the coachman not to get up. I will saddle Kalmyk [his favourite horse at that time] myself. Forgive me, Sergéy, if I have ever offended you!' and he went off to church.

From that day, for a couple of years, he always went to church, seldom missing a Sunday. The whole village was surprised, and asked, 'What has the priest told the Count that has suddenly made him so fond of church-going?'

It used to happen that the Count would come into my hut when I was teaching my little boy religion.

'What are you teaching him?' he would ask.

And I used to say, 'To pray.'

'Ah!' said he, 'that is right. A man who does not pray to God is not a real man.'

The publication of *Anna Karénina* was renewed in the first four numbers of the *Russian Messenger* for 1876. On 1st March Tolstoy writes to Fet:

Things are not yet right with us. My wife does not get over her last illness, coughs, grows thin, and first has fever and then headaches. And therefore the house lacks well-being and I lack mental tranquillity, which I particularly need now for my work. The end of winter and beginning of spring is always my chief time for work, and I must finish my novel, which now wearies me . . . I always hope a tooth will come loose in your jaw, or in your thrashing machine, and cause you to go to Moscow. Then I shall spin a cobweb at Kozlóvka [the nearest station to Yásnaya] and catch you.

In April Fet wrote to say that he had been seriously ill, had thought he was dying, and 'wished to call you to see how I departed'. On 29th April Tolstoy replies in a letter, notable as giving us a glimpse of the progress he had made in the fierce five-year inner struggle with doubt which preceded the production of his *Confession*:

I am grateful to you for thinking of calling me to see your departure, when you supposed it near. I will do the same when I get ready to go *thither*, if I am able to think. No one will be so necessary to me at that moment as you and my brother. When death draws near, intercourse with people who in this life look beyond its bounds is precious and cheering; and you and those rare *real* people I have met in life always stand on the very verge and see clearly, just because they look now at Nirvana – the illimitable, the unknown – and now at Sansara; and that glance at Nirvana strengthens their sight. But worldly people, however much they may talk about God, are unpleasant to you and me and must be a torment when one is dying, for they do not see what we see, namely the God who 'is more indefinite and distant, but loftier and more indubitable', as was said in your article.

You are ill and think of death, and I am alive and do not cease thinking of and preparing for the same thing . . . Much that I have thought, I have tried to express in the last chapter of the April number of the *Russian Messenger* [*Anna Karénina*, Part V, Chap. XX].

The passage referred to, telling of the death of Lévin's brother, is evidently based on that of Tolstoy's own brother Dmítri; and many other characters in *Anna Karénina* are also drawn more or less closely from life. For instance, Agáfya Miháylovna, the servant, was a real person and that was her real name. She died at Yásnaya only a few years ago. Yásnaya Polyána itself in many of its details is also described in the novel.

On 12th May Tolstoy again writes to Fet:

It is already five days since I received the horse, and every day I prepare, but never make time, to write to you. Here the spring and summer life has begun and our house is full of guests and of bustle. This summer life seems to me like a dream: it contains some slight remains of my real, winter life, but consists chiefly of visions, now pleasant and now unpleasant, from some absurd world not ruled by sane sense. Among these visions came your beautiful stallion. I am very much obliged to you for it. Where am I to send the money to? . . .

An event which occupies me very much at present is Sergéy's examination, which begins on the 27th . . . What a terrible summer! Here it is dreadful and mournful to look at the wood, especially at the young trees. They have all perished.

On 18th May he wrote again:

I have been slow in answering your long and cordial letter because I have been unwell and dispirited as I still am, but I will write at least a few lines. Our house is full of people: my niece Nagórny with two children, the Kuzmínskis with four children; and Sónya [his wife] is still poorly, and I dejected and dull-minded. Our one hope was for good weather and that we have not got. As you and I resemble one another, you must know the condition in which one feels oneself to be, now a God from whom nothing is hid and now stupider than a horse. In that state I am at present. So do not be exacting. Till next letter, Yours,

L. TOLSTOY

The Kuzmínskis referred to above were Tánya, her husband, and their family. They spent every summer at Yásnaya, in the annexe.

Passing into his 'summer condition', Tolstoy's attention to *Anna Karénina* slackened, but before the end of the year he set energetically to work to finish it. The interest aroused by the book was extreme, and it is said that Moscow ladies used to send to the printers to try to find out what the continuation would be.

On 21st July Tolstoy writes inviting Fet's brother, Peter Afanásevich, a great lover of horses, to accompany him to Samára; and in the same letter which was addressed to Fet he makes an allusion to the troubles of the Slavs in Turkey, where fighting had been going on for a twelve-month between the Turks and Herzegovinians. Peter Afanásevich had gone as a volunteer, and had returned after the failure of the insurrection.

21st July 1876

I am very much to blame, dear Afanásy Afanásevich, for having been so slow in writing to you. I prepare to write every day but cannot find time . . . Strákhov was here a week ago, and we philosophised to the point of weariness . . . I press the hand of Peter Afanásevich. I should like to hear his stories about Herzegovina, in the existence of which I do not believe!

I am arranging to go to Samára in September. If Peter Afanásevich has no plans for September, will not he go with me to see the Kirghíz and their horses? How jolly it would be!

Mention has already been made of the fact that Tolstoy, who understood horses very well, was at this time interested in horse-breeding as a source of revenue. To buy them he visited Orenbourg, where he met General Kryzhanóvski, a friend who had been one of his superior officers in Sevastopol and was now Governor-General of this northern Province. They spent the time very pleasantly together, recalling their past experiences.

To his wife, who had found it hard to consent to his absence, he wrote in September:

I know that it is hard for you and that you are afraid, but I saw the effort you made to control yourself and not to hinder me and, were it possible, I loved you yet more on that account. If only God grants you to spend the time well, healthily, energetically, and usefully! . . . Lord have mercy on me and on thee!

In a letter of 13th November Tolstoy writes to Fet:

Pity me for two things: (1) a good-for-nothing coachman took the stallions to Samára and, wishing to take a short cut, drowned Guneba in a bog within ten miles of the estate; (2) I sleep and cannot write; I despise myself for laziness and do not allow myself to take up any other work.

Twenty-eight years after the loss of Guneba, the Countess, in speaking to me of her husband's qualities as a man of affairs, remarked that his schemes were very good, but that he generally spoilt them by lack of care in details. 'For instance,' she remarked, 'it was quite a good idea of his to send a very fine stallion which cost 2,000 rubles to our estate in Samára. There were no such horses in the district; but he must needs entrust it to a drunken Tartar who made away with it and said he had lost it.'

On 7th December 1876 Tolstoy wrote to Fet acknowledging a poem, 'Among the Stars', which the latter had sent him:

That poem is not only worthy of you, but is specially, specially good, with that philosophic-poetic character which I expect from you. It is excellent that it is said by the stars . . . It is also good, as my wife remarked, that on the same sheet on which the poem is written, you pour out your grief that the price of kerosene has risen to 12 kopeks. That is an indirect but sure sign of a poet.

The reader is already aware of Tolstoy's devotion to music. Though at times it was crowded out of his life by other interests, he always returned to it with ardour when opportunity offered. Behrs tells us that generally, when playing, Tolstoy chose serious music.

He often sat down to the piano before beginning to work . . . He always accompanied my youngest sister [Tánya] and enjoyed her singing very much. I noticed that the sensation music evoked in him expressed itself by a slight pallor and a scarcely perceptible grimace, suggestive of something like terror. Hardly a day passed in summer without my sister singing and without the piano being played. Occasionally we all sang together, and he always played the accompaniments.

As Tolstoy's spiritual crisis approached, the attraction of music for him seemed to increase, and in December 1876 he made acquaintance with the composer Chaykóvski, who had held the post of Director of the Moscow Conservatoire, the first seeds of which Tolstoy had helped to plant nearly twenty years before.

Chaykóvski had from his youth up been a devoted admirer of Tolstoy, whose skill in reading the human heart appeared to him almost super-human. He was therefore highly gratified when of his own accord Tolstoy sought his acquaintance. At first their intercourse did not appear to lessen the composer's reverence, for on 23rd December 1876 he wrote to a friend:

Count L. N. Tolstoy spent some time here recently. He visited me several times and spent two whole evenings with me. I am tremen-dously flattered, and proud of the interest I have inspired in him, and for my part am completely enchanted by his ideal per-sonality. Chaykóvski induced Nicholas Rubinstein, then Director of the Moscow Conservatoire, to arrange a musical evening for Tolstoy's sole benefit; and at this concert, Rubinstein, Fitzenhagen, and Adolph Bródsky (who is now Principal of the Manchester College of Music) were among the chief performers.

One of the pieces performed was Chaykóvski's 'Andante in D Major', which so affected Tolstoy that he wept. 'Never, perhaps, in my life,' says Chaykóvski, 'was I so flattered, or my vanity as a composer so touched, as when Leo Nikoláevich, sitting next to me and listening to the quartet performing my Andante, burst into tears.'

After Tolstoy had returned to Yásnaya he wrote to Chaykóvski, sending him a collection of folk-songs, and saying:

I send you the songs, dear Peter Ilych. I have again looked them through. They will be a wonderful treasure in your hands. But for God's sake work them up and use them in a Mozart-Haydn style, and not in a Beethoven-Schumann-Berlioz, artificial way, seeking the unexpected. How much I left unsaid to you! I really said nothing of what I wanted to say. There was no time. I was enjoying myself. This last stay of mine in Moscow will remain one of the best of my reminiscences. Never have I received so precious a reward for my literary labours as on that wonderful evening.

Chaykóvski replied:

Count, I am sincerely grateful to you for sending the songs. I must tell you candidly that they have been taken down by an unskilful hand, and bear only traces of their pristine beauty.

The chief defect is that they have been artificially squeezed and forced into a regular, measured form. Only Russian dance music has a rhythm and a regular and equally accentuated beat; but folk-ballads have of course nothing in common with dance songs. Moreover most of these songs are, arbitrarily it seems, written in a solemn D major, which again does not suit a real Russian song that almost always has an indefinite tonality approximating closest of all to ancient Church music. In general, the songs you have sent me cannot be worked up in a regular and systematic way: that is to say, one cannot make a collection of them, because for that they would have to be taken down as nearly as possible in the way in which the people perform them. That is an extremely difficult thing, demanding fine musical feeling and great historico-musical erudition. Except Balakírev, and to some extent Prokúnin, I do not know anyone competent for the task. But as material for symphonic treatment your songs can be of use, and are even very good material, of which I certainly will avail myself in one way or other.

The intercourse between these two men, each so great in his own field and each such an admirer of the other's genius, was however not continued.

Chaykóvski's expectations had been pitched too high, and he felt a certain disappointment that his 'demigod' was, after all, but human. He had dreaded to meet the novelist lest the latter should penetrate the secret recesses of his soul; but, says Chaykóvski:

He who in his writings was the deepest of heart-seers, proved in personal contact to be a man of simple, whole, and frank nature, showing very little of the omniscience I had feared . . . It was plain he did not at all regard me as a subject for his observation, but simply wanted to chat about music, in which he was interested.

Tolstoy – who had boasted of not reading newspapers and had lived so detached from politics and the events of contemporary history – began at this time to feel keenly interested in a question of foreign policy.

Following the insurrection in Herzegovina, another had broken out in Bulgaria in May 1876, but had been quickly suppressed by the Turks, who burnt some sixty-five villages, the Bashi-Bazouks committing unspeakable atrocities on the defenceless inhabitants. At the commencement of July, Servia and Montenegro declared war on Turkey but, in spite of help rendered by Russian volunteers, they were quickly crushed by the Turks and would have been completely at their mercy had not Russia, on 31st October, issued an ultimatum demanding an armistice, which Turkey conceded. On 10th November Alexander II made a speech in the Moscow Krémlin, in which he declared that he would act independently of other powers unless satisfactory guarantees of reform were obtained from the Sultan forthwith. These events led up to the war which broke out between Russia and Turkey in April 1877.

Before this, however, in a letter of 13th November 1876, Tolstoy wrote to Fet:

> I went to Moscow to hear about the war. This whole affair agitates me greatly. It is well for those to whom it is clear, but I am frightened when I reflect on the complexity of the conditions amid which history is made, and on how some Madame A. – with her vanity – becomes an indispensable cog in the machine!

Early in 1877 the Russo-Turkish imbroglio led to a split between Tolstoy and Katkóv. Tolstoy at bottom and in his own way was certainly a reformer, and his alliance with Katkóv, who was very reactionary, had always been rather like the yoking of an ox with an ass. At this time Katkóv was ardent for the liberation of the Slavs from Turkish tyranny, laudatory of those who volunteered for the war, and eager for the aggrandisement of Russia. Tolstoy, with his knowledge of the realities of war and insight into the motives that actuate those who fight, had his doubts about the heroic and self-sacrificing character of the volunteers and the purity of the patriotism of the press; and he expressed these doubts plainly in the concluding chapters of *Anna Karénina*: as, for instance, where he makes Lévin say of 'the unanimity of the Press':

> 'That's been explained to me: as soon as there's a war their incomes are doubled. So how can they help believing in the destinies of the people, and the Slavonic races . . . and all the rest of it?'

The result was that when the final chapters of that novel were appearing in the *Russian Messenger*, during the first months of 1877, Katkóv returned some of it to Tolstoy with numerous corrections and a letter saying that he could not print it unless his corrections were accepted.

Tolstoy was furious that a journalist should dare to alter a word in his book, and sent a sharp reply to Katkóv, which resulted in a rupture.

Tolstoy issued the last part of *Anna Karénina* not in the magazine but separately in book form, besides of course issuing the whole work in book form as usual; and Katkóv had to wind up the story as best he could by giving a brief summary of the concluding part.

These events throw light on the following letter to Fet:

23rd March 1877

You can't imagine how glad I am to have your approval of my writings, dear Afanásy Afanásevich, and in general to receive your letter. You write that the *Russian Messenger* has printed someone else's poem while your *Temptation* lies waiting. It is the dullest and deadest editorial office in existence. They have become terribly repulsive to me, not on my own account but for the sake of others . . .

My head is now better, but as it gets better it has to work that much harder. March and the beginning of April are the months when I work most, and I still continue to be under the delusion that what I am writing is very important, though I know that in a month's time I shall be ashamed to remember that I thought so. Have you noticed that a new line has now been started, and that everybody is writing poetry: very bad poetry, but they all do it. Some five new poets have introduced themselves to me lately.

The dislike Tolstoy felt of the artificially stimulated war fever (though, to do Katkóv and his friends justice, one must admit that Russia had much excuse for then intervening in defence of the Slav population of Turkey) was connected with the religious impulse that was beginning to reshape his life; but it does not appear that he actually disapproved of the war after Russia had officially commenced it. What he primarily objected to was that private individuals should push the Government into war.

An influence which has left its traces in the latter part of *Anna Karénina* (particularly Part VII, Chap. XXI) was Tolstoy's intercourse about this time with some of the most prominent followers of Lord Radstock, the ardent and persuasive Evangelical preacher, who frequently visited Russia and obtained considerable influence in certain aristocratic Petersburg circles. One of these people, Count A. P. Bóbrinski, who had been Minister of Ways of Communication, made Tolstoy's acquaintance and held animated religious discussions with him. Both Bóbrinski and Colonel Páshkov (another very prominent Radstockite) cherished hopes of winning Tolstoy over to Evangelical

Christianity and making him the spokesman of their cause. Tolstoy, as the event proved, was quite capable of throwing himself whole-heartedly into a religious movement, but he needed a faith much more intelligible than the scheme of Redemption by the blood of Jesus: one that faced the facts of life, dealt explicitly with the bread-and-butter problem, and told men how to regard the fact that some people have to overtax their strength without ever reaching an assured maintenance, while others have a superabundance provided from birth without needing to do a stroke of work. His profound contempt for Evangelical doctrine flashed out twenty years later, in the 17th Chapter of Book II of *Resurrection*.

It was a little before this that Fet told Tolstoy the following story. Sauntering in a churchyard, he had come upon an epitaph which touched him more than any he had ever read. The tombstone was in the form of an obelisk of plain grey sandstone. On one of its four sides were deeply cut the words:

> *Here is buried the body of the peasant girl Mary.*

On another side:

> *Here also is buried an infant of the female sex.*

On the side opposite the name of the deceased stood these words ill-spelt:

> *This, my dear, is the last adornment I can give thee*

and below stood the name of

> *Retired non-commissioned officer So-and-so.*

In his next letter Tolstoy writes:

18th October 1876

This, my dear, is the last adornment I can give thee is charming! I have told it twice, and each time my voice has broken with tears.

In Tolstoy's next letter to Fet, dated 11th January [1877], we get a glimpse of one of the reasons that led this strenuous worker to prefer a country life:

DEAR AFANÁSY AFANÁSEVICH – One does not strike or cut off the head that owns its fault! I confess I am quite at fault towards you. But truly in Moscow I am in a condition of irresponsibility; my nerves are out of order, the hours turn to minutes, and the people I do not want turn up as though on purpose and prevent my seeing those I do want.

Among the people whom Tolstoy, in his search for truth, did want to know, were some of the leading scientists of that day – a day when many men thought that Darwin had opened the gateway to a knowledge which would solve the mysteries of life and death, of the here and the hereafter. The great literary fame Tolstoy enjoyed made it easy for him to make such acquaintances.

One of the scientists he got to know was a celebrated professor of chemistry, A. M. Butleróv, whom to his amazement he found to be much concerned with table-turning and spiritualism, occupations Tolstoy at that time held in contempt.

A letter to Fet, dated 14th April, gives some inkling of what was going on in Tolstoy's mind:

I value every letter of yours, especially such as this last! You would hardly believe how pleased I am at what you write 'On the existence of the Deity'. I agree with it all and should like to say much about it, but cannot in a letter, and am too busy. It is the first time you have spoken to me about the Deity – God. And I have long been thinking unceasingly about that chief problem. Do not say that one cannot think about it! One not only can, but must! In all ages the best, the real people, have thought about it. And if we cannot think of it as they did, we must find out *how*. Have you read *Pensées de Pascal* – i.e. have you read it recently with a mature headpiece? When (which God grant) you come to see me, we will talk of many things and I will give you that book. Were I free from my novel – of which the end is already in type and I am correcting the proofs – I would at once on receipt of your letter have come to you.

In the middle of this summer Tolstoy, bringing with him N. Strák-hov, paid Fet an unexpected visit. The latter had at this time engaged as governess a Mlle Oberländer, an excellent pianist, and in his *Recollections* he tells us that on this visit:

The Count, a sensitive aesthete by nature, was greatly taken by the piano playing of Mlle Oberländer. He sat down to play duets with her, and they played through almost the whole of Beethoven.

Fet quotes Tolstoy's comment on the lady's performance:

When we were young, such pianists travelled across Europe giving concerts. She reads any piece of music as you read poetry, finding just the suitable expression for each note.

Towards the end of July, Tolstoy, accompanied by N. Strákhov, visited for the first time the Monastery of Óptina in the Kalúga Government, about 135 miles westwards of Yásnaya. A prominent figure in the monastic world at that time was the *Staretz* Father Ambrose, with whom Tolstoy had some long conversations. Among others whose acquaintance Tolstoy made there was a monk who had formerly been an officer in the Horse Guards. One of the works Tolstoy left for publication after his death is a novel called *Father Sergius*, the hero of which is a man of the world who becomes a monk, acquires a reputation for sanctity, and then yields to temptation and ends as an outcast. His visits to the Óptina monastery, three times repeated, supplied Tolstoy with material which years later he utilised in that work.

A visit which greatly interested Tolstoy was paid him about this time by an itinerant story-teller, expert in folklore, wielding beautifully the simple language of the people, such as Tolstoy loved and has utilised in his stories. He took down some of this traveller's tales, and from them subsequently worked up into literary form *What Men Live By*, *The Three Hermits* (both included in *Twenty-Three Tales*), and some others. The theme of *What Men Live By* is that of an angel sent by God to do penance on earth for a well-intentioned act of disobedience. It is one of the most widely disseminated of the world's legends and has appeared and reappeared in the literature of many countries through many centuries.

In the latter part of 1877 a number of Turkish prisoners of war were located in an abandoned sugar-factory between Túla and Yásnaya. Tolstoy visited them, and found that they were fairly well treated. Being himself much concerned about religion, he naturally talked to them on that subject, and was much impressed to find that each of them had a copy of the Koran in his kit.

On 6th December another son, Andréy, was born.

All through this year, amid bustle and activity of various kinds, spiritual problems continued to torment Tolstoy and his health began to show signs of the strain. Here is a note to Fet, dated 2nd September:

Just now I am constantly out hunting and am busy arranging how to place our educational staff for the winter. I have been to Moscow looking for a teacher and a tutor. Today I feel quite ill.

Matters did not improve as the months went on, for on 27th January [1878] he writes again:

Most unfortunately your suppositions, dear Afanásy Afanásevich, are wrong. Not only am I not at work, but the reason I failed to answer you was because I have been ill all this time. Lately I have even been in bed for some days. A chill in various forms, teeth and side, and the result is that time passes – my best time – and I do no work.

Then follows a touch showing how in many matters his wife's mind was still at one with his own, though she did not share his spiritual struggles, and in regard to the education of the children there was already some disagreement between them:

On reading it I said to my wife, 'Fet's poem is charming, but there is one word that is wrong.' She was nursing and bustling about at the time; but at tea, having quieted down, she took up the poem to read and at once pointed out the words 'as the Gods' – which I considered bad.

On 25th March 1878 he writes:

Last week, after seventeen years' absence, I went to Petersburg to buy some land in Samára from General B . . .

There I met a pair of Orlóv Generals who made me shudder. It was just as though one were standing between two sets of rails with goods trains passing. To enter into the minds of these Generals I had to recall the rare days of drunkenness I have experienced, or the days of my very earliest childhood.

After completing *Anna Karénina* Tolstoy again took up *The Decembrists*, which he had laid aside in favour of *War and Peace* fourteen years before. A second cousin of Tolstoy's mother, Prince S. G. Volkónski, had been a prominent Decembrist; and Tolstoy had at his disposal family diaries and journals throwing much light on that conspiracy. While in Petersburg he made personal acquaintance with some survivors of the movement, and also applied to the Commandant of the Petropávlov Fortress – who happened to be an officer under whom he had served in the Crimea – for permission to see the Alexis dungeons in which the Decembrists had been confined. The

Commandant received him very politely, allowed him to see over other parts of the fortress, but told him that though anyone could enter the dungeons, only three persons in the whole Empire – the Emperor, the Commandant, and the Chief of the Gendarmes – could leave them after having once entered.

Finally, after writing three fragments of it, Tolstoy abandoned this novel to which he had devoted much time. The subject was one he could not have dealt with frankly without getting into trouble with the Censor, and he had been refused permission to study the State Archives, but in the following passage Behrs gives another, and a curiously characteristic, reason for Tolstoy's decision:

> He affirmed that the Decembrist insurrection was a result of the influence of French nobles, a large number of whom had emigrated to Russia after the French Revolution. As tutors in aristocratic families they educated the whole Russian nobility, which explains the fact that many of the Decembrists were Catholics. The belief that the movement was due to foreign influence and was not a purely national one, sufficed to prevent Tolstoy from sympathising with it.

Another letter to Fet again shows the direction in which his mind was working:

6 April 1878

I have received your delightful and long letter, dear Afanásy Afanásevich. Do not praise me. Really you see in me too much good and in others too much bad. One thing in me is good – that I understand you and therefore love you. But though I love you as you are, I am always angry with you for this, that 'Martha is anxious about many things; but one thing is needful.' And in you that one thing is very strong, but somehow you disdain it and are more concerned about arranging a billiard room. Don't suppose that I refer to poems, though I expect them to come too! But it is not of them I speak, they will come in spite of the billiards; I am speaking of a conception of the world which would make it unnecessary to be angry at the stupidity of mortals. Were you and I pounded together in a mortar and moulded into two people we should make a capital pair. But at present you are so attached to the things of this life that should they someday fail you it will go hard with you, while I am so indifferent to them that life becomes uninteresting and I depress others by an eternal pouring 'from the void into vacuum'! Do not suppose that I have gone mad; I am merely out of sorts, but hope you will love me though I be black.*

The prolonged mental struggle through which Tolstoy passed with much suffering during the years 1874–8 was evident to those about him at least from 1876 onward. Not merely did he go regularly to church, and shut himself up in his study morning and evening to pray, but his former high spirits subsided and his desire to become meek and humble was plainly noticeable. One result of his altered attitude was that he felt keenly that it was wrong to have any enemy. Accordingly he wrote to Turgénev to that effect, and held out to him the hand of friendship.

To this Turgénev replied:

Paris. 8th May 1878

DEAR LEO NIKOLÁEVICH – I only today received your letter, addressed *poste-restante*. It gladdened and touched me very much. With the greatest readiness will I renew our former friendship, and I warmly press the hand you hold out to me. You are quite right in supposing me to have no hostile feelings towards you. If such ever existed they have long since disappeared, and the recollection of you remains only as of a man to whom I am sincerely attached, and of a writer whose earliest steps it was my good fortune to be the first to hail and each new work from whom has aroused in me the liveliest interest. I am heartily glad of the cessation of the misunderstandings that arose between us.

I hope to be in the Government of Orël this summer, and in that case we shall of course see one another. Till then I wish you all that is good, and once more press your hand in friendship.

On 13th June, on the point of starting for Samára with his elder sons and their tutor, Tolstoy writes to Fet:

I have seldom enjoyed a summer as much as this year, but a week ago I caught cold and fell ill, and only today have I come to life again.

Rather later in the summer the Countess, with the daughters and the younger children, joined her husband in Samára.

Hardly were the Tolstoys back from Samára before Turgénev wrote

* Alluding to a proverbial Russian saying: 'Love me when I am black, anyone can love me when I'm white.'

from Moscow that he would be in Túla the following Monday, 7th August. Tolstoy, accompanied by his brother-in-law, drove thither to meet him and brought him to Yásnaya, where he passed a couple of days. Both writers were delighted to feel that their seventeen-year disagreement was ended, and the Countess, who when a girl had known Turgénev well, was equally pleased to welcome him to the house.

A lady who was staying with them at the time tells us that the two writers spent much of their time in philosophic and religious conversation in Tolstoy's study, but

When they came out into the sitting-room their conversation became general and took a different turn.

'Of an evening we often play *vint* [a game similar to bridge] – do you?' Turgénev enquired of Tolstoy.

'No, we never play cards,' replied the Count, and turned the conversation to another topic.

Knowing him to be fond of chess the Countess Tolstoy asked Turgénev to play a game with her eldest son, a lad of fifteen, saying, 'He will always remember having played with Turgénev.'

Turgénev condescendingly agreed and began a game while continuing to talk to us.

'In Paris I often used to play chess and was considered a good player. They called me *le chevalier du pion*. I am fond of pawns . . . Do you know the new phrase, now in fashion among the French – *vieux jeu*? Whatever you say, a Frenchman replies, "*Vieux jeu!*"

'Eh! but one must not joke with you,' he exclaimed suddenly, turning to his youthful opponent. 'You have all but done for me.'

And he began to play carefully, and only won the game with difficulty, for young Tolstoy really played chess excellently.

Turgénev had the gift of words, and spoke readily and smoothly, but seemed to prefer narrating to conversing. He told us of his confinement in the Hauptwerk of the Spásski police station in Petersburg for his article on the death of Gógol, and described how dull it was . . .

Tolstoy also narrated, and I liked his stories better. They were more strongly sketched, often humorous, and always original. In them there was much that was simple, unexpected, and touching.

. . . I. S. Aksákov used to say, with reference to Tolstoy's gigantic power, that he had 'a bear-like talent', but I will add that his soul is as meek 'as a dove' and enthusiastic as a youth; and that the union of those two qualities explains the new direction he has since taken – a direction which so distressed Turgénev.

This was the last summer Behrs, now a young man of twenty-three, passed with Tolstoy before taking up official work in the Caucasus. His evidence fully supports that of others who had seen Tolstoy in contact with children, peasants, or native races: to all of these Tolstoy extended his charm of comprehension, consideration, and sympathy.

Whenever Tolstoy went out with his gun and his dogs Behrs used to accompany him; and together they would ride twenty-four miles from Yásnaya to visit Count Sergéy Tolstoy at Pirogóvo. Leo Tolstoy took his brother-in-law on these visits, Behrs says, 'for my sake if not for his own, since he knew what pleasure it gave me to be with him.' The remark he made when he heard that Behrs had obtained an official appointment in the Caucasus is characteristic: 'You are too late for the Caucasus. The whole country already stinks of officials.' Characteristic too of the feeling Tolstoy inspired among those who knew him most intimately is Behrs' concluding remark: 'I at least am aware of nothing in his life that needs concealment.'

At the beginning of September Turgénev, on his return from his estate, again visited Yásnaya, but he arrived at an unfortunate time when there was illness in the house and paid but a short visit.

A letter to Fet on 5th September shows that Tolstoy still found himself unable to be quite intimate with his fellow novelist:

Turgénev on his return journey came to see us and was glad to receive your letter. He is still the same, and we know the degree of nearness possible between us.

I have a terrible desire to write something, but feel a depressing doubt whether this is a false or a true appetite.

The last sentence must refer to the *Confession*, most of which was not written till the following year.

In October he again wrote to Fet:

I do not know how, or in what spirit, to begin to write to you, dear Afanásy Afanásevich; anyway there are no words for it but, 'I am to blame, I am to blame, and I am altogether to blame!' Though it is always superfluous for apologisers to explain their reasons, I yet will write mine because they are true and explain my condition. For a month past, if not longer, I have been living amid the fumes not of external occurrences (on the contrary we are living quietly by our-selves), but of what goes on inside – something I know not how to name. I go out shooting, read, reply to questions put to me, eat and sleep, but can do nothing, not even write a letter, a score of which have accumulated.

Apparently while in low spirits he wrote to Turgénev asking him not to refer to his (Tolstoy's) writings – for the latter replied on 15th October, saying: 'I am glad you are all physically well, and hope the "mental sickness" of which you write has now passed.' He then continues:

Although you ask me not to speak of your writings, I must still remark that it has never happened to me to laugh at you 'even a little'. Some of your things pleased me very much; others did not please me at all, while others again, such as *The Cossacks* for instance, afforded me great pleasure and excited my wonder. But what ground was there for laughter? I thought you had long since got rid of such 'reflexive' feelings. Why are they current only among authors, and not among musicians, painters, and other artists? Probably because in literary work more of that part of the soul is exposed which it is not quite convenient to show. But at our (already mature) age as authors, it is time we had grown accustomed to it.

This displeased Tolstoy, who in his next letter to Fet expressed his vexation with Turgénev, though the latter apparently had not intended to give offence:

22nd November 1878

DEAR AFANÁSY AFANÁSEVICH – I will go to Moscow and have 'I am to blame' printed on my notepaper. But I don't think I am to blame for not replying to the letter in which you promised to come and see us. I remember my joy at that news and that I replied immediately. If not, still please don't punish me, but come . . .

Yesterday I received a letter from Turgénev; and do you know, I have decided that it will be better to 'keep farther away from him and from sin' [a common Russian saying]. He is an unpleasant sort of quarrel-maker.

My congratulations to you on your birthday. I will not in future omit to congratulate you on the 23rd, and hope not to forget it for the next dozen times. That will be enough for either of us. *Au revoir.*

Fet was destined to live four years beyond the span Tolstoy allotted him, and Tolstoy himself for another thirty-two years – and what strenuous years they were – in which he wrestled with life's great problems one after another, and flung down before the world his opinions (right, wrong, or motley) on dogmatic theology, Christ's Christianity, religion in general, economic and social problems, the famine, the employment of violence, war, conscription, Government, patriotism, the sex-problem, art, science, food-reform, and the use of stimulants and narcotics, besides producing a series of simple stories for the people, as well as more complex ones for the rest of society, six plays, a great novel, and that stream of weighty and interesting essays and letters which he poured forth from Yásnaya decade after decade!

On 1st October 1878 Turgénev wrote to Fet from Bougival, again saying that he intended to translate *The Cossacks* into French and adding, 'It will give me great pleasure to assist in acquainting the French public with the best story that has been written in our language.'

In another letter from Bougival in December he remarked:

> I was very glad to come together again with Tolstoy and I spent three pleasant days with him; his whole family are very sympathetic and his wife is charming. He has grown very quiet, and has matured. His name begins to gain European celebrity – we Russians have long known that he has no rivals.

The course of the story has swept us a little past Tolstoy's fiftieth birthday – the point at which I intended to close this first volume of his *Life*. Besides some brief survey of his writings during his first twenty-five years of authorship, all that now remains is to give a summary of that remarkable work, his *Confession*, which shows us vividly, though with some amount of involuntary artistic heightening, what had been going on in his mind and soul from 1874 to 1879, the year in which it was written.

By way of brief preface to his *Confession* it will be in place to say a few words about two tendencies which, each in its own way, influenced Tolstoy. On the one hand was the religious life of the people with all its medieval traditions. Tolstoy had only to go a short walk from his house to reach the highroad on which pilgrims going afoot to the shrines of the Saints could always be met, and he had many a conversation with these pilgrims at the rest-house they frequented.

Among them were some to whom the things of this world were certainly less precious than obedience to the will of God as they understood it; and Tolstoy's stories show us how closely he observed them and how near some of them were to his heart. On the other hand he was influenced by the quite modern and very remarkable movement that was at this time beginning to make itself felt in Russia; a movement having its roots in conditions of life which greatly disturbed him, and which took as one of its watchwords the motto 'Towards the People' – a sentiment that harmonised with his own attitude.

In 1875 public attention was aroused by the trial of the Dolgúshin group of propagandists, and the trial of 'The Moscow 50', in March 1877, revealed the fact that a number of girls of wealthy families were voluntarily living as factory hands, working fourteen hours a day in overcrowded factories, that they might come into touch with working people, teach them, and carry on a social and political propaganda among them. Then followed the historic trial of 'The 193' in 1878.

These and many other indications showed that in spite of the repressive measures of the Government a steadily increasing number of Russians felt – what Tolstoy felt strongly – that the existing order of society resulted in the mass of the people having to live in conditions of blighting ignorance and grinding poverty, while a parasitic minority who lived in plenty, and sometimes in extravagant superfluity, rendered no service at all equivalent to the cost of their maintenance. The mere statement that those who had received an education, thanks to the work of the masses, owe service to the masses in return, sufficed to rouse to action some of the young men and women of that day. They left their wealthy homes, lived the simplest lives, ran fearful risks, and according to their lights – not always very clear ones – devoted themselves to the service of the people.

While this was going on around him a man of Tolstoy's temperament could not be at rest.

Already in 1875 Mihaylóvski had published a remarkable series of articles on *The Right and Left Hand of Count Tolstoy*, in which he pointed out that his works reveal the clash of contrary ideals and tendencies in the writer's soul, and that especially his educational articles contained ideas quite in conflict with certain tendencies noticeable in his novels. With remarkable prevision Mihaylóvski predicted an inevitable crisis in Tolstoy's life, and added:

One asks oneself what such a man is to do, and how he is to live? . . . I think an ordinary man in such a position would end by suicide or drunkenness, but a man of worth will seek for other issues – and of these there are several.

One of these he suggested would be to write for the people (Tolstoy's *Readers* had already been published), or to write so as to remind 'Society' that its pleasures and amusements are not those of the mass of mankind, and thus to arouse the latent feelings of justice in some who forgot the debt they owed to their fellows.

In fact the trial of 'The 193', or the movement from which it arose, had a vital though indirect influence on Tolstoy, who had engaged V. I. Alexéev, a graduate of Petersburg University, as mathematical master for his son. Alexéev had been a member of the Chaykóvski group which carried on an educational propaganda in elementary Socialism in the early 1870s. (He must not be confused with P. I. Chaykóvski, the great composer, previously mentioned.) The activities of this group were so restricted and they were so hampered by the police, that some of its members, feeling a need of freer activity, migrated to Kansas, USA., where for two years they carried on an agricultural colony. Dissensions arose among them and their experiment failed. Alexéev returned to Russia. Chaykóvski settled in England, where he spent many years, and only returned to Russia after the amnesty of 1905, to be again arrested and to spend more than a year in prison awaiting a trial which ended in his acquittal. In 1918, when I was in North Russia, he was head of the Provisional Socialist Government of that region, at whose invitation the Allied troops entered Archangel.

Tolstoy noticed that Alexéev was a man who shaped his life in accord with his beliefs, and he respected him accordingly, and through him made acquaintance with some of the best representatives of the immature Socialist movement then brewing in Russia. We have here a remarkable example of the indirect way in which thoughts influence the world. Auguste Comte wrote a philosophy. Filtering through the minds of G. H. Lewes and J. S. Mill it reached Nicholas Chaykóvski when he was a schoolboy of fourteen in a Gymnasium in Petersburg. 'It fascinated me to such an extent,' says he in his reminiscences, 'that, while sitting in school, I longed to get back to our lodgings and to my chosen reading. The more I progressed the more was I absorbed. This study powerfully affected my mind and systematised my ideas.' A few years later Chaykóvski, having read much in the meantime, formed his group, which sowed the seeds of changes that were yet to come. Progress however was slow and he felt 'the ineffectiveness of ordinary political and socialistic propaganda among a deeply religious peasantry still hopeful of benefits from above'. This forced him to reconsider the whole situation. 'I met,' adds he, 'some friends with whom I began to work upon the rather Utopian idea of formulating a new religion, and for the sake of more effective experiment we were soon compelled to transfer ourselves with this stupendous mission to the plains of Kansas.'

Wishing to transform society Chaykóvski had seen the need of some systematic outlook on life – 'a new religion' in fact. Dissatisfied with his own outlook on life, Tolstoy was seeking a new religion, which when he found it led him to demand great changes in society. The novelist and the propagandist, who never met in the flesh, had therefore much in common, though Tolstoy disliked the works of Comte and Mill which had influenced Chaykóvski, and (except Mill's *Autobiography*, which interested him) could hardly speak of them with tolerance. Detesting the methods of violence to which those who followed Chaykóvski felt themselves driven, Tolstoy was still unable to doubt the sincerity of the faith that actuated many of them, for they had all to lose and nothing to gain by joining the revolutionary movement. Sophie Peróvski, one of 'The 193' (subsequently hanged in Petersburg for her part in the assassination of Alexander II), was the daughter of the Governor-General of that city and a niece of the Minister of Education. Dmítri Lisogúb, a landowner, devoted his whole fortune of some £40,000 to the movement, and was hanged in Odessa. Prince Peter Kropótkin risked his all to give lessons to work-men, and escaped abroad having lost position, fortune, and the right to live in his native land. Tolstoy, an older man with a strong character and definite views of his own, could not join the Socialist movement, but that he was indirectly influenced by it is beyond doubt.

The state of Russian life was such that men of sensitive consciences could not be at rest (as indeed when and where in the wide world can they?), and the work Tolstoy had already done marked him out as one in whose soul the struggle that was moving others would assuredly be fought out strenuously. No one, however, and certainly not he himself, as yet knew what effect that crisis would have upon him, or what his course of life would be in the years to come.

I I

Confession

We have now come to Tolstoy's *Confession*, or 'An Introduction to a Criticism of Dogmatic Theology and an Investigation of the Christian Teachings' as the Russian title runs. In the preceding chapters passages from the first pages of it have already been quoted. I will keep as close to Tolstoy's words as possible but, having to condense, must omit much and must paraphrase some passages to avoid repetition. As the *Confession* can, and should, itself be read in this edition, I will here give only a skeleton of the argument, treating what Tolstoy tells of his own experience rather more fully.

Many men at the age of adolescence, or at any rate while their minds were still maturing, have experienced the change known as 'Conversion'. That is to say they have more or less suddenly turned round and looked at life from a fresh point of view: what had been latent in them has become dominant and worldly things have become subordinate to spiritual.

What is unusual about Tolstoy's conversion is that it came so late in life and so gradually, and that the intellect played so great a part in it.

Some men take to religion at the prompting of the heart, others at the prompting of the brain. Tolstoy belonged chiefly to the latter category, not from lack of heart but because strong as were his emotions his intellectual power was stronger still.

His *Confession* was written in 1879, and in it he says: 'Five years ago something very strange began to happen to me: At first I experienced moments of perplexity and arrest of life, as though I did not know how to live or what to do; and I felt lost and became dejected. But this passed and I went on living as before. Then these moments of perplexity recurred oftener and oftener and always in the same form. They were always expressed by the questions: What is it for? What does it lead to?

'At first it seemed to me that these were aimless and irrelevant questions. I thought it was all well known and that should I ever wish to deal with the solution, it would not cost me much effort; just at present I had no time for it, but when I wanted to I could find the answer. The questions however began to repeat themselves frequently, and more and more insistently demanded replies; and like drops of ink always falling on one place, they ran together into one black blot.

'That occurred which happens to everyone sickening with a mortal, internal disease. At first trivial signs of indisposition appear to which the sick man pays no attention, then these signs reappear more and more often and merge into one uninterrupted period of suffering. The suffering increases and, before the sick man can look round, what he took for a mere indisposition has already become more important to him than anything else in the world – it is death!

'That was what happened to me. I understood that it was no casual indisposition but something very important, and that if these questions constantly recurred it would be necessary to answer them. And I tried to do so. The questions seemed such stupid simple childish questions, but as soon as I touched them and tried to solve them, I at once became convinced (1) that they are not childish and stupid but the most important and deepest of life's questions; and (2) that try as I would I could not solve them. Before occupying myself with my Samára estate, the education of my son, or the writing of a book, I had to know *why* I was doing it. As long as I did not know why, I could do nothing, and could not live. Amid the thoughts of estate management, which greatly occupied me at that time, the question would suddenly occur to me: "Well, you will have 16,000 acres of land in Samára Government and 300 horses, and what next?" . . . And I was quite disconcerted and did not know what to think. Or when considering plans for the education of my children, I would say to myself: "What for?" Or when considering how the peasants might be made prosperous, I suddenly said to myself, "But what business is it of mine?" Or when thinking of the fame my works would bring me, I said to myself, "Very well: you will be more famous than Gógol, or Púshkin, or Shakespeare, or Molière, or than all the writers in the world – and what will it lead to?" And I could find no reply at all. The questions would not wait, they had to be answered at once, and if I did not answer them it was impossible to live. But there was no answer.

'I felt that what I had been standing on had broken down, and that I had nothing left under my feet. What I had lived on no longer existed, and I had nothing left to live on.

'My life came to a standstill. I could breathe, eat, drink, and sleep, and I could not help doing these things; but there was no life, for there were no wishes the fulfilment of which I could consider reasonable . . . Had a fairy come and offered to fulfil my desires, I should not have known what to ask . . . If in moments of intoxication I felt something which I cannot call a wish but a habit left by former wishes, in sober moments I knew this to be a delusion, and that there is really nothing to wish for. I could not even wish to know the truth, for I guessed in what it consisted. The truth was that life is meaningless. I had, as it were, lived, lived, and walked, walked, till I had come to a precipice and saw clearly that there was nothing ahead of me but destruction. It was impossible to stop, impossible to go back, and impossible to close my eyes or avoid seeing that there was nothing ahead but suffering and real death – complete annihilation.

'It had come to this, that I, a healthy, fortunate man, felt I could no longer live: some irresistible power impelled me to rid myself, one way or other, of life. I cannot say I *wished* to kill myself. The power which drew me away from life was stronger, fuller, and more widespread, than any mere wish.

'The thought of self-destruction came to me now as naturally as thoughts of how to improve my life had come formerly. And it was so seductive that I had to be wily with myself lest I should carry it out too hastily: "If I cannot unravel matters, there will always be time." And it was then that I, a man favoured by fortune, hid a cord from myself lest I should hang myself from the crosspiece of the partition in my room where I undressed alone every evening; and I ceased to go out shooting with a gun lest I should be tempted by so easy a way of ending my life. I did not myself know what I wanted: I feared life, desired to escape from it, yet still hoped something of it.

'And all this befell me at a time when all around me I had what is considered complete good fortune. I was not yet fifty; I had a good wife who loved me and whom I loved; good children, and a large estate which without much effort on my part improved and increased. I was more respected by my relations and acquaintances than at any previous time. I was praised by people, and without much self-deception could consider that my name was famous. And far from being insane or mentally unwell, on the contrary I enjoyed a strength of mind and body such as I have seldom met with among men of my kind: physically I could keep pace with the peasants at mowing, and mentally I could work for eight to ten hours at a stretch without experiencing any ill results from such exertion . . .

'My mental condition presented itself to me in this way: my life is a stupid and spiteful joke someone has played on me. Though I did not acknowledge a "someone" who created me, yet that form of representation – that someone had played an evil and stupid joke on me by placing me in the world – was the form of expression that suggested itself to me most naturally.

'Involuntarily it appeared to me that there, somewhere, is someone who amuses himself by watching how I live for thirty or forty years, learning, developing, maturing in body and mind, and how – having now with matured mental powers reached the summit of life from which it all lies before me, I stand on that summit – like an arch-fool – seeing plainly that there is nothing in life, and that there has been and will be nothing. And he is amused . . .

'But whether that "someone" laughing at me existed or not, I was none the better off. I could give no reasonable meaning to any single action, or to my whole life. I was only surprised that I could have avoided understanding this from the very beginning – it has been so long known to all. Today or tomorrow sickness and death will come (they have come already) to those I love or to me; nothing will remain but stench and worms. Sooner or later my deeds, whatever they may have been, will be forgotten, and I shall not exist. Then why go on making any effort? . . . How can man fail to see this? And how go on living? That is what is surprising! One can only live when one is intoxicated with life; as soon as one is sober it is impossible not to see that it is all a mere fraud and a stupid fraud! That is precisely what it is: there is nothing either amusing or witty about it, it is simply cruel and stupid.

'There is an Eastern fable told long ago, of a traveller overtaken on a plain by an enraged beast. Escaping from the beast he leaps into a dry well, but sees at the bottom of the well a dragon that has opened its jaws to swallow him. And the unfortunate man, not daring to climb out lest he should be destroyed by the enraged beast, and not daring to drop to the bottom of the well lest he should be eaten by the dragon, seizes a twig growing in a crack in the well and clings to it. His hands grow weaker, and he feels he will soon have to resign himself to the destruction that awaits him above or below; but he still clings on, and sees that two mice, a black and a white one, go regularly round and round the stem of the twig to which he is clinging, and gnaw at it. And soon the twig will snap and he will fall into the dragon's jaws. The traveller sees this and knows that he will inevitably perish; but while still hanging he looks around and finds some drops of honey on the leaves of the twig and reaches them with his tongue and licks them. So I too clung to the twig of life, knowing that the dragon of death was inevitably awaiting me, ready to tear me to pieces; and I could not understand why I had fallen into such torment. I tried to lick the honey which formerly consoled me, but the honey no longer gave me pleasure, and the white and black mice of day and night gnawed at the branch by which I hung. I saw the dragon clearly and the honey no longer tasted sweet. And this is not a fable, but the real unanswerable truth intelligible to all.

'The deception of the joys of life which formerly allayed my terror of the dragon, now no longer deceives me. No matter how much I may be told: "You cannot understand the meaning of life so do not think about it, but live," I can no longer do it: I have already done it too long. I cannot now help seeing day and night going round and bringing me to death. That is all I see, for that alone is true. All else is false.

'The two drops of honey which diverted my eyes from the cruel truth longer than the rest: my love of family and of writing – art as I called it – were no longer sweet to me.

'Family . . . said I to myself. But my family – wife and children – are also human. They too are placed as I am: they must either live in a lie, or see the terrible truth. Why should they live? Why should I love them, guard them, bring them up, or watch them? That they may come to the despair I feel, or else be stupid? Loving them, I cannot hide the truth from them: each step in knowledge leads them to that truth. And the truth is death.

' "Art, poetry?" . . . Under the influence of success and praise, I had long assured myself that this was a thing one could do though death was drawing near – death which destroys all things, including my work and its remembrance; but I soon saw that that too was a fraud. It was plain to me that art is an adornment to life, an allurement to life. But life had lost its attraction for me – so how could I attract others? As long as I was not living my own life but was borne on the waves of some other life – as long as I believed that life had a meaning – though one I could not express – the reflection of life in poetry and art of all kinds afforded me pleasure; it was pleasant to look at life in the mirror of art. But when I began to seek the meaning of life and felt the necessity of living on my own account, that mirror became for me unnecessary, superfluous, ridiculous, or painful. I could no longer soothe myself with what I saw in the mirror, for what I saw was that my position was stupid and desperate. It was all very well to enjoy the sight when in the depth of my soul I believed that my life had a meaning. Then the play of lights in life – comic, tragic, touching, beautiful, and terrible – amused me. But when I knew life to be meaningless and terrible, the play in the mirror could no longer amuse me. No sweetness of honey could be sweet to me when I saw the dragon, and saw the mice gnawing away my support.

'Nor was that all. Had I simply understood that life has no meaning I could have borne it quietly knowing that that was my lot. But I could not satisfy myself with that. Had I been like a man living in a wood from which he knows there is no exit I could have lived, but I was like one lost in a wood who horrified at having lost his way rushes about wishing to find the road, yet knows that each step he takes confuses him more and more, and still cannot help rushing about.

'It was indeed terrible. And to rid myself of the terror, I wished to kill myself. I experienced terror at what awaited me – knew that that terror was even worse than the position I was in, but still I could not patiently await the end. However convincing the argument might be that in any case some vessel in my heart would give way, or something would burst, and all would be over, I could not patiently await that end. The horror of darkness was too great and I wished to free myself from it as quickly as possible by noose or bullet. That was the feeling which drew me most strongly towards suicide.

*　　*　　*

' "But perhaps I have overlooked something or misunderstood something? It cannot be that this condition of despair is natural to man!" thought I, and as a perishing man seeks safety I sought some way of escape.

'I sought everywhere; and thanks to a life spent in learning, and thanks also to the connections I had with the scholarly world, I had access to scientists and scholars in all branches of knowledge, and they readily showed me all their knowledge not only in books but also in conversation, so that I had at my disposal all that knowledge had to say on this problem of life . . .

'The question which at the age of fifty brought me to the verge of suicide, was the simplest of questions lying in the soul of every man, from a foolish child to the wisest elder: it was a question without answering which one cannot live, as I had found by experience. It was, What will come of what I am doing today or shall do tomorrow? What will come of my whole life?

'Differently expressed the question is: Why should I live, why wish for anything, or do anything? It can also be expressed thus: Has life any meaning that the inevitable death awaiting one does not destroy? All human knowledge I found divided into two kinds. One kind, such as chemistry, mathematics, and the exact sciences, did not deal with my question. They were interesting, attractive, and wonderfully definite, but made no attempt to solve the question; while on the other hand the speculative sciences, culminating in metaphysics, dealt with the question, but supplied no satisfactory answer.

'Where philosophy does not lose sight of the essential question its answer is always one and the same: an answer given by Socrates, Schopenhauer, Solomon, and Buddha.

' "We approach truth only in so far as we depart from life," said Socrates when preparing for death. "For what do we, who love truth, strive after in life? To free ourselves from the body and from all the evil that is caused by the body! If so, then how can we fail to be glad when death comes to us? The wise man seeks death all his life and therefore does not fear death."

'And Schopenhauer also says that life is an evil; and Solomon (or whoever wrote the books attributed to him) says: "Vanity of vanities, all is vanity. What profit hath man of all his labour under the sun? . . . There is no remembrance of former things, neither shall there be any remembrance of things that are to come, with those that shall come after . . . Therefore I hated life, because the work that is wrought under the sun is grievous to me; for all is vanity and vexation of spirit."

'And Sakya Muni, when he learnt what age and sickness and death are, could find no consolation in life and decided that life is the greatest of evils; and he devoted all the strength of his soul to free himself from it and to free others, and to do this so that even after death life shall not be renewed any more but be completely destroyed at its very roots. So speaks all the wisdom of India.

'These then are the direct replies that human wisdom gives when it replies to the question of life: "The life of the body is an evil and a lie. Therefore the destruction of the life of the body is a blessing and we should desire it," says Socrates.

' "Life is that which should not be – an evil; and the passage into Nothingness is the only good in life," says Schopenhauer.

' "All that is in the world: folly and wisdom, and riches and poverty, and mirth and grief – are vanity and emptiness. Man dies and nothing is left of him. And that is stupid," says Solomon.

' "To live in the consciousness of the inevitability of suffering, of becoming enfeebled, of old age, and of death, is impossible – we must free ourselves from life, from all possible life," says Buddha.

'And what these strong minds said, has been said and thought and felt by millions upon millions of people like them. And I have thought it and felt it.

'One cannot deceive oneself. It is all – vanity! Happy is he who has not been born: death is better than life, and one must free oneself from life.

'Then I began to consider the lives of the men of my own kind, and I found that they met the problem in one or other of four ways.

'The first way was that of ignorance. Some people – mostly women, or very young or very dull people – have not yet understood the question of life; but I having understood it could not again shut my eyes.

'The second way was that of the Epicureans, expressed by Solomon when he said: "Then I commended mirth, because a man hath no better thing under the sun, than to eat, and to drink, and to be merry."

'That is the way in which the majority of people of our circle make life possible for themselves. Their circumstances furnish them with more of comfort than of hardship, and their moral obtuseness makes it possible for them to forget that the advantage of their position is an accidental advantage, and that not everyone can have a thousand wives and a thousand palaces like Solomon, and that for every man with a thousand wives there are a thousand without wives, and that for each palace there are a thousand people who have to build it in the sweat of their brows, and that the accident that has today made me a Solomon may tomorrow make me Solomon's slave. The dullness of these people's imagination enables them to forget what gave Buddha no peace – the inevitability of sickness, age, and death, which today or tomorrow will destroy all these pleasures. I could not imitate these people, I had not their dullness of imagination and could not artificially produce it in myself.

'The third escape is that of strength and energy. It consists in under-standing that life is an evil and an absurdity, and in destroying it. It is a way adopted by a few exceptionally strong and consistent people. I saw that it was the worthiest way of escape and I wished to adopt it.

'The fourth escape is that of weakness. It consists in seeing the truth of the situation and yet clinging to life as though one still hoped something from it; and I found myself in that category.

'To live like Solomon and Schopenhauer, knowing that life is a stupid joke played upon us, and still to go on living: washing oneself, dressing, dining, talking, and even writing books, was to me repulsive and tormenting, but I remained in that position.

'I now see that if I did not kill myself it was due to some dim consciousness of the invalidity of my thoughts. And I began to feel, rather than argue, in this way: "I, my reason, has acknowledged life to be unreasonable. If there be no higher reason (and there is not: nothing can prove that there is) then for me reason is the creator of life. If reason did not exist there would be for me no life. How can reason deny life when it is the creator of life? Or to put it the other way: were there no life my reason would not exist; therefore reason is life's son. Life is all. Reason is its fruit, yet reason denies life itself!" I felt that there was something wrong here.

'Nothing prevents our denying life by suicide. Well then, kill yourself and cease discussing. If life displeases you, kill yourself! You live and cannot understand the meaning of life – then finish it; and do not fool about in life, saying and writing that you do not understand it. You have come into good company where people are contented and like what they are doing; if you find it dull and repulsive – go away!

'Indeed what are we who are convinced of the necessity of suicide yet do not decide to commit it, but the weakest, most inconsistent, and to put it plainly, the stupidest of men, fussing about with our own stupidity as a fool fusses about with a painted doll?

' "There is something wrong," said I to myself; but what was wrong I could in no way make out. It was long before the fog began to clear and I began to be able to restate my position.

'It had seemed to me that the narrow circle of rich, learned, and leisured people to which I belonged formed the whole of humanity, and that the milliards of others who have lived and are living were cattle of some sort – not real people . . . And it was long before it dawned upon me to ask: "But what meaning is, and has been, given to their lives by all the milliards of common folk who live and have lived in the world?"

'I long lived in this state of lunacy, which in fact, if not in words, is particularly characteristic of us liberal and learned people. But whether the strange physical affection I have for the real labouring people compelled me to understand them and to see that they are not so stupid as we suppose, or whether it was due to the sincerity of my conviction that I could know nothing beyond the fact that the best I could do was to hang myself, at any rate I instinctively felt that if I wished to live and understand the meaning of life I must seek this meaning not among those who have lost it and wish to kill themselves, but among those milliards of the past and the present who knew it and who support the burden of their own lives and of ours also.

'And on examining the matter I saw that the milliards of mankind always have had, and still have, a knowledge of the meaning of life; but *that* knowledge is their faith, which I could not but reject. "It is God, one and three, the creation in six days, the devils and angels, and all the rest, that I cannot accept as long as I retain my reason," said I to myself.

'My position was terrible. I knew I could find nothing along the path of reasonable knowledge except a denial of life; and in faith I could find nothing but a denial of reason, still more impossible to me than a denial of life.

'Finally I saw that my mistake lay in ever expecting an examination of finite things to supply a meaning to life. The finite has no ultimate meaning apart from the infinite. The two must be linked together before an answer to life's problems can be reached.

'It had only appeared to me that knowledge gave a definite answer – Schopenhauer's answer: that life has no meaning and is an evil. On examining the matter further I understood that the reply is not positive, it was only my feeling that made it seem so. The reply, strictly expressed as the Brahmins and Solomon and Schopenhauer express it, amounts only to an indefinite answer, like the reply given in mathematics when instead of solving an equation we find we have reached an identity: $X = X$, or $O = O$. The answer is, that life is nothing. So that philosophic knowledge merely asserts that it cannot solve the question, and the solution remains, as far as it is concerned, indefinite. And I understood further that however unreasonable and monstrous might be the replies given by faith, they had this advantage, that they introduce into each reply a relation between the finite and the infinite, without which relation no reply is possible.

'Whichever way I put the question that relation appeared in the answer. How am I to live? – According to the law of God. What real result will come of my life? – Eternal torment or eternal bliss. What meaning has life that death does not destroy? – Union with the eternal God: heaven.

'Faith still remained for me as irrational as it was before, but I could not but admit that it alone gives mankind a reply to the questions of life, and that consequently it makes life possible.

'Where there is life, there since man began faith has made life possible for him; and the chief outline of that faith is everywhere and always one and the same. Faith does not consist, as is usually supposed, in agreeing with what someone has said; faith is a knowledge of the meaning of human life as a result of which man does not destroy himself but lives. Faith is the strength of life. If a man lives, he believes in something. If he does not see and recognise the visionary nature of the finite, then he believes in the finite; if he understands the visionary nature of the finite, he must believe in the infinite. Without faith he cannot live.

'What am I? – A part of the infinite. In those few words lies the whole problem.

'I began dimly to understand that in the replies given by faith the deepest human wisdom is stored up.

'I understood this, but it made matters no better for me.

'I was now ready to accept any faith if only it did not demand of me a direct denial of reason – which would be a falsehood. And I studied Buddhism and Mohammedanism from books, and most of all I studied Christianity both from books and from living people.

'Naturally I turned first of all to the Orthodox of my circle, to learned people, to Church theologians, to monks, to theologians of the newest shade, and even to Evangelicals* who profess salvation by faith in the Redemption. And I seized on these believers and questioned them as to their beliefs and their understanding of the meaning of life.

'But in spite of my readiness to make all possible concessions, I saw that what they gave out as their faith did not explain the meaning of life but obscured it.

---

* Readers of *Resurrection* (Book II, Chapter 17) will remember the vivid description of an Evangelical meeting addressed by Kiesewetter, who spoke in English. The original from whom Tolstoy drew Kiesewetter was (as he himself wrote me) Baedeker, a well-known Evangelical preacher who lived in England but visited Russia frequently.

'I remember the painful feeling of fear of being thrown back into my former state of despair, after the hope I often and often experienced in my intercourse with these people.

'The more fully they explained their doctrines to me the more clearly did I see their error . . . It was not that in their doctrines they mixed many unnecessary and unreasonable things with the Christian truths that had always been near to me, that was not what repelled me. I was repelled by the fact that these people's lives were like my own, with only this difference – that such a life did not correspond to the principles they expounded in their teachings.

'No arguments could convince me of the truth of their faith. Only deeds which showed that they saw a meaning in life which made what was so dreadful to me – poverty, sickness, and death – not dreadful to them, could convince me. And such deeds I did not see among the various bodies of believers in our circle. On the contrary, I saw such deeds done by people of our circle who were the most unbelieving, but never by the so-called believers of our circle.*

'And I understood that the belief of these people was not the faith I sought, and that their faith is not a real faith but an Epicurean consolation in life.

'And I began to draw near to the believers among the poor, simple, unlettered folk: pilgrims, monks, sectarians, and peasants. Among them too I found a great deal of superstition mixed with the Christian truths, but their superstitions seemed a necessary and natural part of their lives . . . And I began to look well into the life and faith of these people, and the more I considered it the more I became convinced that they have a real faith which is a necessity to them and alone gives their life a meaning and makes it possible for them to live . . . In contrast with what I had seen in our circle, where the whole of life is passed in idleness, amusements, and dissatisfaction, I saw that the whole life of these people was passed in heavy labour, and that they were content with life . . . While we think it terrible that we have to suffer and die,

---

* This passage is the more noteworthy because it is almost the only reference (and even this is indirect) made by Tolstoy at this period to the revolutionary or 'To-the-People' movement in which many young men and women were risking and sacrificing home, property, freedom, and life itself, from motives that had much in common with his own feeling that the upper layers of 'Society' are parasitic, and prey on the vitals of the people who support them.

these folk live, and suffer, and approach death, with tranquillity, and in most cases gladly.

'And I learnt to love these people. The more I came to know their life the more I loved them and the easier it became for me to live. So I went on for about two years, and a change took place in me which had long been preparing and the promise of which had always been in me. The life of our circle, the rich and learned, not merely became distasteful to me but lost all meaning for me, while the life of the whole labouring people, the whole of mankind who produce life, appeared to me in its true light. I understood that *that* is life itself, and that the meaning given to that life is true, and I accept it.

'I then understood that my answer to the question, "What is life?" when I said that life is "evil" was quite correct. The only mistake was that that answer referred to *my* life, but not to life in general. My life, a life of indulgence and desires, was meaningless and evil . . . And I understood the truth which I afterwards found in the Gospels, that men love darkness rather than the light because their deeds are evil; and that to see things as they are one must think and speak of the life of humanity, and not of the life of the minority who are parasites on life.

'And indeed the bird lives so that it must fly, collect food, and build its nest; and when I see the bird doing that, I joy in its joy. The goat, hare, and wolf, live so that they must feed themselves, and propagate, and feed their families, and when they do so I feel firmly assured that they are happy and that their life is a reasonable one. And what does man do? He should earn a living as the beasts do, but with this difference – that he would perish if he did it alone; he has to procure it not for himself but for all. When he does *that*, I have a firm assurance that he is happy and that his life is reasonable. And what had I done during the whole thirty years of my conscious life? I had not only not been earning a living for all, I had not even earned my own living. I had lived as a parasite, and when I asked myself what use my life was, I found that my life was useless. If the meaning of human life lies in supporting it, how could I, who for thirty years had occupied myself not with supporting life but with destroying it in myself and in others – how could I obtain any other reply than that my life was senseless and an evil? It was both senseless and evil.

'The conviction that a knowledge of life can only be found by living, led me to doubt the goodness of my own life . . . During that whole year while I was asking myself almost every moment whether I should not end matters with a noose or a bullet – all that time, beside the course of thought and observation about which I have spoken, my heart was oppressed with a painful feeling I can only describe as a search for God.

'I went over in my mind the arguments of Kant and Schopenhauer showing the impossibility of proving the existence of a God and I began to refute them. Cause, said I to myself, is not a category such as are Time and Space. If I exist there must be some cause for it, and a cause of causes. And that first cause of all is what men have called "God". And as soon as I acknowledged that there is a force in whose power I am, I at once felt that I could live. But I asked myself: What is that cause, that force? How am I to think of it? What are my relations to that which I call "God"? And only the familiar replies occurred to me: "He is the Creator and Preserver." This reply did not satisfy me, and I felt I was losing within me what I needed for my life. I became terrified and began to pray to him whom I sought, that he should help me. But the more I prayed the more apparent it became to me that he did not hear me and that there was no one to whom to address myself. And with despair in my heart that there is no God at all, I said: "Lord, have mercy, save me! Lord, teach me!" But no one had mercy on me and I felt that my life was coming to a standstill.

'But again and again I returned to the same admission that I could not have come into the world without any cause or reason or meaning, I could not be such a fledgeling fallen from its nest as I felt myself to be. Or granting that I be such, lying on my back in the high grass, even then I cry because I know that a mother has borne me within her, has hatched me, warmed me, fed me, and loved me. Where is she – that mother? If she has deserted me, who is it that has done so? I cannot hide from myself that someone bore me, loving me. Who was that someone? Again "God"?

' "He exists," said I to myself. And I had only for an instant to admit that, and at once life rose within me and I felt the possibility and joy of living. But again from the admission of the existence of a God I went on to seek my relations with him; and again I imagined *that* God – our creator in three persons who sent his son, the Saviour – and again *that* God, detached from the world and from me, melts like a block of ice, melts before my eyes and again nothing remains, and again the spring of life dries up within me and I despair and feel that I have nothing to do but to kill myself. And the worst of all is that I feel I cannot do it.

'Not twice or three times, but tens and hundreds of times I reached those conditions first of joy and animation and then of despair and consciousness of the impossibility of living.

'I remember that it was in early spring, I was alone in the wood listening to its sounds. I listened and thought ever of the same thing, as I had constantly done during those last three years. I was again seeking God.

' "Very well, there is no God," said I to myself; "there is no one who is not my imagination but a reality like my whole life. He does not exist and no miracles can prove his existence, because the miracles would be my perceptions, besides being irrational."

' "But my *perception* of God, of him whom I seek," asked I of myself, "where has that perception come from?" And again at this thought the glad waves of life rose within me. All that was around me came to life and received a meaning. But my joy did not last long. My mind continued its work.

' "The conception of God is not God," said I to myself. "The conception is what takes place within me. The conception of God is something I can evoke or can refrain from evoking in myself. That is not what I seek. I seek that without which there can be no life." And again all around me and within me began to die, and again I wished to kill myself.

'But then I turned my gaze upon myself, on what went on within me, and I remembered that I only lived at those times when I believed in God. As it was before, so it was now; I need only be aware of God to live, I need only forget him, or disbelieve in him, and I die . . . "What more do you seek?" exclaimed a voice within me. "This is he. He is that without which one cannot live. To know God and to live is one and the same thing. God is life. Live seeking God and then you will not live without God." And more than ever before all within me and around me lit up, and the light did not again abandon me.

'And I was saved from suicide . . . And strange to say the strength of life which returned to me was not new but quite old – the same that had borne me along in my earliest days.

'I quite returned to what belonged to my earliest childhood and youth. I returned to the belief in that Will which produced me and desires something of me. I returned to the belief that the chief and only aim of my life is to be better, that is, to live in accord with that Will. And I returned to the belief that I can find the expression of that Will in what humanity, in the distant past hidden from me, has produced for its guidance: that is to say, I returned to a belief in God, in moral perfecting, and in a tradition transmitting to us the meaning of life . . .

'I turned from the life of our circle, acknowledging that theirs is not life but only a simulacrum of life, and that the conditions of superfluity in which we live deprive us of the possibility of understanding life . . . The simple labouring people around me were the Russian people, and I turned to them and to the meaning they give to life. That meaning, if one can put it into words, was the following. Every man has come into this world by the will of God. And God has so made man that every man can destroy his soul or save it. The aim of man in life is to save his soul, and to save his soul he must live "godly", and to live "godly" he must renounce all the pleasures of life, must labour, humble himself, suffer, and be merciful . . . The meaning of this was clear and near to my heart. But together with this meaning of the popular faith of our non-sectarian folk among whom I live, much was inseparably bound up that revolted me and seemed to me inexplicable: sacraments, Church services, fasts, and the adoration of relics and icons. The people cannot separate the one from the other, nor could I. And strange as much of it was to me, I accepted everything, and attended the services, knelt morning and evening in prayer, fasted, and prepared to receive the Eucharist, and at first my reason did not resent anything. What had formerly seemed to me impossible did not now evoke in me any resistance . . .

'I told myself that the essence of every faith consists in its giving life a meaning which death does not destroy. Naturally for a faith to be able to reply to the questions of a king dying in luxury, of an old slave tormented by overwork, and of all sorts of people, young and old, wise and foolish – its answers must be expressed in all sorts of different ways . . . But this argument, justifying in my eyes the queerness of much on the ritual side of religion, did not suffice to allow me in the one great affair of life – religion – to do things which seemed to me questionable. With all my soul I wished to be in a position to mingle with the people, fulfilling the ritual side of their religion, but I could not do it. I felt that I should be lying to myself and mocking at what was sacred to me were I to do so. At this point however our recent Russian theological writers came to my rescue.

'According to the explanation these theologians gave, the fundamental dogma of our faith is the infallibility of the Church. From the admission of that dogma follows inevitably the truth of all that is professed by the Church. The Church as an assembly of true believers united by love, and therefore possessed of true knowledge, became the basis of my belief. I told myself that divine truth cannot be accessible to a separate individual, it is revealed only to the whole assembly of people united by love. To attain truth one must not separate, and not to separate one must love and must endure things one may not agree with.

'Truth reveals itself to love, and if you do not submit to the rites of the Church you transgress against love, and by transgressing against love you deprive yourself of the possibility of recognising the truth. I did not then see the sophistry contained in this argument. I did not see that union in love may give the greatest love, but certainly cannot give us divine truth expressed in the definite words of the Nicene Creed. I also did not perceive that love cannot make some particular expression of truth an obligatory condition of union. I did not then see these flaws in the argument, and thanks to it I was able to accept and perform all the rites of the Orthodox Church without understanding most of them.

'When fulfilling the rites of the Church I humbled my reason, submitted to tradition, united myself with my forefathers – the father, mother, and grandparents I loved, and with all those millions of the common people whom I respected. When rising before dawn for the early Church services I knew I was acting well, if only because I was sacrificing my bodily ease to humble my mental pride and for the sake of finding the meaning of life. However insignificant these sacrifices might be I made them for the sake of something good. I fasted, prepared for communion, and observed the fixed hours of prayer at home and in church. During Church service I attended to every word and gave the words a meaning whenever I could.

'But this reading of meanings into the rites had its limits . . . If I explained to myself the frequent repetition of prayers for the Tsar and his relatives by the fact that they are more exposed to temptation than other people and therefore more in need of being prayed for, the prayers about subduing enemies and foes under his feet (even though one tried to say that sin was the foe prayed against) and many other unintelligible prayers – nearly two-thirds of the whole service – either remained quite incomprehensible or, when I forced an explanation into them, made me feel that I was lying, and thereby quite destroying my relation to God and losing all possibility of believing . . .

'Never shall I forget the painful feeling I experienced the day I received the Eucharist for the first time after many years. The service, confession, and prayers were quite intelligible and produced in me a glad consciousness that the meaning of life was being revealed to me. The communion itself I explained as an act performed in remembrance of Christ and indicating a purification from sin and the full acceptance of Christ's teaching. If that explanation was artificial I did not notice its artificiality, so happy was I at humbling and abasing myself before the priest – a simple, timid country clergyman – and clearing all the dirt out of my soul and confessing my vices, so glad was I to merge in thought with the humility of the Fathers who wrote the prayers of the Office, so glad was I of union with all who have believed and now believe, that I did not notice the artificiality of my explanation. But when I approached the altar gates and the priest made me say that I believed that what I was about to swallow was truly flesh and blood, I felt a pain in my heart: it was not merely a false note, it was a cruel demand made by someone or other who evidently had never known what faith is.

'I now permit myself to say that it was a cruel demand, but I did not then think so: only it was indescribably painful to me. At the time I found in my soul a feeling which helped me to endure it. This was the feeling of self-abasement and humility. I humbled myself, swallowed that flesh and blood without any blasphemous feelings, and with a wish to believe. But the blow had been struck, and knowing what awaited me I could not go a second time.

'I continued to fulfil the rites of the Church and still believed that the doctrine I was following contained the truth, when something happened to me which I now understand, but which then seemed strange.

'I was listening to the conversation of an illiterate peasant, a pilgrim, about God, faith, life, and salvation, when a knowledge of faith revealed itself to me. I drew near to the people, listening to their opinions on life and faith, and I understood the truth. So also was it when I read the Lives of the Saints which became my favourite books. Putting aside the miracles and regarding them as fables illustrating thoughts, this reading revealed to me life's meaning. There were the lives of Makarius the Great, of the Tsarevich Joasafa (the story of Buddha), and there were the stories of the traveller in the well, and the monk who found some gold. There were stories of the martyrs, all announcing that death does not exclude life; and there were stories of ignorant, stupid men, and such as knew nothing of the teaching of the Church, but who yet were saved.

'But as soon as I met learned believers or took up their books, doubt of myself, dissatisfaction, and exasperated disputation, were roused within me, and I felt that the more I entered into the meaning of these men's speech the more I went astray from truth and approached an abyss. How often I envied the peasants their illiteracy and lack of learning! Those statements in the creeds which to me were evident absurdities, for them contained nothing false. Only to me, unhappy man, was it clear that with truth falsehood was interwoven by finest threads and that I could not accept it in that form.

'So I lived for about three years. At first when I did not understand something, I said, "It is my fault, I am sinful"; but the more I fathomed the truth the clearer became the line between what I do not understand because I am not able to understand it, and what cannot be understood except by lying to oneself.

'In spite of my doubts and sufferings I still clung to the Russian Orthodox Church. But questions of life arose which had to be decided, and the decision of these questions by the Church contrary to the very bases of the belief by which I lived, obliged me at last to own that communion with Orthodoxy was impossible. These questions were: first the relation of the Orthodox Eastern Church to other Churches – to the Catholics and to the so-called sectarians. At that time, in consequence of my interest in religion I came into touch with believers of various faiths: Catholics, Protestants, Old-Believers, Molokáns, and others. And I met many men of lofty morals who were truly religious. I wished to be a brother to them. And what happened? The teaching which promised to unite all in one faith and love – that very teaching, in the person of its best representatives, told me that these men were all living a lie, that what gave them their power of life is a temptation of the devil, and that we alone possess the only possible truth. And I saw that all who do not profess an identical faith with themselves are considered by the Orthodox to be heretics, just as the Catholics and others consider the Orthodox to be heretics. And I saw that the Orthodox (though they try to hide this) regard with hostility all who do not express their faith by the same external symbols and words as themselves; and this is naturally so, first, because the assertion that you are in falsehood and I am in truth is the most cruel thing one man can say to another, and secondly, because a man loving his children and brothers cannot help being hostile to those who wish to pervert his children and brothers to a false belief . . . And to me who considered that truth lay in union by love, it became self-evident that the faith was itself destroying what it ought to produce.

'As people of many different religions behave to one another in this same contemptuous, self-assured manner, the error of such conduct was obvious; and I thought on the matter and read all I could about it and consulted all whom I could. And no one gave me any explanation except the one which causes the Súmski Hussars to consider the Súmski Hussars the best regiment in the world, and the Yellow Uhlans to consider that the best regiment in the world is the Yellow Uhlans . . . I went to archimandrites, archbishops, elders, monks of the strictest Orders, and asked them, but none of them made any attempt to explain the matter to me, except one man who explained it all and explained it so that I never asked anyone any more about it.

'I asked him why we should not unite on those main points on which we could agree, and leave the rest for each to decide as he pleases. My interlocutor agreed with my thoughts, but told me that such concessions would bring reproach on the spiritual authorities for deserting the faith of our forefathers, and this would produce a split, and the vocation of the spiritual authorities is to safeguard in all its purity the Greco-Russian Orthodox faith inherited from our forefathers.

'And I understood it all! I am seeking a faith, the power of life, and they are seeking the best way to fulfil before men certain human obligations. . . . And I noticed what is done in the name of religion and was horrified, and I almost entirely abjured Orthodoxy.

'The second relation of the Church to a question of life was with regard to war and executions.

'At that time Russia was at war. And Russians in the name of Christian love began to kill their fellow-men. It was impossible not to think about this, and not to see that killing is an evil, repugnant to the first principles of any faith. Yet they prayed in the churches for the success of our arms and the teachers of the faith acknowledged killing to be an act resulting from the faith. And besides the murders during the war, I saw, during the disturbances which followed the war, Church dignitaries and teachers and monks of the lesser and stricter Orders who approved the killing of helpless erring youths. And I took note of all that is done by men who profess Christianity, and was horrified.

'And I ceased to doubt and became fully convinced that not all was true in the religion I had joined. Formerly I should have said that it was all false, but I could not say so now, for I had felt its truth and had lived by it. But I no longer doubted that there is in it much that is false. And though among the peasants there was less admixture of what repelled me, still I saw that in their belief also falsehood was mixed with the truth.

'But where did the truth and where did the falsehood come from? Both the falsehood and the truth were contained in the so-called holy tradition and Scriptures. Both the falsehood and the truth had been handed down by what is called the Church.

'And whether I liked to or not, I was brought to the study and investigation of these writings and traditions, which till then I had been so afraid to investigate.

'And I turned to the examination of that same theology which I had once rejected with such contempt . . . On it religious doctrine rests, or at least with it the only knowledge of the meaning of life I have found is inseparably connected . . . I shall not seek the explanation of everything. I know that the explanation of everything, like the commencement of everything, must be concealed in infinity. But I wish to understand in a way which will bring me to what is inevitably inexplicable. I wish to recognise anything that is inexplicable as being so not because the demands of my reason are wrong (they are right, and apart from them I can understand nothing), but because I recognise the limits of my intellect. I wish to understand in such a way that everything that is inexplicable shall present itself to me as being necessarily inexplicable, and not as being something I am under an arbitrary obligation to believe. I must find what is true and what is false and must disentangle the one from the other. I am setting to work upon this task. What of falsehood I find in the teaching and what I find of truth and to what conclusions I come, will form the following parts of this work, which if it be worth it, and if anyone wants it, will probably someday be printed somewhere.'

*   *   *

Those closing words, in which Tolstoy expresses the hope that his work 'will probably someday be printed somewhere', are a reminder of the difficulties and dangers that had to be encountered in Russia by anyone who set out to challenge the authority of the Orthodox Church, the affairs of which were managed by the Holy Synod presided over by a Procurator who could call on the secular powers to enforce his decisions.

Confession is a work the whole of which is very well worth reading. Its autobiographic value is great. Without it one could not understand the break that occurred in Tolstoy's life at the age of fifty. It also furnishes a striking instance of Tolstoy's artistic power – making others share his own intimate feelings – and illustrates the fact that this power was not confined to his novels, stories, and plays, but is present even more conspicuously in some of the works we call didactic.

Writing his *Confession* was a brave deed few men would have had the courage to perform. In it he challenges both the authorities that compelled the allegiance of his contemporaries. It was the time when, following the publication of *The Origin of Species* and *The Descent of Man*, materialism was rampant among the intelligentsia, who were confident of being able to explain man by mechanics if not today then assuredly tomorrow, and who – while conforming externally to the established Church – looked on anyone who held a religious belief as obviously credulous, superstitious, or ignorant. So Tolstoy by this work invited the contempt of educated and learned Russia, while at the same time by challenging both the theory and practice of the Orthodox Russian Church (and incidentally of all established Churches) he ran the risk of drawing upon himself the undesirable attentions of the Holy Synod. Moreover he could not hope that his friends would approve of his turning aside from fiction to an enquiry into life's great problem – that of our relation to the infinite.

It had been generally supposed that what was written in the form of a novel was 'art', while what was written as autobiography, or as an essay, was not art. It needed such books as *Confession* and *What Then Must We Do?* to show that the transmission of feeling (which is the very essence of art) depends not on the classification of a book, but on the way it is written.

But if Tolstoy could not hope for the approval of the scientists of the day, or of the ecclesiastics, or of his literary friends, neither could he look for sympathy in his own family. His wife adhered to the Russian Church, and her disapproval of his unorthodoxy was a first cause of the dissension between them which increased as time went on. His dearest friend, Countess Alexándra Tolstáya, was deeply pained by what she regarded as the spiritual pride he showed in condemning the tenets of the Church to which he was born. The stream of disapproval was general, and only a man of great integrity of purpose and strength of will, and one convinced of the supreme importance of the matter in hand, would have persevered in writing a work the publication of which in Russia was sure to be, and in fact was, prohibited; and which had for years to be produced and distributed clandestinely. This was done by those interested in his message, and conscious that it was one many people would be eager to read.

It was indeed a notable achievement to produce so forcible a statement of the fact that we are all so made that of necessity we approve and disapprove in a way not explicable by the physical and chemical constituents of our bodies. Society was divided into those who accepted certain dogmas because they felt religion to be a necessity of their being, and others who rejected all religion, because they considered those dogmas absurd. For a man, especially for a man of Tolstoy's eminence and persuasive power, to come between the contestants and say clearly: You are right – religion is necessary; you are right – the dogmas of popular religion are false; was a great achievement. Had Tolstoy written no other book his name would stand out as that of a great writer, a clear thinker, and one who rendered a valuable service to mankind by showing a middle course between the two extremes.

Works: 1852–78

Tolstoy's writings during the first twenty-five years of his literary career may be divided into six sections.

First came a series of seventeen stories and sketches beginning with *Childhood* and ending with *Family Happiness*. Next his series of educational articles in the *Yásnaya Polyána* magazine. Thirdly *The Cossacks* (the finest story he had yet written) and *Polikúshka*. Fourth came *War and Peace*. Fifth the *ABC Book*, the *Readers*, and another article on Education; and sixth came *Anna Karénina*.

Putting the educational works aside the list can be reduced to nineteen stories and sketches followed by two great novels.

The nineteen sketches and stories, 'trials of the pen' as he called them, covered a wide range, from charmingly realistic sketches of childhood to vigorous presentations of Cossack life, and they showed their writer as an amazingly accurate observer of physical facts and qualities, manners, tones, and gestures, and possessed of a yet more wonderful knowledge of the hearts and minds of all sorts and conditions of men, from the shamefaced child to the officer dying on the field of battle.

What is most remarkable in *Childhood*, *Boyhood* and *Youth*, and in an even earlier posthumously published fragment, *The Story of Yesterday*, is, as Prince Mirsky has observed, that Tolstoy from the very start adopted a manner of his own differing from that of his predecessors. His stories are as straightforward as everyday life, and as unsensational. It is the play of feeling – the intimate revelation of the hearts and minds of his characters – that constitutes their charm. They therefore call for very exact translation and for more deliberate and observant perusal than sensational stories do, which rely on intricate plots; and many a hasty reader taking up a story by Tolstoy for the first time and expecting a different sort of book may have experienced disappointment, though a sensitive reader will have found in it a charm lacking in commonplace fiction.

After *Childhood* came *The Raid*, one of the four stories he wrote of army life in the Caucasus: the others being *The Wood-Felling*, *Meeting a Moscow Acquaintance in the Detachment*, and finally *Hadji Murad* (published posthumously) which, though a more finished story, bears a striking resemblance to the sketches written fifty years before. These four stories are also intimate and sympathetic psychological studies revealing the secret feelings of the characters he observed.

Next after *The Raid* came *Boyhood*, a continuation of *Childhood*, and then *Reminiscences of a Billiard-Marker*, dealing with the temperament of a gambler as observed by a marker at a public billiard room.

After this came the three *Sevastopol* sketches, the first two written during the siege itself, and the third immediately after the town had been abandoned. Here Tolstoy again introduced a new method and set a new standard of war literature. His sketches concern themselves not with laudation of war, but with the portrayal of the feelings of those who risked and sometimes lost their lives in the struggle. The exactness of the description in *Sevastopol* made the ordinary run of war stories seem childish. Its influence has been great and may last as long as war – and man's doubts of the legitimacy of war – endure.

Next we have *The Snow Storm*, spoken of in a previous chapter, and *Two Hussars*, a rollicking story somewhat in the style of Charles Lever. Standing alone of its kind among Tolstoy's works, it exhibits a bold type of Russian officer, gifted, dashing, attractive, but quite unrestrained and reckless.

A Landlord's Morning is a convincing study of the relations of a well-meaning proprietor with the serfs he wishes to help. Its condemnation of serfdom is the more convincing because the picture is seen from the landlord's side.

Throughout these stories, and in fact throughout all Tolstoy's writings, one can observe an autobiographical element, but though he utilises his own experiences, and the feeling expressed by his heroes is often his own, the stories are works of imagination and one has to be constantly on one's guard against writers who devise a formula and proceed to fit it on to Tolstoy, giving their attempts plausibility by quoting words 'he himself has said', without warning their readers that the words they quote are those of imaginary characters, and that Tolstoy had so complex a character, with so many phases, that to fit a formula on to him is not to explain him but to misrepresent what he really was.

After *A Landlord's Morning* came *Youth*, a sequel to *Childhood* and

Boyhood, and then *Lucerne* – closely describing an actual occurrence at the Schweizerhof Hotel, when Tolstoy's acute susceptibility to music, combined with his ready response to immediate want – natural in a humane man from a country with no organised system of relief for destitution – came sharply in conflict with the lack of artistic sensibility, and the reluctance to encourage vagrancy, that he encountered among the English and other guests at the hotel.

His next story, again influenced by the hold music had on him, was *Albert*, based on his experience with Rudolf, the talented but drunken violinist he had encountered in Petersburg and had taken to Yásnaya Polyána.

Three Deaths is an admirable study of the death of a wealthy woman, of a peasant post-boy, and of an old tree, all observed with characteristic penetration and described with masterly skill.

Family Happiness, the most finished novel he had yet produced and the one which by its construction came nearest to an ordinary English novel, appeared next. It has already been mentioned, based as it is on his own affair with Valérya, he presents the story from the woman's side. It is noteworthy that he often looked at things through the eyes of a peasant, a child, a girl, an old woman, a dying man, or even a horse – a method made possible by the strength of his imagination and the penetrating power of his observation and reflection.

Next came *The Cossacks*, largely based on his own life in a Cossack village. This full-blooded story has been much praised, and is an admirable work, but owing to circumstances already mentioned, its intended sequel was never written.

Last in the series we have *Polikúshka*, a very remarkable work in which we find an early example of that caustic humour of which Tolstoy made much use later on and at the touch of which all that is pretentious, artificial, or insincere seems to wither to dust. It is amazing how in a few words in this story a whole group of people are characterised and brought to life with all their peculiarities; and how tragedy and humour blend in this convincing tale of serfdom.

His great novels bear out the promise of his short stories, with the added power of maturity.

Prince Mirsky gave a lecture to the Tolstoy Society, of which I only have rough notes, but he put the matter so well that, as far as I can, I will here reproduce the substance of what he said of Tolstoy's earlier period of literary work: 'Tolstoy heralded a change in the texture of novels, from the old dramatic method (which was still the method of Dostoévski) to a new method – "the point-of-view method". The dramatic method consists of giving the actions and words of the characters without an explanation. Tolstoy, in his earlier period, never gives the actions or words of his characters without an explanation. With him the psychological explanation is the important thing. What is important is not what his people do, it is why they do it that matters. This first period of his work, covering the years 1852–77, falls into two parts: a preparatory period, and a period of fulfilment. The first is the period before *War and Peace*; the second that of *War and Peace*, and *Anna Karénina*.

'In the first period Tolstoy was only preparing himself for his great works. His first object was the formation of a technique of analysis by which he could lay his finger on the mechanism of the internal preparation of human action. It is amusing how he revels in the classification of various types of character, for example in the stories written about 1855, especially the Caucasus and Sevastopol stories. He was gradually perfecting an instrument of analysis which allowed him to go far deeper than anyone before him into the lower layers of consciousness. This gives Tolstoy the specious appearance of a man who was particularly near to unreasoning life. This is a very easy but a very bad fallacy to fall into. In the early stories Tolstoy's analysis does not result in the creation of character. This is particularly true of *Sevastopol* and the moralising stories between that and *War and Peace*. His analysis is abstract in that it isolates the psychological fact, that it loses all its actual appearance, all the form in which it appears in actual life. But on the other hand he goes to the original fact, and by a new combination of these divided particles of reality creates a new concrete reality. His work during this preparatory period is on the whole free from all considerations of construction.

'Turning to the second period, that of the great novels, in *War and Peace* this instrument of analysis is fully perfected and is now only a means to an end, not an end in itself. The nearest approach to *War and Peace* in the period before Tolstoy would be the old family novels of Charlotte Yonge for example, taken, that is, purely as a literary form. Compare the construction of *War and Peace* and *The Daisy Chain*. The differences are two. First, Tolstoy has gone through a period of preparation in his early work which Miss Yonge had not, and he had an instrument of construction superior even to Stendhal's. Secondly,

Tolstoy placed his novel in an historical setting. This is one of the most vital points of *War and Peace*, though it has often been said that Tolstoy had no sense of 'historicity'. But he had another sense of history, an acute sense of the uninterrupted stream of happenings, of time. It is this placing of the family novel, based on a thoroughgoing explanatory analysis of action in this stream of time, that gives *War and Peace* its peculiar place in the history of the novel. Tolstoy created something that may be said to be no longer a novel – it is the open form of the novel as opposed to the closed form. Flaubert, in *Madame Bovary*, was bringing this (the closed) form to perfection. It had a beginning, a middle, and an end, a single *jet* ending in a definite solution of the conflicts inside the novel. Tolstoy in *War and Peace* transcends the limit of the novel and does what had previously been done by the epic. It is as though we had observed a section of a flowing river from one spot to another, conscious that the river neither began nor ended at these points.

'Thus *War and Peace* must be put in a group not with *Madame Bovary*, *Vanity Fair*, or *The Mill on the Floss*, but with the *Iliad*, in the sense that when the novel is finished nothing is finished, the stream of life flows on. Take for example the appearance of Prince Andrew's son – the novel ends on the beginning of a new life. There are all the time openings out of the story on to the outer world. This is a thing that had never been attempted by historical novelists before Tolstoy. Another thing which differentiates *War and Peace* is its religion, which is quite different from the religion of Tolstoy's last years. The religious message of *War and Peace* is that the only fundamental obligation of man is to be in tune with life. This relation between the individual and the whole again gives *War and Peace* its openings.'

*   *   *

Tolstoy's works from the first interested Russia, and now interest the world, because in greater measure than any of his predecessors he possesses the capacity to feel intensely, note accurately, and think deeply. The combination which makes him so interesting is the scientific accuracy of his observation (which never allows him to take liberties with his characters or events in order to make out a case for the side he sympathises with) and the fact that he is mightily in earnest. Life to him is important, and art is the handmaid of life. He wants to discern what is good and what is bad; to help the former and resist the latter. His work tends to evolve order out of life's chaos, and as that is the most important thing a man can do, his books are among the most interesting and important in modern literature. He makes no pretence of standing aloof, cutting off his art from his life, or concealing his desire that kindness should prevail over cruelty. Life interests him, and therefore the reflection of life interests him, and the problems of art are the problems of life: love and passion and death and the desire to do right.

The chief subject appearing again and again throughout the stories he wrote before *War and Peace* is the mental striving of a young Russian nobleman to free himself from the artificial futilities of the society in which he was born, and to see and do what is right. The search is only partially successful. The indictment of society is often convincing, but the heroes' failures and perplexities are frankly admitted. Sometimes there is no hero. In *Sevastopol*, for instance, he exclaims: 'Where in this tale is the evil shown that should be avoided? Where is the good that should be imitated? Who is the villain, who the hero of the story? All are good and all are bad;' and in *Lucerne* he says: 'Who has in his soul so immovable a *standard of good and evil* that by it he can measure the passing facts of life?'

This searching for what is good and rejecting what is false – resulting in a strong distrust and dislike of the predatory masterful domineering types of humanity and in general of what has usually been regarded as the heroic type, and in a friendly compassion for all that is humble, simple, forbearing, and sincere – is the keynote of Tolstoy's early tales. They are studies of life. The characters seem to have an independent life of their own; they speak for themselves, and at times like Balaam, bless what they were apparently expected to curse. For instance, when Prince Nekhlyudov insists on bringing the wandering musician into the Schweizerhof Hotel in *Lucerne*, we feel how uncomfortable he thereby makes the poor singer, though that is evidently not what Tolstoy set out to make us feel.

War and Peace, besides being maturer than the preceding tales, was composed during the early years of Tolstoy's married life when he felt more content with himself and with life in general, and his attitude towards existing things was more tolerant and sympathetic than it had been or than it was in later years.

He told me that in *War and Peace* and *Anna Karénina* his aim was simply to amuse his readers. One is bound to accept the statement, but it is only necessary to read either of those books to see that in them

Tolstoy's ardent nature found vent for all its likes and dislikes, strivings, yearnings, hopes, and fears.

I asked Tolstoy why in *What is Art?* he relegates these novels to the realm of 'bad art', and his answer showed, as I expected, that he did not consider them at all bad, but condemned them merely as being too long, and written in a manner chiefly adapted for the leisured, well-to-do classes who have time to read novels in several volumes because other people do their rough work for them. Of *War and Peace* he said, 'It is, one would think, harmless enough, but one never knows how things will affect people', and he went on to mention with regret that one of Professor Zahárin's daughters had told him that from his novels she had acquired a love of balls and parties – things of which, at the time of our conversation, he heartily disapproved.

The mighty drama of the Napoleonic advance from 1805 to 1812 comes into the novel in so far as it affected the members of the Rostóv and Bolkónski families.

The main theme of the novel, if one may select a main theme from the many latent in the story, is Tolstoy's favourite thesis. He tacitly asks: What is good and what is bad? With what must we sympathise and what must we reject? And the reply is that the predatory, artificial types, exemplified historically by the invading French, as well as by such Russian characters as Hélène, Anatole, and Dólokhov, are repugnant to him, while he loves the humble, the meek, and the sincere: Márya and Platon Karatáev, Natásha (so impulsive and charming in her youth, so absorbed in her family later), and Pierre (who is often humble, always sincere, and devoted to ideas and ideals).

The book introduces many characters, all of them so distinctly drawn that we know them better than we know our personal acquaintances. It treats of life's deepest experiences from the cradle to the grave, and to read it with care is to know life better, and see it more sanely and seriously, than one did before.

Tolstoy is probably justified in claiming that his history is truer than the historians' history of the battles of Schöngraben, Austerlitz, and Borodinó. N. N. Muravyóv, a Commander-in-Chief who distinguished himself in more than one war, declared he had never read a better description of a battle than Tolstoy's account of Schöngraben, and added that he was convinced from his own experience that during a battle it is impossible to carry out a Commander-in-Chief's orders.

When he wrote the book Tolstoy believed war to be inevitable. The idea that it is man's duty to resist it and to refuse to take part in it came to him later.

Yet his inveterate truthfulness and personal knowledge of war, caused him to describe it so exactly that the result is tantamount to a condemnation. As Kropótkin remarked, *War and Peace* is a powerful indictment of war. The effect the great writer exercised in this direction upon his generation could be actually seen in Russia. It was apparent during the Russo-Turkish war of 1877–8, when it was impossible to find in Russia a correspondent who would have described how 'we peppered the enemy with grape-shot', or how 'we knocked them down like ninepins'.

Tolstoy told me he considered the defect of the book, besides its length, to be the intrusion of a philosophic argument into the story. He still held the opinions he had held when he wrote it as to the influence or impotence of 'great' men and all that he then said about destiny and free will, but he realised that the novel would have been better without these abstract disquisitions.

The characters in the book are not strictly copied from life, but in the main Tolstoy's father's family and to some extent his wife's are represented by the Rostóvs, and his mother's family by the Bolkónskis. To a large extent the old Prince N. Bolkónski is drawn from Tolstoy's grandfather, Prince N. Volkónski; the daughter, Princess Márya, from Tolstoy's mother, the old Count Ilyá A. Rostóv from Tolstoy's grandfather, Count Ilyá A. Tolstoy; his son Count Nicholas Rostóv from Tolstoy's father, Count Nicholas Tolstoy; Natásha from Tolstoy's sister-in-law, Tatiána Behrs; Sónya from his 'auntie' Tatiána Érgolskaya. Dólokhov is a combination of Count Theodore Tolstoy, a famous and eccentric traveller, and R. I. Dórokhov, a notorious daredevil of Alexander I's days.

Many even of the minor characters, such as Mlle Bourienne, and Ivánushka, the woman pilgrim in man's clothes, are copied from people connected with the Volkónskis' home at Yásnaya Polyána.

The novel covers nearly the whole range of Tolstoy's own experience of life: in it we have the aristocracy and the peasants; town life and country life; the commanders, officers, and privates of the army, in action and out of action; the diplomatists and courtiers; flirtation, love, balls, hunting, and a reform movement which is mainly talk. What Tolstoy does not show is what he did not know – the middle-class world: the world of merchants, manufacturers, engineers, and men of business. Of course these in Russia a hundred years ago played a com-

paratively small part; there was practically no political activity such as
that of our County Councils, Borough Councils, and Parliament. But
that all this was absent from Tolstoy's mind, and that his outlook on life
was confined to the aristocracy which consumed and the peasantry
which produced will in the sequel help us to understand the social
teaching to which he ultimately came. His brother-in-law tells us that
Leo Tolstoy

> has in my presence confessed to being both proud and vain. He was
> a rampant aristocrat, and though he always loved the country folk,
> he loved the aristocracy still more. To the middle class he was
> antipathetic. When after his failures in early life he became widely
> famous as a writer, he used to admit that it gave him great pleasure
> and intense happiness. In his own words, he was pleased to feel that
> he was both a writer and a noble.
>
> When he heard of any of his former comrades or acquaintances
> receiving important appointments, his comments reminded one of
> those of Suvórov [the great Field-Marshal of Catherine the Great's
> time], who always maintained that at Court one received promotion
> for cringing and flattery but never for good work. Sometimes he would
> ironically remark that though he had himself not earned a Generalship
> in the artillery, he had at any rate won his Generalship in literature.

A simple world of nobles and peasants, with little organisation and
that of a poor kind: a world the evils of which were mitigated by much
kindliness and good intention, and in which on the whole the less the
Government interfered with anybody or anything the better – such was
old Russia as it existed under Alexander I, and as it still existed when
Tolstoy was young. He has described it with extraordinary vividness,
and has made it possible for us to picture to ourselves a country and an
age unlike our own. What effect the limitation of his outlook referred
to above had on the subsequent development of his opinions need not
here be considered. It does not spoil the novel, for no novel can show
the whole of life, but it had a serious effect on the formulation of his
later philosophy. Of certain important types of humanity he had hardly
any conception. Of the George Stephenson type, for instance, which
masters the brute forces of nature and harnesses them to the service of
man – doing this primarily from love of efficient work – he knows
nothing; nor does he know anything of the Sidney Webb type, which
sets itself the difficult task of evolving social order out of the partial

chaos of modern civilisation; nor of the best type of organisers in our great industrial undertakings: men whose hearts are set on getting much work well done with little friction and little waste, and to whom the successful accomplishment of a difficult project gives more satisfaction than any effortless acquisition of wealth could do. Tolstoy over-simplified life's problems. He made a sharp contrast between the predatory and the humble types, and there is much truth in his presentation. He is right that life is supported by the humble and rendered hard by the predatory types, but he has omitted from his scheme of things the man of organising mind: the man who knows how to get his way and generally gets it (or a good deal of it) but does this mainly from worthy motives; the man who is not perfect, who may take more than is good for him and may have some of the tendencies of the predatory type, but who on the whole is worth, and more than worth, his salt, and but for whom there would be greater chaos and less order in the world. Tolstoy said in one of his later writings that the cause of the Russian famines was the Greek Church; and he was right. All that stupefies, and all that impedes thought, tends to make men inefficient even in their agricultural operations. But by parity of reasoning he might have seen that the introduction of thought into methods of production, distribution, and exchange, which has during the last hundred and fifty years so revolutionised our Western world, should not be condemned as bad in itself, however ugly many of its manifestations may be and however often we may see the organising and the predatory types exemplified in one and the same person.

I cannot comment on *War and Peace* better than I did in a preface I wrote to a former edition of that novel, where, following the lines of what N. Strákhov had written, I said: 'The work was begun when Tolstoy was thirty-five, and he was generally in good spirits while writing it.

'Nothing can be simpler than most of the occurrences of *War and Peace*. Everyday events of family life: conversations between brother and sister, or mother and daughter, separations and reunions, hunting, holiday festivities, dances, card-playing, and so forth, are all as lovingly shaped into artistic gems as is the battle of Borodinó itself. Whatever the purpose of the book may be its success depends not on that purpose but on what Tolstoy did under its influence, that is to say it depends on a highly artistic execution.

'If Tolstoy succeeds in fixing our gaze on what occupied his soul, it is because he had full command of his instrument – which was art. Not many readers probably are concerned about the thoughts that directed and animated the author, but all are impressed by his creation. Men of all camps – those who like as well as those who dislike his later works – unite in tribute to the extraordinary mastery shown in this remarkable production. It is a notable example of the irresistible and all-conquering power of art.

'But such art does not arise of itself, nor can it exist apart from deep thought and deep feeling. What is it that strikes everyone in *War and Peace*? It is its clearness of form and vividness of colour. It is as though one saw what is described and heard the sounds that are uttered. The author hardly speaks in his own person; he brings forward the characters and then allows them to speak, feel, and act; and they do it so that every movement is true and amazingly exact, in full accord with the character of those portrayed. It is as if we had to do with real people, and saw them more clearly than one can see in real life. We not only distinguish the form of expression and the feeling of each actor, but their manner, their favourite gestures, and their way of walking. The important Prince Vasíly on one occasion, in unusual and difficult circumstances, had to walk on tiptoe. The author knows just how each of his characters walks. "Prince Vasíly", we are told, "could not walk well on tiptoe, and his whole body jerked at each step." With similar clearness and distinctness the author knows the movements, feelings, and thoughts of all those whom he depicts. When once they are before us he does not interfere with them, but lets each behave as is natural to him.

'Similarly Tolstoy usually describes scenes or scenery only as reflected in the mind of one of his characters. He does not describe the oak that stood beside the road, or the moonlight night when neither Natásha nor Prince Andrew could sleep; but he describes the impressions the oak and the night made on Prince Andrew. The battles and historic events are usually described not by informing us of the author's conception of them, but by the impression they produce on the characters in the story. The battle of Schöngraben is described chiefly by the impression it made on Prince Andrew; Austerlitz by its impression on Nicholas Rostóv; the Emperor's appearance in Moscow by the excitement it produced in Pétya; and the effect of the prayer against invasion by the feelings of Natásha. Tolstoy nowhere appears behind the actors or draws events in the abstract; he shows them in the flesh and blood of those who supplied the material for the events.

'In this respect the work is an artistic marvel. Tolstoy has seized not some separate traits but a whole living atmosphere, which varies around different individuals and different classes of society. He himself mentions the 'loving family atmosphere' of the Rostóvs' house, but there are other instances: the atmosphere surrounding Speránski, or that surrounding the Rostóvs' "uncle"; that of the Big Theatre in Moscow when Natásha went to the opera; of the military hospital Nicholas visited; of a crowded bridge when the French were preparing to fire on it, and so on. The characters who enter each of these atmospheres, or pass from one of them to another, inevitably experience their influence, and so do we with them.

'In this way the highest objectivity is attained; we not only have before us the actions, figures, movements, and speech of the actors, but their whole inner life is shown us by equally clear and distinct traits – their souls and hearts are bared to our view. Reading *War and Peace* we *contemplate*, in the full meaning of that word, the object the artist has depicted. Tolstoy is an admirable realist who shows us alike the excellent and the contemptible traits in his characters. He does not spare us Natásha's infatuation for Anatole, or pretend that as the mother of a family she retained her youthful charm; and while he thus treats his most attractive characters he does full justice to the courage, firmness, and leadership of the rascally card-sharper Dólokhov. Again, no one can doubt his sympathy for his country exposed to Napoleon's invasion, yet he never yields to the temptation to offer incense at the shrine of patriotic pride while depicting Russia's deliverance from a foreign yoke. How faithfully he deals with the shady aspects of Russian army life and its many defects!

'The finest shades of spiritual life and its profoundest upheavals are alike depicted with clearness and fidelity. The feeling of holiday dullness in the Rostóvs' house at Otrádnoe, and the feelings of the Russian army in the heat of the battle of Borodinó; Natásha's youthful perturbations, and the excitement of old Bolkónski when his memory was failing and he was on the verge of apoplexy; are all vivid, living, and exact, in Tolstoy's narration.

'That is where the author's interest centres and consequently his reader's interest also. However important and great the events treated of – whether it be the Krémlin crowded with people on the occasion of the Tsar's visit, or the meeting of the two emperors, or a terrible battle with guns roaring and thousands of men dying – nothing deflects the author, or his readers with him, from steady observation of the inner spirit of the individual characters. It is as if he were concerned only with the effect the occurrences produce on the soul of man – only with what each soul felt and contributed to the event.

'Tolstoy undertook to present the most heroic period of Russian history, and he emerged triumphant from the contest with the difficulties of his theme.

'We have before us a marvellous panorama of the Russia that withstood Napoleon's invasion and dealt a death-blow to his power. The picture is painted without exaggeration and shows many of the shadows and ugly, pitiful features belonging to the mental, moral, and political relations of that day. But at the same time the strength that saved Russia is indicated in a manner that by contrast with the present makes the book painful reading for lovers of Russia today.

'The soul of man is depicted in *War and Peace* with unparalleled reality. It is not life in the abstract that is shown, but creatures fully defined with all their limitations of place, time, and circumstance. For instance, we see how individuals *grow*. Natásha running into the drawing-room with her doll, in Book I, and Natásha entering the church, in Book IX, are really one and the same person at two different ages, and not merely two different ages attributed to a single person, such as one often encounters in fiction. The author has also shown us the intermediate stages of this development. In the same way Nicholas Rostóv develops; Pierre from being a young man becomes a Moscow magnate; old Bolkónski grows senile and so forth.

'The spiritual peculiarities of Tolstoy's characters are so clearly perceptible, so individual, that we can notice the *family likeness* of those who are blood relations. Old Bolkónski and Prince Andrew are evidently of similar nature, though one is young and the other old. The Rostóv family, despite the great divergence of its members, presents features common to them all, and so remarkably reproduced that they merge into shades one feels but cannot describe. For instance, we can feel that even the unsympathetic Vera may be a real Rostóv, while the much more attractive Sónya's mentality evidently springs from a different root.

'The non-Russians present a very trying test, for had Tolstoy been content to give a conventionally Russian view of the nationalities presented, we, from our English point of view, should at once note the artificiality of such a presentation. But take, for instance, the French

Mlle Bourienne or Napoleon himself; the Austrian and German generals Mack and Pfuel, or Adolph Berg, and (though we today may feel more respect for German military capacity than Tolstoy felt in the 1860s) we readily recognise the Frenchness of the Frenchman and the Germanity of the Germans. As to the Russians in the book, not only is every one of them thoroughly Russian but even the class and condition to which each of them belongs is readily distinguishable. For instance, Speránski, little as we see of him, is from head to foot a 'Seminarist', the product of a theological college.

'And all that passes in their minds, each feeling, passion, or agitation, is distinct and true. Tolstoy never makes the common mistake of representing a single state of mind as always prevailing in the soul of any of his heroes. Think for instance of Natásha, whose spirit is so intense and full; in her soul everything is ardent: her vanity, her love of her betrothed, her gaiety, her thirst for life, her deep affection for her relations, and so on. Or think of Prince Andrew when he stood over the smoking shell. " 'Can this be death?' thought Prince Andrew, looking with a quite new, envious glance at the grass, the wormwood, and the streamlet of smoke that curled up from the revolving black ball. 'I cannot – do not wish – to die; I love life, love this grass, this ground, this air.' . . . He thought this *and at the same time remembered that men were looking at him.*" Or take the feeling of animosity Prince Andrew nursed towards Kurágin, with its strange contradictions, or the changes of feeling in the Princess Márya: religious, amorous, filially devoted, and so forth.

'The dignity of man is hidden from us either by all kinds of defects or by the fact that we esteem other qualities too highly and therefore measure men by their cleverness, strength, beauty, and so forth. Tolstoy teaches us to penetrate beneath their externality. What can be simpler, more ordinary, and, so to say, meeker than the figures of Nicholas Rostóv and the Princess Márya? They have no brilliance, no ability, and do not stand out from the most ordinary level of ordinary folk. Yet these simple people, who go quietly along the simplest of life's roads, are evidently admirable souls. The irresistible sympathy with which the author has surrounded these two, who seem so small but are really the peers of any in spiritual beauty, is one of the masterly achievements of *War and Peace*. Nicholas Rostóv is evidently a man of very limited ability, but, as the author says, "he had that common sense of mediocrity which showed him what he ought to do".

'And really Nicholas does many stupid things and does not show much understanding of people or circumstances, but he always understands what ought to be done, and this invaluable wisdom always preserves the purity of his simple and ardent nature.

'Is there any need to speak of the Princess Márya? Despite her weakness, this figure (which represented what Tolstoy treasured as the image of the mother he had lost before he was two years old) attains such purity and mildness that at times she seems to wear the halo of a saint.

'Then again Tolstoy is most masterly in the presentment of what is hidden in the soul of man beneath the play of passion, beneath his egotism, avarice, and animal desires. Very pitiful, very senseless, are the passions which lead Pierre and Natásha astray; but the reader sees that behind it all these people have hearts of gold, and one never for a moment doubts that when a demand comes for self-sacrifice, or when there is a call for boundless sympathy with what is good and admirable, these hearts will yield warm and ready response. The spiritual beauty of these two is remarkable. Pierre – a grown-up child with an enormous body and terrible sensuality, impracticable and unreasonable as a child – unites in himself a childlike purity and tenderness of soul with a mind that is naïve but for that very reason lofty, and a character to which everything dishonourable is not merely foreign but even incomprehensible. He has a childlike absence of fear and unconsciousness of evil. Natásha is a girl gifted with such fullness of spiritual life that, in Pierre's words, *she does not deign to be clever*, that is, she has neither the time nor the desire to convert this fullness of life into abstract forms of thought. Her measureless plenitude of life – which at times brings her into a state of " intoxication" (to translate exactly the word employed in the Russian original) – leads her into the terrible mistake of her senseless passion for Kurágin – a mistake afterwards redeemed by severe suffering. Pierre and Natásha were people who by their very natures were bound to commit many mistakes and encounter much disillusionment. As if in contrast to them the author introduces the happy couple Véra and Adolph Berg – people who commit no mistakes, encounter no disillusionment, and arrange their life most comfortably. One cannot but be amazed at the restraint with which Tolstoy, exhibiting all the paltriness and pettiness of these souls, never once yields to the temptation of treating them with ridicule or anger. This is true realism and real truth! With similar truthfulness are the Kurágins, Hélène and Anatole, depicted; these heartless creatures are exhibited unsparingly, but with no desire to belabour them.

'Amid all the diversity of people and events, we feel the presence of some firm and indestructible principles on which their lives rest. Family, social, and marital obligations are clearly discernible. The conceptions of good and evil are clear and durable. Having shown us the artificial life of the higher spheres of society and of the various staffs surrounding exalted personages, Tolstoy sets in contrast two firm and real spheres of life – family life and life in the active army. The two families, the Rostóvs and the Bolkónskis, present us with life directed by clear, indubitable principles, in the fulfilment of which the members of these families set their duty and honour, their dignity and satisfaction. Similarly army life (which Tolstoy in one place compares to a swarm) presents us with a quite definite conception of duty and human dignity; so that the simple-minded Nicholas on one occasion even prefers to remain in the regiment rather than return home, where he does not see clearly what his conduct should be.

'Tolstoy is peculiarly Russian and may at times be read to find the differences of thought and feeling that separate Russians from ourselves; but what is more remarkable is the way his penetration to the very souls of men convinces us that his Russians are of one nature with ourselves, and that the power that created us made "of one blood all nations of men", however we may vary superficially.'

War and Peace presents us with a complete picture of human life; a complete picture of the Russia of those days; a complete historic picture of the struggle of nations; and a complete picture of the things in which men set their happiness and greatness, their sorrow and their shame. It is a work so amazingly great that though many have *felt* its greatness, few have *understood* how great it is. Tolstoy is one who reveals the secrets of life and death. The meaning of history, the strength of nations, the mystery of death, the reality of love and family life – such are the subjects he deals with. Are these matters so easy that every casual reader may take up the book in an idle hour expecting to fathom them? Is it strange that *War and Peace* should prove both a touchstone testing the quality of its critics and a stumbling-block to many who undertake to judge it?

In judging of such a work one should tread with caution, but we think a Russian critic judged well when he said that the meaning of the book is best summed up in Tolstoy's own words, 'There is no greatness without simplicity, goodness, and truth.'

Napoleon was too generally accepted as a great man for Tolstoy not to feel sceptical of his quality, and Napoleon was precisely of the selfishly aggressive type, pouring out the lives of others like water, whom Tolstoy (who also hated Peter the Great) instinctively detested. But while one admits this, one recognises that his act of indictment is admirably drawn and contains much truth. Tolstoy was scrupulously careful as to the actual incidents of the historic scenes depicted, and never puts a remark into the mouth of an historical character for which he had not good warrant.

Outside Russia, *Anna Karénina* is perhaps more popular than *War and Peace*. The former is a long novel, but not nearly as long as the latter, and though it contains philosophic disquisitions, these fit better into the story and are shorter and clearer than the philosophic chapters in *War and Peace*. In arrangement, again, *Anna Karénina* is more like the novels we are accustomed to, though instead of one hero and one heroine it has two pairs of lovers, living quite different lives and not very closely connected.

It deals with the passionate love of a beautiful and attractive woman; and it has a further interest in the fact that Lévin, to a greater degree than any of the author's other characters, represents Tolstoy himself; though Tolstoy has made Lévin a very simple fellow in order to get a more effective contrast between him and the representatives of high life in Moscow and Petersburg.

Anna Karénina was introduced to the English reading public by Matthew Arnold in an essay which is one of the best ever written about Tolstoy. It is so good that I may be excused for mentioning a point on which it is misleading.

A sentence in it which has done harm is that in which he speaks about translations: 'I use the French translation; in general work of this kind is better done in France than in England, and *Anna Karénina* is perhaps also a novel which goes better into French than into English.'

It is true enough that the early English translations of Tolstoy were very poor. But Arnold was wrong in supposing that *Anna Karénina* would naturally go better into French than into English. Had he been able to read the original he would have seen that in Tolstoy's novels there are two sets of people: a Court set who continually speak French and are Frenchified, and a plain, homely, straightforward Russian (I had almost said, English) set who seldom use French phrases, and are sharply contrasted with the others. This contrast can be made clear in an English version, but is difficult to deal with in a version where the characters have all to speak French. The case is worse than that, however: Arnold did not say, as he fairly might, that up to his time the French versions were less bad than the English; he speaks as though it were in the nature of things that translations into French must be better than translations into English. A statement of that kind diverts attention from the fact that the French translations of Tolstoy are for the most part unsatisfactory, while some English translations are good. I recently received a letter from Mme Guermanova of the Moscow Art Theatre in which she – who often reads passages from Tolstoy's novels to literary gatherings in the different countries she visits – mentions that she cannot find adequate French versions of her favourite passages, but that she likes our versions and would willingly make use of them. For people to assume that they have read a reliable version because they have read it in French (often without so much as noticing the translator's name) is silly.

W. D. Howells who stood sponsor for Tolstoy in America as Matthew Arnold did in England, very truly says:

> It is Tolstoy's humanity which is the grace beyond the reach of art in his imaginative work. It does not reach merely the poor and the suffering; it extends to the prosperous and the proud, and does not deny itself to the guilty. There had been many stories of adultery before *Anna Karénina*, nearly all the great novels outside of English are framed upon that argument, but in *Anna Karénina* for the first time the whole truth was told about it. Tolstoy has said of the fiction of Maupassant that the whole truth can never be immoral; and in his own work I have felt that it could never be anything but moral.

Arnold is rather shocked that Anna should yield so quickly and easily to the persuasions of Vrónski. He is quite sure that she ought to have resisted. But here we come to a matter on which many Russians disapprove of Tolstoy on just the opposite ground. Kropótkin in his *Ideals and Realities in Russian Literature* has stated their case, and this is the substance of what he says:

> *Anna Karénina* produced in Russia an impression which brought Tolstoy congratulations from the reactionary camp and a very cool reception from the advanced portion of society. The fact is that the

question of marriage and of the separation of husband and wife, had been most earnestly debated in Russia by the best men and women, both in literature and in life. Levity towards marriage such as is continually unveiled in the Divorce Courts was decidedly condemned, as also was any form of deceit such as supplies the subject for countless French novels and plays. But after levity and deceit had been condemned, the right of a new love – appearing perhaps after years of happy married life – was seriously considered. Chernyshévski's novel, *What to do?* may be taken as the best expression of the opinions on marriage which became current among the better portion of the young generation. Once married, it was said, don't take lightly to love affairs or flirtation. Not every fit of passion deserves the name of a new love; and what is called love is often merely temporary desire. Even if it be real, before it has grown deep there is generally time to reflect on the consequences that would result were it allowed to grow. But when all is said and done, there are cases when a new love does come, and comes almost inevitably: as for instance when a girl has been married almost against her will under the continued insistence of her lover, or when the two have married without properly understanding one another, or when one of the two has continued to progress towards an ideal, while the other, after having worn the mask of idealism, falls back into the Philistine happiness of warmed slippers. In such cases separation not only becomes inevitable, but is often to the interest of both. It would be better for both to live through the suffering a separation involves (honest natures are improved by such suffering) than to spoil the entire subsequent life of one – or both in most cases – and to face the evil consequences which living together under such circumstances would be sure to produce on the children. That at any rate was the conclusion to which, both in literature and in life, the best portion of Russian society came.

And into the society Kropótkin describes in that statement comes Tolstoy with *Anna Karénina*. The epigraph of the book is 'Vengeance is mine, I will repay', and death by suicide is the fate of poor Anna, who was married young to an old and unattractive man and had never known love till she met Vrónski. Deceit was not in her nature. To maintain a conventional marriage would not have made her husband or child happier. Separation and a new life with Vrónski, who seriously loved her, was the only possible outcome. At any rate, continues Kropótkin, if the story of *Anna Karénina* had to end in tragedy, it was not in consequence of an act of supreme justice. The artistic genius of Tolstoy, honest here as everywhere, itself indicated the real cause, in the inconsistency of Vrónski and Anna, After leaving her husband and defying public opinion – that is, as Tolstoy shows, the opinion of women not honest enough to have a right to a voice in the matter – neither she nor Vrónski had the courage to break right away from that society, the futility of which Tolstoy describes so exquisitely. Instead of that, when Anna returns with Vrónski to Petersburg, their chief preoccupation is, how Betsy and other such women will receive her if she reappears among them? 'And it was the opinion of the Betsies – surely not Superhuman Justice – which brought Anna to suicide.'

Whether Matthew Arnold's view or Kropótkin's be accepted, Tolstoy at any rate does full justice to Anna's charm: 'her large, fresh, rich, generous, delightful nature which keeps our sympathy' and even our respect; there is no nonsense about her being a degraded or vile person. And after all, Tolstoy's view of marriage sanctity is a very old and a very widely held one; and it is surely good to have that side of the case put so artistically, so persuasively, so well, as he puts it. If ultimately the idea that two uncongenial people ought to live out their lives together because they have been married has to be abandoned, let it not be abandoned without the best advocates being heard in its defence.

As to what Tolstoy meant by the epigraph 'Vengeance is mine, I will repay' – this was better understood by Dostoévski than by Kropótkin. Here is a condensation of what Dostoévski wrote:

Anna Karénina as an artistic production is perfection. It appears most opportunely as a thing to which European literature of our epoch offers no equal. Moreover its idea is something of our own, native to us, distinguishing us from the whole European world – it is our national 'new word' or at least its beginning, a word such as one does not hear in Europe, yet which, for all her pride, she greatly needs. In *Anna Karénina* a view of human guilt and criminality is presented. People are taken in abnormal circumstances. Evil exists antecedently. Seized in a vortex of falsehood they commit crimes and inevitably perish. It deals, as we see, with a favourite and very ancient European theme. But after all how is the question solved in Europe? It is there solved always in one of two ways. The first reply is that the law has been given, written, formulated and constituted, during thousands of years. Evil and good are already defined and weighed. He who does not follow it, he who infringes it, pays with liberty, property, or life – pays literally and inhumanly. The other contrary reply is: Since society is abnormally arranged it is impossible to hold individuals responsible for the consequences. Therefore the culprit is not responsible and crime does not yet exist. To have done with crime and human guilt we must end the abnormality of society and its arrangements. The world of Western Europe offers no other replies to the problem of man's guilt and delinquency.

But the Russian author's [Tolstoy's] view clearly considers that no abolition of poverty, no organising of labour, will save humanity from abnormalities, and consequently from guilt and delinquency. This is expressed with terrible profundity and force in an immense psychological study of the soul of man, and with a realism of artistic presentation unequalled among us. It is made so clear and intelligible as to be obvious, that evil lies deeper in humanity than our Socialist physicians imagine – that no arrangement of society will eliminate evil; that the human mind remains the same, abnormality and sin proceed from it, and that finally, the laws of the soul of man are still so unknown, so unimagined by science, so undefined, and so mysterious, that there are not as yet, and cannot be, physicians or ultimate judges, but there is only He, who says: 'Vengeance is mine, I will repay!' To Him alone all the secrets of this world and the ultimate fate of man are known.

And that he may not perish in despair through failing to understand his path and destiny, man is here shown the way of escape. It is indicated with genius in the wonderful scene in the earlier part of the novel, where the heroine is at death's door and the culprits and enemies are transformed into higher beings, into brothers forgiving one another everything – into beings who by mutual and complete forgiveness free themselves from falsehood, guilt, and crime, and thereby justify themselves with full consciousness that they have acquired a right to do so. But further in the last part of the novel, in that dark and terrible picture, followed up step by step, of the fall of a human soul, there is so much instruction for a human judge and for him who holds the scales and weights, that in fear and amazement he will certainly exclaim: 'No, Vengeance is not always mine, and I cannot always repay!' And he will not inhumanly hold a miserably fallen offender guilty for having spurned the issue long since indicated by the light or even for having consciously rejected it.

As an example of the injustice Tolstoy has suffered at the hands of bad translators, it may be mentioned that in a German version the epigraph of this novel was rendered as: '*Mein ist die Rache, ich spiele As*,' 'Vengeance is mine, I play the ace.'

Anna Karénina contains passages – the ball, the officers' steeplechase, the mowing, the death of Lévin's brother, and others – which for artistic beauty are unsurpassed and, one is tempted to say, unsurpassable. Towards the end, it contains in admirably concise form much of what Tolstoy has said in his *Confession*, of his quest after the meaning of life, his thoughts of suicide, and how he learnt from a talk with a peasant that man should live for his soul and for God.

His treatment in this novel of the Russian volunteers who went to fight for Serbia was a bold slap in the face to the Russian jingoes who were having things all their own way at that time; but it is curious to note the precise position that (speaking through the mouth of Lévin) Tolstoy then took up. He did not say that Russia ought not to fight to free the Christian populations of Turkey, he merely said that no individual Russian had any business to volunteer for the Serbian or Bulgarian army or take any action urging the Russian Government towards war.

Of Lévin we are told: 'He, like Miháylich and the peasants, whose feelings are expressed in the legendary story of the invitation sent to the Varyági by the early inhabitants of Russia, said: "Come and be princes and rule over us. *We gladly promise complete submission*. All labour, all humiliations, all sacrifices, we take on ourselves, but *we do not judge or decide*." ' And Lévin goes on to repudiate the idea that the Russian people have 'now renounced this privilege that had been bought at so costly a price' – the privilege, that is, of not taking any part in Government.

The connection between the roots of Tolstoy's opinions – manifested in these writings of his first fifty years – and his opinions in their ultimate rigid and dogmatic form as expressed during the last three decades, is in general so closely connected; the dogmas of the later period grew so naturally out of the sympathies and experiences of the earlier time, that this point – at which there is a clean line of cleavage (the difference between obeying Government and disobeying it) – is particularly worthy of note. When finishing *Anna Karénina* Tolstoy had not yet reached the conclusion that all Governments employing force are immoral, but his later teachings were dominated by that view.

Apart from the special points I have referred to, the general effect and influence of Tolstoy's fiction is very well summed up by W. D. Howells, who says:

Up to his time fiction had been a part of the pride of life, and had been governed by the criterions of the world which it amused. But Tolstoy replaced the artistic conscience by the human conscience. Great as my wonder was at the truth in his work, my wonder at the love in it was greater yet. Here, for the first time, I found the most faithful picture of life set in the light of that human conscience which I had falsely taught myself was to be ignored in questions of art as something inadequate and inappropriate. In the august presence of the masterpieces, I had been afraid and ashamed of the highest interests of my nature as something philistine and provincial. But here I stood in the presence of a master who told me not to be ashamed of them, but to judge his work by them, since he had himself wrought in honour of them. I found the tests of conduct which I had used in secret with myself, applied as the rules of universal justice, condemning and acquitting in motive and action, and admitting none of those lawyer's pleas which baffle our own consciousness of right and wrong. Often in Tolstoy's ethics I feel a hardness, almost an arrogance (the word says too much); but in his aesthetics I have never felt this. He has transmuted the atmosphere of a realm hitherto supposed unmoral into the very air of heaven. I found nowhere in his work those base and cruel lies which cheat us into the belief that wrong may sometimes be right through passion, or genius, or heroism. There was everywhere the grave noble face of the truth that had looked me in the eyes all my life, and that I knew I must confront when I came to die. But there was something more than this, infinitely more. There was that love which is before even the truth, without which there is no truth, and which if there is any last day, must appear the Divine justice . . .

As I have already more than once said, his ethics and aesthetics are inseparably at one; and that is what gives a vital warmth to all his art. It is never that heartless skill which exists for its own sake and is content to dazzle with the brilliancy of its triumphs. It seeks always the truth, in the love to which alone the truth unveils itself. If Tolstoy is the greatest imaginative writer who ever lived, it is because, beyond all others, he has written in the spirit of kindness, and not denied his own personal complicity with his art.

As for the scope of his work, it would not be easy to measure it, for it seems to include all motives and actions, in good and bad, in high and low, and not to leave life untouched at any point as it shows itself in his vast Russian world. Its chief themes are the old themes of art always – they are love, passion, death, but they are treated with such a sincerity, such a simplicity, that they seem almost new to art, and as effectively his as if they had not been touched before . . .

He comes nearer unriddling life for us than any other writer. He persuades us that it cannot possibly give us any personal happiness; that there is no room for the selfish joy of anyone except as it displaces the joy of some other, but that for unselfish joy there is infinite place and occasion. With the same key he unlocks the mystery of death; and he imagines so strenuously that death is neither more nor less than a transport of self-surrender that he convinces the reason where there can be no proof. The reader will not have forgotten how in those last moments of earth which he has depicted, it is this utter giving up which is made to appear the first moment of heaven. Nothing in his mastery is so wonderful as his power upon us in the scenes of the borderland where his vision seems to pierce the confines of another world.

None of the above opinions, however, goes more clearly and deeply to the heart of the matter than what Vita Sackville-West said in the *Nation* at the time of the centenary of his birth. She says:

How organic in growth is *Anna Karenina*! How naturally does one episode branch out of another episode! What a sense of continuity and naturalness are we given! and this in spite of the author, as it were; in spite of the difficulty he has created for himself by running two parallel stories in the same book; and if we say this about *Anna*, what are we to say of that stupendous and complicated *tour de force*, *War and Peace*? We say all this, and remain amazed. Still, the question persists – how is it done?

The whole secret of Tolstoy's supremacy as a novelist lies in one word: intensity. Whatever he felt, saw, undertook, or recorded, he experienced with a maximum of intensity difficult for an English mind (perhaps for any non-Russian mind) to appreciate. It was an intensity which he did not reserve for his fiction only; it was the very essence of the whole man, whether he cut a cockerel out of a railway ticket, denounced the doctrines of the Orthodox Church, made boots, started a school on highly original lines for peasants, scythed a meadow, demolished Shakespeare, played at 'Numidian Cavalry' with the children, or tore himself away from his home and his family. Nature had squandered on Tolstoy enough material to make half a dozen equipped men. To everything he brought the same vigour, and does not appear to have been more interested in literature than in anything else. 'I saw clearly,' he said, 'that art is only the ornament and charm of life.' We are left therefore with the impression of a man who, although the greatest of novelists, used fiction as but one outlet amongst many for his energy; but who at the same time must write fiction as though it were as important as life itself . . .

Again, although he is always preoccupied with large and serious ideas, his concentration on reality is such that we never get lost in a fog. We are never disconcerted even by an unfamiliar harmony, as in Chekhov; or confused and battered by the convulsions of the soul as in Dostoevski. Tolstoy, for all his extreme sensitiveness, is never 'difficult'. *War and Peace*, complicated though it is, is not difficult in the sense that *The Possessed* or *The Brothers Karamasov* is difficult. Essentially robust, of all the great Russians, Tolstoy is the least neurotic.

Nevertheless, his method keeps him walking always on a tight rope. Had his intensity failed him for a moment, he must have fallen. It is only by the strength of his own persuasion that we are persuaded . . . What other novelist would dare to take such liberties with his art? It is Tolstoy's own superb and wanton insolence, justifiable only by the measure of its success; but thanks to that peculiar quality of his genius – his intensity – its success is always beyond question. A novel? Nonsense! Literature? A fig for literature! This is life. And when was life neat, congruous, rounded-off? . . . In the hands of a lesser man, following his method, characters would turn to photographic plates, and incidents to careful records; in Tolstoy's hands, the figures of men and women grow into the round; they pulsate with actual arteries; are furnished with the apparatus of digestion; suffer, joke, and die. It is the life-principle at work. To write like Tolstoy, it is necessary to be Tolstoy all through. It is the element which makes his genius the least baffling, but at the same time the most inimitable.

Tolstoy of the later phase, the last three decades, with which the second volume of this work will deal, differed from the Tolstoy of the first fifty years; but the later Tolstoy grew out of the earlier as the branches of a tree grow from its roots.

The difference lay chiefly in this: that from about the year 1878 Tolstoy became sure of himself, succeeded in formulating his outlook on life, and proceeded to examine and pass judgement on all the main phases of human thought and activity. His work was sometimes hasty and often harsh; he painted, in black and white, subjects really composed of many shades of colours; but what other man has even attempted so to examine, to portray, and to tell the frank truth about, so many great problems?

No one truly concerned to leave the world better than he found it – be his line of work what it may – can afford to ignore what Tolstoy has said on his subject.

No such combination of intellectual and artistic force during the last century provoked the attention of mankind. No one so stimulated thought, or so successfully challenged established opinions. Tolstoy altered the outlook on life of many men in many lands, and caused some to alter not their ideas merely but the settled habits and customs of their lives. Only those who neither know nor understand him can question his sincerity.

Those who have spoken scornfully of him are people who have not taken the trouble to understand him, or who felt themselves convicted by what he said. On the other hand, the small minority who swallowed his opinions whole, did so under the hypnotic influence of his force, fervour, and genius. To analyse his opinions and disentangle what in them is true from what is false, is a task that has not been adequately performed, but for which the time is ripe, and which, bold as the undertaking may be, it is a duty to attempt.

Tolstoy's marvellous artistic power, his sincerity, and the love that is so strong a feature of his work, have often been dwelt upon; but what really gives him his supreme importance as a literary force is the *union* of these three things, with a quite extraordinary intellectual force.

It is not given to any man to solve all the problems of life, but no one has made so bold and interesting an attempt to do so as Tolstoy, or striven so hard to make his solutions plain to every child of man.

PART TWO

THE LATER YEARS

I

The Transition Stage

*The Diary of Tolstoy's Wife** was published too late for use in Part One of this *Life*. To some extent it modifies the impression given by others who have described the first sixteen or eighteen years of their marriage as exceptionally happy. Her Diary makes it plain that at least the seeds of the later differences existed from the first.

It is true that the Countess, as she herself remarks, 'used to write it when depressed', and she repeatedly refers to her happiness:

> It is funny to read my own diary. What contradictions, what an unfortunate woman I seem to be! Yet is there anyone more fortunate than I? Do any happier and more harmonious marriages exist? Sometimes alone in my room, I laugh with joy and cross myself: God grant it may long, long remain thus! It is always when we quarrel that I write my diary. There are still days when we sometimes quarrel, but the quarrels result from such delicate psychological causes that if we did not love one another we should not quarrel. I shall soon have been married six years and I love him more and more. He often says that this is not love, but that we have so grown together that we cannot live apart. But I still love him in the same restless, passionate, jealous and romantic way, and his tranquillity sometimes angers me.

There are many entries to set against the cheerful ones, but it is plain that they loved one another intensely, though the Countess found it hard to adapt herself to her husband's way of life on the lonely country estate, with his often absorbing literary work, and she was greatly upset if he left home even for a couple of days. She was exacting, exceedingly jealous without cause, and wished to monopolise Tolstoy's attention.

---

* *Diary of Tolstoy's Wife*, 1861–91, Victor Gollancz Ltd, London, 1928. The citations here given are, however, from the Russian.

With all this, she was devoted to her husband and to his interests as she understood them, and was the devoted mother of a rapidly increasing family. He was often so absorbed in his farming and in his literary work that she felt herself neglected, and on at least one occasion during the first years of their marriage Tolstoy's tenacious adherence to his opinions caused him to act harshly. It should be remembered that there is only the wife's account of the incident to judge by, and we know that she often wrote to relieve her feelings and said more than she really meant. Her account of the incident is that when their eldest son was five weeks old her breasts were sore, and it became too painful for her to continue to nurse him. Tolstoy, who considered the feeding of children by their mothers a matter of enormous importance, wished her to persist in suckling the baby. He did not expressly demand it in words, but she felt his dissatisfaction, and on 3rd August 1863, noted in her diary:

> Had a talk with him and seem to be more at ease, just because what I suspected has proved true. It's monstrous not to nurse one's child – who denies it? But how is one to help physical incapacity? I feel instinctively that he is unjust to me. Why should he go on tormenting me again and again? I got angry . . . and just as he now wants to wipe me off the face of the earth because I am suffering and do not perform my duty, so I should like not to see him, since he does not suffer, but writes. This is another way I had not thought of in which husbands are dreadful. It even seems to me at this moment as if I did not love him. Can one love a fly that stings every moment? I can't put things right . . . What a weakness it is that he can't be patient for a short time till I recover! After all, I am suffering ten times more than he. I had to write this because I am angry.
>
> It has begun to rain, I am afraid he will catch cold. I am no longer angry – I love him. God protect him!

Under this (they read one another's diaries) Tolstoy wrote:

> Sónya, forgive me, only now do I realise that I am to blame, and how much to blame. There are days when one seems to live not by one's own will, but to be subjected to some irresistible external law. That is how I, actually I, have been during these days in respect to you. I had always thought that though I have many defects, there was a one-tenth part of feeling and magnanimity in me. I have been harsh and

cruel, and to whom? To the one being who has given me the greatest happiness of my life and who alone loves me! Sónya, I know that such things are not forgotten or forgiven, but I know and understand better than you do all my meanness. Sónya, my darling, I am to blame and I am horrid, but there is a fine man within me who sometimes falls asleep. Love him and don't reproach him. Sónya!

But he then ran a wavy line through it, and the wife writes:

Lëvochka wrote this, asking my forgiveness. But then he got angry about something and struck it all out. That was the time when I had terrible pains in my breasts and *could not* feed Serëzha, and that made him angry. Just as if I did not *want* to do what was my chief, my greatest desire. I deserved those few lines of tenderness and repentance·from him, but in another moment of irritation with me he struck them out and deprived me of them before I had read them.

What made Tolstoy angry and caused him to strike it out we do not know, and it is not safe to explain what happened in 1863 by what happened some thirty years later. Were I to judge by what I saw in the 1890s of the Countess's irritable criticisms of her husband when she was upset, I should assume that the provocation under which he erased his note was considerable. It was questions such as this: to what extent his wife's life and conduct should be subjected to 'principles' Tolstoy believed in, that eventually caused the breach between them. That, however, did not come till much later. In her Diary we have an unusually frank and emotional record, but it leaves us with no good reason to suppose that at this period Tolstoy and his wife were less happy than more ordinary couples usually are. Not many marriages – were the limelight turned on their more difficult moments – would stand scrutiny even as well as theirs; nor can the Countess's account be altogether relied on, for it is plain that she was too highly strung fully to control herself or her words.

In the account of her marriage, given in an article accompanying the Diary, what she says of the circumstances under which Tolstoy handed her his letter proposing marriage differs a little from her sister Tánya's account quoted in Part One of this *Life*. One's first inclination is to accept hers, but she wrote it half a century after the event and after passing through troubles which for a time unbalanced her mind. Tánya's account, moreover, is so circumstantial, and she and the song she sang were so closely concerned in the event, that we are almost compelled to accept her story in preference to the Countess's.

The wife's Diary begins on 8th October 1862, when she had been married a fortnight. The perusal of the diary of Tolstoy's bachelor life, which he had felt it his duty to hand to her before marriage, had greatly upset her, and she refers again and again to the effect it had on her. She was from the first excessively highly strung, sensitive, and lacking in balance. She wished to mould herself to suit her husband, but her strong personality rendered this impossible. Her first entry, on 8th October 1862, already speaks of her 'peculiar feeling of strength and love' when she saw her husband, but she adds:

> I never will and never can show what is going on in me. I have so much silly self-love that if I should see in him the least doubt or misunderstanding of me, all would be lost . . . But he is splendid – a dear! He is indignant at everything evil and can't endure it.

She was jealous of his interest in the peasants and in his school, from which after his marriage he soon had to transfer his attention. On 23rd November 1862 she writes:

> He disgusts me with his People, I feel that it is either I – I as representative of the family – or the People and his ardent love of them. This is egotism. Granted that it be so, I live for him, and by him, and expect the same from him, or else it is too narrow, too stifling, for me here: I ran away today because everybody and everything seemed disgusting. Auntie, and the students [the University students who taught in the school], and N. P. [a poor gentlewoman living there with Auntie Tatiána] – and the walls and life here, and I almost laughed with joy when I ran out of the house on the quiet and alone. L. was not repulsive to me, but I suddenly felt that he and I are on opposite sides, that is, that his People cannot engross me *entirely* as they do him, and that I cannot engross him entirely as he engrosses me . . . He looked gloomy. I nearly cried. He did not say anything to me. It is terrible to live with him – what if he again suddenly begins loving the People . . . I shall die, for he loves me as he loved his school, nature, and the People – perhaps also his literature – a little of everything and then something new.

On 16th December 1862:

I think I'll put an end to myself someday from jealousy. 'More in love than ever' [words from Tolstoy's pre-marriage diary, relating to Aksínya, who is here referred to]. And she – nothing but a peasant woman, thickset and fair, it is awful! I looked eagerly at a dagger and a gun. One blow – it's easy – while I have no baby. And she is here, only a few steps away. I am simply beside myself. I'll go for a drive. I may see her directly. So that's how he loved her! I could burn his diary and his whole past.

Love is difficult, but I love so that it takes away my breath; I'd give my life, my soul, to prevent its ceasing on either side. The world I live in would be close and small but for him. Yet it is impossible to unite our two little worlds into one. He is so clever, active, and gifted, and then there is that long awful past of his, while mine is so short and insignificant.

At times she reproaches herself for offences of which we have no record – probably caprice or cantankerousness – thus on 9th January 1863:

Never in my life have I been so miserable from a consciousness of guilt. I never imagined that I could be so guilty. I am so unhappy that tears choke me all day. I am afraid to speak to him or look at him. Never has he been so dear and precious to me and I have never seemed to myself so insignificant and hateful. He is not angry, he still loves me, and his expression is so gentle and holy. One might die of joy and humility with such a man. I am feeling very ill. A moral cause makes me physically ill. I was in such pain that I thought I should have a miscarriage. I was like one mad. I prayed all day long, as if that would lessen my guilt, or as if in that way I could undo what I have done . . . Yesterday I was in a mood to be capricious. I have never been so to such a degree before. Can it be that I have such a disgusting character, or is it my wretched nerves and pregnancy? Never mind, it is best so, because I know now that I shall *guard our happiness* if I have not entirely ruined it already. It is awful. It might be so joyful and good. He is well now; oh, what have I done!

11th January 1863:

My jealousy is an innate disease and perhaps it comes from the fact that, loving him, I love nothing else and have given myself entirely to him and can only be happy through him and with him. I fear losing him as old people, who cannot have another, fear losing an only child on whom their whole life depends . . . There are days – many of them – when I love him till it hurts. It is so today. It's always so when I feel guilty.

On 14th January 1863 she notes:

Happiness has come back to me . . . I live entirely in him and for him, but it is often hard when I feel that I am not *everything* to him, and that if I ceased to exist he would find consolation in something, because he has many resources in himself, while mine is a very poor nature . . .

17th January 1863:

I have just been in a bad temper, and angry that he should love everybody and everything while I want him to love only me. Now that I am by myself I have come to see that I have again been capricious; he is good, with his kindness and wealth of feeling. When one considers it, the source of my perversity, grief, and so on, is the selfish wish that he should live for, think for, and love, only me . . . my misfortune is jealousy.

There are often gaps of months between one entry and another in the Diary, and there are plenty of indications that her life was, in general, a happy one during these first years, and that the situation was not much misrepresented by those friends and relations who at the time described the Tolstoys as a singularly happy couple, which was Tolstoy's own view of the matter, though he must have been aware that his wife did not always feel tranquil or content and was not always at one with him.

On 26th March 1863 she writes:

I am always in a hurry to tell him what worries or vexes me, but sometimes I'm afraid I'm spoilt. Lëva gives me too much happiness. I love his gaiety, his spirit, his kind, kind face, his meekness, and when he is vexed it is all so well expressed that he *hardly* ever hurts one's feelings.

On 22nd September 1863 an entry occurs that seems strange when one remembers that already in his Caucasus stories and in *Sevastopol* Tolstoy had expressed a consciousness of the evil of war, and in *War and Peace* (though accepting it as an inevitable catastrophe) had stripped it of all romance, and especially that in later life he was the most outstanding of peace advocates. Yet he now thought of re-entering the army! A letter to Fet has already been quoted, in which he says: 'What do you think of this Polish business? [the insurrection of 1863]. It looks bad! Shall not we – you and I and Borísóv – have to take our swords down from their rusty nails?' The corresponding entry in his wife's diary, on the eve of the first anniversary of their marriage, reads:

It will be a year tomorrow. Expectations of happiness then, now of unhappiness. Till now I thought it a joke, but I see it is almost a fact. To the war! How strange! He's out of his mind. No, that's wrong – merely inconsistent! I don't know whether it is consciously or unconsciously that he seems to try with all his might to arrange our life so that I should be thoroughly unhappy. He has put me in such a position that I have to live continually thinking that tomorrow, if not today, I may be left with a child, perhaps with two, and without a husband . . . Everything is a joke to him, a momentary fancy! Marries one day, is pleased, produces children, next day wants to go to the war and abandon them. I ought to hope now that my child will die, for I shall never survive him. I don't believe in this love of the fatherland, this enthusiasm at thirty-five. Are not children the fatherland too, are they not also Russians? – Abandon them because it is pleasant to gallop on horseback, enjoy the glory of war, and hear bullets whistle! . . . Why did I marry him? . . . There is no war yet, he is still here. So much the worse for me, having to wait and suffer – if only something were settled! But I love him, that is the chief trouble. When I look at him and see him sad, it breaks my heart.

The Polish insurrection was crushed without Tolstoy having to join the army, but the incident is a reminder of the many-sidedness of his nature, in which a deep-seated patriotism dwelt at strife with the pacifism that eventually overwhelmed it.

The fluctuating character of the relations between Tolstoy and his wife are indicated by an entry in his own diary, on 4th October 1863, after he had expressed some censure of her: 'All *that* has passed and is untrue. I am happy with her, but exceedingly dissatisfied with myself.'

On 19th December 1863 the Countess notes:

At this moment I should like to go to a dance or to some kind of amusement. Later on I shall be vexed with myself, but I can't help this humour. It annoys me that Leo cares little, and does not even feel and understand, how much I love him; and for that I should like to pay him out! He is old and too preoccupied, while today I feel so full of youth that I want to do something crazy. Instead of going to bed I'd like to turn somersaults. But with whom?

On 16th September 1864 Tolstoy wrote in his diary:

It is nearly a year since I wrote in this book and it has been a good year. My relations with Sónya have established themselves and become durable. We love, that is, are dearer to one another than any other people in the world, and we see one another clearly. We have no secrets and nothing to be ashamed of . . .

On 15th March 1865 the Countess writes:

We are on very good terms, and I am again quite at ease with him and do not doubt his love, nor feel jealous, nor anything like that . . . Sometimes he tells me about his literary thoughts and plans, and that always makes me awfully glad. I always understand him. But what does it lead to? I shall not write them.

On 3rd May 1865 the Countess even expressed jealousy of her sister Tánya, of whom in general she was very fond, and who was in fact on the eve of becoming engaged to Tolstoy's brother, Sergéy.

I have been quarrelling with Leo, am spiteful, and not amiable, but will improve. The children are ill. I am angry with Tánya, she worms herself too much into Lëvochka's life: they go to Nikólskoe, shooting, riding, or on foot. Yesterday jealousy broke out for the first time. Today I feel it painfully. I lend her my horse and think it is kind of me to do so; I am always too partial to myself. They've gone shooting in the woods alone. Heaven knows what thoughts come into my head.

19th June 1866:

We have a new manager. His wife is young and pretty – a Nihilist. She and Leo have long and animated conversations about literature and convictions, in general conversations that are long and out of place – painful to me and flattering to her. He used to preach that an outsider, especially a handsome young person, should not be admitted into the family circle, and he is himself the first to do it.

After some more entries of the same kind during the next six weeks, she writes on 10th August: 'My jealousy of M. I. (the manager's wife) has weakened very much and was almost unfounded. Everything is well and natural, except for a coldness in the relations between Leo and myself.'

On 12th November 1866, when Tolstoy was in Moscow, she writes:

When I do not write in my diary for a long time, I am always sorry that I do not write about my happy times . . . It seems so sad and empty without Lëvochka. I think no one could be more spiritually intimate than he and I are. We are awfully happy in everything – in our own mutual relations, in our children, and in our life generally . . .

Every day now – today as well – I am copying Leo's novel [*War and Peace*] (without reading it previously). This is a great pleasure for me. Mentally I live through a whole world of impressions and thoughts while copying it. Nothing affects me so much as his ideas and his talent, and this has begun quite recently. Whether I have changed or the novel is really very good, I don't know . . . We have often talked about the novel, and for some reason he has great faith in and listens to my criticisms, which makes me proud.

In 1872, without any more precise date, she notes:

The winter has been a happy one. We have again lived heart to heart, and Lëvochka's health has not been bad.

As we draw nearer to the period of what for convenience' sake may be called Tolstoy's 'Conversion' we find repeated indications of the change that showed itself in him, and which the Countess did not at all understand.

12th October 1875:

It hurts me, I cannot endure to see him as he is now – gloomy, letting himself go, sitting unoccupied, without work, without energy or pleasure, for days and weeks, as if he had reconciled himself to that condition. It is a sort of mental death, and I don't want it for him, and he himself can't live like that for long. Maybe my opinion is trivial and wrong, but it seems to me that the setting of our life – the setting he himself created, for to me it is burdensome – the awful loneliness and monotony of our life, contributes to this mutual apathy of ours. When I think of the future when the children are grown up, of their lives, of the different requirements they will have, of their having all to be educated, and then think of Lëvochka, I see that he with his apathy and indifference will not be a help to me, he cannot put his heart into anything, and the whole moral responsibility, all the sufferings and failures of the children, will fall on me, but *how* can I bear it all alone and help the children, especially with the pain of seeing that everything in Lëvochka has died down and that nothing can revive it?

Later entries, though still written chiefly when the Countess was upset, continue generally to confirm the impression of a happy family life.

1st November 1878:

I went to Túla with D. A., Serëzha, and Tánya [a visitor and the two eldest children] . . . We bought material for Tánya's winter coat . . . Lëvochka was working at home and came out to meet us. When returning it is such a joy to see his grey overcoat in the distance . . . We finished *Les trois mousquetaires* [Dumas's novel, which the family were reading aloud in French] with much interest this evening. Lëvochka sat long at the piano improvising. He has a gift for that too.

24th November 1878:

All is gloomy in my soul. Terrible jealous thoughts and suspicions about Lëvochka pass through my mind. Sometimes I feel this to be a kind of madness, and whisper: 'Lord, help me!' Yes, I should go mad were anything like that to happen.

Meanwhile, almost unrealised by his wife, a great change had come over Tolstoy's view of life, and having reached a fresh understanding of it he felt, he tells us, as though while walking from home he had suddenly understood that the errand he had started on was unnecessary, and had turned back. All that had formerly been on his right hand now appeared on his left, and all that had been on his left was now on his right. What he had desired – honour, riches, and self-aggrandisement – now seemed evil, while poverty, humility, self-sacrifice, and the service of others seemed good.

Those who have followed his earlier career will find it hard to detect the external signs of so great and sudden a change. The stories and novels he had previously written foreshadowed the views he now preached, and his work in the schools at Yásnaya had pointed much in the same direction. No sudden break was apparent in his external life: what followed evolved from what had gone before, so that it is less natural to speak of his crossing the Rubicon than of his gradual ascent of a mountain.

His works however clearly indicate that at this time a profound change did occur. His stories written before his *Confession* are works of observation. He had watched life and noticed the workings of his own mind with marvellous clearness, and remembered it all to the smallest details with extraordinary accuracy. Those earlier stories almost always centred in himself. Nikólenka Irtényev in *Youth*; Nekhlyúdov in *A Landlord's Morning*, *A Billiard Marker's Memoirs*, and *Lucerne*; Olénin in *The Cossacks*; Pierre and to some extent Prince Andrew in *War and Peace*, as well as Lévin in *Anna Karénina*, were all to a large extent Tolstoy himself. He had not felt sufficiently sure about things, nor had he possessed any sufficiently clear chart of life, to abandon the coast-lines familiar to him and steer right out into the ocean. But after he had found or framed his religion and drawn his map of life – after what we call his Conversion – he wrote differently. Much of his work then became professedly didactic, and merely incidentally artistic; and even the stories, novels, and plays he produced, from *Iván Ilytch* to *Resurrection*, differ from his previous ones. They were no longer self-centred works of observation, but rather studies illustrating the operation of certain moral forces. He had lost none of his artistic power of causing his readers to share his feelings, his technical cunning remained undiminished, and his work remained marvellously true to life – but its centre of gravity had shifted.

This change does not show itself in the fragments of *The Decembrists*, which he wrote a little before 1878 (his second and third attempts at that abortive novel), nor in the fragmentary *First Recollections*, from which I have quoted freely and which was written about this time.

His *Confession*, also written at about this period, was not finally completed till later, but as it narrates his mental struggles in the years 1874–8, I have already dealt with it in my first volume.

In the spring of 1878 he read Renan's *Life of Jesus*, and what he wrote about it to his friend N. N. Strákhov, who had given him the book, throws light on his own attitude towards the study that was to be his chief occupation during the next few years:

Today I fasted, and read the Gospels and Renan's *Life of Jesus*. I read it through, and wondered at you [who admired it] all the time I was reading . . . If Renan has any thoughts of his own, they are the two following: (1) that Christ did not know *l'évolution et le progrès*, and in this respect Renan tries to correct him and criticises him from the height of that conception . . . Buf if Christian truth is high and deep it is so only because it is subjectively absolute . . . (2) Renan's other new thought is that as Christian teaching exists there must have been a man of some kind behind it, and this man certainly sweated and obeyed nature's calls. For us, all human demeaning realistic details have vanished from the life of Jesus for the same reason that all details about all Jews and others who ever lived have vanished, as all vanishes that is not eternal. In other words, the sand that was not wanted has been washed away by an unalterable law and the gold has remained . . . It may be that to know a plant one has to know its surroundings, or even that to know man as a political animal one must know his surroundings and growth and development, but to understand beauty, truth, and goodness, no study of surroundings will help or has anything in common with the matter under consideration. In the one case things go along a level; in the other they go in quite a different direction: up and down. Moral truth may and can be studied, nor is there any end to its study, but as carried on by religious people it goes deep, while this study of Renan's is merely a childish, trivial, and mean prank.

In other words, Tolstoy then considered that in the Gospels we can find absolute truth, and that to understand them it is not necessary to undertake any minute study of the conditions of time and place in which Jesus lived. We shall see later on how this view affected his own work.

That summer he again began to keep a Diary, after having discontinued it for nearly thirteen years, and the very first entry, on 22nd May 1878, relates to the religious questions that now filled his mind.

I went to Mass on Sunday and could find a meaning that satisfied me in the whole service, except that 'vanquish his enemies' is blasphemy. A Christian should pray for his enemies, not against them.

On 5th June follows an entry which shows the closeness of his observation of Nature:

A hot midday. 2 o'clock. I walk in the rich high meadow-grass. Quiet, and sweet and strong scent of St John's wort and clover surrounds me and intoxicates. In the hollow towards the wood the grass is yet higher and the same intoxication reigns, the paths in the wood smell like a conservatory.

Immense plane leaves. By the cut timber a bee gathers honey from a cluster of yellow flowers one after another. From the thirteenth, humming, it flies away full.

That day Tólstoy caught a bad cold, and was ill for a week. Then he went to Samára, taking the two elder boys with him. The Countess with the daughters and the younger children joined him there later in the summer. In a letter written while going down the Volga he says:

I am again writing on board the same steamer. The children are well and asleep and have been good. It is ten o'clock at night, and tomorrow at four, all being well, we shall be at Samára and shall reach the farm by evening. Today has again passed quietly, peacefully, and pleasantly. I was interested in a talk with some Priestless Old Believers from Vyátsk Province, peasants and tradesmen – very simple, wise, decent and serious folk. We had an excellent talk about Faith.

Further light is thrown on his transitional state of mind by an account given by V. I. Alexéev of his first acquaintance with Tolstoy:

I was literally starving. Through some acquaintances a place as tutor at Count Tolstoy's was offered me. I was so frightened by the Count's title that at first I declined. But they persuaded me, and I set out for Yásnaya Polyána and settled in a peasant's hut in the village. I used to go to Leo Nikoláevich's* house to give lessons. Subsequently I moved into a detached wing of his house. From the very first his affability overcame my fears, and very friendly relations were established between us. Leo Nikoláevich was then still sincerely Orthodox. I myself was at that time an atheist, and also frank and sincere about it. It seemed to me that one chief motive of his Orthodoxy was his fondness for the peasants and his wish to share in the life of the people, to study it, to understand it, and to help them. Nevertheless, when talking to him I frequently expressed surprise

* This use of Christian name and patronymic (instead of surname) is the usual, polite Russian fashion.

that with his culture, intellect and sincerity he could go to church, pray, and observe the Church rites. I remember a conversation one clear and frosty day in the sitting-room of his house at Yásnaya. He was sitting opposite a window which through the frosty tracery admitted the slanting rays of the setting sun. After hearing me, he remarked: 'Look now at that tracery lit up by the sun. We only see the sun's reflection in it, but yet we know that beyond it, somewhere afar, is the real sun, the source of light that produces the picture we see. The people see that reflection in religion, but I look further and see – or at least know – that there exists a very source of light. That difference in our relation to the facts does not prevent our communion; we both look at this reflection of the sun, only our reason penetrates it to different depths.'

I noticed however that from time to time a dissatisfied feeling crept into his soul. Once on returning from church he said to me: 'No, I can't do it! It oppresses me. I stand among them, and hear their fingers tap against their sheepskin coats as they make the sign of the cross, and at the very same time I hear them, both men and women, whispering about the most everyday affairs having no connection with the service. Their talk on village matters, and the women's gossip, whispered to one another at the most solemn moments of the service, show that their relation to it is one of complete unconsciousness.'

Of course I treated with all possible delicacy the process going on in him, and only expressed my opinions frankly when he questioned me.

Sometimes we started a conversation on economic and social themes. I had a copy of the Gospels, left from the days of my Socialist propaganda among the people. Passages relating to social questions were underlined in it, and I often pointed these out to Leo Nikoláevich. The ferment constantly going on in him gave him no peace and at last brought on a crisis.

We have mention of the days when Tolstoy was approaching this crisis and writing his *Confession*, in a letter from his wife to her sister Tatiána Kuzmínski:

8th November 1878:
Lëvochka has now quite settled down to his writing. His eyes are fixed and strange, he hardly talks at all, has quite ceased to belong to this world, and is positively incapable of thinking about everyday matters.

Many indications are given in other letters of the fact that the strain of mental and spiritual effort was affecting his health. For instance, on 16th February [1879] he wrote to Fet:

I am still poorly, dear Afanási Afanásyevich, and so did not at once reply to your letter enclosing the excellent poem. This one is quite beautiful. Should it ever be broken and fall to pieces, and only the fragment *Too many Tears* be found, people will place that in a museum and use it as a model.

I am neither ill nor well, but the mental and spiritual vigour I need are lacking. Not as in your case! The tree is dry!

On 5th March the Countess again wrote to her sister:

Lëvochka reads, reads, reads . . . writes very little, but sometimes says: 'Now it is clearing up,' or, 'Ah, God willing, what I am going to write will be very important!'

On 17th April Tolstoy wrote again to Fet:

There is a prayer which says: 'Not according to our merits, but according to Thy mercy.' So, I to you. I have received your long and good letter. I will certainly soon go to Kiev and come to Vorobëvka [Fet's place] and will then tell you everything; for the present I will only reply to your fears.

Heaven knows where my *Decembrists* are now. I do not think about them, and were I to do so and to write, I flatter myself that my breath alone, of which the story would smell, would be unendurable to those who shoot men for the good of humanity . . . But I should mention that even now [the war with Turkey was just over] I conscientiously abstain from reading the newspapers and consider it a duty to wean everyone from that pernicious practice . . . An elderly and good man sits in Vorobëvka, and after melting two or three pages of Schopenhauer in his brain and pouring them out again in Russian, he plays a game of billiards, shoots some woodcock, admires the colts out of Zakrása [a mare], and sits with his wife drinking excellent tea, smoking a cigar, loving everyone and loved by all; when suddenly a stinking, damp sheet of paper is brought, nasty to handle and harmful to the eyes, and it at once evokes in his heart angry condemnation and a feeling of estrangement: the feeling that 'I love nobody and nobody loves me', and then he begins to talk and talk, and gets angry and suffers. One should give it up! Then things would go much better.

On 25th May he wrote apologising for having postponed his promised visit to Fet. The delay he says was caused by the boys' examinations:

> . . . Another cause has been the beautiful spring. It is long since I so enjoyed God's world as I have done this year. One stands open-mouthed, delighting in it and fearing to move lest one should miss anything . . . My wife has gone to Túla with the children, and I am reading good books and shall presently go for a three or four hours' walk.

In June he at last set out for Kiev, which with its great catacomb-Monastery was one of the chief places of pilgrimage in Russia. Thousands flocked there every year seeking spiritual nourishment. Of Tolstoy's interest in such pilgrims we get a glimpse in a letter from Strákhov to Danílevski, the writer, which also shows that Tolstoy had by that time shaken off his indisposition:

> I found Tolstoy in excellent spirits this time. With what vivacity he is carried away by his ideas! Only young people seek truth as ardently as he, and I can say positively that he is now in the very prime of his strength. He has abandoned all his plans and is writing nothing, but works tremendously. One day he took me with him and showed me one of the things that occupy him. He walks to the high-road (a quarter of a mile from his house), and there at once finds men and women pilgrims. With them he starts conversation, and if he chances upon good specimens and is himself in good form he hears wonderful tales. About a mile and a half away lies a small hamlet in which are two rest-houses for pilgrims . . . We entered one of them. Some eight people were there – old men and women supping, praying, or resting – doing whatever they liked. There is always someone talking, narrating, or explaining, and it is very interesting to listen. Besides the religious side, to which he is much devoted (he observes the fasts and goes to church on Sundays), Tolstoy is also concerned with the language. He has come to appreciate the beauty of our folk-language wonderfully. Every day he discovers new words and expressions, and every day he denounces our literary language more and more, calling it not Russian but Spanish. All this, I am convinced, will yield rich fruit . . .

His journey to Kiev was not a success. In a letter to his wife from thence he writes on 14th June:

All morning, till three o'clock, I went about among the churches, catacombs, and monks, and am very dissatisfied with my expedition. It was not worth coming. At seven o'clock I went to the Monastery to see Anthony, the *Skímnik* [a monk of the strictest Order], and got little from him that was of any use.

Tolstoy was equally disappointed next day and did not remain long in the holy city, which has earned the reputation of being one of the most dissolute in Europe.

On his way home he paid his promised visit to Fet, and after reaching Yásnaya wrote to him, on 13th July:

Do not be vexed with me, dear Afanási Afanásyevich, for not writing to thank you for the pleasant day I spent at your place, and for not answering your last letter. It is probably true that I was out of spirits while with you (forgive me for it) and I am still not in good spirits. I am ever capricious, tormenting myself, troubled, correcting myself, and learning; and I wonder whether, like V. P. Bótkin, I shall not 'fill up a gap' and then die [Bótkin, conscious of a gap in his erudition, read up the history of India just before his death]; but still I cannot refrain from turning myself inside out.

We still have measles in the house. It has picked out half the children already, and we are expecting the rest to take it.

On 28th July he wrote again:

Thank you for your last kind letter, dear Afanási Afanásyevich, and for the apologue about the hawk, which pleases me, but which I should like more fully explained. If I am that hawk, and if, as indicated by what follows, my too distant flights mean that I reject real life, then I must justify myself. I reject neither real life nor the labour necessary for its maintenance, but it seems to me that the greater part of my life and yours is taken up with satisfying wants which are not natural but have been invented by us, or artificially inoculated by our education, and have become habitual, and that nine-tenths of the work we devote to satisfying these demands is idle work. I should very much like to be firmly convinced that I give people more than I take from them, but as I feel myself much disposed to value my own work high and other people's work low, I do not hope by simply intensifying my labour and choosing what is most difficult, to assure myself that their account with me does not land them in a loss (I am sure to tell myself that the work I like is the most necessary and difficult). Therefore I wish to take as little from others as possible, and to work as much as possible for the satisfaction of my own needs, and I think this is the easiest way to avoid making a mistake.

The next letter, of 31st August 1879, was less argumentative:

DEAR AFANÁSI AFANÁSYEVICH – Of course I am again to blame towards you, but of course not from lack of love for you or remembrance of you. Strákhov and I had in fact been talking about you and judging and disposing of you as we all judge one another, and as God grant others may judge me. Strákhov was highly pleased with his visit to you and yet more so with your translation [of Schopenhauer].

I have successfully recommended to you *The Arabian Nights* and Pascal; the one and the other, I will not say pleased but suited you. I now have a book to offer you which no one has yet read and which I read the other day for the first time, and continue to read with exclamations of delight. I hope it will be to your taste, especially as it has much in common with Schopenhauer: it is the *Proverbs* of Solomon, *Ecclesiastes*, and the *Book of Wisdom*. It would be difficult to find anything more modern, but if you read it, read it in Slavonic. I have a new Russian translation which is very bad. The English version is also bad. If you had the Greek, you would see what it is like . . .

Since Strákhov's visit we have had guests one after the other, private theatricals and all the devils let loose. Thirty-four sheets in use for the guests and thirty people at dinner, and all went off well, and all – including myself – were gay.

The following brief notes occur in his Diary, dated 28th October:

There are worldly people, heavy and wingless. Their sphere is down below. There are strong ones among them: Napoleon. They leave terrible traces among men and cause an uproar, but it is all on the earth. There are those whose wings grow equably and who slowly rise and fly: monks. There are light people, winged, who rise easily from among the crowd and again descend: good idealists. There are strong-winged ones who, drawn by carnal desires descend among the crowd and break their wings. Such am I. Then they struggle with broken wings, flutter strongly, and fall. If my wings heal I will fly high. God grant it . . .

There are those who have heavenly wings, and purposely – from love to men – descend to earth (folding their wings) and teach men to fly. When they are no more needed they fly away: Christ.

During this period of storm and stress in Tolstoy's soul one comes again and again on signs of change and growth and altered habits. Up to this time he had submitted to the Church, and even when his doctor advised him on grounds of health not to observe the Fasts, instead of deciding the matter for himself he went to the Troítsa Monastery of St Sergius (forty-four miles north of Moscow) to consult, and obtain permission from, the famous monk, Leoníd. A little later the Church's hold on him had so weakened that he entirely abandoned fasting. V. I. Alexéev tells the story as follows:

The Countess, like her husband, observed the Fasts, and made the children do so. When she noticed that her husband was wavering she increased the strictness of the Fast, so that everyone in the house fasted except the French tutor, M. Nief, and myself. I told the Countess that though I did not fast, I could eat anything that was served up, but she always ordered meat to be cooked for us two tutors. And so one day fast-food was handed to everyone else, and some nice cutlets were served for us. We helped ourselves and the footman left the dish on the window-sill. Then Leo Nikoláevich, turning to his son, said: 'Ilúsha [Ilyá, the second son], give me a cutlet.' The lad brought it and Leo Nikoláevich ate the meat with a good appetite, and gave up fasting from that day forth.

Before the end of the year Tolstoy had definitely concluded that it was impossible to reconcile the demands of the Church with the demands of his own reason and conscience.

In November the Countess wrote to her sister:

Lëvochka is always working, as he expresses it, but alas! he is writing some sort of religious polemic. He reads and thinks till his head aches, and all to prove that the Church is not in accord with the teaching of the Gospel. Hardly ten people in Russia will be interested in it, but there is nothing to be done. I only wish he would get it done quicker, and that it would pass like an illness! No one on earth can control him or impose this or that mental work upon him, it is not even in his own power to do so.

His wife's letters as well as her Diary give us a glimpse of the trouble sure to occur from the close union of two people of strong individuality, one of whom changes his outlook on life and wishes to change his way of life accordingly. I once knew a lady who said that no man should change his opinions after he was married! The Countess Tolstoy must often have felt inclined to say something like that when she saw her husband consumed by a fervent devotion to conclusions not her own, and to which, since they went on continually evolving and developing, it was the more difficult for her to adjust herself.

She gave birth to a tenth child on 20th December 1879 – a boy, who was christened Michael. As three had died in infancy, there were now seven children in the family.

It has been mentioned that after their marriage the Tolstoys had not many visitors except relations; but with the growth of the younger generation this altered and Yásnaya Polyána began to swarm with young people. Tolstoy's change of outlook on life also made him more accessible to all sorts and conditions of men, though it caused him to reject some acquaintances whom almost anyone else would have been glad to know.

Prince D. Obolénski has recounted that Tolstoy allowed him to introduce friends without obtaining special permission to do so each time. On one occasion, however, to Obolénski's dismay, Tolstoy definitely avoided an introduction he was anxious to give, and this in reference to General Skóbelev – then at the height of his fame after the Turkish War and the capture of Plevna. A similar case occurred later, when Tolstoy refused the acquaintance of the painter, V. V. Vereshchágin. Light is thrown on his feelings towards these men by his references to them in the Preface to *Sevastopol*.* The passage in Vereshchágin's *Memoirs* where that artist mentions persuading General Stnúkov to hasten the hanging of two Turks that he might sketch the execution, aroused Tolstoy's profound indignation.

In December, Tolstoy received a letter from Turgénev, who wrote from Paris:

---

* Strictly speaking, it is a Preface to Ershóv's *Recollections of Sevastopol*, but it has been used in English as a Preface to Tolstoy's *Sevastopol*.

The Princess Paskévich, who has translated your *War and Peace*, has at last sent 500 copies here, of which I have received ten. I have given them to the most influential critics (Taine and About, among others) . . . The translation is somewhat feeble but has been done with zeal and love. A couple of days ago I read with real pleasure, for the fifth or sixth time, that truly great production of yours.

Tolstoy was by this time so absorbed in other concerns that the fate of the French translation of his novel seems to have interested him less than it did Turgénev; indeed it never was Tolstoy's way to trouble himself much about the fate of a book after it had once left his hands.

Turgénev, an ardent admirer of Púshkin, returned to Russia in 1880, to take part in the celebration of the eightieth anniversary of that poet's birth. Aware of Tolstoy's dislike of jubilees and public celebrations, the committee requested Turgénev to use his influence to persuade Tolstoy to be present at the unveiling of the Púshkin Monument in Moscow; and with this purpose Turgénev visited Yásnaya the week after Easter.

He was very cordially received. A woodcock-shooting expedition was arranged in his honour in the woods near by. In the dusk of the spring evening the Countess stood beside him awaiting the flight of the birds. While he was getting his gun ready, she asked him: 'Why have you not written anything for so long?' Turgénev glanced round, and in his touchingly frank way, with a guilty smile, said: 'Are we out of hearing? Well, I will tell you . . . Whenever I have planned anything it has been when I have been shaken by the fever of love! Now that is over: I am old and can no longer either love or write.'

To Tolstoy, also, Turgénev spoke of the change that had come over him – him to whom love-affairs had formed so large a part of the joy of life. 'I had an affair the other day,' said he, 'and, will you believe it, I found it dull!' 'Ah,' exclaimed Tolstoy, 'if only I were like that!' It was indeed a matter on which their views differed radically, and on which the younger man's struggle for self-mastery was still not fully achieved.

On returning to the house they found awaiting them Prince L. D. Urúsov, Vice-Governor of Túla, a cousin of Prince S. S. Urúsov previously mentioned. He was one of Tolstoy's most intimate friends and shared his outlook on life. Turgénev, too, was glad to see Urúsov, though the two seldom met without strenuous dispute.

Tolstoy's profoundly artistic nature again and again caused him to long to turn, and sometimes actually to turn, from didactic or philosophic work to the creation of works of art, and a little before this he had hit on the idea of writing short prose-poems. Having composed one he sent it, signed in the name of an old servant, to Aksákov's paper, *Rus*. The manuscript came back declined with thanks, on the ground that its author was 'not yet sufficiently expert in expression!' Resigning himself to his failure Tolstoy passed on the idea to Turgénev, and to it we owe the latter's *Poems in Prose*.

One of these, *The Dog*, he had brought with him, and after the shooting-party had returned to the house, he read it aloud. Its attitude towards death and to man and dog were not in tune with Tolstoy's or Urúsov's feelings: and, the reading ended, an awkward pause ensued. Soon, however, Urúsov and Turgénev were warmly discussing the need of a religious outlook on life. Turgénev sat at the head of the table, Tolstoy on his right hand and Urúsov on his left. The latter kept emphasising his remarks by vigorously pointing a forefinger at Turgénev, and gradually becoming increasingly animated, he balanced his chair more and more on its front legs, till it suddenly slipped from under him and he sprawled on his back on the floor, continuing to argue in that position, until a general roar of laughter compelled him to pause. Hastily resuming his seat, he then continued his contention as though nothing had occurred.

Next day Turgénev and Tolstoy went for a walk together, and apparently Turgénev took this opportunity to broach his mission. Tolstoy's admiration for Púshkin, whom he regarded as the foremost Russian writer, and the fact that this was the first time it had been permitted to pay public honour to the memory of a Russian man of letters, led Turgénev to assume that his host would surely agree to take part in the Jubilee. But to Tolstoy the feasting, the expense, the artificiality, and the fictitious enthusiasm accompanying such affairs, were profoundly repugnant, and he met the request with a definite refusal.

We have no account of what passed between the two men that day, but the Countess has recorded that:

The dinner-bell had sounded. All had assembled, but neither Turgénev nor Leo Nikoláevich appeared. At last, after long waiting, I guessed where to look for them. Not far from the house, in the wood among the old oaks, stood a small hut Leo Nikoláevich had built for himself in order, in summer, to have solitude for his work and to escape from flies, children, and visitors. I ran to that hut, which was built on four pillars, and ascended the steps, and through the open door saw the two writers hotly disputing.

No rupture of friendly relations occurred, but so great was Turgénev's dismay at Tolstoy's uncompromising refusal, that when, shortly afterwards, Dostoévski – the third of the trio of great Russian novelists then living – wished to visit Yásnaya and consulted Turgénev on the matter, the latter spoke of Tolstoy's mood in such a way that Dostoévski abandoned his intention; and he died a year later without having ever met Tolstoy, whose writings he had from the first so greatly admired and to whose *Anna Karénina* he had publicly referred as the most palpable proof Russia could offer to the Western world of her capacity to contribute something great to the solution of the problems confronting humanity.

From this time onward Turgénev, without ceasing to be interested in Tolstoy personally, and while continuing to praise him enthusiastically as a novelist, never missed an opportunity of expressing his distrust of, and regret concerning, those new interests which were so profoundly stirring the depths of Tolstoy's nature, and were destined to move the minds of men in many lands more profoundly than his novels had ever done. The power and importance of these the elder writer realised as little as a man suffering from colour-blindness realises the values in a picture. The same clash of feeling between those to whom Tolstoy's later work is important and those to whom it is not, shows itself continually. Generally those who condemn it have shown, as Turgénev did, a touch of contemptuous irritability which suggests that at the back of their minds there lurks a suspicion that to consider the purpose of man's life is, after all, more important than to enjoy the anaesthetics of art.

To Polónski, Turgénev wrote in December 1880: 'I am very sorry for Tolstoy . . . However, as the French say, *Chacun a sa manière de tuer ses puces*' [Everyone kills his fleas his own way]. A few months later he wrote:

It is an unpardonable sin that Leo Tolstoy has stopped writing – he is a man who could be extraordinarily useful, but what can one do with him? He does not utter a word, and worse than that he has plunged into mysticism. Such an artist, such first-class talent, we have never had, nor now have, among us. I, for instance, am considered an artist, but what am I worth compared to him? In contemporary European literature he has no equal. Whatever he takes up becomes alive under his pen. And how wide the sphere of his creative power – it is simply amazing! Whether he describes a whole historic epoch as in *War and Peace*, or a man of our day with high spiritual interests and aspirations, or simply a peasant with a purely Russian soul, he always remains a master. He depicts a lady of the higher circles and she is lifelike; and so is a semi-savage Circassian. See how he describes even an animal! . . . how, for instance, he depicts the mental condition of a horse! But what is one to do with him? He has plunged headlong into another sphere: has surrounded himself with Bibles and Gospels in nearly all languages, and has written a whole heap of papers. He has a trunk full of these mystical ethics and of various pseudo-interpretations. He read me some of it, which I simply do not understand . . . I told him, '*That* is not the real thing;' but he replied: 'It is just the real thing.' . . . Very probably he will give nothing more to literature, or if he re-appears it will be with that trunk . . . And he has followers: Gárshin, for instance, is undoubtedly one.

The mention in the above letter of Tolstoy's capacity to enter into the mind of a horse, recalls an event that occurred during one of Turgénev's visits to Yásnaya. Coming on an old worn-out horse grazing in a field, Tolstoy went up to it and stroked it and began to voice its thoughts and sad feelings so vividly and convincingly, that Turgénev at last exclaimed: 'I am sure, Leo Nikoláevich, you must once have been a horse yourself!'

*   *   *

The remark at the end of Tolstoy's *Confession*, to the effect that he was setting to work to disentangle the truth he found in the Church teaching from the falsehood, and that this would form the next part of his work, 'which if it be worth it, and if anyone wants it, will probably someday be printed somewhere', indicates the difficulty in which he now found himself with reference to the publication of his works. Books calling in question the bases of the Church faith had hardly a chance of being published in Russia. A capricious Censor might now and then happen to pass one such work, or some part of it, but the business was dangerous and uncertain and might easily involve all concerned not merely in material loss but also in serious danger. Tolstoy was working primarily to clear matters up for himself. He never had been accustomed to trouble himself much about the fate of his writings, and in later life he felt that that was not his business, and that his books would someday or other be sure to circulate. This faith saved him much worry, and enabled him to go on working under conditions in which another man's hands would have dropped.

For the present he put aside his almost completed *Confession*, and proceeded to write *A Criticism of Dogmatic Theology*, which was followed in turn by a voluminous *Union and Translation of the Four Gospels*, and a fourth book, *What I Believe* (called *My Religion* in some of the earlier, incorrect editions) – the whole series occupying him for several years almost to the exclusion of other work. All this involved a tremendous concentration of effort, and was done with no possibility of pecuniary profit, no apparent chance of publication in Russia, nor any definite plan for publication abroad. Were all other evidence lacking, this alone would prove both Tolstoy's sincerity and his sense of the importance of the matters with which he was dealing.

On 31st May 1880, we find him again apologising to Fet.

Before telling you how ashamed I am, and how I feel myself to blame towards you, let me first of all say that I am tremendously grateful to you, dear Afanási Afanásyevich, for your kind, admirable and, above all, wise letter. You had cause to be displeased with me, and instead of expressing the displeasure which might well exist, you have told me its cause good-naturedly, and above all in such a way that I feel you still care for me . . .

On 8th July he writes again to the same correspondent.

It is now summer and a charming summer, and as usual I go crazy with life and forget my work. This year I struggled long, but the beauty of the world conquered me. I enjoy life and do hardly anything else. Our house is full of visitors. The children have got up theatricals, and it is noisy and merry. I have with difficulty found a corner, and snatched a moment, to write you a word . . .

In August, Strákhov, again visiting Yásnaya, wrote to Danílevski:

At Yásnaya Polyána, as always, most strenuous mental work is going on . . . I am carried away and subdued by it so that it even oppresses me. Tolstoy, following his unalterable path, has reached a religious frame of mind, which partially found expression in the latter part of

Anna Karénina. He understands the Christian ideal wonderfully. It is strange how we pass the Gospels by without seeing their simplest meaning. He is now engrossed in studying their text, and he has explained much in it with striking simplicity and acuteness. I greatly fear that from lack of practice in the exposition of abstract thought . . . he will not succeed in expressing his arguments briefly and clearly, but the contents of the book he is composing are truly magnificent.

While working so hard at his books, Tolstoy did not abstain from rendering practical help to the peasantry around him. Arbúzov, in his *Recollections* of his master, tells of an event that occurred in this year, 1880:

The peasants who had been serfs of a neighbouring landlord, Khom- yakóv, happened to discover that their former owner had appropriated 175 acres of land that by right belonged to the village Commune. They applied to Tolstoy for assistance, and he took much trouble on their behalf and eventually enabled them to recover the land. Wishing to show their gratitude they reaped his hay and grain crops for him, intending not to charge anything for this service, but seeing that they had worked well, he paid them at more than the usual rate for the time they had given, and also treated them to a good dinner with plenty of vodka.

It was an immense advantage to the peasants of the district to have a man of education and influence to whom they could turn in time of trouble. Much of the help Tolstoy gave was of such an everyday nature that though it left its trace on the hearts and lives of those who received it, it is nowhere recorded, and now escapes observation.

It was always his practice to listen to and advise those who came to consult him; and some came every day. He wrote innumerable petitions, statements, and letters of introduction for them, and no doubt his inveterate dislike of law and jurisprudence largely grew out of experience of the extreme difficulty of obtaining elementary justice for the poor, ignorant, and oppressed peasants.

2

Theology and the Gospels

The problem before Tolstoy was that of separating what is true from what is false in the teachings of the Church and in the Bible.

He had learnt by experience that man needs guidance and requires a chart to enable him to steer his course through life, but he was too sincere to adopt a creed merely because he needed one, or to accept anything he saw no sufficient reason to believe. Other men have felt the need for religion as keenly as he, and not a few have shared his courage and truthfulness, but he alone, in recent times, combined this profoundly religious spirit and fearless truthfulness with a genius for literary expression which secured for his words the attention of the world. Owing moreover to the personal risk he ran, in Russia, his words became heroic deeds, causing the blood of those who heard them to flow faster in their veins.

He first carefully examined the dogmas of the Orthodox Russian Church as stated in the Creeds and in the Dogmatic Theology of Makarius, Metropolitan of Moscow. These, including as they do the doctrine of the Trinity, the miraculous birth of Christ, and the scheme of Redemption and Atonement, do not differ essentially from the dogmas of the Catholic or Protestant Churches.

The conclusion Tolstoy slowly and reluctantly reached was that they, and the whole theology in which they are embedded, are utterly false. The more he looked into the matter the more shocked was he at the levity with which the Churches have accepted conclusions based on evidence which, he says, will not stand the simplest tests of logic. He found it difficult to understand why the theologians say such strange things, and why they support their assertions by arguments that insult human intelligence. But he tells us that he gradually traced out the shallow verbal tricks by which their tenets are pieced together, and found himself driven to the conclusion that dogmatic theology is a fraud, which endures only because it is screened from exposure by the authority of the Church; and examining further what the Church itself is, he came to the conclusion that it is 'power in the hands of certain men'.

Tolstoy charged the Church with lack of intellectual integrity, and from the end of the 1870s, when he finally discriminated between the Church dogmas and Christ's teaching, he never ceased to regard the influence of the Church as a terrible obstacle to man's moral progress and to the spread of any right understanding of religion.

He maintained that though many people credulously accept and repeat the Church dogmas, nobody really believes them, for they mean nothing at all, and a statement must have a meaning before it can be believed. For instance, the statement that someone went up a hill and then rose up into heaven and sat down there, may have had a meaning when people lived on a flat earth with a burning hell below and a solid firmament up above; but with our conception of astronomy, if a man begins to rise from the top of a hill there is nowhere for him to stop. And if he tried to sit down he would have nothing to sit on, and would tumble back again. For people who believe in the solar system to say they believe in the Ascension, is merely to talk nonsense.

Faith is a great virtue, but to be faithful to a belief you must have a belief, and a real belief is not attainable by credulity (which is a vice), but by vigorous mental effort.

Tolstoy's denunciations of the Church are at times as unstinted as those of the late Mr Bradlaugh. In his *Appeal to the Clergy*, written in 1902 (*Essays and Letters*), for instance, he says:

> Drive a wedge between the floor-boards of a granary, and no matter how much grain you pour in, it will not stay there. Just so a head into which has been driven the wedge of a Trinity, or of a God who became man and redeemed the human race by his sufferings and then flew up into the sky, can no longer retain any reasonable or firm understanding of life.
>
> However much you may put into that granary, all will run out, and whatever you may put into a mind which has accepted nonsense as a matter of faith, nothing will remain in it . . .

It may be true, and I think is true, that Tolstoy goes to an extreme in his denunciations of the Churches; for if one hunts back carefully and sympathetically enough one may discover that doctrines which will not *now* stand the simplest tests of common sense, meant something genuine to those who first formulated them; and the Churches have done good as well as evil. Had there been no Churches or Monastic Orders, or Priests or Popes, the world would hardly have been better than it is. On the whole, the tendency of religious communities, Church or Chapel, as long as they retain any vitality, is to keep people in moral touch with one another and to make it easier for them to abstain from flagrant wrongdoing.

Tolstoy, however, in his direct way, took theology at its own valuation and asked whether it is really true in its plain, literal sense, as it is given to and accepted by children and uneducated people. And having come to the conclusion that it is not, he denounced it as a fraud which every honest man should expose, and no decent man should trade in.

Had his nature not been profoundly religious he might have stopped there, and contented himself, as Voltaire and Bradlaugh did, with ridiculing and denouncing the superstitions by which mankind are hood-winked, but being differently made he hastened on to constructive work, and proclaimed the power and worth of the teaching of Jesus even more ardently than he condemned the Church's teaching.

His book, *A Criticism of Dogmatic Theology*, was completed about the year 1880, but only printed in 1891, when a carelessly edited and produced Russian edition was issued at Geneva. A better edition was published by A. Chertkóv at Christchurch, in 1903.

This book is probably the least read of Tolstoy's works. There is no satisfactory English translation. Those who are at the pains to read the original Russian will, however, find that this attack on a Church directed by a Holy Synod controlled by Pobedonóstsev and guarded by gendarmes, is a remarkable and fervent piece of work.

In it Tolstoy tells us that he came to see that, far from coinciding with Christ's teaching, the dogmas the Churches are concerned to enforce are expressly designed to divert men's minds from the things Jesus cared for and spoke most about. It is abundantly plain from the Gospels that he constantly spoke of love and pity, and of man's duty to man and to that Father in heaven who sends the Spirit of Truth to be our Comforter, but he never talked about the Fall of Adam, or the scheme of Redemption, or said that God was a Trinity, or asserted that God was his Father in any sense in which he may not be our Father too; nor did he say that the Holy Spirit was the third person of a Trinity. It is true he often identified himself with his heavenly Father, as when, in John's Gospel, he said, 'I and the Father are one,' and 'Before Abraham was, I am;' but he also wished us to be identified with him in the same way: 'I am in my Father, and ye in me, and I in you;' and again, 'That they may be one, even as we are one; I in them, and they in me.' He also taught his disciples to pray to 'Our Father'; and in the Synoptic Gospels, making a very clear distinction between himself and God, he said: 'My God, my God, why hast Thou forsaken me?' and in another passage he said, 'Why callest thou me good? None is good save one, even God.'

The Gospels often attribute to Jesus language evidently not used literally, as when he says he is 'the door', or 'the vine', and it lies with the reader to take his words reasonably or unreasonably. This applies equally to the statement that he was the 'Son of God'. To make this mean that God was his father in the same way that Mary was his mother, would be absurd; whereas to admit that God was his Father in a mystic sense makes it extremely difficult to differentiate between God's Fatherhood of Jesus and his Fatherhood of the rest of humanity, and as soon as that is admitted, a door is opened enabling Christians to unite with the rest of humanity.

In a very admirable short article in *Essays and Letters* entitled *How to Read the Gospels*, Tolstoy remarks that:

> To understand any book one must choose out the parts that are quite clear, dividing them from what is obscure or confused. And from what is clear we must form our idea of the drift and spirit of the whole work. Then, on the basis of what we have understood, we may proceed to make out what is confused or not quite intelligible. That is how we read all kinds of books. And it is particularly necessary thus to read the Gospels, which have passed through a multiplicity of compilations, translations, and transcriptions, and were composed eighteen centuries ago, by men who were not highly educated and were superstitious.

It must strike anyone who reads the Gospels with an open mind and compares them with the Church Creeds, that if Jesus knew that God would go on punishing mankind for Adam's sin until atonement was made, and if Jesus approved of this and made it the chief aim of his life and death to appease such a God, and if, moreover, he knew that men's eternal salvation depends on these things and on their believing rightly about them, it is singularly unfortunate that he forgot to mention the matter and left us to pick it up from obscure remarks made years later by St Paul, whom he never met, and whose mind, character, and work, differed considerably from his own.

The following summary of his views was submitted by me to Tolstoy and received his approval.

Each one of us has a reason and a conscience that come to us from somewhere: we did not make them ourselves. They oblige us to differentiate between good and evil; we *must* approve of some things and disapprove of others. In this respect we are all alike, all members of one family, and sons of one Father. Dormant or active, in each of us there is a higher and better nature, a spiritual, divine nature. If we open our hearts and minds we can, to some extent, discern good from evil in relation to our own conduct: the law is 'very nigh unto you, in your mouth and in your heart'. The purpose of our life on earth should be to serve not our lower, animal nature but that Power to which our higher nature recognises its kinship. Jesus identifies himself with his higher nature, speaks of himself and of us as Sons of the Father, and bids us be perfect as our Father in heaven is perfect.

This, then, is the answer to the question: What is the meaning and purpose of my life? There is a Power enabling me to discern what is good; I am in touch with it, my reason and conscience flow from it, and the purpose of my conscious life is to do its will – that is, to do good.

Nor do the Gospels leave us without an application of this teaching to practical life. The Sermon on the Mount had always attracted Tolstoy, but much of it had also perplexed him, especially the text: 'Resist not him that is evil, but whosoever smiteth thee on the right cheek, turn to him the other also.' This seemed to him unreasonable and shocked all the prejudices of aristocratic, family, and personal 'honour', in which he had been brought up. But he tells us that so long as he rejected and tried to explain away that saying he could get no coherent sense out of the teaching of Jesus or out of the story of his life.

As soon as he admitted to himself that perhaps Jesus meant that saying seriously, it was as though he had found the key to a puzzle – the teaching and the example fitted together and formed one complete and admirable whole. He saw that in these chapters Jesus is very definitely summing up his practical advice: pointing out, five times over, what had been taught by 'them of old times', and following it each time by the words, 'but I say unto you', and giving an extension, or even a flat contradiction, to the old precept.

Here are the Five Commandments of Christ, an acceptance of which, or even a comprehension of, and an attempt to follow which, would alter the whole course of men's lives in our society.

1 'Ye have heard that it was said to them of old time, Thou shalt not kill; and whosoever shall kill shall be in danger of the judgement: but I say unto you, that everyone who is angry with his brother shall be in danger of the judgement.'

Let me mention in passing, and as it were in parenthesis, that in the Russian version, as in our Authorised Version, the words, *without a cause* occur after the word 'angry'. This makes nonsense of the whole passage, for no one ever is angry without supposing that he has some cause! Comparing different Greek texts, Tolstoy found that those words are an interpolation (the correction has also been made in our English Revised Version), and he found other passages in which the current translations obscure Christ's teaching, as for instance the popular libel which represents him as having flogged people in the Temple with a scourge: a matter again corrected in our Revised Version. Three of the Gospels do not mention that Jesus had a scourge at all, and the one that mentions it only says, 'He made a scourge of cords, and cast all out of the temple, *both the sheep and the oxen*; and he poured out the changers' money, and overthrew their tables; and to them that sold doves he said, Take these things hence . . .' Not a single Gospel, in the Revised Version, says that he struck anyone!

Returning to the first great guiding rule for a Christian, we find then that it is: *Do not be angry*.

Some people will say, 'We do not accept Christ's authority, so why should we not be angry?'

But test it any way you like: by experience, by the advice of other great teachers, or by the example of the best men and women in their best moods, and you will find that the advice is good.

But, finally, one may say, 'I cannot help being angry, it is my nature: I am made so.' Very well; there is no danger of your not doing what you must do; but religion and philosophy exist to help us to think and feel rightly and to guide us, in so far as our animal nature allows us to be guided. If you can't abstain from anger altogether, *abstain from it as much as you can*.

2 'Ye have heard that it was said, Thou shalt not commit adultery: but I say unto you, that everyone that looketh on a woman to lust after her hath committed adultery with her already in his heart.'
   This second great rule of conduct is: *Do not lust*.
   It is not generally accepted as good advice. In all our towns things

exist – ways of dressing, ways of dancing, certain entertainments, pictures, and theatrical posters – which would not be there if everyone agreed that lust is a bad thing, injuring our lives.

Being animals we probably cannot help lusting, but the fact that *we* are imperfect does not prevent the advice from being good; so lust as little as you can, if you cannot be perfect pure.

3 'Again, ye have heard that it was said to them of old time, Thou shalt not forswear thyself, but shalt perform unto the Lord thine oaths: but I say unto you, Swear not at all . . . But let your speech be, Yea, yea; Nay, nay.'

How absurd! says someone. Here are five great commandments to guide us in life: the first is, 'Don't be angry,' the second is, 'Don't lust.' These are broad, sweeping rules of conduct; but the third is, 'Don't say damn!' What is the particular harm or importance of using a few swear-words?

But that is not the meaning of the commandment. It too is a broad, sweeping rule, and means: *Do not give away the control of your future actions*. You have a reason and a conscience to guide you, but if you set them aside and swear allegiance elsewhere: to Tsar, Emperor, Kaiser, King, Queen, President or General – you may someday be ordered to commit the most awful crimes; perhaps even to kill your fellow men. What are you going to do then? Break your oath? or commit a crime you never would have dreamt of committing had you not first sworn an oath?

The Emperor of Germany, Wilhelm II, once addressed some naval recruits just after they had taken the oath of allegiance to him. (It had been administered by a salaried servant of the Prince of Peace, on the book which says, 'Swear not at all.') Wilhelm II reminded them that they had taken the oath and that if he called them out to shoot their own fathers they must now obey!

The whole organised and premeditated system of wholesale murder called war, is, Tolstoy says, based and built up in all lands on this practice of inducing people to entrust their consciences to the keeping of others.

4 'Ye have heard that it was said, An eye for an eye, and a tooth for a tooth: but I say unto you, *Resist not him that is evil*; but whosoever smiteth thee on thy right cheek, turn to him the other also.'

That means, says Tolstoy, do not use physical violence against men who act in a way you disapprove of. Ultimately, taken in conjunction with other Commandments, it means much more than that.

There are two opposite ways of trying to promote the triumph of good over evil. One way is that followed by the best men, from Buddha in India and Jesus in Palestine, down to our own time. It is, to seek to see the truth of things clearly, to speak it out fearlessly, and to endeavour to act up to it, leaving it to influence others as the rain and sunshine act upon the plants. The influence of men who live in that way spreads from land to land and from age to age. But there is another plan, much more often tried, which consists in making up one's mind what *other people* should do and then using physical violence if necessary to make them do it.

People who act like that – Ahab, Attila, Caesar, Napoleon, and the Governments and militarists of today – influence people as long as they can reach them and even longer; but the effect that lives after them and spreads farthest is a bad one, inflaming men's hearts with anger, patriotism, and malice.

These two lines of conduct are contrary to each other, for you cannot persuade a man while he thinks you mean to hit or coerce him.

This Fourth Commandment, as Tolstoy understood it, is very precise and definite and leads to extremely far-reaching conclusions. The words which follow: 'If any man would go to law with thee, and take away thy coat, let him have thy cloke also . . . Give to him that asketh thee, and from him that would borrow of thee turn thou not away,' involve, he says, a complete condemnation of all legal proceedings in which force is actually or implicitly employed to oblige any of those concerned, whether as principals or witnesses, to be present and take part. This teaching involves nothing less than the entire abolition of all compulsory legislation, Law Courts, police, and prisons, as well as of all forcible restraint of man by man. The Tightness or wrongness of using physical force to restrain human beings is the crux of the whole matter and is a point I will deal with later.

The last of these Five Commandments is the most sweeping of all:

5   'Ye have heard that it was said, Thou shalt love thy neighbour and hate thine enemy; but I say unto you, Love your enemies . . . that ye may be sons of your Father which is in heaven: for He maketh His sun to rise on the evil and the good, and sendeth rain on the just and

the unjust. For if ye love them that love you . . . what do ye more than others? Do not even the Gentiles [foreigners] the same? Ye therefore shall be perfect, as your heavenly Father is perfect.'

The meaning of these Five Commandments – backed as they are by the example of Jesus and the drift and substance of his most emphatic teaching – is too plain, Tolstoy says, to be misunderstood; and it is becoming more and more difficult for the commentators and expositors to obscure it, though to many of them the words 'Ye have made void the word of God because of your traditions,' apply. What Jesus meant us to do, the direction in which he pointed us, and the example he set us, are unmistakable.

One great superiority of Tolstoy's interpretation over the Orthodox one, lies in the fact that his statement, whether it be a right or wrong presentation of the mind of Jesus, means something clear and definite and links religion to daily life.

He discriminates between what we know and what we do not know, and makes no assertions about the personality of God, or His nature, or the creation and redemption of the world. For Tolstoy's statement that man owes a duty to a Higher Power which reveals itself through the workings of our reason and conscience, is a fact of personal experience, confirmed by the testimony of the saints and sages of all religions. Socrates and Emerson (and their predecessors and successors), faced by the necessity of supposing either that we live in a moral chaos where nothing is right or wrong, or in a moral order to which we can in some measure conform, chose the latter alternative, and became assured by experience that they had chosen right. By arriving at the conclusion that we are parts of a moral universe, and that only in so far as we discern that order and adjust ourselves to it has life any meaning and purpose that is not defeated by deaths, Tolstoy reached the ultimate root of religion. Through strife and suffering, to have found it by his own effort, and to have proclaimed it in the teeth of those who denounced him as heretic and atheist as well as of those who sneered at him as a superstitious dotard, is an achievement entitling him to rank among the prophets.

Superstitions – beliefs credulously accepted and passed on unverified – immensely hinder the spread of true religion. Yet such is the force of reaction that few men educated in them can throw them off without, at least for a while, losing their consciousness of dependence on and co-operation with the unseen Power that makes for righteousness. A man who has rejected his early beliefs but retains his old religious ardour, and is as eager to fight the battle of the Lord as he was when he still believed that God wrote His Law on tablets of stone and handed them to Moses on the top of a mountain, is as rare as he is valuable, and Tolstoy was such a man.

He saw quite clearly that we cannot make the precise statements of the old theology without landing ourselves in inextricable confusion; for, as J. S. Mill said, it is inconceivable that an all-powerful and all-good God can have created a world in which evil exists. Yet we believe that evil does exist and that it is our duty to help to get rid of it.

Only by confining ourselves, as mathematicians do, to what is 'necessary and sufficient', and by refraining from precise and definite statements concerning things we do not really know, can we get an intellectually honest religion. That there is a Moral Law, with which our natures can be brought at least partly into accord, is, as I have said, not a thing to be credulously accepted but a matter of experience; and no fact in history is more obvious than that those who have most widely, profoundly, and enduringly influenced the minds and hearts of men have firmly believed that they were co-operating with forces beyond the ken of our five senses.

In the early 1880s, in Russia – that country of strange contradictions – beside the dominance of the official Church maintained by the police, and of the peasants' naïve devotion to the Church, a rampant Materialism prevailed as a sequel to the success of the Darwinian movement, and many highly educated men were fully persuaded that Science was about to reveal the origin of life and, more than that, to explain the soul of man by the integration and disintegration of atoms. Under these circumstances it was as difficult for the views Tolstoy proclaimed to obtain a hearing from the arrogant worshippers in the temples of Science as from the scandalised followers of Mother Church.

That marks the greatness of his service. No progress was possible without an emancipation from the petrified ecclesiasticism that masqueraded as religion, and for any spiritual progress it was necessary that those intoxicated with the successes achieved by biological science should learn that we cannot obtain moral guidance for a race endowed with reason and conscience, by studying species comparatively destitute of the one and of the other. Almost alone, Tolstoy maintained the need of religion while unflinchingly denouncing its existing forms.

In his treatment of the Bible, he ranked the Old Testament with the Scriptures of other nations: that is to say, he regarded it as religious literature of varying quality, containing much that is excellent and some of the best literary art the world has produced, but much also that is crude, primitive, and immoral.

In the New Testament, he frankly disliked and disapproved of much in the Epistles of Paul, whom he accused of having given a false bias to Christianity, which enabled the Church to ally itself with the State and prevented the majority of men from understanding what Jesus meant. Paul's mind was of an administrative, organising type, foreign and repugnant to Tolstoy's anarchistic nature, which instinctively resented anything that, aiming at practical results, tolerates imperfect institutions.

Tolstoy is particularly indignant at Paul's approval of Government. 'The powers that be are ordained of God,' says Paul, and thereby provokes Tolstoy's, indignant query: 'Which powers? Those of Pugatchév* or those of Catherine II?' For Tolstoy maintains that man owes allegiance to God alone and that it is impossible to yield obedience to earthly potentates without being ready, at their bidding, to act contrary to His laws. The alliance of Church and State under Constantine was, he holds, tantamount to the abandonment of Christianity, which he says is by its very nature opposed to all rule that employs physical violence.

The Gospels he regarded as by far the most important Scriptures, and above all he valued the words of Jesus. The parables (except one or two obscure ones) he held to be exquisite works of religious art, and the Sermon on the Mount an expression of sacred and eternal truth.

Regarding a future life, Tolstoy's views changed after he began to write of these things in the early 1880s. At first he saw no reason for believing in a life after death; but after he had transferred his interest from personal matters to 'the service of God', that is, to matters of universal interest, the consciousness that his most real 'self' was part and parcel of the Infinite grew so strong within him that it appeared inconceivable that it should cease at the death of his body. But observing carefully the distinction between what we know and what merely seems plausible or possible, he refrained from assertions as to the kind of

* A rebel leader who for a while held the Vólga Provinces under his sway.

existence that will succeed the death of our bodies. Whether there be a personal immortality, whether we shall merge into the Infinite as raindrops fall into the ocean, whether reincarnation awaits us, whether groups of those who have been nearest in soul to one another will become one, or what other experience the future may have for various types of men – he held to be beyond our ken, nor did he think it desirable or important that we should know these things. For whatever the future may have in store, we shall best prepare for it by helping to establish the Kingdom of God on earth, here and now.

He was not interested in Spiritualism, though as a young man he had experimented with it, nor even in Psychical Research. Of the former he spoke scornfully, holding that mankind having made a useful discrimination between matter and spirit, should not be in a hurry to obliterate it. He maintained that attempts to investigate the spirit-world on the physical plane are based on a confusion of thought.

In treating of the Gospel miracles Tolstoy was interested only in what moral they convey, for he felt that if we see a man walking on the water, we may be perplexed, but not therefore assured that he is going to speak the truth; for ability to walk on the water is a physical matter, whereas truth-telling is spiritual.

He tells the story of the Feeding of the Five Thousand somewhat as follows: A popular preacher went out into the country, and the people flocked to hear him. They carried baskets with them, and presumably did not take them empty. When meal-time came, Jesus (whose teaching was of love and service to one's neighbour) had the people arranged in groups of fifty, and set a practical example by having the few loaves and fishes his party had with them distributed not to his own group but to the others. This example was imitated by the rest, with the result that none of the five thousand went away hungry, and twelve basketfuls of scraps were gathered up after all had eaten.

The lesson of the story, read in this way, is obvious; whereas if we suppose that Jesus multiplied the loaves of bread and the fishes like a conjurer, he set an example we cannot imitate.

For the most part, Tolstoy, regarding the miracles as mentally indigestible, simply omits them from the translation he made of the Gospels.

A suggestion he does not refer to, but which goes far towards explaining some at least of the Gospel miracles, is that they grew out of the parables. The parable of the barren fig tree which was to be hewn down if it did not bear fruit, may, for instance, easily have given rise to the perplexing story of the fig tree blasted by Christ's curse, and other miracles admit of similar explanation. This assumes, as Tolstoy himself did, that the Gospels were not supernaturally inspired.

The point of which Christian Scientists make so much, namely the effect of religion on health, is one Tolstoy disregarded altogether. He was concerned about the soul, and believed that sickness, weakness, and death, play a necessary and beneficent part in our spiritual progress. He was therefore neither impressed nor attracted by the promises of perpetual health held out by Mrs Eddy.

No doubt he chose the main and chief side of religion, but still, by disregarding the Gospel stories of physical cures, he perhaps missed what is neither an accidental, nor unimportant, nor altogether incredible, part of the narrative: for unquestionably the mind influences the body, and even in the Tolstoyan Movement I knew nervous, irritable, and sickly people who, when their hearts were lit up and their minds illumined by Tolstoy's wide, generous, and noble ideas and ideals, became physically as well as mentally sounder than before.

Moreover, though it is a matter about which I know little, my impression is that the investigations of the Psychical Research Society, as well as the records of many religious movements, indicate that there are forces at work around us of which science today is profoundly ignorant.

Returning to the consideration of Christ's Five Commandments, I would say that striking as are Tolstoy's remarks on oaths, and valuable as is his protest against militarism (with which I shall deal in another chapter), he may have been mistaken as to what really was in the mind of Jesus when he said, 'Neither shalt thou swear by thy head, for thou canst not make one hair white or black.'

Oaths were originally based on the idea that a man could call on the Higher Powers to destroy him for speaking falsely. As soon as he no longer believed in such divine intervention, and did not think that if he staked his head on the truth of what he said the gods would enforce the penalty, such oaths lost their meaning and became objectionable.

The desirability of remaining free to do from day to day just what seems to us right at the moment, unfettered by agreement with our fellow men, is again a maxim in Tolstoy's teaching that raises problems of great complexity, which, I think, he solved in too summary and rigid a fashion. It is true, as he says, that much wrongdoing goes on in the world not because those who commit it wish to do so, but because they are bound by the conditions of service they have accepted. It is evident that many who slay and destroy in war would never dream of doing so unless they had been ordered to by emperors, kings, or ministers who, in their turn, never would have ordered it had they themselves had to do the dirty work, or even to witness a thousandth part of the suffering they cause. The same is true of inhumanities committed under legal, business, and professional codes.

But where Tolstoy errs, it seems to me, is in assuming that if everyone refused to be bound by oath or agreement (for he sometimes spread the doctrine out so that it condemned *any definite arrangement* among men as to their future work or future actions), things would go on better than they do at present.

One cannot escape Tolstoy's condemnation by merely adopting the method, optional in English Law Courts, of affirming instead of swearing, for it is the *being bound* by agreement, and therefore not being free to act as one's conscience may dictate at a given moment, that he objected to. The promise to 'speak the whole truth' at a trial appeared to him objectionable, for a witness might suddenly feel that it was unkind to the prisoner to recount what really took place or to expose the fact that another witness had lied.

An individualist conception of man's duty is largely prevalent in the East and tinges the thought of many among ourselves, and the real clash of moral conviction between Tolstoy, who represented that thought, and let us say Gladstone – who represented in this matter the social frame of mind prevalent in the West – arises over the question whether it may sometimes be right to act not as one would if matters lay solely between oneself and God, but in the way that does most to promote unity and co-operation with one's fellows, and therefore ultimately to forward the establishment of the kingdom of heaven.

These words of Gladstone's show my meaning:

> For years and years, well into advanced middle life, I seem to have considered actions simply as they were in themselves, and did not take into account the way in which they would be taken and understood by others. I did not perceive that their natural and probable effect upon minds other than my own formed part of the considerations determining the propriety of each act in itself, and not infrequently – at any rate in public life – supplied the decisive criterion to determine what ought and what ought not to be done.

Tolstoy would have us regard only our duty to our conscience and to God. He assured us that if each man would do that, we should think and act in unison, and with the best results for ourselves, our neighbours, our country, and the whole of mankind. I wish it were so! But neither my judgement nor that of others is infallible. If it were, how easy it would be to tread the path of progress in step, chanting songs we all understood and enjoyed! But the test of theory is practice, and in practice we find that only by adjusting our actions to the limitations of our fellows, and by their having regard to our own, can we advance together towards the aims we all desire. That is the justification of democracy, and that is why men can best serve God by living in the main stream of humanity and not as wandering friars.

One of Tolstoy's arguments on the matter is that if a man once begins to consider what others are, or are not, prepared for, he quickly drops from the plane of principle to that of mere expediency, and lower still, to that of party or personal advantage; and so the salt in him loses its savour. Only by keeping his mind fixed on the divine Law can man maintain the integrity to which compromise is fatal.

But, again, the answer is that Tolstoy over-simplifies life's problems. If good results really followed from each man taking his own line, how easy life would be! But we find that men who do so, lose touch with reality and are in danger of falling from cloudland headlong to the bottom of the muddiest of earth's ditches; and so experience of life teaches us humility, and we come to believe that only by rubbing shoulders with the common man and consorting with the publicans and sinners can we achieve real and solid progress.

The principle which lies at the root of Tolstoy's Non-Resistance principle, namely the non-use of physical force, is one to be dealt with separately later on. Here I will only say that, however true it may be that the *lessening* use of physical force in government, in industrial undertakings, in prisons, in schools, and in homes, is a sign of moral progress – there is yet no such clear moral distinction between the use of physical and mental violence as he supposed, and an impulsive blow may often cause less anguish and imply less venom than a malevolent reproach.

Tolstoy was too rigid and too definite in these matters, and I do not think it reasonable to suppose that Jesus meant so much more than he said. 'Sweet reasonableness' has been rightly predicated of him as he is depicted in the Gospels; but it belongs to that spirit to be aware that human nature and human affairs are complex and difficult and need constant care and much careful weighing, and that convenient as it would be to have a few stark and rigid rules as criteria for human conduct, yet to frame such rules and deduce enormously far-reaching conclusions from them, indicates a misapprehension of the real nature of things, and savours more of the spirit of some fierce Old Testament prophet than of him who would not break a bruised reed nor quench the smoking flax. The tests of conduct are not really clear or obvious.

In the path Tolstoy would have us pursue, short and simple as his exposition sounds, there lies, indeed, a very grave practical obstacle. He says that if everyone would obey God's Law, human law would be unnecessary and we should all live in peace and amity. But even with everyone trying his best to obey that law it would still remain true that the abolition of human tribunals would not lessen, but would enormously increase, our difficulties. For friction between well-intentioned people who have to work together often arises, not from anyone wishing to do wrong, but from the fact that people see things differently. One man knows more, another less; one likes change, and another dislikes it; one is shy, overcautious and slow, while another is rash and impulsive; this man readily understands what is said, that one generally misunderstands it; and what to one looks blue, to another looks green. If they are to work together we must make it easy for them by setting up an *external* tribunal; for *definiteness of arrangement* in the long run promotes the growth of goodwill. A clear, firm law and a well-recognised trade-custom (harsh and faulty as our actual arrangements often are) are better for mankind than a haziness of arrangement that necessitates arguing out each point each time it crops up among each separate group of workers.

The proof of the pudding is in the eating. Where the great majority of individuals respect an external, man-made law, and consent to bind themselves by agreements limiting their individual freedom, and settle their disputes by appeals to a tribunal – society is able to exist; whereas though well-meaning men of much more than average ability have tried the experiment again and again, communities conducted on anarchist principles never have endured.

The moral aspect of the case is more important even than its material side, for it is our duty to minimise the friction that arises when hard work has to be done, and experience shows that when men have to co-operate, and their opinions clash, it is cruel and wasteful to condemn them to hammer out conclusions between themselves by argument. It is much more humane to let them – and even in the ultimate resource to compel them to – submit their disagreements to the arbitration of a third party, as is done by our Courts of Law. Nothing frets and worries men more than an unsettled quarrel which they cannot get heard and adjudicated.

Another point to elucidate is that the real objection to some of Tolstoy's doctrines – and especially to some of the tremendous and quite logical deductions he makes from those doctrines – is not, as people are fond of saying, that his ethics are too far ahead of us and only suitable to a better race of men a thousand or more years hence, but on the contrary the objection is that Tolstoy overlooked and disregarded the ethical bases which underlie the superstructure of modern government, law, custom, trade, and property. Such an intellectual misconception as this usually depends on some moral flaw; and since my aim is not to produce a panegyric, but to tell the truth as I see it about this man – whom I respected and loved, and to whom I am profoundly indebted – let me here say what the moral flaw vitiating this part of Tolstoy's work seems to me to be. It is his impatience with the results achieved by human efforts in the past, and his distrustful hostility towards all movements which did not square with his theories and with the commandments he formulated. In a word, he trusted his own conclusions too implicitly, and distrusted the motives, efforts, and conclusions of other men too much.

Nevertheless, let it be borne in mind that the government, law, and customs, mankind has evolved are still so defective that the onslaughts of one who regarded them as fit only for destruction, may and do contain much that is worthy of careful attention. We of the Western world, who believe government, law, property, and trade, to be useful, are far too apt to condone barbarities still habitual among us, on the ground that they are sanctioned by law and custom or are necessary for business; and therefore no one should condemn Tolstoy's conclusions lightly or hastily, but should rather digest them, recognising that they contain much that is sound and wholesome.

His *Union and Translation of the Four Gospels*, a large work, was written simultaneously with or immediately after the completion of his *Criticism of Dogmatic Theology* and, like it was printed in Geneva, but not till much later. It was subsequently reprinted more carefully in three volumes issued in Moscow in 1908. Till then it had not been allowed to circulate in Russia, but after 1905 many previously prohibited books were for a while tolerated.

In a preface, dated August 1891, to his *Four Gospels*, Tolstoy says:

My friends have offered to print this book composed by me ten years ago, and I have consented, in spite of the fact that the work is far from being finished and there are in it many defects. To correct and complete it is, I feel, beyond my power, for the concentrated, constant, and enthusiastic spiritual effort of which I was conscious during the whole time I was writing it cannot now be renewed. But I think that, such as it is, the book may be of use if it communicates to others even a small part of the enlightenment I experienced while at work on it, and of my firm confidence in the truth of the path it revealed.

Some years later he again wrote of it:

At the risk of suggesting the hackneyed quip that an author is always mistaken in his appreciation of his own works, I persist in saying that it is a thousand times more important than anything I have ever written. And I know I am not mistaken in this case, for it cost me the greatest and most joyous effort, was the turning-point of my whole life, and has served as the basis of all I have written since.

The order of the chapters and verses of the various Gospels he arranged at his own discretion, omitting anything he did not understand or disapproved of. The result is a striking and consistent narrative, representing the personality and teaching of Jesus as Tolstoy believed them to have been.

But can we rely on it? Has not everyone who has made an independent study of Christ's teaching and personality – Strauss, Renan, Reuss, Hausrath, Farrar, Harnack, and all the rest of them – each produced a more or less plausible portrait and account of his own, the validity of which remains doubtful because they all disagree and the material they work on is so scanty? That material consists of four little books, written we know not by whom, nor when, nor where, which are not always in accord with one another. There is so much those booklets do not tell us at all, and so much that they do not tell definitely or completely.

That is one of the secrets of the immense popularity of Jesus. Beyond what is clear in his teaching and example there remains a wide domain in which each of us, Catholic or Anabaptist, Evangelical or Unitarian, can picture him as he likes, and men differing radically from one another can all regard him as being of their mind.

Be that as it may, Tolstoy at any rate felt certain that he understood just what Jesus meant, and knew just how Jesus lived and worked, and that his example can and should be followed by us all.

Lowell says that:

New occasions teach new duties; time makes ancient
                                                    good uncouth;
They must upward still and onward, who would keep
                                                    abreast of Truth.

But Tolstoy speaks of no new duties to meet new conditions: his cry is always, Back to Christ! Back to the simple, frugal life of the simple country peasant!

Certainly his presentation is vivid and lifelike, and it may be that Jesus really thought and felt just as Tolstoy says he did; but I doubt it. I admit that the views he attributes to Christ made themselves heard in the early Church, and with sundry modifications and variations reappeared again and again among the anti-ecclesiastical sects: the Bogomílites and Paulicians in the East, the Molokáns and Doukhobórs in Russia, and the Lollards, Moravian Brethren, Mennonites, Anabaptists and Quakers in the Western world.

But as I have said, it seems to me that as Tolstoy expresses them, some of these doctrines are too rigid, too logical, too precise and too unqualified to be true, and in special cases, for instance in regard to Christ's injunction to 'Render unto Caesar the things that are Caesar's', I cannot make the interpretation square with the evidence. I admit that if men are to give their hearts and souls and minds and strength to God, it does not leave much for Caesar, except the minted coins; but even so, I do not see where any Gospel justification can be found for Tolstoy's injunction – repeated in many of his writings – to pay no taxes voluntarily, but to let the tax-collectors seize what they want, refraining from resistance merely as (on the Non-Resistance theory) one ought to refrain from resisting a robber.

Again, Tolstoy ignores the many indications in the Gospels that seem to show that Jesus expected the end of the existing order of things within the lifetime of his generation. Such an anticipation would surely influence his views on law, government, and property, and should at least be taken into account.

When Tolstoy set out to show what the Gospels really mean, he did not adopt the historic method of trying to decide when and where the documents were produced and studying the influences which tended to make them what they are, but taking them as they stand he proceeded to interpret them in accord with his inner consciousness of right and wrong. But the task of showing that such and such texts must have meant so and so, led him unconsciously to trench on the domain of the historical student and to attempt the work of the scholarly critics, for which he hardly possessed the necessary equipment or the tolerant, impartial, balanced accuracy of mind such work requires. His performance is therefore that of an amateur of genius, pouring floods of light on certain questions and overwhelming many hoary sophistries by a strong rush of common sense, but at times stumbling over obstacles a less impetuous man might have avoided.

What helps to perplex a thoughtful reader of Tolstoy's work on the Gospels, is the necessity of considering not merely whether Jesus meant what Tolstoy says he meant, but whether, if he meant it, he was right or wrong in so doing. The ultimate, and much the most important, question is not, What did Jesus say? but, What is the truth of the matter, apart from who said it?

I once mentioned to Tolstoy a charge that has been brought against him, to the effect that in his translation of the Gospels he takes unjustifiable liberties. He replied that he had studied Greek very seriously, and while writing his work had consulted first-rate scholars; but he added that he did not, at the time we were discussing it, attach the importance he had done when he wrote the book to verbal niceties, and he admitted that sometimes, in his anxiety to counteract the bias he detected in the Orthodox Slavonic and Russian translations, he strained the meaning too much in a contrary direction. He compared his task to that of a man who has to demagnetise a steel bar by exposing it to an opposite influence.

At the period we have now reached, early in the 1880s, Tolstoy regarded the teaching of Jesus as unique, and far above all other human wisdom. The force of many passages in Tolstoy's writings rests on citations of 'the very words of Christ himself', and he draws deductions of vast importance from the precise phraseology of certain texts and the exact etymology and context of certain Greek words. This opinion of his about Jesus changed very slowly and gradually, in a way not clearly indicated in his works, but of which he has told me in conversation. Chiefly by becoming better acquainted with the Eastern Scriptures (especially those of India and China), he ultimately reached the conclusion that what is vital lies at the root of all the great religions, which are separated and divided from one another by their superstitious accretions. Without ceasing to believe that the Gospels contain essential truth, and without ceasing to insist on his own interpretation of the teachings of Jesus as being in the main correct, he came to attach less and less importance to Christ's personality and to the exact phraseology and actual words of the Gospels.

How far he went in this direction is shown in a letter to Birukóv, written about the year 1900, after Tolstoy had read Professor Verus's *Vergleichende Uebersicht der vier Evangelien*. In this letter he says:

> In this book it is very well argued (the probability is as strong *against* as *for*) that Christ never existed. The acceptance of this supposition or probability is like the destruction of the last outwork exposed to the enemy's attack, in order that the fortress (the moral teaching of goodness, which flows not from any one source in time or space but from the whole spiritual life of humanity in its entirety) may remain impregnable.

To anyone fresh from reading Tolstoy's works of 1880–5, this may come with rather a shock, though it does not imply the least weakening of his faith in the reality of things unseen and the importance of things spiritual.

A matter all his readers must notice, is the stress he lays on the importance of manual labour, and on the moral duty of *doing* as contrasted with merely talking or writing. He extols the production of the necessaries of life as of more primary importance than study, reflection, talk, reading, writing, or the organisation of other people's industry. Again and again he pours out the vials of his wrath on those who, on any pretext whatever, shirk the primary duty of supporting themselves and others. Yet at the same time we have his unstinted and enthusiastic laudation of the Sermon on the Mount, which after all was *talk*, and talk preceded by forty days in the wilderness without labour to produce those necessaries about which Tolstoy is so greatly concerned. Christ's sermon was no doubt worth incalculably more than the tables and benches he might have made in the time, but by admitting that fact we reduce Tolstoy's contention from the realm of the absolute to that of the comparative, which is perhaps its proper place.

I am much more concerned to draw attention to the value of Tolstoy's work than to dwell on any flaws in it; but he was so terribly strenuous, and often caused such acute distress to people of tender conscience who came under his spell, that perhaps it is well occasionally to let his over-strenuousness in one direction counteract his over-emphasis in another.

From the two large works of which I have spoken some smaller ones sprang. Out of discarded scraps of *A Criticism of Dogmatic Theology*, a secretary (of whom I shall have something to tell in a subsequent chapter) pieced together an article on *Church and State*, which circulated in manuscript, as it could not be printed in Russia. Then a tutor in the family, wishing to copy out for himself Tolstoy's work on the Gospels, had only time to write down the summary given of the various chapters, without the translation itself, and in this way *The Gospel in Brief* came into being. In a preface to that book, Tolstoy referred to the danger he was running, and said that those who have concealed Christ's teaching from men and substituted their own misrepresentations have only two courses open to them: either humbly to repent and abjure their lies, or to persecute those who expose them, including himself – 'a fate for which, while finishing my book, I prepare with gladness, though with fear for my weakness'.

The *Gospel in Brief*, being shorter and simpler, has been much more widely read than the parent work from which it was extracted.

Neither *A Criticism of Dogmatic Theology* nor the *Union and Trans-lation of the Four Gospels* will be included in the twenty-one volumes of this Centenary edition. Both works contain much valuable matter, but the task of preparing readable English translations of them presents enormous difficulties. The statements in the *Dogmatic Theology of Makarius*, which Tolstoy was criticising, do not always tally with the statements in our Church Catechism, and a further element of con-fusion is introduced by the habit prevalent among us during the last half-century, of presenting the Church dogmas under various plausible guises which make it hard to know just what they mean; and as Tolstoy takes them in the cruder forms in which the rigid Orthodox Russian Church offered them, and proceeds to tear them to pieces, English Churchmen may be tempted to say: 'Oh, that is not the way we under-stand the dogma!' Then again Tolstoy's translation of the Gospels is printed in three parallel columns, first the Greek text, then the Russian version, and thirdly his own translation, and much of the book is taken up by his comments on the text, and especially by his exposure of errors in the authorised Russian version, as well as by comments on the explanations offered by Reuss and other commentators. But as the Russian version sometimes corresponds to our Authorised or Revised version and sometimes differs from them both, there is again a complication which calls for much tact, if both the translation of the Russian version of the Gospels and of Tolstoy's interpretation are to be so worded as to exhibit their divergences without straining either of them. In fact the work calls for an acute understanding both of the Greek and the Russian versions, as well as of what Tolstoy himself says and of his attitude towards the problems dealt with. An uncommon delicacy of perception, and very great exactitude and dexterity in phraseology would be needed, as well as an acute consciousness of preconceptions likely to cause English readers to misunderstand Tolstoy's points.

That a scholar, suitably equipped, could extract from these works many ideas shedding light on perplexing problems, I feel sure; for there is hardly another instance in modern times of a man of powerful intelligence, considerable linguistic attainment, and great literary skill, who at the zenith of his intellectual powers put all else aside to devote himself for years to finding intelligible guidance for man's daily life, not from the teaching of the Christian Church but from the Gospels. That is what distinguishes Tolstoy's work from that of any of the scholars, commentators, and theologians who have worked the same ground. He went to the matter not primarily as a scholar, a Churchman, or a critic, but as a man needing guidance for his life, who thought he could find it in the Gospels. The practical aim he had in view, his acute literary scent for what the writers of the Gospels must have meant, and his assurance that they wished to talk sense, enabled him (whatever mistakes he may have made) to find a common-sense meaning in the Gospel narratives, which come as a surprise – like a douche of cold water – to anyone accustomed to accept the orthodox interpretations. Tolstoy's efforts at 'perfecting himself' are noticeable in his gradual development of a clear, persuasive, philosophic style. When he began to write argumentatively, as in the philosophic parts of *War and Peace* and in his educational articles, he was far from showing complete mastery of a suitable style, but by the time he wrote *Confession* he gave us a masterpiece, persuasive and lucid in the highest degree. It is, in form, autobiographic, and the facts are not invented, but primarily and chiefly it is a rhetorical, hortatory appeal – in the best sense of those words. It is written to persuade us of the importance of a religious attitude towards life. In *A Criticism of Dogmatic Theology* and the *Union and Translation of the Four Gospels* he had to deal with more intricate and perplexing problems of arrangement and presentation, and was not so conspicuously successful, but eventually he attained a marvellous control of his medium, and in essay after essay, such as *Religion and Morality*, *Reason and Religion*, *What is Religion?* he wrote with a lucidity which reminds one of his remark that it was his aim to 'make his meaning clear to every cabman'.

An aftermath of Tolstoy's studies of the Gospels was his book *The Teaching of Jesus*, expressly designed for children, and written in 1908.

A work written in 1884, which has had a large circulation in many languages and gives the gist of the faith Tolstoy then held, is *What I Believe*. It contains many interesting autobiographical touches. In substance it is to some extent a recapitulation of what he had said in his *Four Gospels*. To show his understanding of the Second and Fifth of Christ's Commandments, I quote two passages.

Tolstoy explains that the verse in the Sermon on the Mount, translated in our Bibles: 'But I say unto you that everyone that putteth away his wife, saving for the cause of fornication, maketh her an adulteress,' really means: 'But I say unto you that everyone that putteth away his wife, besides the sin of dissoluteness which causes him to want to be rid of her, places her in a position in which she is liable to become an adulteress,' and should be so translated.

I reserve comment on this to a later chapter, and pass on to the other quotation, which deals with patriotism:

Christ showed me that the fifth snare depriving me of welfare, is the separation we make of our own from other nations. I cannot but believe this, and therefore if in a moment of forgetfulness feelings of enmity towards a man of another nation may arise within me, yet I can no longer in my calm moments fail to acknowledge that feeling to be a false one, and cannot justify myself as I used to do by claiming the superiority of my own people to others, basing this on the errors, cruelties, and barbarities of another nation. I now know that my union with other people cannot be severed by lines of frontier, or by Government decrees about my belonging to this or that nation. I now know that all men everywhere are equals and brothers.

Remembering all the evil I have done, suffered, and seen, resulting from the enmity of nations, it is clear to me that the cause of it all lay in the gross fraud called patriotism and love of one's country . . .

I now understand that my welfare is only possible if I acknowledge my unity with all people in the world without exception. I believe this; and that belief has changed my whole valuation of what is good and evil, lofty and mean. What seemed to me good and lofty – love of fatherland, of one's own people, of one's own State, and service of it to the detriment of the welfare of other peoples, as well as military exploits – became to me repulsive and pitiable. What seemed to me bad and shameful – rejection of fatherland and cosmopolitanism – now appeared to me, on the contrary, good and noble.

If now, in a moment of forgetfulness, I might co-operate with a Russian rather than with a foreigner, and might desire the success of the Russian State or nation, I can no longer in calm moments submit to that temptation which ruins me and other people. I cannot acknowledge any States or nations, cannot take part in any quarrel between nations and States, either by writing, or (still less) by serving any Government. I cannot take part in those affairs which are based on the diversity of nations, in the collection of Customs and taxes, nor in the preparation of military stores and ammunition, nor in any activity for creating armaments, nor in military service, nor, least of all, in war itself against other nations, and I cannot help others to do so.

Much in these views is true, but is not part of the truth left out of sight? I will try to answer that question further on in this book.

Years later, when his views had broadened and he was ready to generalise more sweepingly, Tolstoy wrote a series of admirable essays on Religion, of which I will also speak in their proper place.

To sum up my own appreciation of Tolstoy's work on religion, I think, in the main, he clears the ground admirably of old superstitions, and the essential root of religion is ever present to his mind: a consciousness of the purposelessness of human life apart from dependence on and co-operation with a Something greater than ourselves that makes for righteousness. But like other ardent men bent on furthering the spiritual welfare of mankind, he sets up superstitions of his own in place of those he overthrows. His superstitions are the 'principles' of Non-Resistance, No-Government, No-Human-Law, and No-Property.

The true theory of Non-Resistance should, to my mind, deal

primarily, not with a repudiation of the externalities of physical force or legal compulsion, but with furthering the inward and spiritual grace that sheds its warmth both on the evil and the good.

One of Tolstoy's achievements was the way he succeeded in turning their own guns upon his opponents. Adherents of the Church often charge it against the unorthodox as a sin, that they do not believe the doctrines of the Church, but none of them is more impressive than Tolstoy when he indicts all who neglect to use the reason God has given them, and credulously accept and repeat statements they have not tried to verify. Unfortunately he does not stop there, but employs the goad of moral indictment to drive people willy-nilly into accepting his views.

The skill with which, starting from the words of Christ – 'Resist not him that is evil,' he has framed a complete Christian-anarchist theory, is amazing. If one grants him his premises (which is just what one should not do) the whole process of deduction is remarkably logical, and for good or evil the conclusions are of the utmost importance.

When reading Tolstoy I am often reminded of Walter Bagehot, just because the two men are so unlike one another. There is a passage in *Physics and Politics* in which, after pointing out how the man of today has inherited from remote ancestors a tendency to act impulsively, immediately, and strongly, and to do much that he had better have left undone, Bagehot goes on to say:

Even the abstract speculations of mankind bear conspicuous traces of the same excessive impulse. Every sort of philosophy has been systematised, and yet, as these philosophies utterly contradict one another, most of them cannot be true. Unproved abstract principles without number have been eagerly caught up by sanguine men, and then carefully spun out into books and theories, which were to explain the whole world. But the world goes clear against these abstractions, and it must do so, as they require it to go in antagonistic directions. The mass of a system attracts the young and impresses the unwary; but cultivated people are very dubious about it. They are ready to receive hints and suggestions and the smallest real truth is ever welcome. But a large book of deductive philosophy is much to be suspected. No doubt the deductions may be right; in most writers they are so; but where did the premises come from? Who is sure that they are, the whole truth, and nothing but the truth, of the matter in hand? Who is not almost sure beforehand that they will contain a strange mixture of truth and error, and therefore that it will not be worth while to spend life in reasoning over their consequences? In a word, the superfluous energy of mankind has flowed over into philosophy, and has worked into big systems what should have been left as little suggestions.

That applies exactly to Tolstoy's theory of Non-Resistance. Had he given half the time to considering the objections to it that he spent on advocating and extending it by further and further deductions – how much perplexity he would have saved his readers!

But I do not wish to close this chapter on a note of discord, and will therefore turn to a matter which is common ground to an enormous number of men.

Tolstoy prayed regularly and ardently, but he did not believe in a personal God – that is to say, he was not prepared to make definite statements on a matter he could not verify – and he disapproved of all petitions to the Deity for material advantages or even for such more subtle gains as peace of mind or soul.

He says there are two kinds of prayer: the 'continual prayer' which consists in reminding oneself of the religious truths one has grasped, and of striving to live up to the best one has perceived; and the 'occasional prayer' achieved most often in moments of solitude when one feels drawn nearer to God and penetrates more deeply than before into the spiritual nature of things.

Owing to the limitations of human thought and language, Tolstoy found that in practice he used a more personal note in his prayers than in a philosophic argument he would have been inclined to defend.

Writing to a friend in 1901, he said:

I do not at all think that it would be good for everybody, or that it is necessary for all to do so, but I have long since formed the habit of praying every morning in solitude . . .

But besides that prayer I also pray when I am alone, and I read the thoughts of the Saints and Sages, not Christians only nor the ancients only, and I meditate, seeking out what in God's sight there is of evil in my heart and trying to rid myself of it.

I also try to pray in active life, when I am among other people and passions assail me. Then I try to remember what went on in my soul when I prayed in solitude, and the more sincere my prayer was the more easily do I refrain from evil.

3

Letter to the Tsar

Tolstoy's new ideas diverted his attention completely from his former occupations of farming, and breeding horses, cattle, pigs, and poultry. His affairs fell into disorder, for his stewards took advantage of his preoccupation; and the united revenue from the Yásnaya Polyána, Nikólskoe, and Samára estates, the capital value of which amounted altogether to not less than five or six hundred thousand rubles (£50,000 or £60,000), shrank to some £500 a year; a sum quite insufficient to meet the expense of his large and growing family, the children's education, and the generous hospitality the Tolstoys were accustomed to extend to friends, relations, and visitors. The care and responsibility of managing the estates began to devolve on the Countess, who in addition to these cares was now troubled about her husband's health.

On 3rd February [1881] she wrote to her sister:

Lëvochka has quite overworked himself. His head is always aching but he cannot tear himself away. Dostoévski's death produced a great impression on him and on us all: just to have become so celebrated and so generally beloved, and then to die! It has set Lëvochka thinking of his own death, and he has become more absorbed and more silent.

The same day she wrote to her brother in the Caucasus:

If you only knew and heard Lëvochka now! He has altered very much. He has become a most sincere and firm Christian. But he has gone grey, his health is worse, and he has become quieter and more depressed.

On 1st March 1881, Alexander II was assassinated in Petersburg by agents of the Revolutionary Executive Committee. The action was abhorrent to Tolstoy, but he was extremely troubled by the thought of the impending execution of five of the conspirators, among whom was a woman, Sophie Peróvski. Many years later, he wrote to Birukóv:

The trial of the murderers and the preparations for their execution produced on me one of the strongest impressions of my life. I could not get rid of the thought of them, and not so much of them as of those who were preparing to share in their murder – especially Alexander III. The happiness he might experience by pardoning them was so plain to me! I could not believe they really would be executed, yet I feared and tormented myself on behalf of their murderers. I remember that with such thoughts in my mind I lay down on my leather sofa one day after dinner and unexpectedly fell asleep; and in a dream, or half-dream, I thought of them and of the murder that was in preparation, and I felt as clearly as though I had been awake, that not they were being executed but I, and yet that not Alexander III, the hangmen and judges, but I, was executing them and in a nightmare-terror I awoke, and immediately wrote my letter to the Tsar.

The letter was in keeping with the religious reflections that absorbed Tolstoy at the time, and was written in a far humbler tone than that in which twenty years later he reproved Nicholas II, much as the Hebrew prophets of old reproved their kings. The letter actually sent differed somewhat from the draft Tolstoy retained, which – as the only version available – is here quoted:

I, an insignificant, unrecognised, weak and worthless man, write to advise the Russian Emperor how to act in the most complex and difficult circumstances that have ever occurred. I feel how strange, improper, and audacious this is; and yet I write . . .

I write from a country solitude, and have no certain information. What I know, I know from the papers and from rumours, and I may therefore be writing unnecessary futilities about what is in reality quite different. If so, pray forgive my self-confidence and believe that I write not because I think highly of myself, but only because I am already so much to blame towards men that I fear to be again at fault if I fail to do what I can and ought.

I will write not in the usual tone of letters written to an Emperor – with flowers of servile and false eloquence that only obscure both feeling and thought – but simply as man to man.

My real feeling of respect for you, as man and Tsar, will be more evident without such adornments.

Your father, a Russian Tsar, a kind man who had done much good and had always wished his people well, has been inhumanly mutilated and slain, not by personal enemies but by enemies of the existing order, who killed him for the supposed welfare of mankind.

You have succeeded to his place and have before you these enemies who poisoned your father's life and destroyed him. They are your enemies, for you are in your father's place, and for the sake of the imaginary general good they seek they must wish to kill you too.

He goes on to remark that in the Tsar's soul there must be a desire for vengeance on his father's murderers, and the thought that such vengeance is expected of him puts him in a position of terrible tempt-ation, but that his primary duty is not as Tsar but as man. By following the teaching of Christ the temptation would be destroyed; and he quotes Matthew 5:43–5:

'Ye have heard that it was said, Thou shalt love thy neighbours, and hate thine enemy; but I say unto you, Love your enemies . . . do good to them that hate you . . . be sons of your Father which is in heaven . . .'

Tolstoy goes on to admit that the world is far from the divine truth expressed in Christ's teaching, and that it is audacious of him – who has yielded to far weaker temptations – to expect such strength of soul from the Tsar, yet he urges him to return good for evil. He says:

To forgive the most horrible offenders against human and divine laws and to return them good for evil will seem to many people at best idealism or insanity, and some will treat this advice as a sign of ill-intent. They will say; 'Do not pardon, but extirpate the canker. Extinguish the fire.' But one need only call on those who say so to prove their opinions, and the senselessness and ill-intent will be found to be on their side.

About twenty years ago a group was formed of people – mostly young – who hated the existing order of things and the Government. They imagined some other order, or even no order, and by all sorts of godless and inhuman methods, incendiary fires, robberies, and murders, they tried to destroy the existing order of society. For twenty years the struggle against this ferment has been carried on, but like mother-of-vinegar it continually breeds more and more, and has not merely not been destroyed but grows greater, and these people have reached a most terrible state of cruelty and audacity, harmful to the course of life of the State.

Those who wished to fight against this plague by external means have employed two methods: the one, that of cutting away by severity of punishment what was diseased and rotten; the other, that of letting the disease take its course under regulation. The latter were the Liberal measures intended to satisfy the disturbed and calm the attack made by these hostile forces.

For those who regard the matter from the material side there are, he says, only these two ways: decisive methods of extermination (executions, police, the Censor, &c.) or Liberal indulgence (partial freedom, moderation in penalties, a Constitution, &c.). Both these remedies have failed, and therefore the performance of the will of God should not be regarded with contempt, even if considered merely as a cure for everyday ills. Besides which both the old methods are bad for those who apply them, while the new method gives joy to man's soul.

He continues:

The third advantage Christian forgiveness has over coercion or the artificial direction of harmful elements, relates to the present moment and has particular importance. Your position, and that of Russia, is now like that of a sick man at a crisis, One false step, the application of one harmful or unnecessary remedy, may quite destroy the patient. Just so at the present time a single action in one or other direction – either vengeance for evil by cruel executions, or the calling together of Representatives – may involve our whole future. Now in this coming fortnight while the criminals are being tried and sentenced, a step will be taken which will select one of three paths now before us: the path of suppression of evil by evil; the path of Liberal connivance (both of them paths that have been tried and lead nowhere), or the path of the Christian performance of the will of God by the Tsar as a man.

Monarch! By some fatal and terrible error, fearful hatred arose in the souls of the Revolutionaries against your father, which led them to commit a terrible murder. That hatred may be buried with him. The Revolutionaries might blame him, though unjustly, for the death of some dozens of themselves. On your hands is no blood. You are the innocent victim of your position. You are pure and innocent before yourself and before God; but you stand at the parting of the ways. A few days, and if those triumph who say and think that Christian truth is mere talk and that in political life blood must be spilt and death must reign, you will pass for ever from that blessed condition of purity and life in God and will enter on dark paths of State-necessity, justifying everything – even the infringement of the law of God and man.

If you do not pardon but execute the criminals you will have uprooted three or four out of hundreds, but evil breeds evil and in place of those three or four, thirty or forty will grow up and you will have let slip for ever the moment which is worth a whole age – the moment when you might have fulfilled the will of God but did not do so – and you will pass for ever from the parting of the ways where you could have chosen good instead of evil, and will sink for ever into that service of evil called the Interest of the State.

Forgive! Return good for evil, and from among a hundred evil-doers dozens will turn from the devil to God, and the hearts of thousands and millions will quiver with joy and emotion at the example shown of goodness from a throne, at a moment so terrible for the son of a murdered father.

Monarch! If you were to do this: were to call these people and give them money and send them away somewhere to America, and write a manifesto headed with the words 'But I say, Love your enemies,' I do not know how others would feel, but I, poor subject, would be your dog and your slave! I should weep with emotion every time I heard your name, as I am now weeping. But what do I say? – 'I do not know how others'! – I know that at those words kindliness and love would pour forth like a flood over Russia . . .

By killing and destroying the Revolutionaries one cannot contend against them. Not their number is important but their ideal. To struggle against them one must struggle spiritually. Their ideal is a sufficiency for all, and equality and freedom. To contend against them one must oppose their ideal by one that is superior to theirs and includes it. In France and England the struggle against them is also going on and is also fruitless.

There is only one ideal which can be opposed to them: the one from which (misunderstanding it and blaspheming it) they start: the ideal which includes their own – the ideal of love, forgiveness, and the return of good for evil. One word of forgiveness and Christian love spoken and carried out from the height of the throne, and the path of Christian rule which is before you, waiting to be trod, can destroy the evil which is corroding Russia. As wax before the fire, all

Revolutionary struggles will melt away before the man-Tsar who fulfils the law of Christ.

Except in regard to its attitude of humble loyalty, that letter represents very much the attitude Tolstoy maintained to the end towards public affairs. It asserts that what is right – the law of Christ – is clear, indubitable, known to us all, and immediately applicable. It shows indifference towards, and disapproval of, Constitutional Government, and a strong inclination to over-simplify political and social problems. It also shows – what is very attractive – his assurance that the moral criterion is superior to every other, and it expresses his abhorrence of the slaughter of man by man. It is his sincerity, his interest in the great questions that affect our lives, and his intensity of feeling and expression, that make Tolstoy so interesting even when he deals with politics, but in relation to politics Tolstoy, like the Slavophils, represents a phase of thought which even in the East is now beginning to pass away and yield to the Western conception, that man must shape his own fate and must expect no God to grant him good government unless he helps himself thereto, and resolutely tackles rough political work which at first may often seem to yield him nothing but soiled hands. I quite believe that Alexander III would have acted nobly and wisely had he pardoned the conspirators. Certainly many Russians would have shared Tolstoy's feeling and with whole-hearted devotion would have adored the merciful Tsar. But no act of pardon however generous could evade the ultimate issue: Was Russia still to be ruled autocratically, or were the people to begin to have a say in shaping the conditions under which they lived?

To forgive the Tsaricides would have been excellent had Alexander III been inclined to limit his autocratic power, but *that* was the point of supreme importance.

It is curious to note in Tolstoy's letter the assumption that Liberal methods had already been sufficiently tried in Russia and had completely failed. It is true that many Liberal measures had, with the consent of the Tsar and in his name, been passed in the early 1860s. Their record forms one of the brightest pages in Russian history. It is also true that they were succeeded by a long period of reaction and were far from fulfilling the ardent expectations of their promoters. But why speak of them as having failed? It would be truer to say that they were but the first steps upon a path that would have had to be followed much farther before the fertile land to which it led could have been reached.

The history of Russia shows that, broken up into small states, she fell an easy prey to Tartar hordes who swept over her, burning, slaying, and outraging. Slowly the Grand Dukes of Muscovy spread their dominion until, while still nominally tributary to the Tartar Khans, they made themselves practically masters of Central Russia. Then they threw off the yoke, and claimed the title of Tsar or Caesar. And long after the Tartars had ceased to be terrible the Tsardom was still essential to hold Russia together and enable her to withstand not only the Turks, but also the Poles, to whom in 1612 Moscow was in thraldom, the Swedes, who in 1709 were in the heart of Central Russia at Poltáva, and the French, during whose invasion in 1812 Moscow again passed out of Russia's control. In those times the *quantity* of Government may well have seemed more important than its quality. The essential thing was to have a centre round which all the forces of the country could gather, for any native rule was preferable to a foreign yoke. The Tsardom afforded such a centre, but it might be compared to a suit of mail donned by a youth to save himself from assassination. After the danger has passed, if the growing lad still fears to abandon his cramping suit of mail it ultimately proves as fatal to him as the dagger of an assassin. After Russia became a great European Power the task of governing her score of different races, with different languages, different religions, and different customs, completely outgrew the ability of any Autocrat – whether he wished to rule according to the precepts of the Sermon on the Mount or not. Rash and violent as was their action, and little as they foresaw the effects that the Tsar's assassination would have, what Sophie Peróvski and her fellow-conspirators aimed at was to get rid of a Government under which the people were not allowed to make their wants heard, and under which the ever-growing abuses of the administration could not be exposed. To spare five conspirators while continuing to deny elementary liberty to 120,000,000 subjects was not good enough. That the case could not be so met was shown by the fact that the conspirators themselves cared more for the abolition of the irresponsible power of the Autocrat than they did for their own lives.

The Russian people, of whom Tolstoy was one, never have faced the fact that there are only two ways of getting a nation to carry out undertakings that demand effort and simultaneous exertion from many different men. The required direction has to come either from an

Autocrat (or a Dictatorship) or from a Government which the people have a right to influence by discussion, remonstrance, and ultimately even by displacing. Under either system it is possible for the rulers or the ruled to aim at guiding themselves by the Sermon on the Mount, but when it comes to definite directions as to what is to be done for the public interest – these cannot be quoted from the Gospels, for the Gospels do not contain the necessary enactments. The difference between Russia's experience and our own is that for some generations past we have tried Governments which allow a large measure of freedom of the press, of speech, of criticism of the rulers, and of voting to decide who are to carry on the government, and – far from perfect as the results have been – most of us are disposed to think that this has proved more satisfactory than the despotic or arbitrary rule of one man or of a junta.

The Russian people, on the contrary, have had no experience of parliamentary government, they have been ruled by Tartar Khans, endured the yoke of Polish usurpers, suffered under the interregnum of the Troublous Times, and afterwards gladly accepted the Autocracy of the Tsars. Eventually the actual power of control fell into the hands of the 'Third Department' (instituted by Nicholas I for the suppression of administrative abuses). This conglomerate of the gendarmerie, the secret police, the spy-system, and certain special troops, under a Head who reported direct to the Tsar and acted independently of other Ministers, controlled the press and public meetings, could arrest whom it pleased and deal with them by administrative action, and in alliance with the Church could and did harass dissenters and treat freedom of conscience as a crime. It intensified and personified the evils of despotism, and in 1917 was dismissed by the Provisional Government of Prince Lvov and Milukóv, after Raspútin's excesses had rendered the rule of Nicholas II abhorrent to the nation and led to the Revolution. It was then seen how little the Russians valued constitutional liberty. As Macaulay had remarked, the real condemnation of despotism lies in the evils that come after it. A man who has not been allowed to enter the water is unlikely to be able to swim, and a nation that has not been allowed to concern itself with politics is unlikely to be able to judge whether a government that allows it to express its wishes is, or is not, preferable to one which tells it what its wishes are to be. So when the Provisional Government had dismissed the Third Department and allowed freedom of the Press and of public meetings, and arranged for the only free general election (the one for a Constituent Assembly) that ever took place in Russia – and when that election returned a two-third majority opposed to Bolshevism – Lénin, who had meanwhile arrived from Switzerland and come to terms with the Head of the Third Department (which had not disintegrated), was able promptly to dismiss the Constituent Assembly and to rule Russia in the autocratic manner to which it was accustomed. The 'Third Department' became the Cheká, and when that grew too unpopular its name was changed to G.P.U. (State Political Administration), but its nature remained what it had been, and no subsequent election gave Lénin or his successors any trouble, for the Cheká had the people by the throat even more thoroughly than its predecessors under the Tsars had. It can arrange for the election of whatever representative it pleases, for it controls the Press and public meetings, and employing administrative orders can out-Herod Herod. The former Tsars were at least to some small degree restrained by tradition and by regard for the Church, though they largely controlled even that through the Head of the Holy Synod – a layman appointed by the Autocrat.

To return however from this digression to Tolstoy's appeal. He gave it to Strákhov to hand to Pobedonóstsev, formerly Alexander III's tutor and now Head of the Holy Synod, who had great personal influence with the Tsar. Tolstoy also wrote to Pobedonóstsev asking him to hand the document to the Tsar. After reading the appeal Pobedonostsev declined to have anything to do with it, and returned it to Strákhov. The latter then entrusted it to Professor K. Bestúzhev-Rúmin, who handed it to the Grand Duke Sergius, and so it ultimately reached the Tsar, who said that he would have pardoned the conspirators had the attack been directed against himself, but did not consider he had a right to pardon his father's murderers. This reply was informally conveyed to Tolstoy. Pobedonóstsev did not answer the letter addressed to him till 15th June, long after the Tsaricides had been hanged. He then wrote:

Do not be offended, most respected Count Leo Nikoláevich, first that till now I have left unanswered the letter N. N. Strákhov handed me from you. This occurred not from impoliteness or indifference, but from the impossibility of finding one's bearings quickly in the bustle and confusion of thoughts and occupations that overwhelmed me, and have not ceased to overwhelm me, since 1st March.

Secondly, do not be offended that I avoided the performance of your commission. In such an important affair everything must be done according to one's faith. And after reading your letter I saw that your faith is one, and mine and that of the Church another, and that our Christ is not your Christ.

Mine I know as a man of strength and truth, healing the feeble; but in yours I thought I discerned the features of one who is feeble and himself needs to be cured. That is why, in accordance with my faith, I could not fulfil your commission.

Yours with sincere respect and devotion,

K. POBEDONÓSTSEV

Speaking several years later of the executions of the Tsaricides, Tolstoy said:

Repaying deeds of horror by deeds of horror begets deeds of horror. I remember with what a shudder in my soul I heard of the impending execution of the five accomplices in that really terrible, shocking, and inhuman deed. I could not sleep. I could not rest anywhere; I wished to go to Petersburg and do as people used to do in olden times: see the Tsar face to face and beg and implore him not to let the execution take place. Something inexpressibly powerful called on me to do so, but weakness caused me to act in the modern way: I wrote a letter and forwarded it through some acquaintances. It is true that I tried to pour out my whole soul in that letter, but it did not express anything like what I felt.

Afterwards when I heard of what had been done, I could not drive from my eyes those hanging attenuated figures. The image of the woman Sophie Peróvski especially oppressed me. I clearly pictured to myself how she placed her head in the noose, and how she involuntarily adjusted it, moving her head till the noose lay under her windpipe; and then, when the stool had been pushed from beneath her feet and the cord pressed the soft gristle of her throat tight to the hard vertebrae of her nape, she suddenly felt a rush of blood to her head and writhed with her whole body . . . I suffocated and repeatedly swallowed saliva to assure myself that my throat was not yet squeezed up . . . I saw those protruding eyes fixed in amaze on the inexorable nearness of something terrible, and the blue face under the black cap . . . The horror of it all! The horror! . . .

Men forget one thing. The dreadful, monstrous, cruel things they do to others strike quite a different spot from the one they aim at. It is wonderful how the soul of the victim is protected from these cruelties. At the moment when the most cruel thing of all, death, draws near, and you already seem to feel its breath – all your sufferings melt away as darkness melts before the dawn.

This is, so to speak, His protection. He has arranged it so that at the very moment when it seems to men that they are inflicting on another the most terrible of all things, that terrible thing no longer exists for the victim, but recoils entirely upon those who inflict it. It is amazing, but true.

I remember once when a bear attacked me and pressed me down under him, driving the claws of his enormous paw into my shoulder, I felt no pain. I lay under him and looked into his warm, large mouth, with its wet, white teeth. He breathed above me and I saw how he turned his head to get into position to bite into both my temples at once, and in his hurry or from excited appetite, he made a trial snap in the air just above my head and again opened his mouth – that red, wet, hungry mouth, dripping with saliva. I felt I was about to die, and looked into the depths of that mouth as one condemned to execution looks into the grave dug for him. I looked, and I remember that I felt no fear or dread. I saw with one eye, beyond the outline of that mouth, a patch of blue sky gleaming between purple clouds roughly piled on one another and I thought how lovely it was up there . . .

I often remembered that moment afterwards, and now whenever I think of death I picture that situation to myself, because I have never been nearer to death than then. I recall it, reflect on it, make comparisons, and see that death – real, serious, all-absorbing death – is, thank God, not dreadful. Everything becomes torpid then, all that causes fear ceases to growl above one's head, and one's soul is serene and at peace.

It was not only with men such as Pobedonóstsev – whose name soon became as closely identified with the oppression practised by the Orthodox on the dissenters as Tolstoy's was with the struggle for freedom of conscience – that Tolstoy's new views brought him into conflict. He was ardent in his new faith and it often led him to be severe on the ordinary conduct and occupations of his fellows. By natural temperament he was very strenuous, and he always expressed himself emphatically, yet it was part of his new religion to live in amity with all men, to give no offence, and to be humble and forgiving.

There is abundant evidence that the conflict was fierce between his desire to propagate his faith and his wish not to offend those who differed from his views, and that even in his private life he was torn by conflicting influences.

In his Diary, in the staccato style there adopted, he notes on 5th May 1881:

One's family is one's flesh. To abandon one's family is the second temptation: to kill oneself. But do not yield to the third temptation. Serve not the family but the one God. One's family is the indicator of the place one must occupy on the economic ladder. It is one's flesh: as a weak stomach needs light food, so a pampered family needs more than a family accustomed to privations.

We shall find many indications of this struggle later on, as well as of his efforts to be of service to those less favourably situated than himself. On 7th May, after visiting the local prison, he notes:

I was in Túla. In the prison, fifteen Kalúga peasants have been kept more than a month for having no passports. They ought to be sent to Kalúga and from thence to their homes. But for two months they have been detained on the pretext that the Kalúga prison is over-full.

On 12th May he again wrote to Fet, and this was apparently the last letter of the long and intimate correspondence from which I have quoted extensively:

I remember when I received your letter, dear Afanásy Afanásyevich, how surprising it seemed that you should look so far ahead – to 12th May. It seemed specially strange for on that day I had heard of Dostoévski's death. But now 12th May is here, and we are still alive. Please pardon my silence, and do not punish my wife and me by cancelling your visit to us. Please do not be angry with me. I have greatly overworked myself and have grown much older this year, but have not to plead guilty to any change in my attachment to you.

On 15th May he again visits the prison and notes the 'terrible stench' there. He then adds:

In the evening Písarev and Samárin. Samárin with a smile: 'They [the Terrorists] ought to be hanged!' I wished to hold my tongue and ignore him; I wished to pitch him out by the scruff of his neck. I spoke out. 'The State! . . . But I care not what game you play, so long as it is not one that causes evil . . .'

21st May: A dispute. Tánya, Serëzha and Iván Mikháylovich. 'Good is relative,' i. e. there is no goodness. Only instincts.

22nd May: Continuation of conversation about the relativity of goodness. The good I speak of is that which we consider good for ourselves and for all . . .

28th May: Fet all day.

29th May: Talk with Fet and my wife. 'The Christian teaching is not practicable.' 'Then it is stupid?' 'No, but not practicable.' 'But have you tried to practise it?' 'No, but it is not practicable!'

In some of the letters quoted the reader may have detected signs that the cordial intimacy between Fet and Tolstoy was waning. From this time forth they drifted somewhat apart. The Christian teaching had brought, if not a sword, at least estrangement. In a life which was singularly successful, noble, and useful, and which, as Kropótkin says, made Tolstoy 'the most touchingly loved man in the world', there was this tragedy: that his zeal for the Gospel he had discovered, and which he was convinced will save the world, alienated him from many friends, brought discord into his family life, strained his relations with his wife, and left him spiritually alone.

On 10th June he set out on a second pilgrimage to Óptin Monastery; and this time he went on foot, wearing bast-shoes of peasant make. He was accompanied by his servant, Sergéy Arbúzov, part of whose duty it was to give ten or fifteen kopeks (3*d.* or 4*d.*) to each beggar they met on the way.

As was his custom when away from home, Tolstoy wrote frequently to the Countess. The day after starting he wrote from the village of Krapívni as follows:

I got here worse than I expected, having blistered my feet. I slept, and feel better in health. Here I have bought hemp shoes and shall get along better in them. It is very pleasant, useful, and instructive.

You cannot imagine how new, important, and useful for the soul (for one's view of life) it is to see how God's world lives: the real, big world, not the one we have arranged for ourselves and out of which we do not emerge even when we travel round the world . . . I take great care of myself and today bought grapes for my stomach's sake. If you had seen a girl of Márya's age [ten years old] where we slept last night, you would have fallen in love with her. She says nothing, understands everything, is always smiling, and no one looks after her. The chief new feeling is that of recognising oneself, and being in the eyes of others only what I am and not what I plus my belongings am. Today a peasant in his cart overtook us. 'Eh, old fellow, where is God taking you?' 'To Óptin.' 'Are you settling down to live there?' And so we began a conversation . . . If only the big and little children don't upset you. If only the visitors are not unpleasant, if only you yourself are well, if only nothing goes wrong, if only I do everything that is right and you also, then all will be well!

At night the travellers put up at any hut they chanced to reach, whose master or mistress would take them in.

One evening they reached a large village and stopped at the house of the Elder and asked for a samovar. The Elder was paying some twenty-five peasants who had been making bricks for him, and apparently was not paying them fairly, yet when he had finished he said to them: 'And now stand us a bottle of vodka. Here are some pilgrims who will have a drink with us !'

On hearing this, Tolstoy went out into the outhouse, and said to Arbúzov: 'What a wretched man that Elder is, preying on his own peasants!'

The Elder, who was half-drunk, also came into the outhouse and sprawled there.

An old woman with a baby in her arms came and bowed at his feet and implored him.

'Nazár Vasílevich, have pity on me, a poor widow, or I must just lie down and die!'

The Elder only grinned at her, and the woman began begging still harder till the Elder shouted at her: 'Clear out of my sight! If I see another trace of you I will send for the clerk!'

Tolstoy called the woman to him and asked what was the matter. She told him she had had five sons and five shares of the Communal land, but that now the Commune had taken three shares from her and wanted to take her homestead also.

Tolstoy made a note of the case and pacified the woman, promising to see what he could do for her.

At this the Elder began to shout at him, asking what he meant by it, and finished up by demanding to see his passport.

Arbúzov produced Tolstoy's passport from his bundle, but the Elder said: 'I can't read it without spectacles. Show it to my son Vasíly, who is in the house. He has been a coachman in Petersburg and can read well.'

When Vasíly had read, 'Count Leo Nikoláevich Tolstoy', he whispered something in his father's ear, and the latter instantly disappeared, the house became empty, and even the vodka the peasants had brought vanished.

Arbúzov adds:

When the samovar was ready, Vasíly invited us into the hut, where there was no one left but his mother. The Count asked what had become of the Elder and all the workmen. The woman replied that her husband had driven off to the neighbouring District Court and the workmen had gone to their homes.

'What a pity it is they choose such Elders,' said the Count to me, 'who spoil everything for themselves and get into trouble!'

The woman brought us a jug of milk and ten eggs. The Count invited her and her son to drink tea with us but they declined. I asked her to bring a bundle of straw that we might sleep on the floor, but she offered us her own bed, which the Count declined. After tea and supper we lay down to sleep, and there was no one in the hut except the old woman and her son.

Next morning I asked to have the samovar heated, and when all was ready I woke the Count . . . We drank tea, ate, and paid the hostess, though she did not wish to accept anything. At parting the Count said to Vasíly that the way his father was going on would probably lead to bad results.

Next evening in the twilight it thundered and lightened and the travellers were overtaken by a severe storm. Tolstoy was seized with severe spasms in his stomach and, wet through, lay down on the wet ground and said: 'I am at death's door!' When with much difficulty he got to a house, the owner refused to let them in and they had again to set off in the dark, but at last found shelter and a friendly welcome.

They reached the Monastery when the bell was ringing for supper, at six o'clock in the evening of the fifth day of their journey. So humble was their appearance that they were not admitted to the better-class refectory, but were sent to the room where the dirtiest and most ragged tramps ate. Arbúzov says:

I looked at the Count, but he, not at all disdainful of his neighbours, ate with pleasure and drank some *kvás*, which he seemed to like very much.

After supper we went for the night to the third-class hotel. The monk in charge, seeing that we wore bast-shoes, did not give us a room to ourselves but sent us to the common night-dormitory, where there was all sorts of dirt and insects.

'Father,' said I to the monk, 'here is a ruble for you – only let us have a room.'

He consented and gave us a room, saying that there would be three of us in it. The third man was a cobbler. I got a sheet and a small pillow out of my bundle and arranged a bed for the Count on the sofa. The cobbler lay on the other sofa, and I made myself up a shakedown on the floor not far from the Count. The cobbler soon fell asleep and snored loudly, so that the Count jumped up in alarm and said to me: 'Sergéy, wake that man and ask him not to snore.'

I went to the sofa, woke the cobbler, and said: 'My good fellow, you snore very loud and are startling my old man. It frightens him to have someone snoring in the same room with him.'

'Well then do you want me not to sleep all night, for the sake of your old man?'

However, it so happened that the cobbler snored no more.

Next day they rose at nine and drank tea. Arbúzov went to Mass, while Tolstoy went to see how the monks mowed, ploughed, and carried on their handicrafts.

Visiting the Monastery bookshop to see what spiritual food was supplied to the people, he met an old woman asking for a copy of the Gospels for her son. The monk in charge replied that it was not a suitable book for such folk, and proceeded to offer her descriptions of the Monastery and of miracles performed by the Saints. Thereupon Tolstoy purchased a copy of the Gospels for a ruble and a half (3s.) and gave it to the woman, telling her to read it and to let her son read it.

The monk was amazed that a man dressed like a pauper should be so free with his money, and sent to inform the Archimandrite, who despatched another monk to make enquiries. This monk happened to be from Yásnaya Polyána and at once recognised Tolstoy, much to the latter's regret.

The news that Tolstoy was in the Monastery soon spread, and

the Archimandrite sent for him. When he found that he had been recognised, Tolstoy said to Arbúzov:

'Since they have found me out, there is no help for it! Give me my boots and another blouse. I will change my things and go to see the Archimandrite and Father Ambrose.'

Before the Count had time to change, two monks came to take his things to the first-class hotel, in which everything was upholstered with velvet. The Count for a long time declined to move, but at last consented.

He had a four-hours' conversation with Father Ambrose, and, if we may trust Arbúzov's evidence, was delighted with him and afterwards remarked: 'Father Ambrose is quite a holy man. I talked with him and my soul felt light and joyous. When one speaks with such a man one really feels the nearness of God.'

*   *   *

The following extracts from Tolstoy's Diary relate to the days immediately after his visit to Óptin, from whence he returned by train and carriage.

In his Diary on 26th June 1881, he notes:

Very many poor. I am not well. Have not slept nor eaten anything solid for four days. Have tried to feel happy. It is difficult, but possible. I am conscious of making progress towards it.

28th June: A talk with Serëzha about God, in continuation of yesterday's. He and they think that to say, 'I do not know that, it can't be proved, I don't need it,' shows wisdom and education. Whereas it shows ignorance. 'I do not know any planets, nor an axis on which the earth turns, nor those unintelligible ecliptics, I do not wish to accept such things on faith, and I see that the sun and the stars move.' Yes, to prove the revolution of the earth and its course and mutation, and the precession of the equinoxes, is very difficult, and much remains obscure and hard to imagine, but the advantage is that all is brought into unison. So it is with moral and spiritual matters: the great thing is to bring into unison the problems, What to do? What to know? and What to hope? All humanity strives to bring these into unison and suddenly to divide what has been brought into unison is considered by some people a service to boast of.

Whose fault is this? Men have carefully taught them theology and Church rites, knowing in advance that these would not stand the tests of maturity, they have taught them much totally disconnected knowledge. And they are all left without unity, with disjointed knowledge, and think this a gain!

Serëzha admitted that he loves the life of the flesh and believes in it. I am glad to have the case clearly put ...

We had an immense dinner with champagne. The two Tányas [his sister-in-law and daughter] were dressed up. Sashes costing five rubles on each of the children. While we were still at dinner a cart was already starting for the picnic, and passed among peasant carts that were carrying people tortured by overwork.

I went to them – but had not the strength to speak out.

3rd July – I cannot get over my illness. Weakness, indolence, and sadness. Activity is essential: its aims – enlightenment, amendment, and union. Enlightenment I can direct towards others, amendment towards myself – union with those who are enlightened and amending.

On 6th July that year, 1881, comes a notable entry in the Diary:

6th July: Talk with X. An economic Revolution not only may, but must, come. It is wonderful it has not come already.

To a children's magazine which the Countess's brother was publishing, Tolstoy contributed *What Men Live By*, the precursor of his series of admirably simple and beautiful stories, primarily intended for peasants and children, that have become popular among all classes and in all languages, and are collected in the volume of *Twenty-Three Tales*. Of these, Carmen Sylva, Queen of Rumania, wrote:

Of all the works this great man and artist has written, his short stories have made the strongest impression upon me. I regard them as the most perfect tales ever written. In these popular stories thought of the highest purity reaches us which to my mind is far more eloquent than the subtlest style. The highest art is presented; and like Dante, Shakespeare, and the Bible, it will survive all time, for here is Eternal Truth ... If Tolstoy had written nothing but these short stories he would still rank among the greatest men of the world. When writing them he cannot have had a single base thought, but must have been a friend of suffering humanity and a real Christian.

What Men Live By is kindliness and love. The tale was told to Tolstoy by the itinerant story-teller mentioned in the first volume of this *Life*, but the idea of an angel sent to earth by God, and whose actions men could not understand, is one that has been used a thousand times. It appears in various guises in the *Talmud*, the *Apocrypha*, the *Koran* and the *Arabian Nights*, as well as in Voltaire's *Zadig* and elsewhere.

Tolstoy himself felt scruples about having used it, for he disliked supernatural machinery, and never elsewhere introduces an angel. Of all his works hardly any has received more general approval.

Turgénev, at the Countess's request, contributed to her brother's magazine his touching story *The Quail*, and on 9th July Tolstoy went to visit him. Having mistaken Wednesday for Thursday he arrived a day too soon, and finding no conveyance awaiting him at the station, hired a trap to drive to Turgénev's house. The driver lost his way in the dark, and they did not arrive till one o'clock in the morning.

Though Tolstoy was not expected, neither Turgénev nor the poet Polónski, who was staying with him, had gone to bed. Polónski was writing in his room when horses were heard outside, and on going into the hall he saw a sunburnt peasant in a blouse with a leather belt, paying the driver. He looked at him but did not recognise that the peasant was Tolstoy, until the latter raised his head and looking at him inquiringly, said: 'Is that you, Polónski? . . . '

The three writers at once began an animated conversation which continued till three in the morning. Turgénev at times became so excited that even his neck and ears went quite red. Tolstoy's tone and manner struck Polónski (who had not seen him for twenty years) as surprisingly soft and of winning simplicity, though he adhered to his views with firmness.

'He seemed to me,' said Polónski, 'to be reborn: imbued with a different faith and love . . . He did not impose his views on us and listened quietly to Turgénev's objections. In a word, he was no longer the Count I had known in his youth.'

Next day, an hour before dinner time, Turgénev was informed that his man-cook was drunk and that there was no one to prepare the dinner. At first this news perplexed him, for not only was he among the most hospitable of mortals, but good eating was a matter to which he attached great importance. At last he decided to cook the dinner himself, and rubbing his hands, began to recount how he would cut up the carrots and chop the meat to make cutlets. Bent on this achievement he set off to the kitchen, only to be turned back by one of his servants, Zahár, who explained: 'That's not your business! . . . Go away, and God be with you! We will get dinner ready without you.'

9th–10th July 1881 – At Turgénev's. Polónski, kind-hearted and poor, quietly occupied with art and literature, and judging no one, was tranquil. Turgénev fears the name of God, but acknowledges Him. He too is naïvely tranquil, living in luxury and idleness of life.

After Tolstoy's departure Turgénev frequently spoke kindly and affectionately of him as a man and with enthusiasm of him as an author. One day Turgénev appeared with a book in his hand and read to his guests the chapter in *War and Peace* which tells how two battalions of the 6th Chasseurs marched past Bagratión to battle with the French [Vol. I., Book II, Chap. XVIII]. ' . . . They had not yet reached Bagratión, but the ponderous tread of the mass of men marching in step could be heard.'

Turgénev read the whole chapter to the end admirably and with enthusiasm, and when he had finished raised his head and said: 'I know nothing in any literature of our time superior to that description. That is how descriptions should be written! . . . ' and though everyone agreed with him he continued to demonstrate how highly artistic it is.

Immediately after this visit Tolstoy went to his Samára estate. But to busy himself with the management of property was becoming intolerable, and his Diary gives constant indications of his disquiet. For instance he, who was so keen a horseman, jots down:

16th July: I walked and rode to inspect the horses. An unendurable occupation. Idleness. Shame.

22nd July: The husband of the woman from Pávlovka died in hospital, and their son died of hunger. The little girl was saved by giving her milk. The shepherd at Patróvski: poverty, pale and grey.

A talk with A, A. about those landlords who are for holding the land and those who are for distribution. Orlóv-Davídov's peasants: one *desyatína* a head [less than three acres]. They cannot even afford *kvas*, while he owns 49,000 *desyatínas*.

On 24th July he wrote to his wife:

Harvest prospects are excellent. What would be sad, if we could not give at least a little help, is that there are so many poor in the villages and it is a timid poverty, unaware of itself.

The Countess replied:

Let the management of the estate go on as has been arranged. I do not wish anything altered. There may be losses – we have learnt to be accustomed to them; but even if there are large profits the money will reach neither me nor the children if it is given away. At any rate you know my opinion about helping the poor: we cannot feed thousands of Samára and other poor people, but if one sees and knows that so-and-so is poor and has no corn or horse or cow or hut, &c., one must give all that at once, and one cannot refrain from giving, because one feels sorry for them, and because it ought to be done.

The problem of poverty, comparatively simple in primitive communities where the way of life is fixed by custom and each inhabitant is well known to his neighbours and more or less manageable in a wealthy and well-arranged community under some organised plan of administration, is a heart-breaking affair during a transition period such as that in which Tolstoy was living or we ourselves are still faced with. It is obviously too large to be dealt with by any individual's strength or means, while to shut one's eyes to it is to blind oneself to the most urgent of social problems. In the succeeding years we shall see how it oppressed Tolstoy, what efforts he made to deal with it, and how vividly he was able to state the problem – because he did not shrink from facing the facts.

During this stay in the Province of Samára he saw a good deal of the Molokáns, Sabbatarians, and other sectarians, who interested him much. He also met A. S. Prugávin – 'a very interesting and sedate man' – who was studying the varieties of religious beliefs among the Samára peasants. On 24th July, Tolstoy writes to his wife:

The Molokáns are most interesting. I have been to a prayer-meeting of theirs and heard their explanation of the Gospels, and took part in the discussion. They have also visited me and asked me to tell them how I understand things; and I read them extracts from my manuscript. The seriousness, interest, and healthy clear sense of these half-educated people is amazing.

A little later, feeling how heavy a burden he had allowed to fall upon his wife who was expecting her eighth child that autumn, he wrote:

You will be going to Moscow today. You would not believe how troubled I am at the thought that you may be overtaxing your strength, and how I repent of having given you little or no help.

In this respect the kumys has done good: it has brought me down from the point of view from which, carried away by my work, I involuntarily regarded everything. I now see things differently. I still have the same thoughts and feelings, but am cured of the delusion that others can and should see everything as I do. I am much to blame towards you, darling – unconsciously, involuntarily, as you know, but still none the less to blame.

My excuse is that in order to work with the intensity with which I worked, and to get something done, one has to forget all else. And I forgot you too much, and now repent. For heaven's sake and our love's sake, take care of yourself! Put off as much as you can till my return; I will gladly do everything and will not do it badly, for I will take pains.

In a subsequent letter he writes with approval of a family he was staying with, the members of which did most of their own housework, keeping but one servant. Speaking of these people who aimed at a simple life, he adds:

They are admirable people and strive with all their might and all their energy towards the very best and justest way of living, while life and their family pull in another direction – and the result is a middle course. Looking at it from outside, I see that, good as this mean is, it is yet far below what they aim at. One applies the lesson to oneself and learns to be satisfied with a mean.

About this time his family were reminded of Tolstoy's former life in the Caucasus by the arrival at Yásnaya of a Cossack – a nephew of Epíshka (Eróshka in *The Cossacks*). This man had known Tolstoy at Starogládovsk, and riding all the way from the Caucasus to ask the Emperor to give him some post or other, had turned aside to visit Tolstoy in passing.

The Countess wrote to her husband of this event, and in a letter written just before his return, we find her reproaching him for staying too long in Samára. She was however delighted to hear that he was thinking of writing a story:

What a joyful feeling seized me when I read that you again wished to write something poetic!

You have felt what I have long waited and longed for. In that lies salvation and joy; that will again unite us and will console you and light up your life. That is the real work for which you were created, and outside that sphere there is no peace for your soul. I know that you cannot force yourself, but God grant you may cherish that gleam and that this divine spark in you may again kindle and spread. The thought enchants me.

On his way home Tolstoy notes in his Diary:

1st August: At Ryazhk every month a man is killed on the railway. To the devil with all machines, if a man [must be sacrificed]!

He reached home just when there were many visitors and great preparations for amateur theatricals. This jarred on him after the primitive simplicity he had enjoyed in Samára, and he noted in his Diary:

18th August: A Play. Empty people. The days 19, 20 and 21 must be struck out of my life.

On the 22nd, Turgénev visited Yásnaya. The Countess writes of his stay:

In the evening my children and nieces got up a quadrille. The children's merriment infected Turgénev. He danced in the quadrille with my niece, and then took off his coat, and sticking his thumbs into his waistcoat, to the children's great delight, began to perform strange figures with his legs, saying, 'That's how they dance the *cancan* in Paris.'

He was very merry that evening, praising everything and everybody. Looking at me kindly, he said to Leo Nikoláevich, 'How well you did, my dear fellow, to choose such a wife!'

Tolstoy felt differently about Turgénev's behaviour, and noted laconically in his Diary:

Turgénev, *cancan*: it is sad. Meeting peasants on the road was joyful.

On 1st September he notes:

I often wish to die. My work does not absorb me.

His eldest son, Sergéy, was now eighteen and about to enter the

University. Educational opportunities were also needed for the other children, with whose tuition Tolstoy, owing to his religious pre-occupations, had almost ceased to concern himself. Moreover the eldest daughter, Tánya, was seventeen. In the ordinary course of events it was time for her to be brought out into Society, and it had been decided long before that the family should move to Moscow that winter. In mid-September 1881 they did so, and settled in a hired house.

Greatly as Tolstoy now disliked the idea, he had to consent to it, and not till he was in Moscow did he quite realise how painful town life would be to him after so many years spent in the country.

On 5th October he noted in his Diary:

A month has passed. The most tormenting in my life. The move to Moscow. All are busy arranging – when will they begin to live? All of it not for the sake of living but to be like other people. Unfortunates! Life is lacking.

Smells, stones, luxury, destitution, and vice. Malefactors have come together, robbed the people, collected soldiers, and set up Law Courts to protect their orgies, and they feast. The people can do nothing but, by taking advantage of the passions of these others, lure back from them what has been stolen. The men-peasants are cleverest at that. Their wives remain in the villages while they wax our parquet floors, and rub our bodies in the baths, and ply as cabmen.

On 14th October the Countess wrote to her sister:

Tomorrow we shall have been here a month and I have not written a word to anyone. For the first fortnight I cried every day, because Lëvochka not only became depressed, but even fell into a kind of desperate apathy. He did not sleep and did not eat and sometimes literally wept, and I really thought I should go mad. You would be surprised to see how I have altered and how thin I have grown. Afterwards he went to the Province of Tver and visited his old acquaintances the Bakúnins [a Liberal, artistic, Zémstvo-literary household] and then went to a village to see some sectarian Christian, and when he returned he was less in the dumps. Now he has arranged to work in a wing of the house, where he has hired himself two small quiet rooms for a month. Then he goes across the Maiden's Field and over the river to the Sparrow Hills, and there saws and splits wood with some peasants. It is good for his health and cheers him up.

The sectarian Christian referred to was Sutáev, a very remarkable peasant, whose thoughts and feelings were strikingly in accord with Tolstoy's. The fact that Tolstoy left home to find Sutáev on the evening of the very day he first heard from Prugávin of his existence, indicates the strength of the craving he felt for spiritual fellowship.

Sutáev and his sons had abandoned their occupation as tombstone-makers in Petersburg because they considered competitive business immoral. In accord with the Gospel injunction, they forgave their debtors: that is to say, did not collect the money due from their customers. Sutáev retired to the country, undertook the duties of village herdsman, and made it his aim to treat the beasts better than they had been treated before, using, for instance, no whip when he drove a horse. His sons on conscientious grounds refused to serve in the army, and suffered imprisonment for this refusal. His whole family rejected the Church, disapproved of the State, and organised a Commune among themselves. When asked how if people wanted to marry, they could get on without a priest, Sutáev told of his daughter's marriage:

> When the matter was decided and we met in the evening, I spoke to them about how people ought to live, then we made their bed, put them to sleep together, put out the light, and that was the whole wedding.

Tolstoy was charmed by Sutáev. The simplicity, seriousness, and conscientiousness, of this type of peasant, their fearlessness in facing the great problems of conduct, their scorn of conventional shams, their industry, tenacity, and endurance, the usefulness and frugality of their lives, as well as their concise and pithy way of expressing themselves, evoked his unbounded admiration, and no disappointment at the practical results of their efforts ever seemed to diminish that admiration.

At the conclusion of Tolstoy's visit to Sutáev the latter harnessed a horse to drive his guest to the Bakúnins. On the way the two men became so absorbed in discussing the imminence of the Kingdom of God that they did not notice what the horse was doing and their cart upset into a ravine! Fortunately neither of them was seriously hurt by the accident.

The influence Sutáev had on Tolstoy depended not so much on what he said, as on the fact that he had altered his life to accord with his perception of what was right, which was just what Tolstoy himself was finding it extremely difficult to do. The latter's distress of mind, perplexity, striving, and sufferings, as well as the firmness of his conviction that he was at last treading the path to peace, can best be shown by quoting from letters he wrote at this time. Here is one addressed to V. I. Alexéev:

Thanks for your good letter, dear V. I.! We, as it were, forget that we love each other. I do not wish to forget it – or that I am much indebted to you for the tranquillity and clearness of outlook on life I have reached. You were the first man (touched by education) of my acquaintance, who not in words but in spirit confessed the faith that has become for me a clear and steadfast light. That made me believe in the possibility of what had always dimly stirred in my soul. And therefore as you have been, so you will always remain, dear to me. The lack of clearness and continuity in your life disconcerts me, as does your last letter – full of worldly cares, but I myself was so recently full of them and am still so weak in my own life, that I ought to realise how complex is the interweaving of one's life with one's past temptations, and that what is essential is one's faith, not external forms. And I am glad to think that you and I have the same faith . . .

I have become convinced that only one's life can show the path – only the example of one's life. The effect of that example is very slow, very indefinite (in the sense that one cannot possibly, I think, know whom it will influence) and very difficult. But it alone gives a real impulse. Example is the proof of the possibility of Christian – that is of reasonable and happy – life under all conceivable conditions. That alone moves people, and that alone is necessary both to me and to you – so let us help one another to give it. Write to me, and let us be as truthful as possible with one another.

Later on, V. I. Alexéev married a fine lady, became Principal of a School, and abandoned his Simple Life tendencies, but he had helped Tolstoy to realise that life is full of things that destroy and spoil happiness and the continuance of which depends on us. Tolstoy's own experience showed him that the attempt to change life's conditions is the most interesting of occupations, and that a reformer who plays his part manfully, using his powers for the highest aims he sees, though he end by being burnt at the stake, may yet have enjoyed life more abundantly than others who tread conventional paths. His grasp of this truth made Tolstoy powerful and attractive; but it was very difficult for him – a landed proprietor with strong family ties, an artistic temperament, and deeply rooted prejudices – to emancipate himself; and his strenuous efforts caused him at times to lose balance and attribute paramount importance to questionable opinions.

Among the few congenial spirits he met at this time were Nicholas Fëdorovich Fëdorov, Librarian to the Rumyántsev Museum in Moscow, and Orlóv, a teacher in a school for the children of the employees of one of the railways. Of these men Tolstoy speaks in another letter to V. I. Alexéev:

Thank you, dear Vasíly Ivánovich, for your letter. I think of you constantly and love you very much. You are dissatisfied with yourself, what then must I say of myself? It is very hard for me in Moscow. I have been here more than two months and it is still just as hard. I now see that though I knew of the mass of temptations amid which people live, I did not believe in them and could not realise them – just as one learnt from Geography that there is a Caucasus, but only really knew it when one got there. And the mass of this evil oppresses me – brings me to despair – inspires distrust, and it amazes me that no one sees it. Perhaps to find an honest path in life for myself I needed this experience. It seems at first as though one must choose one of two things: either let one's hands drop and suffer passively, yielding to despair, or make peace with evil, befogging oneself with cards and chatter and bustle. But fortunately I cannot do the latter, and the former is too painful, so I seek an outlet. The outlet that presents itself to me is preaching, in print and viva voce. But here stand vanity, pride, and possibly self-deception – and one dreads them. Another issue is to help others, but there the immensity of the number of unfortunates crushes one. It is not here as in a village, where a natural group has been formed. The only issue I see is to live well, always turning one's kindly side to everyone, but I have not yet learnt to do that as you do it. When I break down I remember you. I seldom manage to be like that: I am fiery, get angry and indignant, and feel dissatisfied with myself. But there are some real people even here; and God has let me meet two such: Orlóv is one, and the other and chief is Nicholáy Fëdorovich Fëdorov . . . Do you remember my telling you of him? . . . When I speak to him of carrying out the Christian teaching, he says: 'Yes, *that* of course,' and I know he does perform it. He is sixty and poor; he gives away everything, and is always bright and gentle. Orlóv is a man who has suffered [politically]: he was two years in prison over Necháev's affair, and is sickly. He also is ascetic in his life, provides for nine people, and lives rightly. He is a teacher in a railway school. Orlóv and Fëdorov have read my book, *The Gospel in Brief*, and we are in full agreement with Sutáev to the smallest details. So it should be well. I am also writing stories in which I try to express my ideas. Again that should be well, yet I lack tranquillity. I am oppressed by the triumph of indifference and conventionality and the obduracy of evil and deception. I have been at home all the time; in the mornings I try to work, but it goes badly. At two or three o'clock I go across the Moskva River to saw up timber. When I have the strength and wish to do it, it refreshes me, strengthens me, and I see something of real life, into which – if but for a moment – I dive and am refreshed. But when I don't go (some three weeks ago I relaxed and ceased to go and quite sank into the dumps), then irritability and spleen overcome me. In the evenings I sit at home and am possessed by visitors and conversations, which though interesting, are empty. I now want to shut myself off from them. I have reread this letter and see it is terribly stupid, but I fear I cannot write a better one and so I send it off. I will be sure to write better next time. Please write oftener.

There is something very sad in the further story of Tolstoy's relations with Fëdorov. Their friendship lasted some years and was then broken off owing to the fact that Tolstoy could not accept certain views Fëdorov deemed vitally important. This led the latter in his writings to refer to Tolstoy with virulence; but Tolstoy, who greatly admired the asceticism of Fëdorov's life and was convinced of his sincerity, never spoke of him otherwise than with high respect, and never showed any signs of the contemptuous irritability he often displayed when dealing with men of higher rank and world-wide reputation.

Unity of views was extremely difficult to obtain among men who were shaping life anew, and unity of action was still further from their reach. At the end of November we learn by a letter of Strákhov's that Tolstoy had reproached him with understanding his feelings but not sharing them. Strákhov replied that that reproach 'puts me to shame, and continually troubles my conscience'; but he frankly adds:

I lack the strength of feeling you possess and do not wish to force myself, or to pretend. Where can I obtain devotion and ardour such as you feel? . . . Be indulgent to me and do not reject me because of this difference. I know your aversion to the world, for I share the feeling, but I feel it in a slight degree which neither stifles nor torments me, though I have no attachment to the world, or if I have any I now try to destroy it and to sever the last threads . . . Do not be stringently exacting with me. To you I owe probably the best moments of my life. Do not look only at what is bad in me but also at what may be found of good. Correct me, however; I hearken to you willingly, as you know.

Thanks to Strákhov's frank and conciliatory attitude good relations were maintained.

On 31st October of this year, 1881, another son was born, and christened Alexéy.

It may not be out of place to close this chapter by quoting the novelist Boborykin's account of Tolstoy's appearance when he first visited him, at about the time now reached:

Tolstoy had then the appearance of a kindly, middle-aged man, not yet perceptibly grey; a person not yet quite rusticised, but already noticeably unwilling to submit to fashion or even to the proprieties obligatory on the master of a hospitable, aristocratic house. He wore no waistcoat, but only a pea-jacket over his shirt, and as it grew hot in the room, he took off his coat. Just then the Countess entered to ask whether we would have tea.

She jokingly made a remark to her husband about his attire, to which, without resuming his coat, he good-naturedly replied that it was too hot in the room. This seemed to put the Countess somewhat out of countenance.

I then saw her for the first and last time. She was a very fine woman, elegantly dressed, with a handsome face, a light step, and a pleasant voice.

4

Riches and Poverty

We have seen how Tolstoy strove to grasp the meaning and purpose of life and to realise the relation of the finite to the infinite. This phase of his development culminated with the completion of his studies of theology and the Gospels, and the writings of *What I Believe*. The next great problem he tackled was the economic question: Why are the many poor?

He was sure that it is our business to establish the Kingdom of God on earth. He was also convinced that by conforming to the laws of God miserable lives can be made happy. In Moscow he was horrified to see how wretchedly a large part of the population lived, and how callous the religious, learned, wealthy, and governing classes were to the fate of their less fortunate brethren.

With characteristic impetuosity, self-reliance, energy, and ignorance of the nature of the case he had begun to deal with, he seized the occasion presented by the approaching decennial Census, in January 1882, to issue an ardent appeal to Society in general. The 2,000 students and others about to engage in conducting the Census should, he said, take that opportunity to become acquainted with the destitute in Moscow, to whom organised relief should be extended. *What Then Must We Do?* – one of the most soul-stirring of his works – grew out of this appeal, and out of the experience that followed it. It was written while the emotions aroused in him by that experience were red-hot, which accounts on the one hand for a certain excess of emphasis and rashness of conclusion noticeable in some chapters, and on the other for the interest the description of his experiences arouses in every sympathetic reader.

Tolstoy subsequently poured scorn on his newspaper article, *On the Census in Moscow*, but a couple of its most characteristic sentences must be recorded.

The first shows the Franciscan attitude he adopted towards money, an attitude which often caused his followers much perplexity. He says that:

'To do good' is generally understood to mean 'to give money'. But in my opinion 'to do good' and 'to give money' are not only not one and the same thing, but are two things quite different and for the most part opposite. Money in itself is an evil. And therefore he who gives money does evil. The delusion that to give money is to do good, has arisen because for the most part when a man does good he also frees himself from evil, including money . . .

That he was, however, not very clear on this point is indicated by another sentence, in which he explains the relation he wished to see established between the helpers and the helped:

It may be the smallest part of the matter that we, the Census clerks and organisers, may distribute a hundred six penny-bits to people who are hungry; yet that will be no small thing, not so much because the hungry will be fed, as because clerks and organisers will have dealt with a hundred poor people as with human beings . . .

There is an obvious contradiction in first saying that 'he who gives money does evil', and then approving of the distribution of a hundred sixpenny-bits; but Tolstoy himself often explained that though no good may come of one's gift, one has still no right to refuse to give of one's superfluity to him that is in need.

His argument on that point is not convincing, but in the next passage, together with his amazing optimism, one sees his talent for going with sublime simplicity to the root of a great matter:

. . . However little may be accomplished it will be of importance. But why not hope that everything will be accomplished? Why not hope that we may bring it about that in Moscow there will not be one person unclothed, hungry, or selling himself for money, not one unfortunate crushed by Fate who does not know where to find brotherly aid? What is wonderful is, not that this has not yet been done, but *that these things exist side by side with our superfluity of leisure and wealth and that we can live quietly knowing of them*!

His practical proposals were ludicrously inadequate to meet the evil, but the words I have italicised strike a note which deserves to be heard long after all the blunders of all the reformers of our time, and all the clamours raised by their opponents, have been forgotten.

What Then Must We Do? was not finished till February 1886, but it tells of what happened in January 1882. Besides explaining Tolstoy's view of the social problem, it is autobiographically of such value that I should have to quote the first twelve sections of it in full, were it not available in this edition. Its autobiographical chapters are intensely interesting and everyone interested in Tolstoy should certainly read them, and though much in the following economic part may not be convincing, Tolstoy offers acute reflections that go very deep.

As an epigraph he quoted Luke 3:10–11:

And the multitudes asked him, saying, *What then must we do?* And he answered and said unto them, 'He that hath two coats, let him impart to him that hath none; and he that hath food, let him do likewise . . . '

He says: 'I had spent my life in the country, and when in 1881 I came to live in Moscow the sight of town poverty surprised me . . . after coming to Moscow I had for the sake of exercise formed the habit of going to work at the Sparrow Hills with two peasants who sawed wood there.'

He vividly describes the workmen and beggars he got to know and then tells of a visit to a night lodging-house for the destitute. He says: 'I went upstairs. There men were taking their places. Among them I saw one of those to whom I had given money. On seeing him I suddenly felt dreadfully ashamed and hurried away; and feeling as if I had committed a crime, I left the house and went home. There, ascending the carpeted steps to the cloth-carpeted hall and taking off my fur coat, I sat down to a five-course dinner served by two lackeys in dress clothes with white ties and white gloves.

'Thirty years ago in Paris I once, in the presence of thousands of spectators, saw how they cut a man's head off with a guillotine. I knew that the man was a dreadful criminal; I knew all the arguments written in defence of that kind of action, and I knew it was done deliberately and intentionally; but at the moment the head and body separated and fell into the box I gasped, and realised not with my mind nor with my heart but with my whole being, that all the arguments in defence of capital punishment are wicked nonsense, that however many people may combine to commit murder (the worst of all crimes) and whatever they may call themselves, murder remains murder, and that this crime had been committed before my eyes and I by my presence and non-intervention had approved and shared in it. In the same way now, at the sight of the hunger, cold, and degradation of thousands of people, I understood not with my mind or my heart but with my whole being, that the existence of tens of thousands of such people in Moscow while I and thousands of others over – eat ourselves with beefsteaks and sturgeon, and cover our horses and floors with cloth and carpets is a crime – no matter what all the learned men in the world may say about its necessity – a crime, committed not once but constantly; and that I with my luxury not merely tolerate it but share in it . . . and therefore I felt and feel, and shall not cease to feel, that as long as I have any superfluous food and someone else has none, and I have two coats and someone else has none, I share in a constantly repeated crime.

'That evening after I returned from Lyápin House I told my impressions to a friend. He, a town dweller, began to explain with some satisfaction that it was the most natural thing in a city, and that it was merely my provincialism that caused me to see anything peculiar in it. Things had always been so, and would and must always be so; it *is* an inevitable condition of civilisation. In London it is still worse . . . so there is nothing wrong in it, and one must not be dissatisfied with it. I began to answer my friend, but did it so warmly and irritably that my wife ran in from an adjoining room asking what had happened. It seems that, without noticing it, I had cried out with tears in my voice and waved my arms at my friend, exclaiming: "One cannot live so; one cannot; one cannot!" They took me to task for my unnecessary ardour, telling me that I cannot talk quietly about anything, but become unpleasantly excited, and they proved to me in particular that the existence of such unfortunate people cannot justify my spoiling the lives of those about me.

'I felt that this was quite just, and I was silenced; but in the depth of my heart I felt that I too was right, and I could not feel at ease.

'Town life, which had seemed strange and foreign to me before, now became so repulsive that all the pleasures of the luxurious life I formerly enjoyed became a torment to me. And try as I would to find in my soul some justification for our way of living, I could not without irritation behold either my own or any other drawing-room, nor any clean, elegantly laid table, nor a carriage with well-fed coachmen and horses, nor the shops, theatres, and assemblies. I could not help seeing beside them the hungry, cold, downtrodden inhabitants of Lyápin lodging-house. I could not escape the thought that these two things were connected, and the one resulted from the other.

'When I spoke of my impressions to intimate friends and acquaintances, they all gave me to understand that the sight had acted so strongly on me merely because I – Leo Tolstoy – am a very kind and good man. I willingly believed them . . .

' "Really," said I to myself, "the fault probably lies not in my luxury, but in the inevitable conditions of life. An alteration in my life cannot cure the evils I have seen. By altering my life I shall only make myself and those near me unhappy, while the destitute will remain as badly off as ever. Therefore the task for me is not to change my own life, as I thought at first, but as far as I can to aid in improving the position of those unfortunates who have evoked my sympathy. The fact of the matter is that I am a very good, kind man, and wish to benefit my neighbours." . . . So I began to devise a plan of philanthropic activity in which I could exhibit my goodness. I should mention, however, that when devising this philanthropic activity I felt all the time in the depth of my soul that it was not the right thing, but as often happens, reasoning and imagination stifled the voice of conscience.

'It chanced that preparations were being made at that time for the Census. This seemed a good opportunity for starting the charity in which I wished to exhibit my goodness. I knew of many philanthropic organisations and societies in Moscow, but all their activities seemed falsely directed and insignificant in comparison with what I aimed at. So I planned the following: to arouse sympathy for town poverty among the rich; to collect money, enrol people willing to help in the affair, and besides compiling the Census, to visit all the dens of destitution with the Census-takers, and get in touch with the unfortunates and investigate their needs, helping them with money and work, or by getting them back to their villages, as well as by putting their children to school and the old folk into refuges and almshouses. More than that, I thought that from among those engaged in this work a permanent society could be formed which, dividing the districts of Moscow among its members, would see that poverty and destitution should not be allowed to breed, but be constantly nipped in the bud, and would perform the duty not so much of curing town poverty as of preventing it. I already imagined that there would be none left in the town who were in want, much less totally destitute, and that I should have accomplished all this; and that we, the rich, could afterwards sit at ease in our drawing-rooms, eat five-course dinners, and drive in carriages to theatres and assemblies, untroubled by such sights as I had witnessed at Lyápin House.

Having formed this plan, I wrote an article about it, and before sending it for publication I went about among my acquaintances from whom I hoped to receive help . . .

'At the last house I went to that day, in the evening, I found a large gathering. The hostess of that house has for some years been engaged in philanthropy. Several carriages stood at the entrance, and several footmen in expensive liveries were sitting in the hall. In the large drawing-room, round two tables on which stood lamps, sat married and unmarried ladies in expensive clothes with expensive ornaments, dressing little dolls. Several young men were there also, near the ladies. The dolls these ladies were making were to be disposed of at a lottery for the poor.

'The sight of this drawing-room and of the people collected in it impressed me very unpleasantly. Not to mention that the fortunes of the people there assembled amounted to some millions of rubles, or that the interest on the cost of the dresses, lace, bronzes, jewellery, carriages, horses, liveries, and footmen, would a hundred times exceed the value of their work – the cost of this one gathering alone: the gloves, clean linen, and conveyances, with the candles, tea, sugar, and biscuits provided, must have exceeded a hundred times the value of the things produced. I saw this, and could therefore understand that here at any rate I should find no sympathy for my plan, but I had come to make the proposal, and, difficult as I felt it, I said my say . . .

'After returning home that day I lay down to sleep, not merely with a foreboding that my plan would come to nothing, but with a sense of shame and a consciousness that I had been doing something very horrid and shameful all day.

'At my request they allotted me for the Census the district containing Rzhánov House. I had heard of it as a den of most terrible poverty and vice and had therefore asked the organisers to let me take that district.

*   *   *

'On the first appointed day the student Census-takers began work in the morning, but I, the philanthropist, did not join them till towards noon. I could not get there sooner because I only rose at ten and then drank coffee and had to smoke to help my digestion.

'In the first lodging I did not find a single person on whom to expend my beneficence . . . All the people were of the kind whose case one would have to look into more carefully before helping them. I did not find any unfortunates who could be made fortunate by a mere gift of money. Ashamed as I am to admit it, I began to feel disappointed at not seeing in these houses anything like what I had expected. I thought I should find people of an exceptional kind, but when I had been to all the lodgings I became convinced that the inhabitants of these houses are not at all exceptional, but are just such people as those among whom I live. Among them as among us there were some more or less good and more or less bad, more or less happy and more or less miserable; and the unhappy were just such as exist among ourselves – people whose unhappiness depends not on external conditions, but on themselves – a kind of unhappiness bank-notes cannot cure.

* * *

'Strange as it may seem to say so, I did not here experience anything like the feeling I had at Lyápin House. On the contrary, during the first round both I and the students had an almost pleasant feeling. Why do I say, "almost pleasant"? That is untrue; the feeling produced by inter-course with these people, strange as it seems to say so, was simply a very pleasant one.

'The first impression was that the majority of those who lived here were working people and very good-natured ones.

'We found most of them at work; washerwomen at their troughs, carpenters at their benches, bootmakers on their stools, and so on . . . We came prepared to see nothing but horrors; and instead of horrors we were shown something good, that involuntarily evoked our respect. There were so many of these good people that the tattered, fallen, idle ones, scattered here and there among them, did not destroy the general impression.

[Tolstoy then describes the sort of people he found at Rzhánov House, and speaks in particular of educated people who had sunk from former prosperity.]

' . . . One had been in this plight for a year, another for five, and a third for thirty years. One of them need only be decently dressed to go to see a well-known person favourably disposed towards him; another need only be dressed, pay some debts, and get to the town of Orël; a third need only redeem his things from pawn and find a little money to continue a lawsuit he is bound to win, and then all again will be well. They all say they only need some external thing in order to resume the position they consider natural and happy for themselves!

'Had I not been befogged by my pride as benefactor I need only have looked a little into their faces – young and old – generally weak and sensual, but good-natured, to understand that their misfortune could not be repaired by external means, and that unless their views of life were changed they could not be happy in any position, and that they were not peculiar people in specially unfortunate circumstances, but were just such people as surround us and such as we are ourselves. I remember that I found intercourse with this kind of unfortunates particularly trying; and I now understand why. In them I saw myself as in a looking-glass. Had I thought of my own life and that of the people of our circle, I should have seen that between us and these people there was no essential difference.

'If those now about me do not live in Rzhánov House, but in large flats or houses of their own in the best streets, and if they eat and drink dainty food instead of only bread with bullock's liver or herrings, this does not prevent their being similarly unfortunate. They too are dissatisfied with their position, regret the past, and want something better; and the better positions they desire are just like those the dwellers in Rzhánov House want: namely, positions in which they can do less work and make others do more for them. The difference is merely in degree. Had I then reflected, I should have understood this; however I did not reflect, and only questioned these people and noted them down, intending, after learning the details of their various circumstances and needs, to help them later on. I did not then understand that such men can only be helped by changing their outlook on life; land to change another man's outlook one must oneself have a better one and live in accord with it, while I was myself living according to the view that had to be altered before these people could cease to be unhappy.

'I did not see that, metaphorically speaking, they were unhappy not because they lacked nourishing food but because their digestion was spoilt; and that they were demanding not what was nourishing but what excited their appetites. I did not see that the help they needed was not food, but a cure for their spoilt digestion. Though I anticipate, I will here remark that of all the people I noted down I really helped none, though what they asked – and what seemed as though it would set them on their feet – was done for some of them. Of these I know three particularly well. All three after being repeatedly set on their feet, are now again in just the position they were in three years ago.

[Tolstoy then tells of an incident that occurred among the prostitutes, of whom there were many in Rzhánov House.]

'This incident led me into a fresh error – that of supposing that it would be possible to help these unfortunates also. It seemed to me then, in my self-deception, that this would be quite easy. I said to myself: Let us note down these women also, and afterwards when we have noted everybody down, we (who "we" were I did not stop to consider) will attend to them. I imagined that we (those very people who have for several generations led, and are still leading, these women into that condition) could one fine day take it into our heads suddenly to rectify it all. Yet had I but remembered my talk with the loose woman who was rocking the child whose mother was ill, I might have understood how insensate such an undertaking was.

When we saw that woman with the child, we thought it was her own. In reply to the question, Who she was, she said simply that she was a wench. She did not say, "A prostitute." Only the landlord of the lodging used that terrible word. The supposition that she had a child of her own suggested to me the thought of extricating her from her position. So I asked: "Is that your child?"

' "No, it's this woman's."

' "How is it you are rocking it?"

' "She asked me to. She is dying."

Though my supposition had proved erroneous, I continued to speak to her in the same sense. I began to ask her who she was and how she came to be in such a position. She told me her story willingly and very simply. She was of Moscow birth, the daughter of a factory workman. She had been left an orphan, and an aunt (now dead) had taken charge of her. From her aunt's house she began to frequent the taverns. When I asked whether she would not like to change her way of life, my question evidently did not even interest her. How can the suggestion of anything quite impossible interest anybody? She giggled and said: "Who would take me with a yellow ticket?" [The passports issued to prostitutes by the police.]

' "Well, but suppose we found you a place as cook somewhere?" said I.

'That idea suggested itself to me because she was a strong, flaxen-haired woman, with a kindly, stupid, round face. There are cooks like that. My words obviously did not please her. She said: "A cook! But I can't bake bread!" and she laughed – She said she could not, but I saw by the expression of her face that she did not want to be a cook and despised that position and calling.

'This woman, who like the widow in the Gospels had sacrificed her all for a sick neighbour, considered, as her companions did, that the position of a worker was degrading, and despised it. She had been brought up to live without working, and in the way that was considered natural by those around her. Therein lay her misfortune – the misfortune that had led her into, and kept her in, her present position. That was what led her to sit in taverns. And which of us – man or woman – can cure her of that false view of life? Where among us are people who are convinced that an industrious life is always more to be respected than an idle one – people convinced of this and who live accordingly – valuing and respecting others on the basis of that conviction? Had I thought of this I might have understood that neither I nor anyone I knew could cure this disease.

'I should have understood that those surprised and attentive faces peering over the partition showed merely surprise at hearing sympathy expressed for them, but certainly no hope of being cured of their immorality. They do not see the immorality of their lives. They know they are despised and abused, but cannot understand why. They have lived from childhood among other such women, who, they know very well, have always existed and do exist, and are wanted by society-so much wanted that Government officials are appointed to see that they exist properly. [This refers to the licensing, inspection, and medical examination of prostitutes and brothels.] They know moreover that they have power over men and can often influence them more than other women can. They see that their position in society, though they are always abused, is recognised both by women and men and by the Government, and they cannot even understand what there is for them to repent of, and wherein they ought to amend. During one of out rounds a student told me of a woman in one of the lodgings who traded in her thirteen-year-old daughter. Wishing to save the girl, I purposely went to that lodging. The mother and daughter were living in great poverty. The mother, a small, dark, forty-year-old prostitute, was not merely ugly, but unpleasantly ugly. The daughter was equally unpleasant. To all my indirect questions about their way of life, the mother replied curtly and with hostile distrust, evidently regarding me as an enemy. The daughter never answered me without first glancing at her mother, and evidently trusted her completely. They did not evoke in me cordial pity – rather repulsion; but yet I decided that it was necessary to save the daughter, and that I would speak to some ladies who take an interest in the wretched position of such women, and would send them here. Had I but thought of the long, past life of that mother: of how she bore, nursed, and reared that daughter – in her position assuredly without the least help from others and with heavy sacrifices – had I thought of the view that had been formed in her mind, I should have understood that in her action there was absolutely nothing bad or immoral: she had done, and was doing, all she could for her daughter – that is to say, just what she herself considered best. One might take the daughter from her mother by force, but one could not convince the mother that it was wrong of her to sell her daughter. To save her, one ought long ago to have saved her mother – saved her from the view of life approved by everybody, which permits a woman, without bearing children and without working, to serve only as a satisfaction for sensuality. Had I thought of that, I should have understood that the majority of the ladies I wished to send here to save that girl, themselves live without bearing children and without work, serving merely to satisfy sensuality, and deliberately educate their daughters for such a life. One mother leads her daughter to the taverns, another takes hers to Court or to balls; but both share the same view of life: namely, that a woman should satisfy a man's lusts and that for that service she should be fed, clothed, and cared for. How then can our ladies save that woman or her daughter?

'I visited Rzhánov House several times before the final Census-round was made, and the same thing happened each time. I was besieged by a crowd of suppliants, among whom I was quite lost. I felt the impossibility of achieving anything, because there were too many of them, and therefore I felt angry with them for being so numerous; but besides that, taking them separately, they did not attract me. I felt that each of them was telling me lies or not telling the whole truth, and saw in me merely a purse from which money might be extracted. And it seemed to me very often that the money a man wheedled out of me would do him more harm than good. The oftener I went to the place and the more I got to know the people there, the plainer the impossibility of doing anything became, but I did not abandon my enterprise till the last night of the Census . . .

'That night we visited lodgings I already knew and in which I also knew some of the lodgers; but most of the people were new and the spectacle was new and terrible – more terrible than that I had seen at Lyápin House. All the lodgings were full, all the bunks were occupied, and often by two people. The sight was horrible from the way they were crowded together, and from the mingling of women and men. All the women who were not dead drunk were sleeping with men. Many women with children were sleeping with strange men on the narrow bunks. Terrible was the sight of these people's destitution, dirt, raggedness, and terror. And terrible, above all, was the immense number of them in this condition. One tenement, another, a third, a tenth, a twentieth, and no end to them! Everywhere the same stench, the same stifling atmosphere, the same overcrowding, the same mingling of the sexes, the same spectacle of men and women drunk to stupefaction, and the same fear, submissiveness, and culpability on all faces; and again I felt pained and ashamed of myself as I had done in Lyápin House, and I understood that what I had undertaken was horrid, stupid, and therefore impossible. And I no longer questioned anyone or took notes about anything, well knowing that nothing would come of it.

'I suffered profoundly. At Lyápin House I had been like one who happens to see a horrible sore on a man's body. He is sorry for the man and conscience-stricken at not having pitied him before, but he may still hope to help him. But now I was like a doctor who has come to the sufferer with his medicines, has uncovered the wound and chafed it, but has at last to admit that he has done it all in vain and that his medicine is of no use . . .

'So ended my charitable activity, and I departed for the country, vexed with others – as is always the case – because I had myself done something stupid and wrong. My charity came to nothing and quite ceased, but the flow of thoughts and feelings in me did not cease but went on with redoubled force.'

*   *   *

'What did it all mean?

'I had lived in the country and had been in touch with village poverty. Not out of the humility which is more like pride, but to state the facts which are necessary to make the whole trend of my thoughts and feelings comprehensible, I will mention that in the country I did very little for the poor, but the demands made on me there were so modest that even the little I did was of use to the people and created an atmosphere of love and satisfaction around me, amid which it was possible to soothe the gnawing consciousness of the wrongness of my way of life. When we moved to town I hoped to live in just the same way. But there I met poverty of quite a different kind. Town poverty was less truthful, and more exacting and more cruel than village poverty.

Above all, there was so much of it in one place that it produced a terrible impression on me. What I saw at Lyápin House made me at once realise the odiousness of my life. That feeling was sincere and very strong. But despite its sincerity and strength I compromised, for I was at first weak enough to fear the revolution it demanded in my life. I believed what everyone told me and what everyone has been saying since the world began – that there is nothing wrong in riches and luxury, which are God's gifts, and that one can help the needy without ceasing to be self-indulgent. I believed this and wished to do so. And I wrote the article in which I called on the rich for help. They all acknowledged themselves morally bound to agree with me, but evidently either did not wish, or were unable, to give anything for the poor. I began to visit the poor and saw what I had lot at all expected. On the one hand in those dens – as I called them – I found people whom it was out of the question for me to help, for they were workers accustomed to work and endure, and therefore possessing a far firmer hold on life than my own. On the other hand, I saw unfortunates whom I could not help because they were just like myself. The majority of the unfortunates I saw were unfortunate only because they had lost the capacity, the wish, and the habit, of working for their bread. That is to say, their misfortune consisted in being like me.

'I could not find any unfortunates – sick, cold, or hungry – whom one could help at once, except one starving woman. And I became convinced that, cut off as I was from the life of the people I wished to help, it would be almost impossible for me to find such unfortunates, for every case of real want was met by the very people among whom these unfortunates live, and above all I became convinced that money would not enable me to alter the wretched life these people lead . . . And I threw up the whole thing and, with a feeling of despair, left for the country.

'There I wished to write an article about my experience and to explain why my undertaking had not succeeded . . . and I began it, thinking it would contain much that was of value.

'But try as I would, in spite of an abundance and superabundance of material, since I wrote under the influence of irritation and had then not yet got rid of all that hindered my seeing the matter in a right light, and above all because I was not yet simply and clearly conscious of the cause of the whole matter (a very simple cause rooted in myself), I could not manage the article and I did not finish it till the present year [the winter of 1885–6].'

*   *   *

'One of the obstacles to all efforts to relieve the destitute was their untruthfulness.

At first I blamed them for this (it is so natural to blame others), but a single word from a remarkable man – namely, Sutáev – who was staying with me at the time, explained the case to me and showed me where the cause of my failure lay.

' "It's all useless," said he.

' "Why?"

' "The whole Society you're starting will be no use and no good will come of it," he repeated with conviction.

' "Why not? Why will it be no use to help thousands, or even hundreds, of unfortunates? Is it wrong to clothe the naked and feed the hungry, as the Gospel tells us to?"

' "I know, I know! But you're not doing the right thing. Is that the way to help? You go out walking, and a man asks you for twenty kopeks [fivepence]. You give it. Is that charity? Give him spiritual charity – teach him! But what have you done? Merely got rid of him!"

' "No, that's not what we are talking about. We want to find out the need that exists, and to help with money and work, and to find employment for those who require it."

' "You won't do anything with those people that way."

' "What do you mean? Are they to be left to die of cold and hunger?"

' "Why should they die? Are there so many of them?"

' "Many of them!' said I, thinking he treated the matter so lightly because he did not know what an immense number there were. 'Do you know that in Moscow alone there are, I suppose, some twenty thousand cold and hungry people? And in Petersburg and in other towns . . . !"

He smiled.

' "Twenty thousand! And how many homes are there in Russia alone? A million?"

' "Well, what of it?"

' "What of it!" His eyes gleamed and he became animated. 'Why, let us divide them among us. I am not rich, but I will at once take two. There is that lad you had in your kitchen. I have asked him, but he won't come. If there were ten times as many we could place them all. You take one, I'll take another. We could go to work together. He would see how I work and would learn how to live. We would sit at one table and he would hear a word now from me and now from you. That is charity, but your scheme is quite useless."

'That simple remark struck me. I could not but acknowledge its justice . . .

'Indeed, when I drive out in an expensive fur coat, perhaps in my own carriage, and a man who has no boots sees my two-thousand-ruble-lodgings, or merely sees that I give five rubles without regret because it comes into my head to do so, he knows that if I give away rubles like that, it is because I have collected many and have a lot of superfluous ones I have not given away, but on the contrary have extracted with ease from other people. What can he see in me but a man who has taken what ought to be his? And what feeling can he have towards me but a wish to get back as many as possible of the rubles I have taken from him and from others? I want to get into touch with him and complain that he is not frank; but I fear to sit on his bed lest I should get lice or disease, and I daren't let him into my room. When he comes, hungry, to see me, he has to wait in the hall (if he is lucky) or in the porch. Yet I say he is to blame that I cannot get into touch with him and that he is not frank!'

*   *   *

Of Sutáev, the peasant spoken of above, and of his visit to Tolstoy, mention is made in a letter from the Countess to her sister, on 30th January 1882:

> Yesterday we had a stiff evening party, the Princess Golítzin with her daughter and husband, Mme Samárin with her daughter, young Mansúrov, Homyakóv, the Sverbéyevs, &c. Such evenings are very dull, but we were helped by the presence of a peasant-sectarian, Sutáev, about whom all Moscow is now talking and who is taken everywhere and preaches everywhere. There is an article about him by Prugávin in *Russian Thought*. He is really a remarkable old man. Well, he began to preach in the study and everyone ran there out of the drawing-room, and so the evening passed off . . .
>
> . . . What a quantity and variety of people come to see us – authors and painters, *le grand monde*, Nihilists, and all sorts of others!

In *What Then Must We Do?* Tolstoy mentions Sarah Bernhardt, and I am tempted to reproduce the account given by N. Káshkin, a Professor of the Theory of Music at the Moscow Conservatoire, of his visit to

Tolstoy in the winter of 1881, when Sarah Bernhardt was acting at the Big Theatre in Moscow. Her arrival had been preceded by an amount of advertising never before known in Russia. All the tickets had been sold out. Speculation in them ran high and they changed hands at fancy prices:

> At the very height of the scramble for tickets I happened to be at the Tolstoys' house one evening, and at the tea-table in the presence of visitors, the Count, among other conversation, indignantly told how one aristocratic Moscow family, taking advantage of their acquaint-ance with the Governor General, Prince V. A. Dolgorúki, obtained a box on the ground-floor and then re-sold it at a high price. Tolstoy was altogether in an excited state, and spoke much about dramatic art.
>
> It was not simple table-talk, but a whole lecture on the subject, evidently premeditated. And it was delivered powerfully and well. The Count entirely condemned the contemporary theatre and exhaustively proved the falsity of dramatic art in general. When he had finished, none of us said anything for some time. Then he addressed me across the table.
>
> 'Are you going to see Sarah Bernhardt?'
>
> 'Of course!' replied I.
>
> This evoked from Tolstoy something like an angry exclamation and he even struck the table slightly with his fist. But after a little while, amid general silence, his face lit up a most good-humoured smile, and he said: 'And do you know, I am awfully sorry that I'm not going!'

The Countess's diary indicates the effect Tolstoy's social experiences and reflections had on the relation between him and her. More will be said on that subject later, but here are some passages she wrote at this period:

> *28th February 1882*
>
> We have been in Moscow since 15th September 1881. We live near the Prechístenka . . . in Prince Volkónski's house. Serëzha goes to the University, Tánya to the Art-School in Myasnítskaya Street, and Ilyá and Lëla to Polivánov's High School close to the house. Life in Moscow might be very enjoyable if only Lëvochka were not so unhappy here. He is too impressionable to endure it, and besides, his Christian mood can't reconcile itself to the conditions of luxury,

indolence, and strife in this town life. He returned to Yásnaya yesterday with Ilyá, to work and rest.

Tolstoy's sense of acute discord between his own and his family's manner of life and the way he began to think they ought to live, met with scant comprehension and still less sympathy from the Countess.

The intensity and sincerity of his feelings on this and other subjects and the unusual and sometimes impulsive frankness with which he expressed and published them, are very apparent to those who care to notice and understand what went on, but the conflict within him occasioned by his love of his wife on the one hand and the ardour of his new convictions on the other, caused acillations which enabled the mean and venomous detractors who swarm round the feet of great men to indict Tolstoy, on the one hand for distressing his wife, and on the other for not abandoning with sufficient rapidity and completeness the whole way of life to which he and his family were accustomed. The problems that arose were complex and difficult and I am far from thinking that he always acted wisely, or that there were not occasions on which he failed to show due consideration for his wife. So impulsive, so ardent, and so strenuous a man was sure to make some mistakes, and the very strength of his affection for his wife rendered the position the more terrible for him when he found that he could not act as seemed to him right without a bitter conflict with her, since she had too strong a personality to submit to what seemed to her unreasonable, and unfair to the family.

I make no protest against such comment as Bernard Shaw makes in the article printed in Part One of this *Life*, for while he blames Tolstoy's disregard of his wife's sufferings on a certain occasion, he gives ample recognition to Tolstoy's great achievements; but when one encounters the petty swarm of Tolstoy's venomous detractors, one involuntarily recalls Krylóv's fable of 'Mos'ka and the Elephant' (Mos'ka being a pug-dog). Krylóv tells of an elephant led through a town, accompanied by many sightseers. Mos'ka turned up from somewhere and barked furiously at the elephant. 'Why bark yourself hoarse?' asked an onlooker, 'it has no effect on the elephant.' 'That may be,' replied Mos'ka, 'but the other dogs will think, "Mos'ka must be strong, since he barks like that at an elephant!"'

In considering the complex and painful conflict that developed between Tolstoy and his wife, it is not easy to be fair to both sides and, while speaking of that conflict, to keep in view the abundant evidence of the affection that united them and enabled them to live faithfully together for forty-eight years. To select bits of evidence of bitter conflict, or to frame an apparently powerful indictment of either husband or wife, is easy, and has been done by writers who aimed at effect and did not scruple to ignore facts fatal to the conclusions they wished to arrive at.

Remembering that there are two sides to the case and that the due presentation of either of them calls for many qualifications, let us note what the Countess says in her diary, in a passage written at Yásnaya Polyána:

26th August 1882

Twenty years ago, happy and young, I began writing this book – the whole story of my love for Lëvochka. There is hardly anything in it but love. And now, after twenty years, I am sitting up alone all night reading it, and weeping over my love. For the first time in his life Lëvochka has run away from me and is remaining in his study for the night. We quarrelled over trifles. I attacked him for not troubling himself about the children, not helping to attend to Ilyá who is ill, and not making their jackets. But it isn't a matter of jackets, the matter is that he is growing cold towards me and the children. Today he suddenly exclaimed that his most passionate wish is to go away from the family. To my dying day I shall not forget that sincere cry of his, but it is as if he had torn my heart from me. I pray to God for death. To live without his love is dreadful for me, and I felt this acutely when his love went from me. I can't show him how strongly I still love him as of old, as I have loved him for twenty years. That would humiliate *me* and annoy *him*. He is imbued with Christianity and thoughts of self-perfecting. I am jealous of him . . . Ilyá is ill, lying in the drawing-room in a high fever. He has typhus and I keep watch to give him quinine at frequent intervals, which I am afraid of missing. I will not lie down tonight on the bed my husband has deserted. God help me! I want to take my life, my thoughts grow confused, it is striking four.

I thought: 'If he does not come, it will mean that he loves another.' He has not come . . . duty! – I used to know so well what my duty was, but now?

He came, but we only made it up twenty-four hours later. We both wept, and I saw with joy that the love I had mourned for on that dreadful night had not died. I shall never forget that lovely morning, clear, cold, sparkling with silvery dew, when after a sleepless night I went along the path through the wood to the bath-house. It is long since I have seen nature in such triumphant beauty. I sat for a long time in the icy water with the idea of catching cold and dying. But I did not catch cold, and returned home and began nursing little Alësha, who was glad to see me and smiled.

There we have a glimpse of the acute suffering endured by both husband and wife, and the gulf that separated them is indicated by her complaints that he did not help her in nursing their sick boy and making the children's jackets, and in her groundless suspicion that he was in love with some other woman, while she ignored the distress he was suffering on account of the contrast between the actual conditions of their life and what he thought they ought to be. We have here also a foretaste of the Countess's mental instability, and even of the suicidal tendency that became prominent later.

She felt the need of her husband's support and that she could not live without him, but she wanted him to devote himself completely to her and the family; while he felt his obligations to society at large so acutely that her demands seemed to him inadmissible and unendurable. It was a state of things deserving of compassion, pity, and sympathy, but it has been made a parade-ground on which reckless writers exhibit their capacity for virulent abuse, scathing invective, and calumny in which malice is balanced by mendacity.

The next year, on 5th March 1883, in Moscow, the Countess wrote:

In the quiet of the first week of Lent the whole of last winter passes through my mind. I went a little into society, enjoyed Tánya's successes, the success of my own youthful appearance, and all the pleasures society affords. Yet no one would believe that sometimes – oftener even than enjoyment – I experienced moments of despair and said to myself: 'It's not right, I am not doing right!' But I could not, simply could not stop. It is so plain to me that even in trifles I do not act by my own will, but by the will of God, or Fate, or whatever one likes to call that higher power.

Two days ago, that is, on the 2nd, I weaned Alësha, and I am again experiencing the mental pain of first severance from a loved child. Again and again it is repeated, and there is no escaping it.

Life in our own house, at some distance from the noisy part of the city, is much easier and better than last year. Lëvochka is calm and kind; sometimes the former reproaches and bitterness recur, but they are less frequent and shorter. He is growing kinder and kinder.

God sees, but no one else will know, what went on in my heart, but during the summer and autumn I did not want to come to Moscow for I did not feel I had the strength to bear all the burden and responsibility of town life . . .

It is time to finish this chapter. We have seen Tolstoy possessed of his new faith and faced by the great social problem – poverty among a large city-population living in complex economic conditions. He tried to solve it, and though he did not succeed, his experience was not wasted. It affected his own life and has affected the lives of others, for it would be hard to name a book that did more than *What Then Must We Do?* to make it plain that existing conditions are unendurably wrong, and that we should not rest till they are changed.

Tolstoy's impetuous rush at a practical solution had little result, and he soon ceased to try to deal with the problems of destitution and unemployment, except by persuading people to be industrious and frugal and abstain from acquiring or holding property or taking any share in Governments 'which exist to oppress the people'. He never unravelled the economic tangle, and with reference to the destitute and un-employed soon came to feel that what they most need is a change of heart and mind such as would make them wish to be of service to others. The main ground of his distrust and dislike of all Socialistic or other attempts to deal systematically with the problem and to organise society so that there should be no neglected parts, and so that the feeble and unfortunate may not be trodden into the mud, was that he disliked the official interference it involves, even more than the interference with individual freedom resulting from the scramble for subsistence that now rules the fate of the workers and the weak. He had an inveterate distrust of officialism, and it seemed to him that efforts to organise the external conditions of men's lives divert attention from man's spiritual needs. He saw an antithesis between the attempt to organise society and the attempt to reform oneself and to live a good life.

To me, a Westerner, it seems that to attempt to mitigate the hard fate of the weak and industrially inefficient in the only ways that really promise to reach the mass of mankind in our times, is more likely to benefit than to injure our souls, and that the depression resulting from the age-long failure of unorganised individualist effort to grapple with this gigantic problem is even more detrimental than an excessive devotion to the practical work of organisation.

But while I differ from Tolstoy on that point, I recognise that he accomplished two great things: he presented the problem in a way that makes it difficult for any reader to remain unaware of it, and he aroused the sense of personal responsibility.

He was profoundly right when he pointed out how much character and outlook on life – or 'religion' as he rightly termed it – has to do with matters often regarded as purely economic. The best possible organisation of society will not work unless the officials are imbued with a sense of duty, and they are not likely long to be so imbued unless they have an outlook on life making it reasonable for them to exert themselves in the service of others.

Tolstoy aroused in many hearts the desire to straighten the crooked places of the earth. He carried 'conviction of sin' to people whom no Church dignitaries would have reproached, and whom the late Samuel Smiles would have admired. But in many cases the steam he generated ran to waste for lack of an efficient engine. One did not expect him to attend to all the good projects that are devised, but one regretted that he threw cold water on efforts essentially complementary to his own. Still, as he once said to me of an eminent man he admired, but whose shortcomings he perceived, 'God needs our limitations.' Perhaps he could not have done his own work of arousing men to a recognition of the fact that the best use of individual life is to make the life of humanity better, had he associated himself with any political party. Moreover, the danger Tolstoy saw of our enslavement by a bureaucracy is real, even if the contrary danger, of not dealing systematically with society's festering wounds, be more terrible and more urgent.

Though I think that the only machine strong enough to meet the social need is a Governmental machine, it remains true that unless the steam to drive it be generated in the consciences of men, it can never work, for under any system the price of liberty must be eternal vigilance.

5

Renunciations

The early 1880s were such important years in Tolstoy's life that they must inevitably fill a large space in his biography.

With the accession of Alexander III to the throne and of Pobedonóstsev to the Procuratorship of the Holy Synod, Russia entered on a period of political, social, and moral stagnation in which it seemed as though all that breathed of life, sincerity, freedom, or progress, must die of suffocation. There was no liberty of the Press or of public meeting, and no discussion of political or religious problems was tolerated. Those who accepted and supported the existing order of things without criticism were officially esteemed to be 'well-intentioned' (*blagonaméreny*), and all who were not 'well-intentioned' were dangerous and subject to persecution. The spy and *agent-provocateur* flourished, and those Russians who rejected Orthodoxy or desired a Constitution were regarded, and frequently treated, as malefactors.

It was at this time that Tolstoy's outspoken, unflinching appeal to men's reason and conscience came like a breath of fresh air in a plague-stricken country and aroused many to life. Though it was forbidden, Tolstoy discussed all the vitally important subjects and did it frankly. Blind obedience to external authority was demanded by the Powers that be; Tolstoy bowed to no authority but reason and conscience. The Government relied on the brute force of Cossacks and gendarmes; Tolstoy denounced all physical force as iniquitous, and in the last decades of the nineteenth century dealt deadly blows to the moral authority of the Greek Church and to belief in the right divine of Tsars to govern wrong. But Tolstoy ceased to be a popular force among Russian Progressives from the time their movement became a definitely political struggle. The task of rousing an apathetic community by a moral appeal is a different one from that of shaping the political form in which the new feeling is to express itself, and it can seldom happen that the same man is equally fitted for both tasks.

*　　*　　*

Leaving wife and family in Moscow [1882], Tolstoy, as we have seen, betook himself to the solitude of Yásnaya to recover mental tranquillity after his slumming experiences. From thence he wrote to his wife:

> I think that I could nowhere be better off or more tranquil. You, who are always at home and occupied with family cares, cannot feel the difference town and country make to me.
>
> However there is no need to speak or write in a letter about that, for I am now at work on that very subject and, if I succeed in writing it, you will read it in clearer form. The chief evil of the town for me and for all thinkers (this is not what I am writing about) is that one has either continually to dispute and expose false arguments, or to agree to them without disputing, which is still worse. And to dispute about, and expose, rubbish and lies is the emptiest of occupations and there is no end to it because lies are innumerable. One busies oneself with disputations and begins to imagine that that is work: whereas it is the very greatest waste of time. If one does not dispute one may clear up something for oneself in a way precluding all possibility of doubt. But that is only done in quietness and solitude. I know that intercourse with one's fellows is also necessary, and very necessary, and in one way my three months in Moscow have given me very much (not to mention Orlóv, Nikoláy Fëdorovich and Sutáev), enabling me to know people more intimately. Even Society, which from afar one coldly condemns, has given me a great deal. And I am sorting out all this material. The Census and Sutáev explained much to me. So do not feel troubled about me. Anything may happen to one anywhere, but here I am in the best and safest conditions.

In February he returned to Moscow for a short visit, but seems again to have been dissatisfied with the life and to have disagreed with his wife. He returned almost at once to Yásnaya, and having written to the Countess, received the following reply from her, dated 3rd March:

> ... The first, most dismal and saddest thing when I awoke, was your letter. It gets worse and worse. I begin to think that if a happy man suddenly sees only what is terrible in life and shuts his eyes to what is good, it must be the result of illness. You ought to undergo a cure; I say it without any *arrière pensée*. This seems clear to me. I am terribly sorry for you, and if you would consider my words and your own position without irritation you would perhaps find a way out.

That state of melancholy used to befall you long ago: you say, 'From lack of faith I wished to hang myself!' And now? You are not without faith now, then why are you unhappy? Did you not know before that hungry, sick, unhappy and bad people exist? Look more carefully and you will find merry, healthy, happy and good people also. May God help you – but what can I do in the matter?

In the calm of lonely country life Tolstoy soon recovered tranquillity, and we find him, after receiving an affectionate letter from his wife, writing to her:

It made me very glad. Do not trouble about me and, above all, do not accuse yourself. 'Forgive us our debts as we forgive . . .' As soon as one has forgiven others one is oneself in the right. And your letter shows that you have forgiven and are not angry with anyone. And I have long ceased to blame you. I only did that at first. I do not myself know why I have been so run down. Perhaps it was age, perhaps ill-health . . . but I have nothing to complain of. Life in Moscow gave me very much and made plain to me my line of activity – if any still lies before me – and it brought you and me closer together than before . . .

I fear that we may change rôles, I shall become healthy and animated while you will be gloomy and run down. You say: 'I love you, but you do not want that now.' It is the one thing I do want! No one else can so cheer me, and your letter has cheered me. One's liver counts for something, but one's spiritual life goes its own way. My solitude was very necessary to me and has freshened me up, and your love gladdens me more than anything in life.

It was I think during Tolstoy's next visit to Moscow that he made one of the few close friendships of his life, one which afforded him great pleasure and spiritual refreshment as well as much encouragement in his work.

Nikoláy Nikoláevich Gay, a celebrated Russian painter of French origin, had retired to a small estate in the Ukraine some time before this in a state of great dejection. He had ceased to paint and had come to feel life hardly worth living. In his *Memoirs* he tells us what it was that aroused him from this apathy:

In 1882 a word of the great writer L. N. Tolstoy, *On the Moscow Census*, happened to fall into my hand. I read it in a newspaper. In it I found words precious to me. Tolstoy, visiting cellars and finding wretched people in them, writes: 'Our lack of love for the lowest is the cause of their wretched condition.'

As a spark kindles inflammable material so that word set me aflame . . .

I went to Moscow to embrace that great man and work for him.

I arrived: bought canvas and paints, and drove to his house . . . I saw him, embraced him, and kissed him. 'Leo Nikoláevich, I have come to do anything you like. Shall I paint your daughter?' – 'No, in that case better paint my wife.' I did so. But from that moment I understood all. I loved that man unboundedly, he had revealed everything to me. I could now name what I had loved all my life – he had named it for me, and above all, we loved the same thing. For a month I saw him every day.

A letter from the Countess to her sister tells of the impression Gay made on her:

The famous artist, Gay, is painting my portrait in oils – and it is very good. But what a dear, naïve man he is, charming! He is fifty, bald, with clear light-blue eyes and a kindly look.

There were many points of resemblance between the two men who had so suddenly struck up a friendship destined to last unimpaired till Gay's death in 1894. They were nearly of the same age; each in his own line had done great things, and both after achieving fame had found that it did not satisfy them or supply a meaning to life. Both had then spent years in painful struggles to find the truth, and now they were united in the conviction that they had found a simple truth capable of regenerating the world.

It was in this year (1882) that the critic N. K. Mihaylóvski, who had sided with Tolstoy in the educational battle the latter fought in 1875 and had predicted the spiritual crisis toward which Tolstoy was drifting, made his personal acquaintance.

At the request of Saltykóv ('Stchedrín') then editor of the monthly *Fatherland Notes*, Mihaylóvski called to ask Tolstoy not to forget an offer he had made the year before to contribute to that magazine.

'The Count', says Mihaylóvski, 'had not yet begun to make boots':

This did not prevent him from impressing one as a simple, sincere man, in spite of his social polish. Strange as that last expression may seem in relation to Count Tolstoy, it is nevertheless quite applicable.

Real good manners do not consist in gloves or correct French. That he was a man of the world was shown first of all by the easy, confident way in which the Count put aside the business part of our conversation. When I said to him that we had heard rumours that he had written, or was writing, a tale, so would he not please let us have it? he replied: 'Oh no! I have nothing of the kind. It was only that Strákhov found a story among my old papers and made me polish it up and finish it. It has already been placed.' And then he passed on lightly and freely to a conversation about *Fatherland Notes*, and said many pleasant things about us, without however referring by a single word to his offer; thereby as it were inviting me not to speak about it. I of course obeyed that unexpressed wish. So that I have never understood either his motives for making the offer . . . or his motives for evading its fulfilment. Apparently the one and the other were simply done on the spur of the moment, like so many of Tolstoy's actions.

The talk passed from literature and social problems to Tolstoy's letter to the Emperor on behalf of the Tsar's assassins. Mihaylóvski says:

I was glad to hear an account of the affair from the Count himself, and yet more glad that by its simplicity and sincerity it fully corresponded to the idea I had formed of him before I saw him.

I had often to be in Moscow at that time, and at each visit I allowed myself the pleasure of calling on Count Tolstoy. He is one of the pleasantest men to talk to I have ever met. We disputed much and warmly, and I seem now to hear his voice. 'Come, we are beginning to get warm; that is not well! Let us each smoke a cigarette and rest a bit.' We smoked cigarettes, and that of course did not end our dispute, but the very fact of interrupting it for a few moments really calmed it.

I may have no further occasion to mention Mihaylóvski, so I will here quote his comparison of Proudhon and Tolstoy, who, as the reader will remember, had met one another in Brussels in 1861:

It was easy for Proudhon to believe in the people and demand of others a similar belief, he was believing in himself. There is no such immediate union between Tolstoy and the peasantry. It was easy for Proudhon to see the evils of civilisation when those evils weighed directly on him and those near to him. Count Tolstoy experienced no such pressure. It was easy for Proudhon to say, as Tolstoy puts it, that 'among the labourers there is more strength and more consciousness of right and goodness than among the lords, barons, bankers, and professors'. It was easy for Proudhon to say that – for his father was a cooper, his mother a cook, and he himself a compositor, and he was entitled to say to a Legitimist: 'I am descended from fourteen generations of peasants; show me a family that has had as many honourable ancestors!' But Count Tolstoy is rather in the position of the Legitimist who received that rebuff. Setting aside the question of the correctness or incorrectness of the conclusions arrived at by Proudhon or by Count Tolstoy, and granting that they may both be as far from the truth as the cavemen are from Count Tolstoy, note only the following: that all his circumstances, all the conditions of his life from the cradle upwards, drove Proudhon to the conclusions which he considered true, while all the conditions of Count Tolstoy's life on the contrary drove and drive him away from the conclusions he holds true. If he still arrived at them in spite of a ll that, then however he may have contradicted himself, you must recognise that he is an honourable and powerful thinker in whom we may feel confidence, and whom we are bound to respect.

Among the very few men intimate with Tolstoy who understood and appreciated his views but were strong enough to hold their own opinions and defend them against him, N. N. Strákhov, of whom repeated mention has been made in the previous part of this *Life*, was remarkable. In their intercourse it was by no means always Tolstoy who was teacher and Strákhov pupil. In fact it may safely be said that the latter influenced and instructed the former considerably, and there are pages in Tolstoy's didactic works which are mainly a repetition of Strákhov's views.

There is, for instance, a striking similarity to views subsequently expressed by Tolstoy, in the following letter from Strákhov to him, dated 31st March 1882:

The whole movement which fills the last period of history – Liberal, Revolutionary, Socialist, and Nihilist – has always in my eyes had merely a negative character. Denying *it*, I deny a negation. I have often thought about it and been amazed to find that Liberty and Equality – those idols of many: those standards of battle and Revolution – do not in reality contain any attractive or positive content which could give them real value or enable them to become positive aims. Beginning before the Reformation and down to our time, all that people are doing (as you say) is not rubbish, but a gradual destruction of certain forms composed in the Middle Ages. For four centuries this disintegration has been going on and it must end in a complete collapse. During those four centuries nothing positive has appeared, or now exists, anywhere in Europe. The newest thing is in America and is the selling of votes and the buying of places, &c. Society is held together by its old elements: remains of beliefs, patriotism, and morality, which little by little are losing their bases . . .

People live in this strange position. Life today contains a contradiction. It is possible only because man generally is able to exist without internal harmony . . .

Another letter from Strákhov, dated 21st April, though it formed part of a controversy between the two writers, again contains a statement of views which might well have been written by Tolstoy himself:

What does a Christian say? 'I want no property, I want no dominion over others, I do not want to judge, or kill, or take taxes.' [Exactly Tolstoy's view.] These are holy aspirations which it is impossible to condemn. But what is said by those objectors whom I reject? 'I do not wish anyone to have dominion over me. I do not wish to be judged, or killed, or to pay taxes.' The difference is great, and how can the two things be confused? The source of the one set of wishes is self-denial, the source of the other sheer egotism . . . The Christian's wishes can always be fulfilled, for their essence lies in a change within us, but the wishes of the egotist are unattainable for they require alterations in the whole world, and alterations impossible for the world . . .

Tolstoy's ardour in controversy has often been mentioned and accounts largely for the comparatively small number of close and intimate friends he retained from among the many who appreciated, admired, loved him, and acknowledged spiritual and mental indebtedness to him. Even in the case of Strákhov, who rendered him many services, was much attached to him, and on many important matters agreed with him, there was considerable tension, and it was only due to Strákhov's devotion to Tolstoy that the friendship endured till the death of the former in 1896.

In one letter Strákhov says:

When I left you and went to the Crimea I often recalled your saying, 'He that is not with me, is against me,' and the words in your letter, that I am 'worse than a Positivist'; and I thought, 'He is excommunicating me from the Church! But what can I do? I think as I do, because I cannot think otherwise and do not shuffle with myself. Well, let him reject me – I will remain true to him.' Forgive me for still wishing to express my affection for you, but I am almost ready to be silent and respect you in secret.

Quite another phase of Tolstoy's many-sided nature shows itself in a letter he wrote to his wife from Yásnaya early in April of this same year, 1882, describing the awakening of spring, and the kind of life he was living:

I went out today at eleven and was intoxicated by the beauty of the morning. It was warm and dry. Here and there in the frost-glaze of the footpaths little spikes and tufts of grass show up from under the dead leaves and straw; the buds are swelling on the lilacs, the birds no longer sing at random but have already begun to converse about something, and round the sheltered corners of the house and by the manure heaps bees are humming. I saddled my horse and rode out.

In the afternoon I read, and then went to the apiary and the bathing-house. Everywhere grass, birds, honey-bees; no policemen, no pavement, no cabmen, no stinks, and it is very pleasant – so pleasant that I grow sorry for you and think that you and the children must certainly come here earlier, and I will remain in Moscow with the boys. For me with my thoughts it is equally good or bad everywhere, and as to my health, town can have no effect on it, but it has a great effect on yours and the children's.

In May the Countess with her daughters and the younger sons really moved to Yásnaya as Tolstoy had suggested, while he remained in Moscow with the older lads who went to school and the University. He was at this time planning to get his *Confession* published in the magazine, *Russian Thought*, and he wanted to be within reach of the printer while revising the proofs. The attempt to publish the book was baffled by the Spiritual Censor, who had the sheets destroyed after they had already been printed. *Confession* was the first of a long series of Tolstoy's works which were for many years known in Russia only from 'illegal' copies smuggled into the country, or copied by hand, or hecto-graphed or lithographed in secret. The book was, however, printed in Russian at Geneva and immediately translated into other languages.

Since the beginning of 1882, Turgénev had been very ill and many troubles had befallen him. 'It is as if a wheel had seized me and was beginning to drag me into the machine,' wrote he to Polónski. But his interest in Tolstoy did not wane: it was still the same feeling of extreme admiration for the novelist, mixed sentiments towards the man, and perplexity at, as well as dislike of, the new interests and studies that had become all-important to Tolstoy. To D. V. Grigoróvich, Turgénev wrote on 29th March 1882: 'I hope you and L. Tolstoy have again come together. He is a very queer fellow but undoubtedly a genius, and the kindliest of men.'

At Turgénev's desire, Tolstoy sent him a copy of *Confession*. He asked him to read it without anger, and to try to regard it from its author's point of view. Turgénev replied:

> I will certainly read your article in the way you wish. I know it to be written by one who is very wise and very sincere; I may not agree with him, but first of all I will try to understand him and to enter fully into his position. That will be more instructive and interesting than to measure him by my own foot-rule or search for differences between us. To be angry would be quite unthinkable: only young folk get angry, who imagine that there is no light but what they see from their own window . . .

Having read the book, he wrote to D. V. Grigoróvich on 31st October 1882:

> A few days ago I received, through a very charming Moscow lady, that *Confession* of Leo Tolstoy's which the Censor has forbidden. I read it with the greatest interest. It is remarkable for its sincerity, truthfulness, and strength of conviction. But it is built on false premises and ultimately leads to the most sombre denial of all human life . . . This too is in its way a kind of Nihilism.
>
> I am surprised that Tolstoy, who among other things rejects art, surrounds himself with artists, and I wonder what he can get from conversation with them? Yet all the same he is perhaps the most remarkable man in contemporary Russia.

That Tolstoy's outlook on life 'ultimately leads to the most sombre denial of life', is a statement that has often been made, but of which he was himself a palpable contradiction. For though it is true that he suffered greatly and alienated many friends by his strong views and scathing criticism – it remains true that in general his nature was kindly and genial, his outlook hopeful, and his influence stimulating. Life in his vicinity was stirring and interesting and his keen humour and the good spirits which bubbled up after each fit of depression were always infectious. It is a secret hidden from many but well illustrated by Tolstoy's life, that exertion for impersonal aims and strenuous concern for life's widest interests tend to promote the enjoyment of the common joys and relaxations of life.

Among Tolstoy's amusements, *The Post-Box*, instituted in the autumn of 1882, must be mentioned. The young Tolstoys' cousins, the Kuzmínskis, spent every summer at Yásnaya; and the following letter to Birukóv from Tolstoy's sister-in-law, T. A. Kuzmínski (the Tánya of earlier days), tells how *The Post-Box* arose:

As both our families were numerous and contained many young people between fifteen and twenty years of age, plenty of things were always happening, and it often occurred that we wanted to make fun of something, publish some secret, or praise or blame something, and so it was agreed among the young folk that during the week anyone might write anything he or she liked, without of course signing their names. On Sunday evenings, at tea, someone would read all these productions aloud. It was always one of us three elders: Leo Nikoláevich, my sister, or myself, who read . . . The contributions were long or short notes in prose or verse; and the themes were most varied: sad, poetic, or humorous. Secrets were exposed, occurrences described. Sometimes a whole sheet was written in imitation of a newspaper, with leading articles and paragraphs about arrivals. But for the most part the works appeared in separate scraps. My sister nearly always wrote in verse. Leo Nikoláevich also sometimes wrote for us, and was much interested in *The Post-Box*, and always listened to it all with attention. I have kept some of his productions: for instance, *The Register of the Mentally Afflicted*, in which he described us all as lunatics, naming each of us by a number. He began with himself. He did it all comically, with Latin names for the diseases, &c.

The following is a translation of one of his contributions:

It was fine and sunny weather,
We were happy all together
    Here at Yásnaya.

Of a sudden, thought Tatiána*
That in Yásnaya Polyána
    One can't always stay.

'Soon or later,' thought Tatiána,
'All the kids must in some manner
    Get certificates.'

'Yes! the girls must have good teaching,
Very thorough and far-reaching.
    Get them a Ma'm'selle!'

Books and papers were obtained,
And the girls were to be trained,
    If they liked or not.

First the lessons went not badly,
But things turned out very sadly
    With the Scripture tales.

Mary stuck, in spite of trying;
Véra loudly kept on crying:
    'Scripture I can't bear!'

Véra having vainly striven
To make out why man was driven
    From his Paradise,

Said, 'From Scripture we must learn
How from Eden God did turn
    Eve and Adam both.

But to learn it quite affronts me;
Cannot anyone at once see,
    Que ce n' est pas vrai?

---

* Tatiána Kuzmínski, writer of the above letter.

Think! for what He turned out Adam?
Have we not been told by Madam?
    – *Pour curiosité!*

From the Garden they were turned
'Cos they had become too learn'd;
    Surely, then, I won't!'

And her mother's quite perplexed
What she is to answer next;
    Really, it is hard!

*   *   *

After it had been decided that the family had to winter in Moscow as a regular thing, Tolstoy, as a matter of convenience and economy, decided to purchase a town-house, and succeeded in finding one for about 36,000 rubles [£3,600], which, after much alteration, suited very well. This house has already been mentioned in an extract from the Countess's Diary quoted in the last chapter. It was a large wooden house with a considerable garden and its own water-supply from a well. It was situated in a side-street, in the south-western outskirts of the town, not far from the river Moskvá. The Countess once told me that it was well chosen and cheaply bought, but that in the extensive alterations he made, her husband, with characteristic inattention to details, quite overlooked the fact that they must have rooms for the servants.

The following letter to her sister tells of the Countess's first impressions of the new house:

We came to Moscow on 8 October. The journey went well. In Moscow Lëvochka met us with two carriages: at home a dinner was ready, and tea, and there was fruit on the table. But after the journey and a week's packing I was so tired and had become so irritable that everything displeased me . . . Lëvochka was at first very merry and animated, now he is learning Hebrew and has become more gloomy.

A letter from Strákhov to Danílevski, dated 5th November, says:

Tolstoy is in good spirits. He has bought a house in Moscow, settled down in it, and writes that he is at peace. He is learning Hebrew. I am very glad on his account, though I always fear for him: he lives so ardently and with such effort and such strong emotions.

A letter of Tolstoy's to V. I. Alexéev, written about this time, tells us something of the family which was then fast growing up:

Some of the family have been ill, but now it is all right and more or less as of old. Serëzha works much and believes in the University. Tánya, semi-kind, semi-serious, and semi-wise, does not grow worse but rather better. Ilúsha [Ilyá] is idle and growing, and his soul is not yet strangled by the organic processes [of puberty]. Lëlya [Leo] and Másha seem to me better; they did not catch my harshness as the elder ones did, and I think they are growing up under better conditions and are better and kinder than the elder ones. The laddies are fine little chaps and healthy. I am fairly quiet, but often feel sad at the triumphant, self-assured insanity of the life around me. It often seems strange that it is granted to me to perceive their insanity so clearly, while they are quite unable to understand either it or their mistakes, and so we stand face to face, not comprehending one another, and wondering at and condemning one another. But they are a legion, while I am alone. They are seemingly gay, and I am seemingly sad. All this time I am very assiduously engaged on Hebrew and have almost mastered that language. I already read and understand it. The Moscow Rabbi, Minor, teaches me. He is a very good and wise man. I have learnt a great deal, thanks to this occupation, and above all I am kept very busy. My health grows weaker and I very often wish to die, but I know this to be an evil desire: the second temptation. Evidently I have not outlived it.

Goodbye, my dear fellow – God grant you what I enjoy in my good moments – there is nothing, as you know, better than that!

Tolstoy's desire to learn Hebrew arose from his Scripture studies. His teacher says that Tolstoy took to the work with great zeal and grasped the language with unusual rapidity, but read only what he wanted. Anything that did not interest him he skipped. Minor adds:

We began at the first words of the Old Testament and, with various omissions of the kind indicated, read on to Isaiah, at which point his study ceased. The prophecies about the Messiah in that Prophet were all he required. He only concerned himself with grammar in so far as it seemed to him necessary . . . He also knows the Talmud. In his tempestuous striving after truth he questioned me at almost every lesson about the moral views in the Talmud and about the Talmudist explanations of the biblical legends . . .

For about half an hour we would work as pupil and teacher, once a week I went to the Count and once a week he came to me. After half an hour the lesson became a conversation.

To Minor's surprise Tolstoy soon began to read and understand so well, and to penetrate the meaning of the text so acutely, that on several occasions the master had to admit, after a dispute, that his pupil had seized a meaning he himself had overlooked.

The Countess, however, remembering the physical breakdown that accompanied Tolstoy's enthusiasm for Greek ten years previously, strongly disapproved of these studies and wrote to her sister:

Lëvochka is learning to read Hebrew and I am very grieved about it; he is spending his strength on trifles. From this work both his health and spirits have deteriorated, and this torments me still more and I cannot hide my dissatisfaction.

In another letter she says:

Lëvochka – alas! has bent all his strength to learning Hebrew and nothing else occupies or interests him. No! evidently his literary activity is at an end, and it is a great, great pity!

We get a glimpse of Tolstoy as he was at this time, from the recollections of Boborykin, the novelist:

Tolstoy began with quiet humour and frankness (which showed how far he was removed from the life and habits of his family) to speak of the monstrous life of 'the gentlefolk', and of how cruelly they treat their servants and how in general they 'delight the devils'.

'The other day I said to our ladies,' remarked he, ' "Are you not ashamed to live so? A *bal costumé* at the Governor-General's . . . Dressing up and exposing your bare arms and shoulders!" With furs and warm rooms they can stand it; but the old coachman has to wait for them till four in the morning in twenty degrees of frost [Réaumur]. Pity might at least be felt for him!'

This introduction set the tone of the conversation. Here was a man who was passing through a period of passionate repudiation of all the vain, egotistic, predatory and insensate things with which well-fed gentlefolk sweeten their idle existence. And that the first subjects for exposure should be his own 'ladies', was quite in the nature of things.

On a subsequent visit Boborykin attempted to remonstrate with him for having abjured literary art and for not using his artistic powers, but he was met with the reply:

'Do you know, that is like the quondam admirers of some elderly French whore repeating to her, "Oh, how adorably you used to sing *chansonnettes* and pick up your petticoats!" ' This was said so good-naturedly and with such quiet humour that it only remained for me to accept it without protest.

Among other repudiations we find Tolstoy dropping his title, not demonstratively but quite simply. When a peasant called on him and addressed him as 'Your Excellency', Tolstoy replied, 'I am called simply Leo Nikoláevich,' and at once passed on to speak of the matter in hand.

About this time he received from a stranger, M. A. Engelhardt, letters written from the standpoint of a Christian Revolutionary, and he replied to them in an epistle some 5,000 words long, which was, I think, the first of that series of letter-essays dealing with important questions which as the years went by came more and more frequently from his pen. These create a serious difficulty for his bibliographers, since there is no clear line of distinction to be drawn anywhere between them and his books. Books, essays, epistles, letters, and mere notes and jottings of his, copied on the hectograph or printed abroad, soon began to circulate, often without his supervision or control, and with no clear indication of what was, and what was not, intended for publication.

This letter to Engelhardt is on the doctrine of Non-Resistance, and apart from its main argument its commencement is of value as giving a vivid indication of Tolstoy's state of mind at that time:

My DEAR M. A. – I address you as 'dear' not because it is customary to write so, but because since I received your first and especially your second letter, I feel that you are very near to me and that I love you very much. In the feeling I experience towards you there is much that is egotistic. You probably do not think it, but you cannot imagine to what a degree I am alone and to what a degree that which is my real 'I' is despised by all around me. I know that 'he that endureth to the end shall be saved', I know that only in trifles is it granted to man to enjoy the fruits of his own labour or even to see that fruit, and that in the matter of Divine truth, which is eternal, it cannot be given to man to see the fruit of his work, especially during his brief life. I know all that and yet I often despond, and therefore to have encountered you and to have the hope, almost the assurance, of finding in you a man sincerely going the same road to the same goal as myself, is a great joy to me.

Yet more striking – if one remembers how much pride and self-reliance there was in Tolstoy's nature and how great must have been the strain that produced such an outburst – is the conclusion of this letter. It is one of the most touching passages in modern literature. Referring to a question often put, Tolstoy says:

Another question directly and involuntarily follows from this: 'Well, but you, Leo Nikoláevich: you preach – but what about practice?'

That is the most natural of questions; people always put it to me and always triumphantly shut my mouth with it. 'You preach, but how do you live?' And I reply that I do not preach and cannot preach, though I passionately desire to do so. I could only preach by deeds: and my deeds are bad. What I say is not a sermon, but only the refutation of a false understanding of the Christian teaching and an explanation of its real meaning. Its meaning is not that we should, in its name, rearrange society by violence: its purpose is to find the meaning of our life in this world. The performance of Christ's five commands gives that meaning. If you wish to be a Christian you must fulfil those commands. If you do not wish to fulfil them then don't talk about Christianity.

'But' – people say to me – 'if you consider that apart from the fulfilment of the Christian teaching there is no reasonable life, and if you love that reasonable life, why do you not fulfil the commands?' I reply that I am a horrible creature and deserve blame and contempt for not fulfilling them. But yet, not so much in justification as in explanation of my inconsistency, I say: 'Look at my former life and at my present life, and you will see that I try to fulfil them. I do not fulfil one ten-thousandth part it is true, and I am to blame for that; but it is not because I do not wish to fulfil them that I fail, but because I do not know how to. Teach me how to escape from the nets of temptation that have ensnared me, help me, and I will fulfil them; but even without help I desire and hope to do so. Blame me – I do that myself – but blame *me*, and not the path I tread and show to those who ask me where in my opinion the road lies! If I know the road Home and go along it drunk, staggering from side to side – does that make the road along which I go a wrong one? If it be wrong, show me another; if I have lost my way and stagger, help me, support me in the right path as I am ready to support you, and do not baffle me, do not rejoice that I have gone astray, do not delightedly exclaim: "Look at him! He says he is going home yet he goes into the bog!" Do not rejoice at that, but help me and support me!

'For indeed, you are not devils out of the bog, but are also men going home. See, I am alone, and I cannot wish to fall into the bog. Help me! My heart breaks with despair that we have all gone astray, and when I struggle with all my strength, you – at every failure, instead of pitying yourselves and me – flurry me and cry in ecstasy: "See, he is following us into the bog!" '

So that is my relation to the teaching and to its practice. With all my might I try to practise it, and at every failure not merely do I repent, but I beg for help to enable me to perform it, and I gladly meet and listen to anyone who like myself is seeking the road.

The ardent hope of having found a friend treading the same path as himself was, alas, disappointed. Their paths did not converge and the two men never met.

The year 1882 must have been one of the hardest in Tolstoy's life, and at the end of it, on 22nd December, we find him noting in his Diary that he had been back in Moscow for a month and had suffered terribly in spirit, but not in vain:

The thing that formerly seemed hard, namely, that it is not granted me to see the fruits of my work, is now plain to me. It is not only not cruel, but is blessed and wise . . . What one does lovingly not seeing the reward, is surely God's work. Sow, sow! That which is God's will come up; and not you – as man – will reap it, but that in you which has sown.

Tolstoy was rapidly becoming a Saint! There are many traits in him that strongly remind one of St Francis of Assisi, but I do not know how to convey this except by translating reflections and dissertations which would soon fill this book and crowd out the external facts of his life which it is my special purpose to record. More and more he dwelt on the thought of doing God's work, and feared, rather than sought, the praise of his fellow men.

At this point of the story, a new witness must be introduced – the widow of a Frenchman named Seuron, and a grandniece of Weber, the composer. Having a son to support, she took a place as governess with the Tolstoys, which she retained for some six years. Mme Anna Seuron was conventional, narrow-minded, observant, lively and indiscreet, and her testimony has to be treated with great caution. Still she is one of the very few who, after actually living in the family, put their experience on record, and she certainly helps us to understand certain phases of Tolstoy's conduct and character. Her book has proved particularly useful to writers like Merezhkóvski, who without knowing Tolstoy personally when they wrote about him, have sought to depreciate him; for various bits of her hasty writing can easily be twisted to suit a venomous purpose – though she herself is not malignant and again and again testifies to Tolstoy's nobility of character. Indeed, considering that she wrote after the Countess Tolstoy had dismissed her for boxing the ears of the sixteen-year-old Countess Mary, that she wrote with an evident straining after sensational effects and contrasts, and that what she herself wrote was touched up by an editor with an eye to sensational effect, it is surprising how little Tolstoy suffers at her hands.

This was the impression Tolstoy made on her when she first entered the family and found them just established in their new home in Moscow:

He seemed far younger than his age. He came up to me with quick step and gave me his hand: a good, firm hand, the touch of which left a pleasant impression. His very small, steel-grey eyes glittered. At first meeting he always looks one straight in the face . . . and he often produced on me the impression that I was facing the camera.

She adds:

The eldest daughter was being taken out into Society, and the Countess herself, who notwithstanding her large family retained a very attractive appearance, was also fond of Society.

The Count hindered nothing. He was assured that everything in life is but transitory, and that even along that road his family would reach the convictions he held . . .

She remarks that Tolstoy's searchings among the poor in the slums were not long continued. She says:

He had been seized by some feverish desire to descend into the abyss.

He used to return home with a terrible headache, his eyes glittering like tiny bits of steel. He seemed quite ill. 'What must we do? What teach? . . . Words are useless! I will begin by setting an example and will begin with such a small thing that everyone will be able to imitate my work!'

'In the sweat of thy brow shalt thou eat bread,' is said in the Bible. And one day after eight o'clock the Count harnessed himself to the hand-sledge to which a tub was attached, and dragging it from the yard, filled the tub with water from the well, and then slowly, step by step, dragged it to the kitchen. And the next day, and the next, he did the same. By that work he was serving others . . . And once when there was no water, Moscovites might have seen how he, poorly dressed, descended like all the other water-carriers to the river Moskvá. The journey took him a whole hour and he returned home dead-tired . . . Not the work itself was important, but its purpose; and so it was with heating his stove, lighting the samovar, doing his own room, and cleaning his own boots.

This is her description of Tolstoy's breakfast:

His letters would be put by his place at table. He would open them reluctantly and frequently shove them aside unread, so that some of them, at any rate, were simply mislaid.

Taking his handkerchief in his right hand he would lift the lid of the samovar, into which he would pop four eggs. Then he would put coffee into the coffee-pot, pour in water, and wait till it was all ready. Gradually the room fills with children big and little, who all go to kiss their father, and then place themselves round the table, sitting where they like and talking merrily and quite freely. The Countess comes to breakfast unpunctually, always in a hurry, but always animated and amiable. But now the eggs are ready, the Count (always managing to burn his fingers) gets them out of the samovar; then he places the coffee-pot on the top, breaks the eggs into a glass into which he crumbles some bread, and rapidly swallows the lot; whereas the coffee, which has been brewing meanwhile, is drunk slowly. Then comes the moment for all kinds of requests: for instance, that he would receive a tiresome visitor who has already been four times to the house asking to see him, &c.

Of the way in which Tolstoy dressed Anna Seuron tells us:

During the winter he found a peculiar pleasure in walking about in the poorest attire. He would go out in a sheepskin coat and greased high-boots and sheepskin cap, exactly like a peasant, and sticking his hands in his pockets or tucking them into the opposite sleeves, would set off to visit his Society acquaintances or would wander about the town seeking new impressions.

One day when I was unwell, he went to fetch my son from the Institute of Oriental Languages. To avoid any misunderstanding I telegraphed to my son that the Count would call for him at two o'clock. The telegram reached the Principal, and all the masters waited at the entrance. But when the Count came he was not recognised, but was told to 'sit down, old fellow!' on the locker in the hall and allowed to wait.

When my son came ready dressed into the hall and greeted the Count in French, those present opened their mouths with astonishment that a peasant in sheepskin should understand French; and it was only after the two had gone down the steps and out into the street that it occurred to the masters who were waiting to see the Count, that this was he.

Tolstoy's peculiarities in the matter of dress are again and again referred to by Anna Seuron, who watched him just at the time when his striving after simplicity and economy was accentuated by a conscious revolt against conventionality and a deliberate breaking away from former habits, though for the matter of that, he had always been somewhat original and wilful in his dress, and had also at Yásnaya long before this time been in the habit (not exceptional among Russian country landowners) of wearing a blouse with a leather belt – a comfortable attire none the worse for its resemblance to peasants' garb. He is shown in such a blouse in Kramskóy's portrait in 1873, when Tolstoy was commencing *Anna Karénina* and had not yet changed his views on life or his social habits. This pricks the bubble blown by two Irish visitors who went to see him years later, and came home with the tale that on reaching Yásnaya Polyána they saw Tolstoy (whom, by the way, they did not know by sight) walking in the grounds dressed in very 'county' clothes, and on reaching the house were kept waiting before being admitted to his study, where they found him dressed like a peasant. They jumped to the conclusion that Tolstoy had been so impressed by the fact that Irish visitors had arrived, that he had dressed up like a peasant in order to impress them. Had they frankly told him that they fancied they had seen him walking about in town clothes, they might have started an interesting conversation – instead of which they allowed their suspicions to render their visit valueless and their account of it worthless except as throwing light on their own mentality. Anna Seuron says:

> His caps and hats had neither form nor shape. It was all the same to him whether one article of his dress went with the rest or not. It was so even in town, not to speak of the country! Only his blouse had to be specially long to cover the upper part of his trousers, about which he was particularly modest.
>
> In just the same way he was opposed to women wearing low-necked dresses. His daughter (it was only the eldest who went to balls and she only during the first two winters in Moscow) always avoided letting her father see her *décolletée*. A Charity Bazaar he termed an abuse, and regarded giving money to beggars on the street as merely a habit. But all the same there were some old Moscow ladies who, on account of their age, found grace in his eyes when they formed Groups for benevolent purposes.

She adds:

> The Count could be extremely amiable when he liked, but if he happened to meet a stupid man it was all up! He would rise from his seat and simply go away without even saying goodbye, just as if he were frightened or disgusted.

During the winter of 1882–3 Tolstoy paid several visits to Yásnaya to be alone and escape from the bustle of town. The intensity of conflict aroused by his change of outlook had by that time begun to subside. He was training himself to mildness and ceasing to expect others to accept his views or suddenly change their hearts and lives.

Experience, that greatest of teachers, was showing him that he could not himself escape from his position without coercing the wills of those to whom he was closely bound.

This made him realise that a man's external position is no safe indication of the state of his soul. We cannot say, 'That man is a millionaire, therefore he must be cruel and selfish; this man has nothing, therefore he must be a saint.' Life is not as simple as the parable of Dives and Lazarus suggests.

A letter from the Countess to her sister, dated 30th January 1883, says:

> Lëvochka is very tranquil and at work writing some article or other [it was *What I Believe*]. Remarks against town-life and the life of the well-to-do in general burst from him occasionally. That pains me; but I know he cannot help it. He is a leader: one who goes ahead of the crowd pointing the way men should go. But I am the crowd; I live in its current. Together with the crowd I see the light of the lantern every leader (and Lëvochka, of course, also) carries, and I acknowledge it to be the light. But I cannot go faster, I am held back by the crowd, and by my surroundings and habits.

This attitude towards Tolstoy's teaching is worth noting. Most of those who oppose his views have put themselves in the wrong to an astonishing extent by misrepresenting him. On the other hand his wife and some of his admirers have said: 'He is quite right, but we cannot do what he demands. Five hundred years hence people will tread the path he marks out,' What has as yet hardly been done is to separate what is sound from what is unsound in his teaching and to show that he and his followers repeatedly ran their heads against brick walls because his survey of the ground was hasty and inaccurate. In so far as he was right, his principles are applicable today, and in so far as they are inapplicable today I am not sure that they ever will be applicable; for man's brain is not so made that he can frame moral codes for future societies of whose circumstances he is necessarily ignorant. Even a wise and honest man like Tolstoy, when he attempts to frame a moral code for his own society and his own age, begins by ignoring considerations which experience eventually compels him to allow for. This is no reason for not thinking, or for not testing one's opinions in practice, but it is a reason against calling one's opinion a 'principle' before testing it and finding it workable. Nothing surprised me more among Tolstoyans than to find them treating Tolstoy's views as revelations of absolute truth, and indignantly disapproving of attempts to revise them in the light of experience. That however is the typical attitude of religious fanatics in general and is not peculiar to Tolstoyans.

When he returned to Yásnaya in April, Tolstoy witnessed the effects of a fire that had destroyed twenty-one huts together with their sheds and outbuildings. Such calamities are terribly frequent in Russia, where most of the huts are of wood and straw-thatched. The suffering caused to the peasants, who are very poor at the best of times, was appalling, yet they were extremely slow to take precautions, and even when a fire broke out seldom made collective efforts to limit its extent. Each family seemed only concerned to save its own belongings, and even as to these a fatalistic feeling often prevailed: 'How are we to stop it? If it's God's will that it should burn, we can do nothing. Perhaps He will be merciful!'

Tolstoy, always keenly appreciative of the peasants' best side and sympathising keenly with their hard lot, wrote to the Countess:

> One is very sorry for the peasants. It is difficult to picture to oneself what they have endured and are enduring. All the corn has been burned. Reckoned in money their loss must exceed 10,000 rubles. They will get about 2,000 rubles insurance money, and all the rest has to be replaced by these people who are destitute, and it must be replaced unless they are to die of hunger . . . Send Serëzha [his son] to the State Bank to find out what paper or power of attorney will be required to withdraw my shares should they be needed . . .
>
> I have just been among the victims. It is pitiful and terrible and grand – such strength and independence, and their quiet confidence in their own strength. What is chiefly needed now is oats for seed.
>
> Say to my brother Serëzha, that if it will not inconvenience him he might give me a note to Pirogóvo [Count Sergéy Tolstoy's estate] for 800 bushels of oats. Let the price be the highest he sells at. If he agrees, send or bring me that note, or even reply by telegraph whether Serëzha will give me a note for the oats – for if not I must arrange to buy elsewhere.

Anna Seuron relates that the Count gave the timber to rebuild the huts, and adds that the fire somewhat needlessly spared the village schoolhouse, for the Count had by this time forgotten all about his pedagogics.

Little realising the fierce struggle going on in his mind as to the utility of monetary – or of any but spiritual – help for the poor, she gives us strange glimpses of his relation to that problem:

> One day I saw an ancient dame digging potatoes with some sort of stick . . . I advised her to take a spade. 'But we have only three spades in the whole village,' said she. When I spoke of this to the Count he said that that was all right: having to lend one another a spade trains the peasants in Christian love!

If one compared this systematic, pedantic hard-heartedness with the high ideals that lay at the basis of all his teaching it might seem that all that teaching was merely a sickly mystical confusion.

At the same time the Count was very voluble on the subject of help to one's neighbours. Near the house stands a large maple that has been struck by lightning. On one of its remaining healthy branches hangs a bell, which rings for dinner or to sound an alarm. And beneath that bell at times poor people waited for hours to ask for help or advice. In such cases the Count would disappear as though he had been swallowed up by the earth . . . He would simply run away from the petitioners.* But under that famous bell other forces appeared. There the Countess distributed medicines and lint. Other members of the Count's family gave something to the poor and also gave away small change . . . Yet during those years the Count at times displayed the naïvely childish tenderness of heart depicted in his *Childhood*.

I am in general a conscientious translator, but when dealing with Anna Seuron's eccentric narrative I find myself obliged to employ a free method of translation lest I should perplex my readers; yet I cannot afford to dispense with the intimate touches she supplies concerning these years of storm and stress when Tolstoy was attempting first one and then another method of solving the social question by moral rule and personal example. So many people have witnessed and testified to Tolstoy's wonderful patience with, and kindness to, the swarm of petitioners who day by day for many years collected beneath the tree that stands beside his house, that I do not hesitate to reproduce Anna Seuron's account, illustrating as it does the perplexities he was landed in by his rejection of money – a rejection he soon abandoned in practice.

Here is another witness's account of Tolstoy's attitude to this problem, within a year or two of the same time. His servant Arbúzov tells us:

In general during the summer many people of all kinds used to come to Yásnaya Polyána, particularly many pilgrims. The Count used to receive them all and gave money to them all, and it was my business to feed them.

At first the Count used to give these people a great deal of money,

* 'Because he never kept money, denying it in his writings.' *Note by the Countess S. A. Tolstoy when reading the first edition of this book.*

to some three rubles [6s.] and to some five rubles, and this pleased the pilgrims so much that there was no end to the number that invaded us.

They used to tell all sorts of lies to get more money, so that latterly not more than 10 kopeks [2½d.] and a hot dinner was given to any of them.

Of Tolstoy's attempts to avoid the use of money, Anna Seuron has queer tales to tell. I do not vouch for their accuracy but they are founded on fact, and the judicious reader may allow what discount he considers advisable. Though she approaches the matter without much sympathy or comprehension, she succeeds in giving an impression of the spiritual ferment and the startling contradictions which accompanied Tolstoy's attempt to break away from the ordinary ruts of life and to shape his life anew:

> Those oppressed by riches and *ennui* came in carriages, on horseback, and on foot, seeking peace. Sons of good families, who had already skimmed the cream of life; women who had buried the bloom of their illusions in unwomanliness; poor half-developed students who wished to imitate the Count: their intentions were good towards themselves, but what to one brings blessing often to another brings a curse!
>
> Tolstoy has been much blamed for leading the young astray: in other words, because there are people who tread in his footsteps and hope that for them, too, a light will arise. In that error many come to grief! Others succeed in obtaining a kind of ethical satisfaction for themselves. I could give names to show that those who had means were those who came off best. [Prince D. A. Khilkóv, Prince G. A. Dadiáni, V. G. Chertkóv, A. N. Dunáev, &c.] If I have fifty thousand rubles, it only aids digestion to do my own room, or plough my field, but if I torment the soul out of my body merely to be Tolstoyan the thing may well prove indigestible.
>
> Sons of some of the highest aristocracy discarded gold and lands and went into the desert to eat locusts. Ladies from Cronstadt, *dames de classe* [*chaperons* in a girls' school], appeared at Yásnaya and manured the fields in goloshes and white dressing-jackets. But there were very few of these. Most of them came to grief with their madness and good intentions . . . and many of Tolstoy's followers are now boiling in brimstone or are like mice in a trap.

There is a measure of truth in these remarks. Many who tried to discard the stiff stays or supporting irons of convention and external law, and felt encouraged to trust to their own judgement without regard for the opinions and customs of their fellows, went completely to pieces, and again and again in my own experience of these people I have had occasion to recall with approval T. H. Green's wise saying that, 'There is no other enthusiasm of humanity than the one which has travelled the common highway of reason, the life of the good neighbour and the honest citizen.'

Anna Seuron continues:

It was a strange and brightly varied scene in the new-baked Prophet's reception room in those days . . . Like a Delphic Oracle sits the Count, his legs crossed under him *á la Turque*, or with only one leg tucked under him *á la Tolstoy*, and hears the plaints of humanity. He listens to them all: those who do not know what to do with their gold; those whose wives are too much or too little for them; those who, stung by conscience, confess to him; to each he says a few words. But within himself it was not yet light, and just this half-light suited these modern pilgrims. At that time a snapshotting photographer might have immortalised himself at Yásnaya! All classes of society wandered in at those entrance gates near the high-road, which – despite neglect – spoke of grander times. One felt the landowner behind them, and the lake to the left, near the village, had quite a fine appearance.

In the village the Count was loved, it is true, but less than one might have expected. He made no demands on his peasants, but he also did nothing, or but little, for them. He was absorbed in his system which demanded self-help. Yet he said to everyone: 'Love your neighbour as yourself!'

Wise men the world over have broken their teeth on his teaching. How could the Yásnaya peasants become wise on it? The Count ploughed and worked with them, but often when he talked with them and was not in a good temper or did not wish to give something (as also occurred), the sixteenth-century serf-owner awoke in him. Even when a peasant stood close to him it sometimes seemed as though there were a gulf between them. The Count's eyes would become angry and the beggar would go away, shaking his head disconsolately.

In May 1883 Tolstoy went to his Samára estate and underwent a kumys treatment.

As on previous visits, he had many long talks with the local sectarians, especially the Molokáns, and frankly told them his religious beliefs. 'Never mind if I am denounced to the authorities,' he writes to his wife, referring to the danger of being accused of perverting the people from Orthodoxy and being punished by banishment, confinement to his estate, or what note. That danger naturally did not deter him from oral propaganda – a matter less serious than his literary offences.

Besides the sectarians Tolstoy met in Samára he also made acquaintance there with two Revolutionaries who had been involved in the trial of 'The 193' in 1878. His talks with them turned chiefly on Non-Resistance, a matter which always set a gulf between him and the politicals, with whose indignation against the existing régime he otherwise sympathised.

At this time, as subsequently, Tolstoy's condemnation of the Revolutionaries led to many misconceptions. Once a gendarme-officer even ventured to approach Tolstoy with a request for information regarding some political suspects who were known to be acquaintances of his. All that the officer got however was an indignant enquiry whether, because *he* had no conscience or sense of honour, he supposed that no one else had any!

It was while Tolstoy was still in Samára that Turgénev managed with painful effort to indite his last letter. It is written in pencil and remains unsigned:

> *Bougeval. 27th or 28th June 1883*
>
> KIND AND DEAR LEO NIKOLÁEVICH – For long I have not written to you because, to tell the truth, I have been, and am, on my deathbed. I cannot recover: that is out of the question. I am writing to you specially to say how glad I have been to be your contemporary, and to express my last and sincere request. My friend, return to literary activity! That gift came to you from whence comes all the rest. Ah, how happy I should be if I could think my request would have an effect on you! I am played out – the doctors do not even know what to call my malady, *névralgie stomacale goutteuse*. I can neither walk, nor eat, nor sleep. It is wearisome even to repeat it all! My friend – great writer of our Russian land – listen to my request I Let me know you have received this scrap of paper, and allow me yet once more cordially to embrace you, your wife, and all yours . . . I can write no more . . . I am tired.

This greeting – addressed to the great rival by whom Turgénev had often been grievously offended, whom he had never fully understood, and whom latterly he had hardly understood at all – is most touching, but it indicates how unaware Turgénev was of the immense human interest of the tasks which had for a time turned Tolstoy aside from novel-writing. He did not see that if our interest in life as a whole comes 'from whence comes all', it too has a right to exist. If it were possible today to wipe from memory the series of Tolstoy's works from *Confession* (1879) to *I Cannot be Silent* (1908), the interest the world feels in him would be but a fraction of what it is. The problems of life he faced, the guidance for life he offered, the fact that – artist to his fingertips – there yet were things for which he was ready to forgo his art, are what most profoundly stirred the interest and secured the love of multitudes. Turgénev neither foresaw the literary achievements of Tolstoy's later years, nor realised that it was impossible for Tolstoy to devote himself to art until he had made up his mind about the problems that religion deals with.

We cannot accurately weigh the matter nor say just what proportion of the interest in Tolstoy is due to his novels, but I am convinced that those from Turgénev downwards, who expressed regret that Tolstoy occupied himself with religious, moral and social questions, show their own limitations by doing so. Even his novels owe much of their value to that craving for truth and longing for brotherhood which characterised him from childhood to old age, and only those who are attracted by *What Then Must We Do?* can really appreciate what there is in *War and Peace*.

Even after his return to Yásnaya, Tolstoy delayed replying to Turgénev's letter, and on 22nd August (o.s.) the latter died. It was not that Tolstoy meant to leave the letter unanswered but, hurt by Turgénev's disregard for what was now most important to him, he postponed writing till he could do so in a more cordial frame of mind. Like so many other incidents in the relations between these two, it leaves a sense of ineradicable regret, and makes us feel how complex and difficult a matter is intercourse between susceptible people.

In September 1883 the family moved to Moscow, but Tolstoy remained at Yásnaya. He had received a summons to serve as juryman at the District Court in the neighbouring town. The following letter to his wife tells what happened:

Today I have returned from Krapívna. I went there summoned to serve on the jury. I arrived about three o'clock. The Court was already sitting and I was fined a hundred rubles [£10]. When called upon, I said that I could not act as a juryman. I was asked, Why not? I said, On account of my religious convictions. Then I was asked again, Did I definitely decline? I said I could not serve in any case, and I went away. It was all done in a very friendly manner. Today I shall very likely be fined two hundred rubles, and I do not know if that will be the end of it all, but I think it will. I am sure you will not doubt that I really could not act otherwise, but please do not be angry with me for not telling you about it before you left Yásnaya. I would have told you had you asked me, or if the question had come up; but I did not wish to speak specially to you about it . . . I need not have put in an appearance at all. There would have been the same fines, but then I should have been summoned again next time. Now I have told them once for all that I cannot serve. I said it in the mildest manner and even used such expressions that none of the peasants understood what it was about.

Tolstoy's refusal was intended not merely as a protest against the cruelties of the prison and exile systems, but as part of his repudiation of the whole system of public justice: civil or criminal. The act followed logically from the principle of Non-Resistence he had adopted, and which he was convinced that Christ taught.

A very different call reached him about the same time from the Society of Lovers of Russian Literature, who were planning a meeting in memory of Turgénev and wanted him to read a paper on that occasion. He agreed to do so, and set to work to reread Turgénev's novels for that purpose.

In October he wrote to his wife:

My life goes on like a wound-up watch. I wake at nine, walk in the woods, return, drink coffee, settle down to work about eleven, and continue till half-past three, when I again go into the woods till dinner . . . Then I dine, read Turgénev, Agáfya Miháylovna [an old servant] comes [and talks to me], I drink tea, write to you, take a stroll by moonlight, and go to bed. That is the worst time of the day. It is long before I fall asleep.

Again he writes:

I am always thinking about Turgénev. I love him terribly, pity him, and am always reading him. I am living with him all the time: I certainly will write something about him and either read it myself, or will give it to be read.

. . . I have just read his *Enough*. Read it – it is charming.

The Countess writes to her sister:

On 23 October Lëvochka will give a public lecture about Turgénev. It already agitates all Moscow and there will be a tremendous crowd in the University Hall. They have reserved four seats of honour for me in the very middle of the first row.

Her next letter told a different tale:

DEAR TÁNYA – As you have no doubt already seen from the papers and know by rumour, the lecture in memory of Turgénev has been forbidden from your disgusting Petersburg. It is said that Tolstoy [the Minister] forbade it – and what could one expect from him except tactless and awkward freaks? Only think, the lecture was to have been quite innocent and most peaceful. No one thought of letting off any kind of Liberal squibs . . . Everyone is tremendously surprised . . . What danger to the Government could there have been? Now of course people may imagine anything . . .

. . . Everyone without exception is angry about it except Lëvochka, who is even glad to be excused from appearing in public – a thing he is so unaccustomed to. He is always writing, but will not be allowed to print it.

That Tolstoy, who belonged to no Party and disliked politics, and whose pronouncement on Turgénev as a writer would have been of permanent interest, should not have been allowed to deliver a lecture on the subject is truly characteristic of the régime of Alexander III, which sacrificed everything and everybody to the one aim of maintaining itself, and did that in a way which revolted all reasonable men.

But amid the public matters with which Tolstoy was concerned one must not omit to tell of his lighter and more homely traits. Referring to a day in 1883, Anna Seuron says:

This evening, in the big room upstairs, I saw that wise man dance a valse with as much lightness and agility as though he were the Count of former days. And really, quite unconsciously, he sometimes shakes twenty years off his shoulders; and yet he has the peculiar talent of never appearing ridiculous, no matter how he is dressed – even when his sock shows through a hole in his boot.

His light-heartedness on that particular evening, Anna Seuron attributes to the fact that he had just taken his first lesson in the craft of bootmaking. This occupation was part of his effort to produce more and consume less, and had for him an ethical importance quite out of proportion to the value of the footwear he produced. Before long he appeared in high hunting-boots of his own make.

He was pleased when people praised his work, and talked with enthusiasm about the difficulties of bootmaking, and especially the difficulty of threading the waxed end: 'Oh, threading the waxed end requires extraordinary patience!' Sitting on a low bench, and in all respects imitating his teacher, the Count ardently and conscientiously tormented himself, threading the waxed end. Once, twice, three times, twenty times – in vain! At last fortune favoured him and he smiled and nodded his head.

Tolstoy was at this time engaged on the completion of *What I Believe*, which, like all his works, he wrote and rewrote, correcting and altering again and again.

On 9th November 1883 the Countess mentions that the work is nearly ready, and adds:

Lëvochka has gone to Yásnaya Polyána for a week. There he will rest and hunt.

From Yásnaya he writes to his wife:

I am reading Stendhal . . . *Rouge et Noir*. I read it some forty years ago, but remembered nothing except my relation to the author: sympathy with his boldness and a feeling of kinship – but yet an unsatisfied feeling. And curiously enough I feel the same now, but with a clear consciousness of why and wherefore . . .

Of another great novelist, Dostoévski, Tolstoy, replying to a letter from Strákhov (who had written Dostoévski's *Life*), says:

I have read your book . . . It seems to me that you were the victim of a false and fallacious relation – not on your part but on everybody's part – towards Dostoévski: an exaggeration of his importance, and (from routine exaltation) the elevation into a prophet and saint of a man who died in the midst of a most ardent inward struggle between good and evil. He is touching and interesting, but one cannot set on a pedestal for the instruction of posterity a man who was all struggle. From your book I have learnt for the first time the whole measure of his mind. Pressensé's book I have also read, but all his learning is spoilt by a flaw. There are beautiful horses: but if a trotter, worth say 1,000 rubles, suddenly proves restive, then – beautiful and strong as it is – it is worthless. The longer I live the more I value horses that are not restive. You say that you are reconciled to Turgénev. And I have come to love him very much; and, curiously enough, just because he is not restive but gets to his destination – not like a trotter that will not take one to the journey's end and may even land one in a ditch. But Pressensé and Dostoévski are both restive; and so all the erudition of the one and the wisdom and heart of the other, run to waste. Turgénev will outlive Dostoévski and not for his artistic qualities but because he is not restive . . .

This letter evoked a reply from Strákhov, who wrote:

All the time I was writing I had to fight against a feeling of disgust, and tried to suppress my bad feelings . . . I cannot regard Dostoévski as a good or happy man. He was bad, debauched, full of envy. All his life long he was a prey to passions that would have rendered him ridiculous and miserable had he been less intelligent or less wicked. I was vividly aware of these feelings while writing his biography. In Switzerland, in my presence, he treated his servant so badly that the man revolted and said to him: 'But I too am a man!' I remember how I was struck by those words which reflected the ideas current in free Switzerland about the rights of man and were addressed to one who was always preaching sentiments of humanity to the rest of mankind. Such scenes were of constant occurrence; he could not control his temper . . . the worst of it was that he prided himself on the fact that he never really repented of his dirty actions. Dirty actions attracted him and he gloried in the fact. Viskovátov (a professor) told me how Dostoévski had boasted of having outraged a little girl at the bathhouse, who had been brought to him by her governess. Of all his characters those that resemble him most are . . . Svidrigáylov and Stavrógin. Katkóv refused to publish one of the Stavrógin scenes (rape, &c.), but Dostoévski read it here to a great many people. With all this he was given to a sort of mawkish sentimentality and to high-flown humanitarian dreams, and it is these dreams, his literary message and the tendency of his writings, which endear him to us. In a word, all these novels endeavour to exculpate their author, they show that the most hideous villainies can exist in a man side by side with the noblest sentiments. This is a little commentary on my biography: I might have described that side of Dostoévski's character – I can call to mind innumerable incidents which are even more striking than those I have already mentioned – and my story would have been more truthful; but let this truth perish, let us continue to show nothing but the beautiful side of life as we always do – on all occasions.

On 22nd January 1884 Tolstoy finished *What I Believe*, and considering it useless to submit such a work to the Censor, he first tried printing it in a small, expensive edition of only fifty copies; for it sometimes happened that the Censor would pass a small edition of a book obviously not intended for popular circulation, especially if he had to choose between passing a ready-printed book or suppressing it altogether.

Pobedonóstsev, however, prohibited the book. But so great was the interest the news of its existence aroused that the law decreeing that it should be burnt was not complied with. The whole edition was sent to Petersburg, and arbitrarily, and illegally, distributed among influential officials and their protégés.

It soon began to circulate in lithographed and hectographed copies. Before long it was printed in Geneva, and translated into nearly every European language, though it was not allowed in Russia till much later.

The only writings of Tolstoy's passed for publication in 1884 were the three fragments of *The Decembrists* he had written some years previously. They appeared in a *Miscellany* issued by the Committee of the Society to Assist Authors and Scientists in Distress.

When living in Petersburg in 1857 Tolstoy had rendered Druzhínin some assistance in preparing a scheme for the founding of that Society, and now, when it had existed for more than a quarter of a century, he thus again came in touch with it.

One of the first of the friends who entirely shared Tolstoy's views was V. G. Chertkóv, a young ex-Captain of the Guards. It has been his unfortunate experience in life to come into fierce conflict with most of the people he worked with, and it was so in the army. He was the only son of a General influential at Court, the owner of very large estates.

His mother, a friend of the Empress, was one of the Petersburg circle influenced by Lord Radstock, the evangelical preacher. Chertkóv had passed through experiences similar to Tolstoy's own, having been even more exposed to temptation by his position and temperament. He resembled Tolstoy too in intolerance of what he disliked. Springing from the same class, inheriting the same traditions and faced by the same evils, the two men arrived at similar conclusions on the wickedness of war and on many other subjects. Chertkóv always declares that he was not Tolstoy's disciple, but had formed his Non-Resistant and other principles independently, before making Tolstoy's acquaintance or reading his works. This may well be true, for the views Tolstoy systematised and expressed had long been current in fluctuating forms among those Russians who regarded poverty, chastity, and humility as cardinal virtues, distrusted Governments, and condemned wars, violence and punishments. Similar views, of course, existed outside Russia, but they were perhaps nowhere so prevalent as there, and what distinguished Tolstoy was that he systematised, codified, expounded and clearly expressed, what had before been nebulous and ill-defined.

It was in Moscow, towards the end of 1883, that Chertkóv made his acquaintance. An attachment immediately sprang up between the two men which lasted all Tolstoy's life, and whereas to most men Tolstoy's views appeared extreme, Chertkóv always urged him to go yet further and apply his principles yet more rigidly. To the differences in character between the two I shall have occasion to allude later.

In January 1884 Gay again visited Moscow; and Tolstoy, making an exception in his favour, admitted him to his study while he wrote.

Gay's daughter-in-law tells us:

N. N. Gay and his wife came to stay with us in Moscow, in January 1884, and the day after their arrival we all went to see the Tolstoys. Nikoláy Nikoláevich [Gay] kept us there till late at night; he seemed to me to be carried away by his feelings like a girl at her first ball. He gazed with enraptured eyes at Tolstoy, anxious not to miss a single word he said, while Tolstoy treated him tenderly and as it were carefully. During that visit to Moscow, Nikoláy Nikoláevich painted Tolstoy's portrait while the latter was writing *What Then Must We Do?*

While the portrait was being painted and the book composed, Anna Seuron tells us:

At times the Count would stop writing for a while and would set to
work to mend some old shoe, considering a change of occupation as
good as a rest. At such times Gay would lie on the sofa smoking a
cigarette and studying his model. Now and then we heard them both
bursting out into quite youthful laughter, while at other times they
would both appear as though their brows were marked by the wrath
of God.

For several years running the Tolstoy family spent the winters in
Moscow and the summers at Yásnaya; Tolstoy himself doing the same –
except that he managed to spend more time at Yásnaya and less in
Moscow than the others. He was now settling down to a quarter of a
century of steady, unremitting literary work, carried on with remarkable
and almost monotonous regularity. The external conditions of his life
had by this time shaped themselves in much the same form that they
retained until he grew quite old, except that his performance of hard
manual labour as a more or less regular summer occupation continued
for only a few years, for his absorption in other work soon drew him
away from field-labour except as an occasional relaxation.

Let it be mentioned in passing that the extent to which people have
romanced about Tolstoy's manner of life is extraordinary. I have seen it
stated that he lived like a peasant, earned his livelihood by manual
labour, abandoned literature and art to live like a labourer, and so forth.
On the other hand, with equal mendacity, it has been said that he had
his underclothing made of silk and his blouses of fine linen, used scents
and had his hands manicured. The exaggerated accounts of the extent
to which he simplified his life resulted partly from the vigour with
which he expressed his ideas of how men ought to live, in such works as
What Then Must We Do? The fact that he wrote while his mind was
aflame with the ardour of a new conviction had the double effect of
making that book intensely vivid and moving in its appeal, and of
leading many readers to conclude that Tolstoy was able personally to
put all its precepts into regular practice.

Misapprehension has also been caused by Répin's famous portraits of
Tolstoy ploughing (1892) and of Tolstoy in his room, with a large
spade, saw, and scythe, against the wall (1890). These are genuine
portraits by a great artist who selected incidents and backgrounds
suitable for effective pictures, and the result has been much as though
some artist had produced a great picture of Lord Balfour playing tennis,

and that this had created the impression that Lord Balfour devoted the greater part of his life to that game. Yet more misleading is a painting by Jan Styka, who took the well-known figure of a typical Russian beggar in a long cloak with a wallet over his back, and set on it Tolstoy's head (or a head much resembling Tolstoy's) and so made a symbolic picture entitled: 'On the Road to the Infinite'. Trading on the popular misconception of Tolstoy's habits and way of life, a London agent even now supplies copies of this picture to papers that ask for a portrait of Tolstoy, and it is published again and again, with a variety of inscriptions, such as, 'Tolstoy in garments made by himself', 'Tolstoy snapped in Russia twenty years ago', and so forth. Jan Styka merely made a symbolic picture, but the trade use made of it is a fraud on the public.

One result of the popular delusion about Tolstoy's manner of life has been that some writers have denounced him as a poseur who pretended to live like a peasant but did not really do so. Others who visited him reproached him for continuing to be an author instead of living as they expected to find him living. They wanted him to change his way of life and so save them the trouble of altering their preconception of it.

What is regrettable in all this is, that the attention and discussion devoted to Tolstoy's manner of life tends to divert attention from his works and from the consideration of his views. Personalities and denunciations attract attention more readily than ideas or artistic work, though were it not for Tolstoy's opinions and works no one would care how he lived.

One of the questions Tolstoy had to face – now that he had come definitely to regard Church rites, including the Baptismal, the Marriage, and the Burial Services, as regarding incantations – was whether he should tolerate them in his own family. With reference to the grown-up members the case was simple, it was not for him but for them to decide; and in fact his children – except the one whose birth I am about to mention and who is still unmarried – have all accepted, or endured, the Church Marriage Service. The question of baptism and burial was more under his control, but here again the Countess – who remained a member of the Church – had as much right to an opinion as himself, so that in these cases also the legally obligatory ecclesiastical formalities were always observed.

His youngest daughter, Alexandra, was born on 18th June 1884, under very painful circumstances. Tolstoy was passing through one of his periods of acute distress because he felt the conditions of his life to be wrong.

The evening before her birth he left home saying that he could not endure to live in such luxury, and the Countess remained in uncertainty as to whether he would return.

Soon the birth-pangs began, and they were long continued. The Countess sat or lay weeping in the garden, refusing to go to her room; and at five o'clock in the morning, when she heard that her husband had returned, she went to him in his study and asked what she had done to be so punished: 'My fault is only that I have not changed while you have!'

Tolstoy sat gloomy and morose and did not console her. The struggle in his own soul was more important to him than life or death.

The Countess at last retired to her room and the child was born almost immediately; but the mother's milk was spoilt by the anguish she had endured, and she was forbidden to nurse her baby; it was to this that in conversation with me in 1909, when Alexandra was taking Chertkóv's side against her, she attributed the fact that her youngest daughter seemed less hers than any of her other children.

The following is Anna Seuron's account of Alexandra's christening:

Before we moved to town the little Alexandra was christened. The Count treated this ceremony with amazing indifference. Had it not been for me the priest would hardly have known where to baptise the infant. All the members of the family were absent. The Count was in the fields, the Countess sewing in her room. [In Russia, parents are not present at the christening of their children.] Only the nurse and the godfather and godmother stood at the font. I made my son put on his student-uniform, and I changed my own dress out of a feeling of propriety, but it turned out to be quite superfluous: a three-ruble note was thrust into the priest's hand, and in ten minutes the whole thing was over.

Next winter Alexéy died. 'Is it not a punishment?' thought I; 'Lead us not into temptation, but deliver us from the Evil One!'

The governess's readiness to believe that Alexéy died because Alexandra was not baptised with sufficient ceremony, causes her to misdate the former event by a twelvemonth, for Alexéy did not really die till 1886, so that if some deity dealt out vengeance in this particular case, he must at least be acquitted of having yielded to a sudden impulse.

That the friction with his family was not to any great extent due to personal causes but arose inevitably from the clash of Tolstoy's gospel with the established order of life, is indicated by the fact that in other families one or more members of which adopted his ideas, similar friction always showed itself.

For instance, Gay, one of the mildest of men but a devout Tolstoyan, writes on 16th July 1884:

> My dear, kind Leo Nikoláevich – I have many times prepared to write to you but, knowing your exceptional family circumstances, have refrained, not wishing to pain you. If I were to do nasty things the people around me would look indulgently on my nastiness and would be satisfied and happy in their own way. But as soon as a man wants to live in a godly way, not in word but in deed, thunders and grumblings fall upon him. I do not complain, for I know it must be so. But I did not write to you because I lacked the tranquillity solitude has now given me.

In October 1884 Tolstoy went to spend a week with Gay on the latter's farm in the Chernígov Province, in Ukraine. On returning to Yásnaya he wrote to his wife, who was already in Moscow with the family:

> The best impression I had today was caused by meeting two old men on the high-road. They were brothers from Siberia, and now returning from a pilgrimage to Mount Athos and Jerusalem without a penny. Their combined ages are 150 years; neither of them eats meat. They had a house and property worth 1400 rubles [£140], but when they went on pilgrimage the first time, a report got about that they had died, and their property was handed over to a trustee. The trustee made away with it. They returned and began a lawsuit. Then a monk told them it was sinful to do so as their action might cause people to be sent to prison, and that they ought to abandon it or it was no use going to Jerusalem. And they abandoned it and were left penniless. One of them has a son and has built another house. They were very dignified, kindly old men. Talking with them I did not notice how we walked from Rudakóva to Túla.

In his next letter, a few days later, he says:

> I am undertaking a very difficult thing, namely, engaging in farming

with a view mainly to my relations with the people and not to the farming. It is difficult not to be carried away, and not to sacrifice one's relations with people for the sake of the business, but what one must do is to manage the business properly, yet whenever the choice lies between one's profit and one's relations with men . . . to prefer the latter. I am so feeble that I feel my incapacity for it, but it has so come about that it is necessary, and since it came about of itself, I will try it . . .

Today I went round attending to the estate, and then rode on horseback; the dogs stuck to me. Agáfya Miháylovna said that unless they are on leash they attack the cattle, and she sent Váska with me. I wanted to test my feeling about hunting. From forty years' habit, to ride and look for game was very pleasant. But when a hare leapt up I wished him good luck! Above all, I felt ashamed.

It was not till some time after this that Tolstoy finally abandoned a sport he had ardently loved, in which he had risked his life, and which he has described so often and so magnificently in his novels.

Later on in the letter he says:

Don't be angry, darling, that I cannot attribute any importance to those money accounts! Such things are not like, for instance, an illness, marriage, birth, death, the acquisition of knowledge, a good or bad deed, or the good or bad habits of people near and dear to us. They are things we have devised, which we have arranged this way and can rearrange a hundred different ways. I know that to you often, and always to the children, when I speak so it sounds unendurably dull (it seems as though it were all well known), but I cannot help repeating that our happiness or unhappiness cannot in the least depend on whether we lose or acquire something, but only on what we ourselves are. Now if one left Kóstenka a million – would he be happier? That life should not appear insipid one must take a wider and deeper view. What our life together is with our joys and sorrows, will appear to our children real life, and therefore it is important to help them to acquire what gave us happiness, and to help them to free themselves from what gave us unhappiness; but neither languages, nor diplomas, nor Society, and, still less, money, made our happiness or unhappiness. And therefore the question how much our income shrinks cannot occupy me. If one attributes importance to that, it hides from us what really is important.

The Countess's feeling about her husband's way of life is indicated by a letter of hers dated 23rd October 1884:

Yesterday I received your letter and it made me sad. I see that you have remained at Yásnaya not to do the mental work regard as higher than anything in life, but to play at being Robinson Crusoe. You have sent away Andrián [a manservant], who was desperately anxious to stay out the month, and have let the man-cook go, to whom it would also have been a pleasure to do something for his pension, and from morning to evening you will be doing unprofitable physical work which even among the peasants is done by the young men and the women. So it would have been better and more useful had you remained with the children. Of course you will say that to live so accords with your convictions, and that you enjoy it. That is another matter, and I can only say: 'Enjoy yourself!' but all the same I am annoyed that such mental strength should be lost at log-splitting, lighting samovars and making boots – which are all excellent as a rest or a change of occupation, but not as a special employment. Well, enough of that! Had I not written it I should have remained vexed, but now it is past, and the thing amuses me, and I have quieted down, saying: 'Let the child amuse itself as it likes, so long as it doesn't cry.' [A Russian proverb.]

But though the Countess could be vexed, she did not bear malice, and wrote another letter the same day, saying:

All at once I pictured you vividly to myself and a sudden flood of tenderness rose in me. There is something in you so wise, kind, naïve, and obstinate, and it is all lit up by that tender interest for everyone, natural to you alone, and by your look that reaches straight to people's souls.

The story of the conflict between husband and wife – complicated by love, custom, new convictions, and old habits – a conflict that ultimately led Tolstoy to abandon all attempts to manage his estate and caused him to divide his property among the members of his family – is one difficult to tell without seeming biased on one side or the other. Most of those who have dealt with it have approached it as advocates and, picking out some vehement utterances by one or other of that highly strung couple, have succeeded in presenting a seemingly strong case against the husband or the wife. For anyone who did not know Tolstoy and the Countess, and especially for anyone who is regardless of the truth and bent on securing an effect, that is easy; but it is what a fair-minded observer should avoid. The case presented painful, complex, and difficult problems both to husband and wife, the more so because Tolstoy was breaking fresh ground in the formulation and statement of moral principles to which he attached supreme importance and the Countess, too readily, acknowledged to be just, but which were yet profoundly repugnant to her, not merely because they demanded the sacrifice of what she regarded as her own and her children's welfare, but also because at bottom she did not believe them to be rational or right in the form her husband presented them, and above all because she, on whom the practical task of arranging the family affairs was falling, never knew definitely what developments these new principles would take, or what fresh practical application of them would be desired by her husband, to whom progress was the constant goal and whom no settled arrangement could satisfy.

For the present let it suffice to say that Tolstoy's sincere desire to act in accord with the principles expressed in *What Then Must We Do?* was abundantly evident. On more than one occasion, feeling that 'He that hateth not father and mother and wife and child cannot be my disciple', he left home intending never to return, but like St Francis to become a beggar in the service of mankind. Before he had gone far, however, another feeling always drew him back to those whom he could not desert without arousing angry and bitter feelings. On the Countess's side there was the consideration that had she consented to Tolstoy's wish, the property would probably have slipped away in ways that would have done harm to those who scrambled for it. There was no undertaking, no definite work, no man or group of men, whom Tolstoy specially wished to support or assist. How to act and to whom to give would have depended not on any clearly thought-out plan, but on the fluctuating feelings of one whose social outlook had changed completely during the last decade and was still swaying and changing, and whose economic principles were more denunciatory than constructive. I have often heard the Countess blamed for her attitude, and no doubt she dreaded being left with her large family dependent on charity. But what may be pointed out is another feeling which certainly existed in her practical mind – the feeling that to waste and spoil is easy, while to preserve and repair is very difficult when once established and customary rule is abandoned, and that if – as Tolstoy felt – the acquisition, holding, and spending of property is a responsibility, so also must be its distribution or abandonment. The Countess may well have wanted some much clearer scheme for the future of their property than any Tolstoy proposed. In fact she told me that his plans (mentioned in the letter quoted above) never were at all matured or worked out, but were no more than passing suggestions. She well knew the enthusiasm with which he could throw himself into a task, but she also knew the absolute demand of his nature after a while for fresh occupations and fresh interests. So that to her his personal management of the estate did not sound like a solution of the difficulty. If I regret that Tolstoy did not have his own way in the matter, and that his wife prevented his trying to live among the peasants, it is only because so sincere a man would certainly have learnt from experience, and would not have shrunk from confessing any change of view that his experience brought.

Among other things I think he would have learnt to doubt the validity of some of his 'principles', and would have come to see that the property arrangements of the world have come to be what they are, not merely because men are selfish and wicked, but for reasons he had never sufficiently considered; and that though those arrangements may and should be changed, this cannot be accomplished by rejecting or despising the work done by those who went before us, but rather by learning from them and discriminating between what was permanent and what was temporary in their work.

Soon after this, Tolstoy offered to transfer all his fortune, including his copyrights, to his wife – saying that he could not bear the burden. 'So you want to place it on the shoulders of your wife,' replied the Countess, and with tears and sorrow she refused his offer.

Telling me of this many years later, she said she regretted having refused, for it resulted in a prolonged period of hesitation and uncertainty, leading to a division of the property between herself and the children in 1891. Some of the latter let their portions slip through their fingers until, even before the Revolution, there was little left, so she thought she would have done better had she accepted the whole burden and administered it as best she could.

Towards the end of 1884, Tolstoy made acquaintance with P. I. Birukóv, who after finishing at the Naval Academy had decided to abandon the navy because he disapproved of war. He became closely connected with Tolstoy's undertakings, belonged to the inner group of Tolstoyans, and many years later compiled a very accurate and reliable

Russian biography of his hero – a work far better informed than any previous *Life of Tolstoy* had been.

It is in four volumes. One would speak of it as the definitive Russian life of Tolstoy were it not that N. N. Gúsev has recently produced the first two volumes of one which, since it has the advantage of appearing later, may eventually prove an even more detailed and exact record. Both biographies are reliable in their facts, and have this in common, that they are written in complete accord with Tolstoy's religious and social views; they read there fore almost like panegyrics, and hardly attempt the task of discriminating between what is sound and what is doubtful in Tolstoy's pronouncements.

Of the life lived by the Tolstoy family in Moscow at this time, Anna Seuron has given the following sketch:

> Life in the Tolstoy family in 1884 arranged itself very pleasantly. The eldest son was at the University, the next two were also studying, and the younger children were being taught at home. The eldest daughter went out less, but on the other hand the Count's house became a centre of attraction. Under the guidance of Pryánishnikov [an excellent Moscow artist], Drawing Evenings were arranged, and we also had Literary Evenings, to which Fet, Gárshin, and other well-known writers, came. Musical Evenings were also arranged a which an eminent musician used to perform . . .

> Many guests came to the house, not the former ones but fresh ones. Besides relations and near acquaintances, the house was visited by Professors and by Governors of various Provinces – one of whom was once left standing for more than an hour by the coat-stand in the hall.

Tolstoy's neglect of his property did not result in the family being compelled to lead simple lives, though his example and precepts led to their doing things in a plainer, cheaper, and less conventional manner than would otherwise have been the case. But it did, after 1882–3, lead to the Countess becoming the publisher of his works. Here again Anna Seuron tells us what happened.

> It was at this time that the Countess began to make money out of her husband's works. The business grew with amazing rapidity and – by subscription and without subscription – one edition after another appeared. She attended to the proofs herself and worked at them till late at night.

The Count behaved very strangely in this matter. It was his conviction that money was an evil and the cause of moral deterioration. And suddenly he became aware that a vein of gold had been discovered which had its origin in him. At first when mention began to be made of selling the books, he stopped his ears and his face assumed a frightened and pitiful expression, but the Countess held firmly to her purpose of obtaining a secure competence for herself and her children: for with an increasing family and a decreasing income things could not go on much longer . . . At this time letters came from translators in all lands. None of them however got a straightforward reply as to whether the Count authorised or did not authorise their translations. 'I cannot forbid anything to any of them,' said he with a strange smile.

No literary convention exists between Russia and other countries, so that even apart from Tolstoy's disapproval of property – literary or other – anyone could translate what he liked and publish it as he liked, mangling and mutilating as he pleased, and using whatever titles entered his head.

Tolstoy's genius and fame and the fact that his writings were to be had for nothing, tempted several publishers to speculate in translations of his works, but the versions thus commercially produced were for the most part poor in quality, and the confusion created by the rival editions perplexed booksellers, publishers, and the public, alike.

Tolstoy would, I think, have been much more widely read and better understood throughout the world, if in each country some one experienced and respectable firm had been selected and allowed to issue an authorised edition, subject to such conditions regarding price and standard of translation, editing, and so on, as might have been agreed upon.

But this would have involved definiteness of agreement. It would have been dealing with property: whereas Tolstoy's wish was to have nothing to do with property, which he believed to be immoral apart from all question of the motives actuating those who deal with it.

The resulting chaos of inadequate and misleading versions of his works in all languages – often produced by people whose intentions were good – illustrates the fallacy of Tolstoy's view that things will go right of themselves if only we 'abstain from doing wrong'.

To commence the publication of her husband's works, the Countess borrowed ten thousand rubles (£1,000) from her mother, and fifteen thousand rubles (£1,500) from A. Stakhóvich. The book trade in Russia was not nearly so large or highly organised as among ourselves, and for the Countess to become her husband's publisher was not nearly as unwise as the same sort of thing would be in England today.

During the first year she made a gross turnover of sixty thousand rubles (£6,000), which was considered an extraordinarily large sale, and the profit on it sufficed to remove the financial difficulties she had been faced by.

No part of Tolstoy's life is more difficult to describe than the years of transition and repudiation which have to be dealt with in these chapters. He was ill at ease, perplexing to his family and friends, and consequently presents difficulties to his biographer; but we are reaching smoother water, and though the period of storm and stress was not over, it will be possible to tell the rest of the story, till near the end, more concisely and clearly, for he had by this time seen his aim, defined his purpose, more or less tested his strength, and found out what he personally could and could not undertake.

What he liked and what he hated is well indicated in a letter written to the Countess, when in December 1884 he had left the family in Moscow and was paying one of his frequent visits to Yásnaya:

> Yesterday, when I got out [of the railway carriage] and entered the sledge and drove over the thick, soft snow more than a foot deep (there had been a fresh fall) in that quiet softness, with the enchanting starry winter sky overhead and with sympathetic Mísha [the driver], I experienced a feeling akin to ecstasy, especially after being in the railway carriage with a cigarette-smoking landed-proprietress in bracelets, a doctor who fulminated about the necessity of capital punishment, a horrible drunken woman in a torn cloak lying senseless on the seat . . . a gentleman with a bottle in his bag, a student with a pince-nez, and a conductor who (as I was wearing a sheepskin coat) shoved me in the back: after all that – Orion and Sirius above the Crown Woods, the powdery, silent snow, a good horse, good air, good Mísha, and the good God.

*   *   *

I read *The Countess Tolstoy's Later Diary* (*1891–1897*) after this volume was in type, and can only allude to it briefly in the half-pages available at the end of this and a subsequent chapter, but will deal with it more fully in an Appendix.

If there were no other sources of information about Tolstoy, and we took the Countess's *Diary* as an impartial and quite reliable statement, we should be much misled as to the sort of man Tolstoy was, and should have to regard *War and Peace*, *What Men Live By* and his *Reply to the Synod* as grapes growing on thorns or figs on thistles.

Understandingly read, her Diary is, however, a valuable addition to the information obtainable elsewhere, and explains some things that otherwise remained perplexing.

An entry she made on 18th June 1897 deals with her daughter Alexandra's (Sásha's) birth – mentioned in the present chapter. The reader by turning to the Appendix can see what she says about it while the incident is still fresh in his mind.

6

The New Life

So gradually did the successive phases of Tolstoy's life merge like
dissolving views into each other that no attempts to classify them can
be more than approximately satisfactory. One is tempted to say that
by 1885 he had definitely adopted his new path of life: a life of
simple, strenuous work, the mental part of which was directed towards
removing obstacles to moral progress and clearing up the perplexities
that vex the souls of men. Yet the facts refuse to fit neatly into any
such generalisation, and we find the strands of his old life weaving
themselves into the web of his new endeavour. So, for instance, when
Prince L. D. Urúsov – who had been the first translator (into French)
of *What I Believe* – fell ill and was advised to go to the Crimea for a
change, but had no friend to accompany him, we find Tolstoy offering
to be his companion, though this must have seriously interrupted his
work and did not accord with the laborious frugality he aimed at.

A curious incident occurred on this expedition, which was otherwise
uneventful.

It will be remembered that after serving in the Flagstaff Bastion
during the siege of Sevastopol, Tolstoy was sent to the river Belbék, to
the left of the Russian position, where for some time his battery was
stationed at the spot now occupied by the English monument. Here
the hostile forces were not within range of one another, but one day a
small group of horsemen from the camp of the Allies approached the
southern bank of the roadstead, and the Russian commander ordered a
cannon to be fired to frighten them away. Tolstoy himself pointed that
cannon and fired it. He could not see where the ball fell, but the
horsemen immediately dispersed.

And now, going over the ground that thirty years before had been
occupied by the right wing of the Allies, he found a cannon-ball half
buried in the ground. On showing it to a veteran well acquainted with
the siege operations, he was assured that the only battery from which it
could have reached that spot was the one he, Tolstoy, had served in,

and as he knew that the only ball fired from that battery was the one he himself had aimed, it appears certain that he had picked up that identical ball.

He had, as we know, been very seldom separated from his wife, and now, travelling in the South, he felt what he has so often referred to, namely, the danger of desire aroused by luxury and leisure, and he hurried home.

Of the events to be recorded in 1885, the one that had the greatest permanent influence was the founding by Tolstoy and his fellow-workers (Chertkóv, Birukóv, Gortunóv and others) of a publishing business called the *Intermediary* (in Russian, *Posrédnik*), perhaps the most successful of all the practical undertakings inspired by Tolstoy.

Up to that time the literature supplied to the peasants had been wretched: consisting chiefly of legends and Lives of the Saints, in which whatever there might be of moral worth was encumbered by crude superstition, and of penny-dreadfuls and catch-penny booklets of a quality beneath contempt.

To supply the people with literature embodying the best that has been thought and felt, and – with no aim at pecuniary profit – to supply this in the simplest, briefest, and cheapest possible form, was the purpose of the *Intermediary*. Tolstoy felt profoundly that if it is permissible for authors to sit comfortably and write books while consuming food, wearing clothes, and occupying lodgings other men have produced, they should at least see to it that they provide wholesome mental sustenance for those whose toil produces what they consume. For if the bookmen devote themselves to pleasing the privileged classes, and give the labourers only what is mentally indigestible, then they are a burden and an evil to the mass of their fellow men.

Speaking to Danílevski, he said:

More than thirty years ago when some of the current writers, including myself, were beginning to write, the readers in this hundred-million empire amounted only to some tens of thousands. Now, after the spread of town and village schools, there are probably some millions, and these millions of Russians able to read, stand before us like hungry jackdaws with open mouths, and say to us: 'Gentlemen writers of our native land, throw into these mouths literary food worthy of yourselves and of us; write for us, who hunger for living words, and free us from those penny-dreadfuls and the rubbish of the market.' The simple honest Russian folk deserve that we should respond to their call. I have thought much about this, and have decided to make an effort to the best of my ability in that direction.

The *Intermediary* did much admirable work, and in so doing encountered many difficulties. It had not been started long before the Censors perceived that its simple little booklets and stories meant something, and that in so far as they roused people to think and feel they were a danger to the existing order. After they had become aware of this and had detected Tolstoy's influence in the new publishing company, every kind of obstacle was placed in its path. How exacting the Censorship became may be illustrated by the fact that when the *Intermediary* published the Sermon on the Mount as a reading lesson in a primer, the book was refused a licence until the injunction to 'take no thought for the morrow' had been suppressed!

A history of that publishing company, telling of the men who contributed: Gárshin, Semënov, Prugávin, Storozhénko, Strákhov, and others, and of the wisdom of the serpent needed to get anything past the Censors, would fill a volume in itself. After the Petersburg and Moscow Censors had become alert, authorisation for new books and stories was sometimes secured by submitting them to less wide-awake, provincial Censors. Chertkóv was particularly active in this, as well as in obtaining contributions from literary men, but it was Birukóv who chiefly attended to the regular work and managed the firm up to the time of his banishment. After that, the company was carried on by I. I. Gorbunóv, who remained in charge of it till the Revolution and in whose hands its scope and usefulness greatly increased.

Chertkóv being his intimate friend, Tolstoy used to pass on to him anyone who offered to assist their under takings. Chertkóv himself advanced money to start the business, and it naturally happened that much of the public approval it earned was awarded to him. He was a man of striking appearance and forceful personality, the only son of a wealthy and influential mother who was devoted to him. From that time onwards, Chertkóv was always in close touch with publishing businesses, and the public was often reminded of his connection with the *Intermediary* – the pioneer in a much-needed service. His influence with Tolstoy – which subsequently had serious results for the Countess – was largely based on gratitude for the services Chertkóv had rendered. The conflict between him and the Countess eventually became so important that details concerning Chertkóv, which would otherwise not be worth recounting, may have a certain interest. For instance, some of his nearest colleagues told me that he was, in fact, a hindrance rather than a help to the success of the *Intermediary*, which only went ahead well after he withdrew from the business when he left Russia in 1897. One small matter mentioned to me as illustrating his methods, remains in my mind because it related to a publication that had puzzled me when I first encountered it. The *Intermediary* aimed at supplying good reading matter to the peasants at the lowest possible prices; many of its publications being sold at from a farthing to a penny each. The number of works it could publish was constantly limited by the smallness of its funds, but when Chertkóv himself wrote a booklet on the cruelty of hunting, and wanted to push it, though it did not sell on its own merits, he insisted on having a photographic reproduction of a fine stag pasted on to its paper cover regardless of the cost, which the business could ill afford. When he withdrew from the business and called in the money he had lent, he did so on terms that made it difficult for the business to carry on. Having always spoken as if he attached extreme importance to the undertaking, he appeared reckless of its fate as soon as he ceased to direct it himself.

Tolstoy wanted everybody to be friendly, and discouraged complaints, so it was not easy for colleagues in less frequent and intimate touch with him to make him understand why they found it hard to work with Chertkóv, but the latter, who besides having great diplomatic ability was very intimate with Tolstoy, was always able to present his own case in a favourable light. Things were smoothed over at the time, and the outside world heard little of these difficulties. Only after similar occurrences in England, and after Chertkóv's conflicts with the Countess had become public, did people begin to remember his behaviour in regard to the *Intermediary*.

At the time of its greatest activity the *Intermediary* sold as many as three to four million booklets a year. When in hunting for suitable material Tolstoy came upon stories which, though good, were in his opinion not good enough, he passed these 'mongrels' on to Sítin – a publisher who had a large business and with whom the *Intermediary* worked in alliance – inducing him to improve the quality of his publications, and proving to him that he could make as much profit out of good books as out of bad ones.

Even in England (though Morley's Universal Library was started about the time the *Intermediary* came into existence) we are partly indebted to Tolstoy for the spread of the various series of cheap classics that now circulate so largely. When, in 1888, W. T. Stead visited Yásnaya, the two men discussed a Penny Universal Classical Library, and Stead's ventures in that direction resulted from that conversation. One of his assistants, Grant Richards, after starting in business on his own account, brought out the 'World's Classics' Series (which subsequently passed to the Oxford University Press), and the success of that series encouraged the publication of various shilling, ninepenny, and sixpenny collections that have since done much to place good literature within the reach of all classes. The influence exerted by a man like Tolstoy, whose mind was set on serving his fellows, is incalculable and overflows into many channels.

At first, short stories by Tolstoy were the mainstay of the *Intermediary*, though some of these were promptly forbidden, and permission to publish others was withdrawn by the Censor after one or more editions had been allowed. During 1885 he contributed *Two Old Men*, *A Spark Neglected Burns the House*, and *Where Love is, God is*: all now to be found in *Twenty-Three Tales*.

It was in 1884 or 1885 that Tolstoy wrote his essay on *Industry and Idleness*, as preface to a little book written by a peasant-sectarian, Bóndarev, who was living in exile in Siberia. Bóndarev was a first-rate ploughman, who burned with indignation at the contempt often shown to peasants by people rich enough to evade manual labour, and he formulated his religion of work with a lucidity and vigour that evoked Tolstoy's unbounded enthusiasm.

In his essay on *Industry and Idleness* (in *Essays and Letters*) Tolstoy summarises Bóndarev's contention by saying that:

The misfortune and evil in men's lives come from regarding many empty and harmful regulations as religious duties while forgetting, and hiding from themselves and others, that chief, primary, and undoubted duty announced at the beginning of Holy Scripture: 'In the sweat of thy face shalt thou eat bread.' . . . Not only do people fail to acknowledge this law, they acknowledge the very reverse of it. From King to beggar, they are led by their convictions to strive to avoid this law, not to fulfil it . . . Of all the definite duties of man, Bóndarev considers that the chief, primary, and most immutable for every man, is to earn his bread with his own hands – understanding by 'bread-labour' all heavy rough work necessary to save man from death by hunger and cold, and by 'bread', food, drink, clothes, shelter, and fuel . . . All the ills of humanity – except those produced by direct violence – come from hunger, from want of all kinds, and from being overworked; or on the other hand from excess and idleness and the vices they produce. What more sacred duty can man have than to co-operate in the destruction of this inequality – this want on the one hand and this snare of riches on the other? . . . Life and the blessing of life are not to be found in personal happiness, as people generally suppose, but in the service of God and man . . . And do not suppose it possible to serve men, while you consume what others labour to produce and fail to produce your own sustenance with your own hands . . . Whoever you may be, however gifted, however kind to those about you, however circumstanced, can you sit over your tea, your dinner, your political, artistic, scientific, medical, or educational affairs unmoved, while you hear or see at your door hungry, cold, sick, suffering people? No! Yet they are always there, if not at the door, then ten yards or ten miles away. They are there, and you know it! And you cannot be at peace, cannot have any pleasure which is not poisoned by that knowledge!

Bóndarev, be it, remarked in passing, estimated that a competent worker can perform 'bread-labour' sufficient for his own support by working forty days a year.

Tolstoy's literary output in 1885 ran nearly all in that same direction. He wrote an essay-letter to Romain Rolland (who was then a student), on *Manual Labour* and continued to work at *What Then Must We Do?* He made a (somewhat free) translation from the Greek of the moral precepts forming the first part of *The Teaching of the Twelve Apostles*, the famous document brought to light by Bishop Bryennios, in 1883.

He also devoted himself vigorously to fieldwork, and, much to the perturbation of the Countess, disciples began to gather round him.

By contrasting the accounts given by various eyewitnesses we can get a very good idea of what life at Yásnaya was like during this and the subsequent summers.

Anna Seuron tells us:

When making tea the Count would almost count each leaf, yet he was losing thousands by mismanagement of his estates. For a time he quite ceased to take any care of his personal appearance and was absurdly dirty and untidy. He, who had always worn very fine socks, suddenly demanded strips of linen and began to wrap his legs in them as peasants do . . .

One day he announced that though lice, considered as insects, are dirty, yet a poor man should not be considered dirty for being lousy. Being poor he is a natural prey to lice. To be clean requires means – it is a luxury! . . .

It was a most amazing time, and it is quite comprehensible that people who heard reports of his eccentricities should have considered him simply mad.

But he was never saner than at that period. He was testing, internally and externally, just how much he could endure and how hard it is to do without this or that thing. Of course, only those nearest to him could know this.

This again is one of her thumbnail sketches:

Haymaking! What a picture! Counts, Princes, teachers, and all sorts of blue-blooded people tried to work in competition with the peasants. Scythes hacked awkwardly, mowing the sappy grass. Everyone strove to outdo the others. As far as eye could reach, workers were seen everywhere. All the peasants were there, and so was the Countess in a Russian dress; children and governesses – we all helped to turn the hay. The hunting dogs lay around, and an unusually hot sun shone on the smiling meadow. In the distance, on one hill was seen the village and on another the Count's house.

And there he stands, that peasant Count, in a Russian shirt and trousers, his legs wide apart, mowing, and looking at him I see that he is quite engrossed in it. He is listening to the sound of the scythes and enjoying himself . . .

At that time a very original man arrived from America to see the Count. He called himself Frey, but in spite of his name he was a Russian. He was about fifty, yet his appearance was blooming and youthful; he was a vegetarian and for ten years had not even used any salt.

The Countess was beside herself with vexation, for even her daughters came under his influence; they ceased to eat meat, and began to grow pale. However, before the year was over the fit passed, and the vegetarians ate meat with the rest of us.

I can testify that a few years later, when I made their acquaintance, the Countess Mary was a vegetarian, and her elder sister, the Countess Tatiána, very nearly so. Tolstoy, despite the digestive troubles from which he suffered from the time of the Crimean war, and despite his wife's opposition, remained a vegetarian to the end of his days. Anna Seuron's view is that:

> The Count took up these manias only in the spirit of penitence, to subdue his flesh and elevate and enlighten his spirit. There was even a time when he really seemed to wither up and become thin. He tormented himself, and wrote with his heart's blood . . .
>
> Anyone who in the 1880s noticed how the Count suddenly began to grow thin and how his narrow leather belt was continually being tightened a hole or two, could easily have convinced himself that this too was one of the paths to salvation . . .
>
> Yet at the same time he was good-natured and often merry. He would play croquet, run races with his sons, play the piano, and of an evening draw devils on scraps of paper. He laughed at things that seemed serious to other people, sewed new boots and mended old ones, rejoiced in his frugal economies, and played with the little children: in a word, he was a simple, kindly, good family man, who did not know how to count beyond three and would never stir up the mud in any stream.
>
> It happened at times that he threw off from himself Leo Tolstoy the writer, the Count, the shoemaker, the aristocrat, and the father of a family, and became simply himself – for he possessed the capacity of throwing off one skin after another like an onion. The days on which these metamorphoses occurred were of course not marked in the calendar, and it is better so, or one would get still more completely confused. On such days the Count changed completely and was even sceptical about his family tree.

The real name of the remarkable man mentioned by Anna Seuron, and who passed as William Frey, was V. K. Heins. He was Russian by birth. Besides serving in the Finnish Regiment he had passed through two Military Academies – the Artillery and the General Staff. From boyhood he had shown extraordinary ability. He was an excellent mathematician and possessed wide scientific knowledge. Moved by moral impulse he abandoned the brilliant career opening before him and in 1868 emigrated to the United States, where he founded an agricultural-communal Colony which fell to pieces a few years later, as such things generally do. He then betook himself to the Kansas Colony founded by N. Chaikóvski, there reluctantly consented to exchange manual labour for educational work, and showed himself to be an admirable science lecturer. Chaikóvski's Colony came to grief in its turn, and after working in the United States as a common labourer, Frey migrated to England.

Having gone to America a Communist-Socialist, he returned a Positivist-Comtist of the strictest type.

In 1885 he returned to Russia. From the preface to a series of his Letters to Tolstoy we learn how he came to seek the latter's acquaintance, and how much the two had in common, despite a sharp divergence in views on religion. In quite the Tolstoyan spirit, Frey says:

The more I saw of the readiness of Russians to accept, for the guidance of their life, a new religion and morality, the more tormenting to me was the thought of how much energy and life is spent, at times almost uselessly, in struggles against the Government, when self-sacrifice and altruism are so much needed for another struggle (in my opinion a more real one) in which one has not to fight evil with its own weapons, but to meet its weapons with a bold and invincible determination to devote oneself to the service of humanity at all costs and in spite of all injunctions.

Of himself and Tolstoy he says:

Working apparently in different circumstances and under different banners, we have both come to the conviction that religion is the sole key to the solution of the questions of life, for the individual and for society. We have both arrived at the doctrine of altruism, and relying neither on legendary bogeys nor on any promise of eternal life, have found the solution of our doubts in the life of others. Even in small ethical details we have much in common and can therefore understand one another . . .

Last summer I went to Russia, and only there heard for the first time of Tolstoy's activity, of his immense influence on the live parts of Russian society, and of his manuscripts circulating in thousands of copies. Till then I had known nothing of all that. From Tolstoy's treatises I was not able clearly to grasp his world-conception, but in any case I could not ignore such a force. I wrote him (*a*) a profession of my religion, in order to deduce therefrom (*b*) my criticism of his teaching. On receiving my letter Tolstoy at once wrote asking me to come to see him . . . I hastened to avail myself of his invitation and spent five unforgettable days with him (7 to 12 October 1885).

Feinermann, who was then at Yásnaya, tells us:

It was from Frey that Leo Nikoláevich first heard vegetarianism preached, and in him he first saw a man who had consciously abjured all slaughter.

'How good that is! How good! . . . ' said Leo Nikoláevich, enraptured. 'But can vegetable food suffice?'

'Even wheat grains alone suffice,' answered Frey. 'One only need dry them and use them as food.'

'What? Not even ground?' said Leo Nikoláevich aghast.

'Has man any better mill than his own mouth?' answered Frey, and evoked a storm of enthusiasm by his reply.

Leo Nikoláevich's delight was unbounded. He embraced Frey, kissed him, and in every way expressed his goodwill towards him.

'I mention cereals,' continued Frey, 'because at present they seem easier to get. But gramineous food obtained from the fields is not really the most natural to man. Another and a nobler kind of food is naturally his, to obtain which he need not cut or pluck stalks – which is slaughter of plant-life. Fortunately man's very structure teaches him to eat a wonderful food, retaining the odours of the virgin gardens of Paradise . . . Yes! Both the structure of our teeth and the length of our intestines incontrovertibly prove that man is not a beast of prey adapted to rend and swallow other animals. He has not the sharp-pointed, widely-separate teeth of the beasts of prey, and the length of his intestines is far greater than theirs. Those two circumstances prove, better than any treatises, that it is abnormal for man to feed on flesh-meat.

'It is also clear that man is not an herbivorous animal. His intestines are too short for that: they would have to be twice as long, nor are his teeth as broad as those of the herbivora. Man belongs to a category of animals for whom another food is natural – fruits and nuts. He is not a flesh-eating or a grass-eating, but a fruit-eating animal. And of all fruits the best are nuts. Take for instance the monkeys in the forests.

They feed on nuts, and how flexible, agile and strong they are! With a stroke of his arm a gorilla has been known to smash a lion's skull, and his teeth have flattened the barrel of a gun.

'In vain the flesh-eaters argue that the use of meat is a beneficent process for the perfecting of undeveloped creatures, because when the flesh of an animal is assimilated by the human organism it is converted into bright thoughts, inspired feelings, and noble actions. What, they ask, is there immoral in it? On the contrary the cattle should be grateful to us for eating them!

'It is exactly like Nietzsche with his theory of the Superman. He says that the material welfare of the disinherited masses must be sacrificed for the lofty purpose of developing a new type. Very likely the lower mass of humanity suffers in its fields, shafts, mines, factories, and railways, but the material blessings it produces are mysteriously converted into a new and marvellous type of civilised man. Its sufferings are fully compensated for in the general economy of Nature, and the squalor of capitalism is redeemed by the superiority of the Superman!'

'As I listen to you and to your excellent comparison,' remarked Tolstoy, 'I recall a legend a monk in Óptin Monastery told me when I went there to pray: "God at first created the spiritual world, the realm of angels. They sang praises to the Lord and contemplated His excellence. But then the most beloved of the angels, seized by pride and envy, incited a crowd of the heavenly host to rebel against God, Who hurled him with all his adherents into the gloom of the abyss. The fallen angels became evil spirits, and their leader was called Satan.

"Then the angels who remained in heaven submissive to god, besought Him, saying: 'Woe, woe to us! Thou hast deprived us of our comrade, and our number will not be renewed . . .'

' "But the Lord was angry with them and said: 'O ye of little faith! Ye know not My power! Therefore of the most miserable creatures on earth I will now make beings equal to yourselves, and will renew your number!'

' "And in His anger God created man.

' "People live oppressed by heavy toil, and live passionately in lusts and sufferings, but it is not in vain, for among them there are holy spots, the monasteries, and thither fly the gifts and the sons of suffering humanity; and there, by God's will, from that most wretched creature man, angel-like beings are formed to replace those who fell from heaven." . . .

'And outside the wall of the cell I heard the hiss of a large two-handed saw, shh! . . . shh! . . . It was the noise made by hired workmen cutting planks for the houses of the "future angels"!

'Yes, my friend; deception reigns strongly in our life and you are quite right. Thanks, thanks for your wise and honest words! I will certainly follow your example and abandon flesh-meat.'

And from that time Leo Nikoláevich ate nothing that was slaughtered, and at one time went so far as to live on oatmeal porridge.

One day, soon after his conversion to vegetarianism, Tolstoy called on his friend I. I. Raévski at an hotel in Túla. Raévski was having dinner. Tolstoy began to say that one should not eat meat or be a glutton, and that man's proper food is bread and water. The pudding was brought in, and Tolstoy, still talking, drew the dish towards himself to take some. 'Eh! No! . . . ' protested Raévski humorously, 'that's also gluttony!' and Tolstoy pushed back the dish and expressed his penitence.

Anna Seuron tells us:

It was at this time that he renounced hunting and shooting, and of his difficulty in so doing and the strength of the feeling that at times drew him to such sport, let the following incident testify. Once after writing for many hours he came out into the hall and threw his gun over his shoulder, but could not find his hat. As the sun was baking-hot he seized the first head-gear that came to hand and vanished like lightning from the house. Towards evening he returned immersed in thought, his bare head hanging down, and he crept stealthily into the house dragging behind him a slaughtered hare, and hanging from his belt was his eldest daughter's gigantic turkey-red hat, which in his ardour he had seized on going out.

That was the last hare he killed, and his gun would have been rusting till today had it not been for his sons who, though they respect their father's example, avoid following it . . . He never forbade them to shoot or hunt, but only asked them not to be cruel to the game, and never wished to see what they had shot . . .

Again days of trial arrived. The Count seemed possessed by a fever of renunciation. Now had come the turn of tobacco. Oh, unfortunate man! How hard it was to part from tobacco, and from the cigarettes he used to smoke so awkwardly yet with such enjoyment! 'Smoking is harmful,' announced the Count, one morning, 'it is a luxury! Instead of tobacco, barley might be grown to feed the famished.' And his horn cigar-holder was set aside on the shelf, where it lay beside the works of Rousseau, Stendhal, Bernardin de Saint-Pierre, &c.

The Count gained a new, extremely difficult victory over himself. He suffered unendurable torment, positively not knowing what to do with himself. He would pick up a cigarette-end here and there like a schoolboy, to have but a single whiff, or dilating his nostrils he would eagerly inhale the smoke when others smoked in his presence. And after a while, despite his convictions, he again yielded to his inclination, for smoking really soothed his nerves and those who supposed the Count to be an ascetic in the full sense of the word are much mistaken. He has had, and still has, times when he is capable of any amount of self-denial, but with his physique and his senses the Count can never be a Saint.

Difficult, however, as the struggle may have been, Tolstoy finally and completely overcame his craving for tobacco.

Frey went south after his visit to Yásnaya, and when he returned in December, found Tolstoy in Moscow finishing *What Then Must We Do?* – in Chapter XXIX of which he summarises various religious and philosophic systems that, in his opinion, serve to palliate customary and established wrongs and to divert attention from the changes that ought to be made in our way of life.

Among such systems Tolstoy includes the Evangelical teaching of the Fall and Redemption, which he says is employed to supplant Christ's moral indictment of social wrongs; and the Hegelian system, with its principle that 'all that exists is reasonable'.

Chapter XXX is devoted to a destructive criticism of Positivism, which he treats as a similarly 'apologetic' system. This Tolstoy read to Frey, for as one of Frey's main contentions was the necessity of subordinating scientific activity to religious-moral principles, Tolstoy hoped that he would agree that Comte's scientific system usurps the place of religion, and abolishes the control that moral principles should exercise.

Frey accepted Chapter XXIX – the one in which religious and scientific systems diverting man's attention from moral guidance to intellectual abstractions are criticised; but on hearing Chapter XXX, which treats Auguste Comte as the author of a similar creed, he revolted. After passing the night in Tolstoy's study he rose early, and sitting at Tolstoy's writing-table indited an appeal to him to destroy Chapter XXX, modify Chapter XXIX, and not class Positivism among the ruling, justificatory, scientific theories, nor class Comte among the founders of such systems.

Tolstoy as usual stood to his guns. He always continued to feel and express the kindliest sentiments towards Frey as a man who shaped his life in accord with his beliefs, but there was no further personal intercourse between the two, and in February 1886 Frey returned to England, where three years later he died.

As already mentioned, Tolstoy's absorption in his new ideas, the discussions they aroused, and the literary work by which he sought to spread his views, militated against the efficient management of his estates, which for years were much neglected. Anna Seuron tells us:

> That winter the Count quite neglected his fine estate in Samára. It was too far off, there was at that time no direct communication by railway, and moreover from time to time some famished teacher would turn up who would persuade the Count that he (the teacher) was well acquainted with agricultural affairs. If he also professed agreement with the Count's ideas he was sure to secure a place in Samára . . . One way and another matters there took an exceedingly bad turn . . . Hundreds of thousands of rubles were lost, but the estate ultimately proved to be a veritable gold-mine and yielded a revenue in spite of everything . . .
>
> In those days the Count was enough to drive any observer crazy. He behaved with complete unrestraint, like some boa-constrictor who swallows a bird and calmly digests it. Like a ruminant he swallowed, and threw up and re-swallowed, his ideas, and those around him – especially those who opposed him – suffered from this cud-chewing process.

In a sphere in which things commonly considered important seemed of no account, and things unregarded by the 'cultured crowd' were the all-important subjects of attention, the strangest events happened without attracting notice.

Chúrkin, the famous robber and murderer who had killed fifteen people, twice wrote to Tolstoy, and on one occasion, after one of his three escapes from Siberia, frightened Anna Seuron on her way to bathe in the river that runs at one end of the Yásnaya estate about a mile and a half from the house. Tolstoy took these letters as a matter of course and even forgot that Chúrkin had ever written to him.

The visitors at Yásnaya naturally tended to divide themselves more or less sharply into two camps: those who adhered to Tolstoy and favoured manual labour and a peasant-like life, and those who were on the side of the Countess and wished things to go on as heretofore. The two sets were sometimes called the 'dark' and the 'white'.

One of the 'dark' who arrived about this time was a well-built young Jew named Feinermann, some nineteen years old, who has been already mentioned and of whom Anna Seuron tells us:

> One day he appeared upon the scene, no one knew why or wherefore. He announced that he wished to work. The Count, who was pleased by the way he talked, directed him to the village, and the young man stayed there some weeks and conducted himself admirably, helping everywhere with the roughest work and attending the sick in the peasants' huts. There was typhus in the village. Feinermann was quite the hero of the day; but though the children, nephews, and all the young folk, including my own son, tried to set him on a pedestal, the whole affair seemed to me doubtful and ridiculous. The Countess looked at things with a practical eye and tried at any rate to make use of the young man. He said he knew something of tailoring, so she bought some rubles' worth of linen and set him to work to make the Count a pair of trousers. But alas! what were they like? Whichever way you turned them they were no use at all. Feinermann at once fell in the Countess's eyes.
>
> But he was not abashed by his failure . . . He set to at fieldwork, and later on when things were quieter took to spiritual occupations. The Count often asked him to tea, and he really was a pleasant, educated man with good manners. One fine day he announced that he wished to enter the Orthodox Greek Church, and set off to see the priest . . .
>
> This matter went forward in due course without any fuss. Feiner-mann was a quiet fellow and an adroit one. I am convinced that the Count had nothing to do with his conversion and merely let things take their course. The baptism took place but neither the Count nor the Countess was present, and becoming a Christian only improved Feinermann's position by giving him occasion to confess that he had a wife and asking permission for her to join him . . .

Feinermann's reason, the Countess says, for becoming a member of the Orthodox Church was to qualify himself for the post of village schoolmaster at Yásnaya. The Countess, however, considering that he had a bad influence and that the peasants disliked him, made such representations to the authorities as ensured his having to leave.

Anna Seuron says:

Then one fine day Feinermann was summoned to serve in the army . . . and soon he was no longer remembered. He disappeared from our horizon as rapidly as he had appeared on it. Jew or Christian it was all the same to the Count. How could one find strength to follow up all those who came for a short time, hoping to find salvation in his teaching? It would seem that the maxim, 'Each for himself and God for all,' applied here also.

Having thus made Feinermann's acquaintance, let us hear what he has to say of Yásnaya Polyána in 1885. The lady, Márya Alexándrovna Schmidt, mentioned in the following account, had been a *dame de classe* at the St Nicholas Institute for girls in Petersburg, but having come under Tolstoy's influence wished to simplify her life.

Másha, Tolstoy's favourite daughter, ran in: a light and slim maiden with a kerchief on her head, arranged like a young peasant woman's, and wearing a peasant-costume of hand-spun material and an apron. Gently swaying her body she said rapidly: 'Márya Alexándrovna, would you like to see how they lay the sheaves in the barn? Come along!'

And not waiting for a reply, she drew Márya Alexándrovna away with her, but her ringing laughter could still be heard in the distance as she ran along, kissing and clinging to Márya Alexándrovna. 'Ha! ha! ha! my little *dame de classe!*'

The next day we met in the widow Anísya's yard. She had no one to till her strip of land, so Leo Nikoláevich undertook to manure and plough it. We came into the yard with a cart and forks, and began to fork up the broad damp layers of yellow-brown manure that had accumulated from one cow during the winter. Márya Alexándrovna also helped, smoothing the heaps with a fork.

'Your baptism of fire!' chaffed Leo Nikoláevich. 'Don't be abashed that this is your first work! In all agricultural labour this comes first and one must begin with it.'

'But I am so pleased . . . what do you mean?' and her thin brown cheeks flushed red.

And Másha, who was also there, and who with a serious air was all the time carrying bundles of straw from the stack, and spreading it where the ground was cleared, remarked didactically: 'I think it is better to work than to make wise speeches!' and was off for another bundle of straw.

In the evening we all met again in Leo Nikoláevich's large dining-room, and although we had changed our clothes, the 'ladies' (as they called the Countess, her sister, T. A. Kuzmínski, and the governess) made faces, and brought in plates from which thin streams of performed smoke rose from burning pastilles and scented herbs.

'Smoking out the unclean spirit with incense!' laughed Leo Nikoláevich. 'You would do better to come and work with us then there would be no need of this smoking out!'

This scene produced a very strong impression on Márya Alexándrovna. 'How painful!' she afterwards said to me, 'and how painful it must be for him! Who can realise the burden of this tormenting duality better than he himself?'

Márya Alexándrovna paused, and continued: 'He says it is his "cross". I bow down and confess that I should not have the strength to bear such a cross.'

'The enemies of a man are those of his own household,' said I.

'Yes, yes, exactly!' continued she. 'Másha said, "Do you know what Papa hopes for? That he will bring us all round to a new life, and that we shall all believe as he does." Our dear, precious Leo Nikoláevich! What a terrible task he is undertaking! He will not accomplish it. I foresee the worst: he will not only never see his family living a new life, but will not even have a group of friends living round or near him. You are now the only one living here, and I have heard that even you have much to put up with. They are afraid of your influence on the children, the family, the servants, and the peasants. And if even a small community of us collected, the first words of persecution would come from the rooms from which came those pastilles and sweet herbs. Yes . . .'

Leo Nikoláevich came up and hearing what the conversation was about, said: 'It is my sin, there's no denying it. In my heart I have many a time decided to go away and settle over there, at the corner of the forest – you know, where the Vorónka River twists back towards the Záseka. There was an apiary there once, and the beekeeper's hut is still standing. I could live and work and write there. I have felt drawn and even now feel irresistibly drawn thither, but I have said to myself, "That would be anchoritism: it would be like standing on a pillar." And I want to live and serve God and work in His fields with the equipment and encumbrances it has pleased Him to bestow on me. I have weighed and sounded my soul in all sincerity, and always when I imagine myself in my present circumstances of oppression, opposition, and ridicule, subduing my pride and my ambitious desire to show men an example, I feel nearer to Him Who is guiding my life, and am conscious of His hand. But as soon as I imagine myself there, in a state of freedom, living a model life in peace, I lose the sense of closeness to Him, His hand no longer seems near me, a horror of coldness and desolation seizes me, and I say to myself, "No, I will remain where I am." '

And Márya Alexándrovna, who had been planning to go away, also remained. A strong friendship grew up between her and Másha. They worked together in the field, haymaking, and did housework for the peasants – milking their cows, spinning, cooking, and looking after the children.

A neighbour of that Anísya from whose yard we carted the manure, happened to fall ill. The illness lasted some time and proved to be typhus; and Márya Alexándrovna watched beside him for weeks, at the same time helping his wife, the kindly, tall, but delicate old Dómna.

'Where, O Lord, is there another soul so fine?' Dómna used to say, touching the hem of Márya Alexándrovna's garment. 'Why do you take such a burden on yourself? You, who might eat and drink in plenty and live like the gentlefolk! . . . You waste your health here on us, burning like a taper set before a Saint's icon . . .'

The following is Anna Seuron's account of the foregoing incident:

One day he came to lunch straight from manuring a field. At that time several amateurs of that pleasant occupation had assembled at Yásnaya Polyána. All the windows and doors were opened wide or one would have had simply to run away! The Count smiled and looked cheerily around, thoroughly pleased that he smelt of manure, and he seemed so completely convinced that he was doing something very good, that I burst out laughing . . .

Arbúzov tells us that in fieldwork Tolstoy kept pace with the peasants, and that:

Leo Nikoláevich received remuneration for his work, for he ploughed and mowed not as an amateur, but seriously. He worked, like a peasant, *ispolu* [that is, 'half-and-half': an arrangement under which a peasant does fieldwork for half the crop he raises on someone else's land]. When he had earned five stacks, the Count would cart away three for himself, and give two of the five to a poor widow.

When N. N. Gay stayed at Yásnaya, he and Tolstoy worked for three months at bricklaying, and together built a hut and out-buildings for the widow Anísya Kapylova.

The Count and N. N. Gay laid the bricks, while the Countesses Tatiána and Márya plaited straw for the roof. But there was a difficulty about making the brick-oven. I cannot tell you how they laughed over it!

Leo Nikoláevich sat inside and N. N. Gay from outside handed him in the materials. For a long time nothing came of it, but at last they managed to get the oven built.

Much has been written about that hut, but it was not a great success. The clay was not properly wetted, and before long the building became crooked and began to fall to pieces. The surprising thing however is, not that Tolstoy should have shown himself inexpert at house-building, but that he could do so many different things, and yet do several of them so well. Arbúzov adds:

'Later on, Leo Nikoláevich got angry with that same Anísya Kapylova and ceased to help her.'

'Why?'

'Because she began secretly to trade in vodka and make the peasants drunk. Leo Nikoláevich advised her to stop that business, but she did not obey him.'

'And is vodka still sold in Yásnaya?' asked the recorder of Arbúzov's remarks.

'No; now that poison can't be got for any money, because we love our Count very much and respect him, and Leo Nikoláevich hates vodka and tobacco more than anything else. He says: "The man who does not smoke, saves ten years of his life, and the man who does not drink, saves twenty."'

'And does he drink himself?'

'He used to drink, but only a little. When he returned from shooting, for instance, he would have a small liqueur and a tumbler of light wine, half-and-half with water. But now he does not drink anything at all but water and *kvás* [a non-alchoholic beverage].

In the early 1880s I wished to leave, because there was no getting on with the housekeeper and the nurse, but Leo Nikoláevich would not let me go.

'Don't you listen,' said he, 'to those old maids, because when they settle down to old-maidishness they become utter idiots!'

And so I stayed on.

Let Feinermann continue the story of Tolstoy's activities:

We were getting in a second crop of hay on the meadow near the garden. In the forenoon we shook it and raked it together, and towards evening we began gathering it into *kopná* [large cocks carefully built up to stand like stacks].

Leo Nikoláevich, wielding a pitchfork, stood in the middle, while we brought heaps of fresh, sweet hay, rich with flowers and clover, that had ripened a second time that summer, and this – with an easy movement from his waist – he laid round him in the shape of a well that quickly grew upwards.

When he had completed the circle and trodden down the last lot, he would stand erect waiting in triumph for those who carried the hay: 'I am ahead of you! What are you about?'

Márya Alexándrovna worked harder than anyone, and would rush along carefully pressing a large heap to her bosom with the rake, like a mother carrying a baby across a stream.

Másha dragged along after her, dropping half the hay on the way, and behind her another girl, with a pathetic, anxious look, the meek, dreamy Ólga, tripped along, the handle of her rake pressing hard on her little shoulder as she bent beneath *her* load . . .

When he had made a *kopná*, Leo Nikoláevich would jump to the ground and comb down and trim its sides and top with his rake. The sun was nearly setting and we hurried to complete the last cock.

'Let's hurry up!' Leo Nikoláevich kept encouraging us ' "When sun has set man cannot work." That's what the old folk say!'

There was only a little left and the last cock was a very small one with a pointed top.

Having trimmed its sides, Leo Nikoláevich threw the trimmings on the top, and leaning his elbows on the cock heaved a sigh of relief: 'We have just managed to keep pace with the sun! See there! . . . Its last edge touches the railway and the long trail from the engine's wicked funnel tries to cover even that last rosy edge. I think I see someone standing beside the sun and threatening that wicked funnel and the whole of our blasphemous life.'

We gathered round Leo Nikoláevich and, shaking off the stalks and tendrils that clung to our clothes, placed ourselves also beside the rick. It seemed so much our own! Másha stood on Leo Nikoláevich's left side, Márya Alexándrovna on his right. Leo Nikoláevich thrust his arm into his leather belt, forming a half-circle with his arm, and through this semicircle I saw Márya, Alexándrovna's face full of tenderness, like that of a Saint, and my eyes involuntarily looked for a halo around it.

Ólga placed herself behind Másha, and with an effort, stretching her neck so as to see Leo Nikoláevich's face, asked timidly, as though in reply to his last thought: 'But could there be life without evil? Could man exist if there were no evil?'

'A nice thought, Ólga Nikoláevna,' Leo Nikoláevich said with animation, 'but it is not correct! Man comes of good, not of evil. A few days ago I was looking through a collection of ancient legends and read with delight some that dealt with that very point. There are thoughts of striking depth expressed with extraordinary simplicity and artlessness in those legends. Here, for instance, is one which I shall have of course to tell in my own way.' And he began:

*　　*　　*

'The Lord thought of a new creature, a marvellous combination of heaven and earth.

' "Do not create him!" said the Angel of Truth sternly. "He will quickly defile Thy temple and will glorify fraud on earth, temptations will hold sway everywhere."

' "Do not create him!" prayed the Angel of Justice. "He will be cruel, hurting everyone and loving only himself. He will be deaf to the sufferings of others, and the tears of the oppressed will not touch his heart."

' "He will steep the earth in blood," added the Angel of Peace, "and murder will become his occupation. Terrors of devastation will seize the land, and fear of violent death will enter every soul."

'And the countenance of the All-Upholder became overcast. The marvellous combination of heaven and earth seemed mean and evil to the Ruler, and in His eternal fore-will a decision was ripening – "Not to be . . ."

'But now before the Throne of the Life-Giver appeared his youngest, best beloved child, Mercy. She embraced the Father's knees, and begged: "Create him! When all Thy servants leave him, I will find him, help him, and change even his shortcomings into good. I will guard him that he should not stray from the path of truth. I will draw his heart to sympathy and will teach him to show mercy to the weakest!"

'And the face of the All-Upholder became radiant. The marvellous combination of heaven and earth came into being, and took His form and His likeness.'

' "Live!" breathed on him the All-Upholder, "and know that thou art the child of Mercy."

* * *

'That is how man was created, yet you say he is the outcome of evil,' and Leo Nikoláevich looked at Ólga with a kindly, half-reproachful smile.

'A beautiful legend!' said she, in a tone of delight, and smiled with embarrassment.

* * *

The afterglow of sunset was beginning to fade and dark-purple, dome-shaped clouds, towering one above another, floated up and stretched out eastward like gigantic stripes.

'Look, what an angry spectacle is enacted in the heavens! Every-thing is filled with the hope of dawn . . . Beautiful! . . . But before I finish, just one more legend,' said Leo Nikoláevich, as we approached the house.' I am in a legendary mood this evening:

* * *

'A King's daughter is betrothed to a rich man, who grudges nothing to delight his betrothed and supplies her with every kind of pleasure. He builds her marble palaces with golden ornaments, prepares rich feasts in her honour, lavishes pearls and precious stones, upon her . . . But his betrothed remains cold and indifferent and has no inclination for feasts or presents. Why? Because she is a King's daughter.

'So it is with the soul. Earth spreads all its treasures before her and strews her path with carnal pleasures. But the soul remains cold and does not incline her heart to such delights. Why? Because she is God's daughter!'

*   *   *

We parted in deep thought. The meaning of the legends, the tone in which they were told, and the whole atmosphere of labour and faith, imprinted themselves indelibly on the mind as something unusually joyful and elevating.

Márya Alexándrovna did not remain at Yásnaya Polyána long after that.

A Tolstoy Colony had been started in another part of Russia, and she joined it.

Hard times began for her. Her letters spoke of struggles with the hardships of the new life. The land bought for the Colony was covered with spiky thistles, and these had to be pulled up by hand. The Colonists' hands were always bleeding, the work was very exhausting, and above all there were no prospects before them, no hope of soon getting the land cleared.

Besides Márya Alexándrovna there were several other 'searching souls' in the Community, and they were all crushed by the incredible difficulty of their immense labour, which became real torture . . . Márya Alexándrovna bore everything uncomplainingly and with wonderful fortitude. 'However bad it may be here, still the life of ladies and gentlemen is worse!'

Leo Nikoláevich wrote letters of encouragement, and when these were received, it was a holiday for the whole Colony.

Later on when the Colony fell to pieces, Márya Alexándrovna and her friend, also formerly a teacher, settled on a desert part of the Crimean shore and worked like two hermits from morn till late at night in their little kitchen-garden.

'Simpletons!' they called them in the neighbourhood. 'Saints', was Leo Nikoláevich's name for them.

Eventually Márya Alexándrovna settled in a village a few miles from Yásnaya, and remained there till after Tolstoy's death, keeping cows and cultivating a bit of land lent her by Tolstoy's eldest daughter, and living almost as barely as a peasant-woman.

Of Márya Alexándrovna's sincerity, industry, and devotion to Tolstoy and his doctrines, there was no possible doubt. The only question is whether on the whole, by standing aside from educational work, separating herself from her own class, and working at hard manual labour, she really rendered better service to mankind than she could have done in ways less unconventional. Working alone she was not able to maintain herself by agricultural work without help; whereas a gentle, educated, trustworthy woman of good will, such as she was, working in co-operation with others as a small wheel in the complex mechanism of society, should be worth much more than the bare cost of her keep, and I do not think the value of her example and influence need have been less under such circumstances.

In the autumn when fieldwork was over. Gay would come to Yásnaya, and when the Countess had moved to Moscow with her sons, Tolstoy and his daughters would remain there for a while with him.

Tolstoy would then devote himself to literary work, in which Gay helped him. When the post arrived of an evening they would all deal with it together, Tolstoy sorting out the letters into (1) those he would have to answer; (2) those his daughters could answer; and (3) those that could go unanswered.

In the Recollections of Vasíly Morózov we find an account of Tolstoy as seen from another angle. After being one of the best scholars in Tolstoy's school in the early 1860s, Morózov became a cabman in Túla, but occasionally wrote articles for the magazines.

In the 1880s I heard wonderful things about Leo Nikoláevich, from some of my mates from Yásnaya Polyána: how he had become a simple working-man, a ploughman, a mower, a sower, a woodsman, a stovebuilder, a carpenter and a bootmaker. All peasant-craft came natural to him. The tales my mates told me were surprising. My good friend and schoolfellow, Ignát Makárov, said to me, 'You would not know Leo Nikoláevich as he is now, Morózov! You remember when we were at school? He was good to us then, but now he is still better and is so to everybody. You should just see how he works: how he ploughs, how he mows! You know how strong he is! Why if the horse were too weak you might harness *him* to the plough! And how he works with us in the village! He is not afraid of the illnesses that are about – not even of cholera. That's how we have trained him . . . He even boasts of his work. "Ah, Ignát," he says, "I was quite tired out yesterday, but how well I slept!" And I say to him, "The sleep itself is worth working for." And he, "Yes, yes, Ignát! That's true!" . . . You should drive over to Leo Nikoláevich's, Morózov. He would be glad to see you, he often asks: "How is Morózov getting on?" – You come and we will call on him together and he will give us some books. I have already had many good books from him.'

My soul felt light and joyful after this talk with my friend, who understands goodness as I do.

So I got ready to go to Yásnaya Polyána, to visit my relations and see Leo Nikoláevich. Hardly had I got there and put up my horse, when my old aunt of eighty came running out and began telling me how hard it was for her to live in this world.

'I have nothing,' she said, 'not a stick of my own. But the Count be thanked, and God give him health! He stands up for us forlorn ones; he has brought in my hay, and carted the manure, and ploughed the fallow, and done the sowing. God give him health and strength! . . . And see now! He is rebuilding our homestead. He brought the timber himself. The old hut was ready to fall in on us altogether . . .'

After a chat with my aunt, I went to see Leo Nikoláevich, the carpenter. I did not go near at once, but stopped where I could not myself be seen, to watch him. I stood admiring his work. Dear me! What has become of Leo Nikoláevich? Hair and beard are quite grey and he has become wrinkled . . . he has grown old. But look how he sits astride on the top beam, cutting out a place for the cross-rafter to fit into! His shirt-sleeves are turned up, his unbuttoned shirt shows his bare chest, his hair is dishevelled. The locks in his beard shake at each blow of the axe. He has a chisel stuck in his girdle behind, and a handsaw hangs from his waist . . .

After seeing Leo Nikoláevich at his work as a carpenter, I had a talk with him which still remains in my mind.

For me, the meaning of 'Count' and 'His Excellency' has quite gone, but the idea of old Leo the carpenter, old Leo the ploughman, the mower, the oven-builder, has become quite distinct. And his words about goodness remain with me. 'Let me not waste the short time left me! Today I am alive, tomorrow in my grave.'

I became attached to Leo Nikoláevich with my whole soul, and often planned to get an interview with him. He was always repeating, 'Love and goodness,' and praising country life, labour, healthy appetite, and sound sleep.

The next year, 1886, began sadly, with the death, on 18th January, of the four-year-old Alexéy, from croup.

Anna Seuron says:

Thirty-six hours were enough to turn the Count's charming little boy, blooming with health, into a corpse. He caught cold while out for a walk in a north wind. The doctor, mistaking the disease, treated him merely for sore throat, and afterwards admitted his blunder.

The Count behaved fittingly in accord with his later writings. 'For those of firm mind, death is but a reminder.' But when, at the dying child's request he was called to his bedside, he ran along the corridor like a lad of eighteen and yet managed to enter the room with a show of calmness.

The boy glanced at his father, convinced himself that it was really he, and raising his little hand and eyes towards the ceiling, said distinctly: 'I see . . . I see . . . ' – 'What?' asked the Countess, but no reply came.

Though at that time, says Anna Seuron, Tolstoy rejected priests and ceremonies, he nevertheless allowed the funeral to take place in the usual way.

As is customary in Russian families, little was said of the death that had occurred. Alexéy was a slight, wise, meditative boy. The Countess herself possessed something that counts in the spiritual world – a sort of electric spark or spiritual fire, which corresponded to her rapid, lively speech; and the lad had inherited the good qualities of both his parents.

7

What Then Must We Do?

Having convinced himself that there is a connection between the lives of the rich and of the poor, Tolstoy attacked the problem of poverty. His book, *What Then Must We Do?*, already quoted, was finished in February 1886. It is one of his most striking works, and of intense autobiographical interest. No one caring to understand Tolstoy and his views should miss reading it. Its economic conclusions – biased by his surroundings and intimate knowledge of the life of the Túla peasants (a province much poorer than the black earth district to the South) – are one-sided and too scornful of the benefits which science, capital, and organisation can confer, but Tolstoy pierces to the fundamentals of life in many memorable passages, and were it not for the inexorable limit of space and the fact that my readers will have the book at their disposal in this edition, I would quote many more pages of it here.

He says: 'We who share in the unceasing orgy that goes on in the towns may be so accustomed to it that it seems to us natural for one person to live in five enormous rooms, heated by fuel enough to cook the food and warm the lodgings of twenty families; to employ two horses and two attendants to carry us half a mile; to cover our parquet floors with rugs, and to spend, I will not say five or ten thousand rubles on a ball, but even twenty-five rubles on a Christmas Tree, and so on. But a man who needs ten rubles for bread for his family or whose last sheep is being taken to pay a seven-ruble tax, and who cannot obtain the money even by heavy toil, cannot get accustomed to it. We think it all seems natural to the poor. There are even people naïve enough to say that the poor are very grateful to us for feeding them by our luxury. But being poor does not deprive men of reason, and the poor reason as we do. When *we* hear of a man losing or squandering ten or twenty thousand rubles we immediately think: "What a foolish and good-for-nothing fellow he is to squander so much money uselessly, and how well I could have used it for a building I have long wanted, or to improve my farm," and so forth; and the poor reason just in the same way when they see wealth senselessly wasted, and they do it the more insistently since they need the money not to satisfy some caprice but to supply things they urgently need . . .

'The poor have never admitted and never will admit that it is right for some to have a continual holiday while others must always fast and work. At first it astonishes and angers them to see it. Then they grow accustomed to it, and seeing that such arrangements are considered legitimate they themselves try to avoid work and to share in the perpetual holiday.

'One often hears people complain of the conduct of their servants. Servants often really do behave badly, but this is not to be attributed so much to natural perversity as to the example set by their employers. If – as that example often suggests to them – it is good to enjoy oneself and not to work, what can be more natural than that they should seek to share these good things as much as they can? Some succeed and join the ever-feasting ones, others partially insinuate themselves into that position, others again break down without reaching their aim and, having lost the habit of work, fill the brothels and doss-houses . . .

* * *

'What, indeed, is my money, and where has it come from? Part of it I have got from the land I inherited from my father. A peasant sells his last sheep or cow to pay it to me. The other part of my money I have got from my writings – for books. If my books are harmful I only place temptation in the path of those who buy them and the money I receive is ill-gotten; but if my books are of use, the case is still worse. I do not give them to the people, but say, "Give me seventeen rubles [34s. – the price of Tolstoy's *Collected Works* at that time] and then I will let you have them." And as in the former case the peasant sold his last sheep, so here a poor student, a teacher, or any poor man, deprives himself of things he needs, to give me that money. And I have thus got together much money, and what do I do with it? I bring it to town and give some of it to the poor if they also come to town and obey my whims, and clean the pavement, and my lamps and boots, and work for me in factories. For this money I get all I can out of them: that is, I try to give them as little, and to take as much, as possible. And quite unexpectedly, without any particular reason, I suddenly begin giving away this same money to these same poor people; not to all of them, but to some whom I select. How can each of them help thinking that perhaps he may have the luck to be one of those with whom I shall amuse myself when I distribute my mad money? . . .

'Chucking away farthings with one hand to those whom it pleases me to select, while gathering thousands from the poor with the other, I used to call "doing good"! Is it then surprising that I felt ashamed? . . . What I felt from the first at the sight of the hungry and cold people in Lyápin House – namely, that I was to blame for it, and that one could not, could not, *could not*, go on living as I was doing, was the one thing that was really true! . . .

'It was hard for me to realise this, but when I realised it I was horrified at the delusion in which I had been living. I was up to my ears in the mire, yet thought I could drag others out of it.

'What indeed do I want? I want to do good, to arrange that people should not be cold or hungry, but should live in a way fit for human beings.

'I want this, and I see that by violence, extortion, and various devices in which I participate, the workers' bare necessaries are taken from them, while the non-workers (of whom I am one) consume in super-fluity the fruits of the labour of those who toil . . .

'I see that in our time working-folk, especially the old men, the women, and children, simply perish from intense labour and insufficient nourishment . . . while in the case of the lucky ones (of whom I am one) the life of the non-workers reaches such a degree of security as in olden times people only dreamed of in fairy tales. We have reached the condition of the owner of the magic inexhaustible purse – that is to say, a condition in which a man is not only completely freed from the law of labour for the support of life, but is able without labour to avail himself of all life's bounties and to hand on that magic inexhaustible purse to his children, or to whom he pleases . . . I see that the ideal of an industrious life has been replaced by the ideal of a magic purse . . . I sit on a man's neck, choking him and making him carry me, and yet assure myself and others than I am very sorry for him and wish to ease his lot by all possible means – except by jetting off his back! . . .

'And I came to feel that in money itself, in the very possession of it, there is something evil and immoral; and that money itself and the fact that I possess it, is one of the chief causes of the evils I saw around me – and I asked myself, What is money?'

Tolstoy devotes several chapters to the consideration of this question. He says that wherever, on the one hand, we find people consuming luxuriously without producing, and on the other hand people over-worked and wretchedly poor – there slavery exists, and it is always based on violence. Money makes the poor the common slaves of all the rich.

Money does not usually represent work done by its owner. It represents power to make others work. It is the modern form of slavery.

'As soon as I understood what riches are and what money is, I under-stood the truth handed down from remote times by Buddha, Isaiah, Lao-Tsze, Socrates, and to us most clearly and indubitably by Jesus Christ and his forerunner, John the Baptist. In reply to the people's question: "What Then Must We Do?" John the Baptist replied simply, briefly, and clearly: "He that hath two coats, let him impart to him that hath none; and he that hath food, let him do likewise!" The same was said by Christ many times, and yet more clearly. He said: "Blessed are the poor, and woe unto ye that are rich." He said: "Ye cannot serve God and mammon." He forbade the disciples to take money or even two coats. He told the rich young man that, being rich, he could not enter the Kingdom of God, and that it is easier for a camel to go through the eye of a needle than for a rich man to enter the Kingdom of God. He said that he who will not renounce all – house, and children, and fields – to follow him, is not his disciple. He spoke the parable of the rich man, who like our rich men did nothing bad, but merely clothed himself well and ate and drank sumptuously and thereby ruined his soul, and of the pauper Lazarus, who did nothing good, but was saved just by the fact that he was a pauper . . .

'The rejection of the customary methods of exploiting the labour of others brings us inevitably to the necessity, on the one hand, of moderating our requirements, and on the other, of doing for ourselves what others used to do for us . . .

'Finally I came to the following simple conclusion: that in order not to produce suffering and vice, I ought to consume as little as possible of the work of others and do as much work as possible myself. I came by a long road to the unavoidable deduction formulated a thousand years ago by the Chinese in their saying: "If there is one man idle, another is dying of hunger." '

I must omit Tolstoy's dramatic account of the arrest of a prostitute near his house, and the death in the street of a respectable old washer-woman, who, being destitute, had been turned out of her lodging by the police. He continues: 'The day I wrote this down, there was a great ball in Moscow,' and he goes on to tell of the factories that stood near his Moscow house and produced stockings, silks, scents, and pomades – all articles needed for balls, and he describes how he watched the workmen in the street after the factories closed for a holiday.

'I walked around watching these workmen loafing about in the streets, till nearly eleven o'clock. Then their movements began to quiet down. Only a few drunken ones remained, and here and there men and women who were being taken to the police-station. And now from all sides carriages began to appear, all driving in one direction.

'On the boxes were coachmen and footmen, well-dressed and wearing cockades. The well-fed, caparisoned trotters flew over the snow at fourteen miles an hour, and in the carriages were ladies wrapped in circular cloaks and careful of their flowers and coiffures. Everything – from the horses' harness, the carriages, the rubber-tyres, and the cloth of the coachmen's warm coats, to the stockings, shoes, flowers, velvet, gloves, and perfumes – had been made by those people of whom some are sprawling in their bunks in the dormitories, and some are with prostitutes in the doss-house or fill the cells in the lock-up. Past them – on what was all theirs and in what was all theirs – drive those going to the ball; and it never enters their heads that there is any connection between the ball to which they are going and those drunkards at whom their coachmen shout so sternly . . .

'These people amuse themselves at the ball with quiet consciences: amuse themselves from eleven till six in the morning, through the very middle of night, while others are tossing with empty stomachs in doss-houses and some are dying like the washerwoman.

'The amusement consists in married women and girls baring their breasts, padding themselves out behind, and showing themselves in this unseemly condition, in which an unperverted girl or woman would not for the world wish to exhibit herself to a man; and in that semi-nude condition . . . with dresses drawn tight to their hips, in the strongest illumination, women and girls, whose chief virtue has always been modesty, appear among strange men similarly clad in improperly close-fitting garments, whom at the sound of intoxicating music they embrace, and with whom they whirl around. The old women, often exposing their persons as much as the young ones, sit looking on, and eat and drink good things; the old men do the same. No wonder this is done at night when the common people, being all asleep, do not see it. But this is not done to hide it; it seems to the doers that there is nothing it is necessary to hide, that it is very good, and that by this amusement in which they consume the painful labour of thousands, they not only injure no one but actually feed the poor.

'It may be very amusing at balls. But how does this happen? When among ourselves we see that someone has not eaten or is cold, we are ashamed to be merry, and cannot be merry till he has been fed and warmed; and we do not understand people making merry with sports that cause others to suffer. We dislike and do not understand the mirth of cruel boys who squeeze a dog's tail in a cleft stick and make merry over it.

'Then how is it that here, in these amusements of ours, blindness has befallen us and we do not see the cleft stick in which we squeeze the tails of those who suffer from our amusement?

'Not one of the women who drove to this ball in a one-hundred-and-fifty-ruble dress was born at the ball, or at Madame Minanguoit's [the fashionable Moscow dressmaker], and each of them has lived in the country and seen peasants, or knows her own nurse and lady's-maid who have poor fathers or brothers for whom to save a hundred and fifty rubles to build a hut is the aim of a long and laborious life. She knows this – how then can she be merry, knowing that at this ball she wears on her half-naked body the hut that is the dream of her good maid's brother? But granting that this may not have struck her – it would seem that she cannot but know that velvet, silk, sweets, flowers, laces, and dresses do not grow of themselves, but are made by people, or what kind of people make these things, and under what conditions they make them, and why. She must know that the seamstress whom she scolded did not make that dress for her out of love of her; and so she cannot help knowing that it was made for her under compulsion, and that, like her dress, her lace and flowers and velvet were made for the same reason. Perhaps, however, they are so befogged that they do not see even that. But the fact that five or six people, old, decent, often infirm, footmen and maids, have missed their sleep and been put to trouble on her account, she cannot help knowing. She has seen their weary, gloomy faces. She cannot but know also that the frost that night reached 31 degrees below zero, and that in that frost the old coachman sat on the box all night. But I know that they really do not see this. And if the young married women and girls, owing to the hypnotism produced on them by the ball, do not see it, they must not be condemned. They, poor things, are doing what their elders consider right; but can one explain the cruelty shown by those elders?

'The elders always give one and the same explanation: "I do not force anyone; I buy the things and hire people – the maids and the coachmen. There is nothing wrong in buying and hiring . . ."

' "What is there bad in it? People will go on buying and hiring whether I do or not, and will compel others to make velvet and sweets, and cigarettes, they will go on hiring people to wash shirts, even if I don't. So why should I deprive myself of velvet and sweets and cigarettes and clean shirts, if things are so arranged?" I often, almost always, hear this argument . . .

'If I visit savages and they treat me to tasty cutlets, and next day I learn (or perhaps see) that these tasty cutlets are made of a prisoner whom they have killed to make them; then if I do not think it right to eat people, however tasty the cutlets may be, and however general among those I am living with the practice of eating men may be, and however little the prisoners who are kept to serve as food may gain by my refusal to eat the cutlets, still I shall not and cannot eat them again. Perhaps I might even eat human flesh if compelled by hunger, but I should not entertain others at, or take part in, feasts where human flesh was eaten, and certainly should not seek such feasts or feel proud of taking part in them.'

*   *   *

'Only when I began to look on myself as a man like all others, did my path become plain to me . . . Following that path, one must try first of all to feed oneself honestly: that is to say, learn not to sit on the necks of others, but to take every opportunity to serve others with hands, feet, brain, heart, and all the powers one possesses and on which others make demands . . . No one possesses any rights or privileges or can possess them, but only endless and unlimited duties and obligations; and man's first and most unquestionable duty is to participate in the struggle with nature to support his own life and that of others . . . All other activities become legitimate only when this prime demand is satisfied . . .

'In reply to the question: What must I do? I saw that the most indubitable answer was, first, to do all the things I myself need – attend to my own room, heat my own stove, fetch my water, attend to my clothes, and do all I can for myself. I thought this would seem strange to the servants, but it turned out that the strangeness only lasted a week, and afterwards it would have seemed strange had I resumed my former habits . . .

'When I came to understand all this it seemed to me ludicrous. By a long series of doubts, searchings, and reflections, I have discovered the extraordinary truth that man has eyes in order to see with them, ears in order to hear with them, legs in order to walk with them, and hands and a back to work with, and that if he does not use them for their natural purpose it will be the worse for him . . .

'The solution of the terrible contradictions amid which we live is now before us.

'The apparently insoluble question is the old one of the exploitation by some of the labour of others; and in our time that question is expressed by property.

'Formerly men took the labour of others simply by violence – slavery; in our day we do it by means of property.

'Property today is the root of all evils: of the sufferings of those who possess it or are deprived of it, the reproaches of conscience of those who misuse it, and the danger of collision between those who have a superfluity and those who are in need . . .

'Property is the root of all evil; the division and safeguarding of property occupies the whole world . . .'

* * *

In the last chapter of the book Tolstoy states the view he held (in 1886) on woman's duty, and the fact that he changed his mind a year or two later does not deprive his statement of interest, for here – as all through the book – one is aware of the throb of his heart and feels that he is speaking of things that touched his own life. That last chapter, however, hardly forms an integral portion of the book, and I must summarise it very briefly.

Tolstoy says that women have hitherto been doing their duty better than men, and proceeds to make this an argument for obedience to the primal law of 'bread-labour' . . .

'The general infringement of the law by all men would destroy men at once, its infringement by all women would destroy the next generation; but the evasion of the law by some men and some women does not destroy the human race but deprives the offenders of their rational nature as human beings.'

He adds that the evasion of his duty by man began long ago, whereas evasion of her duty by woman used to be almost unknown except when it expressed itself in prostitution or abortion. Among the wealthy classes women continued to do their duty when men had ceased to perform theirs, and woman's influence naturally and rightly grew stronger. 'It is often said that women (Parisian women, especially those who are childless) have become so bewitching, utilising all the arts of civilisation, that they have mastered man by their fascinations. This is just the reverse of the case. It is not the childless woman who has mastered man, but the mother – the one who has fulfilled the law of her nature while man has neglected his.

'The woman who artificially makes herself barren and bewitches man by her shoulders and curls, is not a woman mastering man but a woman who, depraved by man, has descended to his level, like him has abandoned her duty, and like him has lost every reasonable perception of life' . . .

Woman's real work is to bear children; not to imitate those men of the privileged classes who shirk real work and substitute sham work 'in banks, ministries, universities, academies and studios'.

'Within my memory,' says Tolstoy, 'woman's fall – her dereliction of her duty – has begun, and within my memory it has spread more and more widely.

'Woman having forgotten her law, has believed that her strength lies in the charm of her allurements or in her dexterity in imitating the sham work done by man.

'Children are a hindrance to both of these. And so, with the help of science (science is always ready to do anything nasty), within my memory it has come about that among the wealthy classes dozens of methods of preventing pregnancy have appeared, and appliances for preventing childbirth have become common accessories of the toilet.

'Every woman, however she may dress herself and however she may call herself and however refined she may be, who refrains from childbirth without refraining from sexual relations, is a whore. And however fallen a woman may be, if she intentionally devotes herself to bearing children, she performs the best and highest service in life – fulfils the will of God – and no one ranks above her.

'If you are such a woman, you will not, either after two or after twenty children, say that you have borne enough, any more than a workman of fifty will say that he has worked enough while he still eats and sleeps and has muscles demanding work. If you are such a woman you will not shift the nursing and tending of your children on to another mother . . . The woman who performs her duty in spite of weariness, with effort, and risk to health and life, will apply those same demands to others and will demand that they too shall do real work, producing food and the necessaries of life. She will incite her husband to such labour, and by such labour will value and estimate a man's worth, and for such work will prepare her children . . . A real mother, who knows the will of God by experience, will suffer if she sees her child overfed, effeminate, and dressed-up, for she knows that these things will make it difficult for it to fulfil the will of God which she recognises.'

* * *

The book closes with a panegyric of the fruitful mother who knows that real life is a matter of danger and effort and self-sacrifice, and who will guide humanity in the path of duty, service, and unselfishness.

I leave comment on the views there expressed on the duty of motherhood till a later chapter. But to counteract a current misconception I would beg the reader to notice certain dates. *What Then Must We Do?*, which closes with this panegyric of the fruitful mother, was completed in 1886. The youngest of Tolstoy's children, Iván, was born two years later, in 1888; and it was not till the latter part of 1889 that Tolstoy wrote *The Kreutzer Sonata*, and not till 1890 that he added an *Afterword* in which he adopted some (but not all) of the views the abnormal hero of *The Kreutzer Sonata* had expressed. In that *Afterword* Tolstoy says that while writing *The Kreutzer Sonata* he reached the conclusion that chastity is an absolute ideal towards which everyone, married or unmarried, should strive. He explains that: 'Chastity is not a rule or perception, but an ideal, or rather one condition of the ideal. But an ideal is an ideal only when its accomplishment is possible only in *idea*, in thought, when it appears only attainable in infinity and when the possibility of approaching it is therefore infinite. If the ideal were attainable, or if we could even picture its attainment by mankind, it would cease to be an ideal.' In another place he says: 'It may be possible to reject Christ's teaching . . . but once that teaching is accepted, we cannot but admit that it points to the ideal of complete chastity . . . To most people these thoughts will seem strange and even contradictory . . . That feeling forced itself upon me most strongly when I approached the conclusions I now express. I never anticipated that the development of my thoughts would bring me to such a conclusion. I was startled at my conclusions and did not wish to believe them, but it was impossible not to do so. And however they may run counter to the whole arrangement of our lives, however they may contradict what I thought and said previously, I had to admit them.'

These quotations and dates are plainly on record. The mere fact that Tolstoy, who had had a family of thirteen children, came to the conclusion that chastity was an ideal (even though an unattainable one) is regarded by some as showing him to have been inconsistent and insincere. That view has been often expressed by irresponsible writers in articles begotten by malice out of mendacity, and strange to say this very year (1929), in so reputable a paper as *Time and Tide*, a woman writer of distinction published an article in which she said of Tolstoy that: 'He gave Sófya Andréyevna thirteen children, while perpetually explaining in public and in private that he regarded sex as loathsome and that his one desire was to get away from his family.' It would not be easy to devise a statement more glaringly contrary to the facts – for to represent *The Kreutzer Sonata* and the views expressed in the *Afterword* as preceding, instead of succeeding, the birth of every one of Tolstoy's children is no trivial error, though but one of a number of mis-statements made by Miss Rebecca West in the article in question. She balances her ignorance of the well-known facts of his life by a remarkable readiness to disclose to us the secret workings of his soul, and proceeds to tell us that he was actuated by 'cruelty', a quality those who knew him, or have read his works sympathetically or intelligently, would be reluctant to attribute to him.

That so strenuous and impulsive a man as Tolstoy did say and do harsh and inconsiderate things at times must be admitted, but much oftener he showed sympathy and compassion, and while Miss West's suggestions may indicate the working of her own mind, they are quite misleading as to Tolstoy's.

*   *   *

What Then Must We Do? is a work of first-rate importance because of its frank and fresh treatment of the most pressing practical problem of our times – that of poverty – about which Churches, Chapels, and Political Parties have proved strangely impotent.

It contains what is, I think, the most definite and impressive prediction in modern literature, and one that anybody inclined to consider Tolstoy a theorist out of touch with actual life would do well to notice. Writing thirty-one years before the Revolution, he confidently predicted the coming 'workers' revolution with horrors of destruction and murder', and warned his generation that 'the terrible catastrophe draws nearer', and 'one thing only is left for those who do not wish to change their way of life, and that is to hope that things will last my time – after that let happen what may'. His attitude was that of Noah to the deluge. He did not desire it, but foresaw it, and tried to prepare for it.

Tolstoy's indictment: that masked slavery exists among us, and that we tolerate the existence of a caste of the ever-feasting, and hold in bondage a caste of the underfed but ever-working – is true, and his feeling that this is unendurable grows stronger and reaches more people every year. Probably no modern book has done more than *What Then Must We Do?* to make it prevail. It inspires the feeling not merely that these things must be ended but that the greatest and most inspiring work a man can do is to help to end them.

But how? Tolstoy saw the facts of poverty acutely, especially as they existed in the world he lived in, he described them vividly, and conveyed his feeling of moral condemnation strongly, but did he find a true key to the enigma? I think not. His prescription is that all should live barely, should work hard at 'bread-labour', and there should be no Government using physical force to hinder each man from doing what he thinks right. His ideal life is that of the best Russian country peasants when least interfered with by Government. In his condemnation of wealth, and of money as the symbol of wealth, his teaching reminds us of the New Testament, St Francis of Assisi, and the views held by many of the ancient, medieval, and oriental saints and sages, but he takes no account of the modern thought of the Western world, and after spending years in testing the matter practically and theoretically, I do not find myself in accord with him in so far as he ignores, or totally condemns, what the Western world has done during the last century and a half towards dealing with the matter.

To an extent never before accomplished we have mastered the brute forces of Nature and brought them into subjection to man, making them lift his heavy loads and render his work more productive. No doubt man's motives in the fight with Nature are mixed and often selfish. No doubt the distribution of the gain is very unequal. No doubt while organising labour and making it a hundredfold more fruitful, we have introduced in our factory-system evils which did not previously exist and which justify a scathing indictment. But when all is said, I refuse to condemn utterly the work that has been accomplished, for to thrust aside the whole Industrial Revolution as evil is unreasonable, and also ungrateful to those who, from Stephenson to Kelvin and from Robert Owen to Montagu Norman, have brought courage, perseverance, endurance, steadfastness, ingenuity, genius, and often an earnest desire to serve their race, to the task, of rendering the conditions of life on this planet less hard. The Industrial Revolution produced results that are neither all good nor all bad. It made it possible for man to produce with comparative ease and rapidity more than is needed to ensure a decent subsistence for all, though we have not yet ensured that all shall have a chance to enjoy this sufficiency, nor saved every child from the risk of going hungry to school, nor secured care for every sick man and leisure and sustenance for every mother while she bears and suckles the future workers of our race, nor safeguarded, as yet, every feeble member of the body politic from being crushed by demands beyond his strength. But we have accomplished a large part of a great and difficult task. We have harnessed the waterfalls, cut canals, and built railways. Steam is our servant and electricity our handmaid. Vessels cross the ocean with greater facility than the coaches of our forefathers crossed the continents, and the task before us of arranging the possession of the resources of the world and regulating the distribution of its wealth so that poverty may no longer exist, is more nearly within our reach than it was within the reach of our ancestors to prevent the Plague, the Black Death, or devastation by the Danes.

It is true that that splendid achievement can only be accomplished if men desire it, and we owe a debt of gratitude to Tolstoy for the spiritual impulse he gave towards the abolition of poverty, and for the breath of heroic resolve which breathes through his book and is so valuable in this great emprise. But even at his call we cannot consent to abandon the material achievements which have made the remainder of our task not merely possible but comparatively easy.

He was indeed strangely ignorant of industrial and commercial matters and his ignorance found an ally in an ethical arrogance – a readiness ruthlessly to condemn the achievements of those whose work was remote from his own experience, and to impute base motives to men and movements he knew little of. His tendency to oversimplification was, again, a grave defect. To understand the complex phenomena of the transition period in which we live requires much patience, tolerance, and balance, as well as a sense of the evolutionary growth of things – all of which were foreign to his drastic and cataclysmic way of dealing with life's problems.

He would not admit that the utilisation of the power of Government for the systematic organisation of society may be part of our effort after righteousness. To his mind the two things were antagonistic. I disagree, but that does not blind me to the fact that he says much that is true. No Governmental interference or organisation of society will avail unless we can secure that devotion to duty, that thirst after righteousness, and that sense of dependence on something greater than ourselves, which he did so much to arouse. Unless we can draw into the service of the State men of a higher and finer type than many of the present prison and workhouse officials, no rearrangement of external forms will avail. Improvements of organisation may, however, help the growth of a sense that service – even paid official service – to the least of our brethren, is service to the Highest. The change of heart and mind at which Tolstoy aimed must go on among public servants *pari passu* with improvements in the organisations they have to administer.

While dissenting from certain conclusions, I do not overlook the value of Tolstoy's work. It is most true, for instance, that a man's account with humanity should be credited with all he produces and all the service he renders, and debited with all he consumes and all the service he demands. It is true, too, as he says, that 'to make a pipe of oneself' for money to flow through, as is done by the unproductive rich, is a poor way of spending one's life, even if the fertilising stream be conveyed to where it is needed; while if it be not so conveyed, the 'pipes' are merely a nuisance. Tolstoy again does excellently by claiming for the manual labourer the honour due to him and a fair share of the benefits of art and science. What, finally, can be sounder than his contention that the greatest joy of life comes from spending oneself in a noble cause? Even in games (as every chess – or tennis-player knows) the keenest satisfaction comes from strenuous exertion, and this is even more so with regard to work. He who shirks the stress and strain of life's battle misses the best that it can give.

But Tolstoy erred where many noble minds erred before him. He saw a great evil, was indignant and impatient, and jumped at a remedy insufficiently tried: a remedy that does not succeed, but fails, when put to the test. Again and again attempts have been made to cure social ills by persuading people to stand aside from the main streams of human life, and to save their souls by following an isolated course; but all paths of social improvement except the common highway trodden by the common man have proved to be blind alleys. It was so with the Early

Christian Commune of which, after a couple of notices in the Acts, we hear no more. It was so with the great Franciscan movement, which within a century and a half of the death of its noble founder had produced such a multitude of idle and inefficient wanderers living on the toil of those who were doing settled work, that Wyclif was driven to declare that 'the man who gives alms to a begging friar, is *ipso facto* excommunicate'. It was so in the Tolstoy movement also, for not one single Colony or Group formed under the influence of his writings, either in Russia, or elsewhere in Europe or America, was able to hold to his principles and show a satisfactory record. Nor is this strange, for we are in truth 'members one of another', and it is not by separating ourselves from the common mass that we can make life better. In practice it turns out that the man who refuses to specialise – refuses, that is to say, to do chiefly the things he can do best – lives what is really an unnatural life. What in addition to good intentions humanity needs for the due ordering of its common life, are, above all, intelligence, efficiency, reliability, and power of organisation and co-operation. If men possessed of these qualities stood aside from politics, trade, and industry, to make and do all the things they themselves require, the results would be deplorable. The task of the efficient organiser – and he is one of the most valuable of men – is to get good work well done with as little waste, confusion, toil, or contention, as possible. To effect this the co-operation of many people, living in different countries, speaking different languages, and having different customs, is often needed, and to make such cooperation possible, *definiteness* of legal enactments and the impartial arbitration of law are essential. Yet these are things Tolstoy strenuously condemned. If for thousands of years humanity has gone so utterly wrong that we must abandon all our beaten tracks and adopt ways of life which never succeed, and whenever tried immediately create friction and bitterness, the case is lamentable indeed.

Tolstoy grudged the specialist his training, for fear lest – after much had been spent on him – he might never do work really useful to mankind. But that is the sort of risk we have to run. To get men to sit still and think before acting is more important than to spur them to hasty action, and it is not by assuring the thinker that he is a useless parasite that one encourages him to render the service which he is best capable.

Tolstoy however was no slave to his own utterances, and one can find passages in his works which practically admit a large part of what is here contended for.

Much confusion was caused by his denunciation of money: for he omitted to explain how far he considered the actual coins which serve as a medium of exchange more objectionable than the wealth they represent. I remember how much amusement was caused by the conduct of his friend V. G. Chertkóv, who was reported to have ceased to use money but allowed his wife to sign his cheques, and his secretary to accompany him to the station to buy his railway tickets. Naturally the Philistines rejoiced at the story of his vicarious use of money and declared him a humbug, whereas he was probably quite sincere, and merely mistaken. I heard him deliver an impassioned oration on the wickedness of using money. It was nearly thirty years ago, but I still remember two passages in his ardent address. He told us that any man who accepted money for what he wrote was no better than a prostitute, and on the basis of statistics showing a higher death-rate among families living in one room than among those living in more than one, he deduced the conclusion that if you spend £5 on a holiday you are responsible for the death of so-and-so many people, since that money might have enabled them to move from one room to two.

Tolstoy himself was never guilty of such extravagance, but I think he showed a lack of lucidity when he wished to rid himself of property while still continuing to eat, for a man makes a thing his own most effectively when he eats it; and I do not see that the evil is lessened by insisting that others should have the trouble, and bear the guilt, of owning the land, and the foodstuffs, fuel, stove, and utensils, required before the food is ready for him to eat. Property must be possessed by someone or by some corporate body, unless endless confusion is to ensue, and guilt attaches not to the possession but to the misuse of it. Tolstoy said: 'Consume as little as possible,' but it might be wiser to say: 'Consume only what adds to your efficiency.' For there are cases in which a considerable consumption enables a man to hand over to humanity benefits exceeding the value of what he consumes – whether on his training, instruments, books, or laboratory. I need not stress the argument, however, for it is one on which the Western world has made up its mind, and it is more to the point to remember the unpopular truths Tolstoy uttered than to dwell on what is questionable in his economics. All interested in the right ordering of society, who care to use his works as a quarry, will find in them veins of richest ore, which need only be separated from the common earth of irrelevant error for their value to be manifest.

8

A Strenuous Year

Early in 1886 Gay stayed with Tolstoy in Moscow. Besides illustrating some of Tolstoy's short stories, Gay, inspired by *The Gospel in Brief*, produced a series of sketches illustrating the life and teachings of Jesus. This co-operation of pen and pencil gave both men great satisfaction. Feinermann tells us:

> Leo Nikoláevich loved the late artist Gay with an unusually warm, tender, and brotherly affection.
>
> 'Will you believe me,' Leo Nikoláevich said, 'when he sits by me and lays his head on my shoulder and tremblingly strokes my hand, such a gentle feeling of nearness comes to me from him and I am so pained and vexed with myself for not being at all worthy of his love, that I long to be better, greater, higher . . . How well he discerns the invisible windings of the soul and how inimitably in any work he feels the things that escape other people and remain dim and obscure even to the author. I have myself experienced it and notice it in his illustrations to my stories . . .'

And Gay speaking of Tolstoy, said:

> 'He – of course you know whom I mean, because there is only one *he* for me: our dear, priceless, and holy Leo Nikoláevich! – has kindled new life in me and opened before me a vision of Truth's field. And I wish to repay him. I wish to interpret his teaching. He with his pen, I with my brush. I am only anxious not to repeat but to complete him – to represent what cannot be expressed in words. It is difficult to follow such a master of language, but to my great joy the work progresses.'

Gay was loved by the whole Tolstoy family. He helped and taught the eldest daughter, Tatiána, who was studying painting at the Moscow School of Art, and we find the Countess as well as her daughters writing to him affectionately.

At this time Anton Rubinstein, whom Tolstoy greatly admired and placed above all the pianists he had heard, was giving one of his last concerts in Moscow, and Tolstoy was torn by conflicting emotions. On the one hand he knew he would intensely enjoy hearing Rubinstein play, but on the other hand, according to his theory of art, Rubinstein was not a representative of good and universally comprehensible art, and therefore Tolstoy did not want to take a ticket for his concert. Nevertheless when N. Káshkin visited Tolstoy on the eve of the performance, the latter expressed keen regret that he was again going to miss hearing Rubinstein, for tickets were by that time quite unobtainable.

Káshkin replied that for such an auditor as Tolstoy a place could always be found, and offered to procure him a ticket.

Tolstoy was delighted and thanked him warmly; and Rubinstein, when he heard of the case, gave instructions to have a place arranged for Tolstoy, and himself sent him a ticket. The latter, however, did not turn up. He had been very pleased to receive the ticket and had actually put on his overcoat to go to the concert, when suddenly doubts assailed him as to whether he ought to do so. These doubts brought on a nervous attack so severe that a doctor had to be called in.

Subsequently, Rubinstein offered to pay Tolstoy a visit and play for him, but owing to the death of little Alexéy this project was abandoned.

In the early spring of 1886 Tolstoy moved to Yásnaya, but on this, as on several subsequent occasions, his disapproval of railways, his desire not to use money, his love of outdoor exercise, and his wish to be in touch with the life of the people, made him prefer to walk the 130 miles from Moscow to Yásnaya. Anna Seuron, who saw him start on the journey, tells us:

The Count set out for Yásnaya on foot. He prepared for the journey in the following way: over his shoulder he took a linen sack for his food, and in it he also took a pair of broad shoes, a soft shirt, two pairs of socks, some handkerchiefs, and a small vial of stomach-drops, as he often suffers from indigestion. He also took a notebook with a pencil tied to it, in order to jot down anything of interest during the journey. He started, accompanied by three young men, of whom two belonged to very good families and the third was a son of the artist Gay. The two young aristocrats broke down on the road, and only the Count and Gay, after sleeping in hovels, reached their destination on the third day. No one recognised the Count and this afforded him great pleasure.

Feinermann, who saw him arrive at Yásnaya, says:

In the first week after Easter two pilgrims in bast-shoes carrying sacks on their backs, entered the gates of the Yásnaya Polyána park. Both were lively and merry, with faces tanned by sun and wind, and they breathed satisfaction and a glad consciousness of something well done.

One of these pilgrims was Tolstoy, and the other was young Gay.

'I never enjoyed anything so much,' said Tolstoy . . . 'To be among the people, sleeping, eating, and talking with them . . . Ah, what a story I heard about "Nicholas Stick" [Nicholas I] from a dear, lisping old man of over ninety, who lay on the stove with me in a village near Sérpukhov! With what artistic warmth he described the horrors of those terrible times of which I witnessed the very end!

' "In those days, when they took down a man's breeches they never gave him as few as fifty strokes," said he; "and not a week passed without one or two men in the regiment being flogged to death. One was always hearing: 'The stick! the stick!' . . . two hundred, three hundred strokes at a time, and more!" '

Three days later Tolstoy's sketch, *Nicholas Stick*, was ready, but neither the subject nor the title was such as the Censor could be expected to pass.

Another writer has told the story of a hectographed edition of *Nicholas Stick*. The notorious *agent-provocateur* Zubátov, who was then posing as a Revolutionary, got on the track of M. N., who had issued it:

Soon M. N. was arrested. His mother was terribly distressed, and with tears in her eyes begged me to go to Tolstoy and ask him, if questioned, to say that the pamphlet had been published with his consent. I knew this was not so: M. N. had written to ask Tolstoy's permission, but not receiving a reply had issued the booklet without waiting for it. It was a difficult commission to execute, but I went to Tolstoy and told him of M. N.'s mother's request. With great gentleness and tact he hastened to remove my uneasiness. 'Of course it was with my consent,' said he; 'I am always pleased when my works obtain circulation. Tell his mother that I shall say so if I am asked!'

A few days later Tolstoy was requested to call on Prince Dolgorúki, Governor-General of Moscow. He replied that he had nothing to do with that gentleman, who if he wanted to see him had better come to him. Dolgonúki did not do so, but sent his Adjutant, a young man, to reprove and warn the author. This emissary was amiably received like any other visitor, but during the whole interview Tolstoy talked to him about the immorality of his position in the service of such a Government!

The difficult problem of how to shape his own life and how to influence the lives around him, still continued to occupy Tolstoy's thoughts, but the harsh strenuousness noticeable in the first years of his propaganda gradually mellowed. A glimpse of this change shows itself in a letter of 21st May, addressed to Gay:

> I am glad that all is well with you and that you are at *your own work*. It is good to mow and plough, but there is nothing better than to be of use to people while at one's own trade ...
>
> We have moved to the country. I am up to my neck in work and am glad of it. I allow myself to hope it is not useless. Regarding your life – mine and yours (I think of yours, with all your family and the different trends in it) – one's head whirls when one begins to think what will happen and how to arrange everything. But one need only approach the matter with the thought, 'What can I best do for A, for B, and for C, with whom I am in contact?' and all the difficulties are swept away like cobwebs, and everything fits together better than one could have imagined.

Connoisseurs of literary art were at this time bewailing Tolstoy's absorption in non-artistic matters. But the world in general had become interested in him just because he cared for the great problems of religion and duty in relation to property, and dared to be frank and strove to be intelligible. One sign of his increasing renown was the frequency with which foreigners began to apply for permission to visit Yásnaya Polyána, and sought to secure his advocacy for this or that scheme they were interested in. It was, for instance, at this time that George Kennan, on his return from Siberia, visited him.

One day out mowing, when Tolstoy and his fellow-workers had abandoned their scythes and settled down to lunch, his two sons, Andréy and Michael, aged nine and seven, came running to tell him that a foreigner had arrived at the house. This visitor turned out to be the French soldier, poet and patriot, Déroulède, who had come to Russia to promote an alliance hostile to Germany, to secure revenge for 1871 and the restoration of Alsace-Lorraine to France. Needless to say he got scant encouragement from the author of *The Gospel in Brief*. Anna Seuron says:

> No one knew who he was, the tall man of military appearance in a long grey coat buttoned all the way down, whom a relation of the Count's brought to Yásnaya one day.
>
> Déroulède! The name sounded quite strange, for newspapers were very seldom read here. There had even been a time when they were completely banished! Newspaper reading takes time, it stupefies and perverts people. Of course the news of any great event found its way here, but generally speaking nobody knew, or cared to know, the details of what was going on in the world.

Déroulède was voluble, affable, and quick to adjust himself to the situation:

> War and revenge, and arguments *pro* and *contra*, were Chinese literature to the Count; a single twitch of his lips and a single flash from his steely eyes were enough to make Déroulède understand that he must give some other explanation of his visit than his desire to ally Russia with France for a war of revenge, so he fell back on his ardent desire 'to make the acquaintance of Russia's literary luminary'.
>
> Only on these terms was it possible for him to remain three days at Yásnaya. No doubt he hoped one way or other to return to his theme of *revanche*, but every time he attempted it the Count's face turned to stone.
>
> Only once did the Count condescend to expatiate on the horrors of war. He himself under a night sky had seen on a battlefield thousands of motionless corpses with glazed eyes, which looked as though they were demanding an account from those who had sent them to premature death. And when Déroulède announced that 'the Rhine must belong to the French', the Count merely smiled and said: 'Not with blood should the frontiers of a country be drawn, but by reasonable agreement allowing just advantage to both sides.' Déroulède remarked that war is implanted in the very nature of man. The Count replied that 'War should, and could, be avoided; the chief thing is that men should not be willing to evoke and to provoke it'; and thereupon he rose and left the room with rapid steps.

Tolstoy himself narrates that on one occasion in a fit of exasperation he ran out of the room, slamming the door violently behind him – which did not prevent Déroulède, when next they met, from renewing his propaganda of *revanche* as if nothing had happened. At last Tolstoy proposed to his visitor that they should lay before an ordinary, typical peasant the plan that the French and the Russians, being on each side of the Germans, should unite to squeeze the juice out of them. On the matter being explained to him, the peasant, after scratching his head, replied that he thought the Frenchmen and the Russians had better first do some useful work and then go off together to the inn for a drink and take the Germans with them!

That evening Déroulède departed, hopeless of converting Tolstoy to the belief that the best use he could make of his powers would be to persuade people to kill one another, for the Russian writer stoutly maintained that the real danger of war lay in the pestilent patriotic superstitions of men such as Déroulède who, having no useful work to do and no belief in God, invented for themselves spurious excitements and false enthusiasms.

Among the frequent visitors at Yásnaya was young M. A. Stakhóvich, who subsequently played a part in the constitutional liberation movement in Russia. Feinermann tells us that:

The whole family loved young Michael Alexándrovich Stakhóvich, and his visits always gave occasion for noisy undertakings – hunts, drives, and games.

Of good figure, with a budding beard and a cordial kindly smile, he was the heart and soul of all such affairs, and the special friend of Leo Lvóvich [the third son], who was also a great expert at sports and merry-making.

Leo Nikoláevich could not see their lively, healthy faces without emotion, but became affected by their merry mood and would start racing with them along the long birch avenue, and was very pleased indeed when he managed to forge ahead, overtaking any of the runners.

'Grasshoppers!' he would say triumphantly, 'where would you have been, twenty years ago? Then I would have shown you how to run! It's not done by spurting but by lasting; but you – guttapercha images – try to gallop! We'll see what prizes you'll take in life's race – also by galloping and spurting, I suppose!'

And the talk would suddenly take a serious and didactic turn, touching on the great themes of life, the duty of work, and of association with the people.

Young Stakhóvich would become all attention, and thoughtfully with knit brows, still breathing deeply from his exertions, would eagerly drink in the master's words.

He had a really filial affection for Tolstoy.

'I should be glad to, Count! My dearest dream is to live with the people!' said he sincerely.

And with pious reverence he used to come out into the fields, take hold of the smooth handles of the *sokha* [peasant-plough] with inexpert hands, and anxiously try to cut a straight furrow.

Eventually he learnt to plough, and mow, and load the hay on the carts.

A passionate desire to live with the people and like the people seized almost all the members of Tolstoy's family at that time. Even the Countess Sófya Andréevna, who had long resisted rough manual labour and every attempt at simplification, came to the haymaking wearing a homespun peasant-skirt, and raked the fresh and fragrant hay.

And when the more ardent members of the family began to arrange to carry out their wish and live among the peasants in the village, young Stakhóvich threw himself into the plan with his whole soul.

'We have already chosen the huts and everything!' said he joyfully, burning with enthusiasm and imagining how good and how great it would be to know that one was on an equality with milliards of others – doing the one great and important work which supports life and feeds mankind.

'We shall go to bed early, rise early, meet the sun without blushing, and look men straight in the eyes without feeling ashamed, for we too shall be workers. How inexpressible a blessing that will be!'

But the Countess heard of the plan, and at tea, when all had come together after work, there was a stormy scene. She began sharply to condemn the scheme: 'It shall not be!' she firmly announced, addressing her children. 'You were born Counts, and Counts you shall remain!'

That scene depressed us all and we afterwards talked all the evening on the theme that 'a man's enemies are those of his own household . . .'

I remember that Tolstoy that evening said that opposition from relatives gave an indication of the measure of a man's readiness to serve the truth.

'It means that there is in us something that renders it possible for others to suspect us of being insincere and playing at simplification. Only because they see this something do they raise their voices against the undertaking which threatens to undermine their accustomed ways of life. If but for a moment they saw that we really could not endure this life of landlordising, that it stifles us, sickens us, and that we should die if we did not change our life – believe me they would not find a word to say against us.'

It was about this time that Danílevski visited Tolstoy, who took him for a 'little walk' which lasted three and a half hours.

To him Tolstoy spoke of Turgénev and gave what may be considered his final verdict on that writer in the words:

He was to the end of his life an independent, inquiring spirit . . . He was a genuine, self-reliant artist, never lowering himself consciously to serve the passing demand of the moment. He may have gone astray, but even in his errors he was sincere.

Of manual labour, Tolstoy said:

What a delight it is to rest from intellectual occupations by means of simple physical labour! Every day according to the season I either dig the ground, or saw and chop wood, or work with scythe, sickle, or some other instrument. As to ploughing, you cannot conceive what a satisfaction it is to plough . . . It is not very hard work as many people suppose; it is pure enjoyment! You go along, lifting up and properly directing the plough, and you don't notice how one, two, or three hours go by. The blood runs merrily through your veins, your head becomes clear, you don't feel the weight of your feet – and the appetite afterwards, and the sleep! . . .

For me, daily exercise and physical labour are as indispensable as the air. In summer in the country I have plenty of choice. I can plough, or cut grass, but in the autumn in rainy weather it is wretched . . . Sedentary intellectual work without physical exercise and labour is a real calamity. If for a single day I do not walk, or work with my legs and hands, I am good for nothing by evening. I can't read or write or even listen to anyone with attention, my head whirls, there seem to be stars in my eyes, and I have a sleepless night.

And here is Feinermann's sketch of Tolstoy at work:

The barn of Widow Anísya, whom Tolstoy used often to help, collapsed, and a new one had to be built.

'We'll do it,' said Leo Nikoláevich consolingly, and set to work to prepare timber for the walls and roof.

He himself felled aspens of different sizes in the forest, and when they were all carted, stripped and smoothed them with axe and plane. We dug holes and put in the uprights. Our chief instructor was neighbour Prokófey, a wise, practical peasant who knew every kind of peasant work.

As long as the work was on the ground – digging, preparing the rafters, and so on – Leo Nikoláevich was always first and worked from morn to night. With sleeves tucked up he sat astride a beam in a workmanlike manner, and was very pleased when Prokófey came round and ejaculated: 'Take pains! Take pains . . . You'll do.'

'I am taking pains!' Leo Nikoláevich would reply with a smile.

In a week's time the walls were up and the rafters fixed, and the time came to peg the fourteen-foot cross-poles, between which hazel twigs would have to be twined, so that when the roof was thatched each sheaf could be firmly tied on with ropes of straw. The poles had therefore to be fixed pretty near together and secured firmly with large wooden pegs.

But to drive in those pegs it was necessary first to bore a hole through the pole and the rafter, and then to drive in the peg. It was this boring which Leo Nikoláevich found most difficult.

He managed somehow to bore a hole through the first pole, at the lower end of the roof, and, standing on a ladder and often steadying himself with one hand, he managed to drive in the peg, but when he came to the second pole, which could not be reached from the ladder, and he had to climb on to the rafter, Leo Nikoláevich could not at first make up his mind to do it.

'Don't be afraid! Look at me . . .' urged Prokófey.

Leo Nikoláevich climbed up and sat astride the rafter, but scarcely had he taken hold of the drill and bent back to adjust the point, when it dropped from his hands. He became giddy and swayed, and quickly crept down the ladder holding on to the rafter.

'No, I give it up! I shall never learn to do it!'

'Wait a bit before you run away . . .' Prokófey kept taunting him. 'Time enough to turn tail! Watch me do it . . .'

Leo Nikoláevich climbed up again and sat astride the rafter like Prokófey, but hardly had he stuck the point of the drill in before he again began to sway, dropped the drill and, sliding sideways, reached the ladder and again got down.

'No, I won't!' he said; 'do it yourselves!'

Then Prokófey stopped his work and also got down, and taking Leo Nikoláevich's hand, led him aside and said: 'I know why you sway about on the rafter . . . you look down.'

'That's true,' Leo Nikoláevich admitted.

'Well, that won't do! That's what makes your head giddy. You must look up at your work, fix your eyes on the drill and the hole you are boring and go on quietly twisting. Try it! You will see how easy it is!'

Leo Nikoláevich brightened up.

'That would be good, and perhaps you are right.'

Again he climbed up, again sat astride the rafter, took the drill, stuck in the point, and did not take his eyes from it. Turning the drill round and round he bored a hole and drove in the peg successfully.

His delight knew no bounds.

'I've got it! I've got it!' he shouted to Prokófey, and boldly mounting the next rafter, he began boring another hole.

That evening, when, after fixing on the poles, we were returning from work, Leo Nikoláevich said: 'You know, I have learnt more today than one sometimes learns in a year. Prokófey's remark was a small one, but how deep it goes! Only now do I understand fearless-ness in other situations of life also.

'I remember with what surprise and boundless envy I used, during an artillery fight, to gaze at the work of those simple-minded gunners who pointed and loaded the cannons with imperturbable calmness as if a hail of projectiles were not thundering about their heads and shells bursting around them and tearing horses and men to pieces. I did not understand the secret of their courage. I am not speaking of that deep, fundamental secret of entire submission to Him who called us into being; that is too distant and cannot be evoked every time you approach and point the gun. What I did not then understand was another secret, that of simply adapting oneself, which helps one to hold out for hours in such a hell. Now I see that the secret is Prokófey's "Don't look down! Look at your work!" The gunner sees before him only the charge, the sight, and the muzzle; and so he can do his work.'

At this marvellously prolific time Tolstoy wrote several of his best tales for the people: *How Much Land Does a Man Need?*, *Ilyás*, *The Three Hermits*, and the excellent temperance story, *The Imp and the Crust* (all included in *Twenty-Three Tales*), as well as one or two poorer stories drawn from medieval legends and Lives of the Saints, and tinged with that suspicion of all that makes for material success, and with that reliance on Divine interference in mundane affairs, which occasionally mingled with Tolstoy's usually rational outlook on life. I refer particularly to *The Godson* and *The Candle*. The most remarkable of the series of short stories which he wrote this year was, however, *Iván the Fool*, into which he compressed the essence of *What Then Must We Do?*

Of the writing of *Iván the Fool* we learn something from Feinermann, who was for a short time carrying on the village school at Yásnaya, and had evening Readings with the children which were attended by some of the peasants. Tolstoy also came to those Readings:

> He would sit on the edge of the last bench and listen. During the Reading or after it a lively conversation would generally arise among the audience, and Leo Nikoláevich would often take a warm part in it.
>
> He enjoyed this close intercourse with the people and always got something new and elevating out of such conversations.
>
> 'How good it is!' he said to me once at parting. 'How little we know where true happiness lies! An hour of such intercourse is worth more than any number of Society evenings and routs.'
>
> Once we had finished a short story, when Leo Nikoláevich drew a number of written sheets from his pocket and said: 'Now I'll read you something of my own. It is called *A Fairy Tale*;' and in a clear, distinct voice he read his famous story, *Iván the Fool*, and I noticed how it agitated him to read to this audience the story embodying his view of life.
>
> The story was well received.
>
> The elders praised it and the youngsters began to discuss the various incidents and to compare their impressions . . .
>
> Noticing one of the peasants who was particularly moved by the story, Leo Nikoláevich said to him: 'Well now, Konstantín

Nikoláevich, you might repeat the whole story to us! Be so kind as to try! . . . '

'Why not? I can repeat every word of it,' said the man, and began to tell it fluently. But to our surprise it was not a repetition. His tale was far from completely corresponding to the original. Many parts came out quite differently. Both words and phrases were altered, and in one place even the sequence of events were changed.

The crowd began to interrupt, and sharply correct him.

'That's wrong! It's this way! . . . '

But Leo Nikoláevich eagerly caught just these alterations, and stopped the interrupters: 'Don't stop him . . . Let him tell it his own way. It comes out very well!'

The peasant narrator was the poorest man in the village, but had a remarkable gift of words and was very fond of reading.

Leo Nikoláevich took rapid notes and beamed with enthusiasm whenever a vivid phrase, an apt example, or a happy turn of words occurred in the peasant's narration, and *Iván the Fool* was published in the form Konstantín gave it.

'I always do that,' said Leo Nikoláevich. 'I learn how to write from them, and I test my work on them. That is the only way to produce stories for the people. My story, *God Sees the Truth*, was also made that way. It was retold me by one of my pupils.'

Besides the help he got from peasants and schoolboys, Tolstoy also received literary assistance from peasant women. There was one old woman named Anísya, from the neighbouring village, who used to come to see Tolstoy and tell him tales; and he was delighted both with her stories and her way of telling them, and would say: 'You are a real master, Anísya! Thank you for teaching me to speak Russian – and to think Russian!'

Field work, visitors, correspondence, family matters, economic philippics, and stories for the people, did not suffice to exhaust Tolstoy's energies. His new faith seemed to quadruple his mental and moral strength without impairing his physical powers. One is conscious however, through the whole later part of his life, of the struggle continually going on between his artistic nature – craving for opportunities to express itself in accustomed forms by producing works for the intelligentsia, and that other side of his nature which disapproved of everything the peasants could not share equally. The result was, not that Tolstoy ceased to produce works of art, but that in his stories, novels, and plays of this period, his indictment of and dissatisfaction with the life of the middle and upper classes constantly made itself felt.

After *Anna Karénina* the first distinctly artistic work Tolstoy produced, apart from his tales for the people, was *The Death of Iván Ilych*, a wonderful description of the life and painful death of a Judge, who, at the very end of his fatal illness, realises the futility of his past life and the joy of self-surrender for the sake of others. It was finished on 22nd March 1886.

I have already pointed out that in Tolstoy's later artistic works he makes what someone has called 'psychological experiments'. *Iván Ilych* is an example of this. Iván is, as it were, summoned before a moral Court and accused of having lived 'a most ordinary life' which was at the same time 'most horrible'. The experiment of showing that his life was 'most ordinary' and 'most horrible' is carried through in masterly fashion.

Before the summer of 1886 was over, Tolstoy himself was very seriously ill with erysipelas resulting from a sore on his leg. In spite of the pain it gave him when ploughing, and in spite of the Countess's remonstrances, he long refused to pay attention to this sore. But at last realising the danger of further delay, the Countess pretended to have neuralgia and made this an excuse for going to Moscow, where she persuaded an acquaintance, Dr Chírkov, to accompany her at once to Yásnaya. Owing to his dislike of doctors and medicine, Tolstoy received Chírkov with great dissatisfaction. The latter mildly re-proached him for disregarding in practice the law of love of one's neighbour he professed, and after that things went better and the doctor was allowed to examine the ulcer which had formed on the patient's shin. Tolstoy's temperature had risen to 104 degrees Fahren-heit, the leg was much swollen and his life was in imminent danger. A drainage-tube had to be inserted immediately, and this proved to be a very painful operation.

Days of great suffering followed, till one by one the pieces of decayed bone had come away. When the pain was not too great Tolstoy was the gentlest of patients, but at times he shrieked so that those in attendance were ready to run away. At such periods he longed for a doctor and more than once a surgeon from Túla had to be sent for during the night. The patient had to lie up for nine weeks, and for a month was not allowed to engage in any literary occupation.

Anna Seuron remarks that:

The Countess was an excellent nurse, especially during the early and most critical days, she was always in good spirits and extremely quick, perhaps even too quick, for when a man is seriously ill he prefers quiet movements.

During this illness Tolstoy wrote a play. At first he dictated it to his wife, but when it became possible to move him on to a sofa, he demanded a writing-board, pen, and paper.

Anna Seuron says:

When their father wrote the whole family went on tiptoe. Throwing his head back on the leather cushion he often dropped his pencil and his face expressed a double kind of suffering. He was creating the drama, *The Power of Darkness*.

That terrible play was founded on a case that had come before the Túla Law Courts. It exhibits the worst side of peasant life: crime leading to crime in a crescendo of horrors until towards the end, in a very powerful scene, a drunken fellow, an ex-soldier, inspires Nikíta with courage; and in the last act, at a wedding and in the presence of a police-officer, Nikíta publicly confesses his misdeeds.

These scenes when well rendered entirely obliterate the impression of the painful details that have gone before. We forget that the story deals with adultery, poison, and infanticide – and only the impression of the repentance and confession remains.

The scene in the cellar when Nikíta crushes his child with a board so that its 'bones crunched' was one Tolstoy himself could never read without tears.

Of this work he remarked to Feinermann:

When I am writing a novel I paint and, so to say, work with a brush. There I feel freer. When it comes out awkwardly I can change it, add colour and amplify. But a drama is different . . . it is sculptor's work. It has no shadows and half-tones. All must be clear-cut and in strong relief. The incidents must be ready, finished, and the whole work lies in representing these fully-matured moments, these ripe moods of the characters. This is exceedingly difficult, especially when dealing with the life of peasants, which is a foreign land to us – another hemisphere!

The Power of Darkness possesses in a remarkable degree the qualities of a first-rate acting play. It has movement, life, and the clear-cut clash of wills from which the actions follow inevitably.

While on the subject of the play, let me anticipate and tell its fate.

Not till 1895, when Nicholas II was on the throne, was its public performance in Russia permitted. Alexander III expressed his admiration of it when it was given privately at Court by members of the aristocracy, but Pobedonóstsev disapproved of it and wrote to the Tsar condemning it as likely to give Western Europe a bad opinion of the Russian peasantry. The Tsar submitted to his mentor's opinion.

The play was first publicly performed at Antoine's Théâtre Libre in Paris, on 22nd February 1888. Zola was enthusiastic, and took as much pains to secure its success as if it had been his own work. At one of the rehearsals he said: 'Above all, do not strike out a single scene or a single word, and do not fear for its success.'

It was so successful that it was soon produced at no less than three Paris theatres.

In December 1887 Tolstoy wrote to Gay:

I am in Moscow, but nevertheless for the most part quite happy and tranquil. I lack nothing. I have so much work (which one hopes will be of use to people) that I know I cannot finish it all. It is so with you too, I know. And when one knows one cannot finish it the desire for personal reward falls away, while the consciousness of performing a service remains. I sometimes experience that, and it is very good; but as soon as people begin to praise me (as now for my play) a desire for personal reward springs up, together with a stupid self-satisfaction. Such am I! What is to be done? It is true that, as you also know, one is saved by the fact that one has no time to waste and must begin something else.

In that same year, besides the works already named, Tolstoy wrote some other short stories and a number of letter-essays, as well as a short article on Gay's drawing: *Christ's Last Talk with His Disciples*. He also dramatised *The Imp and the Crust*, under the title of *The First Distiller*.

Near the Tolstoys' house in Moscow is a large open plain called, from the nunnery that stands on it, the Maidens' Field, and here at Carnival and other holidays, booths are erected and cheap entertainments are offered to the people. Tolstoy used to go there to watch the crowd and see what plays were given them. He found that the favourite ones were of the blood-and-thunder variety; the most popular of all being one named after Chúrkin, the criminal mentioned in a previous chapter, who combined generosity to the poor with his robberies and murders, and who had escaped from Siberia four times. It was for performance in these booths, and to replace plays of that kind, that Tolstoy wrote *The First Distiller*, and it was performed there. It is very suitable for Temperance Society performances; it is a short and easy piece, and has several times been produced in England.

By this time 'Tolstoy Colonies' were springing up in various parts of Russia, and to one of them Feinermann eventually betook himself. To follow the fortunes of these Colonies would take me far beyond the limits of this work; but, speaking generally, they failed, and besides inflicting privations on those who joined them, occasioned much quarrelling. Later on, similar Colonies were started in England, Holland, and the United States, with a like result. The experience of these communities has been instructive and throws much light on Tolstoy's teachings.

He condemned so many forms of human activity, including all service of Governments (central or local), all service connected with army, navy, church or chapel, all forms of capitalism or landlordism, and all work done for capitalists or landlords, as well as commerce and professional medicine – that those who, impressed by the validity of his indictment of existing economic injustices, came under the sway of his persuasive eloquence, and believed that he had grasped the whole truth and knew the whole solution of the problem, were often led to abandon their accustomed ways of life, to uproot themselves from the places where they were known, to break off their family connections, and to start life anew on fresh lines, abjuring the things that according to him made life hideous, arid, and vile.

But having done this, what were they to do next? Hard manual labour was what he chiefly recommended, but without co-operation and skilled direction such labour does not, in Russia as in most other countries, enable an inexpert man to secure even a bare subsistence.

To form a Colony of like-minded men and women presented itself as a solution of the difficulty, and Tolstoy, if he did not expressly encourage such Colonies, at least regarded them sympathetically and did not denounce them as he denounced the ways in which educated people usually earn a livelihood.

It was when the Colonies got to work that the real defects of

Tolstoyism as a constructive policy became obvious. The preliminary inconsistencies – the buying or hiring of land, for instance – could be passed over as evils incidental to the transition from a bad life to a good one; and the fact that spades, ploughs, and other things had to be bought, could also be excused or palliated; but the insurmountable difficulty arose from the fact that those who took to colony-life were for the most part people who disregarded and disapproved of the regulations enacted not only by the Church but also by the State. To them civil and criminal law was an abomination. They had stepped out of the customary ruts of life to guide their lives solely by the dictates of reason and conscience. There was no longer any trade-custom or accepted routine to guide them, and when they turned to Tolstoy for help it appeared that his teaching did not supply what was needed. Such general indications as it contains furnish no sufficient guidance for the life of a community; and 'reason and conscience' are so differently developed in different people that, where there is neither fixed law and accepted custom nor a Moses wielding a theocratic power, discussion and friction absorb much of the time and energy that should go into work. Misunderstandings arise, co-operation becomes more and more impossible, and people learn by sad experience how essential law and government are if any man is to know what he may expect of his fellows and what others may reasonably demand of him. The chief lesson taught by the failure of the Tolstoy Colonies is, that definiteness in our relations with our fellow men is essential to harmonious intercourse, and that the ultimate and chief reason for the existence and persistence of legal tribunals is not (as Tolstoy supposed) to enable the rich to exploit the poor, the cunning to prey on the simple, and lawyer-sharks to live on the community at large – but to supply men with the nearest approach we can get to impartial arbitration for the settlement of their disputes. If two men quarrel about the ownership of a field, the essential thing is, not that A should have it or that B should have it, but that the quarrel should be *settled*, and the field again become the undisputed possession of somebody, in order that use may be made of it and that both A and B may be free to get on with their business, without having to discuss points they are unable to agree upon. Remove the law, and induce men to believe that no fixed code or seat of judgement should exist, and the only people who will be able to get on at all decently will be those who, like the Russian pre-revolutionary peasantry, follow a traditional way of life, doing their work as their fathers and grandfathers did before them and always travelling in custom's deep-worn ruts.

The root evil of Tolstoyism is that it disdains and contemns the result of the experience gained by our forefathers, who devised a system which in spite of the many defects that still hamper it made it possible for men to co-operate practically and to carry on their diverse occupations with a minimum of friction.

A great stumbling-block in the Tolstoy Colonies proved to be the law of Non-Resistance, which condemns all physical force used to prevent anyone from doing what he likes. It is quite true that wonderful things have frequently been accomplished by men and women relying on forces higher than the physical, and using moral or mental suasion in place of brute violence. Stated *comparatively*, the proposition that it is better to use persuasion than force and that mind is greater than matter, is excellent. But Non-Resistance occasioned harm when a man or a community adopted it as a rigid rule and thereby deprived himself, or itself, of the power to check obvious wrongs in what was sometimes the only way they could be checked.

Without attempting a history of the Tolstoy Colonies, I may mention a few typical instances of the way in which they broke down.

The first occurred in the Schavéevski Colony in the Province of Smolénsk. The colonists adopted a neglected youngster and took him to live with them. He listened to their discussions, readings, and conversations, and learnt that no physical force should be used to anyone, that it is wrong to possess property, and that no colonist should have anything to do with the police or the Law Courts. One morning the colonist who had special charge of the lad awoke and began to dress, but could not find his waistcoat until at last he discovered that the boy was wearing it. The colonist asked for the waistcoat, but the boy refused to give it up. The man explained how wrong it is to steal, but the boy could not see the point of the argument. If property is wrong, why was it any more wrong for a boy to have it than a man? The other colonists were gradually drawn into the dispute, and as it developed it became more and more apparent that the whole battery of Tolstoy's arguments concerning property and judging, as well as his insistence on condoning all offences, claiming no rights, and acknowledging only duties, were on the boy's side in the controversy. He was accusing no one: and was therefore able to assume a tone of moral superiority. He wanted the waistcoat as much as the man did. He was quite willing to discuss the subject; but it was impossible to alter his opinion that he was going to keep the waistcoat and that it was very wrong of anyone to want to take it from him. That particular waistcoat might not have mattered, but the question at stake was, Whether anyone might rely on retaining anything: a pen, a tool, or even a book he had begun to write? It was a question of principle going to the root of the possibility of efficiency and co-operation. The incident showed that the colonists did not know what they really approved or disapproved of. It further showed that in undermining the bases of Church and State, Tolstoy had unwittingly tunnelled much further, and endangered the very bases of any possible code or of any fixed agreement between man and man. If we accept all he has said as valid, any lunatic, drunkard, wayward child, or angry man, may block the traffic in Cheapside indefinitely, and it would not need many such people to plunge a whole community into chaos.

Another case occurred at the Tver Colony. The farm they had bought was a wretchedly poor one with sandy soil, but attached to it was a wood, some eighty acres in extent, situated a mile and a half away. Some time after the colonists had settled on the farm, a man wished to join them, and they set to work to cut timber from their wood to build a house for him and his family to live in. The man however, changed his mind and did not join the colony, and some peasants from the neighbouring village offered to buy the trees that had been felled. One of the colonists then raised the ethical problem whether it was right to sell the trees, seeing that it had been agreed that the colonists would only consider as their own things they worked with or required for their work, and they did not work with or require this timber.

'If,' said he, 'we do not need it, what right have we to consider it ours? It belongs to those who need it, that is, to the peasants who want to buy it. All property not required for one's personal work is kept and held only by violence, and therefore if we claim such property we maintain the principle of violence. Yet what does our colony stand for but a protest against such violence? If we acknowledge and support the evil principle by selling wood we do not require, what sense is there in our whole undertaking?'

His arguments convinced his companions. They collected the peasants who wished to buy timber and explained to them that as it was not they (the colonists) but God who had caused the trees to grow, and as the peasants needed the timber more than they did, it was the peasants who should take it.

The latter, when they had convinced themselves that the colonists had not gone mad and were speaking seriously, were delighted and hastened to remove the timber; but they too were logical, and said: 'Then neither do you require the thicket from which the timber was cut? It also is God's and anyone may cut what he wants in it?'

Having said A, the colonists had to say B, and to admit that they had no right to the thicket.

Winter was coming to an end, and as soon as this news spread, peasants from the surrounding villages hastened to utilise the last days of sledging before the thaw set in and the roads became impassable. Some came with one sledge and some with as many as five. Soon a peasant from the nearest village came running to the colony to say that so many people had gone to the wood that something like a fight had already begun, and it was urgently necessary to arrange some order and not allow everybody to cut trees at one and the same time. The colonists became alarmed, fearing that someone would be killed; but they were so upset at this result of their application of the principle of Non-Resistance that they could not make up their minds to go to the woods themselves to establish order. Something had to be done, however, and they appointed the peasant who had brought the news to the post of forester, with instructions to let only a few people in at a time. (They learnt subsequently that he only let in those who paid him.)

The peasants were dissatisfied. Those who had taken timber were vexed at not having got more while it was to be had for the taking, and those who got none felt aggrieved. Crowds came to the colony to ask for passes to cut trees, and the colonists had to refuse them and felt very much ashamed of themselves for having occasioned such confusion and so much quarrelling. The best peasants blamed the colonists, saying: 'If you wanted to do good you should have divided the wood among the poorest peasants. But now the richest, who have several horses, have carried off most of the timber and the poorest have got nothing!'

* * *

The fact is, that the institution of property does not rest ultimately on selfishness. Bad and selfish use is often made of property, but the institution rests at bottom on something better. If no property existed we should all perish of want. But if property exists it must be controlled by someone or some group of people, otherwise waste, confusion, and friction, will inevitably result.

One of the world's greatest needs is that property should be held (whether by individuals, by groups, by Municipalities, or by Governments on behalf of the whole people) with a sense of responsibility, wisely administered, and its fruits unselfishly used; but by denouncing it as a thing wrong in itself Tolstoy caused many conscientiously sensitive men and women to be ashamed of their plain duty and to neglect both the administration of property and the exercise of their due influence in promoting the good government of their town, district, or nation.

An incident that occurred in the Khárkov Colony has the same moral. The colonists' land and house had been bought in the name of M. Alëkhin, who held it for the use of the Colony, believing that no one had any right to own property, to defend it, or to go to law about it.

One day there appeared on the scene an eccentric fellow named Klóbski, who called himself a 'Teacher of Life'. Having discussed the whole question with Alëkhin and with the colonists, he went to bed. Next morning at breakfast he announced to them: 'Gentlemen! I have to inform you that from today your colony will have neither house nor land. You are astonished?' added he, raising his head and glaring at them. 'Then I will speak more plainly. Your farmhouse, with its outbuildings, garden and fields, now belongs to me. I am master here and request you to clear out! Do you hear? I allow you three days to go!'

The colonists were thunderstruck and did not understand what had happened. The simple fact was that having ascertained that Alëkhin did not consider that his position as trustee for the others gave him any right to use either law or force, Klóbski had made up his mind to take possession of the property.

None of the colonists resisted him and they all cleared out of the place, but two days later Alëkhin called the peasants of the neighbouring village together and presented the property to their Commune, duly signing the legal deeds necessary to give them possession.

Klóbski thereupon, seeing the game was up, departed and the peasants entered into possession. They, at least, felt no qualms of conscience about possessing the property, and the indefiniteness which had occasioned the trouble was at an end.

Tolstoy expressed himself as being pleased with this result. The land had gone to the peasants and the intelligentsia might settle down and work for them. But therein I think Tolstoy was not quite consistent, for if the institution of property is wrong in itself, its possession even by a village Commune for the use of the peasants is wrong, for the original proposition was an absolute one – 'property is robbery' – and not a comparative one depending on the amount of property, or the number of its owners; and what right had a Khárkov village Commune to hold property (as they certainly would hold it) against the yet poorer inhabitants of some other village?

Tolstoyans who tried living by themselves in the villages seem generally to have fared no better than these colonists, and though one does not take Anna Seuron literally, there is some truth in her remarks:

> There were many young men of good family who married peasant girls, or simply lived with peasant girls in some village, and perished in dirt and drink. Some worked themselves to death. These cases are not generally known as the families avoided publicity.

Tolstoy's Christian-anarchist and anti-Government principles of course precluded him from advocating the State-ownership of property, which with people half as honest and unselfish as men must be to run a Communist Colony would meet most of the evils that shocked him in our present society.

It seems strange that he did not learn more from the experience of the Colonies, but it must be remembered that neither he, nor his nearest friends (Gay, Chertkóv, &c.), ever joined a colony, and Tolstoy was so absorbed in his work, so busily engaged in trying to do good to those with whom he came in immediate contact, and so wrapped up in his own thoughts and feelings, that he was as impervious to the experiences of the Communist colonists as he was to those of the constitutional reformers of Western Europe. As a Russian writer has said: 'He listened so intently to the noise in his own ears that he hardly heard what other people were saying!'

9

Effects of the Teaching

By the year 1887 the evolution in Tolstoy's views which had begun more than ten years before was wellnigh complete. His opinions had solidified, and except on one or two questions they altered but little during the succeeding years.

The chief work he wrote at this time was his philosophic essay *On Life*, about which in a letter in June he says: 'I am always at my work, *On Life and Death*. I cannot tear myself away till it is finished.'

The work is so important and comparatively so little known that I should like to repeat here the summary which I gave in the first edition of this book, but as *On Life* appears in this edition, I refrain, and will only draw attention to one point. *What I Believe* (1884), sometimes called *My Religion*, has had a much wider circulation than *On Life* (1887), and the view expressed in the former work, that Jesus 'never asserted a personal resurrection and personal immortality beyond the grave' has been widely accepted as Tolstoy's permanent opinion. But *On Life* presents a different view, and one that Tolstoy held to the end of his life. He there says: 'Men fear the death of the body because the thought of that event causes them to realise their need of a true life, which they feel they do not possess . . . Knowing that we have received and developed our lives from a past we do not see, we should feel no fear of a future we also do not see.' The further argument makes it plain that Tolstoy had come to believe in a future life.

On Life could not be published in Russia, and as Tolstoy received no 'proofs' of it, he did not submit it to that repeated and careful scrutiny and correction to which his works were usually subjected. Being a philosophical work it specially needed such revision, and when it was carelessly printed in Geneva from the rough manuscript, it required much critical acumen on the part of its readers to grasp its full meaning, and the first translation published in English was such rubbish as ought never to have been attributed to any sane writer. In spite of this, however, Mr Bolton Hall of New York, without knowing

Russian, puzzled out the meaning, and wrote a free paraphrase which gave its essence very well. This was a remarkable instance of the clarity of Tolstoy's thought defeating the ineptitude of his translators and reaching readers despite them.

Wishing to make his views public, Tolstoy read a paper on *Life's Meaning* to the Moscow Psychological Society. The meeting was a crowded one as everybody wished to hear Tolstoy, but Materialism was then rampant, and Tolstoy's treatment of the problem was not generally understood by those who heard his paper.

On Life had a great influence on some of its readers. The late Ernest Howard Crosby, who, after sitting as a Republican in the New York State Legislature, went as Judge of the Mixed Courts to Alexandria, was an instance of this. A French translation of *On Life* (made by the Countess S. A. Tolstoy) fell into his hands, and profoundly altered his perception of what is worth striving for in life. He then visited Tolstoy, and the latter told him it would be very hard for him (Crosby) handicapped by 'all the disadvantages of youth, health, and wealth', to do good, but that he must not cease to try. Crosby returned to America, abandoned politics, and wrote three volumes of poems (some of them very good) presenting the Tolstoyan view of life. He also did a good deal of lecturing. Unable to 'get off men's backs' he 'sat on them as lightly as he could', and is well remembered as one of the sanest, most satisfactory, and most friendly of English-speaking Tolstoyans.

In August 1887 Tolstoy's brother-in-law, S. A. Behrs, returned from the Caucasus and visited Yásnaya. The following is his account of the changes he noticed in Tolstoy, with whom as a lad he had been so familiar, but whom he had now not seen for nine years.

Tolstoy, he says, had grown older and greyer, but not unduly so:

His face, however, showed evident signs of the serious mental sufferings he had endured. It was calm, sad, and had a quite new look. Nor was it his face only, but his whole personality, that had completely altered, and not his life only and his relation to everybody but his whole mental activity. If he still retained many of his former views (his hostility to 'progress' and 'civilisation', for instance) the ground for these convictions had greatly changed.

Leo Nikoláevich had become the personification of the idea of love of one's neighbour, and if I may be allowed a paradox I should say that for the sake of this idea he sinned against it: as, for instance, when he was severe with people who misbehaved.

Education, in the sense of knowledge of Nature, men and life, he considers good in so far as it is necessary to enable us to serve our neighbours, but as a manifestation of 'progress' enabling us to enslave our neighbours, education is harmful. He considers that this last is what is aimed at by contemporary society, and that education is only sought for the sake of rising above one's fellows, distinguishing one-self from them and subjecting them to oneself. He has, therefore, ceased to concern himself about his sons' education and is displeased that his wife still attends to it. When his eldest son had taken his degree at the University and asked his father's advice about a future career, the latter advised him to go as workman to a peasant.

Education, he holds, should develop love and compassion for one's neighbour and to that end should stifle sexual desire and not develop it as happens, he considers, in all contemporary society. Love of simplicity and an unexacting mind as to one's surroundings should also be aimed at in education. Sincere politeness is desirable (again as a manifestation of love of one's fellows), but formal politeness is undesirable and is a sure sign of selfishness . . . Leo Nikoláevich himself is now fond of employing a peasant manner of speech at times as an indication of the simplicity he recommends.

Behrs continues:

His former appreciation of the aristocracy has been replaced by sympathy chiefly for the peasants. The lower a man stands in the social scale, the more, in his opinion, he should evoke sympathy. So in *The Power of Darkness* the best person presented is Akím, the cesspool-cleaner.

Tolstoy's former isolation is now replaced by complete accessibility to everyone, except when restrictions are imposed not by him but by his wife, out of consideration for his health.

Concerning his relation to his property he told me that he had wished to free himself from it as from an evil which oppressed him, but he acted wrongly, at first, in wishing to throw the burden on to others, that is to say, he tried to insist on distributing it and thereby caused another evil – namely, an energetic protest from, and the serious discontent of, his wife. In consequence of that protest he offered to transfer all he had to her, and when she at first refused, he offered it, equally in vain, to his children. After that, not wishing to oppose his wife by force, and abandoning the attempt to transfer the burden to others, he adopted the plan of ignoring his property: refused to have anything to do with it or to care about its fate, and ceased to make use of it except that he continued to live in the house at Yásnaya Polyána. Disapproving in principle of giving money in alms, since every coin is a means of enslaving our fellows, he yet considered it impossible to refuse to use money, since his family continued to use his estate. My sister told me that they give away from two to three thousand rubles [£200 to £300] every year to the poor. While I was there a poor peasant whose house had been burnt, came to Leo Nikoláevich and asked him for wood to build a shed. He invited me to come, and we took axes and cut down some trees in the Yásno-Polyána wood, chopping off the branches and tying the trunks on to the peasant's cart. I confess I did this with pleasure, experiencing a joy unknown till then, perhaps in consequence of Leo Nikoláevich's influence but perhaps simply because I was doing this for an unfortunate man who was really ill, worn out, and destitute ... When the peasant had gone, Leo Nikoláevich said to me: 'Can one doubt the necessity and pleasure of rendering such aid?'

Behrs was struck by the fact that Tolstoy had quite given up tobacco and wine, and he notes that Tolstoy never at this time asked others to work for him, accepting little assistance even from members of his own family, and when he did accept any, doing so rather because he knew it gave them pleasure than for his own sake ...

From compassion for animals he has given up hunting, and he told me he has not merely lost all wish to hunt but feels astonished that he could formerly have liked it.

There was one pleasure he allowed himself: in summer he always had flowers on his table, or stuck in his leather girdle, or held in his hand. 'You should see,' says Anna Seuron, 'with what enjoyment he lifts them from time to time to his big nose, and how he then looks round mildly, as if thanking the Creator for giving us flowers.' Behrs tells us that:

When Tolstoy remained in Yásnaya for some days after his family had moved to Moscow he cooked his own food ... He retains his love of exercise, only he now directs it to useful purposes: ploughing, hut-building, journeys on foot, &c ...

The playfulness so enlivening to others, that was formerly always present in Tolstoy, has now quite vanished. There is nothing morose or specially sad about him, but there is hardly a trace of his former liveliness. That characteristic seems to have fallen to pieces and to have been shared among his children. Quite unabashed by his presence they are noisily animated, and this harmonises admirably with his seriousness and throws into relief his strict attitude on moral questions. Their talks, and songs, and piano-playing, and their youthful disposition in general, seemed to me to please him, though he himself took no part in it. Only on the day of my arrival – guessing no doubt my grief at the change I noticed in him – he played tricks with me, to the delight of us all: unexpectedly jumping on my back when I was walking about the room. He is still fond of the society of the little children, but no longer tries to excite them as he used to.

He advised me to leave the Civil Service and change my way of life, and he spoke to me about the happiness that comes of fulfilling the duty of love to one's neighbour. In particular he mentioned young Prince D. A. Khilkóv to me, as an example. Khilkóv had not been personally acquainted with Leo Nikoláevich nor probably with his teaching, yet almost simultaneously with its publication, disregarding his connections and rank, the young prince gave his lands to the peasants and retained only about twenty-five acres for himself. Nor did he even settle on that, but went to work without pay as workman to a peasant. He is diligently making himself expert as a workman, and waiting till he has become so proficient that a neighbouring Jew will offer him five rubles a month to work for him. Only then does Khilkóv intend to marry and settle down on his twenty-five acres.

This Prince Khilkóv was so remarkable a man and so closely connected with Tolstoy, that I may perhaps be allowed to digress in order briefly to tell his story. He had been the youngest Colonel in the Russian army and had fought not merely the Turks but also the dishonest Russian contractors with great zest and courage. Though an excellent administrator, greatly beloved by his men and much interested in his work, he felt so ill at ease after cutting down a Turk with his own hand in a cavalry charge, that he only awaited the termination of the war of 1878 to resign his commission and leave the army. He then, quite on Tolstoy's lines, adopted the way of life mentioned by Behrs in the passage quoted above. Being a man of great ability, tactful and sincere, he soon acquired influence over the neighbouring peasants, but having repudiated the Russian Church he was denounced by the priests and exiled to the Caucasus, where he lived among the Doukhobórs, and when they refused military service in 1895, the authorities, wrongly suspecting him of having influenced them, re-banished him – to the Baltic Provinces this time. From thence Khilkóv was allowed, in 1898, to go into exile abroad, and it was at the Tolstoyan Purleigh Colony, in Essex, that I first made his acquaintance. There will be further occasion to mention him when I speak of the service he rendered to the Doukhobór migration.

If the abolition of poverty could be brought about by adopting the course Tolstoy recommends, or if the adoption of that course led to an inner consciousness of having chosen the true path, Prince D. A. Khilkóv, of all others, should have been the man best able to testify to the fact. No one resigned more, simplified his life more, or tested the Christian-anarchist doctrine in practice more whole-heartedly. But as a result of testing the course Tolstoy was himself prevented from following, Khilkóv came to the conclusion that it did not meet the needs of the case. The people of Russia needed honest and capable leadership by men with a gift for organisation, and it was not by persuading such men to devote themselves to manual labour that the fear of famine could be exorcised or the rule of law substituted for despotic caprice. Khilkóv, after his experiences, became more of a Socialist-Revolutionary than a Tolstoyan. The very fact that he was banished to a distant part of the Empire without trial or even having any definite charge brought against him, showed how impossible it was for isolated individuals – sincerely and devotedly anxious though they may have been to help the people – to make headway against a Government that ignored all law.

To return, however, to what Behrs tells us of Tolstoy:

In accord with the rule of not resisting evil by violence, Leo Nikoláe-vich is anxious that his children's relation to his teaching should be perfectly free. He tells them what he believes, but not even in his tone is there the least attempt to impose it on them . . . He told me himself that he is much afraid of anything that might lead his children to follow his teaching insincerely, or even to follow it sincerely but not spontaneously. They know this very well and therefore act with complete freedom.

On the other hand there is in Leo Nikoláevich's relation to his wife a shade of exactingness and reproach, or even dissatisfaction. He blames her for preventing him from giving away his property and of continuing to educate the children in the old way.

His wife, for her part, considers that she has acted rightly, and is vexed at this attitude of his. She has been the closest witness of all his spiritual sufferings and in general of the gradual development of his thoughts, and in consequence she has again and again had to suffer on her husband's account. She has involuntarily developed a dread and abhorrence of his teaching and its consequences. Feeling how powerless she was to influence his genius or aid him in his spiritual evolution, she was driven to think only of her children, and to oppose those demands of her husband which related to them, that is, in regard to the distribution of his property and to their education. The saying, 'Between two fires,' but feebly describes her position between her husband's spiritual sufferings and demands on the one side, and the impossibility, with her convictions and for the sake of the children, of submitting to those demands on the other. On her alone during a whole decade was his theory tested and amended during its slow growth, and the result has been that a note of contradiction has arisen between them in which mutual reproach makes itself heard. That is the only ground on which disagreement has occurred; in all other respects they are now, as formerly, a model couple.

Many years later, when I was writing the first edition of this book and before the conflict between Chertkóv and herself had driven a greater wedge between husband and wife, the Countess told me that the beginning and the end of her married life had been happy, but the middle had been unhappy. At the period we have reached, she was, as we know, meeting the economic difficulties of the situation by publishing her husband's works, which sold exceedingly well. Anna Seuron tells us:

The Count was at this time tranquil, though his teaching attracted more and more attention to him and his books sold more and more. He still took little part in their publication, but only wished to be left in peace and not interfered with. He was engaged on work of importance. But even then his wife managed to copy out and put in order various scraps of his writings [of an artistic kind, which could be published in Russia], and used to put them on his table with large sheets of clean paper, to tempt him to add some more – which he occasionally did, as it were accidentally. He sometimes allowed himself to be led as if in leading strings, and he then reminded me of a good-natured cannibal or a tame bear led about on a cord. But his smile at such times was a sad one and his eyes would moisten with tears.

At the end of Behrs' *Recollections* are some passages added apparently about the time his book was published (1893) which somewhat modify the effect of what he saw in 1887. He says, for instance:

To protect her children's interest, when Leo Nikoláevich wanted to give away his estates to outsiders his wife was prepared to appeal to the authorities to put his property under guardianship. And when her husband offered her his possessions she accepted a power of attorney giving her the management of all his property except his later works, those written in the spirit of his teaching.

He also says about the elder children's attitude towards their father's teaching:

The eldest son [Sergéy] does not, as far as I know, agree with his father's opinions. When the latter surrendered all personal claim on his property, this son, in obedience to his mother's wish, undertook the management of the estate and at the same time began his service in the office of the local Zémstvo.

The second son [Ilyá] wished to follow the rules laid down in his father's religious and social creed. He left the High School, married, and settled on one of the smaller estates where, though his wife belongs to the gentry, they led a strictly simple life and had no servants.

Ilyá was far from stable in his adherence to his father's principles, but he has written a very readable and reliable book, his *Reminiscences of Tolstoy*.

The third son, Leo Lvóvich (Lion-son-of-a-Lion), 'was continuing his education, but told me that he should do his best to observe the moral laws of the Count'. A few years later, Leo Lvóvich wrote several short stories in which he strongly opposed his father's views. His *Chopin's Prelude*, in particular, was written in reply to *The Kreutzer Sonata*, and a critic alluding to the tone of these writings, spoke of him as 'Tígr Tígrovich' (Tiger-son-of-a-Tiger).

The younger sons, Andrew and Michael, served in the army voluntarily and had little sympathy with their father's views. Andrew in
particular grieved his father in many ways.

The eldest daughter, Tatiána, helped her father a great deal with his
writing and correspondence before her marriage, and there was always
a strong affection between them.

'It is, however, the second daughter,' says Behrs, 'more than all the
rest, who is devoted to her father, and as far as she is allowed rigorously
observes his every rule and maxim.'

This daughter, Mary Lvóvna (Másha), who by marriage became
Princess Obolénski, studied medicine, and in 1886 we hear of her, 'in
print blouse, passing examinations to qualify as a Primary School
teacher'. Helping her father with his correspondence, copying his
writings, teaching village children, and attending to the sick in the
village, her life was crowded with interests and work.

After her elder sisters had married, the youngest daughter, Countess
Alexandra, succeeded them as her father's assistant and typist, and she
also was devoted to him and to his ideas.

Speaking to me one day of trouble he had had with one of his sons,
Tolstoy added: 'I have reason to thank God for my daughters.'

Of Madame Kuzmínski, Behrs says:

My younger sister, who with her family spends every summer at
Yásnaya Polyána, is also one of Leo Nikoláevich's sincerest admirers.
But though she has a deep reverence for the purity of his belief and
understands the spirit of his teaching, she sees its impracticability and
is not afraid to express her opinions frankly. Leo Nikoláevich, for his
part, is wont to answer her objections in that sarcastic tone which has
now replaced the lively humour that was formerly the great charm of
his conversation. I may perhaps be allowed to give a slight, but
characteristic, example of my sister's mocking attacks and the quiet
sarcasm with which they were parried.

In former days Leo Nikoláevich was particularly fond of a certain
sweet dish which we called 'Ankóvski-pie', from the name of the
good doctor who gave us the recipe.

During my last visit I soon learned that the term had assumed a
different meaning and was now employed by Leo Nikoláevich, in
sarcastic moods, to express his disapproval of our undue hankering
after comfort and luxury. I once happened to be with him while he

was clearing up and dusting his study and I helped him. We had thoroughly swept the room out and were standing on the balcony brooms in hand, when my younger sister chanced to pass by. A little later in presence of them all, she laughingly congratulated me on my conversion and declared she had never seen a more zealous disciple. She went on to relate how she saw the Count and me standing, brooms in hand, and how he made the sign of the cross over me, and raising his eyes solemnly, asked me, 'Dost thou renounce Ankóvski-pie and all its evil works?' whereupon I as solemnly replied, 'I do!'

The 23rd September 1887 was Tolstoy's silver wedding-day, but, displeased at the festivities which were being prepared for the event, he enquired: 'Is tomorrow really the jubilee of my wedding-day or is it not rather the jubilee of Ankóvski-pie?'

In August 1887 Répin painted his first portrait of Tolstoy, in which Tolstoy looks like an Old Testament Prophet in spite of a garb little suggestive of such a comparison. Répin, who subsequently became a friend of the family and a frequent visitor, painted Tolstoy repeatedly.

It was in 1887 that Tolstoy wrote *The Empty Drum*, from a folk-tale that had long been current in the region of the Vólga. It is a story after Tolstoy's own heart, admirably expressing the peasants' hatred of military service. His rendering of it is an admirable example of the way in which he voiced feelings current through centuries among large sections of mankind. He also at that time wrote an article entitled *What is True in Art* and began several other things not published till later.

One of these was the tale of Early Christian life, *Walk in the Light While There is Light*. Tolstoy's friend, V. G. Chertkóv, contributed something to that tale. I once asked Tolstoy what value he set on the work, and he replied: 'I never hear it mentioned without feeling ashamed.' Indeed it suffers from a fundamental fault. The characters in it are divided into two groups: the bad heathen and the good Christians. In real life these would inevitably, Tolstoy said, have merged and over-lapped. It was this story, or rather the ideas which for a while swayed Tolstoy's mind and found expression in this story, which led to the founding of the Colonies that by their failure revealed the weakness of one side of Tolstoyism.

Behind all Tolstoy's denunciation of property-holding, Governments, subdivision of labour, and so forth, there always lay the implication that if these things did not exist people would live harmoniously and morally. Those who believed this, naturally asked: 'How then are we to arrange our lives?' One answer Tolstoy gave was, 'Go and live as peasants with the peasants!' But when educated men tried to do this, they usually came to the conclusion that those were not the surroundings in which they could work best. Another suggestion Tolstoy made is that contained in *Walk in the Light While There is Light* – namely, to form a Community and share all things in common.

Various literary societies, universities, and academies had by this time begun to offer Tolstoy honorary memberships or give him other marks of their esteem. He cared little for such things; they added nothing to the esteem and affection in which he was held by those he taught and helped, and I do not suppose that many readers would thank me were I to enumerate the distinctions that were conferred on him. What must be mentioned are the marks of attention of a different kind showered upon him by the Orthodox Russo-Greek Church and by some of its more zealous adherents.

The peasant-writer, S. Semënov, has told how greatly, as a factory worker of nineteen, he was impressed by the stories the *Intermediary* published, and how when he himself began to write he submitted his first efforts to Tolstoy and received encouragement. After their first talk, he says: 'I felt I had become much more manly, life spread out widely before me, and I saw that many problems had arisen for me to solve.'

He returned to his village, and there:

The parish priest explained to my father that I had been caught in a net. Leo Tolstoy was a noxious man and a cunning schemer. He got simple fellows such as myself to write, paid them a few farthings for their works, published these in his own name, and received immense sums for them. My father was so upset by this that he got drunk, spoke to me as to one who was lost, and began to look with disfavour on all I did.

That is only an instance of what continually occurred in different shapes and forms; and if one is at times taken aback by the way Tolstoy speaks of the Church, the opposition his efforts to help humanity met with at the hands of the Church should be remembered.

Towards the end of 1887 my brother-in-law, Dr P. S. Alexéev, returned to Moscow from a visit to America, where he had studied the Temperance movement which up to that time had attracted little attention in Russia. He approached Tolstoy, who was much interested by what Alexéev told him and promptly started a Temperance Society in his own house. He signed the pledge and so did several members of his family. He always remained keen on the subject, and wrote several articles about it.

Afterwards Tolstoy called a meeting in the village of Yásnaya Polyána, at which he spoke of the evils of drunkenness, and induced the peasants to promise to abandon both vodka and tobacco. They even sacrificed their pipes, tobacco and tobacco-pouches, but there was much subsequent backsliding.

Tolstoy's powers did not usually show themselves to the best advantage in matters of organisation or co-operation. His writings, his personal example, and the stimulus and inspiration he gave, were the things in which he was greatest. To the cause of Temperance his chief literary contributions (besides *The Imp and the Crust* and *The First Distiller*, already mentioned) were a pamphlet, and two essays. The first of these, called *Culture's Holiday*, appeared in 1889 and was issued on the occasion of the Moscow University Anniversary (12th January), which was generally celebrated with much feasting and drinking in the restaurants, ending up with general drunkenness, leading, in many cases, to gross debauchery.

Against this custom Tolstoy, in *Culture's Holiday*, delivered his philippic. It provoked considerable resentment and had little apparent success at the time. But it was just Tolstoy's courage in facing Government and people alike, and reproving students and professors not less sternly than he reproved dissolute peasants, that secured him the respect of the world.

But why do I say he was as stern with professors as with peasants? He was much more so! I well remember when walking with him one day, that he had occasion to comment on a drunken peasant, and then added: 'Ah! but you should see how affectionate they are in their cups! Their fundamental good-nature shows itself then. They are full of kindliness and want to embrace you and are ready to give their souls to serve you.' His way of speaking showed how much he sympathised with the tipsy peasants.

His other essay on the question, *Why Do Men Stupefy Themselves?* deals with narcotics as well as stimulants, and mentions the effect of tobacco on his own work. He wrote it as a preface to a book of Dr Alexéev's, published in 1890.

It was Dr Alexéev who, one winter day in Moscow in 1888, first took me to see Tolstoy, with whose works I was at that time only superficially acquainted. We found many people assembled in a large upstairs room simply furnished with a big table, many chairs, and a grand piano. I was struck by the life and animation of the party. After a time, happening to be left alone with Tolstoy at the table, I said: 'I understand, Leo Nikoláevich, that you disapprove of all money-getting? That interests me very much for I am in Russia to try to earn some money.' He immediately took up the subject and began to explain his views to me. I remember that trying to demonstrate the advantages of the factory system, I said, 'Well, you will at least admit that it is necessary to have knives?' 'Not so necessary as to have bread,' replied he, and proceeded to insist on the primary duty of each man producing as much and consuming as little as possible. I was not convinced, but was struck by his earnestness, his willingness to explain his views and the courtesy with which he listened to what one had to say – despite a fondness for tripping up his interlocutor by an unexpected remark. Alexéev told me afterwards that he had never heard me speak Russian so badly as that evening, and indeed I felt ill at ease and conscious that I had no business to be there. Tolstoy, however, said, 'How clearly and well you express yourself!' – referring I suppose to what I said rather than to my accent or inflections – and at parting asked me with emphasis to come and see him again. I did not do so for some years; not until after reading some of his later books I had become keenly interested in his views and anxious to consult him on points that perplexed me.

Then and subsequently, Tolstoy impressed me by his power of vivid, concise and humorous expression, the keenness of his interest in all sorts of things: people, books, information, games, and work of all kinds, and especially in things of spiritual importance, and also by his tact and power of putting people at their ease and getting them to talk on subjects they knew something about. Whoever might be present – a peasant-author, an artist, or a prince – he had a word for each and in his presence all were equal. In fact Tolstoy's good manners, his power of bringing out the best in people and making them conscious of their own worth, were very noticeable.

As oil lubricates the bearings of a complex machine, so manners should facilitate human intercourse, and in Tolstoy's case they did this without any restriction upon the subjects that might be discussed. He was far too intelligent and too much interested in life to bar out any of the topics which earnest men think about.

It was no small thing, in the 1880s and 1890s, that there was at least one house in Moscow where people of all sorts and conditions came together under the influence of a man in whom there was nothing base, and who in the days of blackest reaction kept a heart full of hope and a flaming conviction that iniquity cannot endure and that the present evils are but transitory. Not vainly does Hope rank as a cardinal virtue!

One of the things for which I personally am most grateful to Tolstoy is for having taken me and my enquiries seriously, and for his patience in explaining his meanings to me. I vividly remember a scene that took place one day just outside the front door of his Moscow house. Looking at me with his piercing eyes as though he would read my very soul, he said: 'Are you sincere?' To which I replied: 'I am not sure that I agree with all that you teach, but my desire to understand you and to recognise all the good there is in your views is absolutely sincere.'

On 1st December 1887 Tolstoy wrote to Gay:

I have been in Moscow a week. Here, as in the country, I am still not working with my pen, and, do you know, this abstinence satisfies and makes me happy. From habit and from self-love, and from the wish to befog oneself, one wants to write and to get away from the life around one, but no irresistible force impels me to write, and I have got rid of that indulgent judge within me who formerly approved of anything I scribbled. I abstain from writing and feel a kind of purity, such as one feels from not smoking. Do you still smoke? I do not know how to rejoice sufficiently at having rid myself of that habit.

The last of Tolstoy's children, a son, christened Iván, was born on 31st March 1888, when Tolstoy was in his sixtieth year and the Countess in her forty-fourth.* The Countess had thirteen children (nine sons and four daughters) and three miscarriages. Of the children, three died in infancy.

The year 1888 was not one of Tolstoy's strenuous years. When he

* Anna Seuron post-dates Iván's birth. Speaking of Tolstoy's work in the famine years 1891–2, she says: 'At this time the Lord granted him a son, his youngest and last child, Iván.' This is quite in keeping with her general inaccuracy against which anyone using her book must be constantly on guard.

heard that Gay had set to work earnestly on his picture 'The Exit from the Last Supper', he wrote to him as follows – ending with a remark about Herzen that might very well be applied to himself:

> You are hard at work and may God help you at it! It was high time! I say this to myself more than to you, though I also know that when one is accustomed to work at a certain depth of creation and cannot reach that depth, one cannot force oneself to it. (But then what joy it gives when one does attain it!) I am now in such a state. I have begun a mass of things, all of them things I love – only I cannot dive down to the proper depth but keep floating up to the surface . . . Lately I have been, and still am, reading Herzen . . . What a wonderful writer! Russian life for the last twenty years would have been different had he not been hidden from the younger generation [his works prohibited]. He was an important organ violently extracted from the body politic of Russia.

Kholstomér, the Story of a Horse was published in 1888, in one of the magazines. It had been written early in the 1860s. Almost the only article Tolstoy is known to have completed in 1888 was an essay-letter addressed to Romain Rolland, who was then a student, to which the title *Manual Labour and Mental Activity* has been given. We get a glimpse of the interest his teaching was arousing from the following remarks of a doctor who subsequently joined a Tolstoy Colony in Tver. He tells us that it became the custom for a group of students and others to go to Tolstoy's house in Moscow on Thursday evenings:

> On those evenings we had sharp disputes with Tolstoy . . .
>
> I remember as though it were yesterday, Leo Nikoláevich, drawn up to his full height with flashing eyes, tenaciously defending his point of view against our attacks. How striking he was at such moments and what a pity it is that no artist was there to sketch him as he then was!
>
> In Tolstoy, a lover of the people and political thinker with a tinge of anarchism is conjoined with a moralist-philosopher seeking a path for a new religion free from all superstition. Tolstoy himself prized most highly his religio-philosophic ideas. His popularist-political opinions flowed from his religious *Weltanschauung*, but did not occupy the forefront. For us at that time, however, it was just those popularist and anarchist ideas that were most important and we did not attach particular weight to his religious views. On this

difference all our disputes hinged. We, with our views, could not endure that men who professed to be followers of Tolstoy should continue their former easy way of life. [This evidently refers to V. G. Chertkóv and others like him.] Leo Nikoláevich maintained that the chief thing was to preserve good relations with those about one, and if this involved remaining in the conditions of one's former well-to-do life it was better to sacrifice one's spiritual peace than to provoke anger and bitterness in those near to one.

A. B. used to reply to Tolstoy with particular harshness, quoting the Gospel text: 'A man's foes shall be they of his own household.' – 'And if for the tranquillity of those near me it is necessary that I should become a burglar – must I do that also?' asked he indignantly. In vain Tolstoy replied that it all depends on the plane of religious consciousness one has reached. We held to our view and each time we met the dispute flared up afresh.

Thus two currents of Tolstoyism became more and more distinct. The one, with which our Group (that met at Tolstoy's) sided, might be called the 'Back-to-the-people' tendency. The other had more the nature of a religious movement.

The adherents of that latter current were spiritually nearer to Tolstoy. He considered that they understood him better, and they on their part treated him with great respect, amounting sometimes to veneration. For them almost every thought he expressed was an unquestioned verity.

While the 'Back-to-the-people' Tolstoyans strove with all their might and in despite of all hardships to realise Tolstoy's teaching in their lives, the representatives of the other tendency for the most part did not in externals abandon their former way of life, except that those who were in the army left the service.

The Tolstoyans who were near him in religio-philosophic opinions have remained till now faithful to their views, but it has not been so with the others: very few of them keep to the path they started on twenty years ago. Most of them have changed their opinions and follow other roads.

To the scheme for organising agricultural Colonies for the intelligentsia Tolstoy was favourable enough, though, distrusting as he does everything that is artificially arranged, he warned us of the possibility of failure.

Professor I. I. Yánzhul, an admirer of Tolstoy who was not a Tolstoyan, mentions that calling on the great man one evening about 8 o'clock he found him making a pair of boots in a tiny room adjoining his study. Tolstoy greeted his visitor merrily and pointed to the study, saying, 'Go in there, please! You will find on the table a pile of American newspapers that have just come. Have a look at them while I finish this job and wash my hands.'

On the study table Yánzhul found a bundle of unopened newspapers in various languages, and taking up the largest of them and tearing the wrapper he found that it was the *Sandusky Times*, hailing from a small but flourishing American town of that name. As soon as he opened it he saw Tolstoy's name several times repeated. It turned out that the paper contained a full report of a sermon preached in the Cathedral Church of Sandusky, and devoted to an account of Tolstoy's rendering of the Gospel. Both the sermon and the newspaper leader thereon contained enthusiastic and dithyrambic laudations of Tolstoy; he was proclaimed to be a thirteenth Apostle whose teaching was as important as that of the other twelve and whose Gospel should be read and studied by everybody, &c. &c.

> The contrast between the enthusiastic description of Tolstoy's greatness in the American paper and the humble figure of the Apostle himself who with sleeves turned up and wearing an apron sat on a rough stool in the next room quietly and diligently sewing a boot, was so great that I burst into loud, almost hysterical, laughter. Leo Nikoláevich, somewhat perturbed, asked what had happened. When I told him what I had read in the *The Sandusky Times* of his elevation to the rank of thirteenth Apostle, he laughed most naturally and merrily, and merely remarked: 'Well, that's really quite American.' He then gravely finished his work and went to wash his hands, and when he returned to the study we had a long talk about various matters without his even casting a glance at *The Sandusky Times*.

Very characteristic was the following advice Tolstoy one day gave Yánzhul:

> If your starting-point and deductions are sound, never be afraid of practical objections to your logical conclusions. Otherwise you will never say or produce anything *original*!

As to the boots Tolstoy made, I asked a man to whom he had given a pair and who had worn them, whether they were well made. 'Couldn't be worse,' was his reply; and indeed I suspect that Tolstoy's boot-making was of more value as a spiritual sedative than as a contribution to the solution of the economic problem.

Of his interest in and admiration for Gay's paintings of the life of Christ, frequent mention has been made in this book. His relation to Polénov's great picture 'Christ and the Woman taken in Adultery' was very different. It was in 1888 that that artist, who in his mastery of form and colour was perhaps Gay's superior, completed the work to which he had devoted himself for years, going specially to Palestine to make studies for it and working himself ill over it. The picture was being much talked about and, when it was nearly finished, Tolstoy – though he and Polénov were not acquainted – called one day to see it. He gazed at it for a long time, and then pointing to the chief figure remarked: 'You do not like this one!'

'That is . . . Which one?' ejaculated the artist.

'This one, sitting in the middle . . .'

'But that is Christ!'

'Well, yes . . . You don't like him!' and with those words, Tolstoy departed.

IO

Non-Resistance

Early in 1889 there were signs that Tolstoy was on the point of returning to the practice of Art, from which (except for his short peasant-stories, his drama, and *Iván Ilych*) he had so long abstained.

In a letter congratulating Gay on having got to work on an important picture, he writes:

> I too should like this winter to do something in the line in which I am expert – but apparently God does not wish it. I should like to do it, but even without that I am happy.

Further on in the letter comes a passage suggesting what the subject of the work 'in the line in which I am expert' was to be:

> Animals have sexual intercourse only when offspring may be born of it. Unenlightened man (such as we all are) is always ready for it and has even declared it to be a necessity. And this pretended necessity destroys woman, demanding of her when she is with child or nursing, the unnatural activity of a mistress, which overtaxes her strength. We ourselves by these demands have destroyed the reasonable nature in woman, and then we complain of her unreasonableness, or we develop her with books and lectures. Yes! In all that relates to his animal nature, man has deliberately to attain the level of the beasts . . . I have been thinking much about this, and therefore write of it to you and to your wife.

On 22nd March, appealing once more to Gay to complete his series of illustrations to the Gospels, Tolstoy again expresses the feeling that a true artist who really has something to say must use his gifts to say it:

> You must produce and express what has ripened in your soul, for it is something no one but you will ever express . . .
>
> Yes! As you know, what matters is not that Nikoláy Nikoláevich [Gay] should be praised, but to feel that you are saying something

new and important and something people need. And when one feels that and works for that – as you, I hope, are now working – it is the greatest happiness on earth. One is even ashamed of the privilege.

This view of the duty of expressing in art-forms the feeling that has ripened in one's soul, was evidently not in line with the disregard expressed in some passages of *What Then Must We Do?* for anything not of strictly utilitarian necessity, and one is therefore not surprised to find him at work on the essay that ultimately grew into *What is Art?* It had in fact already simmered in his mind for some years. But the difficulty of stating the relation in which art stands to the rest of life, was such that nearly ten years more passed before he elucidated it to his satisfaction.

That spring, after walking from Moscow to Yásnaya, he wrote to Gay on 24th April:

I have been staying for three weeks with Urúsov . . . There, in solitude, I got a little writing done. Here I have again dried up. I have among other things begun an article on Art, but cannot finish it. But that is not what I must write. And I *must* write. There is something I see, that no one else sees. So at least it appears to me. And before I die I must manage to make others see it. It is the same with you. And to live an honest and clean life, that is to say, not at other people's cost, will not hinder this but the one effort will help the other.

It was all very well for Tolstoy to repeat that assurance to himself and to others, but he was already over sixty, and his actual experience as he grew older was, that when greatly absorbed in literary work, he was not able to do much physical work. Intermittently he did a good deal of field-labour, being particularly well situated at Yásnaya for working either in his study in solitude, or manually in company with the peasants, whose primitive methods of agriculture and building, entailing great expenditure of strength and skill, afforded excellent opportunities for the participation of one like himself – strong, active, dexterous, and fond of physical exertion.

On 24th June he again wrote to Gay:

I am living well, working a little, ploughing and preparing to mow, and I am writing a good deal or rather preparing to write: that is to say, writing and blotting out. I am writing a comedy, and a story, and an essay on Art. It is for the most part well with my soul. Indeed it would be a sin were it not so. Seldom a day passes without joyful proofs that the fire Christ brought to earth is kindling more and more . . .

It was now that Tolstoy commenced *The Kreutzer Sonata*, a story destined to bring upon him a storm of abuse and to evoke more controversy than any of his other writings, but one which at the same time caused those who knew a masterly piece of work when they saw it, to say, 'his train has at last come out of its tunnel'. He had indeed returned to Art – the art, however, of social and moral experiment.

Before speaking of that extraordinary book, which will be dealt with in the next chapter, the subject of Non-Resistance claims our attention.

What is the Tolstoyan doctrine of Non-Resistance?

He originally arrived at it, as we have seen, from the study of the Sermon on the Mount, and especially from verses 38–41 of the fifth chapter of St Matthew's Gospel: 'Ye have heard that it was said, An eye for an eye, and a tooth for a tooth; but I say unto you, Resist not him that is evil: but whosoever smiteth thee on thy right cheek, turn to him the other also. And if any man would go to law with thee, and take away thy coat, let him have thy cloke also.'

In the ultimate form to which Tolstoy developed it, the doctrine of Non-Resistance means that *no physical force must be used to compel any man* to do what he does not want to do, or to make him desist from doing what he likes. This involves disapproval of all central or local Governments that employ a policeman, as well as of all criminal or civil legal proceedings, and all collection of rates or taxes not purely voluntary, as well as of the defence of life or property by physical force. This disapproval applies even when one acts as trustee for others. One must not use, or cause others to use, physical force to prevent a man from committing forgeries, even though they may involve a whole community in confusion and misery. In fact the principle presupposes a society quite differently organised to any that we know; and I believe it never worked even moderately well, except in situations such as Tolstoy's own, where life continued to flow along its accustomed lines because there were people at hand willing to take on themselves the sin of Resistance.

It should be borne in mind that the view Tolstoy held, though never before stated in quite the same way or pushed to quite such sweeping conclusions, is a very ancient one and has been held by many sects in many lands.

In fact, in any society in which efforts towards social improvement are suppressed by brute force it is natural for reformers to voice their detestation of violence by the proclamation of Non-Resistant principles. Physical force is so often the instrument of oppression that there is a natural inclination to identify the one with the other.

At any rate, whether it be reasonable or not, when men who are morally in advance of their generation feel called on to denounce existing wrongs supported by custom and by the laws and Constitution of their country, they are very apt not merely to announce that their warfare is not waged with carnal weapons and that they mean neither to kill nor injure anyone, but also to lay it down as a rule, that good men rely exclusively on appeals to reason and conscience, whereas bad men rely on appeals to physical force, and that one may judge the goodness of a cause by the means employed to forward it.

They are apt to say that to use physical force proves one to be in the wrong, while to rely on mental and moral force shows that one is in the right. A typical instance was that of William Lloyd Garrison, who took up very nearly that position when he attacked Slavery in America. In Tolstoy's case, as in other similar ones, it is impossible to overlook the fact that this position, which he held quite sincerely and instinctively, suited his purpose admirably. He proclaimed to the world that his was a moral and religious cause, and he denounced the use of physical force. He also denounced the established Orthodox Russo-Greek Church as well as the Government that supported it, and especially the whole system of military service – that colossal example of the subordination of reason and conscience to physical force.

The Government and the Church were in no condition to argue with him. Their sins were too glaring, and much, if not all, in his argument was unanswerable. But suppose that without answering him they had suppressed him – exiled or imprisoned him – what point that would have given to his contention! The use of Cossacks or gendarmes against him would have appeared a palpable proof of the justice of his argument, besides making everybody eager to read the books that caused him to suffer.

In some details the Non-Resistance of Garrison differed from that of Tolstoy, and both their theories differed somewhat from that of the Revd Adin Ballou; but the fact remains that similar circumstances caused each of these able and sincere men to adopt similar opinions, and that they had behind them, apparently the teaching of Jesus and certainly the belief of large religious communities existing in various countries and ages.

When writing *What I Believe* – in which Tolstoy formulated his belief in Non-Resistance – he knew that the beliefs he had arrived at had been to some extent expressed by Origen, Tertullian, and other Fathers of the Church, besides being held, more or less, by such sects as the Mennonites, Herrnhuters, and Quakers, who refuse to take part in war. But after the publication of that book he was delighted to learn from correspondents in America and Bohemia and elsewhere, that other people had expressed, and were still expressing, similar beliefs. The works of the Revd Adin Ballou were sent him by a correspondent, to whom Tolstoy replied, referring enthusiastically to Ballou as: 'one of the chief benefactors of humanity'. Of Ballou's writings he said: 'In those tracts I found all the objections that are generally made against Non-Resistance victoriously answered, and I found also the true basis of the doctrine . . .' Yet even Ballou did not go far enough to satisfy Tolstoy.

In the first edition of this book I quoted their correspondence at considerable length. Here I must confine myself to the last letter Tolstoy wrote to Ballou on 26th March 1890.

DEAR FRIEND AND BROTHER – I will not argue with your objections. It would lead to nothing. Only one point, that I did not put clearly enough in my last letter, I might explain to avoid misunderstandings. It is about compromise. I said that compromise, inevitable in practice, cannot be admitted in theory. What I mean is this:

. . . The great sin is to compromise in *theory* – to lower the ideal of Christ [in order] to make it attainable. And I consider the admission of force (be it even benevolent) over a madman (the great difficulty is, to give a strict definition of a madman) to be such a theoretical compromise. In not admitting this compromise I run the risk only of my death, or the death of other men who may be killed by the madman; and death in fulfilling the will of God is a blessing (as you put it yourself in your book); but if I admit the compromise I run the risk of acting quite contrary to the law of Christ – which is worse than death . . . With deep veneration and tender love, I remain your friend and brother,

LEO TOLSTOY

It is interesting to note that Ballou, whom Tolstoy calls 'a champion of Non-Resistance who devoted fifty years of life to its propaganda by word and print', does not understand Christ's injunction as Tolstoy understands it, and this brings us back to the question: Are we primarily concerned to decide what Jesus taught on the subject, or to decide what is right and wrong about it, independently of what Jesus or anyone else may have said, or have been reported to say?

If it be the former question, it cannot here be adequately discussed, for, apart from the question whether we are bound to accept his decisions, we should have: (1) to face the question of the reliability and completeness of the reports of Christ's teaching that have come down to us; (2) to settle whether it is possible to decide exactly what he did teach; and (3) to ascertain whether he had in mind the same political and social problems as face us.

I prefer to deal with the simpler problem: What is true about the use of physical force? and to leave to others the more complex problem of what Christ taught about it. But I may make just this remark: Assuming the record of Christ's teaching to be correct and sufficiently complete, I am forced to the conclusion that he did *not* mean what Tolstoy thought he meant; for among the illustrations of the doctrine, immediately after those of turning the other cheek and not going to law (on which Tolstoy relies) come the words: 'And whosoever shall compel thee to go one mile, go with him twain.' Now no one who knew how to use language, as the writer of the Sermon on the Mount unquestionably did, and who wished specially to emphasise the duty of not using *physical force* even in extreme cases, could have been so inept as to introduce an illustration which has nothing to do with the case, and which diverts attention from the question of physical force to the question of goodwill and kindliness. As far as the Gospel record is concerned, that to my mind is conclusive. But it leaves the larger question untouched, and Tolstoy may have discovered a truth not enunciated in the Gospels. Has he done so?

He thinks we should never use physical force to restrain our fellow man. (He sometimes incidentally remarked that this should apply to animals also.) Ballou, as his books show, thinks you must never use 'injurious force' to your fellow men; and by 'injurious force' he means:

Any moral influence or physical force exerted by one human being upon another, the legitimate effect of which is to destroy or impair life, to destroy, or impair, the physical faculties, to destroy, impair, or pervert the moral and religious sentiments, or to destroy and impair the absolute welfare, all things considered, of the person on whom such influence or force is exerted; whether that person be innocent or guilty, harmless or offensive, injurious or uninjurious, sane or insane, adult or infant.

In a vigorous passage he explains that:

It is not man's imaginations, thoughts and feelings, that determine what is or is not injurious to him. Love itself may 'heap coals of fire on a man's head'. Truth may torment his mind. The most benevolent restraint may be painful to his feelings . . . Such people often prefer an *injury* to a benefit . . . Their wills, feelings, and opinions are not the indices of their own *good*, much less that of others.

Is it good for a wicked man, under specious hypocritical disguises, to perpetrate the most atrocious mischief, unexposed and unreproved? These things are not good for mankind. On the contrary, it is good for them to be crossed, restrained, and reproved, by all uninjurious moral and physical forces, which benevolence prompts and wisdom dictates.

. . . Cannot unreasonable children be nursed, delirious adults controlled . . . hypocrites exposed, and sinners reproved without inflicting injury on them! Then can nothing good be done without doing evil. Imperfection is indeed incidental to all human judgement and conduct; and therefore . . . some mistakes and some accidental injuries might happen. But the reason and common sense of mankind, once fairly pledged to the true principle of action, would seldom fail to discharge these duties to general satisfaction.

Tolstoy's view has one great advantage over Ballou's (as well as over the view I myself hold) for if he be right, we have a perfectly clear, rigid, and, so to say, *mechanical* test of right and wrong. You need not go into motives – which are always complex and baffling – nor need you ask who has forged, or slain, or stolen; the mere, bare fact that one man is holding another, or employing the law to hold him, shows at once that the man who holds is a wrongdoer and that the man who is held is a victim of anti-Christian violence.

If it were so, life would no doubt be much simpler and we should escape the hesitation and regret that often accompany the question: 'Did I judge So-and-so's motives rightly?' But alas! life and human conduct are complex matters, and to reduce them to conformity with external tests is impossible.

Tolstoy's statement of the case has the advantage of being much the most far-reaching and much the simplest and most easily applied. It has only two disadvantages: first, that it throws all human affairs into confusion, and secondly, that it is not true.

Adin Ballou has thought the question out much better and carries us part of the way to the real solution, which is admirably suggested by a memorable passage in Ruskin's *Munera Pulveris*:

> We must understand the real meaning of the word, 'injury'.
>
> We commonly understand by it any kind of harm done by one man to another; but we do not define the idea of harm: sometimes we limit it to the harm which the sufferer is conscious of; whereas much the worst injuries are those he is *un*conscious of; and, at other times, we limit the idea to violence, or restraint; whereas much the worst forms of injury are to be accomplished by indolence, and the withdrawal of restraint.
>
> 'Injury' is then simply the refusal, or violation, of any man's right or claim upon his fellows; which claim is mainly resolvable into two branches: a man's claim not to be hindered from doing what he should; and his claim to be hindered from doing what he should not . . .
>
> Now, in order to a man's obtaining these two rights, it is clearly needful that the worth of him should be approximately known, as well as the *want* of worth, which has, unhappily, been usually the principal subject of study for critic law . . .

But we still have not got quite to the heart of the matter. The true doctrine of Non-Resistance I take to be this – and I ask my readers to weigh it as a matter of first-rate importance:

The old law of 'an eye for an eye', and the desire to give a man two black eyes for being blind, is not merely wrong but also stupid. By desiring to injure others we unquestionably and inevitably injure ourselves. We should obliterate from our minds *all* feeling of revenge, and should not wish to injure anyone, not even a homicidal maniac. If we can cure him and make a good citizen of him, so much the better; but there may be cases (a diminishing number, I hope) in which it may be necessary regretfully to kill him, not 'because he deserves it', nor because we wish to hurt him, but in order, for instance, to prevent his steering a ship on to the rocks and causing all the passengers and crew to perish as well as himself. Our business is, as far as we can, to promote harmony, goodwill, and good order among all men. In doing that we need all, our faculties: moral, mental, and physical; and I know of no *external* rule of conduct that can safely be applied to relieve us of the difficulty of using our judgement – even in complex and difficult cases about which we are far from feeling quite sure that our judgement is right.

That principle is clear and always applicable, and the more fully and immediately it is applied the better for us all. We want to get things right in the world, and the true contrast is not between injuring our fellows or renouncing the use of physical force: it is between wishing to injure and wishing to aid.

Tolstoy's test applies to the action; my test applies to the motive. He has argued the matter at such length and in so many books, that it would more than fill this volume to answer him point by point; but I think that any reasonable man who once grasps the principle can find for himself the reply to each and all of Tolstoy's special arguments. I will therefore here deal only with two, on which he lays great stress, and which he often repeats.

He says that if you strike a man to prevent his committing an outrage, you know you do evil by striking him, but you cannot know that he would have actually committed the outrage. Perhaps at the last instant he might have died or repented. Granted! But that only implies that our judgement is fallible. Is that a reason for not using it? If we are not to use it, what was it given us for? When a man sows corn, he does not know that it will grow. Sometimes it doesn't; and it is clearly an evil to waste time and seed on sowing corn that perishes. But men sow corn because they think (and on the whole think rightly) that it will probably come up; and a man knocks down a drunken man who is kicking a child, and whom he cannot otherwise restrain, because it seems to him probable that if the man goes on kicking the child with his thick boots, the child will get hurt. Perhaps the child would not; but the intervener's error is, at worst, an error of judgement and not of morals. It is never wrong for a man *to do the best he can* under the circumstances in which he finds himself and to use the faculties he possesses.

Another of Tolstoy's arguments is that we must assert that physical force should never be used, even in cases in which a man feels that he *ought* to use it, for if we once admit any exception to the rule it will break to pieces and all sorts of violence will go on being practised in the world.

It is sad that a thinker and moralist of Tolstoy's calibre should come down like this to the level of the expediencies, evasions, and pusil-lanimities of the most ordinary pulpit. Obviously the real question is: Is it true? And not, What will happen if we admit it? And obviously, to persist in overstating a case so that an ordinary man's common sense revolts against it, does not, and will not, act as a restraining influence on those inclined to violence. They will simply continue to do what they do now: reject the whole doctrine, including the parts that are true.

The fact of the matter is that Tolstoy was not really Non-Resistant in the profoundest sense of the term. He tried to obtain a spiritual result by insisting on a negative rule and an external test. His endeavour to assist the Deity in making smooth the rough places of the earth, was sound and sincere, but in his strenuous eagerness he did not leave a fair share of the work to his partner.

Again, with reference to the enforcement of law, it is quite a fallacy – at least as far as Constitutional countries are concerned – to speak as though the law were usually enforced by the police on an unwilling population for the benefit of the wealthy and governing classes. As a matter of fact, the police, in England for instance, are not numerous enough to maintain any sort of order were it not that they have on their side the great bulk of the population, and that, at any moment, a large force of special constables would, if necessary, volunteer to support the law.

It is because men are accustomed to the benefits of law and feel sure that it will not break down, that they are able to devote so much attention to pointing out the flaws – often admittedly very gross and shameful flaws – there are in it.

I have dealt with this subject so fully because, in his later years, Tolstoy devoted a great deal of space to it, and the published replies to him have for the most part been very inadequate, and frequently err by attempting to justify the use of vindictive violence.

I am convinced that Tolstoy's mis-statement of the theory of Non-Resistance has served, more than anything else, to conceal from man-kind his greatness as a thinker, and I always regret that people should devote special attention to that side of his teaching. It is excusable and perhaps inevitable that a strenuous man opposing great evils, should lose his balance on some points and fall into errors that are obvious to Tom, Dick, and Harry. But though Tolstoy constantly contrasts the Law of Love with the Law of Force, disapproving of the latter *in toto*, and including in his disapproval the policeman who regulates the traffic and removes the drunken sailor obstructing it, we need not let this permanently divert our attention from the many profound things he has said with admirable force and lucidity.

The most important parts of a man's work are generally the things about which he is right, and we should use our prophets as we use our mines, seeking and valuing the veins of rich ore and wasting as little time as possible on the worthless matter we encounter in our search.

Tolstoy's writings in 1889 included the Preface to some *Recollections of Sevastopol* written by Ershóv and already alluded to. This was not an article the Censor would pass, and therefore it could not be used for its original purpose and for long remained unpublished, but it is one that all should read who wish to understand how Tolstoy's abhorrence of war grew out of his own experience. It throbs with the pulse of reality. One feels that when writing it Tolstoy, as he says, 'experienced afresh what we lived through thirty-four years ago'.

Contrary to their practice since 1882, the family did not move to Moscow for the winter of 1889 or for some years subsequently.

During the latter part of the year Tolstoy was at work on *The Kreutzer Sonata*, and on his comedy, *The Fruits of Enlightenment*.

It was arranged that the play should be performed at Yásnaya during the New-Year holidays.

Accounts written by some of the performers give us glimpses of what life was like at that holiday gathering. The five elder Tolstoy children were then from twenty-six to eighteen years old.

One of the actors was A. V. Zínger, a lad of nineteen, who was visiting Yásnaya for the first time. He tells us:

> On my arrival I found myself at a large tea-table, at which all the Tolstoy family were assembled, with relations and visitors who had come there for the holidays.
>
> Among strangers, many of them grown-up young ladies, I had a painful feeling of bashfulness, from which I was skilfully saved by the simple, merry conversation of Tatiána Lvóvna, who played the part of chief hostess among the group of young people . . . She also directed the arrangement of the costumes, accessories, scenery, &c.

Tolstoy when a young man had known Zínger's father, a Moscow Professor of Mathematics, a study followed by A. V. Zínger also. At the breakfast-table next morning,

Tolstoy entered, gay and kindly, and joined us, speaking first to one and then to another of the large company, chiefly women . . . Addressing me, he turned the talk to mathematics, saying: 'I think I should have made a very good teacher of mathematics – just because I am very fond of the subject, but have great difficulty in understanding anything in it clearly. To understand, I have to think it over this way and that, and what I have once understood I can explain to anyone, because I can foresee all the difficulties . . .'

'Aye, aye, aye!' . . . said he, when I took a cigarette and lit it, 'that's not the thing! Why do you do that?'

Abashed, I tried to justify myself on the score that smoking assists concentration and clearness of thought.

'No, no! It's just the other way!' said Leo Nikoláevich. 'I know it so well! The reason one seems to think more easily when one smokes, is just because one's critical faculties get befogged . . . And if you add a glass of vodka to it . . . then it's quite bad.'

After the morning coffee Leo Nikoláevich would go to his study, taking with him the manuscript of the play, which he altered and added to every day right up to the performance . . . Work on the preparations hummed from morning to night for a whole week. One of the rehearsals was at N. V. Davydov's in Túla and the Yásnaya half of the troupe drove there in a whole caravanserai of sledges . . .

On other days, by way of recreation, an animated crowd of young people slide down the hills on small hand-sledges and skate on the pond. Returning to the house, I find a stove being put up on the stage for the second Act. In one corner of the large room the curtains and hangings are being sewn, in another the freshly altered manuscript is being compared with the separate parts. Laughter constantly breaks out: the new additions seem particularly humorous . . .

The day of the performance draws near, but there is still no end of work to be done. We sit up till late at night. In the middle of the night we ask to have a samovar heated to make tea, and arrange to go sledging by moonlight, to refresh ourselves.

'Do whatever you like,' says Tatiána Lvóvna, 'only don't disturb the servants, or, if he hears of it, Papa will be displeased.' . . .

For the last rehearsal but one, V. M. Lopátin, whom we had awaited for the role of Third Peasant, came to Yásnaya. His poses, gesticulations, and speech were admirable. After his inimitable way of saying, 'We've so little land . . . we've no room, let's say, to keep even a hen,' the rehearsal was interrupted by peals of laughter, and Leo Nikoláevich was in raptures.

The part of Tánya was well acted by her namesake, Tatiána Lvóvna, and Mary Lvóvna was admirable as the cook.

Two days before the performance, a reading of the newly finished manuscript of *The Kreutzer Sonata* is arranged.

There is such a turmoil in the whole house on account of the play that it is difficult to find a convenient corner for the reading: so the Countess Sófya Andréevna allows us to use her bedroom.

Some fifteen of us assembled in the small room and Leo Nikoláevich himself joins us.

M. A. Stakhóvich settles at a small table with two candles, and reads the introductory chapter with animation, but when he reaches the plot he is taken aback, in the presence of young ladies, by the realism of the language. He stops.

'Countess, I cannot read it without omissions . . .' says he.

'I expected that,' replies she. 'The girls have no business to be here.'

'Read on, read on!' says Leo Nikoláevich, who is listening attentively, 'but it will really be better to let the girls go away.'

The young ladies depart, and the reading continues.

Leo Nikoláevich takes Stakhóvich's place and himself reads the passages where he has scribbled in many fresh insertions difficult to read . . .

After this reading was finished we sit at the tea-table agitated and dazed. Detached comments on the impression received are uttered, disputes flare up. Leo Nikoláevich enters.

'Ah, how glad I should be,' says he, 'if you would speak about *The Kreutzer Sonata* as though I were not here.'

But this does not come off. After a while someone, mustering courage, remarks: 'The impression is too overpowering. Could you not have given us something positive?'

'Oh yes!' said Leo Nikoláevich. 'Tell you how well they lived, how they had children and grandchildren and how they died in the arms of their great-grandchildren? Give you a German fairy-tale like the thousands that have been written without teaching anybody anything?

'In a work of art,' added Leo Nikoláevich, 'it is indispensable that the artist should give something new, something of his own. It is not how it is written that really matters. People will read *The Kreutzer Sonata* and say, "Ah, that is the way to write . . . 'They were travelling by train and conversed . . .'" The indispensable thing is to go beyond what others have done, to pick off something fresh, however small . . . But it won't do to be like my friend Fet, who at sixteen wrote: "The spring bubbles, the moon shines, and she loves me"; and went on writing and writing, till at sixty he wrote: "She loves me, and the spring bubbles, and the moon shines!" '

V. M. Lopátin, who took the role of Third Peasant, was a Justice of the Peace, He has narrated how, after a rehearsal in Túla, he drove with a large sledge party to Yásnaya. He says:

We galloped merrily along the smooth high-road, past the picturesque woods of Kozlóvka-Záseka which rose on both sides of the way, and late at night, tired by the drive and the keen frosty air, we were glad to enter the comfortable and hospitably lighted house at Yásnaya Polyána.

We were heartily welcomed by our hosts. A well-spread supper-table awaited us. But intoxicants were conspicuously absent, their place being ostentatiously taken by decanters of *kvas*. We, frozen travellers, experienced a feeling akin to disillusionment; but the foresight of one of our party had secured in Túla a supply of what was not allowed at Yásnaya, and we escaped cautiously, in turn, to the entrance-hall, and there in a corner under the stairs (stifling our confusion and the gnawings of conscience) we warmed ourselves with drams of vodka.

Lopátin's practice had brought him into frequent contact with just such peasants as those in the play, and he was able to throw himself heartily into his role. At the rehearsal, he says:

I felt I was succeeding, and soon heard Leo Nikoláevich's laugh – a quite Russian, peasant laugh, full of good-natured sincerity – followed by words of approval . . . My acting evidently produced an impression exceeding my expectations. He was satisfied with it, and his satisfaction expressed itself in such almost childlike glee as quite abashed me.

He laughed to tears, imparted his reflections to those about him with animation, slapped his sides, and appreciatively wagged his head, peasant-fashion.

This delight in anything really artistic – any true transmission of feeling – was quite characteristic of Tolstoy.

So pleased was he with Lopátin's performance, that he made several alterations in the play, giving the Third Peasant more to say.

At tea that evening, speaking about dramatic art, Leo Nikoláevich thus defined the meaning and importance of artistic creation:

The peculiarity of an artist's power of observation consists in his capacity to see in what goes on around him, those traits which escape other people's notice. He sees what others see, but does not see it as they do; and then by reproducing in his work just those traits which others have not noticed, he obliges them to see things as he himself sees and understands them.

Therefore in every work of art we find something new to us, and learn from it. 'Now you, for instance,' said Leo Nikoláevich, 'in representing the peasant, reproduce a figure such as each of us has seen in real life, but you have succeeded in noting and conveying something we had not observed and in your presentation I myself see something new to me.'

Tolstoy treated everyone he spoke to as his equal. He argued hotly and strenuously, but it was easy to see how pure and sincere was the joy that gleamed in his eyes when his hearer sympathised with him, or when he saw that his thought was understood . . . I brought away the conviction that every word of Tolstoy's flows from the depth of his soul, and that his theories are the result not only of immense mental work but also of the keenest spiritual sufferings such as immeasurable breadth of imagination can bring to a man.

It seems to me that in Tolstoy's soul a tragedy is being enacted: that his merciless self-analysis prevents him from reaching satisfaction, that he does not find within himself all that he considers necessary for human life and demands from others, that he struggles with himself and that this duality occasions his sufferings.

When at last, on 30th December, the performance was given to an audience as large as the big salon would hold, the play was a triumphant success.

Tolstoy's intention in it is by no means purely comic. It contains two effectively presented ideas, dear to him. His whole work concerning religion had been an attempt to show that essentially it has nothing to do with the supernatural or miraculous and is quite independent of anything of that kind; and the attack on spiritualism presented by the play is in accord with his deliberate and carefully formed opinion. The Professor's speech in Act III starts by confusing the distinction between matter and spirit. Nothing but perplexity can result, Tolstoy maintains, from talking about spiritualism so long as we do not know what we mean by *spirit*, and how to distinguish it from *matter*. 'We who live after Kant cannot get away from the distinction he indicated.' Matter is that which we can know through our five senses, and to that domain belong astral bodies and ghosts, if they can be perceived or investigated by our eyes, ears, or sense of touch; but spirit belongs to quite a different world. The moral law within belongs to the spirit-world, and is distinguishable from *matter* by the fact that it *cannot* be investigated by means of our five senses. So all the usual talk about spiritualism starts with a misuse of terms. If the spiritualists know what they mean by matter and spirit, they should explain themselves, for to ask us to investigate *material* phenomena and pretend they are *spiritual*, is unreasonable. Tolstoy's contention is that this fundamental confusion cannot be cured by any amount of 'investigation', however extraordinary the occurrences perceived may be. The revelations must stand on their own bottom: a message does not become 'spiritual' by being delivered from a pulpit, or carved in stone, or by coming to us when we are in an abnormal physical condition, or by being uttered by somebody 'under control'.

Neither would Tolstoy admit that man's moral and spiritual welfare can be advanced by ocular or aural demonstration that, after seventy years of this life, he is to have (say) seventy thousand years of life elsewhere with a different body. Time and space, like all that pertains to the domain of the five senses, have no part in the spirit-world, the promptings of which are 'very nigh unto' us here and now, but cannot be reached along lines of investigation which depend for their validity on the physical senses.

This treatment of spiritualism might well make the play distasteful to those who hope great things from the careful investigation of psychic phenomena, but here again Tolstoy's artistic instinct saves him. He places the scene amid surroundings in which fraud would naturally play a part, and his characters (except Tánya, who perhaps is rather too much of a French *soubrette* to be quite in the picture) are people who in real life would have been likely to do and say just the things he makes them do and say. Everybody knows that humbug and trickery have been practised in connection with spiritualism. No reasonable spiritualist objects to this being emphasised, and when, in 1909, the students of Birmingham University performed the play, they did so with the hearty approval of that shining light of the Psychical Research Society, their Principal, Sir Oliver Lodge.

The other conviction which the play brings out is Tolstoy's contempt for the empty, useless, and expensive pastimes of the 'cultured' classes, as compared with the serious interests of the agricultural peasantry; and this again he presents with artistic tact, by contrasting the frivolity of a rather amiable and honourable landowning family with the need for land of peasants whose rustic limitations and crudities he does not at all tone down.

The comedy was publicly performed for the first time by an amateur troupe in Túla, in aid of a Home for Destitute Children. Tolstoy himself went to see a rehearsal, but the door-keeper, who did not know him and supposed him to be a peasant, turned him out. The mistake was, of course, soon explained and remedied. During the rehearsal one of the local aristocrats, who played the part of Gregory the footman, was very politely shoving the peasants out of the front door, when Tolstoy stopped him and said: 'No, that's not natural! You must bundle them out as the door-keeper bundled me out just now!' and he recounted what had occurred.

Long before *The Power of Darkness* was allowed, *The Fruits of Enlightenment* was staged at the Alexándrinski Theatre in Petersburg. It was first produced there in September 1891, the very month when (as will be told later) the Tolstoy family were setting out for the Famine district. The Little Theatre in Moscow produced it at about the same time.

Its production at that crisis, when, beyond the officially admitted 'shortness of crops', a terrible famine was becoming apparent, added poignancy to its satire, and the laughter of the public at the animated futilities of the Zvezdíntsev family had a background of anxiety for the fate of the masses, represented by the three peasants whose presence in her house so annoyed Madame Zvezdíntsev. The inanities of Vovó and Professor Krugosvétlov gave the force of a stinging social indictment to the peasants' exclamations of surprise and disapproval.

In reply to an enquiry from Ptchélnikov, Manager of the Office of the Imperial Moscow Theatres, whether they might hope that he would write other pieces for the Little Theatre, Tolstoy replied:

I would do so with great pleasure, and I even feel a special need to express myself in that way, and at the present time [1892] it would be extremely to the point. But I feel certain the Censor would not pass my plays. You would not believe how from the very commencement of my activity, that horrible Censor question has tormented me! I wanted to write what I felt, but at the same time it occurred to me that what I wrote would not be permitted, and involuntarily I had to abandon the work. I abandoned, and went on abandoning, and meanwhile the years passed away . . .

One could hardly find a clearer instance of the effect an irresponsible Dramatic Censorship has on the work of a great writer.

Since then, *The Fruits of Enlightenment* has been reproduced again and again, not only in Russia but also abroad, though it is still but little known in England or America.

II

The Sex Question

Early in 1890 Semënov, the peasant-writer, met Chertkóv returning with Gay from Yásnaya, where they had been staying. Semënov says:

I asked about Tolstoy, and was told that he was well, vigorous, and working. Chertkóv gave no details. He was evidently upset about something, and only from Gay did I learn that things were not going smoothly. 'Is that the kind of life he needs?' said Gay. 'He is thinking for the whole human race, but no consideration is paid to his spiritual needs at all. Continual bustle, trifles, petty demands, all those guests . . . ugh!'

Chertkóv was taking *The Kreutzer Sonata* to Petersburg. It was already circulating in Moscow in lithographed copies, but this was its final revision. *The Fruits of Enlightenment* was then just being printed.

Chertkóv did not approve of such writings. He did not care for works which lacked a religious tendency. In authorship he demanded religious sermonising, and lest this should become a trade he decided that a writer should take no money for his work. 'To do so is a sin!' said he. 'By writing we serve mankind and lead their souls out of darkness, but if we take money it becomes not a service but something very different!' It is in his opinion immoral – just as it would be for a man when saving another from drowning to demand money for so doing.

These remarks addressed by a wealthy man to a peasant who supported his family with difficulty, and whom the few pounds he got for his stories lifted just above actual want, are very characteristic. I remember that years later when one of his colleagues had occasion to remonstrate with Chertkóv on the harshness of his demands, his reply was: 'In our movement we consider principles, but not people', and it was just that lack of consideration for others which often dried up the fountains Tolstoy's magic caused to gush forth. Tolstoy inspired enthusiasm, and many offered him their help in work or money. All these he passed on to Chertkóv, a man of whose sincerity, ardour, and full acceptance of his principles, he felt assured. But Chertkóv was very unpractical and often unreasonable, and the fate of those whom Tolstoy put at his disposal was a hard one. Ultimately the control of Tolstoy's public affairs passed definitely into Chertkóv's hands, whose many scruples – which bore much more severely on others than on himself – were the main reasons why friction was engendered and comparatively little was accomplished.

Those who would understand the psychology of the Tolstoy movement should ponder Fénelon's remark: '*Rien n'est si contraire á la simplicité que le scrupule. Il cache je ne sais quoi de double et de faux; on croit n'être en peine que par délicatesse d'amour pour Dieu; mais dans le fond on est inquiet pour soi, et on est jaloux pour sa propre perfection, par un attachement natural à soi . . .*'*

The sex question dealt with in *The Kreutzer Sonata* is one Tolstoy always regarded as most important and agitating.

At first the book was forbidden, but lithographed copies circulated widely. I still possess one of them, and the sight of it recalls the thrill of excitement the acquisition of a new, prohibited work by Tolstoy used to evoke. There was in Russia no political liberty, no liberty of conscience, no freedom of the press, and no right of public meeting (even private meetings were liable to be interrupted by the police at any moment), but the intelligentsia were all tacitly united in maintaining freedom of thought and conversation (which the Government would also have suppressed had it been possible to do so), and this tacit conspiracy kept the soul of society alive. It is difficult to convey to those accustomed to buy what books they please, and to read them when and where they please, the interest and excitement then produced in Russia by the appearance of each new prohibited book dealing with a vital subject. Gatherings assembled in private houses to hear the forbidden work read aloud – perhaps from the only available copy – and to discuss it, and books so read and discussed had an immense influence.

The interest excited by *The Kreutzer Sonata* was as vivid as that

---

* Nothing is so opposed to simplicity as scrupulosity. Scrupulosity hides a certain duplicity and falseness. We believe that all our anxieties are caused by refined love of God; but at bottom we are troubled about ourselves, and concerned about our own perfection, because of our natural love of self.

aroused by any of Tolstoy's works, though its views met with scant approval.

It is a story told in a railway carriage. Pozdnishév, who has killed his wife, and says of himself, 'You know I am a sort of lunatic', and 'Charcot would certainly have said that I was abnormal', narrates how he came to commit the crime, and maintains that the words of Christ: 'Everyone that looketh on a woman to lust after her hath committed adultery with her already in his heart', apply to all women – especially to one's own wife, and that absolute purity of thought is the only safe and right thing. Sex should be eliminated from human life as far as possible.

Tolstoy's craftsmanship did not fail him. By selecting Pozdnishév – who is nervous and excitable to the verge of insanity – to express his thought, he was able to express it emphatically yet with absolute fidelity to life.

There is something almost uncanny in the way Tolstoy the thinker with a bias for exaggeration exploits his *alter ego*, the artist with so marvellous a sense of balance.

Man, he says, is to blame for regarding woman as an object to gratify his lust. To serve that purpose she is educated and taught to despise old maids, and to look down on those who have chosen the path of purity. To that end her accomplishments are directed, and for that she is dressed up and exhibited: 'It is the same in the street where the brothels are and at the Court balls! . . . '

To Pozdnishév and to Tolstoy the use of preventatives is repugnant:

'She [his wife] was unwell, and the doctors forbade her to have children and taught her how to refrain. To me that was detestable. I struggled against it, but she with light-hearted obstinacy insisted on having her way and I submitted. The last justification of our swinish life – children – was removed, and life become still nastier.'

Tolstoy explains that in the natural course of things the sex-appetite exhausts itself: on the woman's side owing to the strain of child-bearing and nursing and family cares, and on the man's side owing to the burden of supporting the family. Where preventatives are used the normal burdens of matrimony are evaded, the appetites are kept alive, sooner or later either the husband or wife is attracted by someone else and the evil results become manifest.

Whatever truth there may be in that contention, Tolstoy does not seem to have fairly weighed the fearful evils that result from bringing unwanted children into the world, or from overtaxing a wife's strength, or, on the other hand, the detrimental effects on the nervous system of husband or wife and on their mutual relations, of repression resulting from the belief that marital relations are disgusting. In actual life the choice usually is not between using preventatives or practising continence, but between preventatives and an excessive birth-rate. Even when men set themselves to practise continence, as in a monastery, it often happens that they become more obsessed by sex-desire than they would be were they married.

Tolstoy received many letters of enquiry about the meaning of the story, for extremes meet and some people wanted to read into it an advocacy of 'free love'. Shocked at such an interpretation, Tolstoy wrote an *Afterword* to explain his meaning. Since all who wish to understand Tolstoy should read that essay, I will here quote only a few passages showing that what he commended was not free love, but complete and absolute chastity:

> In our society young people devote the best part of their lives – the men to spying out, pursuing, and obtaining (whether in marriage or free union) those best suited to attract them, and the women and girls to enticing and entrapping men into free unions or marriages.
>
> In this way the best powers of many people run to waste in an activity not merely unproductive but injurious. We should understand that no aim we esteem worthy of a man – whether it be the service of humanity, fatherland, science, or art (not to speak of the service of God) – can be attained by means of connection with the object of one's love (either with or without a marriage rite). On the contrary, falling in love and connection – however men may seek to prove the contrary in prose and verse – never facilitate, but always impede, the attainment of any worthy aim . . .
>
> The Christian ideal is that of love of God and one's fellow man . . . whereas sexual love, marriage, is a service of self, and consequently in any case an obstacle to the service of God and man, and therefore from a Christian point of view a fall, a sin . . .

In the *Afterword* Tolstoy sets forward ideals that are admittedly unattainable, for men to strive towards.

The weakness of his position lies in the fact that he selected 'ideals' such as absolute poverty and complete chastity, and when people question their validity and say that such teaching runs counter not merely to the faults of humanity but to humanity itself – to those fundamental things which make man man – Tolstoy, in effect, replies: It is true that people do not and will not act so, but they ought to strive towards it and not consent to lower the ideal!

But this reply begs the question whether the things selected are true ideals – whether it may not be right that a man should have some property – say, the pen he writes with or the book he wishes to finish writing? – and whether it may not be better that a man's qualities and energies should be drawn out by his natural affection for a woman, rather than that he should spend his force on struggling for self-repression?

We know that only a few years before this, in *What I Believe*, he had written:

> I now understand the words of Christ, who said that from the beginning God created them – male and female – and that the twain should become one flesh, and that, therefore, man should not and must not put asunder what God has joined.
>
> I now understand that monogamy is the natural law of humanity which must not be infringed . . . I cannot approve of a celibate life for those who are ripe for marriage. I cannot help to separate husband and wife. I cannot make a distinction between unions called marriages and unions not so named, nor can I fail to consider a union a man has once entered into as being holy and obligatory.

So that the union which was 'holy and obligatory' in 1883 had now in 1890 become 'a fall, a sin'. It is quite right that a man's mind should grow and change, and we should be grateful to a writer who is frank enough to tell us that he no longer holds his former views; yet we have to ask ourselves whether it is certain that one whose opinion yesterday and the day before yesterday was erroneous or incomplete, is altogether infallible today.

The great motive forces in life are love and hunger. Hunger is the more important, for it may cause us to die and consequently cease to love. But sex-attraction is the next most pervasive influence. It is of such importance for good or evil, that many people seem incapable of thinking calmly or reasonably about it, and strongly resent the expression of any view on it that they do not agree with.

It was so at any rate in the case of *The Kreutzer Sonata*, which was denounced from the pulpit as well as in books and pamphlets.

Some people assumed the story to be autobiographical – as though Tolstoy had murdered his wife. It was also said that he attributed an immoral influence to Beethoven's Kreutzer Sonata, and people spoke as though everything uttered by Pozdnyshév had been said by Tolstoy in his own person. It is true that, as in nearly all his stories, Tolstoy utilised in *The Kreutzer Sonata* much that he had seen, felt, and thought; but the tale does not correspond to the facts of his own life. His eldest son, Sergéy – a composer and an accomplished pianist – in an article in *Family Views of Tolstoy* tells us that while writing *The Kreutzer Sonata* his father tried to elucidate to himself what feeling the first *Presto* of that sonata expressed: 'He said that the introduction to the first part warns us of the importance of what is to follow; then the indefinite agitation expressed by the first theme and the restrained, tranquillising feeling expressed by the second theme both lead up to the powerful, clear, and even coarse melody of the concluding part.' Tolstoy rejected the idea that that melody expresses sensuality, for in his opinion music cannot express this or that emotion; it expresses emotion in general, but it is impossible to define what emotion in particular.

Pozdnyshév's presentation of the problem of sex no doubt reflects to a large extent opinions which Tolstoy adopted while writing the book. The *Afterword* shows this, but it is only what is said in the *Afterword* and not all that is uttered by Pozdnyshév that can properly be set down to Tolstoy's account.

In the Bible two contradictory ideals of sexual morality are offered us, neither of which is regarded as reasonable or desirable by the majority of people today. It is important that the reasonableness of any ideal which people are asked to aim at, or any code they are called on to conform to, should be as apparent as are, for instance, the reasons for not stealing or not murdering. But the guidance offered on this tremendously important subject is so far from being obviously reasonable that, afraid of having their minds upset, people instinctively turn and rend those who treat the subject seriously or propound any view that clashes with the hearer's own opinion or prejudice.

Genesis presents an ideal well suited to serve as the morality of a small tribe in a sparsely populated primitive world. Walter Bagehot long ago pointed out that we are descended from ancestors whose tribes were in constant danger of being wiped out by foes, wild beasts, and all sorts of dangers. For them morality consisted in keeping the race alive by producing as many vigorous children as possible. The polygamy of the Jews aimed at that, as did the Mosaic law, with its injunctions to raise up seed to a deceased brother. A man who had many sons was respected and admired: 'Happy is the man that hath his quiver full of them: they shall not be ashamed when they speak with their enemies in the gate.' With twenty strapping lads behind him – or, like a certain Shah of Persia, with a whole regiment of his own sons – he could indeed 'speak like a father' to anyone he met. To such a people the validity of the precept: 'Be fruitful and multiply, and replenish the earth' would be quite comprehensible, whereas we may convince ourselves that now an unchecked increase of population might, within a strictly limited period, inflict greater misery than that caused by the worst war the world has ever endured. Mussolini appears to consider the Old Testament morality applicable to Italy today, but with the population of England and Wales increasing every five years by as large a number as was probably added to it in the whole two hundred and forty-eight years from the Battle of Hastings to the Battle of Bannockburn, it seems plain that the pre-Mosaic morality is unsuited to our country.

As Bagehot indicates, the difficulties of excessive desire we suffer from, as well as the great evil of every great town, arises from the fact that we are descended from people who had to develop their procreative capacity to the utmost. From them we have inherited a 'felt want' much in excess of the 'real want', which would suffice to provide an adequate number of children to replace us.

In sharp contrast with that code and with the text that tells us that: 'the Lord God said, It is not good that the man should be alone; I will make him an help meet for him', we have the morality inculcated by St Paul in the texts: 'It is good for a man not to touch a woman . . . I would that all men were even as I myself . . . I say to the unmarried and to widows, It is good for them if they abide even as I. But if they have not continence, let them marry, for it is better to marry than to burn.'

That ideal is also not held in much esteem today, perhaps because after centuries of experience, the celibate priesthoods and monastic orders are not generally considered to have rendered better service to God or man than has been rendered by people who did not abjure marriage.

It is curious that Tolstoy, with all his intellectual power, never went farther on the sex-question than to make powerful presentments, first in *What Then Must We Do?* of the pre-Mosaic morality, and then in *The Kreutzer Sonata* and its *Afterword*, of the Pauline morality.

The very intensity of his feelings on the subject and his sense of its enormous importance, seem to have prevented him from thinking about it with the clarity which distinguishes his treatment of religion and art.

It has been well said that his pre-eminence as a writer is based on the intensity of his feeling. It is this that arrests our attention and makes what he wrote memorable – so that we find people who have not read *War and Peace* for many years discussing Pierre and Natásha, Andrew, Princess Mary, Nicholas Rostóv and Sónya, as though they had known them all their lives. His intensity causes us to remember what he has said, but the same intensity that sometimes enabled him to penetrate to the very heart of the problems he dealt with, caused him at other times to adopt opinions he had not fully considered, and to express unsound views that he modified subsequently.

It is all to the good that he gave us such forcible presentations of the two biblical codes, but he carries us no farther; and the extraordinary thing is that, because he restated in present-day language the case for aiming at the elimination or, as far as possible, the repression of sex feelings and activity, he has been denounced and abused as though that ideal had never been heard of before, and the example of Jesus in this matter had never been held in esteem.

He has so re-presented these biblical codes to us, that those to whom they do not appeal must consider what code can furnish guidance on this matter, for people left without guidance are in danger of coming to grief.

It seems to me that the guiding principle of such a morality should be, that what makes for the health, happiness, and efficiency of the present and future generations is good, and the contrary is bad.

This principle covers the case of a Jesus or a Buddha, who abstains from marriage, or leaves wife and child, to carry salvation to the race, for they do what is natural to them and their complete devotion to a noble cause makes others healthier, happier, and more useful. It covers too the case of a married couple whose relations with one another promote the health, happiness, and efficiency of themselves, their children, and those about them. Nor does it shut out the many who neither have a great mission entirely absorbing their life, nor are fortunate enough to enjoy lifelong union with a spiritually and physically congenial mate.

We are no longer exclusively concerned about the children, important as they are, but also about ourselves, and the importance of companionship in sexual relations cannot therefore be left out of sight, or treated as of no value.

When morality becomes humane it will perhaps no longer decree that those who cannot have all must have nothing, and for a woman who cannot find a husband with whom she cares to live, to have a child of her own may no longer involve social ostracism.

The principle here suggested does not taboo the sex instinct, but subordinates it to the welfare of the race and the individual. Sex should be the servant, not the master of life. When it impedes the work that needs doing, it becomes an evil, but in so far as it nerves men and women to play the game of life bravely and heartily, it is surely a good.

To be of real use the principles applied in this matter must have in view not merely what men and women ought to be, but what they are and what they may become. We know that if men and women make pleasure the main aim of their life, the results are bad, but is the result generally less deplorable when pleasure is quite left out? The application of a general principle to the circumstances of a given people at a given place and time, is of course a very complex matter, but one must discern a guiding principle before one can even begin to consider its applications.

While, however, I do not agree with Tolstoy on this subject, I realise how inevitably he arrived at his views. From the first his progress was in one and the same direction, namely, towards greater and greater self-control. As a bachelor he struggled against his passions. As a married man he was faithful to his wife. And when at last he found his preaching checked by his wife's disagreement, and by the matrimonial bonds that held him to her, he wished to sacrifice his marital relations rather than his ideals.

What position could he have taken up other than the one he adopted? His own experience and his knowledge of the lives of the Herzens, Ogarëvs, Nekrásovs, Panáevs, and others, preventing his regarding the go-as-you-please doctrine of free love as a satisfactory solution; but neither could he, as a Christian-anarchist rejecting Church and State, consider that a ceremony performed by a priest, or an entry in the books of a registrar, can turn wrong into right.

What then was left, except to adopt the principle of perfect purity in thought and deed?

Many people are shocked that by including in one wholesale condemnation the whole range of physical love – whether merely animal or arising in connection with complete harmony of mind and soul – he should wipe out a distinction that to them makes all the difference. By painting in black and white he misses, they say, a truth which must be sought in the middle shades; for since life is a matter of degree and evolution, rigid rules and strict statements always fail, at some part of their range, to fit the facts. How, they ask, could a man of such experience and insight make such a blunder? And they put it down to his being a dreamer carried away by fancies, or, yet more strangely, to some sudden reaction from the life he had lived as a bachelor twenty-seven years previously. But precisely the same kind of black and white view, treating the sex question as one of physical desire *versus* purity of thought, was put to me as a young man (and probably to hundreds of others who consulted him on the question) by Sir Henry Thompson, a leading member of the English medical profession and Tolstoy's contemporary, who was not a dreamer but a matter-of-fact materialist.

Sir Henry told me, when I was eighteen, that I had reached the age of puberty and required regular weekly intercourse with a woman. He added that one could make acquaintances in the streets for that purpose, but that it would be advisable to use a certain preventative to avoid the risk of contracting a contagious disease.

In reply to the exclamation: 'But is not that immoral?' the doctor replied: 'Oh, I thought you consulted me as a doctor about your health! If you want advice about morality, go to a clergyman.'

He did not explain how I was to cut myself in half and walk in two different directions if the clergyman advised differently. But he admitted that some doctors would not agree with him, and added: 'I have given you what I consider the best advice for your health, but there is a second-best course, if you like to adopt it. It is to be perfectly chaste and keep all your desires under strict control. In that case you will have to be very careful where you go, what you read, what plays you see, what pictures and photographs you look at, and whom you consort with. I am not a religious man and do not know where he got it from, but Jesus of Nazareth was perfectly right when he said that, "Everyone that looketh on a woman to lust after her hath committed adultery with her already in his heart." The physical facts are in exact accord with that saying.'

This is just the Tolstoyan view, only turned inside out. It is the reverse of what Pozdnyshév meant in his reply to the lady who exclaimed indignantly:

'But you are speaking of physical love! Don't you admit the existence of love founded on identity of ideals and on spiritual affinity?'

'Spiritual affinity! Identity of ideals!' repeated he. 'But in that case (excuse my rudeness) why do they go to bed together?'

The advice given by Tolstoy is diametrically opposed to that given by Sir Henry, but the two are at one in their exclusion of the affections as being of any account in the matter. That is where Tolstoy fails as a moralist. In morals, more than in anything else, '*C'est le ton qui fait la musique.*' To treat the natural affections, rooted though they be in our physical nature, as in themselves disgusting and horrid, is very harsh, and harshness is always wrong and always ineffectual.

When we observe real life we find that perfectly chaste people are sometimes very unpleasant, while a tactful prince, or an amiable actress of genius, may be notoriously unchaste and yet receive a good deal of admiration and affection. And I am not sure that the popular judgement in such cases is always and absolutely wrong, for people's services and virtues should be regarded as well as their offences and frailties; and no virtue or vice can be fairly judged except as part of a whole life. But the point I want to make is, that Tolstoy's advice was the only advice he could possibly give. People demand clear guidance on what is really a very complex and intricate problem. It was Tolstoy's nature to go straight for a definite solution. It was his way to simplify, and even to over-simplify. And on this sex question if you are going to give quite clear-cut advice, you can only say 'do' or 'don't'. The doctor said the one, and Tolstoy said the other, and I hold Tolstoy in higher esteem than I do the doctor.

No doubt Tolstoy's own circumstances brought him to the conclusions he arrived at. That is generally the case with us all. His outlook on life had begun to change seriously after fifteen years of marriage and had gone on changing for another twelve. This, as we have seen, produced friction with his wife, and as the pleasures of matrimony meant much to him and so did his new beliefs, he found himself torn between his desire to hold to his views in his wife's despite, and his desire to be her husband. It was difficult to cling to his principles while held in the bonds of matrimony, and to aim at complete chastity was the only solution for a man of his character placed in such circumstances.

The remark frequently made that Tolstoy was inconsistent and insincere because he continued to be a husband after writing *The Kreutzer Sonata* is unjust. For assuming his extremest view to be correct, his position would be parallel to that of a drunkard who had won his way to a state of semi-self-control alternating with periods of inebriety. Would not such a man be justified in testifying to his belief that the use of intoxicants is harmful? And might he not, without being a hypocrite, declare that the police ought not to allow whisky to be seen in public places?

Tolstoy is so interesting just because he honestly tells us what he thinks and feels, regardless of how it reflects on his own conduct. That is a rare and valuable practice which should be recognised and respected. It would be much fairer to say that those who trim their opinions to match their conduct are insincere, for few men are so obtuse as never to let their minds travel nearer to perfection than their bodies can attain.

The eccentricity of Tolstoy's view lies in the corollary-he draws from the admitted fact that there is something charming and beautiful in innocence and purity, and that some of the noblest work in the world has been done by people so devoted to their mission that they had no time or thought for love-making or marriage. The conclusion he draws – namely, that all marital relations and all love tinged by sex are beastly – seems, as I have said, harsh and unsound.

It had a value, however, in enabling him to throw into strong relief the evils of lustfulness, which are truly tremendous.

The publication of *The Kreutzer Sonata* produced a tremendous storm. The Church naturally resented Tolstoy's scornful dismissal of the idea of marriage as a sacrament, while the 'advanced' people, who for a whole generation had been advocating 'free love', were equally furious. From both camps the thunders pealed forth! Archbishop Nikanór of Khersón denounced Tolstoy as a 'wolf in sheep's clothing', and advised his destruction as his teaching was undermining the whole edifice of society. As examples of pure and continent marriage the Archbishop instanced some of the Grand Dukes, whose lives unfortunately were not such as to endure the scrutiny he rashly invited.

The general verdict of Russian society was: 'Tolstoy is getting old. He has lost his vigour and the grapes are sour!' But this suggestion that his doctrine was the outcome of physical debility was wide of the mark. In 1896, when he was nearly seventy, I was speaking to him on these matters. After saying that one should never be discouraged or cease to strive to attain to what is good, he added, 'I was myself a husband last night, but that is no reason for abandoning the struggle; God may grant me not to be so again!' He was physically strong and active for years after that and some of his greatest intellectual achievements still lay before him.

That Tolstoy felt the sting of such comments, one sees by what he wrote of his life as a young man:

It is grievous to me, in my egotism, to have lived my life bestially and to know that now it cannot be retrieved. Grievous, chiefly, because people will say: 'It is all very well for you, a dying old man, to say this, but you did not live so! We too when we are old will say the same.' That is where the chief punishment of sin lies: in feeling that one is an unworthy vessel for the transmission of the will of God – befouled and spoilt.

Many incidents might be quoted showing how greatly Tolstoy's mind was exercised by this question of the relations of the sexes. On one occasion having heard that a young man was engaged to be married, Tolstoy called to him in an agitated voice from the other side of a partition. In reply, the young man was about to come to Tolstoy, but the latter stopped him, saying: 'Remain there, and tell me, if you can – Have you ever known a woman?'

'Not yet,' replied the young man simply, and heard sobs from the other side.

In relation to the sex problem it ought to be said that Tolstoy was lenient with those who misconducted themselves, and that he had little sympathy with Puritan intolerance. He was not one of those who make up for being strict with themselves by being severe on others. I remember, soon after Górki's visit to New York, hearing Tolstoy express indignation as well as amazement at learning that on reaching America, Górki and Madame Andréev (the actress with whom he was travelling) were not allowed to enter the country because they were not married; and when he was over seventy I remember taking a walk with him and a friend of his – a well-known literary man who was still older. The latter was saying that Tolstoy's assertions did not accord with his (the speaker's) own experience of life. He had a mistress and did not consider that it spoilt his life.

'So much the better!' rejoined Tolstoy quietly: 'but what I say is, that a man in such cases has either to seduce a maid, to deceive a husband, or to go with a woman who sells herself.' Many years later, in *The Christian*

Teaching (1897) he again dealt with the sex question and put the matter much more moderately, though still insisting that sexual relations are undesirable. He then said:

> To overcome the habit of this sin a man must first of all refrain from increasing it. If he be chaste, let him not infringe his chastity; if he be married, let him be true to his partner; if he have sexual intercourse with many, let him not invent unnatural forms of vice. Let him refrain from augmenting his sexual sin. If men would do this, many of their sufferings would, come to an end . . .
>
> Although only in rare cases are men able to be altogether chaste, still everyone should understand and remember that he can always be more chaste than he formerly was, or can return to the chastity he has lost, and that the nearer he approaches to perfect chastity according to his powers, the more true welfare will he attain, the more earthly welfare will be added to him, and the more will he contribute to the welfare of mankind.

When the matter is put like that: telling us that the world suffers from excessive lust and the more this is controlled the better for the individual and the race – it is much easier to agree. It is as though a society which habitually over-ate were adjured to eat less. The advice is good; doubt arises only when one is told not to eat at all.

In some of the Russian Tolstoy Colonies, in which young men and young women were kept apart by the wave of ascetic feeling, *The Kreutzer Sonata* started, its effects were bad, and there were cases in which girls became morbidly obsessed by sex-desire. There were cases also in which wives with little natural inclination for matrimony were filled with loathing for the sex relation on reading the book, and since among decent people such a sentiment renders the thing impossible, their husbands found themselves exposed to the difficulties and dangers of marital celibacy.

In the Tolstoyan as in many other religious movements there sprang up a form of mental coercion. When under the stress of Tolstoy's doctrine some person of tender conscience adopted for a while Tolstoy's point of view regarding sex, or property, or Government employ, it was made hard for him ever to readjust himself. As soon as he tried to do so, he was accused of 'going back on his principles' – his 'principles', for the purpose of the persecution, being the views that had temporarily hypnotised him. Any growth his mind might make after that was treated as moral backsliding. In fact, certain Tolstoyans (not differing in this from many other sectarians) claimed the right not merely to chain men's minds, but even to select the particular milestone to which they should be chained.

Certainly, therefore, *The Kreutzer Sonata* did some harm, but on the whole it probably did more good. Quite recently a distinguished Russian scholar told me that when he was a student it was *The Kreutzer Sonata* that caused him to avoid loose living and set him an ideal that resulted in permanently happy marital relations.

To the smug people who say, Do not think about this question – it is all settled! and to the frivolous people who say, Do not think, but amuse yourselves! Tolstoy says: If you are rational beings you dare not avoid thinking about it!

It is difficult to keep one's balance when forces are in motion of such incredible strength as those aroused by sex, but the danger of disregarding them is greater than that of understanding them. At any rate *The Kreutzer Sonata* presents an aspect of the matter that cannot be left out of account and sets before us the honest and strongly felt opinions of a man of genius.

In *Enduring Passion*, Dr M. C. Stopes has suggested that the change in Tolstoy's views on sex probably coincided with the 'change of life' which she believes occurs in men as well as in women, though usually to a slighter extent. This may be so, but we cannot disregard opinions because of the phase of life at which they were conceived or expressed, otherwise we should have to cancel out all that man has thought, after first assigning it to the pre-adolescent, the adolescent, the adult, the change-of-life, or the post-change-of life period – for there is no moment at which the thoughts of men are infallible or may not be somewhat influenced by their physical condition.

Dr Stopes's book provides an illustration of my previous remark, that on this question of sex people seem to find it difficult to tolerate any outspoken presentation of the matter. Tolstoy has been scornfully denounced for his advocacy of chastity and for his scorn of doctors and their lore – as though his attitude indicated some aberration of the intellect, but Dr Stopes has been treated almost as badly for advocating marriage and arguing that to make it successful an acquaintance with recently ascertained facts about the body's secretions is desirable, and that it is unwise to have more children than a mother's strength can endure or the parents' means provide for. Her position is almost the reverse of Tolstoy's, so one might have anticipated a generally cordial welcome for it, yet the curious fact is, that though *Enduring Passion* is having large sales, almost the entire press has deliberately tabooed it, so that, apart from a review in a medical paper, I have seen only two short notices of this remarkable work by an able writer, on a matter of great public and private importance to which she has devoted special study for years past. It seems therefore that the opposition to Tolstoy may be due not so much to the views he expressed, as to the fact that he dared to speak plainly on a subject around which most people prefer an atmosphere of confused obscurity.

It has been stated in the English press that Górki reports Tolstoy as having used grossly improper language in conversation. This report is based on an unfortunate translation of Górki's *Reminiscences*. What Górki really wrote was:

> On the evening of my first acquaintance with him he took me to his study, and placing me opposite him began to speak of *Várenka Olésova* and of *Twenty-Six and One* [stories by Górki]. I was overwhelmed by his tone, and even lost my head – so plainly and sharply did he speak, arguing that bashfulness is not characteristic of a healthy girl. 'If a girl is over fifteen and healthy, she likes to be embraced and touched. Her mind is afraid of what is unknown and of what she does not yet understand – that is what is called modesty and bashfulness. But her body is already aware that the unknown is inevitable, and legitimate, and despite the mind demands the fulfilment of its law. In your book you have described this Várenka Olésova as healthy, but she feels anaemically – which is not true to life.'
>
> Then he began to speak about the girl in *Twenty-Six*, using one improper word after another so simply that it seemed to me cynical, and even rather offended me. Subsequently I understood that he used 'coarse' words only because he found them more precise and pointed, but at the time I found it unpleasant to listen to him. I did not reply, and suddenly he became attentive and affable and began asking me about my life, how I had studied, and what I had read.

Tolstoy never shrank from biblical directness of statement and used words that convey a plain meaning, and no doubt he did so when telling Górki that Várenka was not true to life. But the English translation of Górki's *Reminiscences* by S. S. Koteliansky and Leonard Woolf have, no doubt inadvertently, given a twist to Górki's remarks by translating 'bashfulness is not characteristic' as 'chastity is not natural', and by rendering 'that is what is called modesty and bashfulness' by 'that is what they call chastity and purity', as well as by needlessly introducing the word 'vulgar' in a previous sentence, and using the expression 'a stream of indecent words' and 'unmentionable words' where 'one improper word after another' and 'coarse words' express the meaning better.

Anyone who knew Tolstoy intimately would know that such a description of him gives quite a wrong impression.

*   *   *

During the summer of 1890 Gay painted the young Countess Másha, who was his particular favourite among the children. Writing to Birukóv, he said:

> I painted that portrait with much love and am glad you appreciate it. It is not difficult to paint such a wise, kindly, and animated little head, but without love of those qualities no one could paint it.

In autumn, being again at Yásnaya when Tolstoy was unwell, Gay modelled a bust of him which Tolstoy considered the best that anyone had yet made.

It was in 1890 also that Répin produced his well-known picture 'Tolstoy in his Room', with spade, saw and scythe standing against the walls.

The picture which aroused most interest at Yásnaya that year was, however, not a portrait of Tolstoy, but Gay's 'What is Truth?' which had been exhibited in Petersburg early in the year and prohibited. After exhibiting it privately, Gay brought it to show to Tolstoy, who was deeply impressed by it.

Already in January, when Gay had sent him a drawing of it, Tolstoy had written to him:

> I am always thinking about you and your picture. I am longing to hear how it is received. I am troubled that the figure of Pilate, with that arm, seems wrong somehow. I don't say it is, I only ask. If the connoisseurs say that that figure is correct, I shall be satisfied. About the rest, I know, and have no need to ask anyone's opinion.

Tolstoy was immensely pleased with the treatment of the subject and the thought and feeling it expressed.

Feinermann tells us:

Leo Nikoláevich, when he saw that painting, was so shaken and agitated that for days after he could hardly speak of anything else.

'I am in raptures,' he said. 'That's a master! I confess that I myself only now understand the deep and true meaning of that short passage, which always appeared to me, as it has to all the Bible commentators, unfinished and abrupt. Pilate asked, 'What is Truth?' and then went out to the crowd without waiting for a reply. And everybody reads and understands it that way. But this picture gives a different interpretation. Pilate does not *ask* what truth is, expecting a reply. No! In the form of a question, he contemptuously replies. When Christ says that he has come into the world as a witness of Truth, Pilate, with a laugh and a contemptuous gesture, throws the words carelessly at him: "And what *is* Truth? Truth is a relative thing; everyone takes it his own way!" and evidently considering his retort decisive, he goes out to the crowd. That is the light in which the moment is seized. It is new, it is profound, and how strongly and clearly the picture expresses it! The fat, shaven neck of the Roman Governor, that half-turned, large, well-fed, sensual body, that outstretched arm with its gesture of contempt are all splendid – it is alive. It breathes, and impresses itself on the memory for ever. And the face! . . . Along with all the dignity of that Roman figure there goes a slavish anxiety about himself – the mean trepidation of a petty soul. He is afraid he may be denounced at Rome . . . And this smallness of soul is wonderfully caught by Gay; notwithstanding the toga and his height, and his majestic pose, Pilate appears so petty before the worn-out sufferer who has undergone during the night, arrest, judgement, and insults . . . A wonderful picture! That is the way to paint!'

Gay, touched and deeply moved by Leo Nikoláevich's delight, embraced and kissed him, and said: 'Do not praise it . . . You will praise me so that I shall become proud. I am afraid of that . . . I shan't be able to paint!'

On 20th December he again wrote to Gay:

We have had visitors all this last time . . . I understand your words that 'man is more than canvas',* and they help me to smother my

---

* By which Gay meant to say that he did not grudge letting his painting wait while he talked to a visitor, trying to convert him to the new faith.

regret at the slow progress of my work, which is growing and seizing upon me in winter – my best working time.

During the summer Tolstoy had visited Óptin Monastery with his daughter. He went there, this time, chiefly to see his sister, the Countess Mary Nikoláevna Tolstoy, who was a nun in the Convent of Shámordin near Óptin Monastery, where he also called on K. N. Leóntiev, an author and scholar and an old acquaintance of his, to whom he put the question: 'How is it that you, an educated man, have become an Orthodox believer and have decided to live here?'

Leóntiev replied: 'Live here and you will yourself believe!'

'Naturally! When they shut one up here one has to believe!' replied Tolstoy. Subsequently, at tea, he offered Leóntiev a copy of his *Gospel in Brief*. In reply the latter handed Tolstoy a pamphlet maintaining the identity and exactitude of the Gospels and refuting Tolstoy's treatment of them. Whereupon Tolstoy remarked: 'This is a useful booklet: it advertises my Gospel.'

Leóntiev thereupon flared up, and said: 'How can you, here in the Hermitage, ruled over by such a Saint as Father Ambrose, speak about "my Gospel?" . . . Such talk is only permissible in Tómsk, or some out-of-the-way place like that!'

Tolstoy replied: 'Well, you've plenty of friends . . . Write to Petersburg and perhaps they'll banish me to Tómsk!'

In reality something much worse than being sent to Tómsk very nearly befell Tolstoy ere many months had passed; but before that event – of which I will tell in another chapter – Alexander III granted Tolstoy's wife, the Countess S. A. Tolstoy, an audience. Her object in going to see him was to obtain permission to publish *The Kreutzer Sonata* in the thirteenth volume (which she was then preparing) of her edition of her husband's works.

The Emperor received her very graciously and talked with her for nearly an hour. 'Tell me, Countess,' said he, 'why you make such persistent efforts to obtain permission to publish *The Kreutzer Sonata*. It seems to me that that work, directed as it is against marriage and family, should be quite alien to you. To you as Leo Nikoláevich's wife, it should be unpleasant.'

'Your Majesty, I ask your permission to print *The Kreutzer Sonata*, not as Leo Nikoláevich's wife, but as the publisher of his works. Everything I undertake I try to do as well as possible. To publish Leo

Nikoláevich's works well, it is necessary first of all to publish them complete,' replied the Countess.

She made a very favourable impression on the Emperor, who after asking whether it was true that Tolstoy had a secret printing-press, and being assured that he had nothing of the kind, eventually allowed *The Kreutzer Sonata* to be included in the authorised Russian edition of his works, on the express condition that it should not be issued separately or sold as a separate volume.

When about a year later Tolstoy published a repudiation of all rights in anything he had written after 1881, various publishers hastened to avail themselves of that permission by issuing separate editions of *The Kreutzer Sonata*. The Countess was in no way to blame for this, and would have stopped it if she could. The Emperor, however, when he heard of these publications was much displeased, and remarked: 'Well, if that woman has deceived me, I do not know whom I can trust!'

* * *

The chief things Tolstoy wrote in 1890, besides the *Afterword* to *The Kreutzer Sonata*, was an article on *Timothy Bóndarev*.

All this time the campaign of vituperation, denunciation and insinuation which the ecclesiastics had commenced against him when his *Confession* appeared, continued and even increased; and Pobedonóstev, Head of the Holy Synod, falsely stated in his Annual Report to the Tsar that Tolstoy was no longer able to render assistance to the peasants in consequence of his sons' extravagance. The elder sons thereupon wrote to the newspapers repudiating this accusation.

As the years passed, the demands made by Churchmen for Tolstoy's suppression became more and more clamorous, but the time had not yet arrived for the employment of any weapon more tangible than slander.

I avail myself of this space to add something more about the Countess's *Later Diary*.

Tolstoy had come to disapprove of owning property, and wished to adjust his life to that principle. His wife opposed this, and often ridiculed and misrepresented his opinions and efforts. Such strife makes marital relations between sensitive people unsatisfactory if not impossible. For good relations some harmony of mind as well as of body is essential. So Tolstoy's desire to practise his principles clashed with his wish to be his wife's husband. St Paul's view – that it is well to eliminate sex-influence from one's life – seemed to offer a way of escape from the dilemma, and Tolstoy (always intense in what he did or wrote) produced *The Kreutzer Sonata*, presenting the Pauline view very forcibly.

The book helped to make his wife regard matrimonial relations as objectionable – as indeed they are when acute mental discord is present – and so the strife as to property arrangements (the real root of the trouble) became complicated by other reproaches and revulsions.

This tragic and painful story should not lead critics of Tolstoy to pile up denunciations and misrepresentations, unless indeed they consider any attempt to practise or advocate Gospel precepts such an unpardonable offence that it can only be regarded with scornful condemnation.

12

The Famine

Tolstoy's didactic epistles owe their quality to the fact that he was so tremendously alive, and vibrated with anxiety to put things right in the world. He saw what life's great problems are, even if he did not always see a true solution to them, and he had an ardent faith that if he could but put men on their guard against temptations they would work whole-heartedly, as he himself did, to establish the Kingdom of God.

That in 1891 his opinions were still evolving is shown by such letters as the following – written to V. V. Rakhmánov in March of that year:

> The thoughts and feelings that agitate you, those new horizons you see before you, are just what agitate me, they are those in which I live . . . and in which Khilkóv lives, with whom I have been corresponding zealously . . .
>
> Do not imagine that I defend the point of view I formerly expressed in *What I Believe*.
>
> Not only do I not defend it, but I am glad we have outlived it. When starting on a new road one cannot help rejoicing at what one first sees before one, and it is excusable to mistake what is at the beginning of the road for the journey's aim . . .

Unfortunately very few people possess Tolstoy's abounding energy and tenacity of purpose, and what frequently occurred was, that after being touched by his appeal and induced to abandon their customary occupations, his followers found themselves at a loose end and did not know what to do.

As his teaching spread, more and more people began to change their way of life, and he often found it difficult to know how to advise those who wished to be his disciples. On 21st June 1891, for instance, he wrote to Gay:

> Seekers are wearisome . . . I am told: 'Here is a man who wishes to change his way of life and live a godly life, and therefore wants to see

you and have a talk.' One's first feeling is unpleasant. I sometimes think it is a matter plain enough for anyone and one in which I *cannot* help him, but then I say to myself: 'It is unpleasant – but that is all the more reason for doing what he perhaps requires.' But what to do for him one does not know . . . And one generally feels ashamed . . . This year I have been much weaker physically and have been busy with my writing [*The Kingdom of God is Within You*], which is not finished, but progresses. I am also overwhelmed by visitors of all kinds, and you can't imagine how uncomfortable and conscience-stricken and sad I feel now, at harvest time, to be living in these mean, abominable surroundings [of comfortable ease]. Especially when I remember former years . . .

In March he wrote to Feinermann, who had been living in a Colony of the intelligentsia in the Province of Poltáva, a letter which again indicates that his mind was active and his views growing. He says of the unsuccessful attempt made by these educated men to live together and support themselves by agricultural labour:

You are too hard on your late experiment, or do not define correctly where the mistake lay . . . It lay in raising to the rank of a principle something that cannot be a principle . . . Even Bóndarev's law of 'bread-labour' cannot be a principle . . .

Our one general, basic principle is love, not in words only but in deed and in truth, that is to say, love that involves the spending and sacrificing of one's life for God and one's neighbour.

From that general principle flow the special principles of humility, meekness, and Non-Resistance.

The results of that in all probability (I say in all probability, and not always, because one may be put in prison or something of that kind) will be agricultural work, handicraft, or even factory work, work at any rate of a kind for which there are the fewest competitors and least reward . . .

It seems to me that a serious mistake generally made by the 'intellectual' Colonists was that they underrated, as Tolstoy himself underrated, the world's need of efficient management. If they really knew their job they were qualified to perform a service urgently needed, that of directing and guiding the labour of others less competent than themselves; but for that there was no sufficient scope in a small Colony of educated and eccentric people. On the other hand when – as was usually the case – they were not practically competent and efficient, they wasted time, effort, and material, by starting a separate undertaking of their own when they should have worked under the supervision of men who knew the business.

In April Tolstoy again wrote to Feinermann:

I was very much struck by what you say at the end of your letter about the constant tergiversations that go on among our friends.

. . . That very day I had written to Popóv, who is living with Chertkóv in the Province of Vorónesh, that it seems to me that in our life (by 'our' I mean those who are travelling the same road as ourselves) a painful or rather a seemingly painful time has arrived, demanding effort and firmness and lacking the former joyousness and enthusiasm . . . A time of disillusionment in efforts to realise our plans rapidly and fully, a time of apostasy and indifference – a time not even of persecution (which on the contrary exhilarates) but of contempt.

In fact, as that letter indicates, the first enthusiasm of the Tolstoy movement was dying down. It had become plain that Tolstoy's own place was at home, and it had also become evident that the Colonies started as a result of the interest he had aroused, were neither to be materially successful nor to ease the spiritual struggles of those who joined them.

Under these circumstances Tolstoy became yet more absorbed in writing, and less inclined to encourage changes in external life. The theme that chiefly occupied him was the principle of Non-Resistance in its application to Government, his thesis being the harmfulness of all Government that 'rests on force', and his conclusion – Christian anarchism: the repudiation of all participation in Government, civil or military, and the refusal both of army service and of the payment of taxes.

To those who did not know him personally, the fact that while he escaped the burden of property others paid the taxes for him, gives an air of unreality to this teaching, and even those who like myself were well aware of the intense ardour of his sincerity, had still to remember that the efficacy of his prescription had not been tested, and that he could therefore not speak with the same authority as if he had tried it in practice.

Zínger gives us a glimpse of him at this time, namely on his 63rd birthday, when a large company assembled at Yásnaya. Tolstoy accepted 'congratulations' (the equivalent of our 'many happy returns') in a kindly, jocose spirit, and took an interest in everything and everybody. To Zínger, the mathematician, he remarked:

> I was born in the year 1828 on the 28th day of the month, and 28 has been the luckiest number for me all my life [he left the army when he was 28]. I only lately learnt that 28 is a specially 'perfect' number in mathematics. Now, Mathematician, do you know what 'perfect' numbers are?

Zínger knew what they were, but had forgotten that 28 was one of them.

> 'Yes, yes, it is!' said Tolstoy. ' "Perfect" numbers are those equal to the sum of all the numbers into which they can be divided. 28 divides by 14, 7, 4, 2, and 1. 1+2+4+7+14 = 28. There are very few such numbers.' [Among the first 10,000, only 6, 28, 496, and 8,128.]

It is curious that Tolstoy lived to be 82, which is 28 reversed, Zínger tells us that, when he was talking to Tatiána Lvóvna, who was pouring out tea:

> Leo Nikoláevich, who was passing, listened to our conversation, which – apropos of Sófya Kovalévski, who had lately died – had turned to the role of women in science.
>
>   Tatiána Lvóvna agreed with me that one must not consider woman's incapacity for original scientific research fully proven.
>
>   'In my opinion,' said Leo Nikoláevich, 'if women were as capable of scientific thought as men it would be unjust, for then they would have an unquestionable superiority. Woman has a natural superiority – in her femininity, her *charm*. It is not a question of her fascination for men, but of that special charm which causes children, for instance, always to love a woman most . . . If we were now, for instance, to ask some child or some inhabitant of the moon, whom he would choose to pour out tea: you, me or Tánya, he would be sure to choose Tánya.'

Feinermann, visiting Yásnaya at this time, found Tolstoy beginning to be depressed and agitated about the famine then imminent. Tolstoy said to him:

Have you heard? It has already begun! Here the peasants have not yet finished threshing, while there, in the Province of Vorónesh, they have nothing left to eat, and are already sitting idle in their houses.

It is the first groan of an approaching calamity. I feel it, and ache inwardly, as a rheumatic body aches before rainy weather.

Tolstoy had as yet little thought of organising relief for the famine-stricken, but was preparing to write an article to destroy the optimistic delusion spread by the Government, to the effect that there would be no famine but only a shortness of grain in certain Provinces. A. M. Novikóv, who was for three years tutor in the family, has told how it occurred that Tolstoy was ultimately drawn into active relief work.

Mention has already been made of Raévski, an old friend of Tolstoy's from the days when they were both ardent gymnasts. The two men often disagreed, though they highly esteemed one another.

Raévski, for instance, would tell ironically of Tolstoy's former enthusiasms: how eager he used to be about bee-keeping and farming; at one time fixing the maximum acreage a squire could profitably farm, and saying that 'intensive farming can only be done on 80 acres, with more land than that it will always yield less profit'; and at another time deciding that it is more profitable to invest one's whole capital in large tracts of virgin soil on the borders of civilisation, and himself purchasing a large estate in Samára; now strictly observing the rites of the Orthodox Church, including Fasts and fête-days, like any peasant, and then breaking away from the Church altogether and devising a faith of his own. Raévski also differed sharply from Tolstoy as to the value of the natural sciences. In Tolstoy's eyes almost all that modern science does is useless or false, and its chief achievements merely enable the few to separate themselves yet more widely from the many and increase man's power to slay his brother. Raévski, who had taken Honours in Pure Mathematics at Moscow University, appreciated science and knew the service it has rendered, and is rendering, to mankind.

The conversations at Yásnaya on ethical themes kept the Tolstoyans and semi-Tolstoyans in a constant state of exaltation. Always struggling with himself and analysing himself, Tolstoy reacted on those around him, and as people passed backwards and forwards between the two families, the effect was also felt at the Raévskis'.

Raévski himself, for instance, after hearing the discussions about the wastefulness and harmfulness of smoking, suddenly gave up the use of tobacco. Nor did he long remain indifferent to what Tolstoy was saying about riches, poverty, and personal work. He tried to justify to himself the social position he occupied, by dwelling on the enlightening influence he, as squire, was able to exercise on the peasants, and by his activity on the Zémstvo. All this, however, did not satisfy him, and when the approach of famine revealed a crisis calling for extraordinary exertions, he felt that the time had come to pay the debt he owed to the people, and threw himself with enthusiasm into the work. The true meaning of his privileged position as a landowner now appeared to him to be that his possessions and those of his class represent an insurance fund safeguarding the peasants from starvation. In July 1891, on returning from an Extraordinary Session of the Epifánski Zémstvo (District Council), Raévski invited his three sons and Novikóv to take a census of the crops and stores in a neighbouring district. Novikóv says:

> In August I returned to Yásnaya Polyána. Here thing were much quieter: the famine was less mentioned than the beggars and burntouts. Tolstoy enquired about the famine district and began to say that there are always many hungry but that the only way to help a horse to drag its load is *to get off its back*.
>
> To me those words sounded dull and lifeless. I knew that Raévski was rushing about from one District Council to another, while Tolstoy was sitting at Yásnaya and writing – or preparing to write – that there always is a famine somewhere, and that it is immoral to prepare to feed the famine-stricken and to imagine *that* to be a good and necessary activity while our whole way of life causes more and more people to become destitute. Yet how fine, convincing, and true it all sounded when Tolstoy himself expounded it to us!
>
> But before a month had passed all had changed. Raévski found time, while rushing from one Council to another, to call at Yásnaya. He had determined to try to arouse Tolstoy and induce him to join the ranks of those who were feeding the hungry. He began by describing scenes in the famine district, and he persuaded Tolstoy to go and see them for himself. Such outings always attracted Tolstoy.
>
> He went to the famine district for a couple of days in order to write about it with better knowledge – and he remained there almost continuously for two years.

During that visit Tolstoy suggested to Ráevski to start free eating-houses for the destitute, and the latter promptly made an experiment on a small scale.

Before speaking about the famine I must however mention that, while still at Yásnaya, Tolstoy had written to the papers announcing that – as he received many enquiries and requests concerning the publication, translation, or permission to perform his writings and plays – he wished it to be known that he gave free permission to all who desired to do so, to publish in Russia or abroad, in Russian or in translations, and also to perform on the stage, all the works he had written since 1881, as well as all those he might publish in future.

This announcement dealt with a matter that had been long in dispute between his wife and himself. She retained control of all his works antecedent to and including *Anna Karénina*. Publishers might scramble as they pleased for anything written subsequently, the Countess having only the same right as anyone else. Owing to the circumstances of the case, however, she had the advantage of knowing in advance what was coming.

I do not think that this decision helped to secure the best form of publication for the works, or to safeguard the interests of the public. Certainly it was bad for the publishers and booksellers, for everything that tends to turn trade into a gamble is undesirable, and the right to scramble for the new works of a popular writer offers a temptation to rush books out without due care in their production. The harm that might have resulted was minimised by the Countess's action in herself publishing the works in reliable editions at a very moderate price. Other publishers for the most part realised that the offer was not much use to them, and therefore did not scramble or gamble over it as wildly as might have been expected. As to translations, the announcement left matters where they were before. Russia not having joined the Berne International Convention, works published in Russia can be freely used by foreign translators. No translator's copyright in his own version was infringed by Tolstoy's announcement, for he of course only gave away what was his own.

With reference to the royalties due for the performance of his plays at the Imperial Theatres, a curious case arose. According to the official regulations, a certain sum was paid to the author for each performance of a play, and it was decided that if Tolstoy refused to accept what was due to him, the money should go for the improvement of the Imperial ballet. As the lesser of two evils, therefore, Tolstoy consented to his wife accepting these payments, and she devoted the money to charitable purposes. From the private Russian theatres, which frequently performed his plays, he received nothing.

Whatever we may think of the wisdom of his decision, the repudiation by the world's foremost writer of all personal profit from the works he published during his last thirty years, stands at any rate as a striking proof of his integrity, and one which it is not easy even for the most malicious of his detractors to ignore. He might have drawn a huge income and spent it for the benefit of others – 'making a pipe of himself' – but we should then not have been as sure as we now are that his work was quite unbiased by mercenary motives.

The question of the disposal of his estates was also settled at this time. They were divided up among his wife and children in portions as nearly equal as possible. The share received by the Countess Sófya Andréevna was as much as she had brought as a dowry at the time of her marriage, and like the other shares, it was not much over fifty thousand rubles (about £5,000). Yásnaya Polyána went to her and to Iván, the youngest son, as it had come to Leo Tolstoy himself as youngest son. After Iván's death, in 1895, it passed to his brothers, but their mother managed it, and they did not interfere in any way. The other estates in Central Russia went to the elder children. Most of the Samára estate, of 6,500 desyatínas (about 17,500 acres), went to the younger children: Michael, Andrew, and Alexandra. Mary, following her father's teaching, refused to accept any property, but her mother, feeling sure that the girl would change her mind later, took charge of her portion, and when Mary married in 1897 she accepted it, and at her death in 1906 left it to her husband, Prince Obolénski, whose means were very limited.

This disposition was probably the best Tolstoy could make of the property he had decided to be rid of. Had he tried to deprive the family of it, his wife was prepared to appeal to the Government, which would readily have declared him incapable of managing his affairs.

*   *   *

The position of things when Tolstoy went to the famine district was a curious one.

The Russian Government had stoutly denied the famine and looked askance at all private initiative in the matter. Tolstoy was at strife with the Orthodox Church, and no sooner did he take part in organising relief than the representatives of that Church publicly denounced him as Antichrist. Moreover, he himself disapproved of what he was doing. I remember, after the famine was over, his explaining to me that a man's real, useful activity consists only in what he does with his own brain and hand, and telling me that his famine-relief work did not afford him satisfaction. He used his favourite simile about 'making a pipe of oneself', but it seemed to me that he did not realise how very useful a good water-pipe often is. He saw that a man who pumps water and carries it in a pail to those who want it, does good work, but I never heard him acknowledge that an engineer who plans a water-supply efficiently and gets the pipes well laid to take water into the heart of a city, does any good. The manual labour at the pump appealed to him, while the probability that a Water Company will pay dividends, or that a Municipal Government will earn a profit on its waterworks and thereby 'steal from the people', repelled him, and the strenuousness of his attack, his habit of suspecting the motives of those with whom he disagreed, and the real complexity of the problem, baffled attempts to separate the considerable amount of truth that lies embedded in his philippics, from the large amount of prejudice they contain.

In this connection the words of Jane Addams recur to my mind:

> There is a common sense in the mass of mankind which one cannot neglect with impunity, just as there is sure to be an eccentricity in the differing and reforming individual which we perhaps do well to challenge.

Leaving for the moment Tolstoy's economic theories, let us note his practical activity at this crisis, which evoked more widespread sympathy and warm approval than almost any other incident in his career.

As I have just explained, after 1881 he generally took no money for his writings, but with what he received for his articles on the famine, as well as what other people gave him – helped by his daughters Tatiána and Mary and his niece V. Kuzmínski, and coached by Raévski in practical details – he set to work opening eating-houses and organising other help for those upon whom the terrible calamity of an almost complete failure of the rye-harvest had fallen.

His daughter Mary used to tell of the pleasure it gave her to watch the two 'old men', as she called Raévski and her father, going about together at the seat of the famine, and talking and laughing in friendly comradeship.

For Raévski it was an occasion of spiritual exaltation to find himself fighting the famine hand in hand with Tolstoy and to feel the work supported by the great stream of contributions which flowed in as a result of letters published, in November 1891, by the Countess S. A. Tolstoy in the papers, announcing that her husband and family had settled in the famine district to render help to the starving.

Returning from a Zémstvo meeting that month in bad weather, Raévski met some destitute peasants going on foot from one village to another, seeking work or begging. He gave them a lift, and on coming to a hill, himself go out and walked. It was snowing and his feet got wet, and he had many miles to drive before reaching home.

Next day he was ill, but insisted on going to a Zémstvo meeting in a town some thirty miles distant. He returned home suffering from influenza and died a few days later, having lost his life doing his duty as a County Councillor. Had such experiences come to Tolstoy's notice oftener, or had this one occurred before his views were definitely formed, I think his disapproval of Governmental work might have been modified.

To me it seems that the future welfare of the human race depends largely on the extent to which the spirit of conscientious devotion to the service of man actuates those who hold official positions: those engaged in the very work Tolstoy so disliked and so strongly condemned. It is not their work that is wrong, but the spirit in which it is often done. One need only remember such men as Lincoln, to disprove Tolstoy's view of the necessarily corrupting influence of public life. I even believe that to stand aside from public affairs may do a man more harm than to participate in them, just as it may be worth while getting one's hands tarred in order to fix up a reliable fence.

Raévski's death deeply distressed Tolstoy, who offered to write his obituary; but his wife declined the offer, as her husband had always avoided publicity, and such an article would, she felt, have run counter to his wishes. His works, however, lived after him, for Tolstoy in his organisation of relief made constant use of the knowledge he had gathered from Raévski's experience, and continued throughout that winter and the next to feed the destitute in four districts, till the good harvest of 1893 came and the work drew to its natural close.

A history of the famine of 1891 and 1892, or even of the part played in it by the Tolstoy family, would be a voluminous affair. The two eldest sons worked in the Chern District of the Province of Túla, and Leo Lvóvich worked in the Government of Samára till his health broke down. Tatiána Lvóvna worked with her father and sister at Begíchevka till she fell ill and had to go home for a time. After her recovery she returned to the work. Tolstoy's wife remained with the four little children in Moscow, and acted as a centre to which contributions flowed. Of her Anna Seuron says:

> The Countess took a warm part in helping the sufferers, and was an inestimable support to the Count. Hundreds of typhus patients received linen, who but for their help would have had no change of garments. Quantities of medicine were supplied. Charitable people of both sexes were found who tended the sick, partly for payment, but in most cases gratuitously from a wish to serve their fellows.

All this time the Countess had to attend to a very large correspondence, and in dealing with it showed herself, as usual, prompt, energetic, and practical. Contributions flowed in from all parts: shiploads of grain from America, and large donations from the Society of Friends in England.

The section of the famine district in which Tolstoy worked lay towards the southern part of the Governments of Túla and Ryazán; Begíchevka being about a hundred miles south-east of Yásnaya Polyána; and the following letter from him to Rakhmánov (who was setting out to render aid in another district) will give the reader some idea of the way the work was done:

> If you wish to open a Soup Kitchen in the Lukoyánski District, where things seem to be very bad, do as follows:
>
> When you have chosen a place amid the hungriest villages, collect there a store of flour, bran, potatoes, cabbages, beetroot, peas, lentils, oatmeal, and salt, or what you can get of these things, and then go to one of the villages and choose near the middle of it (if it has not more than thirty or forty houses) one of the very poorest families (or two, if the village is twice as big) and offer to supply the householder with his food if he will bake bread and cook for the destitute, the old folk, the weak, and the children, or the not old but hungry – up to the number of thirty or forty persons. Then make a list, with the Elder's aid, of those who ought to be fed. Give out the provisions, and visit the Soup Kitchen, trying the food, counteracting abuses, and admitting those who are on the list and who apply. The thing is as simple and as easily arranged as though it were a process of nature . . .

I am living here on the estate of my acquaintance Raévski, a very good and practical man (a great Liberal and a friend of the people), with my two daughters Tánya and Másha, and my niece V. Kuzmínski, and they work heartily.

We have started eighteen Soup Kitchens, and our neighbours the Filosófovs have six. A few days ago two other helpers arrived: one a Law-student and the other a Naturalist, who have taken their degrees. Moscow merchants are also opening Soup Kitchens. Everywhere this thing is spreading out like a net. And there is much good in it. There is also evil: namely one's arbitrary discretion, which one cannot quite get rid of, and the false role one plays . . .

In my friend E. A. Brayley Hodgetts' book, *In the Track of the Russian Famine*, Raévski's country-house, in which Tolstoy stayed, is thus described:

Small and humble, like most of the country residences in this district, it did not stand separate and alone like the houses of other country gentlemen, but at the end of a large and populous village. Tolstoy's room was a small one of about ten feet by five. A small iron bedstead occupied the length of one wall. Near the window stood a rough writing-table. There was a shelf of books. The room was destitute of anything approaching to ornament and there was not the vestige of a carpet or curtains, or any of the signs of English comfort. 'That', said my guide [Raévski's manager], 'is the sacred chamber. Here the great man lives and works. That is Count Tolstoy's room when he is here. I occupy it in his absence.'

How the work of feeding the hungry was carried on is told in one of Tolstoy's articles:

Generally both in our eating-houses and in those of our neighbour, Mme N. Filosófov, who is working independently of us, the number of people fed is always one-third of the people in the village . . .

In four weeks, without making any special effort, we opened and started in twenty villages thirty eating-houses, in which about 1,500 people are fed . . .

These eating-houses are particularly interesting because they have served as an object-lesson of the erroneousness of the belief firmly rooted among the peasants themselves, that rye bread is the most appetising, wholesome and cheap form of food. They have shown beyond a doubt that peas, millet, maize, potatoes, beet, cabbage, oats, and pea-soup satisfy hunger better and form a more wholesome and cheaper food than bread. In places where the Zémstvo distributed rye, the eating-houses provided no bread and the people brought a very little of their own with them, or sometimes none at all; yet they got through the winter in good health and with their hunger well satisfied, eating each day about two kopeks' [½d.] worth of cooked food and two or three kopeks' worth of rye bread; whereas when they ate nothing but rye bread, they consumed at least seven and a half kopeks' [nearly 2d.] worth of food.

To give the people two meals a day cost only from thirty to thirty-six pence per person per month.

The following was a sample menu for a week in a village where, thanks to the distribution of rye made by the Zémstvo, the people had rye bread of their own:

Monday, cabbage-soup and porridge; Tuesday, potato-soup, pea-broth, and the same for supper; Wednesday, pea-soup and boiled potatoes, and for supper, peas with *kvas*; Thursday, cabbage-soup, pea-broth, and the same for supper; Friday, potato-soup, millet-broth, and the same for supper; Saturday, cabbage-soup and boiled potatoes, and for supper, potatoes with *kvas*; Sunday, potato-soup and porridge, and for supper, peas with *kvas*.

The author of this menu was guided by what foodstuffs he had at his disposal at the time. With beets, from which during the winter the favourite beet-stew was made, and with oat-broth, this menu can be varied still more without making the food more expensive.

The people highly approved of the food supplied though it contained no meat at all. Brayley Hodgetts, in his book already referred to, gives evidence supported by other witnesses:

'It is excellent food,' the people round us exclaimed in chorus. 'God bless the good Count and all his friends for giving us such good meals! What should we have done without him? We never want to eat better food than this!'

The peasants in this village struck me as being much less distrustful and more honest than in any I had yet visited.

On our way back we met numbers of little boys carrying books. They were coming from the village school, founded by the Count and now captured by the local priest. The boys looked bright and truthful, as healthy boys should, and showed us their books with fearless frankness. It was evident from all I saw, that Count Tolstoy is exercising an influence of the most powerful kind upon these simple folk.

Tolstoy would not have been himself had he been satisfied with what he was doing. Self-indictment, as well as indictment of society, was as natural to him as breathing, and the following letter to Feinermann, written on 9th November 1891, when the work was at its height, is a very characteristic utterance:

There is much here that is not right. Money from Sófya Andréevna, and money that has been collected, and the relation between the feeders and the fed – there is no end to the sin of it all, but I cannot sit at home and write. I feel the necessity of taking part and doing something. I know I am not doing the right thing, but I can't do the right thing and I can't do nothing. I dread the praise of men and ask myself every hour, 'Am I not sinning?' and I try to judge myself strictly and to act as in God's sight and for His sake.

In December he again wrote as follows:

Thank you for letting me have news of how you are living. I am living abominably. I don't myself know how I was trapped into this work of feeding the starving . . . It is unsuitable for me to feed those by whom I am myself fed, but I have been dragged into it and I find myself distributing the vomit thrown up by the rich. I feel that this is abominable and disgusting, but I cannot stand aside; not that I do not think I ought to, for I do think so, but that I have not the strength to do it.

I began by writing an article on the famine in which I expressed my chief idea: namely that it has all come about as a result of our sin in separating ourselves from our brothers and enslaving them, and that there is only one way to save ourselves and mend matters, namely, by changing our lives, destroying the wall that separates us from the people, returning what we have taken from them, drawing nearer to them and uniting with them as a natural result of abandoning our privileges. Over this article, which I sent to *Philosophical Questions*, Grot has been worrying for a month and is still worrying.

It has been toned down, and allowed, and forbidden, but it has not yet appeared. The thoughts evoked by that article led me to settle among the famine-stricken. Then my wife wrote a letter which has caused donations to be sent, and almost without my noticing it I have become a distributor, and am, as it were, under an obligation to the people here.

The misery grows continually, while the aid grows less rapidly, and therefore having once drifted into this position it has become impossible for me to stand aside.

This is what we do: we buy rye and other food, and in the huts of the poorest villagers we arrange – No! not we, for the owners of the huts do everything themselves, we only give the means, that is, the provisions for the meals; and the weak and old, the children, and sometimes the middle-aged too, are fed. There is much evil, and much good too, in it; I say that, not of our work but of the good feeling evoked. The other day a peasant, who has grown rich in Kalúga, offered to let eighty horses be sent from a famine-stricken spot to the Masálski District, where they will be fed through the winter and sent back in the spring.

The Kalúga peasant made the offer and the peasants here collected eighty horses in one day, and are ready to send them off, putting entire trust in their unseen stranger-brothers . . .

['You know, those horses came back in spring, safe and well-fed!' said Leo Tolstoy to me, laughing, when we met later. Of all the things done that winter, that was the best!]

In February 1892 he wrote to another friend:

If I had had any doubt left as to whether money can do any good, using it to buy grain, and feeding some thousands of people, has quite convinced me that one can do nothing but harm with it.

You will say: 'Why then do you go on?'

Because I cannot escape, and because – beyond a feeling of great depression – I experience nothing, and therefore think I am not doing this work for my personal satisfaction.

The oppression comes not from the practical work, which on the contrary is cheering and attractive, and not from dislike of the occupation, but from an inner feeling of being ashamed of myself.

Please don't seek any general meaning in these words of mine: I write simply *au courant de la plume*, to a kindred spirit who I know will understand what I feel from a mere hint.

I much dislike it, or rather am often made uncomfortable, when people who are too well disposed towards me take me too seriously, demanding and trying to find in my actions a complete correspondence to my words.

'How is it you say this and do that?'

No, I am not a Saint and have never given myself out for one. I am a man, often carried away, and sometimes, or rather always, unable to say exactly what I think and feel – not that I do not want to say it, but that I often exaggerate or simply blunder.

That is so in words. In deeds the case is yet worse, for I am only a weak man, of vicious habits, who wishes to serve the God of Truth but constantly goes astray.

When people consider me as one who cannot make a mistake, every error seems like a lie or a piece of hypocrisy.

But if I am understood to be a weak man, the discord between my words and acts is seen to be a sign of weakness, but not as a lie or an hypocrisy. And then I appear to be what I am: a sorry but sincere man, now and always wishing with his whole soul to be really good, to be, that is, a worthy servant of God.

The work of relief spread, and Tolstoy experienced much difficulty in finding competent and reliable helpers. His friend and mine, A. N. Dunáev, a Director of a Moscow bank, told me that Tolstoy said to him: 'Ah, if only you would come and help us organise!' Dunáev replied that it was impossible for him to get away from his bank. 'Yes,' replied Tolstoy, 'do you know what I have noticed? Those who come to help – those who are free to come at the first call – are people who are disengaged because they are inefficient. The sort of men one needs are already engaged in necessary work and cannot be spared from their posts.'

As time went on Tolstoy became more and more dissatisfied with his work, and on 3rd April 1892 he noted in his Diary: 'My work as manager of contributions is terribly repugnant to me.' It must have required a great effort to enable him to persevere with the work, as he did for another year.

An account of the activity of the Tolstoy family during the famine is given in J. Stadling and Will Reason's book, *In the Land of Tolstoi*. Stadling visited Begíchevka in March 1892, and tells how he drove with Tolstoy's daughter, Mary, to a neighbouring village where there was already one eating-house and where she had to arrange to open another one for children. What he saw in the peasants' huts appalled him. It was not merely the hunger, cold, and lack of fuel, but the terrible amount of disease. In one hut he found a man and his wife, four children, a grandather, a cow, a foal, and three sheep, all in one room; and this was by no means exceptional. In hut after hut they found spotted typhus, scurvy, and smallpox, as well as other diseases. He records his conversation as they drove back to Begíchevka:

'What is your impression from your first village visit?' asked the Countess.

'Terrible!' was all I could say. 'Are you not afraid of catching smallpox or typhus?'

'Afraid! It is immoral to be afraid. Are you afraid?' she replied.

'No, I have never been afraid of infection when visiting the poor,' I said. 'It is terrible to see such hopeless misery. It makes me feel sick to think of it.'

'And is it not shameful of us to allow ourselves so much luxury while our brothers and sisters perish from want and nameless misery?' she added.

'But you have sacrificed all the comforts and luxuries of your rank and position and stepped down to the poor to help them,' I rejoined.

'Yes,' she said, 'but look at our warm clothes and other comforts, unknown to our suffering brothers and sisters!'

'But what good would it do them if we dressed in rags and lived on the verge of starvation?'

'What right have we,' she retorted, 'to live better than they?'

I made no reply, but glancing wonderingly into the eyes of this remarkable girl, I saw there a large tear trembling, and something seemed to press on my heart threatening to choke me.

Even Tolstoy's powers of endurance were often taxed to the utmost by the work and the misery that it revealed, and he was sometimes so exhausted that he could with difficulty express the simplest thought, or even name an article he required.

'Tánya,' he would say to his daughter, 'we must be sure, tomorrow, to send . . .', but his usually retentive memory refused to act and he was unable to say what had to be sent, or where to.

His spirits, however, always rose at the least encouragement. Stadling tells how one day on his return from visiting a neighbouring village, he found Tolstoy very cheerful:

He talked and laughed happily and his eyes fairly beamed with joy. The cause of his delight was soon told. He had finally overcome all obstacles and established a children's eating-room. It had cost him many a weary day of struggle against difficulties. The mere procuring of suitable food was hard enough, but there was also the ignorance, superstition, and folly of the peasants and the bitter opposition of the clergy to overcome. The peasants wanted the children's food brought to their homes, but Tolstoy knew well that in that case the children would get but little of it. Then the priests frightened the peasants with tales of learned theologians having conclusively proved from the Book of Revelations that Tolstoy was veritably Antichrist. The story of his branding the peasants on the forehead to seal them to the power of the devil was preached from the pulpit, and it was said that the Count paid the peasants eight rubles apiece as purchase-money. Only the Sunday before a Bishop had delivered a special sermon in the second-class waiting-room at the railway station at Klekótki [the nearest station] before a crowded audience, dishing up all these fables and denouncing the Count in the strongest terms as Antichrist, who was seducing them with food, fuel, and other worldly goods. The Orthodox Church, he said, was strong enough to 'exterminate Antichrist and his works'.

At first a good many of the peasants were really frightened by these sermons, but for the most part they remained, indifferent, arguing that Antichrist would come to destroy and torment men – but this man saved, pitied, and aided them!

Of the series of articles which Tolstoy wrote on the famine, some appeared in abbreviated form in Russia, several in the London *Daily Telegraph*, and all were printed, in Russian, at Geneva. In them he mingles an account of the terrible condition of the people and of what had been done to relieve the distress, with an indictment of the unchristian organisation of society and an urgent appeal to the rich and powerful to renounce their privileges.

In addition to keeping the people alive by feeding them, it was necessary also to help them to get on their feet again. This he attempted to do by supplying them with material for work during the winter (bast with which to plait shoes, for instance) and with seeds and horses to restart farming in the spring. The actual feeding of the destitute presented comparatively little difficulty, but as soon at it came to giving, or even lending, for the improvement of a man's future prospects, the case altered. Supplying horses (costing about fifty shillings each), necessary as it was – since a peasant cannot till his land without a horse – was particularly difficult, because such aid was much too great to be given to each family, and therefore envy, recrimination, and dissatisfaction were provoked among those who did not receive it. Even in the distribution of seed-corn, the available means were so inadequate to the immense need, that the difficulty of deciding who was to be helped and to what extent, seemed insuperable, and the danger that the help given would be misused rendered the problem yet more difficult. At the end of the work, Tolstoy says, 'we did not feel that we had been of any real use to the peasants in these matters'.

His general practice during the famine was to ignore as far as possible the attacks to which he was exposed, and not to complain of the obstacles placed in his way by the priests and officials. Only here and there his opinion of the Government's activity shows itself incidentally, as in his remark that:

There can be none but living help for living men. Such is the law of Nature. To wish to do good without sacrifice, is like wishing to move a body without expenditure of force. The external activity of the Government on behalf of the famine-stricken is an activity without sacrifice, hence its lack of success and the impossibility of its success.

He did not idealise the peasants he was serving, and many passages show that he was quite alive to the considerations upon which the Charity Organisation Society insists; as for instance when he says:

To determine the amount of help needed, we want not lists [such as the Zémstvos were compiling] but a prophet who will predict which of the peasants will be alive and well, and will live at peace with his family, and will find work and will work.

. . . People who have thought little about the relations between the rich and the poor generally assume that all that is needed is that the rich should give to the poor, or should be compelled to part with some of their wealth, and then all will be well. But this is a great mistake . . . How nice and simple it would be to solve things like that! . . . I myself at one time thought it could be done . . . But try distributing money to the city poor! – indeed it has been tried, and what came of it'.

Some seven years ago a Moscow merchant left six thousand rubles to be distributed at two rubles per head among the poor, and such a crowd gathered that two people were crushed to death and most of the money fell into the hands of strong, healthy fellows, while the weak got nothing.

At a free distribution the worst passions are aroused and flare up. A crowd of greedy people come to the front, and the agile, strong, and unscrupulous, get what is distributed . . .

The Government and the County Councils try to find out who are really in want, but all peasants, even those who are not at all in need, on hearing that something is to be given away for nothing, try to pretend to be in need, or even become so in order to get help without working . . . The hope of receiving these gifts weakens the self-reliance of the masses.

In his *Last Account of Money Contributed from April 12 to July 27, 1892*, written at Begíchevka, Tolstoy mentions that there were in all under his supervision two hundred and forty-six eating-houses, in which from ten to thirteen thousand people were being fed; and besides this, there were a hundred and twenty-four kitchens for children, in which two to three thousand were fed.

These figures do not include the relief organised by his sons, in other Provinces.

Besides supplying horses, and seed for oats, potatoes, millet and hemp (which were to be returned in kind after the harvest), bread was baked and sold at sixty kopeks (14 pence) per pood (36 lbs.), and there were many minor claims on the Relief Fund for help in funerals, payment of debts, support of small schools, and the buying of books, buildings, &c.

Of the peasants' condition towards the end of the famine, Tolstoy writes:

If someone from a city during the severe cold of winter came into a peasant-room which had only been slightly heated the day before, and saw the members of the family climbing, not down from the top of the stove but out of the stove itself, in which they spend their days by turns as this is the only way to get warm, or saw people using the roof of their outhouses for fuel, eating nothing but bread baked half of rye meal and half of the worst kind of bran, saw grown-up people disputing and quarrelling because their piece of rye bread is one-eighth of a pound below the agreed weight, or people not leaving their hut because they have nothing to put on – they would be horrified. But we regard such things as quite usual . . . We have become accustomed to suffering, and have ceased to see anything.

His report ends with a touching account of how weary he grew of his work after two years of it.

'Fresh peasants always, from morning to night, standing at the door or under the windows and in the street, with the same phrases: "We have not eaten for two days; we have sold our last sheep. What are we to do? We are at the end of our tether. Must we die?" Until, ashamed as we are to confess it, we have become so tired of it that we look on them as enemies.' He goes on to tell how he wanted to slip out for a walk early one frosty morning, but a tattered, haggard peasant and a fourteen-year-old boy waylaid him, and began the usual story of prolonged distress and of how they had not eaten for three days.

Tired of hearing always the same words and feeling that he needed a walk, Tolstoy tried to pass on, saying, 'Well, well! We'll come and see!' But glancing casually at the boy he saw that:

The boy looked at me with pitiful, beautiful brown eyes full of tears and hope, and at that moment a bright teardrop rolled down his nose and fell on the snow-trodden, boarded floor of the vestibule. The lad's poor, worn face, with his flaxen hair curling in a crown round his head, twitched with suppressed sobs. For me his father's words are a trite and customary annoyance, but to him . . . at this solemn moment when, at last, they have made their way to me and to succour, the summing up of the terrible year he has endured with his father unnerves him, weakened as he is by hunger. To me it is all wearisome, wearisome, and I think only of how to get away quickly for my walk.

To me it is old, but to him terribly new.

Yes, it has wearied us. But they still want to eat, still desire to live, and still long for happiness and love as I see by the charming tear-filled eyes he fixes on me, this poor, dear lad, tortured by want and full of naïve self-pity, desires it!

Tolstoy's indictment of society for indifference to the famine was suppressed in Russia, but the essential part of it is contained in an *Afterword to an account of Relief Supplied* given in *Essays and Letters*. The objection the Church and State authorities felt to Tolstoy's activity led, in February 1892, to an incident which nearly cost him his liberty.

He had recently sent an article to the Russian Review, _The Week_, and had consented to the omission of anything the Censor would not pass, when Dr Dillon, the correspondent of the London _Daily Telegraph_, applied to him for news of the famine. Tolstoy authorised Dillon to go to the editor of _The Week_ and borrow the article for translation. The result was that the _Daily Telegraph_ published in full what the Russian paper only gave in a toned-down form; this supplied the reactionaries with their wished-for opportunity, and the accumulated bile of Tolstoy's ill-wishers, bureaucratic and ecclesiastical, found vent. The _Moscow Gazette_ (one of whose regular contributors and inspirers was Pobedonóstsev) retranslated Tolstoy's article from the English into Russian, intensifying its strenuousness. In its editorials the paper clamoued for Tolstoy's suppression, and Prince Shoherbátov contributed a letter demanding that he should be exterminated. Rumours to the effect that he had already been arrested soon began to circulate.

Some of Tolstoy's family, alarmed for his safety, and seeing that the article as reproduced in the _Moscow Gazette_ did not agree with what Tolstoy had written, were inclined to put the blame on Dillon, and there was a dispute about it in the Press, but presumably it was the _Moscow Gazette_ that really made the mischief.

So much of Tolstoy's life was lived in retirement and detached from politics that it is only now and then necessary for me to remind readers of the conditions that prevailed in Russia, and that naturally prevail where one man can grant to whom he pleases absolute power over the property, liberty, and lives of others; but at the point we have reached Tolstoy was within a short step of the fate that had befallen nearly all Russia's most ardent reformers.

There existed at Súzdal, in the Province of Vladimír and about one hundred miles to the north-east of Moscow, an ecclesiastical Bastille, used in the nineteenth and even in the twentieth century for the incarceration of people objectionable to the Russian Orthodox Church. It is a Monastery built on the plan of the old Schlüsselburg fortress, but twice as big. In its damp and dismal dungeons men were sometimes confined for acts that were not even illegal. Not only were people imprisoned there by Administrative Order without any trial, 'till they repent and amend', but cases occurred in which they were so imprisoned in direct defiance of decisions given by the Civil Courts, and it even happened that some of the prisoners were completely forgotten by the Government that imprisoned them. This had occurred in the case of two Old Believer bishops whose release, after twenty-three years of confinement, Tolstoy had obtained through the intermediacy of Prince L. D. Urúsov, several years before the period with which we are now dealing.

The use that had been made of Súzdal Monastery, and the fact that the Archimandrites in charge rivalled the agents of the secret police in spying on those condemned to live in the Monastery and on those imprisoned in its dungeons, gave point to Belínski's remark that: 'The Church supports the knout and toadies to Despotism,' and went far to justify Herzen's remark that the Orthodox Russian Church was 'an Asiatic Church, always on its knees before worldly power'. The Church – in Russia, even more than in England – has nearly always sided with the Powers that be, regardless of whether the people were protected or oppressed. For centuries it approved of a system of serfdom that degraded and depraved the masses, and connived at the arbitrary caprices of the Tsars, sanctioning by its authority political repression, executions, and arbitrary violence of all kinds. Under the rule of Pobedonóstsev (who was for a quarter of a century practically dictator of the Russian Church) it had become to all intents and purposes an adjunct of the Police Department, and the liberty of those obnoxious to it was in constant danger.

In other lands the Press would have been a safeguard for so celebrated, and at that time so popular, a man as Tolstoy. But in Russia the best magazines and papers, besides being in constant danger of suppression, continually received secret Circulars prohibiting any reference to this or that public question, and many such Circulars were issued concerning Tolstoy and the famine. Writers for the progressive papers were watched by the police and detectives, nor was speech much freer than the printed word. Students were expelled by hundreds and sent into banishment at the extreme north of European Russia, or to Siberia, for attending meetings which in England or America would have been perfectly legal, while the Universities, Technical Institutes, and Academies, were frequently and arbitrarily closed. Popular and talented Professors were deprived of their Chairs for 'political ill-intentionedness', or their positions were made so unendurable that they resigned of their own accord.

'Ill-intentionedness' was suspected in the Zémstvos and Law Courts, and their rights and powers were constantly and systematically cut down by legislative enactments, or more frequently simply by Circulars from the Ministries. All independent activity by educated people was sternly discouraged and corporal punishment was reintroduced for the peasant population. Amid such circumstances it was a strange anomaly for such a man as Tolstoy to be left at liberty.

Prugávin, who made a special study of the attempts to incarcerate Tolstoy, says:

> In these dark days, days of ominous social silence, when it seemed as though all that was alive and could protest had been crushed, the solitary out powerful voice of Leo Tolstoy rang out like a bell . . .
>
> In artistic as well as in publicist writings, he ardently protested against the oppression and exploitation of the labouring masses by the strong, the ruling, and the rich, and against violence of all kinds: war, executions, taxes, and prisons.

The immediate pretext already alluded to, for an attempt to imprison Tolstoy, is thus referred to by his aunt, the Countess A. A. Tolstoy, Maid of Honour of the Bedchamber, who helped to save her nephew from the danger to which he was exposed. She was writing, let it be noted, years after the event and very possibly may not be accurate about some of the details:

> The worst came about purely from Leo Nikoláevich's carelessness, when he allowed an English journalist to get hold – not for publication – of an anti-Government article. That son *de la perfide Albion* immediately published it in his paper, with the statement that Leo Nikoláevich had allowed him to do so . . .
>
> Rumours began to reach me that the Minister of the Interior was planning to confine Leo Nikoláevich in the Súzdal Monastery without leave to write: that is to say, he would be supplied with a limited amount of paper and would only be able to get more by returning [used] as much as he had received.

She called on the Minister and found him apparently in great perplexity.

'I really do not know what to decide,' said he. 'Just read all these accusations laid against Leo Tolstoy! The first I received I put aside, but I can't go on concealing this whole affair from the Emperor!'

'When [the lady narrates] I saw what danger threatened Leo Nikoláevich, I decided to use all my influence to save him. I wrote to the
Emperor that I was anxious to see him, and asked him to fix a time for
me to come. Imagine my delight when I received a reply that he
would himself call on me that very day!

I was much excited while awaiting his visit, and silently invoked
God's aid. At last the Emperor entered. I noticed that he looked
tired and that he was upset about something. On his asking what I
had to say to him, I replied directly: 'In a day or two a report will be
made to you in favour of incarcerating Russia's greatest genius in a
Monastery.'

The Emperor's face instantly changed and he became stern and
profoundly sad.

'Tolstoy?' asked he briefly.

'You have guessed rightly, Sire!' replied I.

'Then he has designs on my life?' asked the Emperor.

I was amazed, but secretly encouraged: I thought that *only that*
would induce the Emperor to confirm the Minister's decision.

I recounted to the Emperor all that I had learned from the Minister
about Leo's offence, and I saw to my great delight that his face
gradually assumed its usual mild and extremely friendly expression.
Soon he rose to leave. I only allowed myself to say one thing at
parting, namely, that it was of course not on the Minister that the
general indignation – both in Russia and abroad – would fall if his
recommendation were acted upon.

Two days later I learnt that . . . having listened to the Minister's
report of what had occurred and of the (alleged) great public excitement, the Emperor, putting aside the Report, replied literally as
follows: 'I request you not to touch Tolstoy. I have no intention of
making a martyr of him and bringing universal indignation upon
myself. If he is guilty, so much the worse for him!'

I also learnt that the Minister returned from Gáchino making a
show of being, as he expressed it, a 'perfectly happy man'. Had his
recommendations been confirmed much reproach would of course
have fallen on him also. He quite understood that and played the part
of a 'happy man' very cleverly.*

---

* I do not think the Countess A. A. Tolstoy makes out her case against
Dillon, for Tolstoy must have known that the article was wanted for

Tolstoy, born a son of the Orthodox Church and having by his writings turned men from that Faith, was actually guilty of a criminal offence. The administrative powers entrusted to the Governor-General of Moscow were more than sufficient to allow of his being disposed of without even the disagreeable formality of a trial, and it is quite conceivable that the greatest Russian writer then living might have died in a damp and stinking dungeon instead of spending the last years of his life in freedom, but for the fact that he had an aunt at Court. That is how Russia was governed.

Many people who possessed portraits of him tore them up as soon as the *Moscow Gazette* began to attack him and it became evident that he was regarded as politically dangerous.

The ecclesiastics and reactionaries who launched venomous, mendacious attacks on Tolstoy were in the line of spiritual succession to those who brought Socrates and Savonarola to their death; and even today they find worthy successors among some of our own writers to Whom Tolstoy's aspirations are repellent, and who rejoice at any indication of his having fallen short of his aims. Their effusions recall the lines spoken by the Goddess of Wisdom in the poem which Macaulay (whom Tolstoy did not much appreciate) wrote when, at the Edinburgh election of 1847, religious bigotry deprived him of his seat in Parliament:

> Amid the din of all things fell and vile,
> > Hate's yell, and envy's hiss, and folly's bray,
> Remember me; and with an unforced smile
> > See riches, baubles, flatterers, pass away.

---

publication. And another perplexing point remains unsolved. The Minister mentioned by the Countess A. A. Tolstoy is Count D. Tolstoy, Minister of the Interior, who died in 1889; whereas the incident with Dillon and the *Moscow Gazette* occurred early in 1892, and popular report names Pobedonóstsev as the Minister who wished to imprison Tolstoy. Possibly his liberty may have been twice endangered.

13

Patriotism

Among Tolstoy's literary works of 1892 is an essay, *The First Step*,* which pleads the cause of vegetarianism powerfully on moral and humanitarian grounds.

Another article he wrote was *A Conversation among Leisured People*. The characters in it discuss the desirability of living rightly, but owing to the obligation the young are under to the old, and the old to the young, and everybody to somebody else, they all object to any change of their conventional way of life, bad as they admit that way of life to be. In it Tolstoy was holding up to scorn the arguments which chafed him when used by his family or friends to check his own desire for a radical alteration of his life.

In that year he also translated into Russian Guy de Maupassant's short story, *Notre Dame des Vents*, adding some touches of his own, and calling it *Françoise*.

Articles on the famine and articles contributed to famine Miscellanies, complete the list of his writings at this time.

The Kingdom of God is Within You was not finished till 14th May 1893, but the following incident – from its last chapter – refers to 1892.

I was just finishing this two years' work, when on 9th September I had to go by rail to the district in the Governments of Túla and Ryazán where the peasants suffered from famine last year and are suffering still more this year. My train stopped at a station where it met a special train conveying troops commanded by a Governor, and armed with rifles, cartridges, and switches to torture and kill those starving peasants . . .

After describing what the trouble was about, Tolstoy continues:

Where the peasants submit – something peculiar and specially Russian takes place. The Governor having arrived at the place of

* Included in *Essays and Letters*.

action makes a speech to the people, rebuking them for their disobedience, and he either quarters troops on the different houses
in the village (where they sometimes stay a month, ruining the
peasants by their keep), or contenting himself with threats, he
graciously pardons the people and departs, or – as happens most
frequently – he announces that the ringleaders must be punished
and arbitrarily selects, without trial, a certain number of persons
and has them tortured in his presence . . .

When I asked a Governor why such tortures were inflicted on
people who had already submitted and when troops were already in
the village, he replied, with the imposing air of one familiar with all
the refinements of Statecraft, that it was done because experience
proves that if peasants are not subjected to torture they soon again
resist the orders of the Authorities, but that the torture of a few
ensures respect for the orders of the Authorities for ever.

So now the Governor of Túla, accompanied by officials, officers
and soldiers, was setting out to perpetrate just this kind of thing. The
decision of the highest Authority was to be carried out in the same
way by murder or torture, and that decision was that a young landowner with a yearly income of a hundred thousand rubles, was to
receive three thousand rubles more for a wood he had taken by fraud
from a whole Commune of peasants who were starving and perishing
of cold. He might squander that money in two or three weeks in the
restaurants of Moscow, Petersburg, or Paris. That was the business
the people I met were engaged on.

After my thoughts had been fixed for two years in one and the same
direction, fate, as though purposely, brought me for the first time in
my life into contact with an occurrence which plainly showed in
practice what had long been clear to me in theory, namely that
the whole order of our lives rests not on a judicial basis as people
occupying advantageous positions like to imagine, but on sheer, brutal
violence: on the murder and torture of men . . .

The Kingdom of God is Within You is a very remarkable work. It deals
with Non-Resistance as applied to Governments, and contains a scathing
indictment not of war only but of violence in all its forms.

The contention of the book is that Governments which employ
force, make war, maintain prisons, pass penal laws, and rob people by
obliging them to pay rates and taxes, are fundamentally immoral, and

exist for the advantage of the rich and powerful, to the detriment of the poor and needy. It further asserts that it is our duty to refuse to have anything to do with such Governments, whether as voters, officials, Ministers, policemen, or soldiers.

To most of us of the Western world such a thesis appears quite unreasonable. But as Tolstoy presents it, it assumes great plausibility and weighs with many people of tender conscience to the extent of seriously influencing their conduct. At every English election, a number of votes are not, or for years were not, used, owing to Tolstoy's influence.

I cannot convey his point of view or show its plausibility better, perhaps, than by recounting an occurrence to which he often alluded as having happened within his own knowledge.

A village Community wished to migrate to Siberia. Unable to secure official sanction and impatient of bureaucratic delays, they eventually resolved to go without permission. They sold up their belongings and set off. In Siberia, whether from ignorance of geography or because they were illegal immigrants, they failed to find suitable land to settle on and wandered further and further till they reached a no-man's land beyond the Russian frontier, yet ignored by Chinese officials. Here they settled, free from taxes, free from conscription, with no drink shop (Governmental or other), and no tithes to pay. The soil was fertile, and after some fifteen years' hard work the penniless immigrants had become prosperous.

One day a Russian Government official lost his way and stumbled upon this Community. The necessary scientific rectification of frontier soon followed, the district became Russian, and all the blessings of civilisation poured in upon it. They paid taxes and arrears of taxes; their young men for that year and for the preceding years went as conscripts; the Government drew a revenue from the vodka sold to them, and a priest collected tithes and levied contributions for his own and his family's maintenance, so that in a few years the Community was again desperately poor.

The story illustrates Tolstoy's view of Government as an almost unmixed evil, but it conceals a sophistry; for the fact is that a village Community of that kind carries with it its own Government: namely its Elder and his assistants, who do not scruple, if necessary, to use physical force to maintain order. It is true that in a very primitive peasant Community with a traditional routine of life and a customary method of communal agriculture, their laws and customs are so in-grained that they need a *minimum* of Government. They are just the people to gain least and suffer most from coming under the control of a bureaucracy. But it would be rash to assume that in the absence of any central Government the various races that compose the Empire would all live in peace and harmony; and the more it happens that men of different creeds and customs come into touch with one another, the more necessary is a definite external law enabling them to co-operate without being tempted to settle their differences by violence.

In writing for Western readers there is however no need to dwell on the weak side of Tolstoy's position. It is more to the point to emphasise its plausibility and to show that it should not be brushed aside without consideration. Let me therefore mention another aspect of the case and, this time, one not specially Russian.

We are often told that Governments exist primarily to protect life and property, but the plain fact is that all the burglars in Europe do not steal as much property in ten years as any civilised and Christian Government seizes and destroys in a single month of anyone of the wars it periodically wages. And all the murderers in the world do not kill nearly as many people in a whole generation as the Government of any one of the most enlightened and Christian countries kills in a single week's hostilities.

We may disagree with Tolstoy's conclusion that Governments do nothing but harm, but if Governments are to exist they must at least learn to behave themselves better than they have done in the past.

The strongest and most impressive part of the book is its scathing denunciation of war. So overwhelming is Tolstoy's indictment that he almost carries the reader with him when he goes on to denounce patriotism, the cause of wars, as in itself a degrading superstition and a vice.

Tolstoy stated the case against patriotism and war powerfully, and it was important to have this well done in order to have some literary counterpoise to the patriotic influence exerted by the classics and the Old Testament – books written when people did not know other nations, but sincerely hated them, and when the foreigner was a natural enemy and men believed that their national God abhorred the 'Gentiles', and desired to see the Hivites and the Amorites smitten hip and thigh.

Tolstoy showed convincingly that Christianity, with its doctrine of the Fatherhood of God, is fatal to patriotism, and that even those who object to the word 'God' and prefer some other phraseology, can frame no rational outlook on life which justifies the sacrifices the modern world offers up on the altar of international jealousy and enmity – sacrifices often as reckless and as blind as those that of old were offered to Moloch or to Mars.

What he did not see, however, was the rational basis that exists for national feeling of a non-malevolent kind. If the world is to be organised, law to prevail, and Governments to rest on the will of the people (all things of which we generally approve), then it is practically necessary that the world should be subdivided into kingdoms of manageable proportion, and once such subdivisions exist, it is natural to remember that 'charity *begins* at home', and our first duty is to see that we get things rightly arranged in our own section.

The extent of Tolstoy's influence in promoting a spirit of peace among men is not easily estimated. What the teachings of Isaiah and of Jesus had not accomplished in two thousand years naturally could not be accomplished in the few years between the publication of his anti-war opinions and the outbreak of the Great War. Considering the restrictions of the Censorship in Russia and the obstacle presented by defective translations in other countries, the influence his opinions and feeling exerted was remarkable. The conscientious objectors to military service who put their case best were everywhere those who learned it from him. The effect of his fundamental challenge to governments on the moral ground that to compel men to learn to slay their fellows is an intolerable wrong, threatened to attain serious proportions, before the establishment of the League of Nations allowed us to hope that governments themselves may promote the cause of peace. That possibility renders the moral problem less urgent, but it would again present itself acutely should the League break down.

The complexity of human affairs is apparent in this matter. Tolstoy protested vehemently and powerfully against an established and customary evil which was quite firmly rooted. His arguments were not all valid, and he scornfully rejected the line of advance along which the greatest progress has actually been made towards the ends he desired. He could not and would not believe that governments could be trusted to do anything effectual towards banishing war, and he relied on the conscience of individuals to refuse to fight and to refuse to support governments. Actually it has been through the governments that the repugnance for war he helped to arouse has operated, and the League of Nations – an institution he never advocated – obtains from his works much of the driving force that enables it to operate successfully, while, on the other hand, it is because people do not accept the whole of his doctrine, and do not distrust Government as he did, that the League is able to function at all. One is reminded of what, as a young officer, he wrote of 'the union of mankind by religion'. 'I understand that to accomplish this the conscious labour of generations will be needed. One generation will bequeath the idea to the next, and someday fanaticism or reason will accomplish it.'

In *The Kingdom of God is Within You*, as in his other books, Tolstoy pushes Non-Resistance further than any other writer of modern times, and he baffles our attempts to bring his conclusions to a practical test, by asserting that human existence is of no value in comparison with the sanctity of this moral law. But by the assumption that it would not matter if our race perished, he evidently transfers the trial of the case to a future state of existence, and besides begging the question, his attitude has the additional disadvantage of tending to make all ordinary human activities appear worthless.

No appeal to experience moved him in the least. Some five years before his death, I wrote an article on *The Right and Wrong of Non-Resistance** and sent it to him. I thought he would either object to it, or explain that I had presented his position incorrectly, or else would have to admit that his case needed restating. But all I got was a mild intimation that he was hurt at my not standing firm to the principle; and when next I visited him, he made a remark I have never understood. He said: 'I have only one thing to object to in your article, that is, that it destroys my position at its roots.' I do not suppose he meant that my arguments had convinced him that his position was wrong, for in his writings he continued to urge it as confidently as ever. I fancy he meant to say: 'If your arguments were sound my principle would be unsound, which is a *reductio ad absurdum*.' He said it gently, quietly, and with obvious premeditation, and I had no opportunity that visit to discuss the matter, for he had been ill, and his daughter Mary asked me not to excite him by discussion. When I next saw him he was over eighty, and one hardly expects a man of that age to abandon a

* *The Humane Review*, April 1905.

principle he has formulated with great effort and to which he has been firmly wedded for many years.

However horrible war may be – and I regard it as on a par with slavery, duelling, and cannibalism – to stop it by the method Tolstoy commends (that of each conscientious man refusing to serve as a soldier or to pay taxes) has the grave disadvantage that if successful it would disintegrate the State, and if attempted by all humane people, would throw the control of affairs into the hands of those who were not humane.

If even on the question of war I do not quite see eye to eye with Tolstoy, the difference becomes yet greater when we pass from war to civil Government. He maintained that even in the most democratically governed countries – England, France, or the United States – Government is an absolute failure, since it does not secure a fair chance for each citizen to develop his powers, choose his way of life, and enjoy the full fruits of his labour. That accusation is just, if one compares what is with what should be. But if we treat matters comparatively, and ask, What practicable way of regulating human affairs incurs fewest objections? then the existence of Governments, and of democratic Governments in particular, may well be defended.

Twenty-five years before Tolstoy formulated his indictment, Gladstone had written:

> Decision by majorities is as much an expedient as lighting by gas. In adopting it as a rule, we are not realising perfection, but bowing to an imperfection. It has the great merit of avoiding, and that by a test perfectly definite, the last resort to violence; and of making force itself the servant instead of the master of authority.

To which these words of Burke may well be added:

> I am aware that the age is not what we all wish, but I am sure that the only means to check its degeneracy is heartily to concur in whatever is best in our time.

The Kingdom of God is Within You was not allowed in Russia at that time, but it circulated and was eagerly read nevertheless. And by a strange caprice of Fate the exposure it contained of the flogging of the peasants by a Governor – though written by one who had himself narrowly escaped imprisonment a short time before – resulted in that Governor's dismissal from his post.

Tolstoy's participation in the famine relief, together with his popularity as a writer and the abundant evidence of his disinterestedness and courage, had made him at that time the most conspicuous and influential unofficial person in Russia. His relations with the political reformers however were then, as they always remained, strangely dual. He cordially sympathised with their protest against oppression and was on their side when ill-treated, but the moment they approached to power or began to prepare for anything like a Parliamentary government, he simply turned his back upon them. The result was that their feelings towards him swung like a pendulum. Sometimes they were keenly sympathetic, at other times they regarded him as a broken reed and poured fierce scorn on all his works.

Prince D. N. Shakhovskóy (in an article written when he was in prison for signing the Vyborg Protest against the dissolution of the First Dúma) recalls Tolstoy's relations with the Progressives, and recounts how, when the second year's famine came on (in 1892), the Press was not allowed to publish appeals for help, and such references as were permitted failed to evoke the aid urgently needed. A private meeting was therefore convened in Moscow, in the apartment of I. I. Petrunkévich, to hear a report by K. K. Arsényev who had just returned from visiting the famine district of Túla. Among those present were P. N. Milukóv (subsequently Leader of the Constitutional Democrats), Professor Grot, and Tolstoy. In the course of the discussion that took place, Tolstoy gave it as his opinion that 'Russian writers have a traditional method of rendering assistance in such cases by the publication of a *Miscellany* to raise funds for the cause, and that is the only thing we can now do.'

Such a publication was in fact agreed upon and successfully carried out.

The general impression at that gathering was 'that the obstacles placed by the Government in the path of all efforts to meet a great national disaster are intolerable, and that it is necessary at all costs systematically to organise the social forces with a view to obtaining greater freedom'. That meeting was the forerunner of the Congresses held during the 1890s by those actively engaged in Local Government work, and these in turn prepared the way for such measures of Constitutional reform as Russia obtained in 1906. Tolstoy neither aimed at, nor approved of, a Constitution, yet beyond doubt his indictment of unbridled Autocracy contributed to the change that then came about.

To the *Miscellany* above referred to Tolstoy contributed an article *On*

How to Help Those Suffering from the Famine. He had no work of fiction ready, but allowed his folk-story, *The Empty Drum* [in *Twenty-Three Tales*], which up to that time had not been allowed to appear in Russia, to be modified sufficiently to induce the Committee of Censors to pass it, a matter fortunately accomplished by merely altering the word 'Tsar' in the story, to 'Chieftain'. This exquisite little story is one after Tolstoy's own heart. It was current from time immemorial among the peasants of the Vólga district, and its appearance among Tolstoy's works is an instance of the extent to which he was the mouthpiece of the thoughts and feelings of the Russian people.

Tolstoy called one evening at the house of D. Anúchin, who had the publication of this *Miscellany* in hand. The maid who opened the door was displeased that a man in a sheepskin overcoat and felt boots should have the impudence to come to the front door, and she administered a suitable reproof. The visitor, learning that Anúchin was not at home, remarked: 'Tell him Count Tolstoy called.' The maid received the message sceptically and reported it ironically, but was much taken aback to learn that the man she had treated so brusquely was not merely a Count, but the most famous of all Counts.

As an instance of the length to which Tolstoy carried his theory of Non-Resistance, Anúchin mentions that he once asked him: 'May I kill a wolf that attacks me?' and Tolstoy replied: 'No, you must not, for if we may kill a wolf we may also kill a dog, and a man, and there will be no limit! Such cases are quite exceptional, and if we once admit that we may kill, and may resist evil, evil and falsehood will reign in the world unchecked as we see is now the case.'

Here once more it is very obvious that Tolstoy was substituting an external test – the fact of slaying – for any more subtle criterion. He was no doubt trying 'to demagnetise the watch', and to counteract the evil doctrine of an eye for an eye and a tooth for a tooth, but he was hardly adopting a method likely to succeed.

In reply to the editor's request for a contribution to an Album of Autographs issued in aid of the Famine Fund, he sent the following characteristic note:

I do not know how to fulfil your wish. Frenchmen have an advantage over us in that respect, for they know how to do such things and are not ashamed of them. But I confess I feel so ashamed that I cannot master the feeling. Who can have any need of a bit of my writing?

For heaven's sake do not imagine that I say what I do not think and feel! I cannot, and never could, either read in public or write in albums. Please excuse me, and do not be angry, and believe in my sincere respect.

For another *Miscellany* issued for the same object, he edited a translation of an article by Henry George. Inconsistent as it may seem with his no-Government beliefs, he had by this time become an ardent adherent of that writer's views on land-taxation. George's *Social Problems* and *Progress and Poverty*, with their deep feeling, lucid statement, broad outlook, indignation at existing inequalities, and absence of practical administrative detail, were books just calculated to secure his warm sympathy.

A glimpse of Tolstoy at the beginning of the winter of 1892–3 is given us by Semënov, who mentions that he had altered considerably during the preceding couple of years. His beard had become quite grey and his hair was thinner. He seemed smaller, but his deep-set eyes still seemed to pierce one's soul. He was then feeling hopeful of the spread of a good spirit among people, and mentioned with great approval a priest, Apóllov, who having become convinced that the dogmas of the Church have no sound basis, had resigned his living though he lacked any other means of subsistence. Tolstoy also spoke very warmly of the schoolteacher Drózhzhin, who for conscience' sake had refused army service. It was the first instance of such conduct that had come under his personal notice, and he attached great importance to it.

At the same interview Tolstoy dropped a characteristically sarcastic reference to his old friend Fet, remarking that: 'Fet says he wants nothing and his demands are very modest. Give him a soft bed, a well-cooked steak, a bottle of good wine, and a couple of good horses – and he wants no more! . . . ' He went on to express sympathy with the famine-stricken peasants, and irritation against the Government and the upper classes. His face showed indignation when he told how in his Province of Túla, and in Ryazan, many peasants wished to migrate to Siberia, but because the landowners needed a supply of cheap labour, 'a Circular from the Minister of the Interior appeared, temporarily forbidding migration!'

Though Tolstoy's main contention was that in order to help the peasants 'one must simply get further away from them and get off their backs; when you have done that, they will recover and find their own road and follow it,' he nevertheless welcomed efforts to assist the people temporarily, and to give them something at once. Every ruble contributed gladdened him; and he remarked that there was an awakening of conscience in society, and that people were opening their purses and contributing their mites. This he called *Zaccheising* [after Zaccheus who gave away half his property to the poor], and he recounted with emotion how one person had brought him an old fur coat and another some jewellery. Yet alternating with this feeling and growing stronger as time went on, was the other feeling to which I have referred, and on 3rd May 1893 he notes in his Diary: 'Was at Begíchevka. Felt indifference to the empty business of relief and repulsion at the hypocrisy.'

It was during the preceding winter that he first made the acquaintance of P. A. Sergéenko, who subsequently wrote many books and articles about him. Sergéyenko tells us that on the occasion of their first meeting, at the tea-table of a mutual friend, the conversation turned on one of the young Tolstoys, who was then looking out for an estate. Someone present said: 'Leo Nikoláevich, tell your son when he finds a suitable estate to come to me for advice before concluding the bargain – or he may do something stupid.'

Tolstoy shrugged his shoulders, and said: 'Why hinder him? The more stupidities he commits the better for him.'

Sergéyenko did not understand this, and asked: 'Why will it be better for him?'

'Because the sooner his teeth are set on edge by estates, and he finally convinces himself by personal experience that nothing good can come from them, the sooner will he understand that only those should possess land who work it themselves.'

Towards the end of January 1893, Semënov took charge of the relief work at Begíchevka, and remained till the winter frost broke up. Tolstoy himself, after a three weeks' visit to Moscow, returned to Begíchevka with his two eldest daughters and there wrote the last pages of *The Kingdom of God is Within You*.

Among other workers at that place were P. I. Birukóv and A. P. Ivánov. The latter was a short, elderly man, much the worse for wear, with a thin, pointed beard, and a thick purple nose. He had once been an officer, but had taken to drink, lost caste, and dropped into the 'golden regiment'. Towards the end of the 1870s he had come to

Yásnaya as a beggar. Up to that time the Countess S. A. Tolstoy had always copied out her husband's writings, but she so disliked his attacks on the Church in *A Criticism of Dogmatic Theology* that she declined to copy it. A. P. Ivánov happened to have a good handwriting, and Tolstoy took him into the house and employed him as an amanuensis. When he had earned a little money he would buy himself clothes and go off; but after wandering about for a while he would again take to drink, pawn all he had, and return to Tolstoy. This happened several times, and on one occasion Tolstoy found him in Rzhánov House in great misery. It was he in fact who narrated to Tolstoy the episode of the washerwoman whose death is narrated in *What Then Must We Do?*, and it was also he who rescued the fragments of *Church and State* from Tolstoy's waste-paper-basket. At Begíchevka, Ivánov copied out *The Kingdom of God is Within You.*

I knew him years later. He was a man with many good qualities and gave me much information about Tolstoy – for whom he felt both sympathy and respect.

One gathers from Semënov that even in the famine district Non-Resistance principles did not work quite smoothly, despite Tolstoy's potent personal influence; for we read of the wood-carters being dis-honest and of someone explaining that: 'People tell them that with you Tolstoyans they can do what they like: you won't defend yourselves and won't employ the law against them.'

Yet, on the whole, Tolstoy's influence seems to have been strong enough to keep the work going with a considerable measure of success.

In spite of all efforts, however, distress and destitution increased day by day, and those who were at work amid it all felt it strange to see the idle, genteel life of the neighbouring gentry who, in their fine com-fortable houses, surrounded by the broad acres of their private estates, lived on in their accustomed way, hunting and visiting and having dinners, music, and dances, and displaying not merely indifference to the increasing destitution of thousands of peasants, but even enmity towards them.

To show how little ground the Government had for suspecting Tolstoy of political conspiracy, it may be mentioned that when two young men and some women Social Democrats came to Begíchevka offering help, but admitting that political propaganda was their chief aim, Tolstoy refused to allow them to remain.

The help given by his group was quite free from any tendency. None of them did any preaching or propaganda. To make the distress of the peasants publicly known and to render relief was their only care.

They were all the time exposed to police supervision and espionage, but they easily detected the spies who appeared upon the scene, and avoided all the traps that were set.

As the months went on and conditions became worse the horses began to starve to death, typhus spread, and the death-rate in the villages rose terribly.

Throughout this long and dreary time no fear of personal danger caused either Tolstoy or his children to refrain from the work, nor did the grey monotony of the misery exhaust their patience, and this in spite of the fact that he gravely questioned whether he was doing 'the right thing'.

The year 1893 at last brought a better harvest. The famine ended and with its close we enter a fresh phase of Tolstoy's life. The preceding fifteen years were a time of great struggle and change in his life and outlook; from now onwards no radical alteration occurred, and his life ran pretty steadily in its groove till towards its end.

Beyond completing *The Kingdom of God is Within You*, which, while it carries his no-government argument to an extreme, contains a valuable and powerful indictment of war, and is one of those of his works which produced the strongest influence on his readers, Tolstoy did not write much in 1893, except the translation, or rather adaptation, of Bernadin de Saint-Pierre's *The Coffee-House of Surat* (included in *Twenty-Three Tales*). *Walk in the Light While There is Light*, which had been begun in 1887, was completed and published in 1893 by Chertkóv's persuasion. Though generally coloured, as was inevitable, by his own strong feelings, Tolstoy very seldom deliberately set himself to write fiction with a propagandist purpose. *Walk in the Light* is a notable exception to this rule.

On 9th August Tolstoy finished a very interesting essay, entitled *Non-Acting*, of which he wrote to Gay:

> I have finished my book, and now throw myself from one thing to another: I have not finished my article on Art, but have written one on Zola's and Dumas's letters on the mental conditions of today. Zola's stupidity, and the prophetic, artistic, poetic voice of Dumas, interested me very much.

This essay appeared in Russian and (as often happened with Tolstoy's works) was badly translated into French. He generally disregarded such occurrences, but on this occasion, feeling specially anxious that his ideas should reach French readers in an intelligible form, he rewrote the article himself in French, rearranging it at the same time. Excepting letters to correspondents, this was, I believe, the only work Tolstoy ever wrote in French – all the rest having been in Russian.

The article is an earnest plea to men of good will to 'stop and think' of the meaning of life and of the work they undertake, before allowing themselves to become immersed in affairs, often useless or even harmful, that absorb them to the exclusion of all opportunity for calm reflection.

The article on Art referred to in the foregoing letter was a preliminary sketch – commenced in 1890 and frequently resumed and reshaped – for the work which ultimately grew into *What is Art?*. The sketch was entitled, *What is and what is not Art, and when is Art important and unimportant?*, and was not printed till 1900, when it was called *Art and Not-Art*, and was mistaken by some critics for a supplement to and modification of Tolstoy's main pronouncement on Art.

I have already referred to some of the changes in Tolstoy's moods and manners that resulted from the alteration in his religious outlook, but one point remains to be mentioned. When young and comparatively unrecognised he had a tendency, as we have seen, to be arrogant and quarrelsome, but in later life, when he had become the most famous man in Russia, he impressed many observers by his modesty and consideration for other people's feelings. Nor was this altogether the result of his Christianity. It resulted largely from his having found his feet and become sure of himself. A certain kind of arrogance is allied to painful self-consciousness and self-dissatisfaction, such as he often experienced in early life. If traces of his old arrogance were at times discernible even late in life, this was generally in relation to people and classes of people – rulers, politicians, scientists, commercial men and manufacturers – with whom he was but little in personal touch. To those whom he knew he was generally considerate and kind. The friction that arose in his own family will be dealt with separately, later on.

Nothing very remarkable happened during 1893; but I will quote an account of a conversation he had with some Russian-Armenian students who called on him to tell him of the oppression of their countrymen in Turkey, and who expressed the idea that their only hope lay in Revolution.

'Come now,' said Tolstoy, 'is their condition really so hopeless? Don't people exaggerate? Even granting that it is all true, still no doubt some Armenians share in the oppression. What I mean is, that the more influential and wealthy of them squeeze their own people not less than the Turks or the Kurds do . . . the question is not one of nationality! . . . If the Turkish Armenians were liberated tomorrow, some other Government would oppress the poor and the weak just the same: and whether it is an Armenian, Russian, or French Government, really does not matter.'

'It may interest you, Leo Nikoláevich,' said one of the company, 'to know that among the Armenians another movement now exists, not content with merely political aims but taking up an economic ground, and having primarily in view the interests of the labouring classes on the lines of Social Democracy . . .'

'Oh, don't talk about that,' said Tolstoy ironically, frowning slightly: 'I can't speak of it without laughing!'

'But,' replied the other, 'the basic idea of Socialism cannot, I imagine, be altogether repugnant to you. On the ground of the brotherhood and equality of man . . .'

'But, allow me . . . ! Where, in a Social-Democratic State, does equality come in? How can it be got? The wealth now held by the minority will have to be administered by someone, who will, of course, be an ordinary human being with certain weaknesses and defects. They aren't going to invite the angels to come and attend to the distribution of wealth, are they? Well, once it has to be done by certain people – let us say by the most eminent – *they* will rule us. Equality will again not be obtained . . . no! that is not what we have to think about, nor should we call on the Turkish Armenians to rebel,' continued Tolstoy, becoming more and more excited and evidently anxious to convince us of the justice of his argument: 'one must preach to them and to their oppressors humane and pure Christian ideas. Only *that* can lighten and improve the condition of the people. And please don't be frightened at the word "Christianity". I mean nothing mystical, but simply the love of man by man: their brotherly, cordial relations. If all the energy of the patriots who preach the struggle for emancipation were directed into that path, it would in my opinion be far better and more useful. I will go even further and say that it is essential to follow that course.'

'But,' someone replied, 'such humanitarian teaching is only possible under normal conditions of life, and among more or less civilised people. Among barbarians such as the Kurds . . .'

'Allow me . . . !' interrupted Tolstoy again. 'Is not a Kurd a man like you and me? And have we any right to kill him? Why do you suppose he will not understand this Christian appeal and will not value it? Believe me, he will understand it a great deal better than some bureaucrat or other – say, for instance, our Chief of Police, Vlasóvski! Personally, I would sooner undertake to preach compassion to a Kurd than to Vlasóvski. I repeat that Armenian patriotism, like every other, is paganism, against which all thinking people must struggle!'

After some time the conversation passed to other topics, and Tolstoy asked one of his student visitors what he was studying at the University. Hearing that it was Western literature, he exclaimed: 'Excellent! Western literature is very rich . . . One only regrets that *vita brevis, ars longa.* There is so much that is good and interesting and acts beneficently on the soul, that one has not time to read it all. I am just now studying a writer who is quite unknown among us – Amiel. My daughter has translated his *Journal Intime.* We are sending it for publication to the *Northern Messenger,* and I am thinking of writing a Preface. Unfortunately very little is known about him. Luckily N. I. Storozhénko has sent me some information or I should not have known how to manage it.'

'Under your editorship, Leo Nikoláevich, a booklet of translations of Guy de Maupassant's stories has appeared,' said one of the visitors. 'Will any more be published?'

'Yes . . . In my opinion, next to Victor Hugo, Maupassant is the best writer of our time. I am very fond of him and rank him above all his contemporaries. I have written a Preface for an edition of his works which will appear shortly. In it I have fully explained my view of his works and especially of his talent.'

'Excuse me, Leo Nikoláevich, but some people are rather surprised that your name should be in any way connected with the popularisation of the works of Maupassant . . . It was thought that you would hardly have sympathised with a writer who chose such themes . . .'

'One must look at Maupassant from the right point of view,' said Leo Nikoláevich. 'Many people judge him wrongly. He is not only a man of remarkable talent, but the only writer who has, at last, understood and presented the whole negative side of the relations of the sexes. That implies real talent! It is true that at first he went wrong and approached the thing from quite another side. But he afterwards understood his mistake and was, as it were, reborn. And no one else has described the sufferings and spiritual torments born of base relations with women as he has done. Do you remember the story in which he describes a sailor's encounter with his own sister in a house of ill-fame? How that story sets one thinking! What a deep trace it leaves on one's soul! Such stories certainly cannot evoke in the reader any love of or interest in profligacy, no matter into what slough the author may lead us.

. . . In Maupassant there was, however, an inner contradiction sure sooner or later to lead him to suicide. With what bitterness he describes a man's spiritual isolation and orphanhood! That gloom never really leaves him, and he more than once describes the fate of a solitary, deserted man whom no one needs. . . . By all means reread Maupassant! You will find much in him that is remarkable and highly instructive,' said Leo Nikoláevich, at parting.

In this conversation and in scores of others that might be quoted, whether with students, peasants, acquaintances, or people Tolstoy chanced to meet, one continually finds an eagerness to impart to them some thought or feeling he valued. Thirty years before this he had defined Education as 'a human activity having for its basis a desire for equality and a constant tendency to advance in knowledge'; and in that sense one may say that his conversation was truly educational: it aimed at placing his collocutors on a level with himself and at increasing their understanding of the matters dealt with.

The death, on 27th January 1894, in Vorónesh prison-hospital, of E. N. Drózhzhin, the schoolmaster who had refused military service, made a very great impression on Tolstoy.

Drózhzhin had been summoned to serve in August 1891, but on the ground that he was a Christian and wished to serve the Prince of Peace, he declined to take the oath which would have bound him to obey those who wished him to learn to slay his fellow men. He was kept in solitary confinement in Kharkov for a year, and then sent to a Disciplinary Battalion at Vorónesh, where he was exposed to cold, hunger, and solitary confinement, for fifteen months, until he became consumptive. He was then reported as unfit for military service, but was sentenced, nevertheless, to nine years' imprisonment. On his way from the Disciplinary Battalion to prison, he was kept standing for a long time in the street one very cold day, without any warm clothing, and contracting inflammation of the lungs, he died three weeks later.

Ever since then Tolstoy was extremely interested in the cases of refusal of military service, news of which reached him from nearly all countries in which conscription existed. How numerous such cases were was not generally known, for the military authorities were concerned to keep them secret. The position of a Christian Government met by a refusal to learn to kill (based on obedience to Christ's commands) is a very difficult one. The fundamental clash between Christianity and patriotism is more vividly revealed by such incidents than by anything else, and both in Russia and elsewhere the example of men willing to die for their faith constitutes a real danger to governments that rely on force. Cases, for instance, have occurred of soldiers being converted by non-resistant prisoners they had been set to guard, and deliberately laying down their arms. A problem deserving the attention of conscriptionists generally is: How, in the case of those who believe they are sent into the world to benefit and not to slay their fellow men, are you going to combine compulsory military service with freedom of conscience? Something might be said for demanding that every man should devote some years to the service of his country at risk to his life. But to forbid a man willing to spend that time in dangerous industrial occupations (such as coupling railway trucks, coal-mining, or work at a blast furnace) to be of use in that way, and to insist that he must train as a man-slayer, is to inflict on him an intolerable moral wrong, more calculated to make him hate his Government than love his country.

14

The Doukhobórs

After the strenuous famine-relief work of the two previous years, came a quiet period of steady literary work.

Tolstoy's popularity at this time was strikingly demonstrated by what happened at the Ninth Congress of Russian Naturalists, held in Moscow in January 1894. Professor V. Zínger, with whom he had long been acquainted, was announced to speak at one of the large public meetings of the Congress, and the Professor's son invited Tolstoy to be present. At first the latter declined, on the ground that he was quite unaccustomed to large assemblies, but ultimately he turned up unexpectedly during the meeting, and as it was difficult to find him a seat, he was asked to go on the platform. Though he had often been rather hard on the Scientists, no sooner were the audience aware of his presence than thunders of applause broke out, long continued and again and again repeated. Tolstoy was much abashed. He rose and bowed, and again a tumult of applause broke out which seemed to shake the walls. Speaking of it afterwards to young Zínger, he said: 'Why did you tell me there would be no ceremony? . . . All those people in evening dress . . . It was not a scientific meeting, but a scientific Carnival!'

How far Tolstoy was from being an old man (counting in years he was sixty-six) is indicated by the almost boyish ardour with which he took to cycling. Bicycles were just coming into use in Russia, and in the large towns only those were allowed to use them who obtained a licence after demonstrating their proficiency to the police. Tolstoy easily performed the necessary horseshoe movement and a figure-of-eight, and rode off triumphantly with the permit and tin label which according to the regulations had to be attached to each bicycle.

The ardour he showed in cycling was however but a faint reflex of his interest in more serious matters. His friend Gay having finished his great picture of the Crucifixion early that year, brought it, on his way to Petersburg, to show to Tolstoy, who asked to be left alone with it. Gay on returning to the room found him in tears. Embracing him, Tolstoy said, 'I feel, dear friend, that *that* was how it really happened! It is the greatest thing you have ever done!'

Of those who complained of the picture as lacking beauty, Tolstoy remarked that what such critics desire is that one should 'paint an execution and make it look like a nosegay!'

Alexander III when he saw the picture said it was horrible, and its publication was prohibited. Tolstoy wrote: 'When first I saw it, I was convinced that it would not be allowed, and when I now imagine an ordinary exhibition, with fine ladies and landscapes and paintings of *nature morte*, it seems laughable to think it could be included.'

Side by side with his many interests there always existed the possibility of his arrest – a thought which did not oppress, but rather stimulated him. On 1st June he wrote to Feinermann:

Two days ago I went with Chertkóv to Krapívna to see Bulygin, who is in prison for refusing to provide horses for the army requisition. He is in the firmest and most cheerful frame of mind, and calmly and involuntarily preaches [to those whom he meets] in prison. I mean to go and see him again tomorrow.

Have you heard that Kudryávtsev has also been taken by the gendarmes and is in confinement somewhere?

I feel it hard to be left at liberty . . . However, one must not seek, any more than one must avoid [persecution].

That month, N. N. Gay, the most sympathetic and humane of his friends, died suddenly. The simplicity, fervour, and genuineness of his artistic nature closely corresponded to one phase of Tolstoy's own more intellectually powerful personality, and his death was a great loss.

Meanwhile the family life at Yásnaya flowed on as usual, and one comes across many references to his children. For instance, Arbúzov tells us how Mary, the second daughter, applied her father's teaching to her own life:

No matter who fell ill in the village, Márya Lvóvna, as soon as she heard of it, would take various little bottles from her store and go to the sufferer's hut and attend on him till he was well. To give one instance out of many: Dómna, the wife of one of the peasants, Vlás Evdokímov, was ill after childbirth. Márya Lvóvna at once began to attend her. The illness lasted all the summer, and Márya Lvóvna looked after the sick woman and helped Vlás in all his domestic affairs, raking the hay, he mowed and carting it to his yard. Later when the rye was ripe, Vlás mowed it and Márya Lvóvna bound the sheaves, and where it grew thick even reaped it with a sickle. In a word, she worked in the field till harvest was over, and every day after work went home and fetched rye-bread and a pot of milk for Vlás and his family and white bread and beef-tea for the sick Dómna. Then, returning home, she would do her own room, have her supper, and go to bed. She did not waste a single half-hour, and during the time of fieldwork never went out to sit on the terrace where the family and the Kuzmínskis used to have tea.

The family spent the winter of 1894–5 in Moscow as usual; and there Semënov (being entrusted by his village Commune with the purchase of some land) visited Tolstoy, and he thus reports a conversation they had about landholding. Tolstoy asked:

'Well, and are you too buying some of the land?'

'I am taking eight desyatínas [nearly 22 acres].'

Tolstoy smiled, and remarked: 'Well, God will forgive you!'

'What do you mean? Is it such a sin?' said I, surprised.

'Of course! Land is God's gift. It can be no one's property. It is as necessary as light and air and should be as free as light and air for all to use.'

'But it is not free. It is divided among people and we have to pay heavily even to be allowed to use it. We are tired of paying rent and have decided to get the freehold.'

'That is why I say, "God will forgive you"; but He will not forgive those who own land and squeeze others with it.'

'How should it be arranged?'

'The land should be freed and all private rights in it cancelled. The ownership of land is a terrible evil, which will be abolished.' And he began to tell me about Henry George and his Single Tax system, which, were it introduced, would cause the land to be in the hands of those only who worked it, so that it would become impossible for anyone to make it a means of exploiting other people.

'But would such a tax not be too heavy for those who work the land?'

'Not at all! The tax would be as much as the land would yield without labour by its fertility and nearness to a market. If it would yield pasture for three rubles, that would be the tax. If a market was near at hand so that one could get a good revenue from having a market-garden, one would have to pay more, and if the land was in the chief street in Moscow one would have to pay a great deal for it, but it would be quite fair, for it is not the owner who gives land its value but the whole community, and the community would only take back what is rightly its own!'

'That is very good, but how is one to get it; how carry the reform through?'

'I think,' said Tolstoy, 'that such a revolution could be carried out by the Tsar. As the emancipation of the serfs was accomplished by the will of the Tsar, so also the abolition of territorial injustice can be accomplished by the same power . . . No other power will do it, because it will be contrary to the interests of the classes who would support a Constitutional power.'

At Christmas that year the children with some of their numerous friends arranged a masquerade in which celebrities personally known to them were personated, including Professor Zakhárin, Anton Rubinstein, Vladímir Solovév, Répin, and above all, Tolstoy himself. V. Lopátin took the latter role, and made up so admirably that when he appeared dressed in a blouse and belt of Tolstoy's (secretly procured for him by Tátiana Lvóvna), with his hands stuck in his belt in front in Tolstoy's customary way, many of the guests mistook him for their host, who – himself taken by surprise – accepted the joke good-humouredly and cordially shook hands with his pseudo self.

Lopátin mentions that he was glad of his opportunities to visit the Tolstoys, for it made it possible for him to convince himself of

the ardour of Tolstoy's desire to find the truth of life, to obtain it from any source, and to induce people to follow the path that alone leads to the accomplishment of man's true destiny. The simplicity of Tolstoy's relation to the thoughts and feelings of every man, his interest in what each one thought and knew, his bitter regret at the divergence between his view of life and the wishes of those about him, and the pure, almost childish, joy with which he glowed at any indication that his spiritual world was understood by anyone else, convinced me of the profound honesty which has made the great artist a great Christian teacher.

The mingling of grave and gay in the family was often very striking. They were so close to life's great problems and dangers, yet there was so much of youth, mirth, art, and high spirits. Contrasts help one to feel vividly, and I have never been more struck by the charm of simple music than when one winter's evening in Moscow, calling to ask Tolstoy's explanation of some question that perplexed me, I chanced upon an assembly of guests, many of them young people. Tolstoy was engaged, and I waited among people I did not know, in the little vestibule at the top of the stairs, before entering the large, plainly furnished room, in which the family usually drank tea and gathered for games or music. The eldest daughter came up to speak to me and put me at my ease, and Mary, accompanying herself on a guitar, struck up a Gypsy song which she sang admirably. Others joined in the chorus. Song followed song, and one felt that their love of music was innate. When I came to know the family better I realised how much amiability, talent, frankness, and charm there was among them, apart from Tolstoy's own overpowering genius. If I felt this, who came as an outsider drawn by interest in Tolstoy's views and who for a long time feared to intrude on the Countess's domain, I think it must have been still more strongly experienced by others.

It was the fashion for Tolstoy's followers to speak of the Countess as the great obstacle to his carrying out his principles, and to suggest that, were he but free to act, wonderful results would follow; but I do not think that either they or he had any clear idea of how he would have lived or what he would have done, had he had only himself to consider.

Certainly the Countess's position was one of great difficulty. She played a very large part in her husband's life and devoted much attention to his material welfare. She never concealed her disagreement with many of his views, and often based her case frankly on grounds of family interest, but judged by ordinary standards, she was for many years an admirable wife – and to apply extraordinary standards in her case because her husband was an extraordinary man, would be unfair.

During 1894 Tolstoy's literary work – besides Prefaces to Maupassant's Tales, Sernënov's stories, and one to a Life of Drózhzhin – included a short book entitled *Christianity and Patriotism*, which besides expounding the views alluded to in a previous chapter, contains very clever ridicule of the patriotic enthusiasm into which crowds in Russia, and even more in France, were being hypnotised by the festivities held in connection with the visits of the French and Russian fleets to

Cronstadt and Toulon. Two other essays written at this time are worthy of particular attention, as they were the commencement of a series of articles on Religion, expressing a broader and maturer view than was expressed in the books he wrote in the years immediately following his Conversion.

The series referred to contains: *Reason and Religion, Religion and Morality, How to Read the Gospels, A Reply to the Synod's Edict of Excommunication*, and *What is Religion*? They occupy in all less than a hundred pages of *Essays and Letters*, but are the final outcome and ripe fruit of the intense struggles of his powerful mind with the greatest of all problems. They were written over a period of eight years, the last of them not appearing till 1902.

Of the origin of the first of them, Feinermann writes:

'I know,' said Tolstoy, 'that I shall be blamed, but still I must repeat: "Reason, reason, reason!" There is no other way to reach the truth. It is only through reason that we can nourish our minds, as it is only through our mouths that we can nourish our bodies. I have received a letter from a certain Baroness – very cordial and sincere. She is interested about religion, and honestly and frankly – though rather confusedly – questions the value of reason. I have been all day considering how to answer her, and the matter is becoming clearer and clearer to me.'

A few days later, on 26th November, the reply was finished. As it is accessible to English readers, I will not summarise it, but will only say that it clears Tolstoy from the charge sometimes made against him of being a mystic – if by 'mystic' is meant one who claims to have received any kind of revelation not accessible to sane men of goodwill generally. It finishes with the statement that man's duty ('the will of God') is known only:

By the use of reason by all men, transmitting both by deed and word to one another the consciousness of truth that is ever more and more elucidating itself to them . . . So I think the clearing-up by each man of all religious truth accessible to him, and its expression in words (for expression in words is one sure sign of complete clearness of thought) is one of the chief and most holy duties of man.

Copies of this epistle were sent to the various Tolstoy Colonies and aroused much discussion and many disputes; for a strong current of mystical dogmatism had sprung up among some of his followers, and this pastoral epistle occasioned splits in the movement. Eventually many Tolstoyans returned to the bosom of Mother Church, and some even became monks and nuns and bitterly reproached Tolstoy for his rationalism.

The next of the series was *Religion and Morality*, finished on 28th December 1894. It was written in reply to an enquiry from a member of an Ethical Society, who asked Tolstoy what he meant by 'religion', and whether morality could exist independently of it. The article contains a classification of religions into three groups: (1) Selfishness – the religion of all the babies, who desire as much milk and warmth and comfort for themselves as possible and do not care what happens to the rest of the world; (2) Patriotism – the religion of all who make the welfare of their family, clan, group, or nation, the chief aim of their life; and (3) those who recognise a supreme Lord or Law whose service transcends any calculable advantage accruing to themselves or their group. Every sane man must of necessity have a 'religion', that is to say, must have some outlook on life enabling him to know why he approves of some things and disapproves of others. His outlook on life, however expressed, explains his rational – as distinct from merely instinctive – motives for action, and tends to shape his course. In actual life many people are more or less swayed by two, or even by all three, of these religions at once, but one or more of them they must have, if their life has any purpose at all.

The conclusion Tolstoy arrived at is, that 'Religion is a certain relation established by man between his separate personality and the universe or its Source, and morality is the ever-present guide to life resulting from that relation.'

Other writings of the year were translations of Mazzini's *Letter on Immortality*, and of *Karma*, a Buddhist legend.

The new year [1895] began very sadly both in public and private affairs. On 30th January, Nicholas II received the representatives of the Local Government bodies, who came to Petersburg to congratulate him on his accession to the throne. When one or two of them in their Addresses ventured respectfully to suggest the necessity of allowing the representatives of the people some voice in public matters, he made the memorable speech in which he said: 'It is not unknown to me that recently in some Zémstvo meetings, voices have been heard of men who have been carried away by insensate fancies concerning the participation of representatives of the Zémstvos in the affairs of the Government of the country. Let all men know that I, devoting my whole strength to the national welfare, will maintain the principle of autocracy as firmly and infallibly as it was preserved by my late never-to-be-forgotten parent.'

He only receded from that position ten years later when the disasters of the Russo-Japanese War had made obvious the impossibility of governing so great an Empire without allowing any free expression of public opinion. Even then it was not till a railway strike had isolated Petersburg from the rest of the country that he granted something like a Constitution, and the concessions he made were so modified shortly afterwards that the Dúma was practically impotent, and he abdicated twelve years later without having ever allowed a responsible Ministry to be formed that could have carried on the Government of the country.

This speech naturally evoked indignation among all who desired emancipation from the thraldom that stifled Russia. Prince D. N. Shak-hovskóy has told how it fell to his lot to call on Tolstoy one very frosty day, and to invite him to attend a private meeting presided over by P. N. Milukóv, at which the situation was discussed by some of the representative Local Government reformers.

On his arrival at Tolstoy's Moscow house, Shakhovskóy was told by the manservant that the Count was in the yard and would not be disengaged for two hours. By a little persistence the Prince managed to get admission to the yard, where he found Tolstoy, axe in hand, breaking the ice in a large water-tub. Hearing the object of the Prince's visit, Tolstoy uttered the words, 'insensate fancies', in such a tone that Shakhovskóy felt that no persuasion was necessary and that he had not to tell Tolstoy of the time and place of the gathering.

That meeting, however, furnished a fresh proof that Russian public opinion was not ripe for political action. The feeling of indignation was strong, but found no outlet. Tolstoy was as indignant as anyone, though he spoke with quiet self-restraint. One of the proposals made was to publish in the Press of Western Europe a protest on behalf of educated Russians against the Tsar's rejection of their claim to be heard. Tolstoy was asked to draw this up and did not definitely refuse, but said that his intervention would not have the desired effect, for any protest from him would be connected with his Christian-anarchist views and would therefore not be regarded as representing a broad public opinion.

Naturally he did not sympathise with any plans for an organised resistance. 'What', said he, 'do we need an organisation for? Don't we form as it is a Masonic Lodge in which two words enable us to understand one another and call us to the common cause? When Shakhovskóy came to me, do you suppose we needed any Masonic signs?'

Following this public calamity came a very great personal grief. Little seven-year-old Ványa (Iván) died on 23rd February. It was the first time Tolstoy and his wife had lost a child that had outgrown early infancy; and what made the loss the more severe, was that Ványa (their youngest) was highly gifted and showed signs of inheriting the best qualities of his parents. To the Countess the blow was a crushing one, and she was in such despair that for a while she prayed to die. She dreaded the thought of going back to Yásnaya, where she would miss the child more even than in Moscow, and plans were formed for going abroad. At this crisis Tolstoy showed his wife great consideration. Much as it would have run counter to his inclination to leave Russia he was ready to do so for her sake, but a private intimation reached them from a relation in Petersburg, that though no obstacle would be placed to Tolstoy's leaving the country, it was improbable that he would be allowed to return. The journey abroad was therefore abandoned. Tolstoy was himself ill at this time and went to a doctor every day for a slight operation, so that the family did not move to the country till June, by which time the Countess was reconciled to a return to Yásanya.

On hearing of his son's death I wrote Tolstoy a letter of condolence, and a little later when sitting in his room one evening I noticed that he paused in what he was saying to another visitor and looked at me to attract my attention. He then went on to speak of death, and said that it was a mistake to exaggerate its sorrow. What is really terrible is not death, but life lived without a purpose. I forget his words, but remember that he made us feel that the ordinary expressions and shows of grief should not be encouraged. There is no doubt an inevitable and irrepressible regret for dear ones removed by death or distance, but our aim should be not to give way to it, and rather to encourage and help the living than pine for the dead or absent.

Feinermann, hearing a false rumour that Tolstoy was going abroad to escape arrest, wrote to him about it and received this reply:

We did prepare to go abroad, but voluntarily, and not in connection with any persecution or the possibility of any . . .

What prompted us towards going abroad was my wife's state of health and her terribly overwrought state of soul after the death of our youngest son, Vánichka. [Diminutive of Ványa, the pet name of Iván.]

Now that she is suffering so much I feel with every nerve of my body the truth of the words that a man and wife are not separate beings, but one . . . I should like tremendously to give her if but a part of the religious consciousness which I possess (feebly, yet sufficiently to enable me sometimes to rise above life's woes) because I know that that alone – the consciousness of God and of one's sonship to him – gives life; and I hope it will be given to her, not of course by me, but by God – though it reaches women with great difficulty.

Early that year he had finished a story with the triumph of unselfishness over death as its theme. Simply and admirably written, *Master and Man* once more proved that his command of his art was unimpaired by increasing years or by stress of soul. It is a country tale of a master (an innkeeper and village merchant) and his man, overtaken by a snowstorm and losing their way. Warmly clad and well fed, the master lies on the almost frozen body of his poor servant and saves his life. When peasants dig them out of the snowdrift next morning, the master himself is found frozen to death. His last moments were full of gladness at having found the pearl of great price that lies in human sympathy.

Semënov, who visited Yásnaya that summer, tells us of the life he found there:

The family life at Yásnaya, as in Moscow, was that of a landowner, gay and frivolous. It did not accord with Tolstoy's own serious view of labour and his disapproval of idleness and luxury, and this involuntarily distressed one. One pitied Tolstoy who had by this time lost his own enthusiasm for fieldwork and for helping the peasants with personal service, and now lived without it. But after lunch Tatiána Lvóvna announced that a woman from the village, who had borrowed some straw from the estate and had undertaken to bind a desyatína of rye, had come to say that she had been summoned to do the work, but could not do it now because one of her family was ill, and asked Tatiána Lvóvna to get the steward to let her postpone the work.

'Let us go and bind the rye for her,' suggested Tatiána Lvóvna.

Half a dozen of us, including Tatiána Lvóvna and Márya Lvóvna, and from among the guests, M. A. Schmidt, Birukóv, a young lad, and myself, volunteered, and went very willingly to the work . . . The rye was soon tied, the sheaves piled up, and we returned home gaily.

That was the only time at Yásanya that I saw personal help, by work, given to the peasants. Other kinds of help – medicine, advice, and money – I noticed every time I was there.

Besides the story already mentioned, Tolstoy wrote this year *Three Parables*, and a vehement protest entitled *Shame*! against the practice – which had been reintroduced and legalised – of flogging peasants.

In this year, too, he wrote the first of his articles on the Doukhobórs, entitled *A Persecution of Christians in Russia*. According to the excellent system of transliteration formulated and introduced by the British Academy, the name of the sect should be written Doukhobór, but as it has become familiar in the older form, and is so written by themselves, I here follow that usage.

There is much that is remarkable and good about them, and much that deserves to be remembered – especially their sturdy endurance of persecution – but to make the story clear, I have to emphasise a point which has been misunderstood and has caused much confusion.

Reading the Tolstoyan pronouncements about the Doukhobórs, or their own statements about themselves, one would suppose them to be the most reasonable and excellent of Christians – regarding all men as brothers and equals, and living in peace and amity with all men without force or law, and needing no government but that of their own reason and conscience and the advice of their chosen Elders. Yet during the more than thirty years we have had them in view, I do not know of a single person, English, Russian, or Canadian, who ever became a Doukhobór, or settled among them as one of themselves, though many have wished to do so. Evidently there is something that needs explanation. What is it?

The reply to the question is, that at the time of the migration, the orthodox Doukhobór believed his Leader, Peter Verígin, to be an incarnation of the Deity (like his predecessors in the Leadership); besides which the sect were an exclusive and secretive people. Taught by the persecutions of the past, they do not disclose this mystery to outsiders, and are consequently cut off from the rest of the world by a double wall of superstition and concealment. An ignorance of this fact at first, and an unwillingness to admit it afterwards, has warped Tolstoyan statements about them. We shall presently see how this came about.

The extent to which the more intelligent Doukhobórs really believed in the divinity of Verígin is open to discussion; just as it is difficult to say how firmly the more intelligent members of the Church of England believe, today, in the Trinity and the Scheme of Redemption. But the practical importance of the doctrine of the divinity of their Leader is shown by the evidence of those who have studied the matter most carefully and impartially, and by the fact that the history of their movement becomes intelligible as soon as one grasps that clue to its perplexities, while it presents a series of insoluble puzzles until one does so.

Since 1844 the Doukhobórs had been a sect resident in the Caucasus. One of their Leaders, Peter Kalmikóv, on his deathbed, in 1864, named his wife, Lukériya Vasílyevna, to succeed him. She took into her favour a handsome young man of the ruling family, named Peter Verígin, separated him from his wife, had him to live near her, and caused him to be regarded as her successor. He, however, on one occasion let his wife come to Tiflis to meet him. Lukériya, hearing of this, fell into a great rage, had a fit, and died without after all formally appointing him her successor. Her relations and near adherents, knowing that she had quarrelled with Peter, doubted the genuineness of his divinity and refused to recognise him. Most of the Doukhobórs, and especially those living farther off who knew least about the quarrel, accepted him as Leader, and a bitter feud commenced between adherents and opponents. The Russian Authorities were appealed to, to decide who was to have possession of the 'Widow's House' – as the Doukhobórs' Communal House to which considerable property was attached – was called.

They decided in favour of the anti-Veríginites, and in 1887 banished Verígin, by Administrative Order, to a small town in the province of Archangel. During his stay there, in spite of the vigilance of the police, Doukhobór emissaries succeeded in visiting him, supplied him with money, and received his instructions.

Precepts of poverty, chastity, and Non-Resistance, as well as a condemnation of war and Government – much resembling Tolstoy's teaching – have been held for centuries by various peasant sects whose spiritual descendants the Doukhobórs of the eighteenth century were. But after they ceased to be a scattered sect and became a compact clan in the nineteenth century, they unconsciously abandoned their principles and submitted to a Theocratic despotism, without however ceasing to talk the language of Christian anarchism. It then became customary for them to serve in the army and hold private property. But now Verígin met exiles who told him of Tolstoy's views and lent him Tolstoy's writings. He must have seen that besides being in accord with early Doukhobór doctrines, Tolstoy's Non-Resistance principles, involving the rejection of conscription, furnished an admirable weapon for use against the Government that was keeping him in exile. Accordingly, he instructed his followers to practise Non-Resistance, to cease holding private property, to share all things in common, to abstain from intoxicants and narcotics, to become vegetarians, and during the 'time of their tribulation' (i.e., apparently, during his exile) to abstain from marital relations. Not all his followers were able to accept so sweeping a reformation, and a fresh split occurred in the sect.

The Government, discovering that the continued ferment among the Doukhobórs was influenced by Verígin, decided to remove him to a yet more inaccessible locality, and sent him, via Moscow, to Obdórsk, in Northern Siberia.

It was at this time that Tolstoy first made acquaintance with the Doukhobórs. He met three of them, who came to Moscow to see their Leader on his way to Siberia. He was naturally delighted to discover people who, apparently of their own accord, carried out the principles he advocated – principles that met with a feeble response among his own class. Here at last were men not merely professing, but apparently practising, the very principles of Christian anarchy dear to him, and *without that disintegrating result* that had been so evident in the Tolstoy Colonies. It never occurred to him to suspect that they were governed by a Theocracy, and had a Moses to hand them down fresh Tables of the Law as and when required. So he wrote that what was occurring among them was 'the germinating of the seed sown by Christ 1800 years ago; the resurrection of Christ himself', and added that the main condition for the attainment of a Christian life among us 'is the existence and gathering together of people who even now realise that towards which we are all striving. And behold, these people exist!'

Verígin's blow aimed at the Russian Government was serious. Nothing could be more awkward for a great military Power than to have the occasional and sporadic refusals of military service to which it was accustomed, reinforced by a collective refusal proceeding from a well-organised sect, basing their action ostensibly on the teachings of Christ.

In accord with instructions from Verígin, the Doukhobórs held a large meeting on 29th June 1895 (the eve of St Peter's, his name, day), at which they publicly burnt the arms they were in the habit of carrying. While so engaged, Cossack troops fell upon them and flogged them cruelly. It would take long to tell of the persecution that followed. Their first martyr was Sherbínin, brutally done to death in a Penal Battalion in August 1896. Hundreds more died from exposure and lack of food, and from banishment to unhealthy places where they could find no work.

The news of this persecution greatly grieved Tolstoy, who was indignant that such things should be possible; and he and Chertkóv arranged for P. I. Birukóv to go to the Caucasus and collect information for publication. Birukóv's intentions were admirable, but he started with a bias, and instead of visiting all sections of the Doukhobórs and learning what their quarrels were about, he contented himself with what was told him by the Veríginites, and drew up a report which missed the very point essential to an understanding of what had happened – a point already known to the Government.

On his return to Moscow, Chertkóv, Tregúbov and he issued an urgent Appeal for help. This was admirable in that it drew attention to the cruelties inflicted on a well-intentioned and industrious peasantry, but it erred by representing them as being highly enlightened and free from superstition. It said:

> The Spirit Wrestlers [i.e. the Doukhobórs] base their mutual relations and their relations to others – and not only to people, but to all living creatures – exclusively on love; and, therefore, they regard all men as equals and brothers. They extend this idea of equality to the Government authorities; obedience to whom they do not consider binding upon them when the demands of the authorities conflict with their conscience; though, in all that does not infringe what they regard as the will of God, they willingly fulfil the wishes of the authorities.

Yet, of twenty thousand Doukhobórs, less than half ultimately followed Verígin, and the Appeal did grave injustice to those Doukhobórs who had been sufficiently enlightened to throw off his yoke – often at the cost of severe persecution at the hands of his followers.

Had the Doukhobórs really carried on their Community peacefully and well for a century with no government but such as was purely voluntary and uninfluenced by force or superstition, they would have demonstrated the possibility of anarchism as a workable social system, and their example would have been invaluable to Tolstoy's propaganda. Unfortunately the facts do not fit that view of the case, and still more unfortunately, the Tolstoyans – anxious that the facts should fit their theory – were extraordinarily blind to what was obvious to other observers.

Had Tolstoy personally been much in contact with the Doukhobórs he would have noticed that something was wrong; but he was well over sixty-five, and though still vigorous in mind and body, was too much engaged with his own work to spare much personal attention for the Doukhobór business, greatly as it interested him. He relied on the reports collected for him, and lent the weight of his authority to what turned out to be a mistaken view of the case. In this connection two letters of his to Peter Verígin,* written in November 1895 and October 1896, are worthy of attention.

Peter Verígin was quite unaccustomed to play second fiddle to anyone, and on coming into communication with the Tolstoyans in exile set himself to go one better than Tolstoy. For instance, he suggested that people ought not to be satisfied with making their own boots, but ought to give up the use of everything that contained any metal, since to obtain metal men have to be sent to labour in the mines. (He apparently confused convict labour in Siberian mines with mining in general.) He also elaborated a suggestion Tolstoy himself had made, that the writing and printing of books is an evil, for the books are often harmful and their production involves an immense expenditure of labour which might be devoted to the production of food and shelter for those who are in need. There was, it will be remembered, in Tolstoy's character a tendency to opposition, and when Verígin wrote these things, Tolstoy replied by pointing out the good books do, and especially the fact that there are already so many harmful books in the world that the evil can now only be met by writing better books. 'One wedge drives out another.' In his reply to Verígin he even goes so far as to say:

To speak frankly, your stubborn contention against books seems to me a peculiarly sectarian method of defending a once adopted and

* See *Essays and Letters*, p. 167.

expressed opinion. And such a peculiarity does not accord with the conception I had formed of your intellect, and especially of your candour and sincerity.

With regard to mining, he said:

As to your argument that to produce books and railroads people have to burrow underground for ore and to work at a furnace, why – all *that* has to be done before one can have even a ploughshare, a spade, or a scythe. There is nothing bad in burrowing underground for ore or working at a furnace, when I was young I would willingly have done both to show my spirit, and so would any good young fellow today, provided the work were not compulsory, nor for life, and were surrounded by the conveniences which will certainly be devised as soon as everyone is expected to work and the labour is not put on wage-slaves only.

Reading these letters one regrets that so many people (including myself) often urged Tolstoy to be more moderate and to recognise the good side of existing industry and institutions. Had he but been surrounded by people who played in another octave and outran him in the adoption of extreme conclusions, we might have had from him many more letters like these, full of sound practical sense and showing an appreciation of things as they are.

Verígin continued to amuse his leisure by writing letters to the Tolstoyans suggesting the moral desirability of setting our horses and cattle free from the slavery of having to serve us, and of ceasing to spoil the earth by tillage. Why not rely on Nature for our support? Why not live in a warm climate, where fruits and nuts ripen of themselves and man is free to spend his time in contemplation? Tolstoy, to show the wrongfulness of modern business and politics, had dwelt on the teaching and example of Christ, and Verígin again went one better by pointing out that, 'We must live as he lived, and we see that Christ did no physical work, nor did the Apostles.' Pushing the idea of simplification to a yet further extreme he suggested that if only we choose our place of residence rightly, clothing is a useless and immoral luxury. 'That the Apostles and Christ wore clothes and ate bread was natural, for there were plenty of clothes and bread, and (one must add) even Christ and the Apostles were not able, all at once, to go naked.'

All this was in its way very good fooling, and no doubt gave Tregúbov and the other Tolstoyans to whom it was addressed plenty to think about. But Peter Verígin had little idea of adopting the practices he commended, and was careful not to write these things to his own followers, yet by a queer irony of fate these letters of his played a part in the subsequent story of his sect.

For a while things remained as I have described: Verígin in exile in Siberia; the Veríginite Doukhobórs refusing army service and severely persecuted; Tolstoy and the Tolstoyans (with whom I was in alliance, and whose views I accepted) sincerely representing this resistance as resulting solely from the fact that the Doukhobórs understood Christianity sanely and adhered to it faithfully.

I remember in Moscow receiving from Chertkóv an urgent request to hectograph a number of copies of an Appeal on behalf of the Doukhobórs, which he told me Tolstoy wanted to have done quickly and to which Tolstoy would write a Conclusion. For a large part of that night, after the servants had retired and the blinds had been carefully drawn so that no one should see us doing what was illegal and might have led to our arrest, my wife and I worked at the task he had set us, and we duly delivered the copies to Tolstoy, only to learn that it was a document Chertkóv had drawn up but Tolstoy did not approve of. It had to be rewritten before he would associate himself with it by writing an appeal for help for the Doukhobórs.

I then got my first glimpse of the fact that Chertkóv felt quite competent to try to make up Tolstoy's mind for him, and had no hesitation about using Tolstoy's name for his own purposes. Tolstoy was not subservient to Chertkóv, but he felt so grateful to him for devoting himself, his energies, and his means, to the promotion of the movement, that he put up with more from Chertkóv than he would have submitted to from anyone else. There were occasions – one of which I shall cite later – when Tolstoy signed documents prepared by Chertkóv of the contents of which he was unaware, or retained no recollection.

The publication, in December 1896, of *Help!*, the article by Birukóv, Tregúbov, and Chertkóv, to which Tolstoy added a Conclusion, led to the banishment of Birukóv and Tregúbov to small towns in the Baltic Provinces, while Chertkóv (whose mother had considerable influence at Court) was permitted to go abroad. He settled in England and remained there for some ten years.

Besides entrusting the management of the Doukhobór migration to

Chertkóv's direction, Tolstoy entrusted to him the publication of his works abroad both in Russian and English, and especially any new writings forbidden in Russia.

The effect of this close relation between Tolstoy and Chertkóv became more important as time went on. Chertkóv had much in common with Tolstoy but had a striking individuality of his own, and exercised considerable influence on his teacher. In spite of my own strong desire to be on good terms with Tolstoy's friend and representative, I failed to get on well with him, and am perhaps a little in danger of not doing him justice. Yet so intimately was he connected with Tolstoy's public activity and private life that I cannot leave him out of the picture.

Once when I was lecturing on Tolstoy in Chicago, a man in the gallery asked: 'What has Tolstoy *done*?' It seemed that the obvious answer was, that he had set people thinking and had stirred their consciences, but I understood that the man meant to say: 'Leaving aside what he has said and written, how has Tolstoy managed his public affairs?' Nor was that an unfair question, for Tolstoy frequently told us to judge the organisers of Churches and States by their works, and it is obviously unfair to try them by their works and him by his aims and aspirations. We must in fairness have one standard for both. He wrote books and consumed food, which means that people had to produce food and paper and books. What, then, did he *do*? How did he manage his business? As regards his private affairs the reader already knows the reply. He handed over his estates to his wife and family, and lived on their hospitality, for they would have been grieved and angry had he left them. Who can grudge freedom from care for his own material support to a man who gave so much to the world? Yet, to hand the management of affairs over to others does not solve – it only postpones or relegates – the moral and other difficulties involved in the maintenance of human existence. The hermits and the monastic Orders in the Middle Ages, who lived on charity, had done much the same thing, and we know that they did not solve the economic problem for us.

His public affairs he handed over into Chertkóv's charge, and again it would be churlish to object to his transferring to other shoulders a burden of business that would have hampered his literary work. But in dealing with property or power the moral responsibility that clings to its acquisition, use, or retention, clings also to its transference, and one cannot help asking whether it was wisely transferred, and whether

Tolstoy's great influence was used well, whether by himself or by another. Therefore the public activity of Chertkóv must interest those interested in Tolstoy.

There is no doubt of Chertkóv's devotion to his teacher or of his genuine disapproval of the existing order of society. The denunciatory side of Tolstoy was well represented by him, but the humble, forbearing, patient, considerate, and enduring side, was not. Descended from serf-owning ancestors, the spoilt and only son of a fond mother who was the widow of a very wealthy landowner, he never had to endure discipline, or undergo training in self-control. Our statesmen and public men are subject to much criticism and plain-speaking and have their conduct judged by recognised standards set by law or custom. But Chertkóv, in the exercise of his power and influence as Tolstoy's representative, was not subject to any such healthy restraint. He acted in Tolstoy's name, and Tolstoy's reputation shielded him from criticism. Then again there is no recognised criterion to try him by, for Tolstoy repudiated all the customary standards of business life, and Chertkóv was in the position one sometimes sees a child in, who invents and alters the rules of his game while he plays it.

It must be added that with regard to the publications the task before him was an unusual and complex one. Many of Tolstoy's later works were forbidden in Russia and the rule about these was not fixed or definite. Works allowed in one edition, might or might not be allowed in another. Russia did not belong to the Berne Convention and therefore anyone in any other country could translate or could use as he liked a Russian author's work, first published in Russia, as soon as it appeared, and by his specific declaration that people might do as they pleased with his works, Tolstoy abandoned even the moral control which, as a matter of courtesy, authors are generally allowed to exercise over their own works in lands where they are not copyright.

Beyond all this, the translation of Tolstoy's works presents certain difficulties: besides a knowledge of Russian and a mastery of the language into which the books are translated, the task often demands a knowledge of peasant and other Russian customs and speech, an understanding of the peasants' outlook on life, and a grasp of Tolstoy's philosophy of life, which is frequently reflected in his works of fiction.

The task of making Tolstoy's prohibited works as accessible and intelligible as possible to those who do not read Russian, was therefore one to tax the ingenuity and industry of the most tactful and methodical of men. Chertkóv did not appreciate its difficulties. For instance before his own banishment, he got Tolstoy to sign a letter handing over the arrangements for the English versions to J. C. Kenworthy, who knew no Russian at all; and this merely because Kenworthy was a prominent advocate of Tolstoyan No-Government, Non-Resistant views and had started a Brotherhood Church at Croydon, and a Brotherhood Publishing Company for the publication of his own and other works with a Tolstoyan tendency. How much trouble and confusion this arrangement produced, may be illustrated by the fact that some years later, when my wife translated *Resurrection*, I received from Kenworthy a demand to hand the book over to him. He wrote that Tolstoy had given it, and my wife's translation of it, to him. Tolstoy, when referred to, denied having done anything of the kind, and I did not know what to make of the claim until, after Kenworthy had been placed under restraint as mentally deranged, the following letter, which throws light on the matter, turned up among his papers.

John C. Kenworthy, Croydon

MY DEAR FRIEND – Sympathising with all my heart with the aims of your Brotherhood Publishing Co., I intend to put at your disposition the first translation of all my writings as yet unpublished, as well as forthcoming. Should you find it in any way expedient, as for instance in order to secure for them a wider circulation, to offer the first publication of any of my works to one of the English periodical papers or magazines, and should any pecuniary profit therefrom ensue, I would desire it to be devoted to the work of your Brotherhood Publishing Company.

As for the further right of publishing my works (i.e. after this the first appearance in English, which I intend placing at your disposal) they are to become public property in accordance with the statement I have formerly made public and now desire to confirm.

Yours truly,

LEO TOLSTOY
Moscow, 4 February 1896

Tolstoy had no recollection of writing this letter; and the arrangement had apparently been made by Chertkóv. J. C. Kenworthy took it to mean that a free gift would be made to him of the first translation of all Tolstoy's writings by whomsoever made. Probably much that was eccentric in his conduct can be traced to the hopes aroused by this curiously indefinite promise, and to his subsequent disappointments over it. The Brotherhood Publishing Company soon passed out of Kenworthy's control, which increased the muddle yet further.

We shall see later on that the publication of Tolstoy's works gave rise to much friction, and Tolstoy himself, as well as many others, suffered from these disputes.

* * *

After the first Moscow performance of the *Power of Darkness* in 1896, a crowd of students went to Tolstoy's house and gave him an ovation. He was much touched by this, for he always prized the opinions of students and of the rising generation. But as usual on such occasions, he felt very awkward and hardly knew what to say to them.

The struggle always going on within him showed itself in curious ways. For instance, when someone wished to make him a birthday present of a new bicycle he went to the shop and selected one that pleased him, but before it had been delivered his conscience troubled him, and he changed his mind, cancelled the order, and continued to use a shabby old bicycle belonging to one of his sons. Apropos of this incident he told me that it was so long since he had any possession of his own that needed looking after and taking care of, that he felt he ought not again to allow himself to be so encumbered.

Tolstoy was continually pestered by demands for money from all sorts of people, and once humorously remarked that he had thought of acquiring an inexhaustible purse to supply the demands made upon him, but found it would take him all his time to get the money out for those who wanted it, so he preferred to do without the purse!

His patience was also often sorely tried by poets and other writers who wanted his opinion on their productions.

Peasant writers of talent who dealt sympathetically with peasant life received however much encouragement from him. One of these, V. Lyapunóv, even became Manager of the Yásanya Polyána estate.

Among writers not of that class, Anton Chékhov was one of Tolstoy's favourites both as a man and as an author. Tolstoy regretted that Chékhov's works express no clear philosophy of life, but highly prized his artistic qualities. He was also much interested in Chékhov's plays; but one day at parting, much to Chékhov's amusement, Tolstoy said to him with a touch of the humour that often flashed out in his conversations: 'You are a very good fellow, and I am very fond of you and as you know I can't bear Shakespeare, but still he did write plays better than you do!'

In my own intercourse with Tolstoy I was struck by the fact that as soon as he was convinced that one was really interested in life's great problems, all barriers of race, nationality, rank, education, and ability, were abolished, and one could talk to him quite frankly and on a footing of equality.

He once remarked to me:

There are two kinds of people – those with whom it is worth talking, and those with whom it is not. Those with whom it is worth talking are the freethinkers. I do not mean the Freethinkers who form a political party in Germany, nor the agnostic English Freethinkers, but I use the word in its simplest meaning. Freethinkers are those willing to use their minds without prejudice and without fearing to understand things that clash with their own customs, privileges, or beliefs. This state of mind is not common, but is essential for right thinking; where it is absent, discussion is worse than useless. A man may be a Catholic, a Frenchman, or a capitalist, and yet be a freethinker; but if he puts his Catholicism, his patriotism, or his interest, above his reason, and will not give the latter free play where those matters are touched, he is not a freethinker. With such a man, if your aim is to get at the truth regardless of consequences, you will find that discussion brings you up against a brick wall of prejudice that blocks all progress.

The password to intimacy with him always was intellectual integrity. Any man he recognised as honest and in earnest, was his friend. Devotion to Non-Resistant and anti-Government views sometimes biased his judgement, but it happened that I had not definitely cleared up my own views on those matters at the time I saw most of him, and was so far under his sway that we did not come into collision about them. I was so much attracted by his writings, and so indignant at the unfair attacks made upon him by opponents, that I did not stop to consider closely the consequences of his anti-political programme. It appeared to me that he was fond of paradox and contradiction, and sometimes said outrageous things, but that as he was certainly a sensible, shrewd, experienced man, it was impossible that he really meant that one should allow a man to kill his wife in a fit of passion rather than use physical force to restrain him. I must have been slow to understand him on this matter, for even after I had left Russia and made my home in England, I had strenuous disputes with Chertkóv about it, and on referring to Tolstoy was dismayed to find that he fully endorsed the views that seemed to me incredible.

Though Tolstoy's suspicion and love of contradiction were easily aroused, there was yet a wonderful charm about him, and I never met anyone with such a capacity for encouraging, interesting, and stimulating others. When he called at our house of an evening, our children were always interested and delighted, and still remember his teaching them how to make complicated paper birds that flapped their wings.

Regretting the suppression by the Censor of many valuable articles he met with in the course of his readings, Tolstoy and some of his friends formed the plan of getting out, month by month, a typewritten magazine called *The Archive*, in which such articles could be reproduced. Only about a dozen copies of each number were typed, and they have since become extremely rare. My own is one of the very few sets now in existence. I remember, one winter evening, hearing him read one of these articles. It was by a veterinary surgeon who had had a place under a Zémstvo, but had found that the regulations intended to prevent cattle disease bore so hard on the peasants that he resigned his post. The moral was, that to serve a Local Government is wrong. After the reading discussion followed, and a young man and woman who had passed their examinations to become teachers in village schools said that they still did not see what better course was open to them than to accept places under the Zémstvo and teach village children. At this Tolstoy grew vehement in his indignation. 'God forgive me,' said he, 'I cannot remain quiet when I hear you speak so! Here we have been reading N.'s article, and have agreed with his arguments point by point, and seen clearly how Government oppresses the peasants – and now, at the end of it all, you calmly say that you intend to act just as though you had never heard a word of it!' That was the first incident that made me seriously consider whether, and in how far, I could accept his outlook on non-resistance and its sequels.

Part of Tolstoy's influence lay in his genius for expressing himself aptly, powerfully, clearly, and humorously, and a large part lay also in the fact that he, and he alone, at that time dared and was able publicly and effectively to indict the régime of oppression against which we all fretted indignantly but impotently. There was an additional reason for my affection and admiration for him. I had left England when I was sixteen. Since then so much of my time and energy had been absorbed in earning my bread and butter that, till the time when I began to know him well, my outlook had been a narrow one and I knew comparatively little of the movements of Russian life and thought. His writings and conversation came as something fresh and immensely inspiring. I stepped out into a world of new interests, and this happened just when the business I was managing had got into smooth water and was running so that I had more means and leisure than before, and was not so crushed by work as to be unable to respond to Tolstoy's stimulus. Then again, no sooner had I made his acquaintance than through him I made acquaintance with other interesting people. 'To him that hath shall be given', and one thing leads to another. Thus one day in July 1896, I received a note from Jane Addams, of Hull House, Chicago, enclosing a letter of introduction asking me to take her, and her friend Miss Mary Smith, to see Tolstoy.

Jane Addams comes of a sterling, earnest, democratic American stock. Her father was a friend of Lincoln's. When young she was laid up for years by illness and it was thought she would never be fit for active work, but on gaining strength she resolved, instead of marrying or using her small income to secure herself as much enjoyment as possible, to settle with a friend in a slum quarter of Chicago and do what they could to help the poor ignorant immigrants there. She was gifted with remarkable capacity for organising, character reading, and fitting the work to the workers who came to help her, and soon an important Settlement grew up around them with many branches and offshoots. They always worked with a minimum of rules, and Miss Addams presided over her colleagues by the divine right of willingness and ability to do work others have not an equal capacity to do.

I did not know all this when I talked to my new acquaintances that hot summer day in Moscow. They had come to Russia chiefly in the hope of seeing Tolstoy, whose *What Then Must We Do?* had impressed them greatly.

A day or two later I gave myself a holiday from business, and as the leisurely train took several hours to do its one hundred and thirty miles, we had a capital opportunity to supplement our previous conversations by a further comparison of Tolstoyan and Hull House economics before we reached the station from whence we drove to Yásnaya. One main difference between us – though I did not then sufficiently recognise it – was that Jane Addams had for years been bringing her theories and hopes to the test of experience, and finding out how much she could accomplish, while I was theorising and, without the ballast of experience to steady me, eagerly urging an extreme programme. I did not know how much I was learning, but several things in my new friends' way of thinking and speaking impressed me then, and subsequently modified my views considerably.

When we reached Yásanya Polyána we found that Tolstoy had gone to Túla to meet an American visitor who had been staying with him and had promised to take some letters for him to Prince D. A. Khilkóv, then in banishment in a small town in the Baltic Provinces where his correspondence was under supervision.

When Tolstoy returned he welcomed us cordially, and good-humouredly related his afternoon's experiences. The young American – who had made himself very much at home during his stay at Yásanya Polyána – among other things deriding Tolstoy's vegetarianism – had written saying he would reach Túla station by a certain train and asking Tolstoy to meet him there. Tolstoy went, hoping for a reply from Khilkóv, but only received back his own letters, opened and read by the Russian authorities! The bearer had considered it safest to take them to his ambassador and enquire whether it would be proper for him to deliver them to the person to whom they were addressed. The authority in question had passed them on with the same enquiry to the Russian officials, who of course read them and refused permission. The young gentleman had now taken the opportunity afforded by the fact that he was travelling south, to return these letters to Tolstoy, and had made Tolstoy ride ten miles to Túla to receive them.

It was a good test of Tolstoy's temper that he did not seem at all upset by the incident, though it increased the difficulty of future com-munications with Khilkóv. Tolstoy was then nearly sixty-eight, but neither his morning's literary work nor his twenty-mile ride had tired him, and he proposed to go for a bathe. We all walked together towards the little river that flows at some distance from the house. And now Tolstoy wanted to know about his visitors: where they had come from, what work they did, and what their views were. As Jane Addams told him of Hull House and of the condition of the immigrants who lived in that part of Chicago, he gently took hold of the loose, puffy silk shoulder of her fashionable dress, and smilingly asked, 'And what is this for?' Miss Addams smiled and said the people she worked among liked to see her well dressed, to which he replied, 'You should not like to be dressed differently from them.' Miss Addams laughingly replied that the immigrants were of many nationalities – Irish, Italian, Greek, Armenian, and others – and that she could not dress in all their national costumes! To which Tolstoy made answer: 'All the more reason why you should choose some cheap and simple dress any of them could adopt, and not cut yourself off by your garments from the people you wish to serve.' Between other people such a conversation might have been unpleasant, but there was not a shade of offence given or felt between these two. I do not think Miss Addams explained to him that it is part of her method to try not to shock the prejudices of those whose sons or daughters work at the Settlement, and that it is easier for her when well dressed to go among well-to-do people and interest them in the work, than it would be if by adopting some special costume she made herself conspicuous and announced that she is not as others are.

Following the path through the wood, we drew near the river. The ladies went one way, and Tolstoy took the rest of us to bathe from a wooden shed built on the edge of the stream. He swam well, being expert at that as at all physical exercises. During that same visit he taught me to ride a bicycle without holding the handlebar.

When we got back, dinner was served in the open air to a large party consisting of the Tolstoy family and the visitors.

To Tolstoy, with his impulsive, strenuous nature, and his tendency to theorise, a method of reform which gains only a slow, partial and at times questionable success made little appeal. He wanted a theoretic solution: clear, complete and absolute! Jane Addams on the other hand, with her practical American character, had studied the actual conditions of the Chicago poor for years, effecting what amelioration she could, and was convinced that each one of us can contribute but a little towards the building up of the future city of God. As a compatriot of hers has said:

> The'ry thinks Fact a pretty thing.
> And wants the banns read right ensuin';
> But Fact won't noways wear the ring
> 'Thout years o' setting up and wooin'.

She had, I now feel sure, a much better perception of the next steps in progress than I or even Tolstoy, and as a result of this she succeeds in achieving considerable results, and does not mind if other people sometimes carry off the credit for them.

After she had left Russia, she wrote me a letter, in which she said:

The glimpse of Tolstoy has made a profound impression upon me – not so much by what he said, as the life, the gentleness, the Christianity in the soul of him . . .

A radical stand such as Tolstoy has been able to make throws all such effort as that of Settlements into the ugly light of compromise and inefficiency – at least so it seemed to me – and perhaps accounts for a certain defensive attitude I found in myself . . .

I am sure you will understand my saying that I got more of Tolstoy's philosophy from our conversations than I had gotten from his books. I believe so much of it that I am sorry to seem to differ so much.

I only knew later on how much Tolstoy's views had influenced her. She returned to Chicago determined to do some hours of manual work each day in the bakery, but when she encountered the many urgent claims on her time and attention at Hull House, she felt that there would be something artificial in neglecting work for which nature had specially fitted her, in order to do what others could do better than herself.

Jane Addams and her companion left by the midnight train, but I remained at Yásanya for another couple of days and had some long walks and rides with Tolstoy.

He told me of his own efforts to do right in money matters. When he was studying, and writing, on economics and trying to be particularly strict with himself and discard all luxurious habits, he had occasion to visit Prince Urúsov, Vice-Governor of Túla. On reaching the house he found that the Prince was away from home, but the head police-officer of the district happened to be there and was exceedingly attentive and polite, offering his services and insisting on accompanying 'his Excellency' back to the station. It was 'Your Excellency' this, and 'Your Excellency' that, and there was no getting rid of the man. At the station he would not hear of allowing Tolstoy to procure his own ticket – he needs must get it for him, and enquired, 'What class is your Excellency pleased to travel?' with an air that seemed to say: 'Surely your Excellency requires at least a special car!' Tolstoy's good intentions were not proof against the strain. He felt that the shock to the police-officer's feelings would be too great if he said 'Third class', and so he compromised by saying 'Second class'!

When speaking of the simplification of life, Tolstoy once said to me: 'There is one thing I cannot do without – I must have a quiet room to work in.' This was a most reasonable and modest demand, but one that like *any* demand, runs fundamentally counter to his doctrine, that man must hold himself ready to yield up all he possesses to anybody who likes to take it.

Another story, told me by someone else, was that Tolstoy was once standing on the platform at a station when a lady, taking him for a peasant, called to him from a railway carriage to take a note to her husband who had gone into the refreshment room while the train was waiting. Tolstoy delivered the note, and the lady gave him fifteen kopeks (3*d*.). A minute later someone came up and, in her hearing, addressed him as Count, and the lady learnt to her dismay that the peasant she had tipped was Count Tolstoy. She humbly apologised and begged him to give her back the fifteen kopeks, but he only laughed and said: 'No, no! That is money I have earned!'

We played lawn-tennis at Yásanya on a rather rough sand court. Tolstoy played it just as a recreation, not – as it is often played in England – as one of life's serious duties, and he was rather near-sighted; but the quickness of his movements was very remarkable, and he surprised me by winning the sets in which we were opposed, though I was in the habit of playing pretty frequently and played moderately well.

His favourite indoor game was chess, which he played in what seemed to me the best possible way. I do not mean that he could often beat a strong club player, but that he took this game also as recreation and not as a study. He spent no time on chess literature and willingly played in a room full of people. To make a special study of chess would have been impossible to one with so many vivid and pressing interests in life. From lack of book-knowledge he was often weak in the openings, but he was ingenious in snatching advantages. In fact in chess, as in all things, he displayed originality and alertness.

Like most people who came under his influence I was violently swung from my former habits and found it difficult to adjust myself to my new perceptions. For instance, on awakening to the immensity and urgency of the reforms which could be accomplished if we utilised our opportunities, from being a frequent attendant at the Moscow chess club I forswore it as a luxury and waste of time. But it so happened that Lasker and Steinitz came to Moscow in 1894 to play a match for the world's championship, and at Tolstoy's someone suggested that we should go to see them play. Tolstoy agreed, but I objected, on the score that professional chess with its jealousies and bickerings and diversion of ability to the service of a mere game, was contrary to the trend of his teaching. Without making any fuss about it, Tolstoy just said to the others, 'Do you know, I think I won't go. Maude, here, thinks it would not be good.' I am now ashamed to have hindered his seeing a first-class example of a game he was always fond of, but nearly everyone swept into the strong current of *his* movement got things out of focus and proportion at least for a while.

A booklet was issued at this time from the printing-office of the Holy Synod, attacking and denouncing Tolstoy and giving publicity to Father John of Cronstadt's opinion that he was mad. It was entitled, *Plody Oucheniya Gr. L. N. Tolstogo*. In Russian that title can either be read to mean: *The Fruits of Count L. N. Tolstoy's Teaching*, or as *The Fruits of Teaching* by L. N. Tolstoy (as though it were a companion volume to *The Fruits of Enlightenment*), and it was sold everywhere by street-hawkers as a new work of Tolstoy's. In this way the Holy Synod's malignant insinuation reached many readers who never patronised its bookshops.

We were naturally very indignant, but when I mentioned the matter to Tolstoy he merely smiled and said: 'Ah, they don't know that Pears' Soap would pay them ten thousand pounds for such an advertisement!'

He read English quite easily and did not speak it badly, but when I tried to get him to talk English, he said: 'No, no! With you I'll talk Russian, when I talk English I have to say not what I wish, but what I can.'

It was in 1896 that I first translated anything of his – an extract from his Diary, which we called *The Demands of Love*. It appeared in the *Daily Chronicle* and A. B. Walkley wrote an essay on it which is reprinted in his *Frames of Mind*. The first long article I translated was Tolstoy's *Letter on Non-Resistance* to E. H. Crosby. I now wonder how I could have gone word by word through that letter without detecting the flaw I now see in its argument, but so it was. In spite of the clue Jane Addams had given me it was years before I got the Non-Resistant argument (as I venture to hope I now have) into its true perspective.

Tolstoy's chief writings during 1896 were: his *Letter to the Liberals*, definitely expressing his non-political attitude; *Patriotism and Peace*; *How to Read the Gospels* (a leaflet I translated with great pleasure and consider excellent); a *Letter to the Ministers of the Interior and of Justice*, protesting against the arrest and persecution of those who distributed his writings, and requesting that he (Tolstoy) and not his helpers, might be prosecuted; and finally an article entitled *The Approach of the End*, which deals with Van der Veer's refusal of army service in Holland.

Part of Tolstoy's work that year was *The Christian Teaching* – an attempt he never finally completed to state his religious perception briefly, clearly, and systematically. He also, that year, wrote part of his novel, *Resurrection*, which has been more read in England than any of his other works.

Yet another book on the stocks was *What is Art?*, a work he had had in hand off and on for fifteen years, and which when at last completed was the best arranged and most carefully thought out of all his didactic works. While writing it he had occasion to go to the theatres frequently, a thing he had not done for many years, and also to read a large number of popular novels in various languages. He also in 1896 went to Petersburg to visit a picture exhibition.

During the first quarter of 1897 I saw much of Tolstoy and of some of his friends. I had then lived in Russia for twenty-three years, always looking forward to the time when I could retire from business and return to England, an event that was hastened by his influence. On the one hand my wife and I came to feel that we could live on much less than we had formerly considered necessary, while on the other, his denunciations of existing conditions made me dissatisfied with the methods of even so clean and honest a business as the one I was engaged in. Tolstoy's indictment of the whole industrial system is so scathing that it seems to wipe out the discrimination between better and worse businesses, and sets one comparing things as they are with things as they should be, rather than with things as we can make them. This I have ultimately come to consider an undesirable attitude of mind, but for some years it influenced me strongly. I returned to England soon after Chertkóv had settled there, and at Tolstoy's request allied myself with him and with the movement led by J. C. Kenworthy.

I was anxious to see the practical application given to Tolstoy's views by the men he most commended. One had to live somehow, and he had, it seemed, proved all the ordinary ways of living – all property, laws, and government, as well as all hiring or owning of land – to be immoral. What then should one do? Churches and Governments stood condemned because the actual results of their activity did not correspond with the aims they professed. The time had come to submit Tolstoy's teachings to the same test.

One could not imitate his own life. His roots were firmly fixed in a distant past, and only one with his antecedents and his genius could live as he did or do his work. As Dryden said of Shakespeare:

> his magic cannot copied be,
> Within that circle none may walk but he.

He had relegated his public work to Chertkóv, who in turn had handed over the English publication to Kenworthy and his Brother-hood Publishing Company. Chertkóv was himself taking up residence near the Brotherhood Colony at Purleigh in Essex. It was with these people that I resolved to try my experiment in a new life, of which mention will be made in the next chapter.

The Third Pan-Russian Missionary Congress, held that year, pro-nounced Tolstoyism to be a well-defined and harmful sect. In coming to this conclusion the missionaries were no doubt influenced by the Doukhobór troubles. But Tolstoyism was not a sect. Tolstoy influenced many people even to the point of causing them to change their way of life, but no sect of Tolstoyans existed anywhere among the Russian peasants, whose demands on life were much too definite and practical for that.

Following the proceedings at the Missionary Congress, Tolstoy received two threatening letters, which said that as his harmful activity had worn out the patience of members of the Church Militant, it had been decided to kill him on or before 3rd April 1898.

These threats disturbed the Countess, but had no effect on Tolstoy nor in fact was any attempt made on his life.

15

Excommunication

During a stay in Russia in September 1897 I began the translation of *What is Art?*, which Tolstoy then thought he had nearly finished, but continued to alter, rearrange, and rewrite, for another six months. During the course of that work I received many letters from him. In the first he mentions having written to ask Chertkóv's consent to my translating the book.

While at work on it I ventured to raise objections on various minor points and found Tolstoy remarkably free from the irritability proverbially attributed to literary men. If my queries wearied him, he never let me feel it. In one letter he says: 'You ask my pardon, but I do not know how to excuse myself to you for the heavy labour you have taken on yourself and are executing so well.' And again:

> You have quite correctly restored the words omitted on page 31, and your correction of the quotation from Spencer is also right. I will make my version agree with yours. Altogether I see you are doing this translation with great attention, for which I am grateful. I am almost sure I shall agree with all your comments, but still send them to me, I too will consider each point carefully . . .
>
> I am now living alone in the country and enjoying the solitude. I have got to the end of my book, but as long as it is still in hand I go on correcting and altering.

In another letter he says:

> Your remark about page 14 has made me reread it more carefully, and on reconsidering that passage I have decided to omit the words . . .
>
> Thank you for sending news of yourself, but why so briefly? I want very much to know more in detail about you and your life, and about your wife and children. Tell the boys that I shall be very grateful to them if they will write to me. They are sure to write just what is most interesting: whom they play with, what people and what animals . . .

A month later, in November, he wrote:

I begin by replying in sequence to your admirable and very useful remarks . . .

With all the rest I am in agreement, and have made alterations in my text accordingly. Please send me more such. I am very sorry to have to disillusion you of the hope of soon finishing this heavy labour. There will be not twelve, but twenty chapters! It is true there are no more long ones . . . Thank Arnold and Bertie for their letters. All that they write – about the beans and the moles and the astonishing animal – interests me very much. Do they work with the Colonists? It is good to get accustomed to work while one is young. It gives one strength and tranquillity and independence.

And in December:

It is long since I wrote to you, dear friend, for I have been, and still am, going through much that is hard for me, I will not say bad, for it is in our power to turn evil into good, but often one is not up to it. Also yesterday we moved to Moscow, which depresses me so by its bustle and immorality. That is why I have been slow in sending you the last chapters, and the second version of XI, XII, and XIII. I have also had an unpleasant misunderstanding about the printing of the work in the magazine, *Philosophical Questions*.

After explaining what had happened and what arrangements he intended to make, and when the English edition might appear, he adds:

Please do not raise difficulties, for I am so tired of the disagreements and unsatisfied demands that have occurred with regard to the publication of my works ever since I placed them at everyone's disposal!

Again, on 16th December:

I continue to be heartily grateful to you for your work, for I sometimes hope the thoughts expressed in this book may prove useful. Yesterday I read . . . an article about your Colony in the *Northern Messenger*, and I felt so strong a wish to be working not only with my brain but with my whole being, amid all the conditions of physical struggle – weariness, fatigue, moral satisfaction and friendliness – the struggle which is a necessity of life and constitutes real life which I have known and love, which shines in my memory like a bright star in a dark sky. May God bless them [the Colonists].

Then came another letter, undated; he said:

I send you all the chapters in final proofs, except Chap. XX, which I hope to send in two days . . . As you will see, I have again altered the sequence. I have not been quite well all this time, and that is why I have made such confusion. Please forgive me.

Finally in March he wrote:

DEAR FRIEND – I am very glad that the complete book will not be out for another month. That makes it possible for me to send you the fresh and *very important* alterations in Chaps. XI and XVI, which I send availing myself of your amiability and long-suffering. I am very sorry that these alterations will not appear in the first edition. Here the issue of *Philosophical Questions*, in which the completion of the work was already printed, has been held back by the Censor and sent to the Spiritual Censor. That I think is equivalent to its complete prohibition. I regret the labour lost, but am glad of the opportunity to make, as I said, very important corrections . . . I do not at once send you the alterations in some of the chapters because it is all being set up in type (Sófya Andréevna is having it set up, and still hopes to be allowed to print it). As soon as it is ready, in a couple of days, I will send you a proof with all the corrections, and will mark the places where, for the last time I hope, alterations have been made . . .

What about the boys? Are you satisfied with them? When one brings children up at home one must always remember that much seems bad in them merely because we (the parents) see it all and know both the bad and the good, which with school education we don't see. School education is the hypocrisy of education. All is disciplined and externally seems good, and we are glad not to see the bad. It is the same with what is learnt at school. There they learn all that is necessary to give them an external polish, but the most essential knowledge is not touched on.

Eventually Tolstoy found himself obliged either to forgo publication of *What is Art?* in Russia altogether or to consent to various alterations which Professor Grot made in the book to meet the requirements of the Censor. In one of his letters to me he says:

You will of course pay no attention to the alterations made by Grot to suit the Censor.

As proof followed proof, each covered with fresh alterations, excisions, and additions, often very illegibly written, it required the closest attention to keep the text correct and to discriminate between changes made voluntarily, and changes made for the Censor which I was to disregard. Ultimately, when at last the book was quite finished, my version was the only clear and reliable record that remained of Tolstoy's real intentions, and he wrote a Preface for it in which he said:

This book of mine, *What is Art?*, appears now for the first time in its true form. More than one edition has already been issued in Russia, but in each case it has been so mutilated by the Censor that I request all who are interested in my views on art only to judge of them by the work in its present shape.

The book contains the results of long consideration of the relation of art to life in general. The ardour of Tolstoy's temperament and the strength of his likes and dislikes make the book excellent reading, but one's attention is at times diverted to particular examples which admit of doubt.

In the Introduction to *What is Art?* in this edition I have dealt with this subject, and will therefore only touch on it briefly here. Tolstoy tells us that art is possible because men (including children, savages, and illiterate peasants) are so made that they can share other people's feelings. That is the fundamental fact that makes art possible. When we sit round a Christmas fire, if someone yawns he is likely to set others yawning. If he yawns intentionally and in such a way as to make others yawn, he acts as an artist does who having experienced a feeling wishes to share it with others by expressing it suitably – in story, song, play, picture, sculpture, carving, ornament, dance, jest, or mimicry.

That is what art is, but the validity of the definition might not have been recognised for a long time among us, had not Bernard Shaw acclaimed it in a pungent review.*

The diffusion of feelings among mankind, which is the main function

---

* Shaw's article is published in a sixpenny pamphlet, *Tolstoy on Art and its Critics*, which also contains other matters, and is issued by the Oxford University Press.

of art, is of supreme importance, because our conduct, beliefs, treatment of one another, and our whole way of life, are moulded by our feelings. It is therefore essential to the welfare of mankind that the nature of art should be understood, and that its right use should be encouraged.

The conception of what is desirable in feelings made prevalent, and therefore in art, varies at different periods and among different nations. That is why art that is vital and highly esteemed in one age, falls into neglect in another. But unless a community has some aims and aspirations its art will drift helplessly and, being used merely as a recreation, will inevitably become commercialised. Instead of true artists expressing individual feelings as their nature urges, editors and producers will demand what they suppose the public wants, and works will be turned out to order by skilled technicians – so many thousand words by such and such a date – with a strong sport and sex interest, or with whatever else the dealers in the temple of art think the public wants.

But whether the feelings conveyed are good, bad, or indifferent does not decide whether a production is really a work of art: *that* depends on the form in which the feeling is expressed. The feeling itself may be of any possible kind, but unless *the form* be adequate it will not be conveyed to others, and *that* is the real test of art. Such conveyance need not require elaborate educational preparation, as nations that produced Burns, Bunyan, and the folk-songs, folk-dances and folklore of England and Scotland, should know.

No critic, I think, has refuted these fundamentals of Tolstoy's position, though many have refuted absurdities they attributed to his book, and have also taken exception, more or less legitimately, to some of the examples he cites.

Non-Resistance is hardly mentioned in *What is Art?*, and when it does appear it is expressed in its most reasonable and attractive form:

Through the influence of real art, aided by science guided by religion, that peaceful dwelling together of men which is maintained by external means – by our law courts, police, charitable institutions, factory inspection, &c. – should be attained by man's free and joyous activity. Art should cause violence to cease.

In connection with the publication of *What is Art?* my eyes were opened to the inefficiency of our Tolstoyan publishing arrangements, by what A. B. Walkley said in a review of the book, of the way it was produced:

> If we do not henceforward know what art is it will not be Tolstoy's fault. His English translator, Mr Aylmer Maude, has issued a final instalment of *What is Art?* (Brotherhood Publishing Co.) which proves to be, if possible, more interesting than either of its predecessors . . . This calmly and cogently reasoned effort to put art on a new basis is a literary event of the first importance. Whether we agree with Tolstoy's conclusions or not – and it is pretty certain that most of us will not – no one who attempts to reason out a theory of art can afford to ignore them. And, that being so, I cannot help thinking it a pity that the English translation has been issued in so unobtrusive – I had almost written surreptitious – a fashion. However we may deplore the fact, a fact it remains that books must be 'pushed' and 'boomed' if they are to catch the attention of readers in this country. Evidently Mr Aylmer Maude is too modest, too anxious to keep himself unspotted from the (commercial) world in the cloistered seclusion of 'Wickham's Farm, near Danbury, Essex'. He has accomplished an admirable piece of work in this translation, scholarly, solid, conscientious. His notes in their pregnant, concentrated brevity are models of what such things should be. For my sins I have to peruse a good many translations in the course of a year. I have never come across anything so good in its way as Mr Maude's version of Tolstoy. But I must say to him what the original of Foker said to Thackeray about his lectures: 'I tell you what it is, Thack, you want a piano.' Mr Maude wants the equivalent of a piano – some form of inviting advertisement, something to make Tolstoy 'go down'.

As a matter of fact I had merely handed my work over to the Brotherhood Publishing Company for their use free of cost, as they had been nominated by Chertkóv as publishers of Tolstoy's works. Subsequently I paid more attention to such matters, and any volumes I have been free to dispose of I have issued through well-known firms. They have consequently had a larger circulation.

In the years 1897–8 it looked as though a considerable Tolstoy movement was springing up. It has often been asked why this disintegrated, and was succeeded by a period of general indifference. I think the fact is that some people were disappointed to find that the rejection of the ordinary ways of carrying on industry and business did not conduce to

efficient or harmonious activity, while zealous partisans of the movement, reluctant to admit that there was a flaw somewhere in the
teaching, preferred to lay the blame on one another. Quarrels
were frequent, and Chertkóv's peculiarities, as well as Kenworthy's
eccentricities (which later on developed into insanity), complicated
and embittered these disputes.

I cannot attempt to describe the Colony. After many disappointments its operations were summed up by one sympathiser in the words:
'There is more tomfoolery to the square yard in this movement than in
any that I have ever known.'

Partly owing to the strain it put upon men's minds, and partly
because all strenuous movements attract some ill-balanced people,
there was much insanity at Purleigh. At least five of those who lived or
stayed at the Colony while I was there, were subsequently under
medical supervision on account of their mental condition. Even those
of us who kept our sanity did not always keep our tempers. We had
undertaken a task perhaps too hard for anyone, certainly too hard for
us. No doubt we learnt much, but not without tribulation.

Failure in their attempt to 'get out of the industrial system' and 'earn
an honest living' (in contradistinction to ordinary industrial and commercial pursuits, which were regarded as dishonest) was the invariable
experience of all the Russian and other Tolstoy Colonies, as of this one
at Purleigh. We ought to have expected and been prepared for that
result, and in fact both Tolstoy and Chertkóv avoided involving themselves in such undertakings though they did not discourage others from
attempting them. For a time Chertkóv lived near the Purleigh Colony
to encourage it, but when he found that the Colonists' milk was a penny
a quart dearer than a neighbouring farmer's he ceased taking it,
and provoked the comment that the Colonists had known others who
'objected to the use of money' in much the same manner.

But there remained another, practical side to the movement: namely,
the side Tolstoy had entrusted to Chertkóv which might still perhaps
show a way of doing the world's work better than the customary
methods practised in business, politics, and law.

That was really what we had set out to experiment upon. We had
been greatly moved by Tolstoy and were fully convinced (as I still am)
that his personal work and influence, far from being a failure, was a
success; but apart from what he scored off his own bat, I wanted to see
whether his principles conduced to a more harmonious and efficient

organisation of human affairs. Slowly, reluctantly, and regretfully, I was forced to admit that they did not.

It is remarkable how seldom the reason for the failure of movements that have really touched men's hearts is told with lucidity. Who, for instance, has properly explained the Franciscan failure to regenerate the world?

It would be very useful to have records of the failure of sincere and earnest movements. Why are they so scarce? Partly because people prefer to tell of days full of hope than of days full of dejection, and partly because the causes of failure are obscured by petty personal conflicts which have no permanent value and are seldom worth the trouble of unravelling or recording. Another cause is that the *odium theologicum* is not confined to the great Churches. As the highwayman demands your money or your life, so the religious zealot in a new movement requires you to accept his 'principles', or he will attack so your character by imputations of mean motives, and there is always a temptation to save yourself by running away, as a prudent man avoids contact with a skunk.

But in spite of all this, I think that those who have lived through a failure should gather up the results of their experience for the benefit of their successors. It costs us years of life to learn such lessons (though wiser heads might learn them quicker), and if we may not teach what we have learned, it would seem that we have laboured in vain.

Let me then, as best I may, sum up what I learned in the Tolstoy movement.

Tolstoy's genius and goodness caused many people, including men of more than average character and ability, to offer him help. Not wishing to be involved in the material cares of organising a movement himself, he advised these people to go and help Chertkóv, a man of noble sentiments, high aims, and great enthusiasm. Chertkóv was wealthy, accustomed to command, had a very strong will of his own, and held the Tolstoyan views on non-resistance, property, and government to their fullest theoretical extent.

The cause of the failure of our movement lay in the confusion which resulted from trying to combine a gospel of poverty, self-abnegation, and brotherhood, with an autocratic administration of large affairs and the irresponsible power of one man.

This came out very plainly in connection with the Doukhobór Migration, though the story needs much preliminary explanation.

On 20th March 1898, Tolstoy had written me:

> I am now quite engrossed in the affairs of the Doukhobórs, who are
> now permitted to emigrate as they wish. It is a great and very difficult
> affair.

In a book called *A Peculiar People* (*The Doukhobórs*), I have dealt at
length with that matter, which occupied much of Tolstoy's time and
attention during the years 1896 to 1900, and I will here only touch on a
few points.

The Russian whose experience, ability, and character best fitted
him to direct the Migration of the Doukhobórs to Canada and their
settlement in that country, was Prince D. A. Khilkóv, who shared in a
high degree the organising capacity of his uncle, Prince Khilkóv, the
Minister of Ways and Communication to whom the efficiency of the
Siberian Railway was due. Prince D. A. Khilkóv was well acquainted
with Doukhobór agriculture, being himself an expert farmer and having
lodged among them in the Caucasus during a term of banishment from
central Russia. On his release from exile in Russia he came to Purleigh
where, instead of welcoming his co-operation, Chertkóv quarrelled with
him violently, suspecting him (wrongly, Khilkóv told me) of having had
a liaison with a woman he had met during his banishment to the Baltic
Provinces.

Chertkóv, who was in control of the funds of the Migration, declined
to allow Khilkóv anything, and as the latter had given his estates to his
peasants in Russia, he had no resources and would have been unable
to reach Canada had not a Purleigh Colonist, Arnold Eiloart, who
happened just then to inherit some money, supplied him with what he
needed.

On 1st October 1898, D. A. Khilkóv and I sailed for Canada. We
had with us two Doukhobór families sent over as pioneers. To explain
the situation I should mention that we, and others, gave our services
gratuitously, and all who were able to do so paid their own expenses.
We considered ourselves members of a Brotherhood movement, in
connection with which an active and urgent collection of money was
carried on by Chertkóv. The money was subscribed on assurances that
the Doukhobórs were desirable and peaceful settlers who would give
no trouble provided their objection to military service was respected.
When arranging matters we assured the Canadians and the Canadian
Government to that effect, and on the strength of these assurances

facilities were given which enabled 7,363 Doukhobórs to settle in Canada.

After my return home, in December 1898, I received a letter from Tolstoy in reply to reports I had sent him of the suitability of Canada for the settlement.

> DEAR FRIEND MAUDE – Thanks for your letter from New York. I think about you continually and rejoice that you are our friend. I have today received a letter from Khilkóv describing the position of affairs and the locations of the settlements. Thanks to you, it seems that all has been admirably arranged . . .
>
> Herbert Archer has been here and I have made his acquaintance – which is the same as saying that I have learnt to love him.
>
> I do not know what news to send you – what you know and don't know. My son Sergéy is at Batoum. Golítzin [the Viceroy] not only has not expelled him but has been obliging to him. Sergéy wishes to sail with the second steamer [the second of the four voyages made with shiploads of Doukhobórs to Canada]. In general, the undertaking seems to have got over the crest of its difficulties and the road should now be downhill.
>
> As for myself, I have been quite absorbed for a couple of months past in my novel [*Resurrection*], which progresses, and of which I begin to see the end.

About the Doukhobórs two contrary opinions have often been expressed, both tenaciously held and both wrong. The one, often expressed in Canadian, American, and English newspapers, is that they are an objectionable and contemptible folk, too stupid to appreciate the privileges Canada offers them. The contrary view, equally mistaken, represents them as highly enlightened, free from superstition, and needing no Government because they are morally so superior to the rest of mankind.

The complex truth is, that they are a sober, hard-working, frugal folk, possessed of many excellent qualities, but hampered by a superstitious belief in the wisdom and power of their Leader and a rooted distrust of all Governments except their own. Moreover Doukhobórs are not all alike. Herbert P. Archer – the only Englishman who managed to live among them, and he not as one of themselves – wrote: 'We have been thinking of the Doukhobórs as a religious people. Really, as always, there are religious Doukhobórs – but not a religious Doukhobór sect. The sect, because it is a sect, is self-centred, self-righteous, and intolerant.'

Tolstoy had written in whole-hearted commendation of the Doukhobórs, and Chertkóv, in *Christian Martyrdom in Russia*, which he edited and published, repeated this praise still more emphatically. The sect was lauded to the skies, but after they reached Canada it became evident that something was wrong. They found it very difficult to know how to manage their affairs. Verígin was still in exile and the Communal arrangements he had bidden them adopt differed from their former way of life. They did not know whether they were all to form one Commune, or whether each village, or each group of villages, was to be a separate Commune. Neither did they know how far they could acknowledge the Canadian Government and obey its behests, without infringing their allegiance to Verígin. They would not admit outsiders to their sect, did not mingle with the Canadians, and objected even to such regulations as the registration of births, deaths, and marriages, and they also quarrelled much among themselves.

To make matters worse, Chertkóv, without consulting those of us who at his instigation had made ourselves morally responsible for the good behaviour of the Doukhobórs, took it into his head, in 1901, to publish in Russian, and to circulate among the Doukhobórs, some letters, referred to in the last chapter, which Verígin had written in exile in Siberia to chaff his fellow exiles who were Tolstoyans.

When copies of these curious letters reached Chertkóv he was attracted by them, and without asking Verígin's consent, proceeded to print them at his own private press and circulated them among the Doukhobórs, who received them as a divine revelation. Some fifteen hundred Doukhobórs then proceeded to set their cattle free, to abandon work on the land, and to start eastward on a pilgrimage to 'find Christ' (since they expected Verígin's return westward from exile). On entering any Canadian town or village they discarded their clothes, and these 'Nudity Parades' did much to antagonise the Canadians.

Verígin was greatly annoyed when he learnt that his letters had been so circulated, but the chief mischief was done before his release from Siberia.

Those who had been asked to regard the Doukhobórs as examples of exceptionally enlightened Christianity were taken aback by the Pilgrimage and the Nudity Parades and expected some explanation – or some admission that a mistake had been made. Nothing of the kind was forthcoming however either from Tolstoy or Chertkóv, but only reiterations of an obviously mistaken view.

To me personally the occurrence was most instructive. In helping to arrange that Migration I had come in contact with three different ways of doing business. I met representatives of the Canadian Pacific Railway – Sir Thomas Shaughnessy and others – who admittedly wanted to make their railway pay, but did their work with great efficiency and were ready to take these people at half the immigrant rate (over two thousand miles for six dollars), knowing that the growth of an agricultural population would make for future prosperity. Then, in the Society of Friends (Quakers) – who were exceedingly generous in the help they gave to this sect persecuted for refusing military service – I met a Committee of capable men giving their time and substance to aid, from religious motives, a people they had only recently heard of. Their work was more disinterested but not quite so efficient. Finally there was our own Tolstoy movement, with the loftiest possible aspirations, but a performance efficient only when we forgot our 'principles', and at other times ludicrously and pathetically inefficient.

The incident of the Verígin letters raised the question whether we, who formed part of the Tolstoy movement, had any sort of control over, or moral responsibility for, the conduct of a movement to which we were giving time and money, or whether we were mere pawns in the hands of Tolstoy's nominee.

Of Chertkóv's ardour and desire to exalt the principle of non-resistance we were fully assured, but his methods seemed unsatisfactory. When, for instance, by supplying certain information he had induced colleagues to make arrangements they disapproved of and would otherwise not have consented to, and it turned out that the statements made were untrue, Chertkóv, taxed with it, replied, with a disarming naïvety that was one of his most attractive qualities: 'Yes, when I want something very much, I do sometimes say the thing which is not.'

With his charm of manner, striking personality, and the prestige of being Tolstoy's lieutenant, he seldom failed to impress people favourably on first acquaintance, and those who were not obliged to work with him often retained that impression more or less permanently. Things however happened which compelled most of his associates to revolt against his influence.

The Doukhobórs declined to make individual entries for the one hundred and sixty acres of free land the Canadian Government offered to each adult male. They wanted the whole domain to be granted as a Communal possession, lest individuals, becoming freeholders, might break away from the community and live separately. Their objection to registration of births, deaths, or marriages – already mentioned – may have been made on a suspicion that someday this might facilitate conscription, though they had been expressly exempted from military service. A Report by a Committee of the Canadian Privy Council, approved by the Governor General on 6th December 1898, states that: 'Arrangements have been completed with Mr Aylmer Maude, the representative of the sect of Russians known as Doukhobórs . . . for the immediate migration to Canada of several thousand of these people . . . The Minister [of the Interior] is of opinion that it is expedient to give them the fullest assurance of absolute immunity from military service . . . The Minister recommends that . . . the Doukhobórs, settling permanently in Canada, be exempted unconditionally from service.'

Having got the Doukhobórs to Canada and obtained for them from the Government a free grant of land and a bonus of £1 a head, the next step should have been to allay their suspicions of that Government and to minimise any occasion for friction.

But Chertkóv under guise of supplying them with a *Handbook* for learning English, gave them advice calculated to produce the opposite effect. He informed them (p. 42 of the *Handbook*) that: 'All governments are based on violence. They are upheld by armies, law-courts, prisons, and police.' (Pp. 49–52) 'The population of Canada consists of the original inhabitants – the Red Indians – and of emigrants from Europe . . . And now 7,500 Doukhobórs from the Caucasus. There are also negroes. The Indians and negroes are very badly treated . . . Civilised nations shed blood everywhere, and oppress those that are weaker than themselves . . . The Europeans call themselves Christians, but they are not true to Christ's teaching.'

(Page 62) 'It concerns the registration of marriages, births and deaths. Do you promise always to fulfil this? We are quite willing to answer accurately when asked. But we cannot promise anything. A promise is the same as an oath. Our religion forbids us to take an oath. Christ said: "Do not swear." A man must be free. A promise ties the conscience and the actions of a man. Even in little things we want to be free.'

(Page 86) 'Do not give any promises. We cannot take an oath. Our faith is just the same as that of Jesus Christ.'

(Pages 92–3) 'We think there ought not to exist any private property in land. In our opinion land, like air and water, should be for the use of all. He owns the land who, for the time being, is working it.'

This *Handbook* and the *Letters of Verígin* increased the perplexities arising from the settlement of an opinionated sect in a new country. When in addition to their Pilgrimages and Nudity Parades some of them began to set fire to agricultural implements and school houses, they were imprisoned, and declared that they were ill-treated. *The New Order*, the London Tolstoyan organ, came out with a large-type headline, *Christian Martyrdom in Canada*.

It was not fair either to the immigrants or to those among whom they settled, to promote distrust and strife in such away, and what was worse was that much of this was done secretly. Intimately connected as I was with the movement, I heard of this *Handbook* only by accident, from Canada, after it had reached the Doukhobórs. I felt bound to publish what I knew of the migration, and did so in 1901 in the first edition of *Tolstoy and His Problems*.

As soon as he had read that book Chertkóv sent one of his assistants to point out four paragraphs which he disapproved of, and to say that unless I withdrew them, and admitted them to be wrong, he would never speak to me again. I did not share his view of those paragraphs, besides which the book was out and could not be withdrawn, and it was plain that if I submitted to him this time, I must not expect to express opinions of my own in future except by his permission.

It was not a light matter to incur excommunication at the hands of Tolstoy's lieutenant, for it interfered with opportunities which I valued of co-operating with Tolstoy. But on the whole I was glad the breach had come in such a clear-cut way as to leave me no option in the matter. I felt sure Tolstoy would remonstrate with me, and was glad to be able to tell him that any obstacle there might be to the resumption of good relations was not caused by me, but that as I was forbidden to address Chertkóv I was helpless in the matter. Few of Chertkóv's other co-workers escaped from him as easily.

Among those who, after rendering good service, complained bitterly of the way they were treated, was L. Sulerzhítski, who was subsequently active in the management of the Moscow Art Theatre, and of whom Stanislávsky in *My Life in Art* speaks with warm appreciation. At Tolstoy's request Sulerzhítski had taken charge of the first vessel that carried Doukhobórs from Batoum to Halifax. It was the *Lake Huron*, of the Beaver Line, and carried 2,100 people, closely packed. This broke all records of migrations across the Atlantic: never before had a ship taken so many people to settle permanently in America.

Sulerzhítski had energy, initiative, and great organising capacity. He saw that the Doukhobórs were accustomed to and needed leadership, and taking on himself the task, he disciplined them and kept them in good order. When the vessel reached Canada the immigration officers reported that they had never known an immigrant ship arrive so clean and in such excellent condition. He remained some time in Canada, exerting himself unsparingly on behalf of the Doukhobórs to the detriment of his own health. When he reached England his stories about them were not to Chertkóv's taste, and though Sulerzhítski was quite without means, had given splendid service gratuitously, and was completely knocked up, Chertkóv would not allow him even what he needed for his return journey to Russia. I was able to help him to get home, but he never recovered from his privations and over-exertion, dying a few years later of nephritis contracted in Canada.

The Doukhobórs proved themselves excellent agriculturists and fruit-growers, and had they not had such a superstitious belief in the divine character of their Leader, and been so badly directed by fanatical advisers, they might have proved – and may yet ultimately prove – excellent settlers; but in March 1929, while writing these final chapters, a reminder reaches me of the attitude adopted from the first by some of them. It is an Open Letter addressed by 'The Doukhobórs – the Christian Community of Universal Brotherhood – Sons of Freedom – to the Executives of all Countries: Judges, Government Inspectors, Police and all other servants of man-made Laws.' They say: 'The time has come to reveal . . . why we reject the Government schools and their orders. We are conscious of our history, and denote it by saying that Christ was the first Doukhobór. We are the direct Spiritual descendants of the Apostles of Christ and his followers, the so-called Christian martyrs of his time. It was the same kind of Government as the Canadian, that crucified Christ two thousand years ago . . . Savage barbarism is practised today as freely as two thousand years ago . . . here is an example: the poor half-starved miners in England – supposed to be the wealthiest nation in the world . . . Take our Government school-education; people are so hypnotised by it that they do not see that its results are demoralising. The present Government schools are nurseries of militarism and capitalism . . . If there are men to be found among educated people like George B. Shaw, Tolstoy, Tagore, Gandhi, and many others, these men received enlightenment through Spiritual Regeneration, heeding the voice of Christ, and if such men are to be given honour, it was not attained by college education.' [How Bernard Shaw found himself in that galley I don't know. Gandhi belongs there by right.] 'Our whole history is marked by cruel persecutions by the churches, governments, and capitalists. These persecutions are on account of our loyalty to Christ's teaching and our uncompromising refusal to submit to any Authority but God's.' [Their own Leader's authority, be it noted, is identical with God's and therefore by obeying him they do not submit to 'man-made laws' but merely obey the dictates of conscience.] 'In 1902 over thirty men were put in jail at Regina . . . tormented and beaten a great deal for abstaining from meat and declining obedience to special humiliating orders . . . the doctors forcibly injected medical mixtures through rubber tubing into their mouths, which led to excruciating pain . . . All were forcibly fed with meat soups scalding hot, whereby lips and faces were burned black.'

After enumerating eleven others 'tortured to death in the cruellest ways' in 1902, 1904, 1907 and 1908 in various prisons, the Open Letter continues: 'In 1925 the Doukhobórs were again attacked by Government officials, a band of 150 intoxicated policemen took away $25,000 worth of chattels and beat men and women for not sending their children to Government schools as a protest against the murder of Peter Verígin by the Materialist Militarists.'

It concludes by asking for the release of Doukhobórs sentenced to prison on 11th February at Nelson, B.C., 'because they were true to the Teachings of Christ'.

The Letter is signed by twelve Doukhobórs, six men and six women, with Birukóv's name gratuitously added.

The Doukhobórs evidently believe they have been ill-used, and possibly some prison officials, confronted with obstinate and alien peasants, may have acted harshly with them; but the reference to the belief current among them that Verígin's death (caused by the explosion of a bomb on a Canadian Pacific train) was arranged by the Canadian Government [the 'Materialist Militarists' of the Letter] is very strange. Chertkóv, when he told them that 'civilised nations shed blood everywhere', hardly expected his statement to be taken so literally.

It should however be understood that though the extremist group of Doukhobórs who get out such manifestos, always profess to speak on behalf of the sect as a whole, they have no right to do so and do not represent the majority of the Doukhobórs.

All the same it is extraordinary to what an extent the doctrine of Non-Resistance, which pleased Tolstoy just because he thought it would promote peace and harmony, has, with the accretions that have grown on to it, become a virulent source of strife and contention.

This mention of Gandhi reminds me that he fully accepts Tolstoy's doctrine and bases his Non-Cooperation movement on it. The Government of India is faced by a greater difficulty in this respect than that caused by the Doukhobórs in Canada. In England the only overt trouble caused by the doctrine of Non-Resistance was in the case of some conscientious objectors to conscription, but in India, Canada, and England alike, an understanding of Tolstoy's doctrine and of the answer to it, would be of value to those who have to execute the laws, when they have to deal with men who, on the basis of non-resistance, reject Government. An understanding of the problem might save much in police, prisons, and troops. For as I have tried to show, there is a convincing reply, but not one which is self-evident or can be convincingly stated without careful consideration of the problem.

I have heard Bernard Shaw say that it is great fun to attend the lectures that are given by the Flat-Earthists. They have a carefully worked out theory and their lecturers are familiar with the objections an ordinary man makes to it. The lecturer states his case and invites questions. Then people in the audience challenge his conclusions, on the basis of such astronomical knowledge as they possess, and the lecturer promptly wipes the floor with them.

So it is with the doctrine of Non-Resistance. Certain ideas, current for ages among many sects, challenge man's right to use force to his fellow men, and these ideas have been stated by Tolstoy more clearly and forcibly than ever before. Anyone who accepts his views and masters the case as he puts it, can floor any ordinary magistrate or judge who attempts to argue with him without previously considering the theory and its refutation.

Chertkóv rendered a service, however unintentionally, by the thoroughness of the practical demonstration he gave the world of the unworkability of Tolstoyan methods. It was instructive to see how completely so masterful a man, holding Non-Resistant principles, could dominate a whole movement and deprive its adherents of any share in its direction. Had he been either less ardent or more considerate, we might have been left in doubt as to whether the new methods were not better than the old, but to revert to autocracy undiluted and unashamed was too evidently to forget the lessons of human experience and return to the starting point of human society.

It is, I am afraid, clear that the collapse of the Tolstoy movement was a result of the system employed; for no one will wish to say that Tolstoy's chosen representative was a worse or less intelligent man than thousands of others who carry on various undertakings needing the co-operation of many people. Nor can we attribute it to the badness of those he came in contact with; for the same fate befell them nearly all – including such men as Prince D. A. Khilkóv, Van der Veer (who had gone to prison for the refusal of military service in Holland), Sulerzhítski, and many others, English and Russian alike.

The root of the trouble was the *lack of definiteness*. We talked about the high moral principles of our movement, but found things being done that were obviously wrong. If anyone was authorised to say what our 'principles' were, it was Chertkóv, but within the course of a few months we found him ardently collecting money, refusing to handle money, desiring to obtain money from *Resurrection*, and (as Kenworthy publicly pointed out) neglecting to account for sums that passed through his hands.

There was no reason to doubt his ardour or suspect him of making money out of the movement; what was doubtful was his common sense and the intellectual validity of his opinions.

We were quite willing to obey Tolstoy, but our devotion was not transferable, and when Tolstoy passed it on to such a lieutenant it dwindled away.

There was no point on which it might not have been possible to frame a plausible case for Chertkóv's action, but when we compared our movement with other groups, it was plain that there was something wrong either in our methods or in our 'principles'.

Little was accomplished in spite of great efforts and exceptional opportunities, but the saddest part of the affair was the amount of quarrelling that went on in it, and the wreckage of human material that resulted.

There was another matter which may help to explain why it failed.

When it became evident that the Brotherhood Publishing Company was useless, Chertkóv, who was himself already printing Tolstoy's prohibited works in Russian, decided to start an English publishing firm, the Free Age Press, which would set an example of moral reformation in the publishing world by printing the words 'No Rights Reserved' on the cover of its books.

What was wanted was to produce a complete edition of Tolstoy's works, readably and reliably translated and so issued in permanent form as to be readily obtainable at Libraries and bookshops. The difficulty lay in the preparation of suitable translations. The work therefore should have been entrusted to someone who knew Russian, but whose native tongue was English. There was no need to found a new publishing company unless adequate translations could be procured. But the Free Age Press which Chertkóv started, instead of paying due attention to the quality of its versions and delaying publication till that had been properly attended to, issued its English translations of Tolstoy's new works simultaneously with its Russian editions, to keep competitors away, and often issued inferior versions which hindered the publication of better ones when these were ready.

Chertkóv induced Tolstoy, who was always ready to assist him, to express approval of the 'no rights reserved' declaration, and having published this, he made 'Tolstoy's wish' a lever to induce those who contributed to the Free Age Press to surrender their copyrights to him. Eventually he used the moral superiority of his method of publishing as a means of inducing Tolstoy to leave his literary inheritance at his (Chertkóv's) disposal, and to deprive the Countess of it.

Now whatever our faults may be, we English are generally a practical people, and those connected with the book-world knew that as long as the Free Age Press had the *first right* of publishing Tolstoy's new writings, and issued them cheaply, there was not much point in putting 'No Rights Reserved' on the covers. It was improbable that anyone would care to reprint them. As a matter of fact, when other firms have issued any of them, they have usually preferred to procure other versions. At that time I translated some articles for the Free Age Press, and did so at first gratuitously. As long as the copyright remained mine I retained the power of using them, should opportunity arise, as the nucleus of a better and more permanent edition. But had I abandoned the copyright, no well-established publisher would probably have ever consented to republish them. When therefore Chertkóv asked for an assignment of my copyrights to him, I declined, pointing out the inconsistency of asking for an assignment of copyright while objecting to the legal protection of property. Tolstoy had renounced his rights in his own works, but had no desire to interfere with his English or other translators. Yet in England Chertkóv, by a dexterous application of Tolstoyan 'principles', endeavoured to take from those who translated Tolstoy's new works, the control of their productions, even when, as in my own case at that time, they were willing to let him have free use of their versions.

After Chertkóv had severed relations with me I only occasionally worked for the Free Age Press, and then for pay, letting him use my versions, but declining to part with the copyrights. As far as the public were concerned the whole announcement of 'No Rights Reserved' much resembled a hoax. No copyright existed in the Russian works first printed in Russia, and as shown in my own case, Chertkóv put the words 'No Rights Reserved' on books the copyright in which was not his to give away; and a curious confusion might have arisen had anyone, on that invitation, proceeded to make an undesirable use of those versions.

There were other rules that might equally well have been deduced from Tolstoy's teaching, for instance, that no money should be used, or that no one should own the stock of books. In fact while proclaiming the principle that 'property is robbery', Chertkóv retained what others wanted, namely, the right of first translation and publication, and ostentatiously gave away what was not wanted, namely the right to reprint a heterogeneous assortment of translations of varying quality.

It gave a sinister meaning to the words 'No Rights Reserved', when one saw how often the reader's right to a satisfactory version was disregarded.

Chertkóv obtained the assistance of several capable people interested in Tolstoy's work, and was particularly fortunate in securing the services of Mr A. C. Fifield as manager of the Free Age Press. Chertkóv had indeed a talent for obtaining strenuous and free, or cheap, service from Tolstoy's sympathisers. Mrs Fifield, under the pen-name of Salome Hocking, gives an excellent sketch of him in *Belinda the Backward*, where his secretary, overworking herself without pay, remarked:

When in his presence I forgot my own affairs completely, and was only conscious of a strenuous desire to do the work he asked of me.

This I learnt later was the attitude of most of the people whom he gathered round him. As long as he desired their help and would exert himself to retain their allegiance, they were his willing slaves. It was only when he tired of them, or indulging in a fit of temper, and putting no restraint on that fatal fluency of speech which resembled nothing so much as a mountain torrent, allowed himself to say whatever anger or contempt suggested to him, that the spell was broken. He had himself cut the invisible bonds which bound his slaves to him, and once their intelligence was freed from the spell he had exerted over them, they often went to the other extreme and became his severest critics.

Anyone who wished to draw a comparison, favourable to ourselves, between the English and Russian type of mind, can hardly do better than compare Macaulay's speeches in Parliament on the Copyright Bills of 1841 and 1842 with Chertkóv's anti-copyright pronouncements. Macaulay understood what he spoke about and based its consideration on the advantage to the public. Chertkóv did not understand it, and based his decision on abstract and unsound arguments.

Opinions about copyright differ greatly, and no doubt at first glimpse it looks as though the public would benefit if authors received no remuneration for their books and claimed no control over them. It is certainly desirable that when a writer's reputation is established and there is still a demand for his writings years after his death, publishers willing to reprint them should be able to do so, and no inheritor should have power to hinder it. But when books first appear and it is not known what reception they will meet with, it would be difficult to get them published at all unless the firm undertaking that risk could control the works at least for a time, without competition from other publishers. The price at which a book can be sold depends mainly on the number of copies produced; but if there are to be rival editions the chance for each of them is reduced, the publisher cannot risk large editions, and may land himself in loss on a small one even though the price of each copy be high. Besides this, where there is copyright control, a book need not be got out before its translator has revised it and made it as perfect as possible; but with a non-copyright work, to forestall competition, speed becomes more important than quality, and consequently both the author and the reader suffer. Bad versions are thus produced which block the way for better ones.

Chertkóv however by securing Tolstoy's approval of his attitude, obtained an important advantage in his struggle with Tolstoy's wife for priority of publication. Besides holding the rights in Tolstoy's writings published before 1881, the Countess also published editions of his later non-copyright works, and, being on the spot, she had sometimes managed to get them first, which in dealing with non-copyright work is the chief thing.

From this time onwards Chertkóv was able to claim a moral superiority for his own methods of publishing, and urged that claim strenuously on Tolstoy.

This laid the foundation for the campaign by which, contrasting the moral basis of his own activities with the immoral basis of Countess Tolstoy's, Chertkóv supplanted her and eventually deprived her of any share in the management of Tolstoy's works or any profit from them, and ultimately secured for himself the control of Tolstoy's literary inheritance. But the story of that final and complete triumph comes later.

I have, however, again been drawn away from the chronological sequence of my story, which has not yet reached the time when the Free Age Press was started.

On 24th December 1898, Tolstoy wrote me:

Chertkóv writes that he cannot and does not wish to attend further to the affairs of the Doukhobórs, part of which consists of the publication and sale of the translations of my novel [*Resurrection*] . . . so we are obliged to place all our hopes on you. Ashamed as I am to ask you to take on yourself a new task after you have just finished your labour for the common cause, I cannot do otherwise. If you agree I will do all I can from here to relieve you of all unavoidable work . . . So then, dear friend, please do not refuse to help us, and reply soon, to set our minds at rest.

I did not at once undertake the work Tolstoy offered me. I wished to do so, but dreaded friction with Chertkóv, for I had a presentiment that his abstention from the business would not prove permanent. Had I then gone at once to Yásanya Polyána I might have been entrusted with the work and saved much of the waste and confusion that resulted from the ill-advised arrangements actually made. The whole business of getting out a complete English edition of Tolstoy's works might perhaps have been arranged then and a quarter of a century's delay avoided. I should, however, almost certainly have incurred the kind of persecution Tolstoy's wife had for years to endure for opposing Chertkóv. Partly for that reason, and partly because after translating

What is Art? and arranging matters in Canada for the Doukhobórs that year, I needed time to attend to business of my own, I, rather pusillanimously, declined Tolstoy's proposal.

Later on, Mrs Chertkóv wrote saying that the burden was falling on her and was beyond her strength, and begged my wife to relieve her of it. My wife undertook the translation of *Resurrection*, and I finally agreed to attend to its publication, after receiving a promise that Chertkóv would not interfere and on the understanding that my wife should be free to copyright her version. After undertaking it however I found that Chertkóv had already promised the book to the Brotherhood Publishing Company, in a way which resulted in nothing being received for the serial rights, and not till its first publisher had defaulted in his payments could I disentangle the matter, get the book properly produced by another firm and secure large sales for it.

Letters must have crossed in the post, for the next one from Tolstoy was evidently written before he received my reply to his previous communication:

> I have received your letter of 31st December, kind friend Maude, and am very glad you are again in England and wish to work at translating my writings. I do not wish for a better translator, both on account of your knowledge of both languages, and your strictness with yourself in everything.
>
> I am now in the country, probably until 8th January. Unfortunately not only have I been unable to finish the last chapter of *Resurrection*, as I had hoped, but I have been so unwell lately with pains in the back and feverishness, that I have not replied to letters. Today, 30th December, old style, I am better and am writing letters, tomorrow I hope to get properly to work and finish, and then shall start revising it and send off the final version to Marx. [The Petersburg publisher.]
>
> Goodbye for the present. Friendly greetings to you and your family.

His next letter says:

> DEAR FRIEND – I have received all three of your letters. I much regret your refusal to take part in the business of publishing the translation of *Resurrection*, though I understand its motives. In this whole business there is something indefinite, confused, and *seemingly* discordant with the principles we profess. Sometimes in bad moments this acts on me

too and I wish to get rid of the affair as quickly as I can, but when I am in a good, serious frame of mind I am even glad of the unpleasantness that is bound up with it. I know that my motives were, if not good, at least quite innocent, and therefore if in men's eyes it makes me appear inconsistent or even something worse, it is all good for me, teaching me to act quite independently of men's judgement and in accord only with conscience. One should prise such experiences. They are rare and very useful . . .

I am very glad your kind wife is making the translation of *Resurrection*. I am now sending another seventeen chapters. There are five more, which I will send in a few days in manuscript. I will begin to send the finally corrected proofs when I have corrected the last five chapters. The work goes slower than I anticipated because I have been ailing all this winter – backaches and general weakness.

The publication of the book, and Tolstoy's revision of it, lasted the whole of the next year. Ultimately the state of his health obliged him to hasten its completion, which partly accounts for the fact that the last chapters are decidedly inferior to the commencement.

When the work was drawing to its close, and Tolstoy, worn out with the distasteful task of correcting the weekly instalments of proofs by fixed dates, was approaching the severe illness which announced itself by an acute attack on 24th December 1899, he wrote to a friend:

I am much absorbed in my work. And regularly as soon as I see the proof-sheets from Marx, I feel sick and have pain . . . I am so occupied with writing the book that I spend my whole strength on it. Other movements of the soul go on within me, and, thank God, I see the light and see it more and more. More and more often I feel myself not the master of my life, but a labourer.

It was to find funds to help the Doukhobór Migration that Tolstoy resolved to complete this novel he had so long had in hand.

He sold the right of first publication to Marx, the editor of the Petersburg paper *Níva*, receiving £2,350 for it.

Availing themselves of Tolstoy's repudiation of copyright, other Russian newspapers began to reprint the weekly instalments of the story as they appeared. Marx naturally objected, and eventually Tolstoy appealed to the newspapers not to reprint till publication in the *Níva* had been completed. They all complied with his request.

The incident illustrates one of the objections to the repudiation of copyright in a new novel for which there is a large demand and for which the author wants money – however unselfishly.

The publisher in such a case may reasonably say to the author: 'What you want me to undertake is more of a gamble than a fair business risk. If you want me to pay you, why not give me what I want for my money, namely, rights in the book? If you consider it wise to throw the book to be scrambled for, do so; but why ask one of us to pay you for what others may take next day for nothing? If your announcement is understood to mean that a new and saleable novel is to be had for the grabbing, it constitutes an invitation to competition and will cause needless work to be expended on hastily setting up rival editions. The start you offer to one of us will be counterbalanced by a heavier printer's bill, since you will go on making alterations until the book is out, and then our rivals will have clean copy to reprint from for nothing.'

Tolstoy often mentioned the trouble and annoyance he experienced over the publication of each new book after adopting his self-denying ordinance; and while heartily respecting the altruism of his motives, I cannot help thinking that – since regulations are made for man and not man for regulations – the trouble and annoyance he experienced may be taken as an indication that the rule he adopted was not a wise one.

The novel itself, which appeared when Tolstoy was over seventy, though not equal to *War and Peace* or *Anna Karénina*, shows that Tolstoy retained much of the power he had shown in those works, on which he expended immensely more time and effort. It gives a vivid and varied description of many phases of Russian life.

On one point *Resurrection* betrays the seeking, unsatisfied feeling that lurked in the philosophy of the earlier novels: we feel at the end that Tolstoy does not know what his hero, Nekhlyúdov, is to do with himself. Had Nekhlyúdov been an author, Tolstoy could have settled him on a country estate, and let him write books, simplify his life, and learn self-control and self-abnegation. But Nekhlyúdov is a man of action – and what was a Tolstoyan man of action to do? Of necessity the book ends where its hero – after seeing the evils of army service and civil service, of Court life, society, the Church, and the law – reads the Sermon on the Mount, notes the injunction not to resist him that is evil, and decides on a new life.

One would dearly like to know what that new life could be. But after all *Resurrection* is truly a wonderful book, instinct with high purpose and pregnant with the mature thoughts of a great and good man. Extraordinarily truthful in its descriptions of life, it sheds a flood of light on evils to which custom renders us callous. There is hardly any subject of social interest it does not touch on, and in particular it moved men in many lands to reconsider the evils of prison life and the convict system.

I will not recount its story, for it is not a book to read about but to read. It is probably as strenuously moral a novel as was ever written, but in dealing with amatory matters it is almost as plain-spoken as the Bible itself, and for a while Mudie's Library and W. H. Smith's bookstalls boycotted it as objectionable. When, however, a dramatised version was staged at His Majesty's Theatre the demand for the book became very large and they pocketed their scruples.

In England and America *Resurrection* has had a larger sale than any other of Tolstoy's works, and in spite of the appearance of an unauthorised version and the failure of one or two of its publishers, the authorised English translation brought in over £3,000.

Neither Tolstoy nor his wife accepted any part of the proceeds, which went first in aid of the Doukhobórs. After they were settled in Canada and their financial affairs had passed into Verígin's control, a Committee (consisting of J. F. Green, G. H. Perris, and myself) administered what remained of the Fund for other public purposes.

Eventually, in 1915, the Committee's funds being exhausted, the sales much diminished, the book out of print, and more money being needed for a further migration of Doukhobórs to Canada, I repurchased the copyright from the Committee, and undertook to reissue the book, thus preparing the way for the present Centenary Edition. Chertkóv was still announcing his intention of producing an English edition of Tolstoy's works, but it was becoming increasingly evident that he would not do so; in which case I wanted to be ready to step into the breach, and I felt that the control of *What is Art?*, prepared with Tolstoy's co-operation and exclusive authorisation, and of *Resurrection*, carrying his explicit authorisation of my wife's version,* formed a useful basis for that undertaking.

Among the short pieces Tolstoy wrote in 1898, was a Preface to a

---

* The wording of which was: 'This English version of *Resurrection* is published by my authority. Leo Tolstoy.'

translation his eldest son, Count Sergéy Tolstoy, made of Edward Carpenter's *Modern Science,* a book Tolstoy highly appreciated.

Though during the whole of 1899 he was busily engaged on *Resurrection,* he found time to write a number of those letter-essays of which in later life he was so prolific. The most remarkable of that year's epistles was the *Letter on the Hague Conference.*

The appeal sent out to the nations by the young Tsar, Nicholas II, to consider the question of the reduction of armaments or other mitigations of war, delighted most of the friends of peace, but Tolstoy poured scorn on the whole affair, maintaining that the Conference could be nothing but an hypocritical arrangement, aiming not at peace but at hiding the only path by which peace could be attained. He declared that Governments never can or will diminish their armaments, but that 'armies will first diminish and then disappear when public opinion brands with contempt those who, whether from fear or for advantage, sell their liberty and enter the ranks of those murderers called soldiers'. Not the reformation of Government but the rejection of Government was his line persistently, and it was never expressed more harshly than on this occasion.

His second daughter, Mary, had married Prince N. L. Obolénski in June 1897, and now, on 14th November 1899, his eldest daughter, Tatiána, married Mr M. S. Sukhotín.

On 5th April 1900, when his health was known to be critical, the Most Holy Synod sent out a 'confidential' Circular to the clergy informing them that 'Count Leo Tolstoy in his writings on religion has plainly shown himself an enemy of the Orthodox Christian Church. He does not acknowledge the One God in Three Persons; the Second Person of the Holy Trinity, the Son of God, he speaks of as a mere man; he refers blasphemously to the mystery of the Incarnation of God the Word; perverts the holy text of the Gospels; disparages the Holy Church, calling it a human institution; denies the ecclesiastical hierarchy, and mocks at the holy sacraments and rites of the Holy Orthodox Church . . . Therefore the Most Holy Synod decrees that the performance of requiems, masses, and liturgies for the repose of Count Leo Tolstoy's soul, in the event of his dying unrepentant, be forbidden.'

This was preliminary to the famous public decree issued the following year. Being a secret document the Circular caused no great commotion even when its contents leaked out and appeared in the foreign press.

At the commencement of that year I had written asking Tolstoy about an interview that appeared in the papers attributing anti-English views to him in connection with the war in South Africa. He replied in January:

> Of course I could not have said and did not say what is attributed to me. What really took place was this: A newspaper correspondent came to see me, as an author wishing to present me with a copy of his book. In answering a question of his as to my attitude towards the war, I mentioned that I had been shocked to catch myself, during my illness, wishing to find news of Boer successes, and that I was therefore glad to have an opportunity in a letter to V., to express my real attitude towards that matter – which is, that I cannot sympathise with any military achievements, not even with a David opposed to ten Goliaths, but that I sympathise only with those who destroy the cause of war: the prestige of gold, of wealth, of military glory, and above all (the cause of all the evil) the prestige of patriotism, with its pseudo-justification of the murder of our brother men.
>
> Of course I do not think it is worth while publishing in the papers a contradiction of the opinions falsely attributed to me. You cannot wish good health to everyone who sneezes [a Russian proverb, arising from the custom of wishing good health to anyone who sneezes], for instance, I have been receiving letters from America lately, some reproaching and others approving of me for having discarded all my convictions! Is it worth while denying such reports, when tomorrow more such items of news can be invented to fill the columns of the newspapers and the pockets of the editors? However, do what you consider necessary.
>
> My health has not been good all this time; but as in order to die there is but one way, namely by being ill – just as in order to move from one place to another there is no way except to get into a carriage or a railway car – I do not object to my illness, especially as it is not painful and allows me to think and even to work. I am now chiefly occupied with an article on the Labour Question. I have already written on that subject, but it seems to me that I have something new to say, and I hope to say it simply and clearly.

The book referred to was *The Slavery of Our Times*, a disappointing sequel to *What Then Must We Do?* The former work left us in doubt about the solution of the problem of poverty, but it dealt with realities and was vivid and moving. *The Slavery of Our Times* is more abstract, and though it gives a definite reply, that reply is 'Non-Resistance' – abstention from all share in Governmental activity. This was in fact the main theme of Tolstoy's writings during his last decade.

When translating *The Slavery of Our Times* I wrote an Introduction to it, and in that connection (before our rupture) received a very characteristic letter from Chertkóv, which showed to what an extent he and I were travelling different roads. My anxiety was lest the value and truth latent in Tolstoy's message should be lost sight of owing to the intransigency of his attitude. Chertkóv's feeling was of quite another kind. I had said: 'To shake ourselves completely free from all share in violence is not possible. Tolstoy himself does not profess to have ceased to use postage stamps which were issued, and the highway that is maintained, by a Government which collects taxes by force; but reforms come by men doing what they can, not what they can't.' Chertkóv wrote urging me to substitute the words very difficult' for the words 'not possible', and he went on to say, of the use of postage stamps and roads: 'What if that is precisely where Tolstoy is inconsistent in his life, as for my part, I *do* believe it is?'

My view was that Tolstoy's teaching of Non-Resistance did not act, because it is not really true to the facts of life. Chertkóv thought that any lack of success it might have resulted from Tolstoy's not going far enough. Nothing could have been more courteous than Chertkóv's remarks about my Introduction, but the nature of the alteration he wanted, and his urgency, showed the difficulty of working under one who held such extreme views.

In reply to a letter in which I told Tolstoy that the Purleigh Colony was breaking up, he wrote me, on 15th December 1899, as follows:

> Forgive me for being so long in replying to your interesting letter. At first I put it off because I was busy, and then I felt ill, and I am still very weak.
>
> The failure of life in the Colony about which you write, is only an indication that the form of life which was chosen by the Colonists for the realisation of their spiritual needs was not adequate. When a definite inner content exists in man, it finds for itself a corresponding form – generally unconsciously, i.e., when one is not thinking about the form and when the form is not defined in words.

About *Resurrection* and its translation . . . all that money business which I undertook and of which I now repent, has been so tormentingly painful, that now that it is over I have decided to have nothing more to do with the matter, but to return completely to my former attitude towards the publication of my writings: that is, while letting others do as they please with them, to stand quite aside from the business myself.

In the spring of 1900 he wrote, in reply to a letter in which I had made some enquiry about his views on taxation:

As to the relation, I do not say of a Christian, but simply of a reasonable man to taxes, there can be no question. In that respect, as with all demands to participate in governmental crimes, a Christian cannot fail to try to free himself from such participation. The degree to which he will be able to free himself will depend on the difference between the strength of the temptations by which he is ensnared and the strength of his convictions . . .

There, you see how dull and matter-of-fact this letter is! I am pressed for time. But that does not mean that apart from business I have not a sincerely friendly feeling towards you.

In another letter he refers to his health, which was beginning to give very serious anxiety to his family and friends:

3 August 1900

DEAR MAUDE – I write to you not with my own hand, because I have been for some time ill with my customary, very weakening illness. I received your letter enclosing one from Percy Redfern,* which pleased me very much by its ardour and sincerity. Ask him to excuse me not replying to him, and convey to him, what I wish for most of my young friends: namely that they should devote their energy more to the ordering of their inner spiritual being than to propaganda.

I received your pamphlet, 'Tolstoy's Teaching', and approved of it very much. It is admirably constructed and gives what is most essential. Your article on *What is Art?* pleased the exceedingly, so clearly and powerfully is the fundamental bought expressed.

---

* The most active member of a Manchester group who are interested in Tolstoy.

Tolstoy's state of health long remained very unsatisfactory, and his work was often interrupted. Mention of his occurs in a letter he sent to me on 23rd November 1900:

> Before moving to Moscow, I visited my daughter Tánya in the country, and there had influenza or something of that kind; that any rate since then for more than a month I have felt very speak and disinclined to work. At first this distressed me, but low I begin to get accustomed to it. One can also learn to have without mental activity, if only one's moral activity does not cease, and that is what I aim at with more or less success.

As the months wore on his state of health became more critical, and on 18th January 1901, he wrote:

> I was quite unwell, kind friend Maude, when I asked P. A. to write to you for me. Now I am better and add these lines to say a few more words. My illness consisted of suppressed feverishness, causing great weakness and times intensifying my usual liver disease.
>
> When I am in a good spiritual state I am glad of my approaching liberation from the body. But when I am carried away my wish to accomplish things I have planned, I regret my pack of strength.

In February 1901 my conflict with the Free Age Press still continuing, Tolstoy wrote definitely taking Chertkóv's side, but treating me with the kindly consideration which, with age, became an increasingly noticeable feature in one who was by nature both impulsive and masterful:

Moscow, 19 February 1901

DEAR FRIEND MAUDE – Of course I much regret that you and Chertkóv have not come to agreement about translating and publishing, but I am distressed most of all that such people as you and he, both living to accomplish the work we are sent to do, and not for your personal ends, have not found the common principle which would unite you on the present question. The considerations which you advance against the Free Age Press and in favour of copyright, are just; but so is the consideration that the manner of publishing should accord with the bases which are preached in the editions. And I think that the latter argument is more important than the former. I think that if you do not agree to that, then your, and your wife's, splendid translations of works that have been already published in bad translations, deserve to find a publisher. If not, still what you have in view to do [namely to try to explain his views in my own words] is very pleasant to me.

My relation to that business is this: Chertkóv has spent, and continues to spend, so much loving work on the correct reproduction and dissemination of my thoughts, which he fully and very sensitively understands, that I can only rejoice at having such an intermediary between myself and my readers. And the chief thing for me is, that after all the labour he has spent, I cannot disappoint his expectations and instead of aiding him hinder his work. My help in his work is limited to the fact that all my new writings (if there are any more) I issue first of all through him, letting everybody, if they care to, make use of them afterwards as they please.

I am very sorry that I and Chertkóv should lose your help and that of your wife, which is very valuable, both on account of your knowledge of the languages, your conscientious work, and the unity of our understanding of life, but what most of all grieves me is that perhaps I, by my inaccuracy and alterations, have been the cause of the dislike you have taken to this work. Please forgive me for that. Above all, do not attribute importance to this affair and do not let dead business impair living intercourse with living people. I press your own and your wife's hands in friendship.

I have no doubt that a wish not to disappoint Chertkóv's expectations, was in fact 'the chief thing' that induced Tolstoy to support the Free Age Press. Gratitude was a strong characteristic of his character. In common with all who worked with him, I always found him very appreciative and inclined even to overestimate any services rendered. Chertkóv seemed to him to have made great sacrifices for the common cause, undergoing exile, and establishing a printing and publishing business to issue Tolstoy's works and to spread his views. Besides this, Chertkóv's ardour for Non-Resistance and his efforts to give it practical application, seemed to Tolstoy – at a distance from the spot – deserving of support. He did not foresee that Chertkóv – with unequalled opportunities for producing a definitive edition in English, the first disposal of all that Tolstoy wrote, considerable funds contributed by a member of the wealthy Russian merchant family, Kónshin, the efficient co-operation of A. C. Fifield to conduct the publishing, and of others ready for Tolstoy's sake to translate, assist, and contribute support –

would fail to accomplish his purpose, and after long hindering others from producing what was wanted, would finally abandon the attempt.

It would be superfluous to revert to these half-forgotten matters if it were not for the remarkable way in which the theory of non-resistance, Chertkóv's applications of it, and the resulting conflicts, were linked with the sad sequence of events that eventually drove Tolstoy from home and led to his death.

Mr Fifield withdrew from the Free Age Press after a couple of years. Its management then passed from hand to hand, its output slackened and eventually ceased. The booklets it had issued went out of print, and they are now unobtainable, or only obtainable second-hand.

Tolstoy's next letter dealt with the same subject, again with the same friendly forbearance:

22nd March 1901

DEAR FRIEND MAUDE – I have received your letter and am glad you have taken my letter in so good a spirit. Really it is not worth while for the sake of any business, and still less for self-love, to deprive oneself of intercourse with one's fellows and especially with those with whom we are at one on the most important and essential things in life.

In a letter received 25th March 1901, n.s., he says:

DEAR FRIEND – I have received your good letter.

All the same I regret, not that you do not work with Chertkóv, but that between you and him there is an unkindly feeling, and on your side a feeling of personal dignity bordering on pride. But it is not for me to judge you.

As to the money your wife wishes to give for useful work [the *Resurrection* Fund], I have no advice to give. The Doukhobórs, thank God, are well off in Canada, and I think there is no particular need in Yakútsk; and there is money put aside to assist the exiles there which is not wanted as yet. There is some also for the migration of the women. So deal with the money as God puts in your heart. – Your loving

L. TOLSTOY

These letters show Tolstoy's kindly spirit at a time of great stress, for the beginning of that year, 1901, was the moment in Russia at which the long smouldering feelings of dissatisfaction began to express themselves publicly, and the cry of patriotism and loyalty no longer sufficed to repress demonstrations of sympathy with the progressive movement. Several indications of this appeared simultaneously. It showed itself among the members of the Zémstvos who met in Moscow, in February and March, at the Congress of Agronomists and at that of the *Maréchaux de la Noblesse*; and it showed itself also in the students' disturbances when, for the first time, the butchers in the streets near the Moscow University refrained from showing hostility to the insubordinate students. The Government met the unrest in the Universities by issuing 'temporary regulations' under which students participating in the disorders could be sent to serve as soldiers. Some dozens of Kiev University undergraduates were actually sentenced to the ranks under these 'temporary regulations', and this evoked many public protests, especially from the other Universities. A large demonstration took place in the square in front of the Kazán Cathedral in Petersburg on 4th March, during which Kleigels, Governor of Petersburg, ordered the Cossacks to charge and beat the crowd. N. F. Ánnenski, the author, was among those who were struck, and P. B. Struve, the publicist, was among those arrested. This called forth the energetic protest of several well-known men, and in particular that of Prince L. D. Vyázemski, who was on the spot.

The Tsar reprimanded Vyázemski for his interference, and Tolstoy thereupon drafted the following address to the Prince, which was signed by many eminent people:

RESPECTED PRINCE LEONÍD DMÍTRIEVICH!
Your courageous, noble and humane action on 4 March in front of the Kazán Cathedral is known to all Russia.

We hope that you, like ourselves, regard the reproof you have received from the Emperor for that action as merely due to the coarseness and cruelty of those who deceive him. You have done a good deed, and Russian society will always remain grateful to you for it.

You preferred to yield to your feeling of indignation against brutal violence, and to the demands of humanity, rather than to the supposed demands of propriety and of your position, and your action evokes universal respect and gratitude, which we express to you by this letter.

Amid these events, indicating the awakening of that new life which

four years later shook the throne of Russia, the Holy Synod, as though
to show the spirit that actuated it at the beginning of the twentieth
century, surprised the world by launching against Tolstoy a decree of
Excommunication. It was dated 22nd February 1901, and after a preliminary reminder of the fact that 'the gates of Hell shall not prevail
against' the Holy Church, it went on to say:

> In our days God has permitted a new false teacher to appear – Count
> Leo Tolstoy. A writer well known to the world, Russian by birth,
> Orthodox by baptism and education, Count Tolstoy, under the
> seduction of his intellectual pride, has insolently risen against the
> Lord and His Christ and against His holy heritage, and has publicly
> in the sight of all men repudiated the Orthodox Mother Church
> which reared and educated him, and has devoted his literary activity
> and the talent given him by God, to disseminating among the people
> teachings repugnant to Christ and the Church, and to destroying in
> the minds and hearts of men their national faith, the Orthodox faith
> which has been confirmed by the universe and in which our fore-
> fathers lived and were saved, and to which till now Holy Russia has
> held, and in which it has been strong.

After recounting Tolstoy's heresies at considerable length, it proceeded to say:

> Therefore the Church does not reckon him as its member, and cannot
> so reckon him until he repents and resumes his communion with her.

The decree produced a tremendous sensation, and in some people it
aroused anger and hatred against Tolstoy, culminating in fresh threats
of murder.

His books were excluded from some of the public libraries. The
newspapers were forbidden to mention demonstrations made in his
honour. The Censor stopped the reproduction of his portrait in an
illustrated paper. Sermons were preached against him, and a Moscow
Temperance Society expelled him from its membership! Even the
telegraph offices began to refuse to accept messages expressing
sympathy with him, and letters of that character were stopped in the
post – whereas abusive letters were duly delivered.

The demand for Tolstoy's forbidden books increased, however, and
people became more eager than ever to obtain and read them.

Semënov, travelling by rail, overheard a conversation between a young woman who was carrying a baby in her arms and an old one who asked:

'Why have they anathematised him?'

'Why,' calmly replied the young one, speaking with assurance, 'he began to preach and write that marriage is unnecessary . . . !'

'How is that? Are we to do without a proper marriage?' asked the elder, her eyes opening wide.

'No, there is to be no marriage. Men and women are not to come together. It is the cause of destruction, and children are born for destruction.'

'Then are we all to be like monks and nuns?'

'Yes; everything else is deadly sin, says he. Well, after he wrote that book a year or two passed and then, lo and behold! a child was born to him! [This happened not to be true, though it is a statement that has been repeated by his own son, Leo Tolstoy, junior.] So then they began to judge him for demanding of people what he himself did not do. So they took him and turned him out of the Church.'

The old woman remained silent, evidently thinking over what she had heard, and the young one pressed her boy to her heart and gave him a sounding kiss on his lips.

On the day the Edict was made public (February 25), as Tolstoy was crossing a public square someone exclaimed, 'See! There goes the devil in human form!' But the crowd instead of hustling or attacking him, as a year or two previously might have happened to anyone denounced by the Church, cheered him very heartily.

Répin's new portrait of him at the Exhibition in Petersburg was decorated by the public with quantities of flowers, and this so displeased the Authorities that they ordered the portrait to be removed from the Exhibition. The schoolboys in the streets greeted Tolstoy and masses of letters and telegrams poured in upon him. Before dinner a deputation of women came to express their sympathy. After dinner the yard was full of students, girls, and workmen, to whom Tolstoy went out and talked, pacifying them, and advising them in the state of unrest then general, not to be led into any rash conduct. On Tolstoy himself the Excommunication had exceedingly little effect, and he greeted friends who came to see him, with the words: 'I positively decline to accept congratulations!'

Another remark he made was: ' "The gates of Hell shall not prevail," and yet when an ex-Lieutenant writes something they make all this commotion!'

It was a moment when, as had been the case during the famine, years before, Tolstoy appeared in the forefront of the movement of emancipation. His house was a centre of inspiration to the timid and desponding, and for the time being the deep-seated divergence between him and the Constitutional reformers dropped out of sight.

His reply to the Synod is a most noble and inspiring document. The reader will find it in full in *Essays and Letters*.

After a statement of what he believed and disbelieved, Tolstoy concluded as follows:

> Whether these beliefs of mine offend, grieve, or prove a stumbling-block to anyone, or hinder anything, or give displeasure to anybody or not, I can as little change them as I can change my body. I must myself live my own life, and I must myself alone meet death (and that very soon), and therefore I cannot believe otherwise than as I – preparing to go to that God from whom I came – do believe. I do not believe my faith to be the one indubitable truth for all time, but I see no other that is plainer, clearer, or answers better to all the demands of my reason and my heart. Should I find such a faith, I shall at once accept it; for God requires nothing but the truth. But I can no more return to that from which with such suffering I have escaped, than a flying bird can re-enter the eggshell from which it has emerged.

That same month (15th March) Tolstoy wrote an *Appeal to the Tsar and his chief Ministers*, which was delivered to them, but was not then published. In it he says, of some disturbances that had occurred:

> Very possibly the disturbances that have now broken out may be suppressed, though it is also possible that the soldiers and police, on whom the Government place such reliance, may realise that they are being called on to commit the terrible crime of fratricide, and may refuse to obey. But even if the present disturbance is suppressed, it will not be extinguished, but will burn in secret more and more fiercely, and will inevitably burst out sooner or later with increased strength and produce yet greater sufferings and crimes . . .

He then enumerated the demands of the people, which may be summarised as:

1 Equal rights for the peasants
2 Abolition of special enactments enabling the Common Law to be overridden
3 Liberty of education, and
4 Religious liberty

'Such,' he continues,

are the modest and easily realisable desires, we believe, of the immense majority of the Russian people. The adoption of these measures would undoubtedly pacify the people and free them from those terrible sufferings and (what is worse than sufferings) crimes, which will inevitably be committed on both sides if the Government busies itself only with the suppression of these disturbances, leaving their cause untouched.

'Only if this is done,' says Tolstoy to the Tsar, 'can your position be safe and really strong.'

Read a few years later, when the long-suppressed discontent had burst out into Revolution, after the disasters of the Japanese War, this letter, which will be found in *Essays and Letters*, appeared truly prophetic.

16

Nearing the End

Tolstoy's character and views are much misunderstood because people will rush to simple conclusions on complex matters. Though he was sincere and wise, he, like other mortals, made mistakes – and did so just because he, too, over-simplified, and wished to solve the complex problems of property, sex, and Government, by the all too simple method of rejecting those things entirely.

By rejecting property, sex, and Government we should rid ourselves of many familiar ills, but it would be at the cost of encountering others that do not trouble us now. A moral as well as an intellectual error is involved in the supposition that our forefathers arranged matters as they did, for no other reason than that they were bad men, and that we ought to make a clean sweep of the institutions they framed.

One must sympathise with Tolstoy's desire to centralise, unify, and simplify, life's teaching; that is what all who take life seriously should aim at, but the dilemma is, that as soon as opinions are reduced to a concise formula – whether it be 'the blood of Jesus', the 'infallible Church', 'the non-use of physical force', or what not – we find that such formulas fail to carry conviction to those who observe the facts of life; and the acceptance of such short and easy solutions of our difficulties becomes a hindrance to the attainment of truth.

Andrew D. White, telling of a visit he paid to Tolstoy, remarks that, from lack of encountering others of similar calibre to his own, in a land which had till then known no public body where the discussion of large public questions was allowed – a Russian thinker, 'having given birth to striking ideas, coddles and pets them until they become the full-grown spoilt children of his brain. He can see neither spot nor blemish in them, and at last virtually believes himself infallible.' He applies these remarks to Tolstoy, and adds that 'his love of humanity, real though it certainly is, is accompanied by a depreciation of the ideas, statements, and proposals of every other human being, and by virtual intolerance of all thought which differs in the slightest degree from his own.' White says all this while fully admitting the influence of Tolstoy's striking and sincere personality, and I cannot deny that if instead of having his works suppressed, Tolstoy had had them fairly criticised, it would have been good both for him and for them.

In the article just referred to, White records several characteristic remarks Tolstoy made to him. For instance, speaking of the Mormons, he remarked that no doubt two-thirds of their religion is deception, but on the whole he 'preferred a religion which professed to have dug its sacred book out of the earth, to one which pretended that it was let down from heaven'.

White noticed Tolstoy's habit of giving copper money to the beggars who swarm in Moscow, even when he knew they wanted it for vodka. In reply to a remonstrance, Tolstoy said that in such cases the results of our actions are not the main thing, but the cultivation of better feelings in the giver.

This is parallel to his feeling that it is not the success of our work that matters, but the spirit in which we do it. It is difficult to define the amount of truth such views contain. To what extent, for instance, may we endanger other people's safety, or sacrifice the success of a business entrusted to us, in order to cultivate a kindlier state of mind in ourselves and in those whom we meet?

No doubt we harsher people of the West have much to learn from Russian warm-heartedness, but what I never could get Tolstoy to feel, was the spirit underlying Abraham Lincoln's words, uttered towards the close of a war he thought it his duty to conduct until the other side was willing to accept fair terms:

With malice towards none, with charity for all, with firmness in the right as God gives us to see the right, let us finish the work we are in . . . and do all which may achieve a just and lasting peace among ourselves and with all nations.

Again and again when I have heard Tolstoy urge people to yield, submit, and forgo, I have felt that there was another side to the matter, and that one should sometimes try to get things straight, if not for one's own sake, then for the sake of others. As Lowell has it:

> Be kind'z you please, but fustly make things fast,
> For plain Truth's all the kindness that'll last.

To synthesise the two truths – that we must get the world's work done efficiently, and that we ought to do it without friction – is as difficult a problem as any we poor mortals have to face. Probably we of the Anglo-Saxon world lay too little stress on the state of mind in which we work, and men of the Slavonic world have thought too little of getting things well done. Even today the USSR is more concerned about maintaining Marxian principles than about seeing that the people secure decent food, clothing, and housing.

White's account of Tolstoy recalls Tolstoy's comment on White's visit to him. They had a long walk together, and on returning home to dinner, after White had gone, Tolstoy asked his family if they knew how the United States is governed. They confessed to not knowing much about it. 'Well,' said he, 'each State elects its wisest and best men to govern it, but the two very wisest and very best men from each State are sent to the Senate at Washington to make laws for the whole country. I have had one of those men with me today. He has learned all the sciences, and knows all the languages, and has read all the books – the only pity is that he has not yet begun to think.'

After the excitement of the early part of 1901, Tolstoy's health, which had seemed to rally, again failed him, and in June he was seriously unwell. On returning from a visit to his eldest daughter, Madame Sukhotín, he reached Yásnaya quite ill. On 24th June, P. A. Boulanger, a friend of Tolstoy's and of mine, wrote me from Yásnaya that Tolstoy was very weak and constantly ill. 'If he works through the morning he is unable to do anything more . . .'

To this letter Tolstoy added a postscript:

I do not want to let this letter go without adding a few words. What B. says of my health and weariness is correct, but it arises chiefly from the fact that I am just finishing an article, *The Only Means*. It deals with the question, What can free the labourers from their ills? I try to show that only their faith in God and in His law as expressed in the Gospels – the golden rule – can do this.

I have worked at it a great deal, and seem to have arrived at the point at which I begin to spoil it. I am completely absorbed in this work, and therefore postpone correspondence. My health is such that I must not complain, for I can, I think, work as well as formerly. That however is for the readers and for you to judge . . .

I want also to write something about the absence of religion and the consequences thereof and also about education, and on one other matter which I do not wish to name.

On 29th June his strength failed him and the action of his heart became very irregular.

His wife sent to Túla for a doctor, though Tolstoy objected as usual, believing that physical sufferings should be utilised to free one's spirit from subjection to the flesh, and to place it, at death, in the hands of the Father unsoiled by the agitations, desires, and passions of physical life. He would not regard illness or death as an evil. 'Illness,' said he, 'is like fire – it destroys but also warms.'

After recovering from a serious crisis, he remarked to his daughter: 'The sledge was at the door and I had only to get in and go, but suddenly the horses turned round and the vehicle was sent away. It's a pity, for it was a good sledge road, and when I'm ready to start again it may be rough.'

The improvement in his health did not last long. On 3rd July he could scarcely speak, and the doctor pronounced his condition very serious.

At intervals he felt better and was even able to go on with his writing, but these intervals were always followed by dangerous relapses, and at last the family decided to send to Moscow for the doctor who had successfully attended him during a previous severe illness in 1899. This doctor diagnosed his complaint as angina pectoris and said it would be necessary to take him to a warmer climate. The summer which was drawing to its close had been cold, and Yásnaya Polyána with its shady, neglected park, was too damp for him to go out in.

On 11th and 12th July he was again able to walk about the rooms, and at once set to work and finished *The Only Means*.

During this illness he was much cheered by his good relations with his brother Sergéy, for whom he had always felt a strong affection, and with whom he came into closer touch during the years preceding Sergéy's death, which occurred on 22nd August 1904.

The Countess Pánin, who had an estate at Gáspra, near Yálta, gladly lent her palace to the Tolstoys when she heard that the doctors recommended a warmer climate, and the Minister of Railways, Prince Khilkóv, promptly gave orders that a special through-car should be coupled to any train selected, to enable Tolstoy to travel to Sevastopol undisturbed.

One cold, dark evening at the end of August, wrapped in a fur coat, he was taken to Túla by his wife, two daughters, and some friends. The roads were in a dreadful state, and by the time the party reached the station at 10 P.M. he felt very ill, but it was thought that the drive back to Yásnaya would be worse for him than the long journey in a warm, dry railway carriage, so they went on.

In the morning it was warm and sunny, he felt better, and the whole party brightened up. At Kharkov station a large crowd had collected to see him. He was distressed by this, but consented to some students being admitted to the car to speak to him, and in response to repeated demands even showed himself at the window.

After that he was again alarmingly ill, but recovered before reaching Sevastopol, where another crowd had assembled, which was kept away from the station by the police. Here he stayed one night, and in the afternoon was sufficiently well to leave his hotel and go for a short walk with Boulanger. They visited the Museum of relics of the siege. An officer they met introduced himself to Tolstoy, who remembered the man's father and mother and how he had danced with the latter forty-five years before. Tolstoy related many episodes of the siege, describing the position of the batteries and recalling some of the defenders, but the sight of his own portrait in the Museum distressed him and turned the current of his thoughts into bitter channels. Complaining of fatigue he went back to the hotel, and on the way remarked: 'What a pity! . . . What is the use of that expensive building and that careful collection of buttons and splinters? One ought to forget all that horror and savagery and shame; yet people try to inflame the recollection . . . It is horrible, horrible! . . . '

From Sevastopol the party drove to Yálta by road. At the first station, where they stopped to change horses, Tolstoy walked on ahead and met a young fellow (apparently a shop-assistant or small tradesman) of whom he enquired the name of some place on the shore below. The stranger answered the poorly and strangely clad old man contempt-uously, and, when the Countess drove up, was amazed to see him get into the carriage and drive off. Turning to Boulanger, who was waiting for a second carriage, the fellow asked who that old man was.

'Count Tolstoy,' was the answer.

'What? Count Tolstoy, the writer? . . . Oh, my God, my God!' exclaimed the other in despair, flinging his cap into the dirty road. 'I would have given all I possess to see him, and how I spoke to him!'

At Yálta the weather was warm and fine and Tolstoy's health improved rapidly.

Having settled in his new surroundings he again began to write. His Caucasian story, *Hadji Murad*, was more or less a recreation for him, but he worked very seriously at *What is Religion?* and *The Soldier's Notes*.

On 23rd September 1901, he wrote to me saying:

My work on religion progresses very slowly and with difficulty, in spite of the fact that the more I think on this subject the more I see its importance, and I very much desire to express what I think about it.

I called the preacher Kiesewetter [this in reply to my enquiry about the Evangelical preacher in *Resurrection*] because I took the type from Baedeker, a German, who used to preach in English.

I am living amid pleasant scenery and climate, with every possible comfort of life, but I feel that mental energy is lacking, though I do not know whether this comes from illness or from material satisfaction.

Chékhov and Górki were both at Yálta and visited him; and Golden-weiser, the pianist, used to play for him, but in general he lived a very quiet life which allowed him to concentrate on his work whenever well enough to do so.

On 20th November, his daughter-in-law, the Countess Ólga K. Tolstoy, wrote me from Gáspra:

All this time Leo Nikoláevich has been suffering a good deal, and was even laid up for one week. He is again feverish, and has rheumatism in hand and foot, so that for some days the pain and weakness prevented his writing anything. He is now much better again and has begun to go out walking a little. But he is still very weak, and after his customary work has not the strength for anything else. That is why he has not written to you for so long. He asks me to transmit to you his great gratitude for your letters and for *Sevastopol*.

In December he seemed again to have recovered, but could not be persuaded to be careful and moderate in the exercise he took. He would not live the 'old man's life' advised by the doctors.

At that time, to my own great distress, I happened to grieve him. There had been much confusion and many complications in con-nection with the publishing of *Resurrection*, and when printing the first audited 'Account of Receipts and Expenditure', I narrated the history of the matter more fully than was perhaps necessary, and of this publication I sent a copy to Tolstoy, who on 23rd December 1901, replied:

> I have received your letter and article. I am very sorry you wrote it. You have thereby grieved and in no way strengthened the feeling of love – and that is the chief business of life – in the soul of Chertkóv, a man near to you, but have on the contrary evoked in him an angry feeling involuntarily experienced though not expressed in any way.
>
> All considerations as to accounts and donations weigh as nothing in comparison with the infringement of love. I understand that there was much that was unpleasant to you, and you did not succeed in restraining yourself, as happens to us all, and therefore I do not condemn you, but, loving you, point out what seems to me your offence.
>
> Please forgive me if I am doing what is unpleasant to you.
>
> I think I already wrote to you how unusually pleased I am with the first volume of your edition. All is excellent – the edition, the notes, and chiefly the translation, and even more the conscientiousness with which all this has been done. I opened it accidentally at *Two Hussars* and read on to the end just as if it were something new that had been written in English.
>
> My health fluctuates, but does not prevent my working, for which I am very grateful. However, even without that I cannot but be grateful to Him who has made possible for me so beautiful a life as that which is at my disposal.
>
> Give my love to your wife and your sister-in-law if they are with you or near you. How are your children? One has not had time to look round before they – the elder ones – are already announcing their own individual qualities and demands. God grant they may be good ones.

The book he speaks of so kindly was *Sevastopol*, the first volume of my first attempt to produce a collected edition of his works.

In January [1902] he had another very bad attack of palpitation of the heart and shortness of breath, and was again seriously ill with angina pectoris, but he continued to work whenever he could, and wrote an article *On Religions Toleration*, evoked by reading a speech made by his friend, M. A. Stakhóvich, at a Missionary Congress at Orël.

On 16th January, believing that he had not long to live, he completed a letter to the Tsar in which he said:

DEAR BROTHER – I consider this form of address most suitable because in this letter I address you as a brother-man rather than as a Tsar, and also because, awaiting the approach of death, I write as it were from the other world. I should not like to die without having told you what I think of your present activity and of what it might be . . .

After recounting the ills from which Russia was suffering, he proceeded to say that neither Orthodoxy nor Autocracy was then any longer suitable for Russia:

With reference to Autocracy, it may have been natural to Russians when they still believed the Tsar to be an infallible earthly deity who himself personally ruled the people, but it is far from natural now, when they all know – or as soon as they get a little education will know – that, in the first place, a good Tsar is only *un heureux hasard* [a lucky accident] and that Tsars may be and have been monsters and maniacs, like John IV and Paul, and secondly, that however good and wise a Tsar may be, he cannot possibly himself rule a nation of a hundred and thirty million people, but that they are ruled by men who surround the Tsar and are more concerned about their own position than about the people's welfare.

Autocracy is an obsolete form of Government which may suit the demands of people cut off from the world somewhere in Central Africa, but not the demands of the Russian people who are growing ever more and more enlightened by the common enlightenment of the whole world, and therefore that form of Government and the Orthodoxy bound up with it, can only be upheld (as is now being done) by violence of all kinds: a state of siege, banishments by Administrative Order, executions, religious persecution, the prohibition of books and newspapers, the perversion of education, and in general by all kinds of evil and cruel deeds.

Such have hitherto been the actions of your reign: beginning with your reply to the Tver Deputation – which provoked the indignation of the whole Russian people – when you called their most legitimate desires 'insensate fancies'; all your regulations concerning Finland; the Chinese seizures; your project of a Hague Conference, which was accompanied by an increase in the army; your restriction of self-government, and strengthening of Administrative despotism; your consent to the institution of a spirit-monopoly – that is, to Government trading in a poison which ruins the people; and finally your obstinacy in maintaining corporal punishment in spite of all the representations made to you in favour of the abolition of that senseless and utterly useless measure, an outrage on the Russian people.

Measures of coercion make it possible to oppress, but not to govern, a people. Indeed, in our time the only means of governing the people is by placing oneself at the head of their movement from evil to good, from darkness to light, and by leading them towards the attainment of the objects nearest to that end.

In order to do that it is necessary, first of all, to let them express their wishes and needs, and having heard them, to fulfil those which respond to the demands, not of one class or section but of the majority – the mass of the working-people.

Then follows an enumeration of those demands: the abolition of special laws making pariahs of the peasants; freedom to migrate; freedom of education; freedom of conscience; and –

above all, the whole hundred million people will say with one voice that they desire freedom to use the land – that is to say, the abolition of private property in land . . .

In any case the first thing that lies before the Government is the abolition of the gag which now prevents the people from expressing its wishes and needs. One cannot do good to a man whose mouth one has tied up in order not to hear what he wants . . .

Forgive me if I have unintentionally offended or grieved you by what I have written in this letter. I am moved only by a desire for the welfare of the Russian people and of yourself . . .

That letter is characteristic in its ardent desire to remedy great evils, its self-reliance, its assurance that everything the Tsar had done (including the calling of a Hague Conference) was quite wrong, but that being a human being, he yet had a soul to which an appeal could profitably be addressed, and that he might yet be persuaded to turn over a new leaf and do what was right.

There is an evident contradiction between the conviction that Government is necessarily and hopelessly wrong, and the suggestion that the Tsar might do great good by legislation. Tolstoy could not have it both ways. If the badness of Government is a matter of degree much of his customary invective loses its point, but if that badness is absolute and inevitable, what was the use of asking a Tsar to do anything, except resign? What attracts one however here, as always, is Tolstoy's courage, sincerity and ardent desire that right should prevail and his freedom from mean and selfish aims.

During all this the constantly fluctuating condition of Tolstoy's health perplexed his doctors, and when a further complication showed itself, Dr Shuróvski was telegraphed for from Moscow, and found the patient suffering from inflammation of the lungs.

News that he was not expected to survive reached the Holy Synod, and Pobedonóstsev issued secret instructions that in the event of Tolstoy's death a priest should immediately enter the house (to which, as it contained a chapel, the clergy had right of access), and on coming out again should announce that Tolstoy had repented, returned to the bosom of Mother Church, confessed, and received the Eucharist before his death. This news would have been cabled round the world to supplement the efforts of the Censor to destroy the effects of Tolstoy's teaching.

By the end of February, however, the patient was better, and before long he was able to go out in a Bath-chair. Presently the family began to think of returning to Yásnaya, but in May he was again at death's door, this time – if the doctors' diagnosis was correct – with enteric fever. Once more his marvellous recuperative power manifested itself, and at last, in June, the homeward journey really began. Too weak to be driven by road, Tolstoy, after waiting a week for calm weather, was taken to Sevastopol by steamer. There he had a few hours to spare, and, suffering from the intolerable heat, asked to be allowed to rest in the quiet station garden. He had not sat there long, before an irate lady sternly ordered him out, saying that 'this was the garden of a high railway official and not the place for goodness-knows-who to loaf about in!'

Before the train started a crowd collected to see the great writer off, and this same lady came eagerly imploring to be allowed to enter his car to apologise for her rudeness. Owing to the crush it was impossible to let her in. 'How could I know it was Tolstoy?' she said in great distress, handing in a bouquet and begging that he should be asked to forgive her.

The chief work Tolstoy wrote during his stay at Gáspra was *What is Religion?*

Whenever, as in this case, Tolstoy chewed the cud of reflection on a great subject – if only he was not drawn astray by his pet prejudices – he produced a masterpiece. Why this admirable essay is not far better known and more quoted than it is, I can only explain by supposing that it – and others like it – were drowned in the stream of his Non-Resistant articles, and thus escaped the attention they deserve.

Lack of space forbids my doing justice to it here, and I must refer the reader to the article itself in *Essays and Letters*.

Tolstoy's definition of religion is that:

> True religion is a relation, accordant with reason and knowledge, which man establishes with the infinite life surrounding him, and is such as binds his life to that infinity and guides his conduct.

As already mentioned, he held that the essentially important religious truths explaining life and guiding conduct exist in all the great religions. Men are separated from one another by their superstitions but united in the central truth. To save religion, Tolstoy was ready to destroy the Churches.

Of faith, he says:

> Faith is neither hope nor credulity, but a special state of the soul. Faith is man's consciousness that his position in the world is such as obliges him to do certain things . . . Thus, for instance, a man who has defined his position in the world as that of a member of a nation chosen by God, which in order to enjoy God's protection must fulfil His demands, will live in such a way as to fulfil those demands; another man, having defined his position on the supposition that he has passed and is passing through various forms of existence, and that his future, for better or for worse, depends more or less on his actions, will be guided in life by that definition; while the conduct of a third man, who has defined his position as that of a chance combination of atoms in which a consciousness has been temporarily kindled which must be extinguished for ever, will differ from that of the two first . . .

Not in Russia alone did Tolstoy's indictment of the Church as the foe of true religion arouse animosity. At Leipzig, on 9th July, Diederichs, the publisher, and Dr R. Lëwenfeld, the translator of Tolstoy's *Reply to the Synod*, were tried for blasphemy, but the prosecution failed, the judge expressing his concurrence with the defendants' plea that Tolstoy was a great moral force.

After *What is Religion?* Tolstoy wrote, I think, nothing of equal scope and importance.

In August 1902 I had the pleasure of again visiting him. The plain, substantial country-house at Yásnaya, roomy withal and well adapted to its purpose, though with old-fashioned, rather plain furniture, worn bare-board floors in many of the rooms, and window-frames that needed repairing and renewing, made a different impression on me each time I went there, according to the people I met, the circumstances, and my own state of mind. On this occasion the large grounds seemed even more neglected and overgrown than of yore, as though announcing that their former master had become absorbed in matters more serious than the trimness of his park.

Tolstoy himself had sufficiently recovered in health to be able to go for a two-hours' walk, though on returning home he was glad to be helped upstairs. At times too he left the company in the large dining-and-sitting-room and went to lie down. Once or twice he even dropped asleep in his chair.

He had, as we know, always been sceptical about medicine and doctors, and it was amusing to hear the Countess tell of his surprise at the time of his great weakness on finding that it really had a stimulating effect when they gave him injections of camphor.

Speaking in his humorous way to his doctors when already convalescent, he said: 'Well, gentlemen, I have always spoken badly of doctors, but now that I have got to know you better I see that I did you great injustice. You are really very good men and know all that your science teaches, the only pity is – that it knows nothing.'

From the time of his return from the Crimea there was always a doctor resident at Yásnaya on his account; but before he would consent to this, he stipulated that the doctor must also be at the disposal of the neighbouring peasants.

During that visit I was particularly impressed by the atmosphere of love and respect that surrounded Tolstoy from all about him, and from the visitors of all sorts and conditions who came to see him. His two younger daughters were then doing most of the work of copying his manuscripts and assisting him with his correspondence. The elder of the two, Mary, Princess Obolénski, was living with her husband in the 'wing' house, from whence they came across for most of their meals. Besides sympathising warmly with her father and sharing his feelings and out look on life, she also shared his frank and friendly manner of speech.

Countess Sófya Andréevna, who was most solicitous about her husband's health and comfort, spoke very frankly both of his qualities and limitations.

Tolstoy's sister, Countess Mary N. Tolstoy, who, after her husband's death and the marriage of her three daughters, had become a nun and lived at the Shámordin Convent, was staying at the house, having obtained leave of absence from her Nunnery on account of her mother's ill-health.

One of the guests was V. V. Stásov, an old man, tall, upright and white-haired, a well-known critic and author, Head of the Imperial Academy Library at St Petersburg, and an old friend of the family. His immense knowledge of books, as well as the great library at his command, enabled him to be of much use to Tolstoy when the latter wanted to read up any subject he was dealing with.

Stásov by no means shared all Tolstoy's views, but felt the highest esteem for him. He remarked to me that among Russia's great writers there were three pre-eminently *intellectual*; namely, Herzen, Griboyé-dov, and Tolstoy.

Another guest, a striking contrast to Stásov – small, alert, black-haired, and much younger – was the sculptor Ginzburg, who was modelling a bust of Tolstoy. I had met him (as well as Stásov) on a previous visit, and was much struck by his wonderful powers of mimicry. With a towel and chair he could represent a nurse and baby, or could become a most lifelike tailor, stitching clothes, giving in either case a complete performance. It was delightful to see how heartily Tolstoy laughed, and how keenly he appreciated this dramatic ability, saying to Ginzburg, 'Ah, if only our theatre realists could be got to understand that what is wanted is not to put real babies on the stage or show the real messes they make, but to convey, as you do, by voice and feature, the real feeling that has to be expressed!'

Another visitor was M. A. Stakhóvich, friend of the Tolstoys from boyhood, and at that time *Maréchal de la Noblesse* of Orël, whom the Minister of the Interior had reprimanded for the speech he had delivered in favour of religious toleration. Stakhóvich questioned the Minister's right to reprove him on the matter, and thereupon received a letter from the Emperor, who merely took exception however to certain expressions Stakhóvich had used. The latter had come to consult Tolstoy as to what reply he should make.

He brought several young relatives with him. It was their first visit to Yásnaya and they evidently felt it to be a great event. Tolstoy did not miss the opportunity of implanting in their minds the seeds of anti-war, vegetarian, and Henry-Georgian principles, and it was curious to see the members of a great landowning family sit so respectfully at the feet of a Christian-anarchist, who only by way of a concession to humanity's weakness admitted anything as mild as the Single Tax – his own principles demanding the yielding up not of land only but of all possessions to anyone who cared to take them.

There was in the whole atmosphere of the house an infectious feeling of the importance of what was going on. There was plenty of mirth, but its savour came from the strenuous life lived there. It felt as though we were invited to share in the immediate regeneration of mankind, and as though the walls of Jericho would probably fall next time we blew our trumpets.

On Sunday afternoon a Jewish clerk living in the neighbourhood asked to see Tolstoy. He had read some of his religious writings and wanted further explanations. To such callers Tolstoy was especially attentive. The man was asked in to tea, and soon a volume of extracts from the Talmud, a New Testament, and an English Concordance were on the table in the large room already mentioned, and questions and interpretations followed. Presently Tolstoy called for general attention, saying: 'Listen to this – I have just discovered something.' He then read the parable from Matthew 22, beginning: 'The kingdom of heaven is likened unto a certain king, who made a marriage feast for his son, and sent forth his servants to call them that were bidden . . . and they would not come.' He read verses 2 to 10; how other servants were sent, and still those who had been invited would not come, and how at last the king sent his servants to the highways, to gather all they could find, 'and the wedding was filled with guests.' Pausing, he asked us whether that made sense, as a parable of the international democratisation of the kingdom of heaven. We agreed that it did. He then went on to read verses 11 to 14, about the man who had not on a wedding garment and whom the king ordered to be cast into the outer darkness where there shall be weeping and gnashing of teeth. When he asked whether that made sense with the rest of the parable, we all said it did not.

'Well,' said Tolstoy, 'I have just found where it comes from. It is part of a story in the Talmud, and must have been copied on to the end of the Gospel parable. Some scribe who knew the Talmud story by heart, was probably engaged to copy the Gospel, and coming on words that occur identically in both, blundered and proceeded to put into the Gospels from memory a passage which makes sense where it stands in the Talmud, but makes nonsense here.'

Another day a telegram arrived from the Grand Duke Nicholas Miháylovich asking for news of Tolstoy's health. This, Tolstoy told me, was a reminder that he had omitted to acknowledge the service the Grand Duke had rendered him by handing to the Emperor the letter he had written from Gáspra.

That same day a workman called who had been injured at a factory and wanted to know how to secure compensation. After seeing him Tolstoy said: 'In such cases I often have contradictory feelings. One sympathises with the man, but yet I constantly feel – as in this case – that he wishes to take unfair advantage of his injury. He makes out that he can do no work at all, while really he could do something if he wished to.'

There were every day a number of pilgrims, tramps, or destitute peasants, who called simply to beg, and did not go empty away. Something, from a penny to a florin, was given to almost everyone, and quite substantial help to some. Tolstoy felt it to be uncivil not to give at least a little to everyone who asked.

In each of the two houses on the estate stood a grand piano, and eminent musicians, knowing Tolstoy's love of music, were frequent visitors at Yásnaya. During my stay Tanéyev performed a new composition of his own. It was in the elaborate style which Tolstoy discountenanced, and did not receive much commendation from him, though in general he said that Tanéyev's compositions are serious and noble.

I asked Tolstoy if he still held firmly to the view of Wagner's later operas expressed in *What is Art?* Yes; he was as resolute as ever. Music acts in two ways: one way is by the transmission of an artist's feelings, that is the real thing, and of that Wagner has comparatively little. The other is by a physical effect on the nerves. Of this physiological effect acting strongly on the senses but not directly on the feelings, there is, Tolstoy maintained, a great deal in Wagner.

He seldom allowed himself to complain of the way he was treated

by critics or translators, but could not refrain from expressing dissatisfaction with a new French edition of his works, which Stock was
publishing. Among English versions he spoke well of Mrs Garnett's
and of my wife's, whose rendering of the French verses in *What is Art?*
he pointed out to Stásov as a *tour de force*.

He was also much vexed by a résumé *La Revue Blanche* had published,
purporting to be a statement of his views on the sex question, and by
the fact that a number of French authors had accepted this statement
as really representing his opinions. He asked me to write out for him a
letter, which he signed for publication, in which he remarked that:
'The opinions there attributed to me are grotesquely absurd, and are
a careless, second-hand, and incorrect summary of a collection of
articles and undated extracts put together and published by my friend,
Vladímir Chertkóv.'

The collection referred to, on which *La Revue Blanche* had based its
article, was one of three booklets Chertkóv published on *The Meaning
of Life*, *Thoughts on God*, and *The Relations of the Sexes*, in which he
assembled various disconnected fragments from Tolstoy's letters,
writings, and diaries, warning the readers, however, that they 'should
bear in mind that the order and mutual connection of the pieces are
ours, not the author's', and that Tolstoy 'did not contemplate their
ultimate collection into one group'. Concerning such collections
Tolstoy said very decidedly: 'However carefully, and with however
good an intent they may be made, I cannot be held responsible for
them.' This same collection was subsequently reproduced in the
carelessly edited Wiener edition of Tolstoy's works, without even the
warning Chertkóv had given that Tolstoy never intended them to be
used in such a manner.

Of Chertkóv himself Tolstoy admitted that he knew him to be a
tyazhely chelovek, literally 'a heavy man', that is to say, one hard to get on
with, but he repeated what he had said in his letters, that Chertkóv had
done so much and sacrificed so much for the common cause and
for him personally, that he could not but support him. It was plain
that Chertkóv's complete acceptance of Non-Resistant principles, his
thorough understanding of and agreement with Tolstoy's views, and
perhaps even the ardour shown by his urging Tolstoy to go to further
extremes, counted for much in his favour.

It was from Tolstoy's daughter Mary, Princess Obolénski, that I got
most sympathy in regard to Chertkóv. Devoted as she was to her father,

she frankly remarked: 'It is my father's weakness that he relies so much on Chertkóv.' Her experience of that gentleman caused her to sympathise with me on the subject, but she thought that, acting as her father's secretary and enjoying his confidence, she would be able to counteract Chertkóv's influence.

Though anticipating by eight years, let me here mention that when first writing my *Life of Tolstoy* I sent it to Tolstoy and his wife for their comments, and repeatedly received help from them both. When mentioning Mary's remark, quoted above, I suppressed Chertkóv's name, but I received the following letter signed by Tolstoy, though not as usual written with his own hand, and differing so much from his ordinary mode of expression that I have always suspected that it was not he who composed it, especially as, even before his health broke down, Tolstoy was sometimes induced to sign letters with the contents of which he was imperfectly acquainted. It ran:

> Sófya Andréevna has read me the passage in your biography about the words of my late daughter, Másha, expressing to you her bad feeling towards Chertkóv and, it would seem, her surprise at my partiality for that man. I think such a statement of her relation to Chertkóv is quite incorrect, since even if there may have been temporary misunderstandings between them, as was in fact the case, yet her general relation to my best friend was always affectionate and full of respect, as could not but be the case from a daughter who loved me ardently towards the man who for many years has been my best helper and friend. I would therefore ask you to omit that passage from your biography.
>
> In general I much regret your unkindly relation to Chertkóv, as for a biographer such a relation is both unnatural and incorrect and must mislead the reader.
>
> I shall be much obliged if you will pay attention to these remarks of mine.
>
> *23rd June 1910*
> LEO TOLSTOY
> *Yásnaya Polyána*

Tolstoy might well have guessed that the person referred to was Chertkóv, and a request to omit the reference lest others should guess to whom it referred would not have surprised me; but if he really composed that letter it is surprising that he should himself have introduced Chertkóv's name and then written as though I had done so, employing moreover a phraseology unlike his usual style.

Something will be said later of the surroundings and influences to which Tolstoy was exposed during those last months of his life.

Following his letter, I received one from his wife, who said:

DEAR MR MAUDE – I think you should not strike out what you have written about Chertkóv and my daughter's feelings towards him. The truth should always be cleared up, and my poor, dead daughter had a true heart and well understood Mr Chertkóv's cunning, despotic temper. Her opinion is of great value to all of us who have at last understood all this man's wickedness . . . Chertkóv profits by the fact that my dear old husband is weak, has lost his will-power, and is under Chertkóv's despotic influence . . . The more the truth is known the better will be the explanation given of the feeling of those who guessed Mr Chertkóv's real value. That is why I should much like my daughter's opinion not to be struck out.

I naturally yielded to Tolstoy's request at the time, but pointed out that it was not I who had introduced Chertkóv's name.

The incident may help to explain how it was that though many people understood Chertkóv's character and methods, and wondered at his influence on Tolstoy, few dared to remonstrate with Tolstoy about it.

This digression however introduces an element as different as possible from the congenial, animated, and happy atmosphere surrounding the family in 1902, when Mary was still alive and Chertkóv was away in England.

Tolstoy had almost completed his Caucasian novel, *Hadji Murad*, as well as a play, *The Live Corpse*, based on an incident told him by his friend, N. V. Davydov, a Judge.

Another unpublished work he had on hand was the story *Father Sergéy*.

Tolstoy said they should not be published during his lifetime, partly to avoid the unpleasant conflict sure to take place over their publication, and partly because if they had to be published he would be tempted to spend much time in polishing them, and this would interfere with weightier matters he wished to attend to before he died. The attention a new novel would receive would also, he said, be a temptation to his vanity ('I have caught myself at it') and would engross him too much.

The Countess mentioned that a foreign publisher had recently offered a million rubles for the permanent copyright of her husband's works, but that he held rigidly to his repudiation of all such rights. Another publisher, Marx, was offering a hundred thousand rubles for a copyright limited to two years, but with no better success. Yet when I spoke to Tolstoy of my own reasons for copyrighting my translations he raised no objection, but said: 'It is a matter I have not considered carefully as to its practical working, and I can only put a note of interrogation to it.' From what he said I was convinced that the action taken by the Free Age Press was not prompted or demanded by him, but that he merely acquiesced in it, and consented to sign the approval Chertkóv published.

Tolstoy's physical weakness was very noticeable at this time, but almost the only sign of mental debility was his temporary abandonment of his favourite game of chess. Cards taxed his attention less, and he played *vint* each evening, winning eighteenpence one day and tenpence the next. The game of patience was a favourite resource of his when unable to get on with his work or to get it off his mind. His daughter told me that he played it one day from two till six o'clock in the afternoon, and on another occasion announced that he was trying whether a work he was writing would be of use to the world. The result of the game indicated that it would not be. 'But I shall write it all the same!' remarked he as he put away the cards.

The subject always nearest his heart, and to which he returned oftenest, was religion. Speaking of his illness he said, with a smile, that he had gained so much by it that 'I can only wish you all to be ill!'

He compared his recovery to being painfully dragged out of a bog into which he had nearly sunk, and into which he had to return before long and again to sink before reaching the other side.

I cannot adequately describe the peaceful yet animated atmosphere of that home, crowded with vital interests, throbbing with life, overrun with visitors, but so influenced by the high and earnest tone of the great man whom they all looked up to, that I felt it more bracing and more peaceful than any circle I was ever in, and I see that, on leaving, I jotted down in my notebook: 'A remarkable and kindly family apart from Tolstoy's genius. His influence is felt in the simplicity, frankness, kindliness, and consideration shown to all in the place.'

Tolstoy seems to have attached importance to my expression of a wish (referred to in a letter already quoted) to explain his views in my own words, for before I reached Yásnaya Polyána, Boulanger called on me at my hotel in Moscow, and told me he had just come from Yásnaya and understood that I was planning a *Life of Tolstoy*. This was the first time the idea occurred to me, and it was a more ambitious project than I then felt ready for, but when I reached Yásnaya everyone – Tolstoy, his wife, his daughter, his sister, and even Stásov and Stakhóvich – made a point of telling me things that came in very usefully later when I undertook the task. At that time I shrank from it for various reasons. I was still perplexed about the theory of non-resistance, and realised how awkward it would be to undertake an 'authorised life' relying on material supplied by Tolstoy, while dissociating myself from so cardinal a tenet of his creed. Then again, a mass of material now readily available, would at that time have had to be read in rather illegible manuscript, and, finally, I foresaw that if I attempted such a life I must do it independently, free to say what I liked, otherwise if I did not confine myself to what Chertkóv approved of, severe conflict would be inevitable. So I did not then undertake the task, and the 'official' biography was entrusted to Birukóv, who dealt conscientiously and well with the enormous mass of material, confining himself to a strictly orthodox Tolstoyan view of the debatable doctrines.

It was a fine moonlight night when I left Yásnaya and set out to catch the midnight train. The undulating country looked beautiful, the air was sweet and still, and as I made my way toward the wayside station full of thoughts of Tolstoy and of the others with whom I had had friendly intercourse, I came to a place near a wood where there was a splendid echo. To test it some sweet voice in the distance sang, 'I – love – you', and the echo answered clearly: 'I – love – you!' It seemed a fitting sequel to a visit which remains in my memory as one of the most enjoyable and stimulating events in my life.

The stuffy, dirty, unpunctual, and overcrowded train which took me back to Moscow seemed specially designed to emphasise Tolstoy's indictment of modern civilisation.

People have spoken much of discord between Tolstoy and his family, but at that time I saw many more proofs of the affection and esteem in which he was held by them. Here, for instance, is a letter of 10th September 1902, from his daughter, Mary – to whom I had sent one which I carelessly addressed to the 'Countess M. L. Tolstoy':

Notwithstanding your mistake in the address, everything reached me safely. You are not the only one who uses my maiden name in addressing me, It is very strange, but though I have been married five years, I very often receive letters addressed to 'M. L. Tolstoy'. The post-office officials are accustomed to this and send them on to me without delay, and I like it very much, for it seems to me to show an unwillingness to separate me from my father . . .

All goes well with us. My father feels well in spite of the fearful weather. He is working very much and successfully.

We had a consultation of doctors recently about the winter, and decided that while he feels well it is better not to go away from here; and so he will spend the winter at Yásnaya Polyána. My husband and I will, of course, also remain here.

On 1st November Tolstoy completed his scathing *Appeal to the Clergy* (*Essays and Letters*) which certainly hits them much harder than the Excommunication hit him. Since Luther indicted the Catholic Church for the sale of Indulgences, probably no denunciation so full of moral indignation against a shameful trafficking in falsehood has ever been hurled at any body of men.

His health remained very uncertain, and on 21st January 1903, his eldest son, Count Sergéy, wrote me:

> At present my father is ill. He had influenza, which passed but weakened him greatly. He is now suffering from his liver, and from occasional weakening of the heart's action . . .

In April, Tolstoy published letters protesting against the Jew-baiting and pogróms in Kishinév and Gómel. In these letters he expressed abhorrence of:

> the real culprit in the whole matter, namely our Government, with its priesthood which stupefies the people and makes fanatics of them, and its robber-band of officials. The Kishinév crime is a direct consequence of the propaganda of lies and violence carried on with such intensity and insistence by the Russian Government.

He contributed *Esarhaddon* and two other short stories for the relief of the sufferers in these riots.

On 6th May, he wrote me:

> How good it would be if your friendly relations with Chertkóv were renewed! As far as I can I will try to co-operate thereto.

My health is better than I expected. I work a little, but less than I expected or desire. I should like now to write things that need not be published during my life, but questions continually crop up to which it seems necessary to reply. Such is the question concerning the activity of the Revolutionaries, and on that theme I have written a small article in the form of an *Afterword* to my letter *To the Working-People*. I now want to write about the materialistic mood people are in, and about Nietzsche, &c.

Of Nietzsche Tolstoy remarked: 'He was a real madman, but what a talent! I was absolutely charmed by his language when I first read him. What vigour and what beauty! I was so carried away that I forgot myself. Then I came to and began to digest it all. Great God, what savagery! It is terrible to drag down Christianity like this!'

'But,' said a visitor, 'Christianity has long been dragged down; Nietzsche only gave it the finishing blow!'

'I know that very well,' said Tolstoy. 'When I first began to speak about Christianity, it was considered so absurd that even our parish priest turned his back on me, and Boborykin [the novelist] and Mikhaylóvski [the critic] ceased to visit us ... Timiryázev once said to me that religion is needed as a scaffolding is needed by those who are building a house; but once the house is built the scaffolding is carted away ... Our house however is not yet finished and they already want to pull down the scaffolding!'

An article Tolstoy wrote in 1890 on the assassination of King Humbert, entitled *Thou Shalt Not Kill!*, was prohibited in Russia, and at Leipzig, in July 1903, on the demand of the Public Prosecutor, the German edition of it was seized for *lése majesté* and was destroyed.

The following is the passage the prosecution relied on:

What, indeed, must be going on in the head of some Wilhelm of Germany – a narrow-minded, ill-educated, vain man, with the ideals of a German Junker – when he can say nothing so stupid or horrid that it will not be met by an enthusiastic '*Hoch!*' and be commented on by the Press of the whole world as though it were something highly important? When he says that, at his word, soldiers should be ready to kill their own fathers, people shout '*Hoch!*' When he says that the Gospel must be introduced with an iron fist – '*Hoch!*' When he says the army is to take no prisoners in China, but to slaughter everybody, he is not put in a lunatic asylum, but people shout

'*Hoch!*' and set sail for China to execute his commands. (*Essays and Letters*, p. 266.)

The day after his seventy-fifth birthday Tolstoy went out riding, and at the crossing of a ravine, wishing to spare his horse, he got off and led it by the bridle. While he was doing so it trod on his foot, and the result was sufficiently serious to prevent his walking for some time afterwards and to oblige him to have recourse to his Bath-chair.

During his last few years Tolstoy's articles generally turned on Non-Resistance, and he came to treat the doctrine that the use of physical force between man and man is always wrong and always indicates malevolence, as an axiom on the basis of which all political, social, and economic questions can be solved. The more of these articles I translated the more I felt that I should prefer to state the case differently, and to lay the accent not on the use of physical force but on the *motive*. Malevolence is always bad, but to use physical force is sometimes the best thing we can do. At last I felt that I ought to tell Tolstoy wherein I disagreed with the articles I was translating. In reply to my letter he wrote me, on 20th January 1904:

> Your last letter . . . has much astonished and, I confess, grieved me. To struggle with all one's strength against evil and to wish to serve one's neighbour, has nothing in common with the principle of Non-Resistance to evil by violence, and I do not at all understand why you contrast the one with the other. However, I have so often written and spoken about that, that you must please forgive me if I do not speak about it any more.
>
> A few days ago I sent Chertkóv a small Preface to the projected *Biography of Garrison*. There I write about this matter and have said all I could; and I can add nothing to it – except to repeat what I wrote long ago. I think if you analyse your arguments you will find the mistake you are making. If you do not find it yourself, no one, and I least of all, can point it out to you.

Having confessed my heterodoxy I did not feel called upon to harp on it. It is after all the things one can agree about that are the most important.

The events then occurring in Russia were such as to grieve Tolstoy profoundly. There was the useless, disastrous, and shameful war with Japan, which outraged not only his religious principles but also a latent patriotism, the existence of which he had hardly suspected in himself until he wept at the news of the fall of Port Arthur.

Bethink Yourselves!, a vigorous denunciation of that war and of war in general, was written in May 1904.

Tolstoy had expressed his ideas in a great variety of literary forms. He had given us stories, novels, plays, sketches, essays, lay-sermons, legends, expositions, translations, disquisitions, and letters of all sorts and sizes, and he now turned his attention to making Collections of extracts from the works of great thinkers, confirming and elucidating his own outlook on life. His first volume of that kind was entitled *Thoughts of Wise Men*, and was finished in 1904.

With the Japanese war came a rapid growth of the Revolutionary movement in Russia, accompanied by enthusiasm and self-sacrifice, but also by venom, confusion, and crime. To some of us the outstanding need of the situation appeared to be the establishment of a Constitutional Government which would make law supreme over the caprice of officials and even over the action of the Tsar, while at the same time checking the excesses of extremists by an authority based on public opinion. Despite her magnificent artistic and literary achievements, we felt Russia to be politically centuries behind Western Europe, and believed that Government by discussion and consent must replace Government by caprice before a good rule could be hoped for.

At that moment of doubt and confusion there was no man in Russia whose word would have been more useful to the Constitutionalists, had he cared to support them, than Tolstoy's. He had repeatedly and scathingly condemned the Tsardom and its methods, not less uncompromisingly had he denounced the Revolutionary movement and the Socialists, as well as all appeals to force. To many it seemed that the logic of the situation must oblige him to throw his weight on the side of the Constitutional reformers – the Zémstvo leaders, the moderate, practical, experienced, workers who were claiming for themselves a larger sphere of national usefulness. But no! On them, too, fell Tolstoy's condemnation, and in a cablegram reply to an enquiry from an American review, he said that the result of the Zémstvo agitation for representative Government would be to delay real social amelioration, which can only result from the moral improvement of everybody.

No doubt the religious and moral regeneration of individuals is a very essential preliminary or concomitant of 'true social amelioration', and it is also true that men often become so absorbed in the business of politics as to lose sight of the ends that political activity should serve, but by setting up an antithesis between politics on the one hand and religious and moral regeneration on the other, Tolstoy was evading the issue Russia had to face – namely that of the Absolutism *versus* Constitutionalism. Religious and moral regeneration may be, has been, and often is, the incentive to political reform, and the contrast Tolstoy dwelt on seems no more valid than it would be for an architect to decline to consider the general plans of a building, on the ground that everything depends on the quality of the bricks of which the edifice is built.

Apart from the trend of his philosophy, there was something in Tolstoy's temperament which inclined him to oppose all movements and associations composed of men with mixed motives and that were not quite what they professed to be. In other words, he was disposed to resist all movements that comprised large numbers of human beings – as Churches and political parties naturally do. Political activity seemed to him a surface matter, to which it is not worth while for a true social reformer to devote attention.

A glimpse of the strain to which he was exposed at this time is given in a letter Princess M. L. Obolénski wrote me from Pirogóvo, on 22nd January 1905:

> I have lately returned from Yásnaya, where I spent two months. My father was well, but he is tormented by demands made on him to take part in current events. The Liberals want to draw him into their camp, the Conservatives into theirs, and the Revolutionists into theirs, and he does not belong to any one of them and only asks to be left in peace. People do not understand or admit his point of view, and think that in consequence of what is happening in Russia he must come down from his Christian standpoint and say something new, and something they want him to say.
>
> In general the war and all that is now happening in Russia is depressing, and weighs like a heavy burden on us all.

During 1905 he wrote a number of articles applying the doctrine of

Zíngeruestions of the hour, and he began a fresh series of short stories including *Kornéy Vasílyev*, *A Prayer*, and *Strawberries*. He also compiled *A Circle of Reading*, to which he attached great importance, and in which, following the path he had taken up a couple of years before, he gathered together freely-rendered quotations and extracts from writers of all lands.

Tolstoy's unwillingness to take on himself the moral responsibility attaching to the management of money matters sometimes worked out very curiously. For instance, the proceeds from the sale of *Resurrection* were undoubtedly mainly the fruits of his labour, yet merely because my wife had translated the book and I was acting as honorary secretary for a '*Resurrection* Fund Committee' which controlled the expenditure of the money received from the English and American editions, I received letters – sometimes even from members of the Tolstoy family – thanking me for donations made from that Fund, as though the generosity had been ours and not Tolstoy's. For instance, on 15th June 1906, his daughter, Princess Obolénski, wrote me:

Nearly every day I have occasion to remember you with gratitude and to receive thanks for you from poor people, and I want to write to you about it. When we returned this year to the country we found ourselves surrounded by peasants who were in great and real need, owing to last year's bad harvest, the war, and other causes. As a result of the extraordinarily dry summer there were, too, continual fires; and thanks to your money, we were often able to ease the position people were in and to help in cases of acute need. There were unfortunate children with no milk, in consequence of the loss of cattle by murrain, for whom we helped to buy a cow; there were burnt-out peasants who were able with the aid of your money to build brick huts instead of wooden ones. (One man in particular was wretched and touching. He had been burnt out two years running, and could not build himself a brick hut because he was always too poor, but after this year's fire he decided at any cost to put up a brick one. He sold everything he had, all his cattle, and hired himself out as a labourer, but when he learnt how much the fire-insurance payment would be, it turned out that he would not have enough. Then he came to us to ask for a loan. My husband talked with him, and when that old peasant-householder, a sober and industrious man, spoke of the fact that he would again have to build a wooden hut, he could not control himself, but wept. He, a bearded man, shook for a long time with sobs over the thirty shillings that he lacked. And it was your money that helped him.) There were soldiers' wives with children, who had simply to be supported till their husbands' return; and so on. And so, receiving continual thanks for this aid, and wishes of all that is good for the donor, I want to pass this gratitude on to you. I still have a good deal of your money, and I know that I shall in future have many opportunities to hear this gratitude expressed; and I personally thank you for having with this money freed me from frequently being obliged to refuse petitioners, when it has not been possible for me to give.

Tolstoy, feeling that his time was short and that there was much he wished to accomplish, continued to work very diligently whenever his health allowed him to do so. On 20th August I received from him a letter which partly expresses the struggle between the weakness of his flesh and the keenness of his spirit:

I am very, very much to blame, dear Maude. Two letters of yours have long lain before me unanswered. Please do not be angry with me on that account. The reason was that I have spells which succeed one another: first of loss of mental energy, when I cannot rouse myself to write the simplest letter, and then of special energy, when I give myself up to my work – of which there is very much. I have just passed through two such periods.

As to your first letter about the £600 [*Resurrection* Fund money] which you offer me, I think this: I do not just now see a possibility of using it unquestionably well. Therefore if you do not find for it any such unquestionably good use, and until you find it, put the money in the Bank. If a chance to use it presents itself to me, I will write you.

As to Stead I shall be particularly glad of his visit. It will remove the misunderstandings which arose accidentally, probably by my fault.

The reader will remember the contretemps, previously recounted, which occurred on the occasion of W. T. Stead's visit to Yásnaya in 1888, and again this time things went awry. Stead was devoting the *Review of Reviews*, 1906, Christmas Annual to Tolstoy, and before going to Yásnaya wrote asking him to contribute something for inclusion in that publication. Tolstoy, averse to the commercial exploitation of literature, looked on this request as an attempt to make money out of him, declined to contribute anything, and withdrew his invitation to Stead to visit him.

The letter to me continued:

> I have not yet read your book [*A Peculiar People: The Doukhobórs*] but will certainly do so. The story of the Doukhobórs is very interesting and important up to the present, and will, I think, be yet more interesting and instructive in the future.

A few days later the even tenor of life at Yásnaya Polyána was disturbed by the Countess falling seriously ill. Tolstoy was greatly distressed. He said to her one day: 'Now that you are laid up and do not go about the house, I miss the sound of your footstep, and, do you know, missing that, I can neither read nor write properly!' When, however, on 2nd September, the doctor in charge announced that an operation they had had in view for some time for the removal of an intestinal gathering must be performed at once or the patient would die, and die in agony, Tolstoy hesitated, preferring that his children and his wife herself should decide the matter. The operation was performed; and after three critical days the Countess began to regain strength, and within a month was quite well: so well that when I visited Yásnaya Polyána a few weeks later, I did not suspect that she had been so near to death's door, and was surprised subsequently to learn how great the danger had been.

When visiting Russia in 1902, I had found people everywhere extremely interested in Tolstoy, the man who had dared to reply to the Synod and to rebuke the Tsar. Now in 1906, what a change! I had been a fortnight in Russia before visiting Yásnaya and not one single person had spoken to me of him as everyone had spoken four years before. Politics had become to most people as the breath of their nostrils, and consequently Tolstoy, who was telling them to leave politics alone, was to the Liberals a stumbling-block, and to the Socialists a snare. But while he was falling into such disesteem among the educated classes, the temporary relaxation of the Censorship, which followed the establishment of the October Constitution, enabled many of his didactic works to be printed and sold for the first time, and his influence was spreading into quarters it had not previously reached.

I had never before been at Yásnaya so late as the end of October, and the autumnal aspect of the scene as I drove through woodland and over pleasant undulating country for the two miles from Záseka station may have had something to do with the impression that came over me when I reached Tolstoy's home.

The last time I had been there it had been full of visitors coming and going day by day. Now I found only members of the family, the atmosphere was quieter, and the pulses of life seemed to throb less strongly. Tolstoy himself had been much better in health that summer, but at the time of my visit was suffering, as he frequently did, from digestive troubles. His daughter Mary asked me not to discuss with him the matters on which we differed, as any agitation was bad for him. Of course I complied, though I regretted missing the chance of discussing *A Peculiar People* with him, for he had not kept his promise of writing to me about it, and in it I had joined issues with his views of Non-Resistance much on the lines taken in the present volume. It seemed to me a matter of capital importance, and if my view was wrong, I wanted to have my error made plain to me.

At lunch some mention of Stolypin caused Tolstoy to tell of his friendship with the Premier's father, who had been his colleague in the attempt to start a paper for the soldiers during the Crimean war. He told with particular pleasure how the elder Stolypin set to work to write his military memoirs, but becoming more and more convinced as he went on that war is a fearful evil, finished by burning all he had written.

He then spoke of the Vyborg Manifesto, in which about a hundred and eighty members of the first Dúma, on the occasion of its suppression, appealed to the people to cease paying taxes and to refuse military service. This, he said, looked like following advice he had often given, but was in fact a totally different thing. The signers of the Manifesto said: 'Do not serve or pay this Government, but serve and pay us when we become a Government,' whereas his advice was: 'Do not pay or serve any Government at all.'

He went on to mention with approval an article written by Uspénski, one of the signers of that Manifesto. Apropos of the demand for religious toleration, Uspénski expressed the view that, as a necessary part of religious toleration one must include toleration of refusals to serve in the army, and that such refusals based on religious conviction should be respected. One newspaper after another refused to publish the article, and when at last it was printed by the *Intermediary*, their premises were promptly searched by gendarmes and the article confiscated. 'It is remarkable,' said Tolstoy, 'that just his right to refuse to kill one's fellow men is the right Governments are least inclined to grant and most afraid to discuss.' Nearly all Tolstoy's own works were, just at that time, being sold freely in Russia except those aimed directly against military service, which were still suppressed.

During the afternoon Tolstoy rode over to Túla on horseback. At the six o'clock dinner vegetarian food was served as usual for him and for some other members of the family. He spent the evening with the family, one sign of the improvement in his health being that he again played chess, and I was told that he did so every evening when he could find a partner.

In an Appendix I give a game he won from me that evening, as well as one I won from him on my next visit.

It seems to me that Tolstoy showed an excellent sense of proportion in his chess playing. He did it well enough to make and to enjoy combinations, but he never sacrificed social family life for the sake of the game. Anyone might interrupt him while he was playing, and he talked and jested so that no one who only knew the game at Yásnaya would consider chess unsociable. On former occasions I (who had made some study of the game) used generally to beat him, but on this occasion he won two games from me rapidly.

After the chess we had a long talk on many subjects. With the Russian Revolution he expressed no sympathy at all. All *that*, he said, has been done long ago in other lands with no particularly good results. 'People should remember that we all have to die, and must spend our strength not on useless strife but on doing what is obviously good. A Revolution must either be something quite new, such as the abolition of *all* Government, or an imitation of what has been done before, and in the latter case it is sure to be bad. No improvement in a people's condition can be effected that does not rest on a *moral* basis,' said he, and for him it was a settled axiom that no political action and no action relying upon force, can rest on a moral basis. That is where he differed from such a man as Prince D. A. Khilkóv, who once wrote to him: 'I admit that we all of us have to die, and that our work on earth should be to fulfil the will of God, as each of us understands that will. But why not admit that it is possible for men sincerely to believe that it is God's will that they should devote themselves to replacing the present Government of Russia by a better one?'

Speaking of Henry George's Single Tax system with approval, Tolstoy maintained (in opposition to a suggestion made by someone present) that such a tax would amply suffice, even in Russia, to meet all the expenses of Government. I had once before asked him how it was that, condemning all Government, he advocated a system which presupposes a great deal of Government both to collect the tax and to spend the money collected. He replied that the question was a very fair one, but that it all depends on a man's plane of consciousness. His own mind worked on a No-Government plane, but as the great majority of men still believed in Governments and legality, 'let them, at least, see that they get good laws', and among the best possible laws would be the Single Tax.

That reply silenced me at the time, but on reflection it seemed insufficient, and I now returned to the charge and put it to him that progress may lead either towards the abolition of Government or towards the organisation of more and better Government, but that we cannot progress in two contrary directions at one and the same time. The adoption of the Taxation of Land Values certainly does not make towards the abolition of Government or the repudiation of the payment of taxes. To this he replied by asking what prevents voluntary payments to a voluntary administration? I did not pursue the matter, but I think that landowners would not much object to a form of taxation which left them free to pay only what they pleased, nor would such taxation be likely to do much to benefit the peasants whose hard fate Tolstoy deplored.

The talk turned to literature, and Tolstoy expressed his keen admiration of Swift and Goldsmith, saying: 'The more I try to read recent English writers, the more I admire Goldsmith, and among all the novelties, I recommend the *Vicar of Wakefield*.'

Speaking of social conditions he said that if one draws the poverty-line, as English writers do, at the point at which a man cannot purchase food enough to maintain himself and his family in full working efficiency, one must class the whole peasant population of Russia among the poverty-stricken.

After I had ceased to live in Russia in 1897, with each succeeding visit to Yásnaya I was more and more conscious that my life in England had drawn me away from Tolstoy's point of view on practical matters, but this did not diminish either my personal affection or my profound respect for him.

The lapse of years made his earnest and whole-hearted nature more transparent than ever. If at times I regretted his isolation, and thought that some of his views would have been modified had he stood nearer to the common experience of ordinary men, I recalled his own remark that 'God needs our limitations!' He could hardly have done his marvellous literary work, nor set so wonderful an example of unworldliness, had he been plunged in the turmoil of everyday life, soiling his hands with the rough work of business or politics.

On 26th November 1906, a great trial befell him. His daughter, Mary, Princess Obolénski, who had been in poor health for some years, died at Yásnaya Polyána of pneumonia after a very short illness. The news of her death inflicted a keen sense of personal loss on many, for all who knew her recognised her charm, ability, sincerity, and kindliness. I only had some three or four intimate talks with her, yet when the news reached me I felt that I had lost a dear, personal friend and that, though I might revisit Yásnaya, her not being there to welcome me, would make it a different place.

In May 1907, his eldest daughter, Tatiána, Madame Sukhotín, wrote me:

> My father read your letter with great interest and pleasure, and told me to write to you and thank you for it. Latterly he himself gets very easily tired, and therefore tries to do less mental work. During the last two months he has had two fainting fits with complete loss of memory, which in general has been getting much weaker with him.
>
> He has been reading Shaw, and has marked just the place about which you write in your letter [namely, the Salvation Array scene in *Major Barbara*] . . .

In the last years the things chiefly to be remarked were the increasing gentleness of the great man, the tenderness of his conscience, and the tenacity with which – unswayed by what was going on in Russia – he held to his principles.

He continued to work at the *Circle of Reading*, revising and improving it from year to year with the same care that he put into his own writings. Indeed, in addition to the matter selected from other writers, the book contains a number of stories and articles by himself.

During these last years he again held classes for village children. He read and told them stories and legends, and spoke of life and its duties. From these classes, in 1908, grew his book, *The Teaching of Jesus*.

His most striking utterance that year was the article, *I Cannot Be Silent*, protesting against the hangings employed by the Government not merely for the suppression, but also after the suppression, of the first Revolution. Tolstoy's detestation of violence and desire to protest against a very terrible present evil were united in that article – which was written with intense feeling and produced a tremendous sensation.

It contains an account of how men were being hanged by the dozen – with cords well soaped 'to tighten better round their throats' – and one is acutely conscious of the suffering Tolstoy's conscience inflicted on him for his own connection with the ruling classes. Towards the end of the article he says:

> I frankly confess it: I hope my exposure of those men will, one way or other, evoke the expulsion I desire from the set in which I am now living and in which I cannot but feel myself to be a participator in the crimes committed around me.
>
> That is why I write this, and will circulate it by all means in my power, both in Russia and abroad, that one of two things may happen: either that these inhuman deeds may be stopped, or that my connection with them may be severed, and I be put in prison, where I can be clearly conscious that these horrors are not committed on my behalf; or, still better (so good that I dare not even dream of such happiness), they may put on me, as on those twelve or twenty peasants [whose fate I have mentioned], a shroud and a cap, and may push me also off a bench, so that by my own weight I may tighten the well-soaped noose round my old throat.

This protest struck a note in harmony with the feelings of the great bulk of intelligent Russians. It served as a bond of spiritual union between Tolstoy and the Liberal elements of society, and paved the way for the strong and general manifestations of sympathy that reached him later that year.

In spite of the risks they ran, a number of Russian newspapers ventured to print the whole or part of Tolstoy's protest, and several of them paid the penalty in fines. One editor was arrested and his printing establishment closed for publishing it.

Tolstoy was eighty years old on 28th August, old style (10th September, new style), 1908. There had been much talk beforehand of how to honour him on that occasion; but he strongly objected to any ceremony, and hearing that an acquaintance of his who had been sent to prison for six months for circulating some of his writings had suggested that the best way to celebrate the jubilee would be by sending Tolstoy himself to prison as the author of works for which others were being punished, he wrote, on 27th March, cordially approving of the suggestion and saying:

> Nothing really would so fully satisfy me, or give me such pleasure, as to be put in prison – in a real, good, stinking, cold, hungry prison . . . Latterly I have felt so thoroughly happy that I often wondered whether there was anything I still could wish for. And I could think of nothing. Now I cannot refrain from longing, with my whole soul, that what you suggest should be adopted, not as a joke, but as a course which would really satisfy all those to whom my writings and their circulation is unpleasant, and would at the same time afford me in my old age, before death comes, true happiness and satisfaction, while releasing me entirely from the threatened burden of the forthcoming jubilee.

After the suppression of the Revolutionary movement of 1905–6, there was a marked change in the official attitude towards Tolstoy's works. In those years, as already mentioned, considerable liberty of printing was allowed, but later on the Authorities became extremely strict and a whole series of prosecutions and confiscations, fines and imprisonments, was directed against those guilty of possessing, lending, distributing, or publishing Tolstoy's anti-Government and anti-army-service works. Tolstoy again and again wrote to those concerned: Ministers, Judges, and Public Prosecutors, calling on them to recognise him as the chief culprit, and to deal with him accordingly. But the Government – always, in his case, 'ready to wound, but yet afraid to strike' – still persecuted his adherents and left him alone. This attitude showed itself especially on the eve of his eightieth birthday. The Holy Synod warned the faithful against honouring the heretic and in-structed the clergy to circulate publications denouncing him. The civil authorities took steps (varying in different provinces) to prevent the municipal authorities, schools, and literary and other societies from doing him honour. His secretary, N. N. Gúsev, was arrested and banished. Father John of Cronstadt prayed for Tolstoy's death, and the ultra-patriotic 'Black Gang' Congress held in July in Moscow under the presidency of the Archimandrite Makarius, announced its determination to take active steps to 'prevent any celebration; to require priests from the pulpit of every church to warn their congregations against taking part in one; to arrange counter-demonstrations in the streets, and forcibly to stop any favourable manifestations.'

For a while it seemed as though celebrations would have to be held in the spirit of Herzen's toast to Mickiewicz, the Polish patriot-poet – when he rose at a banquet and drank 'to the great name which must not be spoken', but as the day approached the Ministers faltered, and eventually indications of respect and affection for Tolstoy were for the most part neither prevented nor punished, and were so numerous and cordial as to be very impressive. Most of the newspapers devoted a great part – and in some cases even the whole – of their space on that day to articles dealing with Tolstoy's career, and some two thousand congratulatory telegrams reached Yásnaya, where the great writer was then recovering from another attack of illness.

Among the truest things said on that occasion was the remark, that whatever conflict there might be between Tolstoy and the political reformers, when it came to a test, the foes of Liberty were found to be his foes and the friends of Liberty his friends.

A letter characteristic of Tolstoy was one he wrote towards the end of the year to a lady member of the sect of Old Believers who had written to him in a spirit of virulent hostility, ending her epistle with the words: 'Yes, Leo Nikoláevich, I would shoot you for your blasphemous writings and would ruthlessly execute all your followers, had I the power!'

His reply, written on 16th December, was as follows:

DEAR SISTER – I received your letter, for which I thank you, because it gave me a great delight. It rejoices me to see in you a truly religious woman, desirous of living according to the law of God. As to the necessity of so living, I am at one with you. That is why our spiritual communion is possible, because we are at one on the main thing. But further on we disagree. I think a man can only fulfil God's law by setting an example of good life, by purifying himself from evil, and increasing the good. All that he does to please God besides this, is a delusion; it is false service and diverts him from the true purpose of life. To progress even by small steps, constant effort and strenuous attention are needed. Therefore a man must spend all his strength in trying to improve, without wasting his force on anything else. God has given man everything needful for moral progress. He has given conscience, which warns us against evil doing, and reason with which to discriminate good from evil.

'The Kingdom of God is won by effort,' said Christ; and that kingdom is not without, but within us.

I like one other thing in your letter. It is your humility when you speak of yourself. But when you speak of your religion this humility disappears. You seem to think that you and those who taught you are the only people who know the truth and that all the rest are lost. I do not think I am the only person who knows the truth and that everyone else is in darkness. I am eighty years old and I am still searching for truth. Your teachers have misled you into the sin of pride and condemnation. Every man in the depths of his soul has something he alone comprehends, namely his attitude toward God. And this sphere is sacred. We must not attempt to invade it or to imagine that we know all that lies hidden in its depths.

All that you write of your life interests me very much. May God help you to fulfil His will alone. Then He will be with you, and when God is with us all is well.

You say you regret not having read enough of my writings. If you are really interested in them I will send them to you with pleasure. Goodbye, and forgive me. Write to me. Your letters are not only interesting to me, but are of use to my soul.

Yours lovingly,

LEO TOLSTOY

Further correspondence resulted in the lady discarding her narrow sectarianism and adopting Tolstoy's point of view.

17

Conflict

Such fierce strife flared up during the last months of Tolstoy's life that these final chapters are not easy to write. Contradictory views are strongly held and a mass of conflicting material surrounds the subject. I will therefore only deal with a few crucial issues.

The inheritance of Tolstoy's literary rights was the main bone of contention. Twenty years previously he had handed over to his wife all he had published before 1881, including *War and Peace* and *Anna Karénina*. His non-resistant principle involved a readiness to yield whatever anyone demanded, and one would hardly have expected him to employ legal formalities to deprive the Countess of manuscripts she had regarded as her own for many years and had deposited in a public museum.

Formulas, however, have a queer way of refusing to work in practice, and confusion arose from the fact that the wife opposed her husband's wish to discard property or to avoid drawing profit from his writings.

Had she left him free to try living among the peasants he would not have insisted on her sharing that life, and the experiment might have convinced him that the services he was rendering to the world would be hindered rather than helped by abandoning his accustomed surroundings. His wife's hysterical and acrimonious opposition to his aspirations and efforts, however, gave the conflict the appearance of a struggle between right and wrong. Tolstoy, whatever mistakes he made and however little one may agree with his non-resistant doctrine, was always sincere, strenuous, and anxious to do God's will. The wife, whom his change of views certainly placed in a very trying position, became perplexed and irritable and made the initial mistake of basing her opposition not on doubts as to the validity of his principles, but on family interest.

The real affection that existed between husband and wife might have enabled them to come to an arrangement, had it not been for the interference of that remarkable man, V. G. Chertkóv. I never knew anyone with such a capacity for enforcing his will on others. Everybody connected with him became his instrument, quarrelled with him, or had to escape. To resist him was difficult. It was fortunate that he cherished non-resistant principles, for his physical as well as his mental powers were redoubtable. But discarding physical violence seemed to leave him the freer to employ mental coercion, and he was expert in its use. People have expressed surprise at the influence he exerted even over Tolstoy and wondered how a man of Tolstoy's strong character and great insight could have been so influenced. The explanation is twofold. It would be outrageously unjust to compare Chertkóv to Judas Iscariot, but the fact that one of Jesus's chosen disciples was a traitor, shows us that even the trusted friend of the greatest and best man may have flaws in his character. At a time in the 1880s, when Tolstoy's religious and social views isolated him from former friends, produced strife in his own family, caused him to be attacked in the Press, suspected by the Government, denounced from the pulpit, and sneered at in scientific circles, Chertkóv – a man of his own class, an ex-officer of the Guards, the only son of a wealthy mother with influence at Court, a redoubtable dialectician and a man of impressive personality – came and announced himself to him as a whole-hearted adherent, busied himself with the publication of Tolstoy's works, and developed an application of the non-resistance theory new to Tolstoy himself. No one understood the ramifications of that doctrine more thoroughly than Chertkóv, or was keener, in theory, to push its applications to the farthest extremes. That Tolstoy should be attracted by him and feel grateful to him was natural enough. Tolstoy was apt, with an artist's eye, to form a rapid estimate of a man's qualities and character at first sight. It was this that enabled him to give so clear an impression of such a multitude of men and women in his novels; but when once such an impression was formed he was slow to abandon it, and was thus at times singularly slow to recognise the fact if his estimate did not accord with the evidence.

It was quite possible to construct an argument to show that Tolstoy ought to make one who shared his views his literary heir rather than the wife who repudiated them and who towards the end of his life became so mentally unbalanced as hardly to be fit to edit his works.

It should also be recognised that Chertkóv, despite his temperamental eccentricities and his harshness to those who opposed him, was an idealist and enthusiast, and the ardour of his temperament commended him to Tolstoy, who was himself intense and had more sympathy with ardent temperaments than with balanced ones.

The questions at issue were intricate, and to attribute the whole blame either to the Countess, to Chertkóv, or to Tolstoy himself, is to misunderstand the matter.

Tolstoy's mistake lay, I think, in his non-resistance theory, which has already been discussed. If the use of physical force to restrain any man be immoral, the further conclusion that we should not rely on a government that employs police and law courts naturally follows, and to hold a copyright (or any other property) must be wrong. Chertkóv's claim was therefore plausible, for he had been the first to proclaim 'no rights reserved' on the works he issued.

Countess S. A. Tolstoy's position – deprived of the control of her husband's great novels after forty-eight years of marriage, during twenty of which she had actively assisted him in his work – was a very painful one, rendered all the worse by the gradual development of hysterical tendencies which had been but slightly noticeable in earlier years (though there are clear indications of them in her Diary). Her derangement eventually increased till the doctors diagnosed paranoia and suicidal tendencies. Her enemies, characteristically enough, would have it that she was only pretending – for to admit that her mind was affected would have weakened the case they urged against her.

Keenly as one sympathises with her, there is no doubt that, even before her mind gave way, her method of defending her interest was ill-judged. Tolstoy was strenuous, and sometimes spoke and acted inconsiderately, but he sought harmony, and strove to meet his wife's demands as far as he conscientiously could by personal self-sacrifice. He did not wish to make her suffer even when she eventually rendered life at Yásnaya unendurable for him.

There is plenty of excuse for her, and one must admit that she could hardly have avoided conflict with her husband's views. But no one acquainted with the facts can fail to see that many of the difficulties were greatly increased by her own conduct, and by her unfortunate way of presenting her case.

Chertkóv, on the contrary, was a masterly controversialist. No one could put a case more persuasively or ingeniously than he. As on the whole I am unable to share his views, it will be best to let him present his own case by quoting a long letter of his. This will be done in the next chapter.

One lesson to be drawn from the painful story of Tolstoy's last days is that efforts to apply non-resistant principles do not enable people to live in harmony with one another. Those principles were formulated in the belief that if the use of physical force as a means of settling disputes were abandoned, better and more friendly and humane relations would result. Tolstoy took this doctrine which had played an important part in the history of many sects in other lands and ages, reduced it to systematic expression, and tested it in practice. He sought the truth and was ready to lay down his life for it. The argument he set out is one not readily refuted, and therefore the practical test is important, not merely for the effect it may have on the Doukhobórs, Indian non-co-operators, and conscientious objectors in our own time, but also for future generations: for a theory which has so often been revived in the past will assuredly not fail to reappear in the future. We have now on record the example of its most talented interpreter, earnestly attempting to carry it out – with what results? That anger, hatred, malice, intrigue, and strife, were provoked; ultimately driving him to resort to the very legal formalities he had so strenuously repudiated.

Extreme Tolstoyans reply to this that the result was due to the wickedness of his wife and other members of his family, and that among better-intentioned people the principle would have worked well.

That reply is unconvincing. I for one cannot admit that Countess S. A. Tolstoy and her children were morally so inferior to the common mass of humanity as to cause the failure of principles which would work well with ordinary people. If we must await the arrival of a different type of humanity before non-resistant principles can be successfully tested, their soundness meanwhile must remain unproven; for the proof of a pudding is in the eating, and legal enactments, the police, and Civil and Criminal codes, might all work excellently among people so superior as always to do justice, love mercy, and walk humbly with their God.

Tolstoy did not spare himself either in formulating what he thought to be true or in trying to practice it. If the test shows that as much suffering and distress can be inflicted under a non-resistance code as under ordinary penal codes, a truth has been reached, though the answer be not what he expected. He laid down his life for it, and though it is reached by 'trial and error' the result is not the less valuable, nor should we be ungrateful to one whose vigour of thought, clarity of statement, and sincerity in practice, led to this solution of the problem. Perhaps no one, without being willing to travel the road that cost Tolstoy his life, could have elucidated the effect of the non-resistant principle applied to life, drawn the deductions involved by its relation to business, politics, and social problems, and left the matter so clearly presented that people can now scarcely fail to perceive the truth. A man may be a prophet and a teacher without being infallible. The progress of human thought needs a succession of thinkers and experimenters, and it is demanding too much of any one man that he should state such a problem, reason it out, test it in practice, and within the scope of a single lifetime settle a matter which has perplexed many generations.

Chertkóv had returned to Russia some time previously and settled on an estate, Telyátenki, within a couple of miles of Yásnaya, but early in 1909 he was, for a while, banished by Administrative Order from that Province, though allowed to live anywhere else. From the time he had returned to Russia the discord between Tolstoy and the Countess had become more acute.

My last visit to Yásnaya Polyána was in September 1909. Chertkóv was living near Moscow, and Tolstoy had come to that city to visit him.

The exertion of travelling and the excitement caused by the crowds assembled at the stations to see him were too much for Tolstoy, and when, after about a fortnight's absence, he returned to Yásnaya, he had two prolonged fainting fits. A few days later I visited him, and when I asked about his health, he replied: 'Always nearer to death, and that is good. At my age one cannot jump and run, and one's memory fails, but what of that? Physical and mental strength decrease, but something else (moral strength) greatly increases. I would on no account exchange what I am now for what I was sixty years ago.'

He complained that his ability to remember names was failing, and when writing he found it difficult to avoid repeating himself, as he could not remember what he had already said, but his conversation was pointed, animated, and vigorous, and he played chess almost as well as he had done when I first played with him, fifteen years before.

He had been reading Bernard Shaw's plays, and remarked that Shaw is original and many of his sayings are quite admirable and deserve to become quotations, but he has the defect of wishing to be original and to surprise his readers. That, Tolstoy said, is a pity. One wishes to merge into the mind of an author one likes, but this is impossible when he is bent on saying unexpected things. He was much interested when I told him the plot of *Blanco Posnet* (then unpublished), which he thought very promising – and he wished to read the play, because as he said, to many people the working of conscience is the only proof of God's existence.

Shaw had sent him a copy of *Man and Superman*, and Tolstoy replied by a letter, undated, which said:

DEAR MR SHAW – Please excuse me for not having thanked you before this for the book you sent me through Mr Maude.

Now on reading it and giving special attention to the passages you marked, I particularly appreciate Don Juan's speeches in the Interlude – the Scene in Hell (though it seems to me that the subject would have gained greatly by being treated more seriously than as a casual episode in a comedy) – and 'The Revolutionists' Handbook'. In the former I was able without any effort to agree fully with Don Juan's remark that he is a hero 'who seeks in contemplation to discover the inner will of the world . . . and in action to do that will by the so-discovered means' – or, in my way of expressing it, 'to recognise the will of God in one's self, and to do it.'

Secondly, I am particularly pleased by your attitude toward civilisation and progress and the very true reflection that, however long the one and the other may continue, they cannot improve the state of mankind unless men themselves alter. The difference of our views is merely this: you think that mankind's improvement will be accomplished when ordinary people become supermen or when fresh supermen are produced; while, in my opinion, it will occur when men disencumber the true religions, including Christianity, from all the accretions which deform them, and when all, uniting in the understanding of life which lies at the base of all the religions, realise their reasonable relation to the world's eternal origin and accept the guidance for life which flows therefrom.

The practical advantage my way of freeing people from evil has over yours is that one can easily imagine very large numbers even of little educated or quite uneducated people accepting true religion and following it, whereas to evolve supermen out of people who now exist, or to breed new ones, would need exceptional conditions which are as far from being attainable as those required for the correction of mankind by progress and civilisation.

Dear Mr Shaw, life is a great and serious affair, and all of us in the short interval of time granted us must try to find our appointed task and fulfil it as well as possible. This applies to everybody, and to you especially with your great gift of original thought and your penetration into the essence of all questions. And therefore, confidently trusting that I shall not offend you, I will tell you what seem to me to be the defects in your book.

The first defect in it is that you are not sufficiently serious. One should not speak jestingly of such a subject as the purpose of human life, the causes of its perversion, and the evil that fills the life of humanity today. I should like the speeches of Don Juan to be not the speeches of a vision, but the speeches of Shaw, and also that 'The Revolutionists' Handbook' should be attributed not to the non-existent Tanner but to a living Bernard Shaw who is responsible for his words. The second reproach is that the questions you deal with are of such enormous importance that, for men with such profound comprehension of the evils of our life and such brilliant capacity for exposition as yourself, to make them the subject of satire may easily do harm rather than help the solution of these grave questions.

In your book I detect a desire to surprise and astonish the readers by your great erudition, talent, and cleverness. Yet all this is not merely unnecessary for the solution of the questions you deal with, but often distracts the readers' attention from the essence of the matter by attracting it to the brilliance of the exposition. In any case I think this book of yours expresses your views not in their full and clear development, but only in an embryonic state. I think that these views, developing more and more, will arrive at the one truth we all seek and towards which we all gradually approach. I hope you will forgive me if there is anything that displeases you in what I have said. I have said it only because I recognise your very great gifts, and for you personally have a most friendly feeling, and so I remain.

LEO TOLSTOY

On returning to England I told Shaw of my conversation with Tolstoy, and Shaw sent him a copy of *Blanco Posnet*, with a letter in which he said:

MY DEAR COUNT TOLSTOY – I send you herewith, through our friend Aylmer Maude, a copy of a little play called *The Showing Up of Blanco Posnet*. 'Showing Up' is American slang for unmasking a hypocrite. In form it is a very crude melodrama, which might be played in a mining camp to the roughest audience.

It is, if I may say so, the sort of play that you do extraordinarily well. I remember nothing in the whole range of drama that fascinated me more than the old soldier in your *Power of Darkness*. One of the things that struck me in that play was the feeling that the preaching of the old man, right as he was, could never be of any use – that it could only anger his son and rub the last grains of self-respect out of him. But what the pious and good father could not do, the old rascal of a soldier did as if he was the voice of God. To me that scene where the two drunkards are wallowing in the straw and the older rascal lifts the younger one above his cowardice and his selfishness, has an intensity of effect that no merely romantic scene could possibly attain, and in *Blanco Posnet* I have exploited in my own fashion this mine of dramatic material which you were the first to open up to modern playwrights.

I will not pretend that its mere theatrical effectiveness was the beginning and end of its attraction for me. I am not an 'Art-for-Art's-sake' man, and would not lift my finger to produce a work of art if I thought there was nothing more than that in it. It has always been clear to me that the ordinary methods of inculcating honourable conduct are not merely failures, but still worse – they actually drive all generous and imaginative persons into a daredevil defiance of them. We are ashamed to be good boys at school, ashamed to be gentle and sympathetic instead of violent and revengeful, ashamed to confess that we are very timid animals instead of reckless idiots, in short ashamed of everything that ought to be the basis of our self-respect. All this is the fault of the teaching which tells men to be good without giving them any better reason for it than the opinion of men who are neither attractive to them nor respectful to them, and who, being much older, are to a great extent not only incomprehensible to them but ridiculous. Elder Daniels will never convert Blanco Posnet: on the contrary he perverts him, because Blanco does not want to be like his brother; and I think the root reason why we do not do as our fathers advise us to do is that we none of us want to be like our fathers, the intention of the Universe being that we should be like God.

The rest of the letter dealt with Shaw's idea of a God who is trying to get things right in the world but has not yet succeeded, and it concluded with the words: 'Suppose the world were only one of God's jokes, would you work any the less to make it a good joke instead of a bad one?'

In reply, Tolstoy wrote:

MY DEAR MR BERNARD SHAW – I have received your play and your witty letter. I have read your play with pleasure and am in full sympathy with its subject.

Your remark that the preaching of righteousness has generally little influence on people, and that young men regard as laudable what is contrary to righteousness, is quite correct. It does not however follow that such preaching is unnecessary. The reason of the failure is that those who preach do not fulfil what they preach – i.e. hypocrisy.

Also I cannot agree with what you call your theology. You enter into controversy against something no thinking person of our time believes in or can believe in – a God-Creator, and yet you seem yourself to recognise a God who has definite aims comprehensible to you.

'To my mind,' you write, 'unless we conceive God as engaged in a continual struggle to surpass himself – as striving at every birth to make a better man than before – we are conceiving nothing better than an omnipotent snob.'

Concerning the rest of what you say about God and about evil, I will repeat the words that, as you mention, I said about your *Man and Superman*, namely that the problem about God and evil is too important to be spoken of in jest. And therefore I will tell you frankly that I received a very painful impression from the concluding words of your letter: 'Suppose the world were only one of God's jokes, would you work any the less to make it a good joke instead of a bad one?'

Yours sincerely,

LEO TOLSTOY

Some weeks after my last visit to him, not many months before his death, Tolstoy speaking of the dearth of good writers everywhere, said: 'There are none now,' and then added with hesitation, 'unless, perhaps, Shaw.'

During my visit he repeated his often expressed opinion that Dickens stands far above all other English writers. Among Russians Gógol resembled him in humour, but had not his broad humane sympathies.

In a different style Ruskin and Emerson were also very good. Among Russian writers Púshkin is first and, like Dickens, has no second. 'It is very remarkable that Púshkin should have given us so many profound thoughts simply and clearly expressed, for he was brought up in a bad, aristocratic, military circle, and died young.'

After making, as he often did, a passing reference to God's guidance, Tolstoy said: 'I speak of a *personal* God, whom I do not acknowledge, for the sake of convenience of expression.' This recalled to mind what he had said to me twelve years before, when he remarked that: 'There are two Gods,' and went on to explain:

> There is the God people generally believe in – a God who has to *serve them* (sometimes in very refined ways, perhaps merely by giving them peace of mind). This God does not exist. But the God whom people forget – the God whom *we all have to serve* – does exist and is the prime cause of our existence and of all we perceive.

He remarked that it is wonderful how ignorant even educated men are of religions other than their own. They know that such religions exist and have some vague information about them, but no real understanding. He was interesting himself in a series of booklets which the *Intermediary* was preparing on Eastern Religions, and writing prefaces for one or two of them.

Afterwards he spoke of the advantage of 'the Anglo-Saxon characteristic of concentrating on and mastering a single subject'.

He said he got his friend Maklakóv to promise to speak in the Dúma on the Land Question from the Henry-George point of view. Next time they met Tolstoy asked him: 'Well, have you spoken yet?' – 'No,' said Maklakóv, 'I have not had time to read up the subject sufficiently.' – 'That,' said Tolstoy, 'is the worst of educated men: they cannot speak about any great question till they have read everything that has been written about it, for fear someone should say: "But have you read Schwarzenburg?" – and then, if they have not read Schwarzenburg, they are done; whereas a good, ignorant merchant like T. [a member of the Dúma, keen on Temperance], who has read nothing, but is keen on his own subject, will stick to his guns and do something with it.'

The land was the one great practical political question for which Tolstoy cared. He spoke emphatically of the shame of people not being able to get land for use while others own land they have never even seen.

He said he wanted to write again to the Tsar. 'It will do no good, but

I feel as though I ought to. If the Tsar would go right on the Land Question there would be no need to guard him. There used to be a Tsar the people seemed at least to respect, but now there is one who needs three rows of soldiers to prevent the people from killing him.'

In spite of my pleasure at seeing Tolstoy again, this last visit to Yásnaya was depressing. Everything centred round the struggle between Chertkóv and the Countess. Chertkóv's interests were zealously guarded by Tolstoy's youngest daughter, Countess Alexandra, who made me feel that she regarded me as belonging to the enemy's camp – though in fact I realised how much of the trouble was due to her mother's injudicious conduct. The hostile welcome Countess Alexandra accorded me was the more noticeable by contrast with the kindness I had always received not only from Tolstoy himself, but also from his elder daughters when they were at home.

Countess S. A. Tolstoy was busily preparing a new edition of her husband's works, and also writing her own memoirs; but now and then, in what she said about her husband and Chertkóv, there were indications of the mental disturbance that became more pronounced a year later.

The eager interest Tolstoy – then in his eighty-second year and wheeled about the room in a Bath-chair – took in life, and the keen pleasure he felt in all that made for the triumph of the causes he had at heart, was remarkable. To the utmost limit of his strength he still worked as perseveringly as ambitious men in their prime strive for fortune or position, and as ardently as young men seek the affection of their lady-love.

During that stay I translated a long letter from him to a Japanese. His correspondent had written in English, and though Tolstoy wrote our language, he was not sure of expressing the exact shades of his meaning correctly. His reply showed that, despite his age, illness, and the distressing domestic circumstances which taxed his strength to the utmost, he retained all his powers of expression. A year later when I was finishing the first edition of this book, he sent me another long letter for the same correspondent, asking me to translate it. When I had done so he offered me the first publication of it, for inclusion in my book. It appeared there as an Appendix, but in this edition will find place among the *Essays*.

Though I was reluctant to admit it at the time, matters were already obviously heading for a catastrophe.

Countess S. A. Tolstoy often behaved as if her object was to hurt and vex her husband, and when she attacked and ridiculed his views she made no attempt to be fair or reasonable. Years before this I had been present when some University students called to consult Tolstoy, and the Countess had repeatedly interrupted his replies in order to state his opinions in a perverted form, as if her aim were simply to annoy him. On such occasions he showed much self-control and forbearance. Among the group of Tolstoyans surrounding Chertkóv a legend grew up representing Tolstoy as an oracle and saint whose efforts to establish the Kingdom of God on earth were baffled by the selfishness of his wife. That legend contains some elements of truth, has the advantage of simplicity, and is of the kind which sometimes becomes more popular than the real truth.

The position of the Countess, as already remarked, was weakened by her mistake in not thinking out Tolstoy's non-resistance principle and its consequences. Had she done so she might have contested its validity. She adopted the easier course of saying that her husband was right but that she was too weak to follow him. She thus put herself in the wrong, and the natural reply was: If you know I am right, you should not hinder me.

In 1909 the family troubles were much aggravated by the young Countess Alexandra's attitude towards her mother. Non-resisters and resisters were in acute opposition, and the temptation to join one of the parties was natural enough. As the wife was flagrantly unreasonable and made life very trying for her husband, it was excusable for the daughter to throw in her lot with her father, but she went much too far in antagonism to her mother. Moderation is a quality often lacking among Russians, and by submitting to Chertkóv and serving his interests Alexandra only acted as many others had done. He had a talent for making people believe that by obeying him they performed a high moral duty. When he spoke, the will of God, the law of Non-Resistance, the teachings of Tolstoy, and service rendered to Chertkóv, merged into each other and became one.

At any rate during that visit it seemed as if every detail of the family life and work had to be viewed in relation to Chertkóv's wishes, as the following instance shows.

I had travelled from Moscow with representatives of Pathé Frères on their way to Yásnaya to cinematograph Tolstoy in his home surroundings. His wife had given them permission during his absence from home. When they arrived Tolstoy was doubtful about letting them take him. His wife wished him to do so, and to be taken with her. Alexandra was strenuously opposed to it, for he had lately been cinematographed with Chertkóv, and the latter would object to his being taken again, especially with his wife. At first Tolstoy listened to his daughter and declined to be taken. The Pathé Frères representatives then asked permission to give a free show to the villagers in the park that evening. This pleased Tolstoy, who changed his mind and said they might take him next morning when he went for his usual ride.

The pictures pleased the villagers, who clamoured for more. The operators had only one film left – a Russian story of the seduction of a peasant girl by a merchant. This they unwisely showed, and Alexandra saw her opportunity. She went at once to her father and told him how the disgusting Frenchmen were perverting the peasants, and again induced him to say that he would not let them take him. Next morning, before her mother was up or knew what was happening, Alexandra had packed the Frenchmen off.

That incident was trivial, but the constant jar on the nerves of both husband and wife was serious. There are more ways of killing a dog than by choking him with butter, and more ways of killing a man than by physical violence. Countess S. A. Tolstoy was then nearing her mental breakdown, and Tolstoy was approaching the state in which he found Yásnaya unendurable and left home to die. Had his daughter understood Chertkóv's character in 1909 as well as she learnt to understand it after her father's death, Tolstoy's end might have been a different one.

An incident that occurred shortly after this, indicates his constant struggle to approach nearer to the standards of conduct he aimed at. An officer called one day [1910] to upbraid him with riding a horse while preaching poverty, Tolstoy pointed out that his horse, Délire, was a very old one. 'But,' said the officer, 'it is also a very fine one!'

Eventually after a long talk the officer departed convinced that he had misjudged Tolstoy, and expressing regret at having to destroy a denunciation he had prepared before making his acquaintance.

Tolstoy, on his part, however, felt pricks of conscience, and gave directions to have Délire unshod.

For a week or two he abstained from riding. Then feeling the need of his accustomed exercise, he took to riding a common peasant horse, but after a couple of months some friends he visited had the pleasure of seeing him arrive once more on Délire. It would have been sad had he been deprived of an exercise that suited him so well, but in his constant struggle for self-mastery lay the secret of his great achievements.

His passionate ardour gave force to his message and enabled his words to change the lives of many men. No other writer's works have been so promptly translated into so many languages or reached such a widespread audience of serious readers during the lifetime of their author, and there are few whose lives can be laid bare with such assurance that the disclosure will not destroy the respect and affection in which they are held.

His genius, sincerity, industry, courage, endurance and tenacity, his remarkable intuition, extraordinary capacity for observation and artistic reproduction, his devotion to the service of truth and goodness, his self-abnegation, his concentration on the most vital branches of human thought, and his unparalleled power of making his meaning plain and his feeling attractive, mark him out as the greatest and most interesting man of his age.

Of modern men who have stimulated the thoughts and consciences of their fellows, and whose words influence us to feel that we must not trust to a self-acting evolution, but must be up and doing to bring in the millennium ourselves, Tolstoy is so much the first, that one forgets to ask who is second.

While piecing together the scattered and sometimes contradictory facts of his life I realised more vividly than before how great was my own debt to him, and how inadequately my record conveys his spiritual value. That side of my subject takes me out of my depth and the message suffers from the deficiencies of the messenger. Part, but only a small part, of what I felt as I drew near the end of my work, I expressed in the following letter to him:

DEAR LEO NIKOLÁEVICH – Lately I have had occasion to read over, for the book I am writing, all the letters I have had from you. They vividly recall how much I owe to you, and how forbearing and kind you have been, and they make me keenly regret not to have done more in return for the encouragement and friendship you have so generously shown me.

I have not tried to make my book a panegyric of you or of your teaching, but while at work on it my sympathy with you, and my wonder at the immense amount you have accomplished, have continually grown.

You are definitely anti-political, whereas it is bred in my bones to feel that the work done by Pym and Hampden, Washington and Abraham Lincoln, and in general the attempt the Western world has made at Constitutional Government – faulty and imperfect as it is, and slow as has been its progress – was not an ignoble effort and has not utterly failed; and that that path may yet lead on to a juster and kindlier society than the world has yet seen.

I know how deep-rooted that difference of feeling and of outlook is, but it is superficial in comparison with the profounder ground common to us both, which you helped me to reach. To both of us the present state of human society is needlessly and intolerably stupid and cruel. We both believe that intellectual integrity applied with kindly goodwill can reach such an understanding of the position as will render reformation possible, and we both in our different ways – you in a great and world-wide way, I in a very small, circumscribed way – have tried to see the truth and make it 'plain to every cabman' – as you once said of the philosophy you wanted to write.

It seems strange that differing so greatly in race, nationality, class, training, occupation, pursuits, and surroundings, you and I should have been able to come into touch with one another, and that you should have taken the trouble to help me and to treat me as a friend; and I am glad to feel that – whatever our differences of outlook may be – there is such fundamental unity as prevents any shade of bitterness between us, even when I grieve you by failing to accept conclusions you highly prize, or when (to my own disappointment) I failed to be able to co-operate with your friend and found myself banished from his courts . . .

To be swept into your strenuous movement was not all gain. You dragged us from our roots, and many of us were spun down the mighty current unable to steer or row the rickety rafts we found ourselves upon. Some died and some are now in lunatic asylums, but I feel that it was worth all the risk and pain; for nothing is so deadly as torpor and nothing so dangerous as decay, and from those evils you saved us.

I owe you so much that I never differ from any of your opinions without regret, or without remembering that perhaps, after all, I am mistaken, but I feel that it would violate the very essence of what I learnt from you, if I subordinated the truth as I see it to any authority – even to your own.

I have in this letter not said half I feel and want to say, but I hope you know that you have my affectionate gratitude always. Perhaps my thanks may be the more acceptable because I was a stranger and an alien and a trader within your gates when you gave me the hand of friendship.

May all that is good be yours in life and death, and may the good seed you have scattered grow up to feed the hungry in many lands.

Tolstoy's life shows what splendid services a man, not exempt from human weaknesses, may render to his race. Though some of his opinions are not acceptable and may not be quite intelligible to those who grow from roots different from his own, he has yet inscribed his name indelibly upon the hearts of men and earned their lasting gratitude.

To realise the continuity of his struggles and the measure of his success, we should let our minds run back to the days when his brother Nicholas first told him of the secret written on a green stick, buried by the road at the edge of a certain ravine, showing how all men may cease to suffer, quarrel or be angry, and may become permanently happy in a loving brotherhood.

In such a message which can destroy all evil in men and give them universal welfare, Tolstoy believed to the end.

18

Home-Leaving and Death

Tolstoy's attempts to leave home, and the wills he wrote, are closely connected with the story of his death.

Around a great man legends spring up, and we must be on our guard against the legends that are already current, if we would understand what happened. There is, for instance, a legend that Tolstoy earned his subsistence by manual labour, living among the peasants. This is untrue, and the extension of it which describes him as leaving home at the age of eighty-two to begin to live such a life is ridiculous.

The stories about his wife living in luxury are also untrue. Tolstoy, in his sensitiveness to the peasants' poverty, spoke sometimes of 'the intolerable conditions of luxury' surrounding him, but any middle-class Englishman visiting Yásnaya Polyána would have been struck by the simplicity of the life there, though few of the family aimed at the asceticism Tolstoy practised.

What towards the end of his life most drew him to escape was the impossibility of maintaining good relations with his wife. Her mind was giving way, and as happens in such cases, faults of disposition that had previously been under control became more pronounced. She talked of her grievances to everyone she met and recorded them in her letters and Diary. Tolstoy, on the contrary, tried to avoid blaming her, preferring to blame himself and find excuses for her. This has caused much misunderstanding of the position, especially as Tolstoy's theory of non-resistance has found little acceptance, and consequently people are predisposed to side with the wife.

At the time of his slumming experiences in Moscow in 1882, and during the four years he was writing *What Then Must We Do?*, he was specially strenuous in his indignation with the life led by the well-to-do and, as he afterwards admitted, was too ready to assume that other people ought to see things as he did. It was at that time – in 1884 – that he started to leave home on the eve of Alexandra's birth. Till the publication of the Countess's *Later Diary* we did not know what particular provocation impelled him to that step, but only that he turned back before reaching the nearest town. There were other occasions on which he almost left home. In June 1897, on the verge of going away, he wrote a letter to his wife that was only handed to her after his death. In it, as usual when he addressed her, he spared her as much as he could, not dwelling on their differences, but stressing general considerations which also counted for something, but were not the main motive of his intention:

DEAR SÓNYA – I have long been troubled by the inconsistency between my life and my convictions. I could not make you change your way of life and the habits in which I had trained you . . . and I have now determined on what I have long wanted to do – to go away . . . Approaching my seventieth year, I long with my whole soul for peace, solitude, and if not for complete harmony, at least to avoid glaring discord between my life and my conviction and conscience.

If I were to do this openly there would be entreaties, upbraidings, arguments, and complaints. I should perhaps lose courage and not carry out my decision – though it must be carried out. And therefore, Sónya, if my action hurts you, please forgive me and in your soul especially let me go with good will . . .

That I have gone away from you does not mean that I am displeased with you. I know that you literally could not see and feel as I do, and therefore, could not and cannot change your life and make sacrifices for what you do not recognise. And therefore I do not blame you, but on the contrary remember with love and gratitude the thirty-five long years of our life together, especially the first half of it when, with the motherly self-devotion which is part of your nature, you so earnestly and unflinchingly carried out what you considered your duty. You have given me and the world what you could – a great deal of motherly love and self-sacrifice, and one cannot but esteem you for it. But in the later period of our life – the last fifteen years – we have grown apart. I cannot think that I am to blame, for I know I have changed not for my own sake or other people's, but because I could do no other. I cannot blame you either for not following me, but think of you and always shall think of you, with love and thank you for what you have given me.

Farewell, dear Sónya,

Your loving, LEO TOLSTOY

In general, however, it seemed he had come firmly to the conclusion he expressed to me and to others, that much as he wished to escape from a life that was irksome, clashed with his convictions, and exposed him to reproach for inconsistency, it would not be right to follow that inclination, since by doing so he would certainly rouse his wife's anger. That he finally went back on this conviction was because, as a result of the struggle over his literary inheritance, life at Yásnaya became literally intolerable, anything like harmony with his wife became impossible, and he felt that for her as well as for himself, his absence would be better than his presence.

An account of his last will must be prefaced by mention of previous attempts to make one.

Early in the 1880s Tolstoy had given his wife an authorisation to publish his collected works, the income from which was the family's chief resource. Later on, when his disapproval of money-making became stronger, he could not persuade her to abandon the business, and did not feel justified in using compulsion, but at last, in 1891, he published an announcement that everything of his published after 1881 might be freely reprinted by anyone.

In his Diary, on 27th March 1895, he made an informal will, in which he asked that all his papers should be handed, for revision and arrangement, to his wife, to Chertkóv, and to N. N. Strákhov. He desired that anything worth preserving in the Diaries of his bachelor life should be extracted, but that those Diaries themselves should be destroyed. Everything in the Diaries of his married life that might give pain to anyone should also be destroyed.

This service he said Chertkóv had promised to perform, and 'in view of his great and unmerited love for me, as also of his great moral sensibility, I feel sure the service will be excellently performed'.

After explaining why he wished the Diary of his bachelor life to be destroyed, he added: 'However, let the Diary remain as it is, for at any rate it may be seen that in spite of the emptiness and vileness of my youth I was still not quite abandoned by God, and, if only in old age, have come to understand and love Him at least a little.

'Of the rest of my papers I ask those who arrange them not to print the whole, but only what may be of use.

'The right of publishing my former writings – the ten [collected] volumes and the "Readers" – I ask my heirs to give to the public – that is, to renounce the copyrights. But I only ask this, and do not make it obligatory . . . That my works have been sold during these last ten years has been the hardest thing for me in life.'

Finally he asks that neither those near to him, nor others, should praise him: 'but if they wish to use my writings they should fathom those parts in which I know that the power of God has spoken through me, and benefit by them in their own lives . . . There were times when I felt that I became the vehicle of God's will. Often I was so unclean, so full of personal desires, that the light of that truth was obscured by my darkness; still sometimes that truth was transmitted through me – and those were the happiest moments of my life. God grant that their passage through me has not defiled those truths, and that despite the pettiness and impurity I have imparted to them, men may be nourished by them. In that alone lies the significance of my works. And therefore I ought only to be blamed and not praised for them.'

The selection of N. N. Strákhov, an eminent critic and his personal friend, was a very wise one, but unfortunately Strákhov died a year later.

On 13th May 1904 Tolstoy wrote to Chertkóv telling him of the 'something in the nature of a will' he had written in 1895, and referring to the fact that Strákhov had died and that his own death could not be far distant, he asked Chertkóv, in view of their 'complete agreement on the religious understanding of life', to undertake in conjunction with Countess S. A. Tolstoy the task of examining and sorting his post-humous papers. He added: 'To tell the truth, I do not attribute the least importance to any of those papers, except the *Diary* of my later years.'

With his wife's growing insistence on her right to inherit his literary property, and the increasing signs that her faculties were failing her, Tolstoy felt driven to make more definite arrangements, and in the summer of 1909, a year before his death, when his nephew-in-law, I. V. Denísenko, President of the Assize Court of Novocherkásk, visited him, he asked Denísenko to draw up a will bequeathing the whole of his works to the public.

Denísenko knew that a will bequeathing property to everybody, and not to some definite person or institution, would have no legal validity, but in view of Tolstoy's objection to legal sanctions he consented to draft such a document, and on 18th September 1909, when staying with Chertkóv at Krëksino near Moscow, Tolstoy signed it, assigning everything he had written since 1st January 1881, as well as anything written previously but not yet published, 'to constitute after my death no person's private property, but to be freely publishable and re-publishable by all who may desire to use them'.

It also declared: 'that all manuscripts and documents extant at the time of my death shall be handed to V. G. Chertkóv, that after my decease he may dispose of them as heretofore, and that they may be freely accessible to all who may wish to make use of them for publication'.

Chertkóv, however, was not satisfied with this, knowing that it lacked legal validity. It was, as Chertkóv subsequently wrote, naturally distasteful to Tolstoy to draw up a formal, official testament, but he feared by showing 'pedantic aversion to that formality' to risk letting his works remain private property. It is curious that Chertkóv, the protagonist of non-resistance, should himself, when it came to the crux of the struggle for his control of Tolstoy's work, have felt no 'pedantic aversion' to the formality necessary to secure that end.

While urging Tolstoy to make a legally binding will, Chertkóv did not, however, wish to be exposed to reproach for depriving the family of the property. As he put it: 'I felt certain that Tolstoy's wife and children would not like to see a non-member of their family made the official legatee' – and he devised a plan to secure the desired end indirectly.

In his final will, of 22nd July 1910, which was drawn up by Chertkóv, Tolstoy left his literary works, published and unpublished, finished and unfinished, together with any revisions, diaries, private letters, rough drafts, detached notes and reflections – 'in brief, anything, without exception, that I may have written . . . no matter where located, or by whom preserved . . . together with the copyright in all my productions, and the manuscripts themselves . . . to the full possession of my daughter Alexandra Lvóvna Tolstoy', or should she predecease him, to his daughter Tatiána Lvóvna Sukhotín.

That will was not composed by Tolstoy himself. It was quite unlike him to attach importance to the rough drafts or discarded revisions of former works, and he would not deliberately have attempted to reclaim the originals of 'private letters' written to his wife, his family, his friends, or strangers. He had no legal or customary right to them.

As supplement to this formal will, he also signed in pencil a memorandum Chertkóv drew up and to which Tolstoy added the words: 'With the contents of this declaration, drafted at my request and which precisely expresses my wishes, I am wholly in agreement.'

The memorandum explained that: 'All manuscripts and papers (including diaries, rough drafts, letters, &c.) which may be extant at the time of my death, shall be handed to V. G. Chertkóv, that after the death of Leo Nikoláevich, V. G. Chertkóv may examine such documents and publish what he may consider suitable of them. As regards the material aspect, L. N. requests the said V. G. Chertkóv to transact all business in connection with the same on the principles on which he has published writings of L. N.'s during the latter's lifetime.'

This last proviso was indefinite enough. Since Tolstoy's death, one ground of Alexandra's disapproval of Chertkóv's management has been his retention of more than appeared to her fair of the profits of the business. The memorandum does not define what he may take. Tolstoy, knowing Chertkóv's publicly expressed opinion that a man who takes money for anything he has written places himself on a level with prostitutes, probably did not imagine that he would accept profit from anyone else's writings.

These instructions were, Chertkóv tells us, intended 'to confine Countess Alexandra's task to that of securing for me unhindered disposal of Tolstoy's literary legacy according to the directions I had received from him.'

When it came to carrying out these understandings, Alexandra considered that Chertkóv was not fulfilling her father's wishes. Friction arose, and the question presented itself whether, since Chertkóv had appealed unto Caesar (that is to the law), he should not be told: 'To Caesar shalt thou go!' – in other words, whether Alexandra should not exercise her legal rights and take control of the property herself. The series of legal conflicts after Tolstoy's death, the claims and counter-claims, and the alliance of Alexandra now with Chertkóv and now with her mother (with whom she became reconciled) were too perplexing to be followed from a distance. The War came, and then – before the quarrels were over – the Revolution, when for a time literary property, like everything else, was nationalised.

I know of no edition of Tolstoy's works that has appeared cheaper or better arranged than that which Countess S. A. Tolstoy issued in fourteen double volumes for fourteen rubles, including all that the Censor then allowed to be published. Russian subscribers were bitterly disappointed with the edition Chertkóv got out with much flourish of trumpets soon after Tolstoy's death. Some, comparing the announce-ments with what they received and with the price charged, declared it to be a swindle. Not having seen that edition myself I cannot say in how far they were justified,

Something should yet be said about the circumstances under which Tolstoy was induced to sign his wills.

F. A. Strákhov has recounted how he was sent to Yásnaya to secure Tolstoy's approval to the will Chertkóv had drafted. He says the business was 'explained to me at a preliminary consultation with Chertkóv and the jurisconsult N. K. Muravëv'. Chertkóv had decided that the will Denísenko had drafted was unsatisfactory, and that Tolstoy should leave his copyrights and the originals of his works to some definite person.

In Strákhov's account of his visit, he mentions that the presence of Countess S. A. Tolstoy at Yásnaya was 'extremely undesirable for the business on which I was going', and he supposed her 'still to be in Moscow where I had met her'. However, to his dismay he encountered her at the station at Yásnaya, she having come from Moscow by the same train as himself. He nevertheless walked to the house and managed to find his way to Tolstoy's room without meeting her. 'In a few words I explained to Tolstoy the necessity of drawing up a formal will leaving the copyright to a specific person, and I placed before him the draft, asking him to read it and sign it if he agreed to its contents. Tolstoy at once began to read the draft . . . and, having read it all, immediately wrote at the end that he agreed to its provisos, but then having considered a little, he added, "This whole affair oppresses me! And there is no need to safeguard the dissemination of one's thoughts by various legalities."

'Having said this, he left the room, and I remained alone, doubtful whether to reply to his remark or to leave Yásnaya without having accomplished anything.'

When Tolstoy returned, Strákhov – feeling bound to try to fulfil the mission on which he had been sent – said: 'I understand and appreciate the moral height from which you judge this affair, but the conditions of today are such that if you do nothing to ensure the public utilisation of your writings, you thereby indirectly aid the establishment of property rights therein by your family. But if you arrange to leave them to an heir (be it even as private property) to whom your publicly expressed wishes will be sacred, you will secure their public usefulness.' He then continued, employing an argument of Chertkóv's who knew to a nicety how to reach the tender spots of Tolstoy's conscience: 'I do not conceal from you how painful it is for us, your friends, when we hear you reproached for having transferred your estates to your wife and children, despite your condemnation of landed property. Equally painful will it be to hear it said that, though you certainly knew that your declaration of 1891 had no legal validity, you did nothing to secure the carrying out of your wishes, and thus abetted the passing on of your copyrights to your family. I cannot express how painful it will be to your friends to hear this said after your death, and during the triumphant monopolisation of your writings by your heirs for fifty years . . .'

'That is a weighty argument,' replied Tolstoy, and he promised to give a decision after he had been for a ride.

Later on they had dinner, Tolstoy sitting as usual at the right hand of the Countess, who evidently had no suspicion of how important an event was taking place in her house.

'As soon as dinner was over and the Countess had left the room, Tolstoy went to his study, taking Alexandra Lvóvna and me with him.

' "I shall surprise you by my radical decision," said he to us with a kindly smile. "I wish to be *plus royaliste que le roi*. I wish, Sásha [Alexandra], to leave *everything* to you *alone* . . .

' "I think it will be best if I leave *everything* to you *alone*" repeated Tolstoy, "and that will be quite natural, as you, the last of all my children to be living with me, sympathise with me and are helping me so much in all my affairs . . ." '

(We know from Chertkóv's statement, quoted above, that he had asked Tolstoy to make such an arrangement, and the Countess Alexandra was the person whose nomination suited him best.)

' "But, Leo Nikoláevich, what is your wish about those writings the income from which has hitherto been enjoyed by Sófya Andréevna and which she is accustomed to consider as your gift to her, and therefore as her own property?" I interposed, amazed at Tolstoy's decision.

' "I can give Sásha private instructions about all that, and she will see that my wishes are carried out; but in the will, let it stand 'everything' to her alone," said Tolstoy, "As to my unpublished works, *Hadji Murad*, &c., I should like the first receipts to be used to redeem the land for the Yásnaya Polyána peasants. That is a thing I have long desired . . . But all these details and minor points I will consider with Chertkóv."

'At the evening tea, while Tolstoy was out of the room, Sófya Andréevna asked me why I had come? Besides the chief affair I had another errand, namely, to submit a draft of alterations Chertkóv had made in Tolstoy's last article, *It is Time to Understand*, so I was able with a light heart to inform her of that, naturally remaining silent about my principal mission.

'An hour later I started for the train to Moscow, first informing Chertkóv by telegraph of the result of my conversation with Tolstoy.'

'The object of my second journey to Yásnaya Polyána was to take to Tolstoy for signature, or better still for him to copy out with his own hand, the text of the will which had been prepared by the lawyer Muravëv.'

Strákhov goes on to explain his anxiety lest Tolstoy should decline to copy out his will, and as to smuggling the necessary witnesses into the house. He was accompanied by A. B. Goldenweiser, the pianist. The latter, 'who had previously been initiated into the affair and expressed his readiness to co-operate, took the document I had prepared, received all necessary instructions from Chertkóv, and entered the train with me.

'At Telyátenki [Chertkóv's place near Yásnaya] I did not find Chertkóv's steward, P. S. Anúrin, who had been selected by him to serve as a witness – he had started early that morning to fetch another witness, M. V. Bulígin.'*

Strákhov mentions that while driving to the Tolstoys' he felt 'some gnawings of conscience' at having to hide himself from Countess Sófya Andréevna. He achieved his purpose, however, and while he was witnessing the will (which Tolstoy copied out), the latter 'shut both doors of his study, one after the other. I confess it felt strange to see him in the role of one taking precautions against unwelcome visitors. I cannot express what a relief I felt when the precious document, quite complete, was rolled up by Goldenweiser and we both left the study.'

Strákhov tells how, having left the house for a few hours, he returned 'now simply in the character of an ordinary guest and dined there as if nothing had happened, watched Tolstoy playing chess with Goldenweiser and Bulígin, and about eleven o'clock, after evening tea, left the house.'

'Bidding farewell to Sófya Andréevna I looked attentively at her face. Complete tranquillity and cordiality towards the departing guests was so clearly expressed on it that I had no doubt of her entire lack of

---

* Bulígin, on hearing what was on hand, declined to act.

suspicion. I drove off with the pleasant consciousness of a carefully accomplished task, destined to have historic consequences. Only a small worm gnawed within me. It was the pricking of conscience, causing me some disquietude as to the conspiratorial character of our conduct.'

This will still failed to give full satisfaction, and yet another was prepared to meet the eventuality of Alexandra dying before her father. This last will, after Chertkóv had had it drafted, Tolstoy copied out, sitting on the stump of a tree in the forest near Chertkóv's house. It was dated 22nd July 1910, and has already been quoted.

Ilyá Tolstoy in his *Reminiscences of Tolstoy* tells the story of Chertkóv's relations with Leo Tolstoy, though without mentioning Chertkóv's name. In his last years Tolstoy devoted much time and care to preparing a compilation from the works of writers in harmony with his own outlook on life. Of this Ilyá says: 'When my father made up his mind to compile the collection of the sayings of the wise, to which he gave the name *A Circle of Reading*, he told one of his friends about it. A few days afterwards this "friend" came to see him again, and at once told him that he and his wife had been thinking over his scheme for the new book, and had come to the conclusion that he ought to call it *For Every Day* instead of *A Circle of Reading*. To this my father replied that he preferred the title *A Circle of Reading*, because the word "Circle" suggested the idea of continuous reading, which was what he meant the title to express. Half an hour later the "friend" again came across the room to him and repeated exactly the same remark. This time my father made no reply. In the evening when the "friend" was preparing to go home, as he was saying goodbye to my father, he held his hand in his and began once more: "Still I must tell you, Leo Nikoláevich, that I and my wife have been thinking it over and we have come to the conclusion . . . " and so on, word for word, the same.

' "No, no. I want to die, to die as soon as possible," groaned my father, when he had seen his "friend" off. "Isn't it all the same, whether it's *A Circle of Reading* or *For Every Day*? No, it's time for me to die; I cannot live like this any longer."

'But after all, in the end, one of the editions of the sayings of the wise was called *For Every Day* instead of *A Circle of Reading*.

' "Ah, my dear, ever since this – [Chertkóv] turned up, I really don't know which of Leo Nikoláevich's writings are by Leo Nikoláevich, and which are by [Chertkóv]!" murmured our old friend, the sincere and far from malicious Marie Alexándrovna Schmidt.

'This sort of intrusion into my father's work as an author bore, in his "friend's" language, the modest title of "anticipatory corrections", and there is no doubt that M. A. Schmidt was right; for no one will ever know where what my father wrote ends and where his concessions to his "friend's" persistent "anticipatory corrections" begin.'

Ilyá Tolstoy also tells us: 'During the last years of his life my father's health grew perceptibly worse. Several times he had the most sudden and inexplicable sort of fainting fits; he used to recover from them next day, but always lost his memory for the time.

'Seeing my brother's children, who were staying at Yásnaya, in the living room one day, he asked with some surprise: "Whose children are these?" Meeting my wife he said: "Don't be offended, my dear, I know that I am very fond of you, but I have quite forgotten who you are." And when he went up to the living-room after one of these fainting fits, he looked round with an astonished air and said: "Where's my brother Mítenka?" – a brother who had died fifty years before. The following day, all traces of the attack would have disappeared.'

Of the reasons that induced Tolstoy at the very end of his life to leave home after having always decided that it would be wrong to do so, Ilyá says: 'From the moment of my father's death I have been racking my brain to discover what could have given him the impulse to take that last step . . .

'Could my father really have fled from home because the wife with whom he had lived for forty-eight years had developed neurasthenia and at one time showed certain abnormalities characteristic of that malady? Was that like the man who loved his fellow men and knew the human heart so well? Or did he suddenly desire, when he was eighty-three and weak and helpless, to realise the ideal of a pilgrim's life? If so, why did he take my sister Sásha and Dr Makovítski with him? He could not but know that in their company he would be just as well provided with all the necessaries of life as at Yásnaya Polyána.

'Knowing my father as I did, I felt that the question of his flight was not so simple as it seemed to others, and the problem long lay unsolved before me, until it was suddenly made clear by the will he left behind him.

' "All this business is very disagreeable to me, and it is quite unnecessary," my father said when he signed the paper that was thrust before him. That was his real opinion about his will, and it never altered to the end of his days . . .

'He was thrust into a position from which there was absolutely no way out. To tell his wife was out of the question; it would have grievously offended his "friends". To have destroyed the will would have been worse still, for his "friends" had suffered for his principles, morally and materially, and had been exiled from Russia, and he felt bound to them. And on the top of all this were his fainting fits, his increasing loss of memory, the clear consciousness of the approach of death, and the continually growing nervousness of his wife, who felt in her heart of hearts the unnatural estrangement of her husband and could not understand it.

'And if she asked him what it was that he was concealing from her, he would either have to say nothing, or to tell her the truth. But that was impossible.

'What was he to do?

'And so it came about that the long-cherished dream of leaving Yásnaya Polyána presented itself as the only means of escape . . . He went away as a choice of evils. "I am too feeble and too old to begin a new life," he had said to my brother Sergéy only a few days before his departure. Harassed, ill in body and mind, he started forth without any object in view, without any thought-out plan, merely to hide himself somewhere, wherever it might be, and get some rest from the moral tortures which had become insupportable to him.'

The repudiation of legal rights in his works has not produced the results Tolstoy desired. Everyone was to be free to publish, republish, translate, and retranslate them. But I had occasion lately to ask Messrs J. M. Dent & Sons about the posthumous works contained in the volume of Tolstoy's *Stories and Dramas* which they have published, and it appears that they hold the exclusive rights in the English language. The Russian text was first published in Paris, in 1926, and under the Berne Convention rights were secured in all associated countries. The English translation rights were then sold to Dent & Sons. In undertaking the publication of this second skim of posthumous works which Tolstoy had regarded as of little worth, they were justified in stipulating for these rights, but the case is a curious one considering Tolstoy's efforts to make all his works 'freely accessible to all who may wish to make use of them'.

Another case, in which I was personally concerned, occurred when the first batch of posthumous works appeared. The chief story among them was *Hadji Murad*, and its translation was entrusted to me conditionally on my signing a contract submitted to me by Messrs Curtis Brown, Ltd, Chertkóv's agents. I did not suspect that the effect of this contract would be to deprive me of my copyright, and I thought that the principle of 'no rights reserved' would at least ensure my being free to republish my own translation in a Centenary Edition. But to my surprise I have since learnt from Messrs L. C. Page & Co., the American publishers of *Hadji Murad*, that they purchased the copyright in my version from Tolstoy's literary executors. So confusion and difficulties resulting from Chertkóv's way of doing business, still act as a hindrance to the satisfactory production of a Centenary Edition of Tolstoy's works.

The stipulation in his will that not only the copyright but also the manuscripts themselves should go to his literary executors, caused much trouble. His wife refused to hand them over, and Chertkóv publicly accused her of having 'abstracted' them during her husband's lifetime! In the cumbrous phraseology he employs he explains that 'to circumvent L. N.'s [Tolstoy's] direction, there became set on foot a mendacious assertion that the diaries and other papers preserved in the Historical Museum – certain originals of the diary, and others – had presumably been given by Tolstoy to his wife. Thanks to this assertion the opponents of Tolstoy's wishes gained an artificial excuse for juridical cavilling'. Alexandra applied to the Director of the Museum, to the Ministry of Popular Instruction, and finally to the Tsar, for the documents, but in each case was told that they could not be surrendered as her mother claimed them.

The Senate, to which Tolstoy's wife on her side appealed, decided that these manuscripts could only be returned to their depositor – that is to herself. These proceedings related only to the manuscripts, for no one disputed Chertkóv's right to publish whatever Tolstoy had written.

Light is thrown on the last months of Tolstoy's life by the memoirs of his secretary, V. F. Bulgákov, the French version of whose Diary – containing many details omitted from the Russian – appeared in *Les oeuvres litres*, No. 35, under the title, *Tolstoï – La véritable tragédie de ses derniers jours*. I will quote a few passages.

On 12th July 1910, when Tolstoy was still alive, Bulgákov drove with Countess Tolstoy to visit Chertkóv's mother at Telyátenki, where Chertkóv, who had been allowed to return to Túla Province, was also staying. Sófya Andréevna begged Bulgákov to ask Chertkóv to return

Tolstoy's Diaries to her. She was willing that they should be copied, if only the originals were returned to her.

'All his former diaries are in my keeping . . . Tell Chertkóv that if he will return these later diaries I shall calm down and will again be friends with him.'

Sófya Andréevna, in tears and trembling all over, looked at me with beseeching eyes; her tears and her emotion were entirely sincere . . .

I confess that I was much moved, and keenly desired that at any price – whether by the restitution of the manuscripts or in any other manner – the peace so necessary for everyone, and above all for Leo Nikoláevich, should be restored at Yásnaya Polyána.

It was in that state of mind that as soon as we reached Telyátenki I went to V. G. Chertkóv. On learning that I came with a commission from Sófya Andréevna he seemed troubled, assumed an anxious air, and led me into the room of his assistant and intimate adviser, Alësha Sergéenko. We both sat down on Sergéenko's bed, and he, his face strained with curiosity, sat on a chair opposite us. I began to explain Sófya Andréevna's request that he would return the manuscripts, and V. G. became violently excited: 'What?' said he, fixing on me his large eyes dilating with emotion – 'then you have told her right away where the diaries are?'

'No, I could not tell her anything, because I do not myself know where they are.'

'Ah! That is excellent!' exclaimed Chertkóv, and rose in great excitement. 'Now you may go, if you please' (he opened the door before me into the corridor). 'They are drinking tea there . . . You, no doubt, are hungry . . . We have something to talk about here!'

The door slammed behind me and I heard the American lock click. Astonished at the reception I had met with, I went along the corridor. Chertkóv and Alësha Sergéenko held council. I learnt later that they had decided not to return the Diaries.

14th July. At Yásnaya the atmosphere is tense. Sófya Andréevna categorically demands Leo Nikoláevich's diaries of the last ten years which are at Chertkóv's, and threatens, if she does not receive them, to poison or drown herself.

Leo Nikoláevich is tormenting himself on her account but endures this great trial very well. He is prepared to make any concessions to calm her. Naturally general peace and concord are infinitely more

important to him than any papers whatever . . . At his request
Alexandra Lvóvna went to Telyátenki to fetch the Diaries, and
she stayed there a long time. As I learnt afterwards from Varvára
[Feokrítov] there was a sudden reunion of the most intimate of
Chertkóv's friends: O. K. Tolstoy [Tolstoy's daughter-in-law and
Chertkóv's sister-in-law], Alësha Sergéenko, M. and Mme Goldenweiser, Alexandra Lvóvna, and Chertkóv himself, who all set to
work in great haste to extract and copy out passages in Leo Nikoláevich's Diary which compromised Sófya Andréevna and which she
might suppress. Then the Diaries were wrapped up, and Chertkóv
himself, saying goodbye to Alexandra Lvóvna on the doorstep outside, blessed her with ironic solemnity, making the sign of the cross
three times in the air with the packet. It was painful for him to part
with those documents.

Tolstoy had yielded to his wife by taking the Diaries back from
Chertkóv, but by way of steering a middle course placed them in a Túla
bank.

On 22nd July Bulgákov recounts the secrecy with which Tolstoy's
will was signed in the forest, the witnesses being chosen intimates of
Chertkóv.

On 1st August Tolstoy had a long talk in his study with P. I. Birukóv,
the author of his authorised Russian biography. Birukóv, on hearing of
the will, expressed the opinion that it was unsatisfactory that the affair
should have the air of a conspiracy, and that he thought it would be
better for Tolstoy to assemble the whole family and announce his
intentions.

Tolstoy agreed, and wrote to Chertkóv to that effect.

2nd August. Alexandra Lvóvna and the Chertkóvs are dissatisfied
with Birukóv's intervention. According to them Birukóv, without
weighing the complexity of the matter, has allowed himself to inter-
vene in a very unsuitable way, and even to give Leo Nikoláevich
advice which was sure to upset him.

The following reply from Chertkóv to Tolstoy in answer to a letter
from the latter after Birukóv's intervention, speaks for itself and
expresses Chertkóv's view of the case. It is a noteworthy document
and indicates the influence Chertkóv had established. The one thing it
omits is any indication of Chertkóv's anxiety to secure for himself

control of Tolstoy's literary legacy, a consideration which counted for much.

That the document may be read without interruption, and that comment may afterwards be made on certain portions of it, letters are inserted here and there to indicate passages I wish to refer to.

11 August 1910

DEAR LEO NIKOLÁEVICH – As you have asked me to remind you of the circumstances which induced you to make a definite posthumous disposition concerning your writings, I here set out for you the whole course of that affair.

I do not know exactly when you first decided not to take payment for your writings and to place them at everybody's disposal. It was before our acquaintance – probably when you gave Sófya Andréevna authority to publish the works printed before 1881. I only know that from the time of my acquaintance with you, in 1883, all your new writings were considered to belong to everybody and there was no talk of their being anyone's property.

In 1891, as you were pestered by letters from various sides asking permission to print or translate one or other of your writings of the second period (i.e., written after 1881), you published in the papers a letter announcing that you do not consider yourself as having property rights in any of the works written after 1881, but allow everyone to use them without payment.

Subsequently you repeatedly referred to that letter in replying to requests you continued to receive, published a similar announcement in the foreign Press, and if I remember rightly, repeated it in the Russian papers.

During the first period of our acquaintance Sófya Andréevna quite recognised the inviolability of your published renunciation of property in your new writings. These she did not touch (A), and did not hinder your disposing of them as you pleased, and you gave me the rough drafts to preserve and to use according to your indication. She interested and occupied herself exclusively with the publication of the works of 'the first period', which you had placed at her disposal.

As it had become common knowledge that you did not take payment for your new writings, many letters began to arrive asking you to give the first publication of some new work of yours for the benefit of this or that philanthropic undertaking, periodical publication, or private person in need of pecuniary aid. Finding it difficult in such cases to decide to whom to give the preference, and knowing that those who approached you with such requests were not the institutions or persons most deserving of support but the more enterprising and impudent, you soon decided, once and for all, to allow the whole benefit of the first publication of all your writings to go solely to the popular publishing firm, the *Intermediary*, which we had then just established, and which needed material assistance for its development. Since then you have handed over to me all your new writings for publication at my discretion in the interest of the *Intermediary*, and you have been in the habit of referring to me all those who addressed themselves to you for literary co-operation.

With your consent I adopted the following method of utilising your writings, when they were not first published by the *Intermediary*: the pecuniary profit from their first publication, that is, the payment for the right to publish them, was given to the *Intermediary*. Sub-sequently that revenue went to cover some (but a very insignificant part) of the very large expense of disseminating in a form as accessible to the poor as possible, those of your works which were forbidden in Russia (B.).

At first the affair went smoothly, but when you again began to write stories – tales such as *Master and Man*, *Hadji Murad*, *Father Sergius*, *After the Ball*, *The Forged Coupon*, &c., a wish to obtain possession of them for her own personal advantage flamed up in Sófya Andréevna (C.), for if they became her personal property they would represent a very large pecuniary value. Her solicitations and pressure on you in this respect as each work you wrote approached completion, became at last so intolerable as often to deprive you of the least desire to write any fiction (D.), and finally induced you completely to refuse to print such works during your lifetime.

Securing your peace of mind to some extent, this decision – which you of course understood as meaning that after your death these works, together with all the rest of your still unpublished writings, would become public property – also satisfied Sófya Andréevna, but for quite the opposite reason. Having become convinced that she would be unable during your life to appropriate these writings, she consoled herself with the thought that they would at present remain unused, but after your death would belong exclusively to your family under the laws of inheritance.

And Sófya Andréevna thought so, because by that time she had already changed her attitude towards your renunciation of ownership in the writings of your second period. As the quantity of such writings increased year by year it became harder and harder for her to reconcile herself to the thought that she would be unable to exploit (E.) them for the profit of her family. At last it came to this, she decided that after your death she would disregard your will and would claim the property rights in all your writings without exception, for on consulting lawyers – among them K. – she had learnt that your published renunciation would be inoperative should the family after your death claim their legal rights of inheritance.

At first Sófya Andréevna avoided openly expressing this intention, and only occasionally and accidentally let it out. But as time went on, being assured of support by your sons – Leo, Andrew and Michael Lvóvich – she began to be franker in this regard, and at last reached the point at which no longer for herself personally but in the name of the whole family – unrestrained even by your presence – she openly declared that your announcement in the Press had no legal validity, and that after your death your writings of the second period would become family property and the right of publishing them would at once be withdrawn from those who have published them during your lifetime.

For their part your sons, whom I have named above, did not trouble to conceal the fact that they reckoned on a revenue from these works which you had handed over for the public benefit . . .

X. [one of the sons], in a room next to yours, holding in his hand the manuscript of your unfinished story *The Forged Coupon*, said: 'For this story we shall get a hundred thousand rubles cash!' . . . X. addressed himself to Denísenko with an enquiry whether while you are still alive it is not possible, without your participation, to sell your writings to some publisher . . . In 1908 X. encouraged Sófya Andréevna in her refusal to allow the Zémstvos to publish a free Jubilee children's miscellany composed of extracts from your writings, and also in her attempt to deprive the *Intermediary* of permission to publish some of your stories for the people.

You for your part, not realising to what an extent Sófya Andréevna and some of your children set at nought the wishes you have expressed concerning your writings, have continued from time to time to set down arrangements in this connection.

So, for example, many years ago already you wrote in your Diary that after your death you wished all your unpublished writings to be examined by me together with Sófya Andréevna in order to select what may be worth publishing. Knowing even then what Sófya Andréevna's views were on those writings, and therefore understanding the complete impossibility of carrying on such mutual activity with her, I yet did not consider it opportune at that time to attempt to disturb your illusions in regard to Sófya Andréevna, which touched my heart.

One day during a walk you felt faint, and your daughter, Mary Lvóvna, was hardly able to get you home. Thinking that you were dying, you dictated a will to her, in which you repeated approximately what you had said in your announcement in the papers and in the notes in your Diary referred to above. The custody of this will you entrusted to Mary Lvóvna; but Sófya Andréevna, who soon got to know of this, assured you that the fact that the will was in the possession of Mary Lvóvna occasioned such unconquerable ill-will in her (Sófya Andréevna) towards Mary Lvóvna (F.) as could only be removed by your giving that paper to her (Sófya Andréevna) for safe custody. To the extreme mortification of Mary Lvóvna, who easily saw through Sófya Andréevna's conduct, you complied with that demand. Sófya Andréevna's relations with Mary Lvóvna after this were not at all improved, but Sófya Andréevna appears to have destroyed your will. At any rate after Mary Lvóvna's death, Sófya Andréevna, supposing no one to know of this will, remarked to me and to others that no disposition of yours about your writings existed except the announcement you had published in the papers, which has no legal validity.

You wrote once or twice more in your Diary something of the nature of a short testament to your family, and always mentioned that your writings of the second period are to remain public property after your death. But Sófya Andréevna on her side continued to assert that those writings would become family property. It came even to this, that Sófya Andréevna not merely in your presence spoke openly of the invalidity of your arrangements concerning your writings, but did not even refrain from indulging in recrimination with you on the subject, as if intentionally wishing that you should know how matters stand, and letting the fact of your not taking any steps appear to sanction her conduct.

In my own Diary a scene of that kind, which occurred in my presence, is noted down word for word. I quote the following extract from it:

'*4th December 1908*

' . . . Sófya Andréevna, addressing Leo Nikoláevich, irritably asserted that the copyright of all his unpublished writings, whenever written, belonged to the family. Leo Nikoláevich objected. She ran to her room, brought out her pocket Diary, and read from it her memorandum to the effect that Leo Nikoláevich had given as public property only those of his writings which had appeared after 1881, but not those which, though written after 1881, had not been published during his lifetime. Leo Nikoláevich again began a rejoinder. She shouted him down. At last, in an authoritative and decided tone, he made her listen to him. (She had just said that she was not concerned for herself, but that her children might claim their rights.)

'Leo Nikoláevich. "You imagine that our children are some sort of scoundrels, who will wish to run counter to my wishes about what is most precious to me."

'Sófya Andréevna. "Well, I don't know about scoundrels, but . . . "

'Leo Nikoláevich – firmly. "No, let me finish. According to you it seems that the greatest injury that can be done me will be done by my children. A greater offence could not be inflicted on me. You know that I had grounds which caused me to renounce these rights – the bases of my faith – and what now? Do you wish these grounds to appear like a hypocrisy? I handed my property over to you, gave you the earlier works, and it seems you expect me to give my very life – that by which I live. As it is, I receive abusive letters every day accusing me of hypocrisy. And you wish me to become in fact a hypocrite and a scoundrel . . . It is amazing that you should torture yourself so needlessly."

'And he left the room and went to his study, closing the door behind him . . .'

After that Sófya Andréevna with those of your sons whom I have named, arranged that as soon as you die they would claim their legal rights of inheritance in all your unpublished writings and papers, and if necessary would address themselves direct to the Tsar for protection against those 'Tolstoyans' who wish to steal their 'family inheritance' from them.

The position arrived at was this: Long before this, you had publicly announced that all your writings since 1881 belong to the whole of humanity. Copies of all you had written during that period, both fiction and other, had been entrusted by you to me for safe custody, that after your death I might proceed to publish them. In case of your death I (or should I also be dead, my substitute) in accord with your wish would immediately have to publish an announcement that on the basis of your renunciation of property rights in your writings of a certain period, your friends were about to publish an edition of those writings in all languages.

But to this Sófya Andréevna, together with some of your sons, would immediately reply, also publicly, that our announcement was a usurpation of their inherited rights, as you had not left any formal will, and that in case anyone, either in Russia or abroad, dared to publish any of your writings, such persons would be prosecuted.

If regardless of this your friends proceeded, as would be their duty, to publish the material received by me from you, and that is kept by me in England, then they or their publisher would at once be exposed to indictment and prosecution at law, with the inevitable result that they would be subjected to heavy monetary penalties and perhaps to imprisonment, for having considered it their duty to carry out your will.

And not only would your nearest and most devoted friends suffer, but around your writings, preaching love and harmony, a scandal unparalleled in literary history would flare up and, above all, enmity and strife between those who are in one or other way most closely connected with you.

And the only cause of all this would be that during your lifetime you had not drawn up a will so definite and irrefutable, even on its formal side, as not to admit of the least doubt (G.).

If, on the contrary, you drew up such a will, you would thereby forestall all these evils and sufferings. On the legal side it would be impossible to deprive it of validity, and you would therefore have done all in your power to prevent any litigation or prosecutions in connection with your writings (H.).

It would be fully understood that of these two alternatives you chose the one which most surely attained its end, relieved the position of your friends, and restrained from sin the opponents of your will.

In Krëkshino [an estate where Tolstoy had visited Chertkóv] in the autumn of 1909 you signed an informal testament in which you left all your writings of the second period at my disposal. It was signed by witnesses from your nearest friends. But on examination by legal advisers it proved not to be drawn up in due form, so that instead of forestalling the probability of a lawsuit, it, on the contrary, invited one.

Then you decided to write a will yourself which would be irreproachable in form, and you drew it in favour of your daughter Alexandra Lvóvna. With a view to avoid offending your family, it was desirable to entrust this affair to some one of your children. Alexandra Lvóvna, according to your supplementary direction, was to hand over the writings left her to my disposal to edit, and to be converted into public property.

But as by that time the avaricious designs of some of your family concerning your writings after your death had become fully known to you, this time you, having first examined the question attentively before your conscience, decided not to make a distinction between the first and the second periods of your authorship, but to leave all your writings without exception for the use of everyone, with the proviso that Sófya Andréevna was for her lifetime to continue to have the benefit of editing your writings of the first period.

Subsequently, namely this summer, you decided to leave your writings not to Alexandra Lvóvna alone, but also to Tatiána Lvóvna in case of Alexandra Lvóvna's death *during your lifetime*, and you wrote a new will accordingly. You did this not only because Alexandra Lvóvna might actually die before yourself, but chiefly to ease her position in the family after your death, for if she alone were mentioned in your will, you would thereby place her in a quite exceptional position among the rest of the family, some of whom would consequently nourish most hostile feelings towards her.

This new will in favour of your two daughters you had to rewrite a few days later in consequence of a slight formal error in the text. So though only the last will is considered valid, the two previous wills, similar in substance and written in your own handwriting, can in due time serve as confirmation of the fact that your will was not written under any momentary impulse or temporary impression, but on the contrary quite deliberately and persistently, since you gave yourself the trouble on different days, over a prolonged interval of time, to set out in your own handwriting one and the same disposition three times over.

All we, your nearest friends and partisans initiated in the details of this affair, were greatly cheered by its successful completion. It was as if a stone had been rolled from the soul of each of us. And this quite understandably.

On the one hand, having a much higher opinion than yourself of the importance of your writings both for individuals and for the further development of human consciousness in general, as in them you are the vehicle not of your personal wisdom but of the Divine wisdom of the whole of humanity, we naturally could not but desire that these writings should really become a general possession, and receive the widest circulation in the most accessible form. But only you could secure this, and only in the way in which you had at last decided to effect it.

On the other hand we also rejoiced on your own account, for if you had not left such a will you would have been reproached by the people for weakness and for conniving at your family's lowest instincts. You would have been accused – and one cannot say unjustly accused – of having publicly expressed your intention of leaving certain of your writings for the free use of all men, and nevertheless – though you knew that some members of your family had decided to obtain possession of these writings for their own profit – of not wishing to take the one step, and that not a difficult one, which alone could secure for mankind the fulfilment of your desire.

Finally in yet another respect your action could not but delight your friends. By entrusting to them the management of your writings after your death in accord with your indications, you involuntarily laid on their shoulders a complicated and in many respects very difficult task, the accomplishment of which, it goes without saying, they will regard as a sacred duty before God, before you, and before mankind. But if at the same time you did not wish as far as depended on you, by means of a formal testament to safeguard them from the complications and prosecutions to which I have referred, you would have made their task a thousand times more difficult, bringing upon their heads such sufferings as they – who carry out your wishes – would certainly not deserve. So that from that side also your formal testament is an act of cordial delicacy towards the friends who are helping you in this affair.

From this same feeling of delicacy towards them, as well as in the true interests of the opponents of your will, you considered it necessary not to announce that will before your death.

Your disposition – when announced after your death as your last testament – will under the immediate impression of your actual death be accepted by everyone, even by those to whom it is personally unprofitable, with at least the respect and resignation always in such cases shown to the 'voice from the grave' of a near relation. Coming as an unalterable *fait accompli* it could no longer provoke those passions, that enmity, strife, and those desperate solicitations, which it would certainly provoke if announced during your lifetime. It is terrible to think into what a circle of envy and enmity your family life – the atmosphere of which is a far from loving one even as it is – would be converted if your last will were prematurely announced to those of your family who are most under the influence of avarice and egotism. And this is not so much because you have disposed of your writings in this way or that, as because, if your family knew of your will before your death, they might still hope by insistent pressure in every possible way, to succeed in getting you, were it but at some moment of your most helpless physical weakness, or even on your deathbed (H.), to renounce what is expressed in that testament.

In such an atmosphere the life of your daughter, Alexandra Lvóvna, would become a real hell, and in such a helpless position her health, precarious in any case, would hardly be able to stand both the hatred directed against herself and the moral coercion (I.) brought to bear on you before her eyes. In any case it would be too cruel on your part to expose her to such torment when there was a possibility of avoiding it.

All these reasons taken together fully explain the joyful relief we felt when, by your last will, you brought to a happy conclusion this protracted affair, so attentively and carefully considered in the true interests of all those whom in one way or other it concerned. And so you can imagine our grief and perplexity when a few days later you disavowed, if not actually at least in principle, all that you had done with our participation.

This unexpected and as with my whole soul I hope but momentary change, was due it seems to me to a misunderstanding. Paul Iván-ovich Birukóv, not having troubled to ascertain from us the real grounds of your action, and regarding the matter from a very narrow point of view, seems to have supposed that the giving of a post-humous character to your will resulted from personal pusillanimity on your part. He imagined that for the sake of personal tranquillity you did not wish to announce the contents of your will to your family during your lifetime.

In this Birukóv was, of course, quite mistaken. You acted so, not at all for your own sake but, as I have reminded you above, out of goodwill both towards your friends whose position you tried to ease, and your family, whom you wished as far as possible to guard from sin. But when Birukóv, looking at the matter solely from the point of view of your separate personality and suspecting you of pusillanimity, asked why you kept your testament secret, you – temporarily for-getting the actual reasons – at once agreed with him that you appeared to be acting so from a wish to avoid personal unpleasantness. And then, when Birukóv remarked that in that case it would have been better not to make a will at all, you – again forgetting the real motives that actuated you – promptly agreed with him about that also. And in this spirit of self-condemnation you have written me the 'penitential' letter which has grieved us all, and as it seems to us is mistakenly penitential.

In that letter you incidentally accuse yourself of having thought ill of your heirs. In reality you did not 'think' anything, but indubitably *knew* from their own words that they intended in resistance to your wishes to appropriate to themselves what you had given for public use.

You say in your letter that you acted badly in not wishing to announce the contents of your will during your lifetime. But as I have already indicated, you acted thus not at all for your own sake but from love and consideration for others. Moreover no moral principle debars a man from leaving some of his instructions to people in the form of a posthumous will, if for some reason the testator considers it better for them that he should act in that way. And in ordinary life it is not for nothing that the majority of wills only become known after the testator's death.

Finally you say in your letter that in drawing up a formal will you have acted badly – by utilising an institution of the Government of which you disapprove. In reality you did not make use of any government institution at all. Your testament had a purely domestic character and was not even witnessed at a notary's. If by 'an institution of the Government' you have in view the formal, external shape in which your will is drawn up, you know you had recourse to that form of wording not at all that your nominee might by the use of that document begin any prosecution or judicial proceeding, but quite the opposite – in order to avoid any process or prosecution. And in regard to the real significance for you of the official expressions employed in your will, no shadow of misunderstanding can remain, for in the supplementary announcement accompanying your testament your dispositions are explained most exactly.

So, for instance, in that 'supplementary note' it is clearly stated that you had recourse to the 'formal' testament not to place anyone in possession of rights in your writings, but on the contrary, to prevent the possibility of their becoming anyone's private property after your death.

With reference to your remark that 'the dissemination of my books will hardly make up for the distrust of them the inconsistency in my actions must evoke' – by which you mean the drawing up of a formal testament – I allow myself frankly to express my profound conviction that on this point you are completely mistaken. The enemies of the Principle you serve will of course always find something to quibble at in your actions. But sensible people will not merely not blame you for your testament, but will on the contrary indubitably regret it if you do not during your lifetime do all in your power to avert the evil which will inevitably flare up around your writings if you do not leave a will fully authoritative and unimpugnable by anyone.

I know however that people's opinions of your actions count for very little with you. The chief thing, as I have tried in the above to remind you, is that in all this affair you have been guided not by what was agreeable or convenient to yourself, nor by any personal preference or aversion of your own, nor have you sought your own tranquillity, but you have been guided solely by the demands of conscience. Having undertaken the accomplishment of what you consider to be your duty before God and man, you have tried to fulfil this as well as possible.

For you and the friends who have helped you to clear up this affair, and who have to carry it out after your death, the case has not altered; and we are all ready, if we survive you, sacredly to carry out your desires without sparing ourselves in that joyful task, in the unquestionable justice of which we cannot cease to believe. But that we may feel firm ground under our feet it is essential that we should know that we are in fact acting in accord with your will, and acting *at one* with you.

In the letter that grieves us, you, however, express yourself as though you do not approve in principle of what you have done, though you do not in fact find it necessary to repudiate your will. It is true that you have since then said to Alexandra Lvóvna – who reminded you of certain details of the affair – that you had really forgotten them when you wrote that letter. But still we are all of us left at the end of the matter with a too indefinite impression (K.) as to your present relation to this question.

And therefore on behalf, not of myself only, but also of the rest of our friends concerned in the matter (L.), I ask you, dear Leo Nikoláevich, to express your final desire definitely after reading this letter of mine in which I have tried to refresh your memory as to the whole course of the affair.

It is unnecessary to say to what a degree we shall all be gladdened and tranquillised if, on reconsidering the whole matter, you find it possible to agree that what was done was the best it was possible to do, and if with full assurance you will confirm your posthumous dispositions concerning your writings.

V. Chertkóv

I have quoted the whole of this letter to let Chertkóv state his case in his own words, and also because it throws much light on the relations that existed during the last weeks of Tolstoy's life between his friend and himself.

No such able or carefully designed statement can be quoted in defence of Countess Sófya Andréevna, who was not in full control of her faculties and, as previously mentioned, said and did much that was injudicious and regrettable. But to maintain a balance, some comment should be made on the points I have marked by the insertion of capital letters.

A. The Countess was, as a matter of fact, keen to publish whatever new works her husband wrote, and did publish those permitted in Russia. Chertkóv's remark that she 'occupied herself exclusively with the publication of the works of the first period' is therefore hardly correct.

B. While mentioning the payments received for the right of first publication of Tolstoy's articles and stories in various periodicals or papers, Chertkóv ignores the great advantage he obtained by having the first publication of Tolstoy's new works for his own 'Free Age Press' series.

C. The contrast drawn between the wrongness of the Countess's desire to control her husband's works, and the rightness of Chertkóv's desire to do so, is unconvincing to those who remember her cheap and clearly printed volumes, generally of from five hundred to six hundred pages, which were sold at a ruble (2s.) each; and I do not share the belief that a welter of rival editions benefits anyone, in comparison with an authorised edition which, selling in larger quantities, can be better and more cheaply produced than those which have to share in a scramble.

D. Here Chertkóv is right. After Tolstoy ceased to sell his works, the disputes and unpleasantness that resulted made him reluctant to write any more fiction. But this unpleasantness resulted as much from Chertkóv's as from the Countess's demands.

E. Chertkóv's sureness that he understood the Countess's thoughts and that it was his duty to inform Tolstoy of them, is remarkable, but not more so than the fact that he was able to influence Tolstoy by so doing. In Chertkóv's eyes the Countess's publications were an 'exploitation' of Tolstoy's works, while his own were the fulfilment of a 'sacred duty' to God and man, though subsequently, as already mentioned, one of Countess Alexandra's grounds for dissatisfaction with Chertkóv's management of Tolstoy's bequest was that he took too large a share of the proceeds of the publications for himself.

F. This presentation of Sófya Andréevna's attitude towards Mary Lvóvna clashes with what she (Sófya Andréevna) herself wrote me in the letter quoted on page 810, but as Chertkóv is writing of matters of which Tolstoy must have had personal knowledge, I merely note the discrepancy without challenging the statement.

G. One can quite agree that definiteness of arrangement is desirable and even essential to the efficient working of affairs. The pity is that, until his own interests were at stake, Chertkóv had elevated the cult of indefiniteness to the rank of a religious principle.

H. Chertkóv's opinion of Tolstoy's physical and mental condition during the last weeks of his life is indicated not only by this passage but by the whole tenor of the letter. He feels it necessary to remind Tolstoy not only of what he (Tolstoy) had done, but of the motives that had prompted him to do it. Chertkóv's assurance that he completely understood what all the people concerned had done and intended to do, what ought to be done, and the results that would follow if his wishes were properly attended to, as well as Tolstoy's own intentions, motives, mistakes, and lapses of memory, is an indication of his (Chertkóv's) mentality and helps to explain why the Countess disliked him, and others found him difficult to work with. The suggestion of a danger that Tolstoy might, on his deathbed, be induced to alter his will, throws a light on Chertkóv's efforts to prevent members of the family knowing where Tolstoy was during his last illness.

I. The concern expressed on Alexandra Lvóvna's account will be intelligible to readers who remember the account of my last visit to Yásnaya.

K. This reference to Chertkóv's 'indefinite impression' of Tolstoy's relation to the question so shortly before his death shows, I think, that the result of the contest between the wife and the friend for the literary inheritance was doubtful to the last. Had the Countess not been so mentally unbalanced that it was at last hardly possible to entrust her with the editorship, or had her hysterical nature not caused her for years previously to press her claims irritably and on grounds that out-raged Tolstoy's feelings and principles, the issue of the struggle might well have been different, despite the extraordinary ability of Chertkóv's pleadings. To do him justice, however, we must recognise that he could hardly have had such influence with Tolstoy had he not been genuinely at one with him on the principle of non-resistance, and had not the 'no copyright' maxim, which was Chertkóv's invention, been a quite logical deduction from that principle.

L. Chertkóv does not mention who 'the rest of our friends' were. Tolstoy's family are indicated as the enemy, Birukóv is ruled out. Apparently 'the rest of our friends' were those living near Chertkóv, submitting to him and sharing his views.

What Tolstoy's wife thought of Chertkóv may be gathered from a letter she wrote him in September 1910.

After reproaching him for having detained Tolstoy with him when she wanted him to return to Yásnaya, she goes on to say of her husband:

In reply to my reproaches he assured me that he felt all that was kindest and most affectionate for me, and would show me how well he had written about me in his Diaries. He made a movement to take them down, but not finding them, was taken aback, having probably forgotten that they had been taken. Then he took me to Sásha [Alexandra] to ask whether she knew where they are? But Sásha lied, and Leo Nikoláevich had to confess that you have them. You saw how that grieved and upset me. I cannot separate myself from my husband with whom I have lived nearly half a century. His Diaries are the holy of holies of his life, and consequently of mine with him; they are the reflection of his soul, which I am accustomed to feel and to love, and they ought not to be in the hands of an outsider. Yet in secret from me they were carried off by people you sent . . . When in a kindly and cordial letter I asked you to return them, you refused harshly, and attributed to me the dishonourable motive of fear lest, by the help of the Diaries, you should *expose* me and my children, and you angrily added: 'Had I wished, I could long ago have *besmirched* you and your children, and if I have not done so it was only out of love for Leo Nikoláevich.'

To 'misunderstand' those words, as you put it, is impossible; it is all plain, and I am not so stupid as that! I have the earlier Diaries at the Museum and it was natural for me to wish to take the last ones also. But you angrily and obstinately refused, and Leo Nikoláevich, with his weak will, submitted to you, and finally you said that you would have run away to America from such a wife or have shot yourself. Then, when going downstairs, you said to my son Leo, in everyone's hearing: 'I don't understand such a woman, who is engaged all her life long in murdering her husband.'

Why do you now seek intercourse with the murderess? You entered on a struggle with me for the possession of the Diaries and found the struggle an unequal one, and grew angry with me. Then I quite sincerely put the question thus: either my life – or the Diaries must be returned to me. Leo Nikoláevich understands that I should certainly carry out my threat, and he promised to return the Diaries to me, but was frightened of you and instead of giving them to me placed them in the Bank. If you wish to be honest you must admit having heard how, after your note about the return of the Diaries, he replied to my request to give me a written promise to return them: 'What sort of note to a wife? I have promised, and shall give them back.' But he did not give them back, but gave them to Tánya to place in the Bank.

Two weeks of struggle for the Diaries have intensified my oppressive nervous condition. Had you not maliciously persisted from the very first, nothing painful would have occurred and all would have been as before. (See how your *non-resistance* has immediately collapsed!)

If you had only returned the Diaries to Leo Nikoláevich at once, and had borrowed one notebook at a time for your work, and returned it when you had finished with it, I should have been tranquil . . . In your letter you evade all the chief questions, which I put clearly and truthfully, and you always speak of *misunderstandings*. That is a pharisaical device. Misunderstandings should be honestly cleared up. You write that you are always willing to do so. But remember how many times, for instance, I have asked you to tell me what arrangement you have made about Leo Nikoláevich's papers and manuscripts after your death, and you have always angrily refused to reply. You are not fond of truth or clarity. But is it not natural for a wife to wish to know that: not from avarice, since you will of course outlive me, but simply from love of my husband in whose mental life and works I am accustomed to feel interested?

Our sons' ill-will, if it exists, has the same cause. You have published Leo Nikoláevich's works – that is to your credit. But why do you constantly take away his *manuscripts*? In that lies your 'avarice' – not mine. You will say that he gave them to you himself. And just in that, as well as in much else, I notice your ever-growing influence on the ever-weakening will of an old man who is already but little interested in worldly affairs. You have subjugated him by your despotic character (about which, i.e. your despotism, your mother agreed with me) . . . Above all I have suddenly understood why Leo Nikoláevich treats me unkindly, harshly, like a stranger – which never used to be the case and which kills me. You *suggest* to him that he should run away from such a wife, or should shoot himself. And you are the *first* person in my life to dare do me such an injustice.

You also speak of some *abnormal* suspicion . . . My suspicions were aroused solely by the fact that latterly *everything* is concealed from me – conversations, meetings, diaries, letters, and the secret transmission of papers in connivance with my daughter Sásha and various secretaries of yours – which during the long course of my married life *never* occurred before. If everything is so zealously hidden from me, there is something to hide, and it involuntarily arouses fear and distrust.

What I have endured during these last three months cannot be compared with any sufferings in all my life. I bore the death of Vánichka more easily, because it was the *will of God*. But in the loss of Leo Nikoláevich's love for me and the interference of an outsider in our affectionate matrimonial life, I feel the *will of the Evil One* . . . Why should there not now be at Yásnaya Polyána what always was there till you came? We have now not long to live in the world – let us finish the last days of our life in the same communion in which we began our young married life without outside influence . . .

Before your interference in our family nothing ever happened in my life like what has now occurred, nor will, I hope, happen after your removal from personal intercourse with my husband.

That is all.

SÓFYA TOLSTOY

Those letters help us to understand Bulgákov's memoirs, further extracts from which follow:

3rd August: This evening, again, frightful scenes. Sófya Andréevna exceeded all limits in her lack of consideration for Leo Nikoláevich, and said mad things to him in justification of her hatred of Chertkóv . . .

5th August: I went to Leo Nikoláevich in his study. 'Sófya Andréevna,' he said, 'is not well. If only Chertkóv could see her just as she is today! One cannot help feeling pity for her, and to treat her as severely as he does – he and many others, and I myself . . . She does it all without any reason! If there were a reason she would be unable to keep it to herself, she would express it . . . She simply feels oppressed here; she can't breathe. One cannot but feel pity for her, and I am glad when I feel it . . .'

14th September: As usual. Sófya Andréevna complained of the malicious and sometimes rude way Chertkóv has treated her . . .

I do not know whether one can rely on what Sófya Andréevna says when she quotes Chertkóv, but it seems clear to me that with a wailing and rather narrow-minded woman one should behave with more consideration than he and Alexandra Lvóvna do. I am sometimes astonished that they do not consider that she inevitably vents on Leo Nikoláevich (who has no part in the conflict and stands outside it) the anger and irritation aroused by her discussions with them.

On 21st September Bulgákov notes that Tolstoy received a letter from A. B. Goldenweiser (one of Chertkóv's intimate associates), containing extracts from the private diary of V. M. Feokrítov (Alexandra's close friend and fellow-worker), describing Sófya Andréevna in the blackest colours. Tolstoy replied very dryly to Goldenweiser, saying that: 'In what Feokrítov has written, and in your opinion on the subject, there is a great and bad exaggeration, disregard of her sickly condition, and a confusion of good sentiments with bad ones.'

22nd September: Sófya Andréevna seemed to be in a state of great agitation. She was exasperated not only with Chertkóv but with Leo Nikoláevich himself. She said aloud that she did not love him any longer and considered him as 'a man who is half a stranger'. She added that she now awaited him without experiencing the joy she was accustomed to feel.

On 23rd September, the forty-eighth anniversary of Tolstoy's wedding, Sófya Andréevna had asked her husband to let Bulgákov photograph them together, and he had consented.

Alexandra Lvóvna was annoyed, not only at his having acceded to his wife's request, but also because since his return from Kochëti [his daughter Tatiána's home] he had not replaced in his study portraits of Chertkóv with Ilyá Tolstoy, and of himself with Alexandra, which his wife had removed, substituting portraits of herself and of Tolstoy's father.

Alexandra Lvóvna had reproached her father for not replacing the photographs, and now, to make matters worse, he allowed himself to be photographed with Sófya Andréevna. The result was a painful scene with his daughter.

Alexandra Lvóvna in the typing room was loudly condemning Leo Nikoláevich to V. M. Feokrítov, who of course agreed with her in everything. Suddenly Leo Nikoláevich entered unexpectedly.

'Sásha [Alexandra], what are you shouting about like that?'

Alexandra Lvóvna told him of her grievance: it was wrong to have allowed himself to be photographed with Sófya Andréevna after promising Sófya Andréevna not to be photographed any more with Chertkóv; it was inconsistent of him to sacrifice the interests of a friend and of a daughter for a brainless wife, and to allow her to remove photographs, &c, &c . . .

Leo Nikoláevich shook his head in reply and saying, 'You're very like her!' returned to his study.

A few minutes later we heard his gong, which was the signal for Alexandra Lvóvna. (Two rings were the signal for me.) Vexed with her father, she did not stir. It was I who went to him. Hardly had I executed his order and left the study than he rang again for Alexandra Lvóvna. She did not move. Then he sent me to find her. She came.

The scene that then occurred between her and her father, as she told me later, was this:

Leo Nikoláevich told her he wanted to dictate a letter, but hardly had she settled at the desk when the old man suddenly let his head fall on the arm of his chair and began to sob.

'I don't want your shorthand any more!' said he to her amid his sobs.

Alexandra Lvóvna threw herself at his feet, asking his forgiveness, and they both wept.

On 25th September Tolstoy noted in his Diary:

I have received a letter from Chertkóv [the letter already quoted] full of reproaches and accusations. They tear me in pieces. Sometimes the idea occurs to me to go far away from them all.

Alexandra attributed the struggle between Sófya Andréevna and Chertkóv for the manuscripts of Tolstoy's works to her mother's 'cupidity'. When Tolstoy heard this he said: 'Some people, like Sásha, want to explain everything by cupidity. But the matter is much more complex! These forty years of life together . . . Habit, vanity, *amour propre*, jealousy, and illness, all play their part here. In her present state she is very much to be pitied! I try to extricate myself from this situation and it is particularly painful when anyone feels, as Sásha does, what there is of egotism in it . . . It makes one uncomfortable . . .'

There is little disagreement as to the actual facts of Tolstoy's home-leaving and death.

On 28th October 1910 he took the decisive step. The incident immediately prompting him to do so was that, after going to bed the previous evening, he heard his wife searching among the papers in his study. The Countess in a letter to me has denied that she was searching for anything, but it is difficult to suppose that Tolstoy was mistaken, for it was only one in a long sequence of similar occurrences. Tolstoy had trained himself to be very patient with his wife when she was irritable or unreasonable, but for all that the clash of wills had gradually produced a tension which now reached breaking-point.

When she had retired Tolstoy rose, collected some manuscripts, took two changes of underclothing, and told his friend and follower, Dr Makovítski, that he had decided to leave home at once.

He bade goodbye to his daughter Alexandra, promising to let her join him later. Then, about five a.m., he left the house and set out for the stables. The night was dark and as he hurried along he stumbled against some bushes, lost his cap, became entangled, and had to return for an electric torch. Having procured this and another hat, he made his way to the stables, roused the coachmen, and told them to harness – closing the door lest the light should be noticed from the house. His daughter, Varvára Feokrítov, and Dr Makovítski, brought his portmanteau and other things into the stable yard, and Tolstoy again took leave of the girls and drove off with Makovítski.

He decided first to visit his sister Mary, at the Shámordin Convent.

About noon the travellers had to change into a train with only one passenger carriage – a crowded, smoky, and over-heated third class. Though it was raining and the wind was sharp, Tolstoy stood for a long time on the open platform at the end of the carriage, and there caught cold.

It was almost night before the slow train reached Kazëlsk, a station three miles from Óptin Monastery and twelve from the Shámordin Convent. As it was late, Tolstoy decided not to go on to his sister's but to spend the night at the Monastery Hotel. When they had driven up to the gate, he said to the monk who came out to them: 'I am Tolstoy . . . Will you admit me for the night?' – 'We admit everyone,' was the reply.

Next morning Tolstoy visited his sister. Widely as their beliefs differed, their affection for one another had remained unbroken. She understood his case and they wept together.

He then engaged a room at the Shámordin Hotel, and there his daughter Alexandra joined him and brought him the news that his wife had tried to commit suicide when she found that he had left home.

During the day he went for a walk, and enquired whether there was no peasant's hut he could rent to live in. He remarked to his sister that were it not for the religious observances it entailed, he would be content to live in such quiet surroundings as the Monastery afforded. That is the only ground for the absurd story, set in circulation after his death, that he left home to enter a Monastery.

He spent the next day, Saturday, with his sister, and parted from her in the evening with no immediate intention of leaving. But Alexandra persuaded him to continue his journey lest her mother should find him.

That night he felt ill, but rose at five o'clock next morning and decided to catch the early train for Rostóvon-Don, from whence he could visit Denísenko, who might procure him a foreign passport to leave Russia.

About midday he fell ill in the train, and Dr Makovítski decided that it was necessary to stop at the next station, which happened to be Astápovo in the province of Ryazán, barely fifty miles south-east of Yásnaya.

Supported by his daughter and the doctor, he descended with difficulty from the train. His temperature had risen to nearly 104°. He coughed, had a cold in his head, and a very irregular pulse. The station-master readily placed his house at his disposal. Tolstoy himself took the disappointment good-humouredly, and remarked half-jokingly: 'Well, it's checkmate . . . don't be vexed!'

The next morning, Monday, he had Chertkóv telegraphed for. He also dictated some thoughts, entered up his Diary, was read to, and even managed to write an account of his flight from home.

In the Diary, among other entries, he wrote:

> God is the illimitable All; man is but a limited manifestation of Him.
>
> Or, even better – God is that illimitable All of which man is conscious of being a limited part . . .
>
> God is not love, but the more love there is in man the more is God made manifest in him, and the more truly does he exist.

Tolstoy thought that no one but Chertkóv knew where he was, but a newspaper correspondent had tracked him to the Convent, and detectives had followed him thence.

From Astápovo Alexandra telegraphed to her eldest brother in Moscow to send Dr Nikítin. She added that her father wished to see his eldest children, but feared the arrival of the others.

His wife, as soon as she learnt from a newspaper correspondent that her husband was at Astápovo, travelled by special train with some of her children to join him, The eldest son, Sergéy, was there before her, and Chertkóv had arrived at nine o'clock that Tuesday morning. He, Alexandra, Varvára Feokrítov, Dr Makovítski and Alexéy Sergéenko were in possession of the house and the patient.

Tolstoy did not know of his wife's arrival and the responsibility for excluding her from the house did not rest with him.

Dr Nikítin when he arrived examined the patient and diagnosed inflammation of the left lung, but this was not very serious, and what Tolstoy really died of seems to have been nervous exhaustion. The long struggle to find a way of applying his principles, and the resulting conflict, had worn him out so completely that he was unable to withstand the attack of illness produced by exposure.

During the night of Monday, 1st November, he suffered from heartburn, groaned and slept badly, but the next day he was particularly animated, and was pleased that his fever had abated.

He began dictating a letter to me in English (though he usually wrote to me in Russian), but got no further than the words: 'On my way to the place where I wished to be alone, I was . . . ' Interrupted at that point, the letter was never completed. It was the last but one he ever attempted to dictate.

At about 5 p.m. he called in Chertkóv and Nikítin, and spoke to them of his uneasiness lest his wife should hear of his illness and come to Astápovo. He had a telegram sent to his children (whom he supposed still to be at Yásnaya) to say that he was very weak, and that an interview with his wife would be disastrous for him. To Chertkóv he added: 'You understand that if she comes here I shall not be able to refuse her . . . ' and began to cry.

He was by this time so enfeebled that he had to be carefully supported when he had occasion to get out of bed, and when put back, his legs had to be lifted from the floor. Once after being helped in this way by three people, he remarked in a weak, sorrowful voice as he lay back breathing rapidly after the exertion: 'The peasants . . . the peasants, how they die!' and his eyes filled with tears.

Later he remarked: 'Evidently I shall have to die in my sins!' – to which Chertkóv replied: 'This is not sin, but love that surrounds you. You have done all you could to escape from sin!'

He asked to have a newspaper read to him, and Chertkóv complied, reading a letter he had published to explain Tolstoy's action in leaving home.

On Wednesday Tolstoy wrote in his Diary for the last time. The final words in it are: 'I see our plans have failed . . . *Fais ce que dois, adv* . . . * It is all for the good of others, and chiefly of myself.'

---

* The commencement of a French motto: 'Do what's right, come what may.'

That night he slept badly, moaned, and was delirious. The action of his heart was weak and irregular and the pulse reached 120–130.

On the Thursday he looked very ill. His lips were dry and white. In general as his illness progressed his cheeks sank in, his lips grew thinner and more bloodless, and his face became more and more worn from the pain he endured. It was however only occasionally that his sufferings became acute. At such moments he would rise convulsively to a sitting posture, letting his legs hang out of bed, his body swaying from side to side. Then he would sink back on to his pillows with a Look of resignation. He set himself to the duty nearest at hand, that of enduring his sufferings patiently. At times he said: 'It is very hard, very heavy,' and seemed to be trying to discern and fulfil the will of his Master.

He who had so long and arduously endeavoured to do his duty maintained the struggle to the end, not however without a certain perplexity as to what that duty might be.

He still wished to be read to and to dictate his thoughts, but frequently relapsed into delirium and occasionally showed the unreasonable irritability of a sick man. He gave impatient instructions about arranging his sheets. His mind wandered, at one time he evidently did not realise what his watch was for, and he began to use words wrongly. He often took hold of his blanket and seemed to be trying to hook it on to his bare breast.

During the Thursday night he hardly slept at all and was excited and constantly delirious. He became incoherent and tossed about in bed. His breath became laboured and his pulse weak.

At 2.30 a.m. the Countess Alexandra awoke Chertkóv with the words: 'Papa is very ill!' When he reached the patient Chertkóv found that he was delirious, wishing to dictate something and persistently demanding that they should read him a passage he fancied he had just dictated. To pacify him, Chertkóv read for some time from *A Circle of Reading*. Tolstoy listened attentively and eventually quieted down.

During the last days the doctors administered injections of camphor, digitaline, codeine and morphia. Tolstoy was at times too ill to object, but when he knew that it was proposed to inject morphia he forbade it.

In addition to the doctors already mentioned, he was attended by Dr Berkenheim, whom he knew very well.

Expressions Tolstoy let fall from time to time indicated that he had no fear of death, which he knew might be at hand.

'Ah well! . . . This also is good.' – 'All is simple and good.' – 'It is good . . . yes, yes!' were some of his utterances.

His eldest son, Sergéy, and his eldest daughter Tatiána (Madame Sukhotín) came in every day to attend him. Some of his conversations with his daughter were very touching, not merely from the deep affection they felt for one another but also because of his real concern for his wife, whom he still supposed to be at Yásnaya, ill and in ignorance of his whereabouts. Madame Sukhotín found herself in a very difficult position. She considered that the excitement of knowing that his wife was there, longing to be admitted, might be too much for him. When her father's questions about his wife became too direct to be evaded, she said that it was better not to speak about the matter just then, but when he was stronger she would tell him everything. Tolstoy, not understanding the cause of this reserve, replied: 'But you must understand how *necessary* for my soul it is to know it!' and his eyes filled with tears. Thereon Madame Sukhotín bade him a hurried goodbye and left the room.

Tolstoy's thoughts dwelt much on his wife, especially on the Friday, and he expressed regret and anxiety lest people should think badly of her. 'I think we have not acted considerately,' said he, and then grew drowsy and again became incoherent.

Just then a telegram arrived from the Metropolitan Antonius of Petersburg, urging Tolstoy to return to the bosom of the Church. He was so weak that it was decided not to trouble him with the message, especially as during his illness in the Crimea in 1902 the same bishop had sent him a similar message, in reply to which Tolstoy had said to his son: 'Sergéy, tell these gentlemen that they should leave me in peace . . . How is it they do not understand that even when one is face to face with death, two and two still make four?'

That evening, Abbot Varsonófi arrived from Óptin Monastery by order of the Holy Synod, and asked to be allowed to say a few words to Tolstoy, or even merely to bless the sick man. Tolstoy's wishes being well known, the Abbot was not admitted.

The action of Tolstoy's heart was by this time very weak, and it was decided to call in Dr Shuróvski and Professor Úsov (two leading Moscow physicians) for a consultation.

The first half of Friday night Tolstoy slept fairly well, but later on he became very restless, moaned, and was much troubled by hiccoughs and heartburn.

On Saturday, about 2 p.m., he sat up in bed, and exclaimed in a loud voice: 'This is the end . . . I give you only this advice . . . there are many other people besides Leo Tolstoy in the world, and you attend only to this Leo . . . !' A heart failure followed. His pulse almost stopped, blue spots appeared on ears, lips, nose nd nails, and his feet and hands grew cold. Artificial respiration was resorted to. Camphor and caffeine were injected. Towards evening he again seemed better and took a little milk and gruel.

His general attitude towards his illness is well expressed in a letter he wrote to Chertkóv some ten days before leaving home. Referring to the fainting fits to which he had latterly been subject, he said:

> Till yesterday I thought little of my attacks or did not think of them at all, but yesterday I vividly imagined how I should someday die of one, and I understood that though physically such a death would be quite painless and good, yet spiritually it would deprive me of the precious moments of dying which may be so beautiful. This led me to the thought that if those last conscious moments are to be cut off from me, it is yet in my power to extend them to all the hours, days, maybe months and years (scarcely years) which may yet precede my death. I can treat all those days and months as seriously and solemnly (not externally, but in my inner consciousness) as I should regard my last moments if I knew death to be at hand.

Now that death was actually approaching, he tried hard to adjust himself to the conditions and to learn whatever lessons this fresh experience could yield, but the failure of his mental powers and the acute physical sufferings he occasionally endured caused him perplexity, which found expression in the exclamation: 'I do not understand what I have to do!'

His consciousness that death was near showed itself in disjointed exclamations such as: 'It's time to knock off . . . all is over!' – 'This is the end, and it doesn't matter . . .'

The manner of his death, no less than his bravery in action more than half a century before at Sevastopol and his fearlessness when bear-hunting, shows how mistaken are those who have tried to explain his philosophic and religious opinions as arising from a fear of death. There are passages in *Confession* which may seem to furnish some ground for such an explanation, but no attempt to explain the mentality of so active a thinker by any single idea can really be satisfactory.

For the most part during his last days his mind was clear, his manner to those about him kind, and his interest in life's problems unabated.

Towards midnight on Saturday he was worse and in his delirium repeatedly exclaimed: 'To escape . . . to escape . . . !' A large injection of morphia was administered, his breathing fell from sixty to thirty-six a minute and his pulse grew weaker and weaker. At 4 a.m., when it had become almost indistinguishable and an injection of a solution of salt no longer took effect, his wife – who had long been waiting anxiously close at hand – was admitted to his deathbed. Controlling her agitation she entered quietly and fell on her knees to kiss his hand. He sighed deeply but gave no sign of being conscious of her presence.

Artificial respiration was again resorted to. Tolstoy lay calm and tranquil, but breathed loudly. One might have thought he was sleeping. About 5 a.m. he raised his knee and tried to turn from the light of a candle that was brought near. For some time he continued to breathe quietly, but then gave vent to a whistling sound. About six o'clock his breathing was scarcely audible. His family and friends assembled round the deathbed. 'The last breaths!' said Dr Shuróvski who stood near the head of the bed. A few minutes past six on the morning of Sunday, 7th November 1910 (the 20th, new style), he died calmly and painlessly.

A detailed account of his last illness is given in his daughter Alexandra's article 'Tolstoy's Home-Leaving and Death' in *Family Views of Tolstoy*.

During the week of his illness at Astápovo that country station had been thronged by representatives of the Government, including the Governor of the Province, a special official sent by the Prime Minister, gendarme officers, important railway officials, swarms of pressmen, photographers, cinematographers, and many others.

Having left the dearly loved place of his birth, a tragic fate decreed that Tolstoy, instead of leading the quiet life of poverty and tranquillity he had often longed for, was to give more trouble and be the occasion of more labour to his fellow men than at any previous moment of his life. Besides his family and friends no less than five doctors were in attendance; the station-master had been turned out of his house, many people were living in railway carriages side-tracked at Astápovo for their accommodation; the local telegraphic arrangements almost broke down under the pressure of work put upon them, while the telegraph wires and cables of the world were kept busy with messages concerning the great man who lay dying amid such unusual circumstances, and thousands of columns of printed matter about him were written, set up in type, printed and circulated. Never before had the deathbed of a recluse received such publicity.

The warm sympathy manifested when the news of his illness and death became public proved that despite all mistakes his life and works had greatly endeared him to his fellow countrymen, and to multitudes of others the world over.

The Holy Synod by forbidding the performance of memorial services in the churches, and a small fringe of reactionaries by fierce denunciations in the Dúma and the Press, made the general feeling the more conspicuous by contrast.

The Tsar, the Dúma, and the Council of State, were at one in expressing sorrow at the loss of Russia's greatest writer. All the leading papers appeared with black borders. The private theatres were closed. Petersburg University had no lectures on the day its Honorary Member, Count Leo Tolstoy, was buried, and educational establishments throughout the land did all that was permitted to honour his memory.

The student demonstrations in his honour (taking the form of protests against capital punishment and the flogging of political prisoners in Siberia) led regrettably to the suppression of such self-government as the Russian Universities had enjoyed for several years. This was the work of a reactionary Ministry, which believed in force as a remedy as firmly as Tolstoy believed in the repudiation of physical force.

To understand the affection and admiration so many people felt for Tolstoy, as well as the opposition and dislike he often provoked, one has to remember that his aim was to strengthen the motives which cause men to live in amity, and that no work man can do is more stimulating and important than that. One has also to remember that, in his ardour, Tolstoy formulated the law of Non-Resistance in a shape obscuring the truth he aimed at, and leading to the repudiation of government, law, and property, and that this broke down in his own practice and in that of his followers. It was pathetic to see how tenaciously – in the teeth of all disappointment and all experience – he clung to his dogma. It would be difficult to explain why so sincere a man, often ready enough to admit his mistakes, could not be prevailed on to reconsider his formulation of that principle, had he not himself supplied a key to the puzzle, in *What is Art?* where he says:

I know that most men – not only those considered clever, but even those who are very clever and capable of understanding most difficult scientific, mathematical, or philosophic problems – can very seldom discern even the simplest and most obvious truth if it be such as to oblige them to admit the falsity of conclusions of which they are proud, which they have taught to others, and on which they have built their lives.

That fits his own case exactly. We have also to remember that he was not content with talk, but eager to get something done, to encourage us to show by external changes in our lives that we value goodwill more than material possessions. He therefore sought a categorical imperative with which to drive men forward. In the last analysis he was not at heart a Non-Resister, and his definition of the principle indicates that fact. He wished by moral suasion to *compel* men to abandon things he thought evil, not realising that moral coercion produces reactions as strong as those aroused by physical force, and equally destructive of goodwill.

By discriminating between the nobility of his aim and the method by which he sought to achieve it, one may understand both his strength and his weakness, and then neither the love he evoked nor the opposition he aroused appear perplexing.

Had he been less great his achievements might have been lost sight of in the confusion aroused by the discussion of his Christian-anarchist views and amid the rancour caused by attempts to put those beliefs in practice.

At the age of fifty he seemed for a time to be sinking into pessimistic apathy such as often afflicts those who have finished their work and no longer see anything worth striving for, but by a great effort, sweating drops of blood, he attained a view of life which – despite any errors it contained – filled his soul with a great purpose and kept him young in spirit to the end. All who knew him, even when he was over eighty, felt him to be more alive than most men are at their prime.

That was an appropriate reward for one who believed life to have a noble purpose and was convinced that he could co-operate with the noble and great who are gone, in the work of straightening the crooked ways and smoothing the rough places of the earth.

The day after his death, the train bearing home his corpse slowly made its way from Astápovo. At every station crowds had assembled to pay their last respects. The train only reached Záseka, the nearest station to Yásnaya, about eight o'clock on Tuesday, 9th November.

Though the Ministry had prohibited the special trains that were to have been run from Moscow for the funeral, the station was crowded by peasants, students, and deputations. Foremost among them were the villagers of Yásnaya Polyána, who carried a banner bearing on a white linen band the words: 'Leo Nikoláevich, the memory of your goodness will never fade among us orphaned peasants.'

The coffin was carried by Tolstoy's sons and by the peasants from the station to the home that had so long been his. The procession was nearly a mile long, and included two choirs of students who sang the chorale 'Eternal Memory'. The body was borne to a wooded knoll where, surrounded by nine oaks, a grave had been dug by the peasants. There were no speeches and no service, but many sobs, and the whole crowd knelt while the body was interred.

The spot chosen for the grave was the one where, three-quarters of a century before, the four brothers had played, and where Nicholas was supposed to have buried the green stick on which was written the secret it was the purpose of Leo Tolstoy's whole life to discover and reveal.

To win men's hearts, he who sincerely seeks that message need not fully succeed in his quest. He may even seem to fail, and yet his example may do more to make life worth living than the most brilliant material success could achieve.

Tolstoy never read the whole message, for no mortal has read it completely. But the fact that he sought it supplies the key to all his writings, from *Boyhood* to *I Cannot Be Silent*, and assuredly the author of *Where Love is God is* proclaimed a large part of it.

The love and gratitude that followed him were abundantly earned, for if he was dogmatic – and the letter killeth – he was inspired, and the spirit giveth life.

An Afterword

A *Life of Tolstoy* need not deal lengthily with the disputes and legal proceedings that resulted from Tolstoy's will. That unlucky quarrel had not ended when the Bolshévik Government seized power and confiscated literary, with all other, property.

Much light was thrown on the dispute by an article on 'Tolstoy's Posthumous Works' by M. A. Stakhóvich in *The Russian Review*, University of Liverpool, of May 1913.

Speaking of the disputes about the manuscripts of Tolstoy's work, 'which proclaims malice to be a crime and disputes sinful', Stakhóvich remarks that, 'Moral logic clearly says to both sides: if you believe in your right to inherit from Tolstoy, then renounce your right, and he who considers himself the more closely associated with Tolstoy's teaching, should of course be the first to renounce.' The article was written in consultation with Tatiána Lvóvna Sukhotín, Tolstoy's eldest daughter, 'spiritually very close to her father, as all know, and not a party to the dispute'. She pointed out that her sister Alexandra's right to *publish*, under Chertkóv's editorship, the manuscripts preserved in the Historical Museum, was not in dispute. The whole quarrel had arisen over the manuscripts themselves. In 1911, the year after Tolstoy's death, his widow proposed that copies should be taken of all the manuscripts in the Museum and placed at Alexandra's and Chertkóv's disposal, and that after the copies had been taken she would present the originals to a public institution for permanent preservation. 'My sister and Chertkóv refused this proposal, as is proved by a letter from my sister which my mother preserved. My mother then proposed a court of arbitration. They did not agree to this either; they rejected any agreement at all and claimed full possession of the manuscripts.

'When my mother would not consent to give them the manuscripts from the Museum, they began to resort to every means to force her to do this; . . . they went to the doctor who was treating my mother for nervous trouble and asked him to certify that she was in an irresponsible state.'

She further says that: 'My father never valued his manuscripts as things in themselves, and frequently gave them to those who asked him for them, attaching no importance at all to them . . . All the manuscripts found after his death at Yásnaya Polyána were collected by my mother and handed over to my sister . . . All that my mother wished was that the manuscripts given to her by my father and collected by her should be under the protection of some public institution, and should not fall into the uncontrolled hands of Chertkóv whom she did not trust, as she feared that they would be altered . . .

'Now my own readiness to hand over to Chertkóv all the manuscripts from the Historical Museum has been shaken; here are a few examples of what he has done, as a result of which not only my faith in him, but also my friendship for him, which is of thirty years' standing, has been shattered.

'In his Diary for 1895, on April 27th, my father wrote some profoundly touching pages on the character of his will. Among other things he wrote . . . "In the diary of my married life I ask to have all matter destroyed the publication of which might be unpleasant to anyone. Chertkóv has promised to do this while I am still alive." And during his last years my father gave Chertkóv his diaries in order that everything which might after his death grieve anyone should be cut out. Chertkóv did destroy all these places in the diaries, but, without telling my father, kept for himself photographs of these suppressed parts. Thus, against my father's wishes, all those parts of his diaries which he wrote in moments of irritation and which later he wished to destroy, remain in Chertkóv's possession.

'After my father's death, P. A. Sergéenko sent proof-sheets of the third volume of my father's letters to Chertkóv for examination, and Chertkóv struck out those passages in which my father wrote not bad but good things of my mother.

'When the report of this reached me I would not believe it, and asked my sister about it. She questioned Chertkóv and told me: "Chertkóv does not remember what he struck out, but his rule is that if you may not speak ill of a person, you should not speak well." If he does not remember what he suppressed in my father's writings, it is strange that he always affirms that he never permits himself to alter anything in them.

'Here is another example of Chertkóv's treatment of my father's text. He prints in the newspapers the two following phrases, written to him by my father on the subject of his will: "You are quite correct. I thank you for your part in this matter." But he omits the sentence which intervened, to this effect: "I am not satisfied with the thing as I have done it – I know it could have been done better, but it must stand, for I did not know how to do it better." Unfortunately I must cite from memory, for not only are my father's letters in Chertkóv's hands, but Chertkóv demanded that the letters he wrote to my father should be returned to him.'

Tatiána Lvóvna adds that when, during Tolstoy's last illness, Alexandra sent a wire via the Chertkóvs, to be forwarded to her brother Sergéy, there was undue delay in re-forwarding it. She may have been mistaken about this, and a year later in the same *Review* an indignant reply appeared on Chertkóv's behalf explaining that he was quite innocent in regard to the telegram, but not saying a single word in reply to the charge of deceiving Tolstoy, disregarding his wishes concerning the use of the diaries, and publishing attacks on his wife. About these matters there can be no doubt: Tolstoy's desire to save his wife from blame was known to everyone, and that Chertkóv has utilised his position as Tolstoy's literary executor to issue successive volumes containing attacks on her is notorious.

With the publication of that reply the Editor of the *Review* closed the correspondence.

Stakhóvich had also mentioned that: 'I saw Tolstoy for the last time on 26th October 1910, ten days before his departure. I knew of the will, as did Tatiána Lvóvna and Birukóv, and he knew that neither they nor I approved of it, as we considered it undoubtedly a violation of his doctrine of non-resistance to evil by force . . . When I was leaving, Tolstoy took me aside and said: "I have a great favour to ask of you: promise me to come without fail to Yásnaya Polyána in November, when Tánya [Tatiána Lvóvna] will be here. Do you promise? This is of great importance to me." Of course I assured him that I would come without fail at his first call. He repeated: "We will talk it over with her. This is of great importance to me." This last conversation indicates to me beyond doubt that he had yielded to outside pressure in the question of a will, and that this was worrying him.'

When Tolstoy died he is thought to have been on his way to visit his nephew-in-law Denísenko, who had drafted the previous will for him and with whom he might conveniently have rediscussed the whole matter; but whether in fact he wished once more to change the form or substance of his will we shall now never know.

The inadequacy of the reply published on Chertkóv's behalf is the more noticeable because he is usually capable of defending himself very stoutly when he has firm ground under his feet. For instance, in his book *The Last Days of Tolstoy* (which, though minimising his own share in the tragedy, is an able apologia of his conduct and a scathing indictment of Countess S. A. Tolstoy), he says that recently, in the Paris *Figaro*, he had come across 'a series of articles by Leo Lvóvich Tolstoy in which he strives to cover his father's memory with shame and ignominy, in contradistinction to that of his mother whose image he idealises till it becomes utterly distorted. He is so careless with the facts, that under the influence of his notorious envy and enmity for his father, he tells absolute untruths about him and definitely slanders him, though perhaps without meaning to do so.'

That statement is quite justified. Leo Lvóvich's vindication of his mother, with which one would naturally be inclined to sympathise, loses its efficacy by the recklessness of his statements. His remark about Chertkóv may be more or less defensible:

The most cowardly characteristic of this clever and cruel man's dealings with my father was that he made use of the most underhand means to attain his object. He told my father, in interviews with him and in his letters, everything he could find that was bad concerning my mother and her children, myself included, and thus created unjust and malevolent feelings . . .

My younger sister – who at that time was working in association with my father – was alone exempt from these accusations, the reason being that Chertkóv needed her in connection with the formalities connected with the will (which gave him liberty to dispose as he thought fit of all the author's rights in future editions of my father's books). Chertkóv desired, after my father's death, to have a free hand and to be left in sole control of my father's writings.

But the impression he makes by these statements is lessened by the fact that his book *The Truth About My Father*, contains such amazing blunders as the following: 'After the publication of *The Kreutzer Sonata* my father and mother had yet another son, little Vánichka.' This is simply not true. Iván (Vánichka) was born on 31st March 1888, while *The Kreutzer Sonata* was finished in December 1889, and no child was born to Tolstoy and his wife after that.

The bias indicated by this blunder has caused Leo Lvóvich to make other similar mis-statements. For instance, in an article written for his father's Centenary, and published in the *New York Herald-Tribune* and other papers in England and the USA, he says that Tolstoy had fourteen children (after correctly giving the number as thirteen in his book). When remonstrated with for this exaggeration, he replied that his mother had two miscarriages which might count as one extra baby. Apparently the author of *The Truth About My Father* defines 'truth' in an unusual manner. Some of his mis-statements may be due to sheer carelessness, as for instance, when in the same article he gives the date of Tolstoy's birth, wrongly, as 10th September. Tolstoy was actually born on 28th August, old style, which in the nineteenth century was 9th September. He says his mother 'married at seventeen', whereas she was eighteen. He misquotes a letter to Fet, and referring to *My Religion*,* misquotes from *Confession* instead, and even underlines words he has gratuitously inserted, as follows: '*My family and art* no longer satisfied me. My family consisted of *miserable wretches like myself.*' This is taken, and altered, from the part *of Confession*, Section IV, which says: 'I had a good wife who loved me and whom I loved, good children, and a large estate.'

What are readers to make of such treatment of a father's work by a son?

He also says: 'My father had only one brother' – whereas he had three. Some of his mis-statements appear purposeless, but the general bias noticeable throughout the book may be explained by the remark: 'I was carried away by my father's new religion until I was about twenty-five. I went so far in this direction that I was even ready, as I have stated elsewhere, to refuse to perform military service. I fell ill with a serious nervous malady that lasted for a long period and ended with my marriage. I then renounced Tolstoyism definitely, and my health was re-established.'

What the relations were between Leo Lvóvich (Tígre Tígrovich as a critic had called him) and his father may be gathered from the remark of a correspondent to his eldest sister towards the end of Tolstoy's lifetime.

'At Yásnaya, Leo Lvóvich and Alexandra Lvóvna were particularly harmful – the former by his hatred of his father, and the latter by her hatred of her mother.'

* See pp. 186–7 of *The Truth About My Father*, London, 1924.

Leo Lvóvich visited Yásnaya not long before his father died, and the note in Tolstoy's Diary is: 'Lëva has come. This is a great trial for me', followed a little later by mention of his son's rudeness to him.

The difficulty of clearing up misunderstandings about Tolstoy's life and opinions is not lessened when a son who was in conflict with him publishes, with an air of authority, statements that will not stand the least investigation.

The Book of Samuel tells us that: The sons of Eli were not sons of his spirit, and that remark recurs to one's mind as one reads *The Truth About My Father*.

Another matter calling for comment, since it has attracted some attention, is the announcement of a forthcoming edition of Tolstoy's works, in Russian, in more than a hundred volumes, to contain not only what he wrote for publication, but all the rejected drafts of published and unpublished works, his private diaries, many thousands of his letters, and more than a thousand written by Chertkóv to him.

Nothing more contrary to Tolstoy's wishes could well have been suggested. He always said: 'Gold is got by sifting, and the true sign of an artist is to know what to strike out.' He also said that he wished to be judged only by what he had chosen for publication and of which he had corrected the proofs. Among his posthumous writing he said there was little of value.

Nobody wants to read a hundred volumes of any man's works, and the proposal of such an edition indicates a lack of sense of proportion on the part of its editors. Such an edition, as Macaulay remarked of the voluminous *Burleigh and his Times*, 'might, before the deluge, have been considered as light reading by Hilpa and Shalum. But unhappily the life of a man is now three score years and ten; and we cannot but think it somewhat unfair to demand from us so large a portion of so short an existence.'

Up to the present (November 1929), fifteen months after the Centenary, only a prospectus and three volumes have appeared, and one of the editors tells me that he certainly does not expect to live to see the edition completed. Should the Soviet Government really publish in full what Tolstoy wrote in condemnation of Governments that employ violence or interfere with religious liberty and the freedom of the Press, it will be one of the strangest occurrences in their strange career. *Qui vivra verra*.

The Countess Tolstoy's Later Diary

Brief mention of this *Diary* has been made on pages 557 and 678.

The Countess seems to me to have gone widely astray in the motives she attributed to her husband and in her scorn of his didactic works, but, if often self-deceived, she does not deliberately misstate plain facts. No sane reader of the *Diary* can continue to believe the silly legends that have often been accepted as to Tolstoy having lived like a peasant, earned his living by manual labour, gone about in a beggar's cloak made by himself, or the supremely absurd story of his usually wearing 'county' clothes but changing into peasant garb to impress his visitors.

From such sensational rubbish the Countess delivers us, confirming what all competent witnesses have said as to the external conditions of his life. Yet more valuable is the evidence she unwittingly furnishes that Tolstoy's life at Yásnaya became wellnigh unendurable, and that he cannot have borne it for the sake of creature comforts but must have done so from a sense of duty and – as he told me himself – in order not to anger his wife.

That the effects of his change of views about property bore very severely on her life and clashed with her sense of family duty is evident. One must sympathise with her though her *Diary* is full of contradictions. Evidently her mind and nerves were unbalanced and at times she was so acutely hostile to her husband as to consider any stick good enough to beat him with. She sets down denunciations one day in flat contradiction to what she recounts the next.

The recurring strife over the property and over the control of her husband's writings, her groundless jealousy, and her disapproval of conjugal intercourse – which may have been partly an effect of *The Kreutzer Sonata* – her dislike and disparagement of his friends, her open contempt for ideals he held sacred and the work to which he was devoting his whole soul, as well as the growth of her suicidal mania, must often have made Tolstoy's life at Yásnaya a very hell, and rendered his eventual escape from it inevitable.

In the first volume of her *Diary*, on 17th January 1863, the Countess had written with much discernment: 'I have just been in a bad temper and angry because he loves everybody and everything, while I want him to love only me . . . Now, *by myself*, I have come to see that I am again being perverse: he is good with his kindness and wealth of feeling. If one comes to think of it, the real source of all my perverseness, grief, and so on, is my selfish wish that his whole life, his thoughts and his love, should belong to me . . . My misfortune is my jealousy.' Had she remembered this in later years things might have turned out differently.

To keep a balance when reading her condemnations of her husband in this second volume of her *Diary*, it is well to read what Tolstoy himself wrote when his love for his wife received its first severe setback at the time of his eldest son's birth. Here is the passage: '5th August 1863. Her character grows worse from day to day. I recognise in her Pólenka [his aunt Ushkóv] and Máshenka [his sister Márya] with their grumblings and querulous rattle. True, this happens when she is unwell, but her unfairness and deliberate selfishness frighten and torment me. Someone told her, and she has imbibed it, that husbands do not love wives who are ailing, and she feels confident that this justifies her. Or is it that she never loved me, but deceived herself? I looked through her diary – covert animosity towards me seems to breathe from under words of tenderness; and it is often so in our life. If that is so, and the whole matter a mistake on her side, it is terrible. To have given up everything – not as other men do, who on marrying give up a dissolute bachelor life at Dusseaux's,* and their mistresses – but to have exchanged all the poetry of love, of thought, and of activity among the people, for poetry of the domestic hearth with its egotism towards all except one's family, and instead of that to have the troubles of an eating-house, baby-powders, and jam-making, together with grumblings, and devoid of all that can brighten family life, without love or a peaceful and dignified family happiness, and with nothing but paroxysms of tenderness, kisses, and so on. It depresses me terribly. I can't yet believe it is so. I am quite well and have not been upset all day – on the contrary. In the morning I come in happy and cheerful, and see the Countess, who is in a temper and whose hair the maid Dúshka is combing, and I recall Máshenka at her bad period, and everything collapses – and as if I had been scalded, I feel frightened of everything, and realise that it is only

* smart restaurants in Moscow and Petersburg

when I am alone that I can be at ease and in a poetic mood. I am kissed with customary tenderness, and then she begins nagging at Dúshka, at Auntie, at [her sister] Tánya, at me and at everything, and I cannot bear it calmly, because all this is not merely wrong but dreadful when compared with what I desire. I don't know what I would not do for the sake of our happiness; but she can debase and defile our relations so as to make it seem as though I grudged her a horse or a peach. No use explaining. There is nothing to explain . . . But as soon as there is the least glimmer of understanding and feeling, I am again quite happy and believe that she understands things as I do. One believes what one greatly desires, and if it torments only myself I am content. And there is in her the same trait as in Máshenka, a kind of unhealthy and capricious self-assurance and a resignation to her supposedly unhappy fate.'

Such a passage is exceptional in Tolstoy's Diary, for generally he is concerned to find all possible excuses for his wife's conduct and to dwell on what he may himself have done wrong and on the good he saw in her – her devotion to the children and so forth. Indeed it helps an understanding of the case to note in his Diary the readiness to make the best of her, and in hers the readiness to show him at his worst.

Two months after the extract quoted above, he wrote: 'It has all blown over and was not true. I am happy with her; but terribly dissatisfied with myself.' The former entry, however, gives an indication of the discord which, fifteen years later, instead of diminishing, increased, and eventually drove a wedge between the two which completely separated them.

The first fifteen years of the Tolstoys' married life were, on the whole, happy ones, and *War and Peace* is far from being a depressing book; but that Tolstoy even then had a perception of the coming trouble and of its cause is shown by the passage in Chapter VIII of the First Book of *War and Peace*, where Prince Andrew exhorts Pierre not to marry, 'or all that is good and noble in you will be lost. It will all be wasted on trivialities'; and by the equally striking passage almost at the end of the book, in Chapter X of the First Epilogue, where Tolstoy tells us how surprised Pierre was to discover Natásha's opinion that 'every moment of his life belonged to her and to their family'.

The fundamental clash did indeed result from the wife's desire that her husband should belong to her absolutely, to the exclusion of everything that hindered her monopolisation of him, and when, after about 1880, he wished to abandon his material interests and those of the family for the sake of ideals she feared and disliked, the conflict was intensified. The feeling that she was being neglected and wronged soured her love for her husband, and in her *Diary* she instinctively noted down everything that could put him in the wrong and justify her resentment. The change of life evidently had a considerable effect on her. On 10th February 1891 she wrote: 'I am not feeling too well myself. I did not sleep all night, and certain things depress me terribly every month.' This, together with the economic strife already dividing them, sufficed to make the later 1880s and the following years very difficult. There are many indications that *The Kreutzer Sonata* added fuel to the fire. It is difficult even for ordinary readers to peruse that powerful work without being inclined, at least temporarily, to regard conjugal relations as repellent, and this influence is particularly apt to operate on women at their critical period and to intensify other causes of dissension between a husband and wife.

On 23rd April 1891 she notes: 'It is cold and bright. Tánya has just gone past, and said that Lëvochka [Tolstoy] told her to tell me that he had gone to bed and had put out the light. Her innocent lips have transmitted words that are far from innocent. I know what they mean and I am vexed.'

On 15th January 1895: 'I have not yet come to myself but feel even more depressed, either from weariness at the sight of Vánichka and [young] Lëva both ill, or because my periods are coming on too often (every three weeks) and this acts on my nerves and on my state of mind.'

On 21st February of the same year: 'I have gone through and am going through, another painful period of my life. I feel disinclined to write, it is so depressing and terrible, and it is so clear to me that from now on my life will decline. I do not at all regret it, and the thought of suicide is more and more persistent. May God preserve me from such a sin.'

The same day she adds: 'The nerve specialist ordered bromide; the dietetic specialist ordered a mixture and Vichy water, while Snegirëv, the gynaecologist, gave me something else, making a cynical remark about my "critical period". I didn't touch any of the medicines. I am no better.'

6th June 1895: 'I could not sleep at night – a pain in my back, a headache, and such terrible melancholy. This depression must be due to my "critical" period.'

Tolstoy's intense absorption in what he wrote, and the indifference and even aversion the Countess generally felt to his works when they were not novels, is apparent in her *Diary*.

On 20th February 1891, after 'an unpleasant talk' with his wife and the two Gays about married life and the pain a husband experiences when his wife misunderstands him, Tolstoy remarked: 'When with pangs of childbirth you produce a new thought, changing your whole spiritual outlook, you are reproached for your sufferings and people want to ignore it'. To this the Countess replied that, 'while he was giving birth to all the spiritual children he had invented, we, with real pain, gave birth to real children, who have to be fed and brought up (and the property has to be looked after), so when is there time to upset one's life for the sake of a husband's spiritual changes – to keep up with which is impossible, and which, after all, are only things to be regretted?'

The clash could not be more clearly stated. The children, physical pain and the property were real to her, while what Tolstoy was creating with utmost stress of soul were 'things to be regretted'. What tragedy, for such a man, could be greater?

An entry on 18th June 1897 throws light on the distressing incident, previously mentioned, of Tolstoy's leaving home just before Alexandra's birth. The Countess writes: 'This is Sásha's birthday. She is thirteen. What a depressing memory I have of her birth! I remember we were all sitting at tea that evening – the Kuzmínskys were staying with us, as well as Madame Seuron, the governess, and her son Alcide (who, poor boy, died later of cholera). We were talking about horses. I told Lëv Nikoláevich that he ran everything at a loss. He had had some wonderful stud horses in Samára and had lost them all: so that neither horses nor money were left, though they had cost thousands. (That was true, but is not the point.) He was always attacking me, who was pregnant – probably my appearance displeased him, and all that last period he had been irritable with me. But this time, one word following another, he grew terribly angry, put some things in a linen bag, and said he was leaving home for good – perhaps going to America – and in spite of my entreaties he went off.

'Just then my labour-pains began. I was suffering – and he wasn't there. I sat alone on a bench in the garden and the pangs grew worse and worse – and still he was not there. Lëva, my son, and Alcide came and asked me to go in and lie down. But I was as though paralysed by sorrow. The midwife arrived and my sister and the girls, who were crying. They took me under the arms and led me upstairs to my bedroom. The pangs became more frequent and stronger. At last, after four in the morning, he returned.

'I went downstairs to him and found him angry and gloomy. "Lëvochka," I said, "the pangs have begun, I am just going to be confined. Why are you so angry? Forgive me, if I am to blame. I may not survive this birth." He remained silent. And suddenly it occurred to me that he might again be feeling jealous or suspicious. And I said: "Whether I live or die, I must tell you that I shall die true to you in body and mind: I have never loved anyone but you . . ."

'He looked round suddenly and gazed fixedly at me, but did not say a single kind word to me. I left him and an hour later Sásha was born.

'I gave her over to a wet nurse. I could not then nurse a baby, as Lëv Nikoláevich had handed all the affairs over to me, so that I had suddenly to bear both the man's and the woman's burdens.

'What a hard time it was! And that was when he turned to *Christianity*. And in that Christianity it was I, of course, who bore the *martyrdom*, not *he*.'

We here get a hint of the provocation given to Tolstoy, and an indication of the fact that he left home not knowing that the birth was so imminent. The incident occurred in 1884, when he was absorbed in the idea that the possession of property by the rich is the cause of the sufferings of the poor, and nothing could have been more distressing to him than his wife's reference to the fact that, years previously, he had lost expensive horses on his Samára estate by mismanagement. With the marked changes of outlook that occurred in his life, his wife's habit of mixing up the past with the present was not merely a source of irritation, but an indication that she did not *wish* to understand or share the thoughts that were so important to him. In this same entry she repeats, as she often did, the opinion of which Tolstoy, years before, had remarked that someone had told it her and that she had imbibed it and used it in self-justification. This time it appears in this form: 'probably my appearance displeased him'. She adds: 'It was I, of course, who bore the *martyrdom*, and not *he*.' In Tolstoy's opinion the reverse was the case, and it is a matter on which neither of them could claim to be an entirely impartial witness.

The Countess wrote her *Diary* with no thought of publication, and largely as a vent for vexation when things went amiss. A wife who wishes to, can generally say things of her husband which sound dreadful and have some grains of truth in them but yet are very misleading. In the case of the Countess it is useful sometimes to set what she wrote one day beside what she wrote on another. For instance: –

On 26th January 1895 she wrote: 'No one will ever know that he [Tolstoy] never gave his wife a rest and never – in all these thirty-two years – gave his child a drink of water, or spent five minutes by his bedside to give me a chance to rest a little, to sleep, or go for a walk, or even just recover from all my labours.'

On 11th August 1897: 'Mary [her daughter] was seized with pains in her stomach. Leo Nikoláevich got out of bed and was going to heat the samovar himself to prepare a fomentation, but found that the kitchen stove was still hot enough to warm the napkins in the oven. I am always amused when he tries to do anything practical, he does it in such a primitive, naïve, and awkward way.'

When he does not attend to the children, she says he 'never' does so, and when he does attend to them, she notes his clumsiness.

After the birth of their eldest son she had described with what touching eagerness and care he warmed the milk and fed the child, and on 28th February 1865 she had written to her sister that towards his son, Sergéy, Tolstoy had 'become very tender and is always occupied with him', but that 'he never even looks at Tánya [his daughter], which offends and surprises me'. But on 21st March 1866 she writes that 'Lëvochka has gone quite mad over Tánya'. And Tolstoy himself wrote to his wife from Moscow on 14th November that year: 'I picture little Tánya to myself and beam at the thought of her.'

On 6th March 1891 she notes: 'After dinner, for exercise, I joined Lëvochka in playing with the children: Sásha, Ványa and Küzka. After dinner every day Lëvochka goes all over the house with them, puts them into an empty basket, carries them about, covered over, and then stops somewhere and tells the one who is in the basket to guess which room he is in.'

On 26th September 1897, she notes: 'I spent our wedding day on the 23rd very pleasantly, though without any special celebration. It was the thirty-fifth anniversary, and difficult and complicated as my life has been at times, I thank God that we have remained faithful to one another and are now living peacefully and even lovingly.'

On 7th November that year, after a visit to his brother Sergéy at Pirogóvo, she writes: 'We wished to leave there on Tuesday, but it was raining and the roads were slippery, so we stayed on. Next day there was a terrible wind and I was afraid Leo Nikoláevich would catch cold, so we again stayed on. But yesterday my boredom reached a climax and we decided to go to Yásnaya. There was again a strong wind. Leo Nikoláevich did the whole twenty-four miles on horseback cheerfully and gaily, while I travelled in a sledge, and was more anxious about him than I have been for a long time; so insignificant did *all* other interests and fancies seem to me compared to the fear of a cold, an illness, or possibly the death, of my husband!

'We reached home in three hours, and did not catch cold, thank God. At Yásnaya Leo and Dora [her son and daughter-in-law] met us affectionately, and what a paradise Yásnaya Polyána seemed to me compared to Pirogóvo! We dined at Leo's [her son's] quarters, and in the evening heated our own stove . . .

'The two of us drank tea together cheerfully. Lëvochka himself made my bed for me, and was still so vigorous after his twenty-four mile ride that he made love to me . . . I note this as an indication of his remarkable vigour, for he is seventy years old! . . . This morning soft fluffy snow was falling. There was no wind, but a slight frost in the pure air. We drank coffee together, tidied up our rooms, received letters from nearly all the children, and were glad of them; we looked at the papers and then I went, again in a sledge, to Yasenkí station and took the train to Moscow. We parted affectionately and Leo Nikoláevich even thanked me for having helped him so much by copying his work on Art. Today we sent off the further chapters, 12th and 13th, to England for Maude to translate.'

Such passages as these last afford some relief to the gloom of the *Diary*, but its general tenor is one of protest and complaint.

Certainly the wife's position was a very trying one, for some of Tolstoy's cherished ideas had never been satisfactorily put in practice and she was certainly not likely to achieve what even his most ardent disciples had not accomplished, but her eagerness to place the worst interpretation on her husband's actions and motives makes her *Diary* distressing reading, and when she deals not with facts, but with what she supposes people may think about herself, her conjectures throw light chiefly on her own state of mind. For instance, she was anxious to get all she could from the sale of her husband's works, and considered it a duty to her children to do so, for the landed estates were not bringing in much revenue. Also, as she mentioned to the Emperor, she wanted to edit her husband's works as well and therefore as completely as possible.

These were solid reasons for her visit to Petersburg and for asking the Censor and the Emperor to allow volume thirteen of her edition to be passed for publication; but when she sits down to her *Diary* to recount her success in this matter she does not mention either of these two main motives, and barely mentions the other articles in that volume, but writes almost exclusively about *The Kreutzer Sonata* which was admittedly the most valuable portion of it – and the line she takes is an impossible one. She does not say that *The Kreutzer Sonata* was too valuable for her to submit to its suppression. What she says is, that she does not know why people suspected the story of being directed against her and describing her own family life, and that her motive in petitioning was that when people heard that she had interceded with the Emperor for the removal of the ban, they would conclude that such suspicions were false.

Possibly some people may really have thought what she supposed they did, but if so, such people would hardly have arrived at the very subtle conclusion she wished them to reach, merely because they learnt that she had asked the Emperor to allow her to publish a very valuable work.

Possessed by the idea that she was wronged, neglected and mis-understood, and troubled by the thought of what people might say of her during her life or after her death, she elaborated a variety of accusations against her husband as a justification of herself and in reply to her own doubts as to the rightness of her conduct.

Tolstoy was a remarkable man and an heroic writer, and many who are not worthy to black his boots – some who have never even read his novels or stories – are eager to seize on and expand any disparagement of him. It is as difficult to plumb the depths of human meanness as it is to reach the height of man's nobility of soul, and Tolstoy's venomous detractors eagerly welcomed this *Diary*.

On 7th February 1891, when Tánya was feverish, Mísha had a head-ache, her son Lëva had not written, and the Countess was feeling generally upset, she notes: 'It is the second evening that I have wanted to drive to Kozlóvka with Lëvochka, but he has always gone on horse-back as if on purpose. He is again gloomy, unnatural and unpleasant. Yesterday in the evening I was very angry with him, though I did not say anything about it. At first he was downstairs, washing himself a long time. I began to think he was ill. Washing is for him an event. He told me that he had such hard places on his feet that they had begun to hurt him under the hard skin. I shrank with disgust ... Then he lay down and read for a long time ... These days of my aversion for the physical side of my husband's life are terribly hard for me – but I cannot, cannot accustom myself – I never shall get accustomed to dirt, and smell'.*

'Washing is for him an event' probably means that he avoided having a bath at home, where it involved giving the servants the trouble of heating the water and carrying it to the bath-tub, and emptying the tub afterwards. Personally Tolstoy was scrupulously clean, except perhaps when so absorbed in field-work – as described in *Anna Karénina*, Part III, Chapters IV to VI – that he paid no attention to anything else for whole days. Having accompanied him myself to the public Russian Baths in Moscow, I know how thoroughly he washed, and when I bathed with him in the river and in the pond at Yásnaya, I saw how he soaped himself before plunging into the water, and am therefore surprised at his wife's remark, though I realise that her *Diary* was for her a vent for letting off the steam of her dissatisfaction. 'The dirt, the smell', thrown in to complete the picture of what she had to put up with, does not apparently relate to her husband personally but to his surroundings, and may be compared with the entry where she unnecessarily excuses herself to herself for living comfortably in Moscow during the winter and not with him at Yásnaya, and recalls an unpleasant week she did spend there with him.

21st October 1897: ' ... I had a cold and stand-offish letter from Leo Nikoláevich. He has tried to be kind to me – but it has not come off. Probably he is vexed that I am living in Moscow and not with him at Yásnaya, where from morning to night I should have been copying for him.' [Tolstoy had told her that he did not want her to copy for him as he had made other arrangements, and she had been offended at the thought that she was being thrust aside, but still when she copies out anything he has written she makes a grievance of it in the *Diary*.] 'But I cannot, I cannot any more! I am tired, and old; broken in spirit, and perhaps I am spoilt. I often remember the week I spent there: dirt in the yard, dirt in the two rooms I occupied with Leo Nikoláevich. Four mousetraps continually clicking with the mice they caught. Mice, mice

---

* This passage is mistranslated in the published English translation of the *Diary* in a way that gives a very unpleasant impression of Tolstoy's personality.

endlessly . . . the cold, empty house, the grey sky, drizzling rain and darkness: the crossing through the mud from house to house with a lantern to dinner and supper at Lëva's [her son's quarters in the "wing" house]; writing, writing from morning to night, smoky samovars, no servants and deadly silence: terribly hard and gloomy is my life at Yásnaya these days. Here [in Moscow] it is better.'

The picture is depressing, but some wives comfortably established in Moscow with family and servants, would have been less distressed about the hardships they had endured for a week in the country than about a husband seventy years old who preferred to stay the winter at Yásnaya so as to work quietly and escape from constant reproaches. She was partly aware of this herself, and on 1st January 1895 had written: 'I fear that whenever I write my Diary I begin condemning Leo Niko-láevich. But I cannot help complaining that the things he preaches for people's happiness complicate life so much that it becomes harder and harder for me . . . When these complications grow too great I get angry, say hard things, feel unhappy at having done so, and repent when it is too late.'

How little she cared for or understood the things that were vital to him can be judged by an entry made when she was vexed because he allowed *Master and Man* to appear in a periodical before she could publish it in book form:

26th January 1895: ' . . . I am vexed that he should have given it to the *Northern Messenger*. One cannot understand him at all. If he had given it freely to the *Intermediary*, everyone would have bought it for twenty kopeks and would have read Tolstoy's story – that I could understand. But now the public will have to pay thirteen rubles [a year's sub-scription to the periodical] before they can read this story. That is why I do not share my husband's *ideas* – because he is not sincere and not truthful. Everything is invented, artificial and far-fetched, and the basis is wrong – it is chiefly vanity everywhere, an endless thirst for fame, an invincible desire to become more and more popular. No one will believe me, but I suffer from it all, and others do not see it – besides, to them it is all the same.'

The poor Countess worked herself up into a paroxysm over this tale, *Master and Man*, and tells in her *Diary* a very painful story of an attempt to commit suicide in her distress at someone getting it before her. She gives herself away by the remark that it would have been better to let the *Intermediary* have it for their cheap series of booklets, for in fact when Tolstoy did let the *Intermediary* have anything of his before the Countess, she was almost as indignant as she was about *Master and Man*, which, by the way, came out promptly in book form in her edition, in another Petersburg edition, and in the *Intermediary*'s series, as well as serially in the *Northern Messenger*. The fact that there should have been all this fuss and such fierce denunciation of her husband's intentions and motives, just because he allowed his new story to appear in a periodical, shows how hard it was for him to carry out his principle of not letting his writings become family property.

There is another entry in the *Diary* the same day which is equally illuminating.

She says: 'It is now past 1 a.m. Lëvochka has gone to some Committee Meeting called by Prince Dmitry Shakhovskóy [a leader of the Liberal movement and later Secretary to the first Dúma], I don't know what about. All the lamps are burning, the servants are waiting, and I have just prepared his oatmeal porridge, and have been pasting some proof-sheets in their places, while they there are *talking*. And tomorrow at 8 o'clock I shall get up to take Vánichka's temperature and give him his quinine, but *he* will be sleeping. Then he will go out to haul the water-tub, without even knowing whether the child is better or its mother overtaxed.'

The meeting about which she was so scornful and cared so little was called to consider Nicholas II's reply to the Zémstvo delegates, who had gone to congratulate him on his accession and expressed a hope that the elected representatives of the people would be allowed to cooperate in the government of the country. Nicholas had stamped his foot and told them to abandon such 'insensate fancies', and the Liberals were faced with the serious problem whether they should abandon all hope of progress towards a constitution under which the people might be allowed to influence the Government's decisions, or do what they could to save the country from the autocratic rule that was steering it headlong to destruction.

Whether such a meeting – attendance at which involved personal danger – should be regarded as proof of indifference to the family's welfare, is a problem it is unnecessary now to discuss.

It is hopeless to try to understand the state of affairs from the wife's *Diary* alone; one has to compare it with Tolstoy's view of the case, which is best shown by a letter, only recently published, which he wrote and handed to his wife on 14th July 1910, a few days before he made his last will and less than four months before his death. It shows that Tolstoy was then still seeking a reconciliation though his power of endurance was near its limit. It also indicates that had the Countess's mental condition at that time made it possible for her to respond reasonably, not only might their long life together have terminated amicably, but she might even have obtained a large part of her desire regarding the control of her husband's works.

This letter was written in reply to her insistent demands that seven notebooks of Tolstoy's Diary, which had been taken away during her absence from home in November 1909, should be recovered from Chertkóv. Tolstoy wrote:

1. I will not give my private Diary of these latter days to anyone; I will keep it myself.

2. I will take back from Chertkóv the Diary of previous years, and will keep it, placing it probably in a Bank.

3. If you are anxious lest certain pages in my Diary, written under a momentary impression and where our conflicts and disagreements are mentioned, should be made use of by hostile biographers, I want first of all to point out that such expressions of transitory feelings, in my Diary as in your own, cannot give at all a correct idea of our true relations, but if you fear it, I will gladly take the opportunity of saying in my Diary, or in a letter, how I understand and appreciate your life.

As I loved you when you were young, and have not ceased to love you in spite of various causes of coldness between us, I love you still. Without speaking of the interruption of our conjugal relations (for that could only render the expression of real love more sincere), these causes of coldness were: (1) my increasing alienation from worldly life, while you could not cease to be interested in it and did not wish to because the principles which led me to my convictions clashed with your feelings profoundly; that was quite natural and I cannot reproach you for it.

Forgive me if what I am going to say is disagreeable to you; but what is happening between us just now is so important that one must not fear to say and to hear the whole truth. Your character has become, these last years, more and more irritable, despotic and unrestrained. The manifestation of these traits could not fail to chill, if not the feeling itself at least its expression . . .

Thirdly, the chief and fatal cause, one for which we are neither of us guilty, is the conflicting ideas we hold as to the sense and aim of life. Everything is opposed in our conceptions of life, in our way of living and our attitude towards other men, and our way of regarding property – which I consider a sin and you consider an indispensable condition of life. In order not to separate myself from you I have submitted to the painful conditions of our life, while you have considered this submission to be a yielding to your views, and the misunderstanding between us has grown greater and greater.

What is important is the fact that I have not ceased to love you and appreciate you despite all the past misunderstandings . . . I cannot reproach you for not having followed me in my unusual spiritual course, for the inner life of every human being is a secret between him and God, and other men must not demand anything of him: and if I have shown myself exacting towards you, I have been mistaken, and confess my error . . .

4. If my present relations with Chertkóv distress you, I am ready to give up seeing him, though I must tell you that this will be disagreeable and painful both for him and for me; but if you demand it, I will do it.

5. If you do not accept these conditions for a peaceable and kindly life, I shall take back my promise not to leave you. I shall go away, but certainly not to Chertkóv's; I will even make it an absolute condition that he shall not come to live near me, but I will certainly go away, for it is impossible for me to live like this any longer. I could have continued this life were I able to bear your sufferings with tranquillity, but I am not able . . . Consider it well, my dear friend, listen to your heart, respond, and you will decide all as it should be decided. As for me, I have decided in any case that I cannot act otherwise. I am not able to . . . Cease, my dear one, to torture not others but yourself, for you are suffering a hundred times more than the others. That is all.

14th July in the morning.

LEO TOLSTOY

A third portion of the Countess's *Diary*, from 1898 to 1905, is in preparation, and there may even be a fourth volume from 1906 onwards. As the end approached she became more and more mentally unbalanced and the *Diary* of those later years may provide yet more painful reading.

Some great men have owed the success of their work largely to the domestic tranquillity their wives have secured for them; but Tolstoy to the age of eighty-two carried on his work in spite of acute suffering inflicted on him by his wife's utter lack of sympathy with what he valued most highly. The search for the 'green stick' of universal welfare, to which he devoted his life, was to her merely an obstacle to the pursuit of financial prosperity for her family.

Poor woman! She did her duty according to her lights for many years. Mated to a mediocre husband she might have passed as a model wife and mother. Let us not judge her harshly if she broke down when tried by tests beyond her strength.

One effect of reading her *Diary*, and of the knowledge that its sequel may prove even more virulent and unbalanced, has been to suggest to me that perhaps there is more excuse than I had quite realised for the apparently insensate animosity with which V. G. Chertkóv pursued her. If he knew the anguish and distress she was causing her husband, of whom he was a fanatical partisan, Chertkóv may have thought himself justified in the intrigues and the 'conspiratorial' methods by which he drove the unhappy woman to distraction.

As the years pass and more and more evidence accumulates, the main outline of Tolstoy's figure becomes increasingly definite and clear, but the fresh evidence that becomes available from time to time may modify our judgement of the comparative responsibility of those who by their insensate bickerings drove him from his home and to his death. On that question the last word has perhaps not yet been spoken, but if there is more evidence to come, let us hope it will not tend to divert attention from the literary inheritance Russia's greatest, frankest, and sincerest writer has bequeathed to mankind.

Chronology

As in the text, dates are given old style, except those relating to Tolstoy's travels in Western Europe.

1645 Peter Tolstoy born.

1725 Peter Tolstoy made a Count.

1727 Peter Tolstoy exiled.

1822 Marriage of Tolstoy's parents.

1828 28 August o.s. (= 9 September n.s.). Birth of Leo Tolstoy.

1830 7 September. Death of Leo Tolstoy's mother.

1837 Death of father.

1838 Death of grandmother.

1841 Death of aunt, Countess Osten-Sáken. Move to Kazán.

1844 Matriculates at Kazán University.

1847 Leaves University.

1849 Passes two examinations at Petersburg University.

1851 20 April. Leaves Yásnaya for Caucasus.
Goes as volunteer on expedition from Starogládovsk.
November. At Tiflis; writing *Childhood*.

1852 13 February. Enters army.
17–18 February. Nearly killed in action.
September. *Childhood* appears in *Contemporary*.

1853 January. Expedition against Shámyl.
16–17 February. Nearly killed by grenade.
March. *The Raid* appears in *Contemporary*.
13 June. Nearly captured by Tartars.

1854 January. Receives his commission.
2 February. Reaches Yásnaya Polyána.
March. War declared: England and France against Russia.
12 March. Tolstoy reaches the army in Bucharest.
June (end). Siege of Silistria abandoned.
14 September. Allies land in Crimea.
October. *Boyhood* appears in *Contemporary*.
November. Tolstoy reaches Sevastopol.

1854 16 November. Stationed at Simferópol.

1855 January. *Recollections of a Billiard Marker* published.

13 April to 27 May. Serves in Sevastopol, in Fourth Bastion.

May. *Sevastopol in December* published.

16 August (n.s.). In battle of Tchérnaya.

September. *Sevastopol in May* published.

The Wood-Felling published.

8 September (n.s.). Malákhov captured by French.

Sevastopol abandoned by Russians.

November. Tolstoy returns to Petersburg.

1856 January. *Sevastopol in August* published.

January (end). Death of Dmítri Tolstoy.

March. Russia concludes peace with England,
France, and Turkey.

March. *The Snow Storm* published.

May. *Two Hussars* published.

Summer. Entanglement with V. V. Arsénev.

November. Grand Duke Michael displeased about Soldiers' Song.

26 November. Tolstoy leaves the Army.

December. *Meeting a Moscow Acquaintance in the Detachment*
published.

December. *A Landlord's Morning* published.

1857 January. *Youth* published.

10 February (n.s.). Leaves Moscow for Paris.

April. Visits Switzerland.

July. At Lucerne.

August. Returns to Yásnaya Polyána.

September. *Lucerne* published.

1858 March. Visits Petersburg. Helps to found Moscow Musical
Society.

August. *Albert* published.

22 December. Nearly killed by a bear.

1859 January. *Three Deaths* published.

4 February. Speaks to Society of Lovers of Russian Literature.

April. *Family Happiness* published.

Winter. Organises School at Yásnaya.

1860 14 July (n.s.). Leaves Petersburg for Berlin.

2 October (n.s.). Nicholas Tolstoy died at Hyères.

December. In Italy.

1861   January. Revisits Paris.
  February and March. Visits London.
  April. Returns to Russia.
  26 May. Challenges Turgénev.
  June. Commences work as Arbiter of the Peace.
1861-2 Winter. Occupied with his school.
1862   February. *Yásnaya Polyána* magazine appears.
  May. Released from office of Arbiter of the Peace.
  May and June. Takes *kumys* cure in Samára Government.
  6 July. Police raid at Yásnaya Polyána.
  16 September. Proposes to Miss S. A. Behrs.
  23 September. Marries.
  3 October. Minister of Interior disapproves of *Yásnaya Polyána* magazine.
1863   January. *The Cossacks* published.
  February. *Polikúshka* published.
  28 June. Eldest son, Sergius, born.
  Autumn. *War and Peace* commenced.
1864   26 September. Breaks his arm while hunting.
  4 October. Birth of daughter, Tatiána.
1865   February. First part of *War and Peace* published.
1866   22 May. Second son, Ilyá, born.
  16 July. Defends soldier at court martial.
1867   Summer. Treated by Zahárin for indigestion.
  Publication of *War and Peace* continued.
1869   20 May. Third son, Leo, born.
  November. *War and Peace* completed.
1869-70
  Studies the drama.
1870-1 Winter. Studies Greek.
1871   12 February. Birth of daughter, Mary.
  June–July. *Kumys* cure in Samára.
  September. Works at *ABC Book*.
1872   January. Restarts school.
  A Prisoner in the Caucasus published.
  February. *God Sees the Truth* published.
  13 June. Son, Peter, born.
  September. Confined to Yásnaya by Investigating Magistrate.
  12 November. *ABC Book* published.

1873   June. Goes with family to Samára.
          28 July. Samára Famine: Tolstoy's appeal.
          September. Kramskóy paints his portrait.
          9 November. Death of son, Peter.

1874   15 January. Speaks on Learning to Read.
          20 June. Death of Aunt Tatiána.
          September. Published article, *On Popular Education*.

1875   January–April. First instalments of *Anna Karénina* published.
          May. New *ABC Book* published.

1875   Summer. Horse races at Samára.
          1 November. Baby daughter, Vavára, born and died.
          December. Death of Pelagéya I. Yúshkov.

1876   January–April & December. Further instalments of *Anna Karénina*.
          September. Visit to Samára and Orenburg.

1877   January–April. Final instalment of *Anna Karénina* published.
          Rupture with Katkóv.
          6 December. Son, Andrew, born.

1878   March. Visits Petropávlov Fortress.
          May. Reconciliation with Turgénev.
          7 August. Turgénev at Yásnaya Polyána.

1878–9 Writing *Confession* (with an addition in 1882).

1879   20 December. Son, Michael, born.

1880   Spring. At work on *A Criticism of Dogmatic Theology*.

1881   March. Letter to the Tsar.
          June. Visits Óptin Monastery.
          Summer. At work on *A Union of the Four Gospels*.
          What Men Live By published.
          31 October. Son, Alexéy, born.

1881–2 Wrote *A Union and Translation of the Four Gospels*.

1882   Slumming in Moscow.
          Autumn. Buys house in Moscow.
          Winter. Studies Hebrew.
          Drops his title. Does manual labour.

1883   January. Writing *What I Believe*.
          September. Refuses Jury Service.

1884   January. *What I Believe* forbidden.
          The Decembrists published.
          18 June. Daughter, Alexandra, born.
          His works published by his wife.

1885 Visits Crimea.

The *Intermediary* founded.

Writes *Where Love is, God is*.

Writes *Two Old Men*.

Autumn. Becomes a vegetarian.

Renounces Hunting and Smoking.

1886 Writes *The First Distiller*, *The Imp and the Crust*, and other stories.

18 January. Death of son, Alexéy.

14 February. Finishes *What Then Must We Do?*

Summer. Haymaking and hut building.

Iván the Fool written.

The Death of Iván Ilych published.

Has erysipelas, and writes *The Power of Darkness*.

1887 Summer. Writes *On Life*.

Autumn. Writes *The Empty Drum*.

1888 22 February. *The Power of Darkness* performed in Paris.

31 March. Son, Iván, born.

1888 Publishes *The Story of a Horse* (written long before).

Winter. Writes *Culture's Holiday*.

1889 Writes Preface to Ershóv's *Recollections of Sevastopol*.

December. Finishes *The Kreutzer Sonata*.

30 December. *The Fruits of Enlightenment* performed at Yásnaya.

1890 Répin's picture: 'Tolstoy in his room'.

Countess Tolstoy obtains the Tsar's permission to publish *The Kreutzer Sonata*.

Tolstoy denounced as Antichrist.

1891 24 January. First performance of *The Fruits of Enlightenment* in Moscow.

Writes *Why Do Men Stupefy Themselves?*

19 September. Renounces copyrights and divides property among his family.

September. Goes to Famine district.

1892 Articles on Famine.

Engaged on Famine Relief work.

Répin paints: 'Tolstoy ploughing and harrowing'.

The First Step.

1893 14 May. Finishes *The Kingdom of God is Within You*.

Publishes *Walk in the Light While There is Light* (written earlier).

Writes *Non-Acting*.

1894 Writes *Christianity and Patriotism*.
Writes Preface to de Maupassant's works.
26 November. *Reason and Religion* finished.
28 December. *Religion and Morality* finished.

1895 23 February. Death of son, Iván.
Spring. Writes *Master and Man*.
Writes *Shame!*
Writes appeal on behalf of Doukhobórs.

1896 Writes *Patriotism and Peace*.
First public performance in Russia of *The Power of Darkness*.
Writes *How to Read the Gospels*.
December. *Help!* published (an appeal for the Doukhobórs).

1897 June. Marriage of second daughter, Mary.

1898 Finishes *What is Art?*

1899 Doukhobór Migration.
14 November. Marriage of eldest daughter, Tatiána.

1899 December. Finishes *Resurrection*.

1900 Spring. Writes *The Slavery of Our Times*.
Summer. Ill-health.

1901 22 February. Excommunication.
March. *Reply to the Synod's Edict*.
15 March. Writes *A Letter to the Tsar and his Assistants*.
Summer. Illness.
August. Taken to the Crimea.
Autumn. Writes *Hadji Murad*, *What is Religion?* and *Notes for Soldiers*.
Winter. Continued illness.

1902 16 January. Letter to the Tsar.
February. Finishes *What is Religion?*
June. Returns to Yásnaya.

1903 April. Protests against Jew-baitings. *Esarhaddon*.

1904 May. Finishes *Bethink Yourselves!*, a protest against the Japanese War.

1905 *The One Thing Needful*, and other articles, seized by police.

1906 Compiles *A Circle of Reading*.
August. Serious illness of Countess Tolstoy.
26 November. Death of his daughter, Mary, Princess Obolénski.

1907 30 January. Seizure by police of editions of Tolstoy's books.

1908 Finishes *I Cannot Be Silent* – a protest against the Courts-Martial.

The Teaching of Jesus (for Children).

The Annexation of Bosnia and Herzegovina.

9 July. Newspapers fined, and an editor arrested, for printing *I Cannot Be Silent.*

Arrest and banishment of Tolstoy's secretary, N. N. Gúsev.

28 August. Jubilee in honour of Tolstoy's 80th birthday.

1909 18 September. Makes his will.

1910 22 July. Signs his last will.

28 October. Leaves home.

31 October. Ill at Astápovo.

7 November. Dies at Astápovo.

9 November (=22 November n.s.). Buried at Yásnaya Polyána.

Index